ACTA UNIVERSITATIS UPSALIENSIS
Studia Semitica Upsaliensia
28

Kingship in the Early Mesopotamian Onomasticon 2800–2200 BCE

Jakob Andersson

UPPSALA
UNIVERSITET

Dissertation presented at Uppsala University to be publicly examined in Ihresalen, Engelska parken, Thunbergsvägen 3H, Uppsala, Saturday, March 24, 2012 at 10:00 for the degree of Doctor of Philosophy. The examination will be conducted in English.

Abstract

Andersson, J. 2012. Kingship in the Early Mesopotamian Onomasticon 2800–2200 BCE. *Studia Semitica Upsaliensia* 28. xxxix+440 pp. Uppsala. ISBN 978-91-554-8270-1.

Thousands of Sumerian and Old Akkadian personal names from 3rd millennium BCE Mesopotamia are known and documented. The present study inspects names containing the royal appellatives, Sumerian lugal and Akkadian *śarrum*. The study aims at uncovering the relationships between personal names and the development of early historical kingship and religious thought in the area.

An overview of Sumerian and Old Akkadian names and name-giving serves as a starting point for semantic investigations of lugal- and *śarrum*-names. Sumerian and Old Akkadian names are to a large extent meaningful, and the literal meaning can be used to arrive at an understanding of the symbolic value, which led to the coining of the name. Discussions rely on comparable passages of contemporary and later written traditions.

To facilitate discussion and comparisons between the languages, names are divided into semantic groups based on characteristic traits found in contemporary royal inscriptions and religious texts. Parallel constructions are noted whenever such constructions are known. Names are assigned human or divine referents when possible. A look at political and religious developments puts the distribution of certain name types over time and space into perspective. Local and regional traditions and types are displayed and related either to royal ideological traits or to theological speculation. Besides locally significant gods, a few other deities can be identified as referents in names. A brief statistical overview of different archives shows that names featuring the figure of the lugal experience an increase in popularity at the expense of other types.

A system of annotation gives approximate numbers for bearers of names belonging to the types investigated. Lists of attestations, which document date and archival context, form the basis for discussions and conclusions and make the material available for inspection and further exploration.

Keywords: Sumerian, Old Akkadian, personal names, onomastic studies, kingship

Jakob Andersson, Department of Linguistics and Philology, Box 635, Uppsala University, SE-751 26 Uppsala, Sweden.

ISSN 0585-5535
ISBN 978-91-554-8270-1

urn:nbn:se:uu:diva-168457 (http://urn.kb.se/resolve?urn=urn:nbn:se:uu:diva-168457)

Printed in Sweden by Edita Västra Aros, a climate neutral company, Västerås 2012.
Distributor: Uppsala University Library, Box 510, 751 20 Uppsala
www.uu.se, acta@ub.uu.se

Table of contents

List of figures viii
Preface ix
Abbreviations xi
Technical Abbreviations xxxvi
1. Introduction 1
  1.1 The aim of the study 2
    1.1.1 Theoretical background 5
    1.1.2 Reasons for the study 8
  1.2 Name and appellative 10
    1.2.1 Names and their contexts of use 10
    1.2.2 Previous research on Mesopotamian onomastics 12
  1.3 Method 16
  1.4 Source materials and scope 19
    1.4.1 Original sources 20
    1.4.2 Scholastic texts 21
    1.4.3 Treatment of sources and collection of data 22
  1.5 Early Mesopotamian cities 25
  1.6 Historical and ideological background 34
    1.6.1 The Early Dynastic period 34
    1.6.2 The Sargonic period 42
    1.6.3 The Late Sargonic period and the Gutian interregnum 44
    1.6.4 The Ur III period 44
2. Names and time of name-giving 46
  2.1 The name 46
  2.2 Name-giving 48
    2.2.1 Early periods 48
    2.2.2 Ur III and later periods 51
    2.2.3 Name change and kyriophores 53
  2.3 Sumerian names: a brief overview 57
    2.3.1 Some formal characteristics of Sumerian names 59
    2.3.2 Sumerian names: speaker and contents 64
    2.3.3 Sumerian lugal-names: who is the lugal? 66
  2.4 Akkadian names: a brief overview 71
    2.4.1 Some formal characteristics of Akkadian names 72
    2.4.2 Akkadian names: speaker and contents 75
    2.4.3 Akkadian *śarrum*-names: who is the *śarrum*? 75

3. Semantic analyses 78
3.1 Semantic analysis of Sumerian lugal-names 79
3.1.1 Dominion 81
3.1.2 Wisdom and awareness 104
3.1.3 Protection 107
3.1.4 Care and attentiveness 118
3.1.5 Creation, fertility and prosperity 126
3.1.6 Cult or gods 138
3.1.7 Qualitative-descriptive 159
3.1.8 Unattributable or unintelligible 174
3.1.9 Non–existent names and misreadings 183
3.2 Semantic analysis of Akkadian *śarrum*-names 190
3.2.1 Dominion 191
3.2.2 Wisdom and awareness 194
3.2.3 Protection 196
3.2.4 Care and attentiveness 199
3.2.5 Creation, fertility and prosperity 201
3.2.6 Cult or gods 202
3.2.7 Qualitative-descriptive 205
3.2.8 Unattributable or unintelligible 212
3.2.9 Non–existent *śarrum*-names and misreadings 214
4. Overview of lexemes 216
4.1 Divinities 216
4.2 Localities 217
4.3 Nouns 218
4.4 Adjectives and verbs 222
4.5 Sumerian verbal prefixes 226
4.6 Akkadian finite verb forms 227
5. Semantic comparison of lugal- and *śarrum*-names 228
5.1 Synchronic perspectives 228
5.1.1 ED I-II 228
5.1.2 ED IIIa 229
5.1.3 ED IIIb 230
5.1.4 ES-LS 230
5.2 Diachronic perspectives 231
5.2.1 Demographics 231
5.2.2 Distribution of appellatives 232
5.3 Diachronic developments 238
5.4 Semantic differences 239
5.5 Semantic similarities 240
5.6 Comparison with Ur III kyriophore names 241
6. lugal- and *śarrum*-names in their historical and cultural settings 243
6.1 The historical setting 243
6.2 ED I-II (c. 2900–2700 BCE) 245

6.3 ED IIIa (c. 2700–2550 BCE) ... 247
6.4 ED IIIb (c. 2550–2335 BCE) ... 250
6.5 ES-MS (c. 2330–2240 BCE) ... 255
6.6 MS-CS (c. 2280–2200 BCE) ... 257
6.7 The names and their referents ... 258
7. Concluding discussions ... 260
7.1 Conclusions ... 260
7.2 Avenues for future research ... 265
Bibliography ... 266
Lists of attestations ... 298
1. List of lugal-names ... 298
2. List of *śarrum*-names ... 414
Indices ... 422
1. Sumerian names ... 422
2. Akkadian names ... 429
3. Persons ... 431
4. Deities ... 432
5. Sumerian words, phrases and signs ... 434
6. Akkadian words and phrases ... 436
7. Texts and text passages ... 437

List of figures

Fig. 1: Map of cities with archives, c. 2800-2200 BCE 24
Fig. 2: Name-bearers, 3.1.1, Dominion. 81
Fig. 3: Name-bearers, 3.1.2, Wisdom and awareness. 105
Fig. 4: Name-bearers, 3.1.3, Protection 108
Fig. 5: Name-bearers, 3.1.4, Care and attentiveness. 119
Fig. 6: Name-bearers, 3.1.5, Creation, fertility and prosperity. 127
Fig. 7: Name-bearers, 3.1.6, Cult or gods. 138
Fig. 8: Name-bearers, 3.1.7, Qualitative-descriptive. 159
Fig. 9: Name-bearers, 3.2.1, Dominion. 191
Fig. 10: Name-bearers, 3.2.2, Wisdom and awareness. 194
Fig. 11: Name-bearers, 3.2.3, Protection 196
Fig. 12: Name-bearers, 3.2.4, Care and attentiveness. 199
Fig. 13: Name-bearers, 3.2.5, Creation, fertility and prosperity. 201
Fig. 14: Name-bearers, 3.2.6, Cult or gods. 203
Fig. 15: Name-bearers, 3.2.7, Qualitative-descriptive. 205
Fig. 16: Relative frequency of appellatives 233

Preface

Sumerian names, representing the oldest substantial corpus of personal names in recorded history, have been studied for over a hundred years now. Yet many of their mysteries remain unsolved. Any work on these names will be indebted to the great number of philologists and archaeologists who laid the foundations for cuneiform onomastic studies. It has not been possible in each and every instance to ascribe a reading or an interpretation to an individual scholar. But just as the unearthing of clay tablets from the occupational layers of Ancient Near Eastern sites is a group effort, so, too, is much of the subsequent work done by philologists.

This book is a humble acknowledgement of many a good piece of advice I have received over the years. It is thus with sense of indebtedness I offer my sincerest thanks to all those who have affected me in my choice of studies, and those without whose continuous support and encouragement this work would probably never have seen the light of day. My academic advisor Olof Pedersén, Uppsala, has been helpful in organizing the sometimes unwieldy data. He has incessantly made me push myself further to make the most out of the time given to me, and for this I am truly grateful.

In Copenhagen and Dianalund, my secondary advisor, friend and devil's advocate, Aage Westenholz, and his wife Inger Jentoft deserve my lifelong gratitude for their untiring hospitality during my visits there. But the gratitude must also befall Westenholz for the many years I was fortunate to spend with him, in class and outside.

For his ongoing assistance and helpful suggestions, I am indebted to Manfred Krebernik. His willingness to act as my opponent during the final seminar held in Uppsala in December 2011, despite a very busy schedule, was most welcome. During two visits to Jena in 2008 and 2009, made possible by means of grants from STINT (Stiftelsen för internationalisering av högre studier) and H. S. Nybergs stipendiestiftelse, I benefitted much from the weekly seminars under the auspices of Krebernik. I wish to thank the other participants, Kamran V. Zand, Mohammed Hajouz and Giulia Ferrero for their criticisms, and along with the aforementioned, Peter Stein, Christa Müller-Kessler and the Jenaer Hilfskräfte for their good cameraderie.

I also wish to express my thanks to those who regularly attended my seminars in Uppsala for taking the time to read and formulate criticisms concerning my material. These include my Assyriological colleagues Hans Ahlberg and Mattias Karlsson, who were both kind enough to offer written critique on different chapters; and also Mats Eskhult, Bo Isaksson, Stig Norin and others. Thanks are due also to teachers and peers from my years at Copenhagen University, Bendt Alster and Mogens Trolle Larsen, Thomas Hertel, Jacob Dahl, Gojko Barjamovic Johansen, Steven Lumsden, Jan Gerrit Dercksen, and Jacob Thøgersen; and at the Department of Linguistics and Philology in Uppsala, Sina Tezel and Lina Petersson.

Since my first few weeks in Uppsala, Åke Sjöberg and his wife Gunnil have showed me boundless kindness and goodwill. Åke opened his library to me, which has been very useful with regards to the time periods following on the Sargonic period.

Aage Westenholz and Walter Sommerfeld have generously allowed me access to their vast collections of photographs. I have furthermore benefitted greatly from the photographs available through the CDLI database, and its industrious directors, associates and contributors.

Needless to say, neither of the above mentioned scholars are in any way to blame for errors and oversights contained or lacking within these pages; the fault is entirely my own.

My language has seen improvement through the kind assistance of Lesley-Ann Brown, Copenhagen, whose diligence is hereby acknowledged.

Friends and family have in various ways supported me despite years of complete physical absence. And so, last but certainly not least among the persons who have influenced me and my work: my wife Rikke Wulff Krabbenhøft. Without her dedication, patience and encouragement, the last few years would have been hollow and void in comparison. Thank you for sharing your life with me.

Abbreviations

Abbreviations mainly follow the conventions of the *Reallexikon der Assyriologie*, with a number of additions.

AAICAB	J. P. Grégoire, *Archives administratives et inscriptions cunéiformes de l'Ashmolean Museum et de la Bodleian Collection d'Oxford*, 4 Vols. (Paris 1996–2002)
AAS	J. P. Grégoire, *Archives administratives sumériennes* (Paris 1970)
ABW	H. Steible & H. Behrens, *Inschriften aus 'Lagaš.'* Die altsumerischen Bau- und Weihinschriften 1. FAOS 5/1 (Wiesbaden 1982)
ABW 2	H. Steible & H. Behrens, *Kommentar zu den Inschriften aus 'Lagaš.' Inschriften ausserhalb von 'Lagaš.'* Die altsumerischen Bau- und Weihinschriften 2. FAOS 5/2 (Wiesbaden 1982)
ADFU	Ausgrabungen der Deutschen Forschungsgemeinschaft in Uruk-Warka (Berlin, Leipzig etc 1936–)
AfO	Archiv für Orientforschung (Berlin, Graz, Horn 1923–)
AGE	K. Tallqvist, *Akkadische Götterepitheta.* Studia Orientalia edidit Societas Orientalis Fennica 7 (Helsinki 1938)
AHw	W. von Soden *Akkadisches Handwörterbuch* (Wiesbaden 1959–1981)
AIHA	F. Rasheed, *Aqdam al-kitābāt al-mišmārīya l-muktašafa fī ḥauḍ Sadd Ḥamrīn* [*The Ancient Inscriptions in Himrin Area*] (Baghdad 1981)
AJSL	*American Journal of Semitic Languages and Literatures* (Chicago 1895–1941)
Amherst	T. G. Pinches, *The Amherst Tablets: Being an Account of the Babylonian Inscriptions in the Collection of the Right Hon. Lord Amherst of Hackney, F.S.A. at Didlington Hall, Norfolk. Part* 1: *Texts of the Period Extending to and Including the Reign of Bûr-Sin (about 2500 B.C.)* (London 1908)
Angim	J. S. Cooper, *The Return of Ninurta to Nippur: an-gim-dím-ma.* AnOr 52 (Rome 1978)
Annäherungen 1	J. Bauer, R. K. Englund & M. Krebernik, *Mesopotamien: Späturuk-Zeit und Frühdynastische Zeit. Annäherungen* 1.

	OBO 160/1 (Freiburg & Göttingen 1998)
Annäherungen 3	W. Sallaberger & A. Westenholz, *Mesopotamien: Akkade-Zeit und Ur III-Zeit. Annäherungen* 3. OBO 160/3 (Freiburg & Göttingen 1999)
AnOr	Analecta Orientalia (Rome 1931–)
AnOr 1	N. Schneider, *Die Drehem- und Djoha-Urkunden der Strassburger Universitäts- und Landesbibliothek in Autographie und mit systematischen Wörterverzeichnissen* (Rome 1931).
AnOr 28	A. Falkenstein, *Grammatik der Sprache Gudeas von Lagaš*. I, *Schrift- und Formenlehre* (Rome 1949)
AnOr 30	A. Falkenstein, *Die Inschriften Gudeas von Lagaš*. I, *Einleitung* (Rome 1966)
Anthroponymie	H. Limet, *L'Anthroponymie sumérienne dans les documents de la 3e dynastie d'Ur*. Bibliothèque de la Faculté de Philosophie et Lettres de l'Université de Liège, Fasc. 180 (Paris 1968)
AOAT	Alter Orient und Altes Testament (Kevelaer, Neukirchen-Vluyn 1969–)
AOAT 3/1	O. Loretz, *Texte aus Chagar Bazar und Tell Brak* (Neukirchen Vluyn 1969)
AOAT 271	M. P. Streck, *Das amurritische Onomastikon der altbabylonischen Zeit* (Münster 2000)
AOAT 278/2	A. Militarev & L. Kogan, *Semitic Etymological Dictionary vol.* 2: *Animal Names* (Münster 2005)
AOAT 296	M. P. Streck & S. Weninger (eds.), *Altorientalische und semitische Onomastik* (Münster 2002)
AOAT 305	R. Borger, *Mesopotamisches Zeichenlexikon* (Münster 2004)
AOAT 348	K. Lämmerhirt, *Wahrheit und Trug: Untersuchungen zur altorientalischen Begriffsgeschichte* (Münster 2010)
AOAT 362	J. Peterson, *Godlists from Old Babylonian Nippur in the University Museum, Philadelphia* (Münster 2009)
AoF	*Altorientalische Forschungen. Schriften zur Geschichte und Kultur des alten Orients* (Berlin 1971–)
AoN	J. Bauer, *Altorientalische Notizen* (Würzburg 1975–1992)
AOS	American Oriental Series (New Haven, CT, 1924–)
APN	K. Tallqvist, *Assyrian Personal Names*. Acta Societatis Scientiarum Fennicae 43/1 (Helsinki 1914)
ARES 1	A. Archi (ed.), *Eblaite Personal Names and Semitic Name-Giving. Papers of a Symposium Held in Rome July 15–17, 1985*. Archivi reali di Ebla. Studi 1 (Rome 1988)
ARET	Archivi reali di Ebla. Testi (Rome 1981–)
ARET 1	A. Archi, *Testi amministrativi: Assegnazione di tessuti (archivio L.2769)* (Rome 1985)

ARET 2	D. O. Edzard, *Verwaltungstexte verschiedenen Inhalts* (Rome 1981)
ARET 3	A. Archi & M. G. Biga, *Testi amministrativi di vario contenuto (archivio L.2769)* (Rome 1982)
ARET 4	G. Biga & L. Milano, *Testi amministrativi: Assegnazioni di tessuti (Archivio L. 2769)* (Rome 1984)
ARET 5	D. O. Edzard, *Hymnen, Beschwörungen und Verwandtes aus dem Archiv L. 2769* (Rome 1984)
ARET 7	A. Archi, *Testi amministrativi: Registrazioni di metalli e tessuti* (Rome 1988)
ARET 8	E. Sollberger, *Administrative Texts Chiefly Concerning Textiles* (Rome 1986)
ARET 9	L. Milano, *Testi amministrativi: Assegnazioni di prodotti alimentari (Archivio L. 2712 - parte 1)* (Rome 1990)
ARET 13	P. Fronzaroli & A. Catagnoti, *Testi di cancelleria: I rapporti con le città (Archivio L. 2769)* (Rome 2003)
ArOr	*Archív Orientální.* Quarterly Journal of African and Asian Studies (Prague 1929–)
AS	The Oriental Institute of the University of Chicago, Assyriological Studies (Chicago, IL, 1931–)
AS 11	T. Jacobsen, *The Sumerian King List* (Chicago, IL, 1939)
AS 17	G. Buccellati, & R. D. Biggs, *Cuneiform Texts from Nippur: The Eighth and Ninth Seasons* (Chicago, IL, 1969)
ASJ	*Acta Sumerologica* (Hiroshima 1979–2006)
Atīqōt	*ʿAtiqot* ES. Journal of the Israel Department of Antiquities, English Series (Jerusalem 1955–)
ATU	A. Falkenstein, *Archaische Texte aus Uruk.* ADFU 2 (Berlin & Leipzig 1936)
AulaOr	*Aula Orientalis* (Barcelona 1983–)
AUCT 2	M. Sigrist, *Neo-Sumerian Account Texts in the Horn Archaeological Museum.* Andrews University Cuneiform Texts 2 (Berrien Springs, MI, 1988)
AWAS	G. J. Selz, *Altsumerische Wirtschaftsurkunden aus amerikanischen Sammlungen.* Altsumerische Verwaltungstexte aus Lagaš, Teil 2. FAOS 15,2, 2 vols. (Stuttgart 1993)
AWEL	G. J. Selz, *Die altsumerischen Wirtschaftsurkunden der Eremitage zu Leningrad.* Altsumerische Verwaltungstexte aus Lagaš, Teil 1. FAOS 15,1 (Stuttgart 1989)
AWL	J. Bauer, *Altsumerische Wirtschaftstexte aus Lagasch.* StPohl 9 (Rome 1972)
BA	*Biblical Archaeologist.* Published by the American Schools of Oriental Research (Atlanta, GA, 1938–1997)
Babyloniaca	*Babyloniaca.* Études de philologie assyro-babylonienne (Paris

	1906/1907–1937)
BagM	*Baghdader Mitteilungen* (Berlin, Mainz 1960–)
BARI	British Archaeological Reports International Series (Oxford 1978–)
BARI S2135	E. L. Cripps, *Sargonic and Presargonic Texts in the World Museum Liverpool* (Oxford 2010)
BBVO	Berliner Beiträge zum Vorderen Orient (Berlin 1982–)
BBVO 5	J.-J. Glassner, *La chute d'Akkade: L'événement et sa mémoire* (Berlin 1986)
BBVO 7	M. Krebernik, *Die Personennamen der Ebla-Texte: eine Zwischenbilanz* (Berlin 1988)
BBVO 11	R. Zettler, *The Ur III Temple of Inanna at Nippur: The Operation and Organization of Urban Religious Institutions in Mesopotamia in the Late Third Millennium B.C.* (Berlin 1992)
BCSMS	*Bulletin of the Canadian Society for Mesopotamian Studies* (Toronto, 1981–2005)
BE	The Babylonian Expedition of the University of Pennsylvania, Series A: Cuneiform Texts (Philadelphia, PA, 1893–)
BE 1/1	H. V. Hilprecht, *Old Babylonian Inscriptions Chiefly from Nippur. Part* 1 (Philadelphia, PA, 1893)
BE 1/2	H. V. Hilprecht, *Old Babylonian Inscriptions Chiefly from Nippur. Part* 2 (Philadelphia, PA, 1896)
BE 3/1	D. W. Myhrman, *Sumerian Administrative Documents Dated in the Reigns of the Kings of the Second Dynasty of Ur from the Temple Archives of Nippur Preserved in Philadelphia* (Philadelphia, PA, 1910)
BFE	M. Krebernik, *Die Beschwörungen aus Fara und Ebla. Untersuchungen zur ältesten keilschriftlichen Beschwörungsliteratur*. Texte und Studien zur Orientalistik 2 (Hildesheim 1984)
Bilinguismo	L. Cagni (ed.), *Il Bilinguismo a Ebla: atti del convegno internazionale* (Napoli, 19–22 aprile 1982). IUO, Ser. Minor 22 (Naples 1984)
BiMes	Bibliotheca Mesopotamica (Malibu, FL, 1975–)
BiMes 3	R. D. Biggs, *Inscriptions from Al-Hiba-Lagash, the First and Second Seasons* (Malibu, FL, 1976). Second printing with addenda (Malibu, FL, 1992)
BiMes 17	V. Donbaz & N. Yoffee, *Old Babylonian Texts from Kish Conserved in the Istanbul Archaeological Museums* (Malibu, FL, 1986)
BIN	Babylonian Inscriptions in the Collection of James B. Nies, Yale University (New Haven, CT, 1917–)
BIN 2	J. B. Nies, & C. E. Kaiser, *Historical, Religious and*

	Economic Texts and Antiquities (New Haven, CT, London, & Oxford 1920)
BIN 3	C. E. Keiser, *Neo-Sumerian Account Texts from Drehem* (New Haven, CT, 1971)
BIN 8	G. G. Hackman, *Sumerian and Akkadian Administrative Texts from Predynastic Times to the End of the Akkad Dynasty* (New Haven, CT, 1958)
BiOr	*Bibliotheca Orientalis* (Leiden 1943/44–)
BPOA 1	T. Ozaki & M. Sigrist, *Ur III Administrative Tablets from the British Museum, Part One.* Biblioteca del Próximo Oriente Antiguo vol. 1 (Madrid 2006)
BRM 4	A. T. Clay, *Epics, Hymns, Omens, and Other Texts.* Babylonian Records in the Library of J. Pierpont Morgan 4 (New Haven, CT, 1923)
BroTa	R. Kutscher, *The Brockmon Tablets at the University of Haifa. Royal Inscriptions* (Haifa 1989)
CAANE 1	P. Matthiae, A. Enea, L. Peyronel, F. Pinnock (eds.), Proceedings of the First International Congress on the Archaeology of the Ancient Near East, Rome May 18th–23rd 1998, 2 vols. (Rome 2000)
CAD	A. L. Oppenheim, E. Reiner et al. (eds.), *The Assyrian Dictionary of the University of Chicago* (Chicago, IL, 1956–2011)
CAJ	Cambridge Archaeological Journal (Cambridge 1991–)
CDLJ	*Cuneiform Digital Library Journal* (Berkeley, CA, & Berlin 2002–) http://cdli.ucla.edu/pub.html
CDLN	*Cuneiform Digital Library Notes* (Berkeley, CA, & Berlin 2003–) http://cdli.ucla.edu/pub.html
CDOG 1	G. Wilhelm (ed.), *Die orientalische Stadt: Kontinuität, Wandel, Bruch.* 9.–10. Mai 1996 in Halle/Saale. Colloquien der Deutschen Orient-Gesellschaft 1 (Saarbrücken 1997)
CHÉU	G. Contenau, *Contribution à l'histoire économique d'Umma.* Bibliothèque de l'École des Hautes Études fasc. 219 (Paris 1915)
CIRPL	E. Sollberger, *Corpus des inscriptions «royales» présargoniques de Lagaš* (Geneva 1956)
CollAn	*Colloquium Anatolicum* (Istanbul 2002–)
CRAIB	*Comptes-rendus des séances de l'Academie des Inscriptions et Belles-Lettres* (Paris 1857–)
CRRA	Compte rendu de la …e Rencontre Assyriologique Internationale (1951–)
CST	T. Fish, *Catalogue of Sumerian Tablets in the John Rylands Library* (Manchester 1932)
CT	Cuneiform Texts from Babylonian Tablets, &c., in the British

	Museum (London 1896–)
CT 1	L. W. King, Cuneiform Texts from Babylonian Tablets, &c., in the British Museum vol. 1 (London 1896)
CT 7	L. W. King, Cuneiform Texts from Babylonian Tablets, &c., in the British Museum vol. 7 (London 1899)
CT 9	L. W. King, Cuneiform Texts from Babylonian Tablets, &c., in the British Museum vol. 9 (London 1900)
CT 31	P. S. P. Handcock, Cuneiform Texts from Babylonian Tablets, &c., in the British Museum vol. 31 (London 1911)
CT 32	L. W. King, Cuneiform Texts from Babylonian Tablets, &c., in the British Museum vol. 32 (London 1912)
CT 36	L. W. King, Cuneiform Texts from Babylonian Tablets, &c., in the British Museum vol. 36 (London 1921)
CT 44	T. G. Pinches, *Miscellaneous Texts* (London 1963)
CT 50	E. Sollberger, *Pre-Sargonic and Sargonic Economic Texts* (London 1972)
CTMMA 1	I. Spar (ed.), *Tablets, Cones and Bricks of the Third and Second Millennia B.C.* Cuneiform Texts in the Metropolitan Museum of Art 1 (New York, NY, 1988)
CTNMC	T. Jacobsen, *Cuneiform Texts in the National Museum, Copenhagen* (Leiden 1939)
CUSAS	Cornell University Studies in Assyriology and Sumeriology (Bethesda, MD, 2007–)
CUSAS 1	S. Monaco, *The Cornell University Archaic Tablets* (Bethesda, MD, 2007)
CUSAS 11	G. Visicato & A. Westenholz, *Early Dynastic and Early Sargonic Tablets from Adab in the Cornell University Collections* (Bethesda, MD, 2010) [CUSAS11-$X_{\#}$ refers to the sign with corresponding number in the list of unidentified signs, p. 124]
CUSAS 13	M. Maiocchi, *Classical Sargonic Tablets Chiefly from Adab in the Cornell University Collections* (Bethesda, MD, 2009)
CUSAS 14	S. Monaco, *Early Dynastic mu-iti Cereal Texts in the Cornell University Cuneiform Collections* (Bethesda, MD, 2011)
CUSAS 17	A. R. George (ed.), *Cuneiform Royal Inscriptions and Related Texts in the Schøyen Collection* (Bethesda, MD, 2011)
DAS	B. Lafont, *Documents administratifs sumériens, provenant du site de Tello et conservées au Musée du Louvre*. Édition Recherche sur les Civilisations, Mémoires 61 (Paris 1985)
DCS	D. Charpin & J. M. Durand, *Documents cunéiformes de Strasbourg conservés à la Bibliothèque Nationale et Universitaire* 1: *autographies*. Récherches sur les grandes civilisations, Cahier 4 (Paris 1981)
Death Rituals	A. C. Cohen, *Death Rituals, Ideology, and the Development*

	of Early Mesopotamian Kingship: Toward a New Understanding of Iraq's Royal Cemetery of Ur. Ancient Magic and Divination 7 (Leiden & Boston, MA, 2005)
Déc 2	E. de Sarzec & L. Heuzey, Découvertes en Chaldée 2 (Paris 1912)
DOG	Deutsche Orient-Gesellschaft (Berlin)
DP	F. M. Allotte de la Fuÿe, *Documents présargoniques* (Paris 1908–1920)
DPA	H. Limet, *Documents de la période d'Agadé appartenant à l'Université de Liège.* Bibliothèque de la Faculté de Philosophie et Lettres de l'Université de Liège, Fasc. 206 (Paris 1973)
EANEL	C. Wilcke, *Early Ancient Near Eastern Law: A History of its Beginnings. The Early Dynastic and Sargonic Periods* (Munich 2003); 2nd expanded edition (Winona Lake, IN, 2007)
Ebla 1975–1985	L. Cagni (ed.), *Ebla 1975–1985: Dieci anni di studi linguistici e filologici. Atti del convegno internazionale (Napoli, 9–11 ottobre 1985).* IUO Series Minor 27 (Naples 1987)
Eblaitica	*Eblaitica*: *Essays on the Ebla Archives and Eblaite Language.* Publications of the Center for Ebla Research at New York University (New York, NY, 1987–)
ECTJ	A. Westenholz, *Early Cuneiform Texts in Jena. Pre-Sargonic and Sargonic Documents from Nippur and Fara in the Hilprecht-Sammlung vorderasiatischer Altertümer, Institut für Altertumswissenschaften der Friedrich-Schiller-Universität, Jena* (Copenhagen 1975)
EDATŠ	F. Pomponio & G. Visicato, *Early Dynastic Administrative Tablets of Šuruppak.* IUO Series Maior 6 (Naples 1994)
EGA	R. M. Boehmer, *Die Entwicklung der Glyptik während der Akkad-Zeit.* Untersuchungen zur Assyriologie und Vorderasiatischen Archäologie 4. Ergänzungsbände zur *ZA* (Berlin 1965)
EK 1	S. Langdon, Excavations at Kish vol. 1: 1923–1924 (Paris 1924)
EK 4	L. Ch. Watelin & S. Langdon, Excavations at Kish vol. 4: 1925–1930 (Paris 1934)
Épithètes	M.-J. Seux, *Épithètes royales akkadiennes et sumériennes* (Paris 1967)
ESP	J. J. M. Roberts, *The Earliest Semitic Pantheon: A Study of the Semitic Deities Attested in Mesopotamia before Ur III* (Baltimore & London 1972)
ETB 2	D. Oates, J. Oates, H. McDonald et al., *Nagar in the Third Millennium BC.* Excavations at Tell Brak vol. 2 (Cambridge & London 2001)

Expedition	*Expedition* magazine of the University of Pennsylvania Museum of Archaeology and Anthropology (Philadelphia, PA, 1958–)
FAOS	Freiburger altorientalische Studien (Wiesbaden etc. 1975–)
FAOS 1	H. Steible, *Rīmsîn, mein König: Drei kultische Texte aus Ur mit der Schlußdoxologie* ^{d}*ri-im-*^{d}*sîn lugal-mu* (Wiesbaden 1975)
FAOS 6	H. Behrens & H. Steible, *Glossar zu den altsumerischen Bau- und Weihinschriften* (Wiesbaden 1983)
FAOS 7	I. J. Gelb & B. Kienast, *Die altakkadischen Königsinschriften des dritten Jahrtausends v. Chr.* (Stuttgart 1990)
FAOS 8	B. Kienast & W. Sommerfeld, *Glossar zu den altakkadischen Königsinschriften* (Stuttgart 1994)
FAOS 19	B. Kienast & K. Volk, *Die sumerischen und akkadischen Briefe* (Stuttgart 1995)
Fs Boehmer	U. Finkbeiner, R. Dittmann & H. Hauptmann (eds.), *Beiträge zur Kulturgeschichte Vorderasiens: Festschrift für Rainer Michael Boehmer* (Mainz 1995)
Fs Civil	*AulaOr* 9 (1991)
Fs Foster	S. C. Melville & . L. Slotsky, (eds.), *Opening the Tablet Box: Near Eastern Studies in Honor of Benjamin R. Foster*. Culture and History of the Ancient Near East 42 (Leiden 2010)
Fs Groneberg	D. Shehata, F. Weiershäuser & K. V. Zand (eds.), *Von Göttern und Menschen. Beiträge zur Literatur und Geschichte des Alten Orients. Festschrift für Birgitte Groneberg*. CM 41 (Leiden & Boston, MA, 2010)
Fs Hallo	M. E. Cohen, D. C. Snell, D. B. Weisberg (eds.), *The Tablet and the Scroll: Near Eastern Studies in Honor of William W. Hallo* (Bethesda, MD, 1993)
Fs Hirsch	C. Römer (ed.), *Festschrift für Hans Hirsch zum 65. Geburtstag gewidmet von seinen Freunden, Kollegen und Schülern. Wiener Zeitschrift für die Kunde des Morgenlandes* 86 (Viennna 1996)
Fs Hrouda	P. Calmeyer, K. Hecker, L. Jakob-Rost & C. B. F. Walker (eds.), *Beiträge zur altorientalischen Archäologie und Altertumskunde: Festschrift für Bartel Hrouda zum 65. Geburtstag* (Wiesbaden 1994)
Fs Jacobsen	S. J. Lieberman (ed.), *Sumerological Studies in Honor of Thorkild Jacobsen on His Seventieth Birthday, June 7, 1974*. AS 20 (Chicago, IL, & London 1974)
Fs Kienast	G. J. Selz (ed.), *Festschrift für Burkhart Kienast zu seinem 70. Geburtstage dargebracht von Freunden, Schülern und Kollegen*. AOAT 274 (Münster 2003)
Fs Kilmer	W. Heimpel & G. Frantz-Szabó (eds.), *Strings and Threads:*

	A Celebration of the Work of Anne Draffkorn Kilmer (Winona Lake, IN, 2011)
Fs Klein	Y. Sefati, P. Artzi, C. Cohen, B. L. Eichler & V. A. Hurowitz (eds.), *An Experienced Scribe Who Neglects Nothing: Ancient Near Eastern Studies in Honor of Jacob Klein* (Bethesda, MD, 2005)
Fs Kramer	B. L. Eichler, J. W. Heimerdinger & Å. Sjöberg (eds.), *Kramer Anniversary Volume. Cuneiform Studies in Honor of Samuel Noah Kramer*. AOAT 25 (Kevelaer & Neukirchen-Vluyn 1976)
Fs Kraus	G. van Driel, Th. J. H. Krispijn, M. Stol, K. R. Veenhof (eds.), *Zikir šumim: Assyriological Studies Presented to F. R. Kraus on the Occasion of his Seventieth Birthday* (Leiden 1982)
Fs Lambert	A. R. George & I. L. Finkel (eds.), *Wisdom, Gods and Literature: Studies in Assyriology in Honour of W. G. Lambert* (Winona Lake, IN, 2000)
Fs Larsen	J. G. Dercksen (ed.), *Assyria and Beyond: Studies Presented to Mogens Trolle Larsen*. PIHANS 100 (Leiden 2004)
Fs Leichty	A. K. Guinan, M. deJ. Ellis, A. J. Ferrara, S. M. Freedman, M. T. Rutz, L. Sassmannshausen, S. Tinney & M. W. Waters (eds.), *If a Man Builds a Joyful House; Assyriological Studies in Honor of Erle Verdun Leichty*. CM 31 (Leiden & Boston, MA, 2006)
Fs Limet	Ö. Tunca & D. Desehelle (eds.), *Tablettes et images aux pays de Sumer et d'Akkad: Mélanges offerts à Monsieur H. Limet*. Association pour la Promotion de l'Histoire et de l'Archéologie Orientales. Mémoires, 1 (Liège 1996)
Fs Łyczkowska	O. Drewnowska (ed.), *Here & There across the Ancient Near East. Studies in Honour of Krystyna Łyczkowska* (Warsaw 2009)
Fs Meyer	J. Becker, R. Hempelmann & E. Rehm (eds.), *Kulturlandschaft Syrien: Zentrum und Peripherie. Festschrift für Jan-Waalke Meyer*. AOAT 371 (Münster 2010)
Fs Moortgat	K. Bittel (ed.), *Vorderasiatische Archäologie. Studien und Aufsätze: Anton Moortgat zum 65. Geburtstag gewidmet* (Berlin 1964)
Fs Moran	T. Abusch, J. Huehnergard & P. Steinkeller (eds.), *Lingering over Words: Studies in Ancient Near Eastern Literature in honor of William L. Moran*. HSS 37 (Atlanta, GA, 1990)
Fs Oates	L. Al-Gailani Werr, C. Curtis, H. Martin, A. McMahon, J. Oates & J. Reade (eds.), *Of Pots and Plans: Papers on the Archaeology and History of Mesopotamia Presented to David Oates in Honour of His 75th Birthday* (London 2002)
Fs Oelsner	J. Marzahn & H. Neumann (eds.), *Assyriologia et Semitica:*

	Festschrift für Joachim Oelsner anläßlich seines 65. Geburtstages am 18. Februar 1997. AOAT 252 (Münster 2000)
Fs Owen	A. Kleinerman & J. M. Sasson (eds.), *Why Should Someone Who Knows Something Conceal It? Cuneiform Studies in Honor of David I. Owen on his 70th Birthday* (Bethesda, MD, 2010)
Fs Pettinato	H. Waetzoldt (ed.), *Von Sumer nach Ebla und zurück. Festschrift Giovanni Pettinato zum 27. September 1999 gewidmet von Freunden, Kollegen und Schülern*. HSAO 9 (Heidelberg 2004)
Fs Röllig	B. Pongratz-Leisten, H. Kühne & P. Xella (eds.), *Ana šadî Labnāni lū allik. Beiträge zu altorientalischen und mittelmeerischen Kulturen. Festschrift für Wolfgang Röllig*. AOAT 247 (Neukirchen-Vluyn 1997)
Fs Römer	T. Balke, O. Loretz & M. Dietrich (eds.) *dubsar an-ta-men. Studien zur Altorientalistik: Festschrift für Willem H. Ph. Römer zur Vollendung seines 70. Lebensjahres, mit Beiträgen von Freunden, Schülern und Kollegen*. AOAT 253 (Münster 1998)
Fs Schretter	R. Rollinger (ed.), *Von Sumer bis Homer: Festschrift für Manfred Schretter zum 60. Geburtstag am 25. Februar 2004*. AOAT 325 (Münster 2005)
Fs Sigrist	P. Michalowski (ed.), *On the Third Dynasty of Ur: Studies in Honor of Marcel Sigrist* (Boston, MA, 2008)
Fs Westenholz	G. Barjamovic, J. L.Dahl, U. S. Koch, W. Sommerfeld & J. Goodnick Westenholz (eds.), *Akkade is King: A Collection of Papers by Friends and Colleagues Presented to Aage Westenholz on the Occasion of his 70th Birthday 15th of May 2009*. PIHANS 118 (Leiden 2011)
Fs Wilcke	W. Sallaberger, K. Volk & A Zgoll (eds.), *Literatur, Politik und Recht: Festschrift für Claus Wilcke*. Orientalia Biblica et Christiana 14 (Wiesbaden 2003)
FT	H. de Genouillac, *Fouilles de Telloh*, 2 Vols. (Paris 1934 & 1936)
FTUM	H. Martin, F. Pomponio, G. Visicato & A. Westenholz, *The Fara Tablets in the University of Philadelphia Museum of Archaeology and Anthropology* (Bethesda, MD, 2001)
GAG	W. von Soden, *Grundriß der akkadischen Grammatik*. AnOr 33 (Rome 1952). 3rd revised edition (Rome 1995)
Genava	*Genava*. Revue d'histoire de l'art et d'archéologie, Musée d'art et d'histoire de Genève (Geneva 1923–1952)
Gudea	F. Thureau-Dangin, *Les cylindres de Goudéa*. Textes Cunéiformes du Louvre 8 (Paris 1925)
Götterwelt	G. J. Selz, *Untersuchungen zur Götterwelt des altsumerischen*

	Stadtstaates von Lagaš. Occasional Publications of the S. N. Kramer Fund 13 (Philadelphia, PA, 1995)
Gs Cagni	S. Graziani (ed.), *Studi sul Vicino Oriente antico dedicati alla memoria di Luigi Cagni*. 4 vols. IUO 61 (Naples 2000)
Gs Diakonoff	L. Kogan, N. Koslova, S. Loesov & S. Tischenko (eds.), *Memoriae Igor M. Diakonoff*. Babel und Bibel 2 (Winona Lake, IN, 2005)
Gs Kutscher	A. F. Rainey, A. Kempinski, M. Sigrist & D. Ussishkin (eds.) *Kinattūtu ša dārâti: Raphael Kutscher Memorial Volume*. Tel Aviv Occasional Publications Series 1 (Tel Aviv 1993)
Gs Sachs	E. Leichty, M. DeJ. Ellis & P. Gerardi (eds.), *A Scientific Humanist: Studies in Memory of Abraham Sachs*. Occasional Publications of the Samuel Noah Kramer Fund 9 (Philadelphia, PA, 1988)
Gs Unger	M. Lurker (ed.), *In Memoriam Eckhard Unger: Beiträge zu Geschichte, Kultur und Religion des Alten Orients* (Baden-Baden 1971)
HANE/S	History of the Ancient Near East /Studies (Padua 1990–)
HANE/S 5	M. Liverani (ed.), *Akkad: The First World Empire. Structure, Ideology, Tradition* (Padova 1993)
HANE/S 10	G. Marchesi, *LUMMA in the Onomasticon and Literature of Ancient Mesopotamia* (Padua 2006)
Hirose	T. Gomi, Y. Hirose & K. Hirose, *Neo-Sumerian Administrative Texts of the Hirose Collection* (Potomac, MD, 1990)
HLC	G. A. Barton, *Haverford Library Collection of Cuneiform Tablets, or Documents from the Temple Archives of Tello*, 3 vols. (Philadelphia, PA, London 1905–1914)
HSAO	Heidelberger Studien zum Alten Orient (Wiesbaden, Heidelberg 1967–)
HSS	Harvard Semitic Series (Cambridge, MA, 1912–)
HSS 3	M. I. Hussey, *Sumerian Tablets in the Harvard Semitic Museum, Part* 1, *Chiefly from the Reigns of Lugalanda and Urukagina of Lagash* (Cambridge, MA, 1912)
HSS 4	M. I. Hussey, *Sumerian Tablets in the Harvard Semitic Museum, Part* 2, *From the Time of The Dynasty of Ur* (Cambridge, MA, 1915)
HSS 10	T. J. Meek, *Old Akkadian, Sumerian, and Cappadocian Texts from Nuzi* (Cambridge, MA, 1935)
HUCA	*Hebrew Union College Annual* (Cincinnati, OH, 1924–)
IAS	R. D. Biggs, *Inscriptions from Tell Abū Ṣ alābīkh*. OIP 99 (Chicago, IL, 1974) [used as siglum for cuneiform texts 1–515 only. For introduction, edition and commentary on individual compositions, see OIP 99]; R. D. Biggs & J. N.

	Postgate "Inscriptions from Abu Salabikh", *Iraq* 40 (1978), 101–117 [cuneiform texts 516–529]
Imgula	Imgula (Münster/Marburg 1996–)
Imgula 5	M. Hilgert, *Akkadisch in der Ur III-Zeit* (Münster 2002)
Iran	*Iran*. Journal of the British Institute of Persian Studies (London 1963–)
IRSA	E. Sollberger & J.-R. Kupper, *Inscriptions royales sumériennes et akkadiennes*. Littératures anciennes du Proche-Orient No. 3 (Paris 1971)
ISET 1	S. N. Kramer, M. Çığ & H. Kızılyay, *İstanbul Arkeoloji Müzelerinde Bulunan: Sumer edebî tablet ve parçaları* 1 (Ankara 1969)
ITT	Inventaire des tablettes de Tello, conservées au Musée Impérial Ottoman, tomes I–V (Paris 1910–1921)
ITT 1	F. Thureau-Dangin, *Textes de l'époque d'Agadé* (*Fouilles d'Ernest de Sarzec en 1895*) (Paris 1910)
ITT 2	H. de Genouillac, *Textes de l'époque d'Agadé et de l'époque d'Ur* (*Fouilles d'Ernest de Sarzec en 1895*), 2 vols. (Paris 1910 & 1911)
ITT 5	H. de Genouillac, *Époque présargonique, époque d'Agadé, époque d'Ur* (Paris 1921)
IUO	Istituto Universitario Orientale. Dipartimento di Studi Asiatici: Series Minor (Naples 1974–); Series Maior (1979–)
JANES	*Journal of the Ancient Near Eastern Society* (*of Columbia University*) (New York, NY, 1968/69–)
JAC	*Journal of Ancient Civilizations* (Changchun 1986–)
JAOS	*Journal of the American Oriental Society* (New Haven, CT, etc. 1843/49–)
JBVO 5	N. Nebes (ed.), *Neue Beiträge zur Semitistik. Erstes Arbeitstreffen der Arbeitsgemeinschaft Semitistik in der Deutschen Morgenländischen Gesellschaft vom 11. bis 13. September 2000 an der Friedrich-Schiller-Universität Jena*, Jenaer Beiträge zum Vorderen Orient 5 (Wiesbaden 2002)
JCS	*Journal of Cuneiform Studies* (New Haven, CT/Boston, MA, etc. 1947–)
JCSMS	*Journal of the Canadian Society for Mesopotamian Studies* (Toronto 2006–)
JESHO	*Journal of the Economic and Social History of the Orient* (Leiden 1957/58–)
JNES	*Journal of Near Eastern Studies* (Chicago, IL, 1942–)
JSOTS 270	J. Day (ed.), *King and Messiah in Israel and the Ancient Near East. Proceedings of the Oxford Old Testament Seminar*. Journal for the Study of the Old Testament Supplement Series 270 (Sheffield 1998)

Kaskal	*Kaskal. Rivista di storia, ambiente e culture del Vicino Oriente antico* (Padua 2004–)
Keš Temple Hymn	See TCS 3
Königsfriedhof	H. J. Nissen, *Zur Datierung des Königsfriedhofes von Ur: Unter besonderer Berücksichtigung der Stratigraphie der Privatgräber*. Beiträge zur Ur- und frühgeschichtlichen Archäologie des Mittelmeer-Kulturraumes 3 (Bonn 1966)
Königsinschriften	S. Franke, *Königsinschriften und Königsideologie: Die Könige von Akkade zwischen Tradition und Neuerung* (Münster & Hamburg 1995)
LAK	A. Deimel, *Liste der archaischen Keilschriftzeichen*. Wissenschaftliche Veröffentlichungen der Deutschen Orient-Gesellschaft 40 (Leipzig 1922) [LAK# refers to the sign with corresponding number in the sign list]
LdE	L. Cagni (ed.) *La Lingua di Ebla*, IUO Series Minor 14 (Naples 1981)
Love Songs	Y. Sefati, *Love Songs in Sumerian Literature: Critical Edition of the Dumuzi-Inanna Songs* (Ramat Gan 1998)
L'uomo	G. Pettinato, *L'uomo cominciò a scrivere: Iscrizioni cuneiformi della collezione Michail* (Milan 1997)
MAD	I. J. Gelb, Materials for the Assyrian Dictionary, 5 vols. (Chicago 1952–1970)
MAD 1	I. J. Gelb, *Sargonic Texts from the Diyala Region* (Chicago, IL, 1952)
MAD 2	I. J. Gelb, *Old Akkadian Writing and Grammar* (Chicago, IL, 1952). Second, revised edition (Chicago, IL, 1961)
MAD 3	I. J. Gelb, *Glossary of Old Akkadian* (Chicago, IL, 1957)
MAD 4	I. J. Gelb, *Sargonic Texts in the Louvre Museum* (Chicago, IL, 1970)
MAD 5	I. J. Gelb, *Sargonic Texts in the Ashmolean Museum, Oxford* (Chicago, IL, 1970)
MAM	Mission archéologique de Mari (Paris 1956–)
MAM 1	A. Parrot, *Le Temple d'Ishtar*. Institut Français d'Archéologie de Beyrouth. Bibliothèque archéologique et historique vol. 65 (Paris 1956)
MAM 3	A. Parrot & G. Dossin, *Les Temples d'Ishtarat et de Ninni-zaza*. Institut Français d'Archéologie de Beyrouth. Bibliothèque archéologique et historique vol. 86 (Paris 1967)
MAM 4	A. Parrot & G. Dossin, *Le «trésor» d'Ur*. Institut Français d'Archéologie de Beyrouth. Bibliothèque archéologique et historique vol. 87 (Paris 1968)
MARI	*Mari: Annales de recherches interdisciplinaires* (Paris 1982–)
MCS	*Manchester Cuneiform Studies* (Manchester 1951–1964)
MDOG	*Mitteilungen der Deutschen Orient-Gesellschaft zu Berlin*

	(Berlin 1898/99–)
MDP	Mémoires de la délégation de Perse etc (Paris 1900–)
MDP 2	V. Scheil, *Textes élamites-sémitiques: première série* (Paris 1900)
MDP 14	V. Scheil & L. Legrain, *Textes élamites-sémitiques: cinquième série* (Paris 1913).
MEE	Materiali epigrafici di Ebla (Naples 1979–)
MEE 3	G. Pettinato, *Testi lessicali monolingui della bibliotheca L. 2769* (Naples 1981)
MEE 4	G. Pettinato, *Testi lessicali bilingui della bibliotheca L. 2769. Parte* 1: *Traslitterazione dei testi e ricostruzione del VE* (Naples 1982). [VE# refers to the lexical entry with corresponding number in the volume]
Menschenbild	Pettinato, G., *Das altorientalische Menschenbild und die sumerischen und akkadischen Schöpfungsmythen*, Ph.D. diss. (Heidelberg 1971)
MesCiv	Mesopotamian Civilizations (Winona Lake, IN, 1989–)
MesCiv 1	P. Michalowski, *The Lamentation over the Destruction of Sumer and Ur* (Winona Lake, IN, 1989)
MesCiv 4	P. Steinkeller & J. N. Postgate, *Third-Millennium Legal and Administrative Texts in the Iraq Museum, Baghdad* (Winona Lake, IN, 1992)
MesCiv 5	A. R. George, *House Most High: The Temples of Ancient Mesopotamia.* MesCiv 5 (Winona Lake, IN, 1993)
MesCiv 7	J. Goodnick Westenholz, *Legends of the Kings of Akkade: The Texts* (Winona Lake, IN, 1997)
MesCiv 14	G. Marchesi & N. Marchetti, *Royal Statuary of Early Dynastic Mesopotamia* (Winona Lake, IN, 2011)
Mesopotamia	Rivista di Archeologia, Epigrafia e Storia Orientale Antica (Turin 1966–)
Mesopotamia	Mesopotamia. Copenhagen Studies in Assyriology (Copenhagen 1972–1984)
Mesopotamia 2	B. Alster, *The Instructions of Suruppak* (Copenhagen 1974)
Mesopotamia 3	B. Alster, *Studies in Sumerian Proverbs* (Copenhagen 1975)
Mesopotamia 7	M. Trolle Larsen (ed.), *Power and Propaganda: A Symposium on Ancient Cultures* (Copenhagen 1979)
Mesopotamia 8	B. Alster (ed.), *Death in Mesopotamia.* CRRA 26 (Copenhagen 1980)
Mesopotamia 9	B. R. Foster, *Administration and Use of Institutional Land in Sargonic Sumer* (Copenhagen 1982)
Mesopotamia 10	M.-L. Thomsen, *The Sumerian Language. An Introduction to its History and Grammatical Structure* (Copenhagen 1984). Third edition, third issue (Copenhagen 2001)
MLVS 1	F. M. T. Böhl, *Oorkonden uit de periode der rijken van Sumer*

	en Akkad (3000–2000 v. Chr.). Mededeelingen uit de Leidsche verzameling van spijkerschrift-inscripties 1 (Amsterdam 1933)
MNS	Å. Sjöberg, *Der Mondgott Nanna-Suen in der sumerischen Überlieferung. I. Teil: Texte*, Stockholm 1960
MO	*Maništūšu* Obelisk, in: I. J. Gelb et al., OIP 104, pl. 67–72
MSL	B. Landsberger et al. (eds.), Materialien zum sumerischen Lexikon/Materials for the Sumerian Lexicon (Rome 1937–)
MSL 12	M. Civil, R. D. Biggs, H. G. Güterbock, H. J. Nissen & E. Reiner (eds.), *The Series lú =* ša *and Related Texts* (Rome 1969)
MSL 13	M. Civil, H. G. Güterbock, W. W. Hallo, H. A. Hoffner & E. Reiner (eds.), *Izi =* išātu, *Ká-gal =* abullu *and Níg-ga =* makkūru (Rome 1971)
MSL 14	M. Civil, M. W. Green & W. G. Lambert (eds.), *Ea A =* nâqu, *with their Forerunners and Related Texts* (Rome 1979)
MSVO	Materialien zu den frühen Schriftzeugnissen des Vorderen Orients (Berlin 1991–)
MSVO 1	R. K. Englund & J.-P. Grégoire, *The Proto-Cuneiform Texts from Jemdet Nasr* 1: *Copies, Transliterations and Glossary* (Berlin 1991)
MSVO 2	R. J. Matthews, *Cities, Seals and Writing: Archaic Seal Impressions from Jemdet Nasr and Ur* (Berlin 1993)
MVN	Materiali per il vocabolario neosumerico (Rome 1974–)
MVN 2	H. Sauren, *Wirtschaftsurkunden aus der Zeit der III Dynastie von Ur im Besitz des Musée d'Art et d'histoire in Genf nebst kleinerer Sammlungen* (Rome 1974)
MVN 3	D. I. Owen, The John Frederick Lewis Collection (Rome 1975)
MVN 6	G. Pettinato, *Testi economici di Lagaš del Museo di Instanbul. Parte* 1: *La. 7001–7600* (Rome 1977)
MVN 7	G. Pettinato, *Testi economici di Lagaš del Museo di Istanbul. Parte* 2: *La. 7601–8200* (Rome 1978)
MVN 10	J.–P. Grégoire, *Inscriptions et archives administratives cunéiformes (1e partie)*, (Rome 1981)
MVN 12	T. Gomi, *Wirtschaftstexte der Ur III-Zeit aus dem British Museum* (Rome 1982)
MVN 15	D. I. Owen, Neo-Sumerian Texts from American Collections, MVN 15, (Rome 1991)
MVN 16	H. Waetzoldt & F. Yıldız, *Die Umma-Texte aus den Archaeologischen Museen zu Istanbul*, vol. 2 (Rome 1994)
MVN 17	G. Pettinato, *Testi economici neo-sumerici del British Museum (BM 12230–BM 12390)*. MVN 17 (Rome 1993)
MVN 21	N. Koslova, *Neusumerische Verwaltungstexte aus Umma aus*

	der Sammlung der Ermitage zu St. Petersburg - Russland (Rome 2000)
NABU	*Nouvelles assyriologiques brèves et utilitaires* (Paris/Rouen 1987–)
Namengebung	J. J. Stamm, *Die akkadische Namengebung*. Mitteilungen der Vorderasiatisch-Aegyptischen Gesellschaft (e.V.) Bd. 44, (Leipzig 1939)
Namenforschung	E. Eichler et al. (eds.), *Namenforschung. Name Studies. Les noms propres*. Handbücher zur Sprach- und Kommunikationswissenschaft vol. 11/1 (Berlin & New York, NY, 1995)
Names	*Names: A Journal of Onomastics* (New York, NY, etc 1952/53–)
NATN	D. I. Owen, *Neo-Sumerian Archival Texts Primarily from Nippur in the University Museum, the Oriental Institute and the Iraq Museum* (Winona Lake, IN, 1982)
NFT	G. Cros, L. Heuzey, F. Thureau-Dangin, *Nouvelles fouilles de Tello* (Paris 1914)
Nik 1	M. V. Nikol'skij, *Dokumenty chozâjstvennoj otčetnosti drevnejšej epochi Chaldei iz sobraniâ N. P. Lichačeva*. Drevnosti Vostočnyâ vol. III/2 (St. Petersburg 1908)
Nik 2	M. V. Nikol'skij, *Dokumenty chozâjstvennoj otčetnosti drevnejšej epochi Chaldei iz sobraniâ N. P. Lichačeva II: Epocha dinastii Agade i epocha dinastii Ura*. Drevnosti Vostočnyâ vol. V (Moscow 1915)
NIN	*NIN*. Journal of Gender Studies in Antiquity (Groningen 2000–)
NTSŠ	R. Jestin, *Nouvelles tablettes sumériennes de Šuruppak au musée d'Istanbul*. Bibliothèque archéologique et historique de l'Institut français d'archéologie d'Istanbul vol. 2, Paris 1957
OAIC	I. J. Gelb, *Old Akkadian Inscriptions in Chicago Natural History Museum: Texts of Legal and Business Interest*. Fieldiana: Anthropology 44/2 (Chicago, IL, 1955), 161–338
OBO	Orbis Biblicus et Orientalis (Freiburg & Göttingen 1973–)
OBO 166	E. Flückiger-Hawker, *Urnamma of Ur in Sumerian Literary Tradition* (Freiburg & Göttingen 1996)
OBO 203	V. Dasen (ed.), *Naissance et petite enfance dans l'antiquité. Actes du colloque de Fribourg, 28 novembre – 1er décembre 2001* (Freiburg & Göttingen 2004)
OECT 4	P. E. van der Meer, *Syllabaries A,* B^1 *and B with Miscellaneous Lexicographical Texts from the Herbert Weld Collection* (London 1938)
OECT 7	S. Langdon, *The Pictographic Inscriptions from Jemdet Nasr Excavated by the Oxford and Field Museum Expedition* (London, 1928)

OIC 22	M. Civil, *Appendix A: Cuneiform Texts*, in McG. Gibson (ed.), *Excavations at Nippur: Eleventh Season*. Oriental Institute Communications 22 (Chicago, IL, 1975)
OIP	Oriental Institute Publications (Chicago, IL, 1924–)
OIP 14	D. D. Luckenbill, *Inscriptions from Adab* (Chicago, IL, 1930)
OIP 47	G. Eisen, *Ancient Oriental Cylinder and Other Seals with A Description of the Collection of Mrs. William H. Moore* (Chicago, IL, 1940)
OIP 53	P. Delougaz & T. Jacobsen, *The Temple Oval at Khafajah* (Chicago, IL, 1940)
OIP 58	P. Delougaz, S. Lloyd, H. Frankfort & T. Jacobsen, *Pre-Sargonid Temples in the Diyala Region* (Chicago, IL, 1942)
OIP 72	H. Frankfort, *Stratified Cylinder Seals from the Diyala Region* (Chicago, IL, 1955)
OIP 97	D. E. McCown, R. C. Haines & R. D. Biggs, *Nippur II: The North Temple and Sounding E*. Excavations of the Joint Expedition to Nippur of the American Schools of Oriental Research and the Oriental Institute of the University of Chicago. (Chicago, IL, 1978)
OIP 99	R. D. Biggs, *Inscriptions from Tell Abū Ṣalābīkh* (Chicago, IL, 1974), with a chapter on the archaeological findings by D. P. Hansen [Introduction, edition and commentary on individual compositions only. For the texts, see IAS]
OIP 104	I. J. Gelb, P. Steinkeller & R. M. Whiting Jr., *The Earliest Land Tenure Systems in the Near East: Ancient Kudurrus*. 2 Vols. (Chicago, IL, 1989, 1991)
OIP 129	A. McMahon (ed.), *The Early Dynastic to Akkadian Transition: The Area WF Sounding at Nippur* (Chicago, IL, 2006)
OLA 5	E. Lipiński (ed.), *State and Temple Economy in the Ancient Near East* vol. 1, Orientalia Lovaniensia Analecta 5 (Leuven 1979)
OLZ	*Orientalistische Literaturzeitung. Monatsschrift für die Wissenschaft vom ganzen Orient und seine(n) Beziehungen zu den angrenzenden Kulturkreisen* (Berlin/Leipzig 1898–)
Onoma	*Onoma. Journal of the International Council of Onomastic Sciences* (Leuven 1950–)
Onomastika	V. V. Struve, *Ономастика раннединастического Лагаша* [*Onomastika rannedinastičeskogo Lagaša*] (Moscow 1984)
OrAnt	*Oriens antiquus: rivista del Centro per la antichità e la storia dell'arte del Vicino Oriente* (Rome 1962–1990)
Orient	*Orient. Reports of the Society for Near Eastern Studies in Japan* (Tokyo 1960–)
OrNS	*Orientalia Nova Series* (Rome 1932–)

OrSP	*Orientalia Series Prior* (Rome 1920–1930)
OrS	*Orientalia Suecana* (Uppsala, Stockholm 1952–)
OSP 1	A. Westenholz, *Literary and Lexical Texts and the Earliest Administrative Documents from Nippur.* Old Sumerian and Old Akkadian Texts in Philadelphia, Chiefly from Nippur, 1. BiMes 1 (Malibu, FL, 1975) [OSP1-$X_{\#}$ refers to the sign with corresponding number in the list of unidentified signs, p. 117–119]
OSP 2	A. Westenholz, *The 'Akkadian' Texts, the Enlilemaba Texts, and the Onion Archive.* Old Sumerian and Old Akkadian Texts in Philadelphia, Chiefly from Nippur, 2. Carsten Niebuhr Institute Publications 3 (Copenhagen 1987)
Pantheon	P. Mander, *Il Pantheon di Abū Ṣalābīkh. Contributo allo studio del pantheon sumerico arcaico.* IUO Series Minor 26 (Naples 1986)
PBS	University of Philadelphia, Publications of the Babylonian Section (Philadelphia, PA, 1911–1930)
PBS 5	A. Poebel, *Historical and Grammatical Texts* (Philadelphia, PA, 1914)
PBS 9	G. A. Barton, *Sumerian Business and Administrative Documents from the Earliest Times to the Dynasty of Agade* (Philadelphia, PA, 1915)
PBS 11/1	E. Chiera, *Lists of Personal Names from the Temple School of Nippur. A Syllabary of Personal Names* (Philadelphia, PA, 1916)
PBS 11/2	E. Chiera, *Lists of Personal Names from the Temple School of Nippur. Lists of Akkadian Personal Names* (Philadelphia, PA, 1916)
PBS 11/3	E. Chiera, *Lists of Personal Names from the Temple School of Nippur. Lists of Sumerian Personal Names* (Philadelphia, PA, 1919)
PBS 13	L. Legrain, *Historical Fragments* (Philadelphia, PA, 1922)
PBS 15	L. Legrain, *Royal Inscriptions and Fragments from Nippur and Babylon* (Philadelphia, PA, 1926)
PDT 1	M. Çığ, H. Kızılyay & A. Salonen, *Die Puzriš-Dagan-Texte der Istanbuler Archäologischen Museen,* 1: Nrr. 1–725. Annales Academiæ Scientarium Fennicæ, B 92 (Helsinki 1954)
Personennamen	A. Poebel, *Die sumerischen Personennamen zur Zeit der Dynastie von Larsam und der ersten Dynastie von Babylon.* Habilitationsschrift (Breslau 1910)
PIHANS	PIHANS. Uitgaven van het Nederlands Instituut voor het Nabije Oosten te Leiden (Leiden 1956–)
POANE	K. Watanabe (ed.), *Priests and Officials in the Ancient Near*

	East. Papers of the Second Colloquium on the Ancient Near East – The City and its Life held at the Middle Eastern Culture Center in Japan (Mitaka, Tokyo) *March 22–24, 1996* (Heidelberg 1999)
Prosopografia	F. Pomponio, *La prosopografia dei testi presargonici di Fara.* Studi Semitici Nova Series 3 (Rome 1987)
PSD	*The Pennsylvania Sumerian Dictionary* (Philadelphia 1984–)
QDLF	*Quaderni del Dipartimento di Linguistica - Università di Firenze* (Florence, 1990–)
QuadSem	Quaderni di Semitistica (Florence, 1971–)
QuadSem 13	P. Fronzaroli (ed.), *Studies on the Language of Ebla* (Florence 1984)
QuadSem 18	P. Fronzaroli (ed.), *Literature and Literary Language at Ebla* (Florence 1992)
RA	*Revue d'Assyriologie et d'Archéologie Orientale* (Paris 1884/85–)
RÉC	F. Thureau-Dangin, *Recherches sur l'origine de l'écriture cunéiforme* (Paris 1898); *Supplément* (1899) [RÉC# refers to the sign with corresponding number in the sign list]
RGTC	Répertoire Géographique des Textes Cunéiformes. Beihefte zum Tübinger Atlas des Vorderen Orients, Reihe B (Geisteswissenschaften), (Wiesbaden 1977)
RGTC 1	D. O. Edzard, G. Farber & E. Sollberger, *Die Orts- und Gewässernamen der präsargonischen und sargonischen Zeit* (Wiesbaden 1977)
RGTC 2	D. O. Edzard & G. Farber, *Die Orts- und Gewässernamen der Zeit der 3. Dynastie von Ur* (Wiesbaden 1974)
RHR	*Revue de l'histoire des religions* (Paris 1880–)
RIAA	L. Speleers, *Recueil des inscriptions de l'Asie antérieure des Musées Royaux du Cinquantenaire à Bruxelles: Textes sumériens, babyloniens et assyriens* (Brussels 1925)
RIME	Royal Inscriptions of Mesopotamia Early Periods (Toronto 1993–2008)
RIME 1	D. R. Frayne, *Presargonic Period (2700–2350 BC)* (Toronto 2008)
RIME 2	D. R. Frayne, *Sargonic and Gutian Periods (2334–2113 BC)* (Toronto 1993)
RIME 3/1	D. O. Edzard, *Gudea and his Dynasty* (Toronto 1997)
RIME 3/2	D. R. Frayne, *Ur III Period (2112–2004 BC)* (Toronto 1997)
RlA	*Reallexikon der Assyriologie* (*und Vorderasiatischen Archäologie*) (Berlin, Leipzig 1928/32–)
Rochester	Sigrist, M., *Documents from Tablet Collections in Rochester, New York*, Bethesda, MD, 1991
RSO	*Rivista degli studi orientali* (Rome 1907–)

RSP	Y. Rosengarten, *Répertoire commenté des signes présargoniques sumériens de Lagaš* (Paris 1967) [RSP# refers to the sign with corresponding number in the sign list]
RTC	F. Thureau-Dangin, *Recueil de tablettes chaldéennes* (Paris 1903)
SAKF	K. Oberhuber, *Sumerische und akkadische Keilschriftdenkmäler des Archäologischen Museums zu Florenz*, 2 vols. Innsbrucker Beiträge zu Kulturwissenschaft Sonderhefte 7, 8 (Innsbruck 1958, 1960)
SAKI	F. Thureau-Dangin, *Die sumerischen und akkadischen Königsinschriften*. Vorderasiatische Bibliothek Bd. 1, Abteilung 1 (Leipzig 1907)
SANE 2/1	J. S. Cooper, *Reconstructing History from Ancient Inscriptions: the Lagash-Umma Border Conflict.* Sources from the Ancient Near East 2/1 (Malibu, FL, 1983). 3rd revised printing (Malibu, FL, 2002)
SANTAG	SANTAG. Arbeiten und Untersuchungen zur Keilschriftkunde (Wiesbaden 1990–)
SANTAG 7	T. Ozaki, *Keilschrifttexte aus japanischen Sammlungen*. SANTAG 7 (Wiesbaden 2002)
SARI 1	J. S. Cooper, *Sumerian and Akkadian Royal Inscriptions,* 1: *Presargonic Inscriptions.* The American Oriental Society Translation Series 1 (New Haven, CT, 1986)
SAT 1	M. Sigrist, *Texts in the British Museum*. Sumerian Archival Texts 1 (Bethesda, MD, 1993)
SAT 2	M. Sigrist, *Texts from the Yale Babylonian Collections, Part 1*. Sumerian Archival Texts 2 (Bethesda, MD, 2000)
SCT	C. H. Gordon, *Smith College Tablets: 110 Cuneiform Texts Selected from the College Collection* (Northampton, MA, 1952)
SET	T. B. Jones & J. W. Snyder, *Sumerian Economic Texts from the Third Ur Dynasty: A Catalogue and Discussion of Documents from Various Collections* (Minneapolis, MN, 1961)
Shepherds	K. Šašková, L. Pecha & P. Charvát, *Shepherds of the Black-Headed People: The Royal Office Vis-À-Vis Godhead in Ancient Mesopotamia* (Plzeň 2010)
SF	A. Deimel, *Schultexte aus Fara.* Wissenschaftliche Veröffentlichungen der Deutschen Orient-Gesellschaft 43 (Leipzig 1923)
SIA	Z. Yang, *Sargonic Inscriptions from Adab*. The Institute for the History of Ancient Civilizations Periodic Publications on Ancient Civilizations 1 (Changchun 1989)
Six City-State Cultures	M. H. Hansen, (ed.), *A Comparative Study of Six City-State Cultures. An Investigation Conducted by the Copenhagen*

	Polis Centre. Historisk-filosofiske Skrifter 27 (Copenhagen 2002)
SKIZ	W. H. Ph. Römer, *Sumerische 'Königshymnen' der Isin-Zeit* (Leiden 1965)
SMS	Monographic Journals of the Near East. Syro-Mesopotamian Studies (Malibu, FL, 1977–)
SMS 5/1	L. Milano, *Mozan 2: The Epigraphic Finds of the Sixth Season* (Malibu, FL, 1991)
SNAT	T. Gomi & S. Sato, *Selected Neo-Sumerian Administrative Texts from the British Museum* (Abiko 1990)
SRU	D. O. Edzard, *Sumerische Rechtsurkunden des III. Jahrtausends: aus der Zeit vor der III. Dynastie von Ur* (Munich 1968)
STA	E. Chiera, *Selected Temple Accounts from Telloh, Yokha and Drehem: Cuneiform Tablets in the Library of Princeton University*, Princeton, NJ, 1922
StEb	*Studi Eblaiti* (Rome 1979–)
StEL	*Studi Epigrafici e Linguistici sul Vicino Oriente Antico* (Verona 1984–)
StOr	Studia Orientalia (Helsinki 1925–)
StPohl	Studia Pohl: dissertationes scientificae de rebus Orientis antiqui (Rome 1967–)
StPohl 1	F. Gröndahl, *Die Personennamen der Texte aus Ugarit* (Rome 1967)
StPohl 2	See *Tierbilder*
StPohl 6	C. Saporetti, *Onomastica Medio-Assira*, 2 vols.: I, *I nomi di persona;* II, *Studi, vocabolari ed elenchi* (Rome 1970)
StPohl 9	See *AWL*
StPohl 10	G. Farber-Flügge, *Der Mythos "Inanna und Enki" unter besonderer Berücksichtigung der Liste der m e* (Rome 1973)
StPohl SM	Studia Pohl Series Maior (Rome 1969–)
StPohl SM 2	A. J. Ferrara, *Nanna-Suen's Journey to Nippur* (Rome 1973)
StPohl SM 13	A. Alberti & F. Pomponio, *Pre-Sargonic and Sargonic Texts from Ur Edited in UET 2, Supplement* (Rome 1986)
StPohl SM 16	R. A. di Vito, *Studies in Third Millennium Sumerian and Akkadian Personal Names: The Designation and Conception of the Personal God* (Rome 1993)
StPohl SM 17	G. Cunningham, *'Deliver Me from Evil': Mesopotamian Incantations 2500-1500 BC.* (Rome 1997)
STTI	V. Donbaz & B. R. Foster, *Sargonic Texts from Telloh in the Istanbul Archaeological Museums.* Occasional Publications of the Babylonian Fund 5. American Research Institute in Turkey Monographs 2 (Philadelphia, PA, 1982)

Subartu 2	F. Ismail et al., *Administrative Documents from Tell Beydar (Seasons 1993–1994)*. Subartu 2 (Turnhout 1996) [Subartu2-$X_{\#}$ refers to the sign with corresponding number in the list of unidentified signs, p. 56f.]
Subartu 4/2	M. Lebeau (ed.), *About Subartu: Studies Devoted to Upper Mesopotamia. À propos de Subartu: Études consacrées à la Haute Mésopotamie*, vol. 2, *Culture, Society, Image* (Turnhout 1998)
Subartu 12	L. Milano et al., *Third Millennium Cuneiform Texts from Tell Beydar (Seasons 1996–2002)*. Subartu 12 (Turnhout 2004)
Sumer	*Sumer. A Journal of Archaeology and History in Arab World* (Baghdad 1945–1973); *Sumer. A Journal of Archaeology and History in Iraq* (Baghdad 1973–)
Šulgi A	J. Klein, *Three Šulgi Hymns: Royal Hymns Glorifying King Šulgi of Ur* (Ramat-Gan 1981), 167–217
Šulgi C	G. R. Castellino, *Two Šulgi Hymns (BC)* (Rome 1973), 243–294
Šulgi D	J. Klein, *Three Šulgi Hymns: Royal Hymns Glorifying King Šulgi of Ur* (Ramat-Gan 1981), 50–123
TCABI	F. Pomponio, G. Visicato, A. Westenholz et al., *Le tavolette cuneiformi di Adab delle collezioni della Banca d'Italia*, Vol. 1 (Rome 2006)
TCL 5	H. de Genouillac, *Textes économiques d'Oumma de l'époque d'Our*. Textes cunéiformes du Musée du Louvre. Département des antiquités orientales vol. 5 (Paris 1922)
TCS 3	Å. Sjöberg, E. Bergmann & G. Gragg, *The Collection of Sumerian Temple Hymns and The Kesh Temple Hymn.* Texts from Cuneiform Sources 3 (Locust Valley, NY, 1969). Individual lines are cited as TH followed by line number.
TCTI 1	B. Lafont & F. Yıldız, *Tablettes cunéiformes de Tello au Musée d'Istanbul datant de l'époque de la III*[e] *dynastie d'Ur*, 1 (*ITT* II/1, 617–1038). PIHANS 65 (Leiden 1989)
TCTI 2	B. Lafont & F. Yıldız, *Tablettes cunéiformes de Tello au Musée d'Istanbul datant de l'époque de la III*[e] *dynastie d'Ur*, 2 (*ITT* II/1, 2544–2819, 3158–4342, 4708–4713). PIHANS 77 (Leiden 1996)
TCVBI	F. Pomponio, M. Stol, A. Westenholz et al., *Tavolette cuneiformi di varia provenienza delle collezioni della Banca d'Italia*, Vol. 2 (Rome 2006)
TCVC	A. Archi, F. Pomponio & M. Stol, *Testi cuneiformi di vario contenuto*. Catalogo del Museo Egizio di Torino, serie seconda – collezioni, vol. 9 (Turin 1999)
TH	The Sumerian Temple Hymns, see TCS 3
Tierbilder	W. Heimpel, *Tierbilder in der sumerischen Literatur*. StPohl 2 (Rome 1968)

TIM	Texts in the Iraq Museum Published by the Directorate General of Antiquities, Baghdad (Baghdad, Wiesbaden, etc., 1964–)
TIM 7	D. O. Edzard, *Altbabylonische Rechts- und Wirtschaftsurkunden aus Tell ed-Dēr bei Sippar* (Wiesbaden 1971)
TIM 9	J. J. A. van Dijk, *Cuneiform Texts. Texts of Varying Content.* (Leiden 1976)
Titles	W. W. Hallo, *Early Mesopotamian Royal Titles: A Philologic and Historical Analysis.* AOS 43 (New Haven, CT, 1957)
TMH	Texte und Materialien der Frau Professor Hilprecht Collection of Babylonian Antiquities im Eigentum der Universität Jena (Leipzig, etc., 1932–)
TMH 5	A. Pohl, *Vorsargonische und sargonische Wirtschaftstexte* (Leipzig 1935)
TMH NF 1–2	A. Pohl, *Rechts- und Verwaltungsurkunden der III. Dynastie von Ur.* TMH Neue Folge 1–2 (Leipzig 1937)
Toronto 1	M. Sigrist, Neo-Sumerian Texts from the Royal Ontario Museum 1. *The Administration at Drehem* (Bethesda, MD, 1995)
TRU	L. Legrain, *Les temps des rois d'Ur: Recherches sur la société antique, d'après des textes nouveaux*, 2 vols., (Paris 1912)
TSA	H. de Genouillac, *Tablettes sumériennes archaïques: matériaux pour servir à l'histoire de la société sumérienne* (Paris 1909)
TSŠ	R. Jestin, *Tablettes sumériennes de Šuruppak conservées au musée de Stamboul.* Mémoires de l'Institut français d'archéologie de Stamboul vol. 3, Paris 1937
TSU	H. Limet, *Textes sumériens de la IIIe dynastie d'Ur.* Documents du Proche-Orient ancien: Épigraphie, I (Brussels 1976)
TUT	G. Reisner, *Tempelurkunden aus Telloh.* Königliche Museen zu Berlin: Mittheilungen aus den orientalischen Sammlungen 16 (Berlin 1901)
Tutub	W. Sommerfeld, *Die Texte der Akkade-Zeit. 1. Das Dijala-Gebiet: Tutub.* Imgula 3/1 (Münster 1999)
UE	Ur Excavations. Publications of the Joint Expedition of the British Museum and of the University Museum, University of Pennsylvania, Philadelphia, to Mesopotamia (London & Philadelphia, PA, 1927–)
UE 2	C. L. Woolley et al., *The Royal Cemetery.* 2 vols. (London & Philadelphia, PA, 1934)
UE 3	L. Legrain, *Archaic Seal Impressions* (London &

	Philadelphia, PA, 1936)
UE 10	L. Legrain, *Seal Cylinders* (London & Philadelphia, PA, 1951)
UET	Ur Excavations. Texts. Publications of the Joint Expedition of the British Museum and of the University Museum, University of Pennsylvania, Philadelphia, to Mesopotamia (London 1928–)
UET 1	C. J. Gadd & L. Legrain, *Royal Inscriptions*. 2 vols. (London 1928)
UET 2	E. Burrows, *Archaic Texts* (London 1935). [UET2-# refers to the sign with corresponding number in the sign list, pl. 1–34]
UET 3	L. Legrain, *Business Documents of the Third Dynasty of Ur*, 2 vols. (London 1937 & 1947)
UET 5	H. H. Figulla & W. J. Martin, *Letters and Documents of the Old Babylonian Period* (London 1953)
UET 7	O. R. Gurney, *Middle Babylonian Legal Documents and Other Texts* (London 1974)
UET 8	E. Sollberger, *Royal Inscriptions*. Part 2 (London 1965)
UHF	M. J. Geller, *Forerunners to UDUG-HUL: Sumerian Exorcistic Incantations*. FAOS 12 (Stuttgart 1985)
UNT	H. Waetzoldt, *Untersuchungen zur neusumerischen Textilindustrie*. Studi economici e technologici 1 (Rome 1972)
Urban Mind	P. J. J. Sinclair, G. Nordquist, F. Herschend & C. Isendahl (eds.), *The Urban Mind: Cultural and Environmental Dynamics* (Uppsala 2010)
Urnamma A	E. Flückiger Hawker, OBO 166, 93–182
Urnamma B	E. Flückiger Hawker, OBO 166, 183–203
Urnamma C	E. Flückiger Hawker, OBO 166, 204–227
Urnamma D	E. Flückiger Hawker, OBO 166, 228–259
Urnamma EF	E. Flückiger Hawker, OBO 166, 260–289
Urnamma G	E. Flückiger Hawker, OBO 166, 290–296
USP	B. R. Foster, *Umma in the Sargonic Period.* Memoirs of the Connecticut Academy of Arts and Sciences (Hamden, CT, 1982)
UVB	...er Vorläufiger Bericht über die von (dem Deutschen Archäologischen Institut und der DOG aus Mitteln) der Deutschen Forschungsgemeinschaft in Uruk-Warka unternommenen Ausgrabungen / unternommenen Ausgrabungen in Uruk-Warka (Berlin etc. 1930–)
VE	The Vocabulary of Ebla, see MEE 4
VS	Vorderasiatische Schriftdenkmäler der Königlichen Museen zu Berlin (vols. 1–16, Berlin 1907–1917); Vorderasiatische Schriftdenkmäler der Staatlichen Museen zu Berlin (vols. 17–

, Berlin etc. 1971–)

VS 14	W. Förtsch, *Altbabylonische Wirtschaftstexte aus der Zeit Lugalandas und Urukaginas. Texte 1–195* (Leipzig 1916)
VS 25	J. Marzahn, *Altsumerische Verwaltungstexte aus Girsu/Lagaš* (Berlin 1991)
VS 27	J. Marzahn, *Altsumerische Verwaltungstexte und ein Brief aus Girsu/Lagaš* (Mainz 1996)
WF	A. Deimel, *Wirtschaftstexte aus Fara.* Wissenschaftliche Veröffentlichungen der Deutschen Orient-Gesellschaft 45 (Leipzig 1924)
WO	*Die Welt des Orients.* Wissenschaftliche Beiträge zur Kunde des Morgenlandes (Wuppertal/Göttingen 1947/52–)
YOS	Yale Oriental Series. Babylonian Texts (New Haven, CT, & London 1915–)
YOS 1	A. T. Clay, *Miscellaneous Inscriptions in the Yale Babylonian Collection* (New Haven, CT, & London 1915)
YOS 4	C. E. Keiser, *Selected Temple Documents of the Ur Dynasty* (New Haven, CT, & London 1915)
YOS 9	F. J. Stephens, *Votive and Historical Texts from Babylonia and Assyria* (New Haven, CT, & London 1937)
YOS 13	J. J. Finkelstein, *Late Old Babylonian Documents and Letters* (New Haven, CT, & London 1972)
YOS 15	A. Goetze & B. R. Foster, *Cuneiform Texts from Various Collections* (New Haven, CT, & London 2010)
YOS 18	D. Snell & C. Lager, *Economic Texts from Sumer* (New Haven, CT, & London 1991)
ZA	*Zeitschrift für Assyriologie und Vorderasiatische Archäologie* etc (Berlin, New York 1886–)
ZATU	M. W. Green, H. Nissen et al., *Zeichenliste der archaischen Texte aus Uruk.* ADFU 11 (Berlin 1987) [ZATU# refers to the sign with corresponding number in the sign list]

Technical Abbreviations

Abbreviations of royal names in ED datings of texts etc. mainly follow those used by E. Sollberger, *CIRPL*, and H. Steible ABW, with some additions.

(°#)	In discussions denotes discrete entries e.g. in lists of PNN or exercise texts dating to the period 2800–2200 BCE
(a#)	In discussions denotes estimated number of persons attested as bearing a variant of a certain name during the period 2800–2200 BCE
3H	Excavation no. of the third American expedition to Lagaš
4H	Excavation no. of the fourth American expedition to Lagaš
4N	Excavation no. of the fourth American expedition to Nippur
5N	Excavation no. of the fifth American expedition to Nippur
6N	Excavation no. of the sixth American expedition to Nippur
7N	Excavation no. of the seventh American expedition to Nippur
A	Siglum for tablets in the Asiatic collection of the Oriental Institute of the University of Chicago
Akg.	Akurgal, 2nd ruler of the 1st Lagaš Dynasty, c. 2470 BCE
Akk.	Akkadian
AO	Siglum for tablets and inscribed objects in the collection Antiquités orientales of the Musée du Louvre, Paris
Ashm	Siglum for tablets in the Ashmolean Museum, Oxford
b.	In lists of attestations: brother
BCE	Before the Common Era
BM	Siglum for tablets in the British Museum, London
CDLI P	Photo in database of Cuneiform Digital Library Initiative, http://cdli.ucla.edu
CN	Canal name
CS	Classic Sargonic, c. 2240–2200 BCE
DN(N)	Divine name(s)
Ean.	Eanatum, 3rd ruler of the 1st Lagaš dynasty, c. 2450 BCE
ED I-II	Early Dynastic I-II, c. 2900–2700 BCE
ED IIIa	Early Dynastic IIIa, c. 2700–2550 BCE
ED IIIb	Early Dynastic IIIb, c. 2550–2335 BCE
Edin	Siglum for tablets in the Royal Scottish Museum, Edinburgh
Eig.	Eiginimpae, ruler of Adab, c. 2520 BCE

En. I	Enanatum I, 4th ruler of the 1st Lagaš dynasty, c. 2420 BCE
En. II	Enanatum II, 6th ruler of the 1st Lagaš dynasty, c. 2370 BCE
Enšak.	Enšakušana, ruler of an ED Uruk dynasty, c. 2350 BCE
Ent.	Enmetena, 5th ruler of the 1st Lagaš dynasty, c. 2400 BCE
Enz.	Enentarzi, 7th ruler of the 1st Lagaš Dynasty, c. 2360 BCE
ES	Early Sargonic, c. 2330–2260 BCE
EŞEM	Siglum for tablets in Eski Şark Eserleri Müzesi, Ancient Orient Museum, Istanbul
f.	In lists of attestations: father
ff.	In lists of attestations: grandfather or forefather
FN	Field name
FPN(N)	Female personal name(s)
GN(N)	Geographical name(s)
h.	In lists of attestations: husband
HG	Siglum for tablets in a French private collection, published by H. de Genouillac, *Babyloniaca* 8 (1924), 37–40, pl. III–XII
IM	Siglum for tablets and inscribed objects in the Iraq Museum, Baghdad
L	Siglum for Girsu tablets in the Arkeoloji Müzeleri, Archaeological Museum, Istanbul
LS	Late Sargonic, c. 2200–2150 BCE
Lug.	LugalANda, penultimate ruler of the 1st Lagaš dynasty, c. 2350 BCE
Lukin.	Lugalkigubnišedudu, ruler of an ED Uruk dynasty, c. 2400 BCE
Lukis.	Lugalkisalsi, ruler of an ED Uruk dynasty, c. 2380 BCE
Luzag.	Lugalzagesi, last ruler of the ED Umma-Uruk dynasty, c. 2340 BCE
M(N)	Month (name)
MA	Middle Assyrian
Man.	*Maniśtūśu*, son of *Śarrukēn* of Akkade, c. 2280–2260 BCE.
MB	Middle Babylonian
MMA	Siglum for tablets in the Metropolitan Museum of Art, New York, NY
MPN(N)	Male personal name(s)
MS	Middle Sargonic, c. 2280–2240 BCE
n(n).	In index section, footnote(s)
NBC	Siglum for tablets in the Nies Babylonian Collection, Yale University, New Haven, CT
Ni	Siglum for Nippur tablets in the Arkeoloji Müzeleri, Archaeological Museum, Istanbul
NS.	*Narām*-Su'en, penultimate ruler of the 1st Akkade dynasty, c.

	2260–2220 BCE
NA	Neo-Assyrian
NB	Neo-Babylonian
o.	obverse
obj.	object
OA	Old Assyrian
OAkk	Old Akkadian
OB	Old Babylonian
PN(N)	Personal name(s)
Poss. pron.	Possessive pronoun
PUL	Siglum for tablets in the collections of the Université de Liège
r.	reverse
RBC	Siglum for tablets in the Rosen Babylonian Collection, Yale University, New Haven CT
s.	In lists of attestations: son
Serota	Siglum for tablets in the private collection of Dr. H. Serota, Chicago, IL
ss.	In lists of attestations: grandson or male descendant
subj.	subject
Śk.	*Śarrukēn*, first ruler of the 1st Akkade dynasty, c. 2330–2300 BCE
Śkś.	*Śarkališarrē*, last ruler of the 1st Akkade dynasty, c. 2220–2200 BCE
Š	Siglum for Šuruppag tablets in the Arkeoloji Müzeleri, Archaeological Museum, Istanbul
TM.75.G	Excavation no. of the 1975 Italian expedition to Ebla
TN	Temple name
translit. only	Text published only in transliteration
U	Signature for Ur excavation finds in collections housed in the Iraq Museum, Baghdad, The British Museum, London & the University Museum, Philadelphia, PA
UCLM	Siglum for tablets in the Phoebe A. Hearst Museum of Anthropology, University of California, Berkeley, CA
UGN	UD.GAL.NUN, a divergent, mainly ED IIIa orthographic tradition used for writing certain literary and lexical works
Ukg.	UruKAgina, last ruler of the 1st Lagaš dynasty, c. 2340 BCE
Ur III	Ur III period, c. 2112–2004 BCE
Urn.	Ur-Nanše, founder of the 1st Lagaš dynasty, c. 2500 BCE
Urz.	Urzae, one of the last 5 rulers of an ED Uruk dynasty, c. 2360 BCE
VAT	Siglum for tablets in the Vorderasiatisches Museum, Berlin
w.	In lists of attestations: wife

W	Siglum for tablets in the Carol McDonald Gardner Rare Book Room, St. Louis Public Library, St. Louis, MO
W.	Excavation no. of the German expeditions to Uruk-Warka
Y	Year
YBC	Siglum for tablets in the Yale Babylonian Collection, Yale University, New Haven CT
YN(N)	Year name(s)

1. Introduction

This study is focused primarily on certain name types in the early literate societies in the Mesopotamian cultural area, about 2800–2200 BCE, and the veneration of human and divine patrons in them. Early historic Mesopotamia consisted of city-states, each of which had its social elite and a divine counterpart, tied together with those of other city-states in a political, economic and religious framework. Most written sources were in the Sumerian language, in cuneiform writing.

In the course of the 3rd millennium BCE, power became concentrated in the hands of strong urban elites.[1] The leaders of this process portrayed their position using a language firmly rooted in religious ideals of the times, even though the process was not uniform in all places and at all times. Local and regional strategies differed, and toward the end of the 3rd millennium the divine nature of the ruler had become religious dogma. By this time, territorial state formations had emerged, ruled successively by the Semitic-speaking Akkade dynasty and the last Sumerian-speaking dynasty of Ur III.[2] Although civil authorities like councils of elders or popular assemblies did exist, they would never be as influential in Near Eastern societies as the palace and the autocratic ruler. The idea of a single king, authorized by divine backing, was an enduring concept in Mesopotamian myth as well as politics, though the extent of the king's influence of course varied with time.

Personal names will be shown to offer insight into developments in ideas concerning the interdependence of human and divine rulership. Ancient Mesopotamian names were meaningful and often convey information on aspects of both civic and private life, of prevalent value systems and their relevance to the people. By delimiting and contextualizing the onomastic material[3] and by comparing it to the historic, literary and material output of

---

[1] Such elites most certainly also existed already by the late 4th millennium. I define urban here as indicative of strong ties to central settlements. Elite implies families wealthy and influential enough to be able to procure materials and people for accomplishing organizational, economic, architectural and military feats characteristic of early Mespotamian kingship. See, generally, section 1.6 and Chapter 6, below.

[2] See A. Westenholz & W. Sallaberger, *Annäherungen* 3, for a closer look at these periods.

[3] In the following, some attempts have been made to make the terminology harmonize with that used within the field of onomastic studies. For a discussion of issues concerning terminology adopted here, see T. Witkowski, *Namenforschung*, 288–294.

Mesopotamian civilizations a number of lingering questions surrounding key figures in the political and religious spheres may find their answers.

1.1 The aim of the study

From around 3000 BCE onwards,[4] written documentation provides information on many different aspects of life in the ancient Near East. Names of people and places are abundant. A number of local calendars were in use in which months were named, for instance, after events in the agricultural cycle or locally significant festivals. Certain objects relevant to individuals could also receive names. The onomastic corpora of these peoples contain many thousands of names of individuals, and several hundred names of divinities, locations and dozens of commemorative objects, specific occasions and moments in time. Sumerian names are by far more common at all times in the south during the 3rd millennium BCE. In the north Akkadian names are more frequent. These all carry the potential for shedding light on the history of ideas in the early literate societies.[5] The crucial point for a survey centered on personal names is that, in most cases, ancient Mesopotamian Sumerian and Akkadian names were both comprehensible and meaningful. In the words of I. J. Gelb:

> The first observation that can be made about ancient Near Eastern personal names is that they are generally easy to understand. The reason for this comprehensibility is that they were usually couched in the current language of the person or persons giving the name. The reason for their being couched in the current language of the name-givers was that the latter customarily formed names for their children in order to express a sentiment, a wish, or gratitude, revolving around their progeny or themselves. [6]

---

[4] The approximate dates are hereafter based on the Middle Chronology, following J. A. Brinkman, *apud* A. L. Oppenheim, *Ancient Mesopotamia*, revised ed., Appendix, p. 335–348. The Middle Chronology is in general held to be too high, but is used here for practical reasons since most scholarly material on the 3rd millennium BCE published in the last 30 odd years has used this chronology. For an overview of chronological considerations for dating texts based on tablet shape, layout and appearance of script, see, e.g. M. Maiocchi, CUSAS 13, 5f.

[5] R. A. di Vito, StPohl SM 16, 18; 123. 'Sumerian' and 'Akkadian' in the following, refer to ethno-linguistic entities whose names can be etymologized and explained using the grammar and lexicon of respective language. The Sumerian language is a linguistic isolate. Akkadian, a member of the Semitic language family, is the more problematic of the two. It is taken to include pre–Sargonic Mesopotamian and north Syrian Semitic onomastic material; a division which will certainly not be to everyone's liking. The question on Sumerian versus Akkadian has been problematized several times; in relation to onomastic material aptly by B. Foster, *OrNS* 51 (1982), 297–354.

[6] I. J. Gelb, *Names* 10 (1962), 47.

Not only, then, were names meaningful, but they performed a function beyond the mere identification of an individual: they expressed, to the best of our knowledge, thanksgiving or well-wishes for the name-bearer. The world view of the ancients was inseparably tied to religious beliefs. Thoughts about important personas in human society, and divine actors on a cosmic scale, found outlets in the onomasticon. But having said this, it is difficult to prove whether the literal meaning of names can and should be taken at face value or rather as elaborations on beliefs current in society at the time when specific names were coined. R. di Vito saw the literal meaning of names as virtually meaningless after the time after their coining.[7] A. Westenholz, on the other hand, regarded the distribution of theonyms in Old Akkadian PNN as evidence of sorts against di Vito's rather pessimistic stance,[8] but he also concedes that the literal meaning was "mostly unimportant."[9] It will be argued here that name-givers made use of a culture-specific set of symbols, governed by and reinforcing social and religious order. This means that the literal meaning is at all times subordinate to the symbolic associations the names evoked, but that the underlying concepts of the name had to be both factual and actual. Factual in the sense that the statement contained in the name had to convey a meaning that was in accordance with reality as perceived by the name-giver; and actual in the sense that the meaning was seen as applicable to the name-giving situation.

This study will attempt to uncover key elements in the systems of beliefs surrounding early human and divine lordship in Mesopotamia. Central to this undertaking will be to pinpoint characteristic ideas – religious, socio-economical or political – that were connected with the ruler, or 'king,' when used about humans; and 'lord,' when signifying male divinities. The appellatives normally thought of as roughly corresponding to these modern translations were lugal with the Sumerians,[10] and *śarrum*[11] with the Akkadians.[12] Sumerian names containing lugal are by far more common than

[7] StPohl SM 16, esp. p. 92f. w. fn. 71, and 270–273.

[8] *Annäherungen* 3, 79.

[9] *Six city-State Cultures*, 34f.

[10] See overviews of ED sign shapes in A. Goetze *JCS* 15 (1961), 110; D. O. Edzard, *ZA* 53 (1959), 11; H. J. Nissen, *Königsfriedhof*, pl. 23; and E. A. Braun-Holzinger, *Frühdynastische Beterstatuetten*, 23. For the Sargonic period, see B. R. Foster, *Iraq* 47 (1985), 24.

[11] The system for rendering sibilants in this study is based on the model of W. Sommerfeld, *Tutub*, 26–28. In transliterations, *ś* denotes an etymological value other than *š* < *θ*. Exact correspondences are at times thorny due to inconsistencies in cuneiform orthography. The word *śarrum* is consistently given as such for Sargonic and earlier Akkadian passages, while words which originally featured *ś* may be given with *š* when referring to citation forms of the major dictionaries. For further reading on the early sibilants, see G. Rubio, *The Akkadian Language in its Semitic Context*, 114f.; ibid. *NABU* 2009/66.; R. Hasselbach, *Sargonic Akkadian*, 135–145; and also the introductory remarks by B. Kienast, *FAOS* 8, vii-viii.

[12] For a problematization of this equation depending on the Hebrew, Greek and Latin terms for 'king,' see D. O. Edzard, CRRA 19, 146f.; and W. G. Lambert, JSOTS 270, 54–57.

śarrum-names, both generally speaking and when seen in relation to other name types within the respective linguistic groups. More space will therefore be devoted to discussing them. The central lines of questioning in the present study explore the place and function of these groups of names within the early Sumerian and Akkadian onomasticons:

- What are the meanings behind names that can be understood and which semantic patterns are visible?
- What kinds of relationships existed between personal names containing the appellative lugal and the development of institutionalized kingship on the one hand, and theological notions on the other?

The only way to obtain answers to the above questions is to note the relative distribution over time and space of the relevant names; and from that point, to try and asses how common the lugal- and *śarrum*-names were in relation to other contemporary onomastic material. The work will, by necessity then, also include many observations on onomastics in general, as well as on language development and on the history of early Mesopotamian religion.

It is regrettable that a study of this size can only superficially treat other significant appellatives current in early Mesopotamian name-giving. Important among these are lu_2, en, munus and nin in Sumerian names, and *baʿlum* and *malkum* in Akkadian names. To arrive at a better picture of the relationships between these appellatives and of the early Mesopotamian onomastic traditions, all of the aforementioned appellatives require dedicated and systematic study.[13]

By contextualizing and contrasting Sumerian and Akkadian names of similar kinds of meaning or structure, some conclusions concerning the differences and similarities between the naming traditions of these two languages will be reached. But diachronic study will most likely also show divergences in naming patterns due to local and regional preferences within these linguistic units, and perhaps even differences based on the socio-economic position of name-bearers. It would be vain to believe that all names can meet with an explanation. This is of course not the case. But in collecting and cataloguing names with a common feature, and in subjecting them to analyses and grouping them into categories, even those that are not fully understood at present, are made available for further scrutiny by the scholarly community. Even being able to assign a small percentage with a

---

[13] A systematic study of these other appellatives is not attempted here. See generally the remarks below, sections 1.6.1.2, 2.3.2, 2.4.3, 5.2.2–5.2.3, and 5.3. For many insightful perspectives on early titulature and its application, both in Sumerian and in Akkadian, see G. Marchesi & N. Marchetti, MesCiv 14, especially p. 103–113.

large degree of certainty to one referent or another, be it a divinity or a human referent, would still add to the knowledge about early 3rd millennium naming practice.

A hypothesis for this work is that names containing the appellatives lugal and *śarrum* will demonstrate local differences resulting from the specific political-ideological or theological peculiarities of the area in which the names were current. A larger degree of uniformity will be expected as Mesopotamia entered into an era of territorial states, and perhaps also with the development of a common literary legacy. Since the sources are not evenly distributed over space and time, any conclusions reached have to take this state of affairs into consideration. Another working hypothesis is that the writing of names ought to have differed between different areas in accordance with the level of acquaintance with the language conveyed by the name in that area in general, and by the scribe writing down the name in particular.

The relevant names are subjected to a philological method, consisting of combined structural and semantic analyses, aided by a number of quantitative investigations of orthography and distribution of key lemmas. The quantitative studies are intended as illustrations or overviews of statistic distribution of certain name types and orthographic patterns. Special attention is paid to local and regional differences between the above-mentioned systems of belief, but also to similarities that could be useful in understanding how both divine and human rulership were regarded, explained, and consolidated over a period of about 600 years, between 2800 and 2200 BCE. Comparative materials are used to clarify ideas expressed in the names. The method will be described in greater detail in section 1.3, and in the introduction to Chapter 3.

1.1.1 Theoretical background

I shall assume, based on the general comprehensibility of names and the existence of observable structural and semantic patterns in Mesopotamian naming practices, that names fulfilled a number of functions over and above the identification of an individual. The primary functions were social in that they designated a person and made him or her available for repeated reference by others who came into contact with that person. But since the language of names is to such a large extent of a religious nature, names also served to confirm the cultural order of society.[14] Although little is known about the act of name-giving in early Mesopotamia, anthropological

[14] In structural functionalist terms I believe that society and religion are interrelated, and that the social structures to a great degree determine those of the religious system, see, e.g. G. Cunningham, *Religion & Magic*, 42.

evidence suggests that, even if it was performed within the context of the closest family, it took place with a degree of formality.[15]

Early Mesopotamian personal names can quite easily be interpreted as if they were meant to be favourable for the individuals bearing them.[16] Objects were often given names relating to their function,[17] and many deities bore names relating to their area of responsibilities, and thus, names were part of the essence of that which was designated.[18] As in many traditional cultures, having children who could offer support in old age was equal to having a life insurance. In later Mesopotamian cultures, and elsewhere also, childlessness was regarded as a punishment of the gods,[19] and there is evidence that children ideally were expected to care for the spirits of their deceased parents in the beyond.[20] While systematic evidence of the honouring of deceased ancestors is wanting for large parts of the population, it is at least attested with respect to royal families during the 3rd millennium.[21] A name with good implications for the future would be to the advantage of everybody in the close family and may be considered to be a relatively basic way of influencing one's own future by means of positive verbal association clothed in religious terms.[22] Name-giving in Mesopotamian societies may, in the words of Mary Douglas, be characterized as expressions of devoutly employed high ritualism.[23] That is, there was a belief in traditionally efficacious symbols and formulae to achieve wanted ends, but these were chosen and manipulated to reflect the social contexts in which they were used. This could be done because of the flexibility inherent in the religious

---

15 See the persuasive comparison of nouns and proper names by M. Lambek, *The Anthropology of Names and Naming*, 120–124.

16 For the early periods this is rarely alluded to, but see for instance Izi G 53–56 quoted in *CAD* s.v. *šumu*: mu du_{10}-ga = MU *ṭa-a-bu*, MU nu-du_{10}-ga = MU *la* MIN, 'favourable' and 'unfavourable name,' respectively, following upon mu sig_5-ga = MU *dam-qu*, mu nu-MIN = MU *la* MIN 'good' and 'bad reputation'; and the epithet mu du_{10} $še_{21}$-a 'named with a good name' used by Eanatum and Enanatum I of Lagaš, FAOS 6, 282f. s.v. sa_4 1b.

17 Z. Bahrani, *The Babylonian World*, 168.

18 See K. Radner, *Die Macht des Namens*, 15f. with many references.

19 See for instance M. Stol, *StEb* 8 (1991), 200, for evidence of this view in name-giving.

20 See generally M. Bayliss, *Iraq* 35 (1973), 115–125.

21 See, in general, G. Jonker, *The Topography of Remembrance*.

22 Thus J. Bauer, *WO* 6 (1970–71), 110: "Man mag bedenken, daß man das Unglück nicht nennt, um es nicht herbeizurufen und ihm Dauer zu verleihen."

23 *Natural Symbols*, 28. Instead of a definition which would separate magic from religion, Douglas chose to characterize symbolic attitudes on the basis of low or high concerns "that efficacious symbols be correctly manipulated and that the right words be pronounced in the right order," *loc. cit.* The extreme of the "high ritualist" end of the spectrum can be seen, for instance, in the highly formalized celebrations of the New Year festivities in 1st millennium BCE Babylonia. See also G. Cunningham, StPohl SM 17, 181.

system itself, as it had developed during the course of countless centuries from pre- and protohistoric times.[24]

Names thus performed a social function. The older generations to some extent could partake in shaping their own future destiny, but primarily that of their descendant. Social bonds between members of the family were confirmed. And by invoking power-laden symbols and religious terms, the family could strengthen the efficacy of the positive associations inherent in the name. The word "symbol" is used to denote not only visibly or materially significant representations but also spoken words.[25] Potent imagery could in theory be borrowed from any aspect of human culture.

Different kinds of sources which could inspire name-giving were available to the vast illiterate or modestly educated masses. A comparison may be drawn to the early 2nd millennium, for which a decent body of incantations in the vernacular Babylonian and Assyrian dialects are known; rarely in more than one copy, though often with associated ideas and formulae. The incantations are regarded by some scholars as couched in the oral poetry of their times, hence more accessible and widely known than the scholarly works of a specialized theological nature.[26]

But names were not limited to the immediate family surroundings. Outside of the home names functioned on another level. They associated the name-bearer with the cultural order to which others in his or her linguistic context also belonged. Names by sheer number and relative uniformity strengthened the commonly accepted cultural and religious concepts. They did this without necessarily being limited to a fixed set of religious dogmas, because they stemmed from a personal perspective on the world. Serving as condensed statements of the physical and mental world order, names, simply put, were social and cultural motors in themselves of considerable flexibility. They borrowed, adapted, and reinforced the symbolic associations of society and culture and helped strengthen the bond between the individual and society.

With this said, the concepts underlying symbolic associations merit explanations, or attempts at explanations. One might characterize this search for meaning as divided into two parts: one being an understanding of the cognitive processes underlying the naming in itself, the other those manifested by the symbols used. The attempts at explanation on the other hand depends to a greater extent on comparative material and is constantly at risk of being fundamentally subjective and intuitive, thereby not being

---

[24] See, e.g. M. Douglas, *Purity and Danger*, 5: "The native of any culture naturally thinks of himself as receiving passively his ideas of power and danger in the universe, discounting any minor modifications he himself may have contributed."

[25] C. Renfrew, *The Ancient Mind*, 8.

[26] G. Barjamovic and M. T. Larsen, *AoF* 35 (2008), 150, and fn. 12.

verifiable.[27] That is, interpreters may claim intimate knowledge of the cultural aspects involved, without openly displaying the underpinnings for their interpretations, or they may accept the material at face value. The material is therefore offered here in the form of a thematic discussion which sets out to present the basis for interpretations, and this form may be a platform for a continuous discussion on the feasibility of such a method. Understanding the processes of the minds of the ancients is an objective in itself,[28] but it is equally relevant to explain the expressions resulting from the combinations of potent symbols to understand the significance of names, over and beyond the mental processes they shed light on.

1.1.2 Reasons for the study

For a good century and a half, Mesopotamian kings and their exercise of kingship have been studied in great detail. Several editions of royal inscriptions and numerous works on the political achievements of single rulers or entire dynasties have been edited and made available to the scholarly as well as a wider public.[29] Still, not much is known today about what people outside of the royal courts thought of the human ruler; arguably – since early historic times at least – *the* single most important person in society. The king would often portray his position as one instated by the gods. Images of divine selection, patronship and continuing support are commonplace in royal inscriptions of different kinds. But to what degree would such imagery be accepted and adhered to by his subjects? And from where did ideas associated with the human regent and his unique position in the world originate?

Much of the work that has been done on royal ideology has focused on the Ur III and Neo Assyrian periods and has perhaps been too eager to point out similarities instead of underlining and trying to understand the differences that existed between the kingship of different historical periods.[30] An exception is the recent work of G. Marchesi and N. Marchetti, *Royal Statuary of Early Dynastic Mesopotamia*.[31] Though their book contains many important insights into the political development of early historic Mesopotamian states, and a handy collection of illustrations of inscribed objects – and to which this work to some extent will be indebted – the index of that volume only contains some 20 writings of contemporary lugal-names.

---

[27] C. Renfrew, *The Ancient Mind*, 6.

[28] C. Renfrew, *The Ancient Mind*, 9.

[29] The ones being the most important for the time periods touched upon here are: *SAKI*; *IRSA*; ABW; *SARI* 1; FAOS 7 and the Toronto RIME series.

[30] See the discussion and an overview of research, S. Franke, *Königsinschriften*, 32–35.

[31] Published in 2011.

A weighty argument for directing one's attention to the period before Ur III is the differences between earlier and Ur III kingship. The Ur III state was a full-blown empire-like administrative regime. And although they stood on the shoulders of the kings of Akkade, the Ur III period was characterized by far more peaceful circumstances than the Sargonic period. The nature of Ur III kingship is documented by historical inscriptions, hymns and personal names alike. The rulers were for the most part deified during their own lifetime, something which only exceptionally was the case in earlier periods. In a few words, attitudes surrounding kingship are better understood with regards to the Ur III period. If ideas concerning kingship from earlier periods influenced the Ur III royal and political ideology it is relevant to investigate this earlier material.

Written sources from the 3rd millennium all the way down to the end of the first millennium BCE share a common outlook on the institution of kingship: it was considered the pinnacle of human civilization and a position which more or less separated evolved cultures from less civilized ones. It is not merely a matter of late historians taking an interest in monarchs of old who once wrote history; the ancient records are replete with observations on the nature of kingship and its repercussions in the world of men.[32]

As the historical documentation of ancient Near Eastern monarchy makes such frequent use of religious terminology, and since monarchs themselves at times could aspire to be divine, the socio-political process can hardly be separated from religious thought and speculations. The interplay between the royal and the divine needs to be considered. Reflexes of the prime royal appellatives as they appear in the onomastic material can be used as a point of departure, but a complete separation between statements that primarily concerned deities and those that concerned human regents or other prominent figures in society can probably never be fully undertaken. Many names may indeed have referred equally well to a divinity as to a historical person, all depending on the context surrounding the people involved in the name-giving event; a context which almost always escapes deeper insight. Comparing the onomastic data with other epigraphic and archaeological materials ought reasonably to offer the best basis for obtaining a more complete understanding of the ideology of rulership in 3rd millennium BCE Mesopotamia, especially from the point of view of the subjects.

This survey is to serve as a complement to the sources which have been predominant in the study of early Mesopotamian kingship: the statements of the rulers and their closest kin themselves, paired with economic and archaeological data. While the latter two categories of source materials can

---

32 Among the many works written on the subject, see e.g. E. Cancik-Kirschbaum, *Das geistige Erfassen der Welt im Alten Orient*, 167–190, with many refs.; A. Westenholz, *Annäherungen* 3, 26–28.

more readily be seen as facts on the ground, they are often silent on motivational factors and on the human need for rationalizing the surrounding world, so prominent in religion and arts. Through names one can attempt to display the forces that fuelled a long-term social and ideological process toward centralization of power, and the lasting dominion of political dynasties. The combined corpus of PNN offers a source of information which, having their origin in the context of families and therefore primarily reflecting their primary concerns, to a large extent was devoid of official bias and royal propaganda.[33] That is to say, that it is unlikely that all individuals carrying names celebrating the king had anything to gain from doing so; as it would entail being brought to the king's attention, either by reputation or when meeting with him face to face. In the cases of some prominent officials, however, the situation may have to be interpreted differently.

1.2 Name and appellative

This investigation makes use of general linguistic terms as well as terminology current in Assyriology. It is necessary first to direct attention toward the ancient vocabularies in connection with names. After this, a survey of previous work on Mesopotamian onomastics follows suit. Further notes on the name types to which this study is devoted are found in sections 2.3.3 and 2.4.3.

1.2.1 Names and their contexts of use

The giving of names may rightfully be considered one of the most basic functions of a language.[34] Proper names dealt with in the following denote primarily human subjects. But proper names could equally well denote a place or an event, such as a festival or another delimited time-span. A name differs from referential markers such as pronouns in that the latter imply contextual knowledge of the subject or object.[35]

The Sumerian and Akkadian words for 'name' were mu and *šumum*, respectively.[36] In Sumerian, mu also denoted 'year.'[37] Though the etymology

---

[33] R. di Vito, StPohl SM 16, 18; A. Westenholz, *Six City-State Cultures*, 34.

[34] See for instance H. H. Hock & B. D. Joseph, *Language History, Language Change, and Language Relationship*, 312.

[35] See for instance W. van Langendonck, *Theory and Typology of Proper Names*, 22. This idea ultimately goes back to John Stuart Mill. See for example O. F. Summerell, *Namenforschung*, 370f., section 7.1.

[36] The meaning (male) offspring, MAD 3 274 s.v. ŠM *šumum*; *CAD* Š/3 s.v. *šumu*, 4.; *AHw*, 1275, B, is anachronistic for the Sargonic period. All instances from 3rd millennium curse formulae referred to in the dictionaries are all more likely to mean 'name,' whereas 'offspring' is rendered by the sign nitaḫ/UŠ. The personal names cited do not contradict this.

of that word may be wholly different, it is perhaps no coincidence that, beginning in the late ED period, the Sumerian basis for year reckoning consisted of year formulae recalling an important event from the previous year.[38]

Name and object were viewed as virtually inseparable; qualities inherent in any named object was manifest in the name itself. By extension, inanimate objects were also given names inseparable from their function, something to which scholars ancient and modern have devoted quite some time and effort.[39]

The cuneiform writing system, orthographic developments over time and local fashions meant that a certain name could be written in a variety of ways. The use of Sumerian word signs, logograms, to convey an Akkadian word is commonplace also outside of the onomastic corpus. Here, name or PN refers both to any given writing of a particular name and to the name in an idealized form combining known, morphologically comparable variants into a standard form which for instance would correspond to the lexical lemmas found in the major Assyriological dictionaries. For instance, Akkadian *i*$_3$-*li*$_2$-*be*-*li*$_2$ and *i*$_3$-*li*$_2$-*be*$_6$-*li*$_2$ are considered as local, phonetically conditioned variants of the same name: /*ʾilī-baʿlī*/ 'my god is my lord.' It can be compared with later *ilī-bēlī*. Sometimes the equation of two readings is conjectured and merits further discussion.

Practices known from later periods like the use of ancestral or family names, and of naming animals, are not attested in the periods touched upon here.[40] Hypocoristic forms of PNN, so-called pet names, are attested with some frequency in later Akkadian onomastic traditions. Such names exhibit structural shortening, or have one or more components substituted for a diminutive morpheme, similar to hypocoristica in modern langauges.[41] A name type commonly referred to as Banana-names, which exhibit reduplication of the second syllable,[42] and a few other types, might in certain

---

[37] The variant term mu an-na, which appears in logographic use in later times, appears to be used with no distinguishable difference in meaning. See *CAD* Š/2 s.v. *šattu*; and see H. Hunger, *JAOS* 116 (1996), 777, note to p. 401.

[38] For the earliest YNN, from Nippur, see A. Westenholz, *JCS* 26 (1974), 154–156.

[39] See the discussions of G. Marchesi & N. Marchetti, MesCiv 14, 148 w. fnn. 94–95; and 162, with references. Ancient examples are the learned explanations of the 50 names granted to Marduk in the Babylonian epic *Enūma eliš*.

[40] J. A. Brinkman, *Fs Leichty*, 23–43, contains a summary of studies on 2nd and 1st millennium ancestral names. On the subject of animal names, see G. Farber, *Fs Kraus*, 34–36; and K. Radner, *Die Macht des Namens*, 35–37. R. Harris noted that, in OB Sippar at least, names of bovines were patterned after slave names, *JCS* 29 (1977), fn. 15, p. 51.

[41] L. Bloomfield *Language*, 157, compares, e.g., the English names Tom (from Thomas), Will (< William), Dan (< Daniel) with names adding the diminutive suffix –y/-ie, as in Maggie (< Margaret) or Billy (< William).

[42] Called iterative names by T. J. Meek, HSS 10, xiii w. fn. 27, xiv; *RA* 32 (1935), 51–55.

cases represent structural abbreviations. Some evidence exists for hypocoristica, both in the Sumerian and the Sargonic onomastic corpora.[43]

On a graphic level, names of people, cities, months and commemorative objects were generally written out in one line of a cuneiform text.[44] Two personal names could be written in the same space on a tablet without the persons being identical. Also, filiations such as indications of family ties, profession or a person's place of origin, could be placed in the same line as the person, or in a following line. Year names, in contrast, were originally quite often written over two or more lines, but should still be considered as a single semantic unit.

The present investigation is concerned mostly with the human onomasticon of mid 3rd millennium Mesopotamia. To enhance a line of argument, a year name (YN)[45] or a geographical name (GN),[46] names of months, statues or other commemorative objects may be drawn into discussions.

1.2.2 Previous research on Mesopotamian onomastics

Studies on the ancient Mesopotamian onomasticon have been around for a good century. They represent several different approaches to the study of the ancient Near East, and their central concerns have been either to document the onomastic source material with references to the texts in which they appear, or to treat the names more extensively by means of discussions.

During the first half of the 20th century a number of important studies were published. First out was H. Ranke's *Die Personennamen in den Urkunden der Hammurabidynastie*,[47] which was superseded by J. J. Stamm when the latter published his *Die akkadische Namengebung* in 1939. Stamm's book dealt with the situations in which names were given, and the different types of names were divided into categories based on their semantic contents. His categories were ingeniously devised and his discussions detailed to the point that the precision of a great deal of his conclusions

[43] See below, 2.3.1.1 (Sumerian names), and 2.4.1 (Akkadian names). S. Langdon, *Encyclopedia of Religion and Ethics* Vol. 9, "Names (Sumerian)," 171, denied the existence of hypocoristica in the Sumerian onomastic tradition entirely.

[44] Exceptions to this rule include an early month name found in G. Visicato & A. Westenholz, *Kaskal* 2 (2005), 55–78 no. 9, noted by the authors, p. 60; the celebratory name of Eanatum in the Stele of the Vultures inscription, as well as the name of the latter monument; and some commemorative objects dedicated by UruKAgina of Lagaš. K. Radner, *Die Macht des Namens*, 43–59, lists 105 objects with names from the time of Eanatum onwards.

[45] ED IIIb and ES YNN are discussed in A. Westenholz, *JCS* 26 (1974), 154–156; Sargonic YNN are collected and commented on in RIME 2, 8; 40; 85–87; 182–186; FAOS 7, 49–61.

[46] I. J. Gelb, *JCS* 15 (1961), 40–41 discusses the linguistic situation in early historical Syria from the extant GNN and draws parallels to the situation in Mesopotamia. On the same subject, see E. Lipiński, *Semitic Languages*, 41f.: 3.1; 570: 67.8.

[47] Munich 1902.

remain firm today. Even though the book has now been around for about 70 years, it is still to all intents and purposes a cornerstone of cuneiform onomastic studies. The one drawback was hardly a fault of the author: the book does not contain many Akkadian personal names from the time before 2100 BCE.

The Finnish scholar K. L. Tallqvist published both a volume on Neo-Babylonian personal names, and one on Assyrian names. The latter was an exhaustive survey of the forms of Assyrian names from all periods based on the textual material known by that time.[48] Both works are to be regarded as *Namenbücher* or catalogs, rather than as critical surveys, which does not necessarily detract from their practical use. Tallqvist's readings and interpretations are to some extent in need of revision, but many have withstood the test of time.

The to-date only substantial treatment of Sumerian personal names is H. Limet's *L'anthroponymie sumérienne* from 1968. Based on the onomasticon of 2100–2000 BCE Sumer, Limet surveyed the meanings of Sumerian names and what set them apart from Akkadian ones. To some extent he also drew older material into the discussions, but the main focus was on the Ur III period. Limet's survey pointed to important differences between Sumerian and Akkadian personal names with regards to subject matter, syntax, and the relationship between name-bearer and name-giving situation. For reasons of accessibility, ease of reference, as well as sheer volume, it remains an invaluable addition to early Mesopotamian onomastic research. His influence will be readily noticeable in many of the interpretations presented in the present study.

K. Fenzel (later Abrahamsohn) tackled the problematic personal names of the oldest texts found at Ur in his 1967 unpublished Ph.D. thesis from the University of Innsbruck, "Präsargonische Personennamen aus Ur (UET II)."[49] Fenzel went about organizing the names by assigning a reading order to the component signs, and then attempted translations and subsequent links to the typology set up for Akkadian names by J. J. Stamm where the author saw fit.

In 1972, the revised version of J. J. M. Roberts' 1969 Harvard dissertation was published under the title *The Earliest Semitic Pantheon*. It combined epigraphic and onomastic data in an attempt to define and describe the by then earliest witnesses to a regional Semitic pantheon. Since the Ebla

---

[48] *Neubabylonisches Namensbuch*, Helsinki 1905; *Assyrian Personal Names*, Leipzig 1914.

[49] See M. Schretter & K. Oberhuber, *Zwischen Euphrat und Tigris*, 24 and fn. 61. The thesis was made available to me in electronic form through the kind and helpful assistance of Miss Martina Schmidl, Vienna, and K. V. Zand. Unfortunately I became aware of this thesis only at a late stage in my research and have therefore not been able to assess and include all of the relevant descussions in it. The manuscript is in a poor state and partly illegible due to age.

archives had not been found at that time,[50] their absence is of course regrettable. But it must be said that the early Syrian and Old Akkadian pantheons are not wholly one and the same. The raw data for reconstructing qualities of deities in the Sargonic period, and the ideas surrounding them, largely consists of personal names. Many of the discussions hence relied solely or to a great extent on the onomastic material. Though Roberts received some strong criticism for parts of his conclusions on the personal god, his investigation managed to illustrate what kinds of information the onomastic material of the period can convey when put to systematic use.

A study in the vein of Roberts' is another revised Ph.D. thesis: R. A. di Vito's book on reflexes of the personal god in 3rd millennium Sumerian and Akkadian names.[51] Names were investigated following a classification largely borrowed from Stamm's work. Di Vito contributed a great deal to the understanding of certain names when presenting diagrams with variants, but he still struggled with the format for the presentation of names to illustrate their importance for the development of personal deities and the individual's attachment to his personal faith. Names derived from the ED IIIb Ebla archives are unfortunately sorted under the preceding time period (Fara). In a similar fashion, entries from the ES *Maništūšu* Obelisk (MO), are attributed to the ED IIIb period. Though strictly speaking a considerable part of the names belong in the period before the accession of the Akkade dynasty, they would have added considerably to the Sargonic period attestations in di Vito's tables and overviews. Furthermore, the mainstay of names in his survey were entered from indices to major publications, and hand copies or photographs were consulted primarily to inspect more suspicious writings.[52]

In 2002, M. Krebernik treated the form and contents of the earliest Sumerian onomasticon in an important article.[53] His study centered on exemplifying the earliest name-giving traditions, primarily using names from before the advent of the Akkade dynasty. Each grammatical or topical type was discussed, and several diagrams show the specifics of productive lemmas and their distribution over time and space. Krebernik's study showed the way for further semantic analyses of the earliest Sumerian personal names.

1.2.2.1 Previous studies on PNN containing royal appellatives

As will become apparent during the course of this study, a considerable share of Sumerian PNN incorporated the appellative lugal, and a great deal

[50] 3rd millennium texts only started to pour out of the ground at Ebla during the middle of the 1970's. See P. Matthiae, *The Royal Archives of Ebla*.

[51] *Studies in Third Millennium Sumerian and Akkadian Personal Names. The Designation and Conception of the Personal God.* StPohl SM 16, Rome 1993.

[52] Ibid., 19 with fn. 3. See W. G. Lambert's criticism, *OrNS* 64 (1995), 133.

[53] "Zur Struktur und Geschichte des älteren sumerischen Onomastikons," AOAT 296, 1–74.

of the Akkadian ones incorporated similar terms. In some places or archives, around 25% of the Sumerian names attested could incorporate lugal.[54] This fact in itself warrants closer inspection of this type of onomastic material.

To try and make sense of the corpus of Sumerian lugal-names, D. O. Edzard[55] devised 5 categories which in his view would cover the contents of the names: 1. a wish or (expression of) admiration; 2. the lugal in cultic functions; 3. the lugal in relation to epithets stemming from his activities and responsibilities; 4. the lugal and his residence; and 5. the lugal and the divine world.[56] Edzard in most cases unfortunately did not ascribe specific names to these different categories. In all he treated 15 different lugal-names. Also, the statements contained in names belonging to categories 2, 3 and 5 can often be seen to overlap. However, ample and clear translations of names in his article allows one to follow the intended line of reasoning.

Similarly, A. Westenholz[57] made an independent effort at defining qualities ascribed to the lugal, without paraphrasing Edzard, departing from a list of about 50 lugal-names. Westenholz suggested six different categories for describing the lugal: 1. strength, dominion and lordship; 2. wisdom; 3. justice and protection (communal or individual); 4. kindness and care; 5. provision of fertility in the land; and 6. cultic functions. Compared to Edzard's categories, Westenholz's are more diverse, and they allow for a more precise semantic categorization of lugal-names.

Neither Edzard nor Westenholz suggested that their divisions of the material into categories should be seen as iconic and self-contained semantic units. They were meant to serve merely as illustrative of traits associated with the figure of the lugal in names. Even so, their respective approaches may be used as an outline for discussions of these types of names and naming in general. Combining the categories suggested by the two provides more accuracy in some respects, especially for the large number of neutral statements on qualities attributable to just about any god, or to any decent individual in society. A considerable number of such general statements which revolve around the persona of the lugal, his physique, strength, and positive qualities will be collected under a separate heading 3.1.7 (compare Edzard's 1st category). The headings selected are by no means fool-proof, and objections to subdivisions may rightfully be raised and other solutions envisaged.[58] The categories outlined serve as a structural aid for discussions

---

[54] An overview with diagrams for the most common appellatives doubling as royal titles can be found below, section 5.2.2.

[55] CRRA 19, 141–149.

[56] Ibid., 142: "Voeu et admiration; le lugal en fonction cultuelle; le lugal pourvu de certaines épithètes dérivant de ses activités et responsabilités; le lugal et sa résidence; le lugal et le monde des dieux."

[57] OSP 1, 6–8.

[58] As this work was drawing to a close, M. Krebernik kindly directed my attention to an article by D. Foxvog, Fs. Kilmer, 59-97, in which Foxvog presents his views on late Early

and will be useful for the sake of comparison. Assigning a name to one category rather than another does not preclude that the name might be shown to have affinity with names discussed under other headings.

1.2.2.2 A study of Akkadian kyriophore names

In 2002, M. Hilgert published a survey of Akkadian kyriophore names of the Ur III period, a name type closely related to those investigated here. His study proved that there is much to be gained by comparing statements of names containing the king's given name with contemporary epigraphic material. Hilgert's basic approach was philological, first looking at the lexemes contained in the names, then dividing the names according to typology. The concluding section of Hilgert's study was devoted to the statements of the names in relation to the royal ideology of the times.[59] He formulated three main categories for the division of the statements relating to the ruler: 1. the connection between the ruler and the divine sphere; 2. the ruler and the ruled; and 3. the ruler and dominion.[60] Compared to Edzard's and Westenholz's categories, the categories may have been overly inclusive, but the study benefits from being very clear with regard to the referent of the names.

Four main factors sets Hilgert's work apart from the present investigation. Firstly, the names he studied are composed with the name of the king, not the appellative 'king.' The second point derives from the first that since the names in Hilgert's study all contain the ruler's given name there is no possible confusion as to whom the names refer to. Thirdly, all Ur III kings except the founder of the dynasty were deified during their lifetime. Finally, the names central to Hilgert's study are all in Akkadian, but this does not detract from its value in respect to the present study.

1.3 Method

This work applies a philological method to the material, using, as far as possible, a hermeneutical approach which limits the basis for comparison to those Near Eastern cultures who wrote using Sumero-Akkadian cuneiform. Chapter 3 consists of a semantic analysis of the personal names relevant to the survey. Sumerian and Akkadian names are considered separately,

---

Dynastic name-giving. It will be seen that his approach of delimiting semantic categories and assigning names to these is in some respects similar to the approach of the present thesis. In other areas, I follow a completely different path than that chosen by Foxvog.

[59] JBVO 5, 39–76. Compare also ibid., Imgula 5, 424f. fn. 52 (Amar-Su'en); 456 w. fn. 50 (*Ibbi*-Su'en); 488–490 (*Šu*-Su'en).

[60] Ibid., 72: "Die Anbindung des Herrschers an die Sphäre des Göttlichen"; "Herrscher und Beherrschte(s)"; "Herrscher und Herrschaft."

meriting different subsections for each language. The level of transparency and the existence of parallels has influenced the treatment of individual names.

Names are divided under nine main headings, devised much along the lines of Westenholz and Edzard, as recounted above, in the previous section. An overview in tabulary format presents the distribution of the number of bearers of names pertaining to each semantic group, across different time periods and across different archival centers. Most of the nine categories concur with functions of the lugal and *śarrum* in royal inscriptions and other source types, but can sometimes equally be ascribed to divinities in religious contexts. The problem of assigning a referent to the appellative; to decide whether the name refers to a human by using a royal title, or to a god, using an epithet, is definitely the main crux of this survey. Different scholars agree that the best procedure for this type of survey consists of establishing existing parallel name forms. The task would then be to isolate names that do not have counterparts with theophores in place of the appellatives, and see what those names have in common.[61] But this approach is not without flaws either. Regional differences, imperfectly preserved names and developments over time must also be considered. Therefore grouping the names into semantic headings will serve to ensure a higher level of certitude for conclusions proposed.

Chapter 4 consists of a tabulary overview of lexemes found in the names. It is followed by Chapter 5, a discussion with comparisons between the two onomastic corpora.

With this as a point of departure for the remainder of the study, characterizations and patterns of action of the lugal and *śarrum* can be seen in a different and more complete light. More specifically, then, the names are placed within a cultural context described in Chapters 2 and 6, in which both literal meaning and symbolic associations make better sense.

Pregnancy and birth were fraught with risk in ancient times, and the rates of survival for newborns can only be guessed at. The survival of mother and child was of the utmost concern for the closest family and no doubt also for the extended family, and a healthy baby ensured the continuation of the family line. To express hopes, wishes and thanksgiving for receiving an offspring about to receive a name, Mesopotamians quite naturally drew on an imagery related to concepts present in their natural, concrete surroundings. These surroundings were acknowledged as a creation in the hands of a large group of gods, who were also responsible for the upkeep of this world. To these gods was ascribed a level of personal interest in their human subjects.

---

[61] A. Westenholz, OSP 1, 6; G. J. Selz, *OLZ* 85 (1990), 303; R. A. di Vito, StPohl SM 16, 86; G. Marchesi, HANE/S 10, 72f. fnn. 381f. (lugal- and NIN-names respectively); 84f.

Naturally the division of secular societies between a religious and a worldly sphere does not apply to ancient Mesopotamia. Yet in modern terms, in name-giving, the asperations of a social group – the family – are given strength by means of a language often borrowed from the sphere of religion. The relationships between gods were believed to be timeless, the dynamic principles which guided life on earth, and the beings that wielded the power of these principles, were all popular themes in names. The question is: can one ever deduce the meaning of such symbolic language other than on a highly rudimentary semantic level? And further, is it necessary to understand the whole picture to make sense out of the diverse statements contained in names? Is it crucial to possess knowledge about how the statements are connected to a referent and his or her *Sitz im Leben* in order to be able to discuss the contents of names?[62] One may perhaps even be so bold as to turn the question around and address it to the ancient Mesopotamians themselves: how much did *they* understand of certain symbolic statements contained in personal names, given that they were fluent or at least well versed in the vernacular of the language used in the name.[63]

No matter how much a name may have been abbreviated, it would still have been recognized as a name since it appeared in predictable contexts. People at home in a cultural setting in which the words of and by themselves were meaningful would also have been able – to a certain extent – to piece the necessary information together into a coherent message, rendering even an abbreviated name meaningful. And while one may question the theological skills or knowledge about the intricacies of the world of an ordinary person in the street, the spread and longevity of certain name forms disclose that they were popular enough so as to warrant their living on for, in a few extraordinary cases, more than a millennium.[64] The continuity displayed by central features of early Mesopotamian name-giving traditions cannot be stressed enough.

The limits of the material are inherent to the types of sources used. Brevity, things taken for granted in the process of transmission, and damage

[62] A brief discussion of material relevant to the name-giving situation can be found below, Chapter 2.

[63] Here description theory could be helpful in explaining parts of the processes inherent in receiving and making sense of the abbreviated type of information conveyed by names. The theory allows for a holistic use of names and designations, and it is not expected of each and every language user to be familiar with all the specific contexts in which a certain word may occur. It is instead through the general comprehensibility of individual words when contextualized that meaning is acquired. See e.g. F. Collin & F. Guldmann, *Meaning, Use, and Truth*, 55f.

[64] Compare e.g. *be-la-śu-nu* (*baʿlaśunu*) '(he is) their lord,' OIP 104 41 o. viii 16' (ES Sippar), and references to later forms *be-el-šu-nu* (MPN), and *be*$_2$*-lat-su-nu*, and *be-le-su*$_2$*-nu* (FPNN), J. J. Stamm, *Namengebung*, 244 (add also K. Tallqvist, *APN*, 59 *be-let-su-nu*), all '(she is) their (m.pl.) mistress.'

to the writing medium, all in their own way hamper understanding of any type of historic material. In discussing the merits of applying information theory on cuneiform sources, M. Civil concludes that there exist several stages in the passing of information from the point of origin to a recipient. The point of origin represents the authority in need of reporting a given circumstance. An encoder puts the fact into writing. The message is housed on a medium, most often, then, a clay tablet. A decoder interprets the message and draws from it the relevant facts of what has transpired and this is finally transmitted to the recipient of the message. Civil identifies a number of factors at play during the process; among others: the need for a code common to those who put information on or extract information from the medium; economizing with writing space; the necessity that the information transmitted must be new to the recipient, and; pieces of information already known by the recipient may be removed from the message without loss of pertinent information.[65] What is put to the medium, what is written on the tablet, therefore depends on the value of the information.

With the above said in mind, the present work is inclusive but not exhaustive, given the restrictions of time and space. Effort has been spent not only to acquire a workable material from which shortened forms could be compared and reconstructed; but also to benefit future work on related subjects. An alternative approach would have been to limit the material and to supply only one instance of each variant form of a name. This would, however, also limit the possibility to gain an immediate impression of the distribution over time and space of a certain name or its variants.

1.4 Source materials and scope

From the period between c. 2800–2200 BCE, in excess of 20,000 cuneiform texts have been found and published in one form or another; all represent potential sources[66] for the present study. The different text categories in which names are found can be divided into two main groups: originals and copies, each with a few subgroups. The terms refer in the following sections only to the place of the individual source in the textual tradition, not its modern form of publication, photo or hand copy.

---

[65] M. Civil, in *L'archéologie de l'Iraq du début de l'époque néolithique a 333 avant notre ère*, 226f.

[66] German "Quelle." The terminology of source materials follows the discussion of I. Hausner, *Namenforschung*, 294–298, esp. section 2.1. With 'source' is intended a textual witness containing a name of relevance to the investigation. In contrast to 'source,' 'text' implies a cuneiform tablet or monumental inscription, whether containing a name or not.

The categories carry different weight as witnesses to contemporary naming traditions depending on their originality. Some sources reflect a living onomastic tradition, others represent scholarly activities which could preserve names that were outdated by the time they were copied, or names that were formed freely from the scribe's own imagination. In the following sections some notions concerning the written materials, their categorization, find contexts and their treatment are discussed.

1.4.1 Original sources

Around 90% of cuneiform texts from the period once served an administrative purpose, and the absolute majority contain personal names. In some cases only one or a few names; in most cases several. Administrative texts from this period are as a rule unique and exist in only one exemplar. Legal documents and sales contracts make for other types of texts belonging to the original source category.

Commemorative inscriptions exist by the hundreds from the ED through the Sargonic periods. They are mostly unique, though royal inscriptions may be found in more than one exemplar. Some early commemorative inscriptions are only attested in copies made in later periods.[67]

Inscribed cylinder seals are attested from the late ED III period onward. Seals and their sealings are often published separately from texts and even when inscribed are often viewed as archaeological rather than textual objects.[68] For the ED and Sargonic periods this is in fact quite logical as tablets dating to these periods were hardly ever sealed.[69] This may in part account for the absence of seal inscriptions in prosopographic notes on certain individuals.[70] The minute script on seals is often hard to read, which can cause some source-specific problems.

---

[67] Commemorative inscription is used to designate both votive and dedicatory inscriptions. 'Votive' denotes inscribed objects donated to deities or temples by private citizens or royalty on behalf of themselves and sometimes of their family. This is in line with the reasoning of J. A. Brinkman, *Materials and Studies for Kassite History* 1, 56 n. 179. For a different view, see A. K. Grayson, *OrNS* 49 (1980), 156–157 n. 80, who argued that the etymological value of votive would entail an *a priori* vow by the donator. The term dedicatory in contrast refers to inscribed objects donated by individuals for the explicit benefit of someone other than the donor him- or herself.

[68] On this phenomenon and on some of the rewards of integrating textual and archaeological data, see McG. Gibson, *Iraq* 34 (1972), 113–123.

[69] Two exceptions are formed by a pair of documents with legal contents: TMH 5 49, discussed by A. Falkenstein, *AfO* 14 (1941–44), 333–336 and by D. O. Edzard, *SRU* 98; and B. R. Foster, *WO* 13 (1982), 20 no. 7. E. Sollberger, *RA* 60 (1966), 71, is a sealed letter referring to legal affairs, discussed also by D. O. Edzard, as *SRU* no. 95. Another sealed letter was treated by H. Neumann, *AoF* 15 (1988), 209f. Sealed administrative texts include BIN 8 47, 247, 283–285.

[70] A case in point is the omission in the otherwise excellent treatment of ED and Sargonic letters by B. Kienast & K. Volk, FAOS 19. Commenting on the letter Um 4, the authors state

Original sources of the administrative type stem for the most part from archival contexts. Seals were definitely used as administrative tools but could also serve as markers of social status. Commemorative inscriptions most often belong to contexts in connection with temples. The original storage context of sales contracts is less certain.

1.4.2 Scholastic texts

The original sources are in contrast to scholastic texts. Some of these are known in several copies with the same or fairly similar wording. To this category belongs, for example, lists of personal names, some with official titles and GNN interspersed among them.[71] This has been taken to mean that they denoted real persons and thus testify to a living onomasticon, albeit from an earlier period than the time to which the actual tablet dates.[72] Names from such lists are in the following always kept apart from names found in original sources; partly because a precise place and period of origin is difficult to ascertain, and partly since certain names crop up in the same sequence in different lists.

Thematic lists collecting names beginning for instance with a specific sign – acrographic lists – are more dubious in their relation to a living onomastic tradition. They begin to appear in the ED IIIa, and early examples are known from Kiš, Ebla and Nippur.[73] A degree of influence may have been exercised on the compilation principles of such texts by lists of divine names, sometimes containing sections arranged acrographically.[74] These

---

that the sender, *ib-ni*-lugal, besides the letter only appears in one economic document, from Umma. The name of *ib-ni-śarrum* is one of the best publicized non–royal PNN from Sargonic times, as his seal AO 22303 features in numerous publications and is even printed on the cover of some of the most used handbooks of the field: J. N. Postgate's *Early Mesopotamia* and several of the volumes in the Parisian series Littératures anciennes du Proche-Orient.

[71] An overview of the two most important traditions is given by M. Krebernik, AOAT 296, 2–4 w. fn. 9 on p. 4.

[72] It is my impression that the time of origin of the so-called Names and Professions List (NPL, N2 in Krebernik's article cited in the previous footnote), known from Abū Ṣalābīḫ and Ebla is later than a list with examples known from Šuruppag, Nippur, Lagaš and elsewhere in ED IIIa and b period copies (N1 in Krebernik's aforementioned article). I hope to address this and other issues in a forthcoming edition of the list from Šuruppag and elsewhere.

[73] MesCiv 14 pl. 23, 3: H+Y is a badly damaged ED IIIa Kiš tablet; the remaining lines all contain names beginning with lugal. MEE 3 59 is a tablet with six cols. of writing on the obv. and three on the rev. The first half of the obv. consists of one col. each of lines beginning with UD, lugal and *śar*, respectively. The rest is a practical vocabulary or the like. MEE 3 67 likewise collects personal names, six of which begin with lugal. Two ED IIIb texts from Nippur, TMH 5 172 consists of two practically identical columns listing names beginning with ur. TMH 5 173 collects ur- and me-names written in UGN orthograhy in one column and in normal orthography in the other. A Sargonic prism edited by W. G. Lambert, *Gs Sachs*, 251–259, lists names beginning with nin. CUSAS 13 188 is a CS text listing 3 lugal-names.

[74] See, e.g. *SF* 1 r. iv (end) and v. Though badly broken, the remains show DNN composed with lugal grouped together.

texts may be termed copies regardless of their origin in time and place and regardless of whether they have been recovered in one exemplar or several. Names recovered exclusively from scholastic texts are always specifically marked as such, and they are in the following consistently dated to the period in which the actual tablet was made and written, and not to the time in which the text may have been composed.

1.4.3 Treatment of sources and collection of data

The names are all assembled from browsing through published texts; they have not been culled from indices. For ED IIIb Girsu texts, the posthumously published *Namenbuch* of V. V. Struve was utilized,[75] but the names were consistently checked against the original publications, and additional forms not given by Struve have been added. Furthermore, the overviews in the form of transliterations by H. de Genouillac,[76] have not been used. When available, photographs have been preferred to hand copies.[77] Necessity has dictated that names from some key texts and areas only published in transliteration be incorporated. These are always clearly stated to be from transliterations, but insofar as they conform to other attested writings, they are rarely awarded less importance than names from sources published in photograph, so *caveat lector*.

The primary database consists of roughly 5800 name entries. Of these, about 5400 date to before the Ur III period, the rest is primarily made up of OB PNN list entries. More than 50% of the total number of names have been checked against photographs, the rest were mostly entered from hand copies. From this data, around 750 different writings of ED and Sargonic names containing the appellative lugal were extracted; the figure for names composed with different forms of *śarrum* amounts to about 90. Sumerian names in discussions are supplemented by names containing other appellatives, such as en and nin. Akkadian *śarrum*-names benefit greatly from comparison with the appellative *baʿlum*,[78] which was also intimately

[75] *Onomastika rannedinastičeskogo Lagaša*, Moscow 1984. A welcome update promising to supersede this scarce work will be published shortly by T. E. Balke.

[76] See ITT 2/2, 1–53; and ITT 5, 31–39.

[77] Thanks are due to A. Westenholz and W. Sommerfeld for granting me access to their collections of photographs of both published and unpublished texts. To Westenholz I also owe thanks for supplying me with photographs of hundreds of texts housed in the collections of Cornell University, Ithaca, N.Y., and edited by him among many others in the series CUSAS, under the auspices of D. I. Owen. The extensive number of photographs in the CDLI database have furthermore been helpful for collating many texts published in hand copies alone.

[78] It has been decided upon to render the word as *baʿlum* to indicate the original stem of the noun, derived from the verb *bêlum* (**bʿl*). The raising of /a/ to /e/ in the environment of syllable-final /ʿ/, with subsequent lengthening of the preceding vowel, is not consistently carried out in Sargonic orthography. See R. Hasselbach, *Sargonic Akkadian*, 84f. An overview of the different views on the 3rd millennium usage of BE in *baʿlum*-names is J.

associated with control and rule. The parallels will be discussed wherever convenient to establish more firmly the many problematic interpretations offered in this survey. Some statistics for the distribution of the above-mentioned appellatives can be seen below in section 5.2.2.

No systematic attempt has been made to survey other language families in the Near East.[79] Identifying foreigners in cuneiform texts is not always difficult, as people are often qualified by an ethnonym or provided with a remark in the form of a geographical name. Surely, the figure of the ruler ought to have been venerated also in adjacent cultures, and equally likely, divine beings would have been described in terms similar to those used in Mesopotamia. Usage of royal titles and epithets in personal names outside of the Sumerian and Semitic cultures treated here is therefore to be expected.

A full set of references is not given for rulers with names composed with the royal appellatives. Therefore, all known instances of, e.g., the name *Śarrukēn*, is not covered by the lists of attestations. All known variant writings of the names are, however, entered in these lists.

When citing or referring to names, units in ration lists or measuring units appearing in the same line of text are as a rule not written out; neither are *Personenkeilen* or similar scribal remarks.

For the semantic analysis, historical, votive, dedicatory and literary texts are drawn into the discussions and they are used to shed light on motifs incorporated in the names and on other aspects worthy of notice in early Mesopotamian royal ideology.[80] Sign values have been assigned largely following the BCE system.[81] In cases where a 1st millennium sign originally represented two or more 3rd millennium signs, the reading is often completed by a reference to an inventory number in a specialised 3rd millennium sign list. In the case of ligatures, parentheses enclose component parts.

Keetman, *NABU* 2007/25. An important contribution to understanding the logic behind the choice of BE for */baʿ/* was made by J. Krecher, *Gs Kutscher*, 107–118, esp. p. 113–115.

[79] R. Zadok has, for instance, pointed out the existence of names composed with the Elamite word *sunki-* 'king,' in the 1st millennium BCE, *StEL* 8 (1991), 232 and 234.

[80] The ED IIIa literary corpus has been described and commented on by M. Krebernik, *Annäherungen* 1, 317–325. The more modest body of ED IIIb literary texts is outlined by J. Bauer, *Annäherungen* 1, 516–518 and n. 106 on p. 516.

[81] For BCE (Borger, Civil, Ellermeier), see R. Borger, *Mesopotamisches Zeichenlexikon*, vi; 464–466, with notes on the development of this system. Exceptions are formed when discussing Uruk III PNN, which uses values common within the study of these texts; and in the case of UGN texts. For the latter I follow the system of K. V. Zand, with the proposed reading of an UGN value in ordinary characters, and with the actual sign(s) written in parenthesis below the line, eg. lugal$_{(PA.NUN)}$.

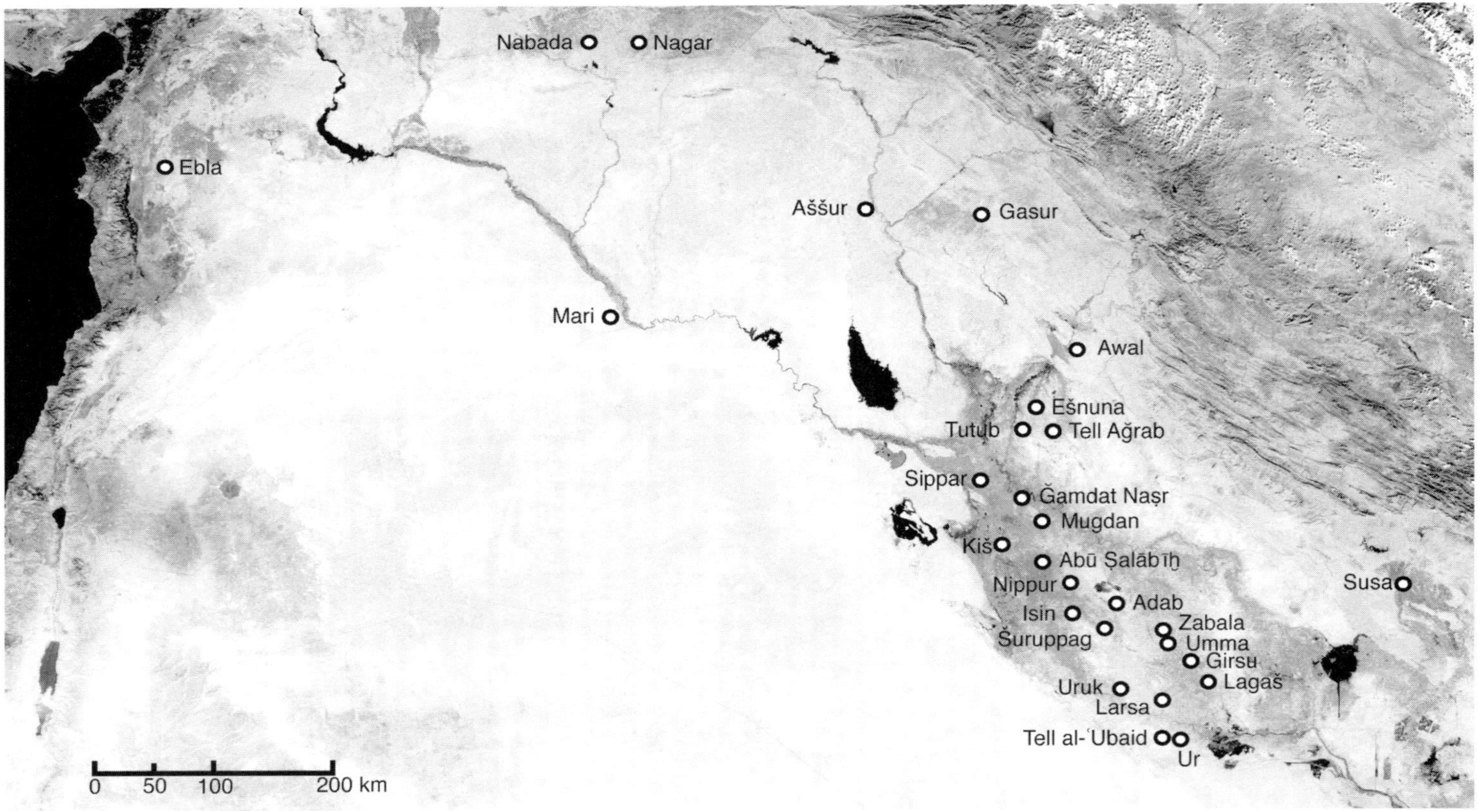

Fig. 1: Map of cities with archives in Mesopotamia and the Near East, c. 2800–2200 BCE

1.5 Early Mesopotamian cities

A comprehensive overview of text finds from the period between 2800 and 2200 BCE is still lacking and this is hardly the place to attempt one. It is still worthwhile to devote some space to discussing finds of provenanced texts used throughout this survey.[82] The discussions begin according to a rough chronological order, and then follow the rivers from the south to the north and northwest. But first, a look back in time to the periods preceding the ED phase of Mesopotamian history may serve to put the text finds from the third millennium into a temporal perspective.

Precursors of cuneiform texts which record the Sumerian and Akkadian languages are represented by various administrative devices. The ubiquitous cylinder seals, trademarks as they are for the emergent bureaucracy of larger Mesopotamia, came to serve several purposes over the millennia in which they were used. The bureaucratic purpose was only one, but at that, probably one of the earliest usages. In combination with tokens imprinted on, and enclosed in, spherical clay balls, or bullae, they could convey information as to the amount and type of goods transmitted from one place to another, or from one part of a bureaucratic entity to another part. Other important material is made up by early tablets containing only numerical annotations.[83]

German expeditions to the site of Uruk (al-Warkā) have extracted the most comprehensive find of texts from the Uruk IV and III periods, c. 3200–2900 BCE. In all, Uruk has yielded around 5400 texts and fragments from these formative stages of the development of writing. About 90 percent of these were found in the Eanna district. Other sites, from the Diyālā on the northeastern rim of the floodplain down to cities in the south-central part of the floodplain have also produced troves of early documents. The site of Ǧamdat Naṣr produced a few hundred tablets dating to the Uruk III period, in part during illicit, in part during controlled excavations in the mid 1920's.[84] But many texts from the late Uruk period are not attributable to a specific location as they were not found during controlled excavations.[85] The majority of texts dating to the Uruk IV and III phases belong to the bureaucratic departments of large-scale households. A smaller portion – less than 15 percent – belongs to the sphere of education or science, like sign lists and texts commonly known as lexical lists.[86]

---

[82] The renderings of modern GNN in the main follow the conventions of the Tübinger Atlas des Vorderen Orients, Sonderforschungsbereich 19, poster no. B II 7, prepared by U. Finkbeiner, W. Röllig and T. Mallmann, under the auspices of W. Denk.

[83] D. Schmandt-Besserat, *Before Writing*, passim; R. K. Englund, *Annäherungen* 1, 17; 42–56.

[84] See especially the texts edited in MSVO 1.

[85] See in general R. K. Englund, *Annäherungen* 1, 24–32. A few hundred such texts were published by S. Monaco, CUSAS 1.

[86] R. K. Englund, *Annäherungen* 1, 17.

In Susa (Šūš) on the Iranian highland plateau another early form of script, Proto-Elamite, developed around 3000 BCE. It was used for administrative purposes, similar to the Mesopotamian script. So far no examples of sign lists or lexical texts exist. During the Uruk period Susa had intimate connections with southern Mesopotamia. Proto-Elamite was certainly inspired by the Uruk period script, but most likely it represents an indigenous development.[87] After a couple of hundred years, this writing system went out of use,[88] and to this day it remains largely undeciphered.

The largest text find from the ED I-II period[89] comes from Ur (Tell al-Muqayyar) in the far south end of the Mesopotamian floodplain. Over the course of five seasons of digging, in layers beneath the so-called Royal Cemetery excavator Sir C. L. Woolley and his team uncovered about 330 archaic-looking tablets and fragments.[90] All these texts were located in a secondary context. Only a handful of texts served other purposes than administrative ones. In layers above the Royal Cemetery excavators came across another batch of tablets: about 50 texts dating to the late ED IIIb and Early Sargonic periods.[91] Important are the inscribed seals – some associated with interments – and large amounts of sealings found in Ur.[92] Other small lots of tablets,[93] and deposits of inscribed votive objects were also found at Ur, and at nearby Tell al-ʿUbaid (ancient Nutur?).[94]

A much smaller number of economic tablets from the ED I-II through the ED IIIb periods were found by the German excavators at Uruk: about 30 pieces; hardly what one would expect given the previous and later political significance of the city of Uruk.[95] A few ED II and IIIa land sale documents

---

[87] T. Potts, *Mesopotamia and the East*, 53–86, especially p. 74f.

[88] The later linear Elamite used mainly for royal inscriptions is not related, save for some graphic similarities, to the earlier Proto-Elamite, with which it is often lumped together. Outside the topic of this survey, it is still important to remember that with deciphering might come the benefit of identifying proper names, see, e.g., F. Vallat, *World Archaeology* 17 (1985–86), 338f.; J. Dahl, *CDLJ* 2005:3, 14: §5.5.

[89] Instead of discarding entirely the term ED II, which lacks general applicability to material culture, I have subsumed it under a collective label ED I-II. For a discussion of the ED II in general, and the basis for its disappearance, see D. R. Frayne, *JCSMS* 4 (2009), 38f.

[90] E. Burrows, UET 2, 1. A number of texts found in these surveys and published among the archaic texts belong, in fact, to the ED IIIa period.

[91] E. Burrows, UET 2, 1. The texts were published in hand copies in the supplement of the volume. A. Alberti & F. Pomponio subsequently treated them in StPohl SM 13.

[92] Primarily published by L. Legrain, UE 3 and UE 10.

[93] For instance those edited by M. Civil, *AulaOr* 6 (1988), 105–106; in part reedited with important additions by G. Visicato & A. Westenholz, *Kaskal* 2 (2005), 55–78. Some 30 further texts await publication by the same authors.

[94] E. Sollberger, *Iraq* 22 (1960), 69–89 collected references to such texts from Ur and al-ʿUbaid in general, including seal inscriptions. The identification of the latter site with ancient Nutur was suggested by P. Steinkeller, *ASJ* 17 (1995), 278–281.

[95] Published in part in A. Falkenstein, *ATU*, pl. 63f.; and by M. W. Green, *ZA* 72 (1982), 163–177. Add also UVB 10 pl. 26 no. 10; UVB 16 pl. 33 (W. 19412,2, literary); UVB 25 pl. 27a.

and a literary text were also either found at the site, or may be attributed an Uruk provenience on other grounds.[96]

Texts from the ED IIIa period are best attested from Šuruppag (Fāra), where also a handful of tablets from an earlier stage of writing were found. Most of the Šuruppag texts served administrative purposes,[97] but a healthy part is made up of scholastic texts, and a considerable number make up witnessed contracts. German and American excavators led by the Deutsche Orient-Gesellschaft (DOG) and the University of Philadelphia respectively, succeeded in unearthing more than a thousand tablets and fragments at the site. The findspots of the German excavation are known for some tablets, and have been surmised for groups of tablets depending on their proposed original archival context.[98] A catalog lists at least 925 entries which can safely be attributed to the DOG excavations. At the division of the finds, most tablets went to Istanbul, while the DOG deposited their share of texts in Berlin.[99] The Philadelphia expedition found over a hundred texts, most in secondary context.[100] Further texts from Šuruppag have surfaced by means of both legitimate excavations and through the antiquities market.[101]

A site which has brought to light more literary works than administrative tablets is Abū Ṣalābīḫ, situated in the northern half of the Babylonian floodplain. The ancient name of the city remains unknown. American and British-led expeditions have each uncovered important textual finds, adding up to a total of more than 500 tablets and fragments.[102] Most of the texts unearthed came from a single architectural unit which ought to have served some official administrative purposes. Excavators speculated whether the building was connected to a temple complex, but no sanctuary was ever identified.[103] The date of the texts is marginally later than those from

---

96 See M. Krebernik, *Annäherungen*, 376f., for an overview.

97 See D. O. Edzard, OLA 5, 153–169.

98 M. Krebernik, *Annäherungen* 1, Faltkarte 2, offers a map of the site with an overview of the areas excavated by the German and American expeditions.

99 243 texts in all were published by A. Deimel in his three volumes on Fara/Šuruppag, LAK (2), *SF* (86) and *WF* (155), which make up the majority of the texts in Berlin. The Istanbul Šuruppag texts have received less complete treatment. 301 texts and fragments were published by R. R. Jestin in his *TSŠ* and *NTSŠ*. A complete edition of all Šuruppag texts from the DOG excavations is foreseen from the hands of H. Steible and M. Krebernik. For an overview of the circumstances surrounding the textual finds of the German expedition, see M. Krebernik, *Annäherungen* 1, 245f. w. fn. 89, p. 246; and ibid. *NABU* 2006/15.

100 The texts were edited in *FTUM*. Only three tablets postdate the ED period.

101 For an annotated list, see M. Krebernik, *Annäherungen* 1, 372–377. Add the texts edited by M. Molina & H. Sanchiz, *StEL* 24 (2007), 1–15, nos. 1 &2; G. Visicato & A. Westenholz, *Fs Cagni*, 1107–1133; and *CUSAS* 11, nos. 341–346; 357–369.

102 Published by R. D. Biggs, *IAS* (texts excavated in 1963 and 1965); R. D. Biggs & J. N. Postgate, *Iraq* 40 (1978), 101–117 (texts excavated in 1975). Tablets found during later seasons await publication by J. N. Postgate and M. Krebernik.

103 D. P. Hansen, in R. D. Biggs OIP 99, 18; J. N. Postgate *BCSMS* 14 (1987), 21. M. Krebernik, *Annäherungen* 1, 255f., provides maps of the excavations and the tell itself.

Šuruppag, but still with a firm date in the ED IIIa.[104] Abū Ṣalābīḫ was largely abandoned after Early Dynastic times and would not become resettled to any larger extent.[105]

The single most comprehensive collection of ED IIIb texts has come from the southeastern city-state of Lagaš. Many thousands of tablets were found by French excavators during their 20 campaigns in Girsu (Tellō).[106] More were dug up after the death of the leader of the first set of excavations, M. de Sarzec, by eagerly enterprising locals. These people later either sold the tablets to the French,[107] or saw them dispersed via the antiquities market networks to end up in collections throughout the world.[108] Eight texts dating to the transition between the ED IIIa and IIIb periods found at Tell K mark the oldest administrative texts from Girsu.[109] Although the exact find spots of the illicitly excavated tablets are lost, prosopographical links to tablets excavated by the French make for a secure identification with Girsu. Important and sizeable finds of Sargonic,[110] Lagaš II and Ur III texts were also made at the site.

At the political capital of Lagaš (Tulūl al-Hibāʾ), American excavators performing four seasons of excavations in the 1970's found further administrative and monumental texts from the ED IIIb;[111] but the numbers are dwarfed by the comparative mass of documents from Girsu. Royal inscriptions from different sites in the Lagaš state make for the largest corpus of such inscriptions from ED Mesopotamia.[112]

Bordering on the Lagaš state to the northwest was Umma (Tell Ǧūḫa), with its satellite Zabala (Buzaiḫ). The two sites have seen only little in the

---

[104] M. Krebernik, *Annäherungen* 1, 257–259.

[105] D. P. Hansen, in R. D. Biggs, OIP 99, 5. There are, however, some indications of settlement in the Sargonic period, H. Crawford, *Sumer and the Sumerians*, 38f.

[106] H. de Genouillac mentions the princely figure of 70.000 tablets and fragments in his introduction to ITT 5, i, most of which belong to the Ur III period. For an overview of the findspots of the ED IIIb period tablets, see R. Opificius, *RlA* 3 (1957–71), "Girsu. B", fig. 1, p. 391. A. Parrot, *Tello*, is a summary of the French excavations.

[107] See for example F. Thureau-Dangin, *RTC*, ii (deuxième série): nos. 19; 24–27; 29–75

[108] See the overview of Girsu texts in worldwide collections, J. Bauer, *AWL*, note 27 p. 40–42. Add to that list texts in the Free Library of Philadelphia, edited in MVN 3. Some of the British Museum texts mentioned by Bauer were edited in CT 50, nos. 26–46 (ED IIIb texts); 49–188 (CS texts). The remaining ED IIIb texts in the Staatlichen Museum zu Berlin were mainly edited in VS 25 and 27. See in general J. Marzahn, VS 27, 5.

[109] A. Parrot, *Tello*, 63, and fig. 15 (upper part) facing page 63, findspot marked as no. 15. The texts were edited by F. Thureau-Dangin, *RTC* 1–8.

[110] B. R. Foster, Mesopotamia 9, 17–19 gives an overview of Sargonic texts from Girsu and a proposed archival context.

[111] G. J. Selz, *Untersuchungen*, 4 w. fn. 20, with previous literature. R. D. Biggs, BiMes 3 contains text finds from the first two seasons; texts from the third and fourth seasons were published by V. E. Crawford, *Iraq* 36 (1974), 29–35; *JCS* 29 (1977), 189–222.

[112] Assembled by E. Sollberger, *CIRPL*; with additions in H. Steible ABW vol. 1.

way of systematic excavations,[113] though texts dug up from the mounds by illicit diggers have almost incessantly managed to find their way onto the antiquities market since the beginning of the 20th century.[114] Texts found outside of controlled circumstances bring their own sets of problems. However, Umma-Zabala texts from the ED IIIb can be identified due to palaeographic peculiarities, i.e. sign shapes. Sargonic texts from Umma, furthermore, are sometimes provided with a local dating system, the so-called mu-iti formula, which draws on an earlier local system of dating.[115] Along with prosopographic analyses, Umma texts can be given a fairly certain provenience, although the exact find context is of course unknown. Some of the earlier texts suffer from an apparent lack of consistency in the reading order of signs, which can make analyses, for instance of PNN, difficult at times.[116] Since the 2003 American-led invasion of Iraq, and the subsequent breakdown of Iraqi control over cultural heritage sites, both Umma and Zabala have suffered massive onslaughts of destructive looting parties, leaving the surface of the sites riddled with holes; a fate shared by many ancient sites in southern Iraq.

A considerable amount of texts from the ED III and the latter half of the Sargonic periods comes from Adab (Bismāyā). During excavations in the beginning of the 20th century American excavators found somewhere in the region of 900 texts. Most were of an economic character, but royal inscriptions were also discovered there.[117] 300 texts were brought back to Chicago, while 600 went to Istanbul.[118] The absolute majority of the Sargonic texts belonged to the $ensi_2$'s archive, located in Mound IV, but Mound III also produced tablets.[119] After the first Gulf War, texts from Adab have trickled out onto the antiquities market.[120] As a consequence, the Adab texts now greatly outnumber other textual finds from these periods, like those from Ur and Nippur (Nuffar) and is second only to the mass of

[113] At present, see McG. Gibson, *Science* 299 (March 2003), 1848f., w. refs.; N. A. al-Mutawalli, *Sumer* 54 (2009), 53–82 (in Arabic).

[114] ED Umma and Zabala texts are hard to tell apart. A good overview of the problems is M. A. Powell, *HUCA* 49 (1978), 1–58 with a breakdown of texts into categories on p. 13–18. A fairly complete list of publications and an overview of texts awaiting publication is given by S. Monaco, CUSAS 17, 1f.

[115] The Sargonic Umma archives texts have been treated extensively by B. R. Foster, *USP*. The older dating system is described by M. A. Powell, *HUCA* 49 (1978), 9–13; the younger by B. R. Foster, *USP*, 1–7. See also R. K. Englund, *JESHO* 31 (1988), 144f. fn. 17.

[116] See note by M. A. Powell, *HUCA* 49 (1978), 13f. Powell states that in cases where the order of signs is jumbled, the order of *writing* of the signs in most cases actually follows the expected order and that this is apparent from studying the texts under a magnifying glass.

[117] Most of the Chicago texts were published by D. D. Luckenbill, OIP 14; and Z. Yang, *SIA*.

[118] I. Schrakamp, *BiOr* 65 (2008), 665 w. fn. 19.

[119] Z. Yang, *SIA*, 27–32; I. Schrakamp, *BiOr* 65 (2008), 665.

[120] Publication of these tablets has begun through F. Pomponio, G. Visicato, A. Westenholz et al., *TCABI*; G. Visicato & A. Westenholz, CUSAS 11; M. Maiocchi, CUSAS 13.

documentation stemming from Girsu. In round numbers, about 2500 texts from Adab from the time before the Ur III period are known to exist.[121]

At Nippur, the religious "capital" of Sumer, American expeditions beginning in the late 1800's uncovered many thousands of texts. A few hundred of them belong to the periods before the Ur III dynasty. Economic texts, a few scholarly tablets, and a wealth of royal and commemorative inscriptions from the ED IIIa down through the Sargonic period and onwards are represented in the material.[122] Later American expeditions to Nippur have also produced small numbers of texts from the pre–Ur III portions of the 3rd millennium BCE.[123]

In late MS to CS times, in the southern part of the floodplain, presumably situated between Umma and Lagaš, an agricultural estate headed by a certain Mesag is known from texts that came through the antiquities market. The published part of the archive of Mesag adds up to about 150 known individual texts.[124] The administration of non-landed holdings belonging to this estate was to an extent written in Akkadian.[125] A few other archives of comparatively modest size are known from southern Mesopotamia. Some of these were located inside cities, others outside of them. A couple of these archives have produced documents in Akkadian.[126]

The Akkadian-speaking northern city-states are represented in part by finds from the northern half of the floodplain. British- and American-led expeditions to Kiš (Inġarra and possibly including finds from Tell al-Uḫaimir), to the northwest of Nippur, uncovered texts ranging from the Uruk III period down to the last few centuries BCE.[127] The size and importance of Kiš is in some respects similar to the situation with Uruk further south. Kiš

---

[121] I. Schrakamp, *BiOr* 65 (2008), 665–667 provides much valuable information on the various collections and discusses the secure assigning of at least large parts of the texts to Adab.

[122] Texts have mainly been published in BE 1/1–2, PBS 9, TMH 5. Many of these were republished by A. Westenholz, in *ECTJ*, with some new texts, OSP 1 and OSP 2 (including some which were published in PBS 9). Westenholz's reeditions are often crucial to the readings used in this thesis, although the reference may be to the original publication.

[123] Including texts published in AS 17, OIC 22, OIP 97 and OIP 129.

[124] Brief surveys of the Mesag tablets have been made by F. Pomponio & G. Visicato, *StEL* 17 (2000), 7f., fn. 7; and E. Salgues, *Fs Westenholz*, 253f. fn. 3, including an overview of published texts. For the debated original location of the archive, see B. R. Foster's notes, Mesopotamia 9, 52; *JAOS* 114 (1994), 445; and the dissenting view of P. Steinkeller, MesCiv 4, 8–10.

[125] B. R. Foster, Mesopotamia 9, 52f.

[126] See A. Westenholz, *Annäherungen* 3, 50 w. fn. 167 for a discussion of these archives, and for refs. to secondary literature.

[127] The texts are strewn across a large number of publications, the ones most important for the relevant parts of the third millennium include a few ED texts published in hand copy in EK 4 and OECT 7, of which a few were republished in *AAICAB* 1/1–2; and a sizeable number of Sargonic texts published in MAD 5. Texts from the Uruk III period have been published as MSVO 1 nos. 205, 207, 224 and 241. An edition by A. Westenholz of the remaining ED texts from Kiš, including some previously published, is in preparation.

must have been a teeming center with respect to both politics, production and trade, but the excavated textual record is disappointingly meager.

Northeast of Kiš lay Mugdan (Umm al-Ǧīr), a site of seemingly little importance to which a group of Classic Sargonic texts dealing with agricultural matters have been attributed.[128]

Sippar (Tell ad-Dēr and Abū Ḥ abba), on the northwest end of the floodplain was a city of great importance. It was located at the junction where trade routes to or from the east met with the Euphrates in an area where several river branches parted with the Euphrates southwards.[129] Like Kiš, Sippar has yielded only a modest number of sources from the 3rd millennium. British excavations during the late 19th century and a subsequent series of 20th century Belgian expeditions have all contributed to the picture of Sippar; though the Old Babylonian and later periods remain infinitely better known than the earliest historic periods. Most of the early textual finds ought to have come from the area of the Ebabbar, the main temple devoted to the cult of the Sun God.[130] The material amounts to about 30 inscribed pieces, such as commemorative inscriptions, contract texts and economic documents.[131]

Situated to the northeast of Sippar, sites in the Diyālā river region have generally been of great help in establishing a chronological sequence for the early 3rd millennium. During six successive years beginning in late 1930, American excavators headed by H. Frankfort carried out work at four different sites in the area of confluence between the Diyālā and the Tigris rivers.[132] The excavations brought more than 300 Akkadian texts belonging to the MS-CS phases to light at three of the four sites: Ešnuna (Tell Asmar),[133] Tutub (Ḫafāǧa),[134] and Tell Ağrab.[135] Clandestine excavations at

---

[128] B. R. Foster, *ASJ* 4 (1982), 7–51. The identification of Mugdan with Umm el-Jīr depends on both archaeological and textual evidence. See Foster's overview, *op. cit.*, 9, and 38, note 7.

[129] C. Woods, *ZA* 95 (2005), 41.

[130] As suggested by A. Westenholz, *Fs Larsen*, 599f. w. fnn. 5 and 6.

[131] For an overview of the 3rd millennium inscribed finds of the early excavations, see C. B. F. Walker & D. Collon, "Hormuzd Rassam's Excavations for the British Museum at Sippar in 1881–1882," in L. de Meyer (ed.), *Tell ed-Dēr* 3, 93–114 and pl. 26–28. Further texts are BE 1/1, pl. VI-VIII; *DP* 1/1 2; and a few texts published in CTMMA 1.

[132] Several volumes of accounts and finds have been published in two of the Chicago Oriental Institute series of publications. Those with the most bearing on the present subject are OIP 44, 53, 58, and 72.

[133] Published in transliteration by I. J. Gelb as MAD 1 1–195.

[134] MAD 1 196–266 (transliteration); reedited by W. Sommerfeld, *Tutub*. A handful of tablets seemingly belong to an earlier phase, i.e. late ED IIIb or ES times, see W. Sommerfeld, *Fs Pettinato*, 288–290, 292.

[135] MAD 1 267–269. A few votive inscriptions were also found during excavations there, for which, see OIP 58, 291 nos. 8–11.

Ešnuna and other mounds in the area have further enriched the picture of the lower Diyālā river basin administration.[136]

Further upstream along the Diyālā lay Awal (Tell as-Sulaima),[137] which was excavated in the late 1970's and early 1980's by Iraqi archaeologists as part of the Ḥamrīn salvage project. During the second and third seasons, archaeologists came across two batches of tablets. The total of texts found amounts to just under four dozen pieces.

In Gasur (renamed Nuzi during the 2nd millennium BCE, modern Yorgan Tepe), in the seasons between 1928 and 1930, American excavators in conjunction with the relatively newly-founded American School of Oriental Research came upon an archive consisting of more than 200 texts, including nine letters, all dating to the CS period.[138] The archive was unfortunately found in a secondary context. Gasur makes for the most northerly situated comprehensive text find from a city under the direct control of the Akkadian central government during CS times.

The Assyrian heartland to the west of Gasur is represented by more than a dozen inscribed objects and tablets found by German excavators in the city of Aššur (Qalʿat aš-Šarqāt) in early March 1912.[139] A few of them consist of scholastic lists of Akkadian personal names and as such they are of great interest for the study of the demographic situation in northern Mesopotamia at the time.[140]

Susa on the Susiana plain to the east of Sumer was for a period under the control of Akkade only later to fall into the hands of a local dynasty.[141] French excavations of the site began in the late 1800's. Besides Sargonic period economic texts,[142] excavators discovered inscribed steles, including

[136] For instance MAD 1 270–336 (Ešnuna). The *OAIC* texts edited by I. J. Gelb are of a probable Diyālā origin. See Gelb's own comments, *op. cit.*, p. 162 and 169–174; and the discussion on a Diyālā provenience of all these texts and more by P. Steinkeller, *OrNS* 51 (1982), 365f.

[137] F. Rasheed, *AIHA*; R. Dsharakian, *ZA* 84 (1994), 1–6; G. Visicato, *JCS* 51 (1999), 17–30. The identification of Awal was made by F. Rasheed on the basis of the number of times the GN Awal is mentioned in the texts from Tell as-Sulaima, *Sumer* 40 (1981), 55f.

[138] R. Dsharakian, ZA 84 (1994), 6–10. The archive was held by the editor of HSS 10, T. J. Meek, to be of ES date, *op. cit.*, ix, but the writing and tablet format of the texts place them quite firmly in a CS timeframe. A recent study of the archive by E. Markina has resulted in a number of joins among the published texts, *Fs Westenholz*, 201–215.

[139] The tablets were found somewhere between the 4th and the 11th of March, judging by the reports of W. Andrae, *MDOG* 48 (1912), 24. See further description of the texts, O. Pedersén, *Archives and Libraries in the City of Assur* 1, 25f., and add OIP 104 pl. 80, no. 45, fragmentary contract on stone. A complete edition of the Aššur tablets by H. Neumann is forthcoming. In the meantime, see Neumann's preliminary study in CRRA 39, 133–138 with many references to previous work.

[140] A few names were incorporated by I. J. Gelb in his MAD 3, and were subsequently included in R. di Vito's StPohl SM 16.

[141] An overview of political and diplomatic connections between Mesopotamia and Elam in the 3rd millennium BCE is given by T. Potts, *Mesopotamia and the East*, 87–142.

[142] Most tablets were published in MDP 14.

the *Maništūšu* Obelisk (MO),[143] *Narām*-Su'en's Victory Stele, and the stele containing the Old Babylonian king *Ḫammurapi*'s famous code of laws, brought to Susa as booty by the Elamite king Šutruk-Naḫḫunte around the middle of the 12th century BCE. Susa represents the eastern limit to the onomastic material treated herein.

West of the Syrian border, Mari (Tell al-Ḥarīrī) has been the subject of continuous excavation since the 1930's.[144] Besides a significant body of commemorative inscriptions on different mediums,[145] a small but important number of administrative texts have been found during excavations there.[146] North of Mari, in the Ḫabūr area lay a few sites which have provided evidence of cuneiform administration. Nagar (Tell Birāk) appears to have been a power centre in the area, and in CS times, it fell under the control of the kings of Akkade.[147] Nabada (Tall Baidar), which was occupied between c. 2900–2100 BCE has yielded in excess of 200 texts, including a literary Sumerian text.[148] Around 40 tablets dating from the latter half of the Sargonic period have been found at Urkeš (Tell Mūzān) to the northeast of Nagar.[149]

Far removed from the southern floodplain, text finds from Ebla (Tell Mardīḫ) in the western half of modern Syria, display a complex palatial bureacracy responsible for an enormous wealth and showing political and economic ties with remote regions, paired with a large scholastic and academic output.[150] Somewhere in the region of 15000 tablets predating the Ur III period were unearthed at Ebla by an Italian expedition, predominantly in the season of 1975.[151]

Further, less comprehensive text finds are known or are believed to have come from a number of further localities like Bad-tibira (Tell al-Madā'in), Isin (Išān al-Baḥrīyāt), Larsa (as-Sankara), Marad (Tell aṣ-Ṣadūm), and

143 The *Maništūšu* Obelisk (MO), of immense importance to the investigation of the earliest Sargonic onomasticon was first edited in MDP 2, but the present work relies on the different order of the sides as established in OIP 104, 116–140.

144 For an overview of excavations, see J.-C. Margueron, *Mari: Métropole de l'Euphrate au IIIe et au début du IIe millénaire av. J.-C.*

145 Key publications include MAM 1, 3 and 4.

146 ED III texts were published and edited by D. Charpin & J.-M. Durand, *MARI* 5 (1987), 65–127; D. Charpin, *MARI* 6 (1990), 245–252.

147 Most of the texts and inscribed objects found at Nagar were edited or reedited in ETB 2.

148 Published in Subartu 2 and 12. The name issue was treated by W. Sallaberger, *NABU* 1998/130. M. Lebeau, *Fs Meyer*, 291–330, provides a summary of the archaeological facts.

149 For a brief overview of Urkeš and its history, see G. Buccellati & M. Kelly-Buccellati, *BA* 60 (1997), 77–96. A few of the texts mentioned by the former, *op. cit.*, 94, were published by L. Milano, SMS 5/1.

150 Ebla texts are mainly published in the ARET and MEE series, with a liberal helping of articles in diverse journals. A helpful tool is G. Conti's *Index of Eblaic Texts (Published or Cited)* from 1992, which is in serious need of an up-to-date complement.

151 Overviews of archival contexts and contents are given by P. Matthiae, CRRA 30, 53–71; ibid., *The Royal Archives of Ebla*; and A. Archi, CRRA 30, 72–86.

Umm al-Ḥafrīyāt. To these must be added a great deal of unprovenanced texts, which have as of yet evaded being assigned a place of origin.

1.6 Historical and ideological background

The basis for a comprehensive view of early Mesopotamian kingship relies on different types of information. Some information can be deduced from texts written with specific purposes in mind, such as historical and commemorative inscriptions, hymns and other literary creations. Other data comes from painstaking work on large and small archives, legal documentation, seal inscriptions and so on. Personal names make for a third type of source material, and it is the kind which will be analyzed and drawn on for the most part of this survey. Here at the onset of the investigation the first two documentary groups are combined to provide an initial framework against which the results of the analytical chapter can be held, and, in the end, combined. A short historical and ideological background picture must first be drawn. This overview serves as an introduction to more in-depth discussions of pertinent facts in Chapter 6.

1.6.1 The Early Dynastic period

The rivers Euphrates and Tigris and their major canals formed a veritable network of life-giving arteries on the Mesopotamian plains on their way to the marshlands of the Gulf delta. Without them, the civilizations of the Sumerian floodplain would never have seen the light of day. The forbidding expanses of desert and steppes would not have been able to sustain human life. But because of these two rivers and their tributaries flowing from the Taurus and Zagros mountain ranges to the north and east, Sumero- Akkadian culture flourished. Over the course of a few millennia, urban locales gradually grew to cultural centers exercising a measure of influence over their immediate surroundings, and over the region at large.[152]

The agrarian-based economy of Mesopotamia was supplemented by horticulture, animal husbandry, fishing, hunting and fowling.[153] The basis for life on the floodplain hinged on the upkeep of canals, major and smaller, which not only offered water for irrigation, but also communication lines navigable by boat.

---

[152] A general overview of environmental issues can be found in O. Pedersén et al., *Urban Mind*, 114–123; 127–132.

[153] J. N. Postgate, *Early Mesopotamia*, 157–172; and H. T. Wright, *The Administration of Rural Production in an Early Mesopotamian Town*, 13–17 give good introductions with key facts.

During the Early Dynastic period the number of large settlements on the floodplain increased, and more people appear to have settled in larger communities. This process reached its apex around the ED III period.[154] It was to some extent related to a general dwindling of the flow of water through the rivers. The concentration of people in urban environments and the steady growth of central settlements presented the burgeoning city-states with a set of managerial problems which had to be addressed with increasingly complex administrative structures. Demographic changes and the strategy for coping with growing numbers of people in cities and towns were addressed by the civic leadership by means of a growing bureaucracy.[155]

Society was hierarchically organized. Economic managerial and administrative offices oversaw a plethora of units involved with production and craftsmanship. Central to the administration were some key architectural and/or economic units and their managers. In ED I-II Ur, two large accounting units were known as AB and e$_2$-gal, though it is not entirely clear how they were distinguished from one another. The former was an earlier invention while the latter represents an innovation, as far as the evidence goes.[156] In slightly later times e$_2$-gal were the households of rulers or local governors, normally translated as "palace."[157] In their hands lay the overarching responsibilities for inter-city cooperation and probably also trade.[158] Over time such units accrued resources in the form of surplus goods, economic wealth and the services of dependent workers who relied on the larger communities for their subsistence, since not all urban dwellers could produce everything needed to sustain themselves.

A central political leadership for the southern floodplain during the earliest part of the 3rd millennium BCE, is not readily identifiable in the sources. Two pieces of evidence may potentially demonstrate an arrangement along political, economical, or religious lines. One is a lexical list of urban centers known from Uruk of around the turn of the 3rd millennium, known also in ED IIIa exemplars. The first four cities listed are Ur, Nippur, Larsa and Uruk. This order corresponds well with a roughly

---

[154] See, e.g., R. McC. Adams, *Heartland of Cities*, 136–141; T. J. Wilkinson *Journal of Archaeological Research* 8 (2000), 242–247.

[155] A detailed overview of these factors can be found with H. J. Nissen, *Grundzüge einer Geschichte der Frühzeit des Vorderen Orients,* 140–182; and G. Visicato, *The Power and the Writing*, 235; 240f. On climatic conditions of the Near East and the eastern Mediterranean area, see M. Finné & K. Holmgren, *Urban Mind*, 46, though it must be noted that the closest points for proxy data were at the head of the Persian Gulf, central Anatolia and the Levant.

[156] A synthesis of the evidence is proposed by W. Sallaberger, *Shepherds*, 31–35.

[157] It is not known exactly when palaces as the architectural base for royalty began to appear in Mesopotamia. For now, see the discussion of G. Marchesi & N. Marchetti, MesCiv 14, 214 w. fn. 15, who cautiously place their appearance in the transition between ED IIIa-b.

[158] G. Visicato in *FTUM*, 121f., with references.

contemporary seal, found rolled over a number of clay tags at the site Ǧamdat Naṣr. On this seal, signs representing a number of important cities appear; the order of the first four are Ur, Larsa, Nippur and Uruk.[159] The order of cities is yet to be satisfactorily explained, but it will be seen that these cities all had important roles to play in the maturing Sumerian kingship, as politically or ideologically important.[160] Variations between the two sources aside, the order of these first entries was hardly coincidental. A number of sealings from Ur, slightly later in time, exhibit greater diversity in organizing the cities.[161]

1.6.1.1 Dynastic seats in the Early Dynastic period

The Sumerian concept of kingship was called nam-lugal, but Sumerian had no specific word for a dynasty. Instead, the type of leadership encompassed by the expression nam-lugal was often pictured as bestowed on an individual basis. In reality, however, already by the turn of ED IIIa-b, a succession of fathers and sons as $ensi_2$ or lugal of a city-state can be observed, notably at Ur, but also in Lagaš.[162] By the end of the 3rd millennium, the idea that nam-lugal rested with a dynasty which was epitomized by the use of the name of their capital had gained influence, a perspective that would continue to influence historiographic works of the early 2nd millennium.[163]

Dynasties of the 3rd millennium would come to be established in Adab, Akšak, Kiš, Lagaš, Mari, Umma, Ur and Uruk.[164] Of these only the latter two were included among the cities on the sealings of the preceding periods. The shifting fortunes of these key players in the power politics on the floodplain can be traced in contemporary and later written sources and their influence was felt also in the neighbouring regions. Nippur, although technically not the seat of a dynasty, would be of utmost importance in the 3rd and 2nd millennia as an ideologically important center.[165] Akšak has never been the subject of excavations and has therefore yielded no texts. Kiš makes for a special case as it was part of a title, lugal Kiš, used by rulers who did not stem from the area. More on this below.

---

159 See brief discussion by R. K. Englund, *Annäherungen* 1, 90–94; and R. J. Matthews, MSVO 2, 34–40. The ED IIIa Šuruppag and Abū Ṣalābīḫ witnesses to the geographical list were treated in part by P. Mander, *OrAnt* 19 (1980), 187–192.

160 A parallel example is furnished by the early OB list of geographical names from Šaduppûm, S. J. Levy, *Sumer* 3 (1947), 50–83. It begins by listing Ur, Nippur, Isin, Uruk and Larsa, cities of key political and ideological importance in contemporary and earlier times.

161 See L. Legrain, UE 3 nos. 390–431, especially no. 429.

162 For a different view, see, e.g. G. J. Selz, *Fs Römer*, 282f., with notes on previous discussions.

163 See e.g. P. Michalowski, *JAOS* 103 (1983), 242f.

164 A detailed overview of most rulers known from the ED and ES periods is given by G. Marchesi & N. Marchetti, MesCiv 14, 118–128, with plenty of references and discussions on individual rulers.

165 See, e.g., G. J. Selz, CRRA 35, 189–225; W. Sallaberger, CDOG 1, 147–168.

1.6.1.2 Leaders of urban communities

In Uruk period texts the highest office is en.[166] According to R. K. Englund, en might have been a manager of any large household, not necessarily a communal leader.[167] Judging by the texts that have been published, the importance of the en to a large extent diminished during the ED I-II period,[168] but echoes of the importance of this office crops up now and then in later times also.[169]

Around ED I-II, the office of lugal appears in documents from the city of Ur.[170] The latter would be the preferred designation of the human ruler in Sumerian society, alongside the title $ensi_2$. The distinction between lugal and $ensi_2$ is not clear, and perhaps it is not even meaningful to separate too strictly between them as they need not have been mutually exclusive.[171] Both en and lugal were also used as designations of deities, primarily in literary texts, but also in the divine and human onomasticon. An epithet $ensi_2$, on the other hand, was only used sporadically in literary texts and the onomasticon.[172]

By ED III, en represented a high clerical office tied to specific deities; and the term would henceforth be associated with such a function, occupied by men or women, depending on the deity.[173] In a few royal inscriptions en was used epithetically by rulers from the city-states of Uruk and Umma where

---

166 Sign ATU383; ZATU134. W. W. Hallo, *Titles*, 3 and fn. 2, noted that the sign EN sometimes appears alone in cases indicating that it should most probably be taken as a title.

167 R. K. Englund, *Annäherungen* 1, 70 and n. 135. The en is sometimes identified as one of three male personae depicted with some regularity in late 4th and early 3rd millennium iconography, see discussion of J.-J. Glassner, StOr 70, 14f.

168 The archaic texts from Ur have yielded one secure instance of the office, UET 2 184 o. ii 4, which may point to the en as responsible for the plowing of the fields listed on the obverse of the tablet. Compare UET 2 227 o. 4'. C. Wilcke's treatment, *Fs Boehmer*, 669–674, of OIP 104 18 ("Le figure aux plumes"), an ED I-II stone tablet from Girsu listing landed property, gives reason to believe that the compound verb nam-en–ak was used to describe divine exercise of authority. Wilcke offered two different interpretations, parts of which offer descriptions of idyllic scenery mixed with building activities and phrases pertaining to the running of an important urban institution.

169 So for instance in an incantation known in exemplars from Ebla and Abū Ṣalābīḫ, where an en takes on a central role in building and maintaining a house or temple. See M. Krebernik, *BFE*, no. 27.

170 E.g. in UET 2 162. See W. Sallaberger, *Shepherds*, 33; H. Steible, *CollAn* 7 (2008), 104 fn. 33. Whereas Steible sees UET 2 205B as referring to a lugal of Lagaš, noted also by E. Burrows, UET 2, 17, I believe that the line on the basis of later parallels represents a PN.

171 M. Powell, *HUCA* 39 (1978), 27–29.

172 One example is the Ur III Ĝirsu FPN nin-$ensi_2$-uru-na 'the queen/lady is the $ensi_2$ of her city,' *TUT* 158 r. iii 7'; D. Foxvog, *ASJ* 18, 88 no. 24 r. iii 23'; abbreviated as nin-$ensi_2$, no doubt referring to the goddess Bau and her sacred precinct Uru-ku_3. See also the OB Keš Temple Hymn, l. 79: ^{d}Šul-pa-e_3-a $ensi_2$-ke_4 nam-en mu-un-⸢x-x⸣ 'Šulpaea the governor [*exercises*] lordhip (there).' A variant has $ensi_2$-gal in place of $ensi_2$-ke_4.

173 P. Steinkeller, *POANE*, 124–129, offers a reconstruction of the early history of en-priestesses along with a valuable set of footnotes containing references to primary sources.

the primary titles otherwise were ensi$_2$ or lugal.[174] And in certain literary compositions, the two titles en and lugal appear in parallelism which give the impression that en, at the time of composition, and in theory at least, was still regarded as a functional correspondence of lugal.[175] Exceptionally, in the Lagaš state the term en was used for a collective of deceased governors, their immediate families, and some other high officials.[176]

The female correspondence to en, lugal and ensi$_2$ was nin, usually 'lady,' but also sometimes to be read ereš 'queen' or nin$_{(9)}$ 'sister.' The title ereš is only rarely attested for named females before the Ur III period.[177] It was often circumscribed, using instead the queen's affiliation to the ruler as an epithet, whether referring to the indigenous queen or to one from outside.[178] This was the case even though the queen sometimes disposed of considerable assets. In the Sargonic period, the title was used unless the queen's name was stated.[179] As with en and lugal, nin was also used to designate goddesses in different text types and in the human onomasticon.[180] However, as the first element in divine names, nin was gender neutral.

---

[174] For Uruk rulers, see discussion of A. Westenholz, *Six City-State Cultures*, 34 w. n. 43; and for Umma, see E. Sollberger, *OrNS* 28 (1959), 339 i 4' en za$_3$ keš$_2$ ^{d}Nin-ur$_4$-ke$_4$ 'the … en of Ninur,' and compare the titles ensi$_2$ and lugal in i 8' and i 10' (Ĝišakidu of Umma).

[175] E.g. in *IAS* 113 o. ii 13: nam$_2$-en$_{(\text{GAL})}$ nam$_2$-lugal$_{(\text{PA.NUN})}$, noted by M. Krebernik, *BFE*, 280 (in a context dealing with Enlil's separation of heaven and earth). The titles are paralleled also in *IAS* 124 o. iv' 8'–10'.

[176] J. Bauer, *AWL*, 470 and 474; J.-J. Glassner, StOr 70, 15. A. C. Cohen, *Death Rituals*, 105, translates en-en-KU.KU as "the lordly ones who are sleeping."

[177] A few women from ED IIIa-b Ur are the only known examples before the Sargonic period, see G. Marchesi, *OrNS* 73 (2004), 175f. Some writings of NIN can be explained as referring to people in the service of, or relations of, the queen: ur-^{d}Dam-gal-nun, ereš, *AAICAB* 1/1 pl. 8 Ashm. 1928-442 o. i 2–3 (ED IIIa Kiš) 'Ur-Damgalnun, (the one of) the queen'; [ur]-ur, dumu lugal-ša$_3$, ereš, TMH 5 3 o. i 5–ii 2 (ED IIIb Nippur) '[Ur]-ur, son of Lugal-ša$_3$, (the one of) the queen'; and šeš ereš, OIP 14 150 r. 6' (CS Adab) 'brother of the queen.' For another interpretation of the Nippur reference, see A. Westenholz, *ECTJ* 13, note to no. 3 ii 2; and T. E. Balke, *Onoma* 32 (1994), 75.

[178] For instance Ajašurmen, wife of Enanatum I of Lagaš, V. E. Crawford, *Iraq* 36 (1974), 34 fig. 15 (3H T14) 2'–5': [aja$_2$]-šurmen(ŠU.ME.EREN), dam en-an-na-tum$_2$, ensi$_2$, [L]agaš$^{\text{ki!(DI)}}$; or *Tašlultum*, wife of *Śarrukēn*, YOS 1 7 2'–4': *taš$_3$-lul-tum*, dam *śar-ru*-gi-, -k(a-ke$_4$). For another example, see G. Marchesi, *OrNS* 73 (2004), 178f.

[179] See for example the texts treated by B. R. Foster, *JANES* 12 (1980), 29–42. The political, economic and possibly religious functions of some of the Old Akkadian queens, have been discussed by F. Weiershäuser, *Die königlichen Frauen der III. Dynastie von Ur*, 195ff.

[180] I am unable to get the point of J. M. Asher-Greve, *NIN* 4 (2006), 8 fn. 28, where she argues that 'queen' should be used instead of the traditional translation of nin as 'lady' when referring to a goddess, merely for the reason that "in non–sexist language "lady" should be replaced whenever possible." If I translate nin as 'lady' in personal names, it is indicative of the level of my understanding of certain personal names and to whom they refer. It is neither intended as an insult to the goddesses who may have been intended by the names, nor to any semantically sensitive peers.

1.6.1.3 Local and regional leadership

The most common expression of control over a geographical area is expressed by means of lugal GN or $ensi_2$ GN, where GN represents the capital of a city-state. The size of these areas may have fluctuated with time, and it is therefore hard at any given time to delimit the exact extent of a ruler's dominion.

Texts from ED IIIa Šuruppag make repeated mention of a group of cities, namely Šuruppag, Uruk, Adab, Nippur, Umma and Lagaš. They may have been headed by a lugal, but it is not entirely clear where this lugal would have resided.[181] G. Marchesi & N. Marchetti have pointed to the likely occurrence of a lugal of Kiš granting land to a subordinate in the south, recorded in a Šuruppag text,[182] which would indicate a form of subordinate role of all the aforementioned cities. Šuruppag has been suggested as the administrative center of the group.[183] At any rate, texts found at Šuruppag listing workers busy at a construction site, KI.UKKIN, and soldiers from the aforementioned cities, indicate that the intentions for these joint operations were of a permanent kind, and involved military activities – but defensive or offensive functions are not necessarily the key reasons for the existence of the site in itself.[184]

Toward the end of the ED IIIb, some rulers of Umma and Uruk made claims to the control of 'the land' lugal kalam-a(k).[185] The title can not have encompassed all Sumerian cities as Lagaš remained independent until the beginning of the Sargonic period,[186] and Adab may have been autonomous until the very last few decades of the ED period.

A few of the earliest known inscriptions, dating to the ED IIIa period, were composed by persons bearing the title lugal Kiš: Mebarasi, Mesilim, and a ruler whose name is unknown, but whose filiation attests to a parent's name Munusušumgal.[187] It is not known with certainty if they all hailed from Kiš. A few ED IIIb rulers of southern city-states who were definitely not

[181] Different perspectives on this group of cities or city-states can be found in T. Jacobsen, *ZA* 52 (1957), 121f. who calls it a "league"; and F. Pomponio & G. Visicato, *EDATŠ*, 14, who refer to it as a "union."

[182] See *NTSŠ* 154 o. i 2: me-nun-si lugal Kiš ĝar aja_2-ki-gal, and the discussion of this line, G. Marchesi & N. Marchetti, MesCiv 14, 101 fn. 38.

[183] So G. Visicato in *FTUM*, 124.

[184] A wealth of information on the textual evidence concerning the activities of this group of cities is found in F. Pomponio & G. Visicato, *EDATŠ*, 10–20.

[185] Enšakušana and Lugalzagesi, see refs. in FAOS 6, 184 s.v. kalam, 2.

[186] A later tradition about the Netherworld made a point of separating between Sumerians, Akkadians, and "a person from Girsu." See A. Cavigneaux & F. al-Rawi, *Iraq* 62 (2000), 2, 7 ll. 23–28.

[187] The dating and internal chronology of these three relies mainly on palaeography, J. S. Cooper, *SARI* 1, 4. Cooper's statement, *op. cit.* 19, note to Ki 2, that lugal-Kiš was a popular PN is probably based on a misreading of piriĝ as kiš, see G. Marchesi & N. Marchetti, MesCiv 14, 100f. fn. 30.

citizens of Kiš in various ways also used the title. As a consequence, the title has been the object of some speculation. T. Jacobsen and J. S. Cooper are among several scholars who have expressed views to the effect that the title lugal Kiš "could be taken by any ruler who claimed hegemony over northern Babylonia,"[188] and that Kiš refers to the city of the same name.[189] According to M. B. Rowton, Kiš is more likely to have represented an expression of a geopolitical nature. Given a foothold in the Kiš area, a military leader would have been in a position to control an economic and military-strategic entrance down to the southern floodplain.[190] Economic documentation from the ED Kiš and Diyālā area is scanty, and little is known of the early political history of that region, so these two sets of theories are not dead certain, though they do offer good suggestions as to why the title was adopted also by rulers further south.[191]

A point which is often overlooked in scholarly literature is the fact that none of the rulers who used the title claimed to be the descendants of a lugal Kiš. And conversely, none of the rulers who mentioned that their father had held nam-lugal Kiš used that same title. In summing up, this kingship of Kiš was different from ED IIIb Sumerian local authority, in that it was seen as an appropriate designation for rulers of different cities, and that it does not seem to have been a hereditary position.

1.6.1.4 Secular vs. religious leadership

To distinguish between religious authorities and civic bureaucracy under a palace is not only difficult, in some places such a distinction was apparently not carried out to any great extent. This, however, is not to say that there could not have existed frictions between the two institutions.

There are a few reasons why the temple and the burgeoning palace economies need not be seen as competitive, but rather as complementary, institutions. First, a brilliant ideological device had probably existed since very early on: the tutelary deity of each urban center was considered the owner of the city or town, its assets and its people. Ownership of cities was expressed by the same word that signified the ruler of the e_2-gal, lugal. Secondly, Sumerian rulers spent a wealth of resources on supporting and enlarging religious structures, thereby undoubtedly strengthening the prestige of religious institutions, while at the same time they made manifest their connections to the divine sphere. In some instances, local rulers could

---

188 J. S. Cooper, *SARI* 1, 18. See also T. Jacobsen, *ZA* 52 (1957), 118.

189 SANE 2/1, 7f. w. fn. 5. Cooper dismisses a suggestion by D. O. Edzard to see Kiš, not as the city, but as representing by extension northern Babylonia.

190 *Fs Kraus*, 318–325.

191 Eanatum of Lagaš stated that he was given nam-lugal of Kiš by the goddess Inana, *CIRPL* Ean. 2. But only after having beaten a coalition consisting of Kiš, Akšak and Mari on the borders of the Lagaš state. More on this below, section 6.4.

be instrumental in assigning cultic staff to temples they had themselves built or restored.[192] In the southeastern floodplain, a handful of rulers are known to have filled priestly or managerial offices linked to temples, prior to, or concurrently with, their acting as $ensi_2$ or lugal. The most famous of these was Lugalzagesi, the last cardinal Sumerian ruler of the Early Dynastic period.[193] Even if this phenomenon should prove to be relevant only for the southeastern part of the Mesopotamian floodplain, the examples show that this area at least, by late ED IIIb allowed for clear links between political offices on the one hand,[194] and managerial temple offices on the other.[195] By late ED IIIb the Girsu ruler UruKAgina seems to have merged the civil and temple households under one office at about the same time as he changed his title from the traditional $ensi_2$ to lugal. This would then not only imply that the two institutions had been regarded as separate entities until that time,[196] but also that they were fundamentally compatible.[197]

This mutually beneficial relationship allowed the Sumerian rulers to define their position as one which was intimately tied to the divine order of the world; epithets could range, for instance, from being engendered by gods through acting on their direct orders, to using titles borrowed from "secular" administration in relation to divinities, underlining the close ties between economy and the religious sphere. This was done without the rulers taking on a divine status in their lifetime, though the associations between the crown and religious concepts clearly were firmly established already by the ED IIIa.

1.6.1.5 Elite funerary cult

The most eye-catching example of elite burials from any time period in Mesopotamia is the burial site in Ur dubbed by its discoverer the Royal Cemetery.[198] It was used as a burial site from late ED IIIa times down into

---

192 As is the case in *CIRPL* Urn. 24 iii 3–6, where a dam ^{d}Nanše is appointed by extispicy. The tradition of instating a princess as high priestess of the Moon God at Ur might also be a practice of the ED III period perpetuated by *Śarrukēn* of Akkade, see A. Westenholz, *Annäherungen* 3, 38 with ref.

193 Lugalzagesi followed in the footsteps of his father U'u, who had been $ensi_2$ of Umma and lu_2-maḫ of the goddess Nisaba prior to his son. This U'u is at present known exclusively from his son's inscriptions from the time when the latter became king of Uruk and lugal of the land (kalam). A survey of the latter is given by P. Steinkeller, *Fs Kienast*, 621–637.

194 J.-J. Glassner StOr 70, 18f.

195 See for instance IL_2, saĝa of Zabala, contemporary of Enmetena of Lagaš, who became the $ensi_2$ of Umma, *CIRPL* Ent. 28 iii 28–29; and about a generation later, Enentarzi, saĝa of Ningirsu, who went on to become $ensi_2$ of Lagaš, e.g. *DP* 1/1 31 i 4–5. A Classic Sargonic example is Lugalajaĝu, a saĝa of Iškur who acted as $ensi_2$ of Adab, CUSAS 17 13 i 1–4.

196 K. Maekawa, *Mesopotamia* 8/9 (1973–74), 77–144; B. R. Foster, *Gs Diakonoff*, 73 fn. 6.

197 See also M. Powell's comments on the quite comparable situation in Umma-Zabala, *HUCA* 49 (1978), 24–27.

198 For the finds, see C. L. Woolley et al., UE 2. H. J. Nissen's *Königsfriedhof*, is very useful for the chronological issues raised by archaeological and inscribed finds from the cemetery.

the post–Sargonic period, and was situated some 200 metres to the southeast of the Ur III ziggurat. The name is perhaps misleading as the definite majority of the several thousand interments on the site belonged to private individuals.[199] 16 tombs stand out from the rest by means of their rich funeral goods and tomb architecture, and the fact that some of these monumental burials exhibit signs of human sacrifice.[200] A. C. Cohen has argued that the ceremonials surrounding these latter burials were intended to cement the elitist ideology of ED Ur royalty. The impressive pomp of mass interments and mourning ceremonies would impress upon all spectators that the palace was set apart from the rest of society, in life and in death.[201] Comparable evidence from other city-states is wanting, but seeming elite burials on a smaller scale have been excavated at Kiš.[202]

Evidence for the ancestral cult of deceased rulers is found in some cities, mainly from Ebla and the Girsu state. How widespread this phenomenon was is hard to assess. The evidence from these latter two city-states implies that the ancestral cult was official business, and so the expenditures for offerings to the dead ended up in official records. At other locations the veneration of deceased ancestors may well have existed, but could rather have been viewed as a private affair, much along the lines of what is known about such practices in the Old Babylonian period.

1.6.2 The Sargonic period

With the advent of the Sargonic dynasty, the political center of gravity moved northwards, toward the area of confluence between the Diyālā and Tigris rivers.[203] The precise location of Akkade remains unknown. However, many thousands of documents and inscriptions from the Ḫabur area in the northwest to Susa in the southeast testify to the policies of Sargonic kings and their importance for the development of royal ideology in Mesopotamia down until the 1st millennium BCE can not be overestimated. The fact that

---

[199] The exact number of burials is unclear. The index of Woolley et al., UE 2, counts around 1850 graves, while Woolley mentions, p. 16, that the number may have been two or three times that amount. H. J. Nissen, *Königsfriedhof*, 2, speaks of 450 previously unpublished burials, which must have been part of Woolley's higher figures. Nissen further notes that a number of graves were erroneously dated in the original publication. S. Pollock, *CAJ* 1 (1991), 173, mentions a round figure of 2000 graves, but adds, p. 175, that Woolley mentioned coming across 4000 more that were too damaged to bother recording them. Several relevant observations were furthermore made by G. Marchesi, *OrNS* 73 (2004), 153–197.

[200] The crania of a number of the retainers buried in full costume along with the main occupants of the tombs exhibit damages caused by a sharp instrument, about an inch in diameter, *NY Times*, Oct. 27 2009, New York Edition, section D4.

[201] *Death Rituals*, 42–44, 121–125, 147f.

[202] See H. Crawford, *Sumer and the Sumerians*, 143–145.

[203] J.-J. Glassner, BBVO 5, 9f.

the names of two kings of Akkade were echoed by those of Akkadian-speaking rulers of the 2nd and 1st millennia serves to illustrate this point.

When the political situation so allowed, the Sargonic kings probably engaged in labour-intensive temple building projects, also in the southern parts of the land. Examples are made up by the temple of Enlil in Nippur and that of the Moon God in the far south.[204] The founder of the dynasty, *Śarrukēn*, originally adopted traditional Sumerian epithets of a religious nature. At some point he, followed by his two sons *Rīmuś* and *Maniśtūśu*, opted for an almost exclusive use of a much simpler – yet still traditional – title, lugal Kiš. He, as well as his successors, underlined the fact that they were supported by Enlil, the leader of the Sumerian pantheon, and ʿAštar, the Semitic goddess of war. *Śarrukēn* seems to have introduced the concept of a standing army to southern Mesopotamia.[205]

The kings of Akkade met staunch opposition from the Sumerian city-states, as witnessed by reports of recurring southbound campaigns and the tearing down of city walls. From a political point of view, the Akkadian kings introduced an order based on personal responsibility toward the ruler.[206] Letters and administrative documents reveal that governors of Sumerian cities travelled to Akkade, doubtlessly to meet with the king personally. The king's officials obviously had great authority, even in giving orders to city governors. Both were sometimes characterized as servants of the king named in their seal inscriptions, which indicates a loyalty to the person of the king rather than to the office. Legally the king was the highest authority in the land with civilians sometimes swearing by his name in oath-taking ceremonies.[207] And during this time there are indications that capital punishment lay in the hands of the king alone,[208] as was ideally the case later during the times of *Ḫammurapi* of Babylon.

Ideologically, the most important idea to gain some degree of acceptance during the Sargonic period was the deification of the living ruler. The evidence for a cult based on the person of the ruler in Sargonic times is

---

[204] See references, A. Westenholz, *Annäherungen* 3, 54 fn. 201f.

[205] See in general the overview by W. G. Lambert, JSOTS 270, 57–59. Contrary to Lambert's characterization of *Śarrukēn*, the latter did actually use the title $ensi_2$ in the Akkadian version of his bilingual Nippur inscription, as parallel to Sumerian $ensi_2$-gal, see T. Jacobsen, *Fs Civil*, 114 n. 9.

[206] Portrayed by A. Westenholz, HANE/S 5, 157–169, as a difference in mentality between Sumerians and Akkadians. I believe Westenholz is in essence right. Difficulties encountered by Akkadian bureaucrats in administering state affairs inevitably led to a jargon foreign to Sumerian bureaucracy. But many of the differences to which Westenholz points might perhaps rather stem from the accountability of officials in relation to their superiors rather than a mentality ingrained in them at home or during their education in scribal schools.

[207] In MS-CS Nippur, an oath was taken simultaneously by the god Ninurta and by the king, OSP 2 74, and p. 85 w. comment to lines 9–10.

[208] Indeed, all of the evidence published so far is circumstantial. See for instance the letter treated by B. Kienast & K. Volk, FAOS 19, 134–136. See also below, p. 95f. w. fn. 493.

mostly derived from seal inscriptions and in particular the preposed divine determinative written in front of the royal name.[209] Beginning in the last century of the 3rd millennium BCE, the statues of these rulers, along with those of the prolific builder Gudea, governor of Lagaš, and those of the Ur III dynasty, are mentioned in texts as recipients of offerings.

1.6.3 The Late Sargonic period and the Gutian interregnum

After the first five kings of the Sargonic dynasty, a period of political turmoil ensued. The Akkadian state shrank and a dynasty based in the borderlands of the eastern mountains, the Gutians, came to power. The extent of their influence over Sumer is unknown. Nippur, Umma and Adab, all seem to have been under their control in one way or another, but the documentation that can be attributed to this period is limited. The best source material consists of a handful of inscriptions authored by Gutian rulers or by local governors under their influence.[210]

In the southeast, the Lagaš state seems to have managed quite well, and written sources attest to a return to old associations between the worldly and the divine spheres of power. A short inscription by an independent sovereign, *Puzur*-Mama, attests to the survival of Early Dynastic ideological traits, as his epithets are very similar to those used by ED IIIb Lagaš rulers.[211] This could either be due to the survival of inscribed pieces of monumental art, or to traditions of ideological tenets in the form of oral or written compositions. Lengthy texts from the governor Gudea testify to large-scale building projects and a blossoming literary tradition. A hymn to the goddess Bau mentioning Gudea was composed during this period.[212]

1.6.4 The Ur III period

The memory of the Sargonic kings remained firm with the Ur III kings. The floodplain was characterized by peaceful circumstances, which meant that

---

[209] But see, e.g. the Bassetkī inscription of *Narām*-Su'en, A.-H. Al-Fouadi, *Sumer* 32 (1976), 63–75; W. Farber, *OrNS* 52 (1983), 67–72, mentioning a "house" built by the citizens of Akkade for *Narām*-Su'en.

[210] E.g. *BroTa* 2 & 3 (OB copies of original inscriptions by Erriduwizir); V. Scheil, *CRAIB* 55 (1911), 319, inscription by Lugalanatum, $ensi_2$ of Umma dated to the reign of Si-u_3-um.

[211] H. de Genouillac, *RHR* 101 (1930), 221 (AO 11253); and the edition with commentary of cols. ii and iii by K. Volk, *ZA* 82 (1992), 28f. As Volk shows, the epithets of *Puzur*-Mama resemble those of Eanatum more than any other Lagaš $ensi_2$. It is thus likely that a monumental inscription of Eanatum had somehow been available to *Puzur*-Mama.

[212] See the edition of a hymn for Bau with a section honouring Gudea, A. Falkenstein & W. von Soden, *Sumerische und akkadische Hymnen und Gebete*, 85–87. Another hymn, Dumu Ana, sometimes taken to refer to a human ruler, was discussed and treated by G. Marchesi, HANE/S 10, 119f., and 132–139, with notes on previous editions.

the kings of Ur could focus much of their attention on intensifying productivity, thereby increasing revenues to the state. Leading cities of the floodplain became the scene of building projects on a grand scale. Prisoners of war were put to work in booming industrial facilities and in production of foodstuffs.[213] Now more than ever, the divine nature of kingship came to the fore in hymns extolling the unique position and function of kingship. To a large extent, these hymns are linguistically influenced by the Lagaš material.[214] Furthermore, the language and wording of the Ur III hymns show much affinity to concepts found in personal names throughout the 3rd millennium.

Consistencies between concepts encountered in pre–Ur III personal names and in late 3rd millennium royal hymns are so great that a continuity of key ideas must be presupposed. To give a proper picture of how this flow of ideas worked, the onomastic, historical and hymnic material of the 21st century BCE would also have to be inspected and judged. Such an undertaking is to a large extent beyond the scope of this study. But part of the purpose of this investigation is to identify older ideological material in a specific group of names, and put them in a perspective which can also shed light on the very beginnings of kingship in ancient Mesopotamia. In Chapter 6, this brief historical background will be discussed along with key findings from the analytical Chapter 3.

---

213 An overview of the Ur III period is found in W. Sallaberger, *Annäherungen* 3.

214 J. Klein, *Three Šulgi Hymns;* E. Flückiger-Hawker, OBO 166.

2. Names and time of name-giving

Sumerian and Semitic names in Mesopotamia during the period 2800–2200 BCE differed from each other in some respects. Within these groups also, names could differ depending, for instance, on temporal or geographic considerations, perhaps also depending on a person's social standing. The traditions which defined name-giving and how much is known about the situations in which names were given vary between the cultures. The Sumerian and Akkadian onomastic materials are both introduced and described in general terms and in respect to traits peculiar to respective language.

2.1 The name

Personal names appear in cuneiform texts throughout the better part of three millennia: from about 3000 BCE to the beginning of the Common Era. They contain a spectrum of statements, ranging from descriptions of references to the child's appearance to condensed statements about the physical world and the way it connected with the social and cultural world of ideas in which the name-givers and -bearers lived and believed.[215] The majority of names from all periods of Mesopotamian name-giving were composed with divine names or objects connected with the divine sphere encompassing a degree of divinity themselves, or with appellatives potentially referring either to humans or to divine denizens of the world.[216]

It is reasonable to assume that every person reaching a certain level of maturity had a name, formal or informal, by which others in the individual's surroundings would know and refer to him or her, and by which he or she could be entered into official documentation. Hardly any evidence for

[215] The Uruk III sign combinations collected by R. K. Englund, *CDLJ* 2009:4, 1–29, esp. p. 18–23, and convincingly argued by him to be names of Uruk III labourers are only briefly examined below, section 2.3. Englund takes an agnostic stance on whether the language of Uruk III texts is Sumerian. The names collected by him are admittedly different from names of the ED I-II period, when the Sumerian basis of substantial parts of the onomasticon is more secure. I hope to be able to publish a more in-depth study of this material in the future.

[216] See for instance A. Westenholz, *AfO* 42-43 (1995–96), 220; D. O. Edzard, *RlA* 9 (1998–2001), "Name, Namengebung. A. Sumerisch," 96, § 2.2; "B. Akkadisch," 106, § 2.2.

namelessness is hinted at by the extant sources, but a form of deliberate anonymity may be the case in some instances.[217] Those beings who had not been accorded names were liminal and potentially dangerous.[218] Some rather specific texts from later Ugarit and other western cultures in certain cases refer to an individual only as 'son of PN,' but these cases no doubt involved people who had names of their own; the administrative context only demanded that the persons be identified with an affiliation due to obligations or privileges in connection with state offices.[219]

Undoubtedly, names were as important to the ancient Mesopotamians as they are in modern societies, and not only for ease of reference in administrative contexts. When factoring in certain features of the terminology surrounding names and naming, this becomes clear. The Sumerian verb $še_{21}$ (in older literature sa_4) 'to name' persons or objects closely associated with persons, was the same as the verb 'to appoint' a person to a function. Both meanings have a correspondence in the Akkadian verb *nabûm*.[220]

The 'name,' Sumerian mu, Akkadian *šumum*, especially of the lugal or an important local god, was invoked in legal proceedings from at least the middle of the Sargonic period onwards.[221] Mere mention of the name in this doubtlessly rather formalized context would then bind the pledger to the contractual agreement.[222] Whether by a divine order or by the earthly legal system, disregard for the sworn arrangement was surely thought to bring

---

[217] See, for instance, the entry mu nu-tuku "having no name," E. Sollberger, *BiOr* 16 (1959), pl. 5 (AO 15540=M. Lambert, *OrAnt* 18 (1979), 225f., copy), o. iv 4 (ED IIIb Umma-Zabala, Luzag. $ensi_2$ 6). The entry is perhaps short for a previously unattested interrogative name missing an appellative, such as: ‹lugal/nin/en›-mu-nu-tuku 'is the ... not famous?' I see no basis for connecting this entry with the OB lemma *munutukû* 'without heir,' for which, see *CAD* M/2 s.v. Compare mu nu-ub-tuku, standing in for a name in anonymous donations (a ru-a) from private individuals in OB Ur, perceived as a name by S. Dunham, *ZA* 75 (1985), 258 and fn. 97. Compare also the MB legal document cited in *CAD* I/J s.v. *jānu*, 1b, where an interrogee stated he did not know his father's name and that his brother had no name. Furthermore, an OB exemplar of the Sumerian King List notes the first Gutian king as mu nu-tuku, while the Ur III version of the list, P. Steinkeller, *Fs Wilcke*, 280, suggests that the Gutians shared power for three years before a lugal emerged from among them.

[218] So, for instance, the nameless demonic beings known under the collective moniker of udug ḫul, Akk. *utukkū lemnūtu*, mu-bi an-ki-a la-ba-an-$ĝal_2$-la-a-meš, MU-*$šu_2$-nu ina šamê erṣeti ul ibašši* "their (the demons') names do not exist in heaven or on earth," quoted by *CAD* s.v. *šumu*, lex. sect. The fate of stillborn children was quite optimistically depicted in the composition Bilgames, Enkidu and the Netherworld, receiving butter and playing with gold and silver buckets (or tables), see A. Cavigneaux & F. al-Rawi, *Iraq* 62 (2000), 7, l. 16.

[219] See A. Alt, *ArOr* 18 (1950), 9–24.

[220] *CAD* N/1 s.v. *nabû* A, lex. sect.; *AHw*, 699f.

[221] See references to oaths by the ruler or by the name of the ruler, A. Westenholz, *Annäherungen* 3, 54 fn. 198.

[222] It is not unlikely, though, that some sort of binding ritual act was performed simultaneously with the uttering of the king's or god's name or in immediate connection to it; enhancing or completing the solemn agreement between the parties.

about some form of penalty from a supreme authority to which all parties in the matter were answerable. Earlier reports on oaths are scanty, but the treaty section in the Lagaš ruler Eanatum's Stele of the Vultures focused on objects belonging to divinities which both the administering and the swearing parties could acknowledge. And as the tutelary deities of Umma and Girsu were seen as affected by the proceedings, they were not featured among the divinities by whom oaths were sworn.[223]

2.2 Name-giving

Information on naming practice is quite sparse and for the most part circumstantial. The point at which children received their names in the early historic periods is still unclear. The person pronouncing the name is in all likelihood a close relative, probably a parent, but that parent would not necessarily be the one who decided upon the name to be given. In the following, what can be said with reasonable safety about naming from the extant sources will be looked at, and evidence from later periods will be drawn on for comparison.[224]

2.2.1 Early periods

When trying to pinpoint facts about Near Eastern name-giving one often has to deal with administrative and contractual sources. Such texts are drawn up with a specific purpose in mind: to document single transactions or sequences of transactions and the parties taking part in these. If age is noted or if age can be deduced from implicit factors in the documents, it is definitely worthy of notice with respect to the question of name-giving even though that often says very little about the *context* in which names were given.

Therefore it is of interest to note that certain Uruk III period documents may have specified the age of named, quite young, children in lists of labourers. These probably sorted under a bureaucratic office. According to some views, some children may have been as young as one or a few years old.[225] A similar practice for (unnamed) animals is known from contemporary administration, and also later, where the age of animals is

[223] A summary of the oath procedures and ritual acts of this treaty is given by C. Wilcke, *EANEL*, 74f.

[224] The following discussion is in part influenced by observations made already by J. J. Stamm, *Namengebung*, 8–10, save that he mainly looked at Akkadian names.

[225] See R. K. Englund, *CDLJ* 2009:4, 13f., and note 35, p. 13; and also the discussion of some of these names, below p. 58f. w. fn. 280.

noted, along with gender and breed.[226] Administrative documents from the Early Dynastic and later periods, however, never express age when writing: 'PN$_1$ child of PN$_2$.' Sizes of rations received by a person disclose an approximate level of physical maturity or the ability to perform labour tasks, as will be shown in section 2.2.2, below.

During the ED and Sargonic periods, adult male and female workers are very often listed by name. Children, when belonging to a worker family, are usually only mentioned as dumu 'child.'[227] Appearing more regularly beginning in the Sargonic period, is a qualifier for the gender of the child, dumu nitaḫ 'boy child,' and dumu munus 'girl child.' Another term is ša$_3$-du$_{10}$ 'immature child.' Infants are listed as dumu ga, amar gaba or just plain gaba 'suckling child,' much depending on local terminology. The exact age groups covered by these terms are unclear and perhaps fleeting, though the ga- or gaba-children are most certainly younger than plain dumu-children.[228]

A rather unique document from Girsu lists family units consisting of adults, servants and children, coming to the temple of Bau via Guabba from around the southern countryside.[229] All persons, regardless of age grouping, are listed by name. The total at the end of the document lists the male providers first, followed by the male servants and the 'boys' ša$_3$-du$_{10}$ nitaḫ. After that, the women, called ama dumu, 'mothers (with) children,' the 'girls' ša$_3$-du$_{10}$ munus, and lastly the female servants.[230]

As for a time of name-giving, some 3rd millennium Sumerian names in themselves appear to refer to specific points in local cultic calendars. When seen in the light of later Akkadian name-giving, such names may arguably be said to refer to a point in time coinciding either with the birth of the child,

---

226 R. K. Englund, *Annäherungen* 1, 176. Later examples include VS 14 160 (ED IIIb Girsu, equids); B. R. Foster, *USP* 74 (CS Umma, equids), commented with more examples, p. 128.

227 This is one of the factors which led S. Langdon to the assumption that Sumerian children only received names when reaching maturity, *Encyclopedia of Religion and Ethics* Vol. 9, "Names (Sumerian)," 171. The other factor was the supposed lack of references to circumstances of birth in Sumerian names, so-called Begrüßungsnamen.

228 At least judging by the evidence from earlier periods. For an OB Kiš example which could point to the opposite, compare V. Donbaz & N. Yoffee, BiMes 17, 62, sections H and N, where a "son" (dumu) receives 2/3 of the rations received by "an infant" (dumu gaba) belonging to another household. The corresponding terms for orphans – not always denoting small children – were nu-siki nitaḫ, nu-siki munus or dumu nu-siki, depending on time and place. See the discussion with many textual references by I. J. Gelb, *JNES* 24 (1965), 239f.

229 The document, Nik 1 19 has been treated and commented on by I. J. Gelb, OLA 5, 61–63.

230 Some of the boys' names are: en-ne$_2$-a-na-ak, lugal-iti-da-tu (o. ii 4–5); and some of the girl's names are nin-si-ĝar-ab-ba, šeš-ku$_3$-ge-še$_3$-mu-ĝal$_2$ (o. ii 8–9), uru-ku$_3$-a-bi$_2$-lu$_5$ (o. iii 13), and ereš-e-rib-ba-ni-gin$_7$-mi$_2$-zi(-du$_{11}$-ga) (o. iv 10). The reconstruction of the latter form depends on the reading of G. Marchesi, HANE/S 10, 189, fn. 199. About a third of the names are either hapaxes, are hardly attested, or contain rare combinations of elements seldom seen in the Sumerian onomasticon. This is probably due to the fact that these people came from the southern countryside.

or with the act of name-giving itself – perhaps both.[231] A few other names may refer to recurring natural phenomena, and could similarly be taken as indications of a time of birth or the time of name-giving.[232]

In essence, these facts represent the basis for a time of name-giving in the earliest periods. The context of naming is of course not worthy of notice to bureaucrats and so such information is not even alluded to. If early official documentation is all but silent on this point, literary sources give no information at all about name-giving with respect to humans. Even without such information, several scholars have assumed that the father was the person responsible for naming his children.[233] Historical texts, on the other hand, often relate to the naming of rulers by gods. The most famous, and definitely the most extensive account of such an event is the one alluded to by Eanatum in his Stele of the Vultures.[234] K. Volk's treatment of the passage suggests that Eanatum's account of his own birth can be used as a model for understanding the procedures around name-giving.[235] After a divine conception, Eanatum is said to have received his name by the goddess Inana, who then placed him on the lap of another goddess, Ninḫursaĝ, for breast feeding. After this, Ninĝirsu examines the child and he (probably) confirms the name given by Inana. Based on that inscription, Volk suggests that the name was given by a midwife, and that later the father confirmed it. Naturally, the circumstances surrounding Eanatum's conception and raising stand out as more ideologically motivated than as descriptions of matter-of-fact child rearing.[236] All Eanatum's other inscriptions featuring this episode in more contracted, epithetical form have the nurturing epithet precede the name-giving epithet. Furthermore, different goddesses are involved.[237] But the sequence of events is not altogether implausible, which is the key issue here. As will be seen presently, later Akkadian textual witnesses have more to offer on this point.

[231] See for instance the discussions of the names lugal-ezem, p. 130f.; and lugal-$^{(ĝiš)}$apin-du$_{10}$ and lugal-apin-ne$_2$, p. 131f.

[232] See discussions of lugal-iti-da(-tu), p. 172; and lugal-še-gu-na, p. 133, below.

[233] K. Volk, OBO 203, 84 fn. 84 mentions specifically H. Limet, *Anthroponymie*, 310; but compare also B. Meissner, *Babylonien und Assyrien* 1, 390 and 395; T. Jacobsen, *CTNMC*, 5; K. Radner, *Die Macht des Namens*, 28.

[234] The stele itself has a name, of which it is said: na-ru$_2$-a, mu-bi, lu$_2$-a nu …, "the name of this stele is not that of a man," *CIRPL* Ean. 1 r. x 23–25.

[235] OBO 203, 71–92, especially p. 83f. Another treatment of the passage, *CIRPL* Ean. 1 o. iv 18–v 29, in a survey of the Near Eastern tradition of royalty with divine parentage is found in M. Stol, *Birth in Babylonia and the Bible*, 83–89.

[236] In the Nippur inscription of Lugalzagesi of Uruk-Umma, the chain of epithets mention him among other things as chosen (mu pa$_3$-da) by the Sun God Utu, as the son born by Nissaba, fed by the wholesome milk of Ninḫursaĝ, and brought up by Ningirim, the lady of Uruk, BE 1/2 87 i 19–33.

[237] See list of writings and attestations in FAOS 6, 282f., and note *CIRPL* Ean. 6 iv 7–10 where Nanše is mentioned instead of Inana.

2.2.2 Ur III and later periods

If 3rd millennium sources divulge little in the way of a time or context of name-giving, later periods do offer more information that can serve as points of comparison. Ur III documentation, for instance, is useful because of its sheer abundance. In texts from this period one may follow individuals appearing in the same archive, sometimes spanning several years. In this period, working class children are called by name in rations disbursement documents, even at a young age, far more regularly than before.

H. Waetzoldt, writing on children's place in Ur III work teams, indirectly touches upon the subject of age and naming. He cites a text in which a mother appears along with her four named children, all five have Sumerian names. All four children are too young to carry out work but they still receive a low amount of rations: 10 sila of barley each, roughly 10 liters worth. The youngest child is qualified as "born afterwards" (eger tu-da), that is, "after the last inspection or accounting."[238] The time frame involved ought to be a year or two at the most, given the regularity of Ur III accounting.

The economic documentation aside, a unique slave sale text from *Šu*-Su'en's first regnal year reports on a boy child, 1 1/2 cubits ($kuš_3$) high (c. 75 cm), being sold. His name was given as ^{d}Nanna-sa_6-ga 'Nanna is favourable.'[239] Considering the height of the boy, an age of 1 1/2–2 years is not improbable.[240] In two other Ur III slave sales documents, one involving a male and a female slave along with a baby boy, the other involving a female slave and her baby girl, only the adults are named. The children are mentioned as clinging to the breasts of their mothers.[241] The boy who appears on his own merited naming in the sales contract while the children who were sold along with parents obviously did not. The latter seem to have been considered part of a package deal and so their names, if they had any by that time, were not seen as necessary for drawing up the sales document.

By the beginning of the 2nd millennium, there are numerous examples of names which refer to a body part of a newborn. These names ought then to be related to phrases uttered by nursemaids, female relatives, older siblings or any member of the entourage surrounding a woman giving birth, if not by the mother herself.[242] Examples include *Aḫa-arši* 'I received a brother,'

238 H. Waetzoldt, *Labor in the Ancient Near East*, 132f.

239 UET 3 26 (=OIP 104 281). The envelope had the height recorded as 1 $kuš_3$. The price of the boy was the modest sum of 2 šeqels (gin_2) of silver, which would be rather low for a child fit for heavier labour.

240 See for instance the dating of a skeleton of about the same height, H. Martin, J. Moon, J. N. Postgate, *Graves 1 to 99*: Grave 11, measurements on site agreeing with dental analysis on an age of 1 1/2–2 years. Conservative measuring of the skeletal parts as published yield a height, when alive, of just under 80 cm.

241 The texts are *NATN* 761, and OIP 104 279. Both are from Nippur.

242 Some examples are given by J. J. Stamm, *Namengebung*, 127–136. The names were characterized by Stamm as "greeting names" (Begrüßungsnamen). M. Stol, *Birth in*

found already in the Ebla texts;[243] *Ikšud-appašu* 'his nose has arrived,'[244] and *Mīn-arnī* 'what have I done to deserve this?,'[245] both from the OB period.

An OB contract from Kiš mentions a servant girl, *Amat-Eššešim*, daughter of *Amat*-Bau, being handed over into the care of the latter's mistress *Ruttīya*. The poignant part of the document is the fact that it was drawn up on the exact same day as the named baby girl was born.[246] A father of the child is not mentioned and is hence taken to be absent totally during the procedings leading up to the handing over of the girl. The name thus, with all certainty, was given by the mother before the baby girl was handed over to her mistress. The day of birth of *Amat-Eššešim* must have coincided with the celebration of the *Eššešum* festival, which occurred a few times per month. Other similar names are known and add to the impression of a name-giving event as early as the first day of a child's life.[247] In fact, the Sumerian word for 'festival,' ezem, forms part of the most common Sumerian lugal-name in the time between 2600 and 2200 BCE, and this could favour a time of birth – or of name-giving – for individuals bearing this name, during a festival.[248]

In another OB adoption contract, a baby boy by the name *Mār*-Ištar, son of a slave girl, is adopted by a man. The period of nursing which would take place in the birth home of the boy is stipulated to two years, while the standard time was three years. This is likely to imply that the boy was around 1 year old by the time of adoption.[249] In the NB period, a 1-year-old girl, or a girl in her first year, was named *Šikkû* 'mongoose.'[250] Two documents from the Achaemenid period record the sale and subsequent cancellation of a male servant along with his three daughters, all named. The

---

Babylonia and the Bible, 131f., argues that some of these names were characteristic of birth complications.

243 Attested also with the opposite word order, M. Krebernik, BBVO 7, 122 and 143.

244 See J. J. Stamm, *Namengebung*, 127f.

245 So A. Westenholz, *AfO* 42/43 (1995–96): "He must have been an ugly child indeed." See also M. Stol, *Birth in Babylonia and the Bible*, 168, for more names of a similar kind.

246 YOS 13 192, edited by J. J. Finkelstein, *op. cit.*, p. 14–16; 8th day of Ab, Samsuditana Y 8. On this text, see also R. Harris, *JCS* 29 (1977), 51 fn. 15.

247 See, e.g. MA *mār-ūmi-ešrā* 'son of the 20th day,' C. Saporetti, StPohl 6/1, 321; and the considerations of A. R. Millard, ARES 1, 163f., on months and festivals as component parts of PNN in Mesopotamia and elsewhere.

248 According to an Eduba dialogue, a schoolboy gives his work month as consisting of 24 days in school, 3 holidays and on average 3 days off for festivals, H. L. J. Vanstiphout, *The Context of Scripture*, 592 ll. 21–25. Whether this can be applied also to the time before the OB period is unclear, but the numbers can not be very far off the mark.

249 See M. Stol, *Birth in Babylonia and the Bible*, 127f., with reference to C. Wilcke.

250 J. N. Strassmaier, *Inschriften von Nabonidus* 75 r. 4: (u_3) ^{munus}*šik-ku-u*$_2$ *mārat šattīšu* (dumu munus mu-*šu*$_2$). Quoted by *CAD* Š/2 s.v. *šattu*, 1k 1'. For *šikkû* in other PNN, see *CAD* Š/2, s.v. Among the latter is at least one other instance of a female bearing this name, made up of a masculine noun. The phenomenon of girls or women bearing or choosing male names is known in other cultures, see e.g. G. vom Bruck, *The Anthropology of Names and Naming*, 226–250.

third daughter, *Šēpēt*-Ninlil-*aṣbat* 'I grabbed hold of Ninlil's feet,' was qualified as *ēniqtu*, 'suckling girl child.'[251]

A few different points concerning the persons in the above-mentioned economic texts and contracts are of interest. In all cases they refer to people from the lower strata of society; either servants or slaves. It seems apparent that there was no need to put to writing the event of a birth within families belonging to the middle or upper classes. In the case of the first OB contract, the mother parting with her baby girl needed to be mentioned, as well as her subordinate status, in order to prevent her from reclaiming her child in the future.

If, with due reservation, this is also applied to the earlier periods and higher strata in society, a possible time of name-giving might be envisaged, ranging from the first day of a child's life up to within a few years of age.[252] At the latest, children ought to have received names during early adolescence when they had grown old enough to take on tasks that merited ration payments from a bureaucratic department of a civic institution. The Mesopotamian material may be compared with early Hebrew society, where the mothers often appear to have been responsible for naming their children, close to the time of birth.[253]

2.2.3 Name change and kyriophores

The practice of renaming or adding additional components to a person's name is known from different areas and time periods in the ancient Near East.[254] A number of instances indicate that certain individuals renamed themselves or were renamed by others. This fact strengthens the idea of a name being associated on an intimate level with its bearer, as the new name can be seen more befitting of the current standing and altered life situation of the bearer. When, for instance, persons show up in official texts bearing names incorporating the name of a ruler – so called kyriophore names[255] –

---

[251] J. N. Strassmaier, *Inschriften von Cambyses* 309 o. 3: ^{munus}*še-pet*-^{d}Nin-lil$_2$-*aṣ-bat*; 388 o. 2: ^{munus}*še-pet*$_2$-^{d}Nin-lil$_2$-*aṣ-bat*, 'I grabbed hold of Ninlil's feet.' Cited by B. Meissner, *Babylonien und Assyrien* 1, 394. Quoted in *CAD* E *s.v.* **ēniqu*. See M. W. Stolper, *JNES* 43 (1984), 306 with fnn. 21, 23 for a brief discussion of the texts.

[252] The names cited by K. Radner, *Die Macht des Namens*, 27 w. fn. 144, as evidence for a Sumerian tradition of Begrüßungsnamen are problematic in the light of parallels. For instance, an-ne$_2$-ba(-ab)-du$_7$ should not be taken as "Bis zum Himmel ist er/sie gesprungen," as the name i$_7$-de$_3$-ba-du$_7$, *CTNMC* 54 o. iv 2, can hardly be taken to mean "he jumped in the river" for joy at the arrival of the child.

[253] See, e.g., J. J. Stamm, *Namengebung*, 10 fn. 1; I. Willi-Plein, *Namenforschung*, 871f.

[254] See in general the short discussion by E. Lipiński, *Semitic Languages*, 569: 67.5.

[255] M. Hilgert, JBVO 5 (2002), 39f. and fn. 5, p. 40, argues for the need to distinguish between theophore and kyriophore names, and contrasts those to the term basiliophore, used about kings who were not necessarily deified. Hilgert's first line of argument is followed here,

who had been in power for only a comparatively short period of time, then there is reason to suspect that renaming had taken place previous to the date of the document being drawn up. Similar to the original name-giving situation, the circumstances surrounding a person's renaming are unknown.

2.2.3.1 Early periods

A few instances from the ED IIIb Lagaš state suffice to show that renaming was practiced then and there. Each of the last few rulers of Girsu, did not stay in power for very long. Therefore, when persons are called ^{d}Utu-palil-Lugal-AN-da[256] 'Utu is the vanguard of LugalANda,' and Uru-KA-gi-na-^{d}En-lil$_2$-le-(i$_3$)-su, Uru-KA-gi-na-^{d}Nin-ĝir$_2$-su-ke$_4$-(i$_3$)-su and Uru-KA-gi-na-^{d}Nanše-(i$_3$)-su,[257] meaning 'UruKAgina is known by DN,' in texts written during the respective reigns of the rulers mentioned in the names, they bear witness to such practice. LugalANda's wife also, Baranamtara, was honoured in a similar way. But names referring to her (personally or in her function as wife of the chief administrator of the city?) substituted her name for a noun of uncertain meaning: PAP.PAP.[258]

Only a few of the persons bearing names of this type seem to have performed important functions; for instance the temple steward (aĝrig) named Enanatum-sipa-zi 'Enanatum is a faithful shepherd' who merited mention in a famous letter. But the chronology involved is somewhat problematic as the person is described as no longer alive, and there is no indication in the letter as to how long the person had been deceased.[259] At any rate the name is, at present, the earliest attested kyriophore name from Mesopotamia.

From ES and CS times two examples merit attention. Two princesses in the Akkadian royal family had Sumerian names, both beginning with the appellative en; and both performed the function of high priestesses (en, Akk. *entum*) of the Moon God in the southern Sumerian city of Ur. Since no other

---

but the term basiliophore will not be used, in part due to the vagaries of the onomastic material and its sometimes inconsistent writing of divine determinatives.

[256] An IL$_2$ known from texts dating between Lug. Y 6 and Ukg. ensi$_2$ Y 1. See V. V. Struve, *Onomastika*, 206, for references.

[257] The men appear in four sources from Ukg. lugal Y 3–4, HSS 3 27 r. iv 1–3; 42 o. i 1–ii 1; both were treated by G. J. Selz as *AWAS* 26 and 42 with commentary ("Höflingsnamen"). See also *op. cit.* no. 124 r. iii 2–4; *DP* 1/2 116 r. i 10–ii 1.

[258] For these names, see G. J. Selz, *Götterwelt*, 272f., and a few examples, below, p. 89, 120, 144 fn. 806. A suggestion by E. Sollberger to read PAP.PAP as variant of munu$_4$(PAP+PAP), seeing in it a phonetic rendering of munus 'woman,' is refuted by Selz, p. 272 fn. 1338. However, the appellative munus replaces PAP.PAP in closely related phrases, and both terms refer to Baranamtara, e.g. *RTC* 47 and *DP* 1/2 89. Compare the discussion of the meaning of geme$_2$, normally 'female servant' or the like, *FTUM*, 121 w. fn. 36.

[259] Found in the letter *CIRPL* Enz. 1, rev. iii 4. The dating of this letter in the latter half of Ukg.'s reign appears solid, see D. R. Frayne, RIME 1, 237, w. refs. The text more than likely refers to events taking place a generation or more before the date of composition.

instances of Sumerian names are attested among those known to have belonged to the royal lineage in Akkade, they are very probably programmatic, and not original names.[260] No doubt, the appellative en of these names referred not to the priestesses, but to the deities whom they served. The name en-ḫe₂-du₇-an-na, 'the en is an adornment of Heaven' is more befitting as epithet of a planetary deity traversing the skies than as referring to a priestess of the Moon God – daughter of a king or not. Hence, a reference to the divinity of en is logically more preferable than viewing it as the professional title of the en-priestess of Nanna.[261] A name like ᵈ*Narām*-ᵈSu'en-*ʾilī*[262] '*Narām*-Su'en is my god' from early on in *Śarkaliśarrē*'s reign might also be taken to be a name acquired in adulthood, but considering the unknown length of *Narām*-Su'en's rule, it is also quite possible that the person bearing the name had had it since early on in life.

Throne names adopted by rulers in connection with their accession were never to become a tradition, even in the most generous sense of the word, judging from the available source material.[263] Only a single possible case from 3rd millennium Mesopotamia presents itself: *Ipḫur*-Kiš, a rebel leader from Kiš under the reign of *Narām*-Su'en. Though he is probably historical, he has left behind no sources of his own, and it may well be that his unusual name refers to the manner in which he was catapulted to power.[264]

[260] Interestingly the en of Enlil in Nippur, *Tuṭṭanābśum*, daughter of *Narām*-Su'en kept her Akkadian name. See family tree of the Akkade dynasty, W. W. Hallo & W. K. Simpson, *The Ancient Near East: A History*, 58; additional children of *Narām*-Su'en are listed in RIME 2, 87. Another daughter is now known, *tar₂-am₃*-A-ka₃-de₃ᵏⁱ, see G. Buccellati & M. Kelly-Buccellati, *Fs Oates*, 14, with an overview of the royal family, note 3, p. 29 At least two more persons belonged to the lineage: ⌜*śu₂*⌝-*mi-ig-ri₂*, BIN 8 121 o. i 7 (dumu lugal); *u-bil*-Aš₁₀-tar₂ (šeš lugal), RIME 2.0.0.1001. "Father" of *Tūtaʾ-śar-libbīś* is to be stricken from Hallo's and Simpson's scheme.

[261] Compare, e.g. M. Krebernik, AOAT 296, 9 fn. 20, who considered the possibility that names of, among others, priests and priestesses, actually did refer to the name-bearer. If all en-names are taken to be similar in scope, then the name en-ᵈNanna-ᵈAmar-ᵈSu'en-ra-ki-âĝa₂ 'the divine en Nanna loves Amar-Su'en,' borne by an en priestess at Karzida, UET 3 1499 r. ii 7, offers the best evidence that en in names of en-priestesses of Nanna denoted, not the official, but the deity under whom the priestess served. But it may be said that, generally, the lack of a substantial corpus of inscriptions by people termed exclusively en (or nin, ama, aja₂, šeš, etc.), make the problems of knowing when the appellative refers to a human and when it refers a divinity much more complex than is the case with lugal-names. Also, in names of en-priests or -priestesses of other divinities, en may indeed prove to denote the official. A further study of this problem could prove most rewarding.

[262] *USP* 31 o. 4: ᵈ⌜*Na*⌝-*ra-am*-ᵈEN.ZU-*i₃-li₂* (2 mu 5 iti 5 u₄, probably of *Śarkaliśarrē* date).

[263] J. J. Stamm, *Namengebung*, 11 w. fnn. 1 and 3. Compare A. Becker, *BagM* 16 (1985), 304–307, who notes that out of 5 known rulers of Uruk in the final half of the ED IIIb period, 4 had names beginning with lugal, but the implications of this are unclear. Most of the royal names cited by Becker, *op. cit.*, 298 fn. 280, are probably not to be seen as throne names. The question is addressed again by E. Frahm, *NABU* 2005/44, who offers some interesting reflections on the MA and NA royal onomasticon, and by K. Radner, *Die Macht des Namens*, 33–35.

[264] See discussion below, section 6.1.

Furthermore, there are no noticeable difference in names after rulers had undergone deification in their own lifetimes.

2.2.3.2 Ur III and later periods

In the latter half of the Ur III period, a handful of examples are known where a high-ranking person appears under two different names; seemingly making a deliberate change sometime during his career. The top Ur III official[265] ir_{11}-$\hat{g}u_{10}$ 'my servant' who was later called ir_{11}-^{d}Nanna 'Nanna's servant,' is one example.[266]

Kyriophore names of this period can be found throughout the region controlled directly by the Ur III state, and also as attributed to persons from neighbouring areas with which the Ur regime was in close political contact.[267] They could be construed both in Sumerian and Akkadian, and in rare cases the linguistic affinity of a name is unknown.[268] The higher echelons of society seem especially well-represented with regards to this specific category of names,[269] but they in fact appear in all strata of society and thus attest to the importance of the king to the people's lives in a very tangible way.

A tradition for deification of Ur III rulers in their own lifetimes definitely led to a considerable increase in the amounts and varieties of kyriophore names in this period. The inception of this tradition of kyriophore names in the Ur III period began under its long-lived, second ruler, Šulgi (c. 2094–2048 BCE), who, it is speculated, assumed divine status somewhere between his 12th and his 20th regnal years.[270] From a preliminary survey of the Ur III onomasticon, the earliest instance of a person bearing a kyriophore name dates from Šulgi's 25th regnal year. The person in question, ^{d}Šul-gi-zi-$\hat{g}u_{10}$ 'Šulgi is my life,' a cook by profession, appears in a text from Nippur.[271] Judging by the date, there is a distinct possibility that he had had this name since childhood, only having the divine determinative added when the effects of Šulgi's deification becomes visible in the sources. It is only a few years after Šulgi's 25th year that dated sources begin to number steadily in

---

[265] See W. Sallaberger, *Annäherungen* 3, 188f., with fn. 228, p. 188, for previous literature.

[266] For a discussion on the assumed identity of Šulgi-*simtī*, wife of Šulgi, 2nd king in the dynasty of Ur III and *Abī-simtī*, wife of Amar-Su'en, see F. Weiershäuser, *Die königlichen Frauen der III. Dynastie von Ur*, 106f.

[267] P. Michalowski, *The Organization of Power*, 55f. A treatment of the Sumerian kyriophores known by the middle of the 1960's, is found in H. Limet, *Anthroponymie*, 175–180.

[268] For the name ḫu-un-^{d}Šul-gi, see the comments by A. Goetze, *JCS* 17 (1963), 18, and fn. 82; and I. J. Gelb, MAD 3, 129f., sub ḪNN, *ḫunnum* "mercy." Other examples are listed in P. Michalowski, *The Organization of Power*, 55 fn. 48.

[269] M. Hilgert, JBVO 5 (2002), 40f.

[270] See the discussions by D. R. Frayne, RIME 3/2, 91; 99.

[271] *NATN* 740 r. 1.

the hundreds.[272] Most names with Šulgi as theophore element are found in texts dating to his last 10 or so regnal years. There is thus no reason to assume *a priori* that names including Šulgi as theophore resulted from a change of name. Kyriophore naming practice continues to be attested well into OB times.[273]

Kyriophore names and names which had bearing on the king and his prerogatives were thus found over considerable geographic areas. The popularity and continuity of this part of Mesopotamian onomastic tradition goes to prove that not only was the king well-known to his subjects, but individuals actually took an interest in the persona of the king and internalized his functions for the benefit of themselves and their loved ones. There can be no doubt that the roots of this practice go back at least to late ED times. As will be shown in Chapter 3, the hymnic material devoted to immortalizing the Ur III kings also rested on much older associations between the lugal and the rest of the physical world, and beyond.

2.3 Sumerian names: a brief overview

Sumerian was the predominant language for written sources in southern Mesopotamia throughout the 3rd millennium and the beginning of the 2nd millennium BCE. The main part of onomastic cuneiform material from the 3rd millennium is best explained as Sumerian. Whether that can be taken as implying that Sumerian-speaking individuals were in the majority in Sumer as a whole during this time is another question. The wealth of administrative documentation is the only basis for judging the question, and this points in the direction of Sumerians as making up the majority of inhabitants on the southern floodplain.[274]

The definition of a Sumerian PN followed here is a name which ideally can be understood on a literal level as conveying sense in Sumerian and which on a structural level conforms to grammatical and syntactic conventions as far as a modern understanding of that language goes. Names, however, are not always completely understandable today. Some contain highly unusual signs with as yet unknown readings,[275] which may not yet have cropped up in contexts other than personal names, at least not in the

---

272 See diagram in W. Sallaberger, *Annäherungen* 3, 149.

273 See M. Stol, *StEb* 8 (1991), 204 fn. 131, for references.

274 The only survey of the demographic picture of southern and northern Mesopotamia respectively has been done by B. R. Foster, *OrNS* 51 (1982), 297–354, who looked at Sargonic period administrative records from a number of different cities. See below, 5.2.1.

275 See for example many of the signs labeled X_1 through X_{22}, in OSP 1, 117–119.

early periods.[276] Certain local writings of names employ signs which can only be explained by means of less opaque variants.[277]

The normal syntactic order of clause components in a Sumerian transitive clause is S(ubject) O(bject) V(erb). This order is consistently adhered to in almost all types of sources, including names. A special case is made up by topicalization in commemorative inscriptions when the indirect, dative object is put at the very beginning of the inscription. In a similar fashion – common in PNN but only rarely in narrative texts – the grammatical object may precede the subject of the predicate,[278] the result being a passive participial chain where the logical subject (grammatical object) is qualified by what follows.[279] The language of the Sumerian onomasticon was to all intents and purposes in accordance with the vernacular encountered in inscriptions and in the administrative texts, but with a tendency toward subject matters which put specific demands on wording.

A number of Uruk III names or personal designations seem to be precursors of names found in later sources. At least, the similarities are too great to be overlooked. Out of the 400 plus writings from this period, identified as possible personal names by R. K. Englund, about a dozen are strongly or vaguely reminiscent of names which can with all certainty be termed Sumerian when appearing in later texts.[280] Already in these Uruk period textual witnesses, a number of points characteristic for the later Sumerian onomasticon present themselves, such as a preoccupation with certain appellatives and the predicates si 'to be just right (for something),'[281] and du$_{10}$ 'to be good, make good.' The appellative lugal also figures, but

---

[276] Like the second component in the name ur-zikum(LAK773)-ma, for instance in ITT 5 9206 o. ii 3 (ED IIIb Girsu); also attested in Sargonic Adab, Girsu (note ITT 1 1241 o. 7', r. 2, person qualified: lu$_2$ ki Ma-ri$_2$-k(a-me)), and Nippur. All names composed with this sign, also in Ur III, seem to be formed as genitive compounds with zikum as nomen rectus.

[277] Like the verb su$_3$ and its functional counterparts su$_{13}$(BU), su$_{20}$(ŠIM), su$_x$(MUŠ), and su$_x$(TAG), though no PN is attested with all these variant writings. See table below, 4.4.

[278] M.-L. Thomsen, Mesopotamia 10, 51f.: §44.

[279] Sometimes referred to as the "Mesanepada-construction," coined by A. Falkenstein, *Das Sumerische*, 54: §40 c. Iβ.

[280] In Englund's list, *CDLJ* 2009:4, 21–23, compare, for instance:

A EN$_a$ with A EN$_a$ DA$_a$, UET 2 357 o. ii 3'; aja$_2$-en-da, e.g. *RTC* 3 o. iii' 1', and munus-en-da, o. iii' 3';

AK EN$_a$ GAL$_a$ with NIN AN GAL$_a$ AK$_a$ (AK-^{d}Nin-gal), UET 2 9 o. ii 4;

AN EN$_a$ DU with en-an-na-tum$_2$, passim in the 3rd millennium;

BAḪAR$_{2a}$ EN$_a$ with AMA UET2-370$_d$, UET 2 248 o. iv 4; and en-eden-ne$_2$(-si), passim in ED IIIb;

DARA$_{4a1}$ SI with SI DARA$_{4b}$ AMA, UET 2 92 o. i 5; and ama-bara$_2$$^!$(DARA$_4$)-ge, OIP 14 61 o. i 2; *WF* 34 o. iii 5; ama-bara$_2$$^!$(DARA$_4$)-si, *TSŠ* 525 o. iii 4; *WF* 26 o. iii 5;

GIR$_{3a/c}$ NI$_a$ with giri$_3$-ni-ba-dab$_5$, passim in ED III-Ur III times;

ḪI NIN SAG with ḪI SAG E$_{2a}$, UET 2 252 o. i 8; and lugal-saĝ-du$_{10}$ (see list of attestations.);

KISAL$_{b1}$ PAP$_a$ SI with KISAL$_{b1}$ SI AMA$_b$, UET 2 252 o. i 4; and nin-kisal-si, OIP 14 5 5.

[281] So I understand most names featuring non–finite forms of this verb, see below, 2.3.2.

never along with a predicate or other qualifying element.[282] More work on this small but significant corpus will no doubt contribute immensely to the understanding of the earliest recorded principles of Sumerian onomasticon and catapult the history of certain well-attested name types as far back in time as seems at present to be possible.

Names in texts from the ED I-II period provide morphologically and phonetically more developed forms of grammatical relationships than what is witnessed by earlier texts. By then, 2800–2700 BCE, writing had been simplified and the inventory of signs had shrunk to a more manageable number, and many signs had obtained phonetic values which made it easier to express morphological traits. Even so, the script never was to become a full representation of spoken Sumerian.[283] The development of the cuneiform script was probably due to the combination of a need for precision from a managerial viewpoint, and ingenuity on the part of the scribal professionals. At least, the developments undergone in the early parts of the 3rd millennium allowed for cuneiform to be adapted for and by other linguistic groups to convey their own languages.[284] The role of names of people, buildings, and points in time like festivals in the initial stages of this process is no doubt an important one.[285]

2.3.1 Some formal characteristics of Sumerian names

PNN in Sumerian texts were identified on a grammatical level with sentient (human) beings, similar to nouns of the animate class. This is apparent from the suffigation of the ergative particle –e to the end of names acting as subjects in transitive clauses, and of the dative particle –ra.[286] Sumerian names come in a variety of forms, ranging from single words and nominal

---

[282] So, e.g. according to D. O. Edzard, CRRA 19, 141f.; J.-J. Glassner, StOr 70, 15; R. K. Englund, *CDLJ* 2009:4, 22. I prefer to see the writing of sole LUGAL as an unmarked genitive construction; unmarked due to the lack at this point in time of phonetic complements to mark the genitive. Compare later Nanna^{na}, 'one of Nanna,' e.g. *WF* 25 o. iv 2, from ED IIIa Šuruppag; and ^{d}En-lil$_2$-la$_2$, 'one of Enlil,' e.g. BIN 8 65 o. ii 6, from ED IIIb Umma-Zabala.

[283] M.-L. Thomsen, Mesopotamia 10, 20. J. Hayes, *Phonologies of Asia and Africa*, 1004: 49.6.

[284] For the adaption of the largely logographic Sumerian to an Akkadian syllabary, see R. Hasselbach, *Sargonic Akkadian*, 27–32, with many references.

[285] D. Schmandt-Besserat went so far as to say that the writing of names was a primary incentive for the development of the script toward a phonetic realization of the spoken language. While this is not unthinkable, her dating of individual steps in this process can not be upheld, and thereby much of the basis for her thesis dissolves. For instance, she considers some of the interments of the Ur royal cemetery with their inscribed objects to be older than the literary texts from Šuruppag and Abū Ṣalābīḫ; and that these funerary furnishings inscribed with names would have paved the way for developments allowing for the writing down of literary works. See CAANE 1/2, 1493–1501; and further, *Archaeology Odyssey* vol. 4 no. 1 (Jan/Feb 2002), 6–7; 63, for her hypotheses.

[286] T. E. Balke, *Onoma* 32 (1994), 76.

phrases, to transitive clauses. The following brief description of forms is arranged according to complexity.

Single element names appear regularly, though as a group their number is fairly limited.[287] The names IL$_2$ (uncl. mng.),[288] ka$_5$-a 'fox,'[289] sa-a 'cat,'[290] maš 'goat('s kid),'[291] and AK (nominal formation derived from ak, 'to create'?),[292] are some examples. With the possible exception of the last name,[293] this group does not seem to be abbreviations of more complex types.

Some professional denominations were introduced into the Sumerian onomasticon during the course of the 3rd millennium, the most wide-spread being gala, a singer of cultic laments.[294] The distribution in the social strata of these names may be limited to the lower classes in society. No such names appear in early commemorative inscriptions. This could, with due reservation, be taken to imply that people bearing such names were rarely in a position to afford the expense of dedicating an inscribed object to a divinity. In ED IIIa administrative texts, titles sometimes appear instead of named persons, serving as identifiers of other, named, persons; indicating that the latter belonged to the bureaucratic sphere of the title office. Without additional graphic or grammatical distinctions, it is often hard to separate between a single noun standing in for a personal name or for a profession.

Phrase names present combinations of nouns with deverbal attributes or predicates like šeš-kal-la 'the brother is precious,'[295] and lugal-mas-su 'the lugal (is) victorious' (or 'a victor'); or genitival noun combinations such as geme$_2$-^{d}Dumu-zi '(female) dependent (of) Dumuzi.'[296] These two groups represent extremely common name types. Names featuring a genitive construction perhaps makes for the single most common type of Sumerian name.[297] Other phrase names are made up by two nouns where the one is qualified, serving as an attribute of the first element: ^{d}En-lil$_2$-sipa 'Enlil is a

---

[287] D. O. Edzard, *RlA* 9 (1998–2001), "Name, Namengebung. A. Sumerisch," 95, § 2.1; T. E. Balke, *Onoma* 32 (1994), 77; 79; M. Krebernik, AOAT 296, 10; all with examples.

[288] *CIRPL* Ent. 28 iii 28–29: u$_4$-ba IL$_2$, saĝa Zabala$_5$^{ki}-kam 'around that time, IL$_2$ was the chief temple administrator of Zabala.'

[289] OSP 2 64 r. 7 (CS Nippur).

[290] BIN 8 86 o. iii 14.

[291] E.g. *TSŠ* 467, o. i 4 (ED IIIa Šuruppag); OIP 104 49 r. iii 8 (ED IIIb Adab, Eig. ^{ni_3}ensi$_2$).

[292] E.g. MVN 10 1 2 (AK, lugal, Umma^{ki}).

[293] Names composed with a named god preceded or followed by AK were frequent in the ED I-II Ur texts, see for instance R. A. di Vito, StPohl SM 16, 115f.; M. Krebernik AOAT 296, 12 and fn. 35.

[294] The phenomenon is common to modern cultures, with names such as Smith, Baker, Müller etc. See H. H. Hock & B. D. Joseph, *Language History, Language Change, and Language Relationship*, 311.

[295] E.g. BIN 8 176 o. 7 (MS-CS Unknown).

[296] E.g. *Amherst* 2 o. iii 2 (ED IIIb Girsu).

[297] H. Limet, *Anthroponymie*, 63–72; M. Krebernik, AOAT 296, 11.

shepherd.'[298] Some names combine nominal elements with dimensional markers, like igi-ĝu$_{10}$-AN-še$_3$-ĝal$_2$ 'my eyes are fixed at the god/the skies.'[299]

A sizeable group of PNN incorporate anticipatory genitive constructions functioning similarly to a subordinate clause: e$_2$-ur$_2$-bi-du$_{10}$ 'the foundation of the house is good,'[300] E$_2$-muš$_3$-ša$_3$-bi-gal 'the *inside* of the Emuš is great.'[301] The end result is a topicalizing construction where the focus is on the first element of the name. The construction is used to the same effect in literary texts and this underscores the literary affinities of Sumerian name-giving.[302] In names this construction can be traced back at least to ED IIIa times. The use of anticipatory genitives outside of literary contexts is quite limited, and, although in part outside the scope of this work, the distribution of this construction in names could produce interesting results.[303]

Clause names, finally, encompass a number of name types. In the ED I-II sources no secure instances of a verbal prefix are attested, apart from the modal negative prefix nu-, and finite forms remain comparatively limited in number until the Ur III period. Predication by verbal root alone continues to be a very common construction throughout the 3rd millennium. The consistency exhibited by this type of predication makes it implausible that they are in each and every instance a product of a graphic convention of shortening the names, but rather that they express an unmarked participle.[304] However, a number of 3rd millennium writings of names do feature unmistakable verbal prefixes mu- and i$_3$-, whereas other writings of the same individuals dispense with these prefixes.[305] The formal aspect aside, the semantic import of such names remain the same, albeit that a punctual action or quality is exchanged for a durative one. In the present work this difference

---

[298] TMH 5 27 o. i 7; ii 7 (ED IIIb Nippur); 180 o. i 7' (MS Nippur). For the construction, see H. Limet, *Anthroponymie*, 73–76.

[299] E.g. *DP* 1/2 113 o. viii 6 (ED IIIb Girsu). Compare igi-AN-še$_3$, *ECTJ* 9 o. ii 2' (ED IIIb Nippur); *TCVBI* 1-1 r. i 6; igi-AN-še$_3$-[(x$^?$)], OSP 2 98 r. i 13 (ES-MS Nippur).

[300] *WF* 33 o. iv 7 (ED IIIa Šuruppag); *DP* 1/2 135 o. i 5 (common in ED IIIb Girsu); OSP 1 46 o. 8 (simug, ED IIIb Nippur); *TCVBI* 7 o. 3 (ED IIIb Zabala); D. Foxvog, *Mesopotamia* 8, 68–69 (UCLM 9-1798) o. i 10 (šeš bil$_2$-lal$_3$-la(-me), ED IIIa-b Adab area economic document, Eig. ensi$_2$). Compare e$_2$-mu-bi-du$_{10}$ Struve *Onomastika*, 47; *ECTJ* 29 r. iii 10 (CS Nippur).

[301] *SF* 33 r. ii 8 (umbisaĝ, ED IIIa Šuruppag colophon).

[302] For investigations on genitive constructions in Sumerian in general, and on the stylistic traits of the anticipatory construction in particular, see G. Zólyomi, *JCS* 48 (1996), 31–47, especially 39–45; E. Haber, *RA* 103 (2009), 1–10. Neither of these studies focus on or address the question of the anticipatory construction in personal names.

[303] See, e.g., the notes by J. Hayes, *ASJ* 13 (1991), 185–194, on the surprisingly limited distribution of the anticipatory genitive in Sumerian, despite its syntactic nature as an SOV language. A similar end result may be observed in some Old Persian dialects under the influence of Aramaic, B. Utas, *Linguistic Convergence and Areal Diffusion*, 70f.

[304] See full discussion of the phenomenon by M. Krebernik, AOAT 296, 22f.

[305] See some kyriophore examples examples composed with the name of UruKAgina given above, p. 54.

is of less importance than the main focus of the name in relation to its content.

Clause names can feature dimensional objects, for instance: en-abzu-ta-mud 'the en (is someone) *born* from the Abzu,'[306] lugal-uru-na-nu_2 'the lugal (is one) lying down in his city.'[307] The predication is hardly ever marked by the expected copula -(a)m.[308]

2.3.1.1 Principles of abbreviation

Personal names in bureaucratic contexts could easily be abbreviated since they were secondary to the bottom line: the number of units at disposal, disbursed, dispatched, rented, borrowed, received or missing. But even when looking at sources where one could expect more precision, and the writing out of otherwise normally abbreviated names, e.g. in commemorative inscriptions on objects presented to gods, serving to remind the divinities of their subjects' piety, one can not detect any distinct differences in the way names were written. That is, names that appear shortened in administrative texts appear that way also in commemorative inscriptions. I. Diakonoff once demonstrated that written contracts from the city Šuruppag dating to the period around 2600 BCE are more generous in supplying grammatical morphemes than the economic texts from the same place and general time period.[309] And indeed, some personal names appearing in those contracts differ from the writings normally encountered in economic documents of the same period.[310] The differences in purpose for these types of text ought to have played a role in their composition. While the one type was meant for purely bureaucratic use within a limited timespan, mainly by the same office that produced it, the other was clearly meant to last for generations.

After a close look at the Sumerian onomastic corpus it is clear that any element in phrase and clause names could be discarded. Nominal predicates could thus be "headless," lacking a logical subject, as in engar-zi '‹x› is a reliable farmer.' The components that suffer the most from abbreviation are

[306] See F. Pomponio, *Prosopografia*, 97, for references (all instances ED IIIa Šuruppag). For the interpretation of mud in the early Sumerian onomasticon, perhaps with a mng. similar to e_3 'to come forth,' see M. Krebernik, AOAT 296, 46.

[307] UET 2, suppl. 14 r. i 4, photo in A. Alberti & F. Pomponio, StPohl SM 13 pl. 2 (ED IIIb Ur).

[308] See examples with H. Limet, *Namenforschung*, 852: 1.2.2; and compare, for the pre–Ur III period, T. E. Balke, *Onoma* 32 (1994), 78f. For the use of the copula, Old Sumerian am_6(AN), later am_3(A.AN), see M.-L. Thomsen, Mesopotamia 10, 275–278: §§ 541–546.

[309] I. Diakonoff, *Fs Jacobsen*, 105f. The names from Šuruppag sales contracts are collected in *FTUM*, 141–162. No other 3rd millennium site has yet provided such a wealth of contemporary sources belonging to both these text categories.

[310] An example of fuller orthography is the unique writing of a divine determinative before the theonym Utu in a contract, contrary to the usage in administrative texts. See the discussion of lugal-UD, p. 146. Compare also lugal-$bara_2$-ge-du_{10}, *WF* 70 r. v 10, against lugal-$bara_2$-du_{10}, twice in a scholastic composition, *SF* 28 and 29; and lugal-$bara_2$-si, *WF* 65 r. v 1.

grammatical ones, such as the case markers. The relative consistency with which this is executed raises a suspicion that it is not merely a matter of orthographic, scribal convention to economize space. Nouns representing subject and object were less prone to be excluded, but ample examples of such practices exist; it is not always possible to say whether what remained was the subject or the object, when lacking the ergative marker. Verbal predicates may have been easier to discard as they most often find themselves at the end of a name, given Sumerian syntax. Verbal prefixes could then be discarded altogether or be left hanging.[311] This latter clause component is especially interesting as it is key in understanding verbal clause names as either punctual or durative in force. The overall situation concerning abbreviations is in some respects similar to that in the earliest known Sumerian literature, from the ED IIIa period, though sentences featuring verbal prefixes without a subsequent verbal root is to my knowledge unattested in literary sources.[312]

Another principle which comes to the fore in some simple, two-component genitive chain names was observed by J. Bauer.[313] A few examples composed with the noun ur are illustrative. In ED IIIb Girsu, a certain ur-šul is for prosopographic reasons identical with a person named ur-^{d}Šul-pa-e$_3$ in other texts.[314] In CS Umma, a person named ur-zu in some texts is identical with ur-^{d}Su'en known from other texts of the same archive.[315] In this case, the fuller form features a double genitive when the syntax of the documentation demands it, while in the abbreviated form the double genitive is, as could be expected, discarded. The single attestation of the name ur-en is suspicious by its mere scarcity, because both ur-lugal and ur-nin abound. The name is rare also in the Ur III period, and is likely to be the result of an abbreviation from a longer form, perhaps ur-^{d}En-lil$_2$ (> ur-$^{‹d›}$En-‹lil$_2$›). Judging by the names ur-šul and ur-zu, the names are shortened on a phonetic basis, and hence the divine determinative is not written out, and what remains after shortening is the first syllable in the theonym (in the latter case zu < ^{d}EN:ZU).

311 See, e.g. the example of the shepherd ^{d}Utu-mu(-gi$_4$), fn. 315, below.

312 Compare the later omissions of all but the first component(s) in parallel verbal chains, as in M. E. Cohen, *Sumerian Hymnology: The Eršemma*, 29f., no. 29; and 139f., no. 10.

313 *AWL*, 498, note to v 3–4.

314 Compare ur-šul in DP suppl. 630 o. ii 1 = ur-^{d}Šul-pa-e$_3$ in VS 27 6 o. vi 11. The first form is about 9 times as common as the second in the ED IIIb Girsu archive.

315 Compare MAD 4 92 o. 1–5: 1 kuš ud$_5$ za$_3$-šuš, ur-zu-kam, ^{d}Utu-mu-gi$_4$, sipa (dated 4 mu 10 iti); MAD 4 109 o. 1–4: 1 kuš ud$_5$ za$_3$-šuš, ur-zu-kam, ^{d}Utu-mu sipa (dated 4 mu 11 iti); and MAD 4 100 o. 5–r. 3: 2 kuš ud$_5$, ur-^{d}Su'en-ka-kam, ^{d}Utu-mu sipa-de$_3$ mu-DU (dated 4 mu 12 iti; all three texts are published in transliteration only). Other texts are cited by W. Sommerfeld, *Fs Westenholz*, 295 fn. 27, who had arrived at the same conclusion concerning the identity of ur-zu/^{d}Su'en. On the nature of the archive, see B. R. Foster, *USP*, 62–78.

The abbreviating may in some cases have been done by those scribes compiling the documents. The phenomenon can be demonstrated in official as well as private archives. Whether the use of names among family members differed from official use is not obvious from the sources. Judging from Sargonic period private letters, no differences from the official usage of names can be detected. Kinship terms or appellatives like 'my lord,' can be used as compliments, which sometimes muddles understanding of the relationship between sender and receiver.[316] It is hard to say whether people writing to one another were in fact related, or if the formal use of names and abundant compliments are results of the level of literacy at the time. Scribes and perhaps someone who read the letter out loud to the recipient, could have acted as mediaries of the message. But the letters may well be faithful reflections of the tone of both familiar and professional interaction.

2.3.2 Sumerian names: speaker and contents

It has been suggested above that Sumerian personal names, with the exception of the simple genitive constructions, are in general impersonal as to voice or reference. Very little in the way of tendencies which would place the name in the mouth of a speaker, or relating it to the name-bearer can be discerned, as formulated by Henri Limet:

> "...dans leur grosse majorité, les noms sumériens sont «objectifs», en ce sens que, pour la plupart, ils énoncent un fait ou une idée de caractère général, sans référence, donc, à un sujet parlant."[317]

The ideas that are called to mind in the names are taken from the social and cultural – most often specifically religious – surroundings of the name-bearer or name-giver. Preoccupation with birth and the place of the child in the family is rare in the earliest times, as opposed to Akkadian name-giving.[318] The logical subject, the appellative explicitly written out or not, in the names, is therefore frequently to be understood as being someone other than the name-bearer him- or herself.[319] Names consisting of a genitive chain in which the first element often can be seen as referring to the individual bearing the name form are an exception.

A common trait of Sumerian names is the extensive use of terms which served as appellatives for prominent persons in society or in the divine realm. Among these, lugal 'king, lord, owner,' and nin 'queen, lady, sister,'

---

[316] Most pre–Ur III letters from Sumer and Akkade known at present, official and private, are edited and commented in B. Kienast & K. Volk, FAOS 19.
[317] H. Limet, *Anthroponymie*, 62. See also R. A. di Vito StPohl SM 16, 21; 82.
[318] M. Krebernik, AOAT 296, 50.
[319] M. Krebernik, AOAT 296, 9.

are among the most common ones. Names formed with en may sometimes denote '(high) priest,' but when referring to a divinity, the noun is culturally specific and untranslatable.[320] Interestingly, nin and en appear in names of both genders, while lugal-names were only exceptionally borne by females.[321] Besides these, original kinship terms such as $aja_{(2)}$ 'father,' ama 'mother,'[322] šeš 'brother'[323] and $nin_{(9)}$ 'sister';[324] and the male designations mes, and šul, both roughly corresponding to '(young) man,' figure prominently.[325] Names containing these and other nouns must be subjected to serious analysis before certitude can be reached as to whom the designation applies. Not all names containing the noun lugal have bearing on the human ruler; neither do names containing the appellative en always have to be interpreted as relating to a religious official.

Some important predicates characteristic of the Sumerian world view recur with high frequency. They seem to share in a view of the universe where the outlines of existence are god-given and already decided upon, and where what abides by these outlines is 'proper, reliable' or 'right,' gi and zi.[326] That which has the capacity to measure up to the inherent potential of a cultural phenomenon, a natural numen or a power-laden place was thought to 'fill' it,[327] si. And so the Sumerian onomasticon is replete with names like ama-$bara_2$-ge-si 'the *mother* is just right for the throne.'[328] For some reason the predicate si does not appear with any regularity in theophore names. A verb of similar import is tum_2, which is in the following regularly given as 'to be befitting,' with respect to someone or something. The verb du_{10}, is in the following most often given as 'to be, make good.' The true sense may, however, in certain cases be a derived one, 'to (make) function properly,' as

---

320 See in part the discussion above, p. 55. An extensive investigation of en in the onomasticon is required to put the results of the present thesis in perspective. Given restrictions in time and scope this has not been attainable but must await further study. For some preliminaries, see D. O. Edzard, CRRA 19, 142f., but note that a name lugal-abzu-si, which Edzard described as non–existent, has since been attested at ED IIIb Nippur.

321 The only likely occurrences of lugal in FPNN in the time between 2800–2200 that I have managed to find are $geme_2$-lugal, from CS-LS Nippur, and lugal-an-na-tum_2, who appears as $geme_2$ in two Sargonic Nippur texts, TMH 5 39 and 44. The latter is, however, less secure, as typically male names (beginning with ur-) appear in close connection to this lugal-an-na-tum_2.

322 VE1044: ama-MU = *u_3-mu-mu*.

323 VE1043: šeš-MU = *a-ḫu-um*.

324 VE1183: nin^{ni} = *a-ḫa-tum*.

325 See G. Marchesi, *OrNS* 73 (2004), 191f., w. fnn. 221f., for a closer analysis of these appellatives.

326 See K. Lämmerhirt's excellent work on these two latter lemmas, AOAT 348, passim.

327 The Akkadian correspondences are *maṣûm* 'to be equal to, sufficient for,' and *malûm* 'to fill,' for which, see *CAD* M/1 s.v.v For previous studies of Sumerian si and its manifold functions, 'to fill' no doubt being the original sense, see e.g. D. O. Edzard, *ZA* 53 (1959), 12–15; P. Michalowski, *Fs Wilcke*, 199–201; M. Krebernik, AOAT 296, 23–32.

328 OSP 1 66 o. 4; and see also GN GAN_2 ama-$bara_2$-ge-si^{ki}, *op. cit.* 114 o. i 2. As in so many other early ama-names, ama appears to be something else than 'mother.'

a complementary form of the verb si, indicating a stronger measure of transitivity. However, the verbs do not seem to occur very often in connection with the same objects.[329]

2.3.3 Sumerian lugal-names: who is the lugal?

The term lugal takes on separate meanings in modern translations depending on the context in which the word is found. Fundamentally, it entails a male being who exercises a measure of control or authority over something, be it a place, a thing, or another being. Hence its use as a title of autonomous rulers, as an epithet of deities under certain circumstances, as the term for 'owner' of a specified object, or even as an honorary term of address in a message. The four main usages and their potential applications in the human onomasticon will in the following be treated in some more detail.

2.3.3.1 The ruler as referent

A traditional way of translating lugal in PNN is 'king.' In certain cases this is the likely idea behind the name in the first place. There is also a possibility that ideas expressed in some names may originally have been associated with a divinity or a human being other than the ruler, but, with time, would come to be associated with the ruler given developments in how nam-lugal was perceived. Associations may also have passed the other way, from originally having denoted a characteristic of the human ruler to being linked to a specific deity. In other names, the idea may be as applicable to a human being as to a divinity.

Thanks to previous research into onomastic features and into the socio-political system of early Mesopotamian state formations, there are some key elements to bear in mind when interpreting the meaning behind personal names. Much depends on the ideas being expressed and whether there are exact or close formal parallels with names featuring theonyms in place of the appellative. The human ruler has been posited by A. Westenholz to be a likely referent in early Nippur names pertaining to the fulfillment of cultic duties and of providing fertility in the land.[330] More recently, Westenholz has argued that the lugal was deeply involved with cultic matters; and that the term denoted an individual with religious duties rather than a political office.[331] G. Marchesi on his part, showed that the lugal is plausibly to be interpreted as the human ruler in certain contexts where a named deity appears.[332] And given close parallels in later royal hymns, the import of

[329] See, first and foremost, the names lugal-bara$_2$-du$_{10}$, lugal-bara$_2$-ga-ne$_2$-du$_{10}$, lugal-bara$_2$-ge-du$_{10}$ and lugal-bara$_2$-si; and perhaps lugal-me-du$_{10}$-ga and lugal-me-si.
[330] OSP 1, 6, 8.
[331] *Six City-State Cultures*, 23–42.
[332] HANE/S 10, 72f. fnn. 381f.

certain other names also may be attributed to the ruler. Though in any given case the existence of parallels, whether incorporating a theonym or another appellative, must always be kept in mind to arrive at an interpretation as to the identity of the referent.

2.3.3.2 A divinity as referent

G. J. Selz has shown that many names which have uncritically been ascribed to the human ruler may in fact rather have had a divinity as referent. He cites a selection of parallel nominal phrase names in which names with the appellative lugal have precise or close correspondences with names incorporating the theonym Ningirsu, the tutelary deity of Girsu.[333] But even if seeming parallel constructions with an appellative on the one hand, and theonyms on the other, can be demonstrated to have existed side by side at the same time and place, the identity of the deity with the appellative is not carved in stone. More than one deity could be characterized in the exact same manner. By far the best type of corroborating evidence would be to have inscriptional material, literary, religious or scholastic texts, preferably contemporary with the name, that would bolster any assumptions made as to the identity of the referent. That is, textual evidence linking a deity with, for instance, a certain kind of quality, action or place, which also surfaces in the onomasticon. In many cases such material exists - in many cases, unfortunately, it does not. However great the difficulties of projecting later expressions of belief back into the 3rd millennium, such associations often offer the best basis for understanding a great deal of not only personal names, but mythical literary themes in general.[334]

Certain divine names feature lugal as first element and may originally have been epithets which developed into free-standing names.[335] The epithet lugal could theoretically apply to any male divinity – given Mesopotamian theology where each god or goddess was responsible for a given part of the physical, cultural or divine world – but this is, of course, not the case. Some deities were widely revered outside of their home communities – most were not. This fact, I believe, is a key to understanding and interpreting lugal-names and for being able to correctly attribute names appearing in several places at the same time. It is also equally important for names which are so far unique and only attested once or twice in one place. The epithet lugal is most often used about gods in a few specific contexts: as the owner, or 'lord'

[333] *OLZ* 85 (1990), 303. A. Westenholz also entertained a similar idea for certain names, concerning An and Enlil, OSP 1, 6.
[334] For some such themes, see M. Krebernik, *Annäherungen* 1, 221f.
[335] For a discussion of such DNN, see D. O. Edzard, *RlA* 7 (1987–90), 108f., "Lugal (in Götternamen)."

of a geographic location, such as a city,[336] a temple,[337] or a cosmologically significant locus;[338] or as the 'lord' of a ruler or a private citizen in commemorative inscriptions on votive objects or in building inscriptions.[339] If some of the gods whose popular appeal was more widespread than others are referred to simply as lugal, without further qualification, then these divinities are perhaps more likely to turn up as the referents more regularly in lugal-names from cities other than those which housed their prime sanctuaries.

After inspecting the early inscriptional and literary material available, a few deities set themselves apart as more likely to be referred to as lugal in the Sumerian onomasticon.[340] The first are An, god of heaven at home in Uruk, and his son Enlil, father of Ninurta, patron god of Nippur. Enlil is said to be the lord of the lands and the father of the gods.[341] The former trait he shared with his father An in inscriptions of Uruk rulers.[342] Enlil was furthermore considered as the one who had settled the gods in their cities,[343] some time in the beginning of history. As rulers of the known world, An and Enlil are prime candidates for being the referents behind a number of lugal-names. In particular perhaps Enlil, whose authority was essentially unchallenged during the 3rd millennium.

---

[336] E.g. W. Schramm, *WO* 7 (1973–74), 16, 1f.: ⸢^{d}En⸣-ki, lugal Eridu^{ki}(-ra) 'for Enki, the lord of Eridu.' An interesting example is ARET 5 20 (=21=*IAS* 278), o. i 5: An nu-gal uru-ka$_{3}$-kam$_{4}$ 'An is the lord of Uruk,' following M. Krebernik, *Fs Röllig*, 187. The phonetic writing /u*r*uk/ for normal Sumerian /u*n*ug/ is consistent with evidence from the CS period, in the gentilic [*u*]*r-ki-um* 'man of Uruk,' MAD 1 172 o. 10', photo and copy in J. Goodnick Westenholz, MesCiv 7, 400f. The reading uru, besides eri, ere, iri, of URU, may find further support in the DN ^{d}⸢Mes⸣-saĝa-⸢uru$_{16}$⸣, *FTUM* 106 o. ii 1', normally featuring UNUG; and, perhaps, in the alternation nin-uru/uru$_{16}$-ni-še$_{3}$-nu-, see notes to lugal-e$_{2}$-ni-še$_{3}$, below, 3.1.1.2. This would of course mean that the sign URU had more than a few possibilities for vocalization, as suggested also by the Akkadian pronounciation /ru/ (ru$_{x}$) of URU×A, e.g. J. Goodnick Westenholz, *op. cit.*, 228 l. 10.

[337] E.g. TH 218: ^{d}Dumu-zi lugal E$_{2}$-muš$_{3}$-a-k(e$_{4}$) 'Dumuzi, lord of the Emuš.'

[338] E.g. TH 463–464: nun-zu ^{d}Ir$_{9}$-ra lugal Mes-lam-ma, ḫuš ki-a lugal u$_{4}$ šu$_{2}$-[x] 'your *prince*, Erra, the lord of the Meslam, fierce one of the Underworld, lord (of the) … sunset.'

[339] E.g BE 1/2 87 iii 38–39: ^{d}En-lil$_{2}$, lugal ki-aĝa$_{2}$-ni '(for) Enlil, his beloved lord'; and the citizen of Lagaš who dedicated a metal dagger for the life of his 'lord' or 'king' Eanatum, V. E. Crawford, *Iraq* 36 (1974), 32 fig. 4 (3H-T7) r. 1: nam-ti lugal-ni e$_{2}$-an-na-tum$_{2}$.

[340] The following overview is influenced to some extent by T. Jacobsen's article from Encyclopedia Britannica, reprinted in *Toward the Image of Tammuz*, 16–38.

[341] *CIRPL* Ent. 28 i 1–3: ^{d}En-lil$_{2}$, lugal kur-kur-ra, ab-ba diĝir-diĝir-re$_{2}$-ne-k(e$_{4}$). See also for the first epithet *IAS* 137 o. ii 2'–3': $^{d(UD)}$en$_{(GAL)}$-lil$_{2(NUN)}$, lugal$_{(PA.NUN)}$ kur$_{(UD)}$-kur$_{(UD)}$: "Enlil, König aller Länder," following M. Krebernik, *BFE*, 280.

[342] E.g. in Lugalzagesi's Nippur inscription BE 1/2 87 i 13–14: igi zi bar-ra, An lugal kur-kur-ra 'looked upon with a graceful eye by An, the lord of the lands.' For more references, see FAOS 6, 222 A 5'.

[343] OIP 99, 46–53, l. 11–14: ^{d}En-lil$_{2}$ a-nun, ki mu-ĝar-ĝar, diĝir gal-gal, za$_{3}$-me mu-du$_{11}$ 'Enlil established places (of worship) for the Anuna(-gods) and the great gods (as one) praised him.' Translation is free and based on key observations by M. Krebernik, *Fs Hrouda*, 151–157.

Enlil's brother Enki, at home in Eridu, was portrayed in later times as the best friend with great insight into the gods' plans that humans could ever have asked for. Wisdom and magic were his traditional areas of expertise. He resided in the Abzu, a power-laden place in close touch with the subterranean waters. Sanctuaries termed Abzu were located also outside of Eridu. The ED Lagaš state appears to have supported up to 9 such Abzus, and others are known from, for instance, Nippur, Ur, and Kiš.[344] M. Krebernik has pointed to the possibility of seeing in early Abzu-names links to ideas surrounding birth, as a body of water which the unborn child and the mother had to cross.[345] And indeed the imagery of a boat laden with cornelian and lapis lazuli figures in an Ur III period incantation with its roots in ED IIIa traditions. The earlier forerunner features only repeated mentions of water and other body fluids.[346]

The Moon God of the city Ur, Nanna (in texts from Ur) or Su'en (in texts from outside of Ur), is one of two or three deities referred to epithetically as lugal without any reference to a specific locus or object in the ED IIIa za$_3$-me hymns from Abū Ṣalābīḫ.[347] He counted as the son of Enlil. Nanna/Su'en's areas of responsibility lay to a great deal in aspects of fertility; especially with cattle, the waning and waxing crescents similar in appearance to the horns of a bull. His journey across the night skies marked the passing of time, and the Mesopotamian calendar was lunar-based.

Nanna's son Utu, is another deity about whom lugal is used epithetically without a governed noun in the za$_3$-me hymns.[348] He was the patron god of Larsa in the south-central floodplain and of Sippar at the northern end of the same. In both places his temple was called the Ebabbar, 'the shining house.'[349] Unfortunately, not much is known about Utu's traits in the early periods.[350] In UD.GAL.NUN literary works he is awarded nam-lugal, probably by Enlil himself, for services rendered to other gods.[351] In later times Utu

---

[344] G. J. Selz, CRRA 35, 195.

[345] AOAT 296, 46, w. ref. to a survey on later incantations pertaining to this theme.

[346] M. Krebernik, *BFE*, 36–47. See also G. Cunningham, StPohl SM 17, 21f., and 69–75; M. Stol, *Birth in Babylonia and the Bible*, 60–63.

[347] R. D. Biggs, OIP 99, 46–53, l. 36: lugal ^{d}Nanna za$_3$-me 'lord Nanna, praise!'

[348] R. D. Biggs, OIP 99, 46–53, l. 38: lugal ^{d}Utu za$_3$-me 'lord Utu, praise!' Compare also the notes in *FTUM*, 107, on a deity ^{d}Lugal-UD in three administrative Šuruppag texts. P. Mander, *Pantheon*, 60, note to no. 187, took the DN as combining the appellative lugal with the name of the Sun God, Utu. Lugal-UD is not found in any of the larger ED IIIa god lists. See also M. Krebernik, *Annäherungen* 1, 321 w. fn. 801, on a deity PA.NUN.UD, which could be taken as UGN for lugal$_{(PA.NUN)}$ Utu, but other readings also present themselves.

[349] TH 176 (Larsa), 491 (Sippar): ^{d}Utu lugal e$_2$-babbar$_2$-ra-k(e$_4$).

[350] This led to Utu's characterization by W. H. Ph. Römer, Historia Religionum 1, 131: "According to Sumerian Texts, the role played by this god appears to have been comparatively subordinate."

[351] *SF* 37 o. iv 19'–20': piriĝ me-te an$_{(UD)}$ ki$_{(UNUG)}$-ta$_{(TA\textit{gunû})}$ bad$_{(LAGAB)}$, ⸢nam$_2$$^?$⸣ [(x$^?$ x$^?$)] mu-še$_{21}$; *SF* 38 o. iii 1–2: ⸢piriĝ⸣ [an$_{(UD)}$] ki$_{(UNUG)}$-ta ⸢bad$_{(LAGAB)}$⸣, [x x x]-še$_{21}$; *IAS* 114 o. iv 1':

presided over the dispensing of justice and the principles that lay the foundations for an ordered society; a trait he to some extent shared with his father. There are also indications that Utu's functions in earlier times were related to the upholding of law and order,[352] functions he would have had in common with his Semitic counterpart Śamaś. The latter is the subject of a hymnic composition going back at least to ED IIIa times, found at both Abū Ṣalābīḫ and Ebla, and composed in an early Akkadian dialect.[353] In it, Śamaś and the god KA.DI gather by the river (and) source (ENGUR) to perform some, unfortunately, unintelligible act.[354] A main theme of the composition seems to be inter-city trade.[355]

Together, Utu and Nanna/Su'en may be seen as the most conspicuous embodiments of the divine world visible to the ancient inhabitants of Mesopotamia – alongside Inana/ʿAštar, who was associated with the planet Venus – and thus it comes as no surprise that they were highly popular among the people in general. In later times, Nanna/Su'en and Utu/Śamaś were two of the three main male deities who were venerated in connection with delivering babies.[356] If there are indications of such responsibilities also in earlier times, this could have left traces in the onomastic material.

Certainly, these are not the only male divinities which might be referred to in lugal-names. However, they were generally regarded as important for human society and they commanded great respect over most of the region that used cuneiform for a vehicle of writing.

Utu nam$_2$-lugal$_{(PA.NUN)}$-še$_3$ nam$_2$-š[e$_{21}$]: 'the 'Lion,' who (by himself) separated heaven from earth, summoned Utu for nam-lugal.' References courtesy of K. V. Zand.

352 See the survey of ED IIIb Girsu PNN by G. J. Selz, *Götterwelt*, 287f. Utu was among the deities invoked in the Stele of the Vultures, along with Enlil, Ninḫursaĝ, Enki and Su'en. Utu's name formed part of the complaint i$_{(3)}$-$^{(d)}$Utu. See passages quoted in *CAD* I s.v. *iutû* (Gudea Cyl. B and *CIRPL* Ukg. 6). A similar word composed with Nanna's name, *inannû*, with the same meaning, is found in later texts. For more on the mng. of i$_{(3)}$-$^{(d)}$Utu, see D. O. Edzard, *Sumerian Grammar*, 169, 15.10.

353 *IAS* 326+342 and ARET 5 6, treated by M. Krebernik, QuadSem 18, 63–149; and W. G. Lambert, JCS 41 (1989), 1–33. Remarks on the composition have been offered by C. Woods, *ZA* 95 (2005), 44; and R. D. Biggs, *LdE*, 127. See also the edition of W. Yuhong, *JAC* 22 (2007), 75–90.

354 ARET 5 6 r. ii 4. The god KA.DI is in later times at least read Ištaran. He is explicitly named in connection with the marking of boundaries in the dispute between Umma and Lagaš, *CIRPL* Ent. 28 i 10. Given the phonetic complement -na in this passage, an older form of Ištaran is likely.

355 As noted already by D. O. Edzard, ARET 5, 30.

356 The third being Asalluḫi/Marduk. See, in general, M. Stol, *Birth in Babylonia and the Bible*, 10f., 63–72, 133. Stol surmises, *op. cit.*, 72, that the reason why Nanna would assist in giving birth was due to his being the tutelary god of Ur, home of the Ur III dynasty. I believe it is rather due to his association with farm animals and their proliferation. For an in-depth analysis of Utu in connection with birth and determining fates, from the OB period onwards, see J. Polonsky, *Fs Leichty*, 297–311.

2.3.3.3 An owner as referent

One of the meanings of lugal is 'owner.' This can be compared with the fact that a significant proportion of Sumerian names are composed with a noun governing a theonym, such as ur-Enlil '*man* of Enlil,' or $geme_2$-Bau 'female servant of Bau.'[357] Similar names composed with the appellative lugal are also known. The relationship between the referent expressed by this noun and the referent of the governed noun is rarely clear. But the grammatical relationship so clearly presented through such names, gives reason to believe that there is a deeper, personal kind of relationship underlying the words. If such was the case, then appellatives appearing in place of the theonyms in parallel names might easily be imagined as representing a divinity. But granted that the human counterparts of these appellatives were also judged as positive influences in the lives of normal people, there is every reason to believe that for instance ur-lugal could be interpreted as a statement from or concerning a thankful subject which was then epitomized in a name given to a child promising future loyalty in return for continuous support.

If the relationship was somehow formalized and an accepted part of the name-giving traditions, pronominal markers -$ĝu_{10}$, -(a)ni, etc., for the first and third person singular, can conceivably be indicators for names of this type, when no other solution presents itself as the more plausible.

2.3.3.4 A term of address

The formula lugal-$ĝu_{10}$ 'Milord,' was quite common in letter incipits.[358] Sometimes replacing the name of the recipient entirely, with all the speculation that this entails.[359] Due to the nature of the Sumerian language and its writing system, the vocative form of a noun is not written in a particular way, but has in theory to be marked by other means, such as the addition of 1st or 2nd person pronominal elements. Of these, the former appears with some frequency while the latter is hardly attested at all. Thus, the possibilities for interpreting lugal in personal names as a term of address is hampered by a number of factors, notwithstanding the fallacies resulting from abbreviation.

2.4 Akkadian names: a brief overview

As a member of the Semitic language family, Old Akkadian personal names as well as toponyms naturally share a lot of traits with formations in other

[357] I have kept the traditional reading of this goddess' name throughout even though a reading ^{d}Ba-ba_6 has met with general acceptance within the field of Assyriology.
[358] B. R. Foster, *USP* 136, provides a partial list.
[359] See discussion by B. Kienast & K. Volk, FAOS 19, 79.

Semitic languages and therefore to a large extent lend themselves to cross-cultural comparisons.[360] Points of common interest in the onomastic material are personal relations, deities, and aspects of their being in themselves or in relation to the name-bearer or -giver. Old Akkadian names often have close parallels in the later Babylonian and Assyrian dialects, although similar name formations for humans and geographic locations belonging to areas further west and north are richly attested in the Ebla archives, and in the Ḫabur area.[361] Quite a few constructions and themes are common to both Sumerian and Akkadian names. One must reckon with a measure of influence or exchange between the two linguistic groups.

2.4.1 Some formal characteristics of Akkadian names

Akkadian names, like Sumerian, exhibit a wide range of types: from single element names over one-participant verbal phrases, on to full transitive clause-type names. In Akkadian texts, neither personal names nor place names were normally declined. In a few cases the nominative case may appear where the genitive would have been expected from the context.[362]

Single element names are more common in Akkadian than in Sumerian. They consist mostly of nouns and adjectives, the latter of which are totally absent as single element names in Sumerian.[363] As a result of this, Akkadian names can to a higher extent be said to describe the name-bearer him- or herself.[364] Some single element names are clearly the result of abbreviation and may be termed hypocoristica. A common type consists of names derived from finite verbal forms where a case ending has been added to the finite

---

[360] A summary of name forms shared by members of the Semitic language family can be found in E. Lipiński, *Semitic Languages*, 570: 67.7. For a handy overview of monographs on the subject of Semitic onomastics, with special attention paid to the Amorite personal names, see M. P. Streck, AOAT 271, 131–138.

[361] For remarks on the early toponymy attested at Ebla, see M.C. Astour, *JAOS* 108 (1988), 545–555; *JAOS* 117 (1997), 332–338. The personal names from Ebla sources in relation to the cities of origin of persons named have been investigated by A. Archi, QuadSem 13 (1984), 225–251; M. Bonechi, *StEL* 8 (1991), 59–79.

[362] See a few instances of the determinative pronoun *šu* in genitive relations in MAD 3, 247, sorted under the demonstrative. The signs *šu* and *śu*$_2$ (demonstrative) are grammatically distinct, but the signs are very similar. The slightest damage to the left side of the sign can be very problematic for establishing a reading and an interpretation. On the name of the daughter of *Narām*-Su'en, written *tu*-DA(-na)-AB-*śum*, see the discussion and the evidence for a reading *Tuṭṭanābśum* 'Sie (die Göttin) bereitet ihm (dem König) immer wieder Gutes,' going back to an interpretation by W. von Soden, and put forward by W. Sommerfeld, *Fs Westenholz*, 290–292, with previous readings.

[363] As noted by T. E. Balke, *Onoma* 32 (1994), 80.

[364] See discussion by D. O. Edzard, *RlA* 9 (1998–2001), "Name, Namengebung. B. Akkadisch", 107, with reference to J. J. Stamm, *Namengebung* 242–273.

verb: *yirʿeum* 'tended one' <*yirʿe*-DN 'DN tended,' using the verb *reʾûm* as an example.[365]

Names composed by a single or two elements make up the main part of the 3rd millennium Akkadian onomasticon. Genitive constructions featuring two nouns or noun plus theophore element, are rare. Instead, the determinative pronouns are used, as in *šu*-ʿAštar 'he of Aštar,' common in the Diyālā area and at Gasur. This may be contrasted with the Sumerian onomasticon, in which a nominal chain is one of the most commonly encountered constructions. In Sargonic times, names containing 3 or 4 elements – including suffixed pronominal elements – existed, but only found more widespread use in the 2nd millennium.[366] For instance ᵈMalik-*zinśu* 'Malik is his rain (i.e. source of abundance).'[367] Many of the more complex names contain a dimensional reference like the terminative suffix (*-iš*): *ʾIliś-takal* 'trust in the god!';[368] or a personal referent, most often a possessive personal suffix, as in *ʾIlak-nuʾʾid* 'praise your god.'[369]

It is rather common for nouns in Old Akkadian names to lack mimation.[370] This is, however, a rule with many exceptions. All names are seemingly not put to writing in exactly the same way throughout the times and places involved here. Examples range from simple orthographic variations to quite distinct morphological alternations. A high-ranking officer *Naḫśum-śanat*, known from CS Nippur, is a case in point. Two different writings of his name are known, all from the same archival context: *na-aḫ-śum-śa-na-at* and *na-ḫaś₂-śi-na-at*.[371] Another example is formed by the name of *Śarrukēn*, for which three contemporary writings, *śar-ru*-gi, *śar-rum₂*-gi and *śar-um*-gi, are attested.[372] Mimation in names and in other sources would require a study of its own.

Unfortunately, knowledge of which syllables a sign actually represented remains a problem. The ligature KA×ŠU in Akkadian contexts had a reading

---

365 The type is discussed by H. Ranke, *AJSL* 23 (1907), 359. Ranke dismissed the form as being hypocoristic. According to him, it was a simply an abbreviation.

366 D. O. Edzard, *RlA* 9 (1998–2001), "Name, Namengebung. B. Akkadisch," 110f.; J. Hilgert, JBVO 5, 67 and fn. 67.

367 ᵈ*Ma-lik-zi-in-śu*, dumu *I-da*-AN, gal.sukkal, /.../, dumu(-dumu) Akkade[ki], MO A xi 9; B xvi 1; C xx' 11; D vii' 16 (ES).

368 E.g. BIN 8 121 o. i 1, r. ii 2. In the Ur III period, prepositions *ana* and *in*(*a*) begin to replace *-iš* in this function in PNN.

369 E.g. HSS 10 155 o. i 9.

370 I. J. Gelb, MAD 2, 145: 1, d.; W. von Soden, GAG § 63d. For the Eblaite onomasticon, see discussion by M. Krebernik, BBVO 7, 31f. For a comparison of forms with and without mimation in the Akkadian Ur III period onomasticon, see M. Hilgert, Imgula 5, 134–144.

371 See A. Westenholz, OSP 2, 94f. with references. The noun *naḫśum* perhaps means 'bounty, riches,' and *śattum*, normally means 'year,' but the exact mng. remains opaque. The associations invoked are clearly highly poetic.

372 Compare also the name *śar-ru-i₃-li₂*, attested from the ES period onwards, with *śar-um-i₃-li₂*, in a text from MS-CS Umma. And see further p. 211, fnn. 1343–1344.

b/pu$_3$, but also *b/pum*. Whichever is meant when occupying final position in a name is basically for a modern reader to decide. This survey for the most part favours short readings of such signs.

The language of Akkadian names is at times archaizing.[373] The normal word order of Akkadian: noun – verbal predicate, strictly observed in administrative and commemorative sources of the times, was not the rule in Sargonic PNN. Instead, the finite forms occupy the first position in sentence type names consisting of a predicate and a subject,[374] at least as long as the predicate was not further embellished by a suffix or a specified object was expressed in the clause.[375]

Another key characteristic is the relative freedom of components in nominal clauses to occupy first or second position with just about equal frequency.[376] In stative names, a morpheme *–a* is regularly found attached to stems of nouns, marking what can be interpreted as predicative forms.[377] This morpheme was only exceptionally used outside of PNN. Word order, subject choice, and nouns uncommon outside of the onomasticon have led some scholars to describe the language of names as close to literary,[378] even if the lack of a decent corpus of Old Akkadian literature – disregarding the historical inscriptions – somewhat takes the edge off such statements. While this may be so, Akkadian names are more tersely formulated than Sumerian ones, but to a large extent, the subject matters show affinities in style and pomp to the Sumerian onomasticon.

At any rate, the freedom which allowed for renewal of name structure and contents, indicates that names were part of a dynamic and living linguistic tradition, which was not just inherited and senselessly repeated until the names had lost much of their original meaning.[379]

---

[373] The archaizing traits of the PNN were one of the strongest reasons why R. Hasselbach opted not to use them for her systematic study *Sargonic Akkadian*, see esp. p. 20f. Hasselbach's decision was supported by the reviewers L. Kogan & K. Markina who at the same time wished for more onomastic material to be drawn into the investigation, exercising "due caution," Babel und Bibel 3, 559.

[374] As was also the case with Ebla names. A survey of finite forms is given by M. Krebernik, BBVO 7 34–65.

[375] See the short overview by D. O. Edzard, *RlA* 9 (1998–2001), "Name, Namengebung. B. Akkadisch", 105, §2.1, II. B. b.

[376] Some tendencies for word placement in names combining nouns and a stative are noted by J. J. M. Roberts, *The Earliest Semitic Pantheon*, 5–8.

[377] Treated as such by I. J. Gelb, *Symbolae Linguisticae in Honorem Georgii Kuryłowicz*, 72–80; MAD 2, 141f.; 146–153; J. J. M. Roberts, *The Earliest Semitic Pantheon*, note 13, p. 11; 128. See also R. Hasselbach, *Sargonic Akkadian*, note 105, p. 21; and for a dissenting view, B. Kienast *Ebla 1975–1985*, 37–47.

[378] For instance D. O. Edzard, *RlA* 9 (1998–2001), "Name, Namengebung. B.", §3.1. M. Hilgert, JBVO 5, 41, was somewhat more cautious in his characterization.

[379] See the discussion by J. J. Stamm, *Namengebung*, 14f.

2.4.2 Akkadian names: speaker and contents

Studies in Akkadian personal names of the 3rd millennium suffer from a dearth of material. Though there are many thousands of texts to draw upon, the Akkadian onomasticon is dwarfed by the significantly higher number of Sumerian names from the same period. Therefore at present, much more can be said about the latter. But with more and more sites in northern Mesopotamia and Syria yielding cuneiform texts from the 3rd millennium, this situation may well change over the next few decades. Given the material available in published form, it is still possible to come to conclusions on similarities and differences in name-giving traditions. For instance, references to a speaker are more common in Akkadian names. Personal suffixes of the third person singular appear already in the ED IIIa, as far back as Akkadian names go. More rarely, verbal attribution to a first and second person subject appear with varying degrees of regularity throughout the Akkadian-speaking area, depending on the time period surveyed.

To a large extent, early Akkadian names, like their Sumerian counterparts, relate to systems of a social and cultural nature surrounding the name-bearer and -giver. The names depict the deeds and qualities of dozens of divinities used as theophore elements, though these are quite often summarily written as diĝir, *ʾilum* or *ʾil*, 'the god.' While Sumerian diĝir could freely represent any divinity, male or female, Akkadian names containing the feminine form *ʾiltum* are rare.[380]

One of the things that separate Akkadian names from Sumerian is the prominence of the lugal in the latter; his dealings and his peers. The corresponding appellative *śarrum* only found limited distribution in Akkadian names.[381] The instances of *śarrum* that do exist, however, become even more interesting precisely due to the scarcity of occurrence.

2.4.3 Akkadian *śarrum*-names: who is the *śarrum*?

Akkadian names surpass Sumerian ones in number, as they are attested for far longer, from about 2600 BCE down to around the beginning of the Common Era and even beyond that. Even though Akkadian name-giving traditions underwent its fair share of changes, certain names remain in attested use over millennia. But material for comparing *śarrum*-names of the earliest periods with those of later times is limited. The *śarrum* was simply

[380] See I. J. Gelb, MAD 3, 26–36: 0 attestations of names composed with *ʾiltum* for the time before Ur III. The note by R. A. di Vito, StPohl SM 16, 12, about a predominance of names composed with *ʾilum* and *ʾiltum* in the Old Akkadian period accredited to Westenholz is a misreading and should of course read *ʾilum* or *ʾil*, and ʿAštar. The reference should be to A. Westenholz, ARES 1, 103.

[381] D. O. Edzard, *RlA* 9 (1998–2001), "Name, Namengebung. B. Akkadisch", 106f., § 2.2.

never as popular in the Akkadian onomasticon as lugal appears to have been in the Sumerian. The usages of these appellatives also differed within their linguistic settings. Whereas Sumerian lugal, as recounted above, was used with at least four different basic senses, *śarrum* seems only to have filled two: those of 'king' in royal titulary contexts, and as 'lord,' in an epithetical sense.[382] The noun *baʿlum* was instead used both in the sense of 'owner,'[383] and as formal address in letters. An etymology of the noun *śarrum* seems at present unattainable. There is no pristine Semitic verb **śarārum/šarārum* attested before the 2nd millennium.[384]

2.4.3.1 The ruler as referent

There is no reason to doubt that many, if not most, names including the appellative *śarrum* do in fact refer to the human ruler. As has been pointed out by A. Westenholz, the ascent of *Śarrukēn* of Akkade brought with it a marked increase of, and a change in focus of *śarrum*-names.[385] It will be seen that these changes were influenced both by the native onomastic traditions and by cross-fertilization with the Sumerian culture of the south. C. Saporetti's study of Middle Assyrian names points in a similar direction, where the latter ascribed 12 names to a human referent, and 16 to a divine referent. Interestingly, the ones attributed to the human ruler by Saporetti exhibit a larger diversity in form and semantic content than the ones ascribed to a divine referent.[386]

2.4.3.2 A divinity as referent

Several names are construed along the pattern of DN-*śar*, or *śar*-DN, giving *śarrum* in its most basic realizable shape, indicating a predication of the theonym: 'the god x is king.'[387] As has been remarked earlier, the unfortunate lack of an Old Akkadian literary corpus results in a number of blind spots with regards to the contemporary world of ideas which comes so vividly, albeit mutely, to the fore in for example cylinder seals.[388]

According to J. Bottéro, the Akkadians adopted the Sumerian pantheon and kept on developing it, adding several hundreds to the already during the

---

[382] Or so I interpret the names formed on the pattern DN-*śar*, see examples below, 3.2.7.6.

[383] The sign LUGAL in Akkadian linguistic settings was predominantly used as a logogram for *śarrum*. B. R. Foster has pointed to passages in which nothing but *baʿlum* can be intended; specifically in situations expressing ownership of immovable property, which would rightly be written lugal had the text been in Sumerian, *USP*, 136.

[384] See also L. Kogan's discussion on the denominative root **śrr* in later West Semitic, Babel und Bibel 3, 239 w. fn. 6.

[385] Mesopotamia 7, 111, and nn. 21f., p. 121.

[386] StPohl 6/2, 160f.

[387] This pattern was common elsewhere also: 6 out of 16 MA names attributed by C. Saporetti to a divine referent feature the stative form, masculine and feminine, StPohl 6/2, 160.

[388] See in general R. M. Boehmer, *EGA*.

3rd millennium known Sumerian divinities. Most of these additions were given Sumerian names.[389] This reworking of the pantheon may in part be due to new inventions as well as a resurfacing of deities which have yet to be discovered in texts from the 3rd millennium. During the Sargonic period about 100 divine beings were revered in personal names.[390] Many were of only marginal importance. Some of the more important deities in the Sumerian pantheon were syncretized with Semitic deities. This goes for Enki, Utu and Nanna/Su'en, who were better known to Akkadians under the names Ea, Śamaś, and Su'en. Enlil retained his name, as did Ninurta and the goddess Nisaba.[391] These and a few other male divinities will be noted in Chapters 3 and 4.

2.4.3.3 The child as referent

The existence in later times of a homonymous *šarrum*, more often *šerrum* 'baby, infant, young child,'[392] with cognates in adjacent regions, opens up for another interpretation of phonetic writings which have previously been interpreted as *śarrum* in 3rd millennium texts. In certain cases to be discussed in Chapter 3, an interpretation as *šarrum* 'child' is a definite possibility.

---

[389] J. Bottéro, *Religion in Ancient Mesopotamia*, 44–48.
[390] See J. J. M. Roberts, *ESP*, passim.
[391] See in general J. Bottéro, *Religion in Ancient Mesopotamia*, 44–48.
[392] *CAD* Š/2 s.v. *šerru*; *AHw*, 1217f. s.v. *šerru*(*m*). See also G. del Olmo Lete & J. Sanmartín, *A Dictionary of the Ugaritic Language in the Alphabetic Tradition* vol. 2, 933 s.v. ṯrrt, with refs. to, e.g. Egyptian and Ugaritic cognates; and F. Gröndahl, StPohl 1, 200 s.v. ṯrry.

3. Semantic analyses

In this chapter the semantics of personal names including the Sumerian and Akkadian appellatives lugal and *śarrum* are examined. The statements about the referents of these appellatives are categorized and discussed under sets of subgroups of varying number, each reflecting qualities, distinct areas of responsibility, or characteristic patterns of actions on the part of the referent of the appellative. In the following, the question whether the referent of a certain name or name type is human or divine is discussed where enough information is available, and the results of this discussion are also resumed in a separate section toward the end of the chapter. Names with similar contents or structure, but featuring other appellatives are drawn on for comparison. Sumerian and Akkadian names are in the end also contrasted in order to compare Sumerian and Akkadian names of the relevant types.

The names composed with the appellatives lugal and *śarrum* are in the following discussed under nine main headings. The headings stem from suggestions by D. O. Edzard and A. Westenholz, who individually divided lugal-names into five and six semantic categories respectively.[393] A combination of the two has proved most fruitful for dividing the material. The headings are as follow:

1. Dominion
2. Wisdom and awareness
3. Protection
4. Care and attentiveness
5. Creation, fertility and prosperity
6. Cult or gods
7. Qualitative-descriptive

Under two additional headings further names are found. The eighth heading collects names which in one way or another are not readily attributable to any of the first seven categories. They may in part be understood but still escape assignment to either of the headings listed above, or they may be totally incomprehensible. The ninth heading collects names which have previously been assigned incorrect readings. In all around 750 different

[393] See above, p. 14–16.

writings of names containing lugal and about 90 featuring *śarrum* have been assigned to the above categories.

The first seven headings correspond quite well to areas of royal activity and ideological tenets found in royal inscriptions from between the 27th century BCE and the end of the Sargonic period. Since, for instance, no lugal proclaimed something similar to a law code until the time of Ur-Namma of Ur (c. 2112–2095 BCE),[394] a name like lugal-di-de$_3$, which addresses a legal function of the lugal, has been entered under the third heading. It might also be imagined to belong under the first heading, as a prerogative of the highest office in the land or city-state; but also as indicative of the field of responsibility of the tutelary deity of a city. This name in particular has been ascribed to a protective function of the lugal, as guarantor of an ordered society, a function which would benefit not only one individual, but the population of the city or country as a whole, hence its placement under the third heading. Other cases where similar considerations come into effect are of course discussed in relation to the names in question.

The subgroups of the main headings are construed in relation to the focus of the name. For instance names bearing on the dominion of the lugal or *śarrum* can be divided into subgroups based on the proximity to a subject and/or an object; from the regalia of kingship used as indicators of the status of ruler to the dominion over the land or the universe. Other categories can be divided along similar lines. The second heading, bearing on the wisdom of the lugal or *śarrum*, is not further subdivided since it involves a limited, but clearly valid, group in and of itself.

A relevant objection that may be raised against this type of division of the material is the fact that a ruler could never be reduced to just one characteristic. A Near Easter ruler, in order to exert lasting hegemony, of course had to be both clever, attentive, caring, skilled in the art of warfare, kind-hearted and pious. The above enumerated semantic categories are therefore not to be seen as mutually exclusive. They individually, first and foremost, represent a recurring focus for whichever feelings on the part of the name-giver or name-givers which found an output through the onomastic traditions.

3.1 Semantic analysis of Sumerian lugal-names

The word lugal was most often written as a ligature, GAL.LU$_2$. Exclusive to Nippur was a semi-phonetic logographic variant GAL.LU.[395] It could appear in

[394] C. Wilcke, *EANEL*, 21–25.

[395] Exchange of LU for LU$_2$ is not limited to writings of this word, A. Westenholz, OSP 1, 5.

the same texts as lugal-names written with the expected LUGAL.[396] A small group of phonetic writings nu-gal comes mainly from cities north of the Sumerian floodplain. No specific function with regards to syntax or reference can be identified, and most of these names have sound parallels in names featuring the normal writing of the appellative.

As a rule, general information on the distribution over time and place of the semantic categories, and of individual names and name types are documented throughout this chapter mostly for parallel formations. The list of attestations for lugal-names from the relevant periods is located in one of the main appendices. The raised parenthesis with an ^{a} followed by a number, e.g. $^{(a1)}$ or $^{(a\geq5)}$ or $^{(>20)}$ refers to an estimated relative distribution of the name, the number indicating number of bearers. In the first case, only one person is attested in the sources as carrying that name; in the second, five or more persons; and in the third, more than 20 individuals may have had the relevant name. A table in the introduction to each of the first 7 semantic categories summarizes the distribution of name-bearers in the different cities which have yielded texts, or which are mentioned in relation to a person bearing a name sorting under the heading in question.

In contrast with these numbers are ones following raised $^{\circ}$ which indicates the number of attestations in scholastic texts. Since some such texts were canonical and saw distribution over large areas, the number after $^{\circ}$ refers to entries from unrelated lists, not to the total number of entries in different manuscripts of the same composition. If the name in question is attested both in documentary sources and in scholastic texts the numbers are separated by a virgule, e.g. $^{(a1/{\circ}1)}$.

Names featuring certain other appellatives sometimes offer evidence for interpretation; mainly names containing en and nin instead of lugal. But other appellatives also, as well as theonyms, may provide clues to both reading and interpretation. These are regularly provided with data such as the city or cities and the period(s) in which that particular name is found.

To a certain extent, the headings of the individual sections which follow are self-explanatory. The most questionable attributions are those of the seventh category, termed Qualitative-descriptive. They encompass names that do not lend themselves to a direct association with a field of action or a clear point of reference in relation to an individual or a place in time or space. Other divisions of the material contained in that specific subsection might be envisaged.

---

[396] E.g. OSP 1 25: GAL.LU once, GAL.LU$_2$ nine times. In all, about 45 writings of GAL.LU in Nippur names are known, as against more than 730 writings of names containing GAL.LU$_2$.

3.1.1 Dominion

Many names quite naturally refer to the lugal as lord and master. This is one of the fundamental aspects of nam-lugal and one of the main implications of the very term lugal. The subcategories of names pertaining to dominion are:

- Ownership
- Family terms, house and indoor loci
- Insignia of power
- Verbal communication and commands
- The city
- Country and people
- The cosmic order

When used to denote 'owner' it could be applied also to citizens in general who in one way or another exercised a right to a locale, an object or a subordinate person. In Sumerian PNN, persons, places and objects all feature as belonging to the lugal. In some names bearing on this type of relationship, it is more than likely that the object standing in direct relation to the lugal is the name-bearer him- or herself. A productive example is made up by ur-lugal, borne by more than 15 people from Nippur and southward throughout the time period at hand. Hegemony is displayed in a substantial group of names which relate the lugal to insignia of kingship or lordship, such as a special headdress or a throne dais. Other names relate to the direct exercise of authority in the land, or to the lugal taking specific actions to subdue opposition from outside.

	ED I-II	ED IIIa-ED IIIb	ED IIIb-ES	ES-MS	MS-CS
Abū Ṣalābīḫ		1			
Adab		6	10	6	15
Gasur					1?
Girsu			41		16
Isin		2	8	1	11
Kiš		1			
Lagaš			2		
Marad		1	2		
Mesag					2
Nippur		1	10	6	17
Šuruppag		28			
Tell Ağrab		1			
Umma-Zabala	1	1	14	8	15
Ur	10		3	2	
Uruk		1	2		1
Unknown		5	1	1	9

Fig. 2: Name-bearers, 3.1.1, Dominion. Estimated minimum number of individual name-bearers.

Fig. 2, above, records the distribution of 263 persons, an estimated minimum number of people bearing 102 variants of names discussed in relation to dominion. Category 1 as a whole shows marked relationships to category 3, Protection.

3.1.1.1 Ownership

As in all other categories, the appellative lugal most often occupies the first position in a name. To this category belong names which express a personal relation between the name-bearer and the referent of the appellative. Another group has lugal functioning as nominal predicate. As these groups contain a limited number of names they make for a good beginning of the study. Also, they can be seen to relate to one of the most commonly expressed themes in royal inscriptions, that of a human or a divinity as governing a locus, like a temple, a city, or the country.

Names belonging to this category are poignant expressions of the benefits of hierarchically ordered society. A set of proverbs is sometimes cited in this connection, as bearing testimony to the ancient Near Eastern attitude towards monarchy:

> A people without a king (is like) sheep without a shepherd. A people without a foreman (is like) water without a canal inspector. Labourers without a supervisor (is like) a field without a ploughman. A house without an owner (is like) a woman without a husband.[397]

The proverb collection from which the quote stems is admittedly late in comparison with 3rd millennium PNN, but the ideas expressed therein no doubt stretch way back into early history. In the onomasticon one finds expressions of this type of reliance upon the lugal, of servitude to him, and the idea that the results of a subject-lugal relationship are beneficial to man.

Structural subordination to a person or divinity is commonly expressed by means of a specific, gender-oriented set of governing nouns in a genitive chain. The earliest attested is ir_{11}-lugal $^{(a2)}$ 'servant of the lugal,'[398] found already in the ED I-II period. As of yet, only one feminine counterpart $geme_2$-lugal is known from before the Ur III period.[399] A likely structural

---

[397] Following W. G. Lambert, *Babylonian Wisdom Literature*, 232 iv 14–21.

[398] The exact phonetic shape of ir_{11} is debated. Important observations were made by J. Krecher, *WO* 18 (1987), 7–19 on complements and phonetic writings; and by C. Wilcke, *ZA* 86 (1996), 31 w. fn. 68, on the history of the sign beginning in the Uruk III period (ZATU268).

[399] *EGA* 773, pl. 23 fig. 264, from CS-LS Nippur. See collection of Ur III Girsu references with H. Limet, *Anthroponymie*, 418.

parallel is lu_2-lugal ^(a3)^ '*man* of the lugal,'[400] known mainly from Nippur, beginning in ED IIIb times.[401] Its relative scarcity accords with the fact that lu_2-DN is not a common name pattern before the Sargonic period.[402]

Servitude to the referent of the appellative lugal also appears neatly in a small number of names using the abstract nominal element nam, as in nam-lugal, of a person or a divinity: nam-lugal-ni ^(a1)^ from MS Adab, probably short for nam-lugal-ni-du_{10} ^(a2)^ 'his kingship is good,'[403] exclusively attested in ED IIIb Lagaš state sources.[404] The translation 'kingship' is based on a later Akkadian parallel which excludes the notion 'ownership,' but which allows for a translation 'lordship.'[405] Add to these, possibly, also lugal-NI:du_{10} ^(a1)^ from ED IIIb Girsu 'his king(ship?) is good.'[406] The latter could well be an unabbreviated, independent form, for instance extolling the qualities of the name-bearer's personal deity or some older, male family member close to the name-bearer.

In keeping with the concept of the lugal as owner, a group of names with a wealth of forms seems to refer to the name-bearer as an object. The fullest attested form is lugal-ni_3-$\hat{g}a_2$-ni-$še_3$ ^(a1)^ 'the lugal ... toward something of his' from CS Umma. It is amply provided with variants leaving out one element

---

400 There is no reason to see lugal in this name as a nominal predicate. Such names are very rare in ED III times. Thus, a translation 'the *man* is lugal (i.e. noble, lordly),' is unlikely. A potential writing ⸢lu_2⸣-[l]u[gal]-la_2 ^(a1)^, perhaps from CS Isin would not be without parallels.

401 H. Limet saw a possible semantic parallel in lugal-lu_2-ni ^(a1)^, attested apart from the Ur III period also in ED IIIb Girsu. Limet's rendering, *Anthroponymie*, 272: "Du roi, son homme (l'homme du roi)," may be correct. There are, however a number of nin-names from Ur III Girsu which give the impression of an abbreviation. Compare, e.g. nin-lu_2-ni-nu!-si-ge, *TUT* 158 r. (!) iv 5; and nin-lu_2-ni-nu-ša-ge, MVN 2 175 r. iii 13, of unknown meaning. A subordination is in any case central to the theme of the names, marked by the suffix -(a)ni.

402 See discussion by G. Marchesi, HANE/S 10, 93 w. fn. 526.

403 Compare nam-ku-li-ni-du_{10} 'his friendship is good,' e.g. V. V. Struve, *Onomastika*, 125 s.v. nam-ku-li-i_3-du(g)$_3$ (ED IIIb Girsu); nam-um-me-ga-ni 'her nursing is ...,' M. Powell, *HUCA* 49 (1978), 34f. no. 1 (A 7554) o. iii 15 (ED IIIb Zabala, Luzag. 7); nam-ušur$_3$-ni-ŠE$_3$ 'her *neighbourliness* is...,' OSP 1 23 o. ii 4'' (MS-CS Nippur). For the Ur III period, see nam-egi-ni-du_{10}, separated for unclear reasons from nam-nin-(a)-ni-du_{10}, H. Limet, *Anthroponymie*, 496f. s.v.v., and s.v. nam-nin-i_3-du_{10}.

404 G. Visicato *StEL* 9 (1992), 5 fn. 22, places one of the sources, BIN 8 12 in Adab, which can not be the case. Among other things, the ligature of gur saĝ+ĝal$_2$ speaks for a Girsu origin. F. Pomponio, *TCABI*, 55 w. fn. 164, discusses a Sargonic school text in the Schøyen collection (now CUSAS 17 10). On the obverse are names of persons holding the office of ensi$_2$ in Adab. The reverese has *ra-am-ra-zu-en-zu*, followed by nam-lugal-ni-du_{10}. The former could, with Pomponio, be a writing of *Narām*-Su'en, and the latter is with all probability also a PN.

405 See Ur III Akk. PN *šar-ru-su$_2$-ṭa-bat$_3$*, UET 3 754 o. ii 18' (cited as OAkk, *CAD* Š/2 s.v. *šarrūtu*, 2e), commented on by M. Hilgert, Imgula 5, 405 fn. 309.

406 V. V. Struve, *Onomastika*, 100: Lugal-du(g)$_3$ (?)-ni; G. J. Selz, *AWEL*, 188, note to o. i 5: lugal-⸢x⸣-ni. A photo of the text (CDLI P221737) shows that the copy in Nik 1 30 does not do the placement of the signs justice. NI might have been placed below lugal due to lack of space.

or more.[407] If the name does not in fact offer evidence of an objectification of a human subject, then the implications are still with all probability an expression of the care invested in things under the lugal's aegis, which could be transferred to include also humans. Another name borne by a small group of persons from the ED IIIb onwards might also bear on this same imagery, lugal-ni$_3$-U.TA $^{(a\geq3)}$,[408] where the latter term, perhaps with a reading za$_x$, is attested in economic contexts as denoting "property, assets," making for a likely interpretation "belonging of the lugal."[409]

In some names expressing personal relations with the lugal, imagery was borrowed from the animal world, as in amar-lugal $^{(a>2)}$ 'calf of the lugal,'[410] and maš-lugal $^{(a\geq3/°1)}$ 'goat('s kid) of the lugal.'[411] The former is limited to ED I-II Ur and Uruk, while the latter is attested also in ED IIIa. The singular ar$_3$-du$_2$:lugal $^{(a1)}$,[412] could belong in the late ED I-II period or the early ED IIIa, and might have had a sense similar to the aforementioned, as ar$_3$-du$_2$ in ED texts appears as a special term in relation with both equids and persons of both sexes.[413] Parallel formations of amar-names, most often construed with a divinity as governed noun, continued down into Ur III times.[414] Some early forms were construed using a GN[415] or an official title.[416] This indicates that the referent in amar-lugal might be a human figure. As was shown above,

---

[407] lugal-ni$_3$-ĝa$_2$ $^{(a1)}$, and lugal-ni$_3$-ĝa$_2$-ni $^{(a\geq5)}$, ED IIIb and CS Girsu with one MS-CS unknown; lugal-ni$_3$-ni $^{(a2)}$ from ED IIIa Šuruppag and ES-MS Umma; and lugal-ni$_3$-ni-še$_3$ $^{(a\geq2)}$, all from the ED IIIb Umma area. Compare ED IIIb Girsu FPN nin-ni$_3$-ĝa-ni, e.g. *DP* 2/1 230 o. v' 9; Ur III abbreviations include ni$_3$-ĝa$_2$-ni, e.g. HSS 4 6 o. i 11'; nin-ni$_3$-ni, e.g. H. Limet, *Anthroponymie*, 510 s.v. nin-ĝar-ni.

[408] ED IIIb Isin; ES to MS-CS Nippur; MS-CS Umma and one unknown. The latter is found in a text (MAD 4 37) which exhibits an inconsistent use of the i$_3$-/e- prefix in otherwise identical verbal chain with a-vowel: i$_3$-da-ĝal$_2$ (o. 5) and e-da-ĝal$_2$ (r. 3). This along with the fact that the overwhelming majority of tablets in H. de Genouillac's tablet acquisition dated June 22 1929 come from Umma makes an Umma provenance also for this text probable.

[409] On the reading and intepretation, with previous literature, see C: Wilcke, *EANEL*, 70 w. fn. 214. In a few cases, ni$_3$-U.TA occurs by itself as a PN, e.g. *TCABI* 70 o. 6 (MS Adab).

[410] Note the unique PN amar-en-ne$_2$-il$_2$-la$_2$, TMH 5 124 ii 5, ED IIIb Nippur, 'calf lifted by the *lord*,' evoking traditional imagery of an animal young held at the bosom of a person or deity.

[411] In ED I-II Ur economic documents the animal is consistently written maš$_2$. The relationship between the two is, then, purely phonetic and the one is only used in an onomastic context. The writing maš takes precedence over maš$_2$ for goat('s kid) in ED IIIb Girsu texts. In other places maš$_2$ seems the most attested one when used in that sense.

[412] Interpreted as ḪAR.TU, lugal, and dated to ED II by G. Marchesi & N. Marchetti, MesCiv 14, 129f. Their reluctance in the commentary to the name, p. 165, to see in this writing a personal name due to the fact that such a name is otherwise unattested is understandable and sound. However, it may be noted that 55% of lugal-names appearing in ED I-II are so far exclusive to that period. As noted by Marchesi and Marchetti, *op. cit.*, fn. 70 p. 165, sole ḪAR.TU/ar$_3$-du$_2$ would most likely make up an abbreviation of an original ar$_3$-du$_2$ plus a theophore. An appellative is just as expected.

[413] See discussion by G. Marchesi & N. Marchetti, MesCiv 14, 165.

[414] Also composed with the deified Šulgi. See, e.g., H. Limet, *Anthroponymie*, 375f.

[415] Some refs. are found in RGTC 1, 79 s.v. I(n)sin; 95f. s.v. Ku'ara.

[416] See, for instance, UET 2, 30, PN no. 189: amar-saĝa.

section 2.2.1, amar was used also in reference to infant children, boys as well as girls. But no woman has been identified as bearing an amar-name so it appears as though amar in PNN was not considered gender neutral. The corresponding Akk. *būr*-names are attested from Late Sargonic times onward, but the logographic use of AMAR for *būr*- makes the identification of an Akkadian name problematic at times.[417] No clear-cut instance links Akkadian *būr*- with any of the Semitic appellatives for lord or ruler. PNN with maš- fell almost completely out of use after the ED period apart from the rare Ur III attestation.[418]

Names with amar- and maš- were part of a name-giving tradition which gradually gave way to the very productive ur-names, as in ur-lugal $^{(a>15/^{\circ}1)}$ '*man* (lit. phps. 'dog') of the lugal,'[419] appearing in sources throughout the period from the area south of Nippur. Writings older than ED IIIb of the name might perhaps rather intend lugal-teš$_2$, but would be hard to identify without poss. pron. -ĝu$_{10}$ 'my,' which appears only beginning in the MS-CS period, specifically at Adab and Nippur. Theoretically, ur-lugal could in some cases be a short form of names where the governed noun is made up by a theophore containing lugal as first sign and missing the divine determinative,[420] but no secure prosopographic evidence for this exists. The hapax ur-lugal-la$_2$ $^{(a1)}$ '*man* of the lugal,' which uncharacteristically marks the genitive, unfortunately is too rare to form a basic rule of restoring the genitive marker when missing. The simpler construction lugal-la$_2$ $^{(a\geq5)}$ '*one* of the lugal,'[421] found primarily at Adab and Isin from the ED IIIa down to CS

[417] See generally MAD 3, 91f.; *CAD* B s.v. *būru* A, 2. b).

[418] E.g. I. J. Gelb, *RA* 66 (1972), pl. III-IV facing p. 28f., r. iii' 10: maš-^{d}Nin-ĝir$_2$-su (Girsu).

[419] E. Chiera, PBS 11/3, 226, no. 809: "The servant of the king"; similarly R. di Vito, StPohl SM 16, 70f., 37.3, 7. A different interpretation of ur as short form of 'hero' ("Held") in this name was offered by G. J. Selz, *Götterwelt*, 17 fn. 2, with refs., but see discussion of A. Cavigneaux, *Die sumerisch-akkadischen Zeichenlisten*, 148. Cavigneaux points to a tradition going back to OB times of equating lu$_2$ and ur (sometimes with an explicit reading /lu/) in the meaning 'man,' in part likely to be influenced by similarities between ur-^{d}DN and lu$_2$-^{d}DN names.

[420] E.g. ur-^{d}Lugal$^{!}$-ba-gara$_2$$^{?\,(a1)}$, C. Wilcke, *ZA* 86 (1996), 36, w. fn. 36; ur-^{d}Lugal-ban$_3$-da $^{(a2)}$, popular in Ur III times, H. Limet, *Anthroponymie*, 551 s.v, and still in use during later periods, A. Poebel, *Personennamen*, 29; K. Tallqvist, *APN*, 243. The case with the ED IIIa name ur-$^{(d)}$Lugal-DU $^{(a\geq1)}$, F. Pomponio, *Prosopografia*, 255f., can be compared with ur-$^{(d)}$Lugal-eden(-na), attested a handful of times before Ur III. The theonym in the latter is not always written with divine determinative, which indicates that it was first and foremost an epithet, later taking on a life of its own. The expected double genitive comes to show in an Ur III source, BE 3/1, 134 o. 7. An overview of the history of Lugal-eden is given in W. G. Lambert, *RlA* 7 (1987–90), 137. Compare lugal-eden(-ne$_2$-si).

[421] For Ur III attestations, see H. Limet, *Anthroponymie* s.v. C. Wilcke saw a possibility to link lugal-la$_2$ in BIN 8 34 o. ii 1 with lugal-a of M. Lambert, *RA* 73 (1979), 5–6 o. vi 5 and 14, *ZA* 86 (1996), 53f. The reason for choosing LAL instead of LA is not clear. At any rate there are no writings with lugal-LA for the genitive in PNN of the periods under scrutiny here. Note, however, the writing GAN$_2$ gi-lugal-la(-ka) for a FN in the Lagaš region, BiMes 3 10 o. i 2, r. iv 4; lugal-la in damaged context, UET 2 suppl. 25 r. ii 9 (ED IIIb-ES Ur); and the difficult

times,[422] may or may not be an abbreviation of this or a similar name. It has parallels for instance in the rather common ^{d}En-lil$_2$-la$_2$.[423] The reason for the use of la$_2$ to mark the genitive in (ur-)lugal-la$_2$ is not clear. More troublesome is the -ra in PN ur-Lugal-ra [(a1)] '*man* of Lugal-ra (?),' for which no explanation can at present be offered.[424] It is worth noting that while ur-nin appears less than half as many times as ur-lugal from the ED IIIb period, only one writing ur-en has so far been attested.[425] Later kyriophore parallels give reason to believe that behind the appellative in many of these names may hide the human ruler.[426]

It is easy to imagine the amar-names as indicative of a society with closer ties to rural environments whereas with time people settled to a larger extent in cities. The symbol favoured to express affection and devotion lost ground and the symbolic import was passed from one animal to another, one which fared better in walled human communities, from amar to ur. It is interesting to note that names combining amar with names of cities and titleholders were not supplanted by ur-names. Part of the valid symbolism was lost and the name type lost much of its original meaning.

An abbreviated writing lugal-nam$_2$ [(a1)] 'the lugal is a prince (?),' possibly belongs among names centered around dominion, but the identity of the second sign may be questioned.[427]

3.1.1.2 Family terms, house and indoor loci

In PNN, the lugal was sometimes described using terms borrowed from kinship terminology, and could at times be pictured in relation to the difficult term 'house' e$_2$. A handful of names picture the lugal as a father-like figure. Such names automatically evoke homely pictures, but it is not evident from the names themselves which aspect of fatherhood is intended; whether, for instance, as leader of a household, as provider, or as one who establishes a secure upbringing for his offspring. What can be said for certain is that family terminology implied a reciprocal exchange of dedication and devotion. But at the same time, it may have been expressive of a one-way

---

[x] siki lugal-la-[(x)]-ga-[(x)], ITT 2/1 r. 7. During the Sargonic period there are examples of both writings in the name of the same person, en-ni$_3$-lu$_5$-la, RTC 81 o. 14; and en-ni$_3$-lu$_5$-la$_2$(-ke$_4$), ITT 1 1261 o. 2.

422 BIN 8 242 is likely to have come from Adab for prosopographical reasons, as Adab is the hitherto only place in which the name, lugal-lu, is otherwise found. Bar the name in o. 2, the other legible names are also more or less common in Adab.

423 See A. Westenholz, OSP 1, 82 (index) s.v.; OSP 2, 196 (index) s.v.

424 Compare ur-$^{(d)}$Lugal-DU (= ra$_2$?).

425 MVN 3 113 o. i 2 (CS Girsu). See above, p. 63.

426 See for instance Ur III PNN: ur-^{d}Amar-Su'en, *Anthroponymie*, 536 s.v.; ur-^{d}Šul-gi(-ra), *op. cit.*, 541 s.v.v. Ur-DUN-gi(-ra); ur-*šar-ru*(-*um*)-*gin$_7$*, *op. cit.*, 560 s.v.v.

427 The seal inscription UET 1 269, from the ES period, shows a narrow sign with two internal horizontals, and ought thus not to be tug$_2$, although it can not be entirely excluded. For the equation nam$_2$ = *rubûm* 'ruler, prince' see MSL 14, 91:168:1 (Proto-Aa).

respect and awe before the authority held by the referent of such appellatives.

Contrary to Akkadian names of later times the connection was not expressed in a plain genitive chain using as nomen regens a proper noun denoting offspring, like dumu.[428] Instead the relation was expressed using a nominal predicate. Names describing the lugal as father appear beginning in the ED IIIb period, and hence do not seem to be part of the earliest layer of ideas associated with the lugal.[429] The oldest attested PNN are lugal-ab-ba-ĝu$_{10}$ (a3),[430] and lugal-aja$_2$-ĝu$_{10}$ (a≥6), 'the lugal is my father.'[431] Both are attested mainly in the ED IIIb period, with single attestations in the Sargonic period. Exclusively Sargonic forms are lugal-ab-ba (a≥1),[432] lugal-abba$_2$ (a1),[433] and lugal-ad-da (a1), 'the lugal is a father.'[434] While, for example, the appellative diĝir exhibits alternation between first and second position in nominal predicate names with similar import,[435] this is only exceptionally the case with lugal.[436] That is, as opposed to diĝir, in this type of names lugal only rarely appears in name-final position; a feature shared with true theophores.

It is not clear what lugal-šeš (a5), literally 'the lugal (is) a brother'[437] is supposed to mean. Perhaps an expression of brotherly support?

A couple of names link the lugal to the noun e$_2$. This e$_2$ is probably in neither case an abbreviation of a TN. The first, lugal-e$_2$-ni-še$_3$ (a≥5), 'the lugal ... for his house'[438] is attested already in ED IIIa Šuruppag, thereafter in ED IIIb Girsu, Umma-Zabala and Ur. Due to parallels with nin these names are probably to be understood as abbreviations of unattested *lugal-e$_2$-ni-še$_3$-nu-

---

[428] For the Akkadian usage, see references with *CAD* M/1 s.v. *māru* 1 d) 3'; C. Saporetti, StPohl 6/1, 309, 317–321; and compare *Mār*-Ištar, above p. 52.

[429] But see the note to the name lugal-A-UR-sikil, below, p. 175 fn. 1028.

[430] Following H. Limet, *Anthroponymie*, 194: "Le roi est mon père"; and R. di Vito, StPohl SM 16, 56, 29.1a, 4. An ED IIIb-ES Adab variant is lugal-abba$_2$-ĝu$_{10}$ (a≥1).

[431] For the erroneous writing A for AN in lugal-diĝir-ĝu$_{10}$, see notes to the latter name.

[432] Similarly H. Limet, *Anthroponymie*, 169; R. di Vito, StPohl SM 16, 58, 30.4a, 2: "(The) lord is father." The word "sea" would often times be indistinguishable from "father." See, e.g. a variant writing of the homonymous DN, M. Krebernik, *RlA* 7 (1987–90), 109 s.v. "Lugal-a'abba „König des Meeres"." However, evidence for (a-)ab-ba in PNN is meager while kinship terms abound. Add to this name, phps., lugal-AB (=abba) (?).

[433] Tentative. The meaning father for abba$_2$ is attested at least once in a female servant sales contract, also from Sargonic Adab, *SIA* 713 o. 4. A translation of abba$_2$ as 'old man,' Akk. *šībum*, could also be considered, perhaps bearing on the sagacity of elderly persons.

[434] H. Limet, *Anthroponymie*, 169: "Le roi est un père."

[435] See R. di Vito, StPohl SM 16, 81–85, discussing names with suffixed -ĝu$_{10}$.

[436] But see Ur III PN ama-lugal, H. Limet, *Anthroponymie*, 374 s.v. Abbreviation originally containing the name of a goddess? Compare ^{d}Nanše-ama-Lugal-an-da, below, p. 141 fn. 788.

[437] Similarly H. Limet, *Anthroponymie*, 173, 202; R. di Vito, StPohl SM 16, 59, 30.4a, 7.

[438] With variant lugal-e$_2$-ni-še$_{3\text{-}90°}$ (a1), only attested at Umma-Zabala. The sign ŠE$_3$ rotated 90°, and sometimes very similar to GAN$_2$ is a local variant of normal ŠE$_3$. On this sign, see M. Powell, *HUCA* 49 (1978), 13, comment to MVN 3 3. Compare abbreviation e$_2$-ni-še$_3$, *WF* 73 r. i 1 (ED IIIa Šuruppag); MesCiv 4 3 o. i 6 & 7 (ED IIIb Umma).

kar$_2$-kar$_2$, ‘the lugal is one who does not cease *working* for his house.’[439] The other name incorporates an anticipatory genitive: e$_2$-lugal-be$_2$-zu $^{(a1)}$ ‘the *house* is known by its master,’ and might well refer to a human, given later parallels.[440] Names with e$_2$ as the first element were popular in the earlier part of the 3rd millennium but would steadily decrease in number as time passed.[441] Here e$_2$ fills the function of a direct object which has been moved to the first position to achieve the wanted focus.

3.1.1.3 Insignia of power

Symbols characteristic of nam-lugal include certain paraphernalia, such as the aga$_{(3)}$, a headdress of sorts, as seen in lugal-aga-zi $^{(a2)}$, and variant lugal-aga$_3$-zi $^{(a\geq4)}$, both: ‘the lugal (wears) the legitimate *crown.*’[442] The aga$_{(3)}$ is common in later royal hymns and is bestowed on the lugal by the gods,[443] though the material of manufacture remains unknown. The names seem so far to be limited to ED IIIb Isin and Girsu texts. Quite possibly unqualified lugal-niĝir could in some cases be read lugal-aga. As will be seen below, several factors indicate that the referent associated with these headdresses should be interpreted as divinities.

Another piece of attire, the men-headdress, is found in the name lugal-men, with a number of variants,[444] attested from ED I-II down through ED period Sumer, with a single attestation from CS Adab. In scholastic texts the name appears at Abū Ṣalābīḫ, Ebla and Kiš.[445] The variant lugal-men-nun $^{(°1)}$

---

[439] See *CAD* N/1 s.v. *naparkû*, lex. sect., for examples of kar$_2$(GAN$_2$)–dag. Compare FPNN nin-e$_2$-ni-še$_3$-nu-kar$_2$-kar$_2$, e.g. VS 25 69 o. viii 17–18; nin-uru-ni-še$_3$-nu-kar$_2$-kar$_2$, Nik 1 2 o. iii 14; iv 7; nin-uru$_{16}$-ni-še$_3$-nu-kar$_2$-kar$_2$, r. ii 4’; nin-uru$_{16}$-še$_3$-nu-kar$_2$-kar$_2$, Nik 1 15 o. iii 1. All names are from ED IIIb Girsu. See, perhaps, lugal-EN-ne$_2$ (uru$_{16}$-ne$_2$?).

[440] Many Ur III parallels to this phrase name exist, most exhibit the direct object in first position, e.g.: TCL 5 6056 r. 19: e$_2$-lu-be$_2$-dug (Umma); MVN 12 202 o. 5: e$_2$-lu$_2$-be$_2$-du$_{10}$ (Girsu); *AAICAB* 1/1 pl. 67f. (Ashm 1924-667) r. ii 24: e$_2$-lu-be$_2$-zu (Umma); D. Foxvog, *ASJ* 18, 88, 24 o. iii 13: e$_2$-lu$_2$-be$_2$-su (Girsu); MVN 16 922 o. 4: e$_2$-lu$_2$-be$_2$-zu (Umma). The syntax is similar, though not identical, with Ur III saĝ-lugal-e-zu and saĝ-^{d}Nanna/^{d}Utu-zu, H. Limet, *Anthroponymie*, 523f. s.v.v.; and saĝ-nin-e-zu, e.g. *CTNMC* 54 o. iv 8 (Girsu). The former was given by Limet, *Anthroponymie*, 325 as “L’esclave que le roi connaît,” while on p. 291 he asserted about this name: “… signification nous échappe.”

[441] So according to I. J. Gelb, OLA 5, 9f.

[442] See also parallel nin-aga$_3$-zi, e.g. HSS 3 38 o. ii 6; and abbreviated forms aga-zi, Nik 1 41 r. ii 2’; aga$_3$-zi, e.g. Nik 1 297, ii 1 (all ED IIIb Girsu).

[443] See e.g. Šulgi D l. 390, where two sources have aga(LAK154, MIR) and aga$_3$(LAK667, TUN$_3$), respectively.

[444] See translation by H. Steible, *CollAn* 7 (2008), 93: “der König (hat) die Krone,” and similarly on p. 97. Variants: lugal-men $^{(a3)}$; lugal-men$_x$(ĜA$_2$×EN) $^{(a\geq6/°2)}$; lugal-men$_y$(LAGAB×EN) $^{(°1)}$. Compare FPN nin-men$_z$(ĜIŠ×EN): UET 2 283 o. iii 5’ (ED I-II Ur); nin-men$_x$: *TSŠ* 150 o. i 5 (ED IIIa Šuruppag). Most, but not all, other names with men$_{(x)}$ are construed as DN-men$_{(x)}$.

[445] The import of the writings lugal-men$_x$-⸢am$^?$⸣ $^{(°1)}$, lugal-me-am $^{(°2)}$, lugal-mi-am $^{(°1)}$, and nu-gal-me-ʾa$_3$-ma $^{(°1)}$, all from scholastic texts, is difficult to establish, save that they come across as partially phonetic variants. It is unclear if the writings stand for men$_{(x)}$ alone or men$_{(x)}$ with qualifying adjective.

adds what may be taken as a qualifying adjective 'sublime.'[446] As with aga, the material used for making the men is unknown but may have varied.[447] The headdress is not found in the titulature of early rulers, but is repeatedly referred to in the Ur III royal hymns.[448] A few names from ED IIIb Girsu associate the men with local royalty, for example the PNN ^{d}Ba-u$_2$-men-zi-PAP.PAP,[449] ^{d}Inana-men-zi-PAP.PAP 'Bau/Inana (is/has/gives) the legitimate men-headdress (of/for) PAP.PAP.'[450] The names imply a form of legitimizing by means of a deity's active involvement, though no such deity is mentioned in the names combining lugal and men. And in no case is it obvious that the men is worn by the queen called PAP.PAP. It is on the other hand likely that men in itself in some other cases should be understood as a symbol representing a deity. Two examples of this is the name of the en-priestesses en-men-an-na 'the en is the men of heaven,' daughter of *Narām*-Su'en;[451] and en-aga$_3$-zi-an-na 'the en is the legitimate crown of heaven,' daughter of Amar-Su'en of Ur.[452] These names surely refer to the Moon God Nanna.[453] The relation between Nanna and his son Utu on one hand, and the men is perhaps also visible in the big god list from Šuruppag, where their names are followed by two rather marginal deities ^{d}Men$_x$(ĜA$_2$×EN) and ^{d}Men$_x$(ĜA$_2$×EN)-bar.[454] PNN construed with men gradually became more and more scarce during Sargonic times. Considering the fact that the men is never expressly

---

446 The entry is damaged in the Abū Ṣalābīḫ version of the Names and Professions List. Compare M. Bonechi, *NABU* 2001/29, who argued that the name should be read lugal-men with a qualifier nun, corresponding to Akk. *rubûm*. Bonechi's arguments that the text has bearing on people from Kiš are interesting. He notes that no king of Kiš by the name lugal-men is known. However, if I should entertain an alternate interpretation of the line, I would suggest reading men-nun lugal (followed by AK-Utu ensi$_2$). Note that according to the Sumerian King List, two kings of the city Kiš have very similar names, en-me(n)-nun-na of the first Kiš dynasty, and men-nun-na of the second, T. Jacobsen, AS 11, 80:23, and 97:30 (the latter misread ĜA$_2$×RU); and C.-A. Vincente, *ZA* 85 (1995), 253, note to ii 1'.

447 See discussion by B. Alster & H. L. J. Vanstiphout, *ASJ* 9 (1987), 32, note to Laḫar and Ašnan l. 17, who contend that the men was made from textile; like a cap or turban, due to its association with Uttu. They further point to the men as being tied onto the head of the bearer. But compare the men$_x$ ku$_3$ 'silver men' in D. Foxvog, Mesopotamia 8, 67–75 o. ii 7; and the men$_x$ saĝ si-ga ku$_3$ luḫ-ḫa "Krone aus geläutertem Silber, die das (ganze) Haupt bedeckt," G. J. Selz, *Götterwelt*, 199 [56]. The latter was perhaps destined for wear by the statue of a deity. There is no arguing that the association of the men with the goddess of weaving, Uttu, suggests a textile headdress, but it is also possible that usage of the term changed with time.

448 One source for Šulgi D l. 295, *ISET* 1, pl. 21 (Ni 4571), r. ii 9', has men written with three *gunû*-strokes on the left hand part, emulating the shape of aga.

449 *DP* 2/1 157 r. i' 6: ^{d}Ba-u$_2$-men$_x$(ĜA$_2$×EN)-⌜z⌝[i]-PAP.PAP. Compare the ED IIIb Nippur PN ^{d}Utu-men-zi, OSP 1 99 o. i 4.

450 See G. J. Selz, *Götterwelt*, 280 w. fn. 1396 for the latter, and parallel formations in PNN and in the names of votive objects of Enmetena and UruKAgina.

451 For inscriptions mentioning Enmenana, see RIME 2.1.4.2018–2020.

452 E.g. CT 36 pl. 2 (BM 114684) l. 23.

453 For the relation men an (ki/uraš)-a, see Å. Sjöberg, *MNS*, 67, 106 and 126. This symbolism exists even today in the English terms lunar and solar corona.

454 *SF* 1 o. i 5–8.

stated as being owned or worn by humans before the Ur III period, names composed with terms for headdresses should be regarded as expressive of a quality or act on the part of a deity, not a human.

Another object associated with rule was for instance the staff/sceptre ĝidri, as in lugal-ĝidri (a1) 'the lugal (holds?) a sceptre,' lugal-ĝidri-du$_{10}$ (a2/°1) 'the lugal (of?) the good sceptre.' The sign ĝidri is written with the pictogram PA, which for example forms part of the diri-compounds ensi$_2$(PA.TE.SI), sipa(PA.LU), maškim(PA.KAS$_4$), and šabra(PA.AL). PA has other readings which could arguably fit this name, and ugula 'foreman' can not be excluded as one of them.[455] The import is one of marked responsibilities in relation to others, and as such the ĝidri features among Lagaš and Akkade rulers' epithets describing the auhority of the lugal, given to him by various gods.[456]

The bara$_2$ which in some names might be interpreted as 'throne dais' is the object in a handful of names which individually are attested no more than a few times each.[457] Fuller writings of such names include lugal-bara$_2$-ge-du$_{10}$ (a1) and lugal-bara$_2$-ga-ne$_2$-du$_{10}$ (a1) 'the lugal makes the/his throne dais good.'[458] They both might correspond to the abbreviation lugal-bara$_2$-du$_{10}$ (°2), attested only in scholastic texts from ED IIIa Šuruppag and Kiš. An early name attested already in ED I-II Ur, and then rarely in the ED IIIa, uses the predicate si, lugal-bara$_2$-si (a3) 'the lugal is just right for the throne dais'[459]; that is, the lugal is one who realizes the full potential of the powers inherent in the throne dais. Some intriguing parallels have been interpreted as featuring a potential missing direct object.[460] The name lugal-bara$_2$-kalam (a1)

---

455 A reading mu$_6$ for PA in lugal-ĝidri was suggested by H. Limet, *Anthroponymie*, 469, perhaps corresponding to Akk. *eṭlum*, for which, see *CAD* E s.v., lex. sect.

456 See references to ĝidri in FAOS 6, 142; Akk. *ḫaṭṭum*, written ^{giš}ĝidri, in FAOS 8, 208.

457 The short form lugal-bara$_2$ (a≥6), was correctly analysed by H. Limet, *Anthroponymie*, 221 as "début d'une phrase qui a servi de nom propre après avoir abrégée."

458 Compare the interpretation of this and parallel with nin by G. J. Selz, *Götterwelt*, 104 fn. 376: "Dem$^?$ Herrn/der Herrin auf dem Thron ist (es$^?$) angenehm." Name correctly identified as containing loc.-term. -e and du$_{10}$, without translation, M. Krebernik, AOAT 296, 34f.; G. Marchesi, *OrNS* 73 (2004), 190 fn. 213, given as "the Lord delights the dais (?)." The short form bara$_2$-ga-ne$_2$ is attested about a dozen times, from the ED IIIb onwards, e.g. TMH 5 102 o. i 7 (ED IIIb Nippur).

459 Compare D. O. Edzard, *RlA* 9 (1998–2001), 95, "Name, Namengebung. A," (-bara$_2$-ge-si): "der König (erfüllt =) nimmt das Thronpostament ein"; M. Krebernik, AOAT 296, 23. A few parallel names supply the expected locative-terminative marker -e on bara$_2$, as in bara$_2$-ge-si, e.g. MO C vii 3. Compare H. Limet, *Namenforschung*, 852: "le roi qui comble le sanctuaire (de bien-faits)"; and H. Steible, *CollAn* 7 (2008), 93 and 97: "der König sitzt (auf) dem Thron."

460 See M. Krebernik, AOAT 296, 23–25, with a number of intriguing examples from the archaic Ur texts. For the name e$_2$-alam-gal-gal-si, Krebernik suggested either seeing an elided subject "[X] ist einer, der das Haus mit großen Statuen füllt," or having e$_2$-alam-gal-gal serve as a dimensional object, *op. cit.*, p. 24f. According to the scheme followed above, the name should rather be interpreted as "the temple is just right for (housing) the great statues (of the gods)." However, not all the names discussed by Krebernik allow for such an interpretation,

might have a different interpretation altogether, as $bara_2$ is sometimes used figuratively to denote a person occupying the throne dais.[461] Thus for instance in Lugalzagesi's Nippur inscription and in the ED IIIb Ur PN $bara_2$-An-ne_2-pa_3-da 'the prince is one chosen by An.'[462] Hence, a translation 'the lugal (is) a prince of the land,' might be ventured, which would rather belong below, under subheading 3.1.1.6, and which would aptly describe a human ruler. The available evidence allows for the extension of $bara_2$, from signifying a locus, to denoting the occupant of the locus, to be traced not much further back than 2400 BCE, or to around the time of the final pre–Sargonic Uruk dynasty. As a loan, $bara_2$ with this interpretation may feature in the CS Mugdan PN *be-li*$_2$-$bara_2$ 'my lord is a prince,'[463] though the metonymic use of Akkadian *parakkum* to signify a person is only attested lexically.[464]

Another outer royal characteristic which made its way into the onomasticon in Sargonic times was the 'splendid robe' of the lugal and nin, as seen in lugal-tug_2-maḫ [(a≥4)] 'the lugal is (one wearing) a splendid robe.'[465] Perhaps the unique name lugal-suluḫu_2(SIG_2.BU) [(a1)], referring to wool from a long-haired breed of sheep, used to make a particular type of ceremonial garment also belongs here.[466] According to E. Flückiger-Hawker, a robe made from suluḫu-hair during the Ur III period was "part of the regalia of

---

so the question must remain open. The name en-me-$bara_2$-si of later traditions is probably a reinterpretation and does not add to the understanding of the earlier names.

461 See in general *PSD* B, $bara_2$ A 2.

462 Note the parallelism in the Lugalzagesi inscription, BE 1/2 87 ii 21–22: $bara_2$-$bara_2$ ki-en-gi, $ensi_2$ kur-kur-ra. The PN $bara_2$-an-ne_2-pa_3-da 'the prince is one chosen by An,' is found in UET 2 suppl. 6 o. 1. It may just be coincidence that the "choosing" deitiy is an Urukean god, but the ties between 3rd millennium Uruk and Ur are numerous. See G. Marchesi & N. Marchetti, MesCiv 14, 157, fnn. 18–19, for a discussion of some related names.

463 MAD 5 74 o. 2; 77 r. 2 (same person in both instances).

464 See, e.g. Malku-*šarru* I 4 *pa-rak-ku* = *šarru*, cited *CAD* P s.v. *parakku* A, lex. sect.

465 If anything is missing, the predicate mu_4 'to dress, wear' is a likely restoration. The lemma tug_2 maḫ is given by H. Waetzoldt, *UNT* xxi w. fn. 34, as "Prachtgewand," and is said to have been worn by Dumuzi; the present name is given on p. xxiii as "der König ist (wie) ein Prachtgewand." Compare J. Krecher, *ZA* 63 (1973), 238: "der König zieht (zum Fest) das ...-Gewand an." H. Limet, *Anthroponymie*, 460 and 474, w. fn. 3, divided the name into -dur_2-maḫ and -TUG_2-maḫ, but indicated that they might have a common reading. Abbreviation lugal-tug_2 [(a1)], attested only in MS-CS Nippur; as commented by A. Westenholz, OSP 2, 197, it may be an abbreviation of the present name or an erroneous writing of -gi_7. No comparable form *nin-tug_2 is known from this or later periods. See further comments by W. Sommerfeld, *Tutub*, 103, for parallel attestations and a discussion of the tug_2 maḫ in economic contexts.

466 OBO 166, 173, note to Urnamma A l. 98 The term appears also in an Inana-Dumuzi composition, Y. Sefati, *Love Songs*, 263, l. 31, there referring to Inana's unkempt hair "which knows no comb." The Ur III variant lugal-suluḫu(SIG_2.SUD), given by H. Waetzoldt, *UNT*, xxiii, as: "der König ist (wie) lange Wolle," is compared by him to the names lugal-si-ĝar and lugal-bad_3. Waetzoldt further, fn. 73 p. xxiii, did not rule out the possibility that shortened forms without appellative referred to the hairs on the newborn baby's head. If so, compare later Akk. *apparrû*/*apparrītu* "(the one with) tufty (hair)," and see J. J. Stamm, *Namengebung*, 266.

kings." The lack of the textile determinative tug_2 is not decisive, as inclusion in PNN of determinatives is inconsistent at best. The exceptions are determinatives used for marking divinity and place, and occasionally even these could be discarded. That kings and queens would distinguish themselves from the lower classes by means of their dress is perhaps to be expected, and the aforementioned names may then well refer to a characteristic of the human ruler. Should the analysis be anywhere near correct, certain people of Sargonic Adab and Nippur may have been keen observers of contemporary fashion introduced by the nobility from Akkade. No parallel formation with a theonym instead of the appellative is in any case known.

3.1.1.4 Verbal communication and commands

A central principle in the Mesopotamian conception of the world was the creative power of spoken words. In short, out of necessity an idea grew about that which was to be created, or *ordered.* Its functions were established as blueprints in the mind of gods, and creation followed by the determining of the name and fate of the new creation. This chain of causes and effects are often taken to have been influenced by the chain of command in human society, with the king at the top of the political and social hierarchy.[467] Divine decrees, when coming from the highest authority, could not be countermanded,[468] so perhaps even in an ED IIIa name of unknown origin: lugal-du_{11}-ga-ni-nu-[$kur_2^?$] (a1) 'what the lugal says can not [be altered?].'[469]

Words, orders and statements were epitomized in names, and lugal-names offer plenty of variations on this theme. Permanence and the correctness of whatever the lugal has decreed, are common associations. So for instance in lugal-du_{11}-ga-ni-zi (a1) 'what the lugal says is reliable,'[470] which is hard to

[467] Following the reasoning of J. Bottéro, *Religion of Ancient Mesopotamia*, 90–95.

[468] OIP 99, 46–53, l. 8–10 (za_3-me hymns): (Enlil) en du_{11}-ga, nu-gi_4-gi, nu-$šar_2$-$šar_2$: "Enlil, lord (whose) words cannot be contested, cannot be *argued against* (?)." For the last line, compare *amata šutābulu*, *CAD* A/1, 27f. c, "to discuss, argue a matter."

[469] According to photo (CDLI P010547), the last sign must be quite small. Restoration kur_2 is likely. See, e.g., TCS 3, 18, l. 20; Urnamma A l. 209; or perhaps $šar_2$, see previous footnote. Another possibility would be a kyriophore name with the addition -nu-[me(-a)], as in lugal-AN-da-nu-me-a (see below, p. 141), but at the same time, the formation lugal-du_{11}(-ga)-ni is not very common this early on; compare, perhaps, lugal-NI-KA from ED I-II Ur, and lugal-KA-ni-nu-$šuba_2$, mentioned below, p. 94.

[470] Probable abbreviations are lugal-du_{11}-ga (a1), and lugal-du_{11}-ga-ni (a4). H. Limet, *Anthroponymie*, 234, explained the probable underlying form of Ur III parallel nin-du_{11}-ga-ni: "La Dame dont la parole (est bonne, ou: est sûre," but no form -du_{11}-ga-ni-du_{10} is known. B. R. Foster, *JAOS* 115 (1995), 538 mentions parallel du_{11}-ga-ni-$še_3$, "implying "At-his-word" or the like." Compare also inim-du_{11}-du_{11}-ga-ni-an-dab_5 'what he says has been understood (?),' VS 25 22 o. ii 2 (ED IIIb Girsu).

delineate from lugal-inim-gi-na $^{(a>12)}$ 'the lugal of permanent word.'[471] Both have close parallels in Akkadian names, for instance the Sargonic *pu*$_3$-*śu*-gi 'his word is reliable,'[472] and OB names featuring the verb *sanāqum*, in the sense "to execute exactly, reliably."[473] The sense of reliability also applied to the words spoken, such as is seen in lugal-inim-zi-da $^{(a\geq10)}$ 'the word (of the) lugal is reliable';[474] and that which had been spoken was also considered beneficial: lugal-inim-du$_{10}$-ga $^{(a3)}$ 'the lugal ... a good utterance,'[475] probably to be completed with the verb du$_{11}$;[476] and lugal-du$_{11}$-ge-du$_{10}$ $^{(a2)}$ 'what the lugal says is good.'[477]

A personal perspective sometimes enters into the names, implying that what was spoken was directed at the name-giver or name-bearer. Examples of this are found from ED IIIb onwards, and include lugal-ĝe$_{26}$-ab-e $^{(a3)}$ 'it was spoken by my lugal,'[478] and lugal-inim-ĝa$_2$-ka-bi $^{(a1)}$ 'the lugal is one *who states my case*,'[479] which both echo sentiments of prayers for offspring

---

[471] H. Limet, *Anthroponymie*, 93, 171, 244: "Le roi dont la parole est sûre;" similarly G. J. Selz, *NABU* 1992/44, "Herr ... des feststehenden Wortes," with parallels. Two identifiable persons from ED IIIb Girsu by this name are attested with the short form lugal-inim. For the homonymous DN attested from OB times onwards, see W. G. Lambert, *RlA* 7 (1987–90), 143 s.v. "Lugal-inimgina": rendered "Lord of the true word." See also J. Peterson, AOAT 362, 60, note to ll. 132f., who read: "Lugal-KA-gin$_6$-na." Compare E. Chiera, PBS 11/3, 213, no. 283: "The king speaks with certainty"; K. Tallqvist, *AGE*, 354 s.v. "lugal-ka-gi-na," given as: "König verschlossenen Mundes (?)."

[472] E.g. MO B iv 8 (ES); MesCiv 4 72 r. 2 (CS Unknown).

[473] See R. Kutscher, *Oh Angry Sea*, 48 w. fn. 5; *CAD* S s.v. *sanāqu* A, lex. sect.; and the collection of names, *loc. cit.*, 4 e.

[474] Abbreviation lugal-inim-zi $^{(a\geq2)}$. A probable variant is lugal-inim-ma-ni $^{(°1)}$ 'the word of the lugal (is ...)' in a scholastic text, which corresponds to three writings with plain lugal-inim, see list of attestations, s.v. I have chosen this interpretation for both the ED IIIa and ED IIIb writings, well aware of the possibility to read *inim-lugal-da-zi, for which, compare ED IIIb Girsu inim-Utu-zi, e.g. VS 25 26 o. iii 4, and notes to inim-lugal-da, below. The three witnesses to the present name, in two different texts from Girsu and Umma-Zabala, consistently write lugal-inim-zi-da.

[475] H. Limet, *Anthroponymie*, 171, 228: "Le roi dont la parole est bonne." Compare E. Chiera, PBS 11/3, 213, no. 293: "The king speaks good words." Abbreviated lugal-inim-du$_{10}$ $^{(a2)}$, seen by H. Limet, *op. cit.*, 232, as an elliptic phrase: "Le roi (qui fait regner) la bonne parole." Another possibility would be to read lugal-ka-du$_{10}$-ga, with roughly the same meaning, see *CAD* P s.v. *pû*, lex. sect.: [KA-du$_{10}$-g]a = *qa-a-du-ka* = *pu-u ṭa-*[*a-bu*]. I can not explain the singular lugal-inim-du$_{10}$.KI $^{(a1)}$ from ED IIIa Adab, CUSAS 11 6 o. ii 4, in which KI does not look like it is part of a scribal note ki lugal-inim-du$_{10}$(-ga)-ta, or the like.

[476] See *CIRPL* Ukg. 41 for a parallel.

[477] Compare Ur III Girsu and Nippur PN lugal-du$_{11}$-ge-du$_7$, H. Limet, *Anthroponymie*, 226: "le roi qui convient à la parole"; alternative translation suggested by W. G. Lambert, *RlA* 7 (1987–90), 133, "Lugal-dug-idu": "The king speaks, it is fitting," adapted here.

[478] Abbreviated lugal-ĝe$_{26}$ $^{(a2)}$. One of the persons named lugal-ĝe$_{26}$-ab-e, the sagi and gala maḫ of the city of Nina appears often in the ED IIIb Girsu documentation under the abbreviated form. A variant form is lugal-ĝe$_{26}$-ab-be$_2$ $^{(a1)}$. Translation follows A. Westenholz, OSP 2, 201(index), note to E$_2$-Diĝir-ĜA$_2$-ab-be$_2$. Note the unique Ur III writing diĝir-ĝe$_{26}$-ab-be$_2$-en$_6$, perhaps 'you are what my god spoke to me about,' BIN 3 576 r. 3 (Puzriš-Dagān).

[479] Following the interpretation of G. J. Selz, *AWAS*, 288f., for the ED IIIb Girsu FPN nin-inim-ĝa$_2$-ka-bi: "Die Her[r]in (ist) der Mund meiner Angelegenheit = bringt meine

or a safe birth having been answered. Perhaps related to these names are lugal-nu-du$_{11}$-ga (a≥3) 'was it not spoken by the lugal?,' in the form of a rhetorical question, and, perhaps, inim-lugal-da (a1) 'the *decision* (rests?) with the lugal.'[480]

A name extant only at MS-CS Nippur, but which has roots in the ED IIIa was lugal-inim-kalag-ga (a1). Whether -a marks kalag as standing in the genitive 'lugal of the strong word,' or as an adjective 'the lugal (is) a powerful word,' is not evident from any writing. In Ebla, the name appears both in normal orthography and written phonetically at the beginning of an acrographic listing of names and phrases all beginning with lugal.[481]

The following names are not entirely understood, but many names featuring the pattern with KA in second position following the appellative belong here. It is likely that these names belong to this category: lugal-inim-ĝal$_2$-la (a2),[482] lugal-KA-ni-nu-šuba$_2$ (a1) 'is the word (?) of the lugal not pure (?),'[483] and ED I-II Ur lugal-NI-KA (a1).[484] At the moment, little can be said about them. And even though this subsection contains a fair share of idioms related to speech, the names are generally not attributable to one referent or the other. It is, however, relevant to note that the association between en and inim or du$_{11}$(-g) was exceedingly rare in all periods, while such names composed with nin or with theophores are found more regularly.

3.1.1.5 The city

There are some indications from literary sources of later times that the lugal interacted with, and sought approval for his ideas, in a city assembly. For instance, in a Šulgi hymn, the weight attributed in the assembly to the king's word is mentioned. Cosmic order was also believed to have rested in the hands of a divine assembly.[485] Little in the way of such information is apparent from pre–Ur III sources. The name lugal-uĝken-ne$_2$ (a≥3) can

Angelegenheit vor." For the sense, compare MB Akkadian name Ištaran-*dābibī* "Ištaran (als Richtergott) plädiert … für mich," D. O. Edzard, *ZA* 88 (1998), 148.

480 The name is not likely to be an abbreviation of lugal-inim-zi-da since one would not expect leaving out the root zi. Compare discussion to that name above, and see also inim-^{d}Sud$_3$-da, *SF* 63 r. iv 6, short for inim-^{d}Sud$_3$-da-zi. F. Pomponio, *StEL* 8 (1991), 144, connected this writing with *inim-lugal-da-zi, see above, note to lugal-inim-zi-da.

481 Variants include lugal-inim-kalag (a≥2/°1) from ED IIIa Šuruppag and Ebla, and the phonetic writing nu-gal-en-nam-gal-ga (°1) in a scholastic text also from Ebla. In CT 50 14 o. ii 2, lu$_2$ in lu$_2$-inim-kalag may stand for lugal. The office responsible for distributing the oil was the office of engar. A person by the name UR-NI in the latter text o. i 3, is attested along with lugal-inim-kalag in *WF* 71 o. v 4 and 7, and both are associated with the engar of the ensi$_2$.

482 Difficult. The reading inim here might indicate a borrowing from legal terminology, see e.g. *CAD* E s.v. *enimgallu* "claim (or claimant)."

483 For a discussion of the nominal and adjectival meanings of šuba$_2$, see E. Flückiger-Hawker, OBO 166, 223, on Urnamma C l. 53. The meaning here remains enigmatic.

484 Compare the normal writing KA-ni in ED IIIa Šuruppag, against only one instance of inim-ma-ni, F. Pomponio, *Prosopografia*, 126 and 129 s.v. The latter writing is found in a contract.

485 See discussion by C. Wilcke, CRRA 19, 182f., with refs.

probably be reconstructed by means of the name uĝken-ne$_2$-si,[486] and the resulting translation of this PN would be something like 'the lugal is just right for the council.'[487] The implication is that the lugal enables the uĝken to function as it is supposed to by reaching a unanimous and fruitful decision. Regardless of the fact that the uĝken is rare in early 3rd millennium sources, the cooperation between different civic institutions clearly would serve the common good. Decisions on when to wage war was hardly a decision which at all times rested with the king alone, without having listened to what military advisors and, for instance, the assembly, had to say on the matter. Two persons acting as leaders of the assembly in Ur III times had military backgrounds, or so later traditions would have it.[488] And in a list including city governors and high ministers these two feature as ab-ba uru 'city elders,' and/or nu-banda$_3$, here clearly used in its function of military rank.[489] If an ab-ba uru also in earlier times was a city representative in the uĝken, then the rare CS Girsu name lugal-ab-ba-uru $^{(a1)}$ 'the lugal is a city elder,'[490] with possible variant lugal-abba$_2$-uru$^?$ $^{(a1)}$,[491] from contemporary Adab, could commemorate situations where the human ruler had acted in the best interest of these cities, utilizing the institutions which could levy troops from the available work forces.

Some names from ED IIIb Umma-Zabala associate lordship with the leading city in the region: Umma$_2$(ḪI×DIŠ)^{ki}-lugal $^{(a1)}$, and Umma$_2$(ḪI×DIŠ)^{ki}-lugal-ĝu$_{10}$ $^{(a1)}$ 'Umma is my lord.'[492] They both stem from the time in which Lugalzagesi was lugal of the land, with his power base in Umma and Uruk. It is tempting to draw a parallel to the famed CS Umma letter which states that a citizen of Akkade must not be put to death since [A]-ka$_3$-de$_3$^{ki} lugal-am$_3$, 'Akkade is lugal,'[493] and also to later traditions that ascribed lordship to

---

486 M. A. Powell, *HUCA* 49 (1978), 52 no. 17 o. 2 (ED IIIb Umma-Zabala). Compare the ED IIIa DN ^{d}Uĝken-du$_{10}$, *SF* 1 r. ii 25, following line count of M. Krebernik, *ZA* 76 (1986), 181.

487 Name read by H. Limet, *Anthroponymie*, 472 as *lugal-ra-ni and *lugal-sanga-ni, both uncommented and left untranslated; correct on p. 475 with translation p. 313: "Le roi … vers l'assemblée." Compare G. J. Selz, CRRA 35, 190 fn. 5: "Leider bieten auch die Ur-III-zeitlichen Namen keinen deutlichen Hinweis für die Namensvollform. lugal-uĝken-ne$_2$ und nin-uĝken-ne$_2$ sind gleichfalls Hypokoristika und beziehen sich inhaltlich wahrscheinlich auf den Herrscher und seine Gemahlin."

488 See C. Wilcke, CRRA 19, 182.

489 A. Goetze, *JCS* 17 (1963), 1–31 (YBC 13087, unpublished). One of the persons, *a$_2$-bi$_2$-la-ša*, is known from other texts as ensi$_2$ of Kazallu, and from his personal seal (wr. *a-bi$_3$-la-ša*), as šagina of the same city, RGTC 2, 94f.

490 Similarly W. W. Hallo, *Titles*, 108: "the king is an elder." Compare H. Limet, *Anthroponymie*, 197: "Le roi … est un sheik (?)."

491 Reading URU very uncertain. There is no trace of right vertical on tablet.

492 On the sign taken to render the name of the city Umma here, ḪI×DIŠ, see R. Borger, AOAT 305, with a list of references; and add W. G. Lambert, *JNES* 49 (1990), 75–80.

493 The letter, T. Donald, *MCS* 9 (1964), 252, has been thoroughly commented and provided with a bibliography of treatments by B. Kienast & K. Volk, FAOS 19, 134–136. Most of the Sargonic texts in Manchester come from Umma, but the provenience and original place of

the city in which a dynasty held nam-lugal.[494] In establishing the reading and understanding of this line of the letter, B. R. Foster referred to names similar to the present two, having a city as head noun in a nominal predicate chain. One name is from the same region as the above-mentioned, Zabala^{ki}-ama 'Zabala is (like a) mother.'[495] The names of the cities appear to be used metonymically for the deity residing in them.[496]

One ED IIIb Ur name relates the lugal to activities in cities or towns. It has a cultic or religious ring to it, lugal-uru-na-nu$_2$ $^{(a1)}$ 'the lugal lies down in his city,' and may in fact rather be sorted under heading 3.1.6.3, dealing with cultic acts and ceremonials. It may be the fuller writing of slightly more common lugal-uru-na $^{(a3)}$.[497] There is, however, nothing formally in the way of interpreting the latter as a qualified nominal phrase name lugal-uru-na as '(he is) lord in/of his city.' One might also consider the name as an abbreviation missing a nominal predicate. If the names uru-na-bad$_3$-bi '(he is) the fortress (i.e. protection) of his city,'[498] or names with an appellative or theonym qualified as bad$_3$-uru-na '(so-and-so is) the fortress of his/her city,'[499] could serve to fill in what is missing, the name might, rather than simply refer to the lugal's dominion over his city, have to do with his protection of the same. A few names of that type are found in section 3.1.3.2, below.

Outside the city and its cultivated surroundings (for which, see 3.1.5.2–3) lay the steppe, eden. A few names revolve around this ominous locus. The semi-arid plain played a liminal and at times ambiguous role. As the haunt of demons and demonic creatures it was manifestly a dangerous place for mankind.[500] At the same time the vegetation that could survive in the steppe offered pastures for flocks of sheep and goats. Names which incorporated eden most probably had this latter aspect in mind, as is apparent the ED IIIa Šuruppag name lugal-eden-ne$_2$-si $^{(a1)}$ 'the lugal is just right for the steppe.'[501]

---

dispatch of the letter is unknown. If the recipient was stationed at Umma, then the sender might deliberately have used a local idiom current and clear to the recipient.

[494] Besides the SKL, see the myth of Inana and Enki, G. Farber-Flügge, StPohl 10, where Inana removes, among other things, nam-lugal from Eridu to Uruk; and further the Lamentation over the Destruction of Sumer and Ur, P. Michalowski, MesCiv 1, 57: 364–368.

[495] B. R. Foster, *RA* 73 (1979), 179.

[496] Inana, at home in Zabala (and pretty much everywhere else in Sumer), is referred to in an ED IIIb Girsu name, ^{d}Inana-ama-ĝu$_{10}$, e.g. *DP* 1/2 116 o. iii 2. See further the Ur III name ^{d}Nanna-lugal, discussed below, p. 141, and compare the modern symbolic usage of the much later female personifications of national spirit in Mor Danmark and Moder Svea from Denmark and Sweden respectively.

[497] Compare H. Limet, *Anthroponymie*, 175, 211: "(Il est) le roi de sa ville."

[498] The saĝa of Enlil in CS times. See A. Westenholz's comments on OSP 2 40 and 41.

[499] E.g. H. Limet, *Anthroponymie*, 458: lugal-bad$_3$-uru-na; 507: nin-bad$_3$-uru-na; FN ^{d}Nin-ĝir$_2$-su-bad$_3$-uru-na, K. Maekawa, *ASJ* 3 (1981), 58 no 6 r. i 6; 59 no. 7 r i 4.

[500] See M. J. Geller, *UHF*, 153, index s.v. edin, for ample, albeit later, references.

[501] Abbreviations: lugal-eden $^{(a1)}$, and lugal-eden-ne$_2$ $^{(a\geq4)}$.

Abbreviations figure most prominently in ED IIIb Girsu, and parallels featuring the appellatives en and e$_2$ are also found.[502] The figure behind this appellative lugal is likely to be identical with the deity whose byname figures in the PN ur-$^{(d)}$Lugal-eden(-na), the earliest attestation of which is also found at Girsu. It is furthermore quite probable that this deity was related to animals grazing on the eden.[503] And so si here may have played a double role, indicating that the lugal encompassed the powers resident in the steppe, and being able to 'fill' it with objects that made full use of the potentials of the steppe; in this case livestock. Of course, the benefits of healthy livestock with plenty of land for grazing is obvious. But bearing in mind the association of people and terms for animal young, especially amar and maš, the meaning may be quite pragmatic, referring to the teeming peoples, and maybe even by extension to the name-bearer him- or herself.

3.1.1.6 Country and people

Names which portray the lugal as keeping enemy forces at bay, or as protecting his home land and its inhabitants, make up a group of considerable size. Names denoting strength and authority are to some extent recognizable, but others may escape detection due to abbreviation, hindering an analysis on semantic grounds.

Names formed with Sumerian a$_2$ are reasonably productive, and carry a wide range of meanings. A concept central to nam-lugal is the subject of a group of names containing the sign a$_2$ "arm," "power, force, ability."[504] Only one name combining the appellative en with the noun a$_2$ is known from the early periods.[505] Along with adjectival or verbal complements, a$_2$ holds key information to the granting of power to be wielded by both humans and divinities. The variant writings of lugal-a$_2$-maḫ $^{(a\geq 8/°1)}$ 'the lugal (possesses) the ultimate authority,'[506] are mostly found in the later ED period. The oldest attestation is around ED I-II in date, the latest from the Ur III period.[507] The

---

502 See, e.g. M. Lambert, *Gs Unger*, 29f. no. 1, r. iii 1: en-eden-ne$_2$-si; *DP* 2/1 195 o. v' 8': e$_2$-eden-ne$_2$-si. See also above, p. 58 fn. 280, for the earliest recorded history of this name type.

503 See discussion by W. G. Lambert, *RlA* 7 (1987–90), 137 s.v. "Lugal-edinna," given as: "lord of the steppe." See also K. Tallqvist, *AGE*, 352 "König der Steppe"; E. Sollberger & J.-R. Kupper, *IRSA*, 318: "maître du désert."

504 *PSD* A/2 s.v. a$_2$ A.

505 The name belongs to an ensi$_2$ of Umma, en-a$_2$-kal-le, of uncertain interpretation, e.g. YOS 9 6, l. 5. In BIN 8 83 o. i 2, the same name occurs, but it probably represents another person.

506 D. O. Edzard, CRRA 19, 142: "le lugal a la plus grande force"; *ZA* 88 (1998), (Enlil) "(ist/hat) höchste Kraft." Variants are: lugal-a$_2$-maḫ$_2$ $^{(a2)}$, from ED IIIa Šuruppag and ED IIIa-b Marad (?); lugal-a$_2^!$(DA)-maḫ$_2$ $^{(a2)}$, from ED IIIa Šuruppag and Nippur. The latter writing is parallelled by an entry in an OB list of PNN, PBS 11/3 25 o. iv' 8'. Compare H. Limet, *Anthroponymie*, 168: "Le roi dont la puissance est grande"; 218: "Le roi dont le bras (ou la puissance) est grand."

507 For Ur III references with the appellative lugal, see H. Limet, *Anthroponymie*, 456 s.v.

names are formed with lugal and nin,[508] alongside certain theonyms. The divinities attested in combination with a$_2$ maḫ are few, but bear on divine power as simultaneously universal and local. Thus, Enlil is one of two gods appearing in names from outside their main cities in the ED and Ur III periods, the other being Utu; the latter limited to names of the ED III period.[509] In a description by Lugalzagesi of his native city Umma, a$_2$ maḫ, much like nam-lugal in the traditions of the SKL, is portrayed as resting with that city.[510] During the Sargonic period, no theophore names, only such construed with lugal and nin, are found. In the Ur III, the deified kings Šulgi and *Šu*-Su'en also figure in names containing a$_2$ maḫ,[511] and their hymns, along with those of Ur-Namma, contain this compound both as nominal forms and as composite verb.[512] Furthermore, one of the variants of Šulgi's 23 regnal YN was named after some unknown event in which the king is said to have been given (šum$_2$-ma) a$_2$ maḫ from the god Enlil.[513]

The combination of the figures that appear in relation to a$_2$ maḫ, along with the Ur III occurrences, make clear that a$_2$ maḫ lay in the hands of a higher authority, and was delegated to the holder of the office of nam-lugal. This empowerment comes to the fore in the Adab and Girsu name lugal-a$_2$-šum$_2$-ma $^{(a2)}$ 'the lugal is granted authority,' the first instance of which belongs in the late ED IIIb or early Sargonic period. The compound is not attested with any other appellative or with theophores.[514] There exists a clear correspondence to an epithetical phrase encountered in ED IIIb Lagaš royal inscriptions. As with a$_2$ maḫ, the earliest occurrences deal with the transfer of power from Enlil or the main deity on a local level.[515] Related to the preceding names is lugal-a$_2$-tuku $^{(a1)}$ 'the lugal is powerful.'[516] The usage of a$_2$ tuku was dependent on the context, but refers in all instances to persons with authority, for good or for bad.[517] No other appellative is attested with a$_2$

---

[508] E.g. *WF* 65 r. i 8 (ED IIIa Šuruppag); TMH 5 159 o. ii 14' (ED IIIb Nippur); MVN 3 52 r. 2 and 6 (ES-MS Isin). No Ur III attestation of this name is known to me.

[509] Enlil: e.g. *FTUM* 43 o. 2 (ED IIIa Šuruppag); Utu: e.g. *WF* 9 r. v 8 (a$_2$-maḫ$_2$); and possibly TMH 5 170 o. i 2 (-a$_2$-[ma]ḫ$^{?}$, ED IIIb Nippur); ^{d}Sud$_3$-a$_2$-maḫ$_{(2)}$, F. Pomponio, *Prosopografia*, 215f. s.v. The name ^{d}Šara$_2$-a$_2$-maḫ appears in an Ur III Umma text, *Rochester* 116 o. 7.

[510] BE 1/2 87 ii 38–42: Umma^{ki}, uru ki-aĝ$_2$, ^{d}Šara$_2$-ke$_4$, a$_2$ maḫ, mu-dab$_6$-il 'Umma, the city beloved by Šara, wielded the utmost authority through (lit. with) him.'

[511] For ^{d}Šul-gi-a$_2$-maḫ, see H. Limet, *Anthroponymie*, 398 s.v. ^{d}DUN-gi-a$_2$-maḫ$_2$ (all attestations from Girsu); and for ^{d}*Šu*-^{d}Su'en-a$_2$-maḫ, see *Hirose* 389 o. 4 (Umma).

[512] See, e.g. E. Flückiger Hawker, OBO 166, 303 (index); Šulgi A ll. 90 and 98; Å. Sjöberg, *Fs Kramer*, 414:33 (*Šu*-Su'en D). More refs. are found with *PSD* A, 10f., 6.1.3 a$_2$-maḫ–sum.

[513] See in general D. R. Frayne, RIME 3/2, 104; and M. Sigrist, *Fs Owen*, 221.

[514] Short form a$_2$-šum$_2$-ma is attested, for instance, in CS Girsu, *RTC* 255 r. 9; and LS-Gutian Nippur, PBS 9 41 o. 3 (ma$_2$-laḫ$_5$); and Ur III Umma, SAT 2 737, seal l. 2 (translit. only).

[515] See references with *PSD*, 10 s.v. a$_2$–sum 6.1.1.

[516] See, e.g., *CIRPL* Ean. 1 o. vi 1: a$_2$-tuku-e; o. v 21: a$_2^{!}$(DA)-tuku-e, qualifying Eanatum, and compare the PN lugal-DA-tuku $^{(a1)}$ from ED I-II Ur.

[517] In texts bearing on proper conduct (lu$_2$) a$_2$-tuku is used idiomatically in contrast to widows and orphans. See refs. to ED IIIb and later passages with *PSD* A/2, 111, a$_2$-tuku A 1.

tuku in PNN, and lugal-a$_2$-tuku is not yet attested later than the MS-CS period, although a form without a head noun occurs in Ur III texts.[518] Many names construed with a$_2$ are general in scope and attest to a quality rather than a specific pattern of action.

The name lugal-gaba-ĝal$_2$ $^{(a1/°1)}$ 'the lugal is influential,'[519] probably also refers to his standing in the land, or in relation to larger groups of people. This attribute sometimes occurs in parallelism with (nam-)nir-ĝal$_2$, for instance in a 3rd millennium royal inscription,[520] and also in an early literary work.[521] Some form of complementarity of the phrases may reasonably be inferred. Names composed with the abstract nam-nir, roughly 'nobility,' or 'authority';[522] or plain nir, roughly 'lord,'[523] appeared with some regularity beginning in the ED IIIa period. The nominal predicate names lugal-nir $^{(a3)}$,[524] and related lugal-nir-ĝal$_2$ $^{(a\geq7/°2)}$ 'the lugal is lord(ly),'[525] lack parallel formations with theonyms before the Ur III period.[526] As with other names referring to dominion, the lugal is portrayed as receiving his authority from

[518] The name is exlusively attested at Girsu, e.g. MVN 12 295 o. 2 (tablet and envelope).

[519] See MSL 12, 181: 37f.: lu$_2$ gaba-ĝal$_2$ = *ša i-ir-tam ma-lu-u$_2$, ra-ap-ša-am i-ir-tim.*

[520] E. Sollberger, *OrNS* 28 (1959), 339 i 3'–4'.: nir-ĝal$_2$ ḫuš saĝ ki-en-gi-ke$_4$, gaba-ĝal$_2$ nu-gi$_4$ kur-kur-ra-ke$_4$, 'fearsome lordly one, head of Kiengi, influential one, unchallenged *in* (lit. of) all lands' (ED IIIb, Ĝišakidu of Umma). Compare PBS 5 36 r. iii' 18'–20': *na-e e-er-tim la i-di$_3$-nu-śum* '(As Enlil) did not give him one who could oppose him' (OB Nippur copy of N.-S. inscription).

[521] Instructions of Šuruppag, *IAS* 256 r. iv 6–7: nir-ĝal$_2$ ni$_3$ du$_{10}$-du$_{10}$, gaba-ĝal$_2$ me nam-nun-kam$_4$, which I would interpret as: 'authority is the best thing (there is), influence is a princely quality.' For another interpretation, and for the somewhat different OB version, see B. Alster, Mesopotamia 2, 17, l. 209; and 46–47 l. 209.

[522] This compound was part of an epithetical byname of Enlil, Nunamnir, attested since the ED IIIa, e.g. OIP 99, 46–53, l. 6–7, and see M. Krebernik's comments to these lines, *Fs Hrouda*, 154. For Akk. correspondences, see *CAD* E s.v. *etellūtu*; and M/2 s.v. *mētellūtu*.

[523] See *CAD* E s.v. *etellu*, lex. sect.

[524] So, e.g. H. Limet, *Anthroponymie*, 167: "Le roi est prince," with further remark, p. 289: "[d]ans le nom Lugal-nir, le terme nir a la même valeur que nir-ĝal$_2$." Compare names composed with the comitative, 's.o. is respected by (lit. with) s.o.,' e.g. nin-da-nir, TMH 5 136 o. i 3 (ED IIIb Nippur); ^{d}Ba-u$_2$-da-nir-ĝal$_2$ and en-da-nir-ĝal$_2$, V. V. Struve, *Onomastika*, 27 (s.v. ^{d}Ba-ba$_6$-da-nir-gal$_2$) and 48 (all ED IIIb Girsu); and further, nir-AN-da-ĝal$_2$, V. V. Struve, *Onomastika*, 157 (ED IIIb Girsu), also in OSP 1 23 o. ix 3 (ES-MS Nippur).

[525] See preceding note. Related to this name may be the DN ^{d}Lugal-nir-ĝal$_2$, discussed by W. G. Lambert, *RlA* 7 (1987–90), 150 s.v. "Lugal-nirgal," rendered: "The princely lord," and in An-Anum taken as byname of Ningirsu. So also K. Tallqvist, *AGE*, 356 s.v., attributing a meaning "Köning und Herr" (sic) to Ningirsu. ED IIIb-ES Adab and Isin texts share a specific form of NIR where the extreme right wedges are not superimposed as in other places. Compare lugal-gaba-ĝal$_2$.

[526] The name aja$_2$-nir, *WF* 74 r. vi 4 "the father is (like) a lord' (ED IIIa Šuruppag), seems unique and might well be an abbreviation. Compare also ab-ba-nir-ĝal$_2$, VS 25 69 o. x 15; with nin-ab-ba-nir-ĝal$_2$, Nik 1 19 r. ii 1 (both ED IIIb Girsu), phps. 'she/the lady (Nanše?) is respected in the Ocean(?).' See also G. J. Selz, *Götterwelt*, 35 fn. 121 on the ED IIIb Girsu FPN nin-e$_2$-Unug^{ki}-ga-nir-ĝal$_2$ "Die Herrin (ist) im Tempel von Uruk angesehen." For Ur III names, see e.g. ^{d}Šara$_2$-nir-ĝal$_2$, H. Limet, *Anthroponymie*, 528 s.v.

another party: lugal-nam-nir-šum$_2$ $^{(a1/°1)}$ 'the lugal is granted authority.'[527] This name lacks any theophore parallel.[528]

The graphic distinction between the signs denoting kalam 'land,' and uĝ$_3$ 'people,' was not strictly adhered to until after the Sargonic period.[529] This can lead to a confusion of readings where no phonetic complement is present.[530] The relation between the land and its inhabitants was a close one, and hardly needs further elaboration. The lugal of course had a special relation to both the land and its population. Already in the ED IIIa this connection appears in a scholastic text with mixed content from Šuruppag: lugal-saĝ-kalam $^{(°1)}$ 'the lugal is exalted in the land.' This can be compared with lugal-bara$_2$-kalam, discussed above, section 3.1.1.3. The people of the kalam, uĝ$_3$, is sometimes portrayed as the object for the lugal's benevolent actions. With all likelihood, all names combining lugal and uĝ$_3$ are variants on an identical theme, as seen in lugal-uĝ$_3$-ĝe$_{26}$-du$_{10}$ $^{(a1)}$,[531] from ED IIIb Girsu and lugal-lu$_{2\text{-}90°}$-uĝu$_3$-du$_{10}$ $^{(a1)}$ from ED IIIb Ur. They follow a pattern common to ED III names in that they feature the appellative without the ergative marker, followed by a direct object marked by the locative-terminative case and an unmarked participial root-only verb. Two parallel

---

527 Compare the phonetic ED IIIb Ebla variant nu-gal-nam-URU-šu-ma $^{(°1)}$; and further the pair lugal-nam-nir $^{(°1)}$ and nu-gal-nam-URU $^{(°1)}$. The phonetic quality of URU in this connection is obviously related to the syllabic value ri$_2$, but even so, does not fit very well with the traditional value /nir/ for NIR. See, however, D. O. Edzard's attempts at reconciling the two, ARET 5, 44f.

528 The DN ^{d}Nam-nir in the Šuruppag PN, amar-$^{(d)}$Nam-nir, F. Pomponio, *Prosopografia*, 34 s.v., is probably identical with ^{d}Nam$_2$-nir, appearing together with Uruk divinities in *SF* 1 o. vii 17. See further M. Krebernik, *RlA* 9 (1998–2001), 140 s.v. "Namnir."

529 LAK729 (kalam) and LAK730 (uĝ$_3$). See M. Krebernik, *Annäherungen* 1, 281, on the ED IIIa period. For the ED IIIb, compare writing of kalam in Lugalzagesi's Nippur inscription, BE 1/2 87 i 39–40: nam-lugal, kalam(LAK729)-ma; and i 42: igi kalam(LAK730)-ma-ke$_4$. For Sargonic examples, see PNN ama-kalam(LAK730)-ma, OSP 2 63 o. ii 4 (MS-CS Nippur); and eren kalam(LAK730)-ma, *SIA* 874 o. 3 (CS Adab); uĝ$_3$(LAK729)-ĝe$_{26}$, OSP 2 68 o. 9 (MS-CS Nippur); uĝ$_3$(LAK729)-IL$_2$, e.g. HSS 10 66 o. 9 (CS Gasur).

530 Abbreviated lugal-KALAM $^{(a\geq3)}$ is slightly damaged in all three instances, but all appear to have LAK729 as the second sign. It is perhaps preferable to see LAK729 here as representing -uĝ$_3$(-e). Compare H. Limet, *Anthroponymie*, 175: "Il est le roi … du pays." As noted by M. Krebernik, AOAT 296, 32 fn. 169, genitive -ka in Limet's example comes from the syntactic position of the name as rectus in a double genitive chain (strike -ma- in Krebernik's analysis.) A GN Lugal-kalam-ma$^{\text{<ki>}}$ appears once, in a sales contract, said to be from Dilbat/Dailem, written in Akkadian, CT 32 pl. 7–8 (BM 22460, reedited as OIP 104 37) r. iii 4'.

531 With variants lugal-uĝ$_3$-e $^{(a3)}$; lugal-uĝ$_3$-ĝe$_{26}$ $^{(a\geq5)}$, and lugal-uĝu$_3$-du$_{10}$ $^{(a1)}$. The second form occurs among a few names listed by M. Krebernik, AOAT 296, 32, as possible abbreviations of phrase names originally incorporating -si, -du$_{10}$ or -e$_3$, and which incorporate locative marker -a instead of loc.-term. -e. A reading /ĝe/ (ĝe$_{26}$) was posited for names beginning in ES times, A. Westenholz apud G. Visicato, *FTUM*, 54; there also used to explain an ED IIIa period name. ĜA$_2$ ergative -(ĝ)e is evidenced in ED IIIb Girsu, for instance in *DP* 2/2 442 o. i 4: ur-saĝ-ĝe$_{26}$, but the sign could also express ĝ plus loc.-term. -e.

formations, lugal-bara$_2$-ga-ne$_2$-du$_{10}$, mes-kalam-ne$_2$-du$_{10}$,[532] and a few OB Akkadian names from Mari,[533] indicate that the country and its human resources were considered his responsibility, in more than just a fleeting sense. Maybe, then, lugal-uĝ$_3$-ĝe$_{26}$-du$_{10}$ and parallels can be translated 'the lugal is one who does good for the (i.e. his) people.' The idea is surely that of providing a safe and benign situation for his people. He is supposed to keep the peace, or organize the defence of the land should hostilities threaten, and to see to the upkeep of the social and religious order. In his role as caretaker of the interest of his people, it is quite logical that he should be portrayed as its father: lugal-aja$_2$-uĝu$_3$ (a1);[534] and literary evidence from later times provide similar imagery, only transposed to the country.[535]

There is a distinct possibility that some abbreviated names, for instance lugal-lu$_2$ (a>10), and lugal-lu$_2$-du$_{10}$ (a3) 'the lugal is one who does good for man' are related to the aforementioned. A few alternative interpretations might be considered. It is, however, not very likely that the latter two represent nominal predicate names.[536] Given the parallel names discussed in the previous paragraph, lu$_2$ is here the direct object of a transitive verb. Another possibility would be to see the adjective du$_{10}$ as ḫi, Akk. *balālum* "to mix."[537] But for a translation 'the lugal mixes (with) man(kind),' or the like, a reduplicated ḫi might have been expected because the action involves multiple participants.[538] Two variants, so far unique to Adab: lugal-lu (a≥3),[539] and lugal-lu-du$_{10}$ (a1), are possibly to be connected with the Nippur orthography in which lu at times interchanges for lu$_2$. This orthographic peculiarity was current also in Isin sources. The sign lu might in the former

---

[532] See discussion of this name, with another explanation by G. Marchesi, *OrNS* 73 (2004), 191. The three writings of mes-KALAM-NI-du$_{10}$, all seem to feature LAK729, that is kalam. In light of parallels, Marchesi's reading *mes-uĝ$_3$-i$_3$-du$_{10}$ is not unavoidable. Read, rather, mes-uĝu$_3$-ne$_2$-du$_{10}$ or mes-kalam-ne$_2$-du$_{10}$, and see also the following note.

[533] E.g. *ṭa$_3$-ab-e-li-ma-ti-šu* 'he is good toward his country,' and *ṭa$_3$-ab-e-li-um-ma-ni-šu* 'he is pleasing toward his people.' See refs. with *CAD* Ṭ s.v. *ṭâbu* 1i; U/W s.v. *ummānu* A 2c.

[534] M. Krebernik, AOAT 296, 17 fn. 58 "der König ist der Vater des Landes/Volkes"; H. Steible, *CollAn* 7 (2008), 97: "der König (ist) der Vater der Bevölkerung."

[535] See, for instance, the byname of Sîn (^{d}30) in a late god list, K. Tallqvist, *AGE* 354 s.v. Lugal-kalam-ma-u$_3$-tu-ud," given as: "König, Erbauer des Landes."; W. G. Lambert, *RlA* 7 (1987–90), 145 s.v. "Lugal-kalamma-utud." Lambert suspected the mng. behind the name to be of extra–Babylonian origin, but the theme is found for instance in an emesal prayer, Å. Sjöberg, *MNS*, 167, 15: u$_3$-[tu]-ud-da-ka-naĝ-ĝa$_2$, Akk.: *bānû māta* "the one creating the land," and comments p. 175; see also *CAD* R s.v. *rašādu*, lex. sect.

[536] As interpreted, for instance, by H. Limet, *Anthroponymie*, 228; R. di Vito, StPohl SM 16, 66, 30.5d, 1; and G. Marchesi, HANE/S 10, 111. Should their interpretations prove to be the correct one,

[537] *CAD* B s.v.

[538] The 2nd millennium composition *Atra-ḫasīs* illustrates a belief in the mixing of substances to create mankind, but this is so far unattested in 3rd millennium texts. See G. Pettinato, *Menschenbild*, 145 (glossar) s.v. *balālu*.

[539] See note to lugal-la$_2$, above, p. 85f. fn. 422, on the provenience of BIN 8 242.

PN also represent true lu, Akk. *duššûm* "to make abundant,"[540] as in the Adab royal name lugal-da-lu, see below, 3.1.5.3. To be sure, lu$_2$ is in itself no uncomplicated term. It encompasses, but is not limited to, concepts which were also attributed to the lugal, such as quality, status, and responsibility.[541]

The lugal was furthermore expected to be vigilant in order to secure such ideal circumstances: lugal-igi-kalam-ma (a1) 'the lugal is the eye of the land,' from ED IIIb Girsu.[542] Judging from later Akkadian parallels it is possible that the referent of this last name – as it stands – is one of the main planetary deities, the Sun- or Moon God.[543] However, a collective 'eye of the land,' meaning the attention of the people, is known from contemporary and later sources,[544] so an interpretation 'the lugal (does something to) the eye of the land,' is not impossible either.

From ED IIIb Girsu comes the name lugal-kalam:ma:dul$_5$ (a1) 'the lugal covers the land,'[545] which implies that a lugal could envelop the land figuratively, either with an object, or with his mere presence, perhaps indicative of his protection. In a name reminiscent of the former kur may be equal to kalam. One such name is featured in an ED IIIa Šuruppag scholastic text, lugal-kur-ra-a$_2$-bad (°1) 'the lugal stretches (his) arm over the land.'[546] It is, however, not entirely certain that kur here refers to the land and not to the mountains. The outstretched arm of a deity is a sign of favour in another, later, context. According to a clay tag, the name of a commemorative object

---

[540] See for instance ⌜lugal-lu⌝ in OB PNN list TIM 9 91 o. iii' 12', following on lugal-sipa!(PA.KU) and lugal-ma$_2$-gur$_8$-re. Compare lugal-lu-lu.

[541] The precise nuance of lu$_2$ is difficult to assess, but T. Jacobsen, *Gs Kutscher*, 69–79, offers much appealing evidence for the general interpretations "person in charge of others," or more specifically, "provider." See also discussions by R. di Vito, StPohl SM 16, 114.

[542] Compare the Ur III PN miscopied as *^{d}Amar-^{d}Su'en-a-kalam-ma in N. Schneider, AnOr 1 (1931), 292 o. i 26. A photo of the text (CDLI P101283) shows that the sign copied as A is really IGI, hence ^{d}Amar-^{d}Su'en-igi-kalam-ma. The sign which must obviously be read kalam is furthermore written using expected LAK729 and not LAK730, against Schneider's copy. The epithet igi-kalam-ma is used about the temple of Lugalmarad, TH 407.

[543] *CAD* I/J s.v. *īnu* (s.), 1., 4' d.

[544] E.g. Lugalzagesi's Nippur inscription, BE 1/2 87 i 36–43: u$_4$ ^{d}En-lil$_2$, lugal kur-kur-ra-ke$_4$, Lugal-za$_3$-ge-si, nam-lugal, kalam-ma, e-na-šum$_2$-ma-a, igi kalam-ma-ke$_4$, si e-na-sa$_2$-a 'when Enlil, the lord of all lands granted kingship over the land to Lugalzagesi, he directed the eye of the land at him,' loosely following C. Wilcke, *Fs Moran*, 464. An alternative understanding of this passage might have bearing on the present name, as igi could correspond to Akk. *panum* "front," "face," but also "concern, opinion," see *CAD* P s.v. *panu* A, and lex. sect. quoting Kagal G 103: *pa-nu i-ša-ru-*[*tu*$_4$], perhaps 'just concerns,' or 'correct opinions.' Hence, the last two lines in the latter inscription might mean '(Enlil) put the concerns of the land in order for him,' which could affect the understanding of the name lugal-igi-kalam-ma. However, the Akk. parallels with *īnum* cannot be completely disregarded.

[545] So J. Bauer, *Fs Hirsch*, 41–46, without translation. Bauer suggested dating the sources to the ED IIIa-b, and that although found in Girsu, they were perhaps foreign to the Lagaš state.

[546] The name possibly appears in abbreviated form in *SF* 28 r. ii 9=29 o. iv 6 as kur-DA-bad. Compare ED IIIa Šuruppag PN a$_2$-(ni)-kur-ra F. Pomponio, *Prosopografia*, 141f., (s.v.v. kur-ra-a$_2$ and kur-ra-a$_2$-ni); and a$_2$-ni-kur-ra from ED IIIb Girsu, V. V. Struve, *Onomastika*, 23f.

from ED IIIb Girsu was: 'Ninĝirsu stretches his arm out like the Anzu for UruKAgina.'[547] But the outstretched arm that offers protection might equally well be perceived as a threat to enemies. If, furthermore, the reading order of a$_2$ and kur-ra were adjusted, lugal-a$_2$-kur-ra-bad could conceivably mean 'the lugal is one who removes the strength of the mountain.'[548] Since no direct parallel is at hand, save abbreviated lugal-kur-ra $^{(a\geq 3)}$ 'the lugal in/over the land/mountains,'[549] which could be derived from such a fuller form, the correct reading remains unknown. Another possible instance is lugal-kur-si $^{(a1)}$, which might be interpreted as 'the lugal is just right for *the land* (?).'[550]

The last few names disclose a telling aspect of the land: it is portrayed as a passive entity, and the lugal is raised above it. The obligations of the land as a whole toward the lugal is hardly ever touched upon in names. When the lugal is pictured as the father of the people, the name only implicitly invokes ideas of loyalty and respect. This makes sense if the outlook of the names is one in which the individual name-bearers are somehow meant to partake in what the name states. Speaking in very general terms, and without overt reference to the kalam, the name lugal-mas-su$_{(2)}$ $^{(a\geq 12)}$ at least implies that the responsibilities of the lugal was as a leader, an enabler, or organizer, and that at the other end of the spectrum, there were individuals ready to carry out the work necessary for maintaining an orderly society. Further names which bear on this relationship between lugal and subjects appear under heading 3.1.3, Protection.

3.1.1.7 The cosmic order

Central to Mesopotamian theology was the concept of nam-tar 'fate, destiny' Akk. *šīmtum*. Two variants of a very early name may, highly tentatively, bear on the lugal's role of governing the cosmos by means of controlling destinies. One name is attested at ED I-II Ur, lugal-$^{su_{13}}$PA.SIKIL-nam-tar $^{(a\geq 1)}$, the other name comes from a slightly later scholastic text edited by A. Deimel among texts from Šuruppag, lugal-$^{su_{13}}$PA$^{!}$(MAŠ).SIKIL-nam-tar $^{(°1)}$.[551] Despite the writing MAŠ for PA in the latter variant, everything speaks in

[547] *CIRPL* Ukg. 40. For more on Anzu, see below, p. 114f., 165–167.

[548] See, e.g. *CAD* N/2 s.v. *nesû* v. "to withdraw," and the D-stem *nussû* "to remove."

[549] Compare the later divine epithet, K. Tallqvist, *AGE*, 355 s.v., "Herr des Berges (der Erde, der Unterwelt) (Tammûz?)," and W. G. Lambert, *RlA* 7 (1987–90), 147 s.v. "Lugal-kurra," referring to a DN from a MA god list.

[550] Compare DN ^{d}Inana-kur-si, *IAS* 90 o. ii' 2' (ED IIIa Abū Ṣalābīḫ), and see a line in the Ur III literary text published by Å. Sjöberg, *OrS* 23-24 (1974–75), 181 o. 4, quoted and discussed by P. Michalowski, *Fs Wilcke*, 200: ^{d}Inana kur-kur-re$_2$ am$_3$-si, given by Sjöberg as "Inanna pervades in (all) lands," and by Michalowski as: "Inana occupies all the foreign lands." The entire text is made up of brief statements like this, featuring the same verbal chain.

[551] See M. Krebernik's notes on the find number 334 of the text *SF* 53 = VAT 12612, *Annäherungen* 1, 412 fn. 1136: "Diese Nummer beinhaltet keinen Tafelfund und muß daher fehlerhaft sein."

favour of these names as being identical. J. Bauer has subjected the compound PA.SIKIL to a careful study and has suggested a reading sug_x, with a possible original meaning "bright beams (?)."[552] M. Krebernik drew attention to the related writing $^{BU\mathit{gun\hat{u}}}$PA.SIKIL and a connection with later u_2-si-na, "evening," "West."[553] The compound $^{su_{13}}$PA.SIKIL might then refer to a locus or a time of the day when destinies were determined. But this association of the western horizon as the place for deciding fates is at odds with other sources, including a Sargonic building inscription from Umma. There, the deciding of destinies is connected with sunrise, hence with the eastern horizon.[554] If either of the suggestions above should be near the mark, the referent is most likely a deity, and in particular, one who distinguishes himself through brilliance and the deciding of fates. Since the origin of the oldest witness of the name is Ur, Nanna might be considered, although he is only rarely described in later literature as a deity concerned with the deciding of fates.[555]

Other names testify more securely to the deciding of fates, like lugal-nam-tar-re_2 $^{(a1)}$ 'the lugal is one who determines fates.'[556] In contrast, in lugal-nam-zi-tar-ra, the lugal himself appears as the beneficiary of the act (see below, 3.1.7.1).

3.1.2 Wisdom and awareness

Under the second heading are collected names which bear on the lugal as possessing or dispensing wisdom. The names which relate to the wise side of the lugal makes for the smallest category and could perhaps be seen as a subcategory of category 7, which bears on general descriptive characteristics of the lugal. No further subdivision is hence called for. This type of name appears first in ED IIIa. Most names are quite rarely attested, some are exclusively known as referring to a single, or a few, persons. The most widely used name belonging to this category is lugal-ni_3-zu which is known from one ED IIIa Šuruppag text and which is attested the most times in texts from Nippur and Isin. No writings of this name are known from Girsu until the latter half of the Sargonic period. Fig. 3, below, records the distribution of 41 persons, the estimated minimum number of people bearing 13 variants of names discussed in this category.

---

[552] J. Bauer, *AoN* 19 (1982), 7 "helle Strahlen."

[553] See M. Krebernik *Annäherungen* 1, 281f. fn. 512.

[554] YOS 1 14. See discussion of the name lugal-ki-gal-la, below, p. 156f.

[555] So Å. Sjöberg, *MNS*, 36f. It goes without saying that the distance in time between the early 3rd millennium and OB and later hymnic traditions could account for this fact.

[556] Compare H. Limet, *Anthroponymie*, 284 (lugal-nam-tar-re): "Le roi (=un dieu?) qui fixe les destins," with fn. 1, relating to the fate-deciding activity of Su'en. Compare also later DN Lugal-nam-tar-ra, K. Tallqvist, *AGE*, 356 s.v., given as: "König des Schicksals"; W. G. Lambert, *RlA* 7 (1987–90), 150 s.v. "Lugal-namtarra."

	ED I-II	ED IIIa-ED IIIb	ED IIIb-ES	ES-MS	MS-CS
Adab			3	1	1
Girsu		1	2		2
Isin		2	3		1
Marad			1		
Nippur			2		4
Šuruppag		8			
Umma-Zabala			1	3	3
Unknown					3

Fig. 3: Name-bearers, 3.1.2, Wisdom and awareness. Estimated minimum number of individual name-bearers.

Wisdom can be conceived as a quality as well as a foundation for action and interaction with the outside world. A person or god can only be considered wise in relation to his or her sphere of responsibilities, past actions or capacity to convey good advice to those in need of enlightenment. In Mesopotamia, the connection of skill and wisdom with the ears is well-known and the god most associated with wisdom during the third millennium was Enki. In the few royal epithets referring to wisdom he is without exception the one related to the granting of wisdom.[557] Personal names, however, mostly focus on wisdom as an innate quality, as seen by the variant forms lugal-^{ĝiš}ĝeštu-su_{20} $^{(a1)}$, lugal-ĝeštu$_2$-su_{20} $^{(a2)}$, and lugal-ĝeštu$_3$-su_{13} $^{(a1)}$, all 'the lugal *is wide* of wisdom.' These names taken together are attested only a handful of times in Šuruppag texts dating to the ED IIIa period, and in an ED IIIa-b text with a possible Isin provenience.

The two names lugal-nam-zu $^{(a1)}$ 'the lugal knows all,' and lugal-ni$_3$-zu $^{(a>20)}$ 'the lugal knows (every)thing,'[558] both share in the same syntactic pattern, as transitive participial phrases, as well as the same general semantic import. The direct objects are neutral nouns with double-duties similar to indefinite pronouns "something, anything," and the different translations rather reflects a wish to separate between the two names than any defined difference in original meaning. This said, ni$_3$ is more common than nam in such constructions in Sumerian – similar in function to a *nomen agentis* – ni$_3$ replacing the object in a two-participant construction.[559] While lugal-nam-zu is attested only in the case of one person, lugal-ni$_3$-zu was at times

[557] For a list of passages, see H. Behrens & H. Steible, FAOS 6, 304 s.v. sum II, b). The Ur III kings seem not to have used this concept in their epithet chains, neither anything similar to it. During the Lagaš II dynasty *Puzur*-Mama revived the connection with Enki, while Gudea simply professes his own broad wisdom as an inherent character trait.

[558] Compare H. Limet, *Namenforschung*, 852: "le roi qui sait tout"; *Anthroponymie*, 325, simply "Le roi … connaît," with Ur III parallels. A variant lugal-ni$_3$-su $^{(a1)}$ is attested once for a person from Girsu, if the copy of MVN 2 298 is correct. More on this name, below, p. 236.

[559] See M.-L. Thomsen, Mesopotamia 10, §§ 56, 59, 511.

widespread, and may also be intended in some cases of the common writing lugal-NIĜ$_2$.

The same construction, though with more concrete objects, is found in the names lugal-inim-zu $^{(a\geq4)}$ 'the lugal is wise (with regards to) word,' and lugal-ku$_3$-zu $^{(a\geq3)}$ 'the lugal is wise.'[560] The former seems related to speech activities, but if it entails the lugal as the active or receiving party is not necessarily clear. The latter name incorporates a term used adjectivally in a rather general sense;[561] it is attested in the latter half of the Sargonic period only, exclusively at Girsu.

Equally generally applicable is the predicate in lugal-gal-zu $^{(a5)}$ 'the lugal is wise,' where gal 'great' either stands in for a noun or carries an unmarked adverbial sense 'knows great(ly).'[562] In royal inscriptions the compound gal–zu is used repeatedly in a modal construction by Eanatum of Lagaš in connection with the oath swearing imposed by him on the 'man of Umma.'[563] The name lugal-gal-zu is attested for a handful of people from late ED Isin and Adab; and the MS-CS Umma area, with one attestation in an OB copy of a *Rīmuś* inscription from Nippur. It is not altogether excluded that the Sargonic references should be read in Akkadian, as the CS parallel *śar-ru*-gal-zu from Umma.[564]

The name type which invokes qualities related to intelligence and wisdom is thus readily attested throughout the late ED and Sargonic periods. The number of attested name forms related to the subject and the number of name-bearers are however not overwhelming in any way. A possible exception is lugal-ni$_3$-zu which in form represents a rather common construction. Another name bearing on an innate quality is the singularly attested lugal-ša$_3$-kuš$_2$ $^{(a1)}$ 'the lugal is sensible,'[565] found at ED IIIa Girsu. A well-known name of a related type is en-ša$_3$-kuš$_2$-An-na 'the divine en is an advisor of An,' an ED IIIb lugal of Uruk. The name of a well-known literary figure, Lugalbanda, may have been given to him on account of his wits. It is at least possible to interpret his name lugal-ban$_3$-da $^{(a2)}$ as 'the lugal is *resourceful*.'[566]

---

560 H. Limet, *Anthroponymie*, 169: "Le roi est sage," further specifying the mng. of ku$_3$-zu as participle, "celui qui sait clairement," with additional parallels, p. 325; similarly E. Sollberger & J.-R. Kupper, *IRSA*, 319; R. di Vito, StPohl SM 16, 64, 30.5a, 12. The name appears also in an OB Ur list of PNN beginning with lugal, UET 7 77 i' 5' ([lugal]-ku$_3$-zu).

561 For the Akkadian equivalent, see *CAD* E s.v. *emqu*, b) 1'–3'.

562 H. Limet, *Anthroponymie*, 169: "Le roi est sage," analyzing gal-zu furthermore as: "celui qui sait grandement." Parallels given there are formed with nin, with the DNN Enlil and Nanna, and with Šulgi.

563 For a list of these passages, see H. Behrens & H. Steible, FAOS 6, 127 s.v. gal- -zu.

564 CT 50 188 o. i 11. For an Umma provenience of the text, see B. R. Foster, *USP*, 124f.

565 See *CAD* M/2 s.v. *muštālu*, lex. sect., ša$_3$-kuš$_2$-u$_3$. For other names composed with kuš$_2$ and composite phrases, see J. Bauer, *AWL*, 94f.; M. Krebernik, AOAT 296, 48 w. fn. 262.

566 So, already, K. Tallqvist, *AGE*, 351: "König der Besonnenheit (oder Regulus?)." For this translation, see *CAD* R s.v. *rīdu* A, s. "common sense, proper attitude." Compare D. O.

At any rate, the dispensing of wisdom to others is thus not a prime focus in names. Only in the name lugal-ad-ĝar-du_{10} [(a1)] 'the lugal (gives/is) good advice,' an act of mediation may be expressed. As du_{10} along with a direct object may indicate the factitive one may also imagine a meaning making the figure behind the appellative a guarantor of good advice, 'the lugal makes advice (a) good (thing).' A genitive construction 'the lugal of good advice,' is not entirely out of the question. Advice being the result of spoken words, this latter name ties in with names extolling the good and reliable qualities of the words or speech of the lugal, treated in section 3.1.1.4, above; and like these, lugal-ad-ĝar-du_{10} can not at the moment be assigned a referent. The same goes for lugal-i_3-$kuš_2$ [(a≥1)] 'the lugal takes counsel,'[567] for which all attestations come from ED IIIb Girsu, and which merely hints at an act of deliberation. Parallel formations are construed with a few theophores and nin, and are found also outside of the Lagaš state.[568]

3.1.3 Protection

The third heading involves the lugal as guarantor of a functioning, just society. Names sorting under this heading have been further subdivided according to the focus expressed:

- Protection of the individual
- Protection of the city
- Protection of the country

To this category belongs a number of names which seem to equate the lugal with defensive structures like the city wall, bad_3, and with the watchtower or 'guard,' en-nu(n). The former is limited to the Lagaš state and the Nippur-Adab area, while names containing the second element are found also at Šuruppag and Isin between ED IIIa and CS times. Fig. 4, below, records the distribution of 126 persons, the estimated minimum number of persons bearing 49 variants of names of this category.

Edzard, *ZA* 55 (1962), 99: "junger König," which is also fully possible. The translation of H. Limet, *Anthroponymie*, 311: "Le roi terrible," implies a mng. corresponding to *ekdu* "fierce." This may perhaps rhyme well when the lugal is compared to a lion or such, but hardly when applied adnominally to the appellative. E. Sollberger & J.-R. Kupper, *IRSA*, 318 chose a translation close to Limet's. The mng. *ekdu* indeed underlies the translation of Ean. 1 o. xx 2–3: amar ban_3-da, ^{d}En-lil_2-k(a), said about Su'en, by e.g. J. S. Cooper, SANE 2/1, 46, followed by C. Wilcke, *EANEL*, 74, fn. 226.

567 Following J. Bauer, *AWL*, 94f., $kuš_2$ reflecting original $ša_3$–$kuš_2$, giving parallel AN-i_3-$kuš_2$ "An/der Gott ist mit sich zu Rate gegangen."

568 E.g. ^{d}Ba-u_2-i_3-$kuš_2$, VS 25 69 o. iv 7 (ED IIIb Girsu); ^{d}Utu-i_3-$kuš_2$, *TCABI* 208 r. 9 (CS Adab); nin-i_3-$kuš_2$, OSP 1 23 o. iv 26, and passim (ES-MS Nippur).

	ED I-II	ED IIIa-ED IIIb	ED IIIb-ES	ES-MS	MS-CS
Adab			6	2	7
Girsu		2	31		11
Isin		1	3		2
Kiš		1			
Lagaš		1			
Nippur			16		6
Šuruppag		4			
Umma-Zabala			5	1	10
Ur	3	1			
Unknown		3	1	1	8

Fig. 4: Name-bearers, 3.1.3, Protection. Estimated minimum number of individual name-bearers.

3.1.3.1 Protection of the individual

The power of the lugal to offer protection to his subjects is a popular theme in names, though a referent for most of them remains uncertain. The simplest consist of two-element nominal phrases, such as lugal-an-dul$_3$ $^{(a\geq8)}$ 'the lugal is protection,'[569] and lugal-bad$_3$ $^{(a\geq8)}$ 'the lugal is a fortress.'[570] M. Krebernik has suggested that the nominal predicate in lugal-ul$_4$-gal $^{(a\geq4)}$, which is of a type quite well-attested in early historical times, may be interpreted as "great thornbush," which would rhyme well with the idea of protection.[571] The interpretation of lugal-palil $^{(a2/°1)}$ 'the lugal is a vanguard,' known only from the ED IIIb period, hinges on it corresponding to Akk. *ašarēdum* and synonyms.[572] The name seems to express faith in the lugal's leadership abilities. Most other PNN featuring palil are construed with deities, both male and female; and one kyriophore construct is also known: ^{d}Utu-palil-Lugal-AN-da. A related name is lugal-en-nu-ĝu$_{10}$ $^{(a1)}$ 'the lugal is my guardian,' attested already at ED IIIa Šuruppag, which has a contemporary

[569] See rare parallel nin-an-dul$_3$, OSP 1 23 o. vii 11 (ES-MS Nippur). The similar wording of *IAS* 357 o. ii' 2', nin an-dul$_3$, probably does not represent a PN. Most other 3rd millennium names featuring an-dul$_3$ are theophores. For a brief list of -an-dul$_3$-names see F. Pomponio & G. Visicato, *StEL* 17 (2000), 9, note to o. 4. The writing lugal-an-«an»-dul$_3$ $^{(a1)}$ in *DAS* 343, CS-LS Girsu is clearly a writing error, as noticed already by the editor B. Lafont, *op. cit.*, 95.
[570] Compare H. Limet, *Anthroponymie*, 171: "Le roi est un rempart"; and 331, w. ref. to names composed with -bad$_3$-uru-na as having become "quasi … un titre royal." The singular writing lugal-UET2-300-si $^{(a1)}$. from ED I-II Ur, is problematic. UET2-300 corresponds to LAK617=bad$_3$. On the one hand si occurs regularly in clause final position. But here the word bad$_3$-si might be considered, which formed part of a wall and which, as pointed out by P. Michalowski, MesCiv 1, 102 note to l. 420, was sometimes described as inhabited by birds. The sign LAK617 is discussed in connection with similar signs by R. D. Biggs, OIP 99, 56; and compare the variant writings of a PN LAK611(EZEM×BAD)-si-DU and bad$_3$(LAK619b)-si-DU in OIP 104 15 o. v 8 and 11 respectively (ED IIIa-b Adab?).
[571] AOAT 296, 21, and fn. 90 p. 22, with parallels.
[572] *CAD* A/2 s.v. *ašaridu*, lex. sect.

parallel formed with nin.[573] Probably of similar import, and with a larger distribution over time, are the names lugal-a$_2$-zi $^{(a1)}$,[574] and lugal-a$_2$-zi-da $^{(a\geq 6)}$, literally 'the lugal on the right side.'[575] The right side being, as in many other cultures, associated with positive attributes.[576] Also, the arm is figurative for strength, hence for protection, which might be the subject of names of the type ^{d}En-lil$_2$-a$_2$-ĝu$_{10}$.[577]

The lugal could also be envisaged as a guardian spirit, a guarantor of good fortune in relation to the name-giver or -bearer. At least, this is the import of a group of names with limited distribution before the Middle Sargonic period. The nominal predicate names lugal-lama $^{(a1)}$,[578] and lugal-^{d}lama$_3$(KAL) $^{(a1)}$, both 'the lugal is a Lama-spirit,' have correspondences in adjectivally qualified ^{nu}lugal-lama-zi-da $^{(°1)}$, and lugal-lama$_3$-zi $^{(a\geq 5)}$ 'the lugal is a reliable Lama-spirit.'[579] Ur III period lugal-^{d}Lama$_3$-ĝu$_{10}$, and names where lugal is substituted for the names of the deified kings Šulgi and Amar-Su'en,[580] opens for the possibility that lugal in the earlier names could refer to the human ruler. An Ur III parallel from Sippar quite expectedly has Utu filling the same function.[581]

A few rarely encountered names contain formulaic references to legalistic terminology. The divine river, a mediary of justice in trials of ordeals, is the object of comparison with the lugal, as in lugal-I$_7$-ĝu$_{10}$ $^{(a2)}$, 'the lugal is my

---

[573] See nin-en-nu-ĝu$_{10}$, WF 31 r. ii 1; 74 r. i 4, and compare lugal-en-nu and lugal-en-nun, below, section 3.1.3.2.

[574] H. Limet, *Anthroponymie*, 168: "Le roi dont la puissance est sûre," interpreted this as an independent name, while on p. 217 it seems he paired it with the abbreviation a$_2$-zi-da.

[575] See examples collected by K. Lämmerhirt, AOAT 348, 27 A$_L$ 1; 424 ex. A3: ⌜a$_2$⌝ zi-da-za, ^{d}Utu, eri-e$_3$ "An deiner (=Eanatums) rechten Seite wird Utu hervorkommen" (Ean. 1 o. vii 6–8); 431 ex. A 37 šar$_2$-ur$_3$ a$_2$ zi-da Lagaš^{ki}-a "(wie mit der) Šarurwaffe, dem rechten Arm von Lagaš" (Gudea Cyl. A xv 23). Compare H. Limet, *Anthroponymie*, 168: "Le roi dont la puissance est noble"; and 217, discussing a mng. "le bras droit," but settling on an interpretation "premier, noble." Still in use in OB times, A. Poebel, *Personennamen*, 29. For parallels, see *PSD* A/2 s.v. a$_2$-zi-da, 5.

[576] Relevant literature can be found in the discussion of K. Lämmerhirt, AOAT 348, 23f.

[577] E.g. OSP 1 25 "ii" 11' (ED IIIb Nippur). See for this name type in general, W. G. Lambert, QuadSem 18, 58, with parallel formation in Akk. *emūqī*. Note *NATN* 858 o. 3: ^{d}Utu-a$_2$-ĝu$_{10}$, and the inscription on the seal l. 3: ^{d}Utu-a$_2$-ĝa$_2$.

[578] The reading lama of LAM is secured from an ED IIIa Abū Ṣalābīḫ UGN text, *IAS* 397, o. ii' 5'–6': nin me-zi-da, lama ^{d}Nin-sun$_2$ 'the lady of the true me-functions, the lama Ninsun.' The epithet lama$_3$ is otherwise commonly associated with this goddess - even in god lists, e.g. *SF* 1 o. i 15 - and the fact that it is missing here can be attributed to the fact that LAM fills that function. Though *IAS* 397 is an UGN text, LAM for lama is a predictable phonetic variant, and hence not a true UGN value.

[579] The qualifier zi serves another function in ^{d}Lama-names of later periods in the same function, rather representing the noun 'life' than the adjective zi(-d). Thus, the name ^{d}lama$_3$-zi-ĝu$_{10}$ in H. Limet, *Anthroponymie*, 449 s.v., should, judging from parallels be seen as a nominal clause, '(the) Lama-spirit is my life.'

[580] H. Limet, *Anthroponymie*, 376 (^{d}Amar-^{d}Su'en-^{d}Lama$_3$-ĝu$_{10}$); 400 (^{d}Šul-gi-^{d}Lama$_3$-ĝu$_{10}$).

[581] TIM 7 1 r. 2: ^{d}Utu-^{d}Lama$_3$-ĝu$_{10}$ (Sippar, Tell ed-Dēr).

river,'[582] i.e. reprieve from a critical state. The first person referent in the poss. pron. suffix -ĝu$_{10}$, 'my,' may cautiously be taken as referring to the name-giver. Looking at OB names, M. Stol has looked at some names in which man may be seen as a party to a legal relationship with the gods,[583] but this is not an apparent motif in the earliest onomastic material. However, a situation in which a child has finally been granted to a mother would certainly be cause for celebration and due thanksgivings. Given that childlessness was considered a punishment, the name lugal-lu$_2$-dadag $^{(a1)}$ and variant lugal-lu-dadag $^{(a1)}$, 'the lugal is one who exonerates man,'[584] may well bear on this general concept. A divine referent for all these names is very likely. Compare also the names lugal-nam-gu$_2$-su$_3$, below, 3.1.3.3, and lugal-nam-dag, further below, section 3.1.6.1.

3.1.3.2 Protection of the city

A small number of nominal sentence-names with a fair distribution in the Girsu and Nippur area make a connection between the lugal and the idea of a town guard, lugal-en-nu $^{(a\geq 9)}$, with variants lugal-en-nun $^{(a4)}$ 'the lugal is a guardian.'[585] It is likely that the qualities of the noun were thought to benefit the township as a whole, as opposed to the similar lugal-en-nu-ĝu$_{10}$, discussed directly above, section 3.1.3.1. It is probably no coincidence that not a single name composed with a specific theonym and en-nu(n) has as of yet been attested, and hence a human referent is likely.[586] The link to the city comes to the fore in the Ur III name uru-na-en-nu-bi '(he/she is) the guardian of his/her city,'[587] which originally may well have incorporated an appellative such as lugal or nin.

---

[582] Once with divine determinative, lu:gal-^{d}I$_7$-ĝu$_{10}$ $^{(a1)}$. All attestations are from Nippur. It is perhaps relevant to note that a few texts referring to the river ordeal have been found at Nippur. Such documents are otherwise not very common, see C. Wilcke, *EANEL*, 46, 3.3.7, and fnn. 118–119.

[583] M. Stol, *StEb* 8 (1991), 199–201.

[584] The combination lu$_2$ dadag(UD.UD) is seen also in the TH 264, in describing the temple of Bau in Uruku.

[585] See, e.g., *CIRPL* Ukg. 17–33, featuring en-nu bad$_3$(-da) as the first line. The terms appear to have been interchangeable also at Ebla. See notes on VE908 en-nun-ak = *na-za-lum*, and en-nu-ak, M. Bonechi, *QDLF* 16 (2006), 87.

[586] OSP 1 28 o. i 9: diĝir-en-nu (ED IIIb Nippur). Compare niĝir-en-nu, ITT 2/1 923 o. 2 (Ur III Girsu). In view of the name *i$_3$-li$_2$-en-nu*, MAD 5 57 o. i 12, diĝir-en-nu may rather be Akkadian. The signs -en-nu could then be seen either as *ennum* 'mercy,' or, for instance, as a logogram for a nominal derivation of *naṣārum*.

[587] *UNT* 88 vii 6 (following column division of H. Waetzoldt, *UNT*, 260–263, translit. only). Compare also the discussion of lugal-uru-na, along with the names uru-na-bad$_3$-bi and bad$_3$-uru-na, above, p. 96.

3.1.3.3 Protection of the country

The largest group of names which deal with the lugal and his protective duties are linked to activities which can be said to benefit the country as a whole. A concept traditionally held as underlying Sumerian royal ideology is the idea of the lugal as a shepherd of the people. Central to this concept is protection of a herd, which symbolizes the people. Provisioning and leadership are also important aspects of this symbolism. The imagery has lasted well into modern times.[588] The name lugal-sipa (a≥8) 'the lugal is a shepherd,' starts to appear in the sources in the ED IIIb and the connection could also be construed as a kyriophore, as shown by the late ED IIIb name Enanatum-sipa-zi,[589] and several Ur III parallels. The noun sipa is not found with the appellatives en or nin in contemporary names.[590] During the time before Ur III, the deities An and Enlil feature most often in names containing sipa, Ninurta once. With the exception of the latter, these names mostly have the deity in the ergative, and so it is reasonable to see 'the shepherd' as someone other than the deity mentioned, and the human ruler is one of the possible referents. From this time and on through the OB period, kings and divinities alike were characterized as shepherds.[591] An important exception being the kings of the Akkade dynasty, as pointed out by S. Franke.[592]

Perhaps related to the protector-provider imagery of shepherding may be the rhetorical question name lugal-da-nu-me-a (a3) '(what would be) without a lugal?,'[593] found only in Girsu. Implicit in the name is that the referent of the appellative is a guarantor of an ordered existence, depending on the capacity of that referent. Literary parallels from later times using the same phraseology point to the universal importance of the divinity addressed. His or her area of responsibilities were expressed as essential for the upkeep of the world order.[594] The name is only attested in the ED IIIb Lagaš state, as is the feminine correspondence nin-da-nu-me-a. An ED IIIa Šuruppag name

---

[588] An in-depth study of the early imagery of the shepherd has been done by J. Goodnick Westenholz, Melammu Symposia 4, 281–310, and pl. 23–26.

[589] See above, p. 54.

[590] An exception is posed by the SKL which lists an otherwise unknown lugal of Larak named en-sipa-zi-an-na. The name is most likely a later construct.

[591] See in general the discussion of C. Zaccagnini, *History of Religions* 33 (1994), 270f.

[592] *Königsinschriften*, 35, 125, 196. Note, however, that later literary traditions associate *Narām*-Su'en with the epithet "shepherd," specifically in contexts describing his kingship. See J. S. Cooper, *The Curse of Agade*, 52 l. 40; J. Goodnick Westenholz, MesCiv 7, 273 l. 11f.

[593] The name is composed as a defective rhetorical question. Compare lugal-AN-da-nu-me-a (a1) '(what would be) without LugalANda?,' (ED IIIb Girsu); and Utu-nu-me, UET 2 28 o. ii 2; 199 o. i 7. For this type of name, see J. Bauer, *AWL*, 192; M. Krebernik, AOAT 296, 49. A diverging interpretation centered around the name-bearer is offered by H. Limet, *Namenforschung*, 852, discussing a parallel, nin-ĝu$_{10}$-da-nu-me-a: "sans ma Dame, peut-il exister?"

[594] Some examples address Utu and Enlil, P. Michalowski, *Fs Civil*, 131–136.

an-dul$_3$-nu-me '(what would be) without protection,'[595] perhaps offers more weight to the interpretation of lugal/nin-da-nu-me-a as bearing specifically on protection.

A small group of names link the lugal to destructive natural forces, specifically such having to do with water. Names like lugal-a-ĝe$_6$ $^{(a \geq 4)}$ 'the lugal is a flood'[596] and lugal-a-ma-ru $^{(a1)}$ 'the lugal is a deluge,'[597] are examples of nominal predicate names which are never construed with another appellative.[598] While the former was part of the natural life cycle of the land, controlled floods being necessary for sustaining life on the floodplain, the latter has far more menacing consequences. When used to describe divine weapons, the import is clearly directed at foreign enemies. So for instance in the CS Girsu name lugal-šar$_2$-ur$_3$-e $^{(a1)}$ 'the lugal (answered? grasped?) Šarur.'[599] Strong connections exist between a-ma-ru, šar$_2$-ur$_3$ and the deities Ningirsu and Ninurta.[600] During Ur III times a-ĝe$_6$ and a-ma-ru were loosely associated with the human king, as a sign of forcing foreign lands to submission.[601]

The chariot of the lugal was not only used for warfare, as seen for instance in traditional imagery on ED plaques.[602] Names featuring the lugal in connection with the chariot are found from the MS-CS period onwards, and are to begin with unique to the southeast corner of the floodplain. No other appellative appears in the same type of construction with gigir$_2$ before

---

[595] *TSŠ* 93 o. iv 1'.

[596] TH 289 has a ĝe$_6$ followed by a-ab-ba(-ka), in broken context, translated as "on the waves of the sea" by Å. Sjöberg, TCS 3, 34, concerning the temple of Nin-mar-ki in Guabba.

[597] H. Limet, *Anthroponymie*, 169: "probablement à completer ... Le roi, ouragan d'Enlil"; 313: "Le roi est un ouragan," with further comment, fn. 1. Still in use in OB times, A. Poebel, *Personennamen*, 29. Compare M. Krebernik, *RlA* 7 (1987–90), 110, "Lugal-amaru," "König (der?) Sintflut."

[598] One would expect the seal of *NATN* 163 lu$_2$-a-ma-ru to harmonize with the writing on the tablet r. 4 lu⌜gal⌝-a-ma-ru, preserving only the bottom wedge of GAL. As copied there is not much room for GAL to the left of LU$_2$ on the seal. Photo (CDLI P120861) is inconclusive.

[599] The name is taken to include a literary allusion to Ningirsu perhaps conversing with, or using, his weapon. The predicate could perhaps be either gi$_4$ 'to answer,' with Šar$_2$-ur$_3$ marked as an inanimate with the loc.-term., or perhaps šu–du$_8$ 'to hold (in the hand). Compare also K. Tallqvist, *AGE*, 358 s.v. "Lugal-ur$_4$-ur$_4$," with note "wahrscheinlich missverstandenes Šar$_2$-ur$_4$" (sic); M. Krebernik, *RlA* 12 (2009–11), 85 s.v. "Šar-ur und Šar-gaz," §2. The name ur-^{d}Šar$_2$-ur$_3$-ra was extant in the Lagaš II-Ur III period, e.g. ITT 2/1 4216 r. 1 and seal l. 4 (Girsu). See furthermore note to lugal-URUDU-da, below, p. 182 fn. 1128.

[600] See refs. in *PSD* A/1 s.v. a-ma-ru, 1.2, 2–3. Iškur also was associated with a-ma-ru, e.g. in TH 338, in broken context.

[601] See for instance *PSD* A/1 s.v. a-ma-ru, 1.2 (*Šu*-su'en); Šulgi D ll. 344–345 (the sign A is missing from parallel lines 228–229). Note the incipit lugal a-ma-ru of a hymn attested only in an Ur III literary catalogue, W. W. Hallo, *JAOS* 83 (1963), 171f. o. ii 9. The section in which the entry appears is expressly stated to be en$_8$-du lugal "royal songs," but whether the incipit referred to a god or a human is not known.

[602] See in general the excellent discussion on this matter by G. J. Selz, *Götterwelt*, 137f.

the Ur III, and then nin appears only exceptionally.[603] A human referent is quite possible. The names may indicate that the focal value of wheeled implements in personal names is one bearing on their significance for the defence of the country. Something that was beneficial and used in support of the homeland was simultaneously a deterrent for outside attacks. The names themselves are mostly construed with the loc.-term. -e, as in lugal-^{ĝiš}gigir$_2$-e $^{(a \geq 4)}$ 'the lugal ... the chariot.'[604] The predicate may, on the basis of a questionable abbreviated ED IIIb writing, have been du$_{10}$ 'to be, make good.'[605] But it is likely that the chariot counted among the objects which could take si 'to be just right (for something),' as predicate.

The name lugal-šilig-e $^{(a1)}$ 'the lugal ... the šilig-axe,'[606] is probably to be seen in the light of this defensive imagery. During the first half of the 3rd millennium the šilig-axe is known from a number of depictions of military scenes,[607] but later traditions associated it with the god Ninurta.[608]

An implement known to be used by both gods and men is the throwing net, used for hunting and warlike purposes alike. Two different terms for nets are extant in lugal-names, with no discernible difference in meaning,[609] lu:gal-sa-par$_2$ $^{(a1)}$,[610] with variants using par$_4$,[611] all: 'the lugal ... the throw

---

[603] The genitival PN ur-^{ĝiš}gigir$_2$ '*man* of the chariot' is during this period also mostly found in Umma and Girsu texts. See further A. Westenholz, *ECTJ*, 59, note on TMH 5 104 r. i 4. Only one Ur III instance of another appellative is known to me, SAT 1 440 r. 2: nin-^{ĝiš}gigir dumu nin-uru$_{16}$-še$_3$ (Girsu, translit. only; mother given as "Nin-en-gi$_7$" in publication).

[604] Attested variants are: lugal-^{ĝiš}gigir$_2$ $^{(a1)}$, lugal-^{ĝiš}gigir$_2$-re $^{(a1)}$, and lugal-^{ĝiš}gigir$_2$-re$_2$$^{?}$ $^{(a1)}$.

[605] MLVS 1, 8 no. 10 (ED IIIb probably Girsu, published in partial transliteration only, but see photo, CDLI P247607) o. i 3–4: 2 kuš gu$_4$, ^{ĝiš}gigir$_2$-du$_{10}$ ba-la$_2$ '2 hides of oxen, Gigirdu *withheld* (?).' The identification as a PN must be considered tentative, since otherwise a predicate is consistently missing from names featuring the ^{ĝiš}gigir$_2$. Compare H. Limet, *Anthroponymie*, 92, 275: "Le roi vers le char."

[606] Compare also lugal-šilig $^{(a1)}$. See the axe type termed ^{ĝiš}šilig in *IAS* 33 o. xi 7', and in general E. Salonen, *Die Waffen der alten Mesopotamier*, 13f. The absence of the ĝiš-determinative can be compared to the usual pre–Ur III writing of lugal-apin-du$_{10}$. There is a remote possibility that šilig should be read banšur$_x$, see e.g. J. Bauer, *AoN* 35. However, in MesCiv 4 30 (MS-CS Umma), the only attested writings of both lugal-šilig-e and lugal-banšur-e appear. Both are qualified as ugula but probably serving in different capacities.

[607] Compare the axes held in the Stele of the Vultures chariot register, E. Salonen, *Die Waffen der alten Mesopotamier*, pl. II, fig. 2–5; and the drawing of an aga-šilig in an OB omen text, CT 31 12, quoted by *CAD* A/1 s.v. *agasalakku*.

[608] In *Angim* l. 133, Ninurta compares his aga-šilig to an ušumgal which disposes of corpses.

[609] See in general E. Salonen, *Die Waffen der alten Mesopotamier*, 97 s.v. *saparru*; and 99 s.v. *šuškallu*(*m*).

[610] Compare the divine byname Lugal-sa-par$_4$ attributed in the OB period to Alla, Ningišzida's vizier, J. Peterson, AOAT 362, 96, note to ii' 1, and references. K. Tallqvist, *AGE*, 356f. s.v. "Lugal-sa-par$_3$," given as: "König des Netzes," suggested a possible link to Dumuzi, while W. G. Lambert underlined that the net invoked by the name was a divine weapon, *RlA* 7 (1987–90), 151 s.v. "Lugal-sapar."

[611] Notably the ED IIIa Kiš variant lugal-sa-par$_4$ $^{(a1)}$ (SA not E$_2$ as copied twice, *AAICAB* pl. 6, Ashm 1928-431, kindly collated by A. Westenholz); and lugal-sa$_x$(ŠU$_2$.SA)-par$_4$ $^{(a1)}$, perhaps from the ED IIIb Umma-Zabala area. See this latter graphic variant also in OIP 104 15 o. ii 4: e$_2$-sa$_x$(ŠU$_2$.SA)-par$_4$. Add these attestations to the list in P. Steinkeller, *ZA* 75 (1985), 42, and

net'; and lugal-sa-šuš-gal $^{(a\geq2)}$ 'the lugal … the great throw net.' Imagery from Girsu stelae of ED and early Sargonic[612] date are well-known illustrations of the use of nets to catch and contain enemies. Nets, as divine weapons, were used in the oath-swearing ceremonies recounted in Eanatum's Stele of the Vultures. Later texts attest to similar procedures in connection with oaths, though not directly with nets at hand. Associations between the just principles of deities and kings remained embedded in the symbolic comparisons with throw nets in the late 3rd millennium and onwards.[613] A single occurrence of lugal-sa-par$_2$-re from the Ur III period shows that the connection lost much of its appeal with time, but at least it provides the loc.-term. dimensional suffix for the object.[614]

Another, more opaque name is known from the ED I-II period onwards and takes on a multitude of variant orthographies. It incorporates the Anzu, a mythological being much revered in the Early Dynastic period. The complex ideas behind the name lugal-^{an}Anzu$_2$(NI$_2$.MI)^{mušen} $^{(a\geq2)}$,[615] are everything but clear, and indeed, the Anzu merits a monograph of its own. However, a few important pointers can be singled out. The Anzu most often appears with the bird determinative ^{mušen}, and its many written attestations indicate that it had a form of popular appeal. It is likely due to the popular appeal of Anzu that it would have appeared as a winged creature in depictions of the time. A number of texts speak of the outstretched wings of the Anzu, sometimes clearly as a sign of protection.[616] And several matching depictions of a lion-headed bird with its wings extended to the sides are known, from the far south of the floodplain to Mari in the northwest. Sometimes the bird-like creature in the pictures spreads its wings over a pair of animals while seated on their hindparts.[617] In other depictions it appears to attack an animal on which it is perched.[618] As with the imagery of throw nets discussed above, it is not improbable that the Anzu represented a divine force beneficient to

---

correct his discussion on orthographies on the following pages accordingly. The writing with par$_4$ is just as old, at least, as the writing with par$_2$, and does not represent a development taking place in OB times. The sign ŠU$_2$.SA equals OSP1-X$_{13}$ and Subartu2-X$_{11}$, but need not have represented a syllabic value beginning with a sibilant each and every time.

612 The *Śarrukēn* Girsu stele was last investigated by L. Nigro, *Iraq* 60 (1998), 85–93.

613 See P. Steinkeller's survey, *ZA* 75 (1985), 39–41; especially the rendering of UET 1 71, where the dub-la$_2$-mah̬ of Nanna in Ur is described as Nanna's place of judgment, the throw net which the enemies of the builder, Amar-Su'en, could not escape.

614 SAT 2 445 r. 1–3: mu lugal-sa-par$_2$-re ama-ka-še$_3$, ur-^{u_2}ninni$_5$, šu ba-ti (translit. only, Umma).

615 This writing is the one at home in ED IIIb Girsu and the Lagaš state, including a single example of the phonetic complement ^{an} written ^{ḫal}. The attested variants are: lugal-^{an}Anzu$_2$ $^{(a1)}$, from MS-CS Nippur; lugal-^{an}Anzu$_x$(IM.MI) $^{(a1)}$, from ED-I-II Ur; lugal-^{an}Anzu$_x$(MI)$^{mušen\ (a3/°1)}$, from ED IIIa Šuruppag, ED IIIa-b Ur, and also found in a list of PNN from Ebla.

616 See the 3rd millennium references collected by K. V. Zand, *Fs Groneberg*, 422f.

617 E.g. H. Frankfort, *Art and Architecture*, 60 fig. 63 (copper frieze from Tell al-ʿUbaid); 67 fig. 70 (silver vase of Enmetena).

618 E.g. H. Frankfort, *Art and Architecture*, 77 fig. 81.

friends and catastrophic to foes. In art the Anzu features as a focal point of the net in which Ninĝirsu captures the enemies subdued by his earthly representative Eanatum on the Stele of the Vultures.[619] On the opposite side of the Anzu's sphere of responsibility is perhaps the small lapis and gold figurine, part of the hoard called the "Trésor d'Ur," found at Mari.[620] The fine pieces of craftsmanship could represent part of an elaborate diplomatic exchange between two key political centers situated on the Euphrates river.[621] The inclusion of the Anzu among the objects might then represent assurances of an alliance and mutual protection. While the nature of Anzu depends on perspective, the idea behind the name lugal-^{an}Anzu$_{2/x}$$^{(mušen)}$ can accordingly be understood to have expressed the dualistic sense of peaceful and warlike protection combined. It seems reasonable to translate the name as a nominal sentence, indicating comparison and not identity, 'the lugal is (like) the Anzu,'[622] and judging from parallel names it is hard to state with certainty to whom the appellative lugal refers,[623] though a human referent is not impossible.

Subjugating the enemy lands was probably the meaning of such names as lugal-kur-dub$_2$ $^{(a\geq4)}$ 'the lugal is one who shatters the mountains,'[624] from the ED III Umma and Girsu area. The name appears to be firmly rooted in the mythology surrounding Ningirsu.[625] The meaning of the latter is reminiscent of the names kur-šu-ni-še$_3$ 'the mountains are in his grasp,' and kur-giri$_3$-ni-še$_3$ 'the mountains (are) at his feet,' though these do not explicitly feature an

---

619 E.g. H. Frankfort, *Art and Architecture*, 73 fig. 75. E. Porada, CRRA 38, 69–72, has also made the connection between the lion-headed bird, Anzu/Imdugud, and warlike activities.

620 See MAM 4, for greater detail as to the contents of this hoard. On different readings of the inscription on the "perle de Mari," see J. S. Cooper, *RA* 80 (1986), 73f., with refs.

621 Connections between Ur and Mari are admittedly not built on firm evidence. See tentatively J. S. Cooper's discussion, *RA* 80 (1986), 73f. In the Ur III period the situation is clearly another, with strong relations between the two cities. See F. Weiershäuser, *Die königlichen Frauen der III. Dynastie von Ur*, 29f., and 106 w. fn. 397 for refs. Note also that two queens of ED IIIb Ur may have come from Semitic-speaking environments: *pu*$_3$-AD and, judging from her inscription, UET 8 2, gan-saman$_3$(ŠE.ŠE$_3$.BU.NUN)-nu. The last mentioned inscription features a sign which ought to be a possessive pronoun, -*śu*$_3$/-*su*$_3$, but see R. D. Biggs, *OrNS* 66 (1973), 56f. fn. 8, for a different opinion.

622 Similarly G. Marchesi, *OrNS* 73 (2004), 183 fn. 173. Compare R. di Vito, StPohl SM 16, 61, 30.4c^a, 1: "(A) lord is Anzud."

623 Most of the pre–Ur III parallels with other appellatives are collected by M. Krebernik, AOAT 296, 20f.; and by K. V. Zand, *Fs Groneberg*, 433–439.

624 Adapted from W. G. Lambert, *RlA* 7 (1987–90), 147 s.v. "Lugal-kur-dub." Lambert's reference there to an ED IIIb PN *me-lugal-kur-dub$_2$ is a misreading for dam lugal-kur-dub$_2$. Compare A. Falkenstein, AnOr 30, 82: "König, der das Bergland erzittern lässt"; and A. Westenholz, *Six City-State Cultures*, 34: "the-lugal-smashes-the-foreign-lands."

625 Later tradition used this name as an epithet of Ninurta, see J. Peterson, AOAT 362, 97, note to ii' 5. The name was sometimes also used for a standard of Ningirsu. Compare also the partial description of a chariot of Ningirsu, related to the road southbound to Eridu, M. Lambert, *RSO* 47 (1973), 3 (AO 24414) ii 8: ^{ĝiš}gigir$_2$ kur dab$_6$ ^{d}Nin-ĝir$_2$-su$_2$-ka 'chariot which encircles the mountains.'

appellative.[626] According to H. Limet, a human referent is not excluded.[627] A passage in a Girsu royal inscription, to the effect that Enanatum I had been granted victory over the foreign countries, adds additional weight to that impression.[628] Another name from the ED IIIa-b Girsu and Umma area can be recreated as *lugal-igi-nim-še$_3$-du 'the lugal goes to the highland.' A preemptive strike or a retaliation against the forces of the highlands toward the east seem to be the general idea in the name, attested in a few variants.[629]

A few terms related to doors appear regularly in contexts which signify the protection of the homeland or the home city from outside threats. They appear sometimes as poetic descriptions of the human king in the Ur III period, and sometimes they refer to acts of divine beings.[630] The names lugal-ig-gal $^{(a3)}$ 'the lugal is a great door,'[631] lugal-igi-tab $^{(a\geq4)}$ 'the lugal is one who seals off (the land),'[632] and lugal-si-ĝar $^{(a\geq3)}$ 'the lugal is a door bolt,'[633] are found in ED IIIb Girsu, and then also in Umma and Adab. All of these cities were situated on the southeastern fringe of Sumer, facing the passage into the floodplain from Susa and Elam. It is reasonable to assume that the names appear in this region due to their position, but it is not clear whether the names refer to defensive actions benefitting first and foremost a city or the whole country.

---

[626] Following A. Westenholz, *Six City-State Cultures*, 34. The names are found e.g. in *DP* 1/2 137 r. iii 5; and *TSA* 47 o. i 5. Compare in the latter text o. v 2, Lagaš^{ki}-giri$_3$-na 'Lagaš (is) at his feet,' and see further kur-mu-gam 'the mountain bends (before him),' BIN 8 104 o. i 2 (ED IIIb Umma-Zabala).

[627] *Anthroponymie*, 169.

[628] F. A. Ali, *Sumer* 29 (1973), 30 (IM 67847, En. I 33) iii 1–8: (u$_4$ Lugal-Uru$_{11}$^{ki}-ke$_4$) en-an-na-tum$_2$-ra, nam-lugal, Lagaš^{ki}, mu-na-šum$_2$-ma-a, kur šu-ni-še$_3$, mu-še$_3$-ĝar-ra-a, ki-bal giri$_3$-⸢ni⸣-še$_3$, [mu-še$_3$-ĝar-r]a-a 'when Lugal-Uru had given nam-lugal of Lagaš to Enanatum, he delivered the foreign lands in his grasp, [plac]ed the rebellious land at his feet.'

[629] See D. O. Edzard, *SRU*, 177: "Lugal-nimše-gena(?)." The writings with the terminative-adverbial -še$_3$ are all from Umma-Zabala texts: lugal-igi-nim-še$_3$ $^{(a\geq1)}$, and lugal-igi-nim-še$_{3\text{-}90°}$ $^{(a1)}$ (the traces of the second sign in *TCVBI* 1-19 o. 3 match expected igi); lugal-nim-DU $^{(a1)}$ is known from ED IIIa Girsu. Compare E. Chiera, PBS 11/3, 227, no. 826: ur-igi-nim-DU.

[630] See the passages cited by J. Klein, *Three Šulgi Hymns*, 160f., note to Šulgi X 121f.

[631] The earliest attested PNN with this nominal predicate feature female appellatives: ama-ig-gal, munus-ig-gal, and nin-ig-gal. See F. Pomponio, *Prosopografia*, 28, 182, 197f. s.v.v. for refs. During the ED IIIb lugal and en predominate, along with a few DN. The phrase seems to have gone out of fashion during the Sargonic period, and is relatively rare thereafter.

[632] For a discussion of the verb igi–tab, see J. S. Cooper, Angim, 111 note to l. 65.

[633] H. Limet, *Anthroponymie*, 331: "verrou," with parallels. Note the opening lines to the Abū Ṣalābīḫ and Ebla Śamaś hymn, which mention the Sun God in connection with the door bolt of heaven. For bilingual passages with the same god, see *CAD* Š/2 s.v. *šigaru*, 1d. The only name featuring a fuller writing is nin-si-ĝar-ab-ba, the ED IIIb PN of a girl from the Guabba district in the state of Lagaš, Nik 1 19 o. ii 8. For the less credible option of seeing si ĝar as a passive participle "endowed (with) horns," see *CAD* Q s.v. *qarnû*, lex. sect.; and an Ur III literary catalogue of songs, W. W. Hallo, *JAOS* 83 (1963), 171f. (YBC 3654), r. i 9: gu$_4$-e si ĝar-re.

Explicit fighting is the subject of lugal-me$_3$ [(a1)] 'the lugal … battle,'[634] and of lugal-me$_3$-TUR-še$_3$-nu-še-ge [(a1)] 'does the lugal not howl fiercely (?) in battle?,'[635] with variant lugal-me$_3$-TUR-še$_3$-nu-še$_{27}$-ge [(a1)]. Both are somewhat opaque, but appear to signal an aptitude (eagerness?) for fighting. In Ur III times, lugal-me$_3$ is exclusively found in Girsu texts, with a form lugal-me$_3$-a found at Nippur. This distribution could indicate that the name belonged to the mythical cycles of Nin̂girsu/Ninurta, at home in these cities.[636]

The function of the lugal in neutralizing threats is the likely idea behind lugal-nam-gu$_2$-su$_3$ [(a≥4)] 'the lugal is one who eradicates oppression.' The referent may well be the human ruler.[637] More questionable is the name lugal-ni$_3$-a$_2$-zi-nu-ak [(a1)] 'the lugal is not one to commit a violent act,'[638] which, compared to the interpretation of some other names featuring modal prefix nu- could be construed as a (rhetorical) question. However, it would be hard to explain such a statement, at least if names are supposed to be in the main positive expressions thought to favour the individual bearing the name. Such a question would be expected to yield an affirmative answer – hardly in keeping with a line of reasoning which expects to see in names positive expressions of hopes for the future of an individual.

In an ordered world, there is still the need for institutions to carry out the due process of law. Texts from the Ur III period describes a belief that deceased kings served as judges in the realm of the dead.[639] Evidence for the living ruler as a legal authority is present also in earlier times. Names such as lugal-di-de$_3$ [(a1)] 'the lugal *passes verdict*,'[640] and lugal-^{d}I$_7$-si [(a1)] 'the lugal is

---

[634] H. Limet, *Anthroponymie*, 169 and 281, sees the name as a genitive compound, due probably to Ur III parallels: "Le roi de la bataille."

[635] Interpretation of TUR/banda$_3$ is difficult; it might qualify the noun me$_3$ or serve as adverbial complement of še$_{(27)}$-ge. See, perhaps, Akk. *ekdiš*, ŠE$_3$ then serves as the adverbial suffix. Compare T. Balke, *Onoma* 32 (1994), 78 fn. 17: "Lord who doesn't agree in smaller battles." Note that TUR.ŠE$_3$ also forms a diri-compound kun/ĝ$_5$, hence, compare lugal-kun$_5$.

[636] For references, see H. Limet, *Anthroponymie*, 469 s.v.v.

[637] The verb su$_3$ is here taken to equate Akk. *sapānum*, often used in connection with non–obliging enemies, see *CAD* S s.v., lex. sect. The proponent of the name ought then to be a heroic character. Compare Urnamma B l. 59 and 61: nam-gu$_2$ maḫ-am$_3$ lil$_2$ am$_3$-mi-(NI)-in-su-ub "He made the wind sweep away the great oppression," following E. Flückiger-Hawker, OBO 166, 197. Abbreviation [lugal]-nam-gu$_2$ [(a1)], gab$_2$-kas$_4$, in *DP* 1/2 124 o. i 1f. was read nam-gu$_2$ by V. V. Struve, *Onomastika*, 125; so also by Y. Rosengarten, *RHR* 156 (1959), 153 fn. 12 who identified this person with lugal-nam-gu$_2$-su$_3$ gab$_2$-kas$_4$ in *DP* 1/2 125 o. i 1f.

[638] Similarly D. O. Edzard, *SRU*, 60, note to v 3: "der König tut keine Gewalttat." V. V. Struve, *Onomastika*, 107 has one instance of the name as lacking -nu-, which is, however, visible on photo of Nik 1 r. iii 3' (CDLI P221710). For the mng. "vehemence, violence" of ni$_3$-a$_2$-zi(-g), see, in part, *PSD* A/2 s.v. a$_2$-zi, and compare the statement in *CIRPL* Ukg. 14 ii' 6': ni$_3$ a$_2$-zi-še$_3$ nu-ak 'I have not acted violently.'

[639] See D. Katz, *The Image of the Netherworld in the Sumerian Sources*, 121f.

[640] See C. Wilcke, *EANEL*, 44: 3.3.5.1: di-bi di ḫe$_2$-be$_2$ "may he speak a judgement for this case." Compare e$_2$-di-de$_3$-ba-gub 'the *house* stood by (for) the verdict,' Nik 1 2 o. i 11; ^{d}Utu-di-de$_3$, ITT 2/2 3159 o. ii 9' (translit. only, CS? Girsu); nin-di-de$_3$ (OSP 1 23 o. iv 36; vi 7,

just right for the river,’[641] may be rare witnesses to that end. Another possibility would be to connect them with Utu. The name lugal-si-sa_2 $^{(a\geq10)}$ ‘the lugal is just,’[642] while being very formulaic may also relate to legal terminology. Perhaps the name lugal-inim-TAR $^{(a1)}$ ‘the lugal is one who decides matters (?),’ is also related to this group.[643]

3.1.4 Care and attentiveness

Central to names under the fourth heading is the view that the actions of the lugal affect people on a personal level. A sense of security on the part of the people, and an interest taken by the lugal in his subjects or in things under his aegis are implicit. Names have been further subdivided as follows:

- Care for the individual
- Care for the city
- Care for the country
- Care for the dead

This category also encompasses names in which a wish is expressed from the point of the name-bearer to be in the presence of the lugal, or to partake in benefits at the disposal of the lugal. Few names of this category were ever widely distributed, but names which featured compounds with $ša_3$, like lugal-$ša_3$-la_2-tuku and lugal-$ša_3$-gid_2. Interestingly, the first is attested exclusively in the ED IIIb Lagaš state, with more than a dozen bearers, most of which can be shown to have been contemporaries; they account for almost half of the number of persons bearing names belonging to this category in that area during that particular time. The other name is found at ED IIIa Šuruppag and also in other Sumerian cities of the ED IIIb period. One single attestation of this lugal-$ša_3$-gid_3 from MS-CS Nippur survives. As with many other names, these fuller writings may underlie a quite common abbreviation, lugal-$ša_3$.

ES-MS Nippur; UET 2 suppl. 33 o. 4, MS-CS Ur). And see the discussion by B. Alster, Mesopotamia 2, 97, on di–gub.

[641] Compare PN I_7-de_3-si, CUSAS 13 o. 2 (CS Adab).

[642] Here the interpretation of H. Limet, *Anthroponymie*, 171, 292: “Le roi est juste,” has been followed. See, similarly, D. O. Edzard CRRA 19, 142; and R. di Vito, StPohl SM 16, 65, 30.5a, 16. The name, used as a divine epithet was seen as a noun with an attribute by K. Tallqvist, *AGE*, 357 s.v.: “Der gerechte König.” Compare the name of a divine counsellor of Ningirsu, interpreted variously by A. Falkenstein, AnOr 30, 83, as: “Herr, der recht leitet”; and W. G. Lambert, *RlA* 7 (1987–90), 151f. s.v. “Lugal-sisa,” as: “The lord who directs.”

[643] Compare Ur III Nippur nin-inim-TAR, BBVO 11 271 (6N-T190+239, translit. only) o. i 24. The predicate phrase (?) may appear as a noun in W. Farber & G. Farber, *WO* 8 (1975), 180 o. iv 6; *WF* 30 o. iii 1: inim-TAR-nin-$ĝa_2$ ‘(it is) the decision of my lady(?)’ (both ED IIIa Šuruppag). In Ur III times this expression is primarily attested with the female Lagaš divinities Bau and Nanše, see H. Limet, *Anthroponymie*, 443 s.v. ka-tar-DN. Is perhaps inim-TAR in these latter names to be linked with inim–sila, for which, see *CAD* Š/1 s.v. *šalāṭu* A “to dominate, to rule, to control.”

Fig. 5, below, records the distribution of 90 persons, the estimated minimum number of persons bearing 31 variants of names sorted under this category.

	ED I-II	ED IIIa-ED IIIb	ED IIIb-ES	ES-MS	MS-CS
Adab			5	2	4
Girsu			28		4
Isin		1	2		
Lagaš			1		
Larsa		1			
Marad			1		
Mesag					3
Nippur		1	5	1	5
Šuruppag		8	1		
Umma-Zabala			7	1	2
Ur			2	2	
Unknown					3

Fig. 5: Name-bearers, 3.1.4, Care and attentiveness. Estimated minimum number of individual name-bearers.

3.1.4.1 Care for the individual

Two sets of names form an aspectual correspondence: those rare ones in which the subject is expressly said to pay attention to the lugal, represented by one name, and those more common in which the lugal directs his attention toward the subject. The distribution of such names serves as a good illustration of the prevalent focus on the benefits a name-bearer could reap when provided with an auspicious name. Among the rare names belonging to the present subcategory is one found exclusively in the ED IIIb period, but with Ur III parallels, igi-lugal-še$_3$ $^{(a2)}$ 'eyes are set on the lugal.'[644] These names correspond to other names in which the name-bearer or -giver may be held to be active.[645] They are likely to have a divine referent.

Much more productive were names in which acts of the lugal were portrayed as beneficient to an individual, whether the name-bearer or the name-giver. The voice of the speaker is of course best shown by personal affixes, either through pronominal suffixes or through infixes in a verbal chain. Empowering of the individual is a theme current in [a$_2$/za$_3$]-lugal-ĝa$_2$-

[644] With variant igi-lugal-še$_{3\text{-}90°}$ $^{(a\geq2)}$. The most plausible interpretation of igi-X-še$_3$-names has been proposed by G. Marchesi, HANE/S 10, 109 and fnn. 563–565. His proposal has been followed here. No genitive markers are present in any writing of a name of this type. The terminative -še$_3$ is irregular for animate nouns, but seems here to be part of a phraseology, as indicated also by a passage in the opening of Gudea Cyl. A i 3: ^{d}En-lil$_2$-e en ^{d}Nin-ĝir$_2$-su$_2$-še$_3$ igi zi mu-ši-bar 'Enlil had directed his just gaze toward the lord Ningirsu.' In later lexical and bilingual passages both the phrases igi ^{d}Utu-še$_3$ and igi ^{d}Utu-ka corresponds to Akk. *ina maḫar* ^{d}Šamaš, see *CAD* M/1 s.v. *maḫru* s., lex. sect. For other names written igi-DN-še$_3$, see, e.g., A. Westenholz, OSP 1, 85: index; Struve, *Onomastika*, 83f.

[645] See e.g. igi-ĝu$_{10}$-AN-še$_3$-ĝal$_2$ 'my eyes are fixed at the god/the skies,' above, p. 61.

ta $^{(a1)}$ 'by the *strength* of my lord,'[646] and related a_2-lugal-ta $^{(a1)}$, both from the ED IIIa. Provisioning and expectations of personal assistance underlies the name lugal-diĝir-$ĝu_{10}$ $^{(a\geq 8)}$ 'the lugal is my god,'[647] which began to appear in the ED IIIb. The ambiguity of reference in this name depends much on the modern appreciation of what the term diĝir entailed. If diĝir is to be seen as a symbolic description for caring and providing, then the term can be likened to elements in names comparing the lugal to a mountain or a walled enclosure, like a fortress.[648] ED IIIb parallels containing the qualified nominal predicate -diĝir-$ĝu_{10}$ are mostly composed with other appellatives. Two theophores and a name mentioning queen PAP.PAP, the wife of LugalANda, are known to have been borne by women from ED IIIb Girsu.[649] Even though the deification of the living ruler was still a couple of generations away, the view of the lugal as a semi-divine personality has compelling parallels from a later example. In one of his cylinder inscriptions, Gudea, $ensi_2$ of the Lagaš state termed himself the 'god of his city,' in a passage which has him utter prayers and showing reverent submission before the gods, he describes himself:[650]

> "The ruler, who is wise, is knowledgeable, kisses the ground over and over before the divinities; with rites and prayer, in submission, he touches the ground; the ruler the (personal) god of his city, says a prayer."

While not attempting to conceal his elevation above the common man, Gudea marks his subordination to the gods, emphasizing his pious stance which so frequently figures in his other inscriptional material. There is no mistaking the attempt to portray the humble attitude of a person acting as an intermediary between the gods and the citizens for whose benefit said acts were performed. In his role as middle-man between the gods and men, the

---

646 Similarly R. di Vito, StPohl SM 16, 72, 39.2, 2 and fn. 18. G. Visicato & A. Westenholz in editing the text (A 33676), *Gs Cagni*, 1113–1117, could draw, for instance, on a contemporary name za_3-nin-$ĝa_2$-ta, *FTUM* 72 o. 3. In accordance with this, adjust the entry in F. Pomponio, *Prosopografia*, 202, *nin-za_3-ta-e_3; photo of *WF* 37 (CDLI P010994) has clear $ĜA_2$ instead of E_3.

647 G. J. Selz contends, *Götterwelt*, 112 fn. 411, that a twice attested alternation lugal-A-$ĝu_{10}$ for lugal-AN-$ĝu_{10}$ in the ED IIIb Girsu archive, would set this name apart from homonymous names during the Ur III, which are more likely to refer to the human king. During the Ur III period the name lugal-diĝir-$ĝu_{10}$ is attested with about a dozen name-bearers. For references, see generally H. Limet, *Anthroponymie*, 459.

648 See also the Sargonic period incantation, W. W. Hallo, *OrNS* 54 (1985), 57 (RBC 2000), reedited by N. Veldhuis, *CDLB* 2003:6, r. 2: diĝir-$ĝu_{10}$ a_2-daḫ-$ĝu_{10}$ ḫa-am_3 'May my god be my helper,' following Veldhuis' edition.

649 For ^{d}Inana-diĝir-$ĝu_{10}$ and ^{d}Ba-u_2-diĝir-$ĝu_{10}$, see, e.g., *DP* 1/2 112 o. v 4 and o. viii 3; for PAP.PAP-diĝir-$ĝu_{10}$, see CT 50 33 o. vii 4. In Sargonic times the construction was comparatively rare.

650 Following D. O. Edzard, RIME 3/1.1.7.CylB i 12–15. For a dissenting view on the interpretation of diĝir uru-na-k(e_4), see, e.g. J. N. Postgate, *JCS* 26 (1974), 49, example 30.

ED lugal fulfilled much the same role, and names comparing him to a god must be seen in the light of the lugal's function, rather than of an essence inherent in him as a person; in the office rather than the man.

Entreaties for intercession by the lugal or proclamations announcing the assistance of the lugal are the subject of a few names. The name lugal-ḫa-ma-ti $^{(a3)}$ 'lord, may (the child) survive for my sake!,'[651] appears for the first time in the ED IIIb and stays in use throughout the 3rd millennium. The verbal chain ha-ma-ti hardly ever appears with an explicitly written theonym as subject in any period though the referent is likely to be a deity; the only clear exception is formed by ^{d}Utu-ḫa-ma-ti, from Ur III Girsu.[652] A unique writing in the style of the former asks for the intercession of the lugal, lugal-ḫa-mu-gi$_4$-gi$_4$ $^{(a1)}$ 'lord, may (the child) return to me!' A name with a few, probably locally conditioned, abbreviated variant writings can be reconstructed as *lugal-e-a$_2$-na-mu-gub 'the lugal (placed him/her) on his arm.' Something in the region of 10 people are known to have carried variants of this name.[653] The lugal as intermediary in delivering a child to his or her parents may be the import of lugal-ma-de$_6$ $^{(a\geq7)}$ 'the lugal brought (him/her) to me,'[654] strongly reminiscent of contemporary *i-di*$_3$-DN and later DN-ma-an-šum$_2$/DN-*iddinam*-names. All these formations are likely to have deities as their referents.

A few names containing compound phrases with ša$_3$ 'heart' may be interpreted as extolling the empathic qualities of the lugal. At least two of them are fairly well attested: lugal-ša$_3$-gid$_2$ $^{(a\geq8)}$ 'the lugal *is considerate*,'[655]

---

[651] Similarly T. Balke, *Onoma* 32 (1994), 73f.: "Oh King! May you leave her(him) alive for me." Compare H. Limet, *Anthroponymie*, 87, 106, 174, 306: "Que le roi me fasse vivre!" An abbreviated form lugal-ḫa-ma $^{(a2)}$ is known from the CS period; and an independent form ḫa-ma-ti is well attested from the ED IIIb down to the Ur III period, e.g. V. V. Struve, *Onomastika*, 79 s.v.; H. Limet, *Anthroponymie*, 429 s.v.

[652] SAT 1 413 o. ii 3 (translit. only, undated).

[653] Attestations range from lugal-a$_2$-na $^{(a\geq5/°1)}$, limited to ED IIIa Šuruppag, and the ED IIIb-CS Umma and Girsu region; lugal-a$_2$-na-gub $^{(a1)}$, from ED IIIb Girsu; to writing lugal-e-a$_2$-na $^{(a\geq3)}$, the writings of which are all from Sargonic Nippur and the Umma state. Prefix mu- comes from three attestations of the Girsu name a$_2$-na-mu-gub, e.g. *DP* 1/2 113 o. vii 15, but no prosopographical link exists between this and other writings treated here. The reconstructed name presupposes a direct object for the verb since lugal is in the ergative, and gub fits with the locative. For a differing opinion, see G. J. Selz, *Götterwelt*, 17, fn. 1: "Der König steht an seiner Seite," which, however, does not account for the ergative particle. Selz also draws comparisons to the Nippur name lugal-da-na, OSP 1 79 o. 2. The Ebla name quoted by Selz as *LUGAL-da-na was given a plausible Semitic etymology from *danānum*, read *da-na*-LUGAL and *da-ni*-LUGAL by B. Kienast, *Ebla 1975–1985*, 41, though I have not seen the texts from which these names were drawn. Note GN E$_2$ ^{d}Nin-a$_2$-na^{ki}, TMH 5 24 o. iv 2' (ED IIIb Nippur); and PN nin-e-a$_2$-na from Ur III Ur (tablet, seal), H. Limet, *Anthroponymie*, 508.

[654] Parallel nin-ma-de$_6$ is found at ED IIIb Girsu, e.g. *DP* 1/2 112 o. viii 1; and ES-MS Umma, Nik 2 53 o. ii 5; theophore ^{d}Šara$_2$-ma-de$_6$ is found at Ur III Umma, e.g. MVN 21 223 o. 14.

[655] Abbreviated, perhaps from ša$_3$-še$_3$ gid$_2$, literal meaning: "to take to heart," Akk. *ana libbim šadādum*, see *CAD* Š/1 s.v. *šadādu*, lex. sect. Compare lugal-ša$_3$-su$_3$, which opens up for the possibility that lugal-ša$_3$-gid$_2$ could be read lugal-ša$_3$-su$_{13}$ without a noticeable change in

attested from the ED IIIa down through the Sargonic period; and lugal-ša$_3$-la$_2$-tuku (a≥13) 'the lugal has compassion,'[656] which was exceedingly popular in the ED IIIb Lagaš state.[657] Both names have correspondences with the appellative nin in place of lugal.[658] lugal-ša$_3$-su$_3$ (a3) 'the lugal is full of compassion (lit. 'heart'),'[659] is more difficult to interpret. The present attempt relies on ša$_3$-la$_2$-su$_3$, attested as an Ur III PN,[660] which must have been a close parallel of ša$_3$-la$_2$-tuku, and su$_3$ may then be a writing for sug$_4$ < si-g, 'to be full,' "to be abundant.'[661] The name lugal-ša$_3$-su$_3$ is attested in ED IIIb Girsu, Umma and Ur; and the latter would fit with later traditions of ascribing this epithetical phrase to the Moon God.[662] It is not found with other appellatives in the onomasticon.

Compassionate action is furthermore the theme of a group of variant writings. The direct object involved, en$_{3/8}$-tar is likely to correspond to a concretization of the basic needs of an individual, hence a translation "provisions,"[663] is no doubt justified. The majority of writings occur with the verb su$_3$ or su$_x$(TAG), and so a translation of lugal-en$_3$-tar-su$_3$ (a≥3),[664] as

---

meaning. 5 out of 11 attestations of lugal-ša$_3$-gid$_2$ are from Nippur sources, and the names are kept apart here due to the fact that no other Nippur name featuring the value su$_{13}$(BU) is known to me. About the single attestation from Marad (?), it is hazardous to say anything with certainty. The attestations from Šuruppag, Umma and possibly Isin, might on the other hand more safely be read lugal-ša$_3$-su$_{13}$ as the value su$_{13}$(BU) is known in names from these places.

[656] H. Limet, *Anthroponymie*, 170, 308: "Le roi (est) compatissant"; 297 fn. 5: "Le roi qui a de la pitié." T. Jacobsen identified an abbreviated form lugal-ša$_3$ as referring once to fuller lugal-ša$_3$-la$_2$-tuku, as both forms appeared in one text, *CTNMC* 2, with qualifier ugula.

[657] One possible Ur III occurrence of lugal-ša$_3$-la$_2$-tuku from outside the Lagaš state is SAT 2 499 o. 4 (Umma, translit. only); given by M. Sigrist, *op. cit.* p. 176 as: (ki) lugal-ša$_3$-naĝa(-ta). This ša$_3$-naĝa is unexpected and can quite easily be emendated to la$_2$-tuku.

[658] For nin-ša$_3$-gid$_2$, only one person is known, H. Steible & F. Yıldız, *Fs Limet*, 149–159 (Š. 1006) o. iii 1; for nin-ša$_3$-la$_2$-tuku, see, e.g. VS 25 69 o. x 3; r. ii 12; r. iv 16, three different women carrying the same name.

[659] Compare singularly attested Ur III Girsu name ša$_3$-ga-ni-en-su$_3$, MVN 6 129 o. 10 (translit. only), possibly bearing witness to the same idea; and see also lugal-ša$_3$-ga, below, p. 181.

[660] See attestations with H. Limet, *Anthroponymie*, 527 s.v. The seal on *PDT* 1 388 l. 5, *lugal-ša$_3$-[ga]-su$_3$, should be held against *PDT* 1 218 r. 4, lugal-ša$_3$-la$_2$ recording a transaction no doubt involving the same persons as no. 388 (both Puzriš-Dagān, translit. only,). Limet, *Anthroponymie*, 473, correctly, has the former as lugal-ša$_3$-[la$_2$]-su$_3$.

[661] Compare the hymnic epithet chains of Bau: ša$_3$ la$_2$ tuku arḫuš$_2$ su$_3$ kalam-ma, and TH 267: (nun-zu nun) ša$_3$ la$_2$ su$_3$ kalam-ma ama kur-kur-ra, both discussed by Å. Sjöberg, TCS 3, 105, note to l. 267. See, further, J. Bauer, *AWL*, 389f., note on PN e$_2$-i$_3$-gara$_2$-sug$_4$.

[662] See Å. Sjöberg, *MNS*, 106, note to l. 5, with Akk. translation *šarrum rēmēnûm*.

[663] See *CAD* P s.v. *piqittu*, lex. sect. The name nin-en$_3$-tar-ĝu$_{10}$ in Ur III times, e.g. TUT o.! ii' 8 (Girsu, date broken), makes it less likely that a meaning can be derived from *šitūlum* (<*ša'ālum*) "to deliberate," *CAD* Š/1 s.v. *šâlu* A. In the latter name, en$_3$-tar rather represents a participial construction parallel to Akk. *pāqidum*.

[664] Variants include: lugal-en$_3$-tar-su$_{13}$ (a1), lugal-en$_3$-tar-su$_x$(TAG) (a1), lugal-en$_8$-tar (a1), lugal-en$_8$-tar-su$_3$ (a≥2), lugal-en$_8$-tar-su$_{13}$ (a1), lugal-en$_8$-tar-su$_x$(TAG) (a1). For the variant lugal-e-tar-su$_3$ (a≥1) from Sargonic Ur, see A. Alberti & F. Pomponio StPohl SM 13, 79f. Compare, phps., lugal-⌜e-tar?⌝ (a1), from ES-MS Umma. The writing lugal-en$_8$-su$_{13}$ (a1) no doubt also belongs to this group.

something along the lines of "the lugal is one who provides (abundantly)," might be suggested.[665] The earliest attestations are from ED IIIb Girsu, but the bulk of attestations lie in the Sargonic period, from Nippur and cities toward the south. This compound is unattested with theonyms and is not found verbatim with other appellatives. A human referent is not excluded. The head noun surfaces in nominal phrase names with en and nin as appellative in ED IIIb Girsu,[666] and in the Ur III period, respectively.[667]

The association of lugal with other positive aspects related to care is furthermore found in other names, such as lugal-lu_2-ti-ti (a2) 'the lugal is one who quickens man,' found at ED IIIb Girsu and Ur. The factitive reduplication of ti with the object lu_2 is repeatedly found in later times in connection with the Moon God,[668] and in contemporary sources mostly with the appellative nin.[669] The object lu_2 is found also in lugal-lu_2-sa_6-ga (a1) 'the lugal is one who is kind to man,'[670] limited to the ED IIIb Umma-Zabala state. Contemporary parallels from Girsu use a theonym, en or sipa 'shepherd,' as head noun.[671] It is likely that these names referred to activities of gods toward people.

Somewhat problematic is the name lugal-mu-da-$kuš_2$ (a5/°1), which in light of its variant writings shows a considerable geographical spread during the ED IIIb period. It would be tempting to see in this MU a direct object or a possessive suffix, but a number of names can be shown with certainty to consist only of appellative and verbal prefix(es), among others names composed with mu- and the modal prefix ḫa-. An abbreviated writing of this name exhibits a structural shortening to plain lugal-mu (a3).[672] Comitative -da

---

[665] For two other suggestions, see H. Limet, Anthroponymie, 171: "Le roi est celui qui se préoccupe, qui prend soin au loin (=pour l'avenir)"; and 240: "Le roi qui s'occupe (de moi?)." The diverging interpretations were noted by A. Alberti & F. Pomponio StPohl SM 13, 80.

[666] For references to the $ensi_2$ of Lagaš en-en_3-tar-zi 'the en is a reliable provider,' see e.g. V. V. Struve, *Onomastika*, 49. His career is outlined by J. Bauer, *Annäherungen* 1, 473–475.

[667] E.g. BBVO 11, 269 (6N-T43, translit only) o. 6: nin-en_3-tar-$\hat{g}u_{10}$ 'the lady is my provider' (Ur III Nippur).

[668] Å. Sjöberg, *MNS*, 106; *CAD* B s.v. *balāṭu* (v.), lex. sect. See also discussion on single and reduplicated ti by A. Poebel, *Personennamen*, 37. The parenthesis in the translation of the name takes into account that reduplicated ti might also refer to plural objects. An extension over time could likewise be considered, making the verbal action habitual.

[669] See V. V. Struve, *Onomastika*, 147 s.v. Note faulty reference to a PN *nin-lugal-ti-ti, E. Chiera, PBS 11/1, 72 no. 413. Photo (CDLI P135735) shows lu_2, not lugal.

[670] Interpretation following G. J. Selz, *Götterwelt*, 98 (226) and fn. 355. Compare H. Limet, *Anthroponymie*, 272 (lugal-lu_2-sa_6-sa_6): "Le roi est quelqu'un de bon." The examples quoted by Limet, p. 272f., should all rather be interpreted as having lu_2 as object for the activity or result of the verb.

[671] See e.g. *DP* 1/2 113 o. iv 15: ^{d}Mes-an-du-lu_2-sa_6-ga; o. v 13: ^{d}Nanše-lu_2-sa_6-ga; o. v 15: Utu-lu_2-sa_6-ga; o. vii 10: ^{d}Ba-u_2-lu_2-sa_6-ga (MPN); o. viii 16 ^{d}Ba-[u_2]-lu_2-sa_6-ga (FPN); Nik 1 3 r. i 3' ^{d}En-lil_2-lu_2-sa_6-ga; VS 14 173 o. i 9: en-lu_2-sa_6-ga; BIN 8 381 o. iii 3: sipa-lu_2-sa_6-ga.

[672] So in the cases of at least three persons known from elsewhere under a fuller writing lugal-mu-da-$kuš_2$. For two of these, see G. Marchesi, HANE/S 10, 75 w. fn. 393. See another example of this practice, above, p. 63 w. fn. 315.

with kuš$_2$ has a sense of 'to be concerned with s.th.'[673] Given a variant, phonetic writing from ED IIIb Ebla, nu-gal-me-ga-šu-u$_3$ $^{(°1)}$,[674] and an Ur III theophore parallel ^{d}Iškur-ma-kuš$_2$,[675] the sense becomes more clear. Behind the prefix -mu- is likely to hide a personal pronominal element for the 1st or 2nd person sing.,[676] which then becomes the object referent of the chain. The verbal root in the Ebla variant seems adamant on the fact that the verb has a vocalic ending, and so is probably a *marû* form; something which a writing with -kuš$_2$ would not automatically exclude.[677] Hence a translation 'the lugal concerns himself with me/you,' is thinkable.[678] Variants found in Nippur and Isin dispenses with the comitative infix, lugal-mu-kuš$_2$ $^{(a\geq2)}$,[679] a verbal chain otherwise only associated with Utu,[680] and yet another phonetic writing is known from Ebla, borne by a person characterized as a singer from Mari, nu-gal-mu-da-kaš$_2$ $^{(a1)}$.[681] Both are more than likely to have carried the same meaning as lugal-mu-da-kuš$_2$(-e), and a divine referent seems the most likely for this set of names.

The same is likely to be the case with a name which expresses the hope of continuing assistance in life. lugal-nam-mu-šub-be$_2$ $^{(a1)}$,[682] from ED IIIb Girsu, with variant writing lugal-nam-mu-šub-e $^{(a1)}$,[683] from contemporary Nippur. The type is known already in ED IIIa Šuruppag and the attested parallels feature the appellative nin or a theonym.[684] This *marû* verbal phrase name with a prohibitive, or rather vetitive, sense, probably features an object

---

673 Compare, for another opinion, J. Bauer, *AWL*, 94f., of kuš$_2$ as reflecting original ša$_3$–kuš$_2$, interpreting -mu- as 1cs poss. pron. -ĝu$_{10}$, and translating: "Mit meinem Herrn… sich beratend," followed by M. Krebernik, AOAT 296, 48 w. fn. 262.

674 P. Steinkeller, *Fs Hallo*, 239; M. Krebernik *Fs Röllig*, 190 w. fn. 13; M. Krebernik, AOAT 296, 48 fn. 262, correct printing error -e$_3$ to -u$_3$.

675 YOS 4 207 r. ii 11'.

676 The case prefix for the 1st person sing. is unknown, but could in later sources take on the form of the 2nd person -e-, see M.-L. Thomsen, Mesopotamia 10, 217 §428.

677 A KVKV-value is missing from R. Borger, AOAT 305, still I refrain from positing a kušu$_x$(DUL$_3$) value for the sign.

678 For a somewhat different interpretation, see G. Marchesi, HANE/S 10, 75 w. fn. 393. His rendering of the name LUM-ma-MU, MesCiv 4 8 o. iii 2' as 'LUM-ma <exerted himself for> me/him' should be held against the fact that lugal-mu-da-kuš$_2$ only has a full parallel in nin-mu-da-kuš$_2$, e.g. VS 14 63 o. i 2. In all other cases the comitative -da- is missing.

679 Judging by the MS-CS date of lugal-kuš$_2$ $^{(a1)}$ it is likely to be abbreviated from original lugal-mu(-da)-kuš$_2$.

680 E.g. *WF* 36 o. iv 7 (ED IIIa Šuruppag), writing Utu-mu-kuš$_2$, all extant writings lack the divine determinative.

681 M. Krebernik, AOAT 296, 48 fn. 262.

682 There is a distinct possibility to see in this and the following name a negative precative, 'may the lugal not forsake …'; and reconstruct a personal infix for the first or second persons, or perhaps an elided object, like a city.

683 Compare nin-nam-mu-šub-e, HSS 3 23 o. ix 15' (ED IIIb Girsu); OSP 1 23 o. iv 9, 38, vii 13 (ES-MS Nippur).

684 See nin-nam-mu-šub-be$_2$, *FTUM* 48 o. i 2; and compare the Ur III Girsu PNN ^{d}Ba-u$_2$-nu-mu-šub-be$_2$, *CTNMC* 54 r. iii 19; and nin-nu-mu-šub-e, *STA* 6 r. vi 7'.

referent in the verbal chain;[685] a translation ‘may the lugal not abandon me/you,’ suggests itself. It is reminiscent of the opening passages in Inana’s Descent, which describes how the goddess abandoned heaven and earth, cultic offices and a number of her temples to journey to the Netherworld.[686] In the present name, however, the sense is more likely one pertaining to involvement on a personal level.[687]

3.1.4.2 Care for the city

Not only were individuals cause for concern for a lugal. His city or its main sanctuary was the probable object for his care and attention in the name lugal-ki-tuš-du$_{10}$ $^{(a\geq 6)}$ ‘the lugal is one who makes the dwelling place pleasant.’[688] the full form known only from ED IIIa Šuruppag, and there it was quite popular. Perhaps similar in scope was lugal-uru-da $^{(a\geq 3)}$, found at ED IIIb Nippur and CS-LS Girsu.[689] The latter name is likely to be completed with the verb kuš$_2$, as in the examples above and below, and as demonstrated by the name nin-uru-da-kuš$_2$.[690] This would yield ‘the lugal (is one who concerns himself) with the city.’[691] If understood correctly, both these names should probably be seen in the light of the responsibilities of the tutelary deities toward their cities, but a human agent is not out of the question. Should, however, URU serve as a verbal prefix, the name lugal-iri/ere-da(-kuš$_2$) would be parallel in meaning to lugal-mu-da-kuš$_2$(-e) in the preceding subsection.[692]

---

685 See M.-L. Thomsen, Mesopotamia 10, 195f., §375, and 198f., §381, with some examples.

686 Following D. Katz, *The Image of the Netherworld*, 251–254, Inana’s abandonment of her cultic offices and temples is indicative of her relinquishing control over these institutions.

687 As is brought home by the later hymn bearing the title nam-mu-un-šub-be$_2$-en, treated by M. E. Cohen, *Sumerian Hymnology: The Eršemma*, 29–35.

688 Compare H. Limet, *Namenforschung*, 852 (tuš read dur$_2$): “le roi qui fait du bien à la demeure”; H. Steible, *CollAn* 7 (2008), 97: “der König (ist) ein guter Ruheplatz.” See also once each nin-ki-tuš-du$_{10}$, *WF* 71 r. viii 5, and ki-tuš-du$_{10}$, *WF* 107 r. iii 5 (both ED IIIa Šuruppag); [x]-ki-tuš-du$_{10}$, UE 3 537 (ES Ur sealing; room enough for nin, too small for lugal). Compare Ur III PN lugal-tuš-du$_{10}$ with H. Limet, *Anthroponymie*, 460; lu$_2$-tuš-du$_{10}$, *TSU* 33 o. 2; for short tuš-du$_{10}$, e.g. MVN 2 18 o. 2.

689 One of the Nippur instances, TMH 5 8 o. ii 1, records a person from Šuruppag. A possible ED IIIa-b Girsu example of the name, *RTC* 2 r. i 1, is damaged and may have featured one more sign. The votive inscription by ḫa-la-^{d}Ba-u$_2$, wife of lugal-uru-da, edited by G. C. Cameron, *JCS* 20 (1966), 125, is by no means from the time of Ur-Nanše. I am not aware of a theophore ḫa-la-name from before the Ur III dynasty.

690 For this name, see J. Bauer, *AWL*, 94f.; M. Krebernik, AOAT 296, 48 w. fn. 262. Compare also sipa-uru-da-kuš$_2$, e.g. *DP* 1/2 113 o. vi 6 (ED IIIb Girsu).

691 A damaged ED IIIa-b Girsu reference, *RTC* 2 r. i 1, may originally have featured a predicate, though this would be a singular occurrence in 3rd millennium sources. The entry *lugal-uru-da-lugal, H. Limet, *Anthroponymie*, 475, is faulty. Read instead: lugal-uru-da šandan(GAL.NI).

692 For the modal verbal prefix iri/ere, of uncertain meaning, see examples in M.-L. Thomsen, Mesopotamia 10, 211 and fn. 94, including an ED IIIb passage.

3.1.4.3 Care for the country

A single attestation of the lugal as caring for the country as a whole is known from ED IIIb Girsu. The land, most often referred to as kalam, is in this name rather referred to using kur, lugal-kur-da-kuš$_2$ [(a1)] 'the lugal is one who concerns himself with the land.' Translating kur as 'mountain(land)' would yield less sense in this name, as it may be regarded as a potential source of danger, and as other names composed with kuš$_2$ all seem to favour an interpretation of caring or of concern in the most positive sense.

3.1.4.4 Care for the dead

Finally, a name with a very tentative translation, lugal-ti-uš$_2$-da-kuš$_2$ [(a1)] 'the lugal is one who concerns himself with the living and the dead,'[693] might point to the reach of the figure of the lugal beyond the world of the living. In later periods the deceased lugals were believed to fill the function of judges among the dead but earlier periods do not offer much in that connection. Since the name is only attested at ED IIIb Girsu, and since the ruling family there is known from official records to have cared for the spirits of deceased ancestors, it is possible that the name, if understood correctly, refers to a human ruler. By making sure that the powerful deceased lords and ladies of the city were cared for, the future survival of the city was secured. Of course, a number of deities whose functions extended also into the realm of the dead might be considered.

3.1.5 Creation, fertility and prosperity

Heading five gathers up names in which the primary function of the lugal is ensuring abundance in the land. Some names do not bear directly on the lugal as being active in making this abundance manifest. Further subdivisions belonging to this heading are:

- The lugal and the procreation of man
- Provisions for the city
- Countryside, produce and farming
- Life and plenty

A name which bears an apparent connection to festivals, lugal-ezem, celebrated on a regular basis in accordance with the agricultural cycle, was the single most popular lugal-name during the periods investigated here. More than 40 persons were called by that name; from the ED IIIa onwards,

[693] The sign read uš$_2$ corresponds to TIL in the survey of P. Steinkeller, *ZA* 71 (1981), 19–28. Since the verbal adjective ti (tila$_3$) is in the sing., uš$_2$ has likewise been interpreted as sing. It is perhaps possible to understand the words as collective objects, but it would not alter the sense of the name given the interpretation offered here.

from Ur in the southwest to Ešnuna in the northeast. Fig. 6 records the distribution of 129 persons, an estimated minimum number of people bearing 47 variants of names sorting under this category and the different cities with which they were associated, divided by periods.

	ED I-II	ED IIIa-ED IIIb	ED IIIb-ES	ES-MS	MS-CS
Adab		2	5	3	8
Ešnuna					1
Girsu			14		9
Girtab				1	
Isin			1		1
Marad				1	
Mesag					1
Nippur			17		10
Susa					2
Šuruppag		18	1		
Umma-Zabala			11	1	10
Ur	3				1
Uruk			1		
Unknown		2		1	4

Fig. 6: Name-bearers, 3.1.5, Creation, fertility and prosperity. Estimated minimum number of individual name-bearers.

3.1.5.1 The lugal and the procreation of man

People in Mesopotamian mythological works are sometimes portrayed as workers on the estates of the gods.[694] The subordinate position of humans was considered part of the state of the world, organized in detail by the gods who each oversaw their specific niche of culture or nature. This perspective led, among other things, to the belief that specific gods were instrumental in the creation of individual humans. This was then the subject matter of a number of Sumerian and Akkadian names. A few names containing the appellative lugal seem to have a bearing on such matters. Though it is not always equally obvious whether lugal here denoted a divine or a human overlord, the former seems more likely, given the subject matter.

A difficult case is made up by the rather rare name AK-lugal [(a2/°1)] 'creation of the lugal,'[695] which, if correctly interpreted, could correspond on a semantic level to Akkadian names construed with the verb *banûm*.[696] The

---

[694] So, for instance, in the myth Enki and Ninmaḫ, Enki is encouraged by the goddess Nammu to create men as substitutes for the gods, so that the gods could enjoy their leisure. This is echoed in later times by the *Atra-ḫasīs* and *Enūma eliš* epics.

[695] Reading order for this name is supported by an ED IIIb Nippur commemorative inscription, A. Goetze, *JCS* 23 (1970), 52 (7N-153); and a LS-Ur III list of PNN, M. E. Cohen, *Fs Hallo*, 79–86 iv 12, followed by ur-lugal.

[696] For a discussion on AK in PNN see M. Krebernik, AOAT 296 12 w. fn. 35, where a sense "created (by)" is considered. Compare ibid., *BFE*, 244, to the effect that AK ought to be a

gods were in contemporary and later texts described as taking active part in the conception of children, mostly of kings but also of commoners.[697] Since this name type went out of use quite early, around ED IIIa, there are no indications as to whether it was considered a genitive compound or not. A name in a similar vein is lugal-mu-daḫ (a1) 'the lugal added (another child),' attested only from Sargonic Girsu.[698] That MU is not the 1st person pron. suff. is evident from parallels with a theonym in place of the appellative.[699] But it is not entirely clear if MU should be taken as a noun 'name' or as a verbal prefix.

A few sentence names might refer to childbirth, such as lugal-eb$_2$-ta-e$_3$ (a1) 'the lugal brought (him/her) out from there,'[700] with a variant expressing the locative, lugal-eb$_2$-ta-ni-e$_3$ (a≥3) 'the lugal brought (him/her) out from in there.' The names may allude to problems in the process of delivery. They are found in the ED IIIb Lagaš and Umma states, and also in post–Sargonic Girsu and Nippur, with some parallels.[701] The verbal chain with locative marker -ni- is attested verbatim in a pair of ED IIIb Girsu royal inscriptions,[702] but this only shows that the name was firmly set in the language of that time and general region. Such comprehensive verbal chains are, however, most unusual to come across in the onomasticon. A shorter parallel is lugal-ab-e$_3$ (a2) 'the lugal brought it out,' attested at ED IIIb Girsu and in a MS-CS text of uncertain provenience.

The birth situation might arguably be the focus of a CS Nippur name: lugal-ša$_3$-zu (a1).[703] The compounded participle ša$_3$-zu otherwise has a meaning 'midwife,'[704] and there are indeed references to a male divinity

---

noun and not a verbal form of ak 'to make.' Both suggestions are possible. For lists of ED I-II Ur and ED IIIa Šuruppag PNN composed with ak, see J. Bauer, *WO* 18 (1987), 6; and *AoN* 21 (1985), 12 note to 29, 2 respectively.

697 See e.g. M. Stol, *Birth in Babylonia and the Bible*, 83–86.

698 See, further, diĝir-mu-daḫ, MVN 3 2 r. iii 5 (ED IIIb Girsu); and compare R. di Vito, StPohl SM 16, 55, 24.6e: "(The) god has helped me," probably intending an original *diĝir-e-a$_2$-mu-daḫ.

699 E.g. Ur III PN ^{d}Nanna-mu-daḫ, see refs. with H. Limet, *Anthroponymie*, 500 s.v. See also nin-mu-daḫ, e.g. *TUT* 162 o. i 2, 19. The problematic ED IIIa Šuruppag name nin-MU-ba-daḫ, MVN 10 84 o. iv 2; *RTC* 13 o. iii 2, is probably not a parallel in the strictest sense.

700 H. Limet, *Anthroponymie*, 79, on the basis of Ur III parallels translates: "Le roi a fait resplendir (quelque chose) parmi …"

701 See *DCS* 5 14 o. 2 (Lagaš II Girsu); TMH NF 1–2 177 o. 5 (Ur III Nippur). See, furthermore, nin-ib$_2$-ta-e$_3$, e.g. W. G. Lambert, *Gs Sachs*, 251–259 iii 16 (Sargonic list of nin-names); ^{d}Ba-u$_2$-ib$_2$-ta-e$_3$, e.g. *UNT* 34 o. ii 15 (Ur III Girsu); and plain ib$_2$-ta-e$_3$, e.g. HSS 4 o. i 16. Compare the Lagaš II and later construction [in]im-^{d}Nin-ĝir$_2$-su-ka-ib$_2$-ta-e$_3$ 'the word of Ningirsu brought him/her out of there,' *RTC* 191 o. 2.

702 *CIRPL* Ent. 28 ii 3 (=29 ii 14), Eanatum established a boundary dike between Lagaš and Umma.

703 Collation from photo (CDLI P216347) shows that the second sign deviates from copied NIĜ$_2$ in next line. Probable abbreviation of lugal-ša$_3$-an-zu.

704 See, e.g. M. Bonechi, *QDLF* 16 (2006), 89, on VE0371: ša$_3$-zu = *wa-a-tum* "ostetrica," nomen agentis from the verb *walādum*.

serving as male midwife in connection with birth incantations.[705] The similar lugal-ša$_3$-an-zu [(a1)] from ED IIIa Šuruppag, may or may not have bearing on the same matter, using instead what looks like a finite verbal form as the predicate.[706] Assisting at birth, adding a measure of divine protection to the hazardous situation was far more often a prerogative of female divinities.[707]

3.1.5.2 Provisions for the city

There are a number of passages in royal inscriptions which characterize the human ruler by means of titles borrowed from the bureaucratic regime. One example is the epithet ensi$_2$-gal, perhaps 'chief tiller,' of a chief god of the pantheon. In inscriptions with claims on regional hegemony, it is always Enlil;[708] in local Lagaš inscriptions it is as expected Ninĝirsu.[709] The title is mentioned in at least one ED IIIb PN, en-ensi$_2$-gal,[710] which with all probability refers not to a human en, but to a divine one. In the bureaucracy the function was one of medium rank.[711] It often appears to be used in parallel with engar 'farmer.'[712] This latter image, of the ensi$_2$-gal as an official with responsibilities toward farming is most likely the concept underlying its inclusion in royal titularies from the ED IIIb and ES periods.

More important than the ensi$_2$-gal in the civic administration was the aĝrig, or 'steward,' used as an epithet by Lugalzagesi in the titulary chain of his Nippur inscription.[713] Names such as lugal-aĝrig [(a2)],[714] and lugal-aĝrig-zi [(a4)] 'the lugal is a faithful steward,'[715] point to this aspect of royalty as part of

[705] See reference to Asalluḫi as midwife, Akk. *šabsû*, M. Stol, *Birth in Babylonia and the Bible*, 70–72. An alternative is to see a petition referring to the heart or mind of the lugal, being, perhaps, unfathomable, distant, or lenient. To this end, see, e.g., Gudea Cyl. A ix 1–2.

[706] Abbreviated form ša$_3$-an-zu(AN:ZU:ŠA$_3$) appears in *FTUM* 103 o. ii 1. Not a DN. See also, in a scholastic Lagaš text, BiMes 3 28 o. iv 4: lugal ša$_3$!(ŠA$_3$×TAB) an-su, and G. Marchesi's notes, *StEL* 16 (1999), 12f. Compare ibid., *OrNS* 73 (2004), 189 w. fn. 201 (ereš-e-an-zu "the Lady knows me"), and add ereš-še$_3$-an-su (/ereš-e/), VS 25 69 o. iv 19 (ED IIIb Girsu). See, furthermore, the list of PNN edited by M. E. Cohen, *Fs Hallo*, 85 (YBC 2124) v 10': ša$_3$-AN-[x] (duplicate NBC 11202 vii 9' has just ⸢ša$_3$⸣-AN).

[707] See, e.g. ED IIIb Girsu FPN nin-ša$_3$-su-ĝu$_{10}$ 'the lady is my midwife,' *DCS* 4 o. iii 4.

[708] See refs. with different translations in FAOS 6, 117 s.v. ensi$_2$-gal (ED IIIb); FAOS 8, 134 (*Śarrukēn*); and 217f. s.v. *iššiakkum* (a) (ED IIIb Mari lugals).

[709] See refs. in FAOS 6, 117 s.v.

[710] See V. V. Struve, *Onomastika*, 49 s.v., for attestations.

[711] D. O. Edzard, OLA 5, 164, showed that the ensi$_2$-gal in ED IIIa Šuruppag did not belong to the upper echelons of the civic administration; but compare the conclusions by I. Schrakamp, *BiOr* 65 (2008), 679, with many references to previous interpretations of the office other than the one followed here. Schrakamp takes as point of departure the situation in Sargonic Adab.

[712] See discussions by T. Jacobsen, *Fs Civil*, 113f. w. fnn. 4–7; and Å. Sjöberg, *Fs Limet*, 125f., note to ii 16. Sjöberg refers to many examples where ensi$_2$ alone carried this meaning.

[713] BE 1/2 87 i 34f.: aĝrig maḫ, diĝir-re-ne-ra 'the august steward for all the gods.'

[714] Compare nin-ĝiskim-ti, e.g. OSP 1 23, o. ii 4' and passim; and Ur III PN lugal-ĝiskim-ti, MVN 21 372 r. 4. No writing combining lugal and ĝiskim-ti is known from ED sources.

[715] Other appellatives attested with the qualified nominal predicate aĝrig are few: aja$_2$, e.g. *DP* 1/1 59 o. ii 14 (ED IIIb Girsu); and in later times: lu$_2$, e.g. Toronto 1 21 r. 1 (Ur III Puzriš-

human lordship. They are attested from various city-states beginning in the transition between ED IIIa-b, and onwards. An interesting point from the time of Gudea is that the latter, at least once, termed himself aĝrig zi of Nanše, and that he had a son by the name lugal-aĝrig-zi.[716] The appellative in the name of this son, then, could realistically be thought to refer to the father, Gudea, regardless of the fact that he never used that title about himself in his known inscriptions. The name, by incorporating a nominal predicate borrowed from civic administration, can plausibly be seen as referring to activities benefitting the relationship between the world and the gods. Hence a strong relationship exists with names of category 6, relating to cult or gods.

A group of names refer to the function of the lugal as providing plenty and stability. The royal name lugal-sila(TAR)-si [(a1)] 'the lugal is just right for the road,'[717] of a lugal from Uruk, seems to allude to the upkeep of roads or thoroughfares, in- or outside the city. That is, as one who is preoccupied with the correct functioning of overland communication lines, enabling movement of people and goods. It can be compared with lugal-uru-si [(a2)] 'the lugal is just right for the city,'[718] attested from ED I-II Ur and once in an OB copy of a Sargonic royal inscription. More widespread is lugal-ezem [(a>40)] 'the lugal … the festival,'[719] the most common lugal-name from the ED IIIa period onwards. In some instances the name may rather represent a genitive compound, 'lugal of the festival.'[720] The only parallel featuring a fuller writing appears to be nin-ezem-ma-ne$_2$-ki-aĝ$_2$, literally 'the lady loves her festival' from ED IIIb Girsu.[721] Celebrations of certain points of the

---

Dagān, translit. only, but see photo CDLI P124434); and nin, e.g. *TSU* 18 o. 2. Compare H. Limet, *Anthroponymie*, 170, 250, 320f., who reads aĝrig as ĝiskim, and who offers two translations of the name, with or without final -da: "Le roi dont le protection est sûre," and "Le roi dont le soutien est fidèle."

[716] RIME 3/1.1.7.Cylfrgms 8+3+5+4 ii' 2'; and 3/1.1.7.100 (inscribed macehead).

[717] Reading suggested by J. S. Cooper, *JNES* 33 (1974), 415: "the king who 'fills' the boulevard"; followed by M. Krebernik, AOAT 296, 27. The idea of bustling roads connecting cities in a network of trade is close at hand. The sign TAR was left untranslated by E. Sollberger & J.-R. Kupper, *IRSA* 319; and by H. Steible, ABW 2, 219f., note to l. 4, with previous literature. Compare en-sila-si, e.g. BIN 8 83 o. i 5 (ED IIIb Umma-Zabala); i$_3$-lu-lu-sila-si 'singing fills the street,' *CHÉU* 53 o. 2; Nik 2 15 (Both ES-MS Umma). See also the short form sila-si, TMH 5 11 o. iii 2 (ED IIIb Nippur).

[718] Compare DN ^{d}Nin-uru-si, e.g. *RTC* 211 (Lagaš II Girsu).

[719] Rendered by A. Westenholz, *Six City-State Cultures*, 34: "the-lugal-(goes)-to the festival."

[720] A few Ur III period writings of this name indicate a genitive compound as -ka is used when the PN forms part of a genitive chain. Thus the translations of E. Chiera, PBS 11/3, 210, no. 218: "The king of the feast"; and E. Sollberger & J.-R. Kupper, *IRSA*, 318: "roi (ou: maître) du festival," could essentially be correct, at least where later forms are concerned. An ED IIIb Nippur example seems to rule this out for earlier periods, BE 1/2 111 2', where the wife of lugal-ezem is the agent of the verb, indicated by -ke$_4$. The name still saw use in the OB period, A. Poebel, *Personennamen*, 29. For more on this name, see below, p. 235.

[721] Nik 1 15 o. i 8. Abbreviation nin-ezem-ma-ne$_2$ in VS 27 33 r. ii 5 (Uru-KA UN:gal). The entry taken as a PN by G. Pettinato, MVN 17 4 r. 19, and index on p. 99, ^{d}Šul-gi ezem-ma

agricultural year with the procurement of specific sets of resources may here echo the securing of the family line through another family member. Also, there is a distinct possibility that the names featuring ezem refer to ongoing festivities taking place at the time of birth, as surmised already by D. O. Edzard;[722] though the Sumerian names are not as accurate as later Akkadian names alluding to a specific festival, a month or a day.[723] Most of these names are plausibly to be ascribed divine referents. Since the ezem-names are related to the agriculturally defined yearly cycle, they have been assigned to this category, although they are closely related to names dealing with cultic matters.

3.1.5.3 Countryside, produce and farming

The Sumerian view of the world was closely tied to its rural origins and the farm country remained the backbone of the economy. Hence, it is not surprising to see the vocabulary in general, and the onomasticon in particular, in several ways make use of imagery borrowed from agriculture and animal husbandry; see for instance names composed with amar, discussed above, 3.1.1.1. As for lugal-names, a handful relate in a rather general way to plowing. The oldest, from ED IIIa Šuruppag, is lugal-engar-zi $^{(a\geq1)}$ 'the lugal is a reliable farmer.'[724] Beginning in the ED IIIb, another name appears: lugal-apin-du_{10} $^{(a\geq8)}$, and a CS variant, only attested once in pre–Ur III sources, lugal-^{ĝiš}apin-du_{10} $^{(a1)}$, both 'the lugal is one who makes the plow good.'[725] The similar ED IIIb Girsu name lugal-apin-ne_2 $^{(a\geq1)}$ 'the lugal … the plow,'[726] is explained by the previous two, as the verb du_{10} takes the loc.-term. ending -e on the direct object. Two Sargonic Nippur writings [x]-apin-ne_2, are clear parallels.[727] Interestingly, the names featuring apin

---

tuš-a (translit. only), must refer to a cultic meal, probably celebrated during the month of the festival of that king. See also, e.g. *TCTI* 2 2721 r. 1f.; HSS 4 3 o. ii 12 and r. iii 10'.

[722] CRRA 19, 142: "Ce serait, pour ainsi dire, le nom d'un enfant né le dimanche."

[723] Such as the OB FPN *Amat-Eššešim*, discussed above, p. 52, and other examples found in J. J. Stamm, *Namengebung*, 271f.

[724] Unattested between ED IIIa and Ur III. D. O. Edzard, CRRA 19, 142: "le lugal est le bon fermier"; H. Limet, *Namenforschung*, 852: "le roi est un fidèle agriculteur." The reading engar zi is based on the appearance of the same combination in Urnamma G l. 19–20, whereas apin in that same hymn is consistently written with the ^{ĝiš} determinative.

[725] Previously often read engar-du_{10}. For the reading used here, see already M. Krebernik, AOAT 296, 37 w. fn. 201 basing his reading on Ur III abbreviated parallels featuring ^{ĝiš} determinative. Compare E. Chiera, PBS 11/3, 211, no. 221: "The king is a husbandman"; H. Limet, *Anthroponymie*, 170, 240: "Le roi est (un) agriculteur." The CS Girsu name lugal-APIN$^{?\ (a1)}$, if read correctly, is most likely an abbreviation of lugal-$^{(ĝiš)}$apin-du_{10}. For du_{10} as a transitive verb with possibly factitive meaning in a related context, see Urnamma G l. 11. Abbreviated form apin-du_{10}, OSP 2, p. 196 (index) s.v. engar-du_{10}.

[726] The original predicate may have been gub or si. Compare H. Limet, *Anthroponymie*, 240 (wr. -apin-e): "Le roi vers la charrue …"

[727] TMH 5 39 o. i 7'; 44 o. ii' 12'. The remains of the first sign in the latter do not look like LU_2 in LUGAL. Compare PN apin-⌜ne_2⌝, OSP 1 24 o. iv 20, in an extremely narrow case.

'plow,' are almost exclusively attested in Girsu and Nippur, cities which both had tutelary deities intimately connected with agriculture.[728] And so it is likely that these names dealt with the respective deities of these cities. Though it may be kept in mind that a ceremony involving the king plowing fields was celebrated in the Ur III and following periods, and that the king could be addressed in hymns as 'the reliable farmer.' Thus lugal-engar-zi may well have had a human referent in mind.[729] None of these names have parallels featuring clear writings of other appellatives before the Ur III period.[730] It is tempting to see these names as indicative of a time of birth for the child bearing such a name, which could then be placed quite firmly in the late summer or early autumn months.[731]

Names concerned with fields, gardens, dikes, canals, and their produce are also well attested, in a multitude of different guises. The irrigation infrastructure is mentioned in a few names from Girsu and Umma: lugal-eg$_2$-ge $^{(a\geq2)}$ 'the lugal … the levee,'[732] and lugal-eg$_2$-pa$_5$-maḫ $^{(a1)}$ 'the lugal is one who makes canal and ditch *magnificent* (?).'[733] Compare in this connection also lugal-i$_7$-maḫ $^{(a1)}$, 'the lugal makes the river *magnificent* (?).' A name which relates the lugal to land in general is in some instances perhaps an abbreviation, but an original, complete form is unfortunately hard to recreate: lugal-GAN$_2$ $^{(a\geq6)}$ 'the lugal, the field,' mostly borne by people from the Umma state and Nippur.[734] The predicate zi is added in a Sargonic Nippur name: lugal-GAN$_2$-zi $^{(a1)}$ 'the lugal is one who puts the fields in

---

[728] The plow was a symbol of Ningirsu and, as suggested by M. Civil, *Fs Kramer*, 85f., an Isin-period text related to plowing may draw upon earlier traditions. The epithet engar-zi an-na, Akk: *ik-ka-ru ki-nu ša$_2$ ^{d}A-nim*, is in later times ascribed to Ninurta, see Å. Sjöberg, *Fs Limet*, 125, note to ii 16. The association of plowing with fertility in general and sexual acts specifically is apparent from, for instance, love lyrics, and is a common metaphor in cultures all around the world, see e.g. M. Stol, *Birth in Babylonia and the Bible*, 1f., but is probably not the underlying theme in these names.

[729] See preceding note and compare also the description of the king in Urnamma G l. 19–20 lugal/ur-^{d}Namma engar zi GAN$_2$ daĝal-la eg$_2$ pa$_5$-re ki […]; and see note on the use of this epithet by OB kings, E. Flückiger-Hawker, OBO 166, 296.

[730] E.g. n[in]-engar-[z]i, BBVO 11, 295 (6N-T632) o. 7 (translit. only, Ur III Nippur); lu$_2$-engar-zi, MVN 21 403 r. 12 (Ur III Umma).

[731] For the time of plowing, see J. N. Postgate, *Early Mesopotamia*, 167–169; D. T. Potts, *Mesopotamian Civilization*, 70–73.

[732] Compare the singularly attested DN ^{d}Lugal-eg$_2$-ga, "Herr(n) des Wassergrabens," on an unprovenanced statue of ED IIIb date, G. J. Selz, *Götterwelt*, 161, with further refs.; and PN nin-eg$_2$-ge, OSP 1 23 o. ix 15; 24 o. iv 10 (both ES-MS Nippur).

[733] See the description of a vessel in a difficult *Ibbi*-Su'en inscription, RIME 3/2.1.5.3, l. 25f.: gi ku$_3$-gi-bi, pa$_5$ maḫ ga$^!$(BI)-lam, 'whose golden drinking (reed) is an artfully (made) main conduit," following D. R. Frayne. Note, furthermore, the epithet of the god Enkimdu in Urnamma A l. 25: lugal eg$_2$ p[a$_5$-re], "lord of embankments and di[tches]," following E. Flückiger-Hawker, OBO 166, 105; and compare note to lugal-engar-zi.

[734] The names e$_2$-GAN$_2$-a, e.g. CUSAS 11 193 o. ii 4 (ED IIIb-ES Adab); and nin-GAN$_2$-a, e.g. PBS 9 15+110 o. i 7 (CS Nippur), are hard to interpret.

order.'[735] A specific locus is mentioned in the ED IIIb Girsu name lugal-GAN$_2$-su$_{11}$-lum-ma-gub $^{(a1)}$ 'the lugal stands in the Date-field,'[736] with variant lugal-su$_{11}$-lum-ma-gub $^{(a1)}$, both used about the same person. The field of Su$_{11}$-lum forms part of a description of a temple dedicated for Nanše; the FN is not provided with a place determinative until after the Akkadian period.[737] Two variants of one name relate the lugal to a garden, though the predicate is left unexpressed, lugal-^{ĝiš}kiri$_6$ $^{(a≥2)}$ 'the lugal ... the garden,'[738] and lugal-kiri$_6$-e $^{(a1)}$ 'the lugal ... the garden.'[739]

Another possible link to fields is found in the rare name lugal-im-nun-ne$_2$ $^{(a1)}$ 'the lugal ... the border (of the) field.' The name incorporates a word denoting a stretch of soil on the edge of land used for agricultural purposes, which may have been used as protection against desertification.[740]

As for produce, only a few different products are specifically named. The name lugal-še $^{(a2)}$ 'the lugal ... grain (?),' is securely attested in Sargonic Umma. Whether it is an abbreviation of the Nippur and Adab name lugal-še-gu-na $^{(a≥3)}$ 'the lugal of grain (and) flax,'[741] is hard to say. The latter seems founded in the beliefs surrounding the god Iškur of Karkara,[742] perhaps modern Tall Ǧidr,[743] located between Umma and Adab. Iškur's character in Pre–Sargonic times is badly understood but his links to wind, rain, and the

---

[735] Following J. Bauer, *AoN* 21 (1985), p. 10 note to (*CIRPL*) 39, 1. Bauer discusses the meaning of this compound as referring to Ninurta/Ningirsu, and this name is at present only attested at Nippur, Ninurta's tutelary city. But compare the discussion of the Instructions of Šuruppag l. 219 and the Nanše hymn l. 60: munus zi gan$_2$ zi-še$_3$ lu$_2$ ši-in-ga-ĝa$_2$-ĝa$_2$ B. Alster, Mesopotamia 3, 27, and the note to the former composition on p. 143. The line is damaged but securely attested also in the ED IIIa Abū Ṣalābīḫ version.

[736] Following G. J. Selz, *Götterwelt*, 185f., with fn. 850: "Der König/Herr steht (auf) dem Felde von Zulum." Note also the entry Lugal-su$_{11}$-lum-ma in the OB Nippur standard god list, W. G. Lambert, *RlA* 7 (1987–90), 157f. s.v. "Lugal-zulumma," given as: "Lord (of the) dates."

[737] See Selz, *Götterwelt*, 185, fn. 849 for references.

[738] The secure attestations of this name are all from Sargonic Umma. In one instance, CT 50 172 r. ii 16 (CS Girsu), most likely not a PN but a note on a payment to the owner of the garden where the transactions recorded in the text took place.

[739] Read by the editors of the text *TCVC* 730, as lugal-⌜nesaĝ$^?$⌝-e, but that noun is written ne-saĝ in o. ii 2 of the same text.

[740] See G. J. Selz, *Götterwelt*, 286 fn. 1423; *AWAS*, 385f. Besides lugal-im-nun-ne$_2$, the name ur-im-nun was used in Ur III Girsu, H. Limet, *Anthroponymie*, 465, 548 s.v.v. The expression im-nun seems limited to Girsu, but the provenience of the text in which the present name occurs is unknown. Judging from other names in the text, e.g. sipa-uru-na in o. i 8, a Girsu origin is not excluded.

[741] What follows the appellative either consists of a qualified noun, še gun$_3$-a 'speckled barley' or 'late barley,' or of two nouns, še 'grain' and gu 'flax.'

[742] The expression is associated with him in the Abū Ṣalābīḫ za$_3$-me hymns, l. 87; parallelled by še gu-nu in TH 332. In the commentary to the latter passage, Å. Sjöberg refers to Enmerkar and the Lord of Aratta, l. 9, where rain brings forth še gu-nu, TCS 3, 117. Rain was of course one of Iškur's attributes. Compare en-še-gu-na, in the agricultural text *WF* 78 o. vii 14 (ED IIIa Šuruppag).

[743] Identification proposed by M. Powell, *JNES* 39 (1980), 47–52.

plenty associated with them, is clear. It is not unthinkable that this name was suitable for a child born just before harvest time, in late spring. A name like lugal-kara$_6$-gal-gal [(a1)] 'the lugal enlarges the grain heap(s),'[744] further underlines the lugal's important role in amassing surplus resources. The name seems not to be a specifically cultic reference, unlike the name lugal-nesaĝ-e, for which, see below 3.1.6.3. None of the produce-names discussed here have parallels featuring other actors than lugal.

In a very general way, many names revolve around the topic of plenty, for instance the royal name lugal-da-lu [(a1)] '(things) flourish with the lugal,'[745] from ED IIIb Adab.[746] The same verb is used in the ED I-II Ur name lugal-lu-lu [(a1)] 'the lugal is one who makes (things) thrive,'[747] with variants expressing the object ni$_3$ 'thing(s),' lugal-ni$_3$-lu-lu [(a1)], attested at ED IIIb Girsu, and lugal-ni$_3$-lu-lu-a [(°1)] in a Sargonic scholastic text. The latter has a perfect parallel in Sargonic ^{d}Utu-ni$_3$-lu-lu-a, but otherwise the names with duplicated verb lu-lu are not found with other agents during this period.[748]

Somewhat better attested are names composed with the nominal compound ḫe$_2$-ĝal$_2$. The word was commonplace both in onomastic and litarary sources and has very positive connotations throughout. The name lugal-ḫe$_2$-ĝal$_2$ [(a6/°1)], 'the lugal … abundance,'[749] was well-known to the point that it ended up in texts found in Ebla; once written phonetically as nu-gal-ḫi-gal [(°1)]. Whether these names are to be understood as a nominal sentence, or whether they may be thought originally to have featured an elided predicate is not possible to say. For lugal-ḫe$_2$-ĝal$_2$-su$_3$ [(a5)] 'the lugal (is one who) extends abundance,'[750] an ED IIIb Girsu parallel with the appellative

---

[744] Compare the reading of G. Marchesi, HANE/S 10, 111: "lugal-kara$_6$-gal, "The Lord Is a Great Granary"," with lexical evidence adduced in fn. 569. Besides GAL in ligature LUGAL, two more GAL are visible on photo in MVN 3 pl. 5–6 o. iii 10. A comparative or superlative adjectival mng. of gal-gal might be considered, but compare, e.g., lugal-lu$_2$-ti-ti.

[745] Similarly D. R. Frayne, RIME 1, 23: "(Things) flourish beside the king." Compare AN-da-lu, *TSŠ* 93 r. iv 3'; NIĜ$_2$-da-lu, *TSŠ* 49 o. iii 4; 704 o. iv 7 (all ED IIIa Šuruppag); $^{d\,aš}$aš$_7$-gi$_4$-da-lu, OIP 14 126 r. 1 (CS Adab); Nibru^{ki}-da-lu, OSP 1 138 o. ii 1; var. -da-lu$_2$, TMH 5 113 r. 1 (both ED IIIb Nippur); e$_2$-da-lu, BIN 8 170 o. 7 (ED IIIb-ES Isin ?); MAD 4 71 r. 7 (CS Unknown). Note Ur III FN kur-da-lu-lu, *SNAT* 183 o. 3 (Girsu).

[746] For a detailed discussion of the date of this lugal in the early ED IIIb, see G. Marchesi & N. Marchetti, MesCiv 14, 130–132.

[747] Compare E. Chiera, PBS 11/3, 236, no. 1201: šeš-lu-lu "The brother makes rich."

[748] For ^{d}Utu-ni$_3$-lu-lu-a, see *STTI* 106 o. 2 (CS Girsu); and compare Šulgi A l. 55: ^{d}Šul-gi lu$_2$ (var. lugal) ni$_3$-lu-lu-me-en ninda ĝiš ḫa-ba-ni-tag "I, Šulgi, the generous provider, presented there meal-offerings," following translation by J. Klein, *Three Šulgi Hymns*, 195. A comprehensive but not complete list of parallels is found with H. Limet, *Anthroponymie*, 252.

[749] Attested throughout Ur III times, H. Limet, *Anthroponymie*, 464 s.v.; down through OB times, A. Poebel, *Personennamen*, 29. The following names with the verb su$_{3/20/x}$ show that this name is not necessarily a genitive compound, such as is the case with what later became a free-standing divine epithet taking on the function of a DN, ^{d}Lugal-ḫe$_2$-ĝal$_2$(-la), for which see W. G. Lambert, *RlA* 7 (1987–90), 141 s.v.: "Lugal-ḫegalla," "Lord of abundance."

[750] There is also a possibility to interpret su$_3$(-g) as parallel to si, Akk. *malû*, see, e.g. *CAD* Ḫ s.v. *ḫegallu*, and Y. Sefati, *Love Songs*, 351, note to 13–14. The associations of ḫe$_2$-ĝal$_2$ and

nin exists, but otherwise fuller writings are rare during the earlier periods.[751] The variants lugal-ḫe$_2$-ĝal$_2$-su$_{20}$ $^{(a1)}$,[752] and lugal-ḫe$_2$-ĝal$_2$-su$_x$(TAG) $^{(a1)}$,[753] probably do not represent deviations in meaning. Whether there is an aspectual difference in names within this group is not clear.

Names revolving around the lugal and his connections with animals are few, apart from when the animal name serves as a nominal predicate in describing the lugal. An exception to this is furnished by the ED IIIa Šuruppag name lugal-ab$_2$-ki-aĝ$_2$ $^{(a1)}$ 'the lugal loves the cow.'[754] There is a definite possibility that the 'cow' is euphemistic for a goddess, and that lugal refers to a male divinity, like the Moon God, who in later times is often associated with cattle.[755] There is also a slight possibility that the cow in this name in actuality is used symbolically for the woman giving birth. The Moon God is known for his assistance at birth in incantation texts of the second millennium.[756] And as suckling children were characterized as amar ga or gaba, the extension of the designation 'cow' to an animate object could be strengthened, but more examples of this would be required.

A few names associate the lugal with vessels for transporting plenty or with places for storaging wealth. Especially prominent are names which relate to waterways. A name which is unfortunately never attested in its full form, but which can be reconstructed on the basis of sound parallels is *lugal-ma$_2$-gur$_8$-e-si 'the lugal is just right for the cargo ship,'[757] for which all witnesses are from the Sargonic period. The term ma$_2$-gur$_8$ was sometimes used figuratively about the Moon God due to his appearance as the new moon, and birth incantations could also use a boat as a vehicle for

---

si/su$_3$(-g) do not, however, help explain the complicated variants with su$_{20}$(ŠIM) and su$_x$(TAG). Compare A. Westenholz, *Six City-State Cultures*, 34: "the-lugal-(provides)-abundance-far-and-wide."

[751] One instance is made up by the canal named ^{i_7} ^{d}Ba-u$_2$-ḫe$_2$-ĝal$_2$-su$_3$, *RTC* 253 r. 11 (date formula, Lagaš II Girsu).

[752] J. Bauer, *ZA* 79 (1989), 9: "Lugal-ḫe$_2$-ĝal$_2$-ŠIM … ist zu lagaschitischem Lugal-ḫe$_2$-gal$_2$-su$_3$, „der König macht den Überfluß weit" zu stellen."

[753] For the reading su-b (sub$_6$) of TAG, see J. Bauer, *WO* 9 (1977–78), 4. Either su$_x$ in this name functions as a local phonetic writing of su$_3$ or the name expresses another, but clearly related, meaning. See, e.g. *CAD* Š/3 s.v. *šuklulu* (v.), lex. sect.

[754] See discussion of lugal-gu$_4$ with ref. to Ur III variant lugal-gu$_4$-e.

[755] See, for instance, *PSD* A/2, ab$_2$ A 4, 3.7, last example (untranslated), fragmentary passage from a hymn to Nanna; and N. Veldhuis, *A Cow of Sîn*, 1, and the account of the first encounter of the Moon God with the bovine bombshell, 8, l. 12: *binûtam kazbat īmuršīma irāmši* 'she was attractive of appearance – as soon as he saw her he fell in love with her.'

[756] See M. Stol, *Birth in Babylonia and the Bible*, 66–70, especially p. 67.

[757] The variants attested are lugal-ma$_2$ $^{(a\geq4)}$; and lugal-ma$_2$-gur$_8$-e $^{(a1)}$. Compare ma$_2$-gur$_8$-si, e.g. Nik 1 306 o. ii 4 (ED IIIb Girsu); and OSP 2 126 o. ii 11 (MS-CS Nippur), and see, already, A. Westenholz, OSP 1, 8; *Six City-State Cultures*, 34. Compare DN Lugal-ma$_2$-gur$_8$-ra, K. Tallqvist, *AGE*, 355 s.v. "Lugal-ma$_2$-gu[r$_8$-ra]," given as: "König des makurru-Schiffes"; W. G. Lambert, *RlA* 7 (1987–90), 148 s.v. "Lugal-magurra."

the woman in labour and her baby.[758] In a literary text from ED IIIa Abū Ṣalābīḫ, a lugal takes a ride (u$_{5}$) on a ship, probably destined for Bad-tibira in the south, to present offerings there.[759] The imagery of unloading a boat is found in lugal-kar-e-si $^{(a1)}$ 'the lugal is just right for the harbour,'[760] attested at Sargonic Umma only, but with antecedent forms from as early as ED IIIa-b. It is uncertain what names mentioning boats alluded to, and hence also who the referent might have been. If a link should be made to the popular motifs on cylinder seals, found practically all across Mesopotamia, of a deity travelling in a boat, then the Moon and Sun Gods might be considered.[761] Parallels are made up mostly by nin-names.[762]

After the transport of the goods to the final destination, foodstuffs that were not directly intended for use in the temple service would end up in storage for distribution through different offices and mediaries, as seems to be the idea behind the ED I-II Ur name lugal-ĝa$_{2}$-si $^{(a1)}$ 'the lugal is just right for the barn.'[763] It is possible that the ED IIIa parallel lugal-e$_{2}$-si $^{(a1)}$ represents a further development on this theme, only with more focus on a societal institution, albeit anonymous. The e$_{2}$ was central to private and official economy alike, and it is of course possible that e$_{2}$ in the latter name refers to a private household or "family." The referents of the names are unknown.

3.1.5.4 Life and plenty

The lugal is sometimes described as one embodying the abstract concept of life, zi or (nam-)ti. For instance, lugal-zi-ša$_{3}$-ĝal$_{2}$ $^{(a1)}$ 'the lugal is one who establishes life,'[764] from ED IIIa Šuruppag, treats the lugal as a source for

---

[758] See, Å. Sjöberg, *MNS*, 27; M. Stol, *Birth in Babylonia and the Bible*, 60–63; and more above, p. 69.

[759] *IAS* 392 o. iv' 3'–4': lugal$_{(PA.NUN)}$ ma$_{2}$-gur$_{8}$ ma$_{2}$ še$_{3}$-⸢u$_{5}$⸣, E$_{2}$-muš$_{3}$ nesa[ĝ] an-še$_{3}$ il$_{2}$ 'the lugal/owner of the ship went for a ride on the ship, in the Emuš he raised the firstling offerings towards the sky.' An incantation from Ebla begins with Enki taking a boat ride. It was directed at illness generally, and was edited by M. Krebernik, *BFE*, 172–175.

[760] Variants include: lugal-kar $^{(a\geq6)}$, all attestations save one from Nippur; lugal-kar$^{!}$(TE) $^{(a1)}$, is Nippur short hand for the former; lugal-kar-e $^{(a1)}$ from CS Adab; lugal-kar-re $^{(a1)}$, and lugal-kar-re$_{2}$ $^{(a1)}$, were limited to Sargonic Girsu and possibly Adab. The writing lugal-kar-si $^{(a3)}$, is found in texts from a few different locations, from the ED IIIa-b onward. In the Ur III the writing lugal-kar-re was the most common, see H. Limet, *Anthroponymie*, 466 s.v.

[761] For a discussion with references to literature on the "boat-god" motif on ED and Sargonic seals from the Ḫabur down to Ur, see D. Ławecka, *Fs Łyczkowska*, 131–143, especially p. 131–134.

[762] E.g. Ur III Umma FPN nin-ma$_{2}$-gur$_{8}$-re-si, N. Schneider, AnOr 1 292 o. ii 18 (SI clear on photo, CDLI P101283; following line not in Schneider's copy); *Rochester* 166 r. 2 (translit. only), which support this reading; nin-kar-re$_{2}$, TMH 5 39 o. ii 15' (MS-CS Nippur); nin-kar-re, H. Limet, *Anthroponymie*, 513 s.v.

[763] Compare nin-ĝa$_{2}$-si, UET 2 2 o. iii 3 (ED IIIa Ur), and see D. Foxvog's discussion of ĝa$_{2}$ as representing "outbuilding, shed, barn," *NABU* 1998/7.

[764] The basic meaning of zi ša$_{3}$ ĝal$_{2}$ is understood in accordance with the discussion of B. Alster & H. L. J. Vanstiphout, *ASJ* 9 (1987), 41, note 9, with refs., that zi ša$_{3}$ ĝal$_{2}$ refers to an

life. The many parallels that exist show that the same perspective applied to a number of loci, persons and divinities.[765] A kyriophore Ur III name offers an angle to the possible interpretation: ^{d}Amar-^{d}Su'en-^{d}Ašnan-gin$_{7}$-zi-ša$_{3}$-ĝal$_{2}$-kalam-ma 'Amar-Su'en establishes life in the land like Ašnan,'[766] comparing Amar-Su'en to a god of agricultural produce. The connection between the two may be further enhanced by the observation of G. Pettinato, who proposed to see zi ša$_{3}$ ĝal$_{2}$ as the result of agricultural work which produced the essentials for human civilization.[767] Another name from ED IIIa Šuruppag ties in nicely with the two aforementioned names, showing that the association with the land at large was an old one: lugal-zi-kalam $^{(a1)}$ 'the lugal is the life (of) the land.'[768] The life-bringing mechanisms may furthermore be alluded to in the name lugal-an-ta-ti $^{(a\geq 1)}$ 'the lugal (bestows) life from above,' from ED IIIb-ES Nippur.[769] If the interpretation is near the mark, it expresses a belief in a recurrent fertilization of the earth from on high. Similar ideas seem to underlie the Ur III names an-na-ḫe$_{2}$-ĝal$_{2}$,[770] and an-ta-ḫe$_{2}$-ĝal$_{2}$,[771] 'plenty in/from heaven.' The first two names might well be ascribed to an earthly leader. Names locating the source of life or plenty in the heavens, by extension, could refer to a human being who by means of ceremonials or rituals could ensure the welfare of the world. This mediary position is the subject of some names in the following category.

---

active life-force and the generation of plenty. See also M. Krebernik, AOAT 296, 17 fn. 58 "der König ist Leben."

[765] For the ED IIIb period, see e.g. V. V. Struve, *Onomastika*, 32f. s.v. bara$_{2}$-zi-ša$_{3}$-ĝal$_{2}$; 67 s.v. e$_{2}$-zi-ša$_{3}$-ĝal$_{2}$; 76 s.v. Ĝir$_{2}$-nun-zi-ša$_{3}$-ĝal$_{2}$. For the Ur III period, zi ša$_{3}$ ĝal$_{2}$ survives in names with e$_{2}$, lugal, nin, deities and the the deified king as first element. From the OB period, see e.g. UET 5, 133 r. 6; 466 o. 8: ^{d}Nanna-zi-ša$_{3}$-ĝal$_{2}$; 682 r. 7: e$_{2}$-zi-ĝal$_{2}$-kalam-ma (TN or PN ?); and the lexical entries in lists of PNN, E. Chiera, PBS 11/3, 212, no. 282: lugal-zi-ša$_{3}$-ĝal$_{2}$, w. parallels, p. 235, no. 1174 (nin); 237, no. 1285a (^{d}Nin-lil$_{2}$).

[766] So according to copy, YOS 15 114 o. i 8 (Umma); The ŠE following the name is read -še$_{3}$ by M. Sigrist, *Rochester* 159, p. 101. The tablet is no longer in its original Rochester collection according to R. K. Englund, *CDLN* 2010:004. Thus no confirmation of either reading has been possible to obtain.

[767] G. Pettinato, *Menschenbild*, 57.

[768] M. Krebernik, AOAT 296, 17 w. fn. 58: "der König ist das Leben des Landes/Volkes," adding that the name might be an abbreviated form which originally sported a verbal element, like -si. Judging from the later writings with -ma, from the Sargonic period onwards, it is more likely a nominal compound predicate name. Otherwise one would have expected -me. See also H. Steible, *CollAn* 7 (2008), 93: "der König (ist) der Lebensodem (für) das Land," and similarly on p. 97. Comparable Ur III names were, for instance, composed with ^{d}Amar-Su'en, ^{d}*Šu*-^{d}Su'en, and ^{d}Ba-u$_{2}$, see H. Limet, *Anthroponymie* s.v.v. ^{d}Šul-gi-zi-kalam-ma appears as a GN from Š 41 on, e.g. CT 9 pl. 25 (BM 19751) r. 3; as a PN in CT 7 pl. 13 (BM 12939) o. ii 3, a singer from Girsu.

[769] Loosely following A. Westenholz, *Six City-State Cultures*, 34: "the-lugal-(brings)-life-from-Heaven."

[770] E.g. SAT 2 625 o. 2 (Umma, translit. only).

[771] E.g. *DAS* 194 r. 1 (Girsu).

3.1.6 Cult or gods

The sixth heading collects names in which the lugal appears in relation to gods, cultic places and ritual objects or acts. Names relating the lugal to divinities can easily be accessed below in table 4.1, and place names are found in table 4.2. Under this heading, names are discussed under a handful of separate subheadings:

- Prayer, petition and purification
- Relations to the divine
- Cultic insignia, acts and ceremonial
- Sacred loci, sanctuaries and installations

A few kyriophores have made their way into this section, though they do not in the strictest sense belong here; they are listed for the sake of completeness. Fig. 7, below, records 262 persons, the estimated minimum number of people bearing 113 variants of theophore lugal-names, and such bearing on cultic topics or in different ways linking the lugal to the divine sphere.

	ED I-II	ED IIIa-ED IIIb	ED IIIb-ES	ES-MS	MS-CS
Abū Ṣalābīḫ		1			
Adab		2	14	2	13
Akšak			1		
Ešnuna			1		
Girsu		3	50		20
Isin		1	3	1	5
Kiš		4	2		
Lagaš			1		
Mesag					3
Nippur		4	25	5	19
Šuruppag		22	1	1	
Umma-Zabala			11	1	17
Ur	6	2	7	1	2
Uruk			2		
Unknown		4		1	4

Fig. 7: Name-bearers, 3.1.6, Cult or gods. Estimated minimum number of individual name-bearers.

3.1.6.1 Prayer, petition and purification

A few lugal-names relate to prayer. The most common word used to signify 'prayer' is šud$_3$, but it could perhaps also signify 'petition,' when addressed to human superiors. Names with šud$_3$ as object appear from the ED IIIa down through the Sargonic periods. The fullest form attested is lugal-šud$_3$-

de_3-ba-$ša_4$ (a1) 'the lugal stands by for prayer,'[772] forming a full transitive clause with the object marked by loc.-term. -e. This name expresses the readiness on the part of the lugal to pay attention to prayer, as is evident from an ED IIIb Girsu inscription. There, a goddess stands by to receive the prayers of a human.[773]

In comparison with the latter name, the name lugal-$šud_3$-du_{10}-ga (a2) 'the lugal of a *good* prayer,'[774] limited to ED IIIb Girsu sources, has been taken to consist of a qualified genitive chain, parallel to lugal-mu-du_{10}-ga. No specific verbal action is apparent, and only an earlier parallel, e_2-$šud_3$-du_{10}-ga, is known.[775] The abbreviated form lugal-$šud_3$-de_3 (a≥7),[776] is quite likely to be an abbreviation of lugal-$šud_3$-de_3-ba-$ša_4$; whereas lugal-$šud_3$ (a>10), could be a short form of any of the two former and also another name, treated below.

Other names also feature the lugal as one who receives prayer and supplication. The MS-CS Nippur PN lugal-inim-e-ĝiš-tuku (a1) 'the lugal is one who pays attention to words,' with variant lugal-inim-e (a1),[777] uses the compound verb ĝiš–tuk, but with loc.-term. -e instead of the expected com. suffix on the direct object. It has therefore been taken to reflect attentive listening rather than a close to passive hearing. It has a close parallel in ED IIIa Šuruppag lugal-$šud_3$-ĝiš-tuku (a1) 'the lugal is one who hears prayers.' The predicate is left out entirely in the name lugal-inim-$še_3$ (a1),[778] belonging to a single person from Isin attested between ES and CS times.[779] Contracted forms like lugal-ĝiš, lugal-KA and lugal-$šud_3$ may be abbreviations of these names. No close parallels with other appellatives serving as subjects are

[772] Full writing of this name attested only once. The ED IIIb Girsu chief scribe so named is attested also with abbreviated forms lugal-$šud_3$ and lugal-$šud_3$-de_3. Compare Ur III Nippur PN e_2-$šud_3$-de_3, BBVO 11, 261f. (4N-T213) o. ii 17 (translit. only, date broken). See also discussion of lugal-di-de_3, section 3.1.3.3, p. 117f.

[773] *CIRPL* Ukg. 54–55 1–3: ^{d}Ba-u_2 $šud_3$ Uru-KA-gi-na-ka-ke_4, ba-$ša_4$, mu-bi 'Bau stands by for the prayers of UruKAgina, is its name.'

[774] Short form lugal-$šud_3$-du_{10} (a2) known from ED IIIb Girsu and Umma-Zabala.

[775] See F. Pomponio, *Prosopografia*, 92, for references. Abbreviated form $šud_3$-du_{10}-ga is found in *TSŠ* 363 o. ii 2.

[776] Compare W. G. Lambert, *RlA* 7 (1987–90), 152 s.v. "Lugal-šudde," given as: "The lord who utters benedictions," in later times equated with Ninurta or Dumuzi. See also Ningišzida's Boat-Ride to Hades, T. Jacobsen & B. Alster, *Fs Lambert*, 337 (MS B) o. 8, used about Ningišzida.

[777] The name lugal-inim-e appears twice in a single text from MS-CS Nippur (OSP 2, 44). From one of the passages it is clear that the name is not marked by ergative -e. Other texts, plausibly from the same archive and around the same period (OSP 2 45; 48; 49), has this name in its fuller form lugal-inim-e-ĝiš-tuku. The reservations by A. Westenholz, OSP 2, 61, note to ii 1 and 8, should be contrasted with the fact that lugal-KA-e is otherwise never so written save to mark the name-bearer as the ergative subject.

[778] Following a suggestion by J. Krecher, *ZA* 63 (1973), 224, referring to Å. Sjöberg, *OrS* 19-20 (1970–71), 155f., with ref. to a literary phrase: lugal inim-$ĝu_{10}$-$še_3$ $ĝeštu_2$-zu, 'Lord, to (my) word (lend) your ear.' Compare lugal-$ŠE_3$-saĝ, p. 181f., below.

[779] J. Krecher, *ZA* 63 (1973), 224, made a connection between two instances, MAD 4 71 and 153, but a third should be added to these due to the stated filiations, see list of attestations.

known. Not knowing in each and every instance whether the word signified ‘prayer’ or ‘petition’ it is difficult to assign a referent to such names. A human referent is in any case not excluded.

A special case is formed by the unique name of a citizen of Nippur temporarily settled in Lagaš during Sargonic times. If understood correctly, it represents an intervention by the lugal to rectify a state of impurity: lugal-nam-dag [(a1)], tentatively: ‘the lugal (removes?) sin.’ While no Nippur parallels exist, some other Girsu names do offer suggestions as to what idea was intended by the name. They would imply that the lugal is qualified as one without flaws or as one who removes guilt.[780] A historical parallel may be seen in the work of Gudea, who in preparation of building the temple of Ninĝirsu banned all wicked words and corporal punishment, and furthermore banished people of compromised purity to ensure the correct circumstances for the founding of the temple.[781] At this point it is not possible to say which alternative is the most likely, or whether this name belongs to any of the following subsections.

With due hesitation, the word šita may also carry a sense of ‘prayer,’ as in the rare name lugal-šita [(a2)].[782] At least, no secure parallel formation connects the lugal with a specific type of priestly office. ŠITA could also be taken to represent a weapon of sorts, for which parallel examples abound, and the missing determinative ĝiš would have ample parallels, for instance in lugal-apin-du$_{10}$, attested once with the determinative. However, two names offer the possibility of a link between šita and prayer, lugal-šita-ĝu$_{10}$ [(a1)], and lugal-šita-uru [(a1)], both from ED IIIb or ES Adab.[783] It is not altogether unlikely that these latter two names represent genitive formations, ‘the lugal (hears) my prayers,’ and ‘the lugal (hears) the prayers of the city.’[784]

3.1.6.2 Relations to the divine

A large number of theophore names are known which associate the lugal with named divinities. The divinities can be both male and female, and in the case of the latter, lugal is most likely never an epithet of these goddesses. By analogy, it is not unlikely that names in which lugal and a male divinity

[780] All parallels are from Girsu. Compare nam-dag-su$_3$ ‘the (lugal/lady, etc.) is free from blame,’ ITT 5 9215 o. 5’; and ⸢nin-nam-dag-nu⸣-tuku ‘the lady is faultless,’ Nik 1 21 o. iii 3 (all ED IIIb); nin-nam-tag-du$_8$ ‘the lady is one who absolves sin,’ *UNT* 34 o. iii 10, undated; and see nin-nam[!](MU)-tag-du$_8$ in *TUT* 158 r. iii 16 (both Ur III).

[781] The sequence is found in Gudea Cyl. A xii 21–xiii 15.

[782] ŠITA corresponds to LAK503, second variant copied by Deimel.

[783] Note that a šita uru is mentioned in other ES Adab texts, *TCABI* 51 and CUSAS 11 310. An abbreviation lugal with official title would be unexpected.

[784] It would have been preferable to have the abstract element nam prefixed to šita in the earlier periods, as in the ED IIIb Girsu name nam-šita-ĝu$_{10}$-bi$_2$-du$_{11}$, e.g. CT 50 36 rev. iii 11 & iv 6 (2 different persons); and Lugalzagesi’s Nippur inscription, BE 1/2 87 iii 17–18: nam-šita-ĝu$_{10}$, ḫe$_2$-na-be$_2$ ‘may (Enlil) utter my prayer to him (An).’

appear in connection with each other express a formalized relationship between two parties. This said, it is very likely that lugal in some, or even many cases, refers to a male god. Often an expected predicate is missing, and in some cases there is an underlying strength in seeing nominal predicate names as being expressions which served to identify the lugal with the key powers of the divinity serving as the predicate. As opposed to Akkadian names of the same general type, lugal never appears in the expected final, predicative position in names featuring a theonym. For the Ur III period, the picture is another, as the name ^{d}Nanna-lugal represents a conspicuous but expected break with earlier Sumerian onomastic traditions,[785] Nanna of course being the tutelary deity of the city which held nam-lugal. On the whole, however, lugal and nin practically never appear as nominal predicates.[786] Simply put, there is no universal key to defining the identity of the lugal; each and every name has to be tried on its own merits and on parallels from texts of different types, not only the onomastic source material.

The best known example of a full sentence name, featuring a negated passive participle is the name of an ensi$_2$ of the Lagaš state in the late ED IIIb period: lugal-AN-da-nu-ḫuĝ-ĝa$_2$ $^{(a1)}$ 'is the lugal not *put in office* by An/a god?.'[787] The name of this ensi$_2$ is most often written lugal-AN-da $^{(a\geq5)}$, a writing which he shared with a few other known individuals. This shortened form could also stand for names such as lugal-AN-da-nu-me-a '(what would be) without LugalANda?,' which, given the provenience and time of the name, refers to the ensi$_2$ himself.[788] Considering the short rule of LugalANda this person must have received or taken this name in adulthood. For the other persons referred to as lugal-AN-da, other fuller writings could be envisaged, such as *lugal-AN-da-nir-ĝal$_2$ 'the lugal is respected with An/the god,' or *lugal-AN-da-maḫ-di 'the lugal is one famous with An/the god.' The only

---

[785] E.g. *NATN* 6 r. 6 (Nippur); and compare ^{d}Nanna-⸢lugal⸣-dalla 'Nanna is a shining lord,' *TRU* 196 r. 1 (Puzriš-Dagān).

[786] Seeming exceptions formed with 1st person poss. pron. suffixes can often also be explained away. The following examples are all from Ur III Girsu: lu$_2$-nin-MU, ITT 2/1 950 o. i 4 (translit. only), must, no doubt, be explained as a phonetic writing of lu$_2$-^{d}Nin-mu$_2$, for which, see *HLC* 2 94 o. ii 7; the cryptic nin-ĝu$_{10}$-nin-ĝu$_{10}$, *HLC* 3 238 o. ii 2, is doubtlessly a phonetic rendering of nin-ĝu$_{10}$-niĝin-ĝu$_{10}$ 'my lady is my all,' as in MVN 2 176 o. i 6.

[787] The verb ḫuĝ is usually seen in the light of Ur III YNN, which talk of the installation of priests and priestesses in the service of specific deities, see J. Krecher, *RlA* 8 (1993–97), 156f. s.v. "Miete. A. 1." The usual Akk. correspondence of ḫuĝ is *agārum*, which, however, did not cover the sense of ḫuĝ in this name or in the YNN. Compare E. Sollberger & J.-R. Kupper, *IRSA*, 318: "le roi n'est pas inactif (au service) du ciel (ou: d'An)"; G. J. Selz, *Götterwelt*, 24: "Der König, der sich für An nicht beruhigt"; B. Meissner, *Babylonien und Assyrien* 1, 396: "Der König ist beim Himmelsgott kein Lohndiener (?)."

[788] See above, p. 111 fn. 593. Other kyriophore ED IIIb Girsu names incorporating the name of LugalANda are known: ^{d}Nanše-ama-Lugal-AN-da $^{(a1)}$ 'Nanše is the mother of LugalANda'; and ^{d}Utu-palil-Lugal-AN-da $^{(a1)}$ 'Utu is the vanguard of LugalANda.' For the former, compare the LugalANda inscription *CIRPL* Ukg. 9 i' 6'–7': ([Lugal-AN-da]) ...[du]mu tu-da, ^{d}Ba-u$_2$.

pre–Ur III formal parallel is lugal-^{d}En-lil$_2$-da $^{(a1)}$ 'the lugal … with Enlil,'[789] where the comitative marker -da is visible.[790] Furthermore, secure readings of diĝir for AN are rather few in number and mostly of a structurally simpler kind. Judging from all this, AN in the name lugal-AN-da-nu-ḫuĝ-ĝa$_2$ is both statistically and logically more likely to have been An, the god of heaven, than an anonymous 'god' or a collective, diĝir.[791] Quite expectedly, then, most of these names underline the fact that the human ruler in part owed his position to close association with a deity. This perspective of nam-lugal is one that frequently comes to the fore in royal inscriptions.

An and Enlil are also featured in a number of other names, full and abbreviated. The eye of An is said to behold the lugal, lugal-igi-An-na-ke$_4$-su $^{(a2)}$ 'the lugal is one known by the eye of Heaven,'[792] i.e. Utu, who was sometimes also portrayed as the (watchful) eye of Enlil.[793] Similar in scope is lugal-An-ne$_2$-su $^{(a1)}$ 'the lugal is one known by An'; which corresponds to the MC-CS name lugal-^{d}En-lil$_2$-le-an-zu $^{(a1)}$ 'the lugal is one whom Enlil knows,' probably from Isin.[794] The meaning of these names may be contrasted to activities of evil spirits who are said to operate at night, when the gods were less watchful. Hence, daylight serves as a backdrop for the undertakings of the human lugal, acting in accordance with the will of the gods. An is also said to love the lugal, lugal-An-ne$_2$-ki-aĝa$_2$ $^{(a1)}$ 'the lugal is one loved by An.'[795] Names which feature An and Enlil as active participants were comparatively common and were often simply abbreviated to lugal-An-ne$_2$ $^{(a\geq 14)}$,[796] and lugal-^{d}En-lil$_2$-le $^{(a\geq 6)}$.[797] It is probably no coincidence that

[789] Compare en-da-nir-ĝal$_2$, e.g. *DP* 2/1 190 r. i 1 (ED IIIb Girsu); ^{d}En-lil$_2$-da-nir-ĝal$_2$ '(s.o.) is respected with Enlil,' BE 3/1 86 r. 7'; and the FN ^{d}*Šu*-^{d}Su'en-^{d}En-lil$_2$-da-nir-ĝal$_2$ '*Šu*-Su'en is respected with Enlil,' e.g. *NATN* 448 r. 10' (both Ur III Nippur); Nin-da-maḫ-di, e.g. *SAKF* 3 o. iii 8 (ED IIIb Umma-Zabala); and ^{d}En-lil$_2$-da-maḫ-di '(s.o.) is one famous with Enlil,' BBVO 11 279 o. 5', 10' (Ur III Nippur).

[790] The OB entry in a lexical list of lugal-names lugal-da-nir-ĝal$_2$, PBS 11/3 25 o. iii' 3', may represent either an abbreviation discarding a head noun: '(s.o.) is respected with the lugal'; or a dropped theonym: 'the lugal is respected with (DN).'

[791] G. Marchesi, HANE/S 10, 68 fn. 319 transcribes "Lugaldiĝirda," without discussion.

[792] One instance of the name, VS 25 r. iii 16, is written in a very compact space but can safely be connected with another, unambiguous writing for the same person. For the interpretation, see Gudea Cyl. A xxiv 5: e$_2$-ninnu igi An-na-ke$_4$ zu, "Eninnu is what heaven's eyes know," following D. O. Edzard, RIME 3/1, 84.

[793] Compare abbreviation, E. Chiera, PBS 11/3, 211f., no. 254: lugal-igi-an-na, "The king is the eye of heaven," also referring to this particular name. Note similarities with ^{d}Utu-*i-i*[*n*]-^{d}En-lil$_2$ and ^{d}Utu-igi-^{d}En-lil$_2$-la$_2$ mentioned by E. Chiera, PBS 11/2, 146, no. 1584.

[794] The oath formula of the text exhibits pa for pa$_3$, known from other Isin texts.

[795] For parallel formations, see G. J. Selz, *Götterwelt*, 131.

[796] An Ur III PN lugal-an-ne$_2$-ba-DU was interpreted by H. Limet, *Anthroponymie*, 86 (wr.: -an-ne-). as phonetic alternation for du$_7$. The matter is complicated in that a person an-ne$_2$-ba-du$_7$ (r. 8) sealed the document, as against two writings of lugal-an-ne$_2$-ba-DU, o. 3, 11. E. Chiera, PBS 11/3, 212 fn. 2, suggested a mng. for this name similar to PBS 11/1 7 r. vi 23: lugal-gaba-ri-nu-tuku, with Akk. translation: *šar-rum ša ma-ḫi-ra la* [*i*]-⌜*šu*⌝-*u*$_2$.

these two deities were named extensively in the onomastic material connected with lugal as they represented the highest authorities in the cosmos, and they seem to have been recognized as such all across Sumer.[798]

Two variants, on the other hand, seem to feature AN as locus, that is, 'heaven.' The name lugal-an-na-tum$_2$ $^{(a>11)}$,[799] and variant lugal-an-tum$_2$ $^{(a2)}$ 'the lugal befits heaven,'[800] found in a number of cities from the ED IIIa onwards, places the lugal in an otherworldly context. A deity with an astral connection is a likely candidate for the identity of the lugal. In comparison, the ED IIIb Ur name lugal-^{d}Nanna-ra-tum$_2$ $^{(a1)}$ 'the king is one who befits Nanna,'[801] refers to an animate object, and hence exhibits the expected dative marker -ra. It is more than likely here to see lugal as the earthly ruler. The name lugal-ra-tum$_2$ $^{(a1)}$, from ED IIIb Nippur, could also belong to this type of name, though it would necessitate restoring an object. Perhaps it is safer to see the name as complete in itself and translate '(he is) fit for a king!,' perhaps bearing on the healthy nature of the child bearing the name.[802]

Similar in meaning to the former group is a rare name from CS Girsu, lugal-ḫe$_2$-du$_7$ $^{(a1)}$ 'the lugal is befitting (of DN/GN?).' Some parallel formations in Sumerian and Akkadian point to the name as involving an inner quality which makes the lugal fitting for service to a god or perhaps a locus.[803] Only Utu appears expressly along with this predicate in the onomasticon, but it is associated with other deities in later literary sources.[804]

---

[797] See, furthermore, lugal-^{d}En-lil$_2$ $^{(a\geq 6/°1?)}$, primarily found in the ED IIIb, denoting persons from Girsu, Nippur and Akšak.

[798] Although the title lugal kur-kur-ra is only attested for An in inscriptions of ED IIIb Uruk lugals I am unaware of any 3rd millennium evidence that would refute the An-Enlil power-dyad. But compare P. Steinkeller, *POANE*, 113f. who pictured Enki as the sole male divinity at the head of a veritable harem of obliging goddesses during proto-historic times.

[799] With Ur III var. lugal-an-na-ab-tum$_2$, H. Limet, *Anthroponymie*, 309: "Le roi qui est digne du ciel"; closely followed by E. Sollberger & J.-R. Kupper, *IRSA*, 318. The CS PN lugal-an-na $^{(a1)}$, of unknown provenience, is an abbreviation of this name.

[800] W. Sallaberger, *Fs Schretter*, 574, features a list of parallel names. G. J. Selz, *Götterwelt*, 23 fn. 50, discusses close parallels, and offers a different interpretation of the name: "Dem König/Herrn hat man (ihn) gebracht." The lack of the dative case is not a critical issue. But more to the point, the implicit introduction of a name-bearer to a king or divine lord begs further explanation or parallels, preferably from outside the onomasticon.

[801] Theoretically the appellative might be considered as preposed to Nanna's name as epithet: '(one) befitting of lord Nanna.'

[802] Compare, for instance en-ra-tum$_2$, e.g. BIN 8 352 r. i 1; (lu$_2$) aja$_2$-en-ra-tum$_2$(-me), e.g. HSS 3 43 o. ii 2; and mes-en-ra-tum$_2$, e.g. VS 25 11 o. v 13' (all ED IIIb Girsu); e$_2$-en-ra, *WF* 151 o. i 4 (ED IIIa Šuruppag); nin-en-ra, OSP 1 23 (ES-MS Nippur).

[803] See Ur III Akkadian kyriophores composed with the verb *wasāmum*, given by M. Hilgert, JBVO 5, 61, w. fnn. 207–210: *wu-sum*$_2$-^{d}Šul-gi "besonders angemessen (gestaltet) ist Šulgi"; and ^{d}*Šu*-^{d}Su'en-*wu-su*$_2$-*um-i-šar-ri* "Šu-Suen ist besonders angemessen (gestaltet) unter den Königen." Compare OB Ur PN *i-na-ša-me-e-wu-sum*$_2$, UET 5 91 r. 11, with en-ḫe$_2$-du$_7$-an-na, 'the en is befitting of An," daughter of *Śarrukēn*; and Ur III Girsu name ĝi$_6$-par$_4$-e-ḫe$_2$-du$_7$ 'he/she is fitting for the ĝipar,' TMH NF 1–2 271 o. i 12, with variant ĝipar$_x$(KISAL), ITT 2/1 3514 o. 4; E. Chiera, PBS 11/3, 213, no. 287: lugal-ḫe$_2$-du$_7$-an-ki "the king is the magnificence of heaven and earth." M. Stol, *Birth in Babylonia and the Bible*, 88, offered

Two, maybe three, goddesses also appear in close connection with the lugal in phrase names parallel to epithets in royal inscriptions. The ED IIIa Šuruppag name lugal-^{d}Sud$_{3}$-ki-aĝ$_{2}$ $^{(a1)}$ 'the lugal is beloved by Sud,'[805] can be compared to CS Adab lugal-^{d}Sud$_{3}$-de$_{3}$ $^{(a1)}$, which contains the expected, though in ED IIIa names largely amissible, ergative marker. In the ED Lagaš state, several names and royal inscriptions attest to Nanše's exalted status. Thus, the name lugal-^{d}Nanše-mu-tu $^{(a1)}$ 'the lugal is one born by Nanše,'[806] is only a confirmation of the distribution of royal ideological tenets in certain layers of society. It no doubt refers to the human ruler in Girsu, as demonstrated amply by G. Marchesi.[807] It echoes passages from royal inscriptions in which regents refer to themselves as dumu (ki-aĝa$_{2}$) DN, or dumu tu-da DN.[808] A name with similar overtones is lugal-^{d}Tu $^{(a1)}$ 'the lugal ... (the goddess) Tu,'[809] probably from ED IIIb Umma-Zabala. ^{d}Tu is most likely a "mother goddess" whose name was later most often written ^{d}Nin-tu.[810] Two abbreviated names should most likely be seen as related to the above: lugal-ša$_{3}$-ge-ib$_{2}$-tu $^{(°1)}$ 'the lugal was born *in* the heart (of DN?),' found only in a later scholastic list of early personal names is problematic;[811] but lugal-mu-tu $^{(a1)}$ 'the lugal is one born (by DN),' from ED IIIb Girsu, is straight-forward by comparison.[812]

A small number of names which presuppose the presence of divine ordinance and selection remind of further passages in royal inscriptions. A name which bears on the lugal as ordered by one or more gods is lugal-inim-

---

another interpretation of *i-na-ša-me-e-wu-sum$_{2}$*, "Made beautiful in heaven," as evidence of the determining of children's destinies before birth. In light of the parallels listed here, that interpretation probably does not apply to this name.

[804] E.g. ^{d}Utu-ḫe$_{2}$-du$_{7}$, OIP 14 150 r. 2' (abba$_{2}$ uru, CS Adab). For literary refs. to other deities, see Å. Sjöberg, *MNS*, 25; K. Tallqvist, *AGE*, 322.

[805] Compare H. Limet, *Namenforschung*, 852: lugal-^{d}Nanše-ki-aĝ$_{2}$ "le roi qui Nanše aime."

[806] Compare parallels en-^{d}Nanše-mu-tu 'the en is one borne by Nanše,' *DP* 2/1 175 o. ii 3; VS 14 86 o. ii 6; PAP.PAP-^{d}Nanše-mu-tu and PAP.PAP-^{d}Ba-u$_{2}$-mu-tu 'PAP.PAP is one borne by Nanše/Bau,' Nik 1 9 o. 7, 9.

[807] HANE/S 10, 72f. fn. 381.

[808] See generally refs. in FAOS 6, 85–91 s.v. dumu, esp. p. 90, A) 3. and 4.

[809] This writing for the goddess appears also in another ED IIIb Umma-Zabala text, M. A. Powell, *HUCA* 49, 1–58, no. 1 o. i 11.

[810] See J. Bauer, *WO* 24 (1993), 163, note to no. 14 VII 5; *Annäherungen* 1, 499f.; and further, M. Krebernik, *Annäherungen* 1, 284 fn. 532, who notes that a pair of ED IIIa Šuruppag god lists feature two ^{d}Tu after another.

[811] The interpretation presupposes a genitive construction following the *ḫamṭu* verbal chain, where the -b- refers back to the loc.-term. -e in /šag-e/. A passive-intransitive understanding of this name is thus taken for granted. See here the discussion of C. Wilcke, *ZA* 78 (1988), 35–49, esp. 40–42 and fn. 140. Other solutions could perhaps be envisaged. The list containing the name in question, M. E. Cohen, *Fs Hallo*, 79–86 (YBC 2124), contains a number of archaic-looking names but also writings more akin to Ur III or later orthographies.

[812] The less certain lu:gal-tu$^{!?}$ $^{(a1)}$ from ES Nippur, if read correctly, could be an even more abbreviated form of this name, or perhaps of lugal-^{d}Tu.

ma-se$_3$-ga (a2) 'the lugal is one instructed (by/of DN),'[813] is found at ED IIIb Nippur and, perhaps, Zabala. Abbreviated variant lugal-inim-se$_3$-ga (a1), is attested in ED IIIb Ur.

A form of vocation and call to office by gods seems also to be the meaning underlying the CS Adab name lugal-gu$_3$-de$_2$-a (a1) 'the lugal is summoned.'[814] The appointment process is sometimes qualified adverbially as zi, and can hence be translated as 'truthful,' and thus in accordance with the overarching ordinances of the world instated by the all-powerful gods. The gods documented by royal inscriptional material as responsible for this call to office are Enlil and Inana.[815]

Divine selection is the theme behind the variants lugal-ša$_3$-pa$_3$-da (a2) 'the lugal is one chosen in the heart (of DN),'[816] and variant lugal-ša$_3$-pa$_3$ (a2), attested at Šuruppag, Girsu and Ur during the ED III period. A few lugal-names featuring the verb pa$_3$ but lacking an indirect object, are likely to be abbreviations of the previous type.[817] A possible reference to the one doing the choosing is contained in two exemplars of a list of PNN from ED IIIa Šuruppag. One text has lugal-mes-nun-pa$_3$ (°1) 'the lugal is one chosen by the noble hero (?),' while the duplicate has lugal-nun-pa$_3$ (°1) 'the lugal is one chosen by the noble one.'[818] It is of course possible, though less likely, that mes nun in the former should be taken as an added description of the referent of lugal. In names where the selection is said to take place in the heart (of DN), a human referent is plausible.

Names in which the lugal may be likened to gods; that is, names which do not feature any remains which could point to their originally having been phrase names, like dimensional suffixes or predicates, are relatively few in number. They seem for the most part to accord well with later practice in royal hymns of the Ur III period, comparing the king to certain divinities. Here, however, in the absence of a corpus of royal hymns, an identification

---

813 Compare epithet used by Ur-Nanše and Eanatum: lu$_2$ inim(-ma) se$_3$(-ga) DN, translated by H. Steible, *Moral und Recht im Diskurs der Moderne*, 76: der auf den Auftrag/Befehl angesetzt wurde von DN"; and see further refs. in G. J. Selz, *Götterwelt*, 111 and fn. 404.

814 See, e.g. the use of *šasûm* in PNN, *CAD* Š/2 s.v. *šasû* (v.), 3'.

815 See references to ED IIIb Uruk and Lagaš inscriptions, FAOS 6, 152 s.v. gu$_3$-zi–de$_2$. Compare also Ur III PNN gu$_3$-zi-de$_2$ and gu$_3$-zi-de$_2$-a, H. Limet, *Anthroponymie*, 426 s.v.v., with comments on p. 235.

816 Compare PN ⸢ša$_3$-ku$_3$-ge⸣-pa$_3$-d[a] (dumu ensi$_2$-ke$_4$, PBS 15 2 1', ED IIIb Nippur) and see ša$_3$ ku$_3$-ge pa$_3$-da$_3$, ^{d}Nanše, nin uru$_{16}$-na-ke$_4$, epithet of Eanatum in *CIRPL* Ean. 60 i 6–8.

817 Including lugal-pa$_3$ (a1/°1), and lugal-pa$_3$-da (a2). The Ebla variant nu-gal-pa$_2$(BA)-da (°1) is phonetic for the latter.

818 The fuller writing appears in *SF* 28 which sometimes exhibits further signs compared to the larger exemplar of the same text, *SF* 29. The rarely attested divinity ^{d}Mes-nun-sa$_6$-aĝ$_2$, e.g. AUCT 2 97 r. i 7 (Ur III Puzriš-Dagān), is hardly intended by the fuller writing. The name of an ED IIIb Ur lugal has traditionally been read as mes-ki-aĝ$_2$-nun, but see G. Marchesi, *OrNS* 73 (2004), 167f. fn. 97, who proposes a more likely reading mes-nun-ki-aĝ$_2$, which forms a nice parallel to the present name, and is more in keeping with other ED IIIa name types.

is not clear-cut, and hence the question of what or who is intended must remain open. The names which appear to be nominal phrase names may be abbreviations for longer ones featuring a predicate or they may simply be elative phrases praising the qualities of the divinity by means of addressing him as lugal, 'lord!' The names are: two variants of lugal-^{d}Dumu-zi $^{(a1)}$,[819] mostly attested in the ED IIIa; lugal-^{d}KA.DI $^{(a1)}$,[820] from MS-CS Nippur; and the contemporary lugal-^{d}Utu $^{(a1)}$, probably from Isin.[821] Less secure are the names lugal-^{d}mes-lam (or ^{d}Lugal-mes-lam?) $^{(a1)}$,[822] and lugal-UD $^{(a\geq6/°1)}$.[823] The names lugal-^{d}Utu and lugal-^{d}KA.DI probably bear on the lugal in relation to the sphere of legal activities, as a source for social justice, see above, 3.1.3.3, end. They might also be condensed writings of longer forms, such as lugal-Utu-gin$_{7}$-e$_{3}$, for which, see below, section 3.1.7.10.[824] The name lugal-AN $^{(a\geq7/°1)}$ 'An/the god ... the lugal (?),'[825] can be an abbreviated form of many different names. As An was considered one of the deities who conferred nam-lugal on humans it is not altogether unlikely that AN does refer to the god An in some instances of this abbreviated name. Similarly, lugal-^{d}En-lil$_{2}$ might rather be a short form of names which, like similar ones composed with An, originally featured an ergative marker, and sometimes a transitive verb, zu 'to know,' or ki–aĝ$_{2}$ 'to love.'

---

[819] Dumuzi is here more likely the nominal predicate than the subject. The PN lugal-dumu-zi $^{(a\geq4/°1)}$, is almost exclusively found in the ED IIIa period, with one reference in the Ebla copy of the Names and Professions List, and is a probable alternative writing of this name, without divine determinative, thus, e.g. H. Steible, *CollAn* 7 (2008), 97; so also M. Krebernik, *Fs Wilcke*, 152f., with the alternative suggestion "der König ist ein 'rechtes Kind.'" The only attestation of lugal-^{d}Dumu-zi is *TSŠ* 131, a small Šuruppag donkey text. A small majority of the other Šuruppag attestations (4 out of 7 in all) are also from donkey texts. However, no direct prosopographical connections between *TSŠ* 131 and the rest of these texts exist.

[820] H. Limet, *Anthroponymie*, 172, discussed similar names as meaning: "Le roi est [DN]," or: "Le (vrai) roi (de la cité), c'est [DN]!"

[821] Oath formula in the text uses pa phonetically for pa$_{3}$, known from other Isin documents. If the name is unabbreviated, ^{d}Utu is the nominal predicate, not the head noun.

[822] Also written lugal-mes-lam $^{(a\geq1)}$ in ED IIIa Šuruppag. An epithet of Nergal lies close at hand, for which see, W. G. Lambert, *RlA* 7 (1987–90), 149 s.v. "Lugal-Meslama," translated: "Lord of (the shrine) Meslam." The ambiguity of the placement of the dinĝir-determinative is perhaps witnessed by the ED IIIb Nippur GN e$_{2}$ Lugal-^{d}mes-lam, TMH 5 24 o. ii 1, compared to MS Nippur GN e$_{2}$ ^{d}Lugal-mes-lam^{ki}, OSP 1 102 o. ii 2.

[823] Not all names can be said with all certainty to refer to Utu, but as has been pointed out by H. Steible, *CollAn* 7 (2008), 101 w. fn. 25, Utu is most often written without the ^{d}-determinative in early texts, including PNN. In ED IIIa Šuruppag economic documentation, ^{d}Utu is written only once, L. Matouš, *ArOr* 39 (1971), p. 14 o. iii 3: di-^{d}Utu. J. Krecher, *ZA* 63 (1973), 213f., saw that text as ED IIIb, in pointing, among other things, to this name. The reading of *WF* 41 o. viii 6 with *EDATŠ*, 170 as: lu$_{2}$-^{d}Utu is not supported by photo (CDLI P010998). Read instead AN.BU.DU$_{3}$, and compare F. Pomponio, *Prosopografia*, 39 s.v.

[824] See also some entries in OB PNN lists, e.g. PBS 11/3 20 r. i 8'f.: lugal-^{d}Utu-gin$_{7}$, ⸢lugal⸣-^{d}Utu-ĝu$_{10}$; and TIM 9 91 o. ii' 6': ⸢lugal⸣-^{d}KA.DI-⸢gin$_{7}$-di⸣-ku$_{5}$ -⸢da-pa-e$_{3}$.⸣

[825] Not necessarily a nominal predicate name, as it was interpreted by H. Limet, *Anthroponymie*, 174; and R. di Vito, StPohl SM 16, 60, 30.4b, 1.

Names which belong, or most likely belong to this category, but which have not been fully understood are: lugal-diĝir-re (a1) "the god … the lugal"; and lugal-dEn-ki-a-DU (a1),[826] from ED IIIa Šuruppag.

3.1.6.3 Cultic insignia, acts and ceremonial

Certain external signs of lordship which bear on the lugal's cultic role have already been mentioned in discussions above. The men, discussed in section 3.1.1.3, for instance, seems to have had a double function of indicating both worldly and cultic responsibilities. But while this outer characteristic of lordship did no more than separate its owner from the surrounding world, other objects presuppose specific acts on the part of the lugal. So, for instance, the name lugal-banšur-e (a1) 'the lugal … the (offering) table,' points to a demand for providing meals for the gods. The loc.-term. suffix -e and the exclusive access to an offering table suggest that the verb missing is si 'to be just right (for something),' indicating special access of the lugal to cultic paraphernalia of this sort. Texts describing allocations of such offerings are known both from contemporary texts and later copies.[827]

That which went to the offering tables of the sanctuaries was sometimes characterized as nidba, and a few variant names exist which associate the lugal with such offerings; most of them are from Nippur, all are of Sargonic date. The earliest form, lugal-nidba$_2$ (a1),[828] may carry a meaning along the lines of: 'the lugal (is just right for) the nidba-offerings (?).' From the ED IIIb and ES period, a handful of independent rulers are known to have provided such offerings for local sanctuaries and for the all–important gods of Nippur.[829] A name with an analogue semantic import is lugal-kadra (a1) 'the lugal (presents) a gift (offering),' attested once at CS Umma.[830] A

[826] Maybe a-DU is to be read a-ra$_2$, and be understood as 'advice,' pointing to a relationship between Enki and the lugal as informed by the god. Another, more or less equally forced interpretation would be to see the name as an abbreviation originally mentioning the Abzu of Enki: lugal(-abzu)-dEnki(-ga-k)a-tum$_2$ 'the lugal befits the Abzu of Enki.' Alternatively, one might consider a wholly different reading: lugal-a-ki-en-DU-am$_6$, freely 'the lugal is water (in) the waterway,' though admittedly, this is without parallel.

[827] E.g. from the reign of *Rīmuś*, BE 1/1 13; A. Westenholz, *ECTJ*, 100, with notes on no. 219, a late 3rd millennium copy of an earlier original.

[828] Slightly later are the MS-CS variants lugal-ni$_3$-nidba$_2$-e (a1), and lugal-nidba$_2$-e (a1). Note the entry lugal(-)nidba-x, in a CS Girsu text edited by B. R. Foster, *JANES* 12 (1980), 30 no. 1 (MLC 114), o. ii 2'. The final sign is not -e, according to Foster, who did not see the entry as a PN, but the copy shows a sign more like lu. A reading of the line as a PN, and a restoration lugal-nidba-si! (?) is possible, and the predicate -si is at any rate the most likely one.

[829] See, e.g., A. Westenholz, *Iraq* 39 (1977), 19–21 (Ukg. lugal 2); TMH 5 84–86 (nidba-offerings of *Śarrukēn*); and compare the statement of Lugalzagesi, BE 1/2 87 iii 7–12: dEn-lil$_2$, lugal-ni, Nibruki-a, nidba gal-gal, e-na-su$_{13}$-[de$_3$], a du$_{10}$ e-na-d[e$_2$-e] 'for his lord, Enlil, in Nippur, he serves up surpassing nidba-offerings (and) pours sweet water.' See also OSP 1 16 (nidba$_2$-offerings from Adab).

[830] For the interpretation, see the note by the editors, W. Sommerfeld, K. Markina & N. Roudik, *Gs Diakonoff*, 195, to l. 9.

special category of offerings may be the nesaĝ (Akk. *nisannu*), as in the name lugal-nesaĝ-e $^{(a\geq4)}$ 'the lugal (is just right for) the firstling (offering),'[831] which is most commonly encountered in the Umma region. But the noun is perhaps to be understood rather as a locus, 'the lugal by the sacristy,'[832] or the like, depending on which verb was associated with nesaĝ.[833]

A small group of ED IIIb names are related to the performance of music. They are all from the Girsu area, and they can with some degree of certainty be linked to a specific context. According to J. Cheng, Sumerian iconography has a preference for depicting musical performances only in relation with banquets, although he notes that according to texts, music was performed also, for instance, during funeral ceremonies.[834] The relevant names all feature the noun tigi, lugal-tigi$_x$(E$_2$.BALAĜ)-mete(TE+ME) $^{(a1)}$ 'the Harp is befitting (of) the lugal,'[835] lugal-tigi$_x$(E$_2$.BALAĜ)-ni-du$_{10}$ $^{(a1)}$ 'the Harp of the lugal is pleasant (sounding).' A parallel of the latter with the appellative nin is also extant.[836] No comparable theophore constructions exist for either of these two names.

Some names combine the lugal with objects which might have served purposes for cultic acts. For instance lugal-gu$_4$ $^{(a2)}$ 'the lugal … the ox,'[837] found in a few different ED IIIb cities, and °lugal-gu$_4$-DU $^{(a1)}$,[838] so far limited to a CS lexical text of unknown provenience. The dedication by royalty of

---

[831] With variant lugal-nesaĝ $^{(a\geq4)}$. For the reconstruction with -si, see the name lugal-nesaĝ-e-si, S. Langdon, *Babyloniaca* 6 (1912), 53 B r. 5 (Ur III Umma).

[832] Compare H. Limet, *Anthroponymie*, 282 (nesaĝ read murub$_4$): "Le roi vers la fête-*murub*."

[833] See discussion with plenty of references, W. Heimpel, *NABU* 1994/83.

[834] J. Cheng, *JNES* 68 (2009), 163–178, with many depictions, esp. p. 164f.

[835] The short form lugal-tigi$_x$(E$_2$.BALAĜ) $^{(a1)}$, belongs to this fuller writing, as against G. J. Selz, *Götterwelt*, 104. Uncertain interpretation. The crux lies in defining the relation between the tigi$_x$ and lugal. If comparable to the following name, there is an underlying anticipatory genitive, lugal(-ak) tigi$_x$(-ni) mete(-am), but this must remain speculative. For the reading tigi$_x$ of E$_2$.BALAĜ, see discussion below of *lugal-e$_2$-balaĝ, etc., p. 185.

[836] Compare also nin-tigi$_x$-ni, T. Gomi, *Orient* 19 (1983), p. 2–3 o. iii 2 (ED IIIa Šuruppag). That the verb du$_{10}$ is used for the effects of musical instruments is clear, for instance, from Gudea Cyl. B 9–15. Another interpretation is offered by G. J. Selz, *Götterwelt*, 104 w. fn. 377: "lugal-e$_2$-balag-i$_3$-du$_{10}$ (Dem) Herrn (des) Hauses ist die Harfe angenehm$^?$." The comparative rarity of this and the two previous names against contemporary nin-tigi$_x$-ni-du$_{10}$ can be explained from the fact that the two or three persons with this latter name are found more often in the e$_2$-MI$_2$ documention. Note unclear [l]u$_2$ tigi$_x$-me in CS Girsu, *STTI* 158 r. 6.

[837] Recreate, with all probability, loc.-term. suffix -e, as in Ur III lugal-gu$_4$-e, H. Limet, *Anthroponymie*, 463 s.v.; given on p. 329 as: "le roi vers le bœuf … (pour le sacrifice?)." Compare lugal-ab$_2$-ki-aĝ$_2$; and, perhaps, ED IIIb Girsu PN nin-maš-e, V. V. Struve, *Onomastika*, 148 s.v. Note the possibility that the bulls refer to a traditional motif associated with Enlil in birth incantations, with witnesses from the ED IIIa and Ur III periods. The last treatment of these are found in M. Stol, *Birth in Babylonia and the Bible*, 60–63.

[838] The name is unique and the interpretation hinges on the multivalent final sign. Is DU a phonetic writing for du$_7$, as in gu$_4$ du$_7$, 'bull without defect,' Å. Sjöberg, TCS 3, 81 note to l. 147, with refs.; or rather gu$_4$ du$_7$, 'goring bull,' or the like, corresponding to Akk. *nakāpum* and derived forms?

utensils to temples and deities is known from early on,[839] but whether the Sargonic name lugal-bur $^{(a\geq3)}$ 'the lugal ... the bowl,' has bearing on this phenomenon is not clear. A likely later parallel supplies a predicate, nin-bur-e-si 'the lady/queen is just right for the bowl.'[840] No fitting theophore parallels exist.

One of the most difficult words in Sumerian is me. It appears regularly in PNN, but its placement in the names vary, and seemingly so also its functions. Another reading of the sign ME is išib, which denoted a priestly role. For some names, me can tentatively be translated as 'rites,' that is, the execution of predefined cultic acts with a specific and expected end-result. In other instances, it is likely that me signifies the dynamic powers which lay at the base of each and every cultural and natural phenomenon. An example of the former is posed by lugal-me-še$_3$-ĝal$_2$ $^{(a1)}$ 'the lugal is present *for* the rites,'[841] from ED IIIb Nippur. Although it is not immediately clear in the latter whether lugal is the one performing or presiding over the rites, other names and literary passages add weight to the assumption that the lugal is the active party in the proceedings. The name lugal-ME-^{d}En-l[il$_2$] $^{(a1)}$ 'the lugal ... the rites of Enlil (?),'[842] from ED IIIb Kiš can be held against Ningirsu's role as išib of An in one of Gudea's cylinders.[843] Another name, lugal-me-gal-gal $^{(a2)}$ 'the lugal (performs) the great rites (?),'[844] relates to the later theology of Ningirsu and Ninurta. In the case of the former, me gal-gal probably refers to rites executed in his honour at a specific festival, known at least from Ur III times.[845] In the case of Ninurta, me gal-gal is linked to an-ki, heaven (and) earth, and thus are more likely to refer to his responsibilities and powers.[846]

---

[839] See, conveniently, J. Goodnick Westenholz, *BiOr* 55 (1998), 44–59, with many refs., for an investigation into different types of inscribed objects and vessels from the Sargonic period.

[840] MVN 21 240 o. 7 (Ur III Umma).

[841] An alternative interpretation, interpreting me-še$_3$ as the interrogative, 'what is the lugal for?,' is implausible.

[842] Collation by A. Westenholz, autumn 2011, confirms the copy by J. P. Grégoire, *AAICAB* 1/1 pl. 5 (Ashm 1928-427 r. i 1) is correct.

[843] Gudea Cyl. A x 13. The passage is one of only six times in the cylinders where Ningirsu is termed lugal, as noted by A. Falkenstein, AnOr 30, 93 note 9.

[844] Compare H. Limet, *Namenforschung*, 852: "Nom+syntagme en relation plus vague ... le roi aux pouvoirs très grands"; and nin-me-gal-[g]al, W. G. Lambert *Gs Sachs*, 259f. ii 12, Sargonic list of nin-names.

[845] In Gudea Cyl. A x 18 Ningirsu in 1st person speaks of the great rites, me gal-gal, performed in his honour at his festival of An. In the Ur III period the festival is commemorated in a month name in Ur and in other places, see W. Sallaberger, *Der Kultische Kalender der Ur III-Zeit*, 7–11. In Gudea Cyl. A, note also i 20: e$_2$-ninnu me-bi gal-gal-la-am$_3$.

[846] See A. Falkenstein, *ZA* 49 (1950), 120 l. 32 (Ur-Ninurta C).

Further names featuring ME are less overt as to meaning; the name lugal-me-si $^{(a\geq1)}$ 'the lugal is just right for the ordinances,'[847] contains the predicate –si; while lugal-me-du$_{10}$-ga $^{(a\geq1)}$ 'the lugal of the good ordinances,'[848] has the appearance of a qualified genitival compound. Other names are even less clear, such as lugal-me-sikil $^{(a1)}$ 'the lugal (is just right for) the pure ordinances (of DN),' which has a parallel featuring the appellative nin;[849] and the ED IIIa entry in a scholastic text lugal-me-zi $^{(°1)}$ 'the lugal … the true me-functions,' which also appears as a theophore featuring Enlil.[850]

That an interpretation išib of ME is fully possible is demonstrated by lugal-šu-luḫ-ku$_3$-An-na $^{(a1)}$ 'the lugal (is one befitting for) the holy handwashing rites of An'[851] known from ED IIIb Ur, and which nicely echoes the role later ascribed to the tutelary deity of Ur, Nanna, in relation to An.[852] A name which is likely to refer to the human lugal is lugal-šu-sikil $^{(a\geq1)}$ 'the lugal is the pure hand (of DN),'[853] from the MS-CS period, and which bears some resemblance to passages in 3rd millennium royal inscriptions.[854]

A most interesting group of lugal-names relate to activities connected with beds: the unique lugal-na$_2$-du$_{10}$-ga $^{(a1)}$ 'the lugal on/of the good bed,'[855] limited to the ED IIIa;[856] and lugal-ni$_3$-^{ba}bara$_3$-du$_{10}$ $^{(a4)}$ with variant lugal-ni$_3$-

---

[847] Abbreviated. An original form incorporating a directional object marked by loc.-term. –e, by or in which the lugal fills the me – whatever they may be in this connection – is envisaged by M. Krebernik, AOAT 296, 23f.

[848] H. Limet, *Anthroponymie*, 172: "Le roi dont les *me* sont bonnes." It is hardly coincidental that a nin-me-du$_{10}$-ga is mentioned just before a lugal-me-du$_{10}$-ga in a difficult passage in a CS Nippur text. The couple ought reasonably to be related to each other. Only two attestations of lugal-me-du$_{10}$-ga predating the Ur III period are known; nin-me-du$_{10}$(-ga) is more common.

[849] *DCS* 9+10 r. iii' 8': nin-me-sikil-An-na (ED IIIb Girsu FPN).

[850] See the ED IIIb Girsu name ^{d}En-lil$_2$-me-zi, VS 27 13 o. iv 10. It is possible that a predicate is missing, as is shown by the ED IIIa Šuruppag name me-zi-pa-e$_3$, e.g. *WF* 41 o. viii 8. It is also possible that ME zi formed part of a genitive chain, governing a divinity, for which, see the later en-me-zi-An-na, e.g. MVN 1 144 o. 5' (Ur III Puzriš-Dagān).

[851] Once abbreviated to lugal-šu.

[852] See the passage from an OB adab-song to Nanna: en šu-luḫ ku$_3$-ga An-e gub-ba-am$_3$-ma "en (responsible) of the holy handwashing rites that An put in place," largely following Å. Sjöberg, *MNS*, 37. The verbal chain is not entirely clear to the present writer.

[853] Interpretation following G. Marchesi, *OrNS* 73 (2004), 180f., with parallels. It is possible that the two known occurrences of this name refer to the same person.

[854] See, for instance, *Šu*-Su'en's priestly functions in YOS 1 20 i 7–11: išib An-na, gudu$_4$ šu dadag(UD.UD), ^{d}En-lil$_2$, ^{d}Nin-lil$_2$-ka, *u*$_3$ diĝir gal-gal-e-ne, 'the purification priest of An, pure-handed gudu$_4$-priest of Enlil, Ninlil and of all the great gods.' For earlier titularies, see Lugalzagesi's Nippur inscription BE 1/2 87 i 6: išib An-na; and see S. Franke on *Śarrukēn*'s borrowing of this part of Lugalzagesi's titulary, *Königsinschriften*, 96–98.

[855] Abbreviation lugal-na$_2$-du$_{10}$ $^{(a1/°1)}$ is found both at Šuruppag, and, in a scholastic text, at Abū Ṣalābīḫ. Contemporary sources and most later lexical entries have $^{(ĝiš)}$na$_2$ or ki na$_2$ as representing 'bed,' but one source equates ki na$_2$-du$_{10}$(-ga) with [*a-šar*] *ma-a-a-lim* (MIN.MIN), 'sleeping place,' *CAD* M/1 s.v. *majālu*, lex. sect.

[856] As noted by F. Pomponio & G. Visicato, *FTUM*, 34, the name is not found outside of Šuruppag. Neither does na$_2$ du$_{10}$(-ga) appear with other appellatives or a theonym.

bara$_4$-du$_{10}$ $^{(a\geq16)}$,[857] attested from the ED IIIa down through the Sargonic periods, both meaning 'the lugal is one who makes joyous (things on) the bedspreads.'[858] The names may deal with what is commonly referred to as the 'sacred marriage,' the union between earthly and divine aspects which served to ensure plenty on earth.[859] The actors in this ceremony were by the late 3rd millennium human actors, one being the deified king, the other a woman representing the divine Inana.[860] However, the earliest history of the sacred marriage is as of yet shrouded in mystery.[861] If the association of these names should prove correct, they would then be linked to a festival of great concern to people in general, which would in part explain the popularity of the name lugal-ni$_3$-bara$_4$-du$_{10}$, borne by more than 15 persons, predominantly in the Nippur, Adab and Isin area. Perhaps this could also be taken as indicative of the time of birth of persons so named, around the time of the celebration of this ceremony. The closest – though not identical – parallels are construed with the appellative nin.[862]

A symbol connected with different activities was a type of standard, uri$_3$. The name lugal-uri$_3$ $^{(a\geq12)}$,[863] known from as early on as ED I-II Ur, has a rare variant in lugal-uri$_3$-da $^{(a1)}$ 'the lugal ... by the standard.' Apart from lugal, and nin, the uri$_3$ appears also in names composed with the theonyms Utu and Nanše, in the Ur III period also with Nanna.[864] As a visible symbol indicative of guidance, uri$_3$ appears in the cylinder inscription of Gudea,[865] and a name mu-ni-uri$_3$ 'his/her name is a standard,'[866] may relate to the same idea.[867] The

---

[857] Described as "Kurzform" of the former, M. Krebernik, AOAT 296, 37 fn. 200.

[858] For the meaning, see the passage in Lugalbanda 1, l. 88 giving ni$_3$-bara$_3$ without tug$_2$-determinative, referring to the setting up of a resting place for Lugalbanda.

[859] Compare na$_2$ du$_{10}$-ga with Akk. *mayyālti mūšim ṭābim* 'bed of the sweet night,' which occurs in a much later source, dating to the late 1st millennium, see *CAD* M/1 s.v. *majāltu*, 1.

[860] See, for instance, two lines from an Iddin-Dagān hymn, D. Reisman, *JCS* 25 (1973), 191: 178–179: "They arrange the cover [^{tug_2}ni$_3$-bara$_3$] on the outside of the bed. So that they (Inanna and the king) might rest comfortably on "the cover [^{tug_2}ni$_3$-bara$_3$] which rejoices the heart.""

[861] Two competent surveys of the background of this ceremony are J. S. Cooper, *Official Cult and Popular Religion*, 81–96; and J. Goodnick Westenholz, *NIN* 1 (2000), 75–89.

[862] For a discussion of these, see J. Krecher, *ZA* 63 (1973), 247; and below, p. 187, *lugal-ni$_3$-bara$_4$-ge and *lugal-ni$_3$-bara$_4$-ga. See P. Steinkeller, *JNES* 52 (1993), 144, for lexical entries.

[863] Compare E. Chiera, PBS 11/3, 214, no. 320: lugal-uru [=uri$_3$] "The king is protector."

[864] nin-uri$_3$, e.g. OSP 1 23 o. iii 5''' and passim; uri$_3$.UD, OSP 1 32 o. ii 1 (ED IIIb Nippur); ^{d}Nanše-uri$_3$, e.g. CT 50 41 o. ii 2 (ED IIIb Girsu); ^{d}Nanna-uri$_3$, e.g. UET 3 1147 o. 3 (Ur).

[865] So in Gudea Cyl. A xx 1 gu$_3$-de$_2$-a-ar inim ^{d}Nin-ĝir$_2$-su-ka uri$_3$-am$_3$ mu-ru$_2$ "Ningirsu's words stood rammed in to Gudea like banners," following D. O. Edzard, RIME 3/1, 81; and see also ibid. CRRA 20, 160f.

[866] E.g. MVN 10 82 o. iv 5 (ED IIIa Šuruppag); TCABI 117 r. 4 (MS Adab).

[867] See E. Chiera's notes on the grouping together in an OB list of PNN, PBS 11/3 25 r. i 10–12 of the names lugal-sipa, lugal-sipa-kalam-ma, and lugal-uri$_3$, PBS 11/3, 197, with the main exception that Chiera understood the sign uri$_3$ ("uru") as indicative of protection. I would rather say that in this case, the common denominator is the aspect of direction and leadership.

form with the comitative signals some form of activity involving the standard but none presents itself.

A reference to an architectural detail by the doorways of temples is lugal-ĝiš-bur$_2$ $^{(a3)}$ ‘the lugal … the *door ornament,*’ limited to the ED IIIb-ES period. The decorations of the ĝiš-bur$_2$ could feature wild animals.[868] No parallels are known that could explain closer the relation between the lugal and this architectural feature.[869]

A few names may arguably sort under this heading, though at present precise interpretations are hard to propose: lugal-LUḪ $^{(a2)}$ ‘the lugal (is) pure (or purifies?) (?),’[870] lugal-na-de$_5$-ga $^{(a\geq1)}$ ‘the lugal is pure (?).’[871]

3.1.6.4 Sacred loci, sanctuaries and installations

Place names occur in the human onomasticon in combination not only with lugal but also with the other popular appellatives en,[872] and nin.[873] A number of names contain references to loci associated with the god Enki, at home in Eridu, in the far south of the floodplain. Names mentioning the Abzu are mostly attested during the ED period. Later on in time, the Abzu became a cultic installation attested in places other than Eridu, but for the ED period it is reasonable to assume that Abzu in the human onomasticon was identical with or symbolically linked to the body of sweet water over which Enki exercised his powers. As stated earlier, M. Krebernik has argued for a possibility to see in early Abzu-names ideas related to birth. The Abzu would then be a body of water which the unborn child and the mother had to cross.[874] Few lugal-names, however, can be connected to such a crossing.

---

[868] This implement or architectural detail is discussed by P. Michalowski, MesCiv 1, 102, note to ll. 420, and 421–424, with refs.

[869] The determinative is definitely part of the word as is indicated by the direct loan into Akkadian, see CAD G s.v. *gišburru*. The fact that the same word was used for a tool of exorcising could indicate that the ĝiš-bur ornament served an apotropaic function similar to lamassu-figures in later Assyrian palaces.

[870] Compare H. Limet, *Anthroponymie*, 333: “Le roi est messager.” W. G. Lambert, *OrNS* 64 (1995), 136, proposes “vizier” as possible translation. It is not clear if that sense is applicable in this or other names of the same type.

[871] Interpretation diffcult. The name could also be taken to mean ‘the lugal is instructed.’ The verb na–de$_5$ was examined by W. Sallaberger, *Fs Klein*, 229–253. He concluded the investigation by proposing an original meaning “to clear, to clarify,” and a set of derived meanings, including “to clarify, enlighten, explain,” and “to clarify, consecrate, purify.”

[872] E.g. en-Kul-aba$_4$-si ‘the en is just right for Kulaba,’ UET 2, PN no. 292f. (ED I-II Ur), given as: “le en réside à Kulaba,” D. O. Edzard, CRRA 19, 144. On inspeciton of a photograph of *IAS* 504 r.1, entry ⌜x⌝ Kul-aba^{ki}, the damaged sign can not be read ⌜lugal⌝, but the remark notes a locus connected with the transactions recorded on the obverse of the text. Compare the remark Bar^{ki} on the reverse of *IAS* 510. In *IAS* 505 r. i’ 4’–5’, lugal, Ereš$_2^{ki}$ refers to the north Mesopotamian town of the same name. See D. R. Frayne, RIME 1, 375; and ibid., *JCSMS* 4 (2009), 47, for the locations of some of these towns on the northern half of the floodplain.

[873] E.g. the ED IIIb Girsu PN nin-e$_2$-Unug^{ki}-ga-nir-ĝal$_2$, V. V. Struve, *Onomastika*, 141 s.v.

[874] AOAT 296, 46, w. ref. to a survey on later incantations pertaining to this theme.

The variant writings of the names lugal-ma$_2$-gur$_8$-e(-si) and lugal-kar-e-si, are two possibilities,[875] but they remain unclear as to referent. None of the early variants mentioning the Abzu is found in more than two cities. Names such as lugal-abzu-si $^{(a1)}$ 'the lugal is just right for the Abzu,' from ED IIIb Nippur, and lugal-abzu-a-gal-di $^{(a\geq1)}$ 'the lord is prominent in the Abzu,'[876] featuring locative marker -a,[877] both indicate a presence at, or an involvement with, the Abzu. For lugal-abzu-a-gal-di the referent is more than likely to have been a deity.[878] Nothing can be said with certainty about the abbreviation lugal-abzu $^{(a2)}$.[879] Provided that the Abzu mentioned in these names was identical with the one found at Eridu, at least a superficial connection exists with the ED IIIb Girsu lugal-Eridu^{ki}-še$_3$ $^{(a1)}$ 'the lugal ... to(wards) Eridu.'[880] This name attests to early mythological and, perhaps, cultic contacts between Girsu and Eridu. In later times, traditions are known which involve journeys, some perhaps only mythological, some no doubt undertaken by the divinities in the form of their statues to visit their kin elsewhere in Sumer.[881]

Eridu was hardly inhabited in historical times, and thus never held political sway over other cities during the times from which documentation survives, so in whatever capacity it appears in personal names, its function as a religious center of one of the most important deities in the pantheon is likely to have been a crucial factor. It appears in administrative texts from ED IIIb Ur where a lugal is said to have provided sacrifices for the city, no doubt intending the main sanctuary there.[882] Cities and towns which appear

---

[875] See above, section 3.1.5.3, p. 135f.

[876] See G. J. Selz, *Götterwelt*, 152 w. fn. 637 for other names construed with gal–di.

[877] Compare abbreviations lugal-abzu-a $^{(a2)}$, and lugal-abzu-da $^{(a2)}$. Abzu with comitative -da also attested in a few other names, abzu:da, UET 2 112 o. v' 5'' (ED I-II Ur); ama-ab-zu-da, OIP 58, 291 no. 3 ii 1 (ED IIIb Tutub); M. Powell, *HUCA* 49, 58 no. 25 o. iv 1' (ED IIIb Umma-Zabala). The comitative seems malplaced in connection with an inanimate such as Abzu. Is Abzu-da, then, to be understood as metonym for Enki, taking on the grammatical form of its metonymic correspondence?

[878] See discussion by G. Marchesi, HANE/S 10, 72f. fn. 381; and compare the name of an UN:gal of ED IIIb Girsu, en-abzu-a-tum$_2$ 'the en befits the Abzu'; and en-da-gal-di, e.g. HSS 3 18 o. vii 11, from the same time and place.

[879] As indicated by A. Alberti & F. Pomponio, StPohl SM 13, 106, the name is abbreviated. Writing: ki lugal-abzu-še$_3$ in UET 2 suppl. 47 o. i 4 does not indicate a genitive compound, as opposed to the byname of Enki from the ED IIIa on, for which, see M. Krebernik, *RlA* 7 (1987–90), 110: "Lugal-abzu," "König des Abzu."

[880] H. Limet, *Anthroponymie*, 173: "Le roi vers Eridu ..." Compare the name of a palm tree planted by UruKAgina during his third year as lugal, lugal-Eridu^{ki}-še$_3$-nu-kuš$_2$ 'the lugal is one who is untiring with regards to Eridu,' *CIRPL* Ukg. 36; and the Ur III Girsu FPN me-Eridu^{ki}-ta, e.g. *TUT* 150 o. i 18.

[881] See the discussion of compositions involving divine journeys in A. J. Ferrara, StPohl SM 2, 1–11, with many references. Note also J. Bauer, *NABU* 2005/31, on a possible journey by Ningirsu to Nippur. Ur III Girsu names composed with Nina^{ki} in a few cases have the ablative -ta, e.g. *HLC* 3 381 o. 3. Neither of these name types are attested from the Sargonic period.

[882] See G. Visicato & A. Westenholz, *Kaskal* 2, 59f. nos 7 and 8; and discussion, p. 63f.

in conjunction with lugal in names are otherwise of various importance and size. The city, or state, of Lagaš, is mentioned in a few lugal-names primarily from the Lagaš state, but also from outside.[883] Nippur appears to be part of an ED IIIa Šuruppag lugal-name, and is definitely part of the name of a merchant appearing in an ED IIIb text from that same city.[884] The importance of Nippur in later times, figuring in epithets of Ur III royalty as synonymous with acceptance by Enlil, may offer a key to understanding the name.[885] Ur, the city of the Sumerian Moon God, is found in the names of two persons from Sargonic times.[886] The important cultic center of Ninḫursaĝ in Keš, somewhere in the region of Adab, is mentioned in the name of at least three people, from ED IIIb Girsu and Sargonic Adab, and is likely to refer to the human lugal.[887] To these should probably be added EZEM×GAL^{ki} a southern city or town in the area between Lagaš and Ur, which also figures in such names from these two cities. The location in this general area is corroborated by external sources, but the name of this urban center, along with its significance meriting inclusion in the onomasticon, is at present unknown.[888] Besides Keš, it is at present difficult to assign a referent to other cities appearing in the lugal-onomasticon, as both divine figures and human rulers may be connected with some of these cities, it is at present not easy to assign referents to this group of names.

---

[883] Variants: lugal-Lagaš $^{(a1)}$, from ED I-II Ur; lugal-Lagaš$^{!}$(ŠIR.BUR) $^{(a1)}$, from CS Girsu; and lugal-Lagaš$^{ki\ (a2)}$, from the ED IIIb Lagaš state. H. Steible, *CollAn* 7 (2008), 104 fn. 33 sees the ED I-II Ur reference not as a PN but as testimony that Lagaš had a lugal by that time.

[884] Lugal-Nibru$^{ki\ (a2)}$. Collation of *TSŠ* 627 indicated by H. Steible, *CollAn* 7 (2008), 93, 95 fn. 14, and 96. Steible seems to regard the writing lugal-Nibru^{ki} not as a name, but as referring to a lugal from outside of Šuruppag, partly due to other officials from Nippur in the same text. Steible indicates, *op. cit.*, 93, that lugal and Nibru^{ki} appear in the same line. This is also indirectly supported by Jestin's copy of *TSŠ* 627 in that the sign representing the amount of thread (SI.NU×U) handed out to lugal-Nibru^{ki} appears next to Nibru^{ki}, and hence the sign lugal was placed above the E$_2$ in Nibru^{ki}. As can easily be seen, all other GN in this text appear in lines separate from the titles they qualify. Thus lugal-Nibru^{ki} is most likely a PN.

[885] See e.g. *CIRPL* Ent. 32 i 4''–8'', where Enmetena states he had been granted an insignium (probably scepter, a small sign like PA is likely) of great authority from Enlil in Nippur.

[886] In lugal-Urim$_2$^{ki}-e $^{(a1)}$, from CS Adab; and lugal-Urim$_x$(AB.URI$_3$)$^{ki\ (a1)}$, CS Unknown. H. Limet, *Anthroponymie*, has the former variant as abbreviation of original lugal-Urim^{ki}-e-ki-âĝa$_2$, giving a translation on p. 171: "Le roi qui aime la ville d'Ur"; 266: "Le roi qui aime Ur." Compare honomymous DN, attributed by W. G. Lambert to Nanna/Su'en, *RlA* 7 (1987–90), 153 s.v. "Lugal-Urim." The DN is with all probability a genitive compound, the PN, according to the writing, is not. See also *lugal-AB.URI$_3$.KI.

[887] lugal-Keš$_3$$^{ki\ (a\geq3)}$, probably with J. Bauer, *Annäherungen* 1, 512, to be interpreted as: "der König (ist nach) Keš (gegangen)." The relation of the human lugal to Keš is seen for instance in the ED IIIa version of Keš Temple Hymn found at Abū Ṣalābīḫ, for which, see the editions of R. D. Biggs, *ZA* 61 (1971); and D. O. Edzard, *OrNS* 43 (1974), 103–113.

[888] The ligature EZEM×GAL might also be dugin$_2$(EZEM×MIR), for which, see J. Bauer, *WO* 18 (1987), 5f.; or EZEM×SIG$_7$, with proposed readings kisig$_2$ or ud(i)nim, discussed by P. Steinkeller, *NABU* 1990/132; and see also R. Borger, AOAT 305, 309, note to no. 281. A damaged writing from ED IIIb Ur lugal-EZEM.GAL-[x] could contain an alternative writing of the name of this GN.

Cultic locations, such as temples, are the focus of a further handful of names, for instance Tiraš in the Lagaš state,[889] and the temple of Dumuzi in Bad-tibira, the Emuš.[890] The latter was, as has already been described above, section 3.1.5.3, the destination of a journey made by an unknown lugal, as recounted in an ED IIIa literary text. The lugal upon arrival presented firstling offerings in the Emuš. Smaller, less important local shrines may hide behind some other names, like for instance an installation called the Muš$_3$-bar, which ought to have been situated in the Lagaš area due both to the archive in which the name was found and other corroborating evidence.[891] A temple by the name of E$_2$-maš occurs in a lugal-name found at Sargonic Adab, but a building by that name is otherwise best attested in Ur III Umma texts.[892] For all these names a divine referent is the most likely.

A number of names refer to installations in or around the main temple area. The idea of a place in which the lugal served his cultic functions was later on called the KI.LUGAL.GUB, loosely 'place (where the) lugal stands (in service).'[893] This "place" is likely referred to also during the pre–Ur III period in a royal name of the dynasty of Uruk, which can be restored from its variants as *lugal-ki-gub(-a)-ni-še$_3$-du$_7$-du$_7$ 'the lugal is the one best suited for the place (where) he serves.'[894] The variants, found from Nippur in

---

[889] lugal-Ti-ra-aš$_2$-še$_3$ $^{(a\geq 2)}$. It is uncertain if the sign -še$_3$ represents the terminative or a phonetic complement /š/ plus the loc.-term. -e, but compare the discussion on lugal-Eridu^{ki}-še$_3$, above, p. 153. A possible further attestation is noted by W. Farber, *JCS* 26 (1974), 198 fn. 12. Other PNN referring to the temple Tiraš are ED IIIb Girsu genitival PNN Ti-ra-aš$_2$-a, *DP* 1/2 138 o. i 4; and ur-Ti-ra-aš$_2$, e.g. VS 27 13 o. 3; emendate UET 3 1411 o. 2 (*ma-ti-ra-aš$_2$), accordingly. The entry: ... Ti-ra-aš$_2$-še$_3$, ba-de$_6$ in *DP* 2/1 163 o. iv 10–r. i 1 (Ukg. ensi$_2$) probably is an abbreviation of the present name. Ur III attestations are also known, see H. Limet, *Anthroponymie*, 474. For *lu$_2$-Ti-ra-aš$_2$-še$_3$ (so on tablet; on seal lugal-Ti-⌜ra⌝-[aš$_2$-e]), *UNT* 64 (BM 14752, translit. only) o. 4, compare H. H. Figulla, *Catalogue of the Babylonian Tablets in the British Museum* 1, 229, who reads lugal also on the tablet.

[890] The variants are: lugal-E$_2$-muš$_3$ $^{(a1)}$, found exclusively at ED IIIb Girsu; lugal-E$_2$-muš$_3$-e $^{(a1)}$, and lugal-E$_2$-muš$_3$-še$_3$ $^{(a1)}$, both attested in the CS Mesag archive. For the genitive construct used as a divine epithet, see generally W. G. Lambert, *RlA* 7 (1987–90), 137 s.v. "Lugal-Emuša." Much information is found in M. Lambert, *RSO* 47 (1973), 2–4; 6–8 (who argued for a development of muš$_3$ < munus); and G. J. Selz, *Götterwelt*, 161f. An OB list of PNN from Ur has the phonetic writing ⌜lugal⌝-E$_2$-muš-e, *UET* 7 77. For the temple E$_2$-muš$_3$(-kalam-ma), see A. R. George, MesCiv 5, 129: 829.

[891] The name lugal-Muš$_3$-bar-ki-aĝa$_2$ $^{(a1)}$, was the name of an ED IIIb gudu$_4$-priest of the deity Eš$_3$-ir-nun. Without parallel formations indicating loc. -a or loc.-term. -e, the agency in relation to the predicate ki-aĝa$_2$, remains obscure. The interpretations 'the lugal is one who loves the Mušbar-temple,' or: 'the lugal is beloved in the Mušbar-temple,' are both possible. See discussion of *lugal-dam-me-ki-aĝ$_2$.

[892] The name figures as lugal-E$_2$-maš-e $^{(a2)}$. Compare the name ur-E$_2$-maš, H. Limet, *Anthroponymie*, 543, for Ur III Umma attestations.

[893] For later KI.LUGAL.GUB see discussion by E. Flückiger-Hawker, OBO 166, 221, on Urnamma C l. 13.

[894] I generally concur with the discussion about lexical matters by H. J. Nissen, *Königsfriedhof*, 123 fn. 358, but still prefer reading DU as gub, not ĝen. My reading thus to all

the north down to Ur in the south, regularly discard one or two elements: lugal-ki-gub-ni-du$_7$-du$_7$ [(a1)],[895] lugal-ki-ni-du$_7$-du$_7$ [(a1)], and lugal-ki-ni-še$_3$-du$_7$-du$_7$ [(a1)],[896] make for the assured writings. The components ki or gub could potentially be done away with in the process of abbreviation without losing the sense of the name.[897] And economizing with dimensional markers, in this case -še$_3$, is common.[898] The writings in which gub is preserved all come from inscriptions authored by Lugalkigubnišedudu himself or by his son. If the reference to KI.GUB is correctly understood, it could implicate that *lugal-ki-gub-ni-še$_3$-du$_7$-du$_7$ refers to activities of the human king.

The stability of the foundations of important buildings were considered crucial for their proper functioning. The event of founding a temple or other central building and to leave inscriptions or precious objects like figurines at the base of the building commemorating this fact, seems to have been a focus of Mesopotamian rulers in general.[899] Whether names invoking the temen 'foundation,'[900] referred to the architectural basis for a building, or to the concept of benefitting from the stability of important civic institutions, is not obvious from the names. The temen is only rarely attested in royal inscriptions.[901]

A word which in the ED period appears with some regularity in personal names from all over Sumer, was sometimes used as synonym of temen: ki-gal, as in lugal-ki-gal-la [(a≥12)], with variants.[902] In Sargonic times its use seems for the most part to have been limited to Nippur. There is as of yet no compelling reason to see in this term a synonym for 'grave' or a euphemism

---

ends and purposes concurs with that of the original editor of the first known inscriptions by this lugal, H. V. Hilprecht, e.g. in BE 1/2, 8–9, and passim.

[895] Compare E. Sollberger & J.-R. Kupper, *IRSA*, 318: Lugal-kigine-dudu "roi qui fonce vers le lieu où il va." Name read by T. Jacobsen, AS 11, 172 fn. 8: *lugal-ki-ni-še$_{13}$-du$_7$-du$_7$ by means of "transposition of the signs GUB and NI." Discussions of previous readings can be found in J. Bauer, *AoN* 21 (1985), 12f.

[896] Compare E. Sollberger & J.-R. Kupper, *IRSA*, 319: Lugal-kiniše-dudu "roi qui fonce vers son but."

[897] See lugal-gub-ba-ni [(a≥5)] 'the lugal … (where) he serves,' from Nippur, and the Mesag and CS Girsu archives; for short lugal-gub-ba [(a1)], a variant found only at ED IIIb-ES Adab.

[898] Perhaps this amissability indicates that the phonetic nature of the terminative after a vowel was rather /(e)š/ than /še/.

[899] See S. Dunham, *RA* 80 (1986), 31–64 for the usage of the word temen and the Akkadian loan *tem(m)ennu*. On the prerogative of building in ED royal inscriptions on statues, see some examples in G. Marchesi & N. Marchetti, MesCiv 14, 147f.

[900] Compare the ED IIIb-ES names lugal-temen [(a≥2)], and lugal-temen-na [(a1)], with the entry en-ne$_2$ temen-na in BiMes 3 27 r. ii 4 (=28 r. i 4), and see G. Marchesi's comments on this composition, *StEL* 16 (1999), 15–17. The Ur III Girsu writing (igi) en-temen-na(-še$_3$), MVN 7 447 o. 3', and r. 4 (translit. only), is singular and rather uncertain. H. Limet, *Anthroponymie*, 209, interpreted the fuller writing lugal-temen-na as a genitive: "Roi du temenos."

[901] The references are collected in FAOS 6, 330 s.v.

[902] Besides lugal-ki-gal-la, found from the ED IIIa down to Sargonic times, the variants cover lugal-ki-gal [(a≥2)], from the ED IIIa-b, and lugal-ki-gal-gal-la [(a1)], attested only at ED IIIa Šuruppag. The extra gal compared to the previous name is inexplicable in this connection.

for the realm of the dead in the early periods, for which meaning later Akkadian sources sometimes used the loanword *kigallu*.[903] However, a building inscription by an ensi$_2$ of Umma, Lu$_2$-^{d}Utu, from LS or Gutian times, contains a dedication to the goddess Ereškigal, who, it might be said, embodied the idea of the Great Beyond 'the lady (of) the Great Earth.'[904] The inscription provides her with the epithet 'the lady of the place of sunset,' i.e. the west, and then goes on to state that the temple was built facing the east, 'where destinies are determined.'[905] D. Katz showed in her treatment of this inscription that the realm of the dead in Sumerian cosmological thought was normally not associated with the western horizon, but with the kur 'mountainland.'[906] Compared to the temen-names, names with ki-gal as second component exhibit a richer inventory of appellatives.[907] However, from the ED IIIa onwards, lugal is the appellative most often associated with this ki-gal, and in the majority of cases ki-gal is marked by an -a, which most probably expresses the locative -a.[908] The exact meaning, which would account for the evolution of this locus, is at present hard to pinpoint. Texts dating back to the Ur III and OB periods often have this word as signifying a pedestal or podium, though sometimes that equation becomes a bit forced.[909]

The courtyard, kisal, was another location popular in personal names. Two different predicates are known for this object: lugal-kisal-a-gub [(a1)] 'the lugal stands in the courtyard,' and lugal-kisal-si [(a≥6)] 'the lugal is just right for the courtyard.'[910] Since the latter is the more common writing, and since the verb si takes the loc.-term. suffix, the abbreviation lugal-kisal [(a≥2)],[911] with all

[903] This interpretation was the reason for H. Limet's translation "Le roi des enfers," in *Anthroponymie*, 263. It is hard to see the name ki-gal-du$_{10}$, *IAS* 502 o. ii 2, from ED IIIa Abū Ṣalābīḫ, as meaning "the grave is a happy (place)." For a collection of references to discussions on ki-gal, see J. Klein, *RA* 80 (1986), 3 fn. 14. For the Akkadian usage of logographic ki-gal, see A. Westenholz, *AfO* 23 (1970), 27–31. For Akkadian *kigallu*, see the entries in *AHw* and *CAD* s.v.

[904] See, e.g. G. J. Selz, *Götterwelt*, 254 w. fn. 1218, though the genitival nature of Ereškigal's name, as well as the other names containing ki-gal might be put in question.

[905] YOS 1 14 1–9: ^{d}Ereš-ki-gal, nin ki u$_4$ šu$_4$-ra, Lu$_2$-^{d}Utu, ensi$_2$, Umma^{ki}-ke$_4$, nam-ti-la-ni-še$_3$, ki ^{d}Utu-e$_3$, ki nam tar-re-da, e$_2$ mu-na-du$_3$.

[906] D. Katz, *The Image of the Netherworld in the Sumerian Sources*, 352–355.

[907] The largest wealth of names composed with ki-gal is found in the ED IIIa period, represented by more than a dozen varieties, and then settles at just over a handful for each of the main remaining periods of the 3rd millennium. For a brief list of different ki-gal-names, see F. Pomponio, *StEL* 8 (1991), 144, though a few readings should be emendated.

[908] This against M. Krebernik, AOAT 296, 32, who saw in this -a a morphological marker of abbreviation. All of Krebernik's examples save the last represent loci, and the last should rather be read lugal-uĝ$_3$-ĝe$_{26}$, and does not belong to this group.

[909] See for instance D. O. Edzard's remarks on the Keš Temple Hymn, *OrNS* 43 (1974), 110, note to l. 87. The line is not included in the archaic version from Abū Ṣalābīḫ.

[910] Compare E. Sollberger & J.-R. Kupper, *IRSA*, 319: "roi qui emplit le parvis." Information on some persons with this name is found with H. Neumann, *AoF* 8 (1981), 80f., and passim. The name formed part of the name of a stele erected by Gudea in Girsu, Cyl. A xxiii 9.

[911] Following H. Limet, *Anthroponymie*, 207, seeing a truncated name: "Le roi … le parvis."

likelihood represents shortening of kisal(-e-si), as suggested by later parallels.[912]

Ĝir$_2$-nun, a stretch of road located to the east of the city-center of Girsu is mentioned in a couple of local names from around the CS period. The names are never provided with a predicate, but the road ought to have filled some role in local religious practice.[913] It could equally well refer to a divinity as to a human ruler and his connection with this landmark.

A handful of names referring to cultic loci are rather generally formulated. Some seem to refer to specific,[914] others to generic locations.[915] The lack of parallels makes attribution to a divinity or a human for these names troublesome, though the safest is to regard them collectively - awaiting evidence to the contrary - as referring to deities.

---

912 Here, a traditional reading of the name has been chosen due to the appearance in the latter text (o. 3 and 14) of the PN ur-ĝi$_6$-par$_4$. Thus, the reading ĝipar$_x$(KISAL), suggested and proven in a number of contexts, see in general J. Bauer, *BiOr* 46 (1989), 639, is not applicable in this name. See also the unpublished ED IIIb-ES name lugal-kisal-le-si referred to by G. Marchesi, *OrNS* 73 (2004), 174 (collated from photo); and strike the Ur III name *en-ĝipar$_x$(KISAL)-re-si referred to *op. cit.* 175. The latter was published by T. Ozaki & M. Sigrist, BPOA 1, as no. 241, and the name in o. 4 is given as en-kisal-e-si; for which, compare the other Ur III writings en-kisal-e-«erasure»-si, UET 3 864 o. 5' (Ur); and lugal-kisal-e-si, S. Levy & P. Artzi, *Atīqōt* 4 (1965), pl. 6 no. 30 o. 6 and r. 3 (Umma).

913 Variant forms (?) are: lugal-Ĝir$_2$-nun (a1), and lugal-Ĝir$_2$-nun-ne$_2$ (a≥1). See W. Heimpel's reconstruction of Gudea's Eninnu with the Ĝirnun-road leading to a weir and bridge crossing the waterway to the east of the main tells of Girsu, *JCS* 48 (1996), 23, fig. 4. Does the name then refer to activities toward the east which entailed a (ritual) crossing of the water to reach some structure outside of Girsu, or does it hint at (martial) movement further east toward Elam? Compare the name of a statue of LugalANda, *CIRPL* Ukg. 9, iii' 3': lugal-AN-da-nu-ḫuĝ-ĝa-˹Ĝir$_2$-nun˺-še$_3$-nu-[kuš$_2$] "LugalANdanuḫunga ermüdet sich nicht hinsichtlich des 'Hohen Weges,'" following G. J. Selz, *Götterwelt*, 19, with discussion.

914 Such names include: lugal-E$_2$.DU$_8$-si (a1), from ED I-II Ur; and lugal-E$_2$.NUN-si (a≥2/°1) 'the lugal fills the reed-sanctuary.' The translation depends on J. Krecher's rendering of VE238: E$_2$.NUN = *šutukkum*, "wohl ... eine Rohrhütte für Riten," *Bilinguismo*, 160. For the E$_2$.NUN, with likely reading agrun, see generally *PSD* A/3, 65–68, esp. 67, 5.2.2–3. The name is found at ED I-II Ur and ED IIIa Šuruppag. Compare the discussion of an E$_2$.NUN of Ningal at Ur, P. Michalowski, MesCiv 1, 105f. note to l. 477. A divinity ^{d}Lugal-agrun-na is found in a few god lists from the OB period on, M. Krebernik, *RlA* 7 (1987–90), 110 s.v. "Lugal-agrunna."

915 Like for instance lugal-ti-ma-nu$_2$ (a1) 'the lugal lies down in the *sanctuary*,' which has the appearance of a phonetic spelling of itima, later ĜA$_2$×MI, Akk. *kiṣṣu*; for the loss of initial i- in (i)tima, see comment to lugal-iti-da, below. Other names of the same general type are lugal-uzug$_x$(AN.ZAG)-še$_3$ (a4) 'the lugal ... *towards* the cella (?),' from the ED IIIa-b; and lugal-za$_3$-ge-si (a2) 'the lugal is just right for the sanctuary.' The interpretation of the locus as sanctuary follows W. H. Ph. Römer, *SKIZ*, 134:200, transl. p. 142, and note to the same line on p. 196. An ED IIIa variant is lugal-za$_3$-si (a1), and other short forms are lugal-za$_3$ (a1), and lugal-za$_3$-ge (a1), both from the Sargonic period. The parallel uru-za$_3$-ge-si, MVN 3 45 r. ii 2 (ES Isin or Nippur?) indicates that whatever action the 'filling' entailed, it could be done by a collective. Hence, a translation of si as 'to be just right for' probably better captures the notions of the verb, and the latter name can be given as 'the city is just right for (having) the sanctuary.'

3.1.7 Qualitative-descriptive

The seventh heading gathers short statements concerned with inner or outer qualities of the lugal as trademark traits or notes on his physical appearance. They are not specific enough to warrant attributing the name to another heading. A large portion of the names is phrase names. In many cases there are hints at qualities or actions which could be attributed to one of the former categories. The names relevant to this category have been divided into the following subsections:

- Favour
- Physical constitution
- Physical strength and prowess
- Aptitude for combat
- Fame and good reputation
- Likeness and equation
- Uniqueness and aloofness
- Similes and kindness
- Justice and dependability
- Light, brilliance and visual phenomena

The most well-attested name is one which links the lugal to the cycle of the month, lugal-iti-da and is most probably a name which refers to the Moon God. About 40 persons are attested as bearing that name. It is found as far north as Kiš, but is mostly attested in Nippur and southwards.

	ED I-II	ED IIIa-ED IIIb	ED IIIb-ES	ES-MS	MS-CS
Adab		5	21	6	21
Akkade				1	
Girsu		3	46		25
Isin		3	5	1	2
Kiš		1			
Lagaš			4	1	4
Marad		1	2		
Mari			1		
Mesag					3
Nippur		1	16	2	18
Šuruppag		16			
Umma-Zabala			16	9	25
Ur	3		3		1
Uruk		1	1		
Unknown		4	1	5	9

Fig. 8: Name-bearers, 3.1.7, Qualitative-descriptive. Estimated minimum number of individual name-bearers.

Fig. 8, above, records the distribution of 287 persons, the estimated minimum number of people bearing 94 variants of names of this category and the different cities with which they are connected.

3.1.7.1 Favour

The lugal as selected or chosen by gods has already been discussed above. Other names, also, focus on praiseworthy attributes of the lugal and his elevated position, such as lugal-a-nun (a2) 'the lugal is a *princely offspring*,' from the ED IIIb and Sargonic Umma and Adab area. The human lugal as one who has received a stamp of approval by gods or men is likely to be the idea behind lugal-mi$_2$-zi-du$_{11}$-ga (a1) 'the lugal is praised,'[916] with variants.[917] The same can be said about a MS-CS Nippur name, lugal-nam-zi-tar-ra (a1) 'the lugal is one (whose) fate is reliably determined.'[918] In both these names, zi has been taken as adverbial complement portraying the lugal as one whose fate is decided in keep with the divine regulations of the world.[919] A divinity is probably intended as the referent of lugal-aja$_2$-da (a1) 'the lugal (is one honoured) with the father,'[920] where aja$_2$ could perhaps refer to An or Enlil.

More opaque is the ED and ES Adab and Isin name lugal-numun-zi (a≥3). Here, zi could be interpreted as an adjective in an elliptic clause missing the verb, or as a participle in a transitive clause with numun serving as object.[921] Based on later literary examples, a set of interpretations may be proposed: 'the lugal (is) a reliable offspring,'[922] or '... (loves) the reliable offspring.'[923]

[916] Interpretation following M.-L. Thomsen, *Mesopotamia* 10, 301. For a passage indicating divine approval, see, e.g., Urnamma C l. 22–23 (approval by Enlil and Enki). The reading was suggested already by E. Sollberger, *BiOr* 16 (1959), 117. Provenience from Adab proposed by A. Falkenstein, *ZA* 55 (1962), 30 fn. 114. The shape of ZI suggests Adab or another site close to Nippur, but the small, rounded tablet is written in an at times rather sloppy hand. M. Powell, *HUCA* 49 (1978), 16f. suggests Zabala as probable provenience, but he also admits there is not much in support of this.

[917] lugal-mi$_2$ (a2), from MS-CS Umma and Girsu; lugal-mi$_2$-du$_{11}$-ga (a1), from CS Adab. The latter also appears in OB lists of PNN, see E. Chiera, PBS 11/3, 210, no. 217.

[918] Once lugal-nam-zi-tar (a1) and very likely referring to the same person.

[919] Compare Lugalzagesi's wish at the end of his Nippur inscription, BE 1/2 87 iii 32–33.: nam sa$_6$-ga, mu-tar-re-eš$_2$-a, šu na-mu-da-ni-bal!(TI)-e-ne 'the propitious fate which they have determined for me, may they not turn it against me.' A variant has correct form of BAL.

[920] Compare ED IIIb Girsu name aja$_2$-da-gal-di, V. V. Struve, *Onomastika*, 12 s.v.

[921] Writings -zi-da-kam and -zi-de$_3$ (erg.) in BIN 8 211 indicate that zi represents expected zid, '(to be) right, true, faithful.' Related names include ama-numun-zi, V. V. Struve, *Onomastika*, 16 (ED IIIb Girsu); ama-še-numun-⌜zi⌝ (MAD 4 73 o. 3, CS Umma); and plain numun-zi (TMH 5 14 o. i 4', ED IIIb Nippur).

[922] Compare, for instance, the OB and later royal self-designations (*zēr šarrūtim*, roughly '(of) royal descent') quoted by *CAD* Z s.v. *zēru* 4b, and Lipit-Ištar A l. 1: lugal mi$_2$ du$_{10}$-ga ša$_3$-ta numun zi-me-en 'I am a respected king, ever since *birth* a reliable offspring,' e.g. *ISET* 1, pl. 46 (Ni 4451), 51 (Ni 9696), 128 (Ni 9923) o. i 1, with Akkadian glosses to zi-me-en: *ki-nu a-na-*[*ku*] (Ni 9696).

A few names contain exclamations of praise. They may be situational, and potentially they refer to circumstances surrounding expectancy or birth. They include the affirmative phrase name lugal-na-nam (a1) 'a lugal (he is) indeed!,'[924] and lugal-za-me (a≥1) 'you are (a) lord!.'[925] Other formations that have bearing on the recognition of a referent as lugal is a type featuring writings of the reflexive pronoun ni_2-te and me-te '(own) self.' A few different variants are seemingly limited to the Girsu and Umma areas, all with a likely translation 'a lord unto himself.'[926] Two CS Umma writings, lugal-ne-te-na (a1), and lugal-ni_2-te-na (a1) may denote the same person.[927] In Girsu and ED IIIb Umma on the other hand, the writings favour an initial /m/: lugal-me-te-na (a2),[928] and lugal-mete(TE+ME)-na (a≥1). The idea behind these names may be that some unknown referent took unilateral action to ensure a positive outcome of a situation. An ED IIIa parallel, in use at Šuruppag and elsewhere, niĝir-me-te-na,[929] might even be suggested to describe the infant itself, 'he is his own herald,' which could refer to a very noisy baby. Quite possibly, the name lugal-ra-tum_2, discussed above, section 3.1.6.2, may be compared to some of the aforementioned names.

[923] See, e.g., Gudea Cyl. B xxiii 19–20: diĝir ama-zu dNin-sun_2-na ama-gan numun zi-da, numun-e ki-$a\hat{g}_2$-am_3 "your mother goddess is Ninsuna, the mother who bore healthy offspring and who loves (her) offspring," following D. O. Edzard, RIME 3/1.1.7.CylB.

[924] Parallel forms to this name are few in number; from the earlier periods dBa-u_2-na-nam and lu_2-na-nam predominate, see V. V. Struve, *Onomastika*, 28; 117. For the interpretation chosen here, see the Ur III PN lu_2-bi-na-nam "he is indeed their master!," for short lu_2-bi. See refs. with H. Limet, *Anthroponymie*, 452 s.v.v. More distant is the variant PN $\hat{g}a_2$-ka-na-nam-ḫe_2-ti from ED IIIb Girsu, *DP* 2/1 230 r. iv 12 (all other attestations lack -na-, V. V. Struve, *Onomastika*, 68), "(because) he/she is verily mine, let him/her live! (?)."

[925] See, e.g. nin-za-me, V. V. Struve, *Onomastika*, 157 (saĝ sa_{10} of Bau, ED IIIb Girsu). It is not clear if theophore constructs like dNin-$\hat{g}ir_2$-su-za-me, *DPA* 44 r. 1 (PUL 52, CS Umma (?), correct reading pointed out by J.-M. Durand, *NABU* 1995/50), and other names of the same type correspond exactly to lugal-za-me. Note discussion by H. Limet, *Anthroponymie*, 75 w. fn. 2, on the gloss to the name dNanna-za-me-en in an OB list of PNN, *lu-u₂ a-na-ku*, *PBS* 11/1 7 o. i 8.

[926] B. Alster, *JCS* 26 (1974), 178–180 argued in favour of mete as combining two lexical items, one of which is an early writing of ni_2-te, largely corresponding to Akk. *ramanum*, 'self.' The /e/ vowel also shows, e.g. in Gudea Cyl. B xviii 16: ne-te-ni bi_2-zu. Compare other names with the component mete(TE+ME), collected by G. J. Selz, *Götterwelt*, 104 fn. 378.

[927] Both texts in which these names figure feature a KA-ku_3 dumu Šeš-tur. The writing is found also in Ur III Umma, e.g., TCL 5 5674 o. ii 24, r. v 16. See remarks by H. Limet, *Anthroponymie*, 175 with fn. 1: "Le roi par lui même …," contemplating the possible origin of this name in the genre of religious hymns.

[928] One example of this name, M. de J. Ellis, *JCS* 31 (1979), 42f. no. 7 o. v 13' has half a line divider inside a case with the names ĝ iš-$ša_3$ and lugal-me-te-na. Two names have been decided upon due to the problematic syntax resulting from reading them as one. Compare BIN 8 82 o. iv 5: [ĝ]iš-$ša_3$ [(x?)]-me-te-na.

[929] E.g. *WF* 18 r. v 11; in *TSŠ* 292 o. i 3', denoting a person from Uruk. Interpreted differently by L. Sassmannshausen, *BagM* 26 (1995), 192: "Der Herold des Fundamentes? (ist er)."

3.1.7.2 Physical constitution

A few names refer to physical traits of the lugal, and are not directly tied to strength or the exercise of power. These names are mostly concentrated to Girsu texts of the Sargonic period. One of them, known also from the ED IIIb, lugal-igi-ḫuš (a≥4) 'the lugal (is) *angry-looking*,' has clear links to the divine cast surrounding Ninĝirsu.[930] Another name, lugal-igi-sa_6 (a1) 'the lugal (is) *friendly-looking*,'[931] appears to be the direct opposite of the former name.[932] But it is also possible to translate these names as something along the lines of: 'the lugal is frightening to behold,' and 'the lugal is pleasing (to) the eye.' At any rate, the referents are most likely divine characters.

The name lugal-a_2-gur-ra (a3) is limited in time to the ED III.[933] The name is cryptic and, if understood correctly, it refers to a physical trait, 'the lugal (has) thick horns'; or the name might focus on the bodily stature of the lugal, 'the lugal is sturdy of frame.'[934] In the case of the first interpretation it is reasonable to see the name as referring to an unknown male divinity,[935] in the case of the second, both a human and a divine lugal might be intended.

The name lugal-ur_2-ra-ni (a1) 'the lugal ... his (her?) lap,' is perhaps too late in date to be included here, as it is found in a text which most likely dates to the Lagaš II dynasty.[936] The name became more popular in Ur III times.[937] The noun ur_2 'lap' might belong to another person or referent.

---

[930] A. Falkenstein, AnOr 30, 82: "Herr mit dem schrecklichen Blick," homonymous with a deified harp of Ningirsu. See also K. Tallqvist, *AGE*, 354 s.v. "Lugal-igi-ḫuš-am_3," translated: "König dessen Augen grimmig sind"; W. G. Lambert, *RlA* 7 (1987–90), 142 s.v. "Lugal-igiḫuš," given as: "The lord with the savage eye/face." Compare H. Limet, *Anthroponymie*, 168, 254: "Le roi dont l'œil est terrible"; 255: "Le roi à l'œil terrible." See also the šu-gar_3 igi ḫuš, of unknown meaning, mentioned in connection with Ningirsu's place of judgement in TH 251–252, and Å. Sjöberg's comments, TCS 3, 102. See further Sjöberg's comments on TH 399, about Numušda.

[931] H. Limet, *Anthroponymie*, 255f.: "Le roi à l'œil favorable." See the rare OB survival lu_2-igi-sa_6, sometimes spelled phonetically as lu_2-gi-sa_3, and the discussion by S. D. Walters, *Water for Larsa*, xx w. fn. 14.

[932] The Ur III form lugal-igi-sa_6-sa_6 is found both at Girsu and Umma, e.g. SAT 2 941 o. 3 (Umma, translit. only).

[933] One individual bearing this name in ED IIIb Nippur (lu:gal-a_2-gur-ra, OSP 1 121 r. ii 3', followed by da-da), is probably identical with the person given as da-da, dumu ⸢a_2-gur-ra⸣, TMH 5 63 o. ii 10–11).

[934] See discussion in *PSD* A/2, 72 s.v. a_2-gur, with reference to VE538.

[935] See references to a number of candidates with *PSD* A/2, 7, A_2 A, 2.3–2.4. Compare also the PN maš-gur-ra '(healthily) fattened lamb,' e.g. VS 14 159 o. vi 4.

[936] The date of the text, *RTC* 221, is debated; the YN mentions the building of the Eninnu of Ningirsu, and fits with building activities of both Ur-Bau and Gudea of the Lagaš II dynasty. The YN does not feature in RIME 3/1. Note, however, the the pre–Ur III names ur_2-ra-ni-$še_3$, R. M. Boehmer, *EGA*, pl. 13 no. 144; and ur_2-ra-ni-du_{10}(-ga), given by G. Visicato, *FTUM*, 27, as: "Her bosom is good."

[937] See, e.g., H. Limet, *Anthroponymie*, 475 s.v.; and 461 s.v. lugal-engar-ra-ni.

3.1.7.3 Physical strength and prowess

A small number of names relate to the lugal as a strong individual. The rare name lugal-kalag-ga $^{(a\geq 2)}$ 'the lugal is strong,'[938] is so far attested only at EDIIIb-ES Adab. It only has a few contemporary parallels, e.g. AN-kalag-ga.[939] An unexpected use of ni_3 in a function similar to an independent pronoun is present in the related name lugal-ni_3-kalag-ga $^{(a1)}$ 'the lugal *is strong*.'[940] This use of ni_3 is not without parallels in the onomasticon.[941] A powerful nature is implied by lugal-šu-maḫ $^{(a\geq 8)}$ 'the lugal (is) forceful,'[942] favoured in the Girsu and Umma region. The name may signal physical strength as well as strength in battle.[943] As the lugal is characterized as physically potent, a name like lugal-lirum $^{(a1)}$ 'the lugal is an athlete/wrestler,' sees him put his strength to use.[944] The iconographic motif of men grappling is a well-known one in Mesopotamian art, and figures both in sculpture in the round and on stone plaques.[945] The idealizing image of the power of the lugal as a constant trait comes to the fore in lugal-nu-šilig $^{(a3/°3)}$ 'the lugal is untiring,' limited to the ED III period. The motif, however, was

---

938 Similarly R. di Vito, StPohl SM 16, 64, 30.5a, 9. Compare epithet of Bilgames in a votive inscription on a macehead, M. Krebernik, *AoF* 21 (1994), 11–12 ll. 2 & 6: lugal KAL.NE-ra ... kalag-ga dumu ^{d}Nin-sun_2-ka-ra, "to (Bilgames), the ... lord, strong one, son of Ninsun." Also a byname of Nergal in later god list, K. Tallqvist, *AGE*, 354 s.v. "Lugal-kalag-ga," given as: "der mächtige König"; W. G. Lambert, *RlA* 7 (1987–90), 145 s.v. "Lugalkalaga," rendered as: "The mighty lord."

939 E.g. *DP* 1/2 117 o. i 11 (ED IIIb Girsu, Ukg. lugal Y 4); TMH 5 80 o. i 7 (reign of *Śarrukēn*); BIN 8 25 o. i 4 (ES-MS Umma). Compare PBS 9 11 r. 5: (e_2) AN-me-me-kalag-ga. Meme may be identical with the deity discussed by J. J. M. Roberts, *ESP*, 45. For Ur III parallels, see the forms attested with H. Limet, *Anthroponymie*, 258, 77, kal.

940 The name appears only in BIN 8 264, belonging to the Mesag archive. Only one out of the six persons listed, the sagi Ur-Inana, is known from other Mesag texts. Concerning the implement urudu ni_3-kalag-ga, Akk. *erû dannu* 'strong copper,' discussed by J. S. Cooper, *Angim*, 150–153, the combination of these two elements seem not to predate the OB period, so it is improbable that lugal-ni_3-kalag-ga refers to the name of a vanquished enemy of Ninurta.

941 Such as the Ur III ama-ni_3-kal-la 'a mother is something precious,' e.g. MVN 2 277 o. ii 15', attested in Umma and Girsu; and nin-ni_3-$ša_3$-An-na-ke_4-ba-du_{10} 'the lady is something (that) gladdens the heart of An,' *CTNMC* 54 o. vi 27.

942 A fuller writing including the verbal roots du_{11} or gi_4 are most probable; lugal-šu-du_{11} or lugal-šu-mu-gi_4 may be complementary forms of this name. For the meaning, see the lexical evidence cited by *CAD* E s.v. *emūqu* "strength (in physical sense as localized in the arms)"; and see similar imagery referring to the arm, a_2, *PSD* A/2, 111, sub a_2-tuku 1.4. The name appears also in the Ur III period, e.g. *NATN* 145 r. 1 (Nippur); also the abbreviation šu-maḫ, *HLC* 2 10 r. i 5.

943 See, e.g. J. Klein, *Three Šulgi Hymns*, 118, note to ll. 354–361.

944 The parallel en-lirum appears once in an ED IIIa Šuruppag contract, see G. Visicato & A. Westenholz, *Gs Cagni*, 1107–1109, no. 1 o. v 3 (translit. only), and note to line on p. 1109.

945 See, in general, Å. Sjöberg, *Expedition* 27/2 (1985), 7–9.

of course one fitting for many rulers eager to portray themselves as superhuman in strength.[946]

3.1.7.4 Aptitude for combat

A couple of names refer to the lugal as brave or competent in exercising the prerogatives of heroic deeds. Neither of them is very informative, and it may well be that the intentended motifs behind the names are different in scope. Abbreviations from longer constructions are hard to establish, but in the case of lugal-u_3-ma $^{(a\geq10)}$ 'the lugal is victorious,' the missing verb is probably gub "to establish."[947]

A rather productive element in names was ur-saĝ, as in lugal-ur-saĝ $^{(a\geq10/°2)}$ 'the lugal is a hero/warrior.'[948] A number of appellatives and theonyms are attested along with this nominal predicate, representing both male and female beings. Exactly which qualities are covered by this expression – bravery, a disposition to tackle situations over and above the ordinary, belligerence, or any combination of the aforementioned qualities – is hard to ascertain. The noun ur-saĝ was also borrowed into the Akkadian onomasticon.[949] For none of the names above does a specific character, human or divine, present itself.

3.1.7.5 Fame and good reputation

Reference to the renown of the lugal is seen in names which in all likelihood contain the noun mu 'name,' for instance the ED IIIb name lugal-mu-da-ri_2 $^{(a2)}$ 'the lugal (has) a lasting name.'[950] The name might testify to the type of traditions which resulted, among other things, in the Sumerian King List or the epic cycle of the early rulers of Uruk. The setting up of objects inscribed with the names of kings and well-to-do citizens was obviously a means of prolonging one's favour with the gods, even beyond the grave, and also a

[946] So for instance the self-lauding Šulgi: "wie bei einem Eselshengst versiegt meine (d.i. Šulgi's) Kraft beim Laufen nicht," following W. Heimpel, *Tierbilder*, 269.

[947] Compare Akk. *irnittam šakānum*. For the phrase u_3-ma(-ni) gub-gub, see e.g. TH 258 (Eninnu of Ningirsu); and W. H. Ph. Römer, *SKIZ*, 112. Note variant lugal-u_3-ma_2 $^{(a1)}$ in BIN 8 46 (possibly ED IIIb Zabala). The shape of U_3 is a bit quaint, but the copy is confirmed by photo (CDLI P221555). The PN u_3-ma-ni is attested at ED IIIb Nippur (e.g. TMH 5 53 o. ii 3), and was popular in the Ur III period.

[948] D. O. Edzard, CRRA 19, 142: "le lugal est un guerrier." Compare H. Limet, *Anthroponymie*, 315: "Le roi est un héros."

[949] See, below, p. 208 w. fn. 1324. J. Goodnick Westenholz, *JAOS* 103 (1983), 327–336, esp. 335f., makes a good case for distinctions between Sumerian and Akkadian heroic figures.

[950] The phrase da-ri_2 appears in a few other places in the ED IIIb period. See, for instance, Eanatum's Stele of the Vultures, *CIRPL* Ean. 1 o. xx 16: da-ri_2 da-gal-$še_3$ in a negated clause in the oath-swearing ceremony with the king of Umma; and Lugalzagesi's Nippur inscription BE 1/2 87 iii 36. A variant Ur III orthography lugal mu da-a-ri "king with a lasting name," is found in Urnamma D 41'. I. J. Gelb, MAD 3, 106, followed by R. di Vito, StPohl SM 16, 215, 30.5a, 8, understood the related writing lugal-da-ri_2 as an Akkadian PN; di Vito in turn also saw lugal-mu-da-ri_2 as an Akkadian name, which is unlikely.

means of establishing a name for oneself. The inscriptions, mu (sar-ra) in Sumerian, *śumum* (*śaṭrum*) in Akkadian, were in the case of kings sometimes provided with a curse formula to insure that no-one would later interfere with the object or the name of the author.[951] It might as well be taken to refer to a divinity, whose lifespan was infinitely less limited than that of a human.

The name attested as lugal-mu-du$_{10}$ $^{(a2)}$,[952] in ED III times, and as lugal-mu-du$_{10}$-ga $^{(a\geq1)}$ 'lugal of a good name,'[953] in the Sargonic period, appears to be formed with a specific referent in mind, but it is at this point not possible to assign this name to either a human or a divinity.

3.1.7.6 Symbolic identification and equation

A simple but effective way of ascribing a given set of qualities to a referent is by means of symbolic identification. This has been explored above in names such as lugal-Anzu. A lot of such names will remain obscure beyond their literal meaning, and sometimes even the literal meaning is beyond grasp due to difficulties in understanding Sumerian generally. However, it is for instance absolutely certain that the most obvious imagery called to mind when comparing the lugal to four-legged animals, to portray him as covered with fur and crawling around on all fours, is not the point intended by the symbolic association. Hence, it is more than likely that the names lugal-nemur$_x$(PIRIĜ.TUR) $^{(a\geq7)}$ 'the lugal is (like) a leopard,'[954] and lugal-piriĝ $^{(a\geq8/°1)}$ 'the lugal is (like) a lion,' all point to other trademark qualities than appearance. A foundation deposit found cast in bitumen in the lowest course of bricks in the White Temple at Uruk contained the bones of the front legs of a pair of feline cubs, one leopard and one lion, with their paws cut off.[955] A millennium or so later, Gudea mentions that the doorways to the Eninnu

---

[951] It was highly irregular until the end of the OB period for anyone but kings to provision private commemorative objects with curses. A rare example is furnished by the inscribed stone water basin dedicated to Inana by *Rīm*-Sîn-Šala-*bāštašu*, queen of Larsa and wife of Rīm-Sîn I, YOS 9 31.

[952] Compare R. di Vito, StPohl SM 16, 105, interpreting MU as -ĝu$_{10}$. One instance of this name is written lugal:mu-du$_{10}$, which would not alter the general meaning of the name.

[953] *STTI* 154 r. 4 has writing lugal-mu-du$_{10}$-ga-ke$_4$ for ergative, indicating an internal genitive construction '*of* a good name.' Compare R. di Vito, StPohl SM 16, 63, 30.5a, 3, who interpreted MU as -ĝu$_{10}$. See also *CIRPL* Ent. 35 vi 6–10: ⌜en-mete(TE+ME)-na-ka, mu-du$_{10}$-ga-ni, ^{d}Nin-ĝir$_2$-su-ke$_4$, da-ri$_2$-še$_3$, ĝeštu$_2$ na-gub⌝ 'Ningirsu will keep the good name of Enmetena in mind forever.'

[954] Reading nemur$_x$(PIRIĜ.TUR) is chosen due to the existence of unqualified piriĝ elsewhere in the corpus, but may prove to be anachronistic. To this end, see parallelism in Šulgi D l. 6, between piriĝ tur ban$_3$-da and piriĝ gal. The name might also be taken as lugal plus qualified noun piriĝ banda$_3$, as did H. Limet, *Anthroponymie*, 168, 329: "Le roi est un lion furieux"; 311: "Le roi est un lion féroce."

[955] For this and other instances associating leopards with the foundations of buildings, or with architectural features, see E. Williams-Forte, *RlA* 6 (1980–83), 603f. s.v. "Leopard. B. Archäologisch," §5.

of Ningirsu had depictions of young lions and leopards resting on their paws.[956]

It should be noted that animal symbolism is not regularly used in self-characterizations of human rulers before the Ur III period; at least not in royal inscriptions. But if people could be characterized as amar 'calf,' in PNN and in economic documents, and as inanimate terms denoting 'property' in PNN, then for subjects to compare a leader of society to a powerful animal would make sense. Associating kings with animals endowed with an aura of strength or force is a common phenomenon in early civilizations. It is possible that other names belong to this group, such as lugal-dara$_3^{?}$(LAK263^{+}) $^{(a1)}$ 'the lugal is (like) a dara$_3$-goat (?),' and lugal-ERIM+X $^{(a1)}$ 'the lugal is (like) the ERIM+X-quadruped,'[957] although they might well be abbreviations of longer names only expressing the appellative along with a direct or indirect object.

In the section dealing with care and attentiveness, a name describing the lugal as the god of a person was discussed.[958] Specifically, the name lugal-diĝir-ĝu$_{10}$ mentions a first person perspective, and thus hints at a motif of personal support. Other names also might contain a measure of symbolic identity, where the appellative is combined with a theonym, with or without an equative marker -gin$_7$.[959]

A name which probably belongs in this category is lugal-ušumgal $^{(a\geq 7)}$ 'the lugal is a *fierce beast* (?).'[960] In late 3rd millennium poetic imagery, ušumgal is mentioned in connection with lions, as if it were a natural occurrence in the fauna of southern Mesopotamia.[961] Later on the ušumgal was predominantly a mythical creature and an honorific epithet of kings and gods.[962] An interpretation similar to that of the Anzu, which could be characterized as beneficient to the allies of the lugal, but detrimental to

[956] See the discussion of R. S. Ellis, *Foundation Deposits in Ancient Mesopotamia*, 42f. and appendix 4. The interpretation of the Gudea passage, Cyl. A xxvi 26–27, follows rather D. O. Edzard's rendering, RIME 3/1, 86. For the sake of argument, I have retained the reading nemur$_x$(PIRIĜ.TUR) with a translation "leopard."

[957] For ERIM+X and proposed readings, see R. D. Biggs, ARES 1, 94 fn. 26. W. G. Lambert, *JCS* 41 (1989), 11–14, suggested a mng. similar to *qurādum*/*qarrādum*. A. Archi, *MARI* 4 (1985), 54, left the name untranslated. M. V. Tonietti, Subartu 4/2, 89f., interpreted this name as Semitic, which is not altogether unlikely.

[958] Above, p. 120.

[959] See, e.g. lugal-UD, lugal-^{d}Utu, and lugal-^{d}KA.DI above, p. 146; and compare discussion of lugal-Utu-gin$_7$-e$_3$, below, p. 173. The amissability of -gin$_7$ in some cases may perhaps be due to its general coordination with, or substitution for, the copula -am$_{(3/6)}$, which is regularly omitted from writings of PNN. See W. Heimpel, *Tierbilder*, 24–42, esp. p. 33–36.

[960] Compare H. Limet, *Anthroponymie*, 168, 283, 329: "le roi est un dragon"; similarly E. Sollberger & J.-R. Kupper, *IRSA*, 319; and R. di Vito, StPohl SM 16, 66, 30.5a, 20. Compare also E. Chiera, PBS 11/1, 78, no. 928: "The king is the only great one."

[961] Gudea Cyl. B iv 17–19 mentions lions (ur-maḫ and piriĝ) as lying down with ušumgal.

[962] Bilingual and Akkadian examples are found in *CAD* U/W s.v. *ušumgallu*. M. Krebernik, *Fs Wilcke*, 153–156, gives a history of interpretation of the DN ^{d}Amaušumgal(-an-na).

whoever opposed him, might be imagined. It is worth noticing that only Anzu appeared as the nominal predicate in theophore names before the Ur III period.[963] The expression had already by the time of Eanatum of Lagaš taken on a potentially hostile overtone.[964] Originally, however, the ušumgal was probably something very different from a predator; something that may have left a few traces in lexical texts and hymns.[965] The referent of the name remains unknown.

Massive landmarks such as the foothills of the mountains were endowed with supernatural powers, marking the boundary between the civilizations of the plains and the ominous highland areas. The function of this stretch of land may hint at an idea of protection as an operative meaning of the name lugal-ḫur-saĝ $^{(a\geq 3)}$ 'the lugal is a *mountain*,' attested at Umma-Zabala, Nippur and Adab, in the late ED IIIb or Early Sargonic periods. There are no indications that the name is either a genitive compound or an abbreviation.[966] The name is not attested in later periods, save as an Ur III DN, possibly construed as a parallel of Ninḫursaĝ.[967] In fact, the noun ḫur-saĝ is not very common in the early Sumerian onomasticon.[968]

3.1.7.7 Uniqueness and aloofness

A small group of names encompass the antithesis of the previous group of names, in which the lugal is subjected to a symbolic identification. In lugal-ni$_3$-da-sa$_2$ $^{(a1)}$ 'what can compare with the lugal?,'[969] and lugal-ni$_3$-nu-da-me

[963] See M. Krebernik on ušumgal and Anzu in ED names, AOAT 296, 20f. w. fn 81; and ibid., *Fs Wilcke*, 155f..

[964] As is evident from the curse formula in *CIRPL* Ean. 63+N. 5 ii' 2'–3': ^{d}Nin-ĝir$_2$-su, ušumgal-ni he$_2$ 'may Ningirsu be his (the malfeitor's) ušumgal.'

[965] In ED Lu A the title ušumgal appears between officials having to do with fattening and caretaking of small livestock. Perhaps the original meaning is implicated in Šulgi T line 10, Å. Sjöberg, *Fs Kramer*, 419, l. 100. There, Ninurta is termed ad gi$_4$-gi$_4$ ušumgal kalam-ma. The term ad gi$_4$-gi$_4$ "adviser," is hardly one which can be attributed to a snarling beast. The development of this early bureaucrat may be similar to those of the maškim and gal$_5$-la$_2$ officials whose titles came to denote demonic beings around the end of the 3rd millennium.

[966] R. di Vito also saw this as a nominal predicate name, StPohl SM 16, 64, 30.5a, 8. Compare the PN ki-ni-ḫur-saĝ-še$_3$-maḫ 'his/her abode is awesome (all the way) to the mountains,' UET 2 2 o. ii 3 (ED IIIa Ur).

[967] The DN ^{d}Lugal-ḫur-saĝ is to my knowledge only attested in the list of offerings *SET* 73 r. i 19, eight lines after Ninḫursaĝ (Puzriš-Dagān, translit. only).

[968] See e$_2$-ḫur-saĝ, e.g. *WF* 22 o. iv 5; ni$_2$-ḫur-saĝ, e.g. *WF* 67 r. iii 5; KA-ni-ḫur-saĝ, *TSŠ* 58 r. v 15 (all ED IIIa Šuruppag); mu-ni-ḫur-saĝ, e.g. BRM 4 45 l. 6 (ED IIIb Uruk); and me-ḫur-saĝ, e.g. *IAS* 506 o. iii' 4' (ED IIIa Abū Ṣalābīḫ). Compare also notes to *śar-ru*-ḫur-saĝ.

[969] Compare lu$_2$-nu-mu-da-sa$_2$ 'no *man* can compare with (him/her),' or: 'no(one) can compare with the *master*,' e.g. *TSŠ* 827 (ED IIIa Šuruppag); a-ba-AN-da-sa$_2$ 'who can compare with An/the god?,' TMH 5 29+ r. iii 11 (MS-CS Nippur). Perhaps AN in the latter is to be analyzed as a prefix and object referent /aba-a-n-da-sa$_2$/, 'who can compare with him/her?' A in the contemporary close parallel a-ba-A-da-sa$_2$, TMH 5 52 o. ii 13, might be interpreted either as 'who can compare with father?' (A=aja$_2$) or, less likely, as a prefix.

(a1) 'the lugal, nothing is beside (him),' the lugal is portrayed as someone who is beyond comparison. Both names are of ED III date.

Similarly, a few names attest to the singular status of the lugal, or to the lugal as taking action alone, lugal-aš$_{10}$ (a4) 'the lugal is one of a kind,'[970] and lugal-aš$_{10}$-ni (a≥4) 'the lugal … by himself.'[971] It is unclear who the intended referent is, but high deities such as Enlil or Nanna, are likely candidates.[972]

Other names are in many ways too general to be understood as referring either to divinities or to men. Only a few of these saw any greater distribution in the onomasticon. Some may be abbreviations of fuller forms. The variants lugal-maḫ (a1/°1) from the ED III period, and lugal-maḫ$_2$ (a≥4), predominantly found in the Sargonic period,[973] are both probably to be interpreted as: 'the lugal is the greatest/sublime.'[974]

The name lugal-u$_4$-su$_{13}$-še$_3$ (a≥2/°1) is likely to be completed with the adjective maḫ,[975] 'the lugal is the greatest for far-off days.'[976] Like the former, the name lugal-gil-sa (a1) 'the lugal is (of) everlasting (value),' involves both a qualitative and a temporal aspect.[977] The use of the attribute gil-sa in the human onomasticon was almost exclusively limited to the ED IIIb period.[978]

Further proclamations of elevated status seem to be the theme of a number of names composed with saĝ 'head, top,' such as lugal-saĝ (a≥8) 'the lugal is exalted,'[979] and lugal-saĝ-rib (a≥1) 'the lugal is preeminent.'[980]

---

[970] With variant lugal-aš (a1), from ED IIIa Uruk.

[971] For the reading, see abbreviated forms aš$_{(10)}$-a-ni, aš$_{(10)}$-ša$_4$-ni and a-ša$_4$-ni discussed by J. N. Postgate, *AfO* 24 (1973), 77; G. J. Selz, *OLZ* 85 (1990), 305. The Akk. term *wēdiššīšu* is found as gloss to aš-ni in Proto-Izi, MSL 13, 23:173. See also GAG § 67, f.

[972] See, e.g. PBS 5 66 o. i 1–3: ^{d}En-lil$_2$, an-ki-še$_3$ lugal-am$_3$, aš-ni diĝir-ra-am$_3$ 'Enlil, who is lord over the heavens and the earth, who alone is god' (OB copy of earlier commemorative inscription of Išme-Dagān of Isin); and other refs. to aš-ni in literary contexts, as attribute of Enlil, Nanna, and Inana with H. Limet, *Anthroponymie*, 168 fn. 2. As a PN, aš-ni is known from ED times onwards, e.g. OSP 1 53 o. i 4 (ED IIIb-ES Nippur)

[973] One instance of lugal-maḫ$_2$ from the ED IIIb Lagaš area may be an abbreviation. Compare lugal-al-sa$_6$, attested for one person from ED IIIb Girsu.

[974] The interpretation follows H. Limet's proposal, *Anthroponymie*, 277, to see maḫ as a descriptive adjective. The possibility remains that lugal-maḫ$_{(2)}$ is an abbreviation.

[975] A single writing of lugal-u$_4$-su$_3$-[(še$_3^?$)] (a1), with su$_3$=BU*gunû* is known from CS Adab.

[976] Paraphrasing *PSD* A/2 s.v. abzu, 1.8.6: (Ningirsu) en abzu-ta u$_4$-su$_3$-še$_3$ maḫ. Note that the name is not attested from the Lagaš state and that all examples have su$_{13}$ for su$_3$. Compare H. Limet, *Anthroponymie*, 171 (-u$_4$-su$_3$-): "Le roi, pour de longs jours (qu'il vive!)" (sic); 295: "Le roi vers des jours lointains"; D. O. Edzard, CRRA 19, 142: "lugal, à des jours lointains (que tu vives)!" Compare singular ED IIIa Adab writing lugal-su$_3$-še$_3$ (a1); and Ur III PN en-u$_4$-su$_3$-[še$_3$], *RTC* 401 o. iii 3 (Girsu).

[977] A thorough investigation of gil-sa (or gi$_{16}$-sa), with many textual references, was made by A. Falkenstein, *ZA* 58 (1967), 5–10.

[978] Compare, e.g. en-gil-sa, father of UruKAgina, ensi$_2$ of Lagaš, MO A xiv 8, and passim; *DP* 2/1 157 o. i 2 (sagi, ED IIIb Girsu).

[979] The name may be abbreviated. Appellative + saĝ is found also in a few Girsu names, such as ED IIIb nin-saĝ-ĝe$_{26}$-tuku 'the servant has acquired a mistress,' e.g. Nik 1 20 o. iv 6; or the

Certainly in the same vein is lugal-saĝ-bi-še$_{3\text{-}90°}$ (a1) 'the lugal takes precedence.'[981] Names of similar import might be: lugal-šu-du$_7$ (a1/°1),[982] and lugal-šu-du$_7$-a (a1) 'the lugal is perfect'[983]; and perhaps also lugal-⸢sukud$^?$⸣-[ra$_2$$^?$] (a1) 'the lugal is lofty.'[984] These names largely lack parallels composed with another appellative or theonym.

3.1.7.8 Similes and kindness

A considerable number of names depict the lugal in terms of his agreeable nature. Such names are very hard to assign any other function than as general expressions of praise. Most such names have parallels with other appellatives or theonyms. They form part of a common and popular group of names which are often construed as similes, comparing the head noun to another, positively charged object. The type goes as far back as ED I-II, as lugal-lal$_3$ (a≥2/°1) 'the lugal is (sweet as) honey (or syrup),' is attested already in the oldest texts from Ur. The association between lugal and lal$_3$ went out of fashion by ED IIIa times and is not found thereafter, though the nominal predicate is found along with other nominal elements after this point.[985] Another commodity favoured for its flavour was wine, as in lugal-ĝeštin (a≥2) 'the lugal is (sweet as) wine,'[986] limited to ED IIIb Girsu. As has been pointed out by M. Krebernik, honey (or syrup) and wine sometimes appear together in literary contexts,[987] and these names are therefore comparable on more than one level. Similar names are lugal-i$_3$-nun (a≥9) 'the lugal (is)

Ur III PNN nin-saĝ-e-ki-aĝ$_2$ 'the lady loves her servant,' e.g. *HLC* 2 22 o. i 7. See later PNN lugal-en-saĝ, SAT 1 420 r. ii 16; and en-saĝ, SAT 1 434 r. ii 1.

980 On the reading rib of KAL alongside usage of this compound in OB titulary chains, see M.-J. Seux, *Épithètes royales akkadiennes et sumériennes*, 439 w. fn. 466.

981 The predicate e$_3$ can with all certainty be appended to the name. See in general the discussion of P. Michalowski, MesCiv 1, 99 note to l. 368; and furthermore RIME 3/2.1.4.1 iii 24–25: (*Šu*-Su'en) kalag-ga-ni, saĝ-bi-še$_3$ e$_3$-a "whose strength is outstanding." For bilingual lexical examples, see A. Cavigneaux, *Die sumerisch-akkadischen Zeichenlisten*, 139. Compare ED IIIb Nippur abbreviation saĝ-be$_6$-e$_3$-a, TMH 5 66 o. ii 3.

982 It is possible that an object me is missing, as can be seen, for instance, in the PN lugal-me-šu-du$_7$ 'the lugal is one who perfects the rites,' UET 7 77 o. ii' 5', OB list of lugal-PNN; and short me-šu-du$_7$, *RTC* 18 o. iii 7; and DN ^{d}Nin-me-šu-du$_7$, for which see *FTUM*, 110.

983 Compare Ur III PN en-ne$_2$-šu-du$_7$-a 'made perfect by the lord (?),' H. de Genouillac, *Babyloniaca* 8 (1924), pl. IX (following p. 40, HG 1) o. 2 (Ur III Girsu).

984 Sign sukud(TA×ŠE) quite damaged; inscribed ŠE not visible. In the Ur III period a homonymous DN ^{d}Lugal-sukud-ra$_2$ is known, see e.g. SAT 1 o. 4 (translit. only). Translation following Å. Sjöberg, *OrS* 19-20 (1970–71), 151, l. 34.

985 See, e.g. ama-lal$_3$, *SIA* 868 o. 5 (CS Adab); mu-ni-lal$_3$ 'his name is (sweet as) honey (or syrup),' *TCABI* 31 o. i 1; and šeš-lal$_3$, CUSAS 11 277 o. i 5 (both ES Adab).

986 Compare aja$_2$-ĝeštin, e.g. UET 2 2 r. ii 5 (ED I-II Ur); ama-‹ĝeš›tin, M. W. Green, *ZA* 72 (1982), 174 no. 12 o. ii' 2' ED I-II Uruk; munus-ĝeštin, e.g. *RTC* 4 o. i 6 (ED IIIa Girsu).

987 AOAT 296, 17–20; and ibid. *Fs Wilcke*, 159f., with parallel name formations.

excellent oil,' lugal-ir-nun $^{(a1)}$ 'the lugal (is) excellent smell,'[988] and lugal-šembi$_3$ $^{(a\geq 2/°2)}$ 'the lugal is ointment.'[989]

Rather general in scope are the names lugal-du$_{10}$ $^{(a\geq 2/°2)}$ 'the lugal is good,'[990] and lugal-du$_{10}$-ga $^{(a1)}$, the latter limited in time to the last part of the Sargonic period. Short names such as these might be taken to be abbreviations of longer names, but no prosopographical links to fuller writings are known. The predicate du$_{10}$ could then be seen as an attribute to a nominal predicate or as a transitive-factitive verb.[991]

The associations evoked by the adjective sa$_6$ were both popular and lasting. It was a highly productive component in names from ED IIIb times and throughout the remainder of the 3rd millennium. Examples include lugal-ni$_3$-sa$_6$-ga $^{(a4)}$ 'the lugal is something favourable'[992]; and the the more concise lugal-sa$_6$ $^{(a\geq 8)}$ 'the lugal is favourable,' found only in the Sargonic period, and lugal-sa$_6$-ga $^{(a\geq 6)}$, limited to the preceding period.[993]

A name which could easily be taken as an abbreviation of a name originally featuring a theonym as subject, or an object is lugal-ki-aĝ$_2$ $^{(a\geq 5)}$ 'the lugal is beloved.'[994] A verbal predicate could be missing from lugal-ḫi-li $^{(a\geq 6)}$ 'the lugal is pleasant.'[995] Other names of this general type represent terse statements describing the lugal in positive terms. are lugal-asila$_x$(A.EZEM)

[988] Compare suggestion by G. J. Selz, *Götterwelt*, 133 fn. 538: "Der König (ist mit) fürstlichem Parfüm (gesalbt)," with parallels.

[989] An ED IIIa Šuruppag source has the defective writing lugal-šembi$_3^!$(DUG×IGI) $^{(a1)}$.

[990] H. Limet, *Anthroponymie*, 228: "Le bon roi"; but compare, ibid., p. 76: "Le roi est bon."

[991] See the discussion by M. Krebernik, AOAT 296, 32–39 with many parallels composed with this productive verbal component, and compare the table below, 4.4.

[992] Apart from an entry in a Sargonic period prism with nin-names, W. G. Lambert, *Gs Sachs*, 259f. ii 21: nin-ni$_3$-sa$_6$-sa$_6$-ga, no close parallels composed with other appellatives are known. See discussion of lugal-ni$_3$-kalag-ga. Compare DN ^{d}Lugal-ni$_3$-sa$_6$-ga, known from later god lists, W. G. Lambert, *RlA* 7 (1987–90), 150 s.v. "Lugal-nišaga/Lugal-nisigga," given as "Lord of pleasant things."

[993] See R. di Vito, StPohl SM 16, 65, 30.5a, 17, with references to names with sa$_6$ (ša$_5$) and sa$_6$-ga collected in one table. For other names composed with sa$_6$, see table 4.4, below.

[994] W. G. Lambert, *OrNS* 64 (1995), 134, refers to H. Limet, *Anthroponymie*, 172, "le roi aimé (des dieux)," with further discussion on p. 265. The lugal-⌈aĝa$_2$⌉ proposed by A. Alberti & F. Pomponio, StPohl SM 13, 107 for UET 2 suppl. 48 o. ii 3 is unclear on photos, though it would be parallel to ^{d}Nanna-aĝa$_2$ in o. i 5, both are otherwise unattested. See table 4.4, below, s.v. ki–aĝ$_2$, for names featuring the same predicate combined with divinities or objects.

[995] H. Limet, *Anthroponymie*, 253, compares the name to a fuller form lugal-ḫi-li-an-na, "Le roi est le charme du ciel." Abbreviation of *lugal-ḫi-li-su$_3$ possible, compare, e.g. lu$_2$-ḫi-li-su$_3$, MVN 3 3 r. vi 11 (ED IIIb Umma-Zabala).

[(a2)], ‘the lugal is joyous’[996] lugal-gi$_7$ [(a3)] ‘the lugal is noble,’ and lugal-ku-li [(a4)] ‘the lugal is a friend.’[997]

A popular group of names, including ones with lugal as appellative, link the individual with an external source for well-being, protection and good luck, teš$_2$, Akkadian *baštum*:[998] lugal-teš$_2$ [(a2)],[999] and, more commonly, lugal-teš$_2$-ĝu$_{10}$ [(a≥13)] ‘the lugal is my pride (and joy).’

3.1.7.9 Justice and dependability

The lugal as a guarantor of an ordered society has already been discussed above, under heading 3.1.3.3. The adjectives gi and zi were seen to be central concepts. In the onomasticon, further links between the lugal and conceptions of righteousness and just behaviour were expressed. In Umma, for instance, the lugal was characterized as ‘a righteous man,’ lugal-lu$_2$-gi-na [(a2)],[1000] while a man in Girsu was called lugal-lu$_2$-zi [(a1)] ‘the lugal is a reliable man.’ Parallels with the noun nitaḫ$_{(2)}$, probably with a very similar meaning: lugal-nitaḫ-zi [(a10)],[1001] and lugal-nitaḫ$_2$-zi [(a≥2)], were both more common seen in relation to number of bearers, but also regarding geographical spread. A possible further name which stressed the quality of reliability of the lugal was lugal-niĝir(LAK154) [(a≥6)] ‘the lugal is a herald.’[1002] The niĝir was an important persona in the early city-states, as shown not least by the

[996] Or a-sil$_x$(EZEM). One of the attestations of this name is found on the incompletely published, pre–Ur-Nanše “bas-relief circulaire” (AO 2350+3288). See L. Heuzey, *Catalogue des antiquités chaldéennes*, no. 5; and Thureau-Dangin, *SAKI*, 2 note a 4. In CS Umma the name is once attested as lugal-asila$_3$(EZEM×A) [(a1)]. Compare discussion on readings, G. Marchesi, HANE/S 10, 110.

[997] Following R. di Vito, StPohl SM 16, 59, 30.4a, 5. The name is booked in MAD 3, 145 s.v. KLL *kullum*, along with *ku$_8$-li$_2$*-SAR in ITT 1 1372 (CS Girsu). The interpretation of this latter name is far from certain. Even though lugal-ku-li appears in the MO as a citizen of Akkade, see below, p. 237, the name of the father is arguably Sumerian and there is therefore no need to posit an Akkadian reading of either element in this specific name.

[998] See G. Marchesi, HANE/S 10, 71 w. fn. 361: teš$_2$ = *baštu*, with ref.; W. Lambert, *OrNS* 64 (1995), 134; and, more generally, *CAD* B s.v. *baštu*.

[999] The same person in MS-CS Adab is twice qualified as muḫaldim “cook” and once receives a shipment of mixed fish. It is uncertain if lugal-teš$_2$-ĝu$_{10}$ in *SIA* 933 is to be identified with this same professional. At any rate, lugal-teš$_2$-ĝu$_{10}$ is rare in Sargonic sources.

[1000] Add name to K. Lämmerhirt, AOAT 348, 529: Materialsammlung ge(-n). Compare R. di Vito, StPohl SM 16, 72, 40.6a, 1: aja-gi-na “Father is sure.”

[1001] See interpretation by G. J. Selz, *Götterwelt*, 287 w. fn. 1429, of this and parallel Utu-nitaḫ-zi: “Utu (ist) ein gerechter Mann,” or: “Utu (ist dem) Manne gerecht.” Compare J. Bauer, *ZA* 79 (1989), 9 fn. 7, with reference to A. Falkenstein, who speculates on the mng. of UŠ as “Gründungsplatte” and translates: “König der das UŠ recht macht.” Bauer further questions the reading of the Ur III DN Lugal-nitaḫ-zi, for which, see W. G. Lambert, *RlA* 7 (1987–90), 150 s.v. Lugal-nitazi. This deity belonged to the circle of the goddess Ninsun of Kuara see P. Steinkeller, *ASJ* 17 (1995), 277 fn. 12. The present reading is chosen on the basis of the parallel lugal-nitaḫ$_2$-zi, as nitaḫ$_2$ is not used to express a value uš.

[1002] Following H. Limet, *Anthroponymie*, 170: “Le roi est un héraut”; and L. Sassmanshausen, *BagM* 26 (1995), 191: “Der König ist ein Herold.” The sign LAK154 may also be read aga, and could then be an abbreviation, or a parallel of, lugal-aga-zi, see p. 88, above.

popularity of the title in personal names.[1003] His duties included – but were surely not limited to – public announcements. All these names might equally well have had a human as a divine referent.

3.1.7.10 Light, brilliance and visual phenomena

The association between the lugal and luminous phenomena is the subject of a variegated group of names. Among them is found one of the Sumerian lugal-names with the largest number of attested bearers: lugal-iti-da [(a>35)].[1004] It appears in the ED IIIb, at Nippur to begin with, and then fans out southward. A fuller parallel makes the identity of the lugal as Nanna or Su'en likely, lugal-iti-da-tu [(a1)] 'the lugal is (re)born each month,'[1005] referring to the lunar cycle in which the moon disappears only to reappear and start the cycle all over. A later tigi-hymn makes the identification with Nanna/Su'en even more likely.[1006] Also, the fact that the cult of the Moon God was next to non–existent at Girsu may help explain why the scribe wrote this name down without abbreviating it. Names containing the theonyms Nanna or Su'en were only rarely attested at Girsu from the ED down through the Sargonic period.[1007] The appearance of the new moon is an important time of the month and it is very probable that lugal-iti-da(-tu) contains an auspicious reference to the point in time when the child was born or the time of name-giving. A damaged name may contain a parallel to the above mentioned names, lugal-iti-da-[zal[?]]-le [(a1)] 'the lugal [brightens?] the month,' though the damage affects the identification of a predicate there.[1008]

The placement of the lugal in the heavens is the theme of a few names, all of them from the Sargonic period: lugal-u_4-an-na [(a1)] 'the lugal is the light of the skies,'[1009] and lugal-si-u_4-a [(a1)], 'the lugal in the high heavens (?).'[1010] One

---

[1003] For lists of names composed with niĝir, see L. Sassmanshausen, *BagM* 26 (1995), 191f.; A. Alberti & F. Pomponio, StPohl SM 13, 109–111.

[1004] Sargonic period abbreviation lugal-iti [(a2)]. A phonetic writing is most likely the case in ES Umma lugal-ti-da [(a1)]. Note the Ur III text *Hirose* 344, with writing lugal-iti-da on tablet, o. 5, and lugal-ti-da on seal, l. 1 (Umma); and compare lugal-ti-ma-nu_2, which is likely to be a phonetic writing of itima, denoting a sanctuary of sorts. See further, below, p. 235.

[1005] See G. J. Selz, *Götterwelt*, 99 fn. 358: "Der König/Herr (=Su'en?) (wird) monatlich geboren"; and the equation iti-da, *arḫišam* "monthly," J. Klein, *Three Šulgi Hymns*, 163, note to Šulgi X 134–140; *CAD* A/2, s.v. *arḫišam*, lex. sect.: itu-itu-da, Akk. *wa-a*[*r-ḫi*]-*ša-am*, in a bilingual inscription of *Samsuiluna*.

[1006] See the passage in a tigi to Inana, CT 36 pl. 33f. (BM 96739) r. 17–18: iti-da uskar-ra [d]Su'en-gin_7 An-ne_2 za[!]-ra ša-mu-ra-an-u_3-tu, lugal [d]Ama-ušumgal-an-na $ša_3$-za ki-$aĝ_2$-bi[!]-im 'each month on the day of the New Moon, like Su'en, An *gives birth* to him for you, the lord, Amaušumgalana is the beloved one of your heart.'

[1007] Only two ED IIIb names are booked in V. V. Struve, *Onomastika*, 169, s.v.v. Nanna[na], and Nanna-$erim_2$-ma. For Sargonic refs., see W. Sommerfeld, *Tutub*, 37.

[1008] The restoration [zal[?]] is offered on the basis that a professional title would be out of place.

[1009] Similarly E. Chiera, PBS 11/3, 212, no. 256. See discussion of literary attestations, Å. Sjöberg, *MNS*, 38f., noting the variant lugal-u_4-an [(a1)]; and that the phrase was associated with Nanna and Ningublaga of Kiabrig in earlier times. See also Ur III Nippur PN [d]Utu-an-na,

of the luminaries is likely to be the referent of these names. An ED I-II Ur name might revolve around the return of the city's tutelary deity Nanna to the night skies after an eclipse, or to the appearance of one of the luminaries in the morning: lugal-u_4-suḫ̮$_3$-gi_4 (a1),[1011] but this interpretation is tentative. The cosmic associations of the name are, however, not in doubt.

It is not always certain that a divinity is intended as the referent of names associating the lugal with natural or numinous phenomena emitting light. An example of this is the ED IIIb Umma name lugal-Utu-gin_7-e_3 (a≥1) 'the lugal goes forth like Utu,'[1012] which compares the (or a) lugal to the Sun God. The use of the verb e_3, 'to go out,' suggests a symbolic association based on the movement of the sun, and especially on his emerging in the morning; his visibility enabling him to fulfill his functions related to justice, ensuring the proper functioning of the cosmos as a whole. This identification between king and the Sun God can be found also in later times, and quite naturally it made its way also into the onomastic material; both Sumerian and Akkadian.[1013] Another name which is echoed in an Ur III hymn is lugal-me-lam_2-su_3 (a1) 'the lugal spreads an ominous sheen.'[1014] In one of Šulgi's self-characterizations he describes himself: 'I am like a magnificent storm wrested free from heaven, spreading an ominous sheen far and wide."[1015] The noun me-lam_2 denotes a brilliance of objects and beings belonging to, or partaking in, the otherworldly sphere.[1016] It was not a very common component in the Sumerian onomasticon until Ur III times.

The composite verb pa–e_3 was popular in Sumerian name-giving from the ED IIIa period onwards. The name lugal-pa-e_3 (a≥14) 'the lugal is shin-

---

NATN 444 o. 7. An OB Nippur list of PNN agrees with the Sargonic writings in not using a divine determinative before the sign UD, PBS 11/3 o. iii' 14, followed by lugal-u_4-an-ki.

1010 Compare the writings si-un_3-na, for a celestial high point or "zenith," e.g. in Enmerkar and the Lord of Aratta, l. 271, H. L. J. Vanstiphout, *Epics of Sumerian Kings*, 70 ("high heaven"); and Urnamma A l. 13; and note the possible value un_5 of UD.

1011 This ED I-II Ur name may refer to a time of day or to a state of either the sun or moon. Compare u_4-e_2-gar_8-e-gi_4-a, *kaṣâtu(m)*, and u_4-ama-bi-$še_3$-gi_4-a, *līlâtu(m)*, "morning" and "evening," respectively. And see the lexical equations $suḫ_3$-bi/ba = *a-ša-a-tum*, "disorder, confusion," and "eclipse," *CAD* E s.v. *ešâtu*, lex. sect.

1012 Besides the occurrences in ED IIIb Umma-Zabala texts, the name lugal-Utu-gin_7-e_3 is reported also to appear in an unpublished MS-CS Umma text (Serota 2, translit. only, given as *Lugal-UD.DIM_2.E_3 by B. R. Foster, *OrNS* 51 (1982), 338 s.v.). The only comparable names are formed with e_2, e.g. e_2-Utu-gin_7-e_3, *WF* 72 r. iii 5.

1013 See, e.g. the references in M.-J. Seux, *Épithètes royales akkadiennes et sumériennes*, 460 s.v. ^{d}utu, and compare *śar-ru-ki*-^{d}Utu, below, p. 211.

1014 Also written lugal-me-lam_2-su_{20}(ŠIM) (a1) in ED IIIa Šuruppag. A possible abbreviation is lugal-me-lam_2 ? (a1) from ED IIIb Isin, but it is rather uncertain, as only the horizontals on the left part of the last sign remain.

1015 Šulgi C l. 3: ud gal an-ta šu ba-ra-gin_7 me-lam_2 su_{13}-su_{13}-me-en_3, copy in G. Castellino, *Two Šulgi Hymns*, 343 fig. 19. Compare Castellino's comments to the line, p. 265f., with ref. to Šulgi B 104.

1016 A. L. Oppenheim, *JAOS* 63 (1943), 31.

ing/splendid,'[1017] therefore has many parallels composed with other appellatives, but also with names of loci. Some early theophore parallels feature Utu and Ašgi of Adab.[1018] A closely related formation is lugal-dalla-pa-e$_3$ (a1/°1?) 'the lugal shines brightly,'[1019] which is uniquely attested with lugal as head noun.

To the above mentioned can be added a handful of names with only minute discernible differences in meaning: lugal-dalla (a7) 'the lugal is bright,'[1020] lugal-šer$_7$-zi (a2/°1) 'the lugal is resplendent,'[1021] and lugal-su$_3$-âĝa$_2$ (a1) 'the lugal is brilliant.'[1022]

3.1.8 Unattributable or unintelligible

Under the eighth and final heading are collected some 220 writings of names which for different reasons are difficult to assign to another heading, and without there being cause for constructing a separate semantic category. They may be understandable in part and may thus be used for comparisons in notes and discussions in other sections and chapters. Out of these names, closer to 130 writings, that is about 60%, are attested only once. A handful of these unique writings are abbreviations for persons known from the same

---

[1017] A likely defective writing is lugal-pa-DU (a1). Compare H. Limet, *Anthroponymie*, 238: "Le roi qui s'avance brilliant"; D. O. Edzard CRRA 19, 142: "le lugal apparaît en éclat"; and R. di Vito, StPohl SM 16, 64, 30.5a, 14: "(The) god is brilliant." Add Fara, Pre–Sargonic and Sargonic attestations to di Vito's table. Compare W. G. Lambert, *RlA* 7 (1987–90), 150 s.v. "Lugal-pa'e/Lugal-urupa'e," given as: "Shining lord." Name of an unspecified divinity in later god list.

[1018] Utu-pa-e$_3$ appears, e.g. in *WF* 87 o. ii 8. Around the turn of ED IIIb and Sargonic times, the name ^{d}Aš$_8$-gi$_4$-pa-e$_3$ appears in Adab sources, e.g. CUSAS 11 278 o. 3. Compare the ED IIIb Adab ruler, e$_2$-igi-nim-pa-e$_3$. E$_2$-igi-nim ought to be a cultic building of sorts, for which, see PN ur-E$_2$-igi-nim, BIN 8 26 o. ii 5'; MVN 3 90 o. ii 4 (both ED IIIb Adab), a temple of Dumuzi?; and E. Sollberger, UET 8, 10, note to no. 53

[1019] The name has been reconstructed on two occurrences, both of which are problematic. A scholastic list of PNN, R. D. Biggs & J. N. Postgate, *Iraq* 40 (1978), 112 o. ii 2, has a cluster of signs which in outline could match PA and IDIGNA. The second sign in BIN 8 53 o. ii 2 is similar to LAK63 (=RÉC28), but is missing a vertical in the left hand part and a horizontal on the right hand side.

[1020] H. Limet, *Anthroponymie*, 168: "Le roi est fort, brillant."

[1021] Compare parallel FPN nin-šer$_7$-zi, e.g. *DP* 1/2 110 (geme$_2$, Girsu, Enz. 3); BIN 8 177 o. 5 (CS Unknown); nin-^{še_3}šer$_7$-zi (*SIA* 989 r. 5, MS-CS Adab). See also ED IIIa Šuruppag name ^{d}Sud$_3$-šer$_7$-zi. For Ur III, see the programmatic name of the en-priestess en-šer$_7$-zi-an-na, UET 3 1320, seal l. 1. The name lugal-šer$_7$-zi appears also in an OB list of lugal-PNN from Ur, UET 7 77 ii' 10'. For the reading šer$_7$(NIR), see J. Bauer, *AfO* 36/37 (1989/90), 80 note to 1 vii 2; *ASJ* 12 (1990), 353–355. A possible variant is lugal-šer$_2$-zi (a≥1), attested twice at ED IIIa Šuruppag. See also, perhaps, the Ebla phonetic writing nu-gal-ḪI-zi (ḪI=šar$_2$?).

[1022] Name appears also in OB list of lugal-PNN, UET 7 77 ii' 4'. Compare DN ^{d}Nin-su$_{13}$-âĝa$_2$, *SF* 1 o. iv 17'; and PN e$_2$-su$_{13}$-âĝa$_2$, from ED IIIa Šuruppag, F. Pomponio, *Prosopografia*, 91f. s.v.; also found at ED IIIb Adab, OIP 104 32, passim. Lexical equivalencies and deities associated with su$_3$-âĝa$_2$ can be found in A. Falkenstein, *ZA* 52 (1957), 304–307; and Å. Sjöberg, *OrS* 19-20 (1970–71) 163f.

archives under fuller names, but which are still difficult to interpret. 14 of the unique writings come from scholastic texts.

No separate table has been construed to illustrate the geographic and temporal distribution of names collected under this heading. The names are listed in alphabetical order.

lugal-a $^{(a5)}$,[1023] lugal-a-a-GUG$_2$-a-ne$_2$-nu-si $^{(a1)}$,[1024] lugal-a-bi$_2$-KU $^{(a1)}$,[1025] lugal-a-DU-nu$_2$ $^{(a1)}$,[1026] lugal-a-MIR-nu$_2$ $^{(a1)}$, lugal-a-RU $^{(°1)}$, lugal-A-SI $^{(a1)}$,[1027] lugal-A-UR-sikil $^{(a1)}$,[1028] lugal-a$^?$-UD $^{(a1)}$, lugal-a$_2$ $^{(a\geq7)}$, ⸢lugal$^?$-a$_2$⸣-da-DU $^{(a1)}$,[1029] lugal-a$_2$-LAK175 $^{(a1)}$, lugal-a$_2$-pa$_3$ $^{(a2)}$, lugal-AB $^{(a>5)}$,[1030] lugal-AB-da-SAĜ $^{(a1)}$,[1031] lugal-ab-du$_{10}$-ga $^{(a1)}$, lugal-AB-x-da $^{(a1)}$,[1032] lugal-al-sa$_6$ $^{(a\geq4)}$ 'it is pleasing to the lugal,'[1033] lugal-al$_6$-sa$_6$ $^{(a1)}$ (see prev.), lugal-alam $^{(a1)}$, lugal-alam-ak $^{(°1)}$,[1034] lugal-am-gal $^{(a1)}$ 'the lugal (is) a great bull,'[1035] lugal-ambar $^{(a1)}$ 'the lugal … the marshes (?),'[1036] lugal-AN-AB $^{(a1)}$, lugal-

---

[1023] Compare lugal-a-a, the normal Ur III orthography, H. Limet, *Anthroponymie*, 169: "Le roi est un père"; and similarly R. di Vito, StPohl SM 16, 58, 30.4a, 1. In Nik 1 44 o. i 3 (and r. i 4?), lugal-a is most likely identical with lugal-a-a-GUG$_2$-a-ne$_2$-nu-si in *DCS* 8 o. i 8, so that lugal-a is not always a nominal predicate name. See also notes to lugal-aja$_2$-ĝu$_{10}$ and lugal-la$_2$.

[1024] Once also lugal-a-a-GUG$_2$-a-ne$_2$ $^{(a1)}$. The name consists of an anticipatory genitive lugal-a(k), plus a noun or nominal nompound a(-)GUG$_2$, the resumpting 3cs poss. pron. suff. with loc. term. -e, and a negated verb. Read, phps., lugal-a-a-gar$_5$-a-ne$_2$-nu-si 'is the lugal not one who is just right for his *meadows*?'(?).

[1025] Writing of a tall and narrow KU may be the result of spacing; read then, perhaps, lugal-a-bi$_2$-dab$_5$$^!$(KU), with an original form *giri$_3$-lugal-a(k)-bi$_2$-dab$_5$, and compare Ur III PN giri$_3$-lugal-ĝa$_2$-i$_3$-dab$_5$ 'I grasped the feet of my lugal,' HSS 4 49 o. i 19 (Girsu); and see R. di Vito, StPohl SM 16, 97. For a discussion of the different interpretations suggested for the PNN *kiš-a-bi$_2$-LUL/tuš, etc., see A. Westenholz, *JAOS* 115 (1995), 536, note to p. 24f.

[1026] Parallel forms collected by J. Krecher, *ZA* 63 (1973), 198f.; J. Bauer, *AfO* 36/37 (1989/90), 80 note to 1 i 7; M. Krebernik, AOAT 296, 48f.

[1027] Compare lugal-SI.A, below, p. 181.

[1028] With all likelihood two different names: lugal-A and ur-sikil/lugal-sikil and aja$_2$-teš$_2$/lugal-teš$_2$ or ur-lugal and aja$_2$-sikil.

[1029] Compare lugal-a$_2$-da(-še$_3$), ITT 5 6722 o. 4 (Ur III Girsu).

[1030] Read, phps. lugal-abba and compare lugal-ab-ba, lugal-abba$_2$, and lugal-ad-da.

[1031] See, perhaps, names of the type lugal-x-da-kuš$_2$; and compare also lugal-AB-x-da.

[1032] AB definitely not part of compound sign abzu since all attestations of this word in ED I-II Ur has the normal sign order ZU:AB.

[1033] The name seems in certain instances to contain a loc.-term. -e for expected dat. -ra or com. -da. See for instance ^{d}En-lil$_2$-al-sa$_6$, for short ^{d}En-lil$_2$-le, OSP 2, index p. 196 s.v.v.; ama-ne$_2$-al-sa$_6$, CT 50 60 o. 7, and Nik 2 68 o. ii 2 (both Sargonic Umma); and the Ur III name nin-be$_2$-al-sa$_6$, SAT 1 o. ii 18 (translit. only). A solution to the Ur III Nippur name ^{d}En-lil$_2$-la$_2$-al-sa$_6$, H. Limet, *Anthroponymie*, 407 s.v., would be to picture -la$_2$- as harmonizing with the following vowels, but this is not altogether satisfactory. R. di Vito, StPohl SM 16, 65, 30.5a, 18, suggested that the predicate qualified the first component, in this case lugal.

[1034] Reading order based on munus-alam-ak (nu-banda$_3$), BiMes 3 14 r. i 1, list of names and professions from ED IIIb Lagaš; the duplicate *SF* 29 r. i 9 leaves out the appellative munus.

[1035] Compare the am gal kur-[ra$^?$], maybe a weapon of Ninurta, or an epithet of one, in *Angim*, l. 28; and Šulgi D l. 29: am zi am gal-še$_3$ tu-da-gin$_7$ "like a rampant wild ox, born to be a great ox," following J. Klein, *Three Šulgi Hymns*, 73. Compare also Šulgi D l. 299 of similar import. Note the DNN ^{d}Am-gal-nun and ^{d}Am-gal-KIŠ, *IAS* 86 o. ii 4 and iii 1. Since the PN is attested at Girsu only, it may hark back to a theologem of Ningirsu so far unattested.

AN-BU ? $^{(a1)}$, lugal-AN-diri $^{(a1)}$, lugal-an-ki-da $^{(a2)}$ 'the lugal … with heaven and earth,'[1037] lugal-an-ki$_2$-dub $^{(°1)}$ 'the lugal makes heaven and earth quake (?)',[1038] lugal-AN-ku$_3$-ge $^{(a1)}$,[1039] lugal-AN-mar $^{(°1)}$, lugal-asal$_2$-RU $^{(°1)}$.[1040]

lugal-bi$_2$-tum$_2$ $^{(a1)}$,[1041] lugal-bu$_3$-la-ni $^{(a1)}$.[1042]

lugal-da $^{(a8)}$,[1043] lugal-DA-gur$^?$ $^{(a1)}$, lugal-DA-gur-ra $^{(a1)}$,[1044] lugal-DA-ḪU $^{(°1)}$ 'the lugal is a DA(or a$_2^!$=ti$_8$)-bird (?),' lugal-DA-KI $^{(a1)}$, lugal-da-MU $^{(a2)}$,[1045] lugal-da-na $^{(a2)}$,[1046] lugal-da-nam $^{(a1)}$, lugal$^?$-da$^?$-tab$^?$-ba$^?$ $^{(a1)}$,[1047] lugal-DA-zi $^{(a2)}$ 'the lugal, right side

---

1036 Compare ED IIIb Girsu PN: ambar-re$_2$-si, e.g. *DP* 1/2 114 r. ii 14; and see DN ^{d}Lugal:ambar in *SF* 1 r. iv 4'''.

1037 Or perhaps lugal-an-ki is to be taken separately as a free-standing genitivally compounded epithet, presupposing a DN, as did A. Poebel, *Personennamen*, 36: (^{d}Utu-)lugal-an-ki-a, "[Utu] ist der Herr des Himmels und der Erde." See also *CIRPL* Ean. 1 o. xvi 21–22: zi ^{d}En-lil$_2$, lugal an-ki-ka.

1038 Uncertain interpretation. The name appears in an Ebla scholastic text, MEE 3 59 o. ii 4. Note the similarity to another Ebla scholastic text ARET 5 24–26, and its rendering of ki in one of the exemplars as gi, hence ki$_2$. In that same text dub$_2$ is rendered in three different ways, including du-bu$_3$, and dub could be yet another phonetic writing of this same verb.

1039 Also attested in the Ur III period, see H. Limet, *Anthroponymie*, 459 s.v. lugal-diĝir-ku$_3$-ge. There are no parallel formations with other appellatives, though an-ku$_3$-ge does appear as short form, see, e.g. *TCTI* 1 896 o. iii 17 (translit. only, Ur III Girsu), a doorkeeper of Ninḫursaĝ; and compare the epithet of the latter goddess in the anonymous and fragmentary Ur III royal inscription BIN 2 10 ii' 4' nin An ku$_3$-g[e] s[a$_4$(-a)] 'lady, named by holy An.' It is of course also possible to see -e as a loc.-term. suffix denoting a placement of the lugal in the holy heavens, that is, as a heavenly body.

1040 Follows on lugal-a-RU in *SF* 28 o. iii 6–7. Corresponds to ^{a}asal:RU in *SF* 29 o. ii 10.

1041 Following OIP 104, 56–63. Compare lugal-gal-bi$_2$-tum$_2$.

1042 Abbreviation bu$_3$-la-ni appears e.g. in ED IIIb Girsu, *DP* 1/1 38 o. i 2; *DP* 1/2 101 o. ii 1; and in CS Adab, *SIA* 640 o. i 8.

1043 E. Chiera, PBS 11/3, 194: "…lugal-da … is an abbreviation of lugal-da-nu-me-a."

1044 It would be tempting to see DA here as an incomplete writing for A$_2$, and relate the name to lugal-a$_2$-gur-ra. That is, however, problematic. The writings of this name in OIP 104 14 and 15 (ED IIIa-b Isin (?)) are all with DA and other names in no. 14 feature clear a$_2$, e.g. a$_2$-kal-le (o. iii 15) and lugal-a$_2$-zi-da (r. vi 5). RA is probably part of the name despite the fact that it on more than one occasion appears before a transitive verb featuring the dative infix -na-. The verb gur together with the comitative has a sense of "renege, go back on (a previous agreement)," J. S. Cooper, *JNES* 33 (1974), 415 (Eanatum's oath swearing passages involving the ensi$_2$ of Umma).

1045 See the final line of a late 3rd millennium incantation of unknown provenience, W. W. Hallo, *OrNS* 54 (1985), 57 (RBC 2000), reedited by N. Veldhuis, *CDLB* 2003:6, r. 8: da-ĝu$_{10}$ ^{d}Nanše al-me-a 'Nanše is at my side,' following Veldhuis' edition. DA, though visible in the copy, was left out entirely by Hallo in his edition. The ED IIIb Nippur attestation of the name is written with normal lugal (coll. from photo), as against five writings with lu:gal ligature in the same text.

1046 See, possibly, the discussion of an enigmatic formula da-na in an administrative context, G. Visicato & A. Westenholz, *Kaskal* 2 (2005), 64f. The Šuruppag attestation was collated from a photo graciously provided by A. Westenholz, and a reading DA is secure.

1047 Very uncertain. If the reading is correct, the name may relate to the lugal as holding a double-bladed weapon, see Šulgi D l. 191, commented by J. Klein, *Three Šulgi Hymns*, 103.

(?),'[1048] lugal-da-x (°1), lugal-da-[x?]-ŠE-UM (a1), lugal-dab$_5$ (a≥8) 'the lugal grasped (?),' lugal-dab$_5$-e (a1) 'the lugal grasps (?),' lugal-dab$_6$ (a2), lugal-dam (a1) 'the lugal … the/a spouse (?),'[1049] lugal-dam-da-[x] (a1),[1050] lugal-dam-MU (a1),[1051] lugal-diĝir-ra (a1) 'lugal of the gods,'[1052] lugal-DU (a≥6), lugal-DU-ME (a1/°1),[1053] lugal-DU-ni (a1), lugal-DU$_3$-UD ? (a1), lugal-du$_8$ (a>10) 'the lugal is one who releases (?)'.[1054]

en-il$_2$-lugal (a1),[1055] lugal-e (a≥7), lugal-e-e (a1), lugal-e-gal-gal (a1), lugal-e$_2$ (a≥4) 'lugal (of?) the *house*,' lugal-e$_2$-ab-ba (a1) 'the lugal in the E$_2$-ab-ba (?),'[1056] lugal-e$_2$-da (a≥3) 'the lugal … with the *house*,'[1057] lugal-e$_2$-ĝiš? (a1),[1058] lugal-e$_2$-pa$_4$ (a1), lugal-eme-UŠ (a1),[1059] lugal-EN-ne$_2$ (a1).[1060]

[1048] Or is the name an independent form similar to the name given by H. Limet, *Namenforschung*, 852: "En.ki.da.zi «la vie avec (le dieu) Enki!»"? I have not been able to locate that name anywhere.

[1049] See comments on lugal-dam-MU; and compare H. Limet, *Anthroponymie*, 173: "Le roi est l'époux," explaining the name "[ces anthroponymes] doi[ven]t être complété[s]: le roi est … l'époux de telle déesse."

[1050] Compare, phps., FPNN dam-da-nu-sa$_2$, e.g. *RTC* 63 o. i 6; and ama-da-nu-sa$_2$, e.g. VS 25 11o. ii 17: '(nothing) compares to the wife/mother' (both ED IIIb Girsu). But the sense would be different in the present name.

[1051] Since dam is largely gender neutral, the intended meaning may be similar to an entry in *SF* 77 o. vii 2: en dam mu-gi$_4$ 'the (divine) en answered (his) wife.' If this is the case, a dative is missing, evident from other names. See notes to lugal-ra-mu-gi$_4$. Compare furthermore nin-DAM-MU, also from ED IIIb Nippur, OSP 1 18 o. i 4. The interpretation by R. di Vito, StPohl SM 16, 56, 29.1a, 7: "(The) lord is my spouse," is hence not inevitable.

[1052] H. Limet, *Anthroponymie*, 140: "(Il appartient) au roi qui est dieu." D. O. Edzard, *AfO* 22 (1968/69), 13, 11.10, read the name as lu$_2$!(LUGAL)-diĝir-ra, and it is rather an unexpected name for a person. The name referred to a village or agricultural estate in Sargonic times, e.g. *STTI* 48 o. 2, and later it was used as an epithet of the storm god Adad, W. G. Lambert, *RlA* 7 (1987–90), 133 s.v. "Lugal-dingirra."

[1053] Writing order in *SF* 28 o. iii 2: lugal-DU.ME; *SF* 29 o. ii 5: lugal-ME.DU.

[1054] H. Limet, *Anthroponymie*, 241, seems to interpret this as an abbreviation of -gaba-ĝal$_2$. No prosopographical evidence from the early periods points to this.

[1055] Difficult. The person is qualified as mu$_6$-sub$_3$, and en-il$_2$ can thus not be a professional title corresponding to lu$_2$-en-il$_2$ in ED Lu C, MSL 12, 14:44. I am not sure whether en-il$_2$ in the ED IIIa Šuruppag texts is a PN, as F. Pomponio, *Prosopografia*, 98, has it; but in the ED IIIb-ES Adab text CUSAS 11 186 o. ii 1 a name en-il$_2$-⌜lu$_2$?⌝-ni is found. Inspection of photo of the latter text is inconclusive as to the identity of the third, damaged sign.

[1056] Name from ED I-II Ur, read phps. lugal-ab-ba-e$_2$?

[1057] Compare PNN e$_2$-da-ḫul$_2$ 'he/she rejoices with the *house*,' e.g. TMH 5 8 o. ii 3; e$_2$-da-lu 'he/she has grown with the *house*,' e.g. MAD 4 71 r. 7; and the FN e$_2$-da-sur-ra 'he/she/it shines with the house.'

[1058] Interpretation as PN not certain; writing ĝiš:⌜e$_2$⌝-l[u]gal.

[1059] Difficult. Read perhaps an unorthographic writing eme for im-mi, lugal-eme-us$_2$. The sign eme is not in common usage in onomastic sources.

[1060] See discussion on PN lugal-e$_2$-ni-še$_3$, above, p. 87f. w. fn. 439, for a possible fuller form.

lu[gal$^?$]-ga $^{(a1)}$, lugal-gal-bi$_2$-tum$_2$ $^{(°1)}$ 'the lugal *performs great deeds* (?),'[1061] lugal-GIM $^{(a1)}$ 'like a lugal,'[1062] lugal-GU$_2$ $^{(a\geq 4)}$, lugal-gu$_2$-gal $^{(a2)}$,[1063] lugal-GU$_2$-ĝu$_{10}$? $^{(a1)}$,[1064] lugal-gu$_7$ $^{(a1)}$, lugal-GUG$_2$ $^{(°1)}$,[1065] lugal-GUR$_8$-[x] $^{(a1)}$.

lugal-ĝir$_2$ $^{(a2)}$, lugal-ĝiš $^{(a>20)}$, lugal-ĝiš-Š[U$^?$] $^{(a1)}$.

lugal-ḫar-an-ne$_2$ $^{(a2)}$, 'the lugal (is just right for?) the road,'[1066] lugal-ḫar:an-ne$_2$ $^{(a1)}$ (see prev.),[1067] lugal-ḪAR-ma-du$_{10}$ $^{(a1)}$,[1068] lugal-ḪAR-sa $^{(°1)}$,[1069] lugal-ḫe$_2$ $^{(a\geq 14)}$, lugal-ḫe$_2$-a $^{(a1)}$, lugal-ḪI-zi $^{(°1)}$,[1070] lugal-ḪU-x $^{(a1)}$.

lugal-i-MU $^{(a1)}$,[1071] lugal-i$_3$-bi$_2$ $^{(a1)}$,[1072] lugal-I$_7$-da $^{(a1)}$ 'the lugal in/of the river,'[1073] lugal-ib-x-GAN ? $^{(a1)}$,[1074] lugal-igi $^{(a\geq 7)}$,[1075] lugal-igi-bi $^{(a1)}$, lugal-igi-il$_2$ $^{(a1)}$ 'the lugal raises (his) eyes,'[1076] lugal-igi-ni $^{(a1)}$, lugal-ildum$_3$ $^{(a\geq 5)}$,[1077] lugal-ildum$_3$-e $^{(a2)}$, lugal-

---

[1061] Sign read by G. Pettinato as tum$_2$, MEE 3, 261, not clear on photo, pl. 37. For the meaning, compare C. Wilcke, *Lugalbanda*, 50 and fn. 156, note to l. 50. See also PN lugal-bi$_2$-tum$_2$, above, p. 176.

[1062] Or, perhaps, lugal-šitim, or lugal-dim$_2$.

[1063] H. Limet, *Anthroponymie*, 167, translates "prince, premier," based on the Akk. correspondence *ašarēdum*, given in an OB list of PNN, PBS 11/1, 7 o. i 8. The interpretation "canal inspector" for this ED III word might be supported by ED LU D, where the profession precedes 'potter,' baḫar$_2$. The name has parallels in nin-gu$_2$-gal, for which, see refs. with F. Pomponio, *Prosopografia*, 197; and the rare en-⌜gu$_2$⌝-gal, CUSAS 11 282 o. 2 (ES Adab).

[1064] R. di Vito, StPohl SM 16, 58, 29.1c, 3: "(The) king is my canal-bank." H. Limet, *Anthroponymie*, 250, suggested for lugal-gu$_2$-ni: "Le roi son pays …," whereby gu$_2$ = *mātum*. Reading and interpretation remain uncertain.

[1065] Name read as lugal-bara$_2$ by E. Chiera, PBS 11/3, 240, no. 1450. Sign is GUG$_2$, not bara$_2$.

[1066] Compare E. Chiera, PBS 11/3, 213, no. 298: "The king is the fear of heaven"; and see nin-ḪAR-an-[x] in *SIA* 640 o. ii 5 (CS Adab, prob. FPN).

[1067] C. Wilcke, *EANEL*, 197 fn. 63, discussed the reading and the possible identification of this person with one of the bearers of the previous name. Add to Wilcke's references also lugal-ḫar-an-na, PBS 11/3 25 o. iv' 17', OB list of lugal-names.

[1068] The verbal chain ma-du$_{10}$ is rare in PNN. Two Ur III names are uru-ĝu$_{10}$-ma-du$_{10}$ and lugal-ma-du$_{10}$, given by H. Limet, *Anthroponymie*, 81, as: "Ma ville m'a rendu heureux, m'a fait du bien," and "Le roi m'a fait du bien," respectively. However, ḪAR would be hard to explain. Read perhaps as a phrase name with anticipatory genitive, *lugal(-ak)-murum-ma(-ni)-du$_{10}$, "the resounding of the lugal is good," bearing on an atmospheric phenomenon?

[1069] Attested only at Ebla. Read perhaps lugal-ḫur-sa, for lugal-ḫur-saĝ, and compare the alternative writings ur-sa/saĝ-da for the same person, also representing a Sumerian name, M. V. Tonietti, Subartu 4/2, 90 fn. 90.

[1070] Compare nu-gal-ḪI-zi, and see in ḪI a phonetic writing of šer$_7$ (šar$_2$)?

[1071] Compare lugal-NI-i-MU, below, p. 180, also of unknown meaning.

[1072] Sumerian? Compare Akk. *be-li$_2$*-NE, e.g. MAD 1 326 o. i 8, o. ii 7 (CS Ešnuna); *śar-ru*-NE, and later Sumerian lugal-i$_3$-bi$_2$-la, e.g. *RTC* 198 o. 6 (Lagaš II Girsu).

[1073] Still in use in OB times, A. Poebel, *Personennamen*, 29. Compare post–3rd millennium DN ^{d}lugal-I$_7$-da, for which, see K. Tallqvist, *AGE*, 354 s.v. "Lugal-id$_2$-da," translated: "König des Flusses"; W. G. Lambert, *RlA* 7 (1987–90), 142 s.v. "Lugal-idda," given as: "Lord of the (cosmic) river."

[1074] Perhaps not a lugal-name. Reading IB, or IB.GAL as professional title, is possible.

[1075] With H. Limet, *Anthroponymie*, 256, the name is an abbreviation.

[1076] Naturally, igi-il$_2$ could be seen as a passive participle, 'the lugal is looked at,' perhaps with a sense of 'admired.' See Å. Sjöberg, *MNS*, 59: "das Auge (den Blick) erheben … ist oft ein Ausdruck des Begehrens oder Auswählens," with many refs.

IM $^{(a5)}$, lugal-IM-ru $^{(a1)}$,[1078] lugal-IM-ru-a $^{(a1)}$ 'the lugal (in?/of?) the neighbourhood (?),'[1079] lugal-IM-SILA$_3$$^{?}$ $^{(a1)}$.[1080]

lugal-KA $^{(a>25)}$, lugal-KA-GAN-ki $^{(a1)}$,[1081] lugal-KA-NIĜ$_2$-U $^{(a\geq1)}$,[1082] lugal-KA-SI-U$_2$-LUM $^{(a1)}$, lugal-KA-U$_2$$^{?}$ $^{(a1)}$, lugal-kas$_4$ $^{(a1)}$, lugal-kas$_4$-e $^{(a4)}$ 'the lugal runs (?),' lugal-kas[kal$^{?}$] $^{(a1)}$, lugal-ki $^{(a\geq10)}$, lugal-ki-NI $^{(a1)}$, lugal-ki-NI-gi$_4$ $^{(a\geq1)}$,[1083] lugal-ki-nu-gi$_4$ $^{(a1)}$ 'the lugal (in) the place of no return (?),'[1084] lugal-KI-ŠIR-PA$^{?}$-⸢x⸣ $^{(a1)}$,[1085] °lugal-KISAL×PAP $^{(°1)}$, lugal-KIŠ$^{?}$-ĜA$_2$×GU$_4$$^{?}$ $^{(a1)}$,[1086] lugal-ku$_3$ $^{(a\geq2)}$,[1087] lugal-kun $^{(a3)}$, lugal-

---

[1077] Only rarely found outside of the Umma-Zabala area. Compare later deity by a similar name, W. G. Lambert, *RlA* 7 (1987–90), 142 s.v. "Lugal-ilduma," given as "Lord of the clan." Once, BIN 8 114 r. (!) i 10 (ED IIIb Umma-Zabala), this name (ildum$_3$ here written NAGAR.MUNU$_4$), is written in the same case as a PN ur-saĝ; a comparison with M. deJ. Ellis, *JCS* 31 (1979), 30–55 no. 6 o. iv 11–14 shows 3 of the same persons as are found, in different order, in BIN 8 114 r. (!) i 7 and 10. Hence, there is no reason to posit a *lugal-ur-saĝ-ildum$_3$.

[1078] The hand copy of the earliest instance of lugal-IM-ru shows damage. Restore probably original NI$_2$(LAK377) for this name according to parallel Utu-NI$_2$-ru, *WF* 41 o. v 7'; 107 o. iv 4. The meaning of IM-ru here as "neighbourhood," "family," or "clan," is therefore not secure. See in general discussion by M. Krebernik, *BFE*, 27f., w. note 27, and 308.

[1079] For alternation between -ri and -ru in im-ri/-ru "family," and other compounds, see M. Krebernik, *BFE*, 309, note 34. The lexical equivalent of *ramûm*, *CAD* R s.v. *ramû* B, is evidently never given as ru, but would merit an interpretation as a descriptive name 'the lugal is endowed with awe/instills fear.' Compare E. Chiera, PBS 11/1, 69, no. 351: "[lugal]-im-ri-a" (glossed *ša-[a-na]*), and fn. 4, offering two proposals: "the king of the storming wind," and "the king who goes by himself." See further Chiera's translation of essentially the same name, PBS 11/3, 212, no. 264: lugal-ni$_2$-ri-a "The only king."

[1080] Name etched into clay after hardening. Reading of last sign and mng. uncertain.

[1081] Compare, phps., FPN GAN-ki, e.g. *DP* 1/2 128 o. ii 6; 129 o. ii 6 (ED IIIb Girsu).

[1082] One attestation from ED IIIb Umma-Zabala, one from ES Umma. For the possibility that both attestations refer to the same individual, see B. R. Foster, *USP*, 43. Foster discusses prosopographical links between ED IIIb texts and the ES mu-iti-archive from his group A. Compare, perhaps, lugal-gu$_7$, from CS Girsu.

[1083] For short: ki-NI-gi$_4$, *FTUM* 83 o. i 2. Writing with appellative and gi$_4$ predicate only attested in texts from ED IIIb Umma-Zabala. Compare e$_2$-ki-be$_2$-gi$_4$, *TSA* 10 r. iv 15 (ED IIIb Girsu); and e$_2$-ki-be$_6$-gi$_4$, TMH 5 29 (with better copy *ECTJ* 29) r. iii 7.

[1084] Known only from an ED I-II Ur text; reading not entirely secure. Name is preceded by a ĜA$_2$ which is hard to explain in this context. Connections to kur-nu-gi$_4$-a of much later times are tentative to say the least.

[1085] PN ? The text lists GN, Adab and Šuruppag, without place determinative ^{ki}, and what looks like PNN, e.g. AN-mud. A reading lugal-GN^{ki} is therefore less likely.

[1086] Damaged and very doubtful.

[1087] Three instances from the CS Adab archives sport damaged signs following ku$_3$. A reading si[mug$^{?}$] for two of the attestations (*SIA* 675 & OIP 14 106) was proposed by Z. Yang, *SIA*, 301; 323. At least one of the texts deals with deliveries of copper, which adds some weight to Yang's assumption. For OIP 14 78, B. R. Foster, *JAOS* 115 (1995), 538, read lugal-ku$_3$-zu, attested elsewhere in the same period, though not in texts from CS Adab. Photos of all three texts have proven inconclusive. The remains of the last sign are not compatible with maḫ, as in lugal-ku$_3$-maḫ, from Ur III Nippur, *NATN* 970 r. 2; and Girsu, *SET* 315 o. 5 (translit. only).

kun$_5$ (TUR.ŠE$_3$) $^{(a\geq3)}$, lugal-kun$_5$ (TUR.ŠE$_3$)-ne$_2$ $^{(a1)}$,[1088] lugal-kur $^{(a\geq7)}$ 'the lugal (is like?) a mountain.'[1089]

lugal-lu$_2$-LAK545-ne-saĝ $^{(a1)}$,[1090] lugal-lu$_2$-saĝ $^{(a1)}$, lugal-lu$_2$-ŠE$_3$-IG-ŠE$_3$ $^{(a1)}$.

lugal-ma$_2$-tab-ba $^{(a1)}$ 'the lugal … a two-pronged boat (?),'[1091] lugal-maš-usu(A$_2$.KAL) $^{(a1)}$, lugal-maškim-e $^{(a\geq2)}$,[1092] lugal-me $^{(a1)}$,[1093] lugal-mes-e $^{(a1)}$ 'the lugal … by the hero,'[1094] lugal-MU $^{(a\geq8)}$,[1095] lugal-mu-da $^{(a3)}$,[1096] lu:gal-mu-dib $^{(a1)}$, lugal-mu-ĝal$_2$ $^{(a1)}$ 'the lugal is present (at/for …),' lugal-mu-LAGAB×PA$^{!?}$ $^{(a1)}$, lugal-mu-ni-da $^{(a1)}$ 'the lugal … with his name (?),'[1097] lugal-mu-še$_3$-ĝal$_2$ $^{(a\geq1)}$, lugal-mu-zu-da $^{(a\geq2)}$,[1098] lugal-muš $^{(a2)}$.

lugal-nagar $^{(a1)}$ 'the lugal (is) a carpenter,' lugal-nagar-zi $^{(a2)}$ 'the lugal (is) a reliable carpenter,' lugal-nam $^{(a\geq3)}$, lugal-nam-DUB ? $^{(a1)}$, lugal-NE-nu-si $^{(a1)}$, lugal-NE-nu-um $^{(a1)}$,[1099] lugal-NI-du$_8$ $^{(a1)}$,[1100] lugal-NI-i-MU $^{(a1)}$,[1101] lugal-ni$_2$-bi-ak $^{(°1)}$, lugal-NI$_2$-D[U$^{?}$]

[1088] Read as *lugal-dumu-gir$_{15}$ -ni by M. Maiocchi, CUSAS 13 108 r. 3, and also on p. 17.

[1089] The discussion by H. Limet, *Anthroponymie*, 271f., on the equation kur = *napāḫu* is probably beside the point, but *napāḫu* does appear in later PNN, *CAD* N/1 s.v., 4c, b'. At least once, Nik 1 3 o. ii 7, the name is short for lugal-kur-dub$_2$, *DP* 1/2 136 o. i 2 (ED IIIb Girsu).

[1090] Copy of *RIAA* 44 is inaccurate in many ways. Photo (CDLI P010547) is clear. Compare DN ^{d}Lugal-LAK545 in Abū Ṣalābīḫ god list, *IAS* 83 r. iv 10, to which, see W. G. Lambert, *RlA* 7 (1987–90), 134, "Lugal-dur(a)": "perhaps … "lord of the (cosmic) bond." See also the discussion on DUR(LAK545) by G. Marchesi N. Marchetti, MesCiv 14, 161 fn. 44.

[1091] Name perhaps referring to the appearance of the moon at the beginning of the month, as in Enūma eliš V 16, quoted by *CAD* Q s.v. *qarnu*, 3.

[1092] The exact meaning of maškim here is open to question. Compare Urnamma EF l. 35: ^{d}Ur-^{d}Namma-ke$_4$ maškim (with phon. var. maš-gi-i…) im-me "Urnamma is in charge," following E. Flückiger-Hawker, OBO 166, 283.

[1093] All attestations of this name can with reasonable certainty be ascribed to the reign of LugalANda of Lagaš. On G. J. Selz's, FAOS 15/1, 401, remarks on a possible identification on phonetic grounds with lugal-me$_3$-TUR-še$_{(3)}$-nu-še$_{(27)}$-ge, compare J. Bauer, *AfO* 36/37 (1989/90), 87 note to 175 K, who finds lugal-me more likely to be an abbreviation of lugal-me-gal-gal. No prosopographical ties between either name are known to me.

[1094] Compare H. Limet, *Anthroponymie*, 316: "Le roi est un héros."

[1095] At least four persons from ED IIIb Girsu are associated with the abbreviated writing lugal-mu for lugal-mu-da-kuš$_2$ and lugal-mu-še$_3$-ĝal$_2$. See further H. Limet, *Anthroponymie*, 93 and 175: "Mon roi (…)" where Limet discusses the name as an end result of a process in which both verbs and qualifiers could be disposed of.

[1096] The name was taken as variant of Akk. *śar-ru-mu-da* by R. di Vito, StPohl SM 16, 216f., 30.5a, 18. If the name is to be read in Sumerian – which is likely given the fact that two attestations come from the ED IIIb south – compare lugal-mu-da-kuš$_2$, lugal-mu-da-ri$_2$, and theophore parallel ^{d}Utu-mu-da-ḫul$_2$, e.g. *DP* 2/1 191 r. iii 4 (ED IIIb Girsu).

[1097] Compare mu-ni-^{d}I$_7$-da, CUSAS 14 258 o. i 3 (ED IIIb Umma-Zabala); and the more commonly attested mu-ni-da, e.g. *DP* suppl. 487 r. ii 2 (ED IIIb Girsu).

[1098] Suggestion by I. J. Gelb, apud G. Eisen, OIP 47, 81, note no. 33, to read ZU as su$_2$ does not add to the understanding of this name.

[1099] See discussion of *lugal-*bi$_2$-nu-um*.

[1100] Read lugal-i$_3$-du$_8$ 'the lugal released (?)'; or lugal-ni-du$_8$ 'his lugal is one who opens(?).' The former could potentially be interpreted as referring to the profession "door-opener," making the lugal an opener of doors (to the world of the living). Parallel names formed with other professions are well-known.

[1101] Compare lugal-i-MU, above, p. 178, likewise of unknown meaning.

$^{(a1)}$,[1102] lugal-ni$_3$-gur$_8$ $^{(a1)}$, lugal-ni$_3$-UET2-276 $^{(a1)}$, lugal-NIĜ$_2$ $^{(a>12)}$, lugal-nu-KI-SAĜ $^{(°3)}$,[1103] lugal-nun-DU $^{(a1)}$.

lugal-pa$_4$-zu $^{(a≥1)}$ 'the lugal knows the uncle.'[1104]

lugal-ra $^{(a≥14)}$ '… to the lugal,'[1105] lugal-ra-diri $^{(a1)}$, lugal-ra-mu-gi$_4$ $^{(a≥2)}$ '… answered the lugal,'[1106] lu:gal-RA-si ? $^{(a1)}$, lugal-RU $^{(°2)}$.

lugal-^{sa_2}sag$_7$ $^{(a1)}$ 'the lugal is one who vanquishes (evil portents?),' lugal-saĝ-du$_{10}$ $^{(a1)}$,[1107] lugal-si $^{(a1)}$,[1108] lugal-SI.A $^{(a≥1)}$,[1109] lugal-si-DU$_6$-e $^{(a1)}$, lugal-si-NE-e $^{(a≥1)}$,[1110] lugal-sur$_x$(ERIM) $^{(a2)}$, lugal-sur$_x$(ERIM)-ra-sa$_6$ $^{(a1)}$, lugal-sur$_x$(ERIM)-re$_2$-ki-aĝ$_2$ $^{(a1)}$ 'the lugal is one who loves the (work) troops (?).'[1111]

lugal-ša$_3$ $^{(a>27)}$,[1112] lugal-ša$_3$-ENGUR $^{(a1)}$,[1113] lugal-ša$_3$-ga $^{(a1)}$,[1114] lugal-ša$_3$-⸢ĜA$_2$×X⸣ $^{(°1)}$, lugal-ša$_3$-uru $^{(a1)}$ 'the lugal in the midst of the city,' lugal-ša$_3$(-)za$_3$-[x] ? $^{(a1)}$,[1115] lugal-

---

[1102] The sign NI$_2$ corresponds to UET2-389b, DU is a possibility given the remaining wedges.

[1103] One instance, *SF* 63 o. vi 4, was left out by Deimel, visible on photo (CDLI P010654). Sign order is the same in all exemplars. Compare ED Word List C 1–4: ad-gi$_4$ 'advice,' ki-saĝ, ad-ḫal 'secret,' abrig 'steward.' An interpretation saĝ-ki = *sakkû* "rites, ritual regulations," *CAD* S s.v. *sakkû* A, is possible, but the negation nu remains problematic. Compare PNN ur-ki-saĝ (BIN 8 26 o. iii 3', ED IIIb Adab, Meskigala ensi$_2$ Adab^{ki}/Luzag. lugal; *SIA* 667 o. 4', CS Adab (not copied; photo: CDLI P217481); MesCiv 4 60 lower edge, CS, prob. Adab); and ki-saĝ-gam-gam '(s)he nods the head (toward) the ground,' MVN 3 14 o. iii 2 (ED IIIb, unknown).

[1104] According to later lexical tradition pa$_4$ could represent the father, brother or (exclusively male?) offspring. It is quite difficult to see which is intended in earlier PNN, see e.g. *CAD* B s.v. *bukru*, lex. sect.

[1105] The name is an abbreviation, several possible alternatives exist, see e.g. J. Hilgert, Imgula 5, 207 fn. 148.

[1106] A possible abbreviation of (noun)-lugal-ra-mu-gi$_4$. Compare aja$_2$-en-ra-mu-gi$_4$, e.g. Nik 1 211 o. ii 2. There is no room on photo of MVN 10 85 for gal in lu[gal$^?$]-ra-mu-gi$_4$, suggested by F. Pomponio, *Prosopografia*, 160. Copy of Nik 1 41 r. i 5 erroneously leaves out ⸢gi$_4$,⸣ indicated by G. J. Selz, *AWEL*, 207. The earliest attestation of this name is ED IIIb in date.

[1107] Name is copied by L. Legrain, *RA* 32 (1935), 126, with line divider between lugal and saĝ-du$_{10}$. I follow here the renderings of F. Pomponio, *Prosopografia*, 160; and *FTUM*, 152.

[1108] Object or predicate missing. Is si=*qarnum*, *šarūrum*, *malûm*, or *maṣûm*? Compare the homonymous DN, W. G. Lambert, *RlA* 7 (1987–90), 151 s.v. "Lugal-si".

[1109] Compare R. di Vito, StPohl SM 16, 62f., 30.5a, 2: "(The) god is preeminent," interpreting SI.A as dirig, which is certainly possible. See also lugal-A-SI and lugal-a-a-GUG$_2$-a-ne$_2$-nu-si.

[1110] Name appears also in Ur III sources: H. Limet, *Anthroponymie*, 472 s.v. "Lugal-si-bil-e." One of the attestations reads si-NE-e only. Most Ur III references come from the Umma area.

[1111] Variant lugal-sur$_x$(ERIM)-ki-aĝ$_2$ $^{(a1)}$. All attestations are from ED IIIb Girsu. An alternative interpretation could be 'the lugal is beloved by the working (class).' It all depends on the function of -e, as ergative marker on a collective or the loc.-term. marker used on the logical object for ki–aĝ$_2$.

[1112] Attested as abbreviation for several persons named lugal-ša$_3$-la$_2$-tuku in ED IIIb Girsu; including a chief singer, a field measurer, a cook and a scribe. See more, below, p. 236.

[1113] Compare E. Sollberger & J.-R. Kupper, *IRSA* 319: "roi parmi les eaux souterraines (?)."

[1114] The name ought probably to be completed with a poss. pron. suffix -ni, as the abbreviation ša$_3$ -ga-ni is attested from the Sargonic period on. See Nippur refs., A. Westenholz, *OSP* 2, index p. 198. The full form is difficult to reconstruct, but see comm. to lugal-ša$_3$-su$_3$.

ŠE$_3$-saĝ $^{(a1)}$,[1116] lugal-šu $^{(a\geq6)}$, lugal-šu-du$_{11}$ $^{(a1)}$ 'the lugal transformed … (?)',[1117] lugal-šu-gi$_4$-gi$_4$ $^{(a1)}$,[1118] lugal-šu-ĝal$_2$ $^{(a1)}$ (PN?), lugal-šu-mu-gi$_4$ $^{(a1)}$ 'the lugal restored … (to someone),'[1119] lugal-ŠU$_2$ $^{(a1)}$, lugal-šuba$_3$ $^{(a1)}$, lugal-šuba$_3$-zi $^{(a1)}$.[1120]

lugal-tab $^{(a1)}$ (PN?), lugal-TAR $^{(a\geq7)}$,[1121] lugal-TAR-me-te $^{(a1)}$, lugal-ti $^{(a2)}$,[1122] lugal-tir $^{(a\geq1)}$ 'the lugal … the forest,'[1123] lugal-tir-a-DU $^{(a1)}$ 'the lugal stands (?) in the woods,' lugal-TUR-X $^{(a1)}$.[1124]

lugal-u$_2$ $^{(a2)}$,[1125] lugal-u$_2$-dag-dag $^{(a1)}$, lugal-u$_2$-tak$_4$ $^{(a2)}$, lugal-u$_4$-de$_3$ $^{(a\geq2)}$,[1126] lugal-uru $^{(a\geq9)}$,[1127] lugal-URUDU-da $^{(a1)}$,[1128] lugal-UŠ $^{(a4)}$,[1129] lugal-uš-su$_{20}$ $^{(a1)}$, lugal-uš-su$_x$(MUŠ)

1115 Perhaps two names in a single line. The second could be za$_3$-mu. Both names are found in Adab during the ES-MS period, but they are so far never attested in the same text.

1116 Compare lugal-inim-še$_3$, and lugal-saĝ-bi-še$_{3\text{-}90°}$, p. 139 and 169, above, respectively.

1117 A sense 'to touch,' Akk. *lapātum* could also be considered. However, many senses of the verb *lapātum* have negative overtones, e.g. *CAD* L s.v. *lapātu*, and hence the idea of a transformation, a change of state in a positive sense is to be preferred. The slightly later sense of '(handi)work, creation,' attested for the nominal derivative, *CAD* L s.v. *liptu* A s., lex. sect., is seen, e.g. in the name *li-pi$_5$-it-i$_3$-le*, ensi$_2$ of Marad and son of *Narām*-Su'en, YOS 1 10 ii 2.

1118 Compare lugal-šu-mu-gi$_4$.

1119 The interpretation is tentative but is strongly reminiscent of a recurring phrase in ED IIIb Lagaš royal inscriptions, šu-a–gi$_4$, for which, see refs. in FAOS 6, 139b. Also, šu-a-gi$_4$-a was the term used for a type of payment or due, see W. Sallaberger, *Fs Klein*, 249–251; G. Visicato & A. Westenholz, CUSAS 11, 8. Compare ED IIIb Uruk PN šu-na-mu-gi$_4$, *RIAA* 14 o. i 2, an official under Enšakušana. The object "restored" is unclear, but it may be the child.

1120 Compare H. Limet, *Anthroponymie*, 474: "lugal-šuba-zi," w. fn. 1; translated on p. 316 as: "le roi est un héros fidèle."

1121 Compare, perhaps, lugal-sila(TAR)-si, above, p. 130.

1122 Compare E. Chiera, PBS 11/3, 213, no. 312: lugal-ti-la, given as "The king of life."

1123 Neither photo nor copy of the text has been published, but it is unlikely that TIR represents *^{še}šer$_7$. The text, MAD 4 45, is from Umma, and other Umma names include the professional title nagar 'carpenter.' This name, then, is part of a group of names native to that area.

1124 C. L. Woolley assigned a date of ED IIIa or -b to the seal on which the name is found, and suggested a reading *lugal-tur-nir (?), UE 2, 316 fn.1; 588. The date is at any rate too high and should probably rather be ED IIIb-ES. In accordance with the discussion by G. Marchesi, *OrNS* 73 (2004), 185, a reading *lugal-tur is out of the question, but a better reading for the third sign does not present itself.

1125 Appears once as an abbreviation of lugal-u$_2$-tak$_4$.

1126 See, tentatively, the brief discussion by S. Mirelman & W. Sallaberger, *ZA* 100 (2010), 184, note to r. 2' etc.: u$_4$-de$_3$ with gloss di, and the suggested meaning "today." That interpretation would be obscure in this PN. An abbreviation is most likely.

1127 Compare DN in E. Sollberger & J.-R. Kupper, *IRSA* 319: Lugal-uru "'roi de la ville.' Sans doute Nin-Ĝirsu"; similarly K. Tallqvist, *AGE*, 358 s.v.: "König der Stadt", and see dissenting view by H. Steible, ABW 2, 8 note 9 (comm. to *CIRPL* Urn. 24), who preferred to see in Lugal-uru an abbreviation for the DNN Lugal-uru-bar(-ra) or Lugal-uru$_{11}$(URU×KAR$_2$).

1128 Attested only at ED IIIb Umma-Zabala. The name may contain a reference to a copper artefact associated with Ningirsu, receiving oil offerings, alongside ^{ĝiš}šar$_2$-ur$_3$ and šar$_2$-gaz and an anonymous ig 'door,' in *RTC* 196 o. ii 2–6. The URUDU-da and the ig both receive twice the amount of oil as ^{ĝiš}šar$_2$-ur$_3$ and šar$_2$-gaz, which makes it reasonable to assume that the entries cover two distinct objects in each line. Compare Gudea StB v 37–44. Another name related to Ningirsu attested at Umma-Zabala is lugal-kur-dub$_2$.

$^{(a\geq5)}$,[1130] lugal-ušum-AN $^{(a1)}$, lugal-ušur$_3$ $^{(a\geq6)}$, lugal-ušur$_3$-MU $^{(a\geq4)}$, lugal-ušur$_3$-ra $^{(a>7)}$, lugal-ušur$_3$-ra-nu$_2$ $^{(a>3)}$,[1131] lugal-ušur$_4$ $^{(a3)}$, lugal-ušur$_4$-MU $^{(a\geq5)}$, lugal-ušur$_x$(LAL+KU) $^{(a1)}$.

lugal-zi $^{(a\geq7)}$ 'the lugal is reliable (?),'[1132] lugal-zi-de$_3$? $^{(a1)}$.

nu-gal $^{(a\geq3)}$,[1133] nu-gal-AŠ$_2$-DA $^{(a1)}$,[1134] nu-gal-ḪI-zi $^{(°1)}$,[1135] nu-gal-NI-zi $^{(a1)}$,[1136] nu-gal-zi-ga $^{(a1)}$.[1137]

UD-lugal-le $^{(a1)}$ (PN?), za-lugal $^{(a1)}$.

3.1.9 Non–existent names and misreadings

Assyriology has long depended on hand copies of texts made available to larger audiences. With the advent of cheaper photographic reproduction in text publications came the potential for greater accuracy. However, the problems of reproducing three-dimensional script on rounded tablet surfaces, not to mention partially destroyed signs are obvious. Even today, with the possi-

---

[1129] ED IIIa attestation from Šuruppag employs ARAD for later UŠ, in accordance with writing conventions of the times.

[1130] Reading of this and the previous name discussed as parallels, without suggestion as to meaning by J. Bauer, *ZA* 79 (1989), 9. See parallel nin-uš-su$_{20}$, e.g. VS 25 69 o. vii 15 (ED IIIb Girsu).

[1131] Once written lugal-ušur$_3$-nu$_2$ $^{(a1)}$. M. Powell, *OrNS* 43 (1974), 398–403, has a list of different writings, and presents evidence that ušur$_3$ and ušur$_4$ denotes a person.

[1132] Similarly R. di Vito, StPohl SM 16, 66., 30.5a, 21: "Ba'u is faithful." See also the GN bad$_3$-lugal-zi^{ki}, perhaps located in the area east of Girsu, *STTI* 141 o. 9' (CS Girsu), and B. R. Foster, *AfO* 28 (1981–82), 141. The Ur III PN lugal-zi-ĝu$_{10}$ "the lugal is my life," H. Limet, *Anthroponymie*, 477 (-zi-mu), offers another avenue for interpretation. It could also be an abbreviation of a longer name.

[1133] One instance from CS Adab, CUSAS 13 11 o. 3, was discussed by the editor M. Maiocchi as possibly containing a phonetic rendering of the title lugal, which is likely given the context. The person or office of nu-gal is listed as receiving 10 workers, following upon 7 destined for the queen and 4 for the šabra e$_2$. Compare DN ^{d}Nu-gal in the Abū Ṣalābīḫ god list, *IAS* 83 o. iii' 6'; 84 o. i' 4'. Reading nu phonetic for nu$_{11}$? See P. Mander, *Pantheon*, 60, no. 181, and compare note to PN lugal-Unug, above.

[1134] P. Steinkeller, *Fs Hallo*, 239 proposed reading nu-gal-az$_2$-da, for lugal-a$_2$-zi-da.

[1135] Name of a singer from Mari in the Ebla documentation. To be read nu-gal-šar$_2$-zi, and to be interpreted as phonetic for lugal-šer$_7$-zi? See also lugal-ḪI-zi.

[1136] Name of a singer from Mari in the Ebla documentation. Interpreted as "*lugal-i$_3$-zi," said to be parallel with "inim-i$_3$-zi" (read instead inim-ni-zi), P. Mander, *JAOS* 108 (1988), 482. P. Steinkeller, *Fs Hallo*, 245, held the name to be a phonetic writing for lugal-ezem due to an entry in a still unpublished text (TM.75.G.1917) which sported the writing EN:LUGAL, not in itself unproblematic. Compare his discussion *op. cit.*, p. 239. See further M. Krebernik, *Fs Röllig*, 190 w. fn. 13.

[1137] Interpreted as "*lugal-zi-ga," with ref. to lugal-mu-ba-zi-ge, Limet, *Anthroponymie*, 121, P. Mander, *JAOS* 108 (1988), 482. P. Steinkeller, *Fs Hallo*, 237 & 245 (Addendum), pointed out that *lugal-zi-ga has no direct parallel in 3rd millennium Mesopotamia and that a variant in the text mentioned in the previous footnote (TM.75.G.1917) has u$_3$-zi-ga, without LUGAL. Perhaps phonetic for lugal-uzug$_x$(AN.ZAG)-še$_3$?

bilities of internet databases of photographs, nothing outdoes actual handling and inspection of the original tablets.

In the following, some readings of lugal-names extant in secondary literature are corrected. The following names are readings which can now be discarded. Discrepancies from the present work which are the result, for example, of varying diacritic values, or tonal quality of sibilants, are not improved on; nor are values which are readily identifiable or well-established, e.g. -ur-mu > -teš$_2$-ĝu$_{10}$. Notes on the new readings result from collation of photographs and from more general comparison of onomastic materials. The readings have been converted to the standards followed in this work unless otherwise indicated.

*AN-lugal.[1138] In Sumerian contexts related to offerings to be read diĝir lugal(-ak). Attestations are known from Ur, Girsu and Adab.[1139]

*dumu-lugal-nam.[1140] To be read as regens-rectus chain dumu Lugal-nam(-ak).

*lu-ga-lu-mu-ug.[1141] Not a phonetic writing for a Sumerian name. To be understood as *lū-kalūmuk* 'he is indeed your lamb.'

*lugal-a-maḫ.[1142] A parallel makes for an identification with lugal-i$_7$-maḫ certain. Read lugal-i$_7^!$(A)-maḫ, or lugal-i$_5$ -maḫ.[1143]

*lugal-a$_2$-gur-re$_2$.[1144] To be read lugal-a$_2$-gur-ra, as indicated already by A. Westenholz and supported by photo of text.[1145]

*lugal-a$_2$-MUG.GU-pa$_3$.[1146] The elements MUG.GU were correctly identified by J. Bauer as a name lugal-a$_2$-pa$_3$ with the title gu:sur.[1147] P. Steinkeller's suggestion to read lugal-pa$_3$:da$^!$(A$_2$),[1148] might be considered were it for a single case, but all 4 writings, 3 of ED IIIb date, sport the sequence a$_2$-pa$_3$, of uncertain meaning.

[1138] So the editors of *TCABI* 8. The text reads: 1 udu niĝa, diĝir lugal(-ak), <ezem/iti$^?$> ^{d}Šuba$_3$-nun. The last line probably indicates a time of the year, most likely a festival, even though the word ezem is missing. A festival of ^{d}Šuba$_3$-nun, giving rise to a month name, is known from the early Adab calendar, see M. E. Cohen, *The Cultic Calendars of the Ancient Near East*, 201–205; *TCABI*, 62f.

[1139] For ED IIIb Ur, see G. Visicato & A. Westenholz, Kaskal 2 (2005), 65; for an ED IIIa Girsu attestation, see *RTC* 8 o. iii 3: diĝir lugal, listing deities and temples reciving bread offerings.

[1140] So V. V. Struve, *Onomastika*, 40. Read in *DP* 2/2 453 o. i 2: dumu lugal-NAM(-ke$_4$, na bi$_2$-ri).

[1141] *OAIC* 31 r. 1. I. J. Gelb understood the name as lugal- and gave a parallel for the interpretation of umug.

[1142] So V. V. Struve, *Onomastika*, 97.

[1143] Same person appears in Nik 1 3 o. iv 1. See note on variants A maḫ and i$_7$ maḫ in different versions of the Instructions of Šuruppag, J. Bauer, *AoN* 21 (1985), 2f.

[1144] So A. Falkenstein, AnOr 28, 27, fn. 2; D. O. Edzard, *SRU* no. 25.

[1145] See A. Westenholz, *ECTJ* no. 75, and photo (CDLI P020489).

[1146] So H. Steible & H. Behrens, ABW 2, 345 (Anonym 10), l. 3. The name was read by E. Sollberger, *Genava* 26 (1948), 66, as: *mug-gu-pa$_3$ dumu lugal-a$_2$.

[1147] J. Bauer, *OLZ* 80 (1985), 150.

[1148] *NABU* 1990/14. In Steinkeller's note on parallels to this name, correct *DP* 59 to 593.

*lugal-AB.URI$_3$.KI.[1149] Despite the orthographic problems, read lugal-Urim$_x$(AB.URI$_3$)^{ki}. Parallels made up by other important cities and the close graphic similarity between ŠEŠ and URI$_3$ are factors which speak in favour of the identification, while the writing order and one or two missing wedges inside URI$_3$ speak against it.

*lugal-an-na-igi-su-su.[1150] Read lugal-igi-An-na-ke$_4^!$-su.[1151]

*lugal-dam-me-ki-aĝ$_2$.[1152] Read instead lugal-Muš$_3$-bar-ki-aĝa$_2$, as copied. A deity ^{d}Nin-Muš$_3$-bar is attested a handful of times in ED IIIb Girsu.[1153] See also *lugal-muš$_3$-me-ki-aĝ$_2$.

*lugal-dib-ra-na$_2$.[1154] Following G. J. Selz, read lugal-⸢ušur$_3^!$(DIB)⸣-ra-nu$_2$.[1155]

*lugal-du$_{10}$-bar-SU.[1156] Read lugal-mas-su$_2$ «x».

*lugal-dub-saĝ-ki.[1157] With all probability not a lugal-PN.[1158]

*lugal-e$_2$-balaĝ, *lugal-e$_2$-balaĝ-mete(TE+ME), *lugal-e$_2$-balaĝ-ni-du$_{10}$.[1159] Read lugal-tigi$_x$(E$_2$.BALAĜ), etc.[1160]

*lugal-e$_2$-gal.[1161] Read lugal-sa-šuš-gal. No PN combining lugal and e$_2$-gal is known before the Ur III period. A FPN nin-e$_2$-gal-le-si is, however, known from ED IIIb Girsu;[1162] and the e$_2$-gal is mentioned also in the genitival phrase name ur-e$_2$-gal, attested already at ED IIIa Šuruppag.[1163]

*lugal-en$_3$-nu-su$_3$.[1164] Read securely lugal-en$_3$-tar$^!$-su$_3$.

*lugal-engar-du$_{10}$.[1165] On account of a Sargonic and several later parallels with the determinative ^{ĝiš}, read lugal-apin-du$_{10}$.

[1149] So J. Krecher, *ZA* 63 (1973), 252–254, with a well-founded argumentation. Krecher categorically denied that AB.URI$_3$ could stand for Urim$_5$ (ŠEŠ.AB), but no convincing alternative presents itself. I. J. Gelb read the same name, MAD 4 36 r. 6 as lugal-ab Bala-ki.

[1150] So V. V. Struve, *Onomastika*, 98.

[1151] Collation of tablet in Berlin shows J. Marzahn's copy of VS 25 70 to be very accurate, but there is no doubt as to the identity of the person, otherwise given with -ke$_4$-.

[1152] So G. J. Selz, *Götterwelt*, 202 fn. 933, and index p. 402 on *DP* 2/1 220 o. iii 5.

[1153] G. J. Selz, *Götterwelt*, 262f., with notes.

[1154] So V. V. Struve, *Onomastika*, 99.

[1155] G. J. Selz, *AWEL*, 79, on Nik 1 3 o. vii 14.

[1156] So V. V. Struve, *Onomastika*, 100. Nikol'skij's copy of MAŠ as BAR in Nik 1 181 o. iii 2 is faulty. Photo (CDLI P221950) has clear MAŠ.

[1157] So H. de Genouillac, writing on ITT 2/2 4544: "2 chevaux, Lugal-dub-sag-ki le scribe"; followed by G. Visicato, *The Power and the Writing*, 279.

[1158] Since the text is only published in partial transliteration it is hard to assess what the entry means. Read, possibly: '2 calves (for) the lugal. First (accounting), place of the scribe.' Compare ITT 2/2 5762 r. 4': ensi$_2$ dub-saĝ [remainder of reverse broken].

[1159] So V. V. Struve, *Onomastika*, 100.

[1160] Reading tigi$_x$(E$_2$.BALAĜ) following J. Klein, *Three Šulgi Hymns*, 120, note to Šulgi D l. 366–367; and W. Sallaberger, *Der kultische Kalender der Ur III-Zeit*, 142 fn. 668.

[1161] So V. V. Struve, *Onomastika*, 100; G. J. Selz, *AWEL*, 79.

[1162] E.g. *DP* 1/2 110 o. v 2. The similar name nin-e$_2$-gal-NI-si, OSP 1 23 o. vi 8 (ES-MS Nippur) is difficult. A finite verb i$_3$-si is totally unexpected; and although preferable, seeing a poss. pron. suffix -(a)ni + loc.-term. e$_2$-gal-ne$_2$ is not entirely uncomplicated.

[1163] See, for references, F. Pomponio, *Prosopografia*, 249 s.v.

[1164] So V. V. Struve, *Onomastika*, 101.

*lugal-$\hat{g}a_2$-ab-e. G. Visicato & A. Westenholz have demonstrated that parallel names from the Ur III period composed with nin must be taken to include the ergative marker –e. A reading /ĝe/ for ĜA$_2$ was posited from at least the ES period,[1166] but the first secure usage of the value, judging from the evidence presented by lugal-PNN, can be traced back at least to the time of Enentarzi of Lagaš. Read lugal-$\hat{g}e_{26}$-ab-e.

*lugal-ĝeštin$^?$-zi.[1167] The sign read as ĝeštin$^?$ is missing two oblique converging wedges. The reading lugal-nitaḫ$^?$-zi has been adopted here.

*lugal-ĝissu.[1168] A PN *lugal-ĝissu is not yet attested from any period. Otherwise most ĝissu-names have e_2 as head noun, with a few early names featuring the appellative nin in the same position.[1169] Read instead lugal-[a$^?$]-$\hat{g}e_6$.

*lugal-$i_3^!$-$gara_2$.[1170] Read lugal-$u\hat{g}u_3$-du_{10}, and see notes to *lugal-NIĜ$_2$.KAK, above.

*lugal-KA-gu-la.[1171] Read lugal-KA gu-la 'lugal-KA senior,' following B. R. Foster.[1172]

*lugal-kal-⌜a⌝.[1173] Probably not a lugal-PN.[1174]

*lugal-kaskal-du_{10}.[1175] Reading lugal-du_{10} has long been established for this entry in the Abū Ṣalābīḫ and Ebla NPL.[1176] KASKAL is part of filiation ga:$e\check{s}_8$.

*lugal-kur-geštin.[1177] Correct reading lugal-kur-dub_2 was given by C. Wilcke.[1178]

*lugal-kur_6.[1179] Read lugal-$\check{s}a_3$.[1180] Nikol'skij's copy of Nik 1 125 o. ii 11 is accurate.

*lugal-⌜la⌝-zi.[1181] Although the second sign is damaged, lugal-⌜numun⌝-zi is certain.

1165 Traditional reading, e.g. E. Chiera, PBS 11/3, 211; H. Limet, *Anthroponymie*, 170, 240; E. Sollberger & J.-R. Kupper, *IRSA*, 318.

1166 *FTUM*, 54, with notes on earlier interpretations.

1167 Reading forwarded by C. Wilcke, *EANEL*, 172. The second sign in the line MVN 3 62 o. 2 is not entirely clear, but nitaḫ is in several respects the best match.

1168 So the editors of *TCABI* 64. The text preserves only lugal-[x]-MI, but ĝiš in the break is questionable.

1169 E.g. TMH 5 1 o. ii 3: (dumu) e_2-ĝissu-bi (ED IIIb Nippur); BIN 8 39 r. ii 2: nin-ĝissu; 173 o. 6: nin-ĝissu-na-NI (both ED IIIb Isin; same woman in both instances).

1170 Reading of OIP 104 14 r. ii 1 suggested by C. Wilcke, *ZA* 86 (1996), 37.

1171 So I. J. Gelb, MAD 4, 68.

1172 *USP*, 70. For this interpretation, see also TMH 5 11 ii 6: ad-da; r. iii 3: ad-da(-bi_3); and r. iii 4: ad-da gu-la. Note that no other lugal-KA is mentioned in MAD 4 68, but lugal-KA was extremely common and so in need of disambiguating remarks such as this.

1173 So G. Visicato, *The Power and the Writing*, 293.

1174 If the name refers to the owner of the seal *EGA* 462, pl. 11 fig. 118 (BM 104489), the writing surface is wiped clean and does not contain any trace of a name.

1175 So M. Krebernik, AOAT 296, 36 w. fn. 191. Krebernik points out that the Abū Ṣalābīḫ NPL has a propensity to place PN and title in separate cases. But one would then expect a professional title or a GN in the following line. *IAS* 74, especially. col. ii, features a number of lines conflated in the same manner.

1176 So already R. D. Biggs, OIP 99, 62–71, l. 167.

1177 So V. V. Struve, *Onomastika*, 104 with question mark on *DP* 1/2 136 i 11 (ref. to *RTC* 1 col. xi is faulty); OIP 104, 69–72 no. 20 (= PBS 9 2) o. iv 6.

1178 *ZA* 86 (1996), 27 w. fn. 63.

1179 So V. V. Struve, *Onomastika*, 104.

1180 M. V. Nikol'skij's copy of Nik 1 125 o. ii 11 is accurate. Sign is RSP320, 1st variant.

1181 So the editors of *TCABI* 3 r. i 2.

*lugal-Lagaš^{ki}-šakan$_3$-na.[1182] Not a lugal-PN. Read Lagaš^{ki}-giri$_3$-na.[1183]

*lugal-Ma$_2$-gan^{ki}.[1184] Exact reading uncertain; see provisionally lugal-KA-GAN-ki.

*lugal-mu-da-kas$_4$.[1185] The name was posited as normal orthography for the phonetic Ebla writing nu-gal-mu-da-kaš$_2$. Correctly identified as a writing of lugal-mu-da-kuš$_2$ by P. Steinkeller.[1186]

*lugal-mu-na-DU.[1187] Following C. Wilcke, not a PN.[1188]

*lugal-mu-ša$_3$-da.[1189] The line in question contains two PNN, lugal-MU and ša$_3$-da, as is made apparent by the plural copula in the following line.[1190]

*lugal-muš$_3$-me-ki-aĝ$_2$.[1191] Read lugal-Muš$_3$-bar-ki-aĝa$_2$, as copied. See also *lugal-dam-me-ki-aĝ$_2$.

*lugal-ni$_3$-^{ba}bara$_3^{!}$-ga.[1192] The text as copied has no BA. See also the following name.

*lugal-ni$_3$-bara$_4$-ga.[1193] The third sign is a miscopied sa$_6$.[1194] The names combining lugal and ni$_3$-bara$_4$ apparently never end in loc. or genitive -a. Read lugal-ni$_3$-sa$_6$-ga.

*lugal-ni$_3$-bara$_4$-ge.[1195] Misprint for nin-ni$_3$-bara$_4$-ge. The names combining lugal and ni$_3$-bara$_4$ apparently never contain the loc.-term. ending -e.

*lugal-ni$_3$-lul.[1196] Not a lugal-PN. Published photo has clear lu$_2$.

*lugal-NIĜ$_2$-da-nu-tuku.[1197] This person appears in two Šuruppag contracts. The name is damaged in both instances, but in one case the last sign looks like ME more than TUK.[1198]

*lugal-NIĜ$_2$.KAK.[1199] Read lugal-uĝu$_3$-du$_{10}$. The form of uĝ$_3$ is verified by another name in the same text, remembering the commonplace alternation of the forms

---

[1182] So V. V. Struve, *Onomastika*, 104.

[1183] The sign lugal appears neither in *TSA* 47 o. v 2, nor in Nik 1 3 r. i 1'.

[1184] So Sollberger, *BiOr* 16 (1959), 117.

[1185] Form recreated by P. Mander, *JAOS* 108 (1988), 482.

[1186] *Fs Hallo*, 239 and addendum, p. 245. See also M. Krebernik, *Fs Röllig*, 190 w. fn. 13.

[1187] So the editors of *TCABI* 1 o. ii 1.

[1188] *EANEL*, 194.

[1189] So the editors of *TCVC* 725 o. i 3.

[1190] The PN ša$_3$-da is also known from later Umma texts. See, e.g. MAD 4 41 r. 3.

[1191] So V. V. Struve, *Onomastika*, 107.

[1192] So P. Steinkeller, *JNES* 52 (1993), 144 on BIN 8 264 o. 3.

[1193] So P. Steinkeller, *JNES* 52 (1993), 144 on BIN 8 179 r. 1.

[1194] On photo (CDLI P212723), the left part of SA$_6$ has more details than copied.

[1195] So J. Krecher, *ZA* 63 (1973), 247. The text referred to, *SRU* no. 56 o. i 2 was originally published as PBS 9 4, and reedited as OSP 2 50 (translit. only).

[1196] F. Pomponio, *Prosopografia*, 159, referring to MVN 10 85 o. ii 8; followed by *FTUM*, 151; and K. Lämmerhirt, AOAT 348, 649 w. fn. 6.

[1197] So F. Pomponio, *Prosopografia*, 156; *FTUM*, 151.

[1198] *WF* 35 o. v 2.

[1199] So the editors of OIP 104 for no. 14 r. ii 1.

kalam(LAK729) and uĝ$_3$(LAK730).[1200] The sign du$_{10}$ when written on stone sometimes comes off looking like DU$_3$.[1201]

*lugal-niĝir(LAK667)-zi.[1202] In one ED IIIb Girsu text,[1203] the sign LAK154 is used twice with the value niĝir, while this name appears in an adjacent column written with LAK667. Read therefore lugal-aga$_3$-zi.

*lugal-niĝir(LAK154)-gi.[1204] The sign rendered GI is a misreading for zi. Read lugal-aga-zi and see notes on the following name.

*lugal-niĝir(LAK154)-zi.[1205] The adjective zi is, as far as I am aware, never associated with niĝir in any literary or lexical context. But there is ample evidence in literary and possibly also in lexical sources for zi as qualifying aga$_{(3)}$.[1206] Read therefore lugal-aga-zi.

*lugal-nu-zu(?).[1207] With all probability not a lugal-PN. The name appears in an OB copy of a Sargonic royal inscription. The passage is damaged and the text is written in an exceptionally cursive hand. Following C. Wilcke, the name might read ur$^{?}$-$^{d?}$Šakan$_x$(ANŠE.AMA.ŠA.GAN.DU).[1208]

*lugal-pirig-ga$_3$-dug$_x$(sic).[1209] Perhaps the result of slips in reading transliterations (UG and UĜ$_3$)? Read lugal-uĝ$_3$-ĝe$_{26}$-du$_{10}$.[1210]

*lugal-saĝ-kalag-ga.[1211] Sign copied as SAĜ is probably KA.[1212] Read lugal-inim-kalag-ga.

*lugal-SUR.ZA-zi.[1213] According to published hand copy,[1214] read lugal-šuba$_3$-zi.

*lugal-TE+UNU(?).[1215] The name appears in the same text as *lugal-nu-zu(?), above. C. Wilcke's reading lugal-sa$_6$ is no doubt correct.[1216]

*lugal-ti-nu-da-kuš$_2$.[1217] Sign read NU is copied as TIL(LAK17, 2nd variant).[1218] Read tentatively lugal-ti-uš$_2$-da-kuš$_2$ and see note on name.

[1200] OIP 104 14 r. vii 7: mu-ni-kalam(LAK730), and compare PN mu-ni-kalam(LAK730)-ma, e.g. *FTUM* 97 r. ii 5 (ED IIIa Šuruppag); TMH 5 8 o. i 4 (ED IIIb Nippur); and mu-ni-kalam(LAK729)-ma, Nik 1 7 o. ii 5 (ED IIIb Girsu).

[1201] Compare shape of ḪI in OIP 104 15 r. vii 27: [e$_2$]-ur$_2$-bi-du$_{10}$.

[1202] So V. V. Struve, *Onomastika*, 107.

[1203] *DP* 2/1 226.

[1204] So R. Zadok, *Iran* 32 (1994), 38.

[1205] So e.g. A. Alberti & F. Pomponio, StPohl SM 13, 110 (refs. to CT 50 36 and 37 belong to another name); L. Sassmanshausen, *BagM* 26 (1995), 191; C. Wilcke, *EANEL*, 96 fn. 298.

[1206] Refs. to literature on aga$_{(3)}$ zi is found with H. Steible, FAOS 1, 18f.; Å. Sjöberg, *MNS*, 73 note to l. 8. See phps. also Izi Ugarit, MSL 13, 130:229f.: aga-ni$_3$-g[i-na$^{?}$], aga-ni$_3$-z[i-da$^{?}$].

[1207] So D. R. Frayne, RIME 2, 92.

[1208] *ZA* 87 (1997), 23, J iv 10, and copy on p. 31.

[1209] So V. V. Struve, *Onomastika*, 109.

[1210] As is shown clearly in hand copy VS 25 26 o. i 3

[1211] So A. Westenholz, *ECTJ* 63 o. i 5.

[1212] So according to photo of o. i 4 (CDLI P020477).

[1213] So D. O. Edzard, *AfO* 22 (1968/69), 17, 25:2.

[1214] A. Quentin, *Journal Asiatique* 1888, 287 l. 1.

[1215] So D. R. Frayne, RIME 2, 93, iv 31.

[1216] *ZA* 87 (1997), 23, iv 32, and copy on p. 31.

[1217] So V. V. Struve, *Onomastika*, 109.

[1218] *DP* 1/2 135 r. v 4.

*lugal-Unug.[1219] The GN Unug without place determinative ^{ki} would be unexpected. Read instead lugal-abba$_2$.

*lugal-ur$_2$-ni-še$_3$.[1220] Such a writing of normal lugal-ur$_2$-ra-ni is otherwise unattested. The traces accord better with a reading lugal-ni$_3$-ĝa$_2$-ni-še$_3$.

*lugal-uš-gid$_2$.[1221] The third sign shows faint *gunû*-strokes on "snout" and an oblique wedge on the far right.[1222] Read, following J. Bauer: lugal-uš-su$_x$(MUŠ).[1223]

*nin-lu[gal].[1224] Due to a lack of compelling parallels, the line most likely refers to a sister ⸢nin$_{(9)}$⸣ of a person whose name begins with lugal-. The text in question lists other relations of named family members.[1225]

*^{d}Nin-MAR-lugal-ĝu$_{10}$.[1226] Copy is not entirely faithful to the original. The sign read GAL as part of ligature lugal is really KI.[1227] Read instead ^{d}Nin-MAR^{ki}-lu$_2$-ĝu$_{10}$.

*^{d}Su'en-lugal-ni.[1228] The line divider between ^{d}Su'en and the following line is clear. Photo shws that there is hardly any room for GAL before LU$_2$. Read instead: 3 sila$_3$ zi$_3$ gu, ^{d}Su'en, ⸢lu$_2$⸣-ni, nu-eš$_3$, zi-ga, inim-ma.[1229]

*šu-ni-ĝiš-uštil-lugal.[1230] Not a lugal-PN. With lugal in final position, the line probably represents a PN followed by a professional title. Copy not entirely faithful to original.[1231] A more likely reading is: šu-ni aga$_3$-us$_2$ lugal.

*[x]-lugal-uru-bar.[1232] Not a lugal-PN. Restore at the beginning of the line rather a professional title, saĝa, išib or gudu$_4$, and the divine determinative, followed by the theonym Lugal-uru-bar.[1233] The other preserved lines in the section where the name appears predominantly consist of name and title.

*ur-^{d}Nin-ĝir$_2$-su-lugal-sa$_6$-ga.[1234] The posited name refers to two individuals who appear in close association in a few ED IIIb Girsu texts. In other texts their names are written in separate writing cases.[1235] Read ur-^{d}Nin-ĝir-su (and) lugal-sa$_6$-ga.

[1219] So the editors of *TCABI* 57 o i 6.

[1220] So B. R. Foster, *OrNS* 51 (1982), 338 on *USP* 46 r. 2''.

[1221] So V. V. Struve, *Onomastika*, 115 on Nik 1 3 o. iv 11.

[1222] According to photo (CDLI P221710).

[1223] *ZA* 79 (1989), 9.

[1224] So Z. Yang, *SIA*, 289f., translit. of no. 640 o. ii 1.

[1225] E.g. ama PN in o. i 9, 11; ii 3, 7; abba$_2$ PN o. ii 8.

[1226] So V. V. Struve, *Onomastika*, 149 on Nik 1 19 r. iii 4.

[1227] Photo (CDLI P221726) shows faint oblique wedge to the left of the horizontals. Compare shape of lugal in o. ii 6.

[1228] So Z. Yang, *SIA*, 376, translit. of A 1026, o. 2 ("^{d}sin-[lu]gal-ni").

[1229] So according to photo (CDLI P217619). See also lu$_2$-ni nu-eš$_3$ in another zi-ga document, *SIA* 947 r. 4.

[1230] So A. Alberti & F. Pomponio, StPohl SM 13, 70 on UET 2 suppl. 22 o. i 2: "almost certainly a personal name."

[1231] See photos (CDLI P217341, P217341_d).

[1232] So G. J. Selz, *Götterwelt*, 169 on BiMes 3 10 o. vi 1'.

[1233] For all about this aspect of Ningirsu, see G. J. Selz, *Götterwelt*, 169–171.

[1234] So G. J. Selz, *Götterwelt*, 248f. w. fn. 1196 on CT 50 30 o. ii' 9. The size of the rations of barley compared to single recipients in the same text show that two persons are involved.

[1235] CT 50 29 o. i 6 and ii 1. Compare also J. Marzahn & H. Neumann, *AoF* 22 (1995), 110f. (VAT 6121) o. v 2'f. In OIP 14 57 o. ii 3 Ur-^{d}Nin-ĝir$_2$-su is likely to hide behind the writing Ur-niĝ$_2$. For NIĜ$_2$ as a rare writing for nin in early Girsu texts, see G. J. Selz, *Götterwelt*, 218.

3.2 Semantic analysis of Akkadian *śarrum*-names

In this section, Akkadian names are sorted under a heading according to the proposed interpretation of each name. The procedure is similar to that used for Sumerian names in the preceding section. The statements in names are correlated with qualities or distinct patterns of action and the relation to a point of reference: the *śarrum* himself, or, for instance, a subordinate or a locus.

As seen in the treatment of Sumerian names above, the appellative lugal was normally written using the ligature GAL.LU_2, with a semi-phonetic logogram GAL.LU, limited to Nippur sources. Exclusively in texts from northern and northwestern cities, the word could appear as nu-gal. These writings do not in any way reflect a specific syntactic function or any discernible distinction between a human or a divine referent. Depending on grammatical form, *śarrum* also could be written in a number of different ways. Lone SAR is used in a seeming logographic function, especially in ED IIIb names from Ebla and Mari. As such it could theoretically stand for any conceivable grammatical shape the word *śarrum* could take on. In the orthography of later periods SAR could be used to express a stative (the predicative form of the noun), the construct state regens in a genitive chain, and sometimes the absolute state of the noun *śarrum*.[1236] No graphic distinction has been made in the following; SAR is consistently given as *śar*.

Names featuring other appellatives are sometimes helpful for interpretation; mainly names containing *baʿlum* and *malkum* instead of *śarrum*. Other appellatives too, as well as theonyms, provide clues to both reading and interpretation.

The lack of a substantial corpus of Old Akkadian literature paired with the comparative brevity of Akkadian names often makes the attribution to a subcategory more hazardous than is the case with Sumerian names of the corresponding subcategory. Many subcategories to which Sumerian names can be shown to have belonged do not have semantically parallel formations in Akkadian *śarrum*-names. The numbering of subsections is retained however, to enable easier access to corresponding name types in lugal-names. If the focus of the Akkadian onomasticon in general, in comparison to Sumerian names, is to a larger extent directed toward the individual and his or her immediate surroundings and the situation around his/her birth, then this will be readily visible in the treatments below.

[1236] A similar suggestion is forwarded by P. Steinkeller apud R. di Vito, StPohl SM 16, 242.

3.2.1 Dominion

The first heading encompasses names where the imagery relates to the attention directed toward the appellative as a source of authority. Here also, the subject's attention toward the referent of the appellative can be found. There are some potential links to heading 3, depending on how the imagery of fatherhood should be viewed. Fig. 9, below, records the distribution of 5 persons, the estimated minimum number of people bearing 5 variants of *śarrum*-names related to dominion.

	ED I-II	ED IIIa-ED IIIb	ED IIIb-ES	ES-MS	MS-CS
Ebla			2		
Mari			1		
Nagar					2

Fig. 9: Name-bearers, 3.2.1, Dominion. Estimated minimum number of individual name-bearers.

3.2.1.1 Ownership

None of the names which can potentially be linked to a personal relationship between an individual and a *śarrum* specifies the nature of the relation. They all appear to be formed by the appellative combined with a personal suffix in the first person singular: *śar-ri*$_2$ $^{(a1)}$, 'my *śarrum*';[1237] or plural: *śar-ru-ni* $^{(a1)}$ 'our *śarrum*,'[1238] and perhaps *śar-ru-na*$^{?}$ $^{(a1)}$, with the same meaning.[1239] All of these names are from Ebla and Nagar. Brief as they are, these names provide no further information. There is even a possibility to see *śarrum* here as the homonym which in later times most often was written *šerrum*, more rarely *šarrum*, and denoting 'baby, child.'[1240] The names would then strictly speaking not belong to the onomasticon formed around the *śarrum*. A third option is to see the names as vocatives, or as abbreviations of longer names. The first two interpretations have as a likely referent the child who bore the name, hailed as the one to whose needs and interests the mother would tend, or as one welcomed into the family. If the names should turn out to be vocative forms or abbreviations, this is less likely to be the case.

The Akkadian term *śarrum* is formally not used to convey a sense of 'owner,'[1241] and it is not known whether the ownership aspect was in any

[1237] Compare the Diyālā PN *be-li*$_2$, which was borne by about five persons from the MS period onwards; e.g. *AIHA* 42 o. 8.

[1238] Compare, e.g. E. Chiera, PBS 11/2, 137, no. 1013: *a-ḫu-ni* "Our brother."

[1239] As noted by R. Hasselbach, *Sargonic Akkadian*, 150 fn. 11, the pron. suffix *-na* appears only in the onomasticon, and never in the syllabically written Akkadian texts.

[1240] See perhaps also the MA name *šar-ri-ni*, written phonetically and not with either of the common logograms MAN or LUGAL, C. Saporetti, StPohl 6/1, 461; 6/2 160 s.v. *šarru* 're.'

[1241] See further, above, p. 76 w. fn. 383, on the usage of the logogram LUGAL to denote Akk. *ba'lum*, in the sense of 'owner.'

way inherent in the term when used about divinities. It may however have allowed for a managerial aspect. *Śarkaliśarrē* of Akkade described himself as *śar* Akkade *u buʿʿulāti* Enlil 'king of Akkade and of the *subjects* of Enlil,' in a Nippur inscription known in at least three different contemporary exemplars.[1242]

3.2.1.2 Family terms, house and indoor loci

A range of name variants contain the noun *ʾabum*, which invariably serves as the nominal predicate in verbless clauses. The stem is then variably given as marked by predicate *-a*, as in lugal-*a-ba*$_4$ $^{(a\geq 1)}$, and *śar-a-ba*$_4$ $^{(a\geq 1/{}^\circ 1)}$ both: 'the *śarrum* is a father,' and both found exclusively in texts from ED IIIb Ebla.[1243]. Names combining the words *śar*(*rum*) and *ʾabum* thus have *ʾabum* as the second element, which is in keeping with Sumerian names of a similar kind. The semantics of *ʾabum* are not altogether straight-forward, as it may be expected to hold an overtone of a male superior in an organization based on blood-ties or other loyalties.[1244] The noun *ʾabum* is one of the most productive components in the Old Akkadian onomasticon, like its Sumerian counterparts abba, adda, and aja$_2$, and was surpassed in number only by names formed with *ʾilum* and *baʿlum*.[1245]

3.2.1.3 Insignia of power

Certain objects can be connected with the exercise of power by Sargonic dynasts. The horned crown of *Narām*-Su'en, for instance, figures in different iconographic representations, like his Stele of Victory. Furthermore, both *Śarrukēn* and *Narām*-Su'en made a point of having received weapons from different divinities at home in cities of the north, such as Ilaba, Dagān and Nergal. They both also mentioned that they washed their weapons upon

---

[1242] E.g. BE 1/1 2 i 4–8. Treatment and commentary by A. Westenholz, OSP 2, 57f. The sense of the noun *buʿʿulātum* is rendered freely. An abbreviated version is known from a NB period mould of an earlier original, see below, p. 201 fn. 1290, for references.

[1243] The form *śar-a* $^{(a1)}$, used for a merchant from Mari in an Ebla text, probably represents a shortening of *śar-a-ba*$_4$, thus *śar-a-‹ba*$_4$›. See for the translation A. Archi, *MARI* 4 (1985), 54: "Le roi est le père"; similarly R. di Vito, StPohl SM 16, 208, 30.4a, 1. Compare, for a different view, G. Pettinato, MEE 3, 245, who preferred to see *ʾaba* as a theonym: "*šar-a-ba*$_4$ è strutturato in maniera identica a *šar-ma-ni* della riga precedente: *a-ba*$_4$ è quindi il teonimo così produttivo nei nomi del periodo paleo-accadico…" I am not certain what to do with LUGAL E$_2$ BE, I-bu-TUM^{ki}, in ARET 8 21 o. iii 2–3, but it is hard to explain it as a PN. Therefore I suggest, very tentatively a reading LUGAL BE:E$_2$, representing the highest authority in I-bu-TUM. Though the order BE E$_2$ for *baʿl*(*u*) *bētim* is attested in the same text along with *Il*$_2$*-zi*. See the notes by A. Archi on the latter and his function, *Fs Foster*, 31. I have discounted the name *śar-ra-bu*$_3$, e.g. Subartu 2 17 o. ii 2 (ED IIIb Nabada); ARET 13 15 o. iii 4 and 14, due to the variant writing *sa-ra-bu*$_3$, ARET 13 19 o. 1 and 5.

[1244] See for instance the greeting formula in the CS Ešnuna letter MAD 1 191 (=FAOS 19 Es 6) o. 1–8: *en-ma*, *šu-ku*$_8$*-bu*$_3$, [*a*]*-na śi*-ḫur-saĝ, *be-li*$_2$, *u*$_3$ *a-bi*$_2$, *qi*$_2$*-bi*$_2$*-ma* 'Thus (speaks) Šu-Kūbu, say to *Śi*-ḫur-saĝ, my lord and father."

[1245] See I. J. Gelb, MAD 3, 9–12, with a list indicating the different orthographic variants.

reaching the sea during their successful campaigns.[1246] Neither crown nor the divine weapons were connected with the *śarrum* in onomastic material. Though names mentioning a weapon are known, they fail to make a connection either to a god or a human.[1247] In a few ED depictions of royal figures, and perhaps also in one of *Śarrukēn*, the ruler holds a mace.[1248]

As in the preceding period, the scepter was as a sign of acceptance by the gods and of the authority to rule; it was bestowed on the king by Enlil.[1249] The scepter is so far unattested in PNN from the Sargonic period, but appears in Ur III names.[1250]

3.2.1.4 Verbal communication and commands

Sargonic kings hardly ever describe a background for their actions by referring to orders from the gods. The exception is *Narām*-Su'en who claimed to be on a mission, *śiprum*, of ʿAštar.[1251] But the idea may also have been the subject of an epithet used by *Śarrukēn* and *Narām*-Su'en, maškim-gi$_4$, of ʿAštar or of the (great) gods. The exact rendering of the term maškim-gi$_4$ in 3rd millennium Akkadian is not certain. But it ought to have had a sense of 'representative,'[1252] that is, of someone acting at the behest and under instructions of someone else. There are no traces of such empowerment in the human onomasticon. For the names previously read *lugal-*pu*$_5$, *lugal-*pum* and **pu*$_3$-*śar*, see below, 3.2.9.

3.2.1.5 The city

Narām-Su'en claims to have saved his capital from certain destruction when the four corners of the world rebelled against him. And because he managed to secure the foundations of his city, the citizens of Akkade took action to have the king be the protective deity of the city, asking gods of Sumer and Akkade for permission to do so.[1253] This represents the official version of how *Narām*-Su'en came to be deified, which would have far-reaching consequences for southern Mesopotamian royal ideology for the following 600 years or so.

1246 See textual references in FAOS 8, 223f. s.v. *kakkum*.

1247 The references are collected by I. J. Gelb, MAD 3, 142 s.v. KK. See also below, [3.2.3.1].

1248 See discussions by G. Marchesi & N. Marchetti, MesCiv 14, 142 and 148, with references and illustrations on pl. 56.

1249 The sceptre, Akk. *ḫaṭṭum*, was mentioned in inscriptions of *Śarrukēn* and *Maništūšu*. In curse formulae of the Sargonic and Gutian periods, the sceptre is variously connected with Enlil and with ʿAštar, see references in FAOS 8, 208 s.v. *ḫaṭṭum*.

1250 I. J. Gelb, MAD 3, 136 s.v. ḪṬ; and see J. Hilgert, JBVO 5, 49f. s.v. *lubburu*(*m*).

1251 See references in FAOS 8, 297 s.v. *šiprum*.

1252 See, e.g. M. Bonechi, *QDLF* 16 (2006), 80: (lu$_2$) maškim-e-gi$_4$/gi "ambasciatore"; FAOS 8 267f. s.v. *rābiṣum*, and compare lugal-maškim-e, appearing in CS times.

1253 So according to the inscription on the Bassetkī statue base, A.-H. Al-Fouadi, *Sumer* 32 (1976), 63–75 i 20–iii 2.

For names referring to the city and its defences as symbols for the protection of the individual, see below, section 3.2.3.1.

3.2.1.6 Country and people

There are at present no attestations of names linking the *śarrum* to the land or its people. In later times such associations are not uncommon in relation to deities and in kyriophore names.[1254] But references are of course not lacking from inscriptional materials. *Narām*-Su'en, for example, often alludes to the people as part of his dominion; and sometimes it is described more specifically as a gift from Enlil.[1255]

3.2.1.7 The cosmic order

Akkadian names referring to the dominion over the universe are lacking from contemporary *śarrum*-names. However, names proclaiming a deity to be king may be seen as touching upon this subject. They are discussed below, section 3.2.7.6.

3.2.2 Wisdom and awareness

As with Sumerian names falling under this heading the number of names attested are not that many. No more than two distinct nominal predicates make up the repertoire attributing wisdom to the *śarrum*. Akkadian names bear witness to a bit more variation in the placement of the nominal predicate due to the freer syntax. As opposed to Sumerian names treated under the corresponding heading, above, the Akkadian names all refer to wisdom as a characteristic of the appellative, not as something that could be dispensed to others. None of the variants of the names belonging to this category has been attested more than a few times. Fig. 10, below, records 4 persons, the estimated minimum number of people bearing 3 variants of *śarrum*-names related to wisdom.

	ED I-II	ED IIIa-ED IIIb	ED IIIb-ES	ES-MS	MS-CS
Mugdan					1
Sippar				1	
Umma				1	1

Fig. 10: Name-bearers, 3.2.2, Wisdom and awareness. Estimated minimum number of individual name-bearers.

As is common in Akkadian names with appellatives *baʿlum* and *śarrum*, the former is most often provided with the possessive marker -*ī* while the latter

[1254] See, e.g. MAD 3 168f. s.v. M'$_x$T *mâtum*; M. Hilgert, JBVO 5, 51; C. Saporetti, StPohl 6/2, 160f.

[1255] See references in FAOS 8, 260 s.v. *nišū*.

turns up lacking the nominative case mimation. Other than this the two appellatives show striking similarities in qualifying predicates used. The predicates are – as far as can be ascertained – all participles. Some doubt lingers as to the Akkadian identity of the word behind the compound gal-zu, but a logographic writing for a word similar in meaning to the participle *mūdûm* 'knowing, wise' seems likely, given the correspondence between the Sumerian and the Akkadian terms and the fact that no syllabic writings for another Akkadian root with a suitable meaning is attested in the onomasticon. But gal-zu is not likely to be a logographic writing for *mūdûm*. Both writings sometimes appear in the same texts. Also, no name in which the phonetic writing *mu-da-* occupies first position is known. The referent of the predicate ought reasonably to be the figure behind the appellative and no direct object is expressed, nor likely to have been intended. The name thus with reasonable certainty refers to a quality of the appellative and not one of the name-bearer. The names *śar-ru-*gal-zu [(a1)], *śar-ru-mu-da* [(a2)],[1256] *be-li*$_2$-gal-zu,[1257] and *be-li*$_2$*-mu-da*,[1258] are here perceived as roughly parallel in meaning, 'the *śarrum*/my lord is a wise one,' or '(all-)knowing.'[1259]

Two other names probably belong here as well. The writing *śar-ru*$_x$(KU)-*ma-da* [(a1)], known as an ugula$^!$(AŠ$_2$) e$_2$ from ES-MS Umma, is most likely a variant writing for the person known as *śar-ru-mu-da*, and performing the same function in the same archive.[1260] One gal-zu-[*śar*]-*ru-śi*-[*in*] [(a1)] 'their (3fpl) *ś.* is a wise one,' is mentioned as a maškim ⌜lugal⌝ in a text from CS Mugdan. The reconstruction -[*śar*]-*ru-śi*-[*in*] is not entirely certain.[1261]

The verb *edûm* is also used in a finite form along with *baʿlum*, *i-da*-be [(a1)] 'the lord knows,'[1262] and *i-da-be-li*$_2$ 'my lord knows,'[1263] respectively. This double usage of a specific verbal root in both participial and finite forms seems not to have been very widespread in Sargonic names including the appellatives *baʿlum* and *śarrum*, but see, e.g. below, 3.2.5, for names

---

[1256] The definitive transcription and mng. of this name, *Śarru-mūdaʿ* "the king is wise," was established once and for all by E. Sollberger, *JCS* 10 (1956), 16, note to l. ii 1. The G participle *mūdûm* of the verb *edûm* in PNN was different from the only attested syllabic writing outside of names, *me-da-a* (dual.), see R. Hasselbach, *Sargonic Akkadian*, 223. The latter text (MVN 3 104) was of course not published by the time of Sollberger's study.

[1257] E.g. MVN 3 38 o. 6 (MS Ešnuna).

[1258] E.g. MO B xi 7 (ES).

[1259] Similarly R. di Vito, StPohl SM 16, 216f., 30.5a, 18: "(The) god is wise/concerned."

[1260] As suspected already by the editor of the text, B. R. Foster, *USP*, 18. For another case of variation *-mu-da*/*-ma-da* in Mari PNN at Ebla, see P. Steinkeller, *Fs Hallo*, 241. The phonetic value ru$_x$(KU) was later proposed by J. Krecher, QuadSem 18, 300 for the name *ku*$_8$*-ru*$_x$(KU)-*ub-e-la-ak*. See also C. Woods, *ZA* 95 (2005), 30f. for another example.

[1261] The name as given here follows the transliteration of B. R. Foster, *ASJ* 4 (1982), 16f.

[1262] *AIHA* 2 r. i 8. Compare R. di Vito, StPohl SM 16, 195, 25.2c, 1: "(The) god knows (the child)."

[1263] HSS 10 157 r. i 1.

construed with *banûm*. The verb *reʾûm* 'to tend, shepherd,' appears both as participle and as finite verb but not with the same appellative as the subject.

3.2.3 Protection

Names of the third heading invoke the appellative as a source for personal protection. Certain names have ended up here which could perhaps equally well be taken as sorting under the first or seventh headings. Fig. 11, below, records 9 persons, the estimated minimum number of persons bearing 9 variants of *śarrum*-names which can be attributed to this category.

	ED I-II	ED IIIa-ED IIIb	ED IIIb-ES	ES-MS	MS-CS
Adab					1
Akkade				1	
Gasur					1
Girsu					1
Kazallu					1
Mari		1	1		
Sippar				1	
Tutub					1

Fig. 11: Name-bearers, 3.2.3, Protection. Estimated minimum number of individual name-bearers.

3.2.3.1 Protection of the individual

The *śarrum* was one to whom people turned, whether for protection, for comfort or for sustenance. The relationship is seen for instance in *śar-iś-ta₂-kal₂* (a1) and variant, *śar-ri₂-iś-ta₂-kal₂* (a1), both: 'rely on the *śarrum*!,'[1264] from CS Gasur and Girsu, respectively. The name incorporates the object marked by the terminative ending *-iś* and a masculine sing. imperative *takal*. In this it was parallel to other nouns, such as the aforementioned *ʾilum* and *baʿlum*, but also to theonyms.[1265] Also, a high-ranking official by the name *Śuā(i)ś-takal* 'rely on him!,' is known from both northern and southern, and even CS sources - as far afield as Susa.[1266] Considering the personal loyalty which was

[1264] E. Sollberger & J.-R. Kupper, *IRSA*, 336: "fais confiance au roi"; similarly R. di Vito, StPohl SM 16, 197, 27.2d, 1. The form *ti-ka₃-al*, consistent with the vowel pattern of later times, is found in a Sargonic letter, but PNN consistently use the form *takal*, see R. Hasselbach, *Sargonic Akkadian*, 199 w. fn. 143. Compare *be-li₂-iś-ta₂-kal₂*, e.g. *STTI* 33 o. 4 (CS Girsu).

[1265] See in general the formations listed in MAD 3, 295.

[1266] See note on different writings, A. Westenholz, OSP 2, 55 note to no. 40 ii 3. Compare the pronominal element in the name *śu*-NI-*iś-ta₂-kal₂*, MAD 1 86 r. i 10 (translit. only, MS-CS Ešnuna), which could represent either the oblique dual independent pronoun *śuni+iś-*, or *śuʾāyiś-* (*śu-ʾa₅* (NI)-*iś*). The referents of whichever pronoun is chosen remain unknown.

central to the Sargonic chain of command, a human ruler is a quite reasonable assumption for the latter, or for both of these *takal*-names.

A pair of names from the northern floodplain and Syria illustrate the protective aspects of the figure of the *śarrum*. One is *i-mi-śar-ru* (a1) 'the *śarrum* protected,'[1267] from Sargonic Sippar. Finite forms of the same verb is attested also with theonyms Erra, Su'en and Śamaś.[1268] The other, *iš-ṭup-śar* (a1) 'the *śarrum* saved,'[1269] the name of an ED IIIb lugal of Mari, likewise lacks the object. This unexpressed direct object is, however, more than likely to be the child bearing the name.

In nominal predicate names, the *śarrum* is likened to shade, as in *ṣi*$_2$*-la*-lugal (a1),[1270] and a form of walled structure, *dūrum*, most often written with the Sumerian sign bad$_3$.[1271] Though the noun *dūrum* could be taken as a defensive structure benefitting the population of a city, or of the country as a whole, all extant names featuring a further qualification of either the appellative or bad$_3$/*dūrum* are pronominal, and hence refer to the protection of single individuals.[1272]

The element *al* in the name *śar-ru-al-śi-in* (a1) represents the construct of *ālum* 'city,'[1273] and is a further example of the metaphorical use of trademarks of the urban settlement as signs of security. It is less likely to see *al* as the preposition ʿ*al* "on, upon, against," which, however, also appears in personal names.[1274] The referent of the pronominal suffix *śin*(*a*) 'their' might

---

[1267] For this form as a preterite of *amûm* (<**ḥmy*), see M. Hilgert, Imgula 5, 450–452, w. refs. R. di Vito, StPohl SM 16, 229, 39.2g, 1, interpreted *i-mi* as a truncated form of *emēdum*.

[1268] See F. Pomponio, *StEL* 8 (1991), 143, for refs. to parallels; J. J. M. Roberts, *ESP*, 21, s.v. *I-mi*/*me*-Ir$_3$-ra; and 49, s.v. *Īmi*-Su'en. Add also to these refs. *i-mi*[!](DUGUD)-*i*$_3$*-lum*, MVN 3 45 o. i 2 (ES Isin or Nippur ?).

[1269] Compare R. D. Biggs, ARES 1, 93: *iš-ṭup-il* "Il rescued"; R. di Vito, StPohl SM 16, 193, 24.1b, 1: "(The) god preserved (him)." The verb *šaṭāpum* is quite productive in the Mesopotamian onomasticon, including Mari. See, for instance, *iš-ṭup*-be, MO B iv 5, and a few other parallel names in that same text. According to A. Archi, *Eblaitica* 1, 131, the verb occurs only in names of foreigners at Ebla.

[1270] Following A. Archi, *MARI* 4 (1985), 54: "Ombre/protection du roi"; similarly P. Fronzaroli, ARES 1, 9.

[1271] Attested writings are *śar*-bad$_3$ (°1), in an ED IIIb Ebla scholastic text, and *śar-ru*-bad$_3$ (a1) ES Akkade (MO); and phonetically: *śar-ru-du*$_2$*-ri*$_2$ (a1) from MS-CS Adab. Compare *be-li*$_2$-bad$_3$, ITT 1 1103 r. 3 (CS Girsu); *be-li*$_2$*-du*$_2$*-ri*$_2$, MAD 1 163+165 o. ii 26 (collated from photo courtesy of W. Sommerfeld); and be-*śu*$_{13}$-bad$_3$, MAM 3, 329 fig. 346 l. 6. For the interpretation "wall," "fortress," see MAD 3, 106f., with parallels.

[1272] Besides the references listed in the previous note, see, e.g. be-*su*$_{13}$-bad$_3$, MAM 3, pl. 70 (M 2241) 6 (ED IIIb Mari); and FPN *be-li*$_2$-bad$_3$-*ri*$_2$, MAD 5 56 o. i 7 (geme$_2$, CS Kiš).

[1273] Note also the name of an ensi$_2$ appearing twice in unpublished MS Adab texts, *śar-ru*-URU.KI^{li_2}, "il re è la mia città," F. Pomponio, *TCABI*, 55 w. fn. 160. For some theophore parallels, compare ^{d}Su'en-*al-śu*, MO A iv 16; Aš$_{10}$-tar$_2$-*al-śu*, MO D ii' 1; AN-*al-śu*, HSS 10 169 o. 4; Il$_3$-a-ba$_4$-*al-śu*, ITT 2/2 4491 (translit. only). J. J. M. Roberts, *ESP*, 37: *Eštar-ālšu* "Eštar-Is-His-City"; and R. di Vito, StPohl SM 16, 202, 29.1c, 2, both took *-al-* as "city."

[1274] Some instances of this preposition are given by R. Hasselbach, *Sargonic Akkadian*, 168. Compare also, e.g. MO A xiii 5: ^{ĝiš}tukul^{ka_3}-*śu-al-śi-in* 'his weapon is upon them,' and compare the Girsu letter *STTI* 185, edited by B. Kienast & K. Volk, FAOS 19, 116f., r. 6'–7': *lu a-ga-*

refer to a collective of females, like elder sisters. But more likely, *-śin(a)* refers to a noun in the feminine plural, such as *nišū* 'people.'[1275] Two Sargonic PNN that could serve as comparisons are names composed with the noun *rē'ûm* 'shepherd': sipa-*śi-in* from MS-CS Tutub,[1276] and sipa-*ni-śe*$_2$, attested at MS-CS Nippur and CS Gasur.[1277]

Another name of uncertain meaning is *śar-ru*-gu$_2$ $^{(al)}$, where gu$_2$ may be a writing for *kišādum*,[1278] or possibly *kibrum*, both with a meaning 'bank (of river, canal, etc.).' At least *kibrum* is attested in Ur III and later names, almost always with a possessive suffix for the 1st person.[1279] At the moment the exact reading of the name and its nuances remain unclear.[1280]

3.2.3.2 Protection of the city

In a few cases discussed above, the city, *ālum* may feature in personal names composed with *śarrum*. No names are known which combine writings of geographical names with the appellative *śarrum*, nor are there any comparable names composed with *baʿlum*.

3.2.3.3 Protection of the country

A single name from MS-CS Nippur has been proposed as potentially referring to the *śarrum* as a shepherd of the people, thus, as a protector of more than the individual.[1281] As has been noted by Sabina Franke, the shepherd imagery is totally absent from Old Akkadian royal inscriptions.[1282] The editor of the text opted for a reading supported by contemporary parallels. The name is critically damaged. Given what remains, [l]u$_2$(-)sipa-*ni-śe*$_2$, and assuming the first sign would be lugal, it would be without a real

---

ma-lu-śu$_2$, ^{ĝiš}tukul *da-mi*$_3$ *al-śu la a-śa-ka*$_3$*-nu* "Ich werde ihn verschonen (und) die 'Waffe des blutes' gegen ihn nicht erheben," as part of an oath, hence the subjunctive.

[1275] See, phps., the CS Nippur PN *iḫ-bu-ut-al-śi-in* 'he plundered (?) their city,' OSP 2 8 o. 1' for another name possibly including *āl(um)* 'city.' For the verb(s) *ḫabātum*, see J. J. Stamm, *Namengebung*, 318; and *CAD* Ḫ s.v.v. *ḫabātu* A-D.

[1276] *Tutub* 4 (=MAD 1 254) r. i 5.

[1277] OSP 2 146 o. ii 2; HSS 10 153. For the reading of the Nippur attestation, see discussion immediately below, 3.2.3.3.

[1278] See *CAD* K s.v. *kišādu*, 3; and *kibru*, 1d. Note that in the case of the latter, all the evidence cited by the *CAD* in the lex. sect. has the term peš$_{10}$(KI.A). Compare *be-li*$_2$-gu$_2$, e.g. *SIA* 862 r. 1; and the different writings of the same official, *be-lu*-gu$_2$, ITT 1 1472 r. i 4, and *be-lum*-gu$_2$, CT 50 172 r. ii 8 (both CS Girsu).

[1279] See J. J. Stamm, *Namengebung*, 212 and compare the objections raised by K. de Graef, *NABU* 2007/24.

[1280] The entry SAR.A.GU$_2$ in BIN 8 277 o. 6 (MS-CS Unknown) is probably a reference to an edible plant rather than a personal name.

[1281] A. Westenholz, OSP 2, note to no. 146, l. 2': "the signs in our text could … be read as … LUGAL-SIPA-*ni-śe*$_2$ »The King is a shepherd of the people«."

[1282] *Königsinschriften*, 35, 125, 196. See, however, p. 111 fn. 592, above, for references to later traditions pinning the epithet of shepherd to *Narām*-Su'en; quite obviously with a sense of historical criticism.

structural parallel in the entire Sargonic onomasticon.[1283] The regens in a construct chain under normal circumstances only serves as the nominal predicate when the second element is a possessive personal pronoun, as for instance in the MS-CS names gal-zu-sipa-*ni* 'our shepherd is a wise one,' from Umma;[1284] and *be-li*$_2$-*tu*$_3$-*kul*$_2$-*ti* 'my lord is my (source of) support,' from Tutub and Sippar.[1285] Apart from this, secure writings of lugal to convey *śarrum* at Nippur are much fewer in number than phonetic writings. The Nippur name, then, ought best be read as sipa-*ni-śe*$_2$, and the lu$_2$ as referring to someone in the service of this person. The referent of the appellative sipa remains unknown.

3.2.4 Care and attentiveness

The fourth heading summarizes names where positive aspects of the relationship between the name-bearer or -giver and the referent of the appellative are in focus. Fig. 12, below, records 8 persons, the estimated minimum number of people bearing 3 variants of *śarrum*-names related to this category, and the cities with which they were associated.

	ED I-II	ED IIIa-ED IIIb	ED IIIb-ES	ES-MS	MS-CS
Adab					1
Akkade				2	
Awal					1
Girsu					1
Mugdan					1
Umma					1
Unknown					1

Fig. 12: Name-bearers, 3.2.4, Care and attentiveness. Estimated minimum number of individual name-bearers.

3.2.4.1 Care for the individual

Names describing the king as a person's god belonged to a common type of names formed with a number of appellatives, theonyms and the given names of rulers. The latter may be considered the closest to the name *śar-ru-i*$_3$-*li*$_2$ $^{(a\geq6)}$ 'the *śarrum* is my god,'[1286] known from the ES period onwards, as there is no reason to doubt that *śarrum* here refers to the king reigning at the time

[1283] In the Ur III period, however, such names begin to increase in number. See, for instance the kyriophore names of types 4 and 5 in M. Hilgert, JBVO 5, 39–76. For later nominal compound predications with *nišū*, see e.g. the short list in E. Chiera, PBS 11/2, 162, s.v. *nišu*, "people."

[1284] BIN 8 338 o. 2.

[1285] MAD 1 244 r. ii 8' (MS-CS Tutub); CT 44 48 o. 19 (CS Sippar).

[1286] Once *śar-um-i*$_3$-*li*$_2$ $^{(a1)}$, in MS-CS Umma. See also J. J. M. Roberts, *ESP*, 129; R. di Vito, StPohl SM 16, 200, 29.1b, 1. K. Tallqvist, *APN*, 217, untranslated.

of birth of the name-bearer. A literal interpretation should, following G. Marchesi, be avoided, as is evident when comparing *śarru-ʾilī*, for instance, to the kyriophore *śar-ru*-gi-*i₃-li₂* (a1) '*Śarrukēn* is my god,' typical for kyriophores of the Sargonic period; he states:[1287]

> A personal name like *Sar-ru*-GI-*i₃-li₂* does not mean that Sargon was a divine being, but rather that Sargon was the protector or the source of good luck of the name-bearer (i.e., to the king are attributed the functions of a personal god). Thus, reverential names sometimes employed the personal-god language for the purpose of extolling and pleasing the king.

This perspective, from the point of view of the ancients, was a simple and useful way for expressing the hopes and aspirations of a name-giver for the benefit of the one so named. Divinity was certainly not a thing to be taken lightly, but in formulaic utterances such as those manifested in personal names, the figurative understanding of the term *ʾilum* would hardly have been lost on contemporaries. Even a modern-day atheist may be caught appealing to higher powers, in exclamations such as 'good lord!' or 'oh my god!,' well aware of the implications of each and every word individually, but that would not make him or her a religious person.

3.2.4.2 Care for the city

No names are known which could be interpreted as the *śarrum* directing his attention to a specific or unspecified urban center.

3.2.4.3 Care for the country

No names are known which express an explicit link between the *śarrum* and the land or its inhabitants.

3.2.4.4 Care for the dead

In the section of Sumerian names bearing on this issue, a single name was analyzed as perhaps bearing on the existence in Girsu of an ancestral cult for members of the ensi₂ family line. There are no indications for a cult around deceased members of the Akkadian dynasty before Ur III times.[1288] In fact, the Akkadian dynasts, contrary to the earlier Lagaš rulers, were for some reason reluctant to mention their genealogy in monumental inscriptions; a practice which would influence the composing of Ur III royal inscriptions. In the Lagaš state, the cult of some of the ED III governors seems to have

[1287] HANE/S 10, 68 fn. 322, citing other kyriophores. The name ᵈ*Na-ra-am-*ᵈEN.ZU-*i₃-li₂*, is found in *USP* 31 o. 4. Sargonic kyriophores are almost exclusively formed with the qualified nominal predicate *ʾilī*. For the only probable exception, see below, [3.2.7.9], note to the name of *Śarrukēn*.

[1288] For the evidence, see J. G. Westenholz, *Fs Sigrist*, 253–256.

continued uninterrupted down into CS times.[1289] The account of the deification of *Narām*-Su'en mentions a 'house' erected by the citizens of Akkade in his honour, which could be either a temple or a palatial building, but there is no compelling evidence of the fate of this structure post-dating this account. There is on the other hand a mould made from an inscription by *Śarkališarrē*, said by its NB originator to have been cast from an original in the palace (e_2-gal) of *Narām*-Su'en in Akkade.[1290]

3.2.5 Creation, fertility and prosperity

Heading five gathers names focusing on some aspect of creating, or on opulence. Fig. 13, below, records 4 persons, the estimated minimum number of people bearing 3 variants of *śarrum*-names related to such matters.

	ED I-II	ED IIIa-ED IIIb	ED IIIb-ES	ES-MS	MS-CS
Girsu					1
Kiš					1
Nippur				1	
Umma					1

Fig. 13: Name-bearers, 3.2.5, Creation, fertility and prosperity. Estimated minimum number of individual name-bearers.

3.2.5.1 The *śarrum* and the procreation of man

The *śarrum* is hailed as a creator in a few names containing the root *banûm*. An administrator under *Śarkališarrē*, whose seal is preserved, went by the name of *ib-ni*-lugal $^{(a\geq1)}$ 'the *śarrum* created.'[1291] Judging from the artisanry of the seal, he belonged to the very top of Akkadian society. A few other attestations of this name, from MS-CS Umma and Girsu may all refer to the same person. Quite clearly, names with preterite forms of the verb *banûm* only occur with certain appellatives during the Sargonic period: as far as the evidence goes, *śarrum*, *baʿlum*, and *ʾilum*.[1292] During the Ur III period, proper theophore and kyriophore names composed with the 3rd ms preterite *ibni-* become more commonplace.[1293]

A name containing a non-finite form of a verb *banûm* might be linked to the idea of the *śarrum* as a creator. But the name *śar-ru-ba-ni* $^{(a\geq1)}$ is open to speculation. Formally *ba-ni* could denote an active (*bāni-*) or passive

[1289] At least one CS document lists offerings destined for the statue of Enmetena, ITT 1 1081.
[1290] See photograph of the mould in H. V. Hilprecht, *Exploration in Bible Lands*, 517; and D. R. Frayne, RIME 2, 197f., for further publication references and an up-to-date edition.
[1291] Similarly K. Tallqvist, *APN*, 217; R. di Vito, StPohl SM 16, 186f., 17.2, 1.
[1292] See in general MAD 3, 98 for ED IIIb-Ur III PNN, and add the Sargonic references *ib-ni-ba-li*$_2$, Nik 2 42 o. 4 (ES-MS Umma); *ib-ni-be*$_6$*-li*$_2$, OSP 1 83 r. ii 9 (ES-MS Nippur).
[1293] See M. Hilgert, Imgula 5, 417f., with references.

participle (*bani-* verbal adjective or stative) in predicative position.[1294] The known variants accord with those featuring the preterite of the verb 'to create' in having mainly the same appellatives as the head noun.[1295]

3.2.5.2 Provisions for the city

There are no names relating the *śarrum* to economic activities, nor are such names commonplace in the Sargonic Akkadian onomasticon.

3.2.5.3 Countryside, produce and farming

There are no obvious names relating the *śarrum* to agricultural activities, nor are such names commonplace in the Sargonic Akkadian onomasticon. The only exception, and a difficult one, is the doubtlessly Akkadian, ES-MS Nippur name *śar*-ḫa-lu-ub$_2$ [(a1)] 'the *śarrum* ... oak(tree).' In a later mythological text the *haluppu*-tree plays a pivotal role, and a medicinal text lists *ḫaluppu*-seeds as stimulating pregnancy, but the form and function of *śar* in relation to any of these remain enigmatic.[1296] The ḫa-lu-ub$_2$ otherwise appears only rarely in the onomasticon, and it usage is limited to the late ED and Sargonic period.[1297]

3.2.5.4 Life and plenty

No names relating to this aspect of kingship are known. Sumerian names revolving around the central concepts of 'life,' ti and zi, are attested both as lugal-names and in later kyriophore names from the Ur III period. In Akkadian kyriophore personal names of the same period, not a single instance of a name of this type is known.

3.2.6 Cult or gods

The sixth heading collects names in which the appellative was portrayed in relation to gods, cultic places and ritual objects or acts. Most such names are

---

1294 Compare also *be-li$_2$-ba-ni*, e.g. HSS 10 109 o. 7 (CS Gasur), attested for more than a hadful of bearers between ES and CS times. A pron. suff. -*ī* is with all likelihood not the case, as that would imply a reading /*bāniʾī*/, which the writing does not immediately support. Instead, a reading *ba-li$_2$* could be considered, and compared to the name *ba-al-li$_2$*, e.g. BIN 8 335 r. 5 (CS Umma), also known from the Ur III period, see H. Limet, *Anthroponymie*, 382 s.v. Ba-al-NI.

1295 See MAD 3, 98 for references. I follow the editors of *FTUM* in seeing no. 93, with the name E$_2$-a-*ba-ni* in o. 4, as early Ur III in date. S. N. Kramer, *JAOS* 52 (1932), 113, in his survey of the tablet finds of the American excavation at Šuruppag, dated it to the ES period.

1296 Noted by M. Stol, *Birth in Babylonia and the Bible*, 52f. B. Böck discusses this in relation to the myth of Bilgames and the Ḫaluppu-tree as oppositions of life-giving and barren forces, *Sefarad* 69 (2009), 275f. The text in which the name figures, OSP 1 47, is chock-full of rare orthographies, denoting names of boys or young men, summarized as dumu nitaḫ.

1297 I am only aware of the name e$_2$-ḫa-lu-ub$_2$, e.g. M. deJ. Ellis, *JCS* 31 (1979), 30–55 no. 6 o. i 3 (ED IIIb Umma-Zabala, Luzag. Y 7); BIN 8 127 o. 5 (CS Mesag).

made up of descriptive names of the type 'the *śarrum* is like the Sun God.' Such names are taken to be qualitative statements, and do not entail any link between the referent of the appellative and service or a special relation to the gods. The corresponding heading is rather productive where Sumerian names are concerned. A few Akkadian names mention sanctuaries, notably the names of three of *Narām-Su'en*'s children whose names mention the Ulmaš-temple, the main sanctuary of Akkade's prime goddess, ʿAštar.[1298]

There might be further allusions to interaction between gods and the *śarrum*, but they remain implicit in the names and the connections are much less overt than in Sumerian names. See, for example, the discussion of the female PN *tu-ta*$_2$-lugal-*li-bi*$_2$*-iś*, below, 3.2.6.2. Fig. 14, below, records 3 persons, the estimated minimum number of persons bearing 3 variants of *śarrum*-names which possibly deal with relations to the divine.

	ED I-II	ED IIIa-ED IIIb	ED IIIb-ES	ES-MS	MS-CS
Ešnuna					2
Girsu					1

Fig. 14: Name-bearers, 3.2.6, Cult or gods. Estimated minimum number of individual name-bearers.

3.2.6.1 Prayer, petition and purification

No *śarrum*-names relating to these subject matters are known. Such activities were, however, not foreign to accounts of activities of Sargonic kings. In *Śarrukēn*'s account of his Syrian campaign he relates that he knelt in prayer before Dagān in Tuttul, who then gave him the upper land to rule.[1299] On arrival at the upper and lower seas, *Śarrukēn* and *Narām*-Su'en both state that they performed a ceremonial washing of their weapons.[1300] *Śarrukēn* furthermore, in a tragically broken context, speaks of his purifying Nippur for Enlil.[1301] But what kinds of acts it entailed is not clear, nor are similar passages encountered in any of the other Akkadian rulers' inscriptions.

[1298] The inscriptions, with publication refs. were edited as RIME 2.1.4.52–54. For the temple E$_2$-ul-maš, see in general A. R. George, MesCiv 5, 155:1168. A. Westenholz has suggested to me that the temple name might be used as metonym for its inhabitant ʿAštar Ulmašītum. J. J. Stamm, *Namengebung*, 91–93, discussed the phenomenon of metonymy, but remained sceptical.

[1299] PBS 5 34+PBS 15 41 o. v 14'–19': Du$_8$-du$_8$-⌜li⌝^{ki}-⌜a⌝, ^{d}Da-gan-ra, ki-a mu-na-za, šud$_3$ ⌜mu⌝-ša$_4$, kalam igi-nim, mu-na-šum$_2$ = vi 19'–26': *in* Tu-tu-li^{ki}, *a-na*, ^{d}Da-gan, *uś-ka*$_3$*-en*, ⌜*ik-ru-ub*⌝*-śu*$_2$, *ma-*⌜*tam*$_2$⌝, *a-li*$_2$*-tam*$_2$, *i-di*$_3$*-śum*.

[1300] See above, 3.2.1.3, p. 192f.

[1301] PBS 15 41 o. x 3''–6''. The episode takes place after *Śarrukēn*'s defeat of Uruk. Was it done in preparation of a temple building project that never materialized?

3.2.6.2 Relations to the divine

Evidence for an association on a personal level between the *śarrum* and a divinity comes from the Classic Sargonic period, and the name *tu-ta*$_2$*-śar-li-bi*$_2$*-iś* $^{(a1)}$ 'she found a *śarrum* of her liking.'[1302] As pointed out by A. Westenholz, the future queen of Akkade might have been called by this name even before her husband's accession to the throne.[1303] This makes the identity of the speaker of the name more likely to be someone other than the name-bearer herself, perhaps a goddess? Though it is also possible that this woman had been designated as a future spouse of prince *Śar-kalī-śarrē* since childhood. This queen of Akkade was hardly a commoner, but of noble, if not even royal birth. Her name is quite singular structurally and content-wise, and a better knowledge about the substantial royal family in Akkade is at any rate a desideratum.

A name with only a few parallels is *śar-ru-da-di*$_3$ $^{(a1)}$ from CS Girsu.[1304] Free-standing *da-di*$_3$ is common in the second half of the Sargonic period all across the Sumerian- and Akkadian-speaking areas. The word is probably to be understood as *dādum* 'darling, favourite'; and the suffix *-ī* can hardly be anything but the 1cs poss. pron. suffix. There is a remote possibility that *dādi* should be seen as a noun in the construct state, governing an elided noun or theonym which would be a neat parallel for *Śarkaliśarrē*'s epithet dumu *da-di*$_3$ Enlil 'the beloved son of Enlil.'[1305] A writing lugal-*da-di*$_3$ $^{(a1)}$ from Ešnuna makes it less likely that *śarrum* corresponds to later *šarrum* or *šerrum*, which would otherwise have made perfect sense 'the child is my favourite one.'

3.2.6.3 Cultic insignia, acts and ceremonial

As recounted above, section 3.2.1.3, Sargonic kings sometimes mentioned owing their success to weapons of gods. These weapons are never described in any detail.

3.2.6.4 Sacred loci, sanctuaries and installations

As was seen above, *Śarrukēn* purified Nippur for Enlil, and the verb used indicates a cultic significance of sorts. Other than that, the passage remains

[1302] Also written *tu-ta*$_2$-lugal-*li-bi*$_2$*-iś* $^{(a1)}$ in Ešnuna sources. Similarly A. Westenholz, *RlA* 12 (2009–11), 65, s.v. "Šar-kali-šarrī" § 4: "she has found the king of her heart."

[1303] *RlA* 12 (2009–11), 65 § 4. D. R. Frayne, RIME 3, 198, perceived her name as assumed upon marriage.

[1304] Compare R. di Vito, StPohl SM 16, 199, 29.1a, 8. Note comment by W. G. Lambert, *OrNS* 64 (1995), 136, pointing to VE1161: pa$_4$-ĝu$_{10}$ = *da-dum*, and the possibility of understanding *da-di*$_3$ as "my uncle." Compare, perhaps, the Danish bedsteforælder, Norwegian besteforelder, 'grandparent' (lit. 'best parent').

[1305] E.g. BE 1/1 2 i 2; and variant, A. Goetze, *JAOS* 88 (1968), 57 (6N-T658) o. i 1–5: ^{d}En-lil$_2$, lugal, *i*$_3$*-le*, ^{d}*Śar-ka*$_3$*-li*$_2$-lugal-*re*$_2$, dumu *da-di*$_3$*-śu*.

opaque. The reasons for this act are unknown, though the results may have been a more suitable environ in which to perform certain royal duties.

It is known that the Sargonic kings built temples just as their Sumerian counterparts. Their continued support of these temples after construction is nowhere further elaborated on. Some Sargonic kings instated their own children as en-priests and priestesses in a few southern cities.[1306]

3.2.7 Qualitative-descriptive

Descriptive statements on the nature and character of the referent of the appellative sort under heading seven. Such names were common among lugal-names, and so is the case also with *śarrum*-names. Such brief statements will be seen to have been well-suited for Akkadian onomastic practice. Fig. 15, below, records 35 persons, the estimated minimum number of persons bearing 32 variants of *śarrum*-names of this type and their distribution in cities with which they are associated.

	ED I-II	ED IIIa-ED IIIb	ED IIIb-ES	ES-MS	MS-CS
Akkade				1	2
Awal					2
Ebla			2		
Ešnuna					2
Gasur					3
Girsu					5
Kiš					3
Mari			1		
Nippur			1		
Sippar				1	
Susa					2
Šuruppag		1			
Tutub		1			2
Umma					2
Ur				1	
Unknown					3

Fig. 15: Name-bearers, 3.2.7, Qualitative-descriptive. Estimated minimum number of individual name-bearers.

3.2.7.1 Favour

Śarrukēn and his successors, like their Sumerian forebears, underlined the fact that they had been placed in power by gods, although the family relations, thereby the dynastic succession, between the first five Sargonic kings were probably no secret. The name of the fifth and last king of Akkade

[1306] See, above, p. 54f.

belonging to *Śarrukēn*'s bloodline and that of a sibling, *śar-ka*$_3$-*li*$_2$-lugal-*re*$_2$ $^{(a1)}$ '*śarrum* of all *śarrums*,'[1307] and *bi-in-ka*$_3$-*li*$_2$-lugal-*re*$_2$ $^{(a1)}$ 'offspring of all *śarrums*,'[1308] seem to extol another kind of favour, one bearing on lineage. This can be said with some certainty even though the referents of both the governing nouns, and of the "kings" in these names, are unclear. The two names are clearly structurally parallel. And given a degree of latitude in interpretation, the first element in the names could easily also be seeen as parallel, since there is the possibility to see *śar-* here as *šar*, representing later *šarrum*, or *šerrum* 'baby, child.' If this should be the case, chances are that *śarrum*/*šarrum* and *bīnum* or *binnum* both referred to the name-bearers as royal offspring following in the line of earlier kings (of Akkade and Kiš?), indicating dynastic succession.

3.2.7.2 Physical constitution

There are no attestations alluding to the physical build or to specific body parts of the *śarrum*. However, under the following subheading a few names are discussed which have bearing on qualities which relate to his appearance.

3.2.7.3 Physical strength and prowess

Typical for the Sargonic onomasticon is the form *śar-ru-dan* $^{(a2)}$ 'the *śarrum* is powerful,'[1309] which nicely echoes the prime epithet *da-num*$_2$ of *Narām*-Su'en in virtually all of his own inscriptions, and in many of those of his successors. Accounts of the Sargonic king felling cedars or wild bulls on campaigns to the northern regions lay further focus on the physical abilities of the king;[1310] something that is also apparent when studying monumental pieces of royal art. The Victory Stele of *Narām*-Su'en is a famous example. While statues of *Narām*-Su'en's predecessors sport long, flowing gowns, *Narām*-Su'en is depicted on his stele wearing his horned crown and a loincloth. He stands in front of his men, armed to the teeth, looming over an enemy who draws his final breath, one of the king's arrows piercing his throat. Divine symbols crown the scene with their presence.

[1307] So, e.g. B. Meissner, *Babylonien und Assyrien* 1, 396: "Der König aller Könige"; similarly E. Sollberger & J.-R. Kupper, *IRSA*, 336; A. Westenholz, *RlA* 12 (2009–11), 64, s.v. "Šar-kali-šarrī." Compare, e.g., K. Tallqvist, *APN*, 216: "The king of the totality is my king." Once written *śar-ka*$_3$-lugal $^{(a1)}$, in a date formula from Tell Ağrab, MAD 1 268 (FAOS 7 D-60 "Šarkališarrī 1a"), not from Tutub, as stated by B. R. Foster, *ZA* 72 (1982), 19.

[1308] For the textual evidence, see *CAD* B s.v. *bīnu* (*binnu*) B, and compare the feminine form, op. cit., s.v. *bintu*. Two imperfect variants of the name are known, one where *in* is left out, inadvertantly, or due to assimilation of *n* to *k*; and one where the first sign is miswritten as a combination of *in* and NIĜ$_2$. The second writing also has *śar* instead of expected lugal.

[1309] Similarly R. di Vito, StPohl SM 16, 214f., 30.5a, 5. Note also K. Tallqvist, *APN*, 69, *dan-nu-šarru* "mighty is the king." Compare also *be-li*$_2$-*dan*, e.g. HSS 10 65 r. 10 (CS Gasur).

[1310] See FAOS 8, 189 s.v. *batāqum*; 270f. s.v. *rīmum*.

Two names which invoke more fearsome aspects of the figure of the *śarrum* seem to be moulded on the model of names featuring other appellatives and theonyms. Thus, both *śar-ru-la-ba* [(a1)] 'the *śarrum* is a lion,'[1311] and *śar-ru-pa*$_2$*-luḫ* [(a1)] 'the *śarrum* is awe-inspiring,'[1312] are more productive with other appellatives than *śarrum.*[1313] A single name of a foreign prince attested at Ebla, lugal-*na-i-iš* [(a1)], might have as its second component a nominal predicate **naḫiš*, which corresponds to later Akkadian *nēšum* 'lion.'[1314] A nominal formation from the verb *naḫāśum*, "to live, be alive," remains a possibility, but a passive participle or stative form, giving 'the *śarrum* is alive' would be unexpected. At least the Sumerian parallels lugal-piriĝ and lugal-nemur$_x$(PIRIĜ.TUR) testify to the appeal of the lion motif across language barriers.

3.2.7.4 Aptitude for combat

śar-ru-gar$_3$ [(a1)] is probably to be understood as *śarru-qarrād* 'the *śarrum* is *a hero*.'[1315] The meaning and reading of the sign GAR$_3$ has been the subject of speculation.[1316] However, the nominal predicate of a šagina by the name *ʾIlśu-qarrād* is variously written *il*$_3$*-śu*-gar$_3$, *il*$_3$*-śu-qara*$_4$(GA*gunû*)*-ad*, and *il*$_3$*-śu-qa*$_2$*-ra-ad* in the CS Nippur archives.[1317] The rarity with which *ʾil-śu* 'his god' appears in southern archives coupled with the fact that three out of the four attestations feature his title šagina makes it well near certain that a single person is meant by all these writings. Further evidence can be adduced from Sargonic Umma texts, where the names *eś*$_3$*-me-qara*$_4$(GA*gunû*),[1318] and

---

[1311] R. di Vito, StPohl SM 16, 216, 30.5a, 15: "(The) god is (a) lion." See discussion by H. Limet concerning names including *lābum*/*labʾum* as nominal predicate, *DPA*, 57 fn. 6, with refs.; and see discussion of cognates by A. Militarev & L. Kogan, AOAT 278/2, 194–197. Compare *be-li*$_2$*-la-ba*, e.g. MVN 3 30 o. 3 (ES-MS Unknown); *il*$_3$*-śu-la-ba*, MO C v' 16 (ES, mentioned in connection with the township of Ki-babbar^{ki}).

[1312] Following R. di Vito, StPohl SM 16, 217, 30.5a, 21. Also written lugal-*pa*$_2$*-luḫ* [(a1)]. I have opted against a 2ms imperative of *palāḫum* as *śarrum* is in the nominative case. Compare also the proposed reading *be-li*$_2$*-pa*$_2$*-luḫ*, e.g. MAD 1 317 r. i 10 (*be-li*$_2$*-pa*$_2$-[*luḫ*]), and 324 o. 2 6 ([*be-li*$_2$]*-pa*$_2$*-luḫ*, both CS Ešnuna). Compare, perhaps, lugal-ni$_2$-bi-ak, above, p. 180.

[1313] See in general MAD 3 159f. s.v. LBʾ$_x$; and 214 s.v. PLḪ.

[1314] A. Militarev & L. Kogan, AOAT 278/2, 210f. no. 159; and see also L. Kogan, Babel und Bibel 3, 294.

[1315] See also *be-li*$_2$-gar$_3$, e.g. ITT 2/1 3150 o. 8 (CS Girsu). Compare R. di Vito StPohl SM 16, 220, 30.5a, 32: "(The) god is precious$^?$," suggesting a derivation from *waqārum* "to be rare, precious." On this identification, see the excursus of M. Hilgert, Imgula 5, 331–333, with ED, Sargonic and Ur III parallels.

[1316] The meaning inferred here was proposed already by M. Krebernik, *Annäherungen* 1, 261 fn. 213. Krebernik left the question open and referred to problematic writings, leaving the ED IIIb and Sargonic refs. out of the discussion.

[1317] See A. Westenholz, OSP 2, 195 s.v.v. DIĜIR-*su-gar*$_3$ and DIĜIR-*su-ga-ra-ad*, with refs. A parallel writing *il-śu*$_3$-gar$_3$, appears in Abū Ṣalābīḫ colophons, eg. in *IAS* 122 and 298. Compare also the Mari merchant be-*śu*$_3$*-qa*$_2$*-ra-du*, ARET 8 10 o. ix 1 (ED IIIb Ebla).

[1318] *TCVC* 728 o. iii 14; Nik 2 54 o. 3 (*eś*$_3$*-me-*⌜*qara*$_4$⌝).

eś$_3$*-me-qara*$_4$*-ad*,[1319] appear, representing one or two individuals. Comparative evidence in the form of other pre–Ur III PNN including the preterite of *šemûm* show that this verb is used primarily in conjunction with a pronominal suffix, with *ʾilum* or with a named deity, like Su'en or Śamaś.[1320] Note also the names EZEM-*qar-ra-ad* from ED IIIb Adab, most likely to be read *eśme*$_x$(EZEM)-*qarrād*,[1321] and *iś*$_2$*-ma*$_2$*-qar-du*, from ED IIIb Ebla.[1322] A related meaning is probably the case of the common borrowed writing ur-saĝ, as in *śar-ru*-ur-saĝ [(a1)] 'the *śarrum* is a hero.' The logographic writing may hide a loanword, as signalled by some phonetic spellings from Ebla and elsewhere.[1323] The meaning is, at least, semantically related, if not synonymous.[1324] The referent of *śarrum*, based on these more or less parallel formations, is likely to be a deity.

Needless to say, the Sargonic kings were accomplished warriors. Some of the kings prided themselves with having won a specified number of battles; *Sarrukēn* mentioned 34 without closer defining the timeframe involved; *Rīmuś* mentioned three specifically fought on Sumerian soil; and *Narām*-Su'en claimed to have won nine battles in the course of a single year.[1325] But where the names *śar-ru*-gar$_3$ and and *śar-ru*-ur-saĝ are concerned, the frequency of finite forms of *šemûm* along with deities or divine appellatives arguably tips the scales toward a divine and not a human referent, although the latter is not entirely unthinkable.

3.2.7.5 Fame and good reputation

There are no clear attestations of names revolving around the *śarrum* as renowned. Neither was this category very productive among Sumerian lugal-names. But a recurring theme which comes to the fore the most clearly in *Narām*-Su'en's inscriptions is that he had gone places and accomplished feats which no king before him had ever gone or done.[1326]

[1319] BIN 8 338 o. 4.

[1320] The references in MAD 3, 274f. are still representative.

[1321] OIP 14 74 o. ii 6.

[1322] E.g. ARET 4 16 o. v 8; ARET 7 22 o. ii 3.

[1323] See M. V. Tonietti, Subartu 4/2, 90f., w. fnn. 90–93, for discussion and examples.

[1324] R. di Vito, StPohl SM 16, 217f., 30.5a, 23 "My god is (a) hero (warrior)"; D. O. Edzard, *AfO* 22 (1968/69), 14: "*šar-ru-qurād*." The reading *qurād*(*um*) is not certain, though plausible considering, e.g., the correspondence between the Abū Ṣalābīḫ and Ebla recensions of the Śamaś hymn, *IAS* 326+ o. iii 14: ^{d}Su'en ur-saĝ-*śu*$_3$ = ARET 5 6 o. v 5: ^{d}Su'en *qur*$_2$*-da-śu*, as pointed out in passing by R. D. Biggs, ARES 1, 98 fn. 51. The writing *be-li*$_2$-kara$_6$(GUR$_7$), *OAIC* 4 r. 6 (MS-CS Ešnuna), was interpreted by G. Marchesi, HANE/S 10, 111 as "My Lord Is My Granary." The name is unique and GUR$_7$ might represent *qara*$_x$(GUR$_7$), for *qarrā*(*dum*).

[1325] See references in FAOS 8, 276–278 s.v. *šaʾārum*.

[1326] See references in FAOS 8, 240 s.v. *mannāma*; and the comments by S. Franke, *Königsinschriften*, 170–172, 191–193. Franke's suggestion that Enḫeduana was influenced by this aspect of *Narām*-Su'en's self depictions when compiling her temple hymns, something no other person had done before, is definitely to the point and an interesting observation.

3.2.7.6 Symbolic identification and equation

Most Sargonic Akkadian theophore *śarrum*-names feature the appellative *śar*(*rum*) as nominal predicate. When *śar*(*rum*) occupies first position, it is regularly followed by the non-coordinating *-ma*, filling what is sometimes termed an asseverative particle. This particle, which ought to have carried the emphasis, is evidently easily coloured by the following syllable /*ʾi*/; thus, expected *śar-ma-i₃-lum* (a1/°1) 'a *śarrum* indeed is the god!,'[1327] attested at ED IIIa-b Tutub, and in a scholastic Ebla text, corresponds to ED IIIb Mari *śar-me-il* (a1),[1328] and Ebla *śar-mi-lu* (a1). Reduction of syllable final /*l*/ may be demonstrated by Eblaite *śar-ma*-NI (°1),[1329] /*śar-ma-ʾi*/. CS *śar-me*-NI (a1) on the other hand is likely to display a retained /*l*/ along with a suffigated pronoun 'my,' /*śar-ma-ʾilī*/>/*śar-me-lī*/, common during this time.[1330] The singular *śar-ma* (°1), attested only in an Eblaite scholastic list of names may be a hypocoristic form of the same type or a variant on the same theme but without a subject referent for the stative form *śar*. A possible ED IIIa witness from Šuruppag *il-lu-śar* (a1) 'a *śarrum* indeed is the god,'[1331] employs another particle with an asseverative function, *lū*, fully in keeping with the other early names featuring *-ma*.

1327 Compare *be-la-ma*-an, Subartu 2 5 o. v 4 (ED IIIb-ES Nabada). Positioning of *-ma* is debated. On one side, I. J. Gelb, MAD 3, 287; M. Krebernik, *ZA* 81 (1991), 140, and A. Westenholz, e.g. *AfO* 42-43 (1995–96), 221 w. fn. 18 all read /*śar-ma-ʾilum*/; on the other side, H. Steible, ABW 2, 207f.: AnHaf 4; followed by R. di Vito, StPohl SM 16, 134, 212, 291; I. J. Gelb, & B. Kienast, FAOS 7, 29, VP 4; and B. Kienast & W. Sommerfeld, FAOS 8, 327, all have /*śar-ʾilum-ma*/. See, however, Sommerfeld's rendering in *Fs Pettinato*, 288, siding with Gelb's original interpretation. See the important observations of P. Fronzaroli, ARES 1, 12f. about the placement of the asseverative on the first element, termed "prédicat exclamatif." Although the semantic difference is academic and hardly affects interpretation, it should be added that all available evidence supports the reading used here, and to the author's knowledge no evidence to the contrary exists. Note, for instance, *dan-ma-ḫum*, Nik 2 48 r. 1 (ES-MS Umma); *dan-ma*-šeš, *SET* 207 r. 3 (Ur III Umma); and, lastly, the two post–*Šamšī*-Adad OA kings *Šar-ma*-ᵈAdad.

1328 Following R. di Vito, StPohl SM 16, 212, 30.4c, 8. Remove reference in Di Vito's table to a PN **sar-ma*-DIĜIR from the Ur III period. The copy of BIN 3 546 o. 7, has *šar-na-an*, as noted already by A. Westenholz, *AfO* 42/43 (1995–96), 217 fn. 18. For notes on other suggested readings, see M. Stol, *RlA* 12 (2009–11), 61 s.v. "Šar-Il."

1329 For asseverative *-ma* plus elided *ʾi*(‹*l*›) in other Eblaite writings, see e.g. A. Archi, *Eblaitica* 1, 130; and for the reduction generally, see M. Krebernik, BBVO 7, 99–101. G. Pettinato, MEE 3, 245, contends that *ma-ni* is a DN; as does C. H. Gordon, ARES 1, 153, treating the word in other names. A divinity ᵈMa-ni appears already in an Abū Ṣalābīḫ god list, for which, see M. Krebernik, *Annäherungen* 1, 269 w. fn. 408. The adjective *mani*(*yum*) may be the case in J. J. M. Roberts, *ESP*, 129: "*Mani*-(*i*)*lī* Beloved-Of-My-God"; R. di Vito, StPohl SM 16, 223, 36, 2 (*ma-ni*-): "Beloved of (the) god."

1330 See e.g., *be-li₂-me-li₂*, ETB 2 75 o. 5 (CS Nagar). I. J. Gelb, MAD 3, 179 s.v. MNʾ₇ offered an interpretation *menjum* "love," for names ending in *me*-NI, but added the comment "interpretation doubtful."

1331 After R. di Vito, StPohl SM 16, 212, 30.4c, 7. Compare A. Westenholz, ARES 1, 106: "Il is the only king."

Divinities qualified as 'king,' or 'lord,' range from anonymous *ʾilum*,[1332] and pronominal *śū*(-*ma*) 'he (alone),'[1333] to gods written out with their full names. The deities appearing in Akkadian names as 'kings' are: Ea,[1334] Adad,[1335] and Su'en.[1336] A single goddess, Mama, is correspondingly dubbed 'queen,'[1337] *śarrat*(*um*). Compare also *śar-ru-ki*-^{d}Utu, below, section 3.2.7.9.

The name *śar-ru*-ḫur-saĝ $^{(a1)}$ 'the *śarrum* is a mountain,'[1338] has a sound parallel in lugal-ḫur-saĝ. The imposing weight and steadfastness of the *śarrum* may be the effective imagery behind the name.

3.2.7.7 Uniqueness and aloofness

There are no clear-cut matches to Sumerian lugal-names of the corresponding subheading above.

3.2.7.8 Similes and kindness

Simple names construed with *śarrum* as head noun followed by a stative are made up by *śar-ru*-du_{10} $^{(a1)}$ 'the *śarrum* is good,'[1339] and *śar-ru*-sig_5 $^{(a1)}$ 'the *śarrum* is kind.'[1340] The logographic writings should with all probability be read in Akkadian as *ṭāb*, and *damiq*, respectively. There are, as of yet, no attestations of names corresponding to the Sumerian PNN of the type lugal-lal_3 or lugal-i_3-nun.

3.2.7.9 Justice and dependability

A good handful of names relate the just nature of the *śarrum*. The name of the founder of the Sargonic dynasty, *Śarrukēn* 'the *śarrum* is dependable,'[1341]

[1332] Forms include *i_3-lum-śar* $^{(a1)}$ from ES Sippar; and CS Tutub AN-*śar* $^{(a1)}$.

[1333] Writing *$śu_2$-ma-śar* $^{(a1)}$ 'he alone is king' from MS Awal. Compare R. D. Biggs, ARES 1, 96: *śu-ma-a-ba_4* "He is a father," with variant *$śu_3$-ma-* in next name on Biggs' list.

[1334] Variants: E_2-a-*śar* $^{(a2)}$, and E_3-a-*śar* $^{(a1)}$. Pre–Sargonic reference to the latter in R. di Vito, StPohl SM 16, 134 is correct, and table 7 on p. 212 should be emended accordingly. Compare OB variant, A. Poebel, *Personennamen*, 24: E_2-a-*šar-rum*.

[1335] Written ^{d}IM-*śar* $^{(a1)}$. Compare ^{d}Adad-*šar-ru-um*, A. Poebel, *Personennamen*, 24, with variants switching positions of appellative.

[1336] Variants: ^{d}EN:ZU-*śar* $^{(a1)}$, and ZU.EN-lugal $^{(a1)}$. So also J. J. M. Roberts, *ESP*, 48; R. di Vito, StPohl SM 16, 212, 30.4c, 7 and 8. The writing order ZU.EN in this name marks one of two breaks with normal orthography ^{d}ZU:EN in Mesopotamian sources; for Ebla writing *Zu-i-nu* in Kiš PNN, see A. Archi, *Eblaitica* 1, 130. A Sargonic GN Lugal-^{d}EN.ZU^{ki} is attested in a CS Sippar text, CT 1 pl. 1 (Bu. 91-5-9,588 = BM 80452) o. 11.

[1337] Ma-ma-*śa-ra-at* $^{(a1)}$, J. J. M. Roberts, *ESP*, 43: "Mamma-Is-Queen"; followed by R. di Vito, StPohl SM 16, 212, 30.4c, 9. Compare A. Poebel, *Personennamen*, 24: Ma-mi-*šar-ra-at*. On this goddess, see J. J. M. Roberts, *ESP*, 24 w. note 159, p. 84f.; and 43f.

[1338] Compare parallels *śi*-ḫur-saĝ, e.g. MAD 1 293 o. 3 (MS-CS Ešnuna); and Ma-ma-ḫur-saĝ, e.g. *USP* 33 o. 2 (MS-CS Umma).

[1339] R. di Vito StPohl SM 16, 219, 30.5a, 29: "(My) god is good." The same person appears more than 5 times in CS Girsu texts. Compare *be-li_2*-du_{10}, e.g. *TCABI* 36 r. i 3 (ES Adab).

[1340] Similarly R. di Vito, StPohl SM 16, 230, 40.6a, 2.

[1341] Compare R. di Vito, StPohl SM 16, 216, 30.5a, 14: "(The) god is true"; K. Tallqvist, *APN*, 217: *Šarru-kīn*(*u*) "The king is true," with many later variants.

is sometimes perceived as a programmatic name adopted at the accession to the throne, but based on the rarity of throne names such an assumption is unwarranted.[1342] What is clear is that his name represents an innovation compared with the earlier Akkadian onomasticon which predominantly featured *śar*(*rum*) as a predicate. As for a possible development in import, the main problem is that the earliest writings of *śar*(*rum*) are rather few, stereotypical, and quite vague in respect to meaning. A few variant writings of *Śarrukēn*'s name are known;[1343] and he appears furthermore in a number of kyriophore names.[1344]

Other names which revolve around the same subject matter as the former are *i-śar-śar-ri*$_2$ (a1), and *śar-ru-i-śar* (a1) 'the *śarrum* is just.'[1345] Both are formed with predicative forms of the verb *ešērum*. A name which offers a parallel to Sumerian names involving aspects of a just nature or dependability is *śar-ru-ki*-^{d}Utu (a1) 'the *śarrum* is like Śamaś.'[1346] The use of the preposition *kī* corresponds to the use of Sumerian gin$_7$, which is also attested along with the name of Utu.[1347]

3.2.7.10 Light, brilliance and visual phenomena

There is a single possible parallel to the rather productive type of Sumerian names which attach to the lugal the quality of brightness. It is tempting to interpret the ES-MS Ur name lugal-*nu-ru* (a1), as Akkadian 'the *śarrum* is light,'[1348] but the reading is not entirely secure. The lack of mimation in the nominative is not a huge problem,[1349] but it is perhaps all too convenient to have the name appear in a city whose tutelary deity was identified with a luminary, and who himself was often referred to as lugal in different

---

1342 See, for instance, B. Meissner, *Babylonien und Assyrien* 1, 396: "Legitimer König"; also perceived by W. G. Lambert to be a throne name, JSOTS 270 (1998), 58; and, furthermore, the discussion by W. Sommerfeld, *RlA* 12 (2009–11), 45 "Sargon," § 1.

1343 Including: *śar-ru*-gi (a1), *śar-rum*$_2$-gi (a1), and *śar-um*-gi (a1). Compare *be-li*$_2$-gi, attested in at least 8 different archives, e.g. *TCVBI* 1-51 o. 5 (CS Umm al-Ḥafrīyāt). See also the following note.

1344 An MS-CS kyriophore offers the writing lugal-gi-pa-e$_3$ (a1). The predicate is probably to be taken as *šupûm*, *šūpiʾ*(*um*), "brilliant, famous." Compare the entries in two 1st millennium literary catalogues of a hitherto unknown tale about *Śarrukēn* with the incipit *Šarrukēn šūpû*, J. Goodnick Westenholz, *JNES* 43 (1984), 78 fn. 14. In the same text appears a person called plainly lugal-gi (a1). Such a name is otherwise unattested in Sumerian, so there is a real possibility that it also represents an Akkadian reading *śarru*(LUGAL)-*kēn*(GI), whether abbreviated or not. Later kyriophore names incorporating *Śarrukēn* are not uncommon, M. Hilgert, Imgula 5, 393f., offers a list of such names.

1345 R. di Vito, StPohl SM 16, 216, 30.5a, 11: "My god is righteous."

1346 Following J. J. M. Roberts, *ESP*, 52.

1347 Compare the Sumerian names lugal-^{d}Utu-gin$_7$, attested in an OB list of PNN, E. Chiera, PBS 11/3, 213, no. 289; and lugal-Utu-gin$_7$-e$_3$, above, p. 173, section 3.1.7.10.

1348 Compare K. Tallqvist, *APN*, 219: *Šarru-nūri* "The god is my light," with different writings; similarly R. di Vito, StPohl SM 16, 205, 29.1c, 22; and *be-li*$_2$-*nu-ri*$_2$, MAD 1 3 o. i 2 (CS Ešnuna).

1349 See Sargonic and Ur III parallel forms, all with mimation, MAD 3, 192 s.v. Nʾ$_6$R.

Sumerian contexts. Reading nu-ru as a negated participle and interpreting the name as Sumerian nominal phrase name does not make it more intelligible.

3.2.8 Unattributable or unintelligible

Under the eighth and final heading are names collected which for different reasons are difficult to assign to another heading. They may be understandable in whole or in part but still not readily attributable to another heading.

Two variants from the Names and Professions List feature a nominal predicate which is otherwise unknown for the 3rd millennium. The name is given as lugal-GA.NIR (°1) in the Abū Ṣalābīḫ version, and as lugal-KA.NIR (°1),[1350] in the Ebla version. Given that the name is Akkadian, no syllabic value with a velar stop would account for the orthographies GA and KA in these variants. GA in the Abū Ṣalābīḫ source being older, is probably the more correct of the two, leaving KA as a possible hearing error during copying. Alternatively, KA in the Ebla source could be read gu$_3$. Turning to later parallels, a participle of the verb *kašārum* "to replace, compensate," might be considered as the nominal predicate contained in this name. This would yield an interpretation lugal-*ka*$_{(3)}$-*śer*$_7$(NIR) 'the *śarrum* is one who compensates.'[1351] If the name is understood correctly, it would make for a thanksgiving-name with a semantic affinity to names containing the verb *riābum*, with a similar meaning,[1352] but the orthography of the Eblaite name hampers a definite solution to the meaning.

A name from CS Gasur, *en-bu*-lugal (a1), has been interpreted as incorporating imagery of plant life, 'fruit of the *śarrum*.'[1353] The word "fruit," *ʿenbum*, could be used about living beings, denoting "offspring." The later epithet *inbu*(*m*) was used primarily about the Moon God, though in personal names, it was used as poetic description of both gods and goddesses.[1354] However, a couple of factors make an interpretation *ʿenbum* of *en-bu* unlikely. To begin with, the sign EN is at present only known to represent the syllables /*hin*/, /*ḫin*/, and most often /*yin*/, which does not

---

[1350] The entry has been published in transliteration only by A. Archi, *StEb* 4 (1981), 177–204.

[1351] Otherwise a syllabic value šer$_7$ is mostly used in conjunction with phonetic complement še$_3$, as in $^{d\ še_3}$Šer$_7$-da. Later parallels are booked in *CAD* K sub *kašāru* C, and see also M. Stol *StEb* 8 (1991), 193f.

[1352] The underlying root of the verb *riābum* was subjected to a close study by M. Hilgert, Imgula 5, 362–368, using Ur III Akkadian names.

[1353] So I. J. Gelb, MAD 3, 51; followed by R. di Vito, StPohl SM 16, 224, 37.1, 2. Three damaged signs are placed below the sign lugal which must be a qualifier of sorts.

[1354] See *CAD* I s.v. *inbu*, for many references.

support seeing the first syllable as /ˁ*en*/, or the like.[1355] Secondly, the nominative -*u*, would be problematic as a construct state noun ending;[1356] this goes also for the parallel *en-bu*-AN.[1357] The expected -*i*-ending is seen in an ED IIIb Kiš royal name, *en-bi*$_{2}$-Aš$_{10}$-tar$_{2}$,[1358] but nor are these two latter names – with initial EN – likely to be derived from *ˁ*nb*,[1359] although links between the king and ˁAštar are later formulated in precisely this manner.[1360] Thirdly, the sign lugal alone would have to be taken to stand for the genitive *śarri*(*m*), which it never does otherwise in the onomasticon, without a phonetic complement. Thus, while *en-bu* could be a nominal predicate occupying first position, the orthography prevents an interpretation along the line of 'a fruit is the *śarrum*.' A derivation of *en-bu* from *nabûm* "to call, to name," would in comparison offer only the slight problem of the unexpected ending in -*u*, as opposed to expected -*i*, which indeed is demonstrated by the aforementioned *en-bi*$_{2}$-Aš$_{10}$-tar$_{2}$.

Other names which at present escape interpretation are: *i-ba*-lugal [(a1)] 'the *śarrum* drew near (?),' *i-li*$_{2}$*-śar-ru* [(a2)] 'a *śarrum* emerged (?),'[1361] *i-pu*$_{3}$*-śar* [(a2)],[1362] lugal-OSP1-X$_{5}$ [(a1)],[1363] *śar-a-Ti-Gu-Bi-śi-in* [(a1)],[1364] *śar-Ku-Da* [(°1)],[1365] *śar*-NI-*sa* [(°1)],[1366] *śar-*

[1355] See generally R. Hasselbach, *Sargonic Akkadian*, 66f. The sign EN is also amply attested in the onomasticon in nominal formations from a verb *enēnum*, that is, as /*ḥin*/ or /*ḥen*/, see MAD 3, 51–53 s.v. ʾ$_{x}$NN.

[1356] See R. Hasselbach, *Sargonic Akkadian*, 182, along with the critical notes by L. Kogan & K. Markina, Babel und Bibel 3 (2006), 573f. A certain example of st. constr. ending -*u* is furnished by *kal*$_{2}$*-bu*$_{3}$-Aš$_{10}$-tar$_{2}$, OSP 1 47 o. i 3 (ES-MS Nippur), and see other names with UR/*kala*/*ib*-, M. V. Tonietti, Subartu 4/2, 93–95.

[1357] E.g. BIN 8 121 r. i 9 (MS-CS Kazallu).

[1358] BE 1/2 104 5'.

[1359] So, for instance, G. Marchesi & N. Marchetti, MesCiv 14, 123.

[1360] See the Ur III kyriophore ^{d}*Šu*-^{d}Su'en-*i*$_{3}$*-ni-ib*-Aš$_{10}$-tar$_{2}$, M. Hilgert, JBVO 5, 48, w. refs.

[1361] The first element conforms to a 3rd person masc. preterite *yi*-. Attested forms of this name have *i-li*$_{2}$-, against I. J. Gelb, MAD 3, 30; correctly J. Bauer, *WO* 24 (1993), 165. A derivation from the verb *elûm* "to go up, emerge," is a possibility. The note by B. R. Foster, *JAOS* 115 (1995), 539 begs collation.

[1362] Both attestations are Early Dynastic in date. The reading order of *TSŠ* 750 o. 2, as far as the name is indeed the same, is corroborated by the ED IIIb Mari writing in MAM 3 8. R. di Vito, StPohl SM 16, 194, 24.6e, 1, interpreted the name with reservation to be derived from *apālum* "to answer," "(The) king answered." An alternative interpretation would be to see the name as a sandhi writing for *yiḫpuś-śar*(*ru*) 'the *śarrum* made (him).' However, the verb *epēšum* is not found in the Sargonic onomasticon.

[1363] The great majority of names in the text, OSP 1 47, are Akkadian, or at least not Sumerian.

[1364] T. Jacobsen, AS 11, 120 fn. 308 read the name as: *Muati-qu*(*b*)*bîsin* "Muati (has heard) their wail"; followed by E. Sollberger & J.-R. Kupper, *IRSA*, 323, who considered another reading, *op. cit.*, 336: *Šar-addī-qubbišin* "O roi, j'ai négligé leurs (f) plaintes." I. J. Gelb, with reservations, proposed: "O king, I gave their (sisters') laments," MAD 3, 287. A. Westenholz gives the known facts about this person, *RlA* 12 (2009–11), 35 s.v. "Šarʾatigubisin."

[1365] Compare, phps., *Ku-Da*-Al$^{?}$-la, B. R. Foster, *WO* 13 (1982), 15f. no. 1 (ITT 1 1405, translit. only), composed with the theophore Alla.

[1366] Compare, phps., Aš$_{10}$-tar$_{2}$*-ni-sa*, MAD 1 163+ o. iii 17 (translit. only, MS-CS Ešnuna).

ru-Du-Gul (a1),[1367] *śar-ru*-NE (a1),[1368] *śar-ru*-pa-[x] (a1),[1369] *śar-ru-ru* (≥a3)[1370], *śar-ru-um* (a1),[1371] *śar-x-Tu* (°1), *u-Bi-in*-lugal-ri$_2$ (a2).[1372]

3.2.9 Non–existent *śarrum*-names and misreadings

A small number of names have previously been thought to be composed with *śarrum*. Some feature the logogram LUGAL, others the sign SAR. Contextual analysis and comparable onomastic material makes it clear that a reading *śar*(*rum*) can no longer be upheld in the following names.

**aś-ma$_2$*!(SI)-*śar*.[1373] Already M. Krebernik held the reading for uncertain.[1374] Three Šuruppag texts[1375] all feature boat crewmen and skippers, and all share variant writings of this formulaic expression. The writing of proposed *aś* with the sign BAR in at least two of the texts is hard to harmonize with a syllabic reading. On top of that, SI (MA$_2$) in the remainder of these texts is used to denote river-faring vessels. The sign SI (MA$_2$) furthermore consistently stands at either end of the writing cases. Read, then, rather a technical term denoting a type of vessel, in Sumerian.

**il$_2$-e-śar*.[1376] Not a *śarrum*-name. Parallels from, for instance, Nabada and Ebla,[1377] indicate that the present name contains a sandhi writing combining a 3ms preterite of *leʾûm*, and the stative of *ešērum* "to be well; to be straight, fair": */yilʾay+yiśar/*. The combination of these two verbs was traditional and remained in use throughout the 2nd millennium.[1378]

**ki-śar*.[1379] As was suspected by C. Wilcke,[1380] the writing does not represent a PN. The writing KI.SAR-še$_3$ appears in a sales contract of a garden and ki represents a phonetic indicator: ^{ki}kiri$_6$-še$_3$ '(sales price) for a garden.'

*lugal-*a-mi*.[1381] This suggested Akkadian reading for the writing lugal-a-ĝe$_6$,[1382] would imply that Nippur orthography LU:GAL could interchange freely with normal

---

[1367] Compare *be-li$_2$-Du-Gul*, MAD 1 163+165 r. iv' 7 (translit. only). Since the same text contains the writing TU for /*du*/, in *be-li$_2$-du$_2$-ri$_2$*, a reading *tu$_3$-Gul* might be preferred.

[1368] See note to lugal-i$_3$-bi$_2$, above, p. 178.

[1369] See discussion on possible readings, B. Kienast & K. Volk, FAOS 19, 74.

[1370] The name does not make sense. Perhaps a Banana-name?

[1371] See discussion of **śar-ru-um*-Dilmun-*mu-bi$_2$*, below, p. 215.

[1372] Name of two individuals, both persons appear as citizens of Akkade in MO.

[1373] See, e.g. F. Pomponio, *Prosopografia*, 52, s.v. *aš-ma$_2$-sar*.

[1374] *Annäherungen* 1, 261 w. fn. 215–216.

[1375] *WF* 67–69.

[1376] Writing found in CS Adab, *SIA* Y2; and Sargonic Girsu, ITT 2/2 2914 (translit. only).

[1377] See, e.g. *il$_2$-e-i-śar*, common at ED IIIb-ES Nabada, e.g. Subartu 2 21 o. ii 2; and Ebla, ARET 8 10 r. ix 8.

[1378] See the Ur III names listed in MAD 3, 158 s.v. Lʾ$_{3\text{-}5}$ʾ$_7^?$ *laʾium*, *leʾûm*; and the entry in an OB list of PNN: *i-šar-le-e*, OECT 4 155 ii 36.

[1379] Treated as a PN by J. Krecher, *ZA* 63 (1973), 237f., w. notes on previous literature; and also by the editors of OIP 104, pl. 146, no. 185.

[1380] *EANEL*, 102 fn. 324.

[1381] Writing found in A. Goetze, *JCS* 23 (1970), p. 48 (5N-T452), 2'.

[1382] R. diVito, StPohl SM 16, 198, 29.1a, 5.

LUGAL to denote Akk. *śarrum*,[1383] for which there is no corroborating evidence. Read instead lugal-a-ĝe$_6$.

*lugal-*bi$_2$-nu-um*.[1384] Due to parallel DUN-NE(-nu-um), the interpretation of the name as Akkadian is unlikely.[1385] While no better option can be forwarded, read, for the moment, lugal-NE-nu-um.

*lugal-na-da.[1386] A few circumstances speak against seeing the name as Akkadian. The measurements of silver are Sumerian style with the unit after the object measured; the other names that can be read all appear to be Sumerian, and specifically, the name aja$_2$-lal$_3$ (o. 3) speaks for a possible provenience in the Adab-Nippur region. Read, more likely lugal-iti$^!$-da.

*lugal-*pu$_5$*(KA).[1387] Judging from known parallels to this posited name, the placement of *pu$_5$*(KA) would be uncharacteristic in that it is unqualified and occupies a name-final position. The latter sign must temporarily be read KA and the name should be understood as Sumerian, beginning with lugal-du$_{11}$(-ga/-ge etc.), or lugal-inim. See also the following name.

*lugal-*pum*.[1388] See note to the previous name, and read, in Sumerian, lugal-šud$_3$.

**pu$_3$-śar*.[1389] The name should be read consistently in Sumerian, as su$_6$-mu$_2$. As indicated by J. Krecher, in many – if not all – cases the first sign in this name does not represent original KA×ŠU, bu$_3$, but what is later to become KA×SA, with a reading su$_6$, "beard." For some reason it is often (always?) borne by females.[1390]

**śar-be-li$_2$*.[1391] Misreading of a seal belonging to the major domo of the Sargonic queen *Tūta'-śar-libbīś*.[1392] Read *i-śar-be-li$_2$*.

**śar-ru-um*-Dilmun-*mu-bi$_2$*,[1393] *śar-ru-um*-maḫ$_2$-*mu-pi$_5$*.[1394] Whatever the reading and meaning of the final component, *mu*-NE, it only appears in two-element names. There is no reason to see DILMUN/maḫ$_2$ as a logogram with an Akkadian reading. To interpret this line as containing two distinct names would be more in keeping with the rest of the Sargonic onomastic material. At any rate, *śarrum* without further qualification would be unexpected. Read, perhaps, *‹i›-šar-ru-um* and *al-mu*-NE.[1395]

1383 See TMH 5 156 o. 4 (lu:gal-a-ĝe$_6$).

1384 So E. Sollberger, *ZA* 54 (1961), 14 no. 49.

1385 See discussions by A. Westenholz, *OrNS* 44 (1975), 434; and J. Bauer, *AfO* 36/37 (1989/90), 88 note to 221 ii 3K.

1386 So I. J. Gelb, MAD 3, 188 s.v. N'$_1$D *na'ādum* "to praise," and 287 s.v. ŠRR *šarrum* "king"; and A. Westenholz, *JCS* 26 (1974), 71–80 no. 5, transliterated on p. 73f.

1387 See I. J. Gelb, MAD 3, 210 s.v. P *pum* "mouth," "word," written lugal-KA.

1388 See I. J. Gelb, MAD 3, 210 s.v. P *pum* "mouth," "word."

1389 See I. J. Gelb, MAD 3 210 s.v. P *pum* "mouth," "word"; and the suggested interpretations of D. O. Edzard, *SRU*, 116 no. 62 (=*RTC* 12) o. i 6 and notes to line.

1390 See discussion by J. Krecher, *ZA* 63 (1973), 204–206, with many references.

1391 R. M. Boehmer, *Fs Moortgat*, pl. 13 no. 28.

1392 So, e.g. W. W. Hallo & W. K. Simpson, *The Ancient Near East: A History*, 58 fig. 10.

1393 So I. J. Gelb, MAD 3, 55 s.v. '$_6$P'x *wuppûm* ?. Line found in UET 2 suppl. 50 r. 3.

1394 So A. Alberti & F. Pomponio, StPohl SM 13, 115f., with diverging interpretation.

1395 Compare, e.g. *i-śar-ru-um* in *AIHA* 7 o. i 11 (MS Awal).

4. Overview of lexemes

In the following, a selection of lexical items contained in lugal- and *śarrum*-names are arranged in tables organized according to word class. The order of listing of lemmas in the individual tables is alphabetical. The first section gives the names of divinities appearing in the names; the second specific loci, followed by a third section containing nouns and a fourth for verbs and adjectives. Two more sections give the attested verbal prefixes for Sumerian names and the finite forms contained in Akkadian names. In the left column the lemmas are listed, in the right the names in which the lemmas appear. Names which are attested only in scholastic texts are marked by means of °.

For a number of reasons, names where reading and interpretation are in doubt have only been assigned to tables when there are compelling reasons to do so. Names which have been deemed unintelligible in the preceding treatments, 3.1.8 and 3.2.8 have been entered in the tables below whenever enough information is provided in the name itself to allow doing so.

A question mark following a name indicates that the reading of the name is in question. A question mark within parenthesis means that the attribution of a name to a lemma is less secure.

4.1 Divinities

In the two tables below are found names in which divinities and superhuman beings appear associated with the appellatives lugal and *śarrum*. Sumerian and Akkadian names have been assigned to their respective table mainly on the basis of overall observations on orthography, syntax and date. The latter is, however, not indicated in the table. Note that not all references to the (divine) river I_7 may refer to a divine being, and that *il*(*um*) may in some cases be the generic term for a male god in Akkadian.

Sumerian

An	lugal-AN (?), lugal-AN-da (?), lugal-AN-da-nu-ḫuĝ-ĝa$_2$ (?), lugal-AN-da-nu-me-a (?), lugal-AN-ku$_3$-ge (?), lugal-An-ne$_2$, lugal-An-ne$_2$-ki-aĝa$_2$, lugal-An-ne$_2$-su, lugal-igi-An-na-ke$_4$-su, lugal-šu-luḫ-ku$_3$-An-na, ^{d}Nanše-ama-Lugal-AN-da (?), ^{d}Utu-palil-Lugal-AN-da (?)
Anzu	lugal-^{an}Anzu$_2$, lugal-^{an}Anzu$_2$^{mušen}, lugal-^{an}Anzu$_x$, lugal-^{an}Anzu$_x$^{mušen}

Dumuzi	lugal-^{d}Dumu-zi, lugal-dumu-zi (?)
Enki	lugal-^{d}En-ki-a-DU
Enlil	lugal-^{d}En-lil$_2$, lugal-^{d}En-lil$_2$-da, lugal-^{d}En-lil$_2$-le, lugal-^{d}En-lil$_2$-le-an-zu, lugal-ME-^{d}En-l[il$_2$]
Id	lugal-i$_7$-da, lu:gal-^{d}I$_7$-ĝu$_{10}$, lugal-I$_7$-ĝu$_{10}$, lugal-i$_7$-maḫ, lugal-^{d}I$_7$-si
^{d}KA.DI	lugal-^{d}KA.DI
Nanna	lugal-^{d}Nanna-ra-tum$_2$
Nanše	lugal-^{d}Nanše-mu-tu, ^{d}Nanše-ama-Lugal-AN-da
Sud	lugal-^{d}Sud$_3$-de$_3$, lugal-^{d}Sud$_3$-ki-aĝ$_2$
Šarur	lugal-Šar$_2$-ur$_3$-e
Tu	lugal-^{d}Tu
Utu	lugal-UD, lugal-^{d}Utu, lugal-Utu-gin$_7$-e$_3$, UD-lugal-le (PN?), ^{d}Utu-palil-lugal-AN-da

Akkadian

Adad	^{d}IM-*śar*
Ea	E$_2$-a-*śar*, E$_3$-a-*śar*
ʾIl(um) (?)	AN-*śar*, *il-lu-śar*, *śar-ma-i*$_3$*-lum*, °*śar-ma*-NI, *śar-me-il*
Mama	Ma-ma-*śa-ra-at*
Su'en	^{d}EN:ZU-*śar*, ZU.EN-lugal
Śamaś	*śar-ru-ki-*^{d}Utu

4.2 Localities

The following table lists mythological and worldly locations associated with the appellative lugal in personal names. No such name has thus far been securely identified with *śarrum*-names. The names *Ipḫur*-Kiš and *Tarām*-Akkade are examples which show that cities sometimes formed part of personal names. A few others were discussed briefly above, 3.2.6.

Sumerian

abzu	lugal-abzu, lugal-abzu-a, lugal-abzu-a-gal-di, lugal-abzu-da, lugal-abzu-si
Emuš	lugal-E$_2$-muš$_3$, lugal-E$_2$-muš$_3$-e, lugal-E$_2$-muš$_3$-še$_3$
eden	lugal-eden, lugal-eden-ne$_2$, lugal-eden-ne$_2$-si
Eridu	lugal-Eridu^{ki}-še$_3$
EZEM×GAL	lugal-EZEM.GAL-[x] (?), lugal-EZEM×GAL^{ki}-e
Sulumar	lugal-GAN$_2$-su$_{11}$-lum-ma-gub, lugal-su$_{11}$-lum-ma-gub
Ĝirnun	lugal-Ĝir$_2$-nun, lugal-Ĝir$_2$-nun-ne$_2$
(igi-)nim	lugal-igi-nim-še$_3$, lugal-igi-nim-še$_{3\text{-}90°}$, lugal-nim-du
KA.GAN ?	lugal-KA-GAN-ki (?)
Keš	lugal-Keš$_3$^{ki}
kur	lugal-kur, lugal-kur-da-kuš$_2$, lugal-kur-dub$_2$, lugal-kur-ra, °lugal-kur-ra-a$_2$-bad

Lagaš	lugal-Lagaš, lugal-Lagaš^{ki}
Mušbar	lugal-Muš$_3$-bar-ki-aĝa$_2$
Nippur	lugal-Nibru^{ki}
Tiraš	lugal-Ti-ra-aš$_2$-še$_3$
Umma$_2$(ḪI×DIŠ)	Umma$_2$^{ki}-lugal, Umma$_2$^{ki}-lugal-ĝu$_{10}$
Urim	lugal-Urim$_2$^{ki}-e, lugal-Urim$_x$(AB.URI$_3$)^{ki}

4.3 Nouns

The following tables represent selective lists of objects which occur alongside lugal and *šarrum*, regardless of their syntactic function. Syllabically written Akkadian words are given in their Old Babylonian citation forms.

Sumerian

Lemma	Translation	Attested writings
a$_2$	"arm, side" "strength" "authority" "horn(s)"	[a$_2$/za$_3$]-lugal-ĝa$_2$-ta, a$_2$-lugal-ta, lugal-a$_2$, ⸢lugal$^{?}$-a$_2$⸣-da-DU ?, lugal-a$_2$-gur-ra, lugal-a$_2$-LAK175, lugal-a$_2$-maḫ, lugal-a$_2$-maḫ$_2$, lugal-a$_2$$^{!}$(DA)-maḫ, lugal-a$_2$-na, lugal-a$_2$-na-gub, lugal-a$_2$-pa$_3$, lugal-a$_2$-šum$_2$-ma, lugal-a$_2$-tuku, lugal-a$_2$-zi, lugal-a$_2$-zi-da, lugal-e-a$_2$-na, °lugal-kur-ra-a$_2$-bad, lugal-ni$_3$-a$_2$-zi-nu-ak
ab-ba abba$_2$ ad-da aja$_2$	"father, elder"	lugal-ab-ba, lugal-ab-ba-ĝu$_{10}$, lugal-ab-ba-uru, lugal-abba$_2$, lugal-abba$_2$-ĝu$_{10}$, lugal-abba$_2$-uru$^{?}$, lugal-ad-da, lugal-aja$_2$-ĝu$_{10}$, lugal-aja$_2$-uĝu$_3$
aga$_{(3)}$	(a headdress)	lugal-aga-zi, lugal-aga$_3$-zi
bara$_2$	"throne dais" "*prince*"	lugal-bara$_2$, lugal-bara$_2$-du$_{10}$, lugal-bara$_2$-ga-ne$_2$-du$_{10}$, lugal-bara$_2$-ge-du$_{10}$, lugal-bara$_2$-kalam, lugal-bara$_2$-si
da	"side"	lugal-da, lugal-da-gur$^{?}$, lugal-da-gur-ra, lugal-da-tab-ba ?
dam	"spouse"	lugal-dam, lugal-dam-da-[x], lugal-dam-MU
e$_2$	"house, temple" "family"	e$_2$-lugal-be$_2$-zu, lugal-e$_2$, lugal-e$_2$-ab-ba, lugal-e$_2$-da, lugal-e$_2$.DU$_8$-si, lugal-e$_2$-ĝiš ?, lugal-e$_2$-ni-še$_3$, lugal-e$_2$-ni-še$_{3\text{-}90°}$, lugal-E$_2$.NUN-si, lugal-e$_2$-pa$_4$, lugal-e$_2$-si
en-nu(n)	"watchtower, guard"	lugal-en-nu, lugal-en-nu-ĝu$_{10}$, lugal-en-nun
e-tar en$_3$-tar en$_8$-tar	"provision"	lugal-⸢e-tar$^{?}$⸣ (?), lugal-e-tar-su$_3$, lugal-en$_3$-tar-su$_3$, lugal-en$_3$-tar-su$_{13}$, lugal-en$_3$-tar-su$_x$(TAG), lugal-en$_8$-su$_{13}$, lugal-en$_8$-tar, lugal-en$_8$-tar-su$_3$, lugal-en$_8$-tar-su$_{13}$, lugal-en$_8$-tar-su$_x$(TAG)

ĝiš/^{ĝiš}	"wood(en object)"	lugal-^{ĝiš}apin-du$_{10}$, lugal-e$_2$-ĝiš ?, lugal-^{ĝiš}gigir$_2$, lugal-^{ĝiš}gigir$_2$-e, lugal-^{ĝiš}gigir$_2$-re, lugal-^{ĝiš}gigir$_2$-re$_2^{?}$, lugal-ĝiš, lugal-ĝiš-bur$_2$, lugal-ĝiš-Š[U$^{?}$], lugal-^{ĝiš}kiri$_6$
ḫar-an	"road, campaign"	lugal-ḫar-an-ne$_2$, lugal-ḫar:an-ne$_2$
igi	"eye"	igi-lugal-še$_3$, igi-lugal-še$_{3\text{-}90°}$, lugal-igi, lugal-igi-An-na-ke$_4$-su, lugal-igi-bi, lugal-igi-ḫuš, lugal-igi-il$_2$, lugal-igi-kalam-ma, lugal-igi-ni, lugal-igi-nim-še$_3$, lugal-igi-nim-še$_{3\text{-}90°}$, lugal-igi-sa$_6$, lugal-igi-tab
inim	"word"	inim-lugal-da, lugal-inim, lugal-inim-du$_{10}$, lugal-inim-du$_{10}$-ga, lugal-inim-du$_{10}$.KI, lugal-inim-e, lugal-inim-e-ĝiš-tuku, lugal-inim-gi-na, lugal-inim-ĝa$_2$-ka-bi, lugal-inim-ĝal$_2$-la, lugal-inim-kalag, lugal-inim-kalag-ga, °lugal-inim-ma-ni, lugal-inim-ma-se$_3$-ga, lugal-inim-se$_3$-ga, lugal-inim-še$_3$, lugal-inim-TAR, lugal-inim-zi, lugal-inim-zi-da, lugal-inim-zu
iti	"month"	lugal-iti, lugal-iti-da, lugal-iti-da-tu, lugal-iti-da-[zal$^{?}$]-le
kalam	"land"	lugal-bara$_2$-kalam, lugal-igi-kalam-ma, lugal-kalam:ma:dul$_5$, lugal-saĝ-kalam, lugal-zi-kalam
kar	"harbour"	lugal-kar, lugal-kar$^{!}$(TE), lugal-kar-e, lugal-kar-e-si, lugal-kar-re, lugal-kar-re$_2$, lugal-kar-si
ki	"place; earth"	lugal-an-ki-da, lugal-DA-KI, lugal-KA-GAN-ki, lugal-ki, lugal-ki-gal, lugal-ki-gal-gal-la, lugal-ki-gal-la, lugal-ki-gub-ni-du$_7$-du$_7$, lugal-ki-NI, lugal-ki-ni-du$_7$-du$_7$, lugal-ki-NI-gi$_4$, lugal-ki-ni-še$_3$-du$_7$-du$_7$, lugal-ki-nu-gi$_4$, lugal-KI-ŠIR-PA$^{?}$-⸢X⸣, lugal-ki-tuš-du$_{10}$, °lugal-nu-KI-SAĜ
kisal	"courtyard"	lugal-kisal, lugal-kisal-a-gub, lugal-kisal-si
kur	"mountain(land)" "country"	lugal-kur, lugal-kur-da-kuš$_2$, lugal-kur-dub$_2$, lugal-kur-ra, lugal-kur-ra-a$_2$-bad, lugal-kur-si
lama$_{(3)}$	"guardian spirit"	$^{\circ\text{nu}}$lugal-lama-zi-da, lugal-^{d}lama$_3$(KAL), lugal-lama$_3$-zi
lu$_{(2)}$	"man" "provider"	lu$_2$-lugal, ⸢lu$_2$⸣-[l]u[gal]-la$_2$?, lugal-lu, lugal-lu-dadag, lugal-lu-du$_{10}$, lugal-lu$_2$, lugal-lu$_2$-dadag, lugal-lu$_2$-du$_{10}$, lugal-lu$_2$-gi-na, lugal-lu$_2$-LAK545-ne-saĝ, lugal-lu$_2$-ni, lugal-lu$_2$-sa$_6$-ga, lugal-lu$_2$-saĝ, lugal-lu$_2$-ŠE$_3$-IG-ŠE$_3$, lugal-lu$_2$-ti-ti, lugal-lu$_{2\text{-}90°}$-uĝu$_3$-du$_{10}$, lugal-lu$_2$-zi
ma$_2$	"ship"	lugal-ma$_2$, lugal-ma$_2$-gur$_8$-e, lugal-ma$_2$-tab-ba

mas-su$_{(2)}$	"leader"	lugal-mas-su, lugal-mas-su$_2$
me	"(divine) ordinances" "rites" "principles of existence"	lugal-DU-ME, lugal-me, °lugal-me-am, lugal-me-du$_{10}$-ga, lugal-ME-^{d}En-l[il$_2$], lugal-me-gal-gal, lugal-me-še$_3$-ĝal$_2$, lugal-me-si, lugal-me-sikil, °lugal-ME-zi, lugal-tigi$_x$(E$_2$.BALAĜ)-mete(TE+ME)
me-lam$_2$	"ominous sheen"	lugal-me-lam$_2$ (?), lugal-me-lam$_2$-su$_3$, lugal-me-lam$_2$-su$_{20}$
mu	"name"	lugal-mu-da-ri$_2$, lugal-mu-du$_{10}$, lugal-mu-du$_{10}$-ga, lugal-mu-ĝal$_2$ (?), lugal-mu-ni-da, lugal-mu-zu-da (?), lugal-mu-še$_3$-ĝal$_2$ (?)
nam	"(the totality of essence of sth.)"	lugal-nam, lugal-nam-dag, lugal-nam-gu$_2$, lugal-nam-gu$_2$-su$_3$, lugal-nam-MES$^{?}$, lugal-nam-zu, nam-lugal-ni, nam-lugal-ni-du$_{10}$
nam-nir	"nobility", "authority"	lugal-nam-nir, lugal-nam-nir-šum$_2$, °nu-gal-nam-URU, °nu-gal-nam-URU-šu-ma
nam-tar	"fate"	lugal-nam-tar-re$_2$, lugal-nam-zi-tar, lugal-nam-zi-tar-ra, lugal-$^{su_{13}}$PA.SIKIL-nam-tar, lugal-$^{su_{13}}$PA$^{!}$(MAŠ).SIKIL-nam-tar
nesaĝ ne-saĝ	"firstling offerings"	lugal-lu$_2$-LAK545-ne-saĝ (?), lugal-nesaĝ, lugal-nesaĝ-e, lugal-nesaĝ
ni$_2$(-te) me-te mete(TE+ME) ne-te	"self" "fear"	lugal-me-te-na, lugal-mete(TE+ME)-na, lugal-ne-⸢te-na⸣, °lugal-ni$_2$-bi$_2$-ak, lugal-ni$_2$-te-na, lugal-TAR-me-te (?)
ni$_3$ NIG$_2$	"(some)thing" "(every)thing"	lugal-NIĜ$_2$, lugal-ni$_3$-a$_2$-zi-nu-ak, lugal-ni$_3$-^{ba}bara$_3$-du$_{10}$, lugal-ni$_3$-bara$_4$-du$_{10}$, lugal-ni$_3$-da-sa$_2$, lugal-ni$_3$-ĝa$_2$, lugal-ni$_3$-ĝa$_2$-ni, lugal-ni$_3$-ĝa-ni-še$_3$, lugal-ni$_3$-gur$_8$, lugal-ni$_3$-kalag-ga, lugal-ni$_3$-lu-lu, °lugal-ni$_3$-lu-lu-a, lugal-ni$_3$-ni, lugal-ni$_3$-ni, lugal-ni$_3$-ni-še$_3$, lugal-ni$_3$-nidba$_2$-e, lugal-ni$_3$-nu-da-me, lugal-ni$_3$-sa$_6$-ga, lugal-ni$_3$-su, lugal-ni$_3$-U.TA, lugal-ni$_3$-UET 2-276, lugal-ni$_3$-zu
nir	"lord"	lugal-nir, lugal-nir-ĝal$_2$
saĝ	"head, top, prime" (also in composites)	lugal-AB-da-SAĜ (?), lugal-ḫur-saĝ, lugal-lu$_2$-LAK545-ne-saĝ (?), lugal-lu$_2$-saĝ, °lugal-nu-KI-SAĜ, lugal-saĝ, lugal-saĝ-bi-še$_{3\text{-}90°}$, lugal-saĝ-du$_{10}$, °lugal-saĝ-kalam, lugal-saĝ-rib, lugal-ŠE$_3$-saĝ, lugal-ur-saĝ
si-ĝar	"door bolt"	lugal-si-ĝar
si	unknown mng.	lugal-si-DU$_6$-e, lugal-si-NE-e
ša$_3$	"heart, midst, center"	lugal-ša$_3$, lugal-ša$_3$-an-zu, lugal-ša$_3$-ENGUR, lugal-ša$_3$-ga, °lugal-ša$_3$-ge-ib$_2$-tu, lugal-ša$_3$-gid$_2$, lugal-ša$_3$-kuš$_2$, lugal-ša$_3$-la$_2$-tuku, lugal-ša$_3$-pa$_3$, lugal-ša$_3$-pa$_3$-da, lugal-ša$_3$-su$_3$, lugal-ša$_3$-uru, lugal-ša$_3$-za$_3$-[x], lugal-ša$_3$-zu, lugal-zi-ša$_3$-ĝal$_2$
šu	"hand"	lugal-ĝiš-Š[U$^{?}$] ?, lugal-šu, lugal-šu-du$_7$,

	(also in compounds)	lugal-šu-du$_7$-a, lugal-šu-du$_{11}$, lugal-šu-gi$_4$-gi$_4$, lugal-šu-ĝal$_2$ (PN?), lugal-šu-luḫ-ku$_3$-An-na, lugal-šu-maḫ, lugal-šu-mu-gi$_4$, lugal-šu-sikil
šud$_3$	"prayer"	lugal-šud$_3$, lugal-šud$_3$-de$_3$, lugal-šud$_3$-de$_3$-ba-ša$_4$, lugal-šud$_3$-du$_{10}$, lugal-šud$_3$-du$_{10}$-ga, lugal-šud$_3$-ĝiš-tuku
u$_4$	"day, light, storm"	lugal-u$_4$-an, lugal-u$_4$-an-na, lugal-u$_4$-de$_3$, lugal-u$_4$-suḫ$_3$-gi$_4$, lugal-u$_4$-su$_3$-[(še$_3$?)], lugal-u$_4$-su$_{13}$-še$_3$
uĝ$_3$	"people"	lugal-aja$_2$-uĝu$_3$, lugal-KALAM(LAK729), lugal-lu$_{2\text{-}90°}$-uĝu$_3$-du$_{10}$, lugal-uĝu$_3$-du$_{10}$, lugal-uĝ$_3$-e, lugal-uĝ$_3$-ĝe$_{26}$, lugal-uĝ$_3$-ĝe$_{26}$-du$_{10}$
uru	"city"	lugal-ab-ba-uru, lugal-abba$_2$-uru?, lugal-ša$_3$-uru, lugal-uru, lugal-uru-da, lugal-uru-na, lugal-uru-na-nu$_2$, lugal-uru-si
ušur$_{3/4/x}$	(?)	lugal-ušur$_3$, lugal-ušur$_3$-MU, lugal-ušur$_3$-nu$_2$, lugal-ušur$_3$-ra, lugal-ušur$_4$, lugal-ušur$_4$-MU, lugal-ušur$_x$(LAL+KU)
za$_3$	"side, strength"	[a$_2$/za$_3$]-lugal-ĝa$_2$-ta (?)
za$_3$	"sanctuary"	lugal-ša$_3$(-)za$_3$-[x] ?, lugal-za$_3$, lugal-za$_3$-ge, lugal-za$_3$-ge-si, lugal-za$_3$-si

Akkadian

abum	"father"	lugal-*a-ba*$_4$, *śar-a-‹ba*$_4$›, *śar-a-ba*$_4$
ālum	"city" (?)	*śar-ru-al-śi-in* (?)
bānûm	"creator"	*śar-ru-ba-ni* (?)
bīnum/ *binnum*	"offspring"	*bi-in-ka*$_3$*-li*$_2$-lugal-*re*$_2$, *bi-ka*$_3$*-li*$_2$-lugal-*re*$_2$, *bi*!*-ka*$_3$*-li*$_2$*-śar-*[*re*$_2$]
dādum	"loved one (or uncle?)"	lugal-*da-di*$_3$, *śar-ru-da-di*$_3$
dūrum	"wall, fortress"	°*śar*-bad$_3$, *śar-ru*-bad$_3$, *śar-ru-du*$_2$*-ri*$_2$
ilum	"god"	*i*$_3$*-lum-śar*, *il-lu-śar*, *śar-ma-i*$_3$*-lum*, °*śar-ma*-NI, *śar-me-il*, *śar-mi-lu*, *śar-me*-NI, *śar-ru*-gi-*i*$_3$*-li*$_2$, *śar-ru-i*$_3$*-li*$_2$, *śar-um-i*$_3$*-li*$_2$
lābum	"lion"	*śar-ru-la-ba*
libbum	"heart"	*tu-ta*$_2$-lugal-*li-bi*$_2$*-iś*, *tu-ta*$_2$*-śar-li-bi*$_2$*-iś*
mūdûm	"knowledgeable one"	*śar-ru-mu-da*, *śar-ru*$_x$(KU)*-ma-da*
nēšum	"lion"	lugal-*na-i-iš*
nūrum	"light"	lugal-*nu-ru* (?)
qarrādum	"hero"	*śar-ru*-gar$_3$
ṣillum	"shade"	*ṣi*$_2$*-la*-lugal

Logographic

gal-zu	"wise one"	gal-zu-[*śar*]*-ru-śi-*[*in*], *śar-ru*-gal-zu
gu$_2$	"river bank" (?)	*śar-ru*-gu$_2$ (?)
ur-saĝ	"*hero*"	*śar-ru*-ur-saĝ, lugal-ur-saĝ (?)

4.4 Adjectives and verbs

The following tables list verbs occurring in finite and non–finite forms in lugal- and *śarrum*-names. Akkadian statives are listed following the citation forms of their respective Old Babylonian adjective. For Akkadian finite verbs, see table 4.6.

Sumerian

ki–aĝ$_2$	"to love"	lugal-ab$_2$-ki-aĝ$_2$, lugal-An-ne$_2$-ki-aĝa$_2$, lugal-ki-aĝa$_2$, lugal-Muš$_3$-bar-ki-aĝ$_2$, lugal-^{d}Sud$_3$-ki-aĝ$_2$, lugal-sur$_x$-ki-aĝ$_2$, lugal-sur$_x$-re$_2$-ki-aĝ$_2$
su$_3$–aĝ$_2$	"to shine"	lugal-su$_3$-aĝa$_2$
ak	"to make, do"	lugal-alam-ak, °lugal-ni$_2$-bi-ak, lugal-ni$_3$-a$_2$-zi-nu-ak
ban$_3$-da	"small, fierce"	lugal-ban$_3$-da
da-ri$_2$	"lasting"	lugal-mu-da-ri$_2$
dab$_5$	"to seize, grab"	lugal-dab$_5$, lugal-dab$_5$-e
dab$_6$	(?)	lugal-dab$_6$
dadag	"to cleanse,	lugal-lu-dadag, lugal-lu$_2$-dadag
daḫ	"to add"	lugal-mu-daḫ
dalla	"to shine"	lugal-dalla, lugal-dalla-pa-e$_3$
na-de$_5$	"pure"	lugal-na-de$_5$-ga
de$_6$	"to bring, deliver"	lugal-ma-de$_6$
dib	"to pass, go along" (?)	lugal-mu-dib
diri	"to exceed, surpass"	lugal-AN-diri, lugal-ra-diri, lugal-SI.A
DU	(?)	⸢lugal$^{?}$-a$_2$⸣-da-DU ?, lugal-DU, lugal-DU-ME, lugal-DU-NI, lugal-^{d}En-ki-a-DU, °lugal-gu$_4$-DU, lugal-nun-DU, lugal-tir-a-DU
du$_7$	"to be fitting, suitable" (also in idioms)	lugal-ḫe$_2$-du$_7$, lugal-ki-gub-ni-du$_7$-du$_7$, lugal-ki-ni-du$_7$-du$_7$, lugal-ki-ni-še$_3$-du$_7$-du$_7$, lugal-šu-du$_7$, lugal-šu-du$_7$-a
du$_8$	"to loosen, release"	lugal-du$_8$, lugal-NI-du$_8$
du$_{10}$	"to be good, make good"	lugal-ab-du$_{10}$-ga, lugal-ad-ĝar-du$_{10}$, lugal-^{ĝiš}apin-du$_{10}$, lugal-apin-du$_{10}$, lugal-bara$_2$-du$_{10}$, lugal-bara$_2$-ga-ne$_2$-du$_{10}$, lugal-bara$_2$-ge-du$_{10}$, lugal-du$_{10}$, lugal-du$_{10}$-ga, lugal-du$_{11}$-ge-du$_{10}$, lugal-ĝidri-du$_{10}$, lugal-ḪAR-ma-du$_{10}$, lugal-inim-du$_{10}$, lugal-inim-du$_{10}$-ga, lugal-inim-du$_{10}$.KI, lugal-ki-tuš-du$_{10}$, lugal-lu-du$_{10}$, lugal-lu$_2$-du$_{10}$, lugal-lu$_{2\text{-}90°}$-uĝu$_3$-du$_{10}$, lugal-me-du$_{10}$-ga, lugal-mu-du$_{10}$, lugal-mu-du$_{10}$-ga, lugal-na$_2$-du$_{10}$, lugal-na$_2$-du$_{10}$-ga, lugal-NI:du$_{10}$, lugal-ni$_3$-^{ba}bara$_3$-du$_{10}$, lugal-ni$_3$-bara$_4$-du$_{10}$, lugal-saĝ-du$_{10}$, lugal-šud$_3$-du$_{10}$, lugal-šud$_3$-du$_{10}$-ga, lugal-tigi$_x$(E$_2$.BALAĜ)-ni-du$_{10}$, lugal-uĝu$_3$-du$_{10}$, lugal-uĝ$_3$-ĝe$_{26}$-du$_{10}$, nam-lugal-ni-du$_{10}$

du$_{11}$ di e	“to say” “to make, do”	lugal-du$_{11}$-ga, lugal-du$_{11}$-ga-ni, lugal-du$_{11}$-ga-ni-nu-[x], lugal-du$_{11}$-ga-ni-zi, lugal-du$_{11}$-ge-du$_{10}$, lugal-e-e (?), lugal-ĝe$_{26}$-ab-be$_2$, lugal-ĝe$_{26}$-ab-e, lugal-mi$_2$-du$_{11}$-ga, lugal-mi$_2$-zi-du$_{11}$-ga, lugal-nu-du$_{11}$-ga, lugal-šu-du$_{11}$
e$_3$	“to go out”	lugal-ab-e$_3$, lugal-eb$_2$-ta-e$_3$, lugal-eb$_2$-ta-ni-e$_3$, lugal-Utu-gin$_7$-e$_3$
pa–e$_3$	“to appear”	lugal-dalla-pa-e$_3$, lugal-pa-e$_3$
gal	“big, great”	lugal-e-gal-gal, lugal-EZEM.GAL-[x], lugal-EZEM×GAL^{ki}-e, °lugal-gal-bi$_2$-tum$_2$, lugal-gal-zu, lugal-gu$_2$-gal, lugal-ig-gal, lugal-kara$_6$-gal-gal, lugal-ki-gal, lugal-ki-gal-la, lugal-ki-gal-gal-la, lugal-me-gal-gal, lugal-sa-šuš-gal
gi	“to be permanent, true”	lugal-inim-gi-na, lugal-lu$_2$-gi-na
gi$_4$	“to (re)turn”	lugal-ḫa-mu-gi$_4$-gi$_4$, lugal-ki-NI-gi$_4$, lugal-ki-nu-gi$_4$, lugal-ra-mu-gi$_4$, lugal-šu-gi$_4$-gi$_4$, lugal-šu-mu-gi$_4$, lugal-u$_4$-suḫ$_3$-gi$_4$
gid$_2$	“to be long”	lugal-ša$_3$-gid$_2$
gub	“to stand”	lugal-a$_2$-na-gub, lugal-GAN$_2$-su$_{11}$-lum-ma-gub, lugal-gub-ba, lugal-gub-ba-ni, lugal-ki-gub-ni-du$_7$-du$_7$, lugal-kisal-a-gub, lugal-su$_{11}$-lum-ma-gub
gu(-n)	“to be multicoloured”(?)	lugal-še-gu-na
gur	“to bend”	lugal-a$_2$-gur-ra, lugal-da-gur ?, lugal-DA-gur-ra
ĝal$_2$	“to be (in place)” (also in idioms)	lugal-gaba-ĝal$_2$, lugal-ḫe$_2$-ĝal$_2$, lugal-ḫe$_2$-ĝal$_2$-su$_3$, lugal-ḫe$_2$-ĝal$_2$-su$_{20}$, lugal-ḫe$_2$-ĝal$_2$-su$_x$(TAG), lugal-me-še$_3$-ĝal$_2$, lugal-mu-ĝal$_2$, lugal-mu-še$_3$-ĝal$_2$, lugal-nir-ĝal$_2$, lugal-šu-ĝal$_2$ (PN?), lugal-zi-ša$_3$-ĝal$_2$, °nu-gal-ḫi-gal
ĝen/du	“to go”	lugal-nim-du
il$_2$	“to raise”	lugal-igi-il$_2$
kalag	“to be strong, mighty”	lugal-inim-kalag, lugal-inim-kalag-ga, lugal-kalag-ga, lugal-ni$_3$-kalag-ga, °lugal-en-nam-gal-ga
KU	(?)	lugal-a-bi$_2$-KU
ku$_3$	“to be sacred” (also in idioms)	lugal-AN-ku$_3$-ge, lugal-ku$_3$?, lugal-ku$_3$-zu, lugal-šu-luḫ-ku$_3$-An-na
kuš$_2$	“to be tired”	lugal-i$_3$-kuš$_2$, lugal-kur-da-kuš$_2$, lugal-kuš$_2$, lugal-mu-da-kuš$_2$, lugal-mu-kuš$_2$, lugal-ša$_3$-kuš$_2$, lugal-ti-uš$_2$-da-kuš$_2$, °nu-gal-me-ga-šu-u$_3$, nu-gal-mu-da-kaš
lu	“to be abundant”	lugal-da-lu, lugal-lu, lugal-lu-lu, lugal-ni$_3$-lu-lu, °lugal-ni$_3$-lu-lu-a
luḫ	“to clean, wash”	lugal-ka-luḫ, lugal-LUḪ, lugal-šu-luḫ-ku$_3$-An-na
maḫ	“to be great”	lugal-a$_2$-maḫ, lugal-a$_2$-maḫ$_2$, lugal-a$_2^!$(DA)-

maḫ$_2$		maḫ$_2$, lugal-da-pa$_5$-maḫ, lugal-eg$_2$-pa$_5$-maḫ, lugal-i$_7$-maḫ, lugal-maḫ, lugal-maḫ$_2$, lugal-šu-maḫ, lugal-tug$_2$-maḫ
me	"to be (in existence)"	lugal-AN-da-nu-me-a, lugal-da-nu-me-a, lugal-na-nam, lugal-ni$_3$-nu-da-me, lugal-za-me
nu$_2$	"to lie down"	lugal-a-DU-nu$_2$, lugal-a-MIR-nu$_2$, lugal-uru-na-nu$_2$, lugal-ti-ma-nu$_2$, lugal-ušur$_3$-nu$_2$, lugal-ušur$_3$-ra-nu$_2$
nun	"regal" "foremost" "of the highest quality"	lugal-a-nun, lugal-i$_3$-nun, lugal-IM-nun-ne$_2$, lugal-ir-nun, °lugal-men-nun, °lugal-men$_x$(ĜA$_2$×EN)-nun, °lugal-mes-nun-pa$_3$, lugal-nun-DU, °lugal-nun-pa$_3$
pa$_3$	"to find, select"	lugal-a$_2$-pa$_3$, °lugal-mes-nun-pa$_3$, °lugal-nun-pa$_3$, lugal-pa$_3$, lugal-pa$_3$-da, lugal-ša$_3$-pa$_3$, lugal-ša$_3$-pa$_3$-da, °nu-gal-pa$_2$-da
sa$_2$	"to equal, match"	lugal-ni$_3$-da-sa$_2$
si–sa$_2$	"to be fair, true"	lugal-si-sa$_2$
sa$_6$	"to be good, beautiful"	lugal-igi-sa$_6$, lugal-lu$_2$-sa$_6$-ga, lugal-ni$_3$-sa$_6$-ga, lugal-sa$_6$, lugal-sa$_6$-ga, lugal-sur$_x$-ra-sa$_6$
sag$_7$	"to disperse"	lugal-^{sa_2}sag$_7$
se$_3$	"to throw (down)"	lugal-inim-ma-se$_3$-ga, lugal-inim-se$_3$-ga
si	"to be just right (for s.th.)" "to fill"	lugal-a-a-GUG$_2$-a-ne$_2$-nu-si, lugal-A-SI, lugal-abzu-si, lugal-bara$_2$-si, lugal-e$_2$.DU$_8$-si, lugal-E$_2$.NUN-si, lugal-e$_2$-si, lugal-eden$_2$-ne$_2$-si, lugal-ĝa$_2$-si, lugal-^{d}I$_7$-si, lugal-kar-e-si, lugal-kar-si, lugal-kisal-si, lugal-kur-si, lugal-me-si, lu:gal-RA-si ?, lugal-si (?), lugal-sila-si, lugal-UET2-300-si, lugal-uru-si, lugal-za$_3$-ge-si, lugal-za$_3$-si
sikil	"to be pure"	lugal-me-sikil, lugal-$^{su_{13}}$PA.SIKIL-nam-tar, lugal-$^{su_{13}}$PA$^{!}$(MAŠ).SIKIL-nam-tar, lugal-šu-sikil
su zu	"to know"	e$_2$-lugal-be$_2$-zu, lugal-An-ne$_2$-su, lugal-^{d}En-lil$_2$-le-an-zu, lugal-gal-zu, lugal-igi-An-na-ke$_4$-su, lugal-inim-zu, lugal-mu-zu-da, lugal-nam-zu, lugal-ni$_3$-su, lugal-ni$_3$-zu, lugal-pa$_4$-zu, lugal-ša$_3$-an-zu, lugal-ša$_3$-zu
su$_3$	"to sprinkle, strew" "to be, make lasting" "to be empty" "to cut clear" "to fill" (< si)	lugal-e-tar-su$_3$, lugal-en$_3$-tar-su$_3$, lugal-en$_8$-tar-su$_3$, lugal-ḫe$_2$-ĝal$_2$-su$_3$, lugal-me-lam$_2$-su$_3$, lugal-nam-gu$_2$-su$_3$, lugal-ša$_3$-su$_3$
su$_{13}$	"to sprinkle, strew"	lugal-en$_3$-tar-su$_{13}$, lugal-en$_8$-su$_{13}$, lugal-en$_8$-tar-su$_{13}$, lugal-ĝeštu$_3$-su$_{13}$
su$_{20}$	"to sprinkle, strew" (?) "to be, make lasting"	lugal-ĝeštu$_2$-su$_{20}$, lugal-^{giš}ĝeštu-su$_{20}$, lugal-ḫe$_2$-ĝal$_2$-su$_{20}$, lugal-me-lam$_2$-su$_{20}$, lugal-uš-su$_{20}$
su$_x$(TAG)	"to sprinkle, strew"	lugal-en$_3$-tar-su$_x$, lugal-en$_8$-tar-su$_x$, lugal-

	"to be, make lasting"	ḫe$_2$-ĝal$_2$-su$_x$
su$_x$(MUŠ)	"to sprinkle, strew" (?)	lugal-uš-su$_x$
šilig	"to cease"	lugal-nu-šilig
šuba$_2$	"to be pure, clear"	lugal-KA-ni-nu-šuba$_2$
šum$_2$	"to give, grant"	lugal-a$_2$-šum-ma, lugal-nam-nir-šum$_2$, °nu-gal-nam-URU-šu-ma
tab	"to double"	lugal-da-tab-ba ?, lugal-igi-tab, lugal-ma$_2$-tab-ba, lugal-tab
tar	"to cut" "to decide"	lugal-inim-TAR, lugal-nam-tar-re$_2$, lugal-nam-zi-tar, lugal-nam-zi-tar-ra, lugal-$^{su_{13}}$PA.SIKIL-nam-tar, lugal-$^{su_{13}}$PA$^{!}$(MAŠ).SIKIL-nam-tar, lugal-TAR
ti	"to live"	lugal-an-ta-ti, lugal-ḫa-ma-ti, lugal-lu$_2$-ti-ti, lugal-ti, lugal-ti-uš$_2$-da-kuš$_2$
tu	"to give birth" "to bear (a child)"	lugal-iti-da-tu, lugal-mu-tu, lugal-^{d}Nanše-mu-tu, °lugal-ša$_3$-ge-ib$_2$-tu, lu:gal-tu$^{!?}$
tuku	"to have, possess"	lugal-a$_2$-tuku, lugal-DA-tuku, lugal- lugal-ša$_3$-la$_2$-tuku
ĝiš–tuku	"to be aware"	inim-e-ĝiš-tuku, lugal-šud$_3$-de$_3$-ĝiš-tuku
tum$_2$	"to be befitting"	lugal-an-na-tum$_2$, lugal-an-tum$_2$, lugal-bi$_2$-tum$_2$, °lugal-gal-bi$_2$-tum$_2$, lugal-^{d}Nanna-ra-tum$_2$
u$_4$	"to shine"	lugal-si-u$_4$-a
ur$_3$	"to wipe clean"	lugal-Šar$_2$-ur$_3$-e
zal	"to shine" "to pass time"	lugal-iti-da-[zal$^{?}$]-le
zi	"to be right, true, loyal" "to rise"	lugal-a$_2$-zi, lugal-a$_2$-zi-da, lugal-aga-zi, lugal-aga$_3$-zi, lugal-aĝrig-zi, lugal-DA-zi, lugal-du$_{11}$-ga-ni-zi, lugal-engar-zi, lugal-GAN$_2$-zi, °lugal-ḪI-zi, lugal-inim-zi, lugal-inim-zi-da, ° ^{nu}lugal-lama-zi-da, lugal-lama$_3$-zi, °lugal-ME-zi, lugal-mi$_2$-zi-du$_{11}$-ga, lugal-nagar-zi, lugal-ni$_3$-a$_2$-zi-nu-ak, lugal-nitaḫ-zi, lugal-nitaḫ$_2$-zi, lugal-numun-zi, lugal-šer$_2$-zi, lugal-šer$_7$-zi, lugal-šuba$_3$-zi, lugal-zi (?), lugal-zi-de$_3$?

Akkadian stative forms

dannum	"strong"	*śar-ru-dan*
išarum	"true, righteous"	*i-śar-śar-ri$_2$*, *śar-ru-i-śar*
palḫum	"terrifying"	lugal-*pa$_2$-luḫ*, *śar-ru-pa$_2$-luḫ*

Logographic

damqum	"kind, beneficient"	*śar-ru*-sig$_5$
kīnum	"permanent, true"	lugal-gi, lugal-gi-pa-e$_3$, *śar-ru*-gi, *śar-ru*-gi-*i$_3$-li$_2$*, *śar-rum$_2$*-gi, *śar-um*-gi
šūpûm (?)	"resplendent, famous"	lugal-gi-pa-e$_3$ (?)
ṭābum	"good, sweet"	*śar-ru*-du$_{10}$

4.5 Sumerian verbal prefixes

The following is a tabulary overview of verbal prefixes encountered in ED and Sargonic lugal-names. Included are also the modals ḫa-/ḫe$_2$-, na-, and nu-. Frozen nominal forms such as he$_2$-ĝal$_2$ or ḫe$_2$-du$_7$, serving as objects, are not included.[1396] For such forms, see above, 4.4, under the relevant verbal root. Nor are names included which feature a dimensional infix which seems appended to the object referent rather than to the prefix chain.

ab-	lugal-AB-da-SAĜ (?), lugal-ab-du$_{10}$-ga (?), lugal-ab-e$_3$, lugal-ĝe$_{26}$-ab-be$_2$, lugal-ĝe$_{26}$-ab-e
al$_{(6)}$-	lugal-al-sa$_6$, lugal-al$_6$-sa$_6$
an-	lugal-AN-diri (?), lugal-^{d}En-lil$_2$-le-an-zu, lugal-ša$_3$-an-zu
ba-	lugal-šud$_3$-de$_3$-ba-ša$_4$
bi$_{(2)}$-	lugal-bi$_2$-tum$_2$, °lugal-gal-bi$_2$-tum$_2$, lugal-i$_3$-bi$_2$ (?), °lugal-ni$_2$-bi-ak
-da-	lugal-AB-da-SAĜ, lugal-mu-da, lugal-mu-da-kuš$_2$, lugal-ni$_3$-nu-da-me, nu-gal-mu-da-kaš$_2$
e-	lugal-e-gal-gal (?)
eb$_2$-/ib$_2$	lugal-eb$_2$-ta-e$_3$, lugal-eb$_2$-ta-ni-e$_3$, °lugal-ša$_3$-ge-ib$_2$-tu
ḫa-/ḫe$_2$-	lugal-ḫa-ma, lugal-ḫa-ma-ti, lugal-ḫa-mu-gi$_4$-gi$_4$, lugal-ḫe$_2$, lugal-ḫe$_2$-a
i$_3$-	lugal-i$_3$-bi$_2$ (?), lugal-i$_3$-kuš$_2$, lugal-ki-NI-gi$_4$?, lugal-NI-du$_8$?, lugal-NI:du$_{10}$?, lugal-NI-KA ?
(-)ma-	lugal-ḫa-ma, lugal-ḫa-ma-ti, lugal-ma-de$_6$
mu-	lugal-dam-MU (?), lugal-ḫa-mu-gi$_4$-gi$_4$, lugal-mu, lugal-mu-da, lugal-mu-da-kuš$_2$, lugal-mu-daḫ, lugal-mu-dib, lugal-mu-kuš$_2$, lugal-mu-tu, lugal-nam-mu-šub-be$_2$, lugal-nam-mu-šub-e, lugal-^{d}Nanše-mu-tu, lugal-ra-mu, lugal-ra-mu-gi$_4$, lugal-šu-mu-gi$_4$, °nu-gal-me-ga-šu-u$_3$, nu-gal-mu-da-kaš$_2$
na-	lugal-na-nam
nam-	lugal-nam (?), lugal-nam-mu-šub-be$_2$, lugal-nam-mu-šub-e
-ni-	lugal-eb$_2$-ta-ni-e$_3$
nu-	lugal-a-a-GUG$_2$-a-ne$_2$-nu-si, lugal-AN-da-nu-ḫuĝ-ĝa$_2$, lugal-AN-da-nu-me-a, lugal-da-nu-me-a, lugal-du$_{11}$-ga-ni-nu-[x], lugal-KA-ni-nu-šuba$_2$, lugal-ki-nu-gi$_4$, lugal-me$_3$-TUR-še$_3$-nu-še-ge, lugal-me$_3$-TUR-še$_3$-nu-še$_{27}$-ge, lugal-ni$_3$-a$_2$-zi-nu-ak, lugal-ni$_3$-nu-da-me, lugal-nu-du$_{11}$-ga, °lugal-nu-KI-SAĜ, lugal-nu-šilig
-ta-	lugal-eb$_2$-ta-e$_3$, lugal-eb$_2$-ta-ni-e$_3$

[1396] Following the rationale of M. Civil, *ASJ* 22 (2005), 31.

4.6 Akkadian finite verb forms

As far as can be seen, the *śarrum*-names featuring finite verbs are all 3rd person preterite forms. A single verb, *takālum*, is found in the imperative. The stative forms were given above, under 4.4. The verbs are given according to their Old Babylonian citation forms.

amûm	"to protect"	*i-mi-śar-ru*
bâʾum ?	"to come near"	*i-ba*-lugal
banûm	"to create, build"	*ib-ni*-lugal
elûm	"to go up, emerge"	*i-li*$_2$*-śar-ru* (?)
epēšum	"to do, make, build"	*i-pu*$_3$*-śar* (?)
šaṭāpum	"to preserve (life), rescue"	*iš-ṭup-śar*
takālum	"to trust"	*śar-iś-ta*$_2$*-kal*$_2$, *śar-ri*$_2$*-iś-ta*$_2$*-kal*$_2$
watûm	"to find, discover"	*tu-ta*$_2$-lugal-*li-bi*$_2$*-iś*, *tu-ta*$_2$*-śar-li-bi*$_2$*-iś*
*B*ʾ$_x$*n*	(?)	*u-Bi-in*-lugal-*ri*$_2$

5. Semantic comparison of lugal- and *śarrum*-names

During the course of the preceding chapters, it has hopefully been made apparent, that the semantic import of Sumerian lugal-names and Akkadian *śarrum*-names are divergent on many points, and are comparable or identical on a number of points. Differences and similarities deserve to be inspected separately. In Chapter 6, the *Sitz im Leben* of these names will be inspected from the viewpoint of their historical and cultural settings.

Almost a third of the different writings of names containing lugal remain unclear as to semantic import, and about a fifth of the different writings of names containing *śarrum*. About 60% of lugal-names which have as of yet defied interpretation are only attested once. In some cases opaque principles of abbreviation are to blame, but certainly not in all cases. Statistics are bound to be skewed by the fact that Sumerian names during the period investigated are more commonly attested than Akkadian names: writings of lugal-names outnumber *śarrum*-names by almost 8:1. Hence, the relative scarcity of an Akkadian name must be seen in the light of the fact that relatively few northern centers have yielded texts during the 700 or so years covered by this survey. About half of all *śarrum*-names are so far only attested once; and adding those Akkadian names that are attested more times but only with one bearer, this figure becomes even higher.

5.1 Synchronic perspectives

The major trends of individual periods are defined and described. Given the number of unintelligible names and names which can not with certainty be ascribed to a specific semantic category, the following sections are to a large part based on the discussions contained in sections 3.1 and 3.2. Names are treated here regardless of a proposed identity of the referent for lugal.

5.1.1 ED I-II

ED I-II names are best attested at Ur. 55% of the writings of lugal-names found in ED I-II are exclusive to this period. No subcategory is represented by more than four names. Dominion 3.1.1, makes for the largest group, with the names amar-lugal, found also at Uruk, maš-lugal, ur-lugal and ir$_{11}$-lugal. The first belongs to a group that is common during this period. Two names, lugal-bara$_2$-si and lugal-men$_{(x)}$, relate to insignia of power. There are no clear references to wisdom as a characteristic of the lugal, nor to a caring attitude on the part of the lugal, name types which are all well represented in later times. Creation, fertility and prosperity (3.1.5), is represented by four names, counting AK-lugal, lugal-ĝa$_2$-si, lugal-lu-lu and lugal-uru-si, all very general in focus. Most names which relate in a general way to cultic issues (3.1.6), are not very informative, except for lugal-pa$_3$, which could be taken to imply that the lugal was formally selected by some form of mantic practice (see further below, section 6.2). Neither of them mention a divinity by name; the name lugal-E$_2$.NUN is also somewhat unclear. The two names which use nominal predicates about the lugal (lugal-lal$_3$, lugal-ur-saĝ), belong to a quite common group of names. Two clause-names set themselves apart in being uncharacteristically detailed: lugal-$^{su_{13}}$PA.SIKIL-nam-tar, lugal-u$_4$-suḫ$_3$-gi$_4$. Both of these are probably to be explained as expressions of local theology surrounding the main tutelary deity Nanna.

5.1.2 ED IIIa

Archival material for the ED IIIa period is available from about ten different sites. 55% of the writings of lugal-names found in this period are attested only in ED IIIa or ED IIIa-b. Names which bear on the lugal's dominion increase steadily in number; those relating to insignia of power (3.1.1.3) circle around the throne dais, bara$_2$, the scepter, ĝidri, and the headdress men, which are, however, not all attributable to humans. The first clear instances of the innate power of the words or utterances of the lugal (3.1.1.4) are found; they are mostly connected with the adjectives gi and zi, implying accordance with the will of the gods. The first few names which combine the lugal with the land, kalam and kur, and its inhabitants, uĝ$_3$, make their appearance (3.1.1.6, 3.1.5.4). Names focusing on the lugal's sagacity (3.1.2) are now well-represented in the material, displaying eight different writings. Few parallels to these are known. Some wisdom-names may have human referents, but royal inscriptions which mention wisdom being bestowed by Enki on the human ruler are of a later date. The fertility of the city and its hinterlands (3.1.5.2–3) become popular themes. Divinities are now mentioned in connection with the lugal (3.1.6.2), predominantly Enlil and Dumuzi, and judging from later parallels, An and Utu are probably also mentioned in a number of names. This indicates a development in which the lugal is brought into a relation to marked divine actors. From having expressed acts or describing states through nominal predication names now introduce the lugal as acting alongside gods. Some of the aforementioned names with all certainty refer to a human lugal. The *śarrum*-names of this and the following period mostly feature *śar*(*rum*) as a nominal predicate.

5.1.3 ED IIIb

More than twice as many ED IIIb texts have been published compared with texts dating to the ED IIIa. 47% of the writings of lugal-names found in this period are attested only in ED IIIb texts, or in texts which could possibly belong in the preceding or following periods (ED IIIa-b and ED IIIb-ES).

Names bearing on the dominion of, and the personal relation to, the lugal, reach their high point during the ED IIIb and Sargonic periods, both in the number of forms and the number of bearers attested. Names related to the dominion over the country and its people (3.1.1.6) are also at a high point during the ED IIIb. The protective features of the lugal (3.1.3) become more and more popular in the onomasticon, and a few of these may with some degree of certainty be ascribed to the human lugal. This type is now also attested for *śarrum*-names. About three quarters of all writings of lugal-names designated as having to do with protection of the individual, the city, or the country as a whole are attested during this time. About 40% of names belonging to category (3.1.6), relating to the cult or deities, are attested either for the first time or exclusively in ED IIIb.

5.1.4 ES-LS

61% of the writings of lugal-names found in the Sargonic period are exclusive to this period, or they appear in texts which could possibly belong in the preceding period (ED IIIb-ES). Among names dealing with insignia of power (3.1.1.3), other than headdresses, the Sargonic period has the first occurrences of names composed with terms for different types of robes, lugal-tug$_2$-maḫ and lugal-suluḫu$_2$. Names featuring headdresses, men and aga, on the other hand, all but disappear during this period. In category (3.1.3.3), connecting the lugal to functions of protecting the country, names mentioning the chariot ^{ĝiš}gigir$_2$ of the lugal appear all of a sudden; their distribution seems limited to Umma and Girsu. Writings mentioning the lugal as providing for the needs of the individual, (3.1.4.1), grow in number. Names dealing with the lugal in relation to the cult or deities (3.1.6) experience a downturn during Sargonic times. Only a quarter of all names devoted to this theme are attested during this period. But some new names during this period are worth noticing. For instance lugal-bur, lugal-banšur-e, and names mentioning nidba-offerings, are all seen for the first time, and they are to some extent paralleled by passages in administrative contexts. Names connecting the lugal to sacred loci, sanctuaries and installations (3.1.6.4) tend to focus more on specific locations, such as named cities or temples, rather than on generic place terms. Names praising the lugal as heroic and apt for battle (3.1.7.4) drop in number and are only rarely attested during this period as compared to their relative popularity earlier on. The number of references to light, brilliance and visual phenomena (3.1.7.10) increase, both with regards to attested writings and to the number of bearers; names bearing on the Moon God, e.g. lugal-iti-da, and variants, seem especially popular during this time and continued to be so in Ur III times. The *śarrum*-names become much more variegated than in earlier times.

5.2 Diachronic perspectives

To attempt a survey of how common a certain appellative was in local or regional name-giving is perilous and the pitfalls are many. The following sections can only be regarded as first steps in such a direction. First, an attempt will be made to outline the possibilities of obtaining a fairly reliable estimate on the demographic composition during the 3rd millennium of cities which have produced archival material. To this will be added a few notes on how certain foreign influences in the material can be identified and explained, and on how the gender of people appearing in the written documentation may influence the results.

5.2.1 Demographics

An article published in 1982 by B. R. Foster bearing on the question of "Ethnicity and Onomastics" in Sargonic Mesopotamia contains the hitherto only attempt at establishing figures for the relative sizes of Sumerian- and Akkadian-speaking populations for any given period in third millennium Mesopotamia.[1397] Foster first went about assigning texts from around a dozen sites to archives of a general area, of individual cities, or to archival dossiers from specific sites.[1398] He devised four different categories, based on linguistic or formal criteria, which he used for classifying the onomastic material: Sumerian, Akkadian, reduplicated and unassigned names. Foster then set out to count individuals.

Each name appearing in an archival record is counted by Foster as one occurrence, thereby as one individual. In the short run this would appear to be slightly more problematic than indicated by Foster. Some persons appear frequently in the same archive, some are mentioned in more than one archive, and the same individual may appear in the same archive under two similar, but differently written names, as known from ED archives. Foster

[1397] B. R. Foster, *OrNS* 51 (1982), 297–354. Previous to that, R. D. Biggs had published an article on Semitic names in ED IIIa Abū Ṣalābīḫ. Biggs looked at colophons of literary and lexical texts and found that individuals with Sumerian names were about as common as such bearing Semitic names. This, however, only goes to prove that the works documented by the tablets had undergone a long chain of tradition, and the people mentioned in the colophons may have been active also outside of Abū Ṣalābīḫ.
[1398] Specifics on the the individual sites are found ibid., 300f.

made the assumption that, provided that the material for both Sumerian and Akkadian names is large enough, persons with Sumerian and Akkadian names are equally likely to turn up more than once in the records. A levelling effect might be thus be expected. This would make the total number of attestations stand in relation to the number of individual name-bearers and hence give a reasonably fair image of the composition of the time and the society in which the archive was placed.

A point worthy of notice is that, as Foster pointed out, families where more than one language was used in name-giving appear to have been quite rare. This could be taken as evidence for names as representative of the language spoken by an individual.[1399] Unfortunately, the linguistic identity of a mother in relation to her children often remains unknown. When a parent is mentioned in notes on filiation, it is practically always the father.

The unexpectedly high number of individuals with Akkadian names found in the "Umma C" archive – really a group of archives from CS Umma – begs an explanation.[1400] Looking at the types of texts in which Akkadian names abound, it becomes clear that about 75%[1401] of the Akkadian names from Umma C are culled from texts recording the disbursements of bread and beer. That is, people who received their subsistence from the state, as opposed to rations such as flour. These people were hardly firmly rooted in the Umma area. Persons with Sumerian names are very often qualified as the son of so-and-so, or as performing some specific administrative function; this is only exceptionally the case with persons bearing Akkadian names.

5.2.2 Distribution of appellatives

However tentative, a brief look at the relative distribution of some key appellatives in Sumerian name-giving may be instructive. The results of the following, very brief survey, are not absolute in any way, but depend on the types of texts represented in the archives. The present investigation has attempted to display the wealth of names which contain the appellatives lugal and *śarrum*. In discussing these, other appellatives too have sometimes offered parallels or have supplied variants supporting a reading or a certain

[1399] Ibid., 303. Out of 10000+ individual attestations, Foster points to less than ten instances of family members with both Sumerian and Akkadian names. As far as the evidence goes, all these persons appear to be male. Partial or true bilingualism, adoption or intermarriage between spouses with different linguistic backgrounds are possible explanations. Too little is known about all these factors during this period at any rate. F. R. Kraus' points on the text CT 32 pl. 7–8 (BM 22460, reedited as OIP 104 37), *Sumerer und Akkader*, 84f., are of interest in this connection. Most of his observations on this text remain valid, but correct the sequence in o. iii' 4–5, *i-ku-il* i_3-ḫal ur-^{d}UM.AN, to: *i-ku*^{ku_8}*-il*, *taš*$_2$*-ṭup*-AN.AN, and see in this latter, based on the verbal prefix /*ta*/, the name of a sister of the former.

[1400] See index of names appearing in Umma C, ibid., 323–354.

[1401] About 260 out of 350 attestations, using Foster's model of calculation.

interpretation. Separate investigations of these other appellatives, along with theophore names, however crucial for a full picture, are not possible within the limits of this work.

Foster's study, outlined above, sought to give an estimate of the comparative sizes of linguistic groups in Sargonic Mesopotamian archives. The following is a schematic overview of name forms appearing in different cities. No attempt has been made to distinguish between different archives published together. It is merely meant to indicate the relative wealth of a few of the most commonly encountered appellatives, with a semantic range close to those surveyed in this thesis, found within the same onomastic tradition.

Period/Place	Sum.	en	lugal	nin	Akk.	*baˁlum*	*śar(rum)*
1. ED I-IIIa Ur	780	2,5%	5%	1%	–	–	–
2. ED IIIa Šuruppag	1730	2,5%	5%	3,5%	45	4,5%	4,5%
3. ED IIIb Girsu	1640	4,5%	9%	9%	–	–	–
4. ED IIIb-ES Adab	200	1,5%	18,5%	2%	10	–	–
5. ED IIIb-MS Ur	160	2,5%	22%	8%	15	–	–
6. ED IIIb-MS Nippur	930	1%	11,5%	8,5%	130	6%	1,5%
7. MS Adab	230	2%	13,5%	2,5%	25	–	–
8. MS-CS Adab	160	2%	9%	4%	35	0,5%	0%–
9. CS Adab	400	3%	14,5%	3%	60	8,5%	1,5%
10. CS Girsu	300	3,5%	12,5%	0,5%	–	–	–
11. CS Mesag	260	1,5%	9%	5%	35	14,5%	0%–
12. CS Nippur	400	1,5%	5%	4,5%	75	12%	1,5%
13. Ur III Sumer	3950	1,5%	9,5%	7%	1700	1%	1,5%
Average ED I–Ur III	–	2%	10.5%	4%	–	6,5%	1,5%

Fig. 16: Relative frequency of appellatives en, lugal, nin in Sumerian names, and of baˁlum, and śar(rum) in Akkadian names.

Fig. 16 lists in the left column the periods and places which have supplied the information noted in the rest of the table. The numbers refer to attested numbers of forms of names, and not to the number of name-bearers. Hence, lugal-šu-luḫ-ku$_3$-An-na is given as much weight as ur-^{d}En-lil$_2$. Similarly, en-lu$_2$ and en-lu$_2$-sa$_6$-ga are counted once each even though they refer to the same person. Even though Akkadian names are few in number in southern archives, they have been noted wherever applicable. The percentages of Akkadian names are only noted when the total number of names attested exceed 30. The figures and percentages are rounded.[1402]

[1402] 1. UET 2, excluding the supplement; 2. F. Pomponio, *Prosopografia*; 3. V. V. Struve, *Onomastika*; 4. *TCABI*, texts no. 1–63; 5 A. Alberti & F. Pomponio, StPohl SM 13; 6. OSP 1; 7. *TCABI*, texts no. 65–193; 8. *TCABI*, texts no. 194–263; 9. Z. Yang, *SIA*; 10. *STTI*; 11. S. J. Bridges, *The Mesag Archive*; 12. OSP 2; 13. Sumerian names: H. Limet, *Anthroponymie*; Akkadian names: M. Hilgert, Imgula 5. R. K. Englund, *CDLJ* 2009:4, 19, has higher numbers for all the names beginning with lugal-, en- and nin- than those culled from Limet, which is to

As can easily be seen from the numbers in Fig. 16, lugal is almost consistently more common than en and nin throughout the parts of Sumer inspected. This, even in archives and specific periods in which the sources include many female names, such as ED IIIb-MS Nippur and the Ur III period. M. W. Green drew attention to the fact that at ED I-II Uruk, en may be seen to have filled the same function as lugal in contemporary names at Ur,[1403] though the selection is fairly limited. A measure of local variation in earlier times must be considered, and the general lack of sources from ED I-II and the remainder of the 3rd millennium means that the picture is incomplete. But given the consistency in numbers from ED I-II Ur and ED IIIa Šuruppag, it can be seen that at least outside Uruk, lugal-names were twice as common as en-names.

F. R. Kraus stated that by the ED IIIa, lugal had come to supplant en both in the human and in the divine onomasticon. Furthermore, he meant that theonyms composed with en had stopped being invented around the time of the Šuruppag texts while many theonyms composed with lugal were later products.[1404] If comparing Kraus' observations to the percentages in Fig. 16, it may be argued that concerning the human onomasticon, this process had been underway since the ED I-II period, at least judging by the onomasticon of Ur. E. Burrows made a similar observation regarding ama-names of ED I-II Ur, which would be outnumbered by names composed with nin as time progressed.[1405] Burrows also pointed to close parallels betweeen early ama-names and contemporary lugal-names, and noted that ama-names outnumbered lugal-names 60:40.[1406]

In ED IIIb to CS Girsu the percentage of names containing the relevant titles appears to be fairly consistent. Only the names composed with nin exhibit a drastic drop in numbers. This is due to the different archival scopes of the ED IIIb Bau temple administration and the civic archive of CS times. That names with en in Girsu sources should be so common compared to most other cities in the region could either have to do with its usage as a term for deceased royalty, or with a widespread usage of that word as an epithet for leading gods in the local pantheon. Outside of Girsu the names

---

be expected given the publication of new texts and collations of texts used by Limet in his study. This increase would only marginally influence the percentages of these names in relation to the onomasticon as a whole.

1403 *ZA* 72 (1982), 165.

1404 F. R. Kraus, *JCS* 3 (1951), 66, followed by D. O. Edzard, CRRA 19, 143. Kraus' low count for the lugal-names is due to the fact that the sections containing these names fall in some of the more damaged parts of *SF* 1, and that he used only Deimel's index of *SF* 1. For estimates on the original line count, and on the number of lugal-, en-, and nin-names contained therein, see M. Krebernik's remarks, *ZA* 76 (1986), 163; and compare P. Mander, *Pantheon*, 117.

1405 UET 2, 5, 20. See also W. W. Hallo, *Titles*, 29f.; R. A. di Vito, StPohl SM 16, 88f.

1406 UET 2, 20f.

composed with en relatively steadily lose ground compared to names composed with lugal and nin. It is conceivable that this decrease is connected with a growing association of that appellative with the title of the religious official en. Adab might be an exception, but the increase is probably within a margin of error and so developments in the Adab onomasticon could bear closer scrutiny.[1407] The comparatively high number for nin-names in ED IIIb-MS Nippur is influenced by an ES-MS tablet of considerable size which lists hundreds of female dependents. This tablet alone accounts for more than half the nin-names encountered in published texts from Nippur before the CS period.[1408]

Although the numbers above are rough estimates and only show the distribution of appellatives among groups of people who were documented using their names, the picture that presents itself is still valuable for assessing roughly how common these epithets were in the population at large. The archives used presumably present a cross-section of both urban and rural settlements during the time periods in question.

5.2.3 Brief overview of parallel formations

Throughout the survey comparative materials have been drawn into discussions. It has been seen that lugal-names have close parallels in names construed with other appellatives. Both nin and en feature prominently, as do certain theonyms and proper names of Ur III rulers. A brief digression into the five most commonly encountered lugal-names along with extant, exact parallels, might be illustrative. All names were borne by 20 or more persons.

lugal-ezem (a>40) 'the lugal … the festival'

The closest direct parallel is e_2-ezem from ED IIIa Šuruppag, which is probably an abbreviation of e_2-ezem-du_{10}.[1409] The single writing lu_2-ezem, also at Šuruppag, might be an abbreviation or defective writing of lugal-ezem.[1410] Names composed with ezem suffer a drastic reduction in number during the Sargonic period but regain popularity during the Ur III period.

lugal-iti-da (a>35) 'the lugal is (reborn each) month'

The name has only one parallel, e_2-iti-da, attested once at ED IIIb Nippur.[1411]

lugal-KA (a>25) abbreviation

The name is clearly an abbreviation; the comparable names nin-KA and e_2-KA are known.[1412] Neither is found anywhere near as often as lugal-KA. The sign KA in most cases probably represents inim or du_{11}.

[1407] With a few new volumes of Adab texts published in the CUSAS series, an in-depth study of Adab name-giving practice promises to deliver interesting results. See more on the published Adab archives and texts, above, p. 29f.

[1408] OSP 1 23. Without the 47 names appearing only in this text, the nin-names would have made up about 3,5% of the total Sumerian onomasticon.

[1409] See F. Pomponio, *Prosopografia*, 77 s.v.v. e_2-ezen(-du_{10}).

[1410] So with the editors of *FTUM* 37, note to r. i 1.

[1411] OSP 1 25 "v" 7'.

lugal-ša$_3$ $^{(a>27)}$ abbreviation
As with the preceding name, the comparable names found in contemporary sources are composed with nin and e$_2$, but neither is as commonly attested as lugal-ša$_3$.[1413] Most lugal-names featuring the noun ša$_3$ have it following directly upon the appellative, apart from lugal-zi-ša$_3$-ĝal$_2$.[1414]

lugal-ni$_3$-zu $^{(a>20)}$ 'the lugal knows (every)thing'
The parallel nin-ni$_3$-zu is limited to the Nippur-Adab-Isin area.[1415]

lugal-ĝiš $^{(a>20)}$ abbreviation
Parallel e$_2$-ĝiš is found at Sargonic Adab, Mesag, Nippur and Umma;[1416] nin-ĝiš is found at Sargonic Adab and Nippur.[1417]

It will be readily noticeable from this very brief list, that where parallels to lugal-names exist, the nouns which most often occupy the same position as lugal are e$_2$ and nin. The same situation applies when enlarging the list to encompass the 30 most commonly attested lugal-names. The two most common lugal-names both deal with aspects of time. The festival, ezem, represents a recurring celebration marking specific points of the year; and the year was divided into lunar calendar months, iti. A connection with the time of birth is possible for both these names, and at least lugal-iti-da is very likely to refer to the Moon God Nanna or Su'en.

5.2.4 Northern lugal-names

lugal-names are attested in a wide sweep from Ebla in the far northwest to Susa in the southeast. The same holds true for *śarrum*-names. At Ebla, the names of many foreigners to the city are recorded, but also, a trove of scholastic material has been documented. Only in the scholastic material does the sign LUGAL appear to represent Sumerian lugal.[1418] Otherwise, in PNN, it is used as a logographic writing here taken to represent *śar*(*rum*).[1419] In economic contexts, Sumerian names composed with lugal are written nu-gal, as for instance in the names of singers travelling to Ebla by way of Mari, but perhaps also residents of Mari. Maria Tonietti considered them as possible "stage names" adopted by the singers as status markers, which is not at all impossible.[1420] On the other hand, she also mentions a passage in which a woman from Adab who received a payment in silver is noted as the

---

[1412] For nin-KA, see, e.g. *TCVBI* 1-34 o. i 6; r. i 1 (ED IIIb Umma-Zabala); for e$_2$-KA, see CUSAS 11 186 o. iv 6 (ED IIIb-ES Adab).
[1413] For e$_2$-ša$_3$, see W. Sommerfeld, K. Markina & N. Roudik, *Gs Diakonoff*, 185–231 no. 5 o. 4; for nin-ša$_3$, see, e.g. CT 50 106 r. i 17 (CS Girsu).
[1414] See above, table 4.3.
[1415] E.g. OSP 1 23 o. viii 12 (ES-MS Nippur).
[1416] E.g. USP 19 o. 5 (CS Umma).
[1417] For e$_2$-ĝiš, see OSP 2 80 o. ii' 1 (MS-CS Nippur); for nin-ĝiš, see
[1418] E.g. in the colophons of ARET 5 20 and 21.
[1419] See M. V. Tonietti, Subartu 4/2, 90; and compare G. Marchesi & N. Marchetti, MesCiv 14, 103f. fn. 57.
[1420] In Subartu 4/2, 88 and 97.

mother of a junior singer, who would in his turn also originally be from Adab.[1421] The writing nu-gal is found elsewhere also, but always as a single-component name, which does not add significantly to the understanding of the appellative and its reception outside of the Sumerian linguistic area.[1422]

Apart from the names of Mari singers, sites located north of Kiš have yielded about ten lugal-names. A few additional Sargonic period lugal-names from northern areas are unfortunately damaged, hindering insight into which types of lugal-names were in use there. Apart from this, some texts are of uncertain, but northern, provenience.[1423] The legible names are:

ED IIIa: ar_3-du_2:lugal, (commemorative inscription), Tell Ağrab
ED IIIb: lugal-kisal-si (commemorative inscription), Ešnuna; lugal-UD (commemorative inscription), Mari; lugal-^{d}En-lil_2 (adm.), Akšak
ES: lugal-ku-li, Akkade (MO)
CS: lugal-ezem (adm.), lugal-An-ne_2 (scholastic) Ešnuna;
lugal-a_2 (adm.), Tutub; lugal-ni_3-lu-lu-a, Mugdan (scholastic)

Only the first of the names above is unique; the last represents a variant of a known type. The name lugal-ku-li, found in *Maništūšu*'s Obelisk, is attested for the first time there, but appears later in the south also. Those two that appear in everyday economic documents are nothing out of the ordinary. The Mari-name lugal-UD, need not have belonged to a person from that city,[1424] but others carrying lugal-names were, as was seen above, connected with Mari in one way or another. In Kiš, consistent with an increase in Semitic names, the number of lugal-names diminishes as time progresses. Before the Sargonic period lugal-names found there accorded with those found in the southern cities. At Abū Ṣalābīḫ, a bit further to the south, only two of the lugal-names encountered come from everyday documents, inim-lugal-da, and lugal-šu-$\hat{g}al_2$; the rest are either entries in scholastic texts of different kinds or appear in colophons. The material is quite small and does not really allow for anything but broad generalizations, but for a large part, the northern material does not display a unique tradition concerning lugal-names. With all likelihood, it depended on onomastic developments in centers further south.

[1421] Ibid., 84 ex. [5] (TM.75.G.2429 o. xx 4–12).

[1422] MO C xiv' 8, xvii' 29 (ES, name of an ancestor of people from Marad); HSS 10 158 r. i 5 (CS Gasur). In CT 50 183 o. i 4 (CS Girsu), reconstruct [ur]-⌜d⌝Ama-nu-gal, and compare e_2-Ma-nu-gal, *IAS* 61 o. x 15 (NPL), and ur-$^{(d)}$Ma-nu-gal, *TCABI* 151 o. 7; 170 r. 1.

[1423] So OIP 104 41 o. ix 3' (lugal-[x-x], ES Sippar?); HSS 10 169 o. 8 (lugal-m[a]s-su_2 ?, CS Gasur); CT 44 48 r. 8 (lugal-[x]-da, CS Sippar?). The PN lugal-$\hat{g}$iš appears four times in MVN 3 29 (ES-MS), of unknown, northern provenience.

[1424] See discussion by M. V. Tonietti, Subartu 4/2, 95.

5.3 Diachronic developments

The Sumerian onomasticon of ED I-II is for the largest part structurally comparable with the earliest attested Akkadian onomasticon, though they differ with respect to semantic content. Akkadian names are far more preoccupied with the arrival of the child into the family while Sumerian names focus on societal and religious aspects of existence.[1425] A significant number of names consist of two-element nominal phrases (aja$_2$-ul$_4$-gal), adjectival phrases (amar-du$_{10}$), or passive participles (mes-pa$_3$-da). Constructions that can be identified as containing an active participle feature direct objects, and here is where Sumerian names begin to exhibit more complex patterns than ED III Akkadian names. Also, the double noun genitival constructions (amar-ezem), lack any substantial distribution in the earliest Akkadian onomasticon; *ka$_3$-la-ab*-E$_2$-a in the *Māniśtūśu* Obelisk is a calque of the common Sumerian name type.[1426] Furthermore, Sumerian names featuring dimensional markers (Nanna-gin$_7$-du$_{10}$) are found already by the ED I-II, although in the beginning they are rare. These correspond to a few ED IIIb Akkadian names containing prepositional phrases (e.g. *ma-ki-be-li$_2$*[1427]).

With the above points in mind, it is relevant to note that lugal-names conform structurally to the rest of the Sumerian onomasticon. Extant in about 40 names from ED I-II Ur, lugal-names are less common than names containing the appellatives aja$_2$, ama, amar, and ur. Although many of the names are of a simple structure, they are still difficult to interpret.

The appearance in ED IIIa of names extolling the lugal's wisdom may be due to the limited material available from ED I-II times, but it may also be that this represents a new focus in the figure of the lugal. The appearance in ED IIIb of a range of names portraying the lugal as a father figure indicate a true development in ideas surrounding the lugal. Names focusing on the lugal as a victorious and heroic figure (e.g. lugal-u$_3$-ma, lugal-ur-saĝ), peak during the ED IIIb and then lose ground.

A stronger focus on the lugal and terms signifying brightness and visual phenomena appearing in the Sargonic period continues to be important throughout the 3rd millennium. It may be linked to the introduction of a new set of ideas which were accessible across great layers of society, or to the popularization of an already existing set of ideas.

Although the appellative *baʿlum* often can be used to supply comparisons for *śarrum*-names, the former could be, and was, used to express distinctive, social connections between the speaker of the name and the world around

[1425] See discussion above, p. 64–66, section 2.3.2.
[1426] OIP 104 40 B xi 4.
[1427] CT 7 pl. 4 (BM 22451) 1.

her or him. This was easily done by adding the poss. pron. *-ī* (or *-ni*, *-na*) to the word stem: *baʿlī*. The *śarrum*-names of this type are rare in the Sargonic onomasticon and continue to be so.[1428] In this respect, the appellative *śarrum* behaves more like theonyms, in that these were seldom provided with pronominal suffixes; an exception was the name of the Akkadian Sun God Śamaś.[1429]

5.4 Semantic differences

This chapter has demonstrated ways in which Sumerian and Akkadian names revolving around a comparable subject differ from each other. A name-giving tradition developing in close association with the languages spoken by their users will be deeply indebted to both concepts and formulae extant in their respective languages. Sometimes similarities may be masked by seeming divergent terminology or imagery, and conversely, sometimes related terms or symbolism may overshadow deep-seated differences in semantic associations. But by definition, such considerations only come into play when Sumerian and Akkadian names bear strong resemblances in wording and are syntactically comparable. This is more likely to happen in simple nominal clause names than in structurally more complex names, as the latter type is less common in the Akkadian onomasticon at this point in time. A few points will illustrate some fundamental differences.

Akkadian *śarrum*-names lack reference to symbolic attributes of power, whereas these were quite popular in lugal-names. Also, these emblems might be conceived of as related to the exercise of kingship or power over the land and its inhabitants. The qualities and benefits of the land having an overlord is taken for granted in lugal-names, but has to be made explicit in the Akkadian names which request allegiance to and faith in the *śarrum* (*śarriś-takal*), as well as faith in and reverence to the gods.[1430] A link here exists to the royal ideological traits which make subjects responsible to the king personally rather than to an office. This confirms a suspicion that Sumerian names were linked to age-old, but constantly developing, ideas about the place of man in the world. Such generally held conceptions may indeed have existed amongst Akkadian-speaking societies, but they are harder to identify – in the onomastic material at least.[1431]

[1428] See discussion of names above, p. 191, section 3.2.1.1. Only one name dating to the Sargonic period features a 1st person pronominal suffix, *i-śar-śar-ri*$_2$; the rest are of ED date.
[1429] E.g. *be-li*$_2$-^{d}Utu^{śi}, MAD 1 109 o. 3' (translit. only, MS-CS Ešnuna).
[1430] See, for instance, *Iliś-takal* and *Ilak-nuʾʾid*.
[1431] See discussion on deities appearing in ED and Sargonic seals with boat motifs above, section 3.1.5.3, p. 135f.; and further, section 2.3.3.2, p. 69.

Akkadian names also generally lack reference to the positive relations between a leader and his city or cities, otherwise a rather productive motif in Sumerian names, and not only those featuring lugal as appellative. The understanding of *śarru-ālśin* as 'the *śarrum* is their city,' would not imply a special relationship to towns or cities, but would rather serve to illustrate the protective qualities of the *śarrum*, on a par with other names using for instance bad$_3$/*dūrum*, as a nominal predicate, types which are at any rate known also in Sumerian.

The overt associations between the *śarrum* and cultic, or religious matters in a broad sense, are much less common than is the case with lugal-names. But in some cases, personal markers as personal prefixes or pronominal suffixes might hide a specific deity, for example in the name *Tūta*ʾ*-śar-libbīś*, which perhaps refers to a goddess.

While there are some points in common between the gods mentioned in lugal- and *śarrum*-names, the difference most often lies in the relation between the appellative and the divinity. As has been said, *śar* occurs as a nominal predicate in Akkadian names; hence they give a good indication as to the identity of *śarrum* when used as a divine epithet. In section 4.1, above, the Akkadian divinities qualified as *śar*(*rum*) were displayed in tabulary form: Adad, Ea, ʾIlum and Su'en were all honored as kings in the onomasticon. Śamaś featured specifically in a comparison with the king, similar to a Sumerian construction with Utu. In Sumerian names before the Ur III period the identity of the divine lugal was never so explicitly stated. But still, some of these deities in their Sumerian guises are likely to have been intended as the referents of lugal-names.

5.5 Semantic similarities

It is clear that while the *śarrum* was not as central a figure in the Akkadian name-giving tradition as lugal was in the Sumerian, a considerable overlap between the two figures can be seen. From the known ED writings featuring the logogram LUGAL or the sign SAR, *śarrum*-names fall mainly into three categories: the first has *śar*(*rum*) as a nominal predicate qualifying a deity; the second combines the *śarrum* with qualities of a potentially threatening nature (*śarru*-GAR$_3$, *śarru-paluḫ*); and the third with protection in general. Only the second and third categories were ever in common use in the Sumerian onomasticon. And while threatening qualities of the lugal may be seen as directed outwards, the Akkadian formations do not supply any further information.

The comparison with a father-figure is found with both appellatives, as are names which ascribe the fortunes of an individual to the lugal or *śarrum*, often marking this relationship through the addition of a possessive suffix to the noun 'god.'

The symbolic association of the lugal with large felines is also found in Akkadian names (lugal-pirig̑, lugal-nemur$_x$; *śarru-lāba*; lugal-*na-i-iŠ*) as is the comparison with the god Utu/Śamaś. While the former remain a bit shady as to their symbolic import, the comparison with Utu/Śamaś is likely to deal with the dispensing of justice in the land and the general reliability of the referent, as is also made apparent by other names (e.g. lugal-si-sa$_2$; *śarru-yiśar*; lugal-di-de$_3$). Sumerian names formed with the adjectives gi and zi, and Akkadian names formed with *kēnum*, also bear on this same idea. These adjectives were also commonplace in the onomastica in general.

Wisdom, strength and kindness are further traits which are associated with both the lugal and the *śarrum*.

5.6 Comparison with Ur III kyriophore names

When comparing ED and Sargonic lugal-names with Ur III kyriophores in Akkadian, which have the advantage of being clear as to their referent, it is useful to call to mind M. Hilgert's conclusions on the latter.[1432] Hilgert proposed three main semantic categories which could account for statements in kyriophore Ur III names: the connection between the ruler and the divine sphere; the ruler and the ruled; and the ruler and dominion. All three categories have their correspondence in one or more categories devised for the present study. Hilgert noted that the most eye-catching innovations in structure of such names occurred during the reign of *Šu*-Su'en; innovations which allowed for more detailed information on ideological matters to be conveyed by the names. He also proposed a correlation with a conscious strategy by the latter king to proclaim his greatness already at the beginning of his reign. If Hilgert's interpretation should prove correct, kyriophore names during this period were finely tuned to changes in contemporary royal ideology.[1433]

While this is not the place for discussing Ur III kyriophores in-depth, a few points are worthy of notice. In both Sumerian and Akkadian kyriophores, those construed with Šulgi are the most common. In his names, the association of the king of Ur with other divinities are rare. Such connections become more common only with Amar-Su'en, at least where Sumerian names are concerned. During *Šu*-Su'en's times they are even more plentiful, but by then, kyriophores in Akkadian had become more common than those in Sumerian. As for the relation to earlier traditions, the Sumerian and Akkadian kyriophores composed with Šulgi's name form the closest parallels to ED and Sargonic lugal- and *śarrum*-names alike. A closer

[1432] See above, p. 16.
[1433] M. Hilgert, JBVO 5, 66–70.

investigation would no doubt shed further light on this matter, and the materials for comparison are of the most fruitful kind, as it includes both monumental and hymnic sources. On top of this, there is an overabundance of parallels to be drawn from year names, names of locations, and other types of personal names from texts which are often datable, down to a certain king's regnal year.

6. lugal- and *śarrum*-names in their historical and cultural settings

Sumerian and Akkadian names incorporating the royal titles lugal and *śarrum* are clearly part of the living onomastic traditions. They exhibit expected changes over time and orthographic variations consistent with a great geographical and temporal spread. In many cases, comparable names featuring other appellatives are known; but in a surprisingly large number of cases, no such parallels are so far attested. Thus, while lugal- and *śarrum*-names were part of the onomastic traditions, they both formed subgroups in that larger stream of tradition, with unique and specialized functions. The present chapter is an attempt to put these names in the larger perspective of the times in which they saw use.

6.1 The historical setting

Studies of the political history of the 3rd millennium owe a great deal to Thorkild Jacobsen who in a seminal article[1434] characterized the burgeoning Mesopotamian city-states as autocracies. The principle was "the concentration of political power in as few hands as possible."[1435] He describes the political developments of the 3rd millennium as if inescapably plummeting toward the centralization of all power in the hands of one individual. In reality, any person making claims to singular hegemony over larger areas of land encompassing several originally independent state formations could do so only by emphasizing a set of ideas common to the area to which he laid claim. This set of ideas formed the basis of royal ideology, which remains unclear in many details. However, enough remains in royal inscriptions and literary texts to enable a hazy picture of what these commonly accepted ideas may have entailed. The lugal, Jacobsen argued in a follow-up to the former article[1436]

[1434] *JNES* 2 (1943), 159–172.
[1435] T. Jacobsen, *JNES* 2 (1943), 159f.
[1436] *ZA* 52 (1957), 91–140.

> was chosen for his skill in warfare and physical endurance. He was therefore typically a young man – usually he still lived at home under parental authority – and of noble family; his father was generally a rich landowner on whose servants and retainers the son could draw for followers on his military ventures.[1437]

Parts of this description of the human king is recognizable both in onomastic sources and royal inscriptions. Descriptions of the lugal as vigorous and skilled in warfare are to be expected as both names and commemorative inscriptions were intended to give vent to an ideal view of the world. But in particular, Jacobsen's descriptions of the lugal as a young man, and at that, one living with his parents, find little support in any way, shape or form. The lugal is rather, beginning in the ED III, sometimes described as a fatherly figure, hardly in keeping with the idea of a young man in a modern sense, but more often just characterized as an independent man.[1438] No material evidence exists to support his idea that a lugal, or an $ensi_2$, lived in his father's house; though it must be stated that the hereditary principles of these high offices are not perfectly understood, and that most reigns of pre–Ur III rulers are estimates.

Jacobsen describes the origins of the types of leadership embodied by the en and the lugal as temporary, and ad-hoc solutions to specific situations; in the case of the en situations demanding administrative leadership or the restoration of law and order ("organizer"); in the case of the lugal a situation where a threat from outside had arisen ("war-leader").[1439] Besides the literary texts Jacobsen draws on for evidence, little survives from the 3rd (or 4th) millennium to confirm Jacobsen's views.[1440] But there is indeed an account of a single instance in which a lugal is chosen by an assembly, dating to Classic Sargonic times. That this matter of course was not or was *no longer* common practice may be seen from the name given to or taken by this lugal: *Ipḫur*-Kiš 'Kiš assembled,' a programmatic name known only from the inscriptions of his enemy *Narām*-Su'en.[1441] Though councils, elders, and city-elders are attested, not much is known about them in the early

[1437] T. Jacobsen, *ZA* 52 (1957), 103.

[1438] Or so I interpret names including the appellatives lu_2 and $nitaḫ_{(2)}$ (zi).

[1439] T. Jacobsen, *ZA* 52 (1957), 103; and compare also ibid. *JNES* 2 (1943), 169f. For a criticism of this stance, see G. J. Selz, *Fs Römer*, 291 w. fn. 40.

[1440] A single ED IIIb text from Ur mentions the delivery by the lugal of [x number of animals] to an uĝken:gal. It is not certain from the text itself or from the dossier to which it belongs whether this latter represents a person, an office or an institution. The text was published and discussed by G. Visicato & A. Westenholz, *Kaskal* 2 (2005), 60, no. 9, and p. 64.

[1441] As noted by A. Westenholz, *Six City-State Cultures*, 38. On the career of this person and the circumstances under which he was elevated to the throne of Kiš, see ibid., *Annäherungen* 3, 51–55.

periods.[1442] The paucity of sources attesting to an initial choice of a leader to address a given state of emergency is perhaps only to be expected. With time the royal inscriptions described the selection as lying in the hands of higher authorities: the divine leaders of the local and regional pantheons.[1443] Elements of this selection can be seen already earlier, in names such as lugal-inim-ma-se$_3$-ga 'the lugal is one instructed (by DN),' and lugal-ša$_3$-pa$_3$-da 'the lugal is one chosen in the heart (of DN)' which profess divine acceptance and privilege.

This attachment to religious structures was not limited to a language of power. Evidence for the lugal interacting with the socially and economically important temple institutions in urban centers abound. So much in fact, that G. J. Selz proposed to see lordship on the Sumerian end of the floodplain as bureaucratic-sacred: with firm roots in the administrative organization of the southern urban milieu. He contrasted this with a cultural tradition of the Semitic-speaking areas to the north, whose leadership style he termed dynastic-charismatic. These different ideological strategies Selz ascribed to the different types of demands put on human societies in the south versus the north.[1444] And speaking specifically about nam-lugal, A. Westenholz characterized Sumerian lordship from at least 2500 BCE to be of a religious rather than a political nature. In his opinion, the lugal acted as a chairman of a league of interconnected city-states; as a caretaker of religious ceremonies to the benefit of all those involved. The lugal was not primarily a political leader, although his arbitrations sometimes had real political repercussions, since he both served as arbiter in disputes between cities and as a military leader. At the top of the political hierarchies in the Sumerian city-states were the city-governors, ensi$_2$, whose roles overlapped with that of the lugal only in the state of Lagaš. Westenholz saw the religious tone of the lugal-names, and the practical lack of names formed with ensi$_2$, as supporting this view.[1445]

6.2 ED I-II (c. 2900–2700 BCE)

In the archaic Ur texts, the title lugal was used about one of a number of professionals involved in managing the comprehensive assets of urban institutions.[1446] However, the title does not appear in any of the known Uruk

[1442] See, e.g. C. Wilcke, *EANEL*, 33: 2.1.3.3; A. Westenholz, *Annäherungen* 3, 62f. w. fnn. 257, 259. The same situation applies to the institution of the city council during the Ur III period, W. Sallaberger, *Annäherungen* 3, 179.

[1443] For Nippur's role, see, e.g. the quite different stances of T. Jacobsen, *ZA* 52 (1957), 104–106; and A. Westenholz, *Six City-State Cultures*, 32–36; compared with those of W. Sallaberger, CDOG 1, 148–153; and J. S. Cooper, CRRA 45, 136 w. fn. 21

[1444] *Fs Römer*, 283, and further on p. 328.

[1445] *Six City-State Cultures*, passim, esp. p. 32–35.

[1446] W. Sallaberger, *Shepherds*, 32f. See also P. Charvát, *ArOr* 47 (1979), 18.

and ED period scholastic lists enumerating public offices, nor in lists of cultic professionals. The simplest etymological analysis of the title itself indicates that the one bearing the title was a man (lu_2), and that he was "large" (gal), i.e. prominent; more precisely a man who exercised control over others who under different circumstances could have been eligible to fill his position themselves. Whether this position was hereditary to begin with depends on where it originated. If the original sense was that of 'owner,' it would have been carried by the head of a private household and quite naturally passed down to the next generation, or to a younger brother. In the least it would have remained within the same nuclear or extended family grouping. If on the other hand, the title originated outside the family, in the context of a bureaucratic environment, nam-lugal would not necessarily have been hereditary, or even an appointment held for life.

Much of the resources in local societies of the dawning 3rd millennium BCE ought to have been tied up in landed property, livestock and their surplus yields, and in material and human assets supervised by large urban institutions.[1447] City-state formations consisted of a conglomerate of large estates and institutions. Institutions may be divided into private estates and communal households. The former were governed by representatives of autochthonous families; the latter by bureaucratic and cultic specialists, or by other types of leaders who either inherited their position or were empowered by some form of popular assembly. But then again, the name lugal-pa_3 does in itself indicate that the lugal was regarded as chosen, presumably not by peers, but by higher powers, if the meaning of the predicate in ED I-II is in keeping with later usage of the verb pa_3.[1448] Temples belonged to the latter category and were ideally seen as owned by their main inhabitant;[1449] and by extension, the owner of the temple also exercised lordship over all available resources within the borders of the city or city-state. Thus, during this time or perhaps already during the end of the Uruk period, the title lugal was transferred to male divinities of local significance, and this surfaced also in personal names, as is shown by a few examples from ED I-II Ur.[1450] The very earliest occurrences of lugal are in the form of a PN, where lugal appears to be unqualified, and so they are not very helpful in ascertaining the earliest history of the appellative.[1451]

[1447] The question as to who owned the land and animals that were administered by different institutions is a complex one. For a brief overview of the problem, with a number of references, see B. R. Foster, CRRA 41, 1–10, especially p. 3.

[1448] Compare, for instance, the occurrence of a temple functionary, dam ^{d}Nanše, being selected by means of omen, *CIRPL* Urn. 24 iii 3–6 ur-nimin, dam, ^{d}Nanše, maš be_2-pa_3.

[1449] See, e.g. the repeated references to lugal in the sense of owner of temples, TH 176, 218, 256, 431, 440, 445, 454, 491.

[1450] See discussions of the ED I-II names lugal-$^{su_{13}}$PA.SIKIL-nam-tar, and lugal-u_4-$su\breve{h}_3$-gi_4.

[1451] See above, p. 58f. w. fn. 282.

Society appears to have been highly stratified. The accumulation of surplus wealth and resources combined with craft and academic specializations, and the rights to utilize these, led to the forming of urban elites. The lugal appears as a member of these elites, but he is not markedly set apart from other high officials at this point. In depictions of the time there are no specifically royal distinguishing markers.[1452] A few names which may refer to him in his official role are known from Ur and Uruk.[1453] The symbolism behind these names indicate a responsibility of caretaker or provider for subordinates, who were portrayed as animal young.

6.3 ED IIIa (c. 2700–2550 BCE)

During this period, historical sources in the form of commemorative inscriptions begin to supplement administrative records. The area stretching along the river Euphrates, from eastern Syria down to the southernmost end of the floodplain was a political hotspot of formidable proportions, with a handful of dynastic seats vying for influence. The area from Nippur and downstream is the one best covered by administrative texts, though nowhere is the picture supplied by these documents comprehensive enough so as to grant a complete image of how a city-state worked, or how political alliances were tied and maintained.

Early inscriptional evidence portrays lugals as taking part in ceremonials. This is witnessed by inscribed shallow bowls (Sum. bur) dedicated by lugals of Kiš. Some were dedicated to temples rather than deities.[1454] A number of anonymous inscriptions featuring only the name of a temple should perhaps be seen as additional witnesses to this tradition,[1455] mentioned in the so-called Keš temple hymn,[1456] and which is echoed by the name lugal-Keš$_3$^{ki}, borne by a few individuals from ED IIIb Girsu and Sargonic Adab. The lugal also figures as builder of temples in inscriptions of rulers of local and regional

[1452] G. Marchesi & N. Marchetti, MesCiv 14, 213.
[1453] See discussions of amar-lugal and maš-lugal; and P. Charvát, *ArOr* 47 (1979), 18.
[1454] See T. Jacobsen *apud* J. S. Cooper, *SARI* 1, 15, note to Ad 1. I believe, however, that that particular object should be discounted, since it is dedicated by a local ruler of Adab, and has the "wrong" shape. See also the following note. OIP 14 5 is the best example. Compare also the broken bowls featuring the name of Mebarasi, OIP 53, 147 no. 2 (bowl?), from the ED temple of Su'en in Tutub; who may or may not be identical with the lugal Kiš by that name, who dedicated a bowl in an unknown place, D. O. Edzard, *ZA* 53 (1959), 9 (IM 30590) w. fn. 1 (unknown provenience, confiscated at Kūt al-Imāra). G. Marchesi & N. Marchetti, MesCiv 14, 99 fn. 18, with previous literature, hold the two Mebarasi to be two different persons.
[1455] OIP 14 7, 9, 11, 16 (?), 31. The vessel fragments OIP 14 8 and 17 feature inscriptions which set them apart from the former, they are furthermore classified as vases in the catalogue, *op. cit.*, 1.
[1456] R. D. Biggs, *ZA* 61 (1971), 193–207; D. O. Edzard, *OrNS* 43 (1974), 103–113; G. Gragg, TCS 3, 157–188.

significance alike; though building activities were not reserved for royalty alone.[1457] Names relating the lugal to specific architectural features are unclear as to referent, but the verb du$_3$, which is the normal verb used in conjunction with building work is not attested along with the appellative lugal in the onomasticon of the time.[1458] However, the connection of the lugal to the gods as one who provided them with places for dwelling and organized worship is clear beginning in this period. A number of theophore constructs attest to this connection as one which was readily acknowledged by the people.

As a manager of large-scale construction work, the lugal must have had access to or have been in control of a considerable work force which had to be provisioned, at least for the duration of the work. Whether the disbursements were allocated from private or public funds, is not known.[1459]

Mythical literature of the time was replete with the doings of gods and heroic figures, their relations with one another, and with specific points on the map. The constant reiteration of names of cities and sanctuaries were central concerns of Sumerian religion, which shows in the writings of the learned scribes of the ED IIIa. The lords and kings of the politically more important of these cities were described as if acting alongside, or on behalf of gods who took active part in the mythical events.[1460] With the same institutions functioning in later times and in the same places, and with the work laid down by previous generations of kings, noble folk, and ordinary citizens visible all across the land, it ought to come as no surprise that the makers and shakers of history were in fact central to the world view of ancient Mesopotamians.[1461] But so far, the relation to the people and the land is only attested to a moderate degree in contemporary lugal-names.[1462] Names which focus on the elect position of the lugal begin to appear.[1463] A

[1457] See the discussion with examples of other officials mentioning building activities in statue inscriptions, G. Marchesi & N. Marchetti, MesCiv 14, 162–164. In a Sargonic text, CUSAS 17 13, the builder also mentions part of the staff with which he supplied the temple.

[1458] Compare the name of the fictitious ED Adab ruler Lugalanemundu, who entered into the stream of tradition in the early 2nd millennium BCE, judging by the look of his name.

[1459] A later parallel, the construction work on the Enlil temple in Nippur in CS times would indicate that the temple organization provided part of the workers' diet. The king, on his part, supplied part of the labour force from his dependents. Whether this picture may apply also to much earlier times is of course difficult to know. See, A. Westenholz, OSP 2, 26.

[1460] *IAS* 247 ii' 1'–8': ⸢lugal⸣$_{\text{([PA.NU]N)}}$ Kiš, Kiš-t[a], lugal$_{\text{(PA.NUN)}}$ Adab, Adab-ta, en$_{\text{(GAL)}}$ Aratta Aratta‹-ta›, en$_{\text{(GAL)}}$ Ki-⸢en-gi⸣, Ki-en-gi-ta, $^{\text{d(UD)}}$En$_{\text{(GAL)}}$-ki$_{\text{(UNUG)}}$, [...], "the lugal of Kiš from Kiš, the lugal of Adab from Adab, the en of Aratta ‹from› Aratta, the en of *Kiengi* from *Kiengi*, Enki [...]. For the reading see M. Krebernik, *Annäherungen* 1, 242 fn. 60. Cf. P. Michalowski, *JCS* 40 (1988), 161, who prefers to read Aratta as Šuruppag although the en of Šuruppag is never an important figure in ED or later literature; the en of Aratta is.

[1461] See in general the survey by D. R. Frayne, *JCSMS* 4 (2009), 37–75.

[1462] E.g. lugal-aja$_2$-uĝu$_3$, °lugal-saĝ-kalam, and perhaps °lugal-kur-ra-a$_2$-bad.

[1463] E.g. lugal-ša$_3$-pa$_3$, reminiscent of later epithets mentioning a deity. Compare also lugal-^{d}Sud$_3$-ki-aĝ$_2$, and later lugal-^{d}Sud$_3$-de$_3$.

few names point to distinguishing attributes such as a staff or scepter, and a throne dais.[1464] And also, a number of names which might bear on the human lugal presuppose that his empowerment came from a superhuman source.[1465] The theophore lugal-names composed with the names of An and Enlil prove that he bore the stamp of approval by the most prominent gods in the Sumerian pantheon.

A number of lugal-names are reminiscent of later literary parallels linking them to specific gods. The Moon God Nanna may possibly already be associated with child birth.[1466] Ningirsu of Lagaš is most certainly the referent behind a name which has been found both at Girsu and Umma and which contains traces of ideas surfacing in literary contexts a few hundred years later.[1467]

Two large god lists have been found at Šuruppag and Abū Ṣalābīḫ, respectively.[1468] They may be taken to illustrate systematic theological traditions of their times and may therefore contain clues as to which deities were most often intended when a lugal-name is most likely to have a divine referent, when that referent was not identical with the tutelary deity of the city-state in which the name was found. The lists contain primarily Sumerian deities, but also a few Akkadian and more foreign gods. The Šuruppag list is the larger of the two, and may originally have contained around 560 individual entries;[1469] the Abū Ṣalābīḫ witnesses about 430.[1470] Within these lists, some groups are organized according to importance, others according to their geographical origin. Others are listed together based on some specific theological significance, and some groups are defined by having a sign in common. The most important male divinities that have surfaced in discussions earlier in this survey are listed along with their place in the lists:

Šuruppag: *SF* 1	Abū Ṣalābīḫ: *IAS* 82
1. An	1. [An]
2. Enlil	2. [Enlil]
4. Enki	4. ⸢Enki⸣
5. Nanna	5. ⸢Nanna⸣
6. Utu	8. Ningirsu

1464 See discussions of lugal-ĝidri-du$_{10}$ and °lugal-bara$_2$-du$_{10}$. The name lugal-bara$_2$-si was extant already in ED I-II Ur and the association continued in ED IIIa times.

1465 See, e.g. the discussions on lugal-a$_2$-maḫ$_{(2)}$, which is known already by ED I-II times; and lugal-a$_2$-tuku.

1466 See discussion of lugal-ab$_2$-ki-aĝ$_2$.

1467 See discussions of lugal-kur-dub$_2$ and lugal-me-gal-gal.

1468 *SF* 1 from Šuruppag and *IAS* 82–84, 86–90. *SF* 1 has been treated by M. Krebernik, *ZA* 76 (1986), 161–204 and also by P. Mander, *Pantheon*, 77–102 and passim. The latter is in the main dedicated to the study of the Abū Ṣalābīḫ text. Another article focusing on the Abū Ṣalābīḫ list is A. Alberti, *StEL* 2 (1985), 3–23.

1469 M. Krebernik, *ZA* 76 (1986), 163. P. Mander, *Pantheon*, 117 reckons with a total of around 600 lines.

1470 P. Mander, *Pantheon*, 117f.

46. Ninurta	9. Ašgi
130. Ningirsu	16. Su'en
210+ Ašgi	81. Ninurta? (NAM_2.IB)

It is uncertain when the lists were compiled; if they represent efforts at systematizing an unwieldy pantheon during a time of increased contacts between city-states; or if the cities in which they were found also were the original places of authorship. It is, however, likely that the general organization of the beginning lines reflect the most important gods in the Sumerian pantheon, as perceived there and then. In the Abū Ṣalābīḫ list, Utu must have featured in one of the many damaged lines, for instance in one of the five completely destroyed lines following the tutelary deity of Adab, Ašgi. The same may go for Ninurta, whose presence in l. 81 is mere conjecture. All the deities listed here are ones who figured in discussions above, in Chapter 3, and it is interesting to note the distribution of these deities and the internal differences in order and organization when comparing the lists. The end of the trajectory for some of these gods and their relation to nam-lugal will become a bit more clear in the overview of the next section, which is concerned with the following time period.

6.4 ED IIIb (c. 2550–2335 BCE)

The period ending with the advent of *Śarrukēn* of Akkade has yielded a wealth of written sources. Economic documentation and commemorative inscriptions complement each other, but the number of published literary works from the southern floodplain is small compared to the ED IIIa. This final phase of the Early Dynastic period is characterized by a complex patchwork of political formations involving a few key players.[1471] There are no references to a joint political undertaking similar to the group of cities mentioned in ED IIIa Šuruppag economic and literary sources. Instead, more loosely-knit alliances were formed, sometimes between dynasts,[1472] sometimes between royal houses on the one hand and political and religious officials on the other.[1473] Only around 2400 BCE are there tendencies toward a regional political construct, which would be pursued with even more political fervour in the following, Sargonic period.

[1471] T. Jacobsen, *ZA* 52 (1957), 124–129.

[1472] E.g. *CIRPL* Ent. 45–73, recounting the brotherhood treaty between Enmetena and Lugalkigubnišedudu. Compare also the discussion of possible dynastic contacts between Ur and Mari, above, p. 115 w. fn. 621.

[1473] Such as the $ensi_2$ of Nippur, the $ensi_2$ of Adab and the lu_2-maḫ of Uruk, appearing alongside the ereš-diĝir of Inana as holders of land in Zabala-texts dating to Lugalzagesi. The latter was, of course, himself a lu_2-maḫ of Nisaba. See discussion of M. Powell, *HUCA* 49 (1978), 26f.

Influential cities on the south-central floodplain can be divided into three general geo-political areas. The northernmost encompassed Adab, Nippur and Isin. It bordered in the southeast on the sphere of Uruk, to which Ur and Umma also belonged, and who succeeded each other as the politically dominant city of that area. In the southeast lay the Lagaš state with its political capital Girsu. The central one, encompassing Uruk, Ur, and Umma, is the least documented of the three.[1474] The demographic picture is one of a diminishing number of smaller settlements and a resulting concentration of the population in larger towns and cities.[1475] To some extent onomastic traditions may have followed communication lines. In some cases, lugal-names are exclusive to one of the groups mentioned above,[1476] in others, names and orthographic variants appear in neighbouring city-states which are normally not considered to be close-knit politically.[1477]

Notable changes in the royal ideology of the times is in part perhaps dependent on an increase in number and length of royal inscriptions. But central concepts which link a lugal or ensi$_2$ to divinities by selection, rearing or birth, become more and more commonplace in commemorative inscriptions. This corresponds also to a veritable explosion in number and distribution of lugal-names with reference to close relationships between deities and human rulers.[1478] The first clear examples of kyriophores referring to incumbent rulers and queens also begin to appear during the ED IIIb and express ideas similar to those formed with appellatives in place of the royal proper names.[1479]

Kiš had suffered a loss of importance after the ED IIIa. It became the target of attacks by southern city governors and lugals and there are no indications that they were able to mount successful retaliative strikes. Akšak, a city probably located in the southeast Diyālā area, briefly ascended to a leading position in the northern floodplain but suffered a bitter defeat at the hands of Eanatum of Lagaš, who went on also to strike out against Kiš and other cities in the region,[1480] without establishing lasting dominion over them.

[1474] See above, p. 36, for a brief overview.

[1475] R. McC. Adams, *Heartland of Cities*, 160f.

[1476] See, e.g. the distribution of lugal-gal-zu, lugal-inim-ĝal$_2$-la, lugal-la$_2$, lugal-lu-dadag and lugal-lu$_2$-dadag, for which the earliest witnesses come from Nippur, Adab, and Isin; and also lugal-numun-zi, found only at Adab and Isin.

[1477] See, e.g. lugal-eb$_2$-ta-ni-e$_3$, lugal-eden-ne$_2$, lugal-ḫe$_2$-ĝal$_2$-su$_3$, lugal-kur-dub$_2$, lugal-šud$_3$-du$_{10}$, during this period found only in texts from the Lagaš and Umma states. Compare also lugal-ig-gal, lugal-igi-tab and lugal-si-ĝar, all attested during ED IIIb, and later on also in Umma and Adab. The latter three names all deal with protection of the land or the home city.

[1478] E.g. lugal-^{d}Nanna-ra-tum$_2$, lugal-^{d}Nanše-mu-tu. See further section 3.1.6.2, p. 140–147.

[1479] See generally above, p. 54–56.

[1480] Eanatum's accounts of campaigns undertaken against more northerly situated states sometimes feature listings of states together, adding to the impression of limited military coalitions, especially *CIRPL* Ean. 2 vi 21–vii 2: Kiš^{ki} Akšak^{ki}, Ma-ri$_2^{!}$(URU×DIŠ), An-ta-sur-ra,

It was instead the Uruk region, with Ur and Umma as satellites, which was to establish itself as the uniter of the south under one dynasty. Adab and the Lagaš state may have been among the last to succumb to this aspiring regional state. Though the process is most likely to have been gradual, under the reign of Lugalzagesi a state of some significance with contacts to key institutions around Sumer had materialized.[1481] And although others before him had used the title lugal kalam-a(k), they had not been in control of as large a state as he.

In his only extant Nippur inscription, Lugalzagesi expresses his standing in relation to the highest deities of the Sumerian pantheon. After the dedication to Enlil, his prime titles and genealogy, he portrays himself as:[1482]

> igi zi bar-ra, An lugal kur-kur-ra, ensi$_2$-gal ^{d}En-lil$_2$, ĝeštu$_3$ šum$_2$-ma ^{d}En-ki, mu pa$_3$-da ^{d}Utu, sukkal-maḫ ^{d}Su'en, šagina ^{d}Utu
>
> one looked upon favourably by An, lord of the lands, chief tiller of Enlil, granted wisdom by Enki, chosen by Utu, minister of Su'en, general of Utu

The order of the gods corresponds roughly to that set out above, in section 2.3.3.2, and for a large part it coincides with the order set out by the ED IIIa god lists. Interestingly, Utu is mentioned twice; Nanna is given under his name Su'en which is natural for a lugal residing in another city than Ur itself. More important is the fact that three of the above quoted epithets make use of terminology couched in the economic and political structure of Sumerian society: chief tiller of Enlil, minister of Su'en and general of Utu. These positions would normally sort under the highest economic and political authority of a city-state, the ensi$_2$ or lugal. Thus, the gods involved are not only portrayed as Lugalzagesi's superiors, but they are described in a fashion that would befit divine lugals, and Lugalzagesi depicts himself as an overseer of the financial, (foreign-)political and military affairs of state. Here, G. J. Selz's suggestion to see Sumerian lordship as "bureaucratic-sacred," and A. Westenholz's characterization of the lugal as a ceremonial head of a league of cities with additional military functions, are brought to mind. It may also be noticed that out of the five different deities mentioned, four of them have correspondences in the city list and sealings of Uruk III date:[1483] Nanna/Su'en of Ur, Enlil of Nippur, Utu of Larsa and An of Uruk.

---

^{d}Nin-ĝir$_2$-su-ka-ta, tun$_3$-ŠE$_3$ be$_2$-se$_3$, 'Kiš, Akšak and Mari he *fended off* from the Antasurra (canal) of Ningirsu.'

[1481] Adab was surely part of Lugalzagesi's closest allies during the final phase of the ED IIIb. An example of this close contact is BIN 8 26, which names Meskigala as ensi$_2$ of Adab and Lugalzagesi simply as lugal. Before that point, *RTC* 19, from Girsu, dated to Lug. 3, indicates high-level formal contacts between the royal houses of Lagaš and Adab.

[1482] BE 1/2 87 o. i 13–24.

[1483] See above, p. 35f.

The political and religious ascendancy of these cities and their associated deities can thus perhaps be traced back to the dawn of the third millennium BCE. All of them also figure in one capacity or another in lugal-names.

Against this backdrop of an ever more united homeland being a political reality since a few generations before the end of the ED IIIb, names that celebrate the lugal as one who does good for his people and the land are in keeping with the political developments. Though they had to some extent been around since the ED IIIa, during the present period they are found distributed over a larger area.[1484] In this period the imagery of the shepherd is found, as a symbol of protection, both in royal inscriptions and in a kyriophore Girsu name, which speaks in favour of lugal-sipa as referring to the human ruler.[1485]A connection with names known since ED I-II which described the subjects in terms of animal young is possible.

As was mentioned previously, the literary production of ED IIIb is not nearly as large as that of ED IIIa. Some tendencies are, however, discernible. The inclusivistic pantheon of earlier days largely fell apart into its local components. But the highest deities were, with notable exceptions,[1486] officially revered across the land. This is especially visible in the onomasticon. The lugal-names are no exception, as no new deities are introduced in ED IIIb or Sargonic theophore lugal-names. Those that are mentioned were all present in corresponding names during the ED IIIa, or belong to the pantheon of the area from which the name is attested.[1487] On a regional scale the wealth of forms for names names involving An and Enlil increase. In many cases these names appear to express a link between the human ruler and the highest gods of the pantheon.[1488]

A steadily growing number of lugal-names present early forerunners of concepts which in later times were associated with specific deities. The Moon God is one, and the ideas that come to the fore bear for instance on his luminous qualities, as marking the passage of time, which might in some cases have a bearing on the time of birth around the time of the new moon.[1489] Also, his kind-hearted attitude toward mankind was probably also the subject of certain names.[1490] Such names are found as far north as Nippur. Another deity who figures as lugal in a Nippur and Adab name is Iškur, and the name is related to his functions as weather god in connection with

[1484] See, e.g. lugal-uĝ$_3$-ĝe$_{26}$-du$_{10}$, with variants, and lugal-KALAM.
[1485] See above, section 3.1.3.3, p. 111.
[1486] A case in point is the lack of a cult of Nanna or Su'en in the ED IIIb Lagaš state, although he was included among the deities of the oath-swearing in the Stele of the Vultures; this while neither Umma's nor Girsu's tutelary deities were mentioned. See above, p. 172.
[1487] Thus I take it for granted that Utu was behind many ED IIIa writings of lugal-UD.
[1488] See, e.g. lugal-An-ne$_2$, lugal-^{d}En-lil$_2$(-le), and, probably, lugal-AN-da(-nu-ḫuĝ-ĝa$_2$).
[1489] E.g. lugal-iti-da, and variants.
[1490] See discussion of lugal-ša$_3$-su$_3$ and lugal-lu$_2$-ti-ti.

crops.[1491] The underlying meaning may also be related to a certain time of the year, when the barley fields were nearing harvest time. Utu is as could be expected also featured in lugal-names; though the writing of his name without the divine determinative for large parts of the third millennium can sometimes be problematic. He is furthermore difficult to identify as a referent of lugal in the onomasticon, though with all likelihood, some lugal-names refer to him; either in his capacity as god of justice, or as sharing in traits of his father Nanna/Su'en.[1492]

Another tendency is the steady growth in popularity of certain names relating to the personal care invested in the individual by a lugal, which in these names most likely stands for one or more divinities.[1493]

In the far north, Ebla and Mari both were regional players whose influence was felt way beyond their closest surroundings. Records from Ebla speak of continuous contacts between the two, of an academic[1494] as well as a confrontational kind.[1495] Because of contacts of the former kind Ebla has yielded the largest number of literary and lexical texts from any ED IIIb site, northern or southern. With all certainty, these texts were in part transmitted to Ebla via scholars from Mari. Some compositions have more or less exact correspondences in texts of different genres known from southern ED IIIa sites. These include a body of incantations with predecessors from Šuruppag,[1496] a hymnic composition centered on Utu/Śamaś, and other scholastic texts also known from Abū Ṣalābīḫ.[1497] The Ebla literary trove is deeply indebted to the academic fervour of the ED IIIa. It is quite possible that the universalist agenda which characterized the ED IIIa literary output in Sumer lingered on for a longer period of time in the far northwest.

At Ebla, a text was found in three exemplars, in both normal orthography and in a phonetic rendering, which some scholars claimed was a hymn.[1498] It

1491 See lugal-še-gu-na.

1492 See, e.g. the discussions of the names lugal-di-de$_3$, lugal-^{d}I$_7$-si; lugal-ni$_3$-lu-lu, lugal-ni$_3$-lu-lu-a and ^{d}Utu-ni$_3$-lu-lu-a; and the literature cited in connection with Utu, p. 69f. If more pre–OB texts were found at Larsa, chances are that Utu could be identified as lugal in more, at present anonymous, lugal-names.

1493 See, e.g. lugal-ḫa-ma-ti, lugal-lu$_2$-ti-ti, lugal-ma-de$_6$, and lugal-mu-da-kuš$_2$, with variants.

1494 A well-known case is made up by the singers from Mari, who surface in a number of Ebla economic texts. A few of these have names composed with lugal, sometimes rendered phonetically as nu-gal. See, e.g. P. Steinkeller, *Fs Hallo*, 236–245; M. Krebernik, *Fs Röllig*, 190 w. fn. 13.

1495 A detailed study of Ebla and Mari military activities can be found in the study of A. Archi & M. G. Biga, *JCS* 55 (2003), 1–44.

1496 See M. Krebernik, *BFE*.

1497 For references to treatments of the Utu/Śamaś composition, see above, p. 70 fn. 353. In addition to this, a list of names and professions, and one enumerating geographical names, corresponding to those treated by R. D. Biggs, OIP 99, 62–78, were also found at Ebla.

1498 G. Pettinato, *OrAnt* 19 (1980), 59–67; *BA* 43 (1980), 208–213; followed by R. D. Biggs, *LdE*, 127f. P. Mander, *La parola creatrice in India e nel Medio Oriente*, 13–34, was sceptical

indeed begins with a hymnic introduction, but this introduction is followed by a list of 8 lugal-names, as observed by D. O. Edzard,[1499] who deemed it a school exercise. All but two of the names have parallels in texts from the south.[1500]

6.5 ES-MS (c. 2330–2240 BCE)

The ascent to power of the Sargonic dynasty in many ways transformed the face of royal ideology in Mesopotamia. Many changes were slowly effectuated and a full grasp of the circumstances during the first half of the Sargonic period is at present beyond reach. Nippur, Adab and Umma provide the largest number of sources for the earliest phase of this period.

The background of the dynasty is never alluded to. Later traditions about *Śarrukēn* as a foundling or a cupbearer in the service of a so far unattested king of Kiš[1501] may be as fanciful as the OB assertion that he founded the so far uncharted city of Akkade.[1502]

Important sources for *Śarrukēn*'s rise to power are in the shape of later copies of original inscriptions, most of them found at Nippur,[1503] and that city retained a key ideological position throughout the Sargonic period. In the beginning of his rule over a united north and south, *Śarrukēn* appears to have borrowed elements from late ED royal ideology. In his epithets the divinities ʿAštar, An and Enlil were given pride of place.[1504] Utu/Śamaś figures constantly in curse formulae of his and of his successors.[1505] He furthermore persisted in ED III royal practice, having nidba-offerings presented to the divine dining table, something that no doubt found its way into the name-

to the designation of the text as a hymn, but still saw it as a coherent composition created to express fundamental existential concepts current in the area at the time of authoring.

1499 ARET 5, 43–45, nos. 23–25; so also M. Krebernik, *Fs Röllig*, 186–191,

1500 The name lugal-nam-nir looks like an abbreviation of the following name, lugal-nam-nir-šum$_2$, known to have been borne by a lugal of Kiš. The name lugal-ḪI-zi, with variant nu-gal-ḪI-zi, might with some reservation be linked to southern lugal-šer$_7$-zi. For another solution, see M. Krebernik, *Fs Röllig*, 190 w. fn. 15.

1501 The texts belonging to the later Babylonian literary traditions in the Akkadian language surrounding *Śarrukēn* and his grandson *Narām*-Su'en have been collected and treated by J. Goodnick Westenholz, MesCiv 7.

1502 See variants on this theme in the Sumerian King List, T. Jacobsen, AS 11, 111. An overview of the suggested locations for the city can be found in A. Westenholz, *Annäherungen* 3, 31–34.

1503 See S. Franke, *Königsinschriften*, 86–89, for an evaluation of the sources.

1504 See S. Franke, *Königsinschriften*, 96–98, sub "Die religiösen Titel"; and A. Westenholz, *Annäherungen* 3, 37f.

1505 At least in all cases where the curse section is complete, Śamaś or Utu figures. See, briefly, G. Cunningham, StPohl SM 17, 61–63. For a brief overview of the other deities appearing alongside Śamaś, see E. Markina, *Fs. Westenholz*, 211f. w. fn. 40.

giving of Sargonic Nippur as lugal-nidba$_2$-e.[1506] If his policies managed to sway a number of Sumerians, the continuity of naming practice compared to the previous period may bear witness to this.

But not everyone was at peace with the new king. *Śarrukēn* and his successors had to stave off repeated rebellions in the south while at the same time they managed to retain a measure of control over areas east of the floodplain. *Śarrukēn* also mentioned the instating of citizens of Akkade to the positions of ensi$_2$ in cities across the floodplain, for which only scraps of evidence exist so far.[1507]

The Sargonic period is regretfully a period marked by a lack of literary sources, in either Akkadian or Sumerian.[1508] A large amount of seal cylinders illustrate aspects of Akkadian mythology; but only in a few cases are the gods and goddesses depicted identifiable.[1509] A particularly popular divinity was Śamaś, who features passing between the doors of heaven, ascending over a mountainrange, or enthroned.[1510] There is also a wealth of theophore Akkadian personal names.[1511] A. Westenholz has argued that Akkadian names during the Early Dynastic period, before the accession of *Śarrukēn*, were largely ditheistic; a great majority of theophore names contained the theonyms ʾIl(um) and ʿAštar.[1512] The picture changes somewhat during the Early Sargonic period when more Akkadian names are attested which feature other named gods and goddesses, even though ʾIl(um) and ʿAštar remain in common use. Apart from these, Su'en was especially popular in the north.[1513]

[1506] Compare also, perhaps, the CS Umma name lugal-kadra.

[1507] A. Westenholz, *Annäherungen* 3, 39 w. fn. 118. A problem in identifying citizens of Akkade is brought home when considering that among the 49 citizens of Akkade mentioned in MO, a handful carry Sumerian names, including UruKAgina, former ensi$_2$ of Lagaš.

[1508] A. Westenholz, *Annäherungen* 3, 75 w. fnn. 352–353, has a summary of the sources.

[1509] R. M. Boehmer, *EGA*, features depictions of close to 700 seals of Sargonic date, and descriptions of several hundred more.

[1510] E.g. *EGA*, figs. 392–438, and 440–463.

[1511] Studied in detail by J. J. M. Roberts, *ESP*.

[1512] ARES 1, 99–117, especially p. 103; *Annäherungen* 3, 78–80; see also ibid. *OrNS* 45 (1976), 215f. The picture of the onomastic material in the Ḫabur-area in northern Syria is similar to the situation in southern Mesopotamia before the advent of *Śarrukēn*. As was shown by A. Catagnoti, Subartu 4/2, 41–66, especially p. 61f., it lacked any explicit references to divinities whatsoever. The Ḫabur material is quite distinct in this respect from the Ebla, Mari and southern traditions.

[1513] See A. Westenholz, *Annäherungen* 3, 78 fn. 371. Out of the 34 theophore names in the MO containing specific deities other than ʾIlum and ʿAštar, nine names, or rougly 25%, are composed with Su'en; or close to 12% of the total of theophores in that stele.

6.6 MS-CS (c. 2280–2200 BCE)

The Middle to Classic Sargonic period encompasses roughly the reigns of *Maniśtūśu*,[1514] *Narām*-Su'en and his successor *Śarkaliśarrē*. Not much is known about the reign of *Maniśtūśu*. That he waged war on the southern and southeastern frontiers of the kingdom is clear from contemporary and Old Babylonian copies of his inscriptions.[1515] The inscribed obelisk associated with him is an invaluable source for ES names, first and foremost from cities on the northern end of the floodplain.[1516]

During the time of his son and successor, *Narām*-Su'en, clearly the most notable development to occur is the functional apotheosis of the living ruler. While this may have had less of an impact in *Narām*-Su'en's own time, the consequences for later periods were considerable. He managed to stave off a massive and coordinated attack on the Akkadian heartland. The king had proven that the gods were with him, vanquishing a coalition which had seemed to engage all four corners of the world with the intent to finish off Akkadian rule once and for all. Hence the citizens of Akkade must have reckoned that the fortunes of such a fortuitous king could be transferred also to his capital should *Narām*-Su'en be made a (not *the*) protective god of Akkade. But for the rest of his kingdom, the practical consequences of his deification are everything but clear. No clear-cut correspondence between *śarrum*-names and the deification of the living ruler can be demonstrated. Names such as *śar-ru-i*$_3$*-li*$_2$ and *śar-ru*-gi-*i*$_3$*-li*$_2$, are already attested in *Maniśtūśu*'s time, as the names of citizens of Akkade.[1517]

The city governors were already tied to the ruler by personal oaths of allegiance and they were probably expected to pay visits to Akkade during their terms of office.[1518] This type of loyalty may also have been borne out in a few personal names.[1519]

Narām-Su'en took it upon himself to restore the temple facilities of Enlil in Nippur, something which would have to be finished by his son and successor *Śarkaliśarrē*, in the most faithful manner; a scheme which may have been repeated also for other building projects begun by *Narām*-Su'en.[1520] Such projects bear witness to prolonged interludes when Sumer

---

[1514] For an overview of later traditions surrounding *Maniśtūśu*, see J. Goodnick Westenholz, *Fs Sigrist*, 254.

[1515] See A. Westenholz, *Annäherungen* 3, 44–46.

[1516] Treated in detail by I. J. Gelb et al., OIP 104 40.

[1517] E.g. MO A xii 8, xv 25, and passim. Compare also the discussion, above, p. 199f.

[1518] As illustrated by seal inscriptions, e.g. those of Lugalušumgal of Girsu, *RTC* 165 (time of *Narām*-Su'en), and 162 (time of *Śarkaliśarrē*). The picture of northern cities is a bit different, as A. Westenholz shows, *Annäherungen* 3, 63 w. fn. 279, in that the ensi$_2$'s were sometimes blood relations of the king.

[1519] See discussions of *ibni-śarrum*, *śarriś-takal*; and further, p. 239.

[1520] See in general A. Westenholz, OSP 2, 27–29; ibid., *Fs Oelsner*, 554.

and Akkade must have enjoyed peace. The great rebellion in which the four corners of the world rebelled against the former had already been quelled.

No comprehensive god list dating to the Sargonic period is known.[1521] What can be said about the religion of the times must mainly be drawn from economic sources and monumental inscriptions, from personal names and cylinder seals. A few lugal-names which make their first appearances during this time relate to traditions surrounding the god Ningirsu.[1522] It is at present not possible to say whether they were new inventions or whether their inclusion in the onomasticon represents a popularization of older ideas.

In the Akkadian onomasticon after the Early Sargonic period, a few deities are mentioned more often than others. ʾIlum, ʿAštar and Su'en remain popular, and joining them are among others Ea and Śamaś. Adad and Nergal gain in popularity with time. Other deities are, of course, attested, but less consistently, and the divergences due to local flavours in names appear to be considerable.[1523]

6.7 The names and their referents

It has proved difficult to assign referents to the lugal- and *śarrum*-names, but more so with the former. Thanks to evidence provided by the contemporary and later textual record, some names are more likely to be attributable to the one referent or the other. The human king is more likely to be the subject of names dealing with authority such as lugal-a_2-$šum_2$-ma, lugal-nam-nir-$šum_2$; and names referring to the country and its inhabitants such as lugal-$bara_2$-kalam and lugal-$uĝ_3$-$ĝe_{26}$-du_{10}. Such names are less often formed with the appellative nin, never with en, and during this period there are no direct Akkadian correspondences, although pronominal elements might sometimes be suspected to conceal a collective like the people.[1524] Local ideological traits concerning the person of the human ruler surface in the names lugal-^{d}Nanna-ra-tum_2 and lugal-^{d}Nanše-mu-tu, from ED IIIb Ur and Girsu respectively. Parallels formed with en The lugal as chosen by the gods is the subject behind lugal-$ša_3$-pa_3-da, and his attentiveness to the will of the gods comes to the fore in lugal-inim-ma-se_3-ga. Names focusing on strength, authority, selection and the issuing of orders and commands are intimately associated with the lugal, and are rarely paralleled by formations with en.

[1521] But such lists ought to have existed. See for instance the fragment, A. Westenholz, *AfO* 25 (1974–77), 104, no. 38, AOAT 3/1 75 (MS-CS Nagar).

[1522] E.g. the name lugal-igi-sa_6, a more benign name related to lugal-igi-ḫuš, found already in ED IIIb Girsu; and lugal-$šar_2$-ur_3-e. All these names probably refer to aspects of divine protection.

[1523] See discussion of A. Westenholz, *Annäherungen* 3, 78–84.

[1524] See the name *śar-ru-al-śi-in*, above, p. 197f. w. fnn. 1274–1275, for further examples.

A deity is likely to be the referent behind Umma$_2$^{ki}-lugal-ĝu$_{10}$, with the name of the city or city-state standing in metonymically for a male god, most likely Šara. The Moon God Nanna or Su'en is referred to in lugal-iti-da, the second most common lugal-name during the time-period in question. Ningirsu and his weapon Šarur figure in the name lugal-šar$_2$-ur$_3$-e. He and Ninurta are likely candidates for lugal in lugal-apin-ne$_2$ and lugal-$^{(ĝiš)}$apin-du$_{10}$. Iškur of Karkar figures in the name lugal-še-gu-na.

For *śarrum*-names, certain formations in themselves provide the names of deities associated with qualities of the *śarrum*, Adad, Ea, ʾIlum and Su'en. A female counterpart is made up by the goddess Mama. In a phrase name, the human *śarrum* is furthermore likened to Śamaś.

The king is the likely referent of names like *śar-ru-i$_3$-li$_2$* and *tu-ta$_2$*-lugal-*li-bi-iś*, and perhaps also *śar-ka$_3$-li$_2$-śar-re$_2$*. The *śarrum* is most often associated with positive attributes, and with protective aspects, although it cannot always be stated with certainty whether the referent of such names is either human or divine.

Certain names could be witnesses to an early occurrence of the word *šarrum* or *šerrum* to denote 'child,' e.g. *śar-ri$_2$*, *śar-ru-na* and *śar-ru-ni*, all known exclusively from cities to the northwest of the floodplain. With some hesitation, the royal name *śar-ka$_3$-li$_2$*-lugal-*re$_2$* might also be suggested to belong to these few names on the basis of its close association with the name of a sibling *bi-in-ka$_3$-li$_2$*-lugal-*re$_2$*. The latter is commonly thought of as containing the word *bīnum* or *bin*(*n*)*um*, a poetic term for '(male) offspring.' The names in this latter group could definitely bear closer scrutiny, but comparative evidence will be hard to come by.

7. Concluding discussions

7.1 Conclusions

Clear relationships exist between lugal-names and the development of political leadership on the one hand, and concepts of a religious nature on the other. Interrelationships between political and religious functions of human rulers no doubt strengthened the associations which surface in the onomastic traditions from the investigated periods. For *śarrum*-names the picture is less clear, although some names clearly demonstrate connections between cultural and political ideological layers similar to that found in Sumerian lugal-names. It is tempting to assume that this development in Akkadian name-giving was influenced by Sumerian ideas. But at the same time the Akkadian witnesses are so integrated in a general development of the Semitic Mesopotamian onomasticon that it may well in part have been a result of internal changes within the system itself, or even a deliberate attempt on the part of the upper classes to create new frames of reference in which they themselves partook, and which in the long run could serve real political needs for cultural and social cohesion.

Where lugal-names are concerned, previous studies by D. O. Edzard, A. Westenholz, G. J. Selz and others, all can be proven right to a large extent. The human ruler and the chief deities of influential cities in the areas in which certain names appear to have originated, figure consistently in the material. This study also shows that deities venerated more widely across the land, or in a neighbouring city-state, can be identified in the material. The lugal-names are an integral part of the Sumerian onomastic tradition, and offer insight both into the conceptions of early Mesopotamian kingship as well as theological matters, and attest to the early development of characteristic traits of human and divine lugals identifiable in contemporary and later source materials. And when viewed as a group, lugal-names also help to shed light on name-giving practices of early Mesopotamia.

Names were conceived and presented to the bearer in settings where the names themselves were not considered out of place. Given parallels from later periods, some 3rd millennium names formed with the appellative lugal give the impression that names could be situational, that names could be chosen depending on the time of birth or of name-giving. Some sort of simple ceremonial befitting the name-giving event might be suggested. As there are no indications that naming involved anything but family members or relatives, a setting suitable for name-giving could be created and supervised by laypersons in the comfort of their own homes or in a place to which the family had access.

The deities that appear as lugal in the onomastic material include Nanna/Su'en and Ninurta/Ningirsu. For the former there are contemporary literary correspondences where he is also termed, simply, lugal. Nanna/Su'en's functions as luminary, and his association with cultural phenomena derived from the light he emitted, were no doubt in part reasons for the widespread popularity of such names. The constant "rebirth" of the moon, and his association with cattle, were no doubt relevant for his importance, at least in later times, as a god called upon for assistance at childbirth. As was the case with names mentioning the "rebirth" of the Moon God, those featuring the word for "festival" were also most clearly associated with lugal, and largely lacked parallels composed with other appellatives. It is quite thinkable that dozens of other names, not only such formed with the royal appellatives, also referred to specific points in local calendars or in the natural cycle – given Mesopotamian deities and their close connections with cultural and natural phenomena – and further research on this topic might well provide more insight into such matters.

Ninurta and Ningirsu were both associated with agriculture, which formed the economical backbone of Sumer. The agricultural cycle was important for the calendar, and agricultural chores of the season of birth might be commemorated in certain names. At the same time, these two deities were gods of combat. Names associated with these two in this latter capacity could be found in neighbouring towns and areas also. Later literary works focusing on Ningirsu's warlike aspects, are, for instance, reflected in personal names from the Lagaš state as well as from neighbouring Umma.

The ideas that surface in lugal-names are variegated and show that the naming traditions were deeply embedded in a society where concepts, phrases and idioms circulated in a continuous flow. Certain phrases were general in scope and could be attributed to several subjects; others were no doubt coined as describing a specific figure; in some cases divinities, in others, the human king. To a certain extent it is possible to trace long-term trends of adaptation to fit with developments on the political and the religious scene during the course of the 3rd millennium BCE. For instance, as time progresses, more focus is put on the lugal in relation to the country.

The wording of Sumerian names was, to a much higher extent than Akkadian names, tuned to the world outside of family and filiation. Although lugal-names linking an individual to the lugal in relation to dominion, protection and care, thus indicating a closeness or attachment between lugal and subject, presented quite popular patterns. Some common Sumerian name-types which refer to a name-bearer (ur-lugal, lu_2-lugal) are often genitival in Sumerian, whereas the corresponding constructions are more rarely attested in early 3rd millennium Akkadian names in general, and among Sargonic *śarrum*-names they appear to be completely absent. This strengthens the impression that the efficacy of Sumerian names was thought to lie in their preoccupation with a superhuman reality, while Akkadian ones during this period more often dealt with the arrival of the child into the world, into a social context.

The appellative lugal in the clear majority of cases formally occupies the position at the head of phrases; either serving as the subject or as the prepositioned object, pushed to the fore by topicalizing tendencies. This trait is shared also by names containing other appellatives, and is common in masculine as well as feminine names, though the choice of appellative to some extent depended on the gender of the name-bearer. Before the Ur III period female bearers of lugal-names are exceedingly rare, and the same holds true for *śarrum*-names. This should not be taken to imply that bearers of lugal- or *śarrum*-names were the referents of the appellative, but rather that some gender-sensitive principle applied to these nouns, to a higher extent than, for instance, en-, nin-, and *baʿlum*-names of similar semantic contents.

As identifiers, it can be seen that most names were borne only by one or a few bearers at any given time and place. So lugal-names, although popular, would in most cases have served well to designate individual members of local society. However, sometimes surprisingly many bearers of the same name are attested at about the same time, sometimes in the same archive. There are examples of about a dozen persons carrying the same name, which ought to have been roughly contemporary with each other. Even so, only rarely do more than two namesakes appear on the same tablet. Though one may have to reckon with the possibility of abbreviations which have produced seemingly identical names from originally distinct name patterns, a more likely explanation is that such names resulted from local naming fashions, and that perhaps some other method of disambiguation was involved which does not always appear in documents, or at least, one which does not leap out and present itself to a modern observer.

It has been assumed that part of the function of a name is to provide a good fate for a child. This is not contradicted by those lugal-names which lend themselves to an interpretation. The many references to warlike acts, weapons, or potentially harmful implements were not directed at the world of the name-giver or -bearer, but at potential threats from outside. Battles could be pictured as ongoing on a superhuman level, and actualized by the continuous use of the name, both in conversation and in administration. Also, some name formulae were borrowed from the cultic sphere; and their continuous use thereby regularly confirmed and re-actualized the associations which the name made manifest. This was certainly a factor beyond the control of name-bearers and name-givers, but may actually have served to strengthen the belief in names as potent statements in themselves. The nature of the contents of names as non–finite is seen by the many examples of participial, two-participant constructions, by clear instances of imperfective forms, including modal constructions, and by nominal predicate names where predication expresses a state. Genitive construct names imply a state of continous subordination to a higher authority and conform with the non–finite forms.

The high extent of anonymity for the referent behind the appellative is not a characteristic exclusive to lugal-names, but is common to Sumerian name-giving generally. It is difficult to see appellatives in names which are obvious references to divinities as a substitute for a theonym. There were no discernible taboos surrounding the use of theonyms in other contexts; neither in personal names, nor in the names of objects, nor in place names. Rather, from at least the ED IIIa period onwards, it may be productive to see lugal as epitomizing a system of male sovereignty – human or divine – where actions of any "lugal" could be seen to benefit the bearer in the future, although names were with all likelihood originally coined with a specific referent in mind. One of the positive aspects of nam-lugal lay in the fact that regardless of which person or dynasty that held power at the moment, there were always several layers of heavenly authority above, first on a local scale, then on a regional, and thirdly on a cosmic scale. All these different levels of the divine world were involved in granting legitimacy to whole dynasties and to single rulers. The auspicious results of a pious or reverent reference to a lugal was not lost because of a shift in worldly power, because the *intent* remained the same, as did, perhaps, the belief in the continuity of nam-lugal even through times of hardship. The alternative was potential chaos.

Names appear to confirm royal self-representations in that they acknowledge the lugal and his connections with the divine world and with significant earthly locations. His position in relation to the gods is sometimes pictured in terms of titles of offices, both in names and in monumental inscriptions. Divine selection and acceptance appears to be ubiquitously acknowledged throughout Sumer, and beyond.

It follows from this survey that lugal-names are likely to have referred to deities more often, or at least as often as they could have had a human referent. It has been made clear that a good deal of the names either have clear parallels in names with explicitly written theonyms, or that the contents of the names may be elucidated by direct correspondences in text passages which concern a deity. But some names are clear markers of a belief in the lugal as involved in taking care of central cultural concerns, keeping order and balance in the world. It is also evident that ideas revolving around certain specific actors which merited the use of the epithet lugal about the Moon God, Ningirsu, Ninurta, and other characters, were well-known; some of these names were found over large areas, some were long-lived but mostly of local significance, others were known and used in a few city-states.

From this survey, it is possible to state a few, very general points, on the importance of the literal meaning of names. It was said at the beginning of the study, that the literal meaning was at all times subordinate to symbolic associations invoked by the name. If the symbolic connection, with time, would come to be expressed more clearly by means of another term or phrase, then a previously popular name type would go out of fashion and others would take its place, regardless of whether or not these new types expressed precisely the same sentiments as the superseded name. It is clear that naming fashions changed over time, and that might in itself be taken to imply that both literal and symbolic contents of names were reinterpreted to fit with changes in the mindset of the people. In short, names that were not both factual and actual would not remain in use for long in the human onomasticon.

The popularity of lugal-names compared to names composed with other appellatives is a question worthy of further inquiry. It was suggested that the drop in relative figures of names composed with en could be a consequence of an increasing identification of that appellative with the office of en.

The basis for the Ur III kings on which to mould their royal ideal was a fruitful one. Many passages in royal hymns of that era echo distant ideas of characteristics and functions for which the best parallels are made up of onomastic evidence. The hymns testify to a living tradition of symbolic verbal associations between an appellative, the institution it designated, and imagery of authority. Whereas lugal-names are in many respects brief and idiomatic witnesses to such beliefs, the composers of hymns could embellish upon these age-old associations and breathe new life into them by linking them to a living human being who simultaneously partook in divine essence, and who therefore was in a position to fulfill his royal duties more perfectly than had ever been done before.

If another investigation was to be undertaken, using the same source materials but with another method for organizing the material, say, along lines of linguistic structure, but with the same aims, I believe the results would in the main remain the same, since so much of the understanding of names is based on comparisons with literary, monumental, and material sources. Naming patterns were under the influence of a number of factors, geopolitical and cultural-religious factors were prominent among these.

All said and done, many question marks remain, and new questions have been posed. An investigation into Sumerian names of any type is bound to reveal formal patterns, and formulae favoured for inclusion in names. Identifying traits of specific referents and understanding underlying concepts depend on the existence and wealth of comparative materials, mainly from non–onomastic sources. Just because aja_2, ama, en, lugal, mes, nin and šul are common components in the early Sumerian onomasticon, it does not automatically follow that such names are clear as to the link between subject matter and referent, or that establishing identities of referents is a straightforward affair. In the case of lugal, recourse consists of archival and historical inscriptional material as well as literature. For the other appellatives, literature alone basically offers parallel material, and such material in the main does not revolve around human actors.

7.2 Avenues for future research

Most importantly, a Sumerian *Namenbuch* is a badly needed, and a prerequisite for future comprehensive treatment of early Mesopotamian onomastics. The form, electronic or printed, is subordinate to the practical use such a collection of names would have. The names should not only be listed alphabetically, but component parts should be listed separately in order to obtain a better overview over parallels. It is not necessary – to begin with – for such a *Namenbuch* to be a critical edition complete with analyses and translations. The usual source-critical information should be appended to each entry, along with an indication as to whether the name was culled from transliterations, hand copies, black and white or full colour photograph, or from physical inspection. Publication of texts in transliteration only should not be deemed fit for full inclusion before confirmation by physical inspection or publication in any of the aforementioned acceptable formats. Such a project is obviously enormously time-consuming, but the knowledge that stands to be gained is equally immense.

A special focus on female personal names and how they set themselves apart from male personal names would be a fruitful area for future studies which could either be envisaged as a specific result of a more complete *Namenbuch* project, or as an independent and self-contained study.

The kyriophore names of the 3rd millennium, Sumerian and Akkadian, could bear closer inspection. Because of the abundance of administrative sources and sealed tablets, especially from the Ur III period, an investigation taking into consideration the distribution of such names in the different layers of society could yield interesting results. Connections between the kyriophore names on the one hand, and the corpora of monumental inscriptions and royal hymns from this and the following period on the other, could definitely bear scrutiny.

Another potentially rewarding project would be closer inspection of the occurrences of anticipatory genitive constructions in onomastic compared with other contexts. Their distribution over time and space would certainly result in a better understanding of Sumerian genitive syntax which would complement previous studies on the subject.

Bibliography

Adams, R. McC., *Heartland of Cities*, Chicago & London 1981

Alberti, A., "A Reconstruction of the Abū Salābīkh God-List", *StEL* 2 (1985), 3–23

Alberti, A. & F. Pomponio, *Pre-Sargonic and Sargonic Texts from Ur edited in UET 2, Supplement*. StPohl SM 13, Rome 1986

Ali, F. A., "New Text of Enannatum I", *Sumer* 29 (1973), 27–30

Alster, B., *The Instructions of Suruppak*. Mesopotamia 2, Copenhagen 1974

—— *Studies in Sumerian Proverbs*. Mesopotamia 3, Copenhagen 1975

—— "EN.METE.NA: "His Own Lord", *JCS* 26 (1974), 178–180

Alster, B. & H. Vanstiphout, "Lahar and Ashnan: Presentation and Analysis of a Sumerian Disputation", *ASJ* 9 (1987), 1–43

Alt, A., "Menschen ohne Namen", *ArOr* 18 (1950), 9–24

Andrae, W., "Aus den Berichten aus Assur", *MDOG* 48 (1912), 19–28

Archi, A., "La "Lista dei nomi e professioni" ad Ebla", *StEb* 4 (1981), 177–204

—— "The "Names and Professions List": More Fragments from Ebla", *RA* 78 (1984), 171–174

—— "The Personal Names in the Individual Cities", in P. Fronzaroli (ed.), *Studies on the Language of Ebla*. QuadSem 13, Florence 1984, 225–251

—— "Les rapports politiques et économiques entre Ebla et Mari", *MARI* 4 (1985), 63–83

—— *Testi amministrativi: Assegnazioni di tessuti (archivio L.2769)*. ARET 1, Rome 1985

—— "The Archives of Ebla", in K. Veenhof (ed.), *Cuneiform Archives and Libraries*. CRRA 30. PIHANS 57, Leiden 1986, 72–86

—— "More on Ebla and Kish", in C. H. Gordon, G. A. Rendsburg and N. H. Winter (eds.) *Eblaitica* 1, Winona Lake, IN, 1987, 125–140

—— *Testi amministrativi: Registrazioni di metalli e tessuti*. ARET 7, Rome 1988

—— "The God Ḫay(y)a (Ea / Enki) at Ebla", in S. C. Melville & . L. Slotsky, (eds.), *Opening the Tablet Box: Near Eastern Studies in Honor of Benjamin R. Foster*. Culture and History of the Ancient Near East 42, Leiden 2010, 15–36

Archi, A. & M. G. Biga, *Testi amministrativi di vario contenuto (archivio L.2769)*. ARET 3, Rome 1982

—— "A Victory over Mari and the Fall of Ebla", *JCS* 55 (2003), 1–44

Archi, A, F. Pomponio & M. Stol, *Testi cuneiformi di vario contenuto*. Catalogo del Museo Egizio di Torino, serie seconda – collezioni, vol. 9, Turin 1999

Asher-Greve, J. M., "The Gaze of Goddesses", *NIN* 4 (2003), 1–59

Astour, M. C., "Toponymy of Ebla and Ethnohistory of Northern Syria: A Preliminary Survey", *JAOS* 108 (1988), 545–555

—— "The Toponyms of Ebla. Review of A. Archi et al., *I Nomi di luogo dei testi di Ebla*", *JAOS* 117 (1997), 332–338

Bahrani, Z., "The Babylonian Visual Image", in G. Leick (ed.), *The Babylonian World*, New York, NY, & London 2007, 155–170

Balke, T. E., "About Sumerian Personal Names", *Onoma* 32 (1994), 71–82

Banks, E. J., "The Oldest Statue in the World", *AJSL* 21/1 (1914), 57–59

Barjamovic, G. & M. T. Larsen, "An Old Assyrian Incantation against the Evil Eye", *AoF* 35 (2008), 144–155

Barton, G. A., *Haverford Library Collection of Cuneiform Tablets, or Documents from the Temple Archives of Tello*, 3 vols., Philadelphia, PA, London 1905–1914

—— *Sumerian Business and Administrative Documents from the Earliest Times to the Dynasty of Agade*. University of Pennsylvania. PBS 9, Philadelphia, PA, 1915

Bauer, J., "Review of H. Limet, *L'Anthroponymie sumérienne dans les documents de la 3e dynastie d'Ur*", *WO* 6 (1970–71), 108–111

—— *Altsumerische Wirtschaftstexte aus Lagasch*. StPohl 9, Rome 1972

—— *Altorientalische Notizen*, Würzburg 1975–1992

—— "Altsumerische Beiträge (7–9)", *WO* 9 (1977–78), 1–9

—— "Ortsnamen in den frühen Texten aus Ur", *WO* 18 (1987), 5–6

—— "ŠIM = su_x", *ZA* 79 (1989), 8–9

—— "Zu NIR = $šer_7$", *ASJ* 12 (1990), 353–355

—— "Review of I. J. Gelb et al., OIP 104", *WO* 24 (1993), 161–165

—— "Zwei frühdynastische Verwaltungsurkunden aus Girsu", in C. Römer (ed.), *Festschrift für Hans Hirsch zum 65. Geburtstag gewidmet von seinen Freunden, Kollegen und Schülern. Wiener Zeitschrift für die Kunde des Morgenlandes* 86 (1996), 41–46

—— "Zum Gebrauch des Ablativs im Sumerischen", *NABU* 2005/31

Bauer, J., R. K. Englund & M. Krebernik, *Mesopotamien: Späturuk-Zeit und Frühdynastische Zeit. Annäherungen* 1. OBO 160/1, Freiburg & Göttingen 1998

Bayliss, M., "The Cult of Dead Kin in Assyria and Babylonia", *Iraq* 35 (1973), 115–125

Becker, A., "Neusumerische Renaissance? Wissenschaftsgeschichtliche Untersuchungen zur Philologie und Archäologie", *BagM* 16 (1985), 229–316

Behrens, H. & H. Steible, *Glossar zu den altsumerischen Bau- und Weihinschriften*. FAOS 6, Wiesbaden 1983

Biga, M. G., "A Sargonic Foundation Cone", in Y. Sefati, P. Artzi, C. Cohen, B. L. Eichler & V. A. Hurowitz (eds.), *An Experienced Scribe Who Neglects Nothing: Ancient Near Eastern Studies in Honor of Jacob Klein*, Bethesda, MD, 2005, 29–38

Biga, M. G., & L. Milano, *Testi amministrativi: Assegnazioni di tessuti (Archivio L. 2769)*. ARET 4, Rome 1984

Biggs, R. D., "Semitic Names in the Fara-Period", *OrNS* 36 (1977), 55-66

—— "An Archaic Sumerian Version of the Kesh Temple Hymn from Tell Abū Ṣalābīkh", *ZA* 61 (1971), 193–207

—— *Inscriptions from Tell Abū Ṣalābīkh*, with a chapter on the archaeological findings by D. P. Hansen. OIP 99, Chicago, IL, 1974

——*Inscriptions from Al-Hiba-Lagash, the First and Second Seasons.* BiMes 3, Malibu, FL, 1976. Second printing with addenda, Malibu, FL, 1992.

——"Ebla and Abu Salabikh: the Linguistic and Literary Aspects", in L. Cagni (ed.) *La Lingua di Ebla.* IUO Series Minor 14, Naples 1981, 121–133

——"Early Dynastic Texts" in I. Spar (ed.), *Tablets, Cones and Bricks of the Third and Second Millennia B.C.* CTMMA 1, New York, NY, 1988

——"The Semitic Personal Names from Abu Salabikh and the Personal Names from Ebla", in A. Archi (ed.), *Eblaite Personal Names and Semitic Name-Giving. Papers of a Symposium Held in Rome July 15–17, 1985.* ARES 1, Rome 1988, 89–98

Biggs, R. D. & J. N. Postgate, "Inscriptions from Abu Salabikh, 1975", *Iraq* 40 (1978), 101–117

Bloomfield, L., *Language*, 2nd, revised edition, 4th printing, London 1957

Boehmer, R. M., "Datierte Glyptik der Akkade-Zeit", in K. Bittel (ed.), *Vorderasiatische Archäologie. Studien und Aufsätze: Anton Moortgat zum 65. Geburtstag gewidmet*, Berlin 1964, 42–56

——*Die Entwicklung der Glyptik während der Akkad-Zeit.* Untersuchungen zur Assyriologie und Vorderasiatischen Archäologie. Ergänzungsband zur *Zeitschrift für Assyriologie und Vorderasiatische Archäologie* 4, Berlin 1965

Bonechi, M., "Onomastica dei testi di Ebla: nomi propre come fossili-guida?", *StEL* 8 (1991), 59–79

——"Notes on the Names and Professions List", *NABU* 2001/29

——"Nomi di professione semitici nelle liste lessicali di Ebla", *QDLF* 16 (2006), 79–98

Borger, R., *Mesopotamisches Zeichenlexikon.* AOAT 305, Münster 2004

Bottéro, J., *Religion in Ancient Mesopotamia*, translated by T. L. Fagan, Chicago, IL, & London 2001

Braun-Holzinger, E. A., *Frühdynastische Beterstatuetten.* Abhandlungen der Deutschen Orient-Gesellschaft 19, Berlin 1977

Bridges, S. J., *The Mesag Archive: A Study of Sargonic Society and Economy* (unpublished Ph.D. diss., Yale 1981)

Brinkman, J. A., "Cuneiform Texts in the St. Louis Public Library", in B. L. Eichler, J. W. Heimerdinger & Å. Sjöberg (eds.), *Kramer Anniversary Volume. Cuneiform Studies in Honor of Samuel Noah Kramer.* AOAT 25, Kevelaer & Neukirchen-Vluyn 1976, 41–57

——*Materials and Studies for Kassite History: A Catalogue of Cuneiform Sources Pertaining to Specific Monarchs of the Kassite Dynasty*, vol. 1, Chicago, IL, 1979

——"The Use of Occupation Names as Patronyms in the Kassite Period: A Forerunner of Neo-Babylonian Ancestral Names", in A. K. Guinan et al. (eds.), *If a Man Builds a Joyful House; Assyriological Studies in Honor of Erle Verdun Leichty.* CM 31, Leiden & Boston, MA, 2006, 23–43

vom Bruck, G., "Names as Bodily Signs", in G. vom Bruck & B. Bodenhorn (eds.), *The Anthropology of Names and Naming*, Cambridge 2006, 226–250

Buccellati, G. & R. D. Biggs, *Cuneiform Texts from Nippur: The Eighth and Ninth Seasons.* AS 17, Chicago, IL, 1969

Buccellati, G. & M. Kelly-Buccellati, "Tarʾam-Agade, Daughter of Naram-Sin at Urkesh", in L. Al-Gailani Werr, C. Curtis, H. Martin, A. McMahon, J. Oates &

J. Reade (eds.), *Of Pots and Plans: Papers on the Archaeology and History of Mesopotamia Presented to David Oates in Honour of His 75th Birthday*, London 2002, 11–31

—— "Urkesh: The First Hurrian Capital", *BA* 60 (1997), 77–96

Burrows, E., *Archaic Texts*. UET 2, London 1935

Böck, B., "Proverbs 30:18–19 in the Light of Ancient Mesopotamian Cuneiform Texts", *Sefarda: Revista de estudios hebraicos y sefardíes* 69 (2009), 263–279

Böhl, F. M. T., *Oorkonden uit de periode der rijken van Sumer en Akkad (3000–2000 v. Chr.)*. MLVS 1, Amsterdam 1933

Cameron, G. C., "A Lagash Mace Head Inscription", *JCS* 20 (1966), 125

Cancik-Kirschbaum, E., "„Menschen ohne König …": Zur Wahrnehmung des Königtums in sumerischen und akkadischen Texten", in J. Hazenbos, A. Zgoll and C. Wilcke (eds.), *Das geistige erfassen der Welt im Alten Orient. Sprache, Religion, Kultur und Gesellschaft*, Wiesbaden 2007, 167–190

Castellino, G. R., *Two Šulgi Hymns (BC)*. Istituto di studi del Vicino Oriente, Studi Semitici 42, Rome 1973

Catagnoti, A., "The III Millennium Personal Names from the Ḫabur Triangle in the Ebla, Brak and Mozan Texts", in M. Lebeau (ed.), *About Subartu: Studies Devoted to Upper Mesopotamia. Culture, Society, Image*. Subartu 4/2, Turnhout 1998, 41–66

Cavigneaux, A., *Die sumerisch-akkadischen Zeichenlisten: Überlieferungsprobleme*, Ph.D. diss., Munich 1976

Cavigneaux, A. & F. al-Rawi, "La fin de Gilgameš, Enkidu et les Enfers d'après les manuscrits d'Ur et de Meturan (Textes de Tell Haddad VIII)", *Iraq* 62 (2000), 1–19

Charpin, D., "Un nouveau compte de rations présargonique", *RA* 71 (1977), 97–105

—— "Nouvelles tablettes présargoniques de Mari", *MARI* 6 (1990), 245–252

Charpin, D. & J. M. Durand, *Documents cunéiformes de Strasbourg conservés à la Bibliothèque Nationale et Universitaire* 1: *autographies*. Récherches sur les grandes civilisations, Cahier 4, Paris 1981

—— "Tablettes présargoniques de Mari", *MARI* 5 (1987), 65–127

Charvát, P., "Early Ur", *ArOr* 47 (1979), 15–20

Cheng, J., "A Review of Early Dynastic III Music: Man's Animal Call", *JNES* 68 (2009), 163–178

Chiera, E., *Lists of Personal Names from the Temple School of Nippur. A Syllabary of Personal Names*. PBS 11 No. 1, Philadelphia, PA, 1916

—— *Lists of Personal Names from the Temple School of Nippur. Lists of Akkadian Personal Names*. PBS 11 No. 2, Philadelphia, PA, 1916

—— *Lists of Personal Names from the Temple School of Nippur. Lists of Sumerian Personal Names*. PBS 11 No. 3, Philadelphia, PA, 1919

—— *Selected Temple Accounts from Telloh, Yokha and Drehem: Cuneiform Tablets in the Library of Princeton University*, Princeton, NJ, 1922

Çığ, M., "New Date Formulas from the Tablet Collection of the Istanbul Archaeological Museums", in B. L. Eichler, J. W. Heimerdinger & Å. Sjöberg (eds.), *Kramer Anniversary Volume. Cuneiform Studies in Honor of Samuel Noah Kramer*. AOAT 25, Kevelaer & Neukirchen-Vluyn 1976, 75–82

Çığ, M., H. Kızılyay & A. Salonen, *Die Puzriš-Dagan-Texte der Istanbuler Archäologischen Museen,* 1: Nrr. 1–725. Annales Academiæ Scientarium Fennicæ, B 92, Helsinki 1954

Civil, M., "Appendix A: Cuneiform Texts", in McG. Gibson (ed.), *Excavations at Nippur: Eleventh Season.* OIC 22, Chicago, IL, 1975

—— "The Song of the Plowing Oxen" in B. L. Eichler, J. W. Heimerdinger & Å. Sjöberg (eds.), *Kramer Anniversary Volume. Cuneiform Studies in Honor of Samuel Noah Kramer.* AOAT 25, Kevelaer & Neukirchen-Vluyn 1976, 83–95

—— "Les limites de l'information textuelle", in *L'archéologie de l'Iraq du début de l'époque néolithique à 333 avant notre ère. Perspectives et limites de l'interprétation anthropologique des documents (Paris 13–15 juin 1980).* Colloques Internationaux du Centre National de la Recherche Scientifique vol. 580, Paris 1980, 225–232

—— "Tablillas sargónicas de Ur", *AulaOr* 6 (1988), 105–106

—— "Modal Prefixes", *ASJ* 22 (2000, publ. 2005), 29–42

Civil, M., R. D. Biggs, H. G. Güterbock, H. J. Nissen & E. Reiner (eds.), *The Series lú* = ša *and Related Texts.* MSL 12, Rome 1969

Civil, M., M. W. Green & W. G. Lambert (eds.), *Ea A* = nâqu, *with their Forerunners and Related Texts.* MSL 14, Rome 1979

Civil, M., H. G. Güterbock, W. W. Hallo, H. A. Hoffner & E. Reiner (eds.), *Izi* = išātu, *Ká-gal* = abullu *and Níg-ga* = makkūru. MSL 13, Rome 1971

Clay, A. T., *Miscellaneous Inscriptions in the Yale Babylonian Collection.* YOS 1, New Haven, CT, & London 1915

—— *Epics, Hymns, Omens, and Other Texts.* BRM 4, New Haven, CT, 1923

Cohen, A. C., *Death Rituals, Ideology, and the Development of Early Mesopotamian Kingship: Toward a New Understanding of Iraq's Royal Cemetery of Ur.* Ancient Magic and Divination 7, Leiden & Boston, MA, 2005

Cohen, M. E., *Sumerian Hymnology; The Eršemma.* HUCA Supplements 2, Cincinatti, OH, 1981

—— *The Cultic Calendars of the Ancient Near East*, Bethesda, MD, 1993

—— "Two Versions of a Fara-Period Name-List", in M. E. Cohen, D. C. Snell, D. B. Weisberg (eds.), *The Tablet and the Scroll: Near Eastern Studies in Honor of William W. Hallo*, Bethesda, MD, 1993

Collin, F. & F. Guldmann, *Meaning, Use, and Truth: Introducing the Philosophy of Language*, Aldershot 2005

Contenau, G., *Contribution à l'histoire économique d'Umma.* Bibliothèque de l'École des Hautes Études fasc. 219, Paris 1915

Conti, G., *Index of Eblaic Texts (Published or Cited).* Quaderni di Semitistica. Materiali 1, Firenze 1992

Cooper, J. S., "Review of E. Sollberger, & J.-R. Kupper, *Inscriptions royales sumériennes et akkadiennes*", *JNES* 33 (1974), 414–417

—— *The Curse of Agade*, Baltimore & London 1983

—— *Reconstructing History from Ancient Inscriptions: the Lagash-Umma Border Conflict.* SANE 2/1, Malibu, FL, 1983; 3rd revised printing 2002

—— "Studies in Mesopotamian Lapidary Inscriptions III", *Iraq* 46 (1984), 87–93

—— *Sumerian and Akkadian Royal Inscriptions,* 1: *Presargonic Inscriptions.* The American Oriental Society Translation Series 1, New Haven, CT, 1986

—— "Studies in Mesopotamian Lapidary Inscriptions V", *RA* 80 (1986), 73–74

—— "Sacred Marriage and Popular Cult in Early Mesopotamia", in E. Matsushima (ed.), *Official Cult and Popular Religion: Papers of the First Colloquium on the Ancient Near East – The City and its Life Held at the Middle Eastern Culture Center in Japan (Mitaka, Tokyo), March 20–22, 1992*, Heidelberg 1993, 81–96

—— "Literature and History: The Historical and Political Referents of Sumerian Literary Texts", in T. Abusch, P.-A. Beaulieu, J. Huehnergard, P. Machinist, P. Steinkeller & C. Noyes (eds.), *Historiography in the Cuneiform World*. CRRA 45, 2 vols., Bethesda, MD, 2001, 131–147

Crawford, H., *Sumer and the Sumerians*, Cambridge 1991; 2nd edition 2004

Crawford, V. E., "Lagash", *Iraq* 36 (1974), 29–35

—— "Inscriptions from Lagash, Season Four, 1975–76", *JCS* 29 (1977), 189–222

Cripps, E. L., *Sargonic and Presargonic Texts in the World Museum Liverpool*. BARI S2135 Oxford 2010

Cunningham, G., *'Deliver Me from Evil': Mesopotamian Incantations 2500-1500 BC*. StPohl SM 17, Rome 1997

—— *Religion & Magic: Approaches & Theories*, Edinburgh 1999

Dahl, J. "Complex Graphemes in Proto-Elamite", *CDLJ* 2005:3, 1–15

Deimel, A., *Liste der archaischen Keilschriftszeichen*. Die Inschriften von Fara 1. Wissenschaftliche Veröffentlichungen der Deutschen Orient-Gesellschaft 40, Leipzig 1922

—— *Schultexte aus Fara*. Die Inschriften von Fara 2. Wissenschaftliche Veröffentlichungen der Deutschen Orient-Gesellschaft 43, Leipzig 1923

—— *Wirtschaftstexte aus Fara*. Die Inschriften von Fara 3. Wissenschaftliche Veröffentlichungen der Deutschen Orient-Gesellschaft 45, Leipzig 1924

Delaporte, L. J., "Tablettes de comptabilité chaldéenne", *ZA* 18 (1904), 245–256

Delougaz, P. & T. Jacobsen, *The Temple Oval at Khafajah*. OIP 53, Chicago, IL, 1940

Delougaz, P., S. Lloyd, H. Frankfort & T. Jacobsen, *Pre-Sargonid Temples in the Diyala Region*. OIP 58, Chicago, IL, 1942

Diakonoff, I., "Ancient Writing and Ancient Written Language", in S. J. Lieberman (ed.), *Sumerological Studies in Honor of Thorkild Jacobsen on His Seventieth Birthday, June 7, 1974*. AS 20, Chicago, IL, & London 1974, 99–121

van Dijk, J. J. A., "Textes divers du Musée de Baghdad, III", *Sumer* 15 (1959), 5–14 and plates 1–15

—— *Cuneiform Texts of Varying Content*. Texts in the Iraq Museum Published by the Directorate General of Antiquities vol. 9, Baghdad, Leiden 1976

Donald, T., "Old Akkadian Tablets in the Liverpool Museum", *MCS* 9 (1964), 36 pages, unnumbered

Donbaz, V., "An Inscribed Dagger-Blade from Lagash", *NABU* 1997/52

Donbaz, V. & B. R. Foster, *Sargonic Texts from Telloh in the Istanbul Archaeological Museums*. Occasional Publications of the Babylonian Fund, 5 and American Research Institute in Turkey Monographs, 2, Philadelphia, PA, 1982

Donbaz, V. & N. Yoffee, *Old Babylonian Texts from Kish Conserved in the Istanbul Archaeological Museums*. BiMes 17, Malibu, FL, 1986

Douglas, M., *Purity and Danger: An Analysis of Concepts of Pollution and Taboo*, London 1978
—— *Natural Symbols*, Harmondsworth 1973
Dunham, S., "Sumerian Words for Foundation. Part I: Temen", *RA* 80 (1986), 31–64
—— "The Monkey in the Middle, *ZA* 75 (1985), 234–264
Durand, J.-M., "Documents d'Agadé", *NABU* 1995/50
Dsharakian, R., "Altakkadische Wirtschaftstexte aus den Archiven von Awal und Gasur (III. Jahrtausend v.Chr.)", *ZA* 84 (1994), 1–10
Edzard, D. O., "Enmebaragesi von Kiš", *ZA* 53 (1959), 9–26
—— "Sumerische Komposita mit dem 'Nominalpräfix' nu-", *ZA* 55 (1961, publ. 1963), 91–112
—— "Die Inschriften der altakkadischen Rollsiegel", *AfO* 22 (1968/69), 12–20
—— *Altbabylonische Rechts- und Wirtschaftsurkunden aus Tell ed-Dēr bei Sippar*. TIM 7, Wiesbaden 1971
—— "Problèmes de la royauté dans la période présargonique", in P. Garelli (ed.) *Le palais et la royauté*. CRRA 19, Paris 1974, 141–149
—— "Zur sumerischen Hymne auf der Heiligtum Keš", *OrNS* 43 (1974), 103–113
—— "Die Einrichtung eines Tempels im älteren Babylonien. Philologische Aspekte", in *Le temple et le culte*. CRRA 20, Leiden 1975, 156–163
—— "Die Archive von Šuruppag (Fāra): Umfang und Grenzen der Auswertbarkeit", in E. Lipiński (ed.) *State and Temple Economy in the Ancient Near East* 1. OLA 5, Leuven 1979, 153–169
—— *Verwaltungstexte verschiedenen Inhalts*. ARET 2, Rome 1981
—— *Hymnen, Beschwörungen und Verwandtes aus dem Archiv L. 2769*. ARET 5, Rome 1984
—— "Lugal (in Götternamen)", *RlA* 7 (1987–90), 108–109
—— *Gudea and his Dynasty*. RIME 3/1, Toronto 1997
—— "Review of M. Hölscher, *Die Personennamen der kassitenzeitlichen Texte aus Nippur*. Imgula 1", *ZA* 88 (1998), 146–148
—— "Name, Namengebung (Onomastik). A. Sumerisch", *RlA* 9 (1998–2001), 94–103
—— "Name, Namengebung (Onomastik). B. Akkadisch", *RlA* 9 (1998–2001), 103–116
—— *Sumerian Grammar*. Handbook of Oriental Studies/Handbuch der Orientalistik 71, Leiden & Boston, MA, 2003
Edzard, D. O. & G. Farber, *Die Orts- und Gewässernamen der Zeit der 3. Dynastie von Ur*. RGTC 2. Beihefte zum Tübinger Atlas des Vorderen Orients, Reihe B (Geisteswissenschaften) Nr. 7, Wiesbaden 1974
Edzard, D. O., G. Farber & E. Sollberger, *Die Orts- und Gewässernamen der präsargonischen und sargonischen Zeit*. RGTC 1. Beihefte zum Tübinger Atlas des Vorderen Orients, Reihe B (Geisteswissenschaften) Nr. 7/1, Wiesbaden 1977
Eisen, G., *Ancient Oriental Cylinder and Other Seals with A Description of the Collection of Mrs. William H. Moore*. OIP 47, Chicago, IL, 1940
Ellis, M. deJong, "Cuneiform Tablets at Bryn Mawr College", *JCS* 31 (1979), 30–55
Ellis, R. S., *Foundation Deposits in Ancient Mesopotamia*. Yale Near Eastern Researches 2, New Haven, CT, & London 1968

Englund, R. K., "Administrative Timekeeping in Ancient Mesopotamia", *JESHO* 31 (1988), 121–185

—— "Ur III Sundries", *ASJ* 14 (1992), 77–102

—— "The Smell of the Cage", *CDLJ* 2009:4, 1–29

—— "Recently Published Catalogues of Cuneiform Collections", *CDLN* 2010:004 (no page number)

Englund, R. K. & J.-P. Grégoire, *The Proto-Cuneiform Texts from Jemdet Nasr* 1: *Copies, Transliterations and Glossary*. MSVO 1, Berlin 1991

Englund, R. K., see also Bauer, J., R. K. Englund & M. Krebernik

Falkenstein, A., *Archaische Texte aus Uruk*. ADFU 2, Berlin 1936

—— "Eine gesiegelte Tontafel der altsumerischen Zeit", *AfO* 14 (1941–44), 333–336

—— "Sumerische religiöse Texte", *ZA* 49 (1950), 80–150

—— "sù-ud-ága", *ZA* 52 (1957), 304–307

—— *Das Sumerische*. Handbuch der Orientalistik, erste Abteilung, zweiter Band, erster und sweiter Abschnitt, Leiden 1959

—— "Sumerische religiöse Texte: 4. Ein Lied auf Šulpa'e", *ZA* 55 (1962), 11–67

—— *Die Inschriften Gudeas von Lagaš*. I, *Einleitung*. AnOr 30, Rome 1966

—— "Zum sumerischen Lexikon", *ZA* 58 (1967), 5–15

Falkenstein, A. & W. von Soden, *Sumerische und akkadische Hymnen und Gebete*, Zürich 1953

Farber, G., "Rinder mit Namen", in G. van Driel, Th. J. H. Krispijn, M. Stol, K. R. Veenhof (eds.), *Zikir šumim: Assyriological Studies Presented to F. R. Kraus on the Occasion of his Seventieth Birthday*, Leiden 1982, 34–36

Farber, G. & W. Farber, "Ein neuer Feldkaufvertrag aus Fara", *WO* 8 (1975–76), 178–184

Farber, W., "Von *BA* und anderen Wassertieren", *JCS* 26 (1974), 195–207

—— "Die Vergöttlichung Narām-Sîns", *OrNS* 52 (1983), 67–72

Farber-Flügge, G., *Der Mythos "Inanna und Enki" unter besonderer Berücksichtigung der Liste der m e*. StPohl 10, Rome 1973

Fenzel, K., *Präsargonische Personennamen aus Ur*. Ph.D. diss., Innsbruck 1967

Ferrara, A. J., *Nanna-Suen's Journey to Nippur*. StPohl SM 2, Rome 1973

Figulla, H. H., *Catalogue of the Babylonian Tablets in the British Museum* vol. 1, London 1961

Figulla, H. H., & W. J. Martin, *Letters and Documents of the Old Babylonian Period*. UET 5, London 1953

Finkbeiner, U, W. Röllig & T. Mallmann, Tübinger Atlas des Vorderen Orients, Sonderforschungsbereich 19, poster B II 7: "Mesopotamien: Frühdynastische Zeit", Wiesbaden 1988

Finkelstein, J. J., *Late Old Babylonian Documents and Letters*. YOS 13, New Haven, CT, & London 1972

Finné, M. & K. Holmgren, "Climate Variability in the Eastern Mediterranean and the Middle East during the Holocene", in P. J. J. Sinclair, G. Nordquist, F. Herschend & C. Isendahl (eds.), *The Urban Mind: Cultural and Environmental Dynamics*, Uppsala 2010, 29–60

Fish, T., *Catalogue of Sumerian Tablets in the John Rylands Library*, Manchester 1932

Flückiger-Hawker, E., *Urnamma of Ur in Sumerian Literary Tradition*. OBO 166, Freiburg & Göttingen 1996

Foster, B. R., "Murder in Mesopotamia", *RA* 73 (1979), 179.

—— "Notes on Sargonic Royal Progress", *JANES* 12 (1980), 29–42

—— "The Circuit of Lagash", *AfO* 28 (1981–82), 141

—— *Administration and Use of Institutional Land in Sargonic Sumer*. Mesopotamia 9, Copenhagen 1982

—— "An Agricultural Archive from Sargonic Akkad", *ASJ* 4 (1982), 7–51

—— "Ethnicity and Onomastics in Sargonic Mesopotamia", *OrNS* 51 (1982), 297–354

—— "Notes on Sargonic Legal and Juridical Procedures", *WO* 13 (1982), 15–24

—— "Selected Business Documents from Sargonic Mesopotamia", *JCS* 35 (1983), 147–175

—— "The Sargonic Victory Stele from Telloh", *Iraq* 47 (1985), 15–30

—— "Early Mesopotamian Land Sales. (Review of I. J. Gelb et al., OIP 104)", *JAOS* 114 (1994), 440–452

—— "Review of R. A. di Vito, *Studies in Third Millennium Sumerian and Akkadian Personal Names: The Designation and Conception of the Personal God*," *JAOS* 115 (1995), 537–539

—— "A Century of Mesopotamian Agriculture", in H. Klengel & J. Renger (eds.), *Landwirtschaft im Alten Orient*. BBVO 11. CRRA 41, Berlin 1999, 1–10

—— "Shuruppak and the Sumerian City State", in L. Kogan, N. Koslova, S. Loesov & S. Tischenko (eds.), *Memoriae Igor M. Diakonoff*. Babel und Bibel 2, Winona Lake, IN, 2005, 71–88

—— "The Sargonic Period: Two Historiographical Problems", in G. Barjamovic, J. L.Dahl, U. S. Koch, W. Sommerfeld & J. Goodnick Westenholz (eds.), *Akkade is King: A Collection of Papers by Friends and Colleagues Presented to Aage Westenholz on the Occasion of his 70th Birthday 15th of May 2009*. PIHANS 118, Leiden 2011, 127–137

Al-Fouadi, A.-H., "Bassetki Statue with an Old Akkadian Royal Inscription of Naram-Sin of Agade (B.C. 2291–2255)", *Sumer* 32 (1976), 63–76

Foxvog, D., "Funerary Furnishings in an Early Sumerian Text from Adab", in B. Alster (ed.), *Death in Mesopotamia*. CRRA 26. Mesopotamia 8, Copenhagen 1980, 67–75

—— "Ur III Economic Texts at Berkeley", *ASJ* 18 (1996), 47–92

—— "Sumerian KA-AL Again", *NABU* 1998/7

—— "Aspects of Sumerian Name-Giving in Presargonic Lagash", in W. Heimpel & G. Frantz-Szabó (eds.), *Strings and Threads: A Celebration of the Work of Anne Draffkorn Kilmer*, Winona Lake, IN, 2011

Frahm, E., "Observations on the Name and Age of Sargon II and on Some Patterns of Assyrian Royal Onomastics", *NABU* 2005/44

Franke, S., *Königsinschriften und Königsideologie: Die Könige von Akkade zwischen Tradition und Neuerung*, Münster & Hamburg 1995

Frankfort, H., *The Art and Architecture of the Ancient Orient*, Harmondsworth 1954. Fifth edition with supplementary notes, additional biography and abbreviations by Michael Roaf and Donald Matthews, Yale 1996.

Frayne, D. R., *Presargonic Period (2700–2350 BC)*. RIME 1, Toronto 2008

— *Sargonic and Gutian Periods (2334–2113 BC)*. RIME 2, Toronto 1993

— *Ur III Period (2112–2004 BC)*. RIME 3/2, Toronto 1997

— "The Struggle for Hegemony in "Early Dynastic II" Sumer", *JCSMS* 4 (2009), 37–75

Fronzaroli, P., "Typologies onomastiques à Ebla", in A. Archi (ed.), *Eblaite Personal Names and Semitic Name-Giving. Papers of a Symposium Held in Rome July 15–17, 1985*. ARES 1, Rome 1988, 1–24

Fronzaroli, P. & A. Catagnoti, *Testi di cancelleria: I rapporti con le città (Archivio L. 2769)*. ARET 13, Rome 2003

de la Fuÿe, A., *Documents Présargoniques*. 5 vols., Paris 1908–1920

Förtsch, W., *Altbabylonische Wirtschaftstexte aus der Zeit Lugalandas und Urukaginas. Texte 1–195*. VS 14, Leipzig 1916

Gadd, C. J., Cuneiform Texts from Babylonian Tablets, &c., in the British Museum 36, London 1921

Gadd, C. J. & L. Legrain, *Royal Inscriptions*. UET 1, 2 vols. Text and Plates, London 1928

Gelb, I. J., *Sargonic Texts from the Diyala Region*. MAD 1, Chicago, IL, 1952

— *Old Akkadian Writing and Grammar*. MAD 2, Chicago, IL, First edition 1952. Second, revised edition 1961

— *Old Akkadian Inscriptions in the Chicago Natural History Museum. Texts of Legal and Business Interest*. Fieldiana: Anthropology Vol. 44, No. 2, Chicago, IL, 1955, 161–338

— *Glossary of Old Akkadian*. MAD 3, Chicago, IL, 1957

— "The Early History of the West Semitic Peoples", *JCS* 15 (1961), 27–47

— "Ethnic Reconstruction and Onomastic Evidence", *Names* 10 (1962), 45–52

— "The Origin of the West Semitic *qatala* Morpheme", in S. Drewniak (ed.), *Symbolae Linguisticae in Honorem Georgii Kuryłowicz*. Polska Akademia Nauk – Oddział w Krakowie. Prace Komisji Językoznawstwa vol. 5, Wrocław, Warsaw, Kraków 1965, 72–80

— *Sargonic Texts in the Louvre Museum*. MAD 4, Chicago, IL, 1970

— *Sargonic Texts in the Ashmolean Museum, Oxford*. MAD 5, Chicago, IL, 1970

— "The ARUA Institution", *RA* 66 (1972), 1–32

— "Household and Family in Early Mesopotamia", in E. Lipiński (ed.) *State and Temple Economy in the Ancient Near East*. Proceedings of the International Conference organized by the Katholieke Universiteit Leuven from the 10th to the 14th of April 1978, vol. 1. OLA 5, Leuven 1979, 1–97

Gelb, I. J. & B. Kienast, *Die altakkadischen Königsinschriften des dritten Jahrtausends v. Chr*. FAOS 7, Stuttgart 1990

Gelb, I. J., P. Steinkeller & R. M. Whiting Jr., *Earliest Land Tenure Systems in the Ancient Near East: Ancient Kudurrus*, 2 vols. Text and Plates. OIP 104, Chicago, IL, 1989 & 1991

Geller, M. J., *Forerunners to UDUG-HUL: Sumerian Exorcistic Incantations*. FAOS 12, Stuttgart 1985

de Genouillac, H., *Tablettes sumériennes archaïques. Matériaux pour servir a l'histoire de la société sumérienne*, Paris 1909

— *Textes de l'époque d'Agadé et de l'époque d'Ur* (*Fouilles d'Ernest de Sarzec en 1894*). Première partie. ITT 2/1, Paris 1910

— *Textes de l'époque d'Agadé et de l'époque d'Ur* (*Fouilles d'Ernest de Sarzec en 1894*). Deuxième partie. ITT 2/2, Paris 1911

— *Époque présargonique, époque d'Agadé, époque d'Ur*. ITT 5, Paris 1921

— *Textes économiques d'Oumma de l'époque d'Our.* TCL 5, Paris 1922

— "Choix de textes économiques de la collection Pupil", *Babyloniaca* 8 (1924), 37–40, with 10 plates

— "Nouveaux princes et cités nouvelles de Sumer", *RHR* 101 (1930), 216–221

George, A. R., *House Most High: The Temples of Ancient Mesopotamia.* MesCiv 5, Winona Lake, IN, 1993

— (ed.), *Cuneiform Royal Inscriptions and Related Texts in the Schøyen Collection*. CUSAS 17, Bethesda, MD, 2011

Gibson, McG., "The Archaeological Uses of Cuneiform Documents: Patterns of Occupation at the City of Kish", *Iraq* 34 (1972), 113–123

— "Fate of Iraqi Archaeology", *Science* 299 (March 2003), 1848–1849

Glassner, J.-J., *La chute d'Akkade: L'événement et sa mémoire*. BBVO 5, Berlin 1986

— "Le roi prêtre en Mésopotamie, au milieu du 3° millénaire – Mythe ou réalité?", in *L'ancien Proche-Orient et les Indes. Parallélismes interculturels religieux.* Colloque franco-finlandais les 10 et 11 novembre 1990 à l'Institut finlandais, Paris. StOr 70, Helsinki 1993, 9–19

Goetze, A., "Early Kings of Kish", *JCS* 15 (1961), 105–111

— "Šakkanakkus of the Ur III Empire", *JCS* 17 (1963), 1–31

— "An Archaic Legal Document", *JCS* 20 (1966), 126–127

— "Akkad Dynasty Inscriptions", *JAOS* 88 (1968), 54–59

— "Early Dynastic Dedication Inscriptions from Nippur", *JCS* 23 (1970), 39–56

Goetze, A. & B. R. Foster, *Cuneiform Texts from Various Collections*, YOS 15, New Haven, CT, & London 2010

Gomi, T., *Wirtschaftstexte der Ur III-Zeit aus dem British Museum*. MVN 12, Rome 1982

— "Ein neuer farazeitlicher Feldkaufvertrag in Japan" *Orient* 19 (1983), 1–6

Gomi, T., Y. Hirose & K. Hirose, *Neo-Sumerian Administrative Texts of the Hirose Collection*, Potomac, MD, 1990

Gomi, T. & S. Sato, *Selected Neo-Sumerian Administrative Texts from the British Museum*, Abiko 1990

Goodnick Westenholz, J. "Heroes of Akkad", *JAOS* 103 (1983), 327–336

— "Review of B. Lewis, *The Sargon Legend: A Study of the Akkadian Text and the Tale of the Hero Who Was Exposed at Birth*", *JNES* 43 (1984), 73–79

— *Legends of the Kings of Akkade: The Texts*. MesCiv 7, Winona Lake 1997

— "Objects with Messages: Reading Old Akkadian Royal Inscriptions", *BiOr* 55 (1998), 44–59

— "King by Love of Inanna – an Image of Female Empowerment?", *NIN* 1 (2000), 75–89

— "The Good Shepherd", in A. Panaino & A. Piras (eds.), *Schools of Oriental Studies and the Development of Modern Historiography. Proceedings of the Fourth Annual Symposium of the Assyrian And Babylonian Intellectual Heritage Project Held in Ravenna, Italy, October 13–17, 2001*, Melammu Symposia 4, Milan 2004, 281–310

—— "The Memory of Sargonic Kings under the Third Dynasty of Ur", in P. Michalowski (ed.), *On the Third Dynasty of Ur: Studies in Honor of Marcel Sigrist*, Boston, MA, 2008, 251–260

Gordon, C. H., *Smith College Tablets: 110 Cuneiform Texts Selected from the College Collection*, Northampton, MA, 1952

—— "Notes on Proper Names in the Ebla Tablets", in A. Archi (ed.), *Eblaite Personal Names and Semitic Name-Giving. Papers of a Symposium Held in Rome July 15–17, 1985*. ARES 1, Rome 1988, 153–158

De Graef, K., "Ili-kibrī «Mon dieu est ma grandeur»: un nom hybride accadien-amorite?", *NABU* 2007/24

Grayson, A. K., "Histories and Historians of the Ancient Near East: Assyria and Babylonia", *OrNS* 49 (1980), 140–194

Green, M. W., "Miscellaneous Early Texts from Uruk", *ZA* 72 (1982), 163–177

Green, M. W., H. Nissen et al., *Zeichenliste der archaischen Texte aus Uruk*. ADFU 11, Berlin 1987

Grégoire, J.-P., *Archives administratives sumériennes*, Paris 1970

—— *Inscriptions et archives administratives cunéiformes (1e partie)*. MVN 10, Rome 1981

—— *Archives administratives et inscriptions cunéiformes. Ashmolean Museum, Bodleian Collection, Oxford. Les sources* 1, vols. 1 and 2, Paris 1996 & 2000

Gurney, O. R., *Middle Babylonian Legal Documents and Other Texts*. UET 7, London 1974

Haber, E., "The Stylistic Role of the Anticipatory Genitive Construction in Sumerian Literature", *RA* 103 (2009), 1–10

Hackman, G. G., *Sumerian and Akkadian Administrative Texts from Predynastic Times to the End of the Akkad Dynasty*. BIN 8, New Haven, CT, 1958

Hallo, W. W., *Early Mesopotamian Royal Titles: A Philologic and Historical Analysis*. AOS 43, New Haven, CT, 1957

—— "On the Antiquity of Sumerian Literature", *JAOS* 83 (1963), 167–176

—— "The Date of the Fara Period", in *OrNS* 42 (1973), 228–238

—— "Back to the Big House: Colloquial Sumerian, Continued", *OrNS* 54 (1985), 56–64

Hallo, W. W. & W. K. Simpson, *The Ancient Near East: A History*, New York, NY, 1971

Handcock, P. S. P., Cuneiform Texts from Babylonian Tablets, &c., in the British Museum vol. 31, London 1911

Harris, R., "Notes on the Slave Names of Old Babylonian Sippar", *JCS* 29 (1977), 46–51

Hasselbach, R., *Sargonic Akkadian. A Historical and Comparative Study of the Syllabic Texts*, Wiesbaden 2005

Hausner, I., "Quellen und Hilfsmittel der Namenforschung: Gewinnung historischer Daten", in E. Eichler et al. (eds.), *Namenforschung. Name Studies. Les noms propres*. Handbücher zur Sprach- und Kommunikationswissenschaft vol. 11/1, Berlin & New York, NY, 1995, 294–298

Hayes, J., "Some Thoughts on the Sumerian Genitive", *ASJ* 13 (1991), 185–194

—— "Phonology of Sumerian", in A. S. Kaye (ed.), *Phonologies of Asia and Africa (Including the Caucasus)*, vol. 2, Winona Lake, IN, 1997, 1001–1019

Heimpel, W., *Tierbilder in der Sumerischen Literatur*. StPohl 2, Rome 1968
—— "ne-saĝ", *NABU* 1994/83
—— "The Gates of the Eninnu", *JCS* 48 (1996), 17–29
Heuzey, L., "Deux armes sacrées chaldéennes découvertes par M. de Sarzec", *RA* 3 (1894), 52–58
—— *Catalogue des antiquités chaldéennes: Sculpture et gravure a la pointe*, Paris 1902
Hilgert, M., *Akkadisch in der Ur III-Zeit*. Imgula 5, Münster 2002
—— "Herrscherideal und Namengebung. Zum akkadischen Wortschatz kyriophorer Eigennamen in der Ur III Zeit", in N. Nebes (ed.) *Neue Beiträge zur Semitistik. Erstes Arbeitstreffen der Arbeitsgemeinschaft Semitistik in der Deutschen Morgenländischen Gesellschaft vom 11. bis 13. September 2000 an der Friedrich-Schiller-Universität Jena*. JBVO 5, Wiesbaden 2002, 39–76
Hilprecht, H. V., *Old Babylonian Inscriptions Chiefly from Nippur. Part* 1. BE 1/1, Philadelphia, PA, 1893
—— *Old Babylonian Inscriptions Chiefly from Nippur. Part* 2. BE 1/2, Philadelphia, PA, 1896
—— *Exploration in Bible Lands during the 19th Century*, Philadephia, PA, 1903
Hock, H. H., & B. D. Joseph, *Language History, Language Change, and Language Relationship. An Introduction to Historical and Comparative Linguistics*, Berlin & New York 1996
Hunger, H., "review of M. E. Cohen, *The Cultic Calendars of the Ancient Near East*," *JAOS* 116 (1996), 776–777
Hussey, M. I., *Sumerian Tablets in the Harvard Semitic Museum, Part* 1, *Chiefly from the Reigns of Lugalanda and Urukagina of Lagash*. HSS 3, Cambridge, MA, 1912
—— *Sumerian Tablets in the Harvard Semitic Museum, Part* 2, *From the Time of The Dynasty of Ur*. HSS 4, Cambridge, MA, 1915
Jacobsen, T., *The Sumerian King List*. AS 11, Chicago, IL, 1939
—— *Cuneiform Texts in the National Museum, Copenhagen*, Leiden 1939
—— "Primitive Democracy in Ancient Mesopotamia", *JNES* 2 (1943), 159–172
—— "Early Political Development in Mesopotamia", *ZA* 52 (1957), 91–140
—— *Toward the Image of Tammuz and Other Essays*, Cambridge, MA, 1970
—— "The Term Ensí", *Fs Civil*, 113–121
—— "Notes on the Word lú", in A. F. Rainey, A. Kempinski, M. Sigrist & D. Ussishkin (eds.) *Kinattūtu ša dārâti: Raphael Kutscher Memorial Volume*. Tel Aviv Occasional Publications Series 1, Tel Aviv 1993, 69–79
Jacobsen, T. & B. Alster, "Ningišzida's Boat-Ride to Hades, in A. R. George & I. L. Finkel (eds.), *Wisdom, Gods and Literature: Studies in Assyriology in Honour of W. G. Lambert*, Winona Lake, IN, 2000, 315–344
Jestin, R., *Tablettes sumériennes de Šuruppak conservées au musée de Stamboul*. Mémoires de l'Institut français d'archéologie de Stamboul vol. 3, Paris 1937
—— *Nouvelles tablettes sumériennes de Šuruppak au musée d'Istanbul*. Bibliothèque archéologique et historique de l'Institut français d'archéologie d'Istanbul vol. 2, Paris 1957

Jones, T. B. & J. W. Snyder, *Sumerian Economic Texts from the Third Ur Dynasty: A Catalogue and Discussion of Documents from Various Collections*, Minneapolis, MN, 1961

Jonker, G., *The Topography of Remembrance: The Dead, Tradition and Collective Memory in Mesopotamia*. Studies in the History of Religions. Numen Book Series, 68, Leiden, New York & Cologne 1995

Katz, D., *The Image of the Netherworld in the Sumerian Sources*, Bethesda, MD, 2003

Keetman, J., "BE^{lí}, be-lí, ba_x-lí ?", *NABU* 2007/25

Keiser, C. E., *Selected Temple Documents of the Ur Dynasty*. YOS 4, New Haven, CT, & London 1919

—— *Neo-Sumerian Account Texts from Drehem*. BIN 3, New Haven, CT, 1971

Kienast, B., "^{d}É-a und der aramäische ‹‹Status Emphaticus››", in L. Cagni (ed.), *Ebla 1975–1985: Dieci anni di studi linguistici e filologici. Atti del convegno internazionale (Napoli, 9–11 ottobre 1985)*. IUO Series Minor 27, Naples 1987, 37–47

Kienast, B. & W. Sommerfeld, *Glossar zu den altakkadischen Königsinschriften*. FAOS 8, Stuttgart 1994

Kienast, B. & K. Volk, *Die sumerischen und akkadischen Briefe*. FAOS 19, Stuttgart 1995

King, L. W., CT 1, London 1896

—— Cuneiform Texts from Babylonian Tablets, &c., in the British Museum vol. 7, London 1899

—— Cuneiform Texts from Babylonian Tablets, &c., in the British Museum vol. 9, London 1900

—— Cuneiform Texts from Babylonian Tablets, &c., in the British Museum vol. 32, London 1912

Klein, J., *Three Šulgi Hymns: Sumerian Royal Hymns Glorifying King Šulgi of Ur*. Bar-Ilan Studies in Near Eastern Languages and Culture, Ramat-Gan 1981

—— "On Writing Monumental Inscriptions in Ur III Scribal Curriculum", *RA* 80 (1986), 1–7

Kogan, L., "The Etymology of Israel (with an Appendix on Non-Hebrew Semitic Names among Hebrews in the Old Testament)", in L. Kogan, N. Koslova, S. Loesov & S. Tischchenko (eds.), Вавилон и Библия 3. Древнеближневосточные, библейские и семитологические исследования (Babel und Bibel 3. Annual of Ancient Near Eastern, Old Testament, and Semitic Studies), Winona Lake, IN, 2006, 237–255

Kogan, L., "Animal Names in Biblical Hebrew: An Etymological Overview", in L. Kogan, N. Koslova, S. Loesov & S. Tischchenko (eds.), Вавилон и Библия 3. Древнеближневосточные, библейские и семитологические исследования (Babel und Bibel 3. Annual of Ancient Near Eastern, Old Testament, and Semitic Studies), Winona Lake, IN, 2006, 257–320

Kogan, L. & K. Markina, "Review of R. Hasselbach, *Sargonic Akkadian. A Historical and Comparative Study of the Syllabic Texts*, Wiesbaden 2005", in L. Kogan, N. Koslova, S. Loesov & S. Tischchenko (eds.), Вавилон и Библия 3. Древнеближневосточные, библейские и семитологические исследования (Babel und Bibel 3. Annual of Ancient Near Eastern, Old Testament, and Semitic Studies), Winona Lake, IN, 2006, 555–588

Koslova, N., *Neusumerische Verwaltungstexte aus Umma aus der Sammlung der Ermitage zu St. Petersburg - Russland.* MVN 21, Rome 2000

Kramer, S. N., "New Tablets from Fara", *JAOS* 52 (1932), 110–132

Kramer, S. N., M. Çığ & H. Kızılyay, *İstanbul Arkeoloji Müzelerinde Bulunan: Sumer edebî tablet ve parçaları* 1, Ankara 1969

Kraus, F. R., "Nippur und Isin nach altbabylonischen Rechtsurkunden", *JCS* 3 (1951) in cooperation with the Archeological Museums of Istanbul and The American Schools of Oriental Research, v–228

—— *Sumerer und Akkader, ein Problem der altmesopotamischen Geschichte.* Mededelingen der Koninklijke Niederlandse Akademie van Wetenschappen, Afd. Letterkunde, nieuwe reeks 33 no. 8, Amsterdam & London 1970

Krebernik, M., *Die Beschwörungen aus Fara und Ebla. Untersuchungen zur ältesten Keilschriftlichen Beschwörungsliteratur.* Texte und Studien zur Orientalistik Bd. 2, Hildesheim, Zürich & New York, NY, 1984

—— "Die Götterlisten aus Fara", *ZA* 76 (1986), 161–204

—— "Lugal-a'abba", *RlA* 7 (1987–90), 109

—— "Lugal-abzu", *RlA* 7 (1987–90), 110

—— "Lugal-agrunna", *RlA* 7 (1987–90), 110

—— "Lugal-amaru", *RlA* 7 (1987–90), 110

—— *Die Personennamen der Ebla-Texte: eine Zwischenbilanz.* BBVO 7, Berlin 1988

—— "review of Gelb & Kienast, *Die altakkadischen Königsinschriften des dritten Jahrtausends v. Chr.* FAOS 7", *ZA* 81 (1991), 133–143

—— "Mesopotamian Myths at Ebla: *ARET* 5, 6 and *ARET* 5, 7", in P. Fronzaroli (ed.), *Literature and Literary Language at Ebla.* QuadSem 18 1992, 63–149

—— "Ein Keulenkopf mit Weihung an Gilgameš im Vorderasiatischen Museum, Berlin", *AoF* 21 (1994), 5–12

—— "Zur Einleitung der zà-me-Hymnen aus Tell Abū Ṣalābīḫ", in P. Calmeyer, K. Hecker, L. Jakob-Rost & C. B. F. Walker (eds.), *Beiträge zur altorientalischen Archäologie und Altertumskunde: Festschrift für Bartel Hrouda zum 65. Geburtstag*, Wiesbaden 1994, 151–157

—— "Zur Interpretation von ARET 5, 24–26", in B. Pongratz-Leisten, H. Kühne & P. Xella (eds.), *Ana šadî Labnāni lū allik. Beiträge zu altorientalischen und mittelmeerischen Kulturen. Festschrift für Wolfgang Röllig.* AOAT 247, Neukirchen-Vluyn 1997, 185–192

—— "Namnir", *RlA* 9 (1998–2001), 140

—— "Zur Struktur und Geschichte des älteren sumerischen Onomastikons" in M. P. Streck & S. Weninger (eds.), *Altorientalische und semitische Onomastik.* AOAT 296, Münster 2002, 1–74

—— "Drachenmutter und Himmelsrebe? Zur Frühgeschichte Dumuzis und seiner Familie", in W. Sallaberger, K. Volk & A. Zgoll (eds.), *Literatur, Politik und Recht. Festschrift für Claus Wilcke.* Orientalia Biblica et Christiana 14, Wiesbaden 2003, 151–180

—— "Neues zu den Fāra-Texten", *NABU* 2006/15

—— "Šar-ur und Šar-gaz", *RlA* 12 (2009–11), 84–86

Krecher, J., "Neue sumerische Rechtsurkunden des 3. Jahrtausends", *ZA* 63 (1973), 145–271

—— "Sumerische und nichtsumerische Schicht in der Schriftkultur von Ebla", in A. Archi (ed.) *Il bilinguismo a Ebla. Atti del Convegno Internazionale (Napoli, 19–22 aprile 1982)*, Naples 1984, 139–166

—— "/ur/ „Mann“, /eme/ „Frau“ und die sumerische Herkunft des Wortes urdu(-d) „Sklave“", *WO* 18 (1987), 7–19

—— "UD.GAL.NUN versus 'Normal' Sumerian: Two Literatures or One?", in P. Fronzaroli (ed.), *Literature and Literary Language at Ebla.* QuadSem 18 1992, 285–303

—— "Über einige 'zusammengesetzte Verben' im Sumerischen", in A. F. Rainey, A. Kempinski, M. Sigrist & D. Ussishkin (eds.) *Kinattūtu ša dārâti: Raphael Kutscher Memorial Volume.* Tel Aviv Occasional Publications Series 1, Tel Aviv 1993, 107–118

Kutscher, R., *Oh Angry Sea* (a-ab-ba hu-luh-ha): The History of A Sumerian Congregational Lament. Yale Near Eastern Researches 6, New Haven, CT, & London 1975

—— *The Brockmon Tablets at the University of Haifa. Royal Inscriptions*, Haifa 1989

Lafont, B., *Documents administratifs sumériens, provenant du site de Tello et conservées au Musée du Louvre.* Édition Recherche sur les Civilisations, Mémoires 61, Paris 1985

Lafont, B. & F. Yıldız, *Tablettes cunéiformes de Tello au Musée d'Istanbul datant de l'époque de la IIIe dynastie d'Ur*, 1 (*ITT* II/1, 617–1038). PIHANS 65, Leiden 1989

—— *Tablettes cunéiformes de Tello au Musée d'Istanbul datant de l'époque de la IIIe dynastie d'Ur*, 2 (*ITT* II/1, 2544–2819, 3158–4342, 4708–4713). PIHANS 77, Leiden 1996

Lambek, M., "What's in A Name? Name Bestowal and the Identity of Spirits in Mayotte and Northwest Madagascar", in G. vom Bruck & B. Bodenhorn (eds.), *The Anthropology of Names and Naming*, Cambridge 2006, 115–138

Lambert, M. "Quatres nouveaux contrats de l'époque de Shuruppak", in M. Lurker (ed.), *In Memoriam Eckhard Unger: Beiträge zu Geschichte, Kultur und Religion des Alten Orients*, Baden-Baden 1971, 27–49

—— "L'expansion de Lagash au temps d'Entéména", *RSO* 47 (1973), 1–22

—— "AO 15540", *OrAnt* 18 (1979), 225f.

—— "Grand document juridique de Nippur", *RA* 73 (1979), 1–22

Lambert, W. G., *Babylonian Wisdom Literature*, Oxford 1960

—— "Lugal-dug-idu", *RlA* 7 (1987–90), 133

—— "Lugal-dur(a)", *RlA* 7 (1987–90), 134

—— "Lugal-edinna", *RlA* 7 (1987–90), 137

—— "Lugal-Emuša", *RlA* 7 (1987–90), 137

—— "Lugal-ḫegalla", *RlA* 7 (1987–90), 141

—— "Lugal-idda", *RlA* 7 (1987–90), 142

—— "Lugal-igiḫuš", *RlA* 7 (1987–90), 142

—— "Lugal-ilduma", *RlA* 7 (1987–90), 142

—— "Lugal-inimgina", *RlA* 7 (1987–90), 143

—— "Lugalkalaga", *RlA* 7 (1987–90), 145

—— "Lugal-kalamma-utud", *RlA* 7 (1987–90), 145

—— “Lugal-kur-dub”, *RlA* 7 (1987–90), 147
—— “Lugal-kurra”, *RlA* 7 (1987–90), 147
—— “Lugal-magurra”, *RlA* 7 (1987–90), 148
—— “Lugal-Meslama”, *RlA* 7 (1987–90), 149
—— “Lugal-namtarra”, *RlA* 7 (1987–90), 150
—— “Lugal-nirgal”, *RlA* 7 (1987–90), 150
—— “Lugal-nišaga/Lugal-nisigga”, *RlA* 7 (1987–90), 150
—— “Lugal-nitazi”, *RlA* 7 (1987–90), 150
—— “Lugalpa’e/Lugal-urupa’e”, *RlA* 7 (1987–90), 150
—— “Lugal-sapar”, *RlA* 7 (1987–90), 151
——“Lugal-si”, *RlA* 7 (1987–90), 151
—— “Lugalsisa”, *RlA* 7 (1987–90), 151–152
—— “Lugal-šudde”, *RlA* 7 (1987–90), 152
—— “Lugal-Urim”, *RlA* 7 (1987–90), 153
—— “Lugal-zulumma”, *RlA* 7 (1987–90), 157
—— “An Old Akkadian List of Personal Names”, in E. Leichty, M. DeJ. Ellis, P. Gerardi (eds.), *A Scientific Humanist: Studies in Memory of Abraham Sachs*. Occasional Publications of the Samuel Noah Kramer Fund 9, Philadelphia, PA, 1988, 251–259
—— “Notes on a work of the Most Ancient Semitic Literature”, *JCS* 41 (1989), 1–33
—— “The Names of Umma”, *JNES* 49 (1990), 75–80
—— “The Language of ARET V 6 and 7” in P. Fronzaroli (ed.), *Literature and Literary Language at Ebla.* QuadSem 18 1992, 41–62
—— “Review of R. A. di Vito, *Studies in Third Millennium Sumerian and Akkadian Personal Names: The Designation and Conception of the Personal God*,” *OrNS* 64 (1995), 131–136
—— “Kingship in Ancient Mesopotamia”, in J. Day (ed.), *King and Messiah in Israel and the Ancient Near East. Proceedings of the Oxford Old Testament Seminar.* JSOTS 270, Sheffield 1998, 54–70
Langdon, S., “Two Tablets of the Period of Lugalanda”, *Babyloniaca* 4 (1911), 246–247
—— “The Sumerian Expression si-ni-tum: Capital, Balance Carried Forward”, *Babyloniaca* 6 (1912), 41–53
—— “Names (Sumerian)” in J. Hastings, J. A. Selbie & L. H. Gray (eds.), *Encyclopedia of Religion and Ethics*, Volume 9, Edinburgh 1917, 171–175
—— Langdon, Excavations at Kish vol. 1: 1923–1924, Paris 1924
—— *The Pictographic Inscriptions from Jemdet Nasr Excavated by the Oxford and Field Museum Expedition.* OECT 7, London 1928
van Langendonck, W., *Theory and Typology of Proper Names*, Berlin 2007
Ławecka, D., “North-Babylonian Motifs in Early Dynastic Mesopotamian Glyptics”, in O. Drewnowska (ed.), *Here & There across the Ancient Near East. Studies in Honour of Krystyna Łyczkowska*, Warsaw 2009, 121–148
Lebeau, M., “Tell Beydar/Nabada: An Archaeological Summary, Facts and Datings”, in J. Becker, R. Hempelmann & E. Rehm (eds.), *Kulturlandschaft Syrien: Zentrum und Peripherie. Festschrift für Jan-Waalke Meyer*. AOAT 371 Münster 2010, 291–330

Legrain, L., *Les temps des rois d'Ur: Recherches sur la société antique, d'après des textes nouveaux*, 2 vols., Paris 1912

—— *Royal Inscriptions and Fragments from Nippur and Babylon*. PBS 15, Philadelphia, PA, 1926

—— "Quelques textes anciens", *RA* 32 (1935), 125–130

—— *Archaic Seal Impressions*. UE 3, London & Philadelphia, PA, 1936

—— *Business Documents of the Third Dynasty of Ur*. UET 3, 2 vols., London 1937 & 1947

—— *Seal Cylinders*. UE 10, London & Philadelphia, PA, 1951

Lenzen, H., XVI. vorläufiger Bericht über die von dem Deutschen Archäologischen Institut und der Deutschen Orient-Gesellschaft aus Mitteln der Deutschen Forschungsgemeinschaft unternommenen Ausgrabungen in Uruk-Warka, Winter 1957/58. Abhandlungen der Deutschen Orient-Gesellschaft 5, Berlin 1960

Lenzen, H. & H. J. Nissen, XXV. vorläufiger Bericht über die von dem Deutschen Archäologischen Institut und der Deutschen Orient-Gesellschaft aus Mitteln der Deutschen Forschungsgemeinschaft unternommenen Ausgrabungen in Uruk-Warka, Winter 1966/1967. Abhandlungen der Deutschen Orient-Gesellschaft 17, Berlin 1974

Levy, S. J., "Harmal Geographical List", *Sumer* 3 (1947), 50–83

Levy, S. & P. Artzi, "Sumerian and Akkadian Documents from Public and Private Collections in Israel", *'Atiqot* ES 4 (1965), 1–15; pl. 1–47

Limet, H., *L'Anthroponymie sumérienne dans les documents de la 3e dynastie d'Ur*. Bibliothèque de la Faculté de Philosophie et Lettres de l'Université de Liège, Fasc. 180, Paris 1968

—— *Documents de la période d'Agadé appartenant à l'Université de Liège*. Bibliothèque de la Faculté de Philosophie et Lettres de l'Université de Liège, Fasc. 206 (Paris 1973)

—— *Textes sumériens de la IIIe dynastie d'Ur*. Documents du Proche-Orient ancien: Épigraphie, I, Brussels 1976

—— "Onomastique sumérienne", in E. Eichler et al. (eds.), *Namenforschung. Name Studies. Les noms propres*. Handbücher zur Sprach- und Kommunikationswissenschaft vol. 11/1, Berlin & New York, NY, 1995, 851–854

Lipiński, E., (ed.), *Semitic Languages. Outline of a Comparative Grammar*. OLA 80, Leuven 1997

Loretz, O., *Texte aus Chagar Bazar und Tell Brak*. AOAT 3/1, Neukirchen Vluyn 1969

Luckenbill, D. D., *Inscriptions from Adab*. OIP 14, Chicago, IL, 1930

Lämmerhirt, K., *Wahrheit und Trug: Untersuchungen zur altorientalischen Begriffsgeschichte*. AOAT 348, Münster 2010

Maekawa, K., "The Development of the É-MÍ in Lagash during Early Dynastic III", *Mesopotamia* 8/9 (1973–74), 77–144

—— "The Agricultural Texts of Ur III Lagash of the British Museum", *ASJ* 3 (1981), 37–61

Maiocchi, M., *Classical Sargonic Tablets Chiefly from Adab in the Cornell University Collections*. CUSAS 13, Bethesda, MD, 2009

Mander, P., "Brevi considerazioni sul testo "lessicale" SF 23 = SF 24 e paralleli da Abu-Ṣalabīkh", *OrAnt* 19 (1980), 187–192

—— *Il Pantheon di Abu-Ṣālabīkh. Contributo allo studio del pantheon sumerico arcaico*. IUO Series Minor 26, Naples 1986

—— "Sumerian Personal Names in Ebla", *JAOS* 108 (1988), 481–483

—— "Lugal-inim-kal (Lord: Mighty Word)" in C. Conio (ed.), *La parola creatrice in India e nel Medio Oriente. Atti del Seminario della Facoltà di Lettere dell'Università di Pisa, 29–31 maggio 1991*, Pisa 1994, 13–34

Marchesi, G., "Notes on Two Alleged Literary Texts from Al-Hiba/Lagaš", *StEL* 16 (1999), 3–17

—— "Who was Buried in the Royal Tombs of Ur? The Epigraphic and Textual Data", *OrNS* 73 (2004), 153–197

—— *LUMMA in the Onomasticon and Literature of Ancient Mesopotamia*. HANE/S 10, Padova 2006

Margueron, J.-C., *Mari: Métropole de l'Euphrate au IIIe et au début du IIe millénaire av. J.-C.*, Paris 2004

Martin, H., J. Moon & J. N. Postgate, *Graves 1 to 99*. Abu Salabikh Excavations vol. 2, Hertford 1985

Martin, H., F. Pomponio, G. Visicato & A. Westenholz, *The Fara Tablets in the University of Philadelphia Museum of Archaeology and Anthropology* Bethesda, MD, 2001

Marzahn, J., *Altsumerische Verwaltungstexte aus Girsu/Lagaš*. VS 25 (Neue Folge Heft 9), Berlin 1991

—— *Altsumerische Verwaltungstexte und ein Brief aus Girsu/Lagaš*. VS 27 (Neue Folge Heft 11), Mainz 1996

Marzahn, J. & H. Neumann, "Eine altsumerische Urkunde aus Girsu über Silberzahlungen", *AoF* 22 (1995), 110–116

Matthiae, P., "The Archives of the Royal Palace G of Ebla: Distribution and Arrangement of the Tablets According to the Archaeological Evidence", in K. Veenhof (ed.), *Cuneiform Archives and Libraries*. CRRA 30. PIHANS 57, Leiden 1986, 53–71

—— *The Royal Archives of Ebla*, Milan 2007

Matouš, L., "Einige Bemerkungen zu altsumerischen Rechtsurkunden", *ArOr* 39 (1971), 1–15

McCown, D. E., R. C. Haines & R. D. Biggs, *Nippur II. The North Temple and Sounding E*. Excavations of the Joint Expedition to Nippur of the American Schools of Oriental Research and the Oriental Institute of the University of Chicago. OIP 97, Chicago, IL, 1978

McMahon, A. (ed.), *The Early Dynastic to Akkadian Transition: The Area WF Sounding at Nippur*. OIP 129, Chicago, IL, 2006

Meek, T. J., *Old Akkadian, Sumerian, and Cappadocian Texts from Nuzi*. Excavations at Nuzi Conducted by the Semitic Museum and the Fogg Art Museum of Harvard University, with the Cooperation of the American School of Oriental Research at Baghdad vol. 3. HSS 10, Cambridge, MA, 1935

—— "The Iterative Names in the Old Akkadian Texts from Nuzi", *RA* 32 (1935), 51–55

van der Meer, P. E., *Syllabaries A, B^1 and B with Miscellaneous Lexicographical Texts from the Herbert Weld Collection*. OECT 4, London 1938

Meissner, B., *Babylonien und Assyrien* 1, Kulturgeschichtliche Bibliothek. 1. Reihe, Bd. 3, Heidelberg 1920

de Meyer, L. (ed.), *Tell ed-Dēr* 3: *Sounding at Abū Ḥabbah (Sippar)*, Leuven 1980

Michalowski, P., "History as Charter: Some Observations on the Sumerian King List", *JAOS* 103 (1983), 237–248

—— "Magan and Meluhha Once Again", *JCS* 40 (1988), 156–164

—— *The Lamentation over the Destruction of Sumer and Ur*. MesCiv 1, Winona Lake, IN, 1989

—— "Charisma and Control: On Continuity and Change in Early Mesopotamian Bureaucratic Systems", in McG. Gibson & R. D. Biggs (eds.), *The Organization of Power: Aspects of Bureaucracy in the Ancient Near East*. Studies in Ancient Oriental Civilization 46, 1st edition Chicago, IL, 1987; 2nd edition with corrections 1991, 45–57

—— "Negation as Description: The Metaphor of Everyday Life in Early Mesopotamian Literature", *Fs Civil*, 131–136

—— "A Man Called Enmebaragesi", in W. Sallaberger, K. Volk & A. Zgoll (eds.), *Literatur, Politik und Recht. Festschrift für Claus Wilcke*, Orientalia Biblica et Christiana 14, Wiesbaden 2003, 195–208

Milano, L., "Un nuovo contratto di cessione immobiliare dell'epoca di Fāra", *StEL* 3 (1986), 3–12

—— *Testi amministrativi: Assegnazioni di prodotti alimentari (Archivio L. 2712 - parte 1)*. ARET 9, Rome 1990

—— *Mozan* 2: *The Epigraphic Finds of the Sixth Season*. SMS 5/1, Malibu, FL, 1991

Militarev, A. & L. Kogan, *Semitic Etymological Dictionary vol.* 2: *Animal Names*. AOAT 278/2, Münster 2005

Millard, A. R., "Ebla Personal Names and Personal Names of the First Millennium B.C. in Syria and Palestine", in A. Archi (ed.), *Eblaite Personal Names and Semitic Name-Giving. Papers of a Symposium Held in Rome July 15–17, 1985*. ARES 1, Rome 1988, 159–164

Mirelman, S. & W. Sallaberger, "The Performance of a Sumerian Wedding Song", *ZA* 100 (2010), 177–196

Molina, M. & H. Sanchiz, "The Cuneiform Tablets of the Varela Collection", *StEL* 24 (2007), 1–15

Monaco, S., *The Cornell University Archaic Tablets*. CUSAS 1, Bethesda, MD, 2007

—— *Early Dynastic mu-iti Cereal Texts in the Cornell University Cuneiform Collections*. CUSAS 14, Bethesda, MD, 2011

al-Mutawalli, N. A., "Jukha (Umma) - the First and Second Seasons 1999–2000", *Sumer* 54 (2009), 53–82 (in Arabic)

Myhrman, D. W., *Sumerian Administrative Documents Dated in the Reigns of the Kings of the Second Dynasty of Ur from the Temple Archives of Nippur Preserved in Philadelphia*. BE 3/1, Philadelphia, PA, 1910

Neumann, H., "Eine Inschrift des Königs Lugalkisalsi (VA 4855)", *AoF* 8 (1981), 75–82

—— "Der sumerische Brief UVB 7, Taf. 23c (W 15966c)", *AoF* 15 (1988), 209–210

—— "Assur in altakkadischer Zeit: Die Texte", in H. Waetzoldt & H. Hauptmann (eds.), *Assyrien im Wandel der Zeiten*. CRRA 39. HSAO 6, Heidelberg 1997, 133–138

Nies, J. B. & C. E. Kaiser, *Historical, Religious and Economic Texts and Antiquities*. BIN 2, New Haven, CT, London, & Oxford 1920

Nigro, L., "The Two Steles of Sargon: Iconology and Visual Propaganda at the Beginning of Royal Akkadian Relief", *Iraq* 60 (1998), 85–102

Nikol'skij, M. V., *Dokumenty chozâjstvennoj otčetnosti drevnejšej epochi Chaldei iz sobraniâ N. P. Lichačeva*. Drevnosti Vostočnyâ vol. III/2, St. Petersburg 1908

—— *Dokumenty chozâjstvennoj otčetnosti drevnejšej epochi Chaldei iz sobraniâ N. P. Lichačeva II: Epocha dinastii Agade i epocha dinastii Ura*. Drevnosti Vostočnyâ, vol. V, Moscow 1915

Nissen, H. J., *Zur Datierung des Königsfriedhofes von Ur: Unter besonderer Berücksichtigung der Stratigraphie der Privatgräber*. Beiträge zur Ur- und frühgeschichtlichen Archäologie des Mittelmeer-Kulturraumes 3, Bonn 1966

—— *Grundzüge einer Geschichte der Frühzeit des Vorderen Orients*, Darmstadt 1983

Nöldeke, A., E. Heinrich & H. Lenzen, Zehnten vorläufiger Bericht über die von der Deutschen Forschungsgemeinschaft in Uruk-Warka unternommenen Ausgrabungen. Abhandlungen der Preußischen Akademie der Wissenschaften Jahrg. 1939, Berlin 1939

Oates, D., J. Oates, H. McDonald et al., *Nagar in the Third Millennium BC*. ETB 2, Cambridge & London 2001

Oberhuber, K., *Sumerische und akkadische Keilschriftdenkmäler des Archäologischen Museums zu Florenz*, 2 vols. Innsbrucker Beiträge zu Kulturwissenschaft Sonderhefte 7, 8, Innsbruck 1958, 1960

del Olmo Lete, G. & J. Sanmartín, *A Dictionary of the Ugaritic Language in the Alphabetic Tradition*. Second revised edition. Handbook of Oriental Studies 67, Leiden & Boston 2004

Opificius, R., "Girsu. B. Nach archäologischem Befund", *RlA* 3 (1957–71), 391–401

Oppenheim, A. L., "Akkadian *pul(u)ḫ(t)u* and *melammu*", *JAOS* 63 (1943), 31–34

—— *Ancient Mesopotamia. Portrait of a Dead Civilization*, Chicago, IL, 1964. Revised ed. completed by Erica Reiner, Chicago, IL, 1977

Owen, D. I., *The John Frederick Lewis Collection*. MVN 3, Rome 1975

—— *Neo-Sumerian Archival Texts Primarily from Nippur in the University Museum, the Oriental Institute and the Iraq Museum*, Winona Lake, IN, 1982

—— *Neo-Sumerian Texts from American Collections*. MVN 15, Rome 1991

Ozaki, T., *Keilschrifttexte aus japanischen Sammlungen*. SANTAG 7, Wiesbaden 2002

—— "Six Sumerian Cuneiform Texts in Japan", *JAC* 22 (2007), 1–8

—— "Three Early Dynastic Sumerian Sales Contracts of Immovables Housed in the Okayama Orient Museum", *JAC* 23 (2008), 55–64

Ozaki, T. & M. Sigrist, *Ur III Administrative Tablets from the British Museum, Part One*. Biblioteca del Próximo Oriente Antiguo vol. 1, Madrid 2006

Parrot, A., *Tello: Vingt campagnes de fouilles (1877–1933)*, Paris 1948

—— *Le Temple d'Ishtar*. MAM 1. Institut Français d'Archéologie de Beyrouth. Bibliothèque archéologique et historique vol. 65, Paris 1956

Parrot, A. & G. Dossin, *Les Temples d'Ishtarat et de Ninni-zaza*. MAM 3. Institut Français d'Archéologie de Beyrouth. Bibliothèque archéologique et historique vol. 86, Paris 1967

A. Parrot & G. Dossin, *Le «trésor» d'Ur*. MAM 4. Institut Français d'Archéologie de Beyrouth. Bibliothèque archéologique et historique vol. 87, Paris 1968

Pedersén, O., *Archives and Libraries in the City of Assur* vol. 1, Uppsala 1985

Pedersén, O., P. J. J. Sinclair, I. Hein & J. Andersson, "Cities and Urban Landscapes in the Ancient Near East and Egypt with Special Focus on the City of Babylon", in P. J. J. Sinclair, G. Nordquist, F. Herschend & C. Isendahl (eds.), *The Urban Mind: Cultural and Environmental Dynamics*, Uppsala 2010, 113–147

Peterson, J., *Godlists from Old Babylonian Nippur in the University Museum, Philadelphia*. AOAT 362, Münster 2009

Pettinato, G., *Das altorientalische Menschenbild und die sumerischen und akkadischen Schöpfungsmythen*, Ph.D. diss., Heidelberg 1971

—— *Testi economici di Lagaš del Museo di Instanbul. Parte* 1: *La. 7001–7600*. MVN 6, Rome 1977

—— *Testi economici di Lagaš del Museo di Istanbul. Parte* 2: *La. 7601–8200*. MVN 7, Rome 1978

—— "Ebla e la Bibbia", *OrAnt* 19 (1980), 49–72

—— *Testi lessicali monolingui della bibliotheca L. 2769*. MEE 3, Naples 1981

—— *Testi lessicali bilingui della bibliotheca L. 2769. Parte* 1: *Traslitterazione dei testi e ricostruzione del VE*. MEE 4, Naples 1982

—— *Testi economici neo-sumerici del British Museum (BM 12230–BM 12390)*. MVN 17, Rome 1993

—— *L'uomo cominciò a scrivere: Iscrizioni cuneiformi della collezione Michail*, Milan 1997

Pinches, T. G., *The Amherst Tablets: Being an Account of the Babylonian Inscriptions in the Collection of the Right Hon. Lord Amherst of Hackney, F.S.A. at Didlington Hall, Norfolk. Part* 1: *Texts of the Period Extending to and Including the Reign of Bûr-Sin (about 2500 B.C.)*, London 1908

—— *Miscellaneous Texts*. CT 44, London 1963

Poebel, A., *Die sumerischen Personennamen zur Zeit der Dynastie von Larsam und der ersten Dynastie von Babylon*. Habilitationsschrift, Breslau 1910

—— *Historical and Grammatical Texts*. PBS 5, Philadelphia, PA, 1914

Pohl, A., *Vorsargonische und sargonische Wirtschaftstexte*. TMH 5, Leipzig 1935

—— *Rechts' und Verwaltungsurkunden der III. Dynastie von Ur*. TMH NF 1–2, Leipzig 1937

Pollock, S., "Of Priestesses, Princes and Poor Relations: The Dead in the Royal Cemetery of Ur", *CAJ* 1 (1991), 171–189

Polonsky, J., "The Mesopotamian Conceptualization of Birth and the Determination of Destiny at Sunrise", in A. K. Guinan, M. deJ. Ellis, A. J. Ferrara, S. M. Freedman, M. T. Rutz, L. Sassmannshausen, S. Tinney & M. W. Waters (eds.), *If a Man Builds a Joyful House; Assyriological Studies in Honor of Erle Verdun Leichty*. CM 31, Leiden & Boston, MA, 2006, 297–311

Pomponio, F., *La prosopografia dei testi presargonici di Fara*. Dipartimento di studi semitici, Studi Semitici nuova serie 3, Rome 1987

—— "I nomi personali dei testi amministrativi di Abū Ṣalābīḫ", *StEL* 8 (1991), 141–147

Pomponio F. & G. Visicato, *Early Dynastic Administrative Tablets of Šuruppak*. IUO Series Maior 6 (Naples 1994)

—— "Tavolette cuneiformi del III millennio di una collezione privata", *StEL* 17 (2000), 3–12

Pomponio, F., G. Visicato, A. Westenholz et al., *Le tavolette cuneiformi di Adab delle collezioni della Banca d'Italia*, vol. 1, Rome 2006

Pomponio, F., M. Stol, A. Westenholz et al., *Tavolette cuneiformi di varia provenienza delle collezioni della Banca d'Italia*, vol. 2, Rome 2006

Porada, E., "A Lapis Lazuli Disk with Relief Carving Inscribed for King Rimuš", in D. Charpin & F. Joannès (eds.), *La circulation des biens, des personnes et des idées dans le Proche-Orient ancien*. CRRA 38, Paris 1992, 69–72

Postgate, J. N., "Old Sumerian GE_{23} = aš ?", *AfO* 24 (1973), 77

—— "Two Points of Grammar in Gudea", *JCS* 26 (1974), 16–54

—— "Scratching the Surface at Abu Salabikh: Urban Archaeology Sumerian Style", *BCSMS* 14 (1987), 21–29

—— *Early Mesopotamia: Society and Economy at the Dawn of History*, 2nd, revised ed., London 1994

Potts, T., *Mesopotamia and the East: an Archaeological and Historical Study of Foreign Relations 3400–2000 BC*. Oxford University Committee for Archaeology Monograph 37, Oxford 1994

Potts, D. T., *Mesopotamian Civilization: The Material Foundations*, Ithaca, NY, 1997

Powell, M., "Graphic Criteria for Dating in the Old Babylonian Period", *OrNS* 43 (1974), 398–403

—— "Texts from the Time of Lugalzagesi: Problems and Perspectives in their Interpretation", *HUCA* 49 (1978), 1–58

—— "Karkar, Dabrum, and Tall Ğidr: An Unresolved Geographical Problem", *JNES* 39 (1980), 47–52

Radner, K., *Die Macht des Namens: Altorientalische Strategien zur Selbsterhaltung*. SANTAG 8, Wiesbaden 2005

Ranke, H., "Review of K. Tallqvist, *Neubabylonisches Namenbuch*", *AJSL* 23 (1907), 358–365

Rasheed, F., "Akkadian Texts from Tell Sleima", *Sumer* 40 (1981), 55–56.

—— *Aqdam al-kitābāt al-mišmārīya l-muktašafa fī ḥauḍ Sadd Ḥamrīn* (*The Ancient Inscriptions in Himrin Area*), Baghdad 1981

Reisman, D., "Iddin-Dagan's Sacred Marriage Hymn", *JCS* 25 (1973), 185–202

Reisner, G., *Tempelurkunden aus Telloh*. Königliche Museen zu Berlin: Mittheilungen aus den orientalischen Sammlungen 16, Berlin 1901

Renfrew, C., "Towards a Cognitive Archaeology", in C. Renfrew & E. B. Zubrow (eds.), *The Ancient Mind: Elements of Cognitive Archaeology*, Cambridge 1994, 3–12

Roberts, J. J. M., *The Earliest Semitic Pantheon: A Study of the Semitic Deities Attested in Mesopotamia before Ur III*, Baltimore & London 1972

Rosengarten, Y. "La notion sumérienne de souveraineté divine: Uru-ka-gi-na et son dieu Nin-ĝír-su", *RHR* 156 (1959), 129–160

—— *Répertoire commenté des signes présargoniques sumériens de Lagaš*, Paris 1967

Rowton, M. B., "Sumer's Strategic Periphery in Topological Perspective", in G. van Driel, Th. J. H. Krispijn, M. Stol, K. R. Veenhof (eds.), *Zikir šumim:*

Assyriological Studies Presented to F. R. Kraus on the Occasion of his Seventieth Birthday, Leiden 1982, 318–325

Rubio, G., "Eblaite, Akkadian, and East Semitic", in G. Deutscher & N. J. C. Kouwenberg (eds.), *The Akkadian Language in its Semitic Context: Studies in the Akkadian of the Third and Second Millennium BC*, Leiden 2006, 110–139

—— "On sibilants in third-millennium Akkadian", *NABU* 2009/66

Römer, W. H. Ph., *Sumerische 'Königshymnen' der Isin-Zeit*, Leiden 1965

—— "The Religion of Ancient Mesopotamia", in C. J. Bleeker & G. Widengren (eds.) *Religions of the Past.* Historia Religionum: Handbook for the History of Religions, vol. 1, Leiden 1969, 115–194

Salgues, E., "Naram-Sin's Conquests of Subartu and Armanum",in G. Barjamovic, J. L.Dahl, U. S. Koch, W. Sommerfeld & J. Goodnick Westenholz (eds.), *Akkade is King: A Collection of Papers by Friends and Colleagues Presented to Aage Westenholz on the Occasion of his 70th Birthday 15th of May 2009.* PIHANS 118, Leiden 2011, 253–272

Sallaberger, W., *Der kultische Kalender der Ur III-Zeit.* Untersuchungen zur Assyriologie und Vorderasiatischen Archäologie. Ergänzungsband zur *Zeitschrift für Assyriologie und Vorderasiatische Archäologie* 7, 2 vols., Berlin 1993

—— "Nippur als religiöses Zentrum Mesopotamiens im historischen Wandel" in G. Wilhelm (ed.), *Die orientalische Stadt: Kontinuität, Wandel, Bruch.* 9.–10. Mai 1996 in Halle/Saale. CDOG 1, Saarbrücken 1997, 147–168

—— "Der antike Name von Tell Beydar: Nabada (*Na-ba$_4$-da*^{ki}/*Na-ba-ti-um*^{ki})", *NABU* 1998/130

—— "The Sumerian Verb na de$_5$ (-g) "To Clear"", in Y. Sefati, P. Artzi, C. Cohen, B. L. Eichler & V. A. Hurowitz (eds.), *An Experienced Scribe Who Neglects Nothing: Ancient Near Eastern Studies in Honor of Jacob Klein*, Bethesda, MD, 2005, 229–253

Sallaberger, W. & A. Westenholz, *Mesopotamien: Akkade-Zeit und Ur III-Zeit. Annäherungen* 3. OBO 160/1, Freiburg & Göttingen 1999

—— ""bringen" im Sumerischen: Lesung und Bedeutung von de$_6$(DU) und tum$_2$(DU)", in R. Rollinger (ed.), *Von Sumer bis Homer: Festschrift für Manfred Schretter zum 60. Geburtstag am 25. Februar 2004.* AOAT 325, Münster 2005, 557–576

—— "The City and the Palace at Archaic Ur", in K. Šašková, L. Pecha & P. Charvát, *Shepherds of the Black-Headed People: The Royal Office Vis-À-Vis Godhead in Ancient Mesopotamia*, Plzeň 2010, 31–37

Salonen, E., *Die Waffen der alten Mesopotamier.* Studia Orientalia edidit Societas Orientalis Fennica 33, Helsinki 1965

Saporetti, C., *Onomastica Medio-Assira.* StPohl 6, 2 vols., Rome 1970

de Sarzec, E. & L. Heuzey, *Découvertes en Chaldée* 2, Paris 1912

Sassmannshausen, L., "Funktion und Stellung der Herolde (nigir/*nāgiru*) im Alten Orient", BagM 26 (1995), 85–194

Sauren, H., *Wirtschaftsurkunden aus der Zeit der III Dynastie von Ur im Besitz des Musée d'Art et d'histoire in Genf nebst kleinerer Sammlungen.* MVN 2, Rome 1974

Scheil, V., *Textes élamites-sémitiques: première série.* MDP 2, Paris 1900

—— "Une nouvelle dynastie suméro-accadienne. Les rois «Guti»", *CRAIB* 55 (1911), 318–327

Scheil, V. & L. Legrain, *Textes élamites-sémitiques: cinquième série*. MDP 14, Paris 1913

Schileico, M. W. G., "Notes présargoniques", *RA* 11 (1914), 61–68

Schmandt-Besserat, D., *Before Writing*. 2 vols. *From Counting to Cuneiform*, and *A Catalog of Near Eastern Tokens*, Austin, TX, 1992

—— "The Personal Name in Mesopotamia: Its Impact on the Evolution of Cuneiform", in P. Matthiae et al. (eds.), Proceedings of the First International Congress on the Archaeology of the Ancient Near East, Rome May 18th–23rd 1998, 2 vols., Rome 2000

—— "Signs of Life", *Archaeology Odyssey* vol. 4 no. 1 (Jan/Feb 2002), 6–7; 63

Schneider, N., *Die Drehem- und Djoha-Urkunden der Strassburger Universitäts- und Landesbibliothek in Autographie und mit systematischen Wörterverzeichnissen*. AnOr 1, Rome 1931

Schramm, W. "Ein altsumerischer Tonnagel", *WO* 7 (1973–74), 16–17

Schretter, M. & K. Oberhuber, "Philologische Forschung am Institut für Sprachen und Kulturen des Alten Orients an der Universität Innsbruck nach 1945", in F. Schipper (ed.), *Zwischen Euphrat und Tigris: Österreichische Forschungen zum Alten Orient*. Wiener Offene Orientalistik 3, Wien 2004, 23–35

Sefati, Y., *Love Songs in Sumerian Literature*: *Critical Edition of the Dumuzi-Inanna Songs*, Ramat Gan 1998

Selz, G. J., *Die altsumerischen Wirtschaftsurkunden der Eremitage zu Leningrad*. Altsumerische Verwaltungstexte aus Lagaš, Teil 1. FAOS 15,1 (Stuttgart 1989)

—— "Review of A. Alberti & F. Pomponio, *Pre-Sargonic and Sargonic Texts from Ur edited in UET 2, Supplement*", *OLZ* 85 (1990), 299–308

—— "Enlil und Nippur nach präsargonischen Quellen", in M. deJong Ellis (ed.), *Nippur at the Centennial*. CRRA 35. Occasional Publications of the Samuel Noah Kramer Fund 14, Philadelphia 1992, 189–225

—— "Zum Namen des Herrschers URU-INIM-GI-NA(-K)", *NABU* 1992/44

—— *Altsumerische Wirtschaftsurkunden aus amerikanischen Sammlungen. 1. Abschnitt: Einleitung; Texte aus dem Harvard Semitic Museum*. Altsumerische Verwaltungstexte aus Lagaš, Teil 2. FAOS 15,2, Stuttgart 1993

—— *Altsumerische Wirtschaftsurkunden aus amerikanischen Sammlungen. 2. Abschnitt: Einleitung; Texte aus: Free Library Philadelphia, Yale University Library, Babylonian Section. Indices, Textkopien, Photos*. Altsumerische Verwaltungstexte aus Lagaš, Teil 2. FAOS 15,2, Stuttgart 1993

—— "Über mesopotamische Herrschaftskonzepte. Zu den Ursprüngen mesopotamischer Herrscherideologie im 3. Jahrtausend", in T. Balke, O. Loretz & M. Dietrich (eds.), *dubsar an-ta-men. Studien zur Altorientalistik: Festschrift für Willem H. Ph. Römer zur Vollendung seines 70. Lebensjahres, mit Beiträgen von Freunden, Schülern und Kollegen*. AOAT 253, Münster 1998, 281–34

Seux, M.-J., *Épithètes royales akkadiennes et sumériennes*, Paris 1967

Sigrist, M., *Neo-Sumerian Account Texts in the Horn Archaeological Museum*. Andrews University Cuneiform Texts 2, Berrien Springs, MI, 1988

—— *Documents from Tablet Collections in Rochester, New York*, Bethesda, MD, 1991

—— *Texts from the British Museum*. SAT 1, Bethesda, MD, 1993

—— Neo-Sumerian Texts from the Royal Ontario Museum 1. *The Administration at Drehem*, Bethesda, MD, 1995

—— *Texts from the Yale Babylonian Collections, Part* 1. SAT 2 Bethesda, MD, 2000

—— "Les noms d'année du règne du roi Šulgi", in A. Kleinerman & J. M. Sasson (eds.), *Why Should Someone Who Knows Something Conceal It? Cuneiform Studies in Honor of David I. Owen on his 70ᵗʰ Birthday*, Bethesda, MD, 2010, 219–238

Sjöberg, Å., *Der Mondgott Nanna-Suen in der sumerischen Überlieferung. I. Teil: Texte*, Stockholm 1960

—— "Hymns to Meslamtaea, Lugalgirra and Nanna-Suen in Honour of King Ibbīsuen (Ibbīsîn) of Ur", *OrS* 19-20 (1970–71), 140–178

—— "Miscellaneous Sumerian Texts", *OrS* 23-34 (1974–75), 159–181

—— "Hymns to Ninurta with Prayers for Šūsîn of Ur and Būrsîn of Larsa", in B. L. Eichler, J. W. Heimerdinger & Å. Sjöberg (eds.), *Kramer Anniversary Volume. Cuneiform Studies in Honor of Samuel Noah Kramer*. AOAT 25, Kevelaer & Neukirchen-Vluyn 1976, 411–433

—— Trials of Strength: Athletics in Mesopotamia, *Expedition* 27/2 (1985), 7–9

—— "UET VII, 73: An Exercise Tablet Enumerating Professions", in Ö. Tunca & D. Deheselle (eds.), *Tablettes et images aux pays de Sumer et d'Akkad: Mélanges offerts à Monsieur H. Limet*. Association pour la Promotion de l'Histoire et de l'Archéologie Orientales, mémoires, 1, Liège 1996, 117–139

Sjöberg, Å. & E. Bergmann, *The Collection of Sumerian Temple Hymns and The Kesh Temple Hymn*, with a chapter by G. Gragg. TCS 3, Locust Valley, NY, 1969

Snell, D. & C. Lager, *Economic Texts from Sumer*. YOS 18, New Haven, CT, & London 1991

von Soden, W., *Grundriß der akkadischen Grammatik*. AnOr 33, Rome 1952. 3rd revised edition, Rome 1995

Sollberger, E., "Documents cunéiformes au Musée d'art et d'histoire", *Genava* 26 (1948), 48–72

—— *Corpus des inscriptions «royales» présargoniques de Lagaš*, Geneva 1956

—— "La frontière de Šara", *OrNS* 28 (1959), 336–350

—— "Review of G. G. Hackman, BIN 8", *BiOr* 16 (1959), 113–119

—— "Notes on the Early Inscriptions from Ur and El-'Obéd", *Iraq* 22 (1960), 69–89

—— "Le syllabaire présargonique de Lagaš", *ZA* 54 (1961), 1–50

—— *Royal Inscriptions. Part* 2. UET 8, London 1965

—— "Lettre d'époque sargonique", *RA* 60 (1966), 71

—— *Pre-Sargonic and Sargonic Economic Texts*. CT 50, London 1972

—— *Administrative Texts Chiefly Concerning Textiles*. ARET 8, Rome 1986

Sollberger, E. & J.-R. Kupper, *Inscriptions royales sumériennes et akkadiennes*. Littératures anciennes du Proche-Orient No. 3, Paris 1971

Sommerfeld, W., *Die Texte der Akkade-Zeit*. 1. *Das Dijala-Gebiet: Tutub*. Imgula Bd. 3/1, Münster 1999

—— "Die inschriftliche Überlieferung des 3. Jahrtausends aus Tutub" in H. Waetzoldt (ed.), *Von Sumer nach Ebla und zurück. Festschrift Giovanni Pettinato zum 27. September 1999 gewidmet von Freunden, Kollegen und Schülern*. HSAO 9, Heidelberg 2004, 285–292

—— "Sargon", *RlA* 12 (2009–11), 44–49

—— "Altakkadische Duelle", in G. Barjamovic, J. L.Dahl, U. S. Koch, W. Sommerfeld & J. Goodnick Westenholz (eds.), *Akkade is King: A Collection of Papers by Friends and Colleagues Presented to Aage Westenholz on the Occasion of his 70th Birthday 15th of May 2009*. PIHANS 118, Leiden 2011, 287–299

Sommerfeld, W., K. Markina & N. Roudik, "Altakkadische Texte der St. Petersburger Eremitage", in L. Kogan, N. Koslova, S. Loesov & S. Tischenko (eds.), *Memoriae Igor M. Diakonoff*. Babel und Bibel 2, Winona Lake, IN, 2005, 185–231

Speleers, L., *Recueil des inscriptions de l'Asie antérieure des Musées Royaux du Cinquantenaire à Bruxelles: Textes sumériens, babyloniens et assyriens*, Brussels 1925

Stamm, J. J., *Die akkadische Namengebung*. Mitteilungen der Vorderasiatisch-Aegyptischen Gesellschaft (e.V.) Bd. 44, Leipzig 1939

Steible, H., *Rīmsîn, mein König: Drei kultische Texte aus Ur mit der Schlußdoxologie ^{d}ri-im-^{d}sîn lugal-mu*. FAOS 1, Wiesbaden 1975

—— "Legitimation von Herrschaft im Mesopotamien des 3. Jahrtausends v. Chr.", in G. Dux (ed.), *Moral und Recht im Diskurs der Moderne: zur Legitimation gesellschaftlicher Ordnung*, Opladen 2001, 67–91

—— "Von der Stadt zum Staat: Beiträge der Sumerer zur geistesgeschichtlichen und gesellschaftspolitischen Entwicklung im alten Orient", *CollAn* 7 (2008), 87–113

Steible, H. & H. Behrens, *Inschriften aus 'Lagaš.'* Die altsumerischen Bau- und Weihinschriften. Teil 1. FAOS 5, Wiesbaden 1982

—— *Kommentar zu den Inschriften aus 'Lagaš.' Inschriften ausserhalb von 'Lagaš.'* Die altsumerischen Bau- und Weihinschriften. Teil 2. FAOS 5, Wiesbaden 1982

Steible, H. & F. Yıldız, "Kupfer an ein Herdenamt in Šuruppak ?", in Ö. Tunca & D. Deheselle (eds.), *Tablettes et images aux pays de Sumer et d'Akkad: Mélanges offerts à Monsieur H. Limet*. Association pour la Promotion de l'Histoire et de l'Archéologie Orientales, mémoires, 1, Liège 1996, 149–159

Steinkeller, P., "Studies in Third Millennium Palaeography, 1: Signs TIL and BAD", *ZA* 71 (1981), 19–28

—— "A Note on sa-bar = sa-par$_4$/pàr "Casting Net"", *ZA* 75 (1985), 39–46

—— "The Reber Statue", *NABU* 1990/14

—— "On the reading of PN KIŠ-a-bí-tuš", *NABU* 1990/132

—— "Observations on the Sumerian Personal Names in Ebla Sources and on the Onomasticon of Mari and Kish", in M. E. Cohen, D. C. Snell, D. B. Weisberg (eds.), *The Tablet and the Scroll: Near Eastern Studies in Honor of William W. Hallo*, Bethesda, MD, 1993, 236–245

—— "Review of A. Westenholz, *The 'Akkadian' Texts, The Enlilemaba Texts, and the Onion Archive*. OSP 2", *JNES* 52 (1993), 141–145

—— "A Rediscovered Akkadian City?", *ASJ* 17 (1995), 275–281

—— "On Rulers, Priests and Sacred Marriage: Tracing the Evolution of Early Sumerian Kingship", in K. Watanabe (ed.), *Priests and Officials in the Ancient Near East. Papers of the Second Colloquium on the Ancient Near East – The City and its Life held at the Middle Eastern Culture Center in Japan* (Mitaka, Tokyo) *March 22–24, 1996*, Heidelberg 1999, 103–137

—— "The Question of Lugalzagesi's Origins" in G. J. Selz (ed.), *Festschrift für Burkhart Kienast zu seinem 70. Geburtstage dargebracht von Freunden, Schülern und Kollegen*. AOAT 274, Münster 2003, 621–637

—— "An Ur III Manuscript of the Sumerian King List", in W. Sallaberger, K. Volk & A Zgoll (eds.), *Literatur, Politik und Recht: Festschrift für Claus Wilcke*. Orientalia Biblica et Christiana 14, Wiesbaden 2003

—— "On the Writing of bēlum in Sargonic and Earlier Sources", *NABU* 2004/1

Steinkeller, P. & J. N. Postgate, *Third-Millennium Legal and Administrative Texts in the Iraq Museum, Baghdad*. MesCiv 4, Winona Lake, IN, 1992

Stephens, F. J., *Votive and Historical Texts from Babylonia and Assyria*. YOS 9, New Haven, CT, & London 1937

Stol, M., "Old Babylonian Personal Names", *StEb* 8 (1991), 191–212

—— *Birth in Babylonia and the Bible: Its Mediterranean Setting*, with a chapter by F. A. M. Wiggermann. CunMon 14, Groningen 2000

—— "Šar-Il", *RlA* 12 (2009–11), 61

Stolper, M. W., "The Neo-Babylonian Text from the Persepolis Fortification", *JNES* 43 (1984), 299–310

Strassmaier, J. N., *Inschriften von Nabonidus, König von Babylon (555–538 v. Chr.), von den Tontafeln des Britischen Museums copirt und Autographirt*. Babylonische Texte Hefte 1–4, Leipzig 1889

—— *Inschriften von Cambyses, König von Babylon (529–521 v. Chr.), von den Tontafeln des Britischen Museums copirt und Autographirt*. Babylonische Texte Hefte 8–9, Leipzig 1890

Streck, M. P., *Das amurritische Onomastikon der altbabylonischen Zeit*. AOAT 271, Münster 2000

Struve, V. V., *Ономастика раннединастического Лагаша* (*Onomastika rannedinastičeskogo Lagaša*), Moscow 1984

Summerell, O. F., "Philosophy of Proper Names" in E. Eichler et al. (eds.), *Namenforschung. Name Studies. Les noms propres*. Handbücher zur Sprach- und Kommunikationswissenschaft vol. 11/1, Berlin & New York, NY, 1995, 368–372

Tallqvist, K., *Assyrian Personal Names*. Acta Societatis Scientiarum Fennicae 43/1, Helsinki 1914

—— *Akkadische Götterepitheta*. Studia Orientalia edidit Societas Orientalis Fennica 7, Helsinki 1938

Thomsen, M.-L., *The Sumerian Language. An Introduction to its History and Grammatical Structure*. Mesopotamia 10, Copenhagen 1984. Third edition, third issue, Copenhagen 2001

Thureau-Dangin, F., *Recueil de tablettes chaldéennes*, Paris 1903

—— *Die sumerischen und akkadischen Königsinschriften*. Vorderasiatische Bibliothek Bd. 1, Abteilung 1, Leipzig 1907

—— *Textes de l'époque d'Agadé* (*Fouilles d'Ernest de Sarzec en 1895*). ITT 1, Paris 1910

—— "Notes assyriologiques", *RA* 8 (1911), 135–158

—— "Notes assyriologiques", *RA* 20 (1923), 3–8

Tonietti, M. V., "The Mobility of the N A R and the Sumerian Personal Names in Pre-Sargonic Mari Onomasticon", in M. Lebeau (ed.), *About Subartu: Studies*

Devoted to Upper Mesopotamia. Culture, Society, Image. Subartu 4/2, Turnhout 1998, 83–101

Utas, B., "Semitic in Iranian: Written, Read and Spoken Language", in É. A. Csató, B. Isaksson & C. Jahani (eds.), *Linguistic Convergence and Areal Diffusion: Case Studies from Iranian, Semitic and Turkic*, London & New York, NY, 2005, 65–77

Vallat, F., "The Most Ancients Scripts of Iran: The Current Situation", *World Archaeology* 17 (1985–86), 335–347

Vanstiphout, H. L. J., "The Dialogue Between an Examiner and a Student", in W. W. Hallo (ed.), *The Context of Scripture* 1: *Canonical Compositions from the Biblical World*, Leiden, New York, NY, & Köln 1997, 592–593

— *Epics of Sumerian Kings: The Matter of Aratta*. Edited by J. S. Cooper. Writings from the Ancient World 20, Atlanta, GA, 2003

Veldhuis, N., *A Cow of Sîn*. Library of Oriental Texts 2, Groningen 1991

— "Entering the Netherworld", *CDLB* 2003:6

Vincente, C.-A., "The Tall Leilān Recension of the Sumerian King List", *ZA* 85 (1995), 234–270

Visicato, G., "Impiego e diffuzione di alcune unita' di misura per aridi in periodo presargonico e sargonico: NI-GA e GUR-SAG-GÁL", *StEL* 9 (1992), 3–10

— "The Sargonic Archive of Tell el-Suleimah", *JCS* 51 (1999), 17–30

— *The Power and the Writing: The Early Scribes of Mesopotamia*, Bethesda, MD, 2000

Visicato, G. & A. Westenholz, "Some Unpublished Sale Contracts from Fara" in S. Graziani (ed.), *Studi sul Vicino Oriente antico dedicati alla memoria di Luigi Cagni*. 4 vols. IUO Series Minor 61, Naples 2000, 1107–1133

— "An Early Dynastic Archive from Ur Involving the lugal", *Kaskal* 2 (2005), 55–78

— *Early Dynastic and Early Sargonic Tablets from Adab in the Cornell University Collections*. CUSAS 11, Bethesda, MD, 2010

di Vito, R. A., *Studies in Third Millennium Sumerian and Akkadian Personal Names: The Designation and Conception of the Personal God*. StPohl SM 16, Rome 1993

Volk, K., "Puzur-Mama und die Reise des Königs", *ZA* 82 (1992), 22–29

— "Vom Dunkel in die Helligkeit" in V. Dasen (ed.), *Naissance et petite enfance dans l'antiquité. Actes du colloque de Fribourg, 28 novembre – 1er décembre 2001*. OBO 203, Freiburg & Göttingen 2004, 71–92

Vukosavović, F., "Private Collection of Cuneiform Tablets in Jerusalem", *JAC* 23 (2008), 37–54

Waetzoldt, H., *Untersuchungen zur neusumerischen Textilindustrie*. Studi economici e technologici 1, Rome 1972

— "Compensation of Craft Workers and Officials in the Ur III Period" (translated into English by M. Powell) in M. Powell (ed.), *Labor in the Ancient Near East*. AOS 68, New Haven, CT 1987

Waetzoldt, H. & F. Yıldız, *Die Umma-Texte aus den Archaeologischen Museen zu Istanbul*, vol. 2. MVN 16, Rome 1994

Walters, S. D., *Water for Larsa: An Old Babylonian Archive Dealing with Irrigation*. Yale Near Eastern Researches 4, New Haven, CT, & London 1970

Watelin, L. Ch. & S. Langdon, Excavations at Kish vol. 4: 1925–1930, Paris 1934

Weiershäuser, F., *Die königlichen Frauen der III. Dynastie von Ur*. Göttinger Beiträge zum Alten Orient Bd. 1, Göttingen 2008

Westenholz, A., "*berūtum*, *damtum*, and Old Akkadian KI.GAL: Burial of Dead Enemies in Ancient Mesopotamia", *AfO* 23 (1970), 27–31

—— "Old Sumerian and Old Akkadian Texts in the National Museum of Copenhagen", *JCS* 26 (1974), 71–80

—— "Early Nippur Year Dates and the Sumerian King List", *JCS* 26 (1974), 154–156

—— *Early Cuneiform Texts in Jena. Pre-Sargonic and Sargonic Documents from Nippur and Fara in the Hilprecht-Sammlung vorderasiatischer Altertümer, Institut für Altertumswissenschaften der Friedrich-Schiller-Universität, Jena*, Copenhagen 1975

—— *Literary and Lexical Texts and the Earliest Administrative Documents from Nippur*. OSP 1. BiMes 1, Malibu, FL, 1975

—— "Old Sumerian Administrative Documents in the Pontificial Biblical Institute in Rome", *OrNS* 44 (1975), 434–438

—— "The Earliest Akkadian Religion", *OrNS* 45 (1976), 215–216

—— "Old Akkadian School Texts: Some Goals of Sargonic Scribal Education", *AfO* 25 (1974–77), 95–110

—— "Diplomatic and Commercial Aspects of Temple Offerings as Illustrated by a Newly Discovered Text", *Iraq* 39 (1977), 19–21

—— "The Old Akkadian Empire in Contemporary Opinion", in M. Trolle Larsen (ed.), *Power and Propaganda: A Symposium on Ancient Cultures* (Copenhagen 1979), 107–124

—— *The 'Akkadian' Texts, The Enlilemaba Texts, and the Onion Archive*. OSP 2. Carsten Niebuhr Institute Publications 3, Copenhagen 1987

—— "Personal Names in Ebla and in Pre-Sargonic Babylonia", in A. Archi (ed.), *Eblaite Personal Names and Semitic Name-Giving. Papers of a Symposium Held in Rome July 15–17, 1985*. ARES 1, Rome 1988, 99–117

—— "The World View of Sargonic Officials: Differences in Mentality Between Sumerians and Akkadians", in M. Liverani (ed.), *Akkad: The First World Empire. Structure, Ideology, Tradition*. HANE/S 5, Padova 1993, 157–169

—— "Review of R. A. di Vito, *Studies in Third Millennium Sumerian and Akkadian Personal Names: The Designation and Conception of the Personal God*", *AfO* 42/43 (1995–96), 217–222

—— "Assyriologists, Ancient and Modern, on Naramsin and Sharkalisharri", in J. Marzahn & H. Neumann (eds.), *Assyriologia et Semitica: Festschrift für Joachim Oelsner anläßlich seines 65. Geburtstages am 18. Februar 1997*. AOAT 252, Münster 2000, 545–556

—— "The Sumerian City-State", in M. H. Hansen, (ed.), *A Comparative Study of Six City-State Cultures. An Investigation Conducted by the Copenhagen Polis Centre*. Historisk-filosofiske Skrifter 27, Copenhagen 2002, 23–42

—— "Have you been near Prof. Larsen too long?", in J. G. Dercksen (ed.), *Assyria and Beyond: Studies Presented to Mogens Trolle Larsen*. PIHANS 100, Leiden 2004, 599–606

—— "Šar'atigubisin", *RlA* 12 (2009–11), 35

—— "Šar-kali-šarrī", *RlA* 12 (2009–11), 64–65

Wilcke, C., *Das Lugalbandaepos*, Wiesbaden 1969

—— "Zum Königtum in der Ur III-Zeit", in P. Garelli (ed.) *Le palais et la royauté*. CRRA 19, Paris 1974, 177–232

—— "Anmerkungen zum 'Konjugationspräfix' /i/- und zur These vom „silbischen Charakter der sumerischen Morpheme“ anhand neusumerischer Verbalformen beginnend mit ì-íb-, ì-im- und ì-in-", *ZA* 78 (1988), 1–45

—— "Orthographie, Grammatik und literarische Form: Beobachtungen zu der Vaseninschrift Lugalzaggesis (*SAKI* 152–156), in T. Abusch, J. Huehnergard & P. Steinkeller (eds.), *Lingering over Words: Studies in Ancient Near Eastern Literature in honor of William L. Moran*. HSS 37, Atlanta, GA, 1990, 455–504

—— "Die Inschrift der "Figure aux plumes" – ein frühes Werk sumerischer Dichtkunst", in U. Finkbeiner, R. Dittmann & H. Hauptmann (eds.) *Beiträge zur Kulturgeschichte Vorderasiens: Festschrift für Rainer Michael Boehmer*, Mainz 1995, 669–674

—— "Neue Rechtsurkunden der altsumerischen Zeit", *ZA* 86 (1996), 1–67

—— "Amar-girids Revolte gegen Narām-Su'en", *ZA* 87 (1997), 11–32

—— *Early Ancient Near Eastern Law: A History of its Beginnings. The Early Dynastic and Sargonic Periods*, Munich 2003; 2nd expanded edition Winona Lake, IN, 2007

Willi-Plein, I., "Hebräische Namen", in E. Eichler et al. (eds.), *Namenforschung. Name Studies. Les noms propres*. Handbücher zur Sprach- und Kommunikationswissenschaft vol. 11/1, Berlin & New York, NY, 1995, 870–872

Williams-Forte, E., "Leopard. B. Archäologisch," *RlA* 6 (1980–83), 601–604

Witkowski, T., "Probleme der Terminologie", in E. Eichler et al. (eds.), *Namenforschung. Name Studies. Les noms propres*. Handbücher zur Sprach- und Kommunikationswissenschaft vol. 11/1, Berlin & New York, NY, 1995, 288–294

Woods, C., "On the Euphrates", *ZA* 95 (1995), 7–45

Woolley, C. L. et al., *The Royal Cemetery*. UE 2, 2 vols., London & Philadelphia 1934

Wright, H. T., *The Administration of Rural Production in an Early Mesopotamian Town*. Museum of Anthropology, University of Michigan Anthropological Papers 38, Ann Arbor, MI, 1969

Yang, Z., *Sargonic Inscriptions from Adab*. The Institute for the History of Ancient Civilizations Periodic Publications on Ancient Civilizations 1, Changchun 1989

Yoshikawa, M., "A Clay Tablet in the Okayama Municipal Museum of Near Eastern Art", *ASJ* 3 (1981), 193–197

—— "Sumerian Tablets in Japanese Private Collections (I)", *ASJ* 9 (1987), 303–319

Yuhong, W., "The Sun the Lion: Earliest Hymn to the Sun from Ebla and Abu-Salabikh (2600–2500)", *JAC* 22 (2007), 75–90

Zaccagnini, C., "Sacred and Human Components in Ancient Near Eastern Law", *History of Religions* 33 (1994), 265–286

Zadok, R., "Elamite Onomastics", *StEL* 8 (1991), 225–237

—— "Elamites and Other Peoples from Iran and the Persian Gulf Region in Early Mesopotamian Sources", *Iran* 32 (1994), 31–51

Zand, K. V., "Zu den Schreibungen des Anzud-Vogels in der Fāra-Zeit", in D. Shehata, F. Weiershäuser & K. V. Zand (eds.), *Göttern und Menschen. Beiträge zur Literatur und Geschichte des Alten Orients. Festschrift für Birgitte Groneberg*. CM 41, Leiden & Boston, MA, 2010, 415–442

Zettler, R., *The Ur III Temple of Inanna at Nippur: The Operation and Organization of Urban Religious Institutions in Mesopotamia in the Late Third Millennium B.C.* BBVO 11, Berlin 1992

Zólyomi, G., "Genitive Constructions in Sumerian", *JCS* 48 (1996), 31–47

Lists of attestations

1. List of lugal-names

Entries in the lists of attestations are provided with a heading in bold script. The heading provides the writing encountered in the previous chapters. A raised parenthesis signals the number of bearers (given as $^{(a\#)}$), and/or discrete entries in scholastic lists of PNN (given as $^{(\circ\#)}$). The translation suggested in discussions is then followed by the section or subheading under which the name was treated, followed by page references, including cross references.

Underneath the bold heading, the writing of the name, filiations (if any), date (with ruler and regnal year if known), provenience, publication data, column and line number follow. Attestations are organized according to date and provenience.

Entries are divided into the discrete time periods ED I-II, ED IIIa, ED IIIa-b, ED IIIb, and ES. Later Sargonic references are not further subdivided due to difficulties in assigning a precise date to texts belonging to the second half of the Sargonic period. A few later attestations are also included due in part to the same reasons, or if they form part of an earlier tradition, as in the case of a few scholastic texts. Hence, some references to texts dated to CS-LS, LS-Lagaš II, or LS-Ur III are also listed. Names taken from OB copies of older original inscriptions are marked as (OB) following the date of the original inscription. The date designation OAkk is used for 11 entries from 5 texts which have not been available in copy or photo, and where closer indications of a date have not been given. Names culled from transliterations only are always clearly marked.

Multiple attestations of a name from the same period and place are organized alphabetically after publication. Each and every known instance of lugal-names in Girsu texts is not found in the list. V. V. Struve's *Onomastika* was used to achieve a preliminary set of ED IIIb names, to which further names were added. Neither are attestations entered from H. de Genouillac's summaries, ITT 2/2, p. 1–53; or ITT 5, p. 31–39. For the remainder of sites, a more complete picture has been strived for.

Museum or excavation number are given when texts lack sequential numbering (e.g. *AAICAB*), or when the numbering of illustrations follows a different sequence than the treatment of the texts in the monograph (*DPA*). Also, when a page or plate contains a number of figures, museum numbers are given to tell texts apart.

Abbreviations used in notes on filiations are given in Technical Abbreviations.

[a$_2$-/za$_3$]-lugal-ĝa$_2$-ta $^{(a1)}$ 'by the *strength* of my lord' 3.1.4.1, p. 119–120
[a$_2$-/za$_3$]-lugal-ĝa$_2$-ta IB ED IIIa Šuruppag? G. Visicato & A. Westenholz, *Gs Cagni*, p. 1107–1133 3 r. iii 1

a$_2$-lugal-ta $^{(a1)}$ 'by the *strength* of the lord' 3.1.4.1, p. 120
a$_2$-lugal-ta ED IIIa Adab CUSAS 11 12 o. i 3

AK-lugal $^{(a2/°1)}$ 'creation of the lugal' 3.1.5.1, p. 127, 229
AK-lugal ED I-II Ur UET 2 12 o. i 5
AK-lugal ED I-II Ur UET 2 87 o. i 4('?)
AK-lugal Ama-^{d}Inana ED I-II Uruk *ATU* 614 o. 3
°AK-lugal LS-Ur III Unknown M. E. Cohen, *Fs Hallo*, p. 79–86 (YBC 2124) iv 12

amar-lugal $^{(a>2)}$ 'calf of the lugal' 3.1.1.1, p. 84–85, 229, 247 n. 1453
amar-lugal ED I-II Ur UET 2 85 r. i 3
amar-lugal ^{d}Nesaĝ$_2^{ki}$ ED I-II Ur UET 2 112 o. ii' 2
amar-lugal ED I-II Ur UET 2 181 o. ii' 7
amar-lugal [lu$_2^{?}$ an]še$^{?}$ ED I-II Ur UET 2 193A o. i' 4'
amar-lugal ED I-II Ur UET 2 274 Edge i 2
amar-lugal ED I-II Ur UET 2 341 r. i 3
amar-lugal ED I-II Ur UET 2 354 o. ii 1
amar-lugal ED I-II Uruk M. W. Green, *ZA* 72 (1982), p. 163–177 8 o. ii 4'

ar$_3$-du$_2$:lugal $^{(a1)}$ 'servant of the lugal' 3.1.1.1, p. 84, 237
ar$_3$-du$_2$:lugal ED IIIa Tell Ağrab OIP 58, p. 291 8 5

e$_2$-lugal-be$_2$-zu $^{(a1)}$ 'the *house* is known by its master' 3.1.1.2, p. 88
e$_2$-lugal-be$_2$-zu ED IIIb/Luzag. ensi$_2$ 7 Umma-Zabala BIN 8 86 o. i 13

en-il$_2$-lugal $^{(a1)}$ unkn. mng. 3.1.8, p. 177
en-il$_2$-lugal mu$_6$-sub$_3$ ED IIIa Nippur OSP 1 125 o. i 1

geme$_2$-lugal $^{(a1)}$ ' female servant of the lugal' 3.1.1.1, p. 65 n. 321, 82
geme$_2$-lugal w. U$_3$-ma-ni, ⌜um⌝-mi-a Nibru^{ki} CS-LS Nippur *EGA* 773 pl. 23 fig. 264 4

igi-lugal-še$_3$ $^{(a2)}$ 'eyes are set on the lugal' 3.1.4.1, p. 119
igi-lugal-še$_3$ ED IIIb/Lug. 5(+1?) Girsu VS 25 14 o. vi 7'
igi-lugal-še$_3$ ED IIIb/Lug. 6 Girsu VS 25 37 r. i 2
⌜igi-lu:gal-še$_3$⌝ ED IIIb Nippur OSP 1 45 r. i 1'

igi-lugal-še$_{3\text{-}90°}$ $^{(a\geq2)}$ 'eyes are set on the lugal' 3.1.4.1, p. 119 n. 644
igi-lugal-še$_{3\text{-}90°}$ (lugal-igi-še$_{3\text{-}90°}$) ED IIIb Adab *TCABI* 13 r. i 5
igi-lugal-še$_{3\text{-}90°}$ (lugal-igi-še$_{3\text{-}90°}$) ED IIIb/X Y 28 Umma-Zabala *SAKF* 3 o. iv 7
igi-lugal-še$_{3\text{-}90°}$ (igi-še$_{3\text{-}90°}$-lugal), sipa-anše ED IIIb Zabala (?) BIN 8 46 o. iii 5

inim-lugal-da $^{(a1)}$ 'the *decision* (rests?) with the lugal' 3.1.1.4, p. 93 n. 474, 94, 237
inim-lugal-da ED IIIa Abū Ṣalābīḫ R. D. Biggs & J. N. Postgate, *Iraq* 40 (1978), p. 101–117 516 o. iii 1

ir$_{11}$-lugal $^{(a2)}$ 'servant of the lugal' 3.1.1.1, p. 82, 229
ir$_{11}$-lugal ED I-II Ur UET 2 128 o. iv' 5'
ir$_{11}$-lugal MS-CS Nippur OSP 2 33 o. 1

lu$_2$-lugal $^{(a3)}$ '*man* of the lugal' 3.1.1.1, p. 82–83, 261
lu$_2$-lugal ED IIIb Nippur TMH 5 32 r. i 2
⌜lu$_2$-lugal⌝ ES-MS Nippur OSP 1 54 o. ii 4
lu$_2$-lugal ES-MS Nippur OSP 1 56 r. i 4
lu$_2$-lugal ES-MS Nippur OSP 1 154 o. ii' 6
lu$_2$-lugal CS Umma Nik 2 84 o. 2

lu$_2$-lugal-la$_2$? $^{(a1)}$ '*man* of the lugal' 3.1.1.1, p. 83 n. 400

⌜lu_2⌝-[l]u[gal]-la_2 ? CS Isin ? CUSAS 13 164 o. 7'

lugal-a (identical with lugal-a-a-GUG$_2$-a-ne$_2$ and lugal-a-a-GUG$_2$-a-ne$_2$-nu-si)
lugal-a dub-sar ED IIIb/X Y 1 Girsu Nik 1 44 o. i 3
lugal-a ED IIIb/X Y 1 Girsu Nik 1 44 r. i 4

lugal-a (a5) (abbreviation or genitival PN lugal-a(k)? Compare lugal-la_2) 3.1.8, p. 85 n. 421, 175 w. nn. 1023 & 1028
lugal-a f. Ku_{10}-ku_{10} & Lugal-inim-ĝal_2-la ED IIIb/Urz. lugal Isin M. Lambert, *RA* 73 (1979), p. 5–6 o. vi 5
lugal$^!$-a$^!$ f. Ku_{10}-ku_{10} ED IIIb/Urz. lugal Isin M. Lambert, *RA* 73 (1979), p. 5–6 o. vi 14
lugal-a ES Adab CUSAS 11 317 o. ii 3
lugal-a CS/Śkś Y 2 Nippur OSP 2 100 r. iii 4'
lugal-a b. (?) Ur-Šu-me-$ša_4$ MS-CS Nippur OSP 2 158 o. 4
lugal-a [saĝ apin] CS Mesag BIN 8 152 o. ii 17
lugal-a aga_3-us_2 MS-CS Mesag BIN 8 236 o. 7
lugal-a saĝ-apin CS Mesag M. deJ. Ellis, *JCS* 31 (1979), p. 30–55 16 o. ii 6
lugal-a MS-CS Unknown MesCiv 4 64 r. 2

lugal-a-a-GUG$_2$-a-ne$_2$ (identical with lugal-a-a-GUG$_2$-a-ne$_2$-nu-si) 3.1.8, p. 175 n. 1024
lugal-a-a-GUG$_2$-a-ne$_2$ RU-lugal ED IIIb/Lug. 1 Girsu VS 25 8 o. i 6

lugal-a-a-GUG$_2$-a-ne$_2$-nu-si (a1) unkn. mng. 3.1.8, p. 175 w. nn. 1023–1024, 181 n. 1109
lugal-a-a-GUG$_2$-a-ne$_2$-nu-si dub-sar ED IIIb/Lug. 1 Girsu *DCS* 8 o. i 8

lugal-a-bi$_2$-KU (a1) unkn. mng. 3.1.8, p. 175
lugal-a-bi$_2$-KU MS-CS Ur UET 2 suppl. 48 o. i 11

lugal-a-DU-nu$_2$ (a1) unkn. mng. 3.1.8, p. 175
lugal-a-DU-nu_2 nitaḫ ED IIIb/Ukg. lugal 6 Girsu *AWAS* 122 o. v 7
lugal-a-DU-nu_2 nitaḫ, il_2 ED IIIb/Ukg. lugal 6 Girsu *DP* 1/2 115 o. v 5
lugal-a-DU-nu_2 nitaḫ,il_2 ED IIIb/Ukg. lugal 6 Girsu *TSA* 16 o. iv 4

lugal-a-ĝe$_6$ (a≥4) 'the lugal is a flood' 3.1.3.3, p. 112, 214–215
lugal-a-ĝe_6 ED IIIb Adab CUSAS 11 48 o. i 3
lugal-a-ĝe_6 ED IIIb Adab CUSAS 11 50 o. iv 2
lugal-a-ĝe_6 ED IIIb-ES Adab CUSAS 11 102 o. iii 10
lugal-a-ĝe_6 ED IIIb Nippur A. Goetze, *JCS* 23 (1970), p. 48 (5N-T452) 2'
lu:gal-a-ĝe_6 ED IIIb Nippur TMH 5 156 o. 4
lugal-⌜a-ĝe_6⌝ ED IIIb Umma-Zabala CUSAS 14 142 o. iii 2
lugal-a-ĝe_6 ED IIIb Umma-Zabala CUSAS 14 270 o. ii 6
lugal-a-ĝe_6 ES Adab CUSAS 11 277 o. ii 5
lugal-a-ĝe_6 ES Adab CUSAS 11 319 o. 3
lugal-[a]-ĝe_6 ES-MS Adab *TCABI* 64 o. i 7'

lugal-a-ma-ru (a1) 'the lugal is a deluge' 3.1.3.3, p. 112
lugal-a-ma-ru CS-LS Girsu *RTC* 254 o. ii 20

lugal-a-MIR-nu$_2$ (a1) unkn. mng. 3.1.8, p. 175
lugal-a-MIR-nu_2 ED IIIb Umma-Zabala CUSAS 14 4 r. v 5

lugal-a-nun (a2) 'the lugal is a *princely offspring*' 3.1.7.1, p. 160
lugal-a-nun ED IIIb/Ĝišakidu $ensi_2$ Umma-Zabala CUSAS 14 252 r. i 3
lugal-a-nun ED IIIb Umma-Zabala MVN 3 3 o. iv 10
lugal-a-nun ED IIIb Umma-Zabala MVN 3 3 r. ii 15
lugal-a-nun ES-MS Adab *TCABI* 64 o. ii 3

°lugal-a-RU (a1) unkn. mng. 3.1.8, p. 175
°lugal-a-RU ED IIIa Šuruppag *SF* 28 o. iii 6

lugal-A-SI (a1) unkn. mng. 3.1.8, p. 175, 181 n. 1109
lugal-A-SI ED IIIa Šuruppag *RTC* 14 o. iv 2

lugal-a$^?$-UD (a1) unkn. mng. 3.1.8, p. 175
lugal-a$^?$-UD ED IIIa-b Marada ? *AAICAB* 1/1 (Ashm 1924-467) o. i 2

lugal-A-UR-sikil (a1) two different names in one case: unkn. reading. 3.1.8, p. 87 n. 429, 175
lugal-A-UR-sikil ED I-II Ur UET 2 199 r. i 7

lugal-a-˹x˺ ED IIIa Šuruppag *WF* 149 o. iii 9
lugal-a-˹x˺ MS-CS Nippur TMH 5 39 r. i 8

lugal-a$_2$ (a≥7) abbreviation 3.1.8, p. 175, 184 n. 1146, 237
lugal-a$_2$ s. Ur$_2$-mud ED IIIb Girsu *DP* suppl. 555 r. ii 2
lugal-a$_2$ ED IIIb Nippur OSP 1 25 "ii" 12'
lu[gal$^?$]-a$_2$$^{!?}$ ED IIIb/Luzag. ensi$_2$ X Umma-Zabala BIN 8 82 o. iv 12
lugal-a$_2$ ED IIIb-ES Umma-Zabala ? BIN 8 189 o. 3
lugal-a$_2$ ED IIIb/Luzag. ensi$_2$ [x] Umma-Zabala J. A. Brinkman, *Fs Kramer*, pl. III*-V* (W 2/7) o. ii 10'
lugal-a$_2$ sipa ud$_5$ MS Adab *TCABI* 117 r. 2
lugal-a$_2$ CS Girsu ITT 5 9304 r. 2'
˹lugal˺-a$_2$ CS Girsu *RTC* 84 o. 1
lugal-a$_2$ *Me-ra-num$_2$* CS Tutub MAD 1 233 r. i 2
lugal-a$_2$ CS/Śkś Y 2 Umma CT 50 53 o. 8

˹lugal$^?$-a$_2$˺-da-DU ? (a1) unkn. mng. 3.1.8, p. 175
˹lugal$^?$-a$_2$˺-da-DU ˹ni˺-is-ku CS Adab OIP 14 194 o. 2

lugal-a$_2$-gur-ra (a3) 'the lugal (has) thick horns' or 'the lugal is sturdy of frame' 3.1.7.3, p. 162, 176 n. 1044, 184
lugal-a$_2$-gur-ra ED IIIa Šuruppag>Nippur TMH 5 75 o. ii 10
lugal-a$_2$-gur-ra ma$_2$-laḫ$_4$ ED IIIb/Lug. 3 Girsu Nik 1 17 o. ii 1
lu:gal-a$_2$-gur-ra ED IIIb Nippur OSP 1 121 r. ii 3

lugal-a$_2$-LAK175 (a1) unkn. mng. 3.1.8, p. 175
lugal-a$_2$-LAK175 ED IIIb Umma-Zabala BIN 8 65 o. ii 2
lugal-a$_2$-LAK175 ED IIIb/Luzag. ensi$_2$ 7 Umma-Zabala BIN 8 86 o. iii 12
lugal-a$_2$-LAK175 ED IIIb/Luzag. ensi$_2$ 7 Umma-Zabala M. deJ. Ellis, *JCS* 31 (1979), p. 30–55 6 o. iii 14
lugal-a$_2$-LAK175 Maš-da$_2$, Lugal-a$_2$-LAK175, Ur-e$_2$-me ED IIIb Zabala M. Powell, *HUCA* 49 (1978), p. 1–58 10 o. i 2

lugal-a$_2$-maḫ (a≥8/°1) 'the lugal (possesses) the ultimate authority' 3.1.1.6, p. 97, 249 n. 1465
lugal-a$_2$-maḫ saĝa ED I-II Umma (?) OIP 104 12 B-C i 2
lugal-a$_2$-maḫ ED IIIa Adab CUSAS 11 8 o. ii 4
lugal-a$_2$-maḫ ED IIIa Adab CUSAS 11 10 o. iii 4
lu[gal]-a$_2$-maḫ dub-sar ED IIIa Šuruppag *TSŠ* 931 r. v 1
lugal-a$_2$-maḫ ED IIIa Šuruppag *WF* 41 o. vi 6'
lugal-˹a$_2$˺-[maḫ] ED IIIa Šuruppag *WF* 65 r. v 9
lugal-˹a$_2$-maḫ˺ ED IIIa Šuruppag *WF* 66 r. i 9'
lugal-a$_2$-maḫ a-ru ED IIIa Šuruppag *WF* 72 o. iii 1
lugal-a$_2$-maḫ sukkal ED IIIa Šuruppag *WF* 75 o. iv 2
lugal-a$_2$-maḫ ED IIIa Šuruppag *WF* 84 r. i 2
lugal-a$_2$-maḫ ED IIIa Šuruppag *WF* 85 o. i 2
lugal-a$_2$-maḫ ED IIIa Šuruppag *WF* 86 o. iii 2
lugal-a$_2$-maḫ ED IIIa Šuruppag *WF* 108 r. iii 2
°lu[gal]-a$_2$-maḫ ED IIIb Ebla MEE 3 67 o. i 1

lugal-a$_2$-maḫ ED IIIb Marada ? *AAICAB* 1/1 (Ashm 1924-465) o. i 2
lugal-⸢a$_2^?$-maḫ⸣ ? ES Adab CUSAS 11 320 o. i 3
lugal-a$_2$-maḫ azlag$_7$(-ra) MS Adab *TCABI* 149 o. 5
lugal-⸢a$_2$⸣-maḫ engar CS Adab CUSAS 13 21 r. 6

lugal-a$_2$-maḫ$_2$ (a2) 'the lugal (possesses) the ultimate authority' 3.1.1.6, p. 97 n. 506, 249 n. 1465
lugal-a$_2$-maḫ$_2$ ED IIIa Šuruppag *TSŠ* 290 o. ii 1
lugal-⸢a$_2$⸣-[ma]ḫ$_2$ ED IIIa-b Marada ? *AAICAB* 1/1 (Ashm 1924-462) r. i 4
lugal-a$_2$-maḫ$_2$ ED IIIb Marada ? *AAICAB* 1/1 (Ashm 1924-468) o. i 5

lugal-a$_2^!$(DA)-maḫ$_2$ (a2) 'the lugal (possesses) the ultimate authority' 3.1.1.6, p. 97 n. 506
lugal-a$_2$-maḫ$_2$ umbisaĝ ED IIIa Šuruppag *SF* 27+*TSŠ* 327+*NTSŠ* 294 r. iii 6
lugal-a$_2^!$-maḫ$_2$ ED IIIa Nippur TMH 5 54 o. iii 1
lugal-a$_2^!$-maḫ$_2$ ED IIIa Nippur TMH 5 54 o. iv 5

lugal-a$_2$-na (identical with lugal-a$_2$-na-gub)
lugal-⸢a$_2$-na⸣ šuku dab$_5$-ba, Gir$_2$-nun, gab$_2$-kas$_4$-da, e-da-se$_{12}$ ED IIIb/Ukg. lugal 3 Girsu BIN 8 381 o. ii 3

lugal-a$_2$-na (a≥5/°1) 'the lugal (placed him/her) on his arm' 3.1.4.1, p. 121 w. n. 653
lugal-a$_2$-na ED IIIa Šuruppag *FTUM* 24 o. i 2
lugal-⸢a$_2$⸣-na ED IIIa Šuruppag *FTUM* 25 o. i 3
°lugal-a$_2$-na ED IIIa Šuruppag *SF* 63 r. iii 2
lugal-a$_2$-na ugula ED IIIa Šuruppag M. Molina & H. Sanchiz, *StEL* 24 (2007), p. 1–15 2 o. ii 3
lugal-⸢a$_2$⸣-na ED IIIb/X Y 3 Girsu CT 50 41 o. i 2
lugal-a$_2$-na ED IIIb/X Y 3 Girsu CT 50 43 o. ii 1
lugal-a$_2$-na šu-ku$_6$ e$_2$ mi$_2$ ED IIIb Girsu *DP* 2/2 334 o. i 4
lugal-a$_2$-na aga$_3$-us$_2$ ED IIIb Girsu Nik 1 102 o. ii 3
lugal-a$_2$-na ED IIIb Umma-Zabala CUSAS 14 4 o. i 6
lugal-⸢a$_2$⸣-na CS Girsu CT 50 106 o. ii 6
lugal-a$_2$-na CS Girsu CT 50 137 r. 1
lugal-a$_2$-na CS Girsu CT 50 138 r. 2
lugal-a$_2$-na CS Girsu CT 50 149 r. 5
lugal-a$_2$-na CS Girsu CT 50 150 r. 6
lugal-a$_2$-na CS Girsu ITT 2/1 2984 r. 3
lugal-a$_2$-na CS Girsu ITT 2/1 4378 r. 3
lugal-a$_2$-na CS Girsu ITT 2/1 4636 r. 3
lugal-a$_2$-na CS Girsu ITT 2/2, pl. 87 1xxx o. i 6
lugal-[a$_2^?$]-na CS Girsu ITT 2/2, pl. 87 1xxx r. iii 1
lugal-a$_2$-na ugula CS Girsu *RTC* 90 r. i 5
lugal-a$_2$-na CS Girsu *RTC* 139 r. 5

lugal-a$_2$-na-gub (a1) 'the lugal placed (him/her) on his arm' 3.1.4.1, p. 121 w. n. 653
lugal-a$_2$-na-gub Gir$_2$-nun, gab$_2$-kas$_4$-da, e-da-se$_{12}$ ED IIIb/Ukg. lugal 5 Girsu *DP* 1/2 114 r. iv 12

lugal-a$_2$-pa$_3$ (a1) unkn. mng. 3.1.8, 3.1.9 (s.v. *lugal-a$_2$-MUG.GU-pa$_3$), p. 175, 184
lugal-a$_2$-pa$_3$ f. Ur-saĝ-Utu, gu:sur ED IIIa-b Unknown E. Sollberger, *Genava* 26 (1948), p. 48–72 fig. 5 3
lugal-a$_2$-pa$_3$ ED IIIb Umma-Zabala CUSAS 14 98 o. ii 1
lugal-a$_2$-pa$_3$ ⸢ugula$^?$⸣ ED IIIb Umma-Zabala CUSAS 14 98 r. ii 1
lugal-⸢a$_2$-pa$_3$⸣ ⸢ugula⸣ ED IIIb Umma-Zabala CUSAS 14 100 o. ii 2

lugal-a$_2$-šum$_2$-ma (a2) 'the lugal is granted authority' 3.1.1.6, p. 98, 258
lugal-a$_2$-šum$_2$-ma ED IIIb-ES Adab CUSAS 11 106 o. i 3

lugal-a$_2$-šum$_2$-ma ED IIIb-ES Adab CUSAS 11 140 o. ii 2'
lugal-a$_2$-šum$_2$-ma ES Adab *TCABI* 29 o. ii 5
lugal-a$_2$-šum$_2$-ma CS Girsu CT 50 134 o. 5
lugal-a$_2$-šum$_2$-ma CS Girsu *RTC* 125 o. ii 11
lugal-a$_2$-šum$_2$-ma nagar CS Girsu *RTC* 126 o. ii 13'

lugal-a$_2$-tuku (a1) 'the lugal is powerful' 3.1.1.6, p. 98–99, 249 n. 1465
lugal-a$_2$-tuku ED IIIa Šuruppag H. Steible, *CollAn* 7 (2008), 97 (Š 380, translit. only) "iii 9"
lugal-a$_2$-tuku MS-CS Nippur TMH 5 29 r. iii 9

lugal-a$_2$-zi (a1) 'the lugal on the right side' 3.1.3.1, p. 109
lugal-a$_2$-zi ED IIIb/X Y 4 Girsu VS 27 54 o. ii 5

lugal-a$_2$-zi-da (a≥6) 'the lugal on the right side' 3.1.3.1, p. 109, 176 n. 1044, 183 n. 1134
lugal-a$_2$-zi-da ED IIIa Šuruppag M. Lambert, *Gs Unger*, p. 27–49 1 o. ii 9
lugal-a$_2$-zi-da ED IIIa-b Isin (?) OIP 104 14 r. vi 5
lugal-a$_2$-zi-da ED IIIb-ES Adab CUSAS 11 144 o. ii 3
lugal-a$_2$-zi-da ir$_{11}$ Lugal-ki-gal-la ED IIIb Nippur TMH 5 50 o. i 1
lugal-a$_2$-zi-da ĝiš-šu-ri-ri ED IIIb Nippur OSP 1 46 o. iii 14
lugal-a$_2$-zi-da ED IIIb Nippur OSP 1 103 o. i 4
lugal-a$_2$-zi-da dab$_5$ ku$_3$-gi-[(x$^{?}$)] CS Umma CT 50 75 r. 4
⸢lugal-a$_2$⸣-zi-da f. ⸢Ur-šul$^{?}$⸣ CS/NS. Unknown BIN 8 162 r. 2
lugal-a$_2$-⸢x⸣-[(x)] CS Adab *SIA* 713 o. 4'

lugal-AB (a>5) unkn. mng. 3.1.8, p. 87 n. 432, 175 n. 1030
lugal-AB ED IIIb-ES Adab CUSAS 11 186 o. iv 12
lugal-AB (aga$_3$-us$_2$) ED IIIb/X Y 4 Girsu *DP* suppl. 616 r. i 4
lugal-AB ED IIIb Girsu VS 14 190 r. i 2
lugal-AB aga$_3$-us$_2$ ED IIIb/X Y 2 Girsu VS 25 83 o. ii 2
lugal-AB f. Lugal-nam$_2$ ES Ur UET 1 269 1
lugal-AB CS Girsu *DPA* 22 (PUL 40) o. 7
lugal-AB CS Girsu *STTI* 131 o. 6
lugal-AB CS Mesag M. deJ. Ellis, *JCS* 31 (1979), p. 30–55 16 r. i 5'
lugal-AB MS-CS Mesag MesCiv 4 45 r. 21
lugal-AB CS Mesag T. Ozaki, SANTAG 7 7 o. 7
[lugal]-AB MS-CS Umma MAD 4 74 o. 2
lugal-AB f. KA-ku$_3$ MS-CS Umma MesCiv 4 28 o. ii 18
lugal-AB f. Ur-^{d}⸢Ab⸣-[u$_2$] MS-CS Umma MesCiv 4 28 r. ii 1
lugal-AB ? CS Umma MVN 15 378 o. 4
lugal-AB OAkk Unknown MAD 4 25 (translit. only) o. 3

lugal-ab-ba (a≥1) 'the lugal is a father' 3.1.1.2, p. 87, 175 n. 1030
lugal-ab-ba CS Girsu ITT 1 1053 r. 3
lugal-ab-ba CS Girsu ITT 1 1053 r. 5
lugal-ab-ba CS Girsu *STTI* 122 o. 4

lugal-ab-ba-ĝu$_{10}$ (a3) 'the lugal is my father' 3.1.1.2, p. 87
lugal-ab-ba-ĝu$_{10}$ nu-sig$_2$ nitaḫ ED IIIb/Ukg. lugal 4 Girsu *DP* 1/2 116 o. iv 9
lugal-ab-ba-ĝu$_{10}$ nu-sig$_2$ nitaḫ ED IIIb/Ukg. lugal X Girsu *DP* 1/2 117 o. iii 8
lugal-ab-ba-ĝu$_{10}$ nu-sig$_2$ nitaḫ ED IIIb/Ukg. lugal X Girsu *DP* 1/2 118 o. iii 14
lugal-ab-ba-[ĝu$_{10}$$^{?}$] ED IIIb Girsu ITT 5 9203 o. 6
lugal-ab-ba-ĝu$_{10}$ nitaḫ, lu$_2$ geme$_2$-^{d}Ba-u$_2$ ED IIIb/X Y 4 Girsu Nik 1 15 r. i 1
lugal-ab-ba-ĝu$_{10}$ ED IIIb-ES Umma-Zabala ? *RIAA* 81 o. 1
lugal-ab-ba-ĝu$_{10}$ ED IIIb/Il$_2$ ensi$_2$ Zabala *TCVBI* 1-1 o. i 5
lugal-ab-ba-ĝu$_{10}$ ED IIIb Zabala *TCVBI* 1-21 o. 3

lugal-ab-ba-uru (a1) 'the lugal is a city elder' 3.1.1.2, p. 95
lugal-ab-ba-uru CS Girsu *RTC* 125 o. ii 7

lugal-AB-da-SAĜ (a1) unkn. mng. 3.1.8, p. 175
lugal-AB-da-SAĜ ED IIIa Šuruppag A. Westenholz, *OrNS* 44 (1975), p. 434–438 1 r. i 5

lugal-ab-du$_{10}$-ga (a1) unkn. mng. 3.1.8, p. 175
lugal-ab-du$_{10}$-ga dub-sar ED IIIb Girsu HSS 3 43 o. ii 3

lugal-ab-e$_3$ (a2) 'the lugal brought it out' 3.1.5.1, p. 128
lugal-ab-e$_3$ ED IIIb/Ukg. lugal X Girsu *DP* 1/2 128 o. v 7
lugal-ab-e$_3$ ED IIIb/Ukg. lugal X Girsu *DP* 1/2 129 o. iv 10
lugal-ab-e$_3$ CS Unknown (Girsu$^?$) MVN 2 298 r. i 9

lugal-AB-x-da (a1) unkn. mng. 3.1.8, p. 175
lugal-AB-x-da ED I-II Ur UET 2 199 r. ii 2

lugal-⸢AB(×AŠ$_2$$^?$)⸣-[x] ED IIIb-ES Adab CUSAS 11 83 o. ii 4

lugal-ab$_2$-ki-aĝ$_2$ (a1) 'the lugal loves the cow' 3.1.5.3, p. 135, 148 n. 837, 249 n. 1466
lugal-ab$_2$-ki-aĝ$_2$ ED IIIa Šuruppag? G. Visicato & A. Westenholz, *Gs Cagni*, p. 1107–1133 3 o. vi 1

lugal-abba$_2$ (a≥1) 'the lugal is my father' 3.1.1.2, p. 87, 175 n. 1134, 189
lugal-abba$_2$ ES Adab *TCABI* 57 o. i 6

lugal-abba$_2$-ĝu$_{10}$ (a≥1) 'the lugal is my father' 3.1.1.2, p. 87 n. 430
lugal-abba$_2$-ĝu$_{10}$ ED IIIb Adab CUSAS 11 21 o. ii 3
[lugal]-⸢abba$_2$-ĝu$_{10}$⸣ ED IIIb-ES Adab CUSAS 11 107 o. i 4
lugal-abba$_2$-ĝu$_{10}$ ED IIIb-ES Adab CUSAS 11 142 o. ii 1
lugal-abba$_2$-ĝu$_{10}$ ED IIIb-ES Adab CUSAS 11 198 o. ii 3
lugal-abba$_2$-ĝu$_{10}$ maškim-bi ED IIIb-ES Adab CUSAS 11 203 o. ii 1

lugal-abba$_2$-uru ? (a1) 'the lugal is a city elder (?)' 3.1.1.2, p. 95
lugal-⸢abba$_2$-uru$^?$⸣ CS Adab *SIA* 753 o. 1

lugal-abzu (a2) 'the lord … the Abzu,' abbreviation 3.1.6.4, p. 153
lugal-abzu ED IIIb-ES Umma-Zabala R. D. Freedman, *The Cuneiform Tablets in St. Louis* 48 o. i 8
lugal-abzu ED IIIb Umma-Zabala CUSAS 14 36 o. i 3
lugal-abzu ED IIIb Umma-Zabala CUSAS 14 117 o. i 4
lugal-abzu ED IIIb Ur UET 2 suppl. 47 o. i 4

lugal-abzu-a (a2) 'the lord … in the Abzu' 3.1.6.4, p. 153 n. 877
lugal-abzu-a ED IIIb/Luzag. (?) 7 Umma-Zabala BIN 8 55 o. ii 2
lugal-⸢abzu⸣-a ED IIIb/Luzag. ensi$_2$ X Umma-Zabala BIN 8 82 o. i 12
lugal-abzu-a ED IIIb Umma-Zabala CUSAS 14 40 o. i 3
lugal-abzu-a ED IIIb Umma-Zabala CUSAS 14 112 o. i 3
lugal-abzu-a ED IIIb/Luzag. ensi$_2$ 7 Umma-Zabala M. deJ. Ellis, *JCS* 31 (1979), p. 30–55 7 r. i 7
lugal-abzu-a azlag$_7$ MS-CS Nippur TMH 5 147 r. 3

lugal-abzu-a-gal-di (a≥1) 'the lord is prominent in the Abzu' 3.1.6.4, p. 153
lugal-abzu-a-gal-di lu$_2$ luĝa$_x$(BI×NIĜ$_2$) ED IIIb/Enz. ensi$_2$ X Girsu *DP* 2/1 195 o. iv' 6'
lugal-abzu-a-gal-di aga$_3$-us$_2$ ED IIIb/[Enz. ensi$_2$ X] Girsu *DP* 2/1 231 o. ii' 3'

lugal-abzu-da (a2) 'the lord … with the Abzu (?)' 3.1.6.4, p. 153 n. 877
lugal-abzu-da ED IIIa Unknown F. Vukosavović, *JAC* 23 (2008), p. 37–54 2 o. i 2
⸢lugal-abzu-da⸣ ED IIIa-b Girsu *RTC* 1 o. iii 1

lugal-abzu-si (a1) 'the lugal is just right for the Abzu' 3.1.6.4, p. 65 n. 320, 153
lugal-abzu-si nagar ED IIIb Nippur OSP 1 46 o. iv 6

lugal-ad-da (a1) ‘the lugal is a father’ 3.1.1.2, p. 87, 175 n. 1134

lugal-ad-da sagi MS-CS Isin ? BIN 8 158 r. i 9

lugal-ad-ĝar-du$_{10}$ (a1) ‘the lugal (gives/is) good advice’ 3.1.2, p. 107

lugal-ad-ĝar-du$_{10}$ ED IIIb/Ukg. lugal 6 Girsu *DP* 1/2 135 o. i 4

lugal-aga(LAK154)-zi (a2) ‘the lugal (wears) the legitimate *crown*’ 3.1.1.3, p. 88, 171 n. 1002, 188

lugal-aga-zi ED IIIb Isin BIN 8 80 r. i 5

lugal-aga-zi s. NIM ED IIIb-ES Isin MVN 3 53 o. iii 6

lugal-aga-zi ED IIIb/Urz. lugal Isin M. Lambert, *RA* 73 (1979), p. 5–6 o. v 15

lugal-aga$_3$(LAK667)-zi (a≥4) ‘the lugal (wears) the legitimate *crown*’ 3.1.1.3, p. 88, 188

lugal-aga$_3$-zi muḫaldim ED IIIb/Enz. ensi$_2$ 2 Girsu BIN 8 347 r. ii 12

lugal-aga$_3$-zi lu$_2$ a-kum$_2$ ED IIIb/Lug. 5 Girsu BIN 8 353 o. iii 5

lugal-aga$_3$-zi sagi ED IIIb/Lug. 1 Girsu *DCS* 8 o. iv 1

lugal-aga$_3$-zi lu$_2$ a-kum$_2$ ED IIIb/Lug. 5 Girsu *DP* 1/2 132 r. ii 13

lugal-aga$_3$-zi lu$_2$ igi-niĝin$_2$ ED IIIb/Enz. ensi$_2$ X Girsu *DP* 2/1 195 o. ii’ 6’

lugal-aga$_3$-zi [lu$_2$ a-kum$_2$] ED IIIb/Lug. 4 Girsu *DP* 2/1 226 r. i 4

lugal-aga$_3$-zi ED IIIb/X Y 3 Girsu *DP* suppl. 615 o. iii 3

lugal-aga$_3$-zi sagi ED IIIb/Lug. 3 Girsu *DP* suppl. 623 r. i 5

lugal-aga$_3$-zi sagi ED IIIb/Lug. 3 Girsu *DP* suppl. 624 o. i 3

lugal-aga$_3$-zi gab$_2$-dan$_6$ ED IIIb/Lug. 5 Girsu *DP* suppl. 626 o. i 3

lugal-aga$_3$-zi ED IIIb/X Y 1 Girsu *DP* suppl. 657 o. ii 3

lugal-aga$_3$-zi ED IIIb/Enz. ensi$_2$ 4 Girsu Nik 1 42 r. i 1

lugal-aga$_3$-zi lu$_2$ igi-niĝin$_2$ ED IIIb/Lug. 3 Girsu Nik 1 79 r. i 2

lugal-aga$_3$-zi ED IIIb/Enz. ensi$_2$ 4 Girsu *RTC* 70 r. i 2

lugal-aĝrig (a2) ‘the lugal is a steward’ 3.1.5.2, p. 129–130

lugal-aĝrig ED IIIa-b Unknown T. Ozaki, *JAC* 22 (2007), p. 1–8 1 o. i 2

lugal-aĝrig sipa anše CS Adab *SIA* 639 o. ii 5

lugal-aĝrig-zi (a4) ‘the lugal is a faithful steward’ 3.1.5.2, p. 129–130

lugal-aĝrig-zi ED IIIb Adab CUSAS 11 40 o. ii’ 4

lugal-aĝrig-zi ED IIIb-ES Adab CUSAS 11 140 o. iii 6

lugal-⸢aĝrig⸣-zi ED IIIb Nippur TMH 5 58 r. ii 2

lugal-aĝrig-zi MS-CS Adab OIP 14 176 o. ii 4

lugal-aĝrig-zi s. Lugal-ni$_3$-bara$_4$-du$_{10}$ MS-CS Nippur TMH 5 92 o. 4

lugal-aja$_2$-da (a1) ‘the lugal (is one honoured) with the father’ 3.1.7.1, p. 160

lugal-aja$_2$-da ED IIIa Šuruppag *TSŠ* 401 r. ii 3

lugal-aja$_2$-da ED IIIa Šuruppag *WF* 74 o. ii 4’

lugal-aja$_2$-ĝu$_{10}$ (a≥6) ‘the lugal is my father’ 3.1.1.2, p. 87, 175 n. 1023

lugal-aja$_2$-ĝu$_{10}$ ED IIIb Adab Eig. ^{ni_3}ensi$_2$ OIP 14 51 r. iii 8

lugal-aja$_2$-ĝu$_{10}$ E$_2$-ur$_2$-bi$_2$-du$_{10}$, gudu$_4$-da, e-da-se$_{12}$ ED IIIb/Ukg. ensi$_2$ 1 Girsu *AWAS* 119 r. ii 5’

lugal-aja$_2$-ĝu$_{10}$ a[mar]-gu$_4$-ka i$_3$-ti, U$_2$-u$_2$, saĝa e$_2$-gal-da e-da-ti ED IIIb/Ukg. lugal 4 Girsu *AWAS* 120 r. iv 20

lugal-aja$_2$-ĝu$_{10}$ U$_2$-u$_2$, saĝa e$_2$-⸢gal⸣-da, e-da-⸢se$_{12}$⸣ ED IIIb/Ukg. lugal 1? Girsu *AWAS* 123 o. viii 2’

lugal-aja$_2$-ĝu$_{10}$ saĝ-[apin] ED IIIb/Ukg. lugal 3 Girsu *AWAS* 124 o. i 2

lugal-aja$_2$-ĝu$_{10}$ 2 kam-ma, saĝ-[apin] ED IIIb/Ukg. lugal 3 Girsu *AWAS* 124 o. i 3

lugal-aja$_2$-ĝu$_{10}$ [s]ipa ⸢anše⸣ sur$_x$-ka, nitaḫ ED IIIb/Ukg. lugal 2 Girsu BIN 8 359 o. i 5’

lugal-aja$_2$-ĝu$_{10}$ nitaḫ ED IIIb/Ukg. lugal 2 Girsu *DP* 1/2 113 r. iv 2

lugal-aja$_2$-ĝu$_{10}$ lu$_2$ iti-da ED IIIb/Ukg. lugal 4 Girsu *DP* 1/2 116 o. i 13

lugal-aja$_2$-ĝu$_{10}$ saĝ-apin ED IIIb/Ukg. lugal 4 Girsu *DP* 1/2 117 o. i 4

lugal-aja$_2$-ĝu$_{10}$ [saĝ-apin] ED IIIb/Ukg. lugal 1 Girsu *DP* 1/2 118 o. i 4
lugal-aja$_2$-ĝu$_{10}$ saĝ-apin, nitaḫ ED IIIb/Ukg. lugal 2(+x?) Girsu *DP* 1/2 119 o. ii 1
lugal-aja$_2$-ĝu$_{10}$ s. An-na-bi$_2$-kuš$_2$ ED IIIb/Ukg. lugal 4 Girsu *DP* 1/2 138 o. ii 3
lugal-aja$_2$-ĝu$_{10}$ nitaḫ ED IIIb/Ukg. ensi$_2$ 1 Girsu HSS 3 15 r. ii 3
lugal-aja$_2$-ĝu$_{10}$ nitaḫ ED IIIb/Ukg. ensi$_2$ 1 Girsu HSS 3 16 r. ii 15
lugal-aja$_2$-ĝu$_{10}$ ED IIIb/Ukg. lugal 1 Girsu HSS 3 17 r. v 20
lugal-aja$_2$-ĝu$_{10}$ saĝ-apin ED IIIb/Ukg. lugal 2 Girsu HSS 3 25 o. i 2
lugal-aja$_2$-ĝu$_{10}$ saĝ-apin ED IIIb/Ukg. lugal 2 Girsu HSS 3 25 o. i 3
lugal-aja$_2$-ĝu$_{10}$ [E$_2$]-⸢ur$_2$⸣-[bi]-du$_{10}$, gudu$_4$-da, e-da-ti ED IIIb/Ukg. ensi$_2$ 1 Girsu MVN 3 2 r. iv 18
lugal-aja$_2$-ĝu$_{10}$ ED IIIb/Ukg. ensi$_2$ 1(+X?) Girsu Nik 1 9 o. ii 12
lugal-aja$_2$-ĝu$_{10}$ [saĝ-apin] ED IIIb Girsu Nik 1 16 o. i 2
lugal-aja$_2$-ĝu$_{10}$ E$_2$-ur$_2$-bi-du$_{10}$, gudu$_4$-da, e-da-se$_{12}$ ED IIIb/Lug. 6 Girsu D. Charpin, *RA* 71 (1977), p. 97–105 r. iv 9
lugal-aja$_2$-ĝu$_{10}$ saĝ-apin ED IIIb/Ukg. lugal 3 Girsu *TSA* 18 o. i 2
lugal-aja$_2$-ĝu$_{10}$ saĝ-apin ED IIIb/Ukg. lugal 3 Girsu *TSA* 18 o. i 3
lugal-aja$_2$-ĝu$_{10}$ ED IIIb/Lug. 6 Girsu VS 25 11 r. iii 9
lugal-aja$_2$-ĝu$_{10}$ nitaḫ ED IIIb/Lug. 6 Girsu VS 25 71 r. iii 17
lugal-aja$_2$-ĝu$_{10}$ dam-gar$_3$ saĝa-gal ED IIIb Uruk M. W. Green, *ZA* 72 (1982), p. 163–177 16 o. ii' 10
lugal-aja$_2$-ĝu$_{10}$ saĝa ^{d}Iškur (ensi$_2$ Adab^{ki}) MS Adab M. G. Biga, *Fs Klein*, p. 29–38 i 1
lugal-aja$_2$-ĝu$_{10}$ MS Adab *TCABI* 130 o. 3
lugal-aja$_2$-ĝu$_{10}$ CS Adab CUSAS 13 58 r. 2'
⸢lugal⸣-aja$_2$-ĝu$_{10}$ MS-CS Nippur OSP 2 119 o. 2

lugal-aja$_2$-uĝu$_3$(LAK730) $^{(a1)}$ 'the lugal is the father of the people' 3.1.1.6, p. 101, 248 n. 1462
lugal-aja$_2$-uĝu$_3$ ED IIIa Šuruppag *RTC* 13 o. iii 1

lugal-al-sa$_6$ $^{(a\geq4)}$ 'it is pleasing to the lugal' 3.1.8, p. 168 n. 973, 175
lugal-al-sa$_6$ b. En-lu$_2$-du$_{10}$ ED IIIb/Ukg. lugal 1 Girsu HSS 3 40 o. iv 11
lugal-al-sa$_6$ ED IIIb/Ukg. lugal 1 Girsu HSS 3 40 o. v 2
lugal-al-sa$_6$ gudu$_4$ ^{d}Ama-geštin-na ED IIIb/Ukg. lugal 1 Girsu HSS 3 40 o. vi 10
lugal-⸢al-sa$_6$⸣ gudu$_4$ ED IIIb/Ukg. lugal 1 Girsu HSS 3 40 r. iii 4
lugal-⸢al⸣-sa$_6$ f. Lugal-igi-an-na-ke$_4$-su ED IIIb/Ukg. lugal 1 Girsu HSS 3 40 r. iv 1
lugal-al-sa$_6$ b. En-lu$_2$-du$_{10}$ ED IIIb/Lug. 4 Girsu VS 14 170 r. ii 1
lugal-al-sa$_6$ gudu$_4$ ^{d}Ama-geštin ED IIIb/Ukg. lugal 1 Girsu VS 25 70 r. iii 14
lugal-al-sa$_6$ ED IIIb Nippur TMH 5 164 o. ii 3
lugal-al-sa$_6$ dub-sar maḫ ED IIIb Nippur TMH 5 166 r. ii 2
lugal-al-sa$_6$ lu$_2$ EDIN-gur ES Adab *TCABI* 32 o. ii 3
lugal-⸢al-sa$_6$⸣ h. Ama-e$_2$ MS-CS Nippur TMH 5 52 o. i 8

lugal-al$_6$-sa$_6$ $^{(a1)}$ 'it is pleasing to the lugal' 3.1.8, p. 175
lugal-al$_6$-sa$_6$ ED IIIb Nippur OSP 1 39 r. ii' 3

lugal-alam $^{(a1)}$ unkn. mng. 3.1.8, p. 175
lugal-alam ED I-II Ur UET 2 224 o. ii 4

°lugal-alam-ak $^{(°1)}$ unkn. mng. 3.1.8, p. 175
°lugal-alam-ak ED IIIa Šuruppag *SF* 29 o. vi 5

lugal-am-gal $^{(a1)}$ 'the lugal (is) a great bull' 3.1.8, p. 175
lugal-am-gal CS Girsu *DPA* 1 (PUL 1) r. 4

lugal-ambar $^{(a1)}$ 'the lugal … the marshes (?)' 3.1.8, p. 175
lugal-ambar E$_2$-lu$^{?}$-a, Lugal-ambar ED IIIb Umma-Zabala ? BIN 8 62 o. ii 6

lugal-AN (a≥7/°1) 'An/the god … the lugal (?)' 3.1.6.2, p. 146
lugal-AN ED IIIa Adab CUSAS 11 8 o. iv 3
lugal-AN ED IIIa Nippur OIP 97 2 r. i 3
lugal-AN ED IIIa Šuruppag CUSAS 11 344 r. ii 3
°lugal-AN šitim ED IIIa Šuruppag *SF* 29 o. vi 10
lugal-AN ED IIIa Šuruppag *WF* 65 r. ii 9
lugal-AN ED IIIb-ES Adab CUSAS 11 152 r. i 2
lugal-AN ED IIIb Nippur TMH 5 9 o. iii 2
lu:gal-AN šu-i ED IIIb Nippur TMH 5 67 o. ii 9
lugal-AN ES Adab *TCABI* 28 o. i 8
lugal-AN sipa ⸢udu⸣ CS Girsu *SCT* 2 r. i 9
lugal-AN nu-banda$_3$ CS Umma CT 50 188 r. i 13

lugal-AN-AB (a1) unkn. mng. 3.1.8, p. 175
lugal-AN-AB ED IIIa-b Umma ? YOS 1 2 3

lugal-AN-BU ? (a1) unkn. mng. 3.1.8, p. 175–176
lugal-AN-BU ? ED IIIa Šuruppag *TSŠ* 453/1 r. (?) iii 3'

lugal-AN-da (a≥5) 'the lugal … by An/a god,' abbreviation 3.1.6.2, p. 141, 153 n. 1488
lugal-AN-da Pa$_5$-še-mu[š] ED IIIb Girsu J. Marzahn & H. Neumann, *AoF* 22 (1995), p. 111f. (VAT 6121) o. vi 4'
lugal-AN-da ED IIIb/Enz. saĝa 17 Girsu BIN 8 352 r. iii 3
lugal-AN-da sipa anše ED IIIb/Lug. 1 Girsu *DCS* 8 r. iv 3
lugal-AN-da dumu saĝa ED IIIb/Enz. or En. II Girsu ? *DP* 1/1 31 v 18
lugal-AN-da ED IIIb/Ukg. lugal 5 Girsu *DP* 1/2 136 r. iii 16
lugal-AN-da sipa anše ED IIIb/Lug. 5 Girsu *DP* 1/2 132 r. iv 4
lugal-AN-da ensi$_2$ ED IIIb/Lug. 5 Girsu *DP* 1/2 132 r. v 4
lugal-AN-da ugula ma$_2$ gal-gal ED IIIb/Ukg. ensi$_2$ 1 Girsu *DP* 2/2 434 o. i 2
lugal-AN-da ensi$_2$ ED IIIb/Lug. 3 Girsu E. Sollberger, *Genava* 26 (1948), p. 48–72 1 r. iii 6
lugal-AN-da ensi$_2$ ED IIIb/Lug. 3 Girsu E. Sollberger, *Genava* 26 (1948), p. 48–72 2 r. iv 2
lugal-AN-da ensi$_2$ ED IIIb/Lug. 4 Girsu E. Sollberger, *Genava* 26 (1948), p. 48–72 3 r. iv 4
lugal-AN-da ED IIIb/X Y 6 Girsu E. Sollberger, *Genava* 26 (1948), p. 48–72 5 o. ii 4
lugal-AN-da ensi$_2$ ED IIIb/Lug. 6 Girsu E. Sollberger, *Genava* 26 (1948), p. 48–72 6 r. i 1
lugal-AN-da ensi$_2$ ED IIIb/Lug. 6 Girsu E. Sollberger, *Genava* 26 (1948), p. 48–72 6 r. ii 4
lugal-AN-da ensi$_2$ ED IIIb/Lug. Y X Girsu E. Sollberger, *Genava* 26 (1948), p. 48–72 7 r. ii 5
lugal-AN-da [x] Lugal-al-sa$_6$ (gudu$_4$) ED IIIb/Ukg. lugal 1 Girsu HSS 3 40 o. vi 4
lugal-AN-da ED IIIb/Ukg. lugal 5 Girsu Nik 1 3 r. vi 17
lugal-[AN]-da ED IIIb Girsu Nik 1 4 o. ii 1
lugal-AN-da ED IIIb/Ukg. lugal 1 Girsu Nik 1 25 o. ii 7
[lugal-AN-da] ED IIIb Girsu Nik 1 38 o. i 4
lugal-AN-da sipa e$_2$ gibil ED IIIb/Lug. 6 Girsu Nik 1 164 o. i 2
lugal-AN-da ED IIIb Girsu Nik 1 226 o. ii 2
lugal-AN-da ED IIIb Girsu Nik 1 235 o. i 2
lugal-AN-da s. Amar-A.ḪA^{ki} ED IIIb/Dudu saĝa Girsu W. W. Hallo, *OrNS* 42 (1973), p. 228–238 r. i 3
lugal-AN-da sipa anše ED IIIb/Lug. 6 Girsu *RTC* 54 o. vi 18
lugal-AN-da s. Maš-gur-ra ED IIIb/Lug. 2 Girsu VS 14 159 o. vi 4

lugal-AN-da ensi$_2$ ED IIIb/Lug. 2 Girsu VS 14 159 r. iii 5
lugal-AN-da ensi$_2$ ED IIIb/Lug. 4 Girsu VS 14 173 r. iv 4
lugal-AN-da ED IIIb/Ukg. lugal 3 Girsu VS 27 85 o. i 3
lugal-AN-da f. [(x)]-⸢IGI$^{?}$⸣-⸢x⸣ CS Girsu MVN 3 113 o. i 14

lugal-AN-da-nu-ḫuĝ-ĝa$_2$ (a1) 'is the lugal not put in office by An/a god?' 3.1.6.2, p. 141-142, 253 n. 1488
lugal-AN-da-nu-ḫuĝ-ĝa$_2$ ensi$_2$ ED IIIb/Lug. 2 Girsu *AWEL*, p. 548 1 (Riftin 1) r. i 3
lugal-AN-da-nu-ḫuĝ-ĝa$_2$ ensi$_2$ ED IIIb/Lug. 1 Girsu *RTC* 33 r. ii 2

lugal-AN-da-nu-me-a (a1) '(what would be) without LugalANda?' 3.1.6.2, p. 92 n. 469, 111 n. 593, 141
lugal-AN-da-nu-me-a ED IIIb/(Ukg. 2) Girsu VS 27 4 o. iii 1

lugal-AN-diri (a1) unkn. mng. 3.1.8, p. 176
lugal-AN-diri ED IIIa Šuruppag *TSŠ* 7 o. i' 4'
lugal-AN-diri ED IIIa Šuruppag *WF* 74 o. iv 9'

lugal-an-dul$_3$ (a≥8) 'the lugal is protection' 3.1.3.1, p. 108
lugal-an-dul$_3$ ED IIIa-b Unknown *L'uomo* 3 o. iii 7
lugal-an-dul$_3$ ED IIIb Adab CUSAS 11 28 o. ii 3
lugal-an-dul$_3$ ED IIIb Adab CUSAS 11 52 r. i 4
lugal-an-dul$_3$ s. Kas$_4$-e-ki-aĝ$_2$(-kam) ED IIIb-ES Adab CUSAS 11 83 o. i 4
lugal-an-dul$_3$ Ur-lum-ma, Lugal-an-dul$_3$ ED IIIb-ES Adab CUSAS 11 91 o. ii 6
lugal-⸢an⸣-dul$_3$ ED IIIb-ES Adab CUSAS 11 92 o. i 5
[lugal]-an-dul$_3$ ED IIIb-ES Adab CUSAS 11 94 o. i 2
[lugal-an]-d[ul$_3$] ? ED IIIb-ES Adab CUSAS 11 96 o. ii 4
lugal-an-dul$_3$ ED IIIb-ES Adab CUSAS 11 252 r. i 5
lugal-an-dul$_3$ ED IIIb Adab *TCABI* 5 o. 5
lugal-an-dul$_3$ ED IIIb Adab *TCABI* 6 o. 3
lugal-an-dul$_3$ ED IIIb Girsu ITT 5 9200 o. ii 4
lugal-an-dul$_3$ ED IIIb Girsu ITT 5 9201 o. ii 1
lugal-an-dul$_3$ ED IIIb Girsu ITT 5 9208 r. (?) i 1
lugal-an-dul$_3$ ED IIIb Nippur OSP 1 28 o. i 6
lugal-an-dul$_3$ sagi, MAḪ-zi (or al$_6$-zi) ED IIIb Nippur TMH 5 10 o. 1
lugal-an-dul$_3$ ED IIIb Umma-Zabala CUSAS 14 4 r. iii 6
lugal-an-dul$_3$ ES-MS Unknown MVN 3 58 r. 7
lugal-an-dul$_3$ sipa MS Adab *TCABI* 115 o. 2
lugal-an-dul$_3$ MS-CS Adab CUSAS 13 8 r. 2
lugal-an-dul$_3$ MS-CS Unknown BIN 8 275 o. 2
lugal-an-dul$_3$ MS-CS Unknown BIN 8 289 o. (?) 5
lugal-an-«an»-⸢dul$_3$⸣ kisal-luḫ CS-LS Girsu *DAS* 343 o. 5

lugal-an-ki-da (a2) 'the lugal … with heaven and earth' 3.1.8, p. 176
lugal-an-ki-da f. ^{d}Sud$_3$-a$_2$-maḫ ED IIIa Šuruppag G. Farber & W. Farber, *WO* 8 (1975–76), p. 178–184 o. iv 3
lugal-an-ki-da ED IIIb Umma-Zabala MVN 3 3 r. iii 14

°**lugal-an-ki$_2$-dub** (°1) 'the lugal makes heaven and earth quake (?)' 3.1.8, p. 176
°lugal-an-ki$_2$-dub ED IIIb Ebla MEE 3 59 o. ii 4

lugal-an-ku$_3$-ge (a1) unkn. mng. 3.1.8, p. 176
lugal-an-ku$_3$-ge ĝuruš CS Umma BARI S 2135 40 o. 5'

°**lugal-AN-mar** (a1) unkn. mng. 3.1.8, p. 176
°lugal-AN-mar ED IIIa Abū Ṣalābīḫ *IAS* 330 o. ii 1

lugal-an-na (a1) (abbreviation of the following) 3.1.6.2, p. 143 n. 799

lugal-an-na CS Unknown (Girsu?) MVN 2 298 o. ii 21

lugal-an-na-tum₂ (a>11) 'the lugal befits heaven' 3.1.6.2, p. 65 n. 321, 143
lugal-[an]-na-tum₂ ED IIIb-ES Adab CUSAS 11 157 o. ii 2
lugal-an-na-tum₂ ED IIIb Girsu *RTC* 18 r. iii 1
lugal-an-na-tum₂ f. Ur-[t]u ED IIIb/Urz. lugal Isin M. Lambert, *RA* 73 (1979), p. 5–6 r. i 8
lugal-an-na-tum₂ ED IIIb/X Y 6 Lagaš BiMes 3 20 i 5
lugal-an-na-tum₂ ED IIIb Nippur TMH 5 9 o. i 4
lugal-an-na-tum₂ f. A[d?-d]a? ED IIIb Nippur TMH 5 11 o. ii 3
lugal-an-na-tum₂ ED IIIb Nippur TMH 5 45 o. ii 2'
lugal-an-na-tum₂ ED IIIb-ES Nippur TMH 5 94 o. 3
lugal-an-na-tum₂ CS Adab CUSAS 13 145 o. 6
lugal-an-na-tum₂ CS Adab *SIA* 699+823 r. 10
lugal-an-na-tum₂ šita₂ U CS Girsu *RTC* 96 r. ii 9
lugal-an-na-tum₂ CS-LS ? Girsu *RTC* 198 r. 5
lugal-an-na-tum₂ ugula CS Girsu ITT 1 1350 o. 2
lugal-an-na-tum₂ CS Girsu ITT 5 9270 r. 6'
lugal-an-na-tum₂ CS Girsu CT 50 126 o. 2
lugal-an-na-tum₂ MS-CS Isin ? MVN 3 25 r. 1
lugal-an-na-tum₂ geme₂ zaḫ₃(-me) MS-CS Nippur TMH 5 39 o. ii 12'
lugal-an-na-tum₂ geme₂ zaḫ₃(-me) MS-CS Nippur TMH 5 44 o. iii' 5'
lugal-an-na-tum₂ dumu AN-LUḪ, ĝuruš CS Umma BARI S 2135 40 o. 3'
lugal-an-na-tum₂ ugula CS Umma *USP* 50 o. 4
lugal-an-na-tum₂ ensi₂ Ummaki LS Umma V. Scheil, *CRAIB* 55 (1911), 318–327 1

lugal-An-ne₂ (a≥14) 'An… the lugal' 3.1.6.2, p. 142, 237, 253 n. 1488
lugal-An-ne₂ ED IIIb-ES Adab CUSAS 11 78 o. ii 5
lugal-An-ne₂ ir₁₁ SIG₄-zi ED IIIb/Ukg. lugal Girsu TIM 9 94 iv' 3'
lugal-An-ne₂ niĝir ED IIIb-ES Isin (?) BIN 8 170 r. 1
lugal-An-ne₂ ED IIIb Nippur OSP 1 73 o. 4
lugal-⸢An-ne₂⸣ ED IIIb Nippur TMH 5 203 o. 3
lugal-An-ne₂ ED IIIb Umma-Zabala ? BIN 8 48 o. 4
⸢lugal⸣-An-ne₂ ⸢nu-kiri₆⸣ ED IIIb Umma-Zabala ? BIN 8 120 o. i 5'
lugal-An-ne₂ [nu]-⸢kiri₆⸣ ED IIIb/Luzag. Y X Umma-Zabala M. Powell, *HUCA* 49 (1978), p. 1–58 2 o. ii 12
lugal-An-ne₂ ED IIIb Ur UET 2 suppl. 10 o. i 3
lugal-An-ne₂ s. Ur-me MS Adab *TCABI* 70 o. 1
lugal-An-ne₂ lugal-An-ne₂, [*i*]*g-ru-sa-am* lugal [(x)], «x» Urim₅ki CS Ešnuna MAD 1 172 o. 6
lugal-An-ne₂ CS Girsu CT 50 107 o. 7
lugal-⸢An⸣-ne₂ CS Girsu CT 50 134 r. 1
lugal-An-ne₂ CS Girsu *DPA* 31 (PUL 23) o. 7
lugal-An-ne₂ f. Šeš-šeš CS Girsu ITT 1 1174 o. 4
lugal-An-ne₂ CS Girsu ITT 2/1 4588 o. 7
lugal-An-ne₂ CS Isin MVN 3 1 r. ii 8
lugal-[An-ne₂] MS-CS Nippur OSP 2 58 r. 10
lugal-An-ne₂ [šandan] MS-CS Nippur OSP 2 59 r. 9
lugal-An-ne₂ E₂-lu₂, Lugal-An-ne₂, be₆-da MS-CS Nippur OSP 2 60 o. 9
lugal-An-ne₂ E₂-lu₂, Lugal-An-ne₂, be₆-da MS-CS Nippur OSP 2 60 r. 2
lugal-An-ne₂ 3 FPN saĝ-ba Lugal-An-ne₂-me MS-CS Nippur OSP 2 63 o. ii 5
lugal-An-ne₂ (-e, erg.) MS-CS Nippur PBS 9 11 r. 4
lugal-An-ne₂ MS-CS Umma MAD 4 22 (translit. only) o. 6

lugal-An-ne$_2$? MS Umma MAD 4 68 o. 9
lugal-An-ne$_2$ ⸢ir$_{11}$⸣ Ur-bi ? MS-CS Umma ? *TCVC* 728 o. ii 5
lugal-An-ne$_2$ s. Lugal-iti-da CS Umma *USP* 71 o. 6
lugal-An-ne$_2$ MS-CS Unknown MVN 3 31 r. 3
lugal-An-ne$_2$ MS Unknown MVN 3 37 o. 6
lugal-An-ne$_2$ f. [x-x] CS Unknown MVN 3 108 r. 5
lugal-An-ne$_2$ dub-sar CS-LS Unknown *EGA* 653 pl. 17 fig. 195

lugal-An-ne$_2$-ki-aĝa$_2$ $^{(a1)}$ ‘the lugal is one loved by An’ 3.1.6.2, p. 142
lugal-An-ne$_2$-ki-aĝa$_2$ lu$_2$ umum-ma *DP* 2/1 ED IIIb/Lug. 2 176 o. ii 4

lugal-An-ne$_2$-su $^{(a1)}$ ‘the lugal is one known by An’ 3.1.6.2, p. 142
lugal-An-ne$_2$-su CS Girsu ITT 5 9301 o. 2

lugal-an-ta-ti $^{(a\geq1)}$ ‘the lugal (bestows) life from above’ 3.1.5.4, p. 137
lugal-an-ta-ti ED IIIb Nippur OSP 1 25 “v” 3’
lugal-⸢an-ta⸣-ti ES-MS Nippur OSP 1 23 o. ii 16’

lugal-an-tum$_2$ $^{(a2)}$ ‘the lugal befits heaven’ 3.1.6.2, p. 143
lugal-an-tum$_2$ Ur-saĝ ED IIIa Šuruppag M. Molina & H. Sanchiz, *StEL* 24 (2007), p. 1–15 1 o. iv 7
lugal-⸢an-tum$_2$⸣ (lu$_2$ ganun) ED IIIb Nippur OSP 1 16 r. i 2
lugal-an-tum$_2$ lu$_2$-gan[un] ED IIIb Nippur OSP 1 117 o. i 3
lugal-an-tum$_2$ ED IIIb Nippur TMH 5 154 r. ii 2

lugal-AN-... ED IIIb Nippur TMH 5 14 o. iii 3’
lugal-AN-[x] MS-CS Ur UET 2 suppl. 32 o. 1’

lugal-^{an}Anzu$_2$(NI$_2$.MI) $^{(a1)}$ ‘the lugal is (like) the Anzu’ 3.1.3.3, p. 114 n. 615, 165
lugal-^{an}Anzu$_2$ ir$_{11}$ MS-CS Nippur OSP 2 75 r. 3

lugal-^{an}Anzu$_2$(NI$_2$.MI)^{mušen} $^{(a\geq2)}$ ‘the lugal is (like) the Anzu’ 3.1.3.3, p. 114 w. n. 615, 165
lugal-^{an}Anzu$_2^{mušen}$ engar ED IIIb Girsu J. Marzahn & H. Neumann, *AoF* 22 (1995), p. 111f. (VAT 6121) o. iv 4’
lugal-$^{an!(ḪAL)}$Anzu$_2^{mušen}$ ED IIIb Girsu V. Donbaz, *NABU* 1997/52 A 3
lugal-^{an}Anzu$_2^{mušen}$ nagar ša$_3$ ED IIIb Girsu OIP 14 57 r. i 2
lugal-^{an}Anzu$_2^{mušen}$ ED IIIb/En. I ensi$_2$ Girsu OIP 104 22 r. ii 42
lugal-^{an}Anzu$_2^{mušen}$ ED IIIb/Lug. 4 Girsu VS 25 26 o. i 1

lugal-^{an}Anzu$_x$(IM.MI) $^{(a1)}$ ‘the lugal is (like) the Anzu’ 3.1.3.3, p. 114 n. 615, 165
lugal-^{an}Anzu$_x$ ED I-II Ur UET 2 128 r. i 4

lugal-^{an}Anzu$_x$(MI)^{mušen} $^{(a3/°1)}$ ‘the lugal is (like) the Anzu’ 3.1.3.3, p. 114 n. 615, 165
lugal-^{an}Anzu$_x^{mušen}$ Lagaš^{ki} ED IIIa Šuruppag *WF* 70 r. v 1
⸢lugal⸣-^{an}Anzu$_x^{mušen}$ IB ED IIIa Šuruppag *NTSŠ* 262 r. i 2
lugal-^{an}Anzu$_x^{mušen}$ ED IIIa-ED IIIb Ur UE 2 pl. 197 no. 60 1
°lugal-^{an}Anzu$_x^{mušen}$ ED IIIb Ebla MEE 3 67 o. i 3

lugal-APIN ? $^{(a1)}$ ‘the lugal … the plow’ 3.1.5.3, p. 131 n. 725
lugal-⸢APIN$^?$⸣ Ur-ba, ir$_{11}$ Lugal-⸢APIN$^?$⸣ CS Girsu *RTC* 96 r. i 13’

lugal-^{ĝiš}apin-du$_{10}$ $^{(a1)}$ ‘the lugal is one who makes the plow good’ 3.1.5.3, p. 50 n. 231, 131 w. n. 725, 140, 259
lugal-^{ĝiš}apin-du$_{10}$ nar CS Umma *USP* 41 o. 5

lugal-apin-du$_{10}$ $^{(a\geq8)}$ ‘the lugal is one who makes the plow good’ 3.1.5.3, p. 50 n. 231, 113, 131, 140, 185, 259
lugal-apin-du$_{10}$ ED IIIb Adab CUSAS 11 52 o. iv 7’
lugal-⸢apin$^?$⸣-du$_{10}$ ED IIIb-ES Adab CUSAS 11 252 r. ii 1
lugal-apin-du$_{10}$ ED IIIb Nippur OSP 1 36 o. i 4’

lugal-apin-du$_{10}$ ED IIIb Nippur OSP 1 39 o. iii 4’
lugal-apin-du$_{10}$ tug$_2$-du$_8$ ED IIIb Nippur OSP 1 46 o. iv 4
lugal-apin-du$_{10}$ ED IIIb Nippur TMH 5 4 o. i 1
lugal-apin-du$_{10}$ f. Lugal-ur-saĝ ED IIIb Nippur TMH 5 11 o. i 7
lugal-apin-du$_{10}$ ED IIIb Nippur TMH 5 15 o. ii 7
lugal-apin-du$_{10}$ ED IIIb Nippur TMH 5 56 o. ii 3
lugal-apin-du$_{10}$ muḫaldim ED IIIb Nippur TMH 5 79 o. iii 2
⸢lugal-apin⸣-[du$_{10}$] MS Adab *TCABI* 114 o. 6
lugal-apin-du$_{10}$ dam-⸢gar$_3$⸣ MS-CS Isin ? MAD 4 78 r. 4
lugal-apin-du$_{10}$ MS-CS Nippur OSP 2 95 o. i 10
lugal-⸢apin⸣-[du$_{10}$] MS-CS Nippur OSP 2 96 o. i 3
lugal-[apin]-⸢du$_{10}$⸣ MS-CS Nippur OSP 2 106 o. 6
lugal-apin-du$_{10}$ ĝir$_2$-la$_2$ MS-CS Nippur OSP 2 162 r. 1
lugal-⸢apin⸣-du$_{10}$ muḫaldim, ugula-[b]⸢i⸣ MS-CS Nippur PBS 9 11 r. 7
lugal-apin-du$_{10}$ CS/NS. Nippur PBS 9 15+110 o. ii 5
[lugal]-⸢apin⸣-du$_{10}$ CS Nippur PBS 9 36 o. i’ 4’
lugal-apin-du$_{10}$ CS Nippur PBS 9 77 o. i 2’
[lugal-a]pin-du$_{10}$ CS Nippur PBS 9 79 o. i 2’
lugal-apin-du$_{10}$ MS-CS Nippur PBS 9 105 o. (?) i 1’
lugal-apin-du$_{10}$ CS/NS. Nippur TMH 5 7+184+201a o. i 6
lugal-apin-du$_{10}$ dumu nu-siki MS-CS Nippur TMH 5 34 r. i 14
lu[gal]-apin-du$_{10}$ dumu nu-siki MS-CS Nippur TMH 5 39 o. i 16’

lugal-apin-ne$_2$ $^{(a\geq1)}$ ‘the lugal (is one who makes) the plow (good)’ 3.1.5.3, p. 50 n. 231, 131, 259
lugal-apin-[ne$_2$] AN-palil, azlag$_3$, Lugal-apin-[ne$_2$], e-da-ti ED IIIb/Ukg. lugal 3 Girsu *AWAS* 124 r. ii 18
lugal-apin-ne$_2$ Ur-^{d}Ba-u$_2$, mi$_2$-us$_2$-sa, Lugal-apin-ne$_2$ ED IIIb/Ukg. lugal 1 Girsu *Amherst* 2 o. ii 3
lugal-apin-ne$_2$ Ur-^{d}Ba-u$_2$, mi$_2$-us$_2$-sa, Lugal-apin-ne$_2$ ED IIIb/Lug. 6 Girsu *DP* 1/2 125 o. ii 2
lugal-apin-ne$_2$ ED IIIb/Ukg. lugal 4 Girsu *DP* 1/2 116 r. iv 1
lugal-apin-ne$_2$ ED IIIb/Ukg. lugal 4 Girsu *DP* 1/2 117 r. iii 8
lugal-apin-ne$_2$ ED IIIb/Lug. 3 Girsu *DP* 1/2 124 o. i 9
lugal-apin-ne$_2$ Ur-^{d}Ba-u$_2$, mi$_2$-us$_2$-sa, Lugal-apin-ne$_2$ ED IIIb/Ukg. lugal 3 Girsu *DP* 1/2 126 o. ii 1
lugal-apin-ne$_2$ ED IIIb X Y 4 Girsu HSS 3 19 r. i 9
lugal-apin-ne$_2$ lu$_2$ ni$_3$-^{ba}bara$_3$ ED IIIb X Y 5 Girsu *RTC* 39 r. i 5
lugal-apin-ne$_2$ azlag$_3$ ED IIIb/Lug. 6 Girsu *RTC* 50 o. iii 1
lugal-apin-ne$_2$ Ur-^{d}Ba-u$_2$, mi$_2$-us$_2$-sa, Lugal-apin-ne$_2$ ED IIIb/Ukg. lugal 2 Girsu VS 27 75 o. ii 2

°lugal-asal$_2$-RU $^{(°1)}$ unkn. mng. 3.1.8, p. 176
°lugal-asal$_2$-RU ED IIIa Šuruppag *SF* 28 o. iii 7

lugal-asila$_3$(EZEM×A) $^{(a1)}$ ‘the lugal is joyous’ 3.1.7.8, p. 171 n. 996
lugal-asila$_3$ s. Si-du$_3$ CS Umma *USP* 46 o. 16

lugal-asila$_x$(A.EZEM) $^{(a2)}$ ‘the lugal is joyous’ 3.1.7.8, p. 170–171
lugal-asila$_x$ ED IIIa Girsu L. Heuzey, *Catalogue des antiquités chaldéennes* no. 5 (AO 2350+3288)
lugal-asila$_x$ ED IIIb/Ukg. lugal 6 Girsu *DP* 1/2 135 o. v 13

lugal-aš $^{(a1)}$ ‘the lugal is one of a kind’ 3.1.7.7, p. 168 n. 970
lugal-aš ED IIIa Uruk M. W. Green, *ZA* 72 (1982), p. 163–177 5 o. i 2

lugal-$aš_{10}$ (a4) ‘the lugal is one of a kind’ 3.1.7.7, p. 168
lugal-$aš_{10}$ šu-ku_6 lugal CS Girsu ITT 1 1040 o. 5’
lugal-$aš_{10}$ na-gada CS Girsu ITT 1 1059 o. 6
lugal-$aš_{10}$ lu_2 u_3 Mar-tu-ne^{ki} CS Girsu ITT 1 1475 o. 9
lugal-$aš_{10}$ sipa CS Girsu ITT 5 6710 o. 2
lugal-$aš_{10}$ maškim CS Girsu *RTC* 127 o. v 8’
lugal-$aš_{10}$ maškim CS Girsu *RTC* 127 o. v 27

lugal-$aš_{10}$-ni (a≥4) ‘the lugal is one of a kind’ 3.1.7.7, p. 168
lugal-$aš_{10}$-ni du_3-a-ku_5 ED IIIb/Ukg. lugal 6 Girsu *AWAS* 122 o. iii 3
lugal-$aš_{10}$-ni ki šu-ku_6 CS Girsu *RTC* 91 r. ii’ 5
lugal-$aš_{10}$-[ni$^?$] saĝ-⌜apin⌝ MS-CS Umma ? *TCVC* 733 r. i’ 3’
lugal-$aš_{10}$-ni CS Umma MAD 4 39 o. 7
lugal-$aš_{10}$-ni CS Umma MAD 4 32 o. 8

lugal-bad_3 (a≥8) ‘the lugal is a fortress’ 3.1.3.1, p. 91 n. 466, 108
lugal-bad_3 ED IIIb Adab CUSAS 11 48 o. ii 4
lugal-bad_3 lu_2 igi-niĝin_2 ED IIIb/Ukg. lugal 3 Girsu *AWAS* 124 o. ii 12
lugal-bad_3 [lu_2 igi-niĝin_2] ED IIIb/Ukg. lugal 2 Girsu BIN 8 359 o. ii 10’
⌜lugal-bad_3⌝ nitaḫ ED IIIb/Ukg. lugal 2(+x?) Girsu *DP* 1/2 119 i 1
lugal-bad_3 lu_2 igi-niĝin_2 ED IIIb/Ukg. lugal 2 Girsu HSS 3 25 o. ii 12
lugal-bad_3 lu_2 igi-niĝin_2 ED IIIb/Ukg. lugal 3 Girsu HSS 3 26 o. ii 11
lugal-bad_3 lu_2 igi-niĝin_2 ED IIIb/Ukg. lugal 3 Girsu HSS 3 27 o. iii 4
lugal-bad_3 lu_2 igi-niĝin_2 ED IIIb/Ukg. lugal 3 Girsu *TSA* 18 o. ii 12
lugal-bad_3 GAB_2 ED IIIb Nippur OSP 1 36 o. i 1’
lugal-bad_3 muḫaldim ED IIIb Nippur OSP 1 36 o. i 4’
lugal-bad_3 s. Gu_2-en, …, nu-$kiri_6$ ED IIIb Nippur TMH 5 6 o. ii 6
lugal-⌜bad_3⌝ ED IIIb Nippur TMH 5 21 o. iii 7’
lugal-⌜bad_3⌝ ED IIIb Nippur TMH 5 56 o. i 6
lugal-bad_3 muḫaldim ED IIIb Nippur TMH 5 56 r. iii 3’
lugal-bad_3 ED IIIb Nippur TMH 5 79 o. ii 5
lugal-bad_3 muḫaldim ED IIIb Nippur TMH 5 79 o. ii 6
lugal-bad_3 ED IIIb Nippur TMH 5 164 o. ii 7
⌜lugal-bad_3⌝ ED IIIb Nippur TMH 5 167 o. i 5
⌜lu:gal-bad_3⌝ ED IIIb Nippur TMH 5 174 o. ii 2
lu:gal-bad_3 muḫaldim ED IIIb Nippur TMH 5 174 o. ii 4
lugal-bad_3 ES Adab CUSAS 11 331 o. ii 5
lu:gal-bad_3 muḫaldim ES Nippur OSP 1 31 o. i 5’
lugal-bad_3 CS Girsu ITT 5 9263 o. ii 3
lugal-bad_3 CS Unknown Mesopotamia 9 2 o. 17’
lugal-bad_3 CS Unknown Mesopotamia 9 4 o. 18

lugal-ban_3-da (a2) ‘the lugal is resourceful’ 3.1.2, p. 106
lugal-ban_3-da ED IIIb Marada ? *AAICAB* 1/1 (Ashm 1924-468) r. ii 4
lu[gal]-ban_3-da CS Adab CUSAS 13 56 o. ii 8

lugal-banšur-e (a1) ‘the lugal (is just right for) the (offering) table(?)’ 3.1.6.3, p. 113 n. 606, 147, 230
lugal-banšur-e ugula MS-CS Umma MesCiv 4 30 o. i 1

lugal-$bara_2$ (a≥6) ‘the lugal … the throne dais’ 3.1.1.3, p. 90 n. 457
lugal-$bara_2$ lu_2 il_2, nu-$banda_3$ ED IIIb/Ukg. lugal 1 Girsu *DP* 2/2 374 o. iii 1
lugal-$bara_2$ lu_2 banšur ED IIIb/Ukg. lugal 4 Girsu *DP* suppl. 590 o. v 7
lugal-$bara_2$ ES Adab CUSAS 11 318 o. 3
lugal-$bara_2$ Mar-ḫa-ši$^{‹ki›}$ ES-MS Umma *CST* 8 o. i 2

lugal-bara$_2$ [ugula]-ni ES-MS Umma Nik 2 13 o. 4
lugal-bara$_2$ ES-MS Umma Nik 2 62 o. i 6
⸢lugal⸣-bara$_2$ Mar-ḫa-ši$^{‹ki›}$ ES-MS Umma *USP* 7 r. 8
lugal-bara$_2$ saĝ-apin-na CS Girsu *STTI* 86 o. ii’ 17’
lugal-⸢bara$_2$⸣ CS Girsu *STTI* 151 r. i’ 6’
[l]u[gal$^?$]-bara$_2$ s. Ur$_2$-ra-ni b. Ur-si$_4$ CS Isin *TCVBI* 1-56 o. 8
lugal-bara$_2$ dub-sar MS-CS Nippur OSP 2 44 o. ii 3
lugal-bara$_2$ CS Umma MAD 4 39 o. 5
lugal-bara$_2$ Lugal-bara$_2$, NI-tuk-MU, NIM-me MS Umma *L’uomo* 33 o. i 5

°lugal-bara$_2$-du$_{10}$ (°2) ‘the lugal makes the throne dais good’ 3.1.1.3, p. 62 n. 310, 66 n. 329, 90, 249 n. 1464
°lugal-⸢bara$_2$⸣-du$_{10}$ ED IIIa Kiš MesCiv 14, pl. 23, 3: H+Y r.(?) ii’ 3
°lugal-bara$_2$-du$_{10}$ ED IIIa Šuruppag *SF* 28 o. iii 4
°lugal-bara$_2$-du$_{10}$ ED IIIa Šuruppag *SF* 29 o. ii 7

lugal-bara$_2$-ga-ne$_2$-du$_{10}$ (a1) ‘the lugal makes his throne dais good’ 3.1.1.3, p. 66 n. 329, 90, 101
lugal-bara$_2$-ga-ne$_2$-du$_{10}$ nu-banda e$_2$ Lum-ma-tur-ka ED IIIb/En. I ensi$_2$ 4 Lagaš BiMes 3 10 r. iii 1

lugal-bara$_2$-ge-du$_{10}$ (a1) ‘the lugal makes the throne dais good’ 3.1.1.3, p. 62 n. 310, 66 n. 329, 90
lugal-bara$_2$-ge-du$_{10}$ Unug^{ki} ED IIIa Šuruppag *WF* 70 r. v 10

lugal-bara$_2$-kalam(LAK729) (a1) ‘the lugal is a prince of the land’ 3.1.1.3, p. 90–91, 100, 258
lugal-bara$_2$-kalam(LAK729) ir$_{11}$ sukkal-maḫ MS-CS Umma ? *TCVC* 728 o. iii 9

lugal-bara$_2$-si (a3) ‘the lugal is just right for the throne dais’ 3.1.1.3, p. 62 n. 310, 66 n. 329, 90, 229, 249 n. 1464
lugal-bara$_2$-si ED I-II Ur UET 2 248 o. ii 1
lugal-bara$_2$-⸢si⸣ ED IIIa Adab CUSAS 11 6 o. ii 5
lugal-bara$_2$-si ED IIIa Šuruppag *WF* 65 r. v 1

lugal-bi$_2$-tum$_2$ (a1) unkn. mng. 3.1.8, p. 176, 178 n. 1061
lugal-bi$_2$-tum$_2$ ED IIIa-b Isin (?) OIP 104 15 o. ii 12
lugal-bi$_2$-tum$_2$ ED IIIa-b Isin (?) OIP 104 15 o. vi 18

lugal-bu$_3$-la-ni (a1) unkn. mng. 3.1.8, p. 176
lugal-⸢bu$_3$⸣-la-ni ES-MS Umma Nik 2 17 o. 4

lugal-bur (a≥3) ‘the lugal … a bowl’ 3.1.6.3, p. 149, 230
lugal-⸢bur⸣ CS Girsu CT 50 100 o. 2
lugal-b[ur] šabra CS Girsu ITT 1 1040 o. 4’
lugal-bur CS Girsu ITT 5 6679 r. 2
lugal-bur LS-Lagaš II Girsu ITT 5 6689 o. 2
lugal-bur CS Girsu ITT 5 9268 o. 4’
lugal-bur ^{d}MUŠ-ur-saĝ simug, ir$_{11}$ Lugal-bur CS Girsu ? MVN 10 137 r. 1
lugal-bur aĝrig CS Girsu *STTI* 6 o. 7’
lugal-bur CS Girsu *STTI* 7 r. 8
lu[gal]-bur CS Girsu *STTI* 98 o. 3
lugal-bur CS Girsu *STTI* 118 o. 4
lugal-bur CS Girsu *STTI* 121 o. 3’
lugal-bur CS Girsu *STTI* 182 r. ii 7’
lugal-bur šabra CS Umma CT 50 75 r. 9

lugal-da (a8) unkn. mng. 3.1.8, p. 176

[lugal]-da   ED IIIb-ES   Adab   CUSAS 11   161   r. 2
lugal-da   ED IIIb X Y 2   Girsu   *DP* 2/2   461   r. ii 4
lugal-da   sipa udu-siki   ED IIIb/Ukg. ensi$_2$ 1   Girsu   *DP* 2/1   259   o. i 4
lugal-da   sipa udu-siki   ED IIIb/Lug. 6   Girsu   Nik 1   293   r. i 3
lugal-da   ir$_{11}$ E$_2$-ERIM   ED IIIb/Urz. lugal   Isin   M. Lambert, *RA* 73 (1979), p. 5–6   o. vi 22
lugal-da   ED IIIb   Umma-Zabala ?   BIN 8   104   o. i 1
lugal-da   Pa$_5$-maḫ   ED IIIb   Unknown   MVN 3   14   o. iii 4
lugal-da   ES-MS   Nippur   OSP 1   23   o. iii 13'
lugal-da   ES-MS   Nippur   OSP 1   23   o. vi 17
lugal-da   nagar   MS-CS   Nippur   TMH 5   63   o. i 10
lugal-da   f. Lu$_2$-diĝir-ra, sipa anše lugal-ka   MVN 3   107   r. 4
lugal-da$^?$ CS   Kiš   B. Buchanan, Catalogue 1   307   1

lugal-DA-gur ? (a1)   unkn. mng.   3.1.8, p. 176
lugal-DA-gur$^?$ ED IIIb   Umma-Zabala   MVN 3   3   r. vi 10'

lugal-DA-gur-ra (a1)   unkn. mng.   3.1.8, p. 176 w. n. 1044
lugal-DA-gur-ra   ED IIIa-b   Isin (?)   OIP 104   14   r. viii 4
lugal-DA-gur-ra   ED IIIa-b   Isin (?)   OIP 104   14   r. ix 1
lugal-DA-gur-ra   ED IIIa-b   Isin (?)   OIP 104   14   r. ix 10
lugal-DA-gur-ra   ED IIIa-b   Isin (?)   OIP 104   14   r. ix 16
lugal-DA-gur-ra   ED IIIa-b   Isin (?)   OIP 104   15   l.e. 24

°lugal-DA-ḪU (°1)   unkn. mng.   3.1.8, p. 176
°lugal-DA-ḪU   ED IIIa   Šuruppag   *SF*   29   r. iii 11

lugal-DA-KI (a1)   unkn. mng.   3.1.8, p. 176
lugal-DA-KI   MS-CS   Nippur   OSP 2   88   o. 2'

lugal-da-lu (a1)   '(things) flourish with the lugal'   3.1.5.3, p. 102, 134
lugal-da-lu   lugal Adab^{ki} ED IIIb/Lugaldalu X   Adab   E. J. Banks, *AJSL* 21/1 (1914), p. 57–59   2

lugal-da-MU (a2)   unkn. mng.   3.1.8, p. 176
lugal-da-MU   ED IIIa   Larsa ?   *AAICAB* 1/1   (Ashm 1924-455)   o. i 3
⌜lugal-da⌝-MU   nar   ED IIIb   Nippur   TMH 5   67   o. iii 2

lugal-da-na (a2)   unkn. mng.   3.1.8, p. 121 n. 653, 176
lugal-da-na   ED IIIa   Šuruppag   *TSŠ*   467   r. ii 3
lugal-da-na   ED IIIb   Nippur   OSP 1   79   o. 2

lugal-da-nam (a1)   unkn. mng.   3.1.8, p. 176
lugal-da-nam   ED I-II   Ur   UET 2   143   o. i 1

lugal-da-nu-me-a (a3)   '(what would be) without a lugal?'   3.1.3.3, p. 111–112, 176 n. 1043
lugal-da-nu-me-a   gab$_2$-ra-ni, sipa udu siki-ka   ED IIIb [Ukg. lugal] 6   Girsu   *AWAS*   67   o. vi 5
lugal-da-nu-me-a   sipa u[du siki-ka]   ED IIIb/Ukg. lugal X   Girsu   *AWAS*   69   o. v 11'
lugal-da-nu-me-a   sipa udu [siki]-ka   ED IIIb/Ukg. lugal 3   Girsu   *AWAS*   118   o. vi 9
lugal-da-nu-me-a   sipa udu siki-ka   ED IIIb/Ukg. ensi$_2$ 1   Girsu   *AWAS*   119   r. i 6'
lugal-da-nu-me-a   sipa udu siki-ka   ED IIIb/Ukg. lugal 4   Girsu   *AWAS*   120   r. iii 17
lugal-da-nu-me-a   [gab$_2$]-⌜ra⌝ [udu siki-ka]   ED IIIb [Ukg. lugal 3]   Girsu   *AWAS*   121   r. v 1
⌜lugal-da-nu-me⌝-[a]   [sipa udu siki-ka-me]   ED IIIb/Ukg. lugal 1?   Girsu   *AWAS*   123   o. vii 21
lugal-da-nu-me-a   sipa [udu] siki-ka   ED IIIb/Ukg. [lugal] 6   Girsu   BIN 8   354   o. v 13'
lugal-da-nu-me-a   sipa udu siki-⌜ka⌝   ED IIIb/Ukg. lugal 3   Girsu   BIN 8   391   r. i 10
lugal-da-nu-me-a   sipa udu siki$_2$ ED IIIb/Ukg. lugal 2   Girsu   *DP* 1/2   113   r. iii 5

lugal-da-nu-me-a lu$_{2}$ iti-da ED IIIb/Ukg. lugal 4 Girsu *DP* 1/2 116 o. i 14
⌜lugal-da⌝-[nu-me-a] [sipa udu-siki-ka] ED IIIb/Ukg. lugal 5 Girsu *CTNMC* 3 o. vi 12
lugal-da-nu-me-a (sipa udu siki) ED IIIb/Ukg. lugal X Girsu *DCS* 7 o. vi 5'
lugal-da-nu-me-a saĝ-apin ED IIIb/Ukg. lugal 4 Girsu *DP* 1/2 117 o. i 2
lugal-da-nu-me-a saĝ-apin ED IIIb/Ukg. lugal [X] Girsu *DP* 1/2 118 o. i 2
lugal-da-nu-me-a gab$_{2}$-ra udu siki$_{2}$ ED IIIb/Ukg. lugal 3 Girsu HSS 3 17 r. iv 10
lugal-da-nu-me-a sipa udu siki$_{2}$-ka ED IIIb/Ukg. ensi$_{2}$ 1 Girsu MVN 3 2 r. iii 14
lugal-da-nu-me-a sipa udu siki$_{2}$-ka ED IIIb/Ukg. lugal 6 Girsu MVN 3 7 o. iii 2
lugal-da-nu-me-a (+2 PNN) ba-ug$_{7}$-ge-eš$_{2}$ ED IIIb/Ukg. ensi$_{2}$? Girsu Nik 1 7 o. iii 4
lugal-da-nu-me-a sipa udu siki-ka ED IIIb/Ukg. lugal 2 Girsu Nik 1 13 r. iv 7
lugal-da-nu-me-a sipa udu siki-ka ED IIIb/Lug. 6 Girsu D. Charpin, *RA* 71 (1977), p. 97–105 r. iii 9

lugal-da-tab-ba ? (a1) unkn. mng. 3.1.8, p. 176
lugal-da-tab-ba ? ED IIIb/X Y 28 Umma-Zabala *SAKF* 3 o. i 6

lugal-DA-tuku (a1) (compare lugal-a$_{2}$-tuku 'the lugal is powerful') 3.1.1.6, p. 98 n. 516
lugal-DA-tuku ED I-II Ur UET 2 53 r. 1

lugal-da-zi (a2) 'the lugal, right side (?)' 3.1.8, p. 176–177
lugal-da-zi Ni$_{2}$-zu$_{5}$-kur-še$_{3}$ ED IIIa Šuruppag *TSŠ* 222 o. i 4
lugal-da-zi Ni$_{2}$-zu$_{5}$-kur-še$_{3}$ ED IIIa Šuruppag *TSŠ* 794 r. i 3'
lugal-da-zi Ni$_{2}$-zu$_{5}$-kur-še$_{3}$ ED IIIa Šuruppag *WF* 9 o. ii 6
lugal-da-zi Ni$_{2}$-zu$_{5}$-kur-še$_{3}$ ED IIIa Šuruppag *WF* 18 o. iv 9
lu:gal-da-zi ED IIIb Nippur OSP 1 32 o. ii 2

lugal-da-[x] ED IIIa Adab CUSAS 11 8 o. iii 1
⌜lugal-da⌝-[(x)]-ŠE-UM ED IIIb Ur G. Visicato & A. Westenholz, *Kaskal* 2 (2005), 55–78 6 o. 3
°lu[gal]-da-x ED IIIb Ebla MEE 3 67 o. ii 1
lugal-da-[(x)] [umbisaĝ] ED IIIb Ebla ARET 5 20 r. iii 1'

lugal-dab$_{5}$ (a≥8) 'the lugal grasped (?)' 3.1.8, p. 177
lugal-dab$_{5}$ ES-MS Adab *TCABI* 64 r. iv 2
lugal-dab$_{5}$ IM^{ki}, maškim MS Adab *TCABI* 79 o. 4
lugal-dab$_{5}$ dam-gar$_{3}$ CS Adab CUSAS 13 78 o. ii 14
lugal-dab$_{5}$ CS Adab CUSAS 13 108 o. 10
lugal-dab$_{5}$ CS Adab OIP 14 192 r. 4
lugal-dab$_{5}$ CS Girsu *DPA* 40 (PUL 30) o. 6
lugal-dab$_{5}$ s. Ni$_{3}$-ul CS Girsu ITT 1 1337 o. 1
lugal-dab$_{5}$ ugula, s. Ur-me CS Girsu *RTC* 96 r. ii 8
lugal-dab$_{5}$ CS Girsu *RTC* 96 r. ii 10
lugal-dab$_{5}$ MS-CS Nippur OSP 2 80 o. ii 2
lugal-dab$_{5}$ dub-sar CS Nippur OIP 129 pl. 157 no. 1 1
lugal-dab$_{5}$ dub-sar CS Nippur OIP 129 pl. 157 no. 2 1
lugal-dab$_{5}$ CS Unknown Mesopotamia 9 7 o. 3'

lugal-dab$_{5}$-e (a1) 'the lugal grasps (?)' 3.1.8, p. 177
lugal-dab$_{5}$-e MS-CS Unknown MesCiv 4 53 r. 3

lugal-dab$_{6}$ (a2) unkn. mng. 3.1.8, p. 177
lugal-dab$_{6}$ ar$_{3}$-du$_{2}$ e$_{2}$-ša$_{3}$-ga-ta$^{!}$ ED IIIb Girsu OIP 14 57 o. i 4
lugal-dab$_{6}$ CS Girsu CT 50 85 o. ii 9

lugal-dalla (a7) 'the lugal is bright' 3.1.7.10, p. 174
lugal-dalla saĝa ED IIIb/Ukg. [l]u[gal] 1 Girsu BIN 8 364 r. iii 5
lugal-dalla saĝa ED IIIb X Y 1 Girsu *DP* 1/2 91 o. i 3

lugal-dalla saĝa ED IIIb/Ukg. lugal 4 Girsu *DP* 1/2 98 r. iii 3
lugal-dalla saĝa Pa$_5$-sir$_2$ ED IIIb/Lug. 5 Girsu *DP* 1/2 132 o. v 12
lugal-dalla saĝa Pa$_5$-sir$_2$ ED IIIb/Ukg. lugal 1 Girsu *DP* 1/2 133 o. ii 4
lugal-dalla saĝa Abzu Pa$_5$-sir$_2$^{ki} ED IIIb/Ukg. lugal 2 Girsu *DP* 2/1 206 o. iv 7
lugal-dalla saĝa Pa$_5$-sir$_2$ ED IIIb Girsu *DP* 2/1 216 o. ii 1
lugal-dalla saĝa Pa$_5$-sir$_2$ ED IIIb/Lug. 4 Girsu *DP* 2/1 226 o. v 1'
lugal-dalla lu$_2$ Lugal-dalla ED IIIb Girsu *DP* 2/2 359 o. i 2
lugal-dalla saĝa Pa$_5$-sir$_2$ ED IIIb/Ukg. lugal 3 Girsu *DP* suppl. 631 o. iii 3
lugal-dalla ED IIIb X Y 1 Girsu *DP* suppl. 637 o. i 5
lugal-dalla ED IIIb/Ukg. lugal 2 Girsu Nik 1 146 o. iii 6
lugal-dalla ED IIIb/Ukg. lugal 2 Girsu *TSA* 4 o. iv 6
lugal-dalla saĝa Pa$_5$-sir$_2$-ra^{ki} ED IIIb/Ukg. lugal 2 Girsu *TSA* 5 o. ii 3
lugal-dalla saĝa Pa$_5$-sir$_2$-ra^{ki} ED IIIb/Ukg. lugal 1 Girsu *TSA* 23 r. iv 4
lugal-dalla saĝa ⸢Pa$_5$-sir$_2$⸣ ED IIIb/Lug. 4 Girsu VS 14 173 o. v 2
lugal-dalla saĝa Pa$_5$-sir$_2$-ra^{ki} ED IIIb/Lug. 3 Girsu VS 14 179 o. iii 4
lugal-dalla saĝa Pa$_5$-sir$_2$-ra^{ki} ED IIIb/(Lug.) 2 Girsu VS 25 27 o. iii 4
lugal-dalla saĝa ED IIIb/Ukg. lugal 2 Girsu VS 27 11 r. i 1
lugal-dalla saĝa ED IIIb/Ukg. lugal 4 Girsu VS 27 42 r. i 2
lu:gal-dalla ED IIIb Nippur TMH 5 62 o. i 3
lugal-dalla ED IIIb-ES Ur UET 2 suppl. 19 r. i 4
lugal-dalla lu$_2$ ma$_2$-gur$_8$ ES Adab *TCABI* 61 o. iv 3
lugal-dalla s. Ur-a-MIR CS Umma *USP* 45 o. ii 9
lugal-dalla šitim CS Unknown CUSAS 13 200 r. 1

lugal-dalla-pa-e$_3$ (a1/°1) 'the lugal shines brightly' 3.1.7.10, p. 174
°lugal-⸢dalla$^{!?}$-pa$^?$⸣-e$_3$ ED IIIa Abū Ṣalābīḫ R. D. Biggs & J. N. Postgate, *Iraq* 40 (1978), p. 101–117 522 o. ii 2
lugal-dalla$^!$-pa-e$_3$ ED IIIb-ES Umma-Zabala ? BIN 8 53 o. ii 2

lugal-dam (a1) 'the lugal … a/the spouse (?)' 3.1.8, p. 177
lugal-dam lu$_2$ Ur-abzu CS Girsu *RTC* 95 r. 6

lugal-dam-da-[x] (a1) unkn. mng. 3.1.8, p. 177
⸢lugal⸣-dam-da-[x] ED IIIb Unknown (Adab ?) BIN 8 27 r. i 1

lugal-dam-MU (a1) unkn. mng. 3.1.8, p. 177 w. nn. 1049 & 1051
⸢lugal⸣-dam-MU ED IIIb Nippur OSP 1 28 o. i 4

lugal-dara$_3$$^?$(LAK263$^+$) (a1) 'the lugal is (like) a dara$_3$-goat (?)' 3.1.7.6, p. 166
lugal-dara$_3$$^?$ ĝuruš, dumu gi$_7$ CS Girsu ITT 1 1182 r. 1

lugal-di-de$_3$ (a1) 'the lugal *passes verdict*' 3.1.3.3, p. 79, 117, 139 n. 772, 241, 254 n. 1492
lugal-di-de$_3$ ED IIIb Nippur TMH 5 102 o. iii 3

lugal-diĝir-ĝu$_{10}$ (a≥8) 'the lugal is my god' 3.1.4.1, p. 87 n. 431, 120, 166
lugal-diĝir-ĝu$_{10}$ ED IIIb-ES Adab CUSAS 11 94 o. i 7
⸢lugal⸣-diĝir-ĝu$_{10}$ sipa ⸢an⸣še sur$_x$-ka ED IIIb/Ukg. lugal 3 Girsu *AWAS* 124 o. i 15
lugal-diĝir-ĝu$_{10}$ ED IIIb/Enz. 17 Girsu BIN 8 352 r. iii 4
lugal-diĝir-ĝu$_{10}$ sagi ED IIIb/Enz. or En. II Girsu ? *DP* 1/1 31 v 10
lugal-diĝir-ĝu$_{10}$ sipa anše-sur$_x$-ka ED IIIb/Ukg. lugal 4 Girsu *DP* 1/2 116 o. ii 5
lugal-diĝir-ĝu$_{10}$ sipa anše-sur$_x$-ka ED IIIb/Ukg. lugal 4 Girsu *DP* 1/2 117 o. i 18
lugal-diĝir-ĝu$_{10}$ sipa anše-sur$_x$-ka ED IIIb/Ukg. lugal [X] Girsu *DP* 1/2 118 o. ii 6
lugal-diĝir-ĝu$_{10}$ sipa anše Geme$_2$-^{d}Ba-u$_2$-ka ED IIIb/Ukg. lugal 2(+x?) Girsu *DP* 1/2 119 o. i 8
lugal-diĝir-ĝu$_{10}$ lu$_2$ Ur-saĝ ED IIIb/Ukg. lugal 5 Girsu *DP* 1/2 136 o. i 1
lugal-diĝir$^!$(A)-ĝu$_{10}$ sipa anše-sur$_x$-ka ED IIIb/Ukg. lugal 2 Girsu HSS 3 25 o. i 12
lugal-diĝir-ĝu$_{10}$ sipa anše-sur$_x$-ka ED IIIb/Ukg. lugal 3 Girsu HSS 3 26 o. i 12

lugal-diĝir-ĝu$_{10}$ sipa anše-sur$_{x}$-ka ED IIIb/Ukg. lugal 3 Girsu HSS 3 27 o. ii 4
lugal-diĝir-ĝu$_{10}$ ri-mušen ED IIIb/Ukg. lugal 5 Girsu Nik 1 3 o. i 16
⌜lugal⌝-[diĝ]ir-[ĝ]u$_{10}$ (+2 PNN) ba-ug$_{7}$-ge-eš$_{2}$ ED IIIb/Ukg. ensi$_{2}$? Girsu Nik 1 7 o. i 3
lugal-diĝir-ĝu$_{10}$ sipa anše-sur$_{x}$-ka ED IIIb/Ukg. lugal 4 Girsu Nik 1 16 o. ii 5
lugal-diĝir$^{!}$(A)-ĝu$_{10}$ sipa anše-sur$_{x}$-ka ED IIIb/Ukg. lugal 3 Girsu *TSA* 18 o. i 12
lugal-diĝir-ĝu$_{10}$? ED IIIb/Luzag. ensi$_{2}$ 7 Umma-Zabala M. deJ. Ellis, *JCS* 31 (1979), p. 30–55 6 r. i 4''
lugal-diĝir-ĝu$_{10}$ šu-i, maškim-⌜bi⌝ ED IIIb Ur UET 2 suppl. 35 o. 3
lugal-diĝir-ĝu$_{10}$ ES-MS Adab *TCABI* 64 o. iv 8

lugal-diĝir-ra (a1) 'lugal of the gods' 3.1.8, p. 177
lugal-diĝir-ra f. Lugal-me-du$_{10}$-ga MS Unknown *EGA* 522 2

lugal-diĝir-re (a1) 'the god … the lugal' 3.1.6.2, p. 147
lugal-diĝir-re CS Girsu ITT 2/1 4516 r. 6

lugal-DU (a≥6) unkn. mng. 3.1.8, p. 177
lugal-DU ? ED IIIb Girsu ? BIN 8 12 r. ii 2
lugal-DU saĝa (?) ED IIIb/Luzag. ensi$_{2}$ 7 Umma-Zabala ? BIN 8 86 o. iii 15
lugal-DU ED IIIb Umma-Zabala E. Milone, *Sefarad* 65 (2005), 327–351 16 o. 2
lugal-DU lu$_{2}$ tu-ra ES Adab *TCABI* 26 r. ii 3
lugal-DU Gal-zu CS Adab CUSAS 13 137 o. 4
lugal-DU sipa, dumu uru^{ki} MS-CS Adab OIP 14 167 o. 2
lugal-DU nagar MS-CS Mesag MesCiv 4 45 o. 2
lugal-DU CS/NS.-Śkś Nippur OSP 2 79 o. 2
lugal-DU MS-CS Umma MAD 4 35 (translit. only) o. 9
lugal-DU saĝ-apin-na lugal CS Umma T. Donald, *MCS* 9 (1964) 236 o. i 10

lugal-DU-ME (a1/°1) unkn. mng. 3.1.8, p. 177
lugal-DU-ME ED IIIa Adab CUSAS 11 5 o. ii 1
°lugal-DU-ME ED IIIa Šuruppag *SF* 28 o. iii 2
°lugal-DU-ME ED IIIa Šuruppag *SF* 29 o. ii 5

lugal-DU-ni (a1) unkn. mng. 3.1.8, p. 177
lugal-DU-ni MS-CS Umma *AAS* 3 o. 2

lugal-DU$_{3}$-UD ? (a1) unkn. mng. 3.1.8, p. 177
lugal-DU$_{3}$-UD ? ED IIIb Adab OIP 14 74 o. ii 5

lugal-du$_{8}$ (a≥10) "the lugal is one who releases (?)' 3.1.8, p. 177
lugal-du$_{8}$ ED IIIb Girsu J. Marzahn & H. Neumann, *AoF* 22 (1995), p. 111f. (VAT 6121) o. iii 10'
lugal-du$_{8}$ ED IIIb/Ukg. lugal 6 Girsu *DP* 1/2 135 o. ii 12
lugal-du$_{8}$ sipa šagan$_{x}$ ED IIIb/X Y 4 Girsu *DP* suppl. 587 r. ii 2
lugal-du$_{8}$ ma$_{2}$-laḫ$_{5}$ ED IIIb/X Y 1 Girsu *DP* suppl. 637 r. iii 2
lugal-du$_{8}$ ma$_{2}$-laḫ$_{5}$ ED IIIb/Ukg. lugal 5 Girsu Nik 1 3 r. iv 12
lugal-du$_{8}$ ma$_{2}$-laḫ$_{5}$ ED IIIb/Ukg. lugal 3 Girsu Nik 1 32 o. ii 7
lu[gal]-du$_{8}$ [u]nu$_{3}$ ED IIIb/Ukg. lugal 2 Girsu *TSA* 30 o. i 5
lugal-du$_{8}$ gudu$_{4}$ ED IIIb/Enz. 3 Girsu VS 25 61 o. iii 4
lugal-du$_{8}$ nu-kiri$_{6}$ ED IIIb Nippur OSP 1 113 o. i 2'
lugal-du$_{8}$ ED IIIb Nippur TMH 5 167 o. iii 5
lugal-du$_{8}$ ED IIIb/Luzag. ensi$_{2}$ 6 Umma M. Lambert, *OrAnt* 18 (1979), p. 225–226 (AO 15540) o. i 6
lugal-du$_{8}$ ED IIIb Zabala M. Powell, *HUCA* 49 (1978), p. 1–58 8 r. ii 5
lugal-du$_{8}$ maškim-bi ES-MS Umma *CHÉU* 53 o. 3
lugal-du$_{8}$ dub-sar ES-MS Umma Nik 2 46 r. 1
⌜lugal⌝-du$_{8}$ MS-CS Adab OIP 14 151 o. 3

lugal-du$_8$ lu$_2$ eme CS/Śkś Girsu CT 50 172 r. i 10
lugal-du$_8$ s. Lu$_2$-⸢ba⸣ CS Girsu MVN 3 113 r. iii 3'
lugal-du$_8$ ugula CS Umma CT 50 188 o. i 7
lugal-du$_8$ saĝ-apin-na lugal CS Umma T. Donald, *MCS* 9 (1964) 236 o. i 6
lugal-du$_8$ ir$_{11}$ Me-lam$_2$ MS-CS Umma MesCiv 4 30 o. ii 8
lugal-du$_8$ CS Umma *USP* 48 o. 13'
⸢lugal⸣-du$_8$ OAkk Ur M. Civil, *AulaOr* 6 (1988), 105 (U 4395, translit. only) o. 1
lugal-du$_8$ LS-Lagaš II Girsu *RTC* 255 o. 5
lugal-du$_8$ Lagaš II Girsu *RTC* 201 r. 7

lugal-du$_{10}$ $^{(a\geq 2/°2)}$ 'the lugal is good' (or abbreviation) 3.1.7.8, p. 170, 186
°lugal-du$_{10}$ ga:eš$_8$ ED IIIa Abū Ṣalābīḫ *IAS* 61 o. vii 13
°lugal-du$_{10}$ lu$_2$ [...] ED IIIa Abū Ṣalābīḫ *IAS* 66 o. iii' 4'
°lugal-du$_{10}$ ga:eš$_8$ ED IIIa Abū Ṣalābīḫ *IAS* 69 o. vi' 4
°⸢lugal⸣-du$_{10}$ ⸢lu$_2$ x⸣ [x (x)] ED IIIa Abū Ṣalābīḫ *IAS* 73 (o.) v 6'
°⸢lugal-du$_{10}$⸣ ga:[eš$_8$] ED IIIa Abū Ṣalābīḫ *IAS* 74 o. vi 7'
°lugal-du$_{10}$ šeĝ$_9$ maš-da$_3$ ED IIIb Ebla A. Archi, *StEb* 4 (1981), p. 177–204 (translit. only) o. v 11
°lugal-du$_{10}$ ga:eš$_8$ ED IIIb Ebla A. Archi, *RA* 78 (1984), p. 171–174 o. viii 12
lugal-⸢du$_{10}^{?}$⸣ ? lu$_2$ ma$_2$ addir$_x$ ED IIIb Girsu *DP* suppl. 592 o. ii 10
lugal-du$_{10}$ ED IIIb-ES Uruk M. W. Green, *ZA* 72 (1982), p. 163–177 19a o. (?) ii' 3'
lugal-du$_{10}$ ES-MS Nippur OSP 1 23 o. iv 19
lugal-⸢du$_{10}^{?}$⸣ ? x CS Unknown MAD 4 71 o. 8

lugal-du$_{10}$-ga $^{(a1)}$ 'the lugal is good (?)' 3.1.7.8, p. 170
lugal-du$_{10}$-ga s. U$_2$-DA CS-LS Ur UE 2 pl. 216 no. 379 1

lugal-du$_{11}$-ga $^{(a1)}$ (abbreviation of one of the following names) 3.1.1.4, p. 92 n. 470
lugal-du$_{11}$-ga ES-MS Umma Nik 2 60 o. ii 3

lugal-du$_{11}$-ga-ni $^{(a4)}$ 'what the lugal says' 3.1.1.4, p. 92 n. 470
lugal-⸢du$_{11}$⸣-ga-⸢ni⸣ ED IIIb Nippur TMH 5 152 o. 4
lugal-du$_{11}$-ga-ni sipa ED IIIb Uruk M. Krebernik, *AoF* 21 (1994), p. 5–12 (VA 3123) 4
lugal-du$_{11}$-ga-ni ĝuruš, ir$_3$ dub-sar-ne ES-MS Umma *CHÉU* 54 o. i 2
lugal-du$_{11}$-ga-ni CS Umma W. Sommerfeld, K. Markina & N. Roudik, *Gs Diakonoff*, 225–231 4 o. 6

lugal-du$_{11}$-ga-ni-nu-[kur$_2^{?}$] $^{(a1)}$ 'what the lugal says can not [be altered?]' 3.1.1.4, p. 92
lugal-du$_{11}$-ga-ni-nu-[kur$_2^{?}$] l[u$_2$] dub sar ED IIIa Unknown *RIAA* 44 r. i 3

lugal-du$_{11}$-ga-ni-zi $^{(a1)}$ 'what the lugal says is reliable' 3.1.1.4, p. 92–93
lugal-du$_{11}$-ga-ni-zi Umma^{ki}-*u*$_3$ CS (OB)/NS. Nippur < Umma C. Wilcke, *ZA* 87 (1997), p. 11–32 (HS 1954+) o. v 21

lugal-du$_{11}$-ge-du$_{10}$ $^{(a2)}$ 'what the lugal says is good' 3.1.1.4, p. 93
lugal-du$_{11}$-ge-du$_{10}$ šu-ku$_6$ ab-ba ED IIIb/Ukg. lugal 6 Girsu *DP* 1/2 135 r. iv 5
lugal-du$_{11}$-ge-du$_{10}$ šu-ku$_6$ ab-ba ED IIIb/Ukg. lugal 4 Girsu *TSA* 47 o. ii 4
lugal-du$_{11}$-ge-du$_{10}$ sa$_{12}$-sug$_5$ ED IIIb Isin BIN 8 37 o. i 2

lugal-^{d}Dumu-zi $^{(a1)}$ (perhaps) 'the lugal (is like) Dumuzi' 3.1.6.2, p. 146 w. n. 819
lugal-^{d}Dumu-zi ED IIIa Šuruppag *TSŠ* 131 o. ii 2

lugal-dumu-zi $^{(a\geq 4/°1)}$ (perhaps) 'the lugal (is like) Dumuzi' 3.1.6.2, p. 146 n. 819
°lugal-dumu-zi A.DIM ED IIIa Abū Ṣalābīḫ *IAS* 61 o. xi 12
°lu[gal]-dumu-zi DIM ED IIIa Abū Ṣalābīḫ *IAS* 69 r. ii 7'
lugal-dumu-zi ED IIIa Kiš *AAICAB* 1/1 (Ashm 1928-429) o. i 3'
lugal-dumu-zi saĝa ED IIIa Nippur OIP 97 2 r. ii 2
lugal-dum[u-zi] ED IIIa Šuruppag *NTSŠ* 444 o. ii 6

lugal-⸢dumu-zi⸣ ED IIIa Šuruppag *NTSŠ* 444 o. iii 5
lugal-dumu-zi ED IIIa Šuruppag *WF* 3 r. ii 6
lugal-dumu-zi ED IIIa Šuruppag *WF* 9 o. iv 6
lugal-dumu-zi ED IIIa Šuruppag *WF* 13 o. iv 4
lugal-⸢dumu-zi⸣ ED IIIa Šuruppag *WF* 65 o. v 3
lugal-dumu-zi ED IIIa Šuruppag *WF* 71 o. vii 10
⸢lugal⸣-dumu-zi A-ne-ra ED IIIa Šuruppag *WF* 72 o. iii 9
°lugal-dumu-zi a-MIR(LAK154) ED IIIb Ebla A. Archi, *StEb* 4 (1981), p. 177–204 r. iv 1

lugal-e $^{(a\geq 7)}$ unkn. mng. 3.1.8, p. 177
lugal-e ED IIIb-ES Adab CUSAS 11 186 o. v 9
lugal-e ED IIIb/Luzag. ensi$_2$ X Umma-Zabala ? BIN 8 82 r. i 5’
lugal-e ED IIIb Umma-Zabala CUSAS 14 141 r. 4
lugal-e ED IIIb Umma-Zabala CUSAS 14 147 o. ii 4
lugal-e ED IIIb Umma-Zabala CUSAS 14 158 o. ii 4
lugal-e ED IIIb/Il$_2$ ensi$_2$ Zabala *TCVBI* 1-1 r. i 1
lugal-e ES Adab *TCABI* 25 o. i 4
lugal-e ES Adab *TCABI* 46 o. 3
lugal-e MS Adab *TCABI* 122 o. 3
lugal-e CS Girsu CT 50 95 o. 3
lugal-e f. Ur-^{d}Nin-mug CS Girsu CT 50 98 o. i 8
lugal-e lu$_2$ e$_2$-gal-a nu$_2$ CS Girsu CT 50 101 o. 3
lugal-[e] Girsu lu$_2$ e$_2$-a n[u$_2$] MS-CS CT 50 102 o. 3
lugal-e (ugula) CS Girsu CT 50 105 o. 3
lugal-e engar ki-duru$_5$, dab$_5$-ba CS Girsu *DPA* 33 (PUL 38) o. 13
lugal-e ugula CS Girsu ITT 1 1106 r. 2’
lugal-e Girsu (ugula) ĝuruš MS-CS ITT 1 1352 o. 3
lugal-e Girsu (ugula) ĝuruš, aga$_3$-us$_2$ gibil MS-CS ITT 1 1353 o. 3
lugal-e CS Girsu ITT 2/1 4511 o. 3
lugal-e ugula CS Girsu ITT 5 6677 o. 2
lugal-e ugula CS Girsu ITT 5 9258 o. i 7’
lugal-e CS Girsu ITT 5 9269 o. 2’
lugal-⸢e⸣ f. Ur-⸢KUN$^{?}$⸣ CS Girsu MVN 3 113 o. ii 10
lugal-e CS Girsu *RTC* 93 o. 3
lugal-e CS Girsu *STTI* 9 o. 3
lugal-⸢e⸣ ugula CS Girsu *STTI* 39 o. 2
lugal-e CS Girsu *STTI* 81 o. 3
lugal-e f. Ur-⸢^{d}x-DU-a⸣ CS Girsu *STTI* 105 r. 7’
lugal-e CS Girsu *STTI* 144 o. 3
lugal-e CS Girsu *STTI* 146 o. 3’
lugal-e CS Girsu *STTI* 146 o. 11’
lugal-e MS-CS Umma MAD 4 73 r. 5
lugal-e MS-CS Umma MAD 4 138 (translit. only) r. 4
lugal-e sipa CS Unknown MAD 4 168 o. 6

lugal-e-a$_2$-na $^{(a\geq 3)}$ ‘the lugal (placed him/her) on his arm’ 3.1.4.1, p. 121 w. n. 653
lugal-⸢e⸣-[a$_2$-na] f. Zabala$_6$[^{ki}-a] MS-CS Mesag BIN 8 243 r. 3’
⸢lugal⸣-[e-a$_2$]-⸢na⸣ f. [Zabala$_{5/6}$^{ki}-a] MS-CS Mesag MesCiv 4 45 r. 2
lugal-e-a$_2$-na CS/NS.-Śkś Nippur OSP 2 79 r. 1
lugal-e-a$_2$-na MS-CS Nippur OSP 2 83 o. 6
⸢lugal⸣-[e-a$_2$]-na MS-CS Nippur OSP 2 98 r. i 7
⸢lugal-e⸣-a$_2$-na [x E$_2$]-mi$_2$-kam (?) MS-CS Nippur OSP 2 107 r. 1
lugal-e-a$_2$-na s. Ur-Abzu, b. ^{d}En-lil$_2$-la$_2$ & Si-du$_3$ CS Umma *USP* 47 r. ii 4

lugal-e-e $^{(a1)}$ unkn. mng. 3.1.8, p. 177
lugal-e-e ED IIIa Šuruppag *RTC* 15 o. iv 6

lugal-e-gal-gal $^{(a1)}$ unkn. mng. 3.1.8, p. 177
lugal-e-gal-gal ED IIIa-b Girsu *RTC* 1 o. iii 4

lugal-⸢e-tar$^{?}$⸣ $^{(a1)}$ (probable abbreviation of the following) 3.1.4.1, p. 122 n. 664
lugal-⸢e-tar$^{?}$⸣ Ad-da ugula Lugal-⸢e-tar$^{?}$⸣ ES-MS Umma *USP* 16 o. 6

lugal-e-tar-su$_3$ $^{(a\geq1)}$ 'the lugal provides (abundantly)' 3.1.4.1, p. 122 n. 664
⸢lugal⸣-e-tar-su$_3$ ES-MS Ur UET 2 suppl. 30 o. 8
lugal-e-tar-su$_3$ MS-CS Ur UET 2 suppl. 48 o. ii 14

lugal-e-[x(-x)]-NI-⸢x⸣ ugula-[bi] MS-CS Nippur TMH 5 29 o. ii 18

lugal-e$_2$ $^{(a\geq4)}$ 'lugal (of?) the *house*' 3.1.8, p. 177
lugal-e$_2$ ED IIIb/Lug. 1 Girsu Nik 1 151 o. i 2
lugal-⸢e$_2$⸣ ED IIIb Nippur OSP 1 25 "iii" 7'
lugal-e$_2$ f. Baḫar$_2$ ED IIIb Nippur OSP 1 87 o. 6
lugal-e$_2$ ED IIIb Umma-Zabala CUSAS 14 142 o. iii 7
lugal-e$_2$ ED IIIb Umma-Zabala CUSAS 14 201 o. i 2
lugal-e$_2$ MS-CS Adab CUSAS 13 16 o. 4
⸢lugal-e$_2$⸣ CS Adab CUSAS 13 138 r. 2
lugal-e$_2$ MS-CS Adab *TCABI* 198 o. 6
lugal-e$_2$ MS-CS Adab OIP 14 99 r. 2
⸢lugal⸣-e$_2$ MS-CS Adab OIP 14 108 r. 1
lugal-⸢e$_2$⸣ dub-sar MS-CS Adab OIP 14 120 o. 3
lugal-e$_2$ MS-CS Adab OIP 14 155 r. 1
lugal-e$_2$ MS-CS Adab OIP 14 167 r. 6'
lugal-e$_2$ MS-CS Adab OIP 14 174 r. 1
⸢lugal-e$_2$⸣ CS Adab *SIA* 713 r. 3
lugal-e$_2$ CS Adab *SIA* 842 o. 7'

lugal-e$_2$-ab-ba $^{(a1)}$ 'the lugal in the E$_2$-ab-ba (?)' 3.1.8, p. 177
lugal-e$_2$-ab-ba ED I-II Ur UET 2 348 r. ii 1

lugal-e$_2$-da $^{(a\geq3)}$ 'the lugal … with the *house*' 3.1.8, p. 177
lugal-e$_2$-da kikken$_2$ ED IIIb/Lug. 1 Girsu *DCS* 8 r. iii 3
lugal-e$_2$-da lu$_2$ u$_2$-rum ^{d}Ba-u$_2$ ED IIIb/Ukg. lugal 2 Girsu *DP* 1/2 120 o. iv 7
lugal-e$_2$-da kikken$_2$ ED IIIb Girsu *DP* 2/1 231 o. v' 4'
lugal-e$_2$-da gudu$_4$ ED IIIb/X Y 6 Girsu *DP* suppl. 655 r. i 1
lugal-e$_2$-da ED IIIb Girsu *RTC* 18 o. iii 2
lugal-e$_2$-da kikken$_2$ ED IIIb/Lug. ensi$_4$ 4 Girsu *RTC* 66 o. iv 10
lugal-e$_2$-da s. Lu$_2$-gid$_2$, lu$_2$ luĝa$_x$(BI×NIĜ$_2$) ED IIIb/Lug. 4 Girsu VS 25 34 o. ii 6

lugal-E$_2$.DU$_8$-si $^{(a1)}$ 'the lugal is just right for the E.DU (?)' 3.1.6.4, p. 158 n. 914
lugal-E$_2$.DU$_8$-si ED I-II Ur UET 2 201 o. i 4

lugal-e$_2$-ĝiš ? $^{(a1)}$ unkn. mng. 3.1.8, p. 177
lugal-e$_2$-ĝiš$^{?}$ (ĝiš-e$_2$-lugal) ad-la$_2$? ED IIIa Šuruppag *FTUM* 29 r. i 3'

lugal-E$_2$-maš-e $^{(a2)}$ 'the lugal (is just right) for the Emaš (?)' 3.1.6.4, p. 155 n. 892
lugal-E$_2$-maš-e CS Adab CUSAS 13 21 o. 3'
lugal-E$_2$-maš-e engar Ur-[x(-x)] MS-CS Adab CUSAS 13 22 r. 4'
lugal-E$_2$-maš-e CS Adab CUSAS 13 49 r. 3'
lugal-E$_2$-maš-e engar CS Adab *SIA* 863 o. 6
lugal-E$_2$-maš-e gal$_5$-la$_2$-gal CS Adab *TCABI* 210 o. 4

lugal-E$_2$-muš$_3$ $^{(a1)}$ 'the lugal … the Emuš' 3.1.6.4, p. 155 n. 890
lugal-E$_2$-muš$_3$ ED IIIb/Ukg. lugal 2 Girsu VS 14 5 o. vii 6

lugal-E$_2$-muš$_3$-e (a1) 'the lugal (is just right) for the Emuš (?)' 3.1.6.4, p. 155 n. 890
lugal-E$_2$-muš$_3$-e dumu nitaḫ CS Mesag BIN 8 152 r. ii 13'
lugal-E$_2$-muš$_3$-e f. E$_2$-x-x & Ama-bara$_2$ CS Mesag M. deJ. Ellis, *JCS* 31 (1979), p. 30–55 16 r. ii 15'

lugal-E$_2$-muš$_3$-še$_3$ (a1) 'the lugal … for/to the Emuš' 3.1.6.4, p. 155 n. 890
lugal-E$_2$-muš$_3$-še$_3$ ĝuruš MS-CS Mesag BIN 8 148 r. i 6

lugal-e$_2$-ni-še$_3$ (a≥5) 'the lugal (is one who does not cease *working*) for his house' 3.1.1.2, p. 68 n. 336, 87–88, 177 n. 1060
lugal-e$_2$-ni-še$_3$ lu$_2$ sa$_{10}$ gu$_7$ ED IIIa Šuruppag? MVN 10 84 o. ii 11
lugal-e$_2$-ni-še$_3$ ED IIIa-b Unknown *L'uomo* 3 r. i 1
lugal-e$_2$-ni-še$_3$ du$_3$-a-ku$_5$ ED IIIb/Ukg. lugal 6 Girsu *AWAS* 122 o. ii 4
lugal-e$_2$-ni-še$_3$ nu-kiri$_6$ ED IIIb/Ukg. lugal 5 Girsu *CTNMC* 3 r. iii 9
lugal-e$_2$-ni-še$_3$ ED IIIb/Ukg. lugal 5 Girsu *DP* 1/2 114 o. ii 5
lugal-e$_2$-ni-še$_3$ ED IIIb/Ukg. lugal 6 Girsu *DP* 1/2 115 o. ii 5
lugal-e$_2$-ni-še$_3$ (nu-kiri$_6$?) ED IIIb/Ukg. lugal 4 Girsu *DP* 1/2 116 o. vi 14
lugal-e$_2$-ni-še$_3$ ED IIIb/Ukg. lugal 4 Girsu *DP* 1/2 117 o. vi 7
lugal-e$_2$-ni-še$_3$ s. E-ta$^!$(GU$_4$)-da ED IIIb/Ukg. lugal 4 Girsu *DP* 2/2 339 o. iii 6
lugal-e$_2$-ni-še$_3$ ED IIIb Girsu ITT 5 9203 o. 4
lugal-e$_2$-ni-še$_3$ ED IIIb Ur UET 2 suppl. 12 r. 2
lugal-e$_2$-ni-še$_3$ ED IIIb Ur UET 2 suppl. 42 o. 4

lugal-e$_2$-ni-še$_{3\text{-}90°}$ (a1) 'the lugal (is one who does not cease *working*) for his house' 3.1.1.2, p. 87 n. 438
lugal-e$_2$-ni-še$_{3\text{-}90°}$ ED IIIb Umma-Zabala MVN 3 3 o. vi 16

lugal-E$_2$.NUN-si (a≥2/°1) 'the lugal is just right for the reed-sanctuary' 3.1.6.4, p. 158 n. 914
lugal-E$_2$.NUN-[si$^?$] ED I-II Ur UET 2 159 o. i 2
lugal-E$_2$.NUN-si ED I-II Ur UET 2 201 o. i 3
lugal-⌜E$_2$.NUN⌝-si ir$_{11}$ ED I-II Ur UET 2 259 o. i 3
°lugal-E$_2$.NUN-si ED IIIa Šuruppag *SF* 28 o. iii 3
°lugal-E$_2$.NUN-si ED IIIa Šuruppag *SF* 29 o. ii 6
lugal-E$_2$.NUN-si ED IIIa Šuruppag *WF* 133 o. iv 3

lugal-e$_2$-pa$_4$ (a1) unkn. mng. 3.1.8, p. 177
lugal-e$_2$-pa$_4$ ED IIIb Umma-Zabala M. Powell, *HUCA* 49 (1978), p. 1–58 23 o. ii 2

lugal-e$_2$-si (a1) 'the lugal is just right for the house/temple' 3.1.5.3, p. 136
lugal-e$_2$-si dub-sar, maškim ED IIIa Šuruppag *TSŠ* pl. 33f. "X" o. vi 4
lugal-e$_2$-si (dub-sar aša$_5$) ED IIIa Šuruppag ("gekauft") *WF* 33 r. ii 2
lugal-e$_2$-si dub-sar aša$_5$ ED IIIa Šuruppag ("gekauft") *WF* 33 r. iii 1

lugal-e$_2$ (-x-) BU ED IIIb/Luzag. ensi$_2$ [x] Umma-Zabala J. A. Brinkman, *Fs Kramer*, pl. III*-V* (W 2/7) o. v 4'
lugal-e$_2$-[x(-x)] MS-CS Nippur OSP 2 130 r. i' 7

lugal-eb$_2$-ta-e$_3$ (a1) 'the lugal brought (him/her) out from there' 3.1.5.1, p. 128
lugal-eb$_2$-ta-e$_3$ ED IIIb Umma-Zabala ? BIN 8 57 o. 3
lugal-eb$_2$-ta-e$_3$ ED IIIb/Luzag. ensi$_2$ 7 Umma-Zabala M. deJ. Ellis, *JCS* 31 (1979), p. 30–55 6 o. iv 17

lugal-eb$_2$-ta-ni-e$_3$ (a≥3) 'the lugal brought (him/her) out from in there' 3.1.5.1, p. 128, 251 n. 1477
lugal-eb$_2$-ta-[ni-e$_3$] ⌜niĝir⌝ ED IIIb Girsu Nik 1 317 iii 6'
[lugal-eb$_2$-ta-ni-e$_3$] ? [niĝir] ED IIIb Girsu Nik 1 317 iv 3'
lugal-eb$_2$-ta-ni-e$_3$ ka-ki-kam ED IIIb/Dudu saĝa Girsu W. W. Hallo, *OrNS* 42 (1973), p. 228–238 r. iii 2

lugal-eb$_2$-ta-ni-e$_3$ ED IIIb Umma MesCiv 4 3 o. ii 7
lugal-eb$_2$-ta-ni-e$_3$ ED IIIb/Luzag. ensi$_2$ X Umma-Zabala BIN 8 82 o. ii 13
lugal-eb$_2$-ta-ni-e$_3$ ED IIIb/Luzag. ensi$_2$ X Umma-Zabala BIN 8 82 o. v 18
lugal-eb$_2$-ta-ni-e$_3$ ED IIIb Umma-Zabala M. Powell *HUCA* 49 (1978) 13 o. i 5'

lugal-eden $^{(a1)}$ 'the lugal … the steppe' 3.1.1.6, p. 85 n. 420, 96 n. 501, 97
lugal-eden lu$_2$ ED IIIb/Ukg. lugal 6 Girsu *DP* 1/2 135 o. v 5

lugal-eden-ne$_2$ $^{(a\geq4)}$ 'the lugal … for the steppe' 3.1.1.6, p. 85 n. 420, 96 n. 501, 251 n. 1477
lugal-eden-ne$_2$ gala ED IIIb/Ukg. ensi$_2$ 1 Girsu MVN 3 2 r. v 10
lugal-eden-ne$_2$ (šu-ku$_6$ a du$_{10}$-ga ?) ED IIIb/Ukg. lugal 5 Girsu Nik 1 3 r. i 12
lugal-eden-ne$_2$ ED IIIb Girsu Nik 1 14 o. iii 1
lugal-eden-ne$_2$ gala, ĝuruš ED IIIb/Lug. 3 Girsu Nik 1 17 o. i 1
lugal-eden-ne$_2$ gala ED IIIb/Lug. 6 Girsu D. Charpin, *RA* 71 (1977), p. 97–105 r. iv 17
lugal-eden-ne$_2$ šu-ku$_6$ a du$_{10}$-ga ED IIIb/X Y 4 Girsu *TSA* 47 o. v 4
⌜lugal⌝-e[den-ne$_2$] gala, ĝuruš ED IIIb/Lug. 6 Girsu VS 25 11 r. iv 2
lugal-eden-ne$_2$ gala, ĝuruš ED IIIb/Lug. 6 Girsu VS 25 71 r. iv 6
lugal-eden-ne$_2$ ED IIIb Umma-Zabala CUSAS 14 235 o. ii 3
lugal-eden-ne$_2$ gu$_4$-apin CS/NS. Nippur TMH 5 7+184+201a o. ii 6'

lugal-eden-ne$_2$-si $^{(a1)}$ 'the lugal is just right for the steppe' 3.1.1.6, p. 85 n. 420, 96–97
lugal-eden-ne$_2$-si ED IIIa Šuruppag M. Lambert, *Gs Unger*, p. 27–49 1 o. ii 10
lugal-eden-ne$_2$-si ED IIIa Šuruppag L. Milano, *StEL* 3 (1986), p. 3–12 r. ii 1

lugal-eg$_2$-ge $^{(a\geq2)}$ 'the lugal … the levee' 3.1.5.3, p. 132
lugal-eg$_2$-ge lu$_2$ ED IIIb/Ukg. lugal 6 Girsu *DP* 1/2 135 o. vii 11
lugal-eg$_2$-ge naĝ-ku$_5$? MS-CS Umma MAD 4 93 (translit. only) o. 2
lugal-eg$_2$-ge MS-CS Umma MAD 4 99 (translit. only) o. 3
lugal-eg$_2$-ge MS-CS Umma MAD 4 111 (translit. only) o. 6
lugal-eg$_2$-ge ? MS-CS Umma MAD 4 119 (translit. only) o. 5
lugal-eg$_2$-ge MS-CS Umma MesCiv 4 19 o. 2

lugal-eg$_2$-pa$_5$-maḫ $^{(a\geq3)}$ 'the lugal is one who makes canal and ditch *magnificent* (?)' 3.1.5.3, p. 132
lugal-eg$_2$-pa$_5$-maḫ ED IIIb Girsu *DP* suppl. 612 o. iii 1

lugal-eme-UŠ $^{(a1)}$ unkn. mng. 3.1.8, p. 132
lugal-eme-UŠ (3 PNN) Lugal-eme-UŠ, ba-ug$_7$-ge ED IIIb/Ukg. lugal 4 Girsu *DP* 1/2 138 o. ii 1

lugal-^{d}En-ki-a-DU $^{(a1)}$ uncertain mng. 3.1.6.2, p. 147
lugal-^{d}En-ki-a-DU ED IIIa Šuruppag *WF* 35 o. iii 4

lugal-^{d}En-lil$_2$ $^{(a\geq6/°1)}$ 'the lugal … Enlil' 3.1.6.2, p. 143 n. 797, 146, 237, 253 n. 1488
°⌜lugal⌝-^{d}En-lil$_2$ ED IIIa Abū Ṣalābīḫ *IAS* 462 o. i 5
lugal-^{d}En-lil$_2$ Ur-^{d}Sud$_3$, lu$_2$ ma$_2$, Lugal-^{d}En-lil$_2$ ED IIIa Šuruppag *WF* 79 r. i 3
lugal-^{d}En-lil$_2$ ED IIIb/Lug. 1 Girsu *RTC* 75 r. ii 2
lugal-^{d}En-lil$_2$ lu$_2$ u$_5$ Akšak^{ki} ED IIIb/En. I ensi$_2$ 4 Lagaš BiMes 3 10 o. vi 1'
lugal-^{d}En-lil$_2$ ED IIIb Nippur OSP 1 17 o. ii 5
lugal-^{d}En-lil$_2$ ED IIIb Nippur TMH 5 170 o. ii 3
lugal-^{d}En-lil$_2$ ED IIIb Nippur TMH 5 170 r. i 1
lugal-^{d}En-lil$_2$ saĝa ^{d}Eš-peš ES Adab CUSAS 11 331 o. ii 1
lugal-^{d}En-lil$_2$ CS/NS. Nippur TMH 5 7+184+201a o. i 2

lugal-^{d}En-lil$_2$-da $^{(a1)}$ 'the lugal … with Enlil' 3.1.6.2, p. 142
lugal-^{d}En-lil$_2$-da ED IIIb/Ukg. lugal 5 Girsu *DP* 1/2 136 r. ii 8

lugal-^{d}En-lil$_2$-le $^{(a\geq6)}$ 'Enlil … the lugal' 3.1.6.2, p. 142, 253 n. 1488

lugal-^{d}En-lil$_2$-le šu-i$_2$ ED IIIb/Ukg. lugal 3 Girsu *AWAS* 124 o. ii 14
⸢lugal⸣-^{d}En-[lil$_2$]-«a»-le šu-[i$_2$] ED IIIb/Ukg. lugal 2 Girsu BIN 8 359 o. iii 1
lugal-^{d}En-lil$_2$-le lu$_2$ iti-da ED IIIb/Ukg. lugal 4 Girsu *DP* 1/2 116 o. ii 3
lugal-^{d}En-lil$_2$-le šu-i$_2$ ED IIIb/Ukg. lugal 4 Girsu *DP* 1/2 117 o. iii 15
lugal-^{d}En-lil$_2$-le šu-i$_2$ ED IIIb/Ukg. lugal 2+X Girsu *DP* 1/2 119 o. i 4
lugal-^{d}En-lil$_2$-le sagi ED IIIb/Lug. 5(+1?) Girsu VS 25 14 o. v 6'
lugal-[^{d}En-lil$_2$-le] sagi ED IIIb/Lug. 6 Girsu VS 25 37 o. v 10
[lugal-^{d}En-l]il$_2$-le ED IIIb Nippur *ECTJ* 222 o. 5
lugal-^{d}En-lil$_2$-le ED IIIb Nippur OSP 1 99 o. i 5
lugal-^{d}En-lil$_2$-le ED IIIb Nippur TMH 5 110 o. 4
⸢lugal⸣-^{d}En-lil$_2$-le lu$_2$ gub-ba CS Adab *SIA* 667 o. 12
lugal-^{d}En-lil$_2$-le CS Girsu ITT 5 6688 r. 2

lugal-^{d}En-lil$_2$-le-an-zu (a1) 'the lugal is one whom Enlil knows' 3.1.6.2, p. 142
lugal-^{d}En-lil$_2$-le-an-zu MS-CS Isin ? MVN 3 81 r. 4

lugal-EN-ne$_2$ (a1) unkn. mng. 3.1.8, p. 88 n. 439, 177
lugal-EN-ne$_2$ ED IIIb X ensi$_2$ 5 Girsu VS 27 44 o. i 3

lugal-en-nu (a≥9) 'the lugal is a guardian' 3.1.3.2, p. 109 n. 573, 110
lugal-en-nu ED IIIb/Ukg. lugal 5 Girsu *DP* 1/2 136 r. ii 9
lugal-en-nu ED IIIb Girsu ITT 5 9203 o. 5
lugal-en-nu ED IIIb-ES Isin BIN 8 39 o. ii 6
lugal-en-nu ED IIIb Nippur BE 1/2 114 5'
lugal-en-nu ED IIIb Nippur OSP 1 25 "iii" 3'
lugal-en-nu ED IIIb Nippur OSP 1 26 o. ii' 1'
lugal-en-nu ED IIIb Nippur OSP 1 37 o. ii 2
⸢lugal-en⸣-nu ED IIIb-ES Nippur TMH 5 42 o. i 4
lugal-en-nu f. Ur-gu ED IIIb Unknown BIN 8 44 o. 6
lugal-en-nu ES-MS Unknown BIN 8 163 o. 4
lu[gal]-en-nu CS Adab CUSAS 13 97 o. 4
lugal-en-nu CS Adab *TCABI* 219 r. 2
lugal-en-nu CS Adab *TCABI* 255 o. 4
lugal-en-nu MS-CS Isin ? MAD 4 155 r. 6
lugal-en-nu s. AN-lu$_2$ MS-CS Nippur OSP 2 51 o. 15
lugal-en-nu sukkal ^{d}Dumu-zi-da MS-CS Nippur OSP 2 57 r. 7
lugal-en-nu s. AN-lu$_2$-maḫ MS-CS Nippur OSP 2 63 r. i 12
lugal-en-nu s. AN-lu$_2$ MS-CS Nippur OSP 2 64 o. 4'
lugal-en-nu MS-CS Nippur OSP 2 68 r. 5
lugal-en-nu MS-CS Nippur OSP 2 69 r. 11
lugal-en-nu MS-CS Nippur OSP 2 71 r. 4
lugal-en-nu MS-CS Nippur OSP 2 80 o. ii 7
lugal-en-nu MS-CS Nippur OSP 2 86 o. i 8'
lugal-en-nu MS-CS Nippur OSP 2 91 o. 2'
lugal-en-nu MS-CS Nippur OSP 2 96 o. ii 9
lugal-en-nu CS/Śkś Y 2 Nippur OSP 2 100 r. ii 12'
[lugal]-en-nu MS-CS Nippur OSP 2 101 o. ii' 2
lugal-en-nu niĝir, maškim-bi$_3$ MS-CS Nippur OSP 2 123 o. 9
lugal-en-nu f. Ur-sa$_6$ MS-CS Nippur OSP 2 174 r. 4
lugal-en-nu UN.SUKKAL MS-CS Nippur OSP 2 178 edge
lugal-en-nu MS-CS Nippur PBS 9 28+34 r. ii' 7'
lugal-en-nu CS Umma ? CUSAS 13 201 o. 2
lugal-en-nu MS-CS Unknown MVN 3 61 o. ii 10

lugal-en-nu-ĝu$_{10}$ (a1) ‘the lugal is my guardian’ 3.1.3.1, p. 108–109, 110
lugal-en-nu-ĝu$_{10}$ f. Lugal-za$_3$-si ED IIIa Šuruppag M. Molina & H. Sanchiz, *StEL* 24 (2007), p. 1–15 2 o. ii 6

lugal-en-nun (a4) ‘the lugal is a guardian’ 3.1.3.2, p. 109 n. 573, 110
lugal-en$^!$-nun ED IIIa-b Unknown BIN 2 2 o. iii 95
lugal-en-nun ED IIIb-ES Adab *TCABI* 17 o. i 4’
lugal-en-nun ED IIIb Unknown MVN 3 14 o. iii 7
lugal-en-nun lu$_2$ bappir-ra CS Unknown *L’uomo* 16 o. 6

lugal-en$_3$-tar-su$_3$ (a≥3) ‘the lugal is one who provides (abundantly)’ 3.1.4.1, p. 122–123, 185
lugal-en$_3$-tar$^!$(NU)-su$_3$ (apin-la$_2$) ED IIIb/X Y 4 Girsu *TSA* 7 r. ii 13
lugal-en$_3$-tar-su$_3$ apin-la$_2$ ED IIIb/X Y 2 Girsu VS 25 93 o. i 6
lugal-en$_3$-tar-su$_3$ sipa ensi$_2$-ka MS-CS Adab OIP 14 144 o. 2
lugal-en$_3$-tar-su$_3$ MS Adab *TCABI* 132 o. 2
lugal-en$_3$-tar-su$_3$ muḫaldim, ir$_{11}$ *Qi$_3$-šum* CS Girsu ITT 1 1471 o. 1
lugal-en$_3$-tar-su$_3$ CS Unknown MAD 5 105 o. 5

lugal-en$_3$-tar-su$_{13}$ (a1) ‘the lugal is one who provides (abundantly)’ 3.1.4.1, p. 122 n. 664
[lugal-e]n$_3$-tar-su$_{13}$ MS Adab *TCABI* 80 o. 4’

lugal-en$_3$-tar-su$_x$(TAG) (a1) ‘the lugal is one who provides (abundantly)’ 3.1.4.1, p. 122 n. 664
lugal-en$_3$-tar-su$_x$ MS-CS Nippur OSP 2 80 o. ii 8
lugal-en$_3$-tar-su$_x$ MS-CS Nippur OSP 2 96 o. iv 2’

lugal-⸢en$_3$⸣-tar-⸢x⸣ CS Adab *SIA* 802 r. 8
lugal-en$_3$-tar-[x] ĝuruš CS Girsu?/Nippur? MVN 3 68 o. 5
lugal-en$_3$-tar-[x] s. UŠ-[A]B$^?$, …, ĝuruš dumu nitaḫ CS Girsu MVN 3 113 r. iii 5’

lugal-en$_8$-su$_{13}$ (a1) (defective for lugal-en$_8$-tar-su$_{13}$) 3.1.4.1, p. 122 n. 664
lugal-en$_8$-su$_{13}$ ES Adab CUSAS 11 281 r. 4

lugal-en$_8$-tar (a1) (defective for lugal-en$_{3/8}$-tar-su$_{3/13/x}$) 3.1.4.1, p. 122 n. 664
lugal-en$_8$-tar na[gar ?] MS-CS Unknown MesCiv 4 58 r. 6

lugal-en$_8$-tar-su$_3$ (a≥2) ‘the lugal is one who provides (abundantly)’ 3.1.4.1, p. 122 n. 664
lugal-en$_8$-tar$^!$(ME)-su$_3$ ES-MS Umma Nik 2 67 o. i 2
lugal-en$_8$-tar$^!$(ME)-su$_3$ ES-MS Umma Nik 2 67 o. ii 2
lugal-en$_8$-tar-su$_3$ CS Adab CUSAS 13 61 o. 8
lugal-en$_8$-tar-su$_3$ CS Adab *SIA* 676 o. 5
lugal-en$_8$-tar-su$_3$ CS Umma *AAS* 204 o. 1’
lugal-en$_8$-tar-su$_3$ ugula CS Umma BARI S 2135 40 r. 7’
⸢lugal-en$_8$-tar-su$_3$⸣ CS Umma ? CUSAS 13 201 r. 4
lugal-en$_8$-tar-su$_3$ CS Umma T. Donald, *MCS* 9 (1964) 239 r. 7
lugal-en$_8$-tar-su$_3$ f. Lugal-iti-da CS Umma *USP* 47 r. i 19
lugal-en$_8$-tar-su$_3$ CS Umma *USP* 49 o. 3
lugal-en$_8$-tar-su$_3$ CS Umma *USP* 65 o. 2

lugal-en$_8$-tar-su$_{13}$ (a1) ‘the lugal is one who provides (abundantly)’ 3.1.4.1, p. 122 n. 664
lugal-en$_8$-tar-su$_{13}$ ED IIIb-ES Adab CUSAS 11 103 o. ii 1

lugal-en$_8$-tar-su$_x$(TAG) (a1) ‘the lugal is one who provides (abundantly)’ 3.1.4.1, p. 122 n 664
lugal-en$_8$-tar-su$_x$(TAG) MS-CS Nippur OSP 2 84 o. i 9

lugal-engar-zi (a≥1) ‘the lugal is a reliable farmer’ 3.1.5.3, p. 131–132
⸢lugal⸣-[engar]-zi ED IIIa Šuruppag *NTSŠ* 207 o. ii 6
lugal-engar-zi ED IIIa Šuruppag *NTSŠ* 207 r. i 2
lugal-engar-zi ED IIIa Šuruppag *NTSŠ* 280 o. ii 1

lugal-engar-zi ED IIIa Šuruppag *TSŠ* 8 o. ii 11
lugal-engar-zi ED IIIa Šuruppag *TSŠ* 9+127 o. ii 10
lugal-engar-zi ED IIIa Šuruppag *TSŠ* 102 r. iii 6
lugal-engar-zi ED IIIa Šuruppag *TSŠ* 260 o. ii 6
lugal-engar-zi ED IIIa Šuruppag *TSŠ* 260 o. iii 1
lugal-engar-zi ED IIIa Šuruppag *TSŠ* 704 o. ii 1
lugal-engar-zi ED IIIa Šuruppag *TSŠ* 794 o. iii 1
lugal-engar-zi ED IIIa Šuruppag *WF* 9 o. ii 1
lugal-engar-zi ED IIIa Šuruppag *WF* 13 o. ii 1
lugal-engar-zi ^{d}Gibil$_6$ ED IIIa Šuruppag *WF* 18 o. vi 11
lugal-engar-zi ED IIIa Šuruppag *WF* 53 o. iii 15
lugal-engar-zi ED IIIa Šuruppag *WF* 56 o. ii 1
lugal-engar-zi ED IIIa Šuruppag *WF* 65 r. iv 1
lugal-engar-zi ED IIIa Šuruppag *WF* 124 o. v 8

lugal-Eridu^{ki}-še$_3$ $^{(a1)}$ 'the lugal … to(wards) Eridu' 3.1.6.4, p. 153 w. n. 880, 155 n. 889
lugal-Eridu^{ki}-še$_3$ bir$_3$ suḫ$_5$-ḫa ED IIIb/Ukg. lugal 6 Girsu *DP* 1/2 135 o. i 9

lugal-ERIM+X $^{(a1)}$ 'the lugal is (like) the ERIM+X-quadruped' 3.1.7.6, p. 166 w. n. 957
lugal-ERIM+X Ma-ri$_2$^{ki} ED IIIb Ebla A. Archi, *MARI* 4 (1985), p. 63–83 84 (translit. only) o. v 6bis

lugal-ezem $^{(a>40)}$ 'the lugal … the festival' 3.1.5.2, p. 50 n. 231, 126, 130–131, 183 n. 1136, 235, 237
lugal-ezem b. E$_2$-zi-zi ED IIIa Šuruppag CUSAS 11 344 r. i 2
lugal-ezem dam-gar$_3$ ED IIIa Šuruppag? G. Visicato & A. Westenholz, *Gs Cagni*, p. 1107–1133 5 (translit. only) o. iv 1
lugal-ezem E$_2$-ku[r] ED IIIa Šuruppag *NTSŠ* 569 r. iii' 8'
lugal-ezem ED IIIa Šuruppag A. Westenholz, *OrNS* 44 (1975), p. 434–438 1 r. ii 3
lugal-ezem dub-⸢sar⸣ ED IIIa Šuruppag>Nippur TMH 5 71 o. v 1
lugal-ezem ED IIIa Šuruppag *TSŠ* 1 r. iii 13
lugal-ezem Nam-maḫ$_2$, Lugal-ezem ED IIIa Šuruppag *TSŠ* 1 r. v 14
lugal-ezem ED IIIa Šuruppag *TSŠ* 14 o. ii 10
lugal-ezem ED IIIa Šuruppag *TSŠ* 53 r. i 1
lugal-ezem ED IIIa Šuruppag *TSŠ* 627 o. ii 3
lugal-ezem na-gada ED IIIa Šuruppag *TSŠ* 794 o. ii 3
lugal-ezem ED IIIa Šuruppag *TSŠ* 878 o. ii 1
lugal-ezem ED IIIa Šuruppag *WF* 1 o. v 1
lugal-ezem ED IIIa Šuruppag *WF* 3 o. iii 7
lugal-ezem ED IIIa Šuruppag *WF* 7 o. i 8'
lugal-ezem PA.PA ED IIIa Šuruppag *WF* 7 r. iii 2
lugal-ezem E$_2$-kur ED IIIa Šuruppag *WF* 18 r. vi 1
lugal-ezem PA.PA sila ED IIIa Šuruppag *WF* 25 o. iii 15
lugal-ezem nu-kiri$_6$ ED IIIa Šuruppag *WF* 25 r. iii 13
lugal-ezem sipa ED IIIa Šuruppag *WF* 27 o. iii 9
lugal-ezem Nam-maḫ, Lugal-ezem, e$_2$-geme$_2$ ED IIIa Šuruppag *WF* 27 o. iv 4
lugal-ezem ED IIIa Šuruppag *WF* 59 o. 1
lugal-ezem ED IIIa Šuruppag *WF* 65 r. v 3
lugal-ezem Lugal-ezem, KA-TAR-zi engar ED IIIa Šuruppag *WF* 78 r. vi 3
lugal-ezem luĝa$_3$ ED IIIa Šuruppag *WF* 95 o. iv 6
lugal-ezem ED IIIa Šuruppag *WF* 99 o. ii 2
lugal-ezem luĝa$_3$ ED IIIa Šuruppag *WF* 99* o. ii 2'
lugal-ezem ED IIIa Šuruppag *WF* 104 o. iii 4
lugal-ezem ED IIIa-b Girsu *RTC* 1 r. i 4'

lugal-ezem f. Maš-lugal ED IIIa-b Isin (?) OIP 104 14 o. iii 8
lugal-ezem ED IIIa-b Isin (?) OIP 104 14 r. vi 12–13
lugal-ezem engar ED IIIa-b Isin (?) OIP 104 15 o. i 23
lugal-ezem engar ED IIIa-b Isin (?) OIP 104 15 o. ii 22
lugal-ezem engar ED IIIa-b Isin (?) OIP 104 15 o. iii 20
lugal-ezem engar ED IIIa-b Isin (?) OIP 104 15 o. iv 20
lugal-ezem engar ED IIIa-b Isin (?) OIP 104 15 o. v 19
lugal-ezem engar ED IIIa-b Isin (?) OIP 104 15 o. vi 26
lugal-ezem engar ED IIIa-b Isin (?) OIP 104 15 o. vii 23
[lugal-ez]em engar ED IIIa-b Isin (?) OIP 104 15 r. ii 24
[lugal-ezem] engar ED IIIa-b Isin (?) OIP 104 15 r. iii 23
lugal-ezem engar ED IIIa-b Isin (?) OIP 104 15 r. vi 10
lugal-ezem engar ED IIIa-b Isin (?) OIP 104 15 r. vii 6
lugal-ezem engar ED IIIa-b Isin (?) OIP 104 15 l.e. 4
lugal-ezem lu$_2$-⸢u$_5$⸣ ED IIIb-ES Adab CUSAS 11 107 o. ii 1
lugal-ezem b. Tu-tu ED IIIb-ES Adab CUSAS 11 186 o. ii 3
lugal-ezem s. Bil$_2$-lal$_3$-la, lu$_2$ ni$_3$-sa$_{10}$ ku$_2$ ED IIIb/(Eig. ^{ni_3}ensi$_2$) Adab D. Foxvog, Mesopotamia 8, p. 67–75 (UCLM 9-1798) o. iv 4
lugal-ezem ED IIIb Adab OIP 14 67 o. ii 1
lugal-ezem ED IIIb Girsu ? BIN 8 14 r. ii 3
lugal-ezem s. Ur-^{d}Nanše ED IIIb/Urn. X Girsu *CIRPL* Urn. 20 Upper register, center caption
lugal-ezem saĝa ED IIIb/Lug. 5 Girsu HSS 3 51 r. i 4
lugal-ezem lu$_2$ inim du$_{11}$ ED IIIb/Ukg. lugal 5 Girsu Nik 1 3 o. iii 12
lugal-ezem f. Ma-ma & BA-IR-X-[*t*]*um* ED IIIb/Urz. lugal Isin M. Lambert, *RA* 73 (1979), p. 5–6 r. vi 12
lugal-ezem ED IIIb Nippur BE 1/2 111 2’
lugal-ezem ED IIIb Nippur OSP 1 25 “ii” 3’
lugal-ezem ED IIIb Nippur OSP 1 33 o. i 1’
lugal-ezem s. ⸢Aja$_2$⸣-ul$_4$-gal-ke$_4$ ED IIIb Nippur OSP 1 44 o. 7
lugal-ezem ⸢x⸣ ED IIIb Nippur OSP 1 46 o. ii 7
lugal-ezem ED IIIb Nippur OSP 1 66 r. 1
lugal-ezem s. U$_3$-mu-NI.NI, azlag$_7$ ED IIIb Nippur OSP 1 104 o. 2
lugal-ezem f. Lugal-i$_7$-ĝu$_{10}$, nu-kiri$_6$ ED IIIb Nippur TMH 5 6 o. ii 1
lugal-ezem nagar ED IIIb Nippur TMH 5 10 o. 4
lu:gal-ezem f. Ur-^{d}Nin-urta ED IIIb Nippur TMH 5 11 o. ii 5
lugal-ezem ED IIIb Nippur TMH 5 20 r. 4
lugal-ezem ED IIIb Nippur TMH 5 90 o. ii 1
lugal-ezem f. A-ne-da ED IIIb Nippur TMH 5 134 o. ii 5
lugal-ezem f. Ur-tur ED IIIb/Enšak. Y X Nippur TMH 5 158 o. 6
lugal-ezem ED IIIb Nippur TMH 5 159 o. vi 10’
lugal-ezem s. ⸢x⸣-[x-x], maš[kim-bi] ED IIIb Nippur TMH 5 159 r. i 5
lugal-ezem ugula e$_2$ ED IIIb Nippur TMH 5 176 o. ii 2
lugal-ezem ED IIIb Nippur TMH 5 203 o. 6
lugal-ezem ugula ED IIIb Umma-Zabala ? BIN 8 54 o. i 3
lugal-ezem ugula ED IIIb/Luzag. ensi$_2$ X Umma-Zabala BIN 8 82 o. i 3
lugal-ezem ugula ED IIIb/Luzag. ensi$_2$ X Umma-Zabala BIN 8 82 o. i 6
lugal-ezem ugula ED IIIb/Luzag. ensi$_2$ X Umma-Zabala BIN 8 82 o. ii 7
lugal-ezem ugula ED IIIb/Luzag. ensi$_2$ X Umma-Zabala BIN 8 82 o. iv 16
lugal-ezem ugula ED IIIb Umma-Zabala ? BIN 8 90 o. ii 1
lugal-ezem ED IIIb Umma-Zabala CUSAS 14 4 r. i 1
lugal-ezem ED IIIb Umma-Zabala CUSAS 14 112 o. ii 2

lugal-ezem ED IIIb Umma-Zabala CUSAS 14 159 o. ii 2

lugal-ezem ED IIIb Umma-Zabala CUSAS 14 241 o. ii 5

lugal-ezem ugula ED IIIb Umma-Zabala CUSAS 14 252 o. ii 2

lugal-ezem ugula ED IIIb/Luzag. Y 7 Umma-Zabala M. Powell, *HUCA* 49 (1978), p. 1–58 1 o. iii 4

lugal-ezem ugula ED IIIb Umma-Zabala M. Powell, *HUCA* 49 (1978), p. 1–58 3 o. ii 5

lugal-ezem ? [ug]ula ? ED IIIb/X Y 8 Umma-Zabala M. Powell, *HUCA* 49 (1978), p. 1–58 5 o. i 4'

lugal-ezem ugula ED IIIb Umma-Zabala M. Powell, *HUCA* 49 (1978), p. 1–58 13 o. ii 3

lugal-ezem ugula ED IIIb/Luzag. ensi$_2$ 7 Umma-Zabala M. deJ. Ellis, *JCS* 31 (1979), p. 30–55 6 o. i 8

lugal-ezem ugula ? ED IIIb/Luzag. ensi$_2$ 7 Umma-Zabala M. deJ. Ellis, *JCS* 31 (1979), p. 30–55 7 o. ii 8

lugal-ezem Ur-saĝ-diĝir Lugal-ezem ED IIIb Umma MesCiv 4 3 o. i 2

lugal-ezem AMAR-⸢x⸣ ED IIIb Umma-Zabala MVN 3 3 o. iii 13

lugal-ezem ED IIIb Umma-Zabala MVN 3 3 r. iv 2

lugal-ezem ED IIIb Zabala (?) BIN 8 46 o. i 3

lugal-ezem ED IIIb Zabala (?) BIN 8 46 o. ii 5

lugal-ezem lu$_2$ tu-ra ES Adab *TCABI* 26 r. i 5

lugal-ezem ES-MS Nippur OSP 1 23 o. iv 29

lugal-ezem f. *Puzur*$_4$-pa$_4$-pa$_4$, ... ĝuruš, *be-lu* gan$_2$, Gir$_{13}$-tab^{ki} ES/Man. Unknown (MO) OIP 104 40 B vi 4

lugal-ezem ugula, ... ĝuruš, abba$_2$.abba$_2$ gan$_2$, Gir$_{13}$-tab^{ki} ES/Man. Unknown (MO) OIP 104 B x 6

lugal-ezem ff. *A-ḫu*-ĝiš-erin$_2$, f. *A-ḫa-ar-ši*, ĝuruš, Mar$_2$-da^{ki}, abba$_2$.abba$_2$, gan$_2$ ES/Man. Unknown (MO) OIP 104 C xvii' 5

lugal-ezem ES-MS Umma Nik 2 14 o. iii 5

lugal-ezem [x x] x [x x] ES (recut later?) Unknown *EGA* 354 (translit. only) 1

lugal-ezem CS Adab CUSAS 13 23 o. 1

lugal-ezem CS Adab CUSAS 13 78 o. ii 13

lugal-ezem CS/Śkś Adab OIP 14 117 o. 5

lugal-ezem ugula CS/Śkś Adab OIP 14 117 o. 14

lugal-ezem CS Adab *SIA* 699+823 o. 4

lugal-ezem nu-banda$_3$ baḫar CS Adab *SIA* 863 o. 4

lugal-ezem CS Adab *SIA* 1113 o. 2

lugal-⸢ezem$^?$⸣ ? CS Adab *SIA* 685+734 o. 19

lugal-⸢ezem⸣ MS Adab *TCABI* 79 o. 8

lugal-ezem CS Ešnuna MAD 1 292 r. 5

lugal-ezem *šu* Ur-^{d}Iškur CS Girsu *DPA* 2 (PUL 5) o. 5

lugal-ezem CS Girsu *DPA* 40 (PUL 30) r. 2

lugal-ezem *šu* Ur-^{d}Iškur, ĝuruš CS Girsu *DPA* 43 (PUL 47) o. 5

⸢lugal⸣-ezem maškim CS Girsu ITT 2/1 4438 r. 1

lugal-ezem ad-‹kup$_4^?$› CS Girsu ITT 5 6867 o. 8

lugal-ezem maškim CS Girsu ITT 5 9277 r. 4'

lugal-ezem CS Girsu MVN 3 114 r. 1

lugal-ezem f. Lu$_2$-UN-da CS Girsu MVN 3 113 o. ii 4

lugal-ezem f. Lu$_2$-gu-la CS Girsu MVN 3 113 r. iii 22'

lugal-ezem s. Lugal-ni$_3$-zu(-ke$_4$) CS Girsu *RTC* 81 o. 4

lugal-ezem maškim CS Girsu *RTC* 101 r. 5

lugal-ezem CS Girsu *STTI* 54 r. 6

lugal-ezem CS Girsu *STTI* 143 o. ii 6'
lugal-ezem CS Girsu *STTI* 155 o. 2
lugal-ezem ad-kup$_4$ CS Girsu *STTI* 166 r. i 3'
lugal-ezem sip[a x], …, ĝuruš CS Mesag M. deJ. Ellis, *JCS* 31 (1979), p. 30–55 16 o. iii 18
lugal-ezem ⌜sipa⌝ anš[e] MS-CS Mesag MesCiv 4 33 r. 2
lugal-ezem ku$_3$-⌜dim$_2$⌝ MS-CS Nippur OIP 97 13 r. 3
lugal-ezem Uru$_2$(URU×UD)$^{[ki]}$ MS-CS Nippur OSP 2 118 o. 2
lugal-ezem MS-CS Nippur OSP 2 158 o. 7
lugal-ezem ? ens[i$_2$-gal] MS-CS Umma ? *TCVC* 726 o. iii 18
lugal-ezem Lugal-ezem, Ur-^{d}Inana ga:eš$_8$, mu-DU MS-CS Unknown *L'uomo* 30 o. 5
lugal-ezem CS Unknown Mesopotamia 9 2 o. 10'
lugal-ezem CS Unknown Mesopotamia 9 3 o. 10
lugal-ezem CS Unknown Mesopotamia 9 4 o. 9

lugal-EZEM.GAL-[x] (a1) (compare, perhaps, the following) 3.1.6.4, p. 154 n. 888
lugal-⌜EZEM.GAL⌝-[x] sagi ED IIIb Ur UET 2 suppl. 23 o. i 2

lugal-EZEM×GAL^{ki}-e (a1) 'the lugal … (the town) EZEM×GAL' 3.1.6.4, p. 154 w. n. 888
lugal-EZEM×GAL^{ki}-e CS-LS ? Girsu *RTC* 254 r. i 10

lugal-⌜EZEM×X⌝ ED IIIb Umma-Zabala CUSAS 14 4 o. ii 3

lu[gal$^?$]-ga (a1) unkn. mng. 3.1.8, p. 178
lu[gal$^?$]-ga CS-LS ? Girsu *RTC* 254 o. i 3

lugal-gaba-ĝal$_2$ (a1/°1) 'the lugal is influential' 3.1.1.6, p. 99
°lugal-gaba-ĝal$_2$ ED IIIb Ebla MEE 3 59 o. ii 3
lugal-gaba-ĝal$_2$ sukkal-ĜA$_2$×U$_2$ ES-MS Ur UET 2 suppl. 16 r. i 3'

°lugal-gal-bi$_2$-tum$_2$ (°1) 'the lugal *performs great deeds* (?)' 3.1.8, p. 176 n. 1041, 178
°lugal-gal-bi$_2$-tum$_2$ ED IIIb Ebla MEE 3 67 o. ii 2

lugal-gal-zu (a5) 'the lugal is wise' 3.1.2, p. 106, 251 n. 1476
lugal-gal-zu ED IIIa-b Isin (?) OIP 104 15 r. iii 6
lugal-gal-zu ED IIIa-b Isin (?) OIP 104 15 r. iv 7
lugal-gal-zu ED IIIb Adab Eig. ^{ni_3}ensi$_2$ OIP 14 49 o. iv 6
lugal-gal-zu s. X-ke$_4$ ED IIIb/Urz. lugal Isin M. Lambert, *RA* 73 (1979), p. 5–6 r. i 26
lugal-ga[l-zu] ensi$_2$ Zabala$_3^{ki}$ ES/Rīmuś (OB) Nippur PBS 15 41 r. viii 7'
lugal-gal-zu ⌜nu-banda$_3$⌝-ni ES-MS Umma BIN 8 314 o. 4
lugal-gal-zu lu$_2$ Lugal-gal-zu ES-MS Umma Nik 2 19 o. iii 7
lugal-gal-zu lu$_2$ Lugal-gal-zu nu-banda$_3$-bi ES-MS Umma Nik 2 19 o. iii 12
lu[gal]-gal-zu ES-MS Umma Nik 2 60 o. i 6
lu[gal]-ga[l-zu$^?$] [nu]-banda$_3$-[bi] ES-MS Umma Nik 2 65 r. 6

lugal-GAN$_2$ (a≥6) 'the lugal … the field' 3.1.5.3, p. 132
lugal-GAN$_2$ Lugal-GAN$_2$, Lugal-kar, KAL.EDIN ED IIIb Nippur TMH 5 11 o. iii 6
lugal-GAN$_2$ ED IIIb Nippur OSP 1 27 o. i 9'
lugal-GAN$_2$ (PN?) ED IIIb Umma-Zabala ? BIN 8 114 r. (!) ii 8
lugal-GAN$_2$ ED IIIb/Luzag. ensi$_2$ [x] Umma-Zabala J. A. Brinkman, *Fs Kramer*, pl. III*-V* (W 2/7) r. i 3
lugal-⌜GAN$_2$⌝ ? ED IIIb Umma-Zabala M. Powell, *HUCA* 49 (1978), p. 1–58 21 o. ii 3
lugal-GAN$_2$ ugula ED IIIb/Luzag. (?) Y 7 Zabala BIN 8 61 o. ii 1
lugal-GAN$_2$ CS Adab CUSAS 13 108 o. 12
lugal-GAN$_2$ MS-CS Nippur OSP 2 82 o. 2
lugal-GAN$_2$ MS-CS Nippur OSP 2 89 o. 4
[lugal]-GAN$_2$ MS-CS Nippur OSP 2 90 o. ii 1

⸢lugal⸣-GAN$_2$ MS-CS Nippur OSP 2 96 o. i 13
⸢lugal-GAN$_2$⸣ ? MS-CS Nippur OSP 2 96 o. iii 8’
lugal-GAN$_2$ MS-CS Nippur OSP 2 98 o. ii 5
⸢lugal⸣-GAN$_2$ CS/Śkś Y 2 Nippur OSP 2 100 o. iii 1
lugal-GAN$_2$ MS-CS Nippur OSP 2 101 r. i 2’
lugal-GAN$_2$ CS Susa MDP 14 26 o. 6
lugal-⸢GAN$_2$⸣ f. E$_2$-ĝiš & Lugal-mi$_2$ MS-CS Umma ? *TCVC* 731 o. i 15’

lugal-GAN$_2$-su$_{11}$-lum-ma-gub (a1) ‘the lugal stands in the Date-field’ 3.1.5.3, p. 133
lugal-GAN$_2$-su$_{11}$-lum-ma-gub šu-ku$_6$ a du$_{10}$-ga ED IIIb/X Y 4 Girsu *TSA* 47 o. iv 8

lugal-GAN$_2$-zi (a1) ‘the lugal is one who puts the fields in order’ 3.1.5.3, p. 132
lugal-GAN$_2$-zi MS-CS Nippur OSP 2 153 o. 5
lugal-GAN$_2$-zi nar e$_2$ nin-ke$_4$ MS-CS Nippur OSP 2 177 o. 4

lugal-gi$_7$ (a3) ‘the lugal is noble’ 3.1.7.8, p. 171
lugal-gi$_7$ CS Girsu ITT 2/1 2926 o. 5
⸢lugal⸣-gi$_7$ ⸢ĝuruš$^?$⸣ MS-CS Mesag BIN 8 148 o. ii 8’
lugal-gi$_7$ MS-CS Mesag BIN 8 243 o. 1
lugal-gi$_7$ MS-CS Mesag MesCiv 4 45 o. 10
lugal-gi$_7$ GAN$_2$-ban$_3$-da^{ki} MS-CS Nippur OSP 2 81 r. 5
lugal-gi$_7$? sipa maš$_2$-bar-du$_8$ MS-CS Nippur OSP 2 180 r. 3

lugal-^{ĝiš}gigir$_2$ (a1) ‘the lugal … the chariot’ 3.1.3.3, p. 113 n. 604
lugal-^{ĝiš}gigir$_2$ dub-sar CS Umma BIN 8 335 o. 3
lugal-^{ĝiš}gigir$_2$ dub-sar MS-CS Umma BIN 8 340 o. 4

lugal-^{ĝiš}gigir$_2$-e (a≥4) ‘the lugal … the chariot’ 3.1.3.3, p. 113
lugal-^{ĝiš}gigir$_2$-e CS/Śkś Y 2 Umma CT 50 53 r. 7
⸢lugal⸣-^{ĝiš}gigir$_2$-e CS Umma MVN 15 379 o. 1’
lugal-^{ĝiš}gigir$_2$-e s. E$_2$-abzu CS Umma Nik 2 70 o. 9’
lugal-^{ĝiš}gigir$_2$-e [nu$^?$]-banda$_3$ (?) CS Umma Nik 2 72 r. 7
lugal-^{ĝiš}gigir$_2$-e CS Umma? A. Westenholz, *OrNS* 44 (1975), p. 434–438 10 o. 2
lugal-⸢^{ĝiš}gigir$_2$⸣-e CS Umma *USP* 19 r. 2
lugal-^{ĝiš}gigir$_2$-e s. Ur-^{d}Inana CS Umma *USP* 45 r. i 19
lugal-^{ĝiš}gigir$_2$-e dumu URU.KI CS Umma *USP* 45 r. i 17
lugal-^{ĝiš}gigir$_2$-e s. Ur-lu$_2$, b. Lugal-nesaĝ-e CS Umma *USP* 47 o. ii 9
lugal-^{ĝiš}gigir$_2$-e nu-banda$_3$ CS Umma *USP* 47 r. ii 13
lu[gal]-^{ĝiš}gigir$_2$-[e] CS Umma *USP* 48 o. 4’
lugal-^{ĝiš}gigir$_2$-e f. [X]-KAL CS Umma *USP* 48 r. 10’
lugal-^{ĝiš}gigir$_2$-e CS Umma *USP* 73 o. 9
lugal-^{ĝiš}gigir$_2$-e maškim MS-CS Umma B. R. Foster, *WO* 13 (1982), p. 15–24 8 o. 2

lugal-^{ĝiš}gigir$_2$-re (a1) ‘the lugal … the chariot’ 3.1.3.3, p. 113 n. 604
lugal-^{ĝiš}gigir$_2$-re CS Girsu *DPA* 17 (PUL 49) r. 5

lugal-^{ĝiš}gigir$_2$-re$_2$? (a1) ‘the lugal … the chariot’ 3.1.3.3, p. 113 n. 604
lugal-⸢^{ĝiš}gigir$_2$⸣-[r]e$_2$$^?$ CS Girsu *STTI* 140 o. 6

lugal-gil-sa (a1) ‘the lugal is (of) everlasting (value)’ 3.1.7.7, p. 168
lugal-gil-⸢sa⸣ s. Ur-igi, nu$^!$-banda$_3$ ED IIIb/(Ukg. lugal) 6 Girsu M. Yoshikawa, *ASJ* 9 (1987), p. 303–319 1 o. ii 2
[lu]gal-[gil-sa] ‹nu›-banda$_3$ ED IIIb/(Ukg. lugal) 6 Girsu A. Westenholz, *JCS* 26 (1974), p. 71–80 2 o. ii 3
lugal-gil-sa s. [Ur-igi] ED IIIb/(Ukg. lugal) 3 Girsu VS 14 26 o. i 6

lugal-GIM (a1) ‘like a lugal’ 3.1.8, p. 178
lugal-GIM CS Girsu CT 50 85 o. ii 2

lugal-GU$_2$ (a≥4) unkn. mng. 3.1.8, p. 178
lugal-GU$_2$ CS Adab CUSAS 13 152 r. 5
lugal-GU$_2$ CS Adab CUSAS 13 152 r. 10
lugal-GU$_2$ CS Girsu *STTI* 20 r. 2'
lugal-GU$_2$ ^{d}Šara$_2$-bi$_2$-du$_{11}$, ir$_{11}$ Lugal-GU$_2$ dam-gar$_3$ MS-CS Umma MesCiv 4 30 o. ii 13
lugal-GU$_2$ ugula-bi MS-CS Unknown T. Ozaki, SANTAG 7 4 r. 6
lugal-GU$_2$ (b. Lugal-nu-du$_{11}$-ga) CS Unknown Mesopotamia 9 2 o. 12'
lugal-GU$_2$ b. Lugal-nu-du$_{11}$-ga CS Unknown Mesopotamia 9 2 o. 15'
lugal-GU$_2$ (b. Lugal-nu-du$_{11}$-ga) CS Unknown Mesopotamia 9 3 o. 12
lugal-[GU$_2$] b. Lugal-nu-du$_{11}$-[ga] CS Unknown Mesopotamia 9 3 o. 15
lugal-GU$_2$ (b. Lugal-nu-du$_{11}$-ga) CS Unknown Mesopotamia 9 4 o. 12

lugal-gu$_2$-gal (a2) uncertain mng. 3.1.7.7, p. 178 w. n. 1063
lugal-gu$_2$-gal ED IIIa Šuruppag *WF* 35 o. v 5
lugal-gu$_2$-gal ED IIIb Adab MVN 3 90 o. ii 6

lugal-GU$_2$-ĝu$_{10}$? (a1) unkn. mng. 3.1.8, p. 178 w. n. 1064
lugal-GU$_2$-ĝu$_{10}$? or: muḫaldim ? ED I-II Ur UET 2 28 o. ii 1

lugal-gu$_3$-de$_2$-a (a1) 'the lugal is summoned' 3.1.6.2, p. 145
lugal-gu$_3$-de$_2$-a CS Adab *SIA* 948 o. 3
lugal-[gu$_3$]-⸢de$_2$-a⸣ CS Adab *SIA* 948 r. 3

lugal-gu$_4$ (a2) 'the lugal … the ox' 3.1.6.3, p. 135 n. 754, 148 w. n. 837
lugal-gu$_4$ f. Ur-AN.AN, dub-sar ED IIIb/Meskigala ensi$_2$ X/Luzag. lugal Adab BIN 8 26 r. i 3
lugal-gu$_4$ ED IIIb Adab MVN 3 90 o. i 2
lugal-gu$_4$ ED IIIb/Lug. 1 Girsu VS 25 22 o. i 6

°lugal-gu$_4$-DU (a1) 'the lugal … the ox' 3.1.6.3, p. 148
°lugal-gu$_4$-DU CS Unknown CUSAS 13 188 o. 3

lugal-gu$_7$ (a1) unkn. mng. 3.1.8, p. 178, 179 n. 1082
lugal-gu$_7$ dam-gar$_3$ CS Girsu B. R. Foster, *JCS* 35 (1983), p. 156 (L 3015, translit. only) o. 1

lugal-gub-ba (a1) (abbreviated writing of the following) 3.1.6.4, p. 156 n. 897
lugal-gub-ba ED IIIb-ES Adab CUSAS 11 186 o. iv 9

lugal-gub-ba-ni (a≥5) 'the lugal … (where) he serves' 3.1.6.4, p. 156 n. 897
lugal-gub-ba-ni s. Dur$_x$-kilim, f. Ur-^{d}Er$_9$-ra & Ur-^{d}Nin-tu ED IIIb-ES Adab CUSAS 11 77 o. i 5
lugal-gub-ba-ni Ur-dam, Lugal-gub-ba-ni, Ad-da-b[e$_6$] ED IIIb Nippur TMH 5 11 r. iii 2
lugal-gub-ba-ni ED IIIb Nippur OSP 1 40 o. 1
lugal-[gub]-ba-ni ED IIIb Nippur OSP 1 115 o. i 3
lugal-gub-ba-ni ES/Śk. Nippur TMH 5 151 r. 1
lugal-gub-ba-ni sagi CS Girsu *STTI* 123 r. 2
lugal-gub-ba-ni s. ME-⸢ḪA⸣-[(x$^{?}$)], b. E$_2$-⸢x-x⸣ & ⸢A$_2$-kal$^{?}$⸣-[x] CS Mesag BIN 8 152 r. i 5'
lugal-gub-ba-ni ⸢nagar⸣ MS-CS Mesag BIN 8 245 o. i 3
lugal-gub-ba-ni [na]gar MS-CS Mesag BIN 8 254 o. 8
lugal-gub-ba-ni s. ME-⸢ḪA⸣-[(x$^{?}$)], b. E$_2$-⸢x⸣-[x] & A$_2$-k[al$^{?}$-x] CS Mesag M. deJ. Ellis, *JCS* 31 (1979), p. 30–55 16 r. i 11'
lugal-gub-ba-ni MS-CS Nippur OSP 2 95 o. iii 10
⸢lugal⸣-gub-⸢ba-ni⸣ MS-CS Nippur OSP 2 96 o. i 6
[lu:gal-gu]b-ba-ni MS-CS Nippur OSP 2 102 r. iii' 3'
lugal-gub-ba-ni MS-CS Nippur OSP 2 104 o. i' 6'

lugal-gub-ba-ni MS-CS Nippur OSP 2 110 o. 5
lugal-gub-ba-ni MS-CS Nippur OSP 2 111 o. i' 5'

°lugal-GUG$_2$ (°1) unkn. mng. 3.1.8, p. 178
°lu[gal]-GUG$_2$ LS-Ur III Unknown M. E. Cohen, *Fs Hallo*, p. 79–86 (YBC 2124) ii 15

lugal-GUR$_8$-[x] (a1) unkn. mng. 3.1.8, p. 178
lugal-GUR$_8$-[x] MS-CS Nippur OSP 2 148 r. 1'

lugal-ĝa$_2$-si (a1) 'the lugal is just right for the barn' 3.1.5.3, p. 136, 229
lugal-ĝa$_2$-si ED I-II Ur UET 2 109 o. iv 5

⌜lugal-ĜA$_2$×X⌝ ED IIIa-b Girsu *RTC* 1 o. i 3

lugal-ĝe$_{26}$ (a2) **(in most instances identical with lugal-ĝe$_{26}$-ab-e, sagi)**, p. 93 n. 478
lugal-ĝe$_{26}$ sagi ED IIIb/Ukg. ensi$_2$ 1 Girsu *AWAS* 119 o. vi 6
lugal-ĝe$_{26}$ sagi ED IIIb/Ukg. lugal 4 Girsu *AWAS* 120 o. vii 1
lugal-ĝe$_{26}$ sagi ED IIIb/[Ukg. lugal 3] Girsu *AWAS* 121 o. vii 5'
lugal-ĝe$_{26}$ sagi ED IIIb/Ukg. lugal 6 Girsu *AWAS* 122 o. vii 14
⌜lugal⌝-ĝe$_{26}$ sagi ED IIIb/Ukg. lugal 1? Girsu *AWAS* 123 o. v 11
lugal-ĝe$_{26}$ ED IIIb Girsu *DCS* 4 o. vi 5
lugal-ĝe$_{26}$ lu$_2$ igi-niĝin$_2$ ED IIIb/Enz. ensi$_2$ 3 Girsu *DP* 1/2 110 o. iii 6
lugal-ĝe$_{26}$ sagi ED IIIb/Enz. ensi$_2$ 4 Girsu *DP* 1/2 111 o. i 3
lugal-ĝe$_{26}$ ED IIIb/X Y 1 Girsu *DP* suppl. 657 o. ii 4
lugal-ĝe$_{26}$ sagi ED IIIb/Ukg. ensi$_2$ 1 Girsu HSS 3 16 o. vi 2
lugal-ĝe$_{26}$ sagi ED IIIb/Ukg. ensi$_2$ 1 Girsu MVN 3 2 o. vii 4
lugal-ĝe$_{26}$ ED IIIb/X Y 6 Girsu Nik 1 61 o. i 7
[lugal-ĝe$_{26}$] sagi ED IIIb/Lug. 6 Girsu D. Charpin, *RA* 71 (1977), p. 97–105 o. vii 4

lugal-ĝe$_{26}$-ab-be$_2$ (a1) 'it was spoken by my lugal' 3.1.1.4, p. 93 n. 478
lugal-ĝe$_{26}$-ab-be$_2$ s. Gu$_2$-[ab$^?$]-ba-[ki$^?$-du$_{10}$$^?$] ED IIIb Girsu J. Bauer, *AoN* 1 (1976) 1 (translit. only) o. ii 7

lugal-ĝe$_{26}$-ab-e (a3) 'it was spoken by my lugal' 3.1.1.4, p. 93, 186
lugal-ĝe$_{26}$-ab-e sagi ED IIIb/Lug. 1 Girsu *DCS* 8 o. iv 2
lugal-ĝe$_{26}$-ab-e sagi ED IIIb/Ukg. lugal 5 Girsu *DP* 1/2 114 o. vii 7
lugal-ĝe$_{26}$-ab-e sagi ED IIIb/Lug. 5 Girsu *DP* 1/2 132 o. v 14
lugal-ĝe$_{26}$-ab-e nitaḫ ED IIIb/X ensi$_2$ 3 Girsu *DP* 2/1 176 o. iv 3
lugal-ĝe$_{26}$-ab-e sagi ED IIIb/Lug. 3 Girsu *DP* suppl. 623 r. ii 2
⌜lugal-ĝe$_{26}$-ab-e⌝ sagi ED IIIb/Lug. 4 Girsu VS 14 173 o. v 4
lugal-ĝe$_{26}$-ab-e ED IIIb/Luzag. ensi$_2$ 6 Umma M. Lambert, *OrAnt* 18 (1979), p. 225–226 (AO 15540) o. i 5

lugal-ĝeštin (a≥2) 'the lugal is (sweet as) wine' 3.1.7.8, p. 169
lugal-ĝeštin ED IIIa-b Adab CUSAS 11 17 r. iii 1
lugal-ĝeštin ED IIIb-ES Adab CUSAS 11 252 o. ii 6
lugal-ĝeštin nagar, lu$_2$ šuku dab$_5$-ba ED IIIb/Ukg. lugal 4 Girsu *DP* 1/2 116 o. i 8
lugal-ĝeštin nagar ED IIIb/Ukg. lugal 4 Girsu *DP* 1/2 117 o. i 13
lugal-ĝeštin nagar ED IIIb/Ukg. lugal [x] Girsu *DP* 1/2 118 o. ii 1
[lugal-ĝeštin] nagar, nitaḫ ED IIIb/Ukg. lugal 2+X Girsu *DP* 1/2 119 o. ii 3
lugal-ĝeštin nagar, saĝ-apin ED IIIb/Ukg. lugal 6 Girsu HSS 3 25 o. i 7
⌜lugal-ĝeštin⌝ ⌜nagar⌝, [s]a[ĝ api]n ED IIIb/Ukg. lugal 3 Girsu HSS 3 26 o. i 7
lugal-ĝeštin [nag]ar ED IIIb/Ukg. lugal 3 Girsu HSS 3 27 o. i 14
lugal-ĝeštin na[g]ar ED IIIb/Ukg. lugal 4 Girsu Nik 1 16 o. ii 1
lugal-ĝeštin nagar ED IIIb/Ukg. lugal 3 Girsu *TSA* 18 o. i 7

lugal-^{ĝiš}ĝeštu-su$_{20}$ (a1) 'the lugal *is wide* of wisdom' 3.1.2, p. 105
lugal-^{ĝiš}ĝeštu-su$_{20}$ ^{d}Sud$_3$-ur-saĝ, ugula ED IIIa Šuruppag *WF* 71 r. v 8'

lugal-ĝeštu$_2$-su$_{20}$ (a2) 'the lugal *is wide* of wisdom' 3.1.2, p. 105

lugal-ĝeštu$_2$-su$_{20}$ f. Lugal-uri$_3$ ED IIIa Šuruppag? MVN 10 82 o. v 3
lugal-ĝeštu$_2$-su$_{20}$ f. Lugal-uri$_3$ ED IIIa Šuruppag? MVN 10 83 o. iv 2
lugal-⸢ĝeštu$_2$⸣-su$_{20}$ ED IIIa Šuruppag *WF* 65 o. iii 9

lugal-ĝeštu$_3$-su$_{13}$ (a1) 'the lugal *is wide* of wisdom' 3.1.2, p. 105
lugal-ĝeštu$_3$-su$_{13}$ ED IIIa-b Isin (?) OIP 104 14 o. ii 14

lugal-ĝidri (a1) 'the lugal (holds?) a sceptre' 3.1.1.3, p. 90
lugal-ĝidri šitim, *be-lu bu-dim*, *in* Umma^{ki} CS Umma CT 50 188 o. i 4

lugal-ĝidri-du$_{10}$ (a2/°1) 'the lugal (of?) the good sceptre' 3.1.1.3, p. 90, 249 n. 1464
lugal-ĝidri-du$_{10}$ lu$_2$ di ED IIIa Šuruppag *TSŠ* 45 r. i 4
lugal-ĝidri-du$_{10}$ MS Adab *TCABI* 157 r. 2
lugal-ĝidri-du$_{10}$ 2 geme$_2$ Lugal-ĝidri-du$_{10}$ CS Adab CUSAS 13 66 r. 4
°lugal-ĝidri-du$_{10}$ CS Unknown CUSAS 13 188 o. 1

lugal-ĝir$_2$ (a2) unkn. mng. 3.1.8, p. 178
lugal-ĝir$_2$ ED IIIb Adab CUSAS 11 52 o. ii 5'
lugal-ĝir$_2$ ED IIIb Girsu CT 50 28 o. v 2
lugal-ĝir$_2$ ED IIIb Girsu VS 25 1 r. ii 2

lugal-Ĝir$_2$-nun (a1) 'the lugal … the Ĝirnun(-road)' 3.1.6.4, p. 158 n. 913
lugal-Ĝir$_2$-nun engar ki-duru$_5$, dab$_5$-ba CS Girsu *DPA* 33 (PUL 38) o. 8

lugal-Ĝir$_2$-nun-ne$_2$ (a≥1) 'the lugal … the Ĝirnun(-road)' 3.1.6.4, p. 158 n. 913
lugal-Ĝir$_2$-nun-ne$_2$ CS/Śkś Girsu CT 50 51 o. 3
lugal-Ĝir$_2$-nun-ne$_2$ CS Girsu *DPA* 4 (PUL 6) o. 4
lugal-Ĝir$_2$-nun-ne$_2$ CS Girsu *DPA* 31 (PUL 23) o. 12
lugal-Ĝir$_2$-nun-ne$_2$ CS Girsu *DPA* 32 (PUL 24) o. 7
lugal-Ĝir$_2$-nun-ne$_2$ CS Girsu ITT 2/1 4416 o. 2
lugal-Ĝir$_2$-[nu]n-ne$_2$ PNN [ir$_{11}$] Lugal-Ĝir$_2$-[nu]n-ne$_2$-me CS Girsu *RTC* 96 o. i 5'
lugal-Ĝir$_2$-nun-ne$_2$ PNN geme$_2$ Lugal-Ĝir$_2$-nun-ne$_2$-me CS Girsu *RTC* 96 r. iii 8
lugal-Ĝir$_2$-nun-ne$_2$ CS Girsu *STTI* 128 r. 4

lugal-ĝiš (a>20) abbreviation of a number of possible readings 3.1.8, p. 139, 178, 236, 237 n. 1423
lugal-ĝiš ED IIIb-ES Adab CUSAS 11 102 o. i 5
⸢lugal-ĝiš⸣ ED IIIb-ES Adab CUSAS 11 159 o. i 4
lugal-⸢ĝiš⸣ ED IIIb-ES Adab CUSAS 11 186 o. iv 5
lugal-ĝiš sagi ED IIIb/Ukg. lugal 4 Girsu *DP* suppl. 563 o. iii 4
lugal-ĝiš ED IIIb Isin BIN 8 66 o. 2
lugal-ĝiš ED IIIb Nippur OSP 1 25 "ii" 10'
lugal-ĝiš ? saĝa ES Unknown BIN 8 36 o. i 2
lugal-ĝiš ES-MS Unknown BIN 8 85 o. 6
lugal-ĝiš ES-MS Unknown (north) MVN 3 29 o. i 5
lugal-ĝiš ES-MS Unknown (north) MVN 3 29 o. ii 4
lugal-ĝiš ES-MS Unknown (north) MVN 3 29 r. i 2
⸢lugal⸣-ĝiš ES-MS Unknown (north) MVN 3 29 r. i 7
⸢lugal-ĝiš⸣ ES Adab *TCABI* 41 o. i 5
lugal-ĝiš ES-MS Isin BIN 8 154 o. ii 2
⸢lugal-ĝiš⸣ maškim MS Adab *TCABI* 79 o. 2
⸢lugal⸣-ĝiš MS Adab *TCABI* 188 o. 3
lugal-ĝiš MS Umma *L'uomo* 33 o. i 12
lugal-ĝiš Lugal-ĝiš Ur-saĝ CS/NS. Isin BIN 8 164 r. 3'
[lugal$^?$]-ĝiš ? CS Adab CUSAS 13 24 o. 12'

lugal-ĝiš   CS   Adab   CUSAS 13   66   o. 3
lugal-⸢ĝiš⸣   CS   Adab   CUSAS 13   96   r. 2
lugal-ĝiš   dub-sar, e[n]si$_2$ A[dab^{ki}]   CS   Adab   R. M. Boehmer, *Fs Moortgat*, p. 42–56   30a, b   i 3
lugal-ĝiš   ensi$_2$ Adab^{ki}-ba   CS/Śkś   Adab   *SIA*   650   o. 5
⸢lugal⸣-ĝiš   šu-i   CS   Adab   *SIA*   699+823   r. 4
lugal-ĝiš   CS   Adab   *SIA*   745   o. 4
lugal-⸢ĝiš⸣   (ensi$_2$)   CS   Adab   *SIA*   815   o. 5
lugal-ĝiš   (ensi$_2$)   CS   Adab   *SIA*   885+1062   o. 1
lu[gal]-ĝiš   CS   Adab   *SIA*   886   o. 4
lugal-ĝiš   [ensi$_2$ A]dab[^{ki}]   CS   Adab   *SIA*   886   r. 2
lugal-ĝiš   s. E$_2$-ki   CS   Isin   *TCVBI*   1-56   o. 11
lugal-ĝiš   nitaḫ, ĝuruš   CS   Girsu   *DPA*   45 (PUL 22)   r. 3
lugal-ĝiš   niĝir   CS   Girsu   ITT 1   1452   o. 2
lugal-ĝiš   *Be*$_6$*-li-*⸢*li*⸣   MS-CS   Isin ?   MAD 4   78   r. 2
lugal-ĝiš   *Be*$_6$*-li-li*   MS-CS   Isin ?   MAD 4   150   r. 6
lugal-ĝiš   s. Ne-saĝ ugula   CS   Isin ?   MAD 4   169   r. 4
lugal-ĝiš   s. A$_2$-kal-le   MS-CS   Nippur   OSP 2   50   r. i 5
[lugal-ĝ]iš   s. Šeš-kur-ra šandan   MS-CS   Nippur   OSP 2   55   r. 2
lugal-ĝiš   s. En-lil$_2$-⸢le⸣ aš[gab]   MS-CS   Nippur   OSP 2   59   o. 12
lugal-ĝiš [šandan]   MS-CS   Nippur   OSP 2   59   r. 5
lugal-ĝiš   šandan   MS-CS   Nippur   OSP 2   61   o. ii 6
lugal-ĝiš   šandan   MS-CS   Nippur   OSP 2   62   r. i 7
lugal-ĝiš   šandan   MS-CS   Nippur   OSP 2   63   o. ii 12
lugal-ĝiš   MS-CS   Nippur   OSP 2   80   o. i 5
lugal-ĝiš   MS-CS   Nippur   OSP 2   81   r. 3
lugal-⸢ĝiš⸣   MS-CS   Nippur   OSP 2   98   o. i 3
lugal-ĝiš   sagi   MS-CS   Nippur   OSP 2   137   o. 6
lugal-ĝiš   sagi   MS-CS   Nippur   OSP 2   138   r. 10
lugal-ĝiš   MS-CS   Nippur   PBS 9   55   o. 1
lugal-ĝiš   MS-CS   Nippur   TMH 5   29   o. i 6’
lugal-ĝiš   b. Ur-lugal   MS-CS   Unknown   B. R. Foster, *JCS* 35 (1983), p. 147–175   11   o. 3
lugal-ĝiš   sagi(ŠU.⸢SILA$_3$⸣.DU$_8$)   MS-CS   Unknown   MesCiv 4   57   o. 7
lugal-ĝiš   MS-CS   Unknown   MesCiv 4   59   r. 5
lugal-ĝiš ? ĝuruš   MS-CS   Unknown   MVN 3   68   o. 3
lugal-ĝiš   Ur-PA Lugal-ĝiš, maškim-še$_3$, mu-da-gi$_4$ MS-CS   Unknown   MVN 3   77   r. 12

lugal-ĝiš-bur$_2$ [(a3)]   ‘the lugal … the *door ornament*’   3.1.6.3, p. 152
lugal-ĝiš-bur$_2$ (lu$_2$ u$_2$-rum, ^{d}Ba-u$_2$)   ED IIIb/Ukg. lugal 6   Girsu   *DP* 1/2   135   o. v 11
lugal-ĝiš-bur$_2$ šu-ku$_6$ ED IIIb/Ukg. ensi$_2$ 1   Girsu   *DP* 2/1   194   r. ii 7
lugal-ĝiš-bur$_2$ šu-ku$_6$ Su$_{11}$-lum-ma   ED IIIb/X Y 3   Girsu   *DP* 2/2   335   o. i 1
lugal-ĝiš-bur$_2$ šu-ku$_6$ ED IIIb/X Y 1   Girsu   *DP* suppl.   637   o. iii 2
lugal-ĝiš-bur$_2$ šu-ku$_6$ a du$_{10}$-ga   ED IIIb/Ukg. ensi$_2$ 1   Girsu   HSS 3   6   r. iii 9
lugal-ĝiš-bur$_2$ šu-ku$_6$ a du$_{10}$-ga   ED IIIb/Ukg. lugal 2   Girsu   *TSA*   20   o. iii 6
lugal-ĝiš-bur$_2$ ED IIIb-ES   Ur   UE 2   pl. 205 no. 171   1

lugal-ĝiš-š[U$^?$] [(a1)]   unkn. mng.   3.1.8, p. 178
lugal-ĝiš-š[U$^?$]   CS   Adab   *SIA*   845   o. 2’   A 845

lugal-ḫa-ma [(a2)]   ‘lord, may (the child survive) for my sake!’   3.1.4.1, p. 121 n. 651
lugal-⸢ḫa$^?$-ma$^?$⸣ ? *I*$_3$*-li*$_2$ lu$_2$ Lugal-⸢ḫa$^?$-ma$^?$⸣   CS   Girsu   *RTC*   95   r. 9
lugal-ḫa-ma   ni-is-⸢ku⸣, h. Nin-šer$_7$-z[i]   CS   Nippur ?   BIN 8   177   o. 3

lugal-ḫa-ma-ti (a3) ‘lord, may (the child) survive for my sake!’ 3.1.4.1, p. 121, 254 n. 1493
lugal-ḫa-ma-ti IB ED IIIb Adab OIP 14 62 o. i 5
lugal-[ḫa$^{?}$]-ma-t[i] ? ES Adab CUSAS 11 268 o. ii 10
lugal-ḫa-m[a-ti] Lugal-ḫa-m[a-ti], *I$_3$-lum*-[x] ES-MS Nippur OSP 1 136 o. ii 5
lugal-⸢ḫa-ma-ti⸣ MS-CS Mesag MesCiv 4 43 o. 2’

lugal-ḫa-mu-gi$_4$-gi$_4$ (a1) ‘lord, may (the child) return to me!’ 3.1.4.1, p. 121
lugal-ḫa-mu-gi$_4$-gi$_4$ ED IIIb Umma-Zabala MVN 3 3 r. i 2

lugal-ḫar-an-ne$_2$ (a2) ‘the lugal (fills?) the road’ 3.1.8, p. 178
lugal-ḫar-an-ne$_2$ f. Gala CS Girsu ITT 1 1324 o. 3
lugal-ḫar-an-ne$_2$ CS Isin *TCVBI* 1-56 r. 3

lugal-ḫar:an-ne$_2$ (a1) ‘the lugal (fills?) the road’ 3.1.8, p. 178
lugal-ḫar:an-ne$_2$ saĝ Lugal-ḫar:an-ne$_2$-še$_3$, E$_2$-zi-e šu-ba-ti MS-CS Isin ? MVN 3 81 o. 14

lugal-ḪAR-ma-du$_{10}$ (a1) unkn. mng. 3.1.8, p. 178
lugal-ḪAR-ma-du$_{10}$ dub-sar ED IIIa Šuruppag *TSŠ* 14 o. iii 2

°lugal-ḪAR-sa (°1) (phonetic for lugal-ḫur-saĝ ?) 3.1.8, p. 178 w. n. 1069
°lugal-ḪAR-sa ED IIIb Ebla MEE 3 59 o. ii 6

lugal-ḫe$_2$ (a≥14) unkn. mng. 3.1.8, p. 178
lugal-ḫe$_2$ usan$_5$-du$_3$ ED IIIa Šuruppag? *DP* 1/1 38 r. ii 3
⸢lugal⸣-ḫe$_2$ engar ^{d}Maḫ ED IIIb-ES Adab CUSAS 11 86 o. i 3
lugal-ḫe$_2$ ED IIIb-ES Adab CUSAS 11 117 o. i 3
lugal-ḫe$_2$ ED IIIb-ES Adab CUSAS 11 139 o. i 3
⸢lugal$^{?}$⸣-ḫe$_2$? ED IIIb Adab MVN 3 28 r. iii 12
lugal-ḫe$_2$ gala ED IIIb Girsu J. Marzahn & H. Neumann, *AoF* 22 (1995), p. 111f. (VAT 6121) o. iv 7’
lugal-ḫe$_2$ ED IIIb/X ensi$_2$? 3 Girsu BIN 8 349 o. v 3
lugal-ḫe$_2$ aga$_3$-us$_2$ Ama-diĝir-re$_2$-ne-ka ED IIIb/Lug. 1 Girsu *DP* 2/1 184 o. i 6
lugal-ḫe$_2$ ar$_3$-du$_2$ e$_2$-ša$_3$-ga ED IIIb/Lug. 7 Girsu HSS 3 30 r. i 8
lugal-ḫe$_2$ ⸢ar$_3$⸣-du$_2$ ⸢e$_2$-ša$_3$-ga⸣ ED IIIb/Lug. [ensi$_2$] 3 Girsu *DCS* 6 o. v 10
lugal-ḫe$_2$ muḫaldim ED IIIb/Lug. 5 Girsu *DP* 1/2 132 r. i 10
lugal-ḫe$_2$ [muḫaldim] ED IIIb/Lug. 4 Girsu *DP* 2/1 226 o. vi 8’
lugal-ḫe$_2$ lu$_2$ ti ED IIIb/Ukg. lugal 1 Girsu *DP* suppl. 591 o. v 8
lugal-ḫe$_2$ nu-kiri$_6$ ED IIIb/X Y 5 Girsu *DP* suppl. 593 o. v 5
lugal-ḫe$_2$ muḫaldim ED IIIb/Ukg. lugal 6 Girsu HSS 3 18 o. v 17
lugal-ḫe$_2$ muḫaldim ED IIIb/Ukg. ensi$_2$ 1 Girsu MVN 3 2 o. vii 11
lugal-ḫe$_2$ gala ED IIIb/X Y 5 Girsu Nik 1 111 o. i 4
lugal-ḫe$_2$ ar$_3$-du$_2$ e$_2$-ša$_3$-ga-ke$_4$ ED IIIb/(Lug.) Y 4 Girsu Nik 1 157 r. i 1
lugal-ḫe$_2$ ar$_3$-du$_2$ e$_2$-ša$_3$-ga-ke$_4$ ED IIIb/X Y 5 Girsu Nik 1 197 o. i 2
lugal-ḫe$_2$ ED IIIb/Lug. 6 Girsu D. Charpin, *RA* 71 (1977), p. 97–105 o. vii 11
lugal-ḫe$_2$ muḫaldim ED IIIb/[Ukg. lugal 6] Girsu *TSA* 17 o. 5’
lugal-ḫe$_2$ ar$_3$-du$_2$ e$_2$-ša$_3$-ga ED IIIb/Ukg. ensi$_2$ 1 Girsu VS 14 9 r. ii 1
lugal-ḫe$_2$ muḫaldim ED IIIb/Lug. 4 Girsu VS 14 173 o. vi 11
lugal-ḫe$_2$ ED IIIb/Luzag. (?) 7 Umma-Zabala BIN 8 55 o. i 1
lugal-ḫe$_2$ ED IIIb/Luzag. (?) 7 Umma-Zabala BIN 8 55 o. ii 5
lugal-ḫe$_2$ ED IIIb Umma-Zabala CUSAS 14 157 o. i 2
lugal-ḫe$_2$ ED IIIb/X Y 29 Umma-Zabala M. Powell, *HUCA* 49 (1978), p. 1–58 6 o. i 5
lugal-[ḫ]e$_2$? lu$_2$-eš$_2$-gid$_2$ ED IIIb Zabala BIN 8 76 o. ii 3
lugal-ḫe$_2$ ED IIIb Zabala *TCVBI* 1-4 o. iv 3*
lu[gal]-⸢ḫe$_2$⸣ ED IIIb Zabala *TCVBI* 1-4 r. i 4
lugal-ḫe$_2$ ES Adab CUSAS 11 329 o. 3

lugal-ḫe$_2$ CS Girsu *SCT* 1 o. i 8
lugal-ḫe$_2$ CS Girsu *STTI* 147 o. 10
lugal-ḫe$_2$? CS Adab *SIA* 658 o. 3
lugal-ḫ[e$_2^?$] f. Ur-lugal CS Girsu MVN 3 113 o. iii 14
lugal-ḫe$_2$ engar CS Girsu *RTC* 143 r. 4
lugal-ḫe$_2$ s. DU-DU CS Umma *USP* 47 r. ii 8

lugal-ḫe$_2$-a $^{(a1)}$ unkn. mng. 3.1.8, p. 178
lugal-ḫe$_2$-a MS-CS Nippur OSP 2 143 r. 6

lugal-ḫe$_2$-du$_7$ $^{(a1)}$ 'the lugal is befitting (of DN/GN?)' 3.1.6.2, p. 143
lugal-ḫe$_2$-du$_7$ gur[uš] CS Girsu ITT 1 1365 o. 3

lugal-ḫe$_2$-ĝal$_2$ $^{(a6/°1)}$ 'the lugal … abundance' 3.1.5.3, p. 134
lugal-ḫe$_2$-ĝal$_2$ engar ED IIIa Šuruppag *TSŠ* 49 o. iii 5
lugal-ḫe$_2$-ĝal$_2$ IB ED IIIa Šuruppag *TSŠ* 115 o. iv 1
lugal-ḫe$_2$-ĝal$_2$ ED IIIa Šuruppag *TSŠ* 158 o. iii 5
lugal-ḫe$_2$-ĝal$_2$ ED IIIa Šuruppag *TSŠ* 158 o. v 6
lugal-ḫe$_2$-ĝal$_2$ IB ED IIIa Šuruppag *WF* 6 o. iv 9
lugal-ḫe$_2$-ĝal$_2$ ED IIIa Šuruppag *WF* 34 o. ii 8
lugal-ḫe$_2$-ĝal$_2$ ED IIIa Šuruppag *WF* 41 o. iv 15 (?)
lugal-ḫe$_2$-[ĝal$_2$] Ur-nin, šitim ED IIIa Šuruppag *WF* 77 o. vi 13
lugal-ḫe$_2$-ĝal$_2$ ED IIIb Adab CUSAS 11 50 o. iv 1
lugal-ḫe$_2$-ĝal$_2$ ED IIIb Adab CUSAS 11 55 o. iii 1
lugal-ḫe$_2$-ĝal$_2$ ED IIIb Adab CUSAS 11 59 o. i 6
lugal-ḫe$_2$:ĝal$_2$ [umbisaĝ] ED IIIb Ebla ARET 5 20 r. iv 1
lugal-ḫe$_2$-ĝal$_2$ umbisaĝ ED IIIb Ebla ARET 5 21 r. vii 1'
°lugal-ḫe$_2$-ĝal$_2$ ED IIIb Ebla ARET 5 25 o. ii 2
lu[gal]-ḫe$_2$-ĝal$_2$ ED IIIb Nippur TMH 5 70 o. ii 3
lugal-ḫe$_2$-ĝal$_2$ ED IIIb Nippur TMH 5 79 o. i 5
lugal-ḫe$_2$-ĝal$_2$ šita uru ES Adab *TCABI* 51 o. i 2

lugal-ḫe$_2$-ĝal$_2$-su$_3$ $^{(a5)}$ 'the lugal (is one who) extends abundance' 3.1.5.3, p. 134–135, 251 n. 1477
lugal-ḫe$_2$-ĝal$_2$-su$_3$ [umbisa]ĝ, lu$_2$ dub-ba šu ĝal$_2$-la ED IIIa Unknown *RIAA* 44 r. i 5
lugal-ḫe$_2$-ĝal$_2$-su$_3$ f. Amar-^{d}Saman$_3$, gala ED IIIb/Ukg. lugal 4 Girsu BIN 8 363 o. ii 2
lugal-ḫe$_2$-ĝal$_2$-su$_3$ dub-sar maḫ ED IIIb/En. I ensi$_2$ Girsu OIP 104 23 o. x 3
lugal-ḫe$_2$-ĝal$_2$-su$_3$ dub-sar maḫ ED IIIb/En. I ensi$_2$ 4 Lagaš BiMes 3 10 o. v 2'
lugal-ḫe$_2$-ĝal$_2$-su$_3$ ED IIIb/Meannedu 5 Umma T. Ozaki, *JAC* 23 (2008), p. 55–64 1 o. iii 6
lugal-ḫe$_2$-ĝal$_2$-su$_3$ šitim ED IIIb Umma-Zabala MVN 3 3 o. vi 4

lugal-ḫe$_2$-ĝal$_2$-su$_{20}$ $^{(a1)}$ 'the lugal (is one who) extends abundance' 3.1.5.3, p. 135
lugal-ḫe$_2$-ĝal$_2$-su$_{20}$ šitim ED IIIa Šuruppag *WF* 87 o. iii 3

lugal-ḫe$_2$-ĝal$_2$-su$_x$(TAG) $^{(a1)}$ 'the lugal (is one who) extends abundance' 3.1.5.3, p. 135
lugal-ḫe$_2$-ĝal$_2$-su$_x$ ED IIIb/X Y 28 Umma-Zabala *SAKF* 3 o. iv 4

lugal-ḫi-li $^{(a\geq6)}$ 'the lugal is pleasant' 3.1.7.8, p. 170 w. n. 995
lugal-ḫi-li nimgir-us$_2$ ED IIIb/Enz. ensi$_2$ X Girsu *RTC* 17 r. ii 2
lugal-ḫi-li ES Adab *TCABI* 40 r. 1
lugal-ḫi-li CS Adab *SIA* 632 o. i 4
lugal-ḫi-li CS Adab *SIA* 800+1011 o. 8
[lugal]-ḫi-li ugula ^{giš}[g]⸢u⸣-za-la$_2$ CS Adab *SIA* 646 o. ii 8'
lugal-ḫi-li CS-LS? Adab OIP 14 170 r. 2
lugal-ḫi-li b. An-za$_3$ CS Girsu ITT 1 1370 r. 1
lu[gal]-ḫi-li s. (?) [G]u$_3$-de$_2$-a CS Girsu ITT 5 6680 o. 3

lugal-ḫi-li CS Girsu CT 50 107 o. 13
lugal-ḫi-li dub-sar CS Girsu *RTC* 98 r. 5
lugal-ḫi-li f. Lugal-u$_2$ CS Umma *USP* 46 o. 23

°lugal-ḪI-zi (°1) (phonetic for lugal-šer$_7$-zi (šar$_2$) ? Compare nu-gal-ḪI-zi) 3.1.8, p. 178, w. n. 1070, 183 n. 1135
°lugal-ḪI-zi ED IIIb Ebla ARET 5 25 r. ii 1

lugal-ḪU-x (a1) unkn. mng. 3.1.8, p. 178
lugal-ḪU-x ED IIIb/Luzag. ensi$_2$ 7 Umma-Zabala M. deJ. Ellis, *JCS* 31 (1979), p. 30–55 6 r. ii 8

lugal-ḫur-saĝ (a≥3) 'the lugal is a *mountain*' 3.1.7.6, p. 167, 178 n. 1069, 210
lugal-ḫur-saĝ ED IIIb-ES Adab *TCABI* 14 o. i 3
lugal-ḫur-saĝ ED IIIb-ES Adab *TCABI* 14 o. ii 4
lugal-ḫur-saĝ saĝa ^{d}⌜En-lil$_2$$^{?}$⌝ Nippur ED IIIb A. Goetze, *JCS* 23 (1970), p. 51 (7N-136+155) 1
lugal-ḫur-saĝ ED IIIb/Luzag. ensi$_2$ X ? Umma MesCiv 4 3 r. i 2
lugal-ḫur-saĝ Lugal-ildum$_3$, Lugal-ḫur-saĝ ED IIIb Umma-Zabala ? BIN 8 60 o. i 2
lugal-ḫur-saĝ ED IIIb/Luzag. ensi$_2$ 7 Umma-Zabala M. deJ. Ellis, *JCS* 31 (1979), p. 30–55 6 o. iii 2

lugal-i-MU (a1) unkn. mng. 3.1.8, p. 178, 180 n. 1101
lugal-i-MU engar ED IIIa-b Isin (?) OIP 104 14 r. v 15

lugal-i$_3$-bi$_2$ (a1) unkn. mng. 3.1.8, p. 178 w. n. 1072, 214 n. 1368
lugal-i$_3$-bi$_2$ CS Girsu *RTC* 79 o. 2

lugal-i$_3$-kuš$_2$ (a≥1) 'the lugal takes counsel' 3.1.2, p. 107
lugal-i$_3$-kuš$_2$ ED IIIb/X Y 1 Girsu BIN 8 383 o. i 2
lugal-i$_3$-kuš$_2$ ED IIIb/X Y 1 Girsu *CST* 1 r. ii 2
lugal-i$_3$-kuš$_2$ ED IIIb Girsu CT 50 30 r. ii 6
lugal-i$_3$-kuš$_2^!$(SAĜ) ED IIIb Girsu OIP 14 57 r. ii 3

lugal-i$_3$-nun (a≥9) 'the lugal (is) excellent oil' 3.1.7.8, p. 169–170, 210
lugal-i$_3$-nun dub-sar ED IIIa Šuruppag M. Lambert, *Gs Unger*, p. 27–49 1 r. i 9
lugal-i$_3$-nun sipa anše ED IIIa Šuruppag *WF* 16 r. i 2
lugal-i$_3$-nun ED IIIb-ES Adab CUSAS 11 186 o. v 13
lugal-i$_3$-nun nitaḫ ED IIIb/Ukg. lugal 4 Girsu *AWAS* 120 r. iv 13
lugal-i$_3$-nun ED IIIb Girsu BIN 8 382 o. i 3'
lugal-i$_3$-nun nitaḫ ED IIIb Girsu *DCS* 5 r. iii 9'
lugal-i$_3$-nun nitaḫ ED IIIb/Ukg. lugal 2 Girsu *DP* 1/2 113 r. iv 1
lugal-i$_3$-nun ri-mušen ED IIIb Girsu *DP* suppl. 555 o. ii 4'
lugal-i$_3$-nun nitaḫ ED IIIb/Ukg. lugal 6 Girsu HSS 3 18 r. ii 6
lugal-i$_3$-nun ED IIIb Girsu ITT 5 9201 o. i 6
lugal-i$_3$-nun ED IIIb Girsu ITT 5 9208 r. (?) ii 4
lugal-i$_3$-nun gab$_2$-ra ED IIIb/Ukg. ensi$_2$ 1 Girsu MVN 3 2 r. iv 2
lugal-i$_3$-nun ED IIIb/Ukg. ensi$_2$ 1(+X?) Girsu Nik 1 9 r. ii 9
lugal-i$_3$-nun ri-mušen ED IIIb/X Y 4 Girsu Nik 1 86 o. i 2
lugal-i$_3$-nun gab$_2$-ra ED IIIb/Lug. 6 Girsu D. Charpin, *RA* 71 (1977), p. 97–105 r. iii 11
lugal-i$_3$-nun gab$_2$-ra ED IIIb/Lug. 6 Girsu VS 25 11 r. ii 13
lugal-i$_3$-nun ED IIIb Lagaš BiMes 3 12 o. ii' 1
lugal-i$_3$-nun dub-sar MS-CS Adab OIP 14 114 o. 5
lugal-i$_3$-nun MS-CS Isin ? Nippur ? Adab ? A. Goetze, *JCS* 20 (1968), p. 126–127 r. 3
lu[gal]-i$_3$-nun CS Nippur PBS 9 77 o. ii 13'
lugal-i$_3$-nun MS-CS Nippur TMH 5 29 o. i 9'

lugal-I$_7$-da $^{(a1)}$ 'the lugal in/of the river' 3.1.8, p. 178 w. n. 1073
lugal-I$_7$-da f. ^{d}En-l[il$_2$-(x$^?$)] ED IIIb Girsu Nik 1 102 o. iii 2

lu:gal-^{d}I$_7$-ĝu$_{10}$ $^{(a1)}$ 'the lugal is my river' 3.1.3.1, p. 110 n. 582
lu:gal-^{d}I$_7$-ĝu$_{10}$ ED IIIb Nippur TMH 5 69 o. i 4

lugal-I$_7$-ĝu$_{10}$ $^{(a2)}$ 'the lugal is my river' 3.1.3.1, p. 109–110
lugal-I$_7$-ĝu$_{10}$ ED IIIb Nippur OSP 1 143 o. i 4
lugal-I$_7$-ĝu$_{10}$ s. Lugal-ezem, nu-kiri$_6$ ED IIIb Nippur TMH 5 6 o. i 7

lugal-I$_7$-maḫ $^{(a1)}$ 'the lugal makes the river *magnificent* (?)' 3.1.5.3, p. 132, 184
lugal-I$_7^!$(A)-maḫ lu$_2$ e$_2$-nam ED IIIb/Ukg. lugal 5 Girsu *DP* 1/2 136 o. iv 5
lugal-I$_7$-maḫ lu$_2$ e$_2$-nam ED IIIb/Ukg. lugal 5 Girsu Nik 1 3 o. iv 1

lugal-^{d}I$_7$-si $^{(a1)}$ 'the lugal is just right for the river' 3.1.3.1, p. 117–118, 254 n. 1492
lugal-^{d}I$_7$-si ED IIIb Nippur TMH 5 102 o. ii 2

lugal-ib-x-GAN ? $^{(a1)}$ unkn. mng. 3.1.8, p. 178 w. n. 1074
lugal-ib-x-GAN ? ED I-II Ur UET 2 297 o. i 5'

lugal-ig-gal $^{(a3)}$ 'the lugal is a great door' 3.1.3.3, p. 116, 251 n. 1477
lugal-ig-gal lu$_2$ luĝa$_x$(BI×NIĜ$_2$) ED IIIb/X Y 5 Girsu Nik 1 94 o. i 2
lugal-ig-gal ED IIIb/Enz. 3 Girsu VS 25 61 r. ii 3
lugal-ig-gal aman(MUNU$_4$.SAR) ED IIIb/Enz. 3 Girsu VS 25 61 r. iii 2
lugal-ig-gal CS Girsu *RTC* 111 r. 1
lugal-ig-[gal$^?$] CS Girsu *RTC* 125 r. i 6

lugal-igi $^{(a\geq 7)}$ unkn. mng. 3.1.8, p. 178
lugal-igi ED IIIb/Ukg. lugal 2 Girsu *DP* 1/2 120 r. iii 9
lugal-igi$^?$ Ur-šul, Lugal-igi$^?$, ar$_3$-du$_2$-ni i$_3$-tuš ED IIIb/Ukg. lugal 4 Girsu *DP* 1/2 138 o. v 5
lugal-igi šu-ku$_6$ Su$_{11}$-lum-ma ED IIIb/X Y 3 Girsu *DP* 2/2 335 o. ii 2
lugal-igi simug, lu$_2$ Ĝiš-ša$_3$ simug ED IIIb Umma-Zabala M. Powell, *HUCA* 49 (1978), p. 1–58 18 r. i 5
lugal-igi MS-CS Adab ? BIN 8 242 o. 7
lugal-igi CS Adab *SIA* 772 o. 5'
lugal-igi MS Adab *TCABI* 116 o. 4
lugal-igi sipa ud$_5$ MS Adab *TCABI* 117 r. 3
lugal-igi CS Nippur OSP 2 13 o. 9
lugal-igi OAkk Ur M. Civil, *AulaOr* 6 (1988), 105 (U 4395, translit. only) o. 5
lugal-⸢igi⸣-[x x] CS Umma MVN 15 379 o. 5'
lugal-igi-[x]-⸢se$_3$⸣ ? MS-CS Ur UET 2 suppl. 48 o. ii 9

lugal-igi-An-na-ke$_4$-su $^{(a2)}$ 'the lugal is one known by the eye of heaven' 3.1.6.2, p. 142, 185
lugal-igi-An-na-ke$_4$-su šu-ku$_6$ a du$_{10}$-ga ED IIIb Ukg. lugal 6 Girsu DP 1/2 135 r. i 5
lugal-igi-An-na-ke$_4$-su s. Lugal-al-sa$_6$ ED IIIb/Ukg. lugal 1 Girsu HSS 3 40 r. iii 17
lugal-igi-An-na-ke$^!$(SU)-su gala-maḫ Gir$_2$-su^{ki}, s. Lugal-al-sa$_6$ ED IIIb/Ukg. lugal 1 Girsu VS 25 70 r. iii 16

lugal-igi-bi $^{(a1)}$ unkn. mng. 3.1.8, p. 178
lugal-igi-bi ED IIIb Girsu *DP* 2/2 321 r. i 5

lugal-igi-ḫuš $^{(a\geq 4)}$ 'the lugal (is) *angry-looking*' 3.1.7.2, p. 162, 258 n. 1522
⸢lugal⸣-igi-ḫuš ED IIIb Girsu *RTC* 76 r. i 1
lugal-igi-ḫuš ? CS-LS ? Girsu *RTC* 254 o. ii 17
lugal-igi-ḫuš ? Ambar^{ki}(LAGAB×DIŠ.DIŠ) CS Girsu *SCT* 1 o. ii 2
lugal-igi-ḫuš ? CS Girsu *STTI* 20 o. 6
lugal-igi-ḫuš CS Umma MVN 15 378 o. 6

lugal-igi-ḫuš šabra CS Umma *USP* 61 o. 3

lugal-igi-il$_2$ (a1) ‘the lugal raises (his) eyes’ 3.1.8, p. 178 w. n. 1076
lugal-igi-il$_2$ Na-ri-ri, lu$_2$ Lugal-igi-il$_2$ ED IIIb Nippur TMH 5 23 o. ii 3
lugal-igi-il$_2$ ED IIIb Nippur TMH 5 103 r. 1

lugal-igi-kalam(LAK729)-ma (a1) ‘the lugal is the eye of the land’ 3.1.1.6, p. 102
lugal-igi-kalam-ma ED IIIb Girsu *NFT*, p. 180 (bottom) o. v 2

lugal-igi-ni (a1) unkn. mng. 3.1.8, p. 178
lugal-igi-ni ED IIIb Ur UET 2 suppl. 46 r. i 11

lugal-igi-nim-še$_3$ (a≥1) ‘the lugal (goes) to the highland’ 3.1.3.3, p. 116 w. n. 629
lugal-igi-nim-še$_3$ ED IIIb Umma-Zabala CUSAS 14 4 o. v 3
lugal-igi-nim-še$_3$ ED IIIb/Luzag. ensi$_2$ 7 Umma-Zabala M. deJ. Ellis, *JCS* 31 (1979), p. 30–55 7 r. ii 11
lugal-igi-nim-še$_3$ ED IIIb Zabala BIN 8 75 o. 2

lugal-igi-nim-še$_{3\text{-}90^\circ}$ (a1) ‘the lugal (goes) to the highland’ 3.1.3.3, p. 116 w. n. 629
lugal-⌜igi⌝-nim-še$_{3\text{-}90^\circ}$ ED IIIb/Il$_2$ ensi$_2$ Zabala *TCVBI* 1-19 o. 3

lugal-igi-sa$_6$ (a1) ‘the lugal (is) *friendly-looking*’ 3.1.7.2, p. 162, 258 n. 1522
lugal-igi-sa$_6$ CS Girsu ITT 5 9281 r. 6

lugal-igi-tab (a≥4) ‘the lugal is one who seals off (the land)’ 3.1.3.3, p. 116, 251 n. 1477
lugal-igi-tab ED IIIb/X ensi$_2$? 3 Girsu BIN 8 349 o. v 1
lugal-igi-tab ED IIIb/X Y 6 Girsu *DP* 2/1 153 o. ii 2
lugal-igi-tab šu-i ED IIIb/Dudu saĝa Girsu W. W. Hallo, *OrNS* 42 (1973), p. 228–238 r. ii 4
lugal-igi-tab muḫaldim, maškim-bi ED IIIb/Enz. ensi$_2$ 1 Girsu M. W. G. Schileico, *RA* 11 (1914), p. 61 r. i 1
lugal-igi-tab šabra CS Girsu *STTI* 148 r. ii’ 10’
lugal-igi-tab nar CS Adab CUSAS 13 76 o. 5
lugal-igi-tab CS Adab *SIA* 745 o. 2

lugal-igi-x (x like ĜA$_2$ or ŠE$_{3\text{-}90^\circ}$) ED IIIa-b Unknown *L’uomo* 4 o. i 6

lugal-ildum$_3$ (a≥5) unkn. mng. 3.1.8, p. 178
lugal-ildum$_3$ ED IIIb-ES Adab CUSAS 11 98 o. iv 2’
lugal-ildum$_3$ lu$_2$-eš$_2$-gid$_2$ ED IIIb Umma-Zabala ? BIN 8 54 o. i 4
lugal-ildum$_3$ Lugal-ildum$_3$, Lugal-ḫur-saĝ ED IIIb Umma-Zabala ? BIN 8 60 o. i 2
lugal-ildum$_3$ Lugal-ildum$_3$, Ĝiš-ša$_3$ lu$_2$-šim ED IIIb Umma-Zabala ? BIN 8 62 o. ii 1
lu[gal]-ildum$_3$ ugula ED IIIb/Luzag. ensi$_2$ X Umma-Zabala BIN 8 82 o. ii 17
lugal-ildum$_3$ lu$_2$-⌜eš$_2$⌝-gid$_2$? ED IIIb/Luzag. ensi$_2$ X Umma-Zabala BIN 8 82 r. ii 8 ?
lugal-ildum$_3$ lu$_2$-eš$_2$-⌜gid$_2$⌝ ED IIIb/Luzag. ensi$_2$ 7 Umma-Zabala BIN 8 86 o. v 14
lugal-ildum$_3$ lu$_2$-eš$_2$-gid$_2$ ED IIIb Umma-Zabala BIN 8 90 o. i 6
lugal-ildum$_3$!(NAGAR.MUNU$_4$) Ur-saĝ, lugal aša$_5$ ED IIIb Umma-Zabala ? BIN 8 114 r. (!) i 10
lugal-ildum$_3$ ED IIIb Umma-Zabala CUSAS 14 4 o. iii 1
lugal-⌜ildum$_3$⌝ ED IIIb Umma-Zabala CUSAS 14 4 o. iv 4
lugal-ildum$_3$ ED IIIb Umma-Zabala CUSAS 14 4 r. iii 7
⌜lugal⌝-ildum$_3$ ED IIIb Umma-Zabala CUSAS 14 142 o. ii 6
lugal-ildum$_3$ ED IIIb Umma-Zabala CUSAS 14 270 o. ii 2
lugal-ildum$_3$ nagar-gal ED IIIb/Luzag. ensi$_2$ [x] Umma-Zabala J. A. Brinkman, *Fs Kramer*, pl. III*-V* (W 2/7) o. i 10’
lugal-ildum$_3$ lu$_2$-eš$_2$-gid$_2$ ED IIIb/Luzag. ensi$_2$ [x] Umma-Zabala J. A. Brinkman, *Fs Kramer*, pl. III*-V* (W 2/7) o. iii 3’

lugal-ildum$_3$ lu$_2$-eš$_2$-gid$_2$ ED IIIb/Luzag. ensi$_2$ [x] Umma-Zabala J. A. Brinkman, *Fs Kramer*, pl. III*-V* (W 2/7) o. iii 11’
lugal-ildum$_3$ ED IIIb/Luzag. Y 7 Umma-Zabala M. Powell, *HUCA* 49 (1978), p. 1–58 1 o. ii 6
lugal-ildum$_3$ ED IIIb/Luzag. Y 7 Umma-Zabala M. Powell, *HUCA* 49 (1978), p. 1–58 1 o. v 4
⌜lugal⌝-ildum$_3$ ED IIIb/X Y 8 Umma-Zabala M. Powell, *HUCA* 49 (1978), p. 1–58 5 o. i 2’
lugal-ildum$_3$ [l]u$_2$-eš$_2$-gid$_2$ ED IIIb Umma-Zabala M. Powell, *HUCA* 49 (1978), p. 1–58 9 o. i 5
lu[gal]-ildum$_3$ lu$_2$-eš$_2$-gid$_2$ ED IIIb Umma-Zabala M. Powell, *HUCA* 49 (1978), p. 1–58 24 “r.” ii 1
lugal-ildum$_3$ ED IIIb/Luzag. ensi$_2$ 7 Umma-Zabala M. deJ. Ellis, *JCS* 31 (1979), p. 30–55 6 o. i 4
lugal-ildum$_3$ lu$_2$-eš$_2$-gid$_2$ ED IIIb/Luzag. ensi$_2$ 7 Umma-Zabala M. deJ. Ellis, *JCS* 31 (1979), p. 30–55 6 o. i 11
lugal-ildum$_3$ lu$_2$-eš$_2$-gid$_2$ ED IIIb/Luzag. ensi$_2$ 7 Umma-Zabala M. deJ. Ellis, *JCS* 31 (1979), p. 30–55 6 o. ii 14
lugal-ildum$_3$ lu$_2$-eš$_2$-gid$_2$ ED IIIb/Luzag. ensi$_2$ 7 Umma-Zabala M. deJ. Ellis, *JCS* 31 (1979), p. 30–55 6 o. iii 10
lugal-ildum$_3$ lu$_2$-eš$_2$-gid$_2$ ED IIIb/Luzag. ensi$_2$ 7 Umma-Zabala M. deJ. Ellis, *JCS* 31 (1979), p. 30–55 6 o. iii 15
lugal-ildum$_3$ lu$_2$-eš$_2$-gid$_2$ ED IIIb/Luzag. ensi$_2$ 7 Umma-Zabala M. deJ. Ellis, *JCS* 31 (1979), p. 30–55 6 o. iv 13
lugal-ildum$_3$ lu$_2$-eš$_2$-gid$_2$ ED IIIb/Luzag. ensi$_2$ 7 Umma-Zabala M. deJ. Ellis, *JCS* 31 (1979), p. 30–55 6 o. v 15
lugal-ildum$_3$ lu$_2$-eš$_2$-gid$_2$ ED IIIb/Luzag. ensi$_2$ 7 Umma-Zabala M. deJ. Ellis, *JCS* 31 (1979), p. 30–55 7 o. ii 1
lugal-ildum$_3$ lu$_2$-eš$_2$-gid$_2$ ED IIIb/Luzag. ensi$_2$ 7 Umma-Zabala M. deJ. Ellis, *JCS* 31 (1979), p. 30–55 7 o. ii 4
lugal-ildum$_3$ lu$_2$-eš$_2$-gid$_2$ ED IIIb/Luzag. ensi$_2$ 7 Umma-Zabala M. deJ. Ellis, *JCS* 31 (1979), p. 30–55 7 o. iv 11
lugal-ildum$_3$ ED IIIb Umma-Zabala MVN 3 3 o. viii 14
lugal-ildum$_3$ ED IIIb Zabala BIN 8 74 o. 4
lugal-ildum$_3$ um-mi-a ED IIIb/Il$_2$ ensi$_2$ Zabala *TCVBI* 1-1 r. i 2
lugal-ildum$_3$ ES Umma or Zabala *TCVBI* 1-50 o. 5
lugal-ildum$_3$ ES-MS Umma-Zabala ? BIN 8 25 o. ii 4

lugal-ildum$_3$-e (a2) unkn. mng. 3.1.8, p. 178
lugal-ildum$_3$-e ĝuruš, ir$_3$ dub-sar-ne ES-MS Umma *CHÉU* 54 o. ii 7
lugal-ildum$_3$-e šabra MS-CS Umma BIN 8 287 o. 2

lugal-IM (a5) unkn. mng. 3.1.8, p. 178–179
lugal-IM DUN-a ED IIIb-ES Adab CUSAS 11 161 o. 2
lugal-IM ugula-⌜ni⌝ ES-MS Umma BIN 8 314 o. 7
lugal-IM CS Adab *SIA* 890 o. 5 A 890
lugal-IM CS Girsu *STTI* 115 r. 2
lugal-IM f. E$_2$-zi MS-CS Isin ? MVN 3 81 r. 16

lugal-im-nun-ne$_2$ (a1) ‘the lugal … the border (of the) field’ 3.1.5.3, p. 133
lugal-im-nun-ne$_2$ MS Unknown F. Vukosavović, *JAC* 23 (2008), p. 37–54 5 o. i 4

lugal-IM-ru (a1) unkn. mng. 3.1.8, p. 179 w. n. 1078
⌜lugal-IM-ru⌝ ED IIIa-b Marada ? *AAICAB* 1/1 (Ashm 1924-467) o. ii 1

lugal-IM-ru-a (a1) unkn. mng. 3.1.8, p. 179 w. n. 1079
lugal-IM-ru-a azlag$_7$ ED IIIb Nippur OSP 1 66 o. 2

lugal-IM-SILA$_3$? (a1) unkn. mng. 3.1.8, p. 179
lugal-IM-SILA$_3^?$ f. I$_7$-pa-e$_3$ CS Umma *USP* 45 r. ii 4

lugal-inim (identical with lugal-inim-gi-na sagi), p. 131 n. 471
lugal-inim sagi ED IIIb/Ukg. lugal 5? Girsu VS 14 183 o. ii 4

lugal-inim (identical with lugal-inim-gi-na sipa maš), p. 131 n. 471
lugal-inim sipa maš ED IIIb/X Y 3 Girsu *DP* 1/2 104 o. ii 4

°lugal-inim (identical with lugal-inim-ma-ni, GIN$_2$.TUKU), p. 93 n. 474
°lugal-inim GIN$_2$.⸢ḪUB$_2$⸣ ED IIIa Šuruppag *SF* 29 r. i 11
°[lugal]-inim GIN$_2$.Ḫ[UB$_2$] ED IIIa Šuruppag *SF* 44 o. ii 1
°lugal-inim GIN$_2$.TUKU ED IIIb Nippur PBS 9 64 o. ii 5

lugal-inim-du$_{10}$ (a2) 'the lugal … a good utterance' 3.1.1.4, p. 93 n. 475
lugal-inim-du$_{10}$ ES-MS Nippur OSP 1 108 o. 2
lugal-inim-du$_{10}$ CS-LS ? Girsu *RTC* 192 o. 3
lugal-inim-du$_{10}$ CS-LS ? Girsu *RTC* 193 o. 3

lugal-inim-du$_{10}$-ga (a3) 'the lugal … a good utterance' 3.1.1.4, p. 93
lugal-inim-du$_{10}$-ga ED IIIb-ES Adab *TCABI* 15 o. iii 5
lugal-inim-du$_{10}$-ga ED IIIb-ES Adab *TCABI* 15 r. ii 4
lugal-inim-du$_{10}$-ga ED IIIb-ES Adab *TCABI* 15 r. ii 6
lugal-inim-du$_{10}$-ga uri$_x$ ED IIIb-ES Nippur TMH 5 5 o. 4
lugal-inim-du$_{10}$-ga MS Unknown F. Vukosavović, *JAC* 23 (2008), p. 37–54 5 o. ii 6

lugal-inim-du$_{10}$.KI (a1) (compare the previous two writings) 3.1.1.4, p. 93 n. 475
lugal-inim-du$_{10}$.KI ugula (?) ED IIIa Adab CUSAS 11 6 o. ii 4

lugal-inim-e (identical with lugal-inim-e-ĝiš-tuku), p. 139 w. n. 777
lugal-inim-e MS-CS Nippur OSP 2 44 o. ii 1
lugal-inim-e MS-CS Nippur OSP 2 44 o. ii 8

lugal-inim-e-ĝiš-tuku (a1) 'the lugal is one who pays attention to words' 3.1.6.1, p. 139
lugal-inim-e-ĝiš-tuku MS-CS Nippur OSP 2 45 o. ii 14
lugal-ini[m-e]-ĝiš-tuku MS-CS Nippur OSP 2 48 o. ii 12
lu[gal]-inim-e-[ĝiš]-tuku MS-CS Nippur OSP 2 49 o. ii 10

lugal-inim-gi-na (a>12) 'the lugal of permanent word' 3.1.1.4, p. 93
lugal-inim-gi-na umbisaĝ ED IIIa Unknown *RIAA* 44 r. i 7
lugal-inim-gi-na sagi ED IIIb/Ukg. ensi$_2$ 1 Girsu *AWAS* 119 o. vi 9
lugal-inim-gi-na sagi ED IIIb/Ukg. lugal 4 Girsu *AWAS* 120 o. vii 4
lugal-inim-gi-na sagi ED IIIb/[Ukg. lugal 3] Girsu *AWAS* 121 o. vii 8'
lu[gal]-[inim-g]i-na sagi ED IIIb/Ukg. lugal 1? Girsu *AWAS* 123 o. v 14
lugal-inim-gi-na E-ta-⸢e$_{11}$⸣, sipa maš-da, e-da-ti ED IIIb/Ukg. lugal 1? Girsu *AWAS* 123 o. vii 11
lugal-inim-⸢gi⸣-[na] s[agi] ED IIIb Girsu *DCS* 4 o. vi 8
lugal-inim-gi-na sagi ED IIIb/Ukg. lugal 2 Girsu *DP* 1/2 113 o. vii 12
lugal-inim-gi-na lu$_2$ e$_2$-gal ED IIIb/Ukg. lugal 5 Girsu *DP* 1/2 136 o. vi 5
lugal-inim-gi-na ED IIIb/Ukg. lugal 3 Girsu *DP* 2/1 177 r. ii 4
lugal-inim-gi-na sagi ED IIIb/Ukg. ensi$_2$ 1 Girsu HSS 3 16 o. vi 5
lugal-inim-gi-na ED IIIb/Ukg. lugal 4 Girsu HSS 3 28 r. i 1
lugal-inim-gi-na sagi ED IIIb/Ukg. ensi$_2$ 1 Girsu MVN 3 2 o. vii 7
lugal-inim-gi-na lu$_2$ E$_2$-me-lam$_2$-su$_3$ ED IIIb/Ukg. lugal 5 Girsu Nik 1 3 o. vii 10
lugal-inim-gi-na sipa maš ED IIIb/Ukg. ensi$_2$ 1(+X?) Girsu Nik 1 9 r. i 7
lugal-inim-gi-na sipa maš ED IIIb/Lug. 2 Girsu Nik 1 239 o. i 5

[lugal-inim]-⌜gi-na⌝ sagi ED IIIb/Lug. 6 Girsu D. Charpin, *RA* 71 (1977), p. 97–105 o. vii 7
lugal-inim-gi-na ED IIIb/Ukg. lugal 2 Girsu VS 27 13 o. iv 9
lugal-inim-gi-na ED IIIb Nippur TMH 5 130 o. ii 3
lugal-inim-gi-na Maš-pa$_3$-da^{ki} ED IIIb Nippur TMH 5 159 o. ii 5'
lugal-inim-gi-na ED IIIb Nippur OSP 1 33 r. i 2
lugal-inim-gi-na ED IIIb Umma-Zabala CUSAS 14 142 o. ii 8
lugal-inim-gi-na ED IIIb Umma-Zabala CUSAS 14 270 o. ii 4
lugal-inim-gi-na dumu ensi$_2$, maškim-bi ES Adab CUSAS 11 340 o. 3
lugal-inim-gi-na dam-gar$_3$ MS-CS Isin ? MAD 4 150 r. 6
lugal-inim-g[i-na] MS-CS Nippur TMH 5 29 o. ii 1
lugal-inim-gi-na nagar MS-CS Nippur TMH 5 63 o. i 4
lugal-[inim]-gi-⌜na⌝ [da]m-gar$_3$ MS-CS Nippur OSP 2 66 o. 8
lugal-inim-gi-na dam-gar$_3$ MS-CS Nippur OSP 2 67 r. 1
[lugal]-inim-g[i-na] MS-CS Nippur OSP 2 95 r. i 7
lugal-⌜inim⌝-[g]i-na MS-CS Nippur OSP 2 98 o. iii 2
lugal-inim-gi-na f. [x] MS-CS Unknown BIN 8 293 r. ii 1
lugal-inim-gi-na na-gada CS-LS Girsu *DAS* 274 o. iii 7
lugal-inim-gi-na na-gada CS-LS Girsu *DAS* 274 o. iii 8

lugal-inim-ĝa$_2$-ka-bi (a1) 'the lugal is one *who states my case*' 3.1.1.4, p. 93
lugal-inim-ĝa$_2$-ka-bi ED IIIa Šuruppag M. Lambert, *Gs Unger*, p. 27–49 1 r. iii 5

lugal-inim-ĝal$_2$-la (a2) uncertain mng. 3.1.1.4, p. 94, 251 n. 1476
lugal-inim-ĝal$_2$-la ED IIIa Adab CUSAS 11 10 o. v 2
lugal-inim-ĝal$_2$-la s. Lugal-a, b. Ku$_{10}$-ku$_{10}$ ED IIIb/Urz. lugal Isin M. Lambert, *RA* 73 (1979), p. 5–6 o. vi 7

lugal-inim-kalag (a≥2/°1) 'lugal of the strong word' 3.1.1.4, p. 94 n. 481
lugal-inim-kalag engar ED IIIa Šuruppag *TSŠ* 1 o. vii 8
lugal-inim-kalag engar ED IIIa Šuruppag *WF* 7 o. vi 1'
lugal-inim-kalag engar ED IIIa Šuruppag *WF* 26 o. i 3
lugal-inim-kalag ED IIIa Šuruppag *WF* 41 o. v 12'
lugal-inim-kalag ugula ED IIIa Šuruppag *WF* 41 o. vii 4'
lugal-inim-kalag engar, ensi$_2$ ED IIIa Šuruppag *WF* 71 o. v 7
lugal-inim-kalag E$_2$-UD-nu-dib, ugula ED IIIa Šuruppag *WF* 71 r. iv 1
lugal-inim-kalag ED IIIa Šuruppag *WF* 107 o. vi 7
lugal-inim-kalag ? ED IIIa Šuruppag *WF* 113 o. ii 1'
°lugal-inim-kalag ED IIIb Ebla ARET 5 25 o. ii 1
lugal-inim-kalag ED IIIb Umma-Zabala CUSAS 14 142 o. iv 1
lugal-inim-kalag ED IIIb Umma-Zabala CUSAS 14 201 r. i 1

lugal-inim-kalag-ga (a1) 'lugal of the strong word' 3.1.1.4, p. 94, 188
lugal-inim-kalag-ga MS-CS Nippur TMH 5 63 o. i 5

°lugal-inim-ma-ni (°1) 'the word of the lugal (is …)' **(identical with lugal-inim, GIN$_2$.ḪUB$_2$, GIN$_2$.TUKU)**, p. 93 n. 474
°lugal-inim-ma-ni GIN$_2$.TUKU ED IIIb Lagaš BiMes 3 14 r. i 3

lugal-inim-ma-se$_3$-ga (a2) 'the lugal is one instructed (by/of DN)' 3.1.6.2, p. 144–145, 245, 258
lu:gal-inim-ma-se$_3$-ga ED IIIb Nippur OSP 1 45 r. iii 8'
lugal-[in]im-ma-⌜se$_3$⌝-ga ED IIIb Zabala (?) BIN 8 46 o. iv 3

lugal-inim-se$_3$-ga (a1) 'the lugal is one instructed (by/of DN)' 3.1.6.2, p. 145
[lu]gal-inim-se$_3$-ga dub-sar ES-MS Ur UET 2 suppl. 16 r. ii 1'

lugal-inim-še$_3$ $^{(a1)}$ 'lord, (lend your ear) to (my) word' 3.1.6.1, p. 139, 182 n. 1116
lugal-inim-še$_3$ simug ES-MS Isin MAD 4 153 o. ii 10
lugal-in[im-še$_3$$^?$] f. [L]u$_2$-na-nam simug MS Isin ? MAD 4 170 4
lugal-inim-še$_3$ simug CS Unknown (prob. Isin) MAD 4 71 r. 6

lugal-inim-TAR $^{(a1)}$ 'the lugal is one who decides matters' 3.1.3.3, p. 118
lugal-inim-TAR MS-CS Unknown L. J. Delaporte, *ZA* 18 (1904), p. 245–256 6 r. 5

lugal-inim-zi (identical with lugal-inim-zi-da, nu-kiri$_6$)
lugal-inim-zi (zi-KA-lugal) nu-kiri$_6$ ED IIIa Šuruppag *NTSŠ* 444 r. iii 2

lugal-inim-zi (identical with lugal-inim-zi-da, ma$_2$ gal-gal)
lugal-inim-zi (lugal-zi-KA) ma$_2$ gal-gal ED IIIa Šuruppag *TSŠ* 668 o. ii 5'

lugal-inim-zi $^{(a1)}$ 'the lugal (of) permanent word' 3.1.1.4, p. 93 n. 474
lugal-inim-zi ED IIIa Šuruppag *WF* 29 r. ii 6

lugal-inim-zi-da $^{(a\geq10)}$ 'the word (of the) lugal is reliable' 3.1.1.4, p. 93, 94 n. 480
lugal-inim-zi-da (KA-zi-lugal-da), sa$_{12}$-sug$_5$ ED IIIa Šuruppag *NTSŠ* 147 o. iii 4
lu[gal]-⌜inim⌝-zi-da (lu[gal]-⌜KA⌝-da-zi) ma$_2$ gal-gal ED IIIa Šuruppag *NTSŠ* 165 o. v 5'
lugal-inim-zi-da (lugal-KA-zi-da) nu-kiri$_6$ ED IIIa Šuruppag *NTSŠ* 244 o. i 2
lugal-inim-zi-da umbisaĝ (Jestin: E$_2$) ED IIIa Šuruppag *SF* 27+*TSŠ* 327+*NTSŠ* 294 r. iii 2
lugal-inim-[zi$^?$-da$^?$] ED IIIa Šuruppag *TSŠ* 1 o. i 7
lugal-inim-zi-da (zi-da-KA-lugal) lu$_2$ ma$_2$ gal-gal ED IIIa Šuruppag *TSŠ* 1 o. iv 7
lugal-inim-zi-da (KA-da-zi-lugal) ma$_2$ gal-gal ED IIIa Šuruppag *TSŠ* 9+127 o. i 5
lugal-inim-zi-da ED IIIa Šuruppag *TSŠ* 15 o. ii' 7!
lugal-inim-zi-da umbisaĝ Ur-^{d}Sud$_3$ ED IIIa Šuruppag *TSŠ* 46 r. ii 4
lugal-inim-zi-da umbisaĝ dub mu-sar ED IIIa Šuruppag *TSŠ* 79+80 r. ii 1
lugal-inim-zi-da (z[i]-K[A]-lugal-da) gal-niĝir ED IIIa Šuruppag *TSŠ* 101 o. iii 7
lugal-inim-zi-da ED IIIa Šuruppag *TSŠ* 113 o. ii 6
lugal-inim-zi-da ED IIIa Šuruppag *TSŠ* 181 o. iv 14
[lu]gal-[inim]-zi-d[a] ([lu]gal-zi-[KA]-d[a]) engar ED IIIa Šuruppag *TSŠ* 261 o. iii 1'
lugal-inim-zi-da ED IIIa Šuruppag *TSŠ* 456 o. ii 1
lugal-inim-zi-da ED IIIa Šuruppag *TSŠ* 619 o. ii 1
lugal-inim-zi-da niĝir-gal ED IIIa Šuruppag *WF* 4 o. ii 8
lugal-inim-zi-da ED IIIa Šuruppag *WF* 5 o. iii 7
lugal-inim-zi-da niĝir-gal ED IIIa Šuruppag *WF* 6 o. iii 1
lugal-inim-zi-da niĝir-gal ED IIIa Šuruppag *WF* 7 o. i 2'
lugal-inim-zi-da lu$_2$ ma$_2$$^!$ gal-gal ED IIIa Šuruppag *WF* 11 o. i 2
lugal-inim-zi-da ED IIIa Šuruppag *WF* 12 o. i 2
lugal-inim-zi-da niĝir-gal ED IIIa Šuruppag *WF* 15 r. ii 2
lugal-inim-zi-da ma$_2$$^!$ gal-gal ED IIIa Šuruppag *WF* 18 o. vi 9
lugal-inim-zi-da nu-kiri$_6$ ED IIIa Šuruppag *WF* 25 r. i 5
lugal-inim-zi-da ED IIIa Šuruppag *WF* 34 r. iii 1
lugal-inim-zi-da ED IIIa Šuruppag? CT 50 2 r. ii 3
lugal-inim-zi-da [l]u$_2$ gi-di ED IIIa Šuruppag *WF* 65 o. ii 2
lugal-inim-zi-da ED IIIa Šuruppag *WF* 65 r. v 4
lugal-inim-zi-da ED IIIa Šuruppag *WF* 67 r. iii 10
lugal-inim-⌜zi⌝-da ED IIIa Šuruppag *WF* 68 o. viii 2'
lugal-inim-zi-da ED IIIa Šuruppag *WF* 69 o. vii 11
lugal-inim-zi-da Adab^{ki} ED IIIa Šuruppag *WF* 70 o. ii 4
lugal-inim-zi-da munu$_4$(PAP.PAP) ED IIIa Šuruppag *WF* 71 r. vi 11

lugal-inim-zi-da Lu$_2$-lum-ma, Lugal-da-zi-KA, gal-niĝir ED IIIa Šuruppag *WF* 72 r. i 11
lugal-inim-zi-da (KA-zi-lugal-da) Adab^{ki} ED IIIa Šuruppag *WF* 72 r. iii 1
lugal-inim-zi-da Lum-ma, gal-niĝir, lugal-zi-KA-da engar ED IIIa Šuruppag *WF* 77 l.e. 11
lugal-inim-zi-da (lugal-KA-zi-da) engar ED IIIa Šuruppag *WF* 77 r.e. 6
lugal-inim-zi-da Ur-^{d}Sud$_3$, (Lugal-KA-zi-da) engar, lu$_2$ ma$_2$ gal-gal ED IIIa Šuruppag *WF* 78 r. ii 4
lugal-inim-zi-da ED IIIa Šuruppag *WF* 100 o. i 8
lugal-inim-zi-da ED IIIa Šuruppag *WF* 105 o. i 1
lugal-inim-zi-da (lugal-KA-zi-da) gal-niĝir ED IIIa Šuruppag *WF* 121 o. i 3
lugal-inim-zi-da (KA-zi-da-lugal) nu-kiri$_6$ ED IIIa Šuruppag *WF* 124 r. ii 12
lugal-inim-zi-da ED IIIb Girsu ITT 5 9228 o. vi 2'
lugal-inim-⌜zi⌝-da ED IIIb Zabala(?) BIN 8 45 o. ii 2
lugal-inim-zi-da ED IIIb Zabala(?) BIN 8 45 o. iii 5

lugal-inim-zu $^{(a\geq4)}$ 'the lugal is wise (with regards to) word' 3.1.2, p. 106
lugal-⌜inim⌝-zu ad-da [uru$^?$] ED IIIa Šuruppag? G. Visicato & A. Westenholz, *Gs Cagni*, p. 1107–1133 4 (translit. only) r. i 8
lugal-inim-zu AN-nu-me, Lugal-inim-zu ED IIIa Šuruppag *TSŠ* 1 o. viii 7
lugal-⌜inim⌝-zu AN-nu-me, Lugal-⌜inim⌝-zu ED IIIa Šuruppag *TSŠ* 8 o. iii 4
lugal-inim-zu umbisaĝ PAP IM ED IIIa Šuruppag *TSŠ* 46 r. i 16
lugal-inim-zu AN-nu-me, Lugal-inim-zu ED IIIa Šuruppag *TSŠ* 53 o. iv 9
lugal-inim-zu ED IIIa Šuruppag *WF* 3 o. ii 7
lugal-inim-zu ED IIIa Šuruppag *WF* 100 o. viii 12
lugal-inim-zu AN-nu-me, Lugal-inim-zu ED IIIa Šuruppag *WF* 105 r. i 7
lugal-inim-zu ED IIIa Šuruppag *WF* 119 r. iii 3
lugal-inim-zu Ka$_5$-a, Lugal-inim-zu ED IIIb Umma-Zabala MVN 3 3 o. v 11
lugal-inim-zu ED IIIb Umma-Zabala MVN 3 3 r. i 5
lugal-inim-zu ED IIIb Umma-Zabala MVN 3 3 r. iv 5

lugal-ir-nun $^{(a1)}$ 'the lugal (is) excellent smell' (compare lugal-i$_3$-nun) 3.1.7.8, p. 170
lugal-ir-nun nitaḫ ED IIIb/Ukg. lugal 5 Girsu *DP* 1/2 114 r. v 9
lugal-ir-nun nitaḫ ED IIIb/Ukg. lugal 5 Girsu *DP* 1/2 115 r. iv 16
[lugal]-ir-nun nitaḫ ED IIIb/Ukg. lugal 6 Girsu *TSA* 16 r. iii 11

lugal-iti $^{(a2)}$ 'the lugal (is reborn each) month' 3.1.7.10, p. 159, 172 n. 1004
lugal-⌜iti$^?$⌝ f. Šeš-s[a$_6$$^?$] CS Girsu *STTI* 164 o. ii 4
lugal-⌜iti⌝ Lugal-⌜x-x⌝, dumu Ur-mes, ir$_{11}$ Lugal-⌜iti⌝ CS Umma *USP* 50 o. 3

lugal-iti-da $^{(a>35)}$ 'the lugal (is reborn each) month' 3.1.7.10, p. 50 n. 232, 158 n. 915, 159, 172, 215, 231, 235, 236, 253 n. 1489, 259
lugal-iti-da ED IIIb Adab CUSAS 11 52 o. ii 6'
lugal-iti-da ED IIIb-ES Adab CUSAS 11 155 o. i 5
lugal-iti-da ED IIIb-ES Adab CUSAS 11 186 o. v 12
lu:gal-iti-da ED IIIb Nippur OSP 1 25 "ii" 7'
lugal-⌜iti⌝-[da] ED IIIb Nippur OSP 1 92 o. 2
lugal-iti-da ED IIIb Nippur OSP 1 155 o. i' 3'
⌜lugal-iti-da⌝ s. ⌜Ur-^{d}Dumu⌝-[zi] ED IIIb Unknown TIM 9 98 o. 12
lugal-iti-da ES Adab CUSAS 11 272 o. ii 1
lugal-iti-da ES-MS Adab *TCABI* 64 o. iii 6
lugal-⌜iti⌝-da ES-MS Nippur OSP 1 23 o. vii 9
lugal-iti-da ES-MS Nippur OSP 1 131 o. i 5
lugal-iti-da ES-MS Nippur OSP 1 131 r. iii 1

lugal-iti-da Al-lu-lu-ka ES-MS Umma Nik 2 33 o. 6
[lugal-it]i-da MS Adab *TCABI* 80 o. 6’
lugal-⸢iti⸣-da su-si-kam MS Adab *TCABI* 124 r. 4
lugal-iti-da CS Adab CUSAS 13 2 r. 4
lugal-iti-da sipa CS Adab CUSAS 13 12 o. 7
lugal-iti-da pisaĝ-dub CS Adab CUSAS 13 24 r. 8’
lugal-iti-da CS Adab CUSAS 13 32 o. 4
lugal-iti-da dub-sar MS-CS Adab CUSAS 13 43 o. 4
lugal-iti-da CS Adab CUSAS 13 78 r. ii 6’
lugal-iti-da CS Adab CUSAS 13 86 r. i 9
lugal-iti-da CS Adab CUSAS 13 91 r. 10’
lugal-iti-da sukkal MS-CS Adab OIP 14 144 o. 2
lugal-⸢iti$^{!}$(E)-da⸣ dumu URU.KI MS-CS Adab OIP 14 167 o. 7
lugal-iti-da CS Adab *SIA* 652 r. 5
lugal-iti-da lu$_2$ gub-ba CS Adab *SIA* 667 o. 10
lugal-iti-da lu$_2$ gub-ba CS Adab *SIA* 667 o. 11
lugal-iti-da CS Adab *SIA* 677 o. 5
lugal-iti-da ⸢muḫaldim$^{?}$⸣ CS Adab *SIA* 690+876 o. 3’
lugal-iti-da f. Ur-mes MS-CS Adab *SIA* 705 r. i 11
lu[gal]-iti-da sukkal CS Adab *SIA* 712 r. 3
lugal-iti-da CS Adab *SIA* 713 r. 2
lugal-iti-da CS Adab *SIA* 725 o. 5
lugal-iti-da CS Adab *SIA* 772 o. 2’
lugal-iti-da dub-sar CS Adab *SIA* 972 o. 5
lugal-iti-da CS Adab *TCABI* 228 o. 2
lugal-iti-da su-si-kam CS Adab *TCABI* 231 r. 7
lugal-iti-da su-si CS Adab *TCABI* 232 r. 5
lugal-iti-da CS Adab *TCABI* 234 o. 3
lugal-iti-da dub-sar CS Adab *TCABI* 242 o. 4
lugal-iti-da CS/Śkś Girsu CT 50 51 o. 7
lugal-iti-da CS Girsu CT 50 85 r. i 9
lugal-iti-da [l]⸢u$_2$⸣ [x-x] CS Girsu CT 50 106 o. ii 4
lugal-iti-da CS Girsu CT 50 163 o. 2
lugal-iti-da CS Girsu CT 50 182 o. 4
lugal-iti-da CS Girsu CT 50 184 r. 7’
⸢lugal-iti-da⸣ s. En-TAR CS Girsu (?) CUSAS 13 214 r. 2’
lugal-iti-da engar ki-duru$_5$, dab$_5$-ba-me CS Girsu *DPA* 33 (PUL 38) o. 2
lugal-iti-da Diĝir-da-da/*šu* Lugal-iti-da, ĝuruš CS Girsu *DPA* 43 (PUL 47) o. 4
lugal-iti-da ĝuruš, dumu gi$_7$ CS Girsu ITT 1 1182 o. 5
lugal-iti-da baḫar$_2$ zaḫ$_3$, *in* Lag[aš^{ki}], *u-ša-*[*bu*] CS Girsu ITT 1 1256 o. 5’
lugal-iti-da CS Girsu ITT 1 1364 o. 3
lugal-iti-da gur[uš] CS Girsu ITT 1 1365 o. 5
lugal-iti-da ma$_2$-laḫ$_5$ CS Girsu ITT 1 1436 o. 4
lugal-iti-da CS Girsu ITT 2/1 4455 r. 2
lugal-iti-da CS Girsu ITT 5 9270 r. 4’
lugal-iti-da CS Girsu ITT 5 9270 r. 8’
lugal-⸢iti⸣-da CS Girsu ITT 5 9317 o. 4
lugal-iti-da CS Girsu ? MVN 3 34 o. 5
lugal-iti-da CS Girsu *RTC* 103 o. 5
lugal-iti-da CS Girsu *RTC* 139 r. 6
lugal-iti-da s. Ur-^{d}IM CS Girsu *RTC* 142 o. ii 7
lugal-iti-da [l]u$_2$ Unug^{ki} CS Girsu *RTC* 248 o. 3

lugal-iti-[da] CS Girsu *STTI* 16 r. 5
lugal-iti-da CS Girsu *STTI* 31 o. i 4’
lugal-iti-da CS Girsu *STTI* 72 o. 4’
lugal-iti-da CS Girsu *STTI* 103 r. 5’
lugal-iti-da CS Girsu *STTI* 160 r. 2
lugal-iti-da [s. (?)] Ur-^{d}Iškur CS Girsu *STTI* 180 o. i’ 5
lugal-iti-da MS-CS Isin ? MAD 4 150 o. 4
lugal-iti-da Lugal-iti-da, *Be$_6$-li-li* MS-CS Isin ? MAD 4 155 r. 6
lugal-iti-[da] dub-sar MS-CS Kiš MAD 5 31 o. 2’
lugal-iti-da ? MS-CS Mesag BIN 8 137 o. 2
lugal-iti-da sipa eme$_4$ CS Mesag BIN 8 142 o. 10
lugal-iti-da b. Ur-mes, ⸢aman⸣([MUNU$_4$].S[AR]) MS-CS Mesag BIN 8 148 o. i 9’
lugal-iti-da aman(MUNU$_4$.SAR) CS Mesag BIN 8 152 o. iii 7
lugal-iti-da CS Mesag BIN 8 216 o. 4
lugal-iti-da MS-CS Mesag BIN 8 226 r. 2
lugal-iti-da MS-CS Mesag BIN 8 230 o. 3
lugal-iti-da s. ⸢Az⸣ MS-CS Mesag BIN 8 243 o. 10
lugal-iti-da [am]an([MUNU$_4$].SAR) MS-CS Mesag BIN 8 245 o. i 6
lugal-iti-da saĝ-apin CS Mesag M. deJ. Ellis, *JCS* 31 (1979), p. 30–55 16 o. ii 9
lugal-iti-da s. Az MS-CS Mesag MesCiv 4 45 o. 19
lugal-iti-da šandan ^{d}En-lil-la$_2$ MS-CS Nippur OIC 22 1 o. 2
lugal-iti-da šandan MS-CS Nippur OIC 22 2 o. 7
lugal-iti-da CS Nippur OIP 129 pl. 193 no. 3 o. 9
lugal-⸢iti-da⸣ MS-CS Nippur OSP 2 68 o. 16
lugal-iti-da MS-CS Nippur OSP 2 69 r. 10
lugal-iti-da MS-CS Nippur OSP 2 70 r. i 3’’
lugal-iti-da MS-CS Nippur OSP 2 71 o. 2
lugal-iti-da MS-CS Nippur OSP 2 71 o. 4
lugal-iti-da MS-CS Nippur OSP 2 80 o. iii 1’’
lugal-iti-da MS-CS Nippur OSP 2 84 o. ii 10
lugal-iti-da MS-CS Nippur OSP 2 84 r. iii 5
lugal-iti-da MS-CS Nippur OSP 2 85 r. 3
lugal-iti-da MS-CS Nippur OSP 2 93 o. i 4’
lu[gal]-iti-da MS-CS Nippur OSP 2 94 o. i 10
lugal-iti-da MS-CS Nippur OSP 2 95 o. ii 10
lugal-iti-da MS-CS Nippur OSP 2 96 o. ii 5
lugal-iti-da MS-CS Nippur OSP 2 96 o. iii 4’
lugal-iti-da MS-CS Nippur OSP 2 96 r. i 4’
lugal-iti-da MS-CS Nippur OSP 2 97 r. i 6’
lugal-iti-da E-TUM-AL ? MS-CS Nippur OSP 2 148 o. 3
lugal-iti-da MS-CS Nippur OSP 2 180 o. 2
lugal-iti-da f. Geme$_2$-^{d}En-lil$_2$ CS/NS. Nippur PBS 9 15+110 o. ii 9
lugal-iti-da [si]pa maš$_2$ CS/NS. Nippur PBS 9 25 o. 9
lugal-iti-da MS-CS Nippur PBS 9 28+34 r. i’ 7’
lugal-iti-da MS-CS Nippur PBS 9 28+34 r. ii’ 3’
lugal-iti-da MS-CS Nippur PBS 9 43 o. i 6’
lugal-iti-da CS Nippur PBS 9 77 o. ii 14’
lugal-⸢iti⸣-da CS/NS. Nippur TMH 5 7+184+201a r. i 8’
lugal-iti-da s. Nitaḫ-tur CS/NS. Nippur TMH 5 7+184+201a r. ii 3’
lugal-⸢iti⸣-da MS-CS Nippur TMH 5 29 o. ii 9
lugal-iti-da s. Sipa-^{d}En-lil$_2$-le MS-CS Nippur TMH 5 63 o. ii 1
lugal-iti-da kuš$_7$ ^{d}Šara$_2$ MS-CS Umma BIN 8 329 o. 4

lugal-iti-da kuš$_7$ ud$_5$ CS Umma BIN 8 335 o. 7
lugal-iti-da MS-CS Umma *CST* 21 o. ii 9
lugal-iti-da MS-CS Umma *CST* 21 r. ii 9’
lugal-iti-da maškim MS-CS Umma or Girsu ? CT 50 76 r. 1
lugal-iti-da šitim, *be-lu bu-dim*, *in* Umma^{ki} CS Umma CT 50 188 o. ii 7
⸢lugal-iti-da⸣ CS Umma ? CUSAS 13 201 r. 3
lugal-[iti-d]a ugula, nu-banda$_3$ ⸢NIĜ⸣ [x] gu$_4$ CS Umma T. Donald, *MCS* 9 (1964) 244 o. 10
lugal-iti-da s. [D]a-da CS Umma *USP* 45 o. i 13
lugal-iti-da s. Ur-lu$_2$ CS Umma *USP* 45 r. i 7
lugal-iti-da f. Ur-Niĝin CS Umma *USP* 46 o. 15
lugal-iti-da s. I-mi CS Umma *USP* 47 o. 6
lugal-iti-da [s.] Al-lu$_2$ CS Umma *USP* 47 o. i 16
lugal-iti-da s. Lugal-en$_8$-tar-su$_3$ CS Umma *USP* 47 r. i 18
lugal-iti-da f. Za$_3$-mu CS Umma *USP* 71 o. 5
lugal-iti-da f. Lugal-an-ne$_2$ CS Umma *USP* 71 o. 7
lugal-iti-da sagi-maḫ, Adab^{ki} CS-LS Unknown *EGA* 605
lugal-iti$^{!}$-da h. Nin-An-ne$_2$ MS-CS Unknown A. Westenholz, *JCS* 26 (1974), p. 71–80 5 o. 7
lugal-iti-da dam-gar$_3$ CS Unknown B. R. Foster, *JCS* 35 (1983), p. 147–175 18 r. 2
lugal-iti-da CS Unknown MAD 5 106 o. 4
lugal-iti-da dub-sar CS Unknown MAD 5 108 o. 6
lugal-iti-da sipa CS Unknown MAD 5 108 r. 2
lugal-iti-da nu-eš$_3$ MS-CS Unknown MesCiv 4 52 r. 6
lugal-iti-da ni-is-[ku] MS-CS Unknown MesCiv 4 53 o. 3
lugal-⸢iti⸣-da h. Nin-ME MS-CS Unknown MVN 3 21 o. 2
lugal-iti-da MS-CS Unknown OIP 47 pl. 5 no. 30 1

lugal-iti-da-tu $^{(a1)}$ ‘the lugal is (re)born each month’ 3.1.7.10, p. 49 n. 230, 50 n. 232, 172
lugal-iti-da-tu s. GAN-^{d}Ba-u$_2$ & Ur-^{d}Nin-MAR.KI, b. En-ne$_2$-a-na-ak ED IIIb/X Y 5 Girsu Nik 1 19 o. ii 6

lugal-iti-da-[zal$^{?}$]-le $^{(a1)}$ ‘the lugal [brightens?] the month’ 3.1.7.10, p. 172
lugal-iti-da-[zal$^{?}$]-⸢le⸣ lu$_2$ ildum$_2$ ES-MS Umma Nik 2 15 o. i 9

lugal-KA $^{(a>25)}$ abbreviation 3.1.8 **(see also lugal-inim, lugal-šud$_3^{!}$(KA))**, p. 139, 179, 186 w. n. 1172, 215 n. 1387, 235
lugal-KA f. Ur-PA, sukkal ED IIIb-ES Adab CUSAS 11 77 o. ii 7
lugal-KA ED IIIb-ES Adab CUSAS 11 81 r. ii 4
lugal-KA tug$_2$-du$_8$ ED IIIb-ES Adab CUSAS 11 186 o. iii 4
lugal-KA tug-du$_8$(-ra) ED IIIb-ES Adab CUSAS 11 243 o. i 3
lugal-KA s. Ki-gub ED IIIb/X Y 5 Girsu *DP* suppl. 593 o. v 3
lugal-KA ED IIIb Girsu VS 25 38 o. i 3
lugal-KA ED IIIb/X Y 3 Girsu VS 25 42 o. ii 3
lugal-KA sukkal ED IIIb-ES Isin MVN 3 105 r. i 1
lugal-KA (PN ?) ED IIIb Umma-Zabala ? BIN 8 48 o. 1
lugal-KA (PN ?) ED IIIb Umma-Zabala ? BIN 8 48 o. 3
lugal-KA sipa ED IIIb Umma-Zabala ? BIN 8 62 o. i 8
lugal-KA ED IIIb Umma-Zabala ? BIN 8 78 o. i 5
lugal-KA ED IIIb/Luzag. ensi$_2$ X Umma-Zabala BIN 8 82 o. iv 10
lugal-KA lu$_2$-eš$_2$-gid$_2$ ED IIIb/Luzag. ensi$_2$ X Umma-Zabala BIN 8 82 o. v 19
lugal-KA ⸢sipa⸣ ED IIIb/Luzag. ensi$_2$ 7 Umma-Zabala BIN 8 86 o. iii 1
lugal-KA ugula nu-banda$_3$(-am$_6$) ED IIIb-ES Umma-Zabala ? BIN 8 108 o. i 5
lugal-KA sagi ED IIIb Umma-Zabala ? BIN 8 120 o. i 2’

lugal-KA nagar ED IIIb Umma-Zabala CUSAS 14 147 r. i 1
lugal-KA nagar ED IIIb Umma-Zabala CUSAS 14 158 r. i 2
lugal-KA ED IIIb Umma-Zabala CUSAS 14 235 o. ii 3
lugal-KA tug$_2$-du$_8$ ED IIIb/Luzag. Y [x] Umma-Zabala M. Powell, *HUCA* 49 (1978), p. 1–58 2 o. ii 9
lugal-KA ED IIIb/X Y 8 Umma-Zabala M. Powell, *HUCA* 49 (1978), p. 1–58 4 o. ii 7
lugal-KA ugula nu-banda$_3$(-am$_6$) ED IIIb Umma-Zabala M. Powell, *HUCA* 49 (1978), p. 1–58 19 o. i 6
lugal-KA ED IIIb Umma-Zabala M. Powell, *HUCA* 49 (1978), p. 1–58 20 r. i 4
lugal-KA ugula nu-banda$_3$(-⸢am$_6$⸣) ED IIIb Umma-Zabala M. Powell, *HUCA* 49 (1978), p. 1–58 21 o. ii 4
lu[gal]-K[A] ugula nu-banda$_3$(-am$_6$) ED IIIb Umma-Zabala M. Powell, *HUCA* 49 (1978), p. 1–58 22 o. i 6
lugal-KA ED IIIb/Umma$_2$(ḪI×DIŠ)-nitaḫ-gin$_7$ 3 Umma T. Ozaki, *JAC* 23 (2008), p. 55–64 3 o. iv 12
lugal-KA tug$_2$-⸢du$_8$⸣ ED IIIb/Luzag. ensi$_2$ 7 Umma-Zabala M. deJ. Ellis, *JCS* 31 (1979), p. 30–55 6 o. ii 1
lugal-KA ED IIIb/Luzag. ensi$_2$ 7 Umma-Zabala M. deJ. Ellis, *JCS* 31 (1979), p. 30–55 7 o. iii 3
lugal-KA lu$_2$-eš$_2$-gid$_2$ ED IIIb/Luzag. ensi$_2$ 7 Umma-Zabala M. deJ. Ellis, *JCS* 31 (1979), p. 30–55 7 o. vi 11'
lugal-KA lu$_2$-eš$_2$-gid$_2$ ED IIIb/Luzag. ensi$_2$ 7 Umma-Zabala M. deJ. Ellis, *JCS* 31 (1979), p. 30–55 7 o. vi 12'
lugal-KA apin-us$_2$ ED IIIb/Luzag. ensi$_2$ 6 Umma M. Lambert, *OrAnt* 18 (1979), p. 225–226 (AO 15540) o. i 11
lugal-KA ED IIIb/Luzag. ensi$_2$ 6 Umma M. Lambert, *OrAnt* 18 (1979), p. 225–226 (AO 15540) o. ii 1
lugal-KA ED IIIb/Luzag. ensi$_2$ 6 Umma M. Lambert, *OrAnt* 18 (1979), p. 225–226 (AO 15540) o. ii 5
lugal-KA lu$_2$ ĜIŠ-AB ED IIIb/Luzag. ensi$_2$ 6 Umma M. Lambert, *OrAnt* 18 (1979), p. 225–226 (AO 15540) o. ii 6
lugal-KA gala KA TI ED IIIb/Luzag. ensi$_2$ 6 Umma M. Lambert, *OrAnt* 18 (1979), p. 225–226 (AO 15540) o. ii 11
lugal-KA ED IIIb/Il$_2$ ensi$_2$ Zabala *TCVBI* 1-1 o. ii 2
lugal-KA UB.ME^{ki}, maškim-bi$_3$ ED IIIb-ES Unknown BIN 8 159 r. ii 1
lugal-KA ES Adab CUSAS 11 275 o. ii 3
lugal-KA ensi$_2$ KI.AN^{ki}, šu-du$_8$-a ES (OB)/Rīmuś Nippur PBS 15 41 r. vii 3''
lugal-KA ensi$_2$ KI.AN^{ki}, šu-du$_8$-a ES (OB)/Rīmuś Nippur PBS 15 41 r. viii 12'
lugal-KA ugula-ni ES-MS Umma Nik 2 10 r. 2
lugal-KA nu-banda$_3$ ES-MS Umma Nik 2 14 o. ii 13
lugal-KA lu$_2$-dab$_5$ lugal-KA ES-MS Umma Nik 2 27 o. 5
lugal-KA Zi-zi lu$_2$-dab$_5$ lugal-KA ES-MS Umma *USP* 3 o. 4
lugal-KA sipa anše ES-MS Umma *USP* 5 r. 4'
lugal-⸢KA⸣ Lugal-saĝ ⸢lu$_2$⸣ ^{ĝiš}gi ⸢Lu⸣gal-⸢KA⸣(-ke$_4$) ES-MS Umma *USP* 7 r. 5
lugal-KA MS-CS Adab CUSAS 13 8 o. 2
lugal-KA MS-CS Adab CUSAS 13 8 o. 8
lugal-KA CS Adab CUSAS 13 56 o. ii 16
lugal-KA ir$_{11}$ E$_2$-RU-BI MS-CS Adab ? MesCiv 4 60 r. edge
lugal-KA lu$_2$ a-bul$_5$-la CS Adab OIP 14 143 r. 3'
⸢lugal⸣-KA CS Adab *SIA* 632 o. i 9
lugal-KA CS Adab *SIA* 660 r. 5
lugal-KA f. E$_2$-ur-x-x CS Adab *SIA* 661 r. 2'

lugal-KA lu$_2$ gub-ba CS Adab *SIA* 667 o. 13
[lugal]-K[A$^?$] ni-is-ku CS Adab *SIA* 753 r. 2
lugal-KA MS-CS Adab *TCABI* 196 o. ii 12
lugal-KA f. Ur-^{d}Gir$_3$-ra & Nam-maḫ CS Girsu CT 50 98 o. i 13
lugal-KA ad-kup$_4$, dumu Šuruppag^{ki} CS Girsu ITT 1 1363 o. 5
lugal-KA CS Girsu ITT 1 1425 o. 5
lugal-KA ma$_2$-laḫ$_5$ CS Girsu ITT 2/1 2917 r. 4
lugal-KA ga-eš$_8$ CS Girsu ITT 2/1 4380 r. 1
lugal-KA s. Ur-me-ke$_4$ CS Girsu ITT 2/1 4436 o. 2
lugal-KA ga-eš$_8$ CS Girsu ITT 2/1 4461 r. 3
lugal-KA ga-eš$_8$ CS Girsu ITT 2/1 4512 r. 2
lugal-KA CS Girsu MVN 3 113 o. i 21
lugal-KA f. Ur-^{d}Šakkan CS Girsu MVN 3 113 o. ii 16
lugal-KA engar CS Girsu *RTC* 91 r. ii' 9'
lugal-KA f. Lu$_2$-ba CS Girsu *RTC* 78 o. 6
⸢lugal-KA⸣ CS Girsu *STTI* 11 o. 7
lugal-KA CS Girsu *STTI* 20 r. 3'
lugal-KA CS Girsu *STTI* 26 o. i 9'
lugal-KA s. Da-da CS Girsu *STTI* 85 o. (?) ii 1
lugal-KA CS Girsu *STTI* 163 o. 2
lugal-KA MS-CS Lagaš BiMes 3 25 r. 1
lugal-KA MS-CS Mesag BIN 8 122 o. i 9
⸢lugal⸣-KA MS-CS Mesag BIN 8 122 o. ii 3
lugal-KA MS-CS Mesag BIN 8 131 o. ii 7
lugal-KA ⸢ĝuruš$^?$⸣ MS-CS Mesag BIN 8 148 o. ii 7'
lugal-KA aga$_3$-us$_2$ CS Mesag BIN 8 152 o. i 7
lugal-KA MS-CS Mesag BIN 8 243 o. 2
lugal-KA ir$_{11}$ Lugal-⸢x-x⸣ ⸢n⸣[ar$^?$] MS-CS Mesag BIN 8 267 r. ii 8
lugal-KA MS-CS Mesag MesCiv 4 45 o. 11
lugal-KA MS-CS Nippur OSP 2 82 r. 1
lugal-KA MS-CS Nippur OSP 2 90 o. ii 8
lugal-KA MS-CS Nippur OSP 2 91 o. 3'
lugal-[KA] MS-CS Nippur OSP 2 96 r. ii 3
⸢lugal-KA⸣ MS-CS Nippur OSP 2 96 r. iii 12
lugal-KA MS-CS Nippur OSP 2 97 r. ii 5
lugal-KA MS-CS Nippur OSP 2 112 o. 5
lugal-KA abba$_2$ uru^{ki} MS-CS Susa MDP 14 19 o. 14
lugal-KA MS-CS Umma BIN 8 287 o. 4
lugal-KA MS-CS Umma BIN 8 298 o. 3
lugal-KA f. Niĝin$_3$ CS Umma BIN 8 335 o. 10
lugal-KA s. Ur-lu$_2$ MS-CS Umma BIN 8 393 o. 1
lugal-KA MS-CS Umma *CST* 25 o. 2
lugal-KA CS Umma MAD 4 24 o. 7
lugal-KA MS-CS Umma MAD 4 40 r. 9
lugal-K[A] MS-CS Umma MAD 4 42 (translit. only) r. 4'
lugal-KA CS Umma MAD 4 51 o. 3
lugal-KA MS-CS Umma MAD 4 54 (translit. only) o. 4
lugal-KA MS-CS Umma MAD 4 57 (translit. only) o. 2
lugal-KA (ugula) MS-CS Umma MAD 4 62 (translit. only) o. 2
lugal-KA ugula MS-CS Umma MAD 4 62 (translit. only) r. 1
lugal-KA MS-CS Umma MAD 4 67 (translit. only) r. 6
lugal-KA gu-la MS Umma MAD 4 68 o. 9

lugal-KA MS-CS Umma MAD 4 100 (translit. only) o. 4
lugal-KA MS-CS Umma MAD 4 102 (translit. only) o. 4
lugal-KA MS-CS Umma MAD 4 103 (translit. only) r. 1
lugal-KA MS-CS Umma MAD 4 104 (translit. only) o. 4
lugal-KA MS-CS Umma MAD 4 108 (translit. only) r. 1
lugal-KA MS-CS Umma MAD 4 120 (translit. only) r. 1
lugal-KA MS-CS Umma MAD 4 121 (translit. only) o. 2
lugal-KA MS-CS Umma MAD 4 123 (translit. only) o. 4
lugal-KA MS-CS Umma MAD 4 124 o. 3
lugal-KA MS-CS Umma MAD 4 125 (translit. only) o. 5
lugal-KA MS-CS Umma MAD 4 133 (translit. only) o. 5
lugal-KA MS-CS Umma MAD 4 135 (translit. only) o. 5
lugal-KA MS-CS Umma MAD 4 148 (translit. only) o. 7
lugal-KA saĝ-apin-na lugal CS Umma T. Donald, *MCS* 9 (1964) 236 r. i 3
lugal-⸢KA⸣ CS Umma T. Donald, *MCS* 9 (1964) 237 o. 6
lugal-KA MS-CS Umma MesCiv 4 14 o. 2
lugal-KA eš$_2^!$(DU$_6$)-gid$_2$ CS Umma Nik 2 76 o. i 8
lugal-KA ? MS-CS Umma ? *TCVC* 726 o. ii 12
lugal-KA f. AMAR-si & KA-diĝir-ra MS-CS Umma ? *TCVC* 731 o. ii 15’
lugal-KA eš$_2$-gid$_2$ CS Umma *USP* 22 o. i 6
lugal-KA CS Umma *USP* 24 3
lugal-KA f. Saĝ-lu$_2$-[(x)] CS Umma *USP* 45 o. ii 8
lugal-KA f. Al-lu$_2$ CS Umma *USP* 47 o. i 9
⸢lugal-KA⸣ MS-CS Umma *USP* 69 o. 4
lugal-[KA] CS Umma *USP* 72 o. 3
lugal-KA lugal-KA ⸢*u*$_3$⸣ Ur-zu CS Unknown CUSAS 13 2 r. 12
lugal-KA aga$_3$-us$_2$ lugal CS Unknown W. Sommerfeld, K. Markina & N. Roudik, *Gs Diakonoff*, 225–231 8 r. 2’
lugal-KA sipa MS-CS Unknown B. R. Foster, *JCS* 35 (1983), p. 147–175 4 r. 1
lugal-KA OAkk Unknown MAD 4 25 (translit. only) o. 10
lugal-KA CS Unknown MAD 4 36 o. 2
lu[gal]-KA OAkk Unknown MAD 4 154 (translit. only) o. i 12
lugal-KA CS Unknown (Girsu ?) MVN 2 298 o. ii 4
lugal-KA CS Unknown (Girsu ?) MVN 2 298 o. ii 5
lugal-KA MS-CS Unknown MVN 3 92 o. 3

lugal-^{d}KA.DI (a2) (perhaps) ‘the lugal (is like) Ištaran’ 3.1.6.2, p. 146, 166 n. 959
lugal-^{d}KA.DI MS-CS Nippur TMH 5 29 o. ii 17

lugal-KA-GAN-ki (a1) unkn. mng. 3.1.8, p. 179, 187
⸢lugal-KA-GAN⸣-ki ED IIIb-ES Umma-Zabala BIN 8 77 o. 4
lugal-[K]A-GAN-ki ED IIIb/Luzag. ensi$_2$ X Umma-Zabala BIN 8 82 o. iv 11
lugal-KA-GAN-ki ED IIIb/Unknown Umma-Zabala M. Powell, *HUCA* 49 (1978), p. 1–58 3 o. iii 3
lugal-KA-GAN-ki ED IIIb/Luzag. ensi$_2$ 7 Umma-Zabala M. deJ. Ellis, *JCS* 31 (1979), p. 30–55 6 o. iii 17

lugal-KA-ni-nu-šuba$_2$ (a1) ‘is the word (?) of the lugal not pure (?)’ 3.1.1.4, p. 92 n. 470, 94
lugal-KA-ni-nu-šuba$_2$ niĝir sila ED IIIa Šuruppag *FTUM* 96 r. i 1

lugal-KA-NIĜ$_2$-U (a≥1) unkn. mng. 3.1.8, p. 179
lugal-KA-NIĜ$_2$-U ED IIIb Umma-Zabala MVN 3 3 o. v 3
lugal-KA-NIĜ$_2$-U ĝuruš, ir$_3$ dub-sar-ne ES-MS Umma *CHÉU* 54 o. ii 6

lugal-KA-SI-U$_2$-LUM (a1) unkn. mng. 3.1.8, p. 179

lugal-KA-SI-U$_2$-LUM ED IIIb Zabala BIN 8 76 o. ii 1

lugal-KA-U$_2$ $^{?\ (a1)}$ unkn. mng. 3.1.8, p. 179
lugal-KA-U$_2$$^{?}$ ED IIIb/Luzag. ensi$_2$ 7 Umma-Zabala M. deJ. Ellis, *JCS* 31 (1979), p. 30–55 6 o. v 7
lugal-KA-U$_2$$^{?}$ ED IIIb/Luzag. ensi$_2$ 7 Umma-Zabala M. deJ. Ellis, *JCS* 31 (1979), p. 30–55 7 o. v 12'

lugal-KA×DIŠ$^{?}$? MS-CS Adab CUSAS 13 8 o. 6
lugal-KA-[(x)]-⸢x⸣-[(x)] ED IIIb Ur UET 2 suppl. 40 o. 2
lugal-⸢KA-x⸣-[(x)] ES Adab *TCABI* 26 edge

lugal-kadra $^{(a1)}$ 'the lugal (presents) a gift (offering)' 3.1.6.3, p. 147, 256 n. 1506
lugal-kadra CS Umma W. Sommerfeld, K. Markina & N. Roudik, *Gs Diakonoff*, 225–231 4 o. 9

lugal-kalag-ga $^{(a\geq2)}$ 'the lugal is strong' 3.1.7.3, p. 163
lugal-kalag-ga usandu(MUŠEN.DU$_3$) ED IIIb-ES Adab CUSAS 11 86 o. ii 2
lugal-kalag-ga ED IIIb-ES Adab CUSAS 11 98 o. ii 3
lugal-kalag-ga ugula ES Adab *TCABI* 61 o. i 6

lugal-KALAM(LAK729) $^{(a\geq3)}$ (compare lugal-uĝ$_3$-) 3.1.1.6, p. 100 n. 530, 253 n. 1484
lugal-KALAM-[(x)] s. Ak-[^{d}x$^{?}$] ED IIIb Nippur OSP 1 39 o. i 4'
lugal-KALAM lu$_2$ nagar-gal ED IIIb Umma-Zabala M. Powell, *HUCA* 49 (1978), p. 1–58 18 o. i 2
lu‹gal›-KALAM ^{d}Nin-šubur-an-dul$_3$$^{!}$(SAĜ), ir$_{11}$ lu‹gal›-KALAM tug$_2$-du$_8$ MS-CS Umma MesCiv 4 30 o. ii 11
lugal-KALAM s. (?) [Ur-^{d}]⸢Ĝiš⸣-bar MS-CS Umma ? *TCVC* 728 o. i 2

lugal-kalam(LAK729):ma:dul$_5$ $^{(a1)}$ 'the lugal covers the land' 3.1.1.6, p. 102
lugal-kalam:ma:dul$_5$ ED IIIb Girsu *NFT*, p. 180 (bottom) o. i 2
[lu]gal-⸢kalam⸣:[ma]:dul$_5$ ED IIIb Girsu ITT 5 9228 o. iv 7

lugal-kar $^{(a\geq6)}$ 'the lugal ... the harbour' 3.1.5.3, p. 136 n. 760
lugal-⸢kar⸣ ED IIIb Nippur OSP 1 24 o. iv 3
lugal-kar ED IIIb Nippur OSP 1 29 r. i 3
lugal-kar ED IIIb Nippur OSP 1 29 r. i 6
lu:gal-kar ED IIIb Nippur OSP 1 33 o. i 5'
lu:gal-⸢kar⸣ ED IIIb Nippur OSP 1 33 o. ii 2'
lugal-kar nu-banda$_3$ ED IIIb Nippur OSP 1 35 ii 1'
lu:gal-kar s. Ur-^{d}Iškur ED IIIb Nippur TMH 5 1 o. i 3
lugal-kar s. Lugal-uru-da, lu$_2$ Šuruppag^{ki} ED IIIb Nippur TMH 5 8 o. i 5
lugal-kar KAL.EDIN ED IIIb Nippur TMH 5 11 o. iii 7
lugal-kar ED IIIb Nippur TMH 5 58 r. ii 1
lugal-kar ED IIIb Nippur TMH 5 159 o. i 15'
⸢lugal-kar⸣ lu$_2$ u$_5$ ED IIIb Nippur TMH 5 164 o. ii 7
lugal-kar ED IIIb Nippur TMH 5 168 o. iii 4
lugal-kar ES-MS Nippur PBS 9 49 o. 2
lugal-kar ES-MS Nippur TMH 5 180 o. i 2'
lugal-kar CS Girsu *DPA* 22 (PUL 40) r. 2
lugal-kar f. Uĝ$_3$$^{!}$(LAK729)-IL$_2$ MS-CS Nippur OSP 2 69 o. 6
lugal-kar f. Uĝ$_3$$^{!}$(LAK729)-IL$_2$ MS-CS Nippur OSP 2 69 o. 10
lugal-kar MS-CS Nippur OSP 2 80 o. i 2
⸢lugal⸣-kar MS-CS Nippur OSP 2 95 o. iii 6
lugal-kar CS/Śkś Y 2 Nippur OSP 2 100 r. iii 6'
lugal-[kar$^{?}$] f. ⸢Uĝ$_3$⸣-I[L$_2$] MS-CS Nippur OSP 2 129 o. ii 9'
lugal-kar MS-CS Nippur OSP 2 180 r. 2

lu:gal-k[ar$^?$] dub-sar MS-CS Nippur OSP 2 182 r. 2

lugal-kar$^!$(TE) (a1) ‘the lugal … the harbour’ 3.1.5.3, p. 136 n. 760
lugal-kar$^!$(TE) f. Uĝ$_3$-IL$_2$ MS-CS Nippur OSP 2 70 o. ii 6
lugal-kar$^!$(TE) f. Uĝ$_3$-IL$_2$ MS-CS Nippur OSP 2 70 o. ii 8

lugal-kar-e (a1) ‘the lugal … the harbour’ 3.1.5.3, p. 136 n. 760
lugal-kar-e ⸢sipa anše⸣ CS Adab CUSAS 13 107 o. 4’

lugal-kar-e-si (a1) ‘the lugal is just right for the harbour’ 3.1.5.3, p. 136, 153
lugal-kar-e-si f. Gala, lu$_2$ ma$_2$-gur$_8$-ka CS Umma MAD 4 51 o. 2

lugal-kar-re (a1) ‘the lugal … the harbour’ 3.1.5.3, p. 136 n. 760
lugal-kar-re ĝuruš CS Girsu *DPA* 45 (PUL 22) o. 2

lugal-kar-re$_2$ (a1) ‘the lugal … the harbour’ 3.1.5.3, p. 136 n. 760
lugal-kar-re$_2$ CS Adab ? *TCABI* 262 o. 3*

lugal-kar-si (a3) ‘the lugal is just right for the harbour’ 3.1.5.3, p. 136 n. 760
lugal-kar-si ED IIIa-b Isin (?) OIP 104 14 r. vii 13
lugal-kar-si ED IIIb Umma-Zabala BIN 8 63 o. i 4
lugal-kar-si ED IIIb Umma-Zabala MVN 3 3 r. i 7
lugal-kar-si f. Ur-PA, u$_2$-ḫub$_2$ ES-MS Unknown MVN 3 85 o. 3

lugal-kara$_6$-gal-gal (a1) ‘the lugal enlarges the grain heap(s)’ 3.1.5.3, p. 134 w. n. 744
lugal-kara$_6$-gal-gal ED IIIb Umma-Zabala MVN 3 3 o. iii 10

lugal-kas$_4$ (a1) (see the following) 3.1.8, p. 179
lugal-kas$_4$ CS Isin CUSAS 13 163 r. i 4

lugal-kas$_4$-e (a4) ‘the lugal runs (?)’ 3.1.8, p. 179
lugal-kas$_4$-e nu-banda$_3$ ma$_2$-gid$_2$ CS Adab CUSAS 13 78 r. ii 10’
lugal-kas$_4$-⸢e⸣ s. Ur-d[a] CS Girsu ITT 1 1404 r. 1
lugal-kas$_4$-e MS-CS Nippur OSP 2 146 o. 4’
lugal-kas$_4$-e s. Šeš-šeš CS Unknown *EGA* 913 pl. 29 fig. 350

lugal-kas[kal$^?$] (a1) unkn. mng. 3.1.8, p. 179
lugal-kas[kal$^?$] f. [x-x] MS-CS Umma ? *TCVC* 729 o. 3’

lugal-Keš$_3^{ki}$ (a≥3) ‘the lugal (went to) Keš’ 3.1.6.4, p. 154 n. 887, 247
lugal-Keš$_3^{ki}$ dub-sar ED IIIb/Ukg. lugal 3 Girsu *AWAS* 68 r. ii 4’
lu[gal]-[K]eš$_3^{ki}$ ⸢lu$_2$⸣ šuku dab$_5$-ba ED IIIb/Ukg. lugal 3 Girsu *AWAS* 124 o. iv 16
lugal-Keš$_3^{ki}$ dub-sar ED IIIb/Ukg. lugal 3 Girsu *AWAS* 124 o. v 5’
lugal-Keš$_3^{ki}$ dub-sar ED IIIb/Ukg. lugal 3 Girsu *AWAS* 124 r. iii 6
lugal-Keš$_3^{ki}$ dub-sar ED IIIb/Ukg. lugal 4 Girsu *DP* 1/2 116 o. vi 10
lugal-Keš$_3^{ki}$ lu$_2$ šuku dab$_5$-ba ED IIIb/Ukg. lugal 4 Girsu *DP* 1/2 116 o. v 18
lugal-Keš$_3^{ki}$ dub-sar ED IIIb/Ukg. lugal 4 Girsu *DP* 1/2 116 r. ii 3
lugal-Keš$_3^{ki}$ ED IIIb/Ukg. lugal 4 Girsu *DP* 1/2 117 o. iii 8
lugal-Keš$_3^{ki}$ ED IIIb/Ukg. lugal 4 Girsu *DP* 1/2 117 o. v 18
lugal-Keš$_3^{ki}$ ED IIIb/Ukg. lugal 4 Girsu *DP* 1/2 117 o. vi 4
lugal-Keš$_3^{ki}$ dub-sar ED IIIb/Ukg. lugal 4 Girsu *DP* 1/2 117 r. i 6
lugal-Keš$_3^{ki}$ lu$_2$ šuku dab$_5$-ba ED IIIb/Ukg. lugal 4(+x?) Girsu Nik 1 16 o. v 1
lugal-Keš$_3^{ki}$ dub-sar ED IIIb/Ukg. lugal 4(+x?) Girsu Nik 1 16 o. v 11
lugal-Keš$_3^{ki}$ ED IIIb/Ukg. lugal 4(+x?) Girsu Nik 1 16 r. iii 3
lugal-Keš$_3^{ki}$ saĝ-apin Geme$_2$-tar-sir-sir-ka ED IIIb/X Y 4 Girsu VS 14 39 o. ii 4
lugal-Keš$_3^{ki}$ MS-CS Adab OIP 14 124 o. 2
lugal-Keš$_3^{ki}$ CS Adab *SIA* 800+1011 o. 4

lugal-ki (a≥10) unkn. mng. 3.1.8, p. 179
lugal-ki ED IIIa Girsu PBS 9 2 o. iv 5

lugal-ki ED IIIb Adab CUSAS 11 60 o. i 8
lugal-ki ED IIIb/X Y 6 Girsu Nik 1 178 o. i 2
lugal-ki ED IIIb/Umma$_2$(ḪI×DIŠ)-nitaḫ-gin$_7$ 3 Umma T. Ozaki, *JAC* 23 (2008), p. 55–64 3 o. iv 10
lugal-ki saĝa ED IIIb/Luzag. ensi$_2$ 7 Umma-Zabala BIN 8 86 o. ii 13
lugal-⸢ki⸣ dub-sar ED IIIb Umma-Zabala ? BIN 8 104 o. ii 2
lugal-ki saĝa ED IIIb/Luzag. ensi$_2$ [x] Umma-Zabala J. A. Brinkman, *Fs Kramer*, pl. III*-V* (W 2/7) o. ii 14’
lugal-ki saĝa ED IIIb/Luzag. ensi$_2$ 7 Umma-Zabala M. deJ. Ellis, *JCS* 31 (1979), p. 30–55 6 o. i 2
lugal-ki saĝa ED IIIb/Luzag. ensi$_2$ 7 Umma-Zabala M. deJ. Ellis, *JCS* 31 (1979), p. 30–55 6 o. i 10
lugal-ki saĝa ED IIIb/Luzag. ensi$_2$ 7 Umma-Zabala M. deJ. Ellis, *JCS* 31 (1979), p. 30–55 6 o. ii 15
lugal-ki saĝa ED IIIb/Luzag. ensi$_2$ 7 Umma-Zabala M. deJ. Ellis, *JCS* 31 (1979), p. 30–55 6 o. iii 8
lugal-⸢ki⸣ saĝa ED IIIb/Luzag. ensi$_2$ 7 Umma-Zabala M. deJ. Ellis, *JCS* 31 (1979), p. 30–55 6 o. v 5
lugal-ki saĝa ED IIIb/Luzag. ensi$_2$ 7 Umma-Zabala M. deJ. Ellis, *JCS* 31 (1979), p. 30–55 7 o. iv 14
lugal-ki ĝuruš, lu$_2$ gi sa$_{10}$-sa$_{10}$ ED IIIb Ur UET 2 suppl. 11 o. i 3
lugal-ki ED IIIb Ur UET 2 suppl. 12 r. 3
lugal-ki saĝa ED IIIb Zabala M. Powell, *HUCA* 49 (1978), p. 1–58 7 o. iii 4
lugal-ki ES-MS Adab *TCABI* 64 o. ii 6
lugal-ki ma$_2$-laḫ$_5$ ES-MS Umma Nik 2 19 o. iii 11
lugal-[ki$^?$] ma$_2$-laḫ$_5$-bi ES-MS Umma Nik 2 19 r. i 10
lugal-ki MS-CS Nippur OSP 2 81 r. 2
lugal-ki MS-CS Nippur OSP 2 82 o. 4
lugal-ki MS-CS Nippur OSP 2 104 o. ii’ 4’

lugal-ki-aĝa$_2$ (a≥5) ‘the lugal is beloved’ 3.1.7.8, p. 170
lugal-ki-aĝa$_2$ ED IIIb-ES Adab CUSAS 11 102 o. iii 3
lugal-ki-aĝa$_2$ ED IIIb-ES Nippur TMH 5 94 o. 3
⸢lugal-ki-aĝa$_2$⸣ MS Adab *TCABI* 78 o. 2’
lugal-ki-aĝa$_2$ MS-CS Nippur OSP 2 80 r. ii 2
lugal-ki-aĝa$_2$ MS-CS Nippur OSP 2 99 r. iii 3’
lugal-ki-aĝa$_2$ CS/Śkś Y 2 Nippur OSP 2 100 r. i 9’
lugal-ki-aĝa$_2$ lu$_2$ *Kal$_2$-bum*, šitim CS Unknown CUSAS 13 200 o. 9

lugal-ki-gal (a≥2) uncertain mng. 3.1.6.4, p. 156 n. 902
lugal-ki-gal AN-nu-[me$^?$] ED IIIa Šuruppag *TSŠ* 93 o. iii 7
lu[gal]-ki-gal ED IIIa Šuruppag *WF* 78 o. i 13’
lugal-⸢ki-gal$^?$⸣ ? ED IIIa-b Isin (?) OIP 104 14 r. vi 7

lugal-ki-gal-gal-la (a1) uncertain mng. 3.1.6.4, p. 156 n. 902
lugal-ki-gal-gal-la ED IIIa Šuruppag *TSŠ* 158 o. vi 10

lugal-ki-gal-la (a≥12) uncertain mng. 3.1.6.4, p. 104 n. 554, 156
lugal-ki-gal-la ED IIIa Adab *TCABI* 1 o. iii 3
lugal-ki-gal-la išib ^{d}Nin-ĝir-su ED IIIa Girsu PBS 9 2 r. ii 1
lugal-ki-gal-la AN-nu-me ED IIIa Šuruppag *NTSŠ* 569 o. iii’ 13
lugal-ki-gal-la ED IIIa Šuruppag *TSŠ* 9+127 o. iv 4
lugal-ki-gal-la ED IIIa Šuruppag *TSŠ* 467 o. i 5
lugal-ki-gal-la NI-NI-[x] ED IIIa Šuruppag *TSŠ* 873 o. ii’ 5’

lugal-ki-gal-la AN-nu-me ED IIIa Šuruppag *WF* 25 o. i 11
lugal-ki-gal-la ED IIIa Šuruppag *WF* 47 o. ii 1
lugal-ki-gal-la ED IIIa Šuruppag *WF* 78 r. ii 11
lugal-ki-gal-la ED IIIa-b Unknown *L'uomo* 5 o. ii' 3
lugal-ki-gal-la lu$_2$-u$_5$ ED IIIb-ES Adab CUSAS 11 77 r. i 1
lugal-ki-gal-la ED IIIb/Lug. 1 Girsu *DP* 2/1 191 o. iii 4
lugal-ki-gal-la lu u$_5$ ED IIIb-ES Isin MVN 3 53 o. i 3
lugal-ki-gal-la s. E$_2$-da-ḫul$_2$, lu$_2$ Šuruppag^{ki} ED IIIb Nippur TMH 5 8 o. ii 2
lugal-ki-gal-la Lugal-ki-gal-la, Lugal-ni$_3$-zu ED IIIb Nippur TMH 5 11 o. i 2
lugal-ki-gal-la Lugal-a$_2$-zi-da, ir$_{11}$ Lugal-ki-gal-la ED IIIb Nippur TMH 5 50 o. i 2
lugal-ki-gal-la ED IIIb Umma-Zabala BIN 8 68 o. iv 4
lugal-ki-gal-la ED IIIb Umma (?) CUSAS 11 45 o. iii 2
lugal-ki-gal-la ES/Śk. Nippur TMH 5 181 o. 5
lugal-ki-gal-la CS/NS.-Śkś Nippur OSP 2 79 o. 8
lugal-ki-gal-la MS-CS Nippur OSP 2 93 o. i 10'
lugal-ki-gal-la MS-CS Nippur OSP 2 99 r. ii 5'
lugal-[ki-gal-la] f. Dal-[la] MS-CS Nippur OSP 2 118 o. 7
lugal-ki-gal-la f. Dal-la MS-CS Nippur OSP 2 162 r. 4
lugal-ki-gal-la CS Nippur PBS 9 77 o. ii 12'
⸢lugal-ki⸣-[gal-la] MS-CS Nippur TMH 5 29 o. iii 5'
lugal-ki-gal-la [s. G]ala CS Umma *USP* 46 o. 7

lugal-ki-gub-ni-du$_7$-du$_7$ (a1) 'the lugal is the one best suited for the place (where) he serves' 3.1.6.4, p. 156
lugal-ki-gub-ni-du$_7$-du$_7$ (en Unug^{ki}-ga, Lugal Urim$_5$^{ki}-ma) ED IIIb/Lukin. X Nippur BE 1/2 86 3 etc.
lugal-ki-gub-ni-du$_7$-du$_7$ (en Unug^{ki}-ga, Lugal Urim$_5$^{ki}-ma) ED IIIb/Lukin. X Nippur BE 1/2 86 15 etc.
lugal-ki-gub-ni-du$_7$-du$_7$ f. Lugal-kisal:si (lugal Unug^{ki}-ga, Lugal Urim$_5$^{ki}-ma) ED IIIb/Lukis. X Nippur BE 1/2 86 (b) 2'

lugal-ki-NI (a1) uncertain mng. 3.1.8, p. 179
lugal-ki-NI ED IIIa-b Isin (?) OIP 104 14 r. v 6

lugal-ki-ni-du$_7$-du$_7$ (a1) (compare lugal-ki-gub-ni-du$_7$-du$_7$) 3.1.6.4, p. 156
lugal-ki-ni-du$_7$-du$_7$ a-diĝir-ĝu$_{10}$, dub-sar-maḫ, Lugal-ki-ni-du$_7$-du$_7$ im-DU, maš$_2$-še$_3$ da i$_3$-na-ri ED IIIb Adab CUSAS 11 68 r. ii 3
lugal-ki-ni-du$_7$-du$_7$ ensi$_2$ Unug^{ki}-ga ED IIIb/Ent. X Bad-Tibira *CIRPL* Ent. 53 (translit. only) ii 7

lugal-ki-NI-gi$_4$ (a≥1) unkn. mng. 3.1.8, p. 179
lugal-ki-NI-gi$_4$ ED IIIb/Luzag.$^?$ ensi$_2$ 7 Umma-Zabala BIN 8 116 o. i 5
lugal-ki-NI-gi$_4$ luĝa ED IIIb/Luzag. ensi$_2$ [x] Umma-Zabala J. A. Brinkman, *Fs Kramer*, pl. III*-V* (W 2/7) o. i 13'
lugal-ki-NI-gi$_4$ Ĝiš-ša$_3$ dumu AN-ki-⸢ki$^{!?}$⸣-du$_{10}$, lu$_2$ Lugal-ki-NI-gi$_4$ ED IIIb Umma-Zabala M. Powell, *HUCA* 49 (1978), p. 1–58 18 r. ii 7
lugal-ki-NI-gi$_4$ ED IIIb-ES Umma-Zabala BIN 8 234 o. i 8

lugal-ki-ni-še$_3$-du$_7$-du$_7$ (a1) (compare lugal-ki-gub-ni-du$_7$-du$_7$) 3.1.6.4, p. 156
lugal-ki-ni-še$_3$-du$_7$-du$_7$ ensi$_2$ Unug^{ki}-ga ED IIIb/Ent. X/Lukin. X Bad-Tibira *CIRPL* Ent. 45 ii 7
[lugal]-⸢ki⸣-[x(-x)]-še$_3$-du$_7$-du$_7$ lugal Kiš^{ki}-a ED IIIb/Lukin. X Ur UET 1 3+J. S. Cooper, *Iraq* 46 (1984), pl. Vb 1'

lugal-ki-nu-gi$_4$ (a≥5) 'the lugal (in) the place of no return (?)' 3.1.8, p. 179
lugal-ki-nu-gi$_4$ ĜA$_2$ nu:ki:gi$_4$:lugal ED I-II Ur UET 2 17 r. i 2

lugal-KI-ŠIR-PA$^{?}$-⸢X⸣ $^{(a1)}$ unkn. mng. 3.1.8, p. 179
lugal-KI-ŠIR-PA$^{?}$-⸢X⸣ ED I-II Šuruppag(?) F. Thureau-Dangin, *RA* 6 (1907), p. 143–146 (AO 2753) r. i 4

lugal-ki-tuš-du$_{10}$ $^{(a\geq6)}$ 'the lugal is one who makes the dwelling place pleasant' 3.1.8, p. 125
lugal-ki-tuš-du$_{10}$ simug ED IIIa Šuruppag H. Steible & F. Yıldız, *Fs Limet*, 149–159 (Š 1006) o. iii 4
lugal-ki-tuš-du$_{10}$ dam-gar$_3$ ED IIIa Šuruppag *NTSŠ* 205 o. ii 8
lugal-ki-tuš-du$_{10}$ ED IIIa Šuruppag *NTSŠ* 238 o. ii 2
lugal-⸢ki-tuš-du$_{10}$⸣ dub-sar ED IIIa Šuruppag *NTSŠ* 258 o. iii 2
lugal-ki-tuš$^{!}$-du$_{10}$ ED IIIa Šuruppag *NTSŠ* 276 o. (?) ii 4'
lugal-ki-tuš-du$_{10}$ Lugal-dum[u-zi] ED IIIa Šuruppag *NTSŠ* 444 o. ii 5
lugal-ki-tuš-du$_{10}$ Ur-^{d}Sud$_3$, Ni$_3$-ĝal$_2$-du$_{10}$ ED IIIa Šuruppag *NTSŠ* 569 o. iv' 1
lugal-ki-tuš-du$_{10}$ umbisaĝ ED IIIa Šuruppag *SF* 27+*TSŠ* 327+*NTSŠ* 294 r. iii 5
lugal-ki-tuš-du$_{10}$ ED IIIa Šuruppag *SF* 62 o. vi 3'
lugal-ki-tuš-du$_{10}$ dub-sar ED IIIa Šuruppag *TSŠ* 1 r. iii 9
lugal-ki-tuš-du$_{10}$ KUN.KUN ED IIIa Šuruppag *TSŠ* 104 o. ii 7'
lugal-ki-tuš-du$_{10}$ ašgab ED IIIa Šuruppag *TSŠ* 106 o. ii 3
lugal-ki-tuš-du$_{10}$ ED IIIa Šuruppag *TSŠ* 113 o. ii 2
lugal-ki-tuš-du$_{10}$ Ni$_3$-ĝal$_2$-du$_{10}$ ED IIIa Šuruppag *TSŠ* 668 r. ii 4
lugal-ki-tuš-du$_{10}$ dam-gar$_3$ ED IIIa Šuruppag *TSŠ* 794 o. iv 3
lugal-ki-tuš-du$_{10}$ ED IIIa Šuruppag *TSŠ* 842 r. ii 2'
lugal-ki-tuš-du$_{10}$ ED IIIa Šuruppag *WF* 3 r. ii 5
lugal-ki-tuš-du$_{10}$ Ni$_3$-ĝal$_2$-du$_{10}$ ED IIIa Šuruppag *WF* 5 r. iii 9
lugal-ki-tuš-du$_{10}$ Ni$_3$-ĝal$_2$-du$_{10}$ ED IIIa Šuruppag *WF* 6 r. ii 6
lugal-ki-tuš-du$_{10}$ ED IIIa Šuruppag *WF* 6 r. v 2
lugal-ki-tuš-du$_{10}$ E$_2$-ZU#ZU-SAR ED IIIa Šuruppag *WF* 7 o. vi 11'
lugal-ki-tuš-du$_{10}$ Lugal-dumu-zi ED IIIa Šuruppag *WF* 9 o. iv 5
lugal-ki-tuš-du$_{10}$ Ni$_3$-ĝal$_2$-du$_{10}$ ED IIIa Šuruppag *WF* 9 o. v 4
lugal-ki-tuš-du$_{10}$ Lugal-dumu-zi ED IIIa Šuruppag *WF* 13 o. iv 3
lugal-ki-tuš-du$_{10}$ ED IIIa Šuruppag *WF* 16 o. iv 6
lugal-ki-tuš-du$_{10}$ Ur-^{d}Sud$_3$ ED IIIa Šuruppag *WF* 18 r. i 3
lugal-ki-tuš-du$_{10}$ ašgab ED IIIa Šuruppag *WF* 25 o. iii 9
lugal-ki-tuš-du$_{10}$ A-RU ED IIIa Šuruppag *WF* 25 r. v 4
lugal-ki-tuš-du$_{10}$ dub-sar ED IIIa Šuruppag *WF* 26 o. i 3
lugal-ki-tuš-du$_{10}$ dub-sar ED IIIa Šuruppag *WF* 42 o. i 3
lugal-ki-tuš-du$_{10}$ Ni$_3$-ĝal$_2$-du$_{10}$ ED IIIa Šuruppag *WF* 52 o. i 2
lugal-ki-tuš-du$_{10}$ ED IIIa Šuruppag *WF* 53 r. v 12
lugal-ki-tuš-du$_{10}$ ED IIIa Šuruppag *WF* 65 r. iv 8
lugal-ki-tuš-du$_{10}$ ED IIIa Šuruppag *WF* 66 o. v 8
lugal-ki-tuš-du$_{10}$ ED IIIa Šuruppag *WF* 67 o. iv 11
lugal-ki-tuš-du$_{10}$ ED IIIa Šuruppag *WF* 68 o. iii 15
lugal-ki-tuš-du$_{10}$ ED IIIa Šuruppag *WF* 69 o. ii 14
lugal-ki-tuš-du$_{10}$ munu$_4$(PAP.PAP) ED IIIa Šuruppag *WF* 71 r. vi 9
lugal-ki-tuš-du$_{10}$ ED IIIa Šuruppag *WF* 77 r. v 15
lugal-ki-tuš-du$_{10}$ ED IIIa Šuruppag *WF* 84 r. i 1
lugal-ki-tuš-du$_{10}$ ED IIIa Šuruppag *WF* 86 r. i 2
lugal-ki-tuš-du$_{10}$ ⸢DU⸣-DU ED IIIa Šuruppag *WF* 125 r. i 7
lugal-ki-tuš-du$_{10}$ sagi ED IIIa Šuruppag *WF* 125 r. ii 1
lugal-ki-tuš-du$_{10}$ ED IIIa Šuruppag *WF* 143 o. i 3
lugal-ki-tuš-du$_{10}$ ED IIIa Šuruppag *WF* 143 r. i 5
lugal-ki-tuš-du$_{10}$ ED IIIa Šuruppag *WF* 149 o. i 4

lugal-^{ĝiš}kiri$_6$ $^{(a≥2)}$ 'the lugal … the garden' 3.1.5.3, p. 133
lugal-^{ĝiš}kiri$_6$ (PN ?) CS/Śkś Girsu CT 50 172 r. ii 16
lugal-^{ĝiš}kiri$_6$ usan$_5$-du$_3$ CS/Śkś Y 5 Umma CT 50 61 r. 10
lugal-^{ĝiš}kiri$_6$ s. *Ba-al-ni*, šeš-U MS-CS Umma MesCiv 4 30 o. i 14
lugal-⌜^{ĝiš}kiri$_6$⌝ [nu$^?$]-banda$_3$ CS Umma MVN 15 379 r. 1

lugal-kiri$_6$-e $^{(a1)}$ 'the lugal … the garden' 3.1.5.3, p. 133
lugal-⌜kiri$_6$⌝-e f. Pu$_2$-ta MS-CS Umma ? *TCVC* 730 o. ii 6

lugal-kisal $^{(a≥2)}$ (compare lugal-kisal-si) 3.1.6.4, p. 157
lugal-kisal CS Umma R. K. Englund, *ASJ* 14 (1992), p. 77–102 6 o. 6
lugal-kisal MS-CS Umma BIN 8 316 r. 6
lugal-kisal f. Me-sag$_2$ CS Girsu MVN 3 113 r. iii 16'

lugal-kisal-a-gub $^{(a1)}$ 'the lugal stands in the courtyard' 3.1.6.4, p. 157
lugal-kisal-a-gub gab$_2$-kas$_4$ ED IIIb/Ukg. lugal 3(+X?) Girsu HSS 3 12 o. iv 8

°lugal-KISAL×PAP $^{(°1)}$ unkn. mng. 3.1.8, p. 179
°lugal-KISAL×PAP CS Unknown CUSAS 13 188 o. 2

lugal-kisal-si $^{(a≥6)}$ 'the lugal is just right for the courtyard' 3.1.6.4, p. 157, 237
lugal-kisal-si (um-mi-a) ED IIIa Abū Ṣalābīḫ *IAS* 34 r. ii 3
lugal-⌜kisal⌝-si (um-mi-a) ED IIIa Abū Ṣalābīḫ *IAS* 39 r. i 2'
lugal-k[isal-si] (um-mi-a) ED IIIa Abū Ṣalābīḫ *IAS* 46 o. xii 7
lugal-kisal-si ⌜um-mi-a⌝ ED IIIa Abū Ṣalābīḫ *IAS* 59 o. vi' 12'
lugal-kisal-si (um-mi-a) ED IIIa Abū Ṣalābīḫ *IAS* 117 (o.) vii' 4'
⌜lugal⌝-kisal-si (um-mi-a) ED IIIa Abū Ṣalābīḫ *IAS* 122 r. i 4'
lugal-kisal-si (um-mi-a) ED IIIa Abū Ṣalābīḫ *IAS* 298 r. i 2'
lugal-kisal-si ED IIIa Kiš *AAICAB* 1/1 (Ashm 1924-16) o. ii 5
lugal-kisal-si gala ED IIIa Šuruppag? MesCiv 4 1 o. v 6
lugal-kisal-si f. E$_2$-u$_2$-u$_2$ ED IIIb Adab *TCABI* 11 o. ii 3
lugal-⌜kisal⌝-si umbisaĝ ED IIIb Ebla ARET 5 20 r. iv 2
lugal-kisal-si umbisaĝ ED IIIb Ebla ARET 5 21 r. vii 2'
lugal-kisal-si s. Ar$_3$-du$_2$ ED IIIb Ešnuna OIP 58, p. 291 12 2
lugal-kisal-si lugal Unug^{ki} ED IIIb/Lukis. X Nippur TMH 5 140 o. i 3
lugal-kisal-[si] ED IIIb/Lukin. X Ur UET 1 3 6'
lugal-kisal-si lugal Unug^{ki}-ga, lugal Urim$_5$^{ki}-ma-k(e$_4$) ED IIIb/Lukis. X Uruk? H. Neumann, *AoF* 8 (1981), p. 75–82 3
lugal-kisal:si s. Lugal-ki-gub-ni-du$_7$-du$_7$, lugal Unug^{ki}-ga, lugal Urim$_5$^{ki}-ma-ke$_4$ ED IIIb BE 1/2 Nippur 86 (b) 5'
lugal-kisal-si f. Me-girim$_x$(A.BU.ḪA.DU)-ta ED IIIb Uruk BRM 4 45 3
lugal-kisal-si lugal Unug^{ki} ED IIIb Uruk F. Thureau-Dangin, *RA* 20 (1923), p. 3–5 5

lugal-KIŠ$^?$-ĜA$_2$×GU$_4$ $^{(a1)}$ unkn. mng. 3.1.8, p. 179
lugal-⌜KIŠ$^?$-ĜA$_2$×GU$_4$⌝ ? ED I-II Ur UET 2 76 o. i 2

lugal-ku-li $^{(a4)}$ 'the lugal is a friend' 3.1.7.8, p. 171, 237
lugal-ku-li f. Ur-^{d}Irḫan(MUŠ), dumu.dumu A-ka$_3$-de$_3$^{ki} ES/Man. Unknown (MO) OIP 104 40 A xiii 8
lugal-ku-li f. Ur-^{d}Irḫan(MUŠ), dumu.dumu A-ka$_3$-de$_3$^{ki} ES/Man. Unknown (MO) OIP 104 40 B xviii 11
lugal-ku-li f. Ur-^{d}Irḫan(MUŠ), dumu.dumu A-ka$_3$-de$_3$^{ki} ES/Man. Unknown (MO) OIP 104 40 C xxi' 30
lugal-ku-li f. Ur-^{d}Irḫan(MUŠ), dumu.dumu A-ka$_3$-de$_3$^{ki} ES/Man. Unknown (MO) OIP 104 40 D x' 13
lugal-ku-li CS Girsu ITT 1 1101 o. 4
lugal-ku-li MS-CS Nippur OSP 2 78 r. 4'

lugal-ku-li CS Umma *USP* 20 o. 6

lugal-ku$_3$ $^{(a\geq2)}$ uncertain mng. 3.1.8, p. 179 w. n. 1087
lugal-ku$_3$ ED IIIb-ES Adab CUSAS 11 93 r. ii 5'
lugal-ku$_3$ ED IIIb-ES Adab CUSAS 11 186 o. iii 5
⌜lugal-ku$_3$⌝ si[mug$^?$] CS Adab OIP 14 78 r. i 1'
lugal-ku$_3$ s[imug$^?$] CS Adab OIP 14 106 r. 4
⌜lugal-ku$_3$⌝ s[imug$^?$] CS Adab *SIA* 675 r. 9

lugal-ku$_3$-zu $^{(a\geq3)}$ 'the lugal is wise' 3.1.2, p. 106, 179 n. 1087
lugal-ku$_3$-zu sipa anše ED IIIb-ES Adab CUSAS 11 85 o. ii 1
lugal-ku$_3$-zu lu$_2$ eme CS/Śkś Girsu CT 50 172 r. i 9
lugal-ku$_3$-zu i$_3$-du$_8$ CS-LS Girsu *DAS* 343 o. 3
lugal-ku$_3$-zu CS Girsu ITT 2/2 5758 o. 1
lugal-ku$_3$-zu CS Girsu *RTC* 127 o. iv 9'

lugal-kun $^{(a3)}$ unkn. mng. 3.1.8, p. 179
lugal-⌜kun⌝ CS Adab CUSAS 13 62 r. 13
lugal-kun s. I$_3$-lu$_2$ CS Adab *SIA* 713 r. 7
lugal-kun ir$_{11}$ ereš-diĝir ^{d}Nin-šubur CS Nippur ? BIN 8 177 r. 8
lugal-kun CS Unknown (Girsu$^?$) MVN 2 298 o. ii 3

lugal-kun$_5$ (TUR.ŠE$_3$) $^{(a\geq3)}$ unkn. mng. 3.1.8, p. 117 n. 635, 179–180
lugal-kun$_5$ ED IIIa Nippur TMH 5 54 o. v 4
lugal-kun$_5$ ES-MS Umma ? *SAKF* 1 r. 3
lugal-kun$_5$ ugula CS Nagar P. Michalowski, apud G. Emberling & H. McDonald, *Iraq* 65 (2003), p. 56–60 82 o. i 8'
lugal-kun$_5$ MS-CS Umma MAD 4 57 (translit. only) o. 4
lugal-kun$_5$ ugula MS-CS Umma MAD 4 62 (translit. only) o. 3
lugal-kun$_5$ ugula CS Umma Nik 2 72 r. 5
lugal-kun$_5$ OAkk Unknown MAD 4 154 (translit. only) o. i 2

lugal-kun$_5$ (TUR.ŠE$_3$)-ne$_2$ $^{(a1)}$ unkn. mng. 3.1.8, p. 180 w. n. 1088
lugal-kun$_5$-ne$_2$ gala CS Adab CUSAS 13 108 r. 3

lugal-kur (identical with lugal-kur-dub$_2$ lu$_2$ Inim-du$_{11}$), p. 180 n. 1089
lugal-kur lu$_2$ Inim-du$_{11}$ ED IIIb/Ukg. lugal 5 Girsu Nik 1 3 o. ii 7

lugal-kur $^{(a\geq7)}$ 'the lugal (is like?) a mountain' 3.1.8, p. 180
lugal-kur engar ED IIIb/Lug. 5 Girsu *DP* 1/2 132 o. v 5
lugal-kur lu$_2$-eš$_2$-gid$_2$ ED IIIb/Ukg. lugal 1 Girsu *DP* 1/2 133 r. ii 8
lugal-kur engar ED IIIb/Lug. 4 Girsu VS 14 173 o. iv 13
lugal-kur ED IIIb Girsu Nik 1 4 o. ii 2
lugal-kur ED IIIb/Ukg. lugal 3 Girsu Nik 1 32 o. iii 1
lu[gal$^?$]-kur E$_2$-sar ED IIIb Umma-Zabala ? BIN 8 50 o. i 6
lugal-kur ED IIIb/Luzag. ensi$_2$ 7 Umma-Zabala BIN 8 86 o. iii 7
lugal-kur ĝuruš, ir$_3$ dub-sar-ne ES-MS Umma *CHÉU* 54 o. i 7
lugal-kur ES-MS Umma Nik 2 18 o. 3
lugal-kur engar, še-kin$_x$-ku$_5$ CS Girsu *SCT* 1 o. ii 9
lugal-kur sipa MS-CS Umma MAD 4 159 (translit. only) o. 6
lugal-kur sipa MS-CS Umma MAD 4 159 (translit. only) r. 3
lugal-kur MS-CS Umma MesCiv 4 15 r. 3
lugal-kur kuš$_7$ CS Umma *USP* 56 o. 6
lugal-kur MS Unknown F. Vukosavović, *JAC* 23 (2008), p. 37–54 5 o. ii 4
lugal-kur MS-CS Unknown *DCS* 43 r. 8

lugal-kur-da-kuš$_2$ $^{(a1)}$ 'the lugal is one who concerns himself with the land' 3.1.4.3, p. 126

lugal-kur-da-kuš$_2$ ED IIIb/Eig. ^{ni_3}ensi$_2$ Adab   OIP 14   49   r. ii' 6'

lugal-kur-dub$_2$ $^{(a\geq4)}$ 'the lugal is one who shatters the mountains'   3.1.3.3, p. 115 w. n. 624, 180 n. 1089, 182 n. 1128, 186, 249 n. 1467, 251 n. 1477
lugal-kur-dub$_2$ ED IIIa   Girsu   PBS 9   2   o. iv 6
lugal-kur-dub$_2$ f. Lugal-u$_3$-ma   ED IIIb/Enz. or En. II   Girsu ?   *DP* 1/1   31   iv 1
lugal-kur-dub$_2^!$(BI) ?   ED IIIb/Ukg. lugal X   Girsu   *CTNMC*   1   r. ii 7
lugal-kur-dub$_2$ lu$_2$ Inim-du$_{11}$ ED IIIb/Ukg. lugal 5   Girsu   *DP* 1/2   136   o. i 12
lugal-kur-dub$_2$ sagi   ED IIIb/Enz. Y 2   Girsu   ITT 5   9237   r. i 1
lugal-⸢kur-dub$_2$⸣ h. Dun-dun   ED IIIb/Lug. 1   Girsu   Nik 1   53   r. iii 11
lugal-kur-dub$_2$ s. Šeš-kur-ra-AŠ$^?$ ED IIIb/Dudu saĝa   Girsu   W. W. Hallo, *OrNS* 42 (1973), p. 228–238   r. i 5
lugal-kur-dub$_2$ ED IIIb   Umma-Zabala   MVN 3   3   o. ii 14'

lugal-kur-ra $^{(a\geq3)}$ 'the lugal in/over the land/mountains'   3.1.1.6, p. 103
lugal-kur-ra   ED IIIb-ES   Adab   CUSAS 11   95   o. ii 7
⸢lugal⸣-kur-⸢ra⸣   ED IIIb-ES   Adab   CUSAS 11   97   o. ii 1
lugal-kur-ra   ES   Adab   *TCABI*   60   o. i 2
lugal-kur-[ra]   CS   Adab   CUSAS 13   121   obv 3'
lugal-kur-ra f. Ur-^{d}Ĝiš-bar-e$_3$, lu$_2$-^{d}Nanše & Ur-bara$_2$ CS   Girsu   CT 50   98   o. ii 6

°lugal-kur-ra-a$_2$-bad $^{(°1)}$ 'the lugal stretches (his) arm over the land'   3.1.1.6, p. 102, 248 n. 1462
°lugal-kur-ra-a$_2$-bad   ED IIIa   Šuruppag   *SF*   63   r. iii 5

lugal-kur-si $^{(a1)}$ 'the lugal is just right for *the land* (?)'   3.1.1.6, p. 103
lugal-kur-si h. ⸢Bara$_2$⸣-su$_3$ ED IIIa-b   Unknown   YOS 1   6   3

lugal-kuš$_2$ $^{(a1)}$ (probable abbreviation of lugal-mu-da-kuš$_2$)   3.1.4.1, p. 124 n. 679
lugal-kuš$_2$ saĝa   MS-CS   Isin ? Nippur ? Adab ?   A. Goetze, *JCS* 20 (1968), p. 126–127   o. 5

lugal-la$_2$ $^{(a\geq5)}$ '*one* of the lugal'   3.1.1.1, p. 85–86, 101 n. 539, 175 n. 1023, 251 n. 1476
lugal-la$_2$ sukkal   ED IIIa   Adab   *TCABI*   1   o. iii 1
lugal-la$_2$ ED IIIb-ES   Isin   MVN 3   67   o. ii 6
lugal-la$_2$ f. Lugal-sipa   ED IIIb   Isin   BIN 8   34   o. ii 1
lugal-⸢la$_2^?$⸣ s. Ne-saĝ   ES-MS   Isin   MVN 3   52   o. ii 5
lugal-la$_2$ MS-CS   Adab ?   BIN 8   242   o. 5
lugal-la$_2$ f. [U]r-PA   MS-CS   Adab   CUSAS 13   6   r. 4
lugal-la$_2$ [Ur]-šul-bi   MS-CS   Isin   BIN 8   172   o. 11
lugal-la$_2$ Ur-šul   CS   Isin   MAD 4   151   r. 4
lugal-la$_2$ s. Ur-abzu   MS-CS   Isin ?   BIN 8   158   r. i 6
lugal-la$_2$ s. Ur-gu, ss. (?) Pu$_2$-ta   MS-CS   Mesag   BIN 8   186   o. 10
⸢lugal$^?$⸣-la$_2$ KUM-tuš-še$_3$ MS-CS   Unknown   MVN 3   103   o. 9

lugal-Lagaš(LA.BUR.ŠIR) $^{(a1)}$ 'the lugal … Lagaš'   3.1.6.4, p. 154 n. 883
lugal-Lagaš(LA.BUR.ŠIR)   ED I-II   Ur   UET 2   205B   o. i 2

lugal-Lagaš$^!$(ŠIR.BUR) $^{(a1)}$ 'the lugal … Lagaš'   3.1.6.4, p. 154 n. 883
lugal-Lagaš$^!$(ŠIR.BUR) (ugula)   CS   Girsu   CT 50   96   o. 3

lugal-Lagaš^{ki} $^{(a2)}$ 'the lugal … Lagaš'   3.1.6.4, p. 154 n. 883
lugal-Lagaš^{ki} simug   ED IIIb/Ukg. lugal 4   Girsu   *AWAS*   120   r. i 6
lugal-Lagaš^{ki} simug   ED IIIb/Ukg. lugal 6   Girsu   *AWAS*   122   r. ii 4
lugal-Lagaš^{ki} [šu-ku$_6$ a šeš]   ED IIIb/Lug. 2   Girsu   BIN 8   370   o. iv 1
lugal-Lagaš^{ki} simug   ED IIIb/Ukg. lugal 5   Girsu   *DP* 1/2   114   r. i 13
lugal-Lagaš^{ki} simug   ED IIIb/Ukg. lugal 6   Girsu   *DP* 1/2   115   r. ii 1
lugal-Lagaš^{ki} šu-ku$_6$ ab-ba   ED IIIb/Ukg. lugal 6   Girsu   *DP* 1/2   135   r. iv 9

lugal-Lagaš^{ki} šu-ku$_6$ a dun-a ED IIIb/Ukg. lugal 3 Girsu *DP* 2/1 177 r. iv 2
lugal-Lagaš^{ki} šu-ku$_6$ a šeš ED IIIb/Lug. 1 Girsu *DP* 2/1 191 r. i 1
lugal-Lagaš^{ki} simug ED IIIb/Ukg. lugal 1 Girsu HSS 3 17 r. ii 5
[lugal-Laga]š^{ki} simug ED IIIb/Ukg. lugal 6 Girsu HSS 3 18 o. ix 1'
lugal-Lagaš^{ki} simug ED IIIb/Ukg. lugal 4 Girsu Nik 1 2 r. i 3'
lugal-Lagaš^{ki} simug ED IIIb/Ukg. lugal 4 Girsu *TSA* 14 r. i 3
lugal-Lagaš^{ki} simug ED IIIb/Ukg. lugal 4 Girsu *TSA* 15 r. ii 4
lugal-[La]gaš^{ki} [simug] ED IIIb/Ukg. lugal 6 Girsu *TSA* 16 o. ix 7'
lugal-Lagaš^{ki} šu-ku$_6$ a du$_{10}$-ga ED IIIb/Ukg. lugal 4 Girsu *TSA* 47 o. iii 3

lugal-lal$_3$ $^{(a/\geq 2^\circ 1)}$ 'the lugal is (sweet as) honey (or syrup)' 3.1.7.8, p. 169, 210, 229
lugal-lal$_3$ ED I-II Ur UET 2 89 r. i 3'
lugal-lal$_3$ ED I-II Ur UET 2 224 o. ii 2
⸢lugal-lal$_3$⸣ ED IIIa Adab CUSAS 11 3 o. i 1'
°lugal-lal$_3$ ED IIIa Šuruppag *SF* 29 o. vii 18
°lugal-⸢lal$_3$⸣ ED IIIa Unknown *RIAA* 44 o. ii' 5

lugal-lama $^{(a1)}$ 'the lugal is a Lama-spirit' 3.1.3.1, p. 109
lugal-lama dub-sar MS Unknown *EGA* 583 1

° ^{nu}**lugal-lama-zi-da** $^{(\circ 1)}$ 'the lugal is a reliable Lama-spirit' 3.1.3.1, p. 109
° ^{nu}lugal-lama-zi-da ED IIIa Abū Ṣalābīḫ R. D. Biggs & J. N. Postgate, *Iraq* 40 (1978), p. 101–117 522 o. ii 1

lugal-^{d}lama$_3$(KAL) $^{(a1)}$ 'the lugal is a Lama-spirit' 3.1.3.1, p. 109
lugal-^{d}lama$_3$ Girsu [x (x)] e$_3$ ḪA CS/Śkś B. R. Foster, *JANES* 12 (1980), p. 29–42 1 r. i 5'

lugal-lama$_3$-zi $^{(a\geq 4)}$ 'the lugal is a reliable Lama-spirit' 3.1.3.1, p. 109
lugal-lama$_3$-zi ED IIIb/Luzag.$^{?}$ ensi$_2$ 7 Umma-Zabala BIN 8 116 o. i 2
lugal-lama$_3$-zi f. Me-An-ne$_2$ CS/Śkś Isin MAD 4 15 r. 1
lugal-lama$_3$-zi MS-CS Nippur OSP 2 80 r. ii 3
lugal-lama$_3$-zi MS-CS Nippur OSP 2 118 o. 4
lugal-lama$_3$-zi MS-CS Nippur OSP 2 129 r. ii 3'
lugal-lama$_3$-zi maškim-bi$_3$ MS-CS Nippur OSP 2 134 r. 4'
lugal-lama$_3$-zi ašgab MS-CS Nippur OSP 2 149 r. 8
lu[gal]-⸢lama$_3$⸣-[zi] MS-CS Nippur OSP 2 158 o. 8
lugal-lama$_3$-zi MS-CS Nippur TMH 5 120 o. 9
lugal-lama$_3$-zi MS-CS Unknown BIN 8 180 r. 3
lugal-lama$_3$-zi (saĝ-sug$_5$) CS Unknown BIN 8 213 o. 3
lugal-lama$_3$-zi saĝ-sug$_5$ CS Unknown BIN 8 213 o. 9
lu[gal]-lama$_3$-zi šita uru-ke$_4$ MS-CS Unknown B. R. Foster, *JCS* 35 (1983), p. 147–175 7 o. 6

lugal-lirum $^{(a1)}$ 'the lugal is an athlete/wrestler' 3.1.7.3, p. 163
lugal-lirum gala ED IIIa Šuruppag? MesCiv 4 1 r. ii 1

lugal-lu $^{(a\geq 3)}$ (phonetic for lugal-lu$_2$, or 'the lugal makes (things) thrive'?) 3.1.1.6 or 3.1.5.3, p. 86 n. 422, 101, 102 n. 540
lugal-lu ED IIIb Adab BIN 8 8 o. iii 3
lugal-lu ED IIIb-ES Adab CUSAS 11 105 o. i 2
lu[gal]-lu ES-MS Adab *TCABI* 64 o. i 5'
lugal-lu MS-CS Adab ? BIN 8 242 o. 6
lugal-lu nu-banda$_3$ MS-CS Adab CUSAS 13 10 o. 3
lugal-lu dumu šitim-gal CS Adab CUSAS 13 109 r. 4
lugal-lu lu$_2$ šabra e$_2$ MS-CS Adab MVN 3 23 r. 2

lugal-lu-dadag(UD.UD) $^{(a1)}$ 'the lugal is one who exhonerates man' 3.1.3.1, p. 110, 251 n. 1476
lugal-lu-dadag s. Lugal-mu-kuš$_2$ ED IIIb-ES Isin MVN 3 67 o. i 6
⸢lugal⸣-l[u-dadag$^?$] s. [Lugal]-⸢mu⸣-[kuš$_2$$^?$] ED IIIb-ES Isin MVN 3 67 o. iii 6

lugal-lu-du$_{10}$ $^{(a1)}$ 'the lugal is one who does good for man' 3.1.1.6, p. 101
⸢lugal-lu-du$_{10}$⸣ ⸢nar$^?$⸣ ED IIIb Adab MVN 3 28 r. ii 3

lugal-lu-lu $^{(a1)}$ 'the lugal is one who makes (things) thrive' 3.1.5.3, p. 102, 134, 229
lugal-lu-lu ED I-II Ur UET 2 338 o. ii 2'

lugal-lu$_2$ $^{(a>10)}$ abbreviation 3.1.1.6, p. 101
lugal-⸢lu$_2$⸣ ED IIIa Šuruppag *FTUM* 41 o. ii 25
lugal-lu$_2$ ED IIIa Šuruppag *RTC* 15 r. i 4
lugal-lu$_2$ h. E$_2$-ul-le ED IIIb/Lug. ensi$_2$ Girsu *DP* 1/2 127 o. v 7
lugal-lu$_2$ ED IIIb Nippur OSP 1 128 o. i 4'
lugal-lu$_2$? ED IIIb Nippur OSP 1 128 r. ii 3'
lugal-lu$_2$ h. Giri$_3$-ni ED IIIb Nippur PBS 15 6 3
lugal-lu$_2$ ED IIIb Nippur TMH 5 11 r. i 9
lugal-lu$_2$ ED IIIb Nippur TMH 5 11 r. iii 6
lugal-lu$_2$ ED IIIb Nippur TMH 5 22 o. 2
lugal-lu$_2$ f. Lugal-ša$_3$ ED IIIb Nippur TMH 5 69 o. ii 4
lugal-lu$_2$ ED IIIb Nippur TMH 5 199 o. 3
lugal-lu$_2$ ED IIIb/Luzag. ensi$_2$ X Umma-Zabala BIN 8 82 o. iii 17
lugal-lu$_2$ ⸢GU$_2$⸣$^?$.KI Lugal-[l]u$_2$ ugula ⸢x⸣-[(x$^?$)] ED IIIb/Luzag. ensi$_2$ 7 Umma-Zabala BIN 8 86 o. i 15
lugal-lu$_2$ ED IIIb Umma-Zabala CUSAS 14 87 o. i 5
lugal-lu$_2$ ED IIIb/Luzag. Y 7 Umma-Zabala M. Powell, *HUCA* 49 (1978), p. 1–58 1 o. v 13
lugal-lu$_2$ ES Adab CUSAS 11 273 o. 2
lugal-lu$_2$ ES-MS Nippur OSP 1 136 o. i 4
lugal-lu$_2$ ES-MS Umma Nik 2 44 r. 2
lugal-lu$_2$ MS-CS Adab OIP 14 176 o. i 11
lugal-⸢lu$_2$⸣ CS-LS? Adab OIP 14 198 o. ii 11
lugal-lu$_2$ išib ^{d}Inana, lu$_2$ Nina^{ki} CS Girsu *RTC* 120 o. 3
lugal-lu$_2$ CS Girsu *STTI* 164 o. i 6
lugal-lu$_2$ f. U$_2$-da, Bar-ra-an & E$_2$-ki, ir$_{11}$ ^{d}Nin-MAR.KI-me CS Girsu ITT 2/1 2892 o. 4
lugal-lu$_2$ s. Ne-saĝ MS-CS Isin BIN 8 155 o. 8
lugal-lu$_2$ MS-CS Mesag BIN 8 281 r. 10
lugal-lu$_2$ MS-CS Nippur OIP 97 12 r. 3
lugal-lu$_2$ MS-CS Nippur OSP 2 84 o. ii 2
lu[gal]-lu$_2$ MS-CS Nippur OSP 2 104 o. i' 1'
lugal-lu$_2$ f. Du$_{11}$-ga-ni CS/NS. Nippur PBS 9 25 r. 5
lugal-lu$_2$ CS Unknown MAD 5 106 r. 8
lugal-l[u$_2$] CS Unknown Mesopotamia 9 5 r. 5'

lugal-lu$_2$-dadag(UD.UD) $^{(a1)}$ 'the lugal is one who exhonerates man' 3.1.3.1, p. 110, 251 n. 1476
lugal-lu$_2$-dadag ED IIIb Nippur TMH 5 24 r. i 3'
lugal-lu$_2$-dadag ED IIIb Nippur TMH 5 56 o. ii 5
lugal-lu$_2$-dadag ED IIIb Nippur TMH 5 139 o. 2
lugal-⸢lu$_2$⸣-dadag ED IIIb Nippur TMH 5 167 o. ii 3
lu:gal-[lu$_2$$^?$-da]dag ES Nippur OSP 1 31 o. ii 2'

lugal-lu$_2$-du$_{10}$ $^{(a3)}$ 'the lugal is one who does good for man' 3.1.1.6, p. 101

lugal-lu$_2$-du$_{10}$ nitaḫ, il$_2$ ED IIIb/Ukg. lugal 1? Girsu *AWAS* 123 o. v 6
lugal-lu$_2$-du$_{10}$ il$_2$ ED IIIb/Ukg. lugal 2 Girsu *DP* 1/2 113 o. vii 2
lugal-lu$_2$-du$_{10}$ [ugu]la e$_2$ ED IIIb Umma-Zabala CUSAS 14 134 o. i 6
lugal-lu$_2$-⸢du$_{10}$⸣ ugula ⸢e$_2$⸣ ED IIIb Umma-Zabala CUSAS 14 246 o. i 2
lugal-lu$_2$-du$_{10}$ s. Ad-da MS-CS Nippur TMH 5 52 o. i 9

lugal-lu$_2$-gi-na (a2) 'the lugal is a righteous man' 3.1.7.9, p. 171
lugal-lu$_2$-gi-na ED IIIb/Umma$_2$(ḪI×DIŠ)-nitaḫ-gin$_7$ 3 Umma T. Ozaki, *JAC* 23 (2008), p. 55–64 3 o. ii 13
lugal-lu$_2$-gi-na ES-MS Umma Nik 2 14 o. iii 10

lugal-lu$_2$-LAK545-ne-saĝ (a1) unkn. mng. 3.1.8, p. 180
lugal-lu$_2$-LAK545-ne-saĝ umbisaĝ ED IIIa Unknown *RIAA* 44 r. i 11

lugal-lu$_2$-ni (a1) 'man of the lugal' or abbreviation 3.1.1.1, p. 83 n. 401
lugal-lu$_2$-ni lu$_2$ luĝa$_x$(BI×NIĜ$_2$) ED IIIb/Enz. ensi$_2$ 2 Girsu BIN 8 347 o. i 3
lugal-lu$_2$-ni ED IIIb/Enz. ensi$_2$ 2 Girsu VS 25 83 r. i 4

lugal-lu$_2$-sa$_6$-ga (a1) 'the lugal is one who is kind to man' 3.1.4.1, p. 123
lugal-lu$_2$-sa$_6$-ga ED IIIb-ES Umma-Zabala ? BIN 8 98 o. i 2
lugal-lu$_2$-sa$_6$-ga ED IIIb Umma-Zabala ? BIN 8 104 o. i 5

lugal-lu$_2$-saĝ (a1) unkn. mng. 3.1.8, p. 180
lugal-lu$_2$-saĝ ED IIIb-ES Umma-Zabala BIN 8 92 o. 2

lugal-lu$_2$-ŠE$_3$-IG-ŠE$_3$ (a1) unkn. mng. 3.1.8, p. 180
lugal-lu$_2$-ŠE$_3$-IG-ŠE$_3$ ED IIIb/X Y 1 Girsu *DP* 2/2 284 o. i 3

lugal-lu$_2$-ti-ti (a2) 'the lugal is one who quickens man' 3.1.4.1, p. 123, 134 n. 744, 253 n. 1490, 254 n. 1493
lugal-lu$_2$-ti-ti lu$_2$ ED IIIb/Ukg. lugal 6 Girsu *DP* 1/2 135 r. iii 2
lugal-lu$_2$-ti-ti ĝuruš, lu$_2$ gi sa$_{10}$-sa$_{10}$ ED IIIb Ur UET 2 suppl. 11 o. ii 4
lugal-lu$_2$-ti-ti ED IIIb Ur UET 2 suppl. 12 r. 1

lugal-lu$_{2\text{-}90^\circ}$-uĝu$_3$(LAK730)-du$_{10}$ (a1) 'the lugal is someone who makes the country good' 3.1.1.6, p. 100
lu[gal]-lu$_{2\text{-}90^\circ}$-uĝu$_3$-du$_{10}$ ED IIIb Ur UET 2 suppl. 14 r. ii 5

lugal-lu$_2$-zi (a1) 'the lugal is a reliable man' 3.1.7.9, p. 171
lugal-lu$_2$-zi ulu$_3$-di ED IIIb Girsu CT 50 29 r. ii 1

lugal-LUḪ (a2) 'the lugal (is) pure (or purifies?)' 3.1.6.3, p. 152
lugal-LUḪ nitaḫ CS Girsu *DPA* 46 (PUL 25) o. 6
lugal-LUḪ MS-CS Ur UET 2 suppl. 48 o. i 6

lugal-ma-de$_6$ (a≥7) 'the lugal brought (him/her) to me' 3.1.4.1, p. 121, 254 n. 1493
lugal-ma-de$_6^{!}$(AB) ED IIIb Girsu S. Langdon, *Babyloniaca* 4 (1911), 246–247 (Edin 09-405, 34) r. i 2
lugal-ma-de$_6$ šu-i ED IIIb/X Y 3 Girsu *RTC* 60 o. ii 4
lugal-ma-de$_6$ ED IIIb Isin TIM 9 100 r. 11'
lugal-ma-de$_6$ ED IIIb Lagaš BiMes 3 15 r. iii 1'
lugal-ma-de$_6$ ED IIIb Nippur TMH 5 35 o. i 9
lugal-ma-de$_6$ f. Ur-^{d}En-ki Adab ES *TCABI* 49 o. i 3
lugal-ma-de$_6$ MS-CS Adab CUSAS 13 28 o. 7
lugal-ma-de$_6$ MS-CS Mesag BIN 8 272 r. 2
lugal-ma-de$_6$ MS-CS Nippur TMH 5 29 o. i 3'
lugal-ma-de$_6$ MS-CS Unknown MVN 3 71 o. 2

lugal-ma$_2$ (a≥4) 'the lugal … the ship' 3.1.5.3, p. 102, 135 n. 757, 153, 180

lugal-ma$_2$ h. ⸢bara$_2$$^{?}$⸣-ḫe$_2$-NI-ĝal$_2$ CS Girsu ? M. Yoshikawa, *ASJ* 3 (1981), p. 193–197 r. ii 3'
lugal-ma$_2$ CS Girsu CT 50 122 r. 3
lugal-ma$_2$ CS Girsu ITT 2/1 4444 o. 4
lugal-ma$_2$ h. Na-na MS-CS Susa MDP 14 19 o. 6
lugal-ma$_2$ CS Umma T. Donald, *MCS* 9 (1964) 264 r. 2
lugal-ma$_2$ s. Da-da CS-LS Ur *EGA* 1695 1
lugal-ma$_2$ CS Unknown (Girsu$^{?}$) MVN 2 298 r. i 14

lugal-ma$_2$-gur$_8$-e $^{(a1)}$ 'the lugal is (just right for) the cargo ship (?)' 3.1.5.3, p. 135 n. 757, 153
lugal-ma$_2$-gur$_8$-e CS Adab *SIA* 846 r. 1

lugal-ma$_2$-tab-ba $^{(a1)}$ 'the lugal … a two-pronged boat' 3.1.8, p. 180 w. n. 1091
lugal-ma$_2$-tab-ba lu$_2$ ED IIIb/Ukg. lugal 6 Girsu *DP* 1/2 135 o. v 14

lugal-maḫ $^{(a1/°1)}$ 'the lugal is the greatest/sublime' 3.1.7.7, p. 168
°lugal-maḫ ED IIIa Kiš MesCiv 14, pl. 23, 3: H+Y r.(?) ii' 1
lu:gal-maḫ sagi ED IIIb Nippur OSP 1 94 o. i 2

lugal-maḫ$_2$ $^{(a\geq4)}$ 'the lugal is the greatest/sublime' 3.1.7.7, p. 168 w. n. 973
lugal-maḫ$_2$ ED IIIb Lagaš area CT 7, pl. 4 (BM 90905, prev. 12033) 3
lugal-maḫ$_2$ CS Adab *SIA* 972 o. 4
lugal-maḫ$_2$ MS Adab *TCABI* 175 o. 5
lugal-maḫ$_2$ MS Adab *TCABI* 179 o. 3
lugal-maḫ$_2$ CS Isin ? MAD 4 169 o. 3
lugal-maḫ$_2$ CS Isin ? MAD 4 169 o. 12
lugal-maḫ$_2$ šandan ^{d}En-lil-la$_2$ MS-CS Nippur OIC 22 1 o. 4
lugal-maḫ$_2$ šandan MS-CS Nippur OIC 22 2 r. 2
lugal-maḫ$_2$ MS-CS Nippur OSP 2 90 o. i 2'
lugal-maḫ$_2$ f. E$_2$-sa$_6$-ga MS-CS Nippur TMH 5 52 o. i 6

lugal-mas-su $^{(a\geq6)}$ 'the lugal is a leader' 3.1.1.6, p. 60, 103
lugal-mas-su ED IIIb Girsu *AWEL*, p. 548 3 (Riftin 3) o. ii 3
lugal-mas-su aga$_3$-us$_2$ ED IIIb/Enz. ensi$_2$ 2 Girsu BIN 8 347 o. ii 1
[lugal]-⸢mas-su⸣ ⸢engar⸣ ki-⸢gub⸣ ED IIIb/Lug. [x] Girsu BIN 8 387 o. iii 1
lugal-mas-su engar ED IIIb/Lug. 5 Girsu *DP* 1/2 87 o. ii 5
lugal-mas-su lu$_2$ Ur-saĝ ED IIIb/Ukg. lugal 5 Girsu *DP* 1/2 136 o. i 6
lugal-mas-su saĝ-apin ED IIIb/Lug. 2 Girsu *DP* 2/1 239 r. i 5
lugal-mas-su aga$_3$-us$_2$ ED IIIb/Enz. ensi$_2$ X Girsu *DP* 2/1 195 o. iii' 3'
lugal-mas-su lu$_2$ ^{d}Ba-u$_2$ ED IIIb Girsu *DP* suppl. 568 o. i 2
lugal-mas-su ED IIIb/X Y 4 Girsu *DP* suppl. 587 r. i 8
lugal-mas-su engar ED IIIb/X Y 4 Girsu *DP* suppl. 587 r. iii 1
lugal-mas-su aga$_3$-us$_2$ ED IIIb/X Y 4 Girsu *DP* suppl. 616 o. i 4
lugal-mas-su engar ki-gub, e Uru$_{11}$^{ki}-kam ED IIIb/Lug. 3 Girsu *DP* suppl. 623 o. v 6
lugal-mas-su engar ki-gub ED IIIb/X Y 4 Girsu *DP* suppl. 646 o. i 3
lugal-mas-su ED IIIb Girsu HSS 3 38 o. ii 2
lugal-mas-su ED IIIb/Ukg. lugal 3 Girsu Nik 1 32 o. i 7
lugal-mas-su ugula ED IIIb/Lug. 2 Girsu Nik 1 173 o. ii 1
lugal-mas-su engar ki-gub ED IIIb/Lug. 2 Girsu Nik 1 173 o. iii 4
lugal-mas-su ugula ED IIIb/Lug. 3 Girsu Nik 1 186 o. ii 2
lugal-mas-su ED IIIb/X Y 2 Girsu VS 14 7 o. ii 3
lugal-mas-su MS-CS Nippur OSP 2 95 r. ii 4''
lugal-mas-su maškim MS-CS Umma CT 50 60 r. 10

lugal-mas-su$_2$ $^{(a6)}$ 'the lugal is a leader' 3.1.1.6, p. 103, 185

lugal-mas-su$_2$ engar ED IIIb/Lug. 6 Girsu Nik 1 181 o. iii 2
lugal-mas-su$_2$ dub-sar ED IIIb Umma-Zabala BIN 8 102 o. i 4
lugal-mas-su$_2$ nu-banda$_3$-ni ES-MS Umma Nik 2 10 r. 3
lugal-mas-su$_2$ CS Adab CUSAS 13 65 o. 4
lugal-m[a]s-su$_2$? CS Gasur HSS 10 169 o. 8
lugal-mas-su$_2$ lu$_2$ di-da Ur-lugal MS-CS BIN 8 Isin ? 153 o. 2

lugal-maš-usu(A$_2$.KAL) $^{(a1)}$ unkn. mng. 3.1.8, p. 180
lugal-maš-usu ED IIIa-b Isin (?) OIP 104 14 r. vii 12

lugal-maškim-e $^{(a\geq2)}$ unkn. mng. 3.1.8, p. 180
lugal-maškim-e CS Adab *SIA* 885+1062 o. 3
lugal-maškim-[e] CS Umma *AAS* 202 o. 5
lugal-maškim-e CS Umma ? CUSAS 13 201 r. 5
lugal-maškim-e saĝ-apin-na lugal CS Umma T. Donald, *MCS* 9 (1964) 236 o. ii 13
lugal-maškim-e CS Umma *USP* 22 o. ii 13
lugal-maškim-e ugu[la] CS Umma *USP* 65 o. 4

lugal-me $^{(a1)}$ unkn. mng. 3.1.8, p. 180 w. n. 1093
lugal-me ED IIIb/Lug. 1 Girsu BIN 8 362 o. iii 6
lugal-me s. Ni$_3$-ul-pa-e$_3$ ED IIIb Girsu Nik 1 122 o. i 5
lugal-me ED IIIb/Lug. 4 Girsu Nik 1 156 o. ii 6
lugal-me ‹s.› Ni$_3$-u[l]-pa-⌜e$_3$⌝ ED IIIb/X Y 1 Girsu Nik 1 160 o. iii 1
lugal-me ED IIIb/Lug. 3 Girsu Nik 1 175 o. ii 6
lugal-me ED IIIb/Lug. 4 Girsu *RTC* 27 o. ii 2
lugal-me s. Ni$_3$-ul-pa-e$_3$ ED IIIb/Lug. 2 Girsu VS 14 78 o. ii 1
lugal-me ED IIIb/Lug. [X] Girsu VS 25 36 o. iii 2

°lugal-me-am $^{(°2)}$ uncertain mng. 3.1.1.3, p. 88 n. 445
°lugal-me-am ma$_2$-gur$_8$ ED IIIa Abū Ṣalābīḫ *IAS* 61 o. xii 2
°lugal-[me-am$^?$] ED IIIa Abū Ṣalābīḫ *IAS* 81 (r.) iii' 7'
°lugal-me-am ED IIIb Ebla ARET 5 25 r. i 2

lugal-me-du$_{10}$-ga $^{(a\geq1)}$ 'the lugal of the good ordinances' 3.1.6.3, p. 66 n. 329, 150
lugal-me-du$_{10}$-ga MS-CS Nippur TMH 5 39 r. ii 12
lugal-me-du$_{10}$-ga s. Lugal-diĝir-ra MS Unknown *EGA* 522 1

lugal-ME-^{d}En-l[il$_2$] $^{(a1)}$ 'the lugal … the rites of Enlil (?)' 3.1.6.3, p. 149
lugal-ME-^{d}En-l[il$_2$] ED IIIb Kiš *AAICAB* 1/1 (Ashm 1928-427) r. i 1

lugal-me-gal-gal $^{(a2)}$ 'the lugal (performs) the great rites (?)' 3.1.6.3, p. 149, 180 n. 1093, 249 n. 1467
lugal-me-gal-gal (s. Ur-^{d}En-ki) ED IIIa Šuruppag? MVN 10 82 r. i 1
lugal-me-gal-gal s. Ur-^{d}En-ki ED IIIa Šuruppag? MVN 10 83 o. iv 8
lugal-me-gal-gal (šu-ku$_6$) ED IIIb/Lug. 2 Girsu BIN 8 370 o. iii 4
lugal-me-gal-gal šu-ku$_6$ ab-ba ED IIIb/Ukg. lugal 6 Girsu *DP* 1/2 135 r. iv 2
lugal-me-gal-gal šu-ku$_6$ a dun-a ED IIIb/Ukg. lugal 3 Girsu *DP* 2/1 177 r. iv 4
lugal-me-gal-gal ugula ED IIIb/Ukg. lugal 3 Girsu *DP* 2/1 177 r. iv 5
lugal-me-gal-gal šu-ku$_6$ a šeš ED IIIb/Lug. 1 Girsu *DP* 2/1 191 o. v 5
lugal-me-gal-gal šu-ku$_6$ Gu$_2$-eden-na-ka ED IIIb/Ukg. lugal 3 Girsu *DP* 2/2 303 r. ii* 3
lugal-me-gal-gal šu-ku$_6$ Gu$_2$-eden-na-ka, šu-ku$_6$ ^{d}Ba-u$_2$ ED IIIb/X Y 3 Girsu *DP* 2/2 318 r. i 2
lugal-me-gal-gal (šu-ku$_6$) ED IIIb/Ukg. lugal 2 Girsu *DP* 2/2 324 o. ii 3
lugal-me-gal-gal šu-ku$_6$ Gu$_2$-eden-na-ka ED IIIb/Ukg. lugal 3 Girsu *DP* 2/2 328 o. ii 2
lugal-me-gal-gal ED IIIb/Lug. Y X Girsu E. Sollberger, *Genava* 26 (1948), p. 48–72 7 o. ii 5

lugal-me-gal-gal šu-ku$_6$ u$_2$-rum, ^{d}Ba-u$_2$ ED IIIb/Ukg. lugal 4 Girsu HSS 3 28 r. iii 1
lugal-me-gal-gal šu-ku$_6$ a šeš ED IIIb/Lug. 6 Girsu *RTC* 32 o. iii 4
lugal-me-gal-gal ugula (šu-ku$_6$ a du$_{10}$-ga) ED IIIb/Ukg. lugal 4 Girsu *TSA* 47 o. iii 6
lugal-me-gal-gal šu-ku$_6$ a šeš ED IIIb/Lug. 5 Girsu VS 14 25 o. iv 6

lugal-me-lam$_2$? $^{(a1)}$ compare perhaps the following name 3.1.7.10, p. 173 n. 1014
lugal-me-l[am$_2^?$] ED IIIb/Urz. lugal Isin M. Lambert, *RA* 73 (1979), p. 5–6 r. vi 28

lugal-me-lam$_2$-su$_3$ $^{(a1)}$ 'the lugal spreads an ominous sheen' 3.1.7.10, p. 173
lugal-me-lam$_2$-su$_3$ ED IIIb Umma-Zabala CUSAS 14 4 o. i 4

lugal-me-lam$_2$-su$_{20}$(ŠIM) $^{(a1)}$ 'the lugal spreads an ominous sheen' 3.1.7.10, p. 173 n. 1014
lugal-me-lam$_2$-⸢su$_{20}$⸣ ED IIIa Šuruppag M. Molina & H. Sanchiz, *StEL* 24 (2007), p. 1–15 2 o. iv 1

lugal-me-si $^{(a\geq1)}$ 'the lugal is just right for the ordinances' 3.1.6.3, p. 66 n. 329, 150
lugal-me-si ED I-II Ur UET 2 87 o. v 4'
lugal-me-si ED I-II Ur UET 2 126 o. i 4'

lugal-me-sikil $^{(a1)}$ 'the lugal (is just right for) the pure ordinances (of DN)' 3.1.6.3, p. 150
lugal-me-sikil ED IIIb Umma-Zabala ? BIN 8 63 o. ii 1

lugal-me-še$_3$-ĝal$_2$ $^{(a1)}$ 'the lugal is present *for* the rites' 3.1.6.3, p. 149
lugal-me-še$_3$-ĝal$_2$ ED IIIb Nippur TMH 5 25 o. i 5

lugal-me-te-na $^{(a2)}$ 'a lord unto himself' 3.1.7.1, p. 161
lugal-me-te-na ED IIIb/Luzag. ensi$_2$ 7 Umma-Zabala M. deJ. Ellis, *JCS* 31 (1979), p. 30–55 7 o. v 13'
lugal-me-te$^!$-na ĝuruš CS Girsu *RTC* 91 o. ii' 12'

°lugal-me-zi $^{(a\geq1)}$ 'the lugal … the true me-functions' 3.1.6.3, p. 150
°⸢lugal⸣-me-⸢zi⸣ ED IIIa Šuruppag *SF* 63 o. vi 2
°lugal-⸢me⸣-[x-(x)] ED IIIa Šuruppag *SF* 28 r. ii 5
°lugal-me-[x-(x)] ED IIIa Šuruppag *SF* 29 o. iv 2

lugal-me$_3$ $^{(a1)}$ 'the lugal … battle' 3.1.3.3, p. 117
lugal-⸢me$_3$⸣ CS-LS ? Girsu *RTC* 254 r. ii 16

lugal-me$_3$-TUR-še$_3$-nu-še-ge $^{(a1)}$ 'does the lugal not howl fiercely (?) in battle?' 3.1.3.3, p. 117, 180 n. 1093
lugal-me$_3$-TUR-še$_3$-nu-še-ge ED IIIb/X Y 3 Girsu VS 14 127 o. ii 5

lugal-me$_3$-TUR-še$_3$-nu-še$_{27}$-ge $^{(a1)}$ 'does the lugal not howl fiercely (?) in battle?' 3.1.3.3, p. 117, 180 n. 1093
lugal-⸢me$_3$⸣-TUR-še$_3$-nu-še$_{27}$-ge ED IIIb/Ukg. ensi$_2$ 1 Girsu *DP* suppl. 519 o. ii 1
lugal-me$_3$-TUR-še$_3$-nu-še$_{27}$-ge ED IIIb/Ukg. lugal 1 Girsu Nik 1 155 o. i 5
lugal-me$_3$-TUR-še$_3$-nu-še$_{27}$-ge ED IIIb/Ukg. lugal 1 Girsu Nik 1 155 o. iii 1
lugal-me$_3$-TUR-še$_3$-nu-še$_{27}$-ge ED IIIb/Lug. 4 Girsu A. Deimel, *OrSP* 20, p. 28 (translit. only) o. ii 3

lugal-men $^{(a3)}$ 'the lugal … the men-headdress' 3.1.1.3, p. 88, 89 n. 446, 229
lugal-men ED IIIa-b Marada ? *AAICAB* 1/1 (Ashm 1924-462) r. i 3
lugal-men ED IIIb Nippur TMH 5 159 r. i 2
lugal-men lu$_2$ gub-ba CS Adab *SIA* 667 o. 3'

°lugal-men-nun $^{(°1)}$ 'the lugal … the sublime (?) men-headdress' 3.1.1.3, p. 88f. w. n. 446
°lugal-men-nun ED IIIb Ebla A. Archi, *RA* 78 (1984), p. 171–174 o. i 1

lugal-men$_x$(ĜA$_2$×EN) $^{(a\geq6/°2)}$ 'the lugal … the men-headdress' 3.1.1.3, p. 88 n. 444, 229
lugal-men$_x$ ED I-II Ur UET 2 93 o. iii 10
°lu[gal]-men$_x$ ED IIIa Kiš MesCiv 14, pl. 23, 3: H+Y r.(?) i' 2

lugal-⸢men$_x$$^{?}$⸣ ED IIIa Šuruppag *RTC* 11 o. i 3
lugal-men$_x$ ED IIIa Šuruppag *SF* 16 r. i 6
°lugal-men$_x$ ED IIIa Šuruppag *SF* 29 o. vii 17
lugal-men$_x$ UD-šeš ED IIIa Šuruppag *TSŠ* 1 r. i 15'
lugal-men$_x$ ED IIIa Šuruppag *TSŠ* 14 o. iv 7
lugal-⸢men$_x$⸣ ku$_3$-ĝal$_2$ ED IIIa Šuruppag *TSŠ* 58 r. iv 9
lugal-men$_x$ ED IIIa Šuruppag *WF* 7 o. viii 7'
lugal-men$_x$ engar ED IIIa Šuruppag *WF* 22 o. viii 12
lugal-men$_x$ nitaḫ, s. Ni$_3$-erim$_2$-bar-ra ED IIIb/Ukg. lugal 4 Girsu Nik 1 15 o. iii 6
lugal-men$_x$ lu$_2$ luĝa$_x$(BI×NIĜ$_2$) ED IIIb/X Y 4 Girsu Nik 1 231 o. ii 1
lugal-men$_x$ ED IIIb/X Y 6 Girsu VS 27 97 o. ii 3

°lugal-men$_x$(ĜA$_2$×EN)-am$^{?}$ $^{(°1)}$ uncertain mng. 3.1.1.3, p. 88 n. 445
°lugal-men$_x$-⸢am$^{?}$⸣ ma$_2$-gur$_8$ ED IIIa Abū Ṣalābīḫ *IAS* 69 r. iii 1'
°⸢lugal⸣-m[en$_x$-am$^{?}$] [ma$_2$-gur$_8$] ED IIIa Abū Ṣalābīḫ *IAS* 72 (r.) ii' 2'

°lugal-men$_x$(ĜA$_2$×EN)-nun $^{(°1)}$ 'the lugal … the sublime (?) men-headdress' 3.1.1.3, p. 88f. w. n. 446
°lugal-[men$_x$]-nun ED IIIa Abū Ṣalābīḫ *IAS* 74 o. i 1

°lugal-men$_y$(LAGAB×EN) $^{(°1)}$ 'the lugal … the men-headdress' 3.1.1.3, p. 88 n. 444
°lugal-men$_y$ ED IIIa Unknown *RIAA* 44 o. ii' 4

lugal-mes-e $^{(a1)}$ 'the lugal … by the hero' 3.1.8, p. 180
lugal-mes-e CS Girsu CT 50 85 o. i 16

lugal-^{d}mes-lam $^{(a1)}$ uncertain mng. 3.1.6.2, p. 146 n. 822
lugal-^{d}mes-lam ED IIIa Kiš *AAICAB* 1/1 (Ashm 1928-429) o. ii 2'

lugal-mes-lam $^{(a\geq1)}$ uncertain mng. 3.1.6.2, p. 146 n. 822
lugal-mes-lam na-gada ED IIIa Šuruppag *TSŠ* 704 o. iii 5
lugal-mes-lam Nin-ni$_3$-zu ED IIIa Šuruppag *WF* 74 r. ii 4
lugal-mes-lam ^{d}Sud$_3$-UR-⸢x⸣ ED IIIa Šuruppag *WF* 137 r. i 4

°lugal-mes-nun-pa$_3$ $^{(°1)}$ 'the lugal is one chosen by the noble hero (?)' 3.1.6.2, p. 145
°lugal-mes-nun-pa$_3$ ED IIIa Šuruppag *SF* 28 r. iii 9

lugal-⸢mes$^{?}$⸣-[x] ED IIIa Girsu Déc 2, p. LIVf. 2 (AO 3279+3280+4494) vi 3''

lugal-mete(TE+ME)-na $^{(a1)}$ 'a lord unto himself' 3.1.7.1, p. 161
lugal-mete-na sipa [x] ED IIIb/X Y 4 Girsu *DP* suppl. 587 r. i 4
lugal-mete-na lu$_2$ šu luḫ-ḫa ED IIIb/Lug. 4 Girsu VS 14 72 r. i 3

°lugal-mi-am $^{(°1)}$ uncertain mng. 3.1.1.3, p. 88 n. 445
°lugal-mi-am ma$_2$-gur$_8$ ED IIIb Ebla A. Archi, *StEb* 4 (1981), p. 177–204 r. iv 1

lugal-mi$_2$ $^{(a2)}$ (abbreviation of the following) 3.1.7.1, p. 160 n. 917
lugal-mi$_2$ s. lugal-⸢GAN$_2$⸣, b. E$_2$-ĝiš MS-CS Umma ? *TCVC* 731 o. i 14'
lugal-mi$_2$ ugula CS Girsu *RTC* 97 o. 4
lugal-mi$_2$ ⸢ugula⸣ CS Girsu *RTC* 97 r. 6

lugal-mi$_2$-du$_{11}$-ga $^{(a1)}$ 'the lugal is praised' 3.1.7.1, p. 160 n. 917
lugal-mi$_2$-du$_{11}$-ga CS Adab *SIA* 879 o. 1

lugal-mi$_2$-zi-du$_{11}$-ga $^{(a1)}$ 'the lugal is praised' 3.1.7.1, p. 160
lugal-mi$_2$-du$_{11}$-ga dam$^{!}$-gar$_3$$^{!?}$ ED IIIb Adab (?) BIN 8 31 o. 4

lugal-mu (identical with lugal-mu-da-kuš$_2$, muḫaldim), p. 123 w. n. 672, 180 w. n. 1095
lugal-mu muḫaldim ED IIIb/Lug. 1 Girsu *DCS* 8 r. iv 5
lugal-mu muḫaldim ED IIIb/Ukg. lugal 3 Girsu *DP* 1/2 130 o. vi 12
lugal-mu muḫaldim ED IIIb/Lug. 6 Girsu VS 25 41 r. i 4

lugal-mu (identical with lugal-mu-da-kuš$_2$, sipa anše) , p. 123 w. n. 672, 180 w. n. 1095
lugal-mu sipa anše ED IIIb/Ukg. lugal 2 Girsu Nik 1 13 r. iv 14

lugal-mu (identical with lugal-mu-da-kuš$_2$, sipa anše sur$_x$) , p. 123 w. n. 672, 180 w. n. 1095
lugal-mu sipa anše sur$_x$-ka ED IIIb/Ukg. lugal 3 Girsu HSS 3 9 o. iv 4
lugal-mu sipa anše sur$_x$-ka ED IIIb/Ukg. lugal 3 Girsu HSS 3 11 o. iii 11

lugal-mu (identical with lugal-mu-še$_3$-ĝal$_2$, dub-sar ?), p. 180 w. n. 1095
lugal-mu dub-sar ED IIIb/X Y 1 Girsu Nik 1 44 o. i 4

lugal-mu (identical with lugal-mu-še$_3$-ĝal$_2$, šu-ku$_6$), p. 180 w. n. 1095
lugal-mu šu-ku$_6$ ab-ba ED IIIb/X Y 5 Girsu *CTNMC* 2 o. ii 1
lugal-mu šu-ku$_6$ a dun-a, šu-ku$_6$ ab-ba ED IIIb/Ukg. lugal 3 Girsu *DP* 2/1 177 r. iii 13

lugal-MU $^{(a\geq8)}$ abbreviation 3.1.8, p. 180 w. n. 1095, 187
lugal-MU ED I-II Ur UET 2 281 o. i 4
lugal-MU muḫaldim ED IIIb/Enz. ensi$_2$ 2 Girsu BIN 8 347 r. iii 4
lugal-MU sipa anše ED IIIb/Lug. 1 Girsu *DCS* 8 r. iv 2
lugal-MU lu$_2$ Ur-$^{d\ še_3}$Šer$_7$-da-ka ED IIIb/Ukg. lugal 5 Girsu *DP* 1/2 136 o. iii 3
lugal-MU sipa anše ED IIIb/X Y 2 Girsu *DP* suppl. 577 r. iii 5
lugal-MU lu$_2$ Ur-$^{d\ še_3}$Šer$_7$-da ED IIIb/Ukg. lugal 5 Girsu Nik 1 3 o. iii 9
lugal-MU ED IIIb/X Y 4 Girsu Nik 1 177 o. ii 4
lugal-MU (PN?) ED IIIb Nippur PBS 15 11 3
lugal-MU ši[tim] CS Umma *AAS* 1 o. i 4
lu[gal]-MU ⸢šitim⸣ CS Umma *AAS* 1 o. i 13
lugal-MU CS Umma ? CUSAS 13 201 o. 9
lugal-MU ir$_{11}$ Lugal-KA MS-CS Umma ? *TCVC* 725 o. i 3

lugal-mu-da $^{(a3)}$ (probable abbreviation of either of the following) 3.1.8, p. 180 w. n. 1096
lugal-mu-da ED IIIb Adab CUSAS 11 33 o. i 2
lugal-mu-da A$_2$-kal-le Lugal-mu-da maškim-bi ED IIIb Zabala M. Powell, *HUCA* 49 (1978), p. 1–58 7 o. ii 12
lugal-mu-da ES-MS Nippur OSP 1 23 o. vii 7

lugal-mu-da-kuš$_2$ $^{(a5/°1)}$ 'the lugal concerns himself with me/you' 3.1.4.1, p. lugal-mu-da-kuš$_2$, 123–124, 125, 180 nn. 1095–1096, 187, 254 n. 1493
lugal-mu-da-kuš$_2$ ugula e$_2$, lu$_2$ ku$_3$ lal-a, lu$_2$ še aĝ$_2$ ED IIIb/(Eig. ^{ni_3}ensi$_2$) Adab D. Foxvog, Mesopotamia 8, p. 67–75 (UCLM 9-1798) r. ii 5
°lugal-mu-da-kuš$_2$ ED IIIb Ebla ARET 5 25 r. i 1
lugal-mu-da-kuš$_2$ muḫaldim ED IIIb/[Ukg. lugal] 6 Girsu *AWAS* 67 r. ii' 2'
lu[gal]-mu-da-kuš$_2$ sipa anše sur$_x$-ka ED IIIb/[Ukg. lugal] 6 Girsu *AWAS* 67 o. v 2
lugal-mu-da-kuš$_2$ sipa anše sur$_x$-ka ED IIIb/Ukg. lugal X Girsu *AWAS* 69 o. iii 13
lugal-mu-da-kuš$_2$ sipa anše sur$_x$-ka ED IIIb/Ukg. lugal 3 Girsu *AWAS* 118 o. iii 14
lugal-mu-da-kuš$_2$ muḫaldim ED IIIb/Ukg. lugal 3 Girsu *AWAS* 118 r. ii 4
lugal-mu-da-kuš$_2$ [sipa anše sur$_x$-ka] ED IIIb/Ukg. [lugal] 6 Girsu BIN 8 354 o. iv 11'
lugal-mu-da-kuš$_2$ muḫaldim ED IIIb/Ukg. [lugal] 6 Girsu BIN 8 354 r. ii 8'
lugal-mu-da-kuš$_2$ sipa anše sur$_x$-ka ED IIIb/Ukg. lugal 6 Girsu *DP* 1/2 121 o. iv 13
lugal-mu-da-kuš$_2$ muḫaldim ED IIIb/Ukg. lugal 6 Girsu *DP* 1/2 121 r. iii 1
lugal-mu-da-kuš$_2$ sipa anše ED IIIb/Ukg. lugal 3 Girsu *DP* 1/2 130 r. iii 10
lugal-mu-da-kuš$_2$ muḫaldim ED IIIb/Lug. 5 Girsu *DP* 1/2 132 r. i 5
lugal-mu-da-kuš$_2$ muḫaldim ED IIIb Girsu MVN 3 8 r. ii' 4
lugal-mu-da-kuš$_2$ ED IIIb/Lug. 3 Girsu *DP* 1/1 59 r. ii 19
lugal-mu-da-kuš$_2$ ED IIIb Umma-Zabala CUSAS 14 280 r. ii 5
lugal-mu-da-kuš$_2$ MS-CS Unknown B. R. Foster, *JCS* 35 (1983), p. 147–175 8 o. 10

lugal-mu-da-ri$_2$ (a2) 'the lugal (has) a lasting name' 3.1.7.5, p. 164, 180 n. 1096
lugal-mu-da-ri$_2$ ED IIIb/Ukg. lugal 2 Girsu *DP* 1/2 120 o. v 5
⌜lu:gal⌝-mu-⌜da-ri$_2$⌝ ED IIIb Nippur OSP 1 32 o. i 4

lugal-mu-daḫ (a1) 'the lugal added (another child)' 3.1.5.1, p. 128
lugal-mu-daḫ f. Ur-^{d}Nin-⌜ĝir$_2$⌝-su, dub-sar CS Girsu *RTC* 81 r. 6

lu:gal-mu-dib (a1) unkn. mng. 3.1.8, p. 180
lu:gal-mu-dib ED IIIb Nippur OSP 1 137 r. i 4'

lugal-mu-du$_{10}$ (a2) 'lugal (of) a good name' 3.1.7.5, p. 165 w. n. 952
lugal:mu-du$_{10}$ ED IIIa-b Isin (?) OIP 104 15 o. iii 11
lugal-mu-du$_{10}$ ED IIIb Adab Eig. ^{ni_3}ensi$_2$ OIP 14 51 o. iii' 4

lugal-mu-du$_{10}$-ga (a≥1) 'lugal of a good name' 3.1.7.5, p. 139, 165 w. n. 953
lugal-mu-du$_{10}$-ga CS Girsu *RTC* 126 o. ii 4'
lugal-mu-du$_{10}$-[ga] CS Girsu *SCT* 2 r. ii 10
lugal-mu-du$_{10}$-ga(-ke$_4$) CS Girsu *STTI* 154 r. 4
lugal-mu-du$_{10}$-ga CS Girsu *STTI* 178 o. i 5'

lugal-mu-ĝal$_2$ (a1) 'the lugal is present (at/for) …' 3.1.8, p. 180
lugal-mu-ĝal$_2$ ED IIIa Šuruppag CUSAS 11 341 o. ii' 8

lugal-mu-kuš$_2$ (a≥2) 'the lugal concerns himself (with me/you)' 3.1.4.1, p. 124
lugal-mu-kuš$_2$ engar saĝa ED IIIb Isin MVN 3 36 r. i 1
lugal-mu-kuš$_2$ f. Lugal-lu-dadag ED IIIb-ES Isin MVN 3 67 o. i 7
[lugal]-⌜mu⌝-[kuš$_2$?] f. ⌜Lugal⌝-l[u-dadag?] ED IIIb-ES Isin MVN 3 67 o. iii 7
lugal-mu-kuš$_2$ ED IIIb/Urz. lugal Isin M. Lambert, *RA* 73 (1979), p. 5–6 o. xi 5
[lugal?]-mu-kuš$_2$ lu$_2$ Ur-^{d}Inana ED IIIb Nippur OSP 1 135 o. i 1
lugal-mu-kuš$_2$ ED IIIb Nippur TMH 5 53 o. i 1
⌜lugal⌝-mu-kuš$_2$ ED IIIb Nippur TMH 5 167 o. iii 4

lugal-mu-LAGAB×PA!? (a1) unkn. mng. 3.1.8, p. 180
lugal-mu-LAGAB×PA!? ED IIIb Umma-Zabala CUSAS 14 4 o. iii 3

lugal-mu-ni-da (a1) 'the lugal … with his name (?)' 3.1.7.10, p. 180
lugal-mu-ni-da lu u$_5$ ED IIIb/Meannedu 5 Umma T. Ozaki, *JAC* 23 (2008), p. 55–64 1 o. iii 2

lugal-mu-še$_3$-ĝal$_2$ (a≥1) unkn. mng. 3.1.8, p. 180 w. n. 1095
lugal-mu-še$_3$-ĝal$_2$ [šu-ku$_6$] ED IIIb/Lug. 2 Girsu BIN 8 370 o. iv 4
lugal-mu-še$_3$-ĝal$_2$ šu-ku$_6$ ab-ba ED IIIb/Lug. 1 Girsu *DP* 2/1 191 r. ii 1
lu[gal]-mu-še$_3$-ĝal$_2$ [dub-sar?] ED IIIb Girsu *DP* 2/1 231 o. i' 7'
lugal-mu-še$_3$-ĝal$_2$ šu-ku$_6$ u$_2$-rum, ^{d}Ba-u$_2$ ED IIIb/Ukg. lugal 4 Girsu HSS 3 28 r. i 1

lugal-mu-tu (a1) 'the lugal is one born (by DN)' 3.1.6.2, p. 144
lugal-mu-tu šu-i$_2$ ED IIIb/Lug. 5(+1?) Girsu VS 25 14 r. ii 7
lugal-mu-tu šu-[i$_2$] ED IIIb/Lug. 6 Girsu VS 25 37 r. i 10

lugal-mu-zu-da (a≥2) unkn. mng. 3.1.8, p. 180
lugal-⌜mu⌝-zu-⌜da⌝ ED IIIb Umma-Zabala CUSAS 14 4 o. i 2
lugal-mu-zu-da CS Girsu ITT 1 1408 o. 3
lugal-mu-zu-da MS-CS Unknown OIP 47 pl. 5 no. 33 1

lu[gal]-mu-[x] ED IIIb Nippur TMH 5 134 o. i 2
⌜lugal⌝-mu-[x(-x)] ES-MS Isin ? MAD 4 152 o. ii 1

lugal-muš (a2) unkn. mng. 3.1.8, p. 180
lugal-muš ED IIIb Umma-Zabala CUSAS 14 114 o. ii1
lugal-muš!? CS Girsu *STTI* 166 r. i 1'

lugal-Muš$_3$-bar-ki-aĝa$_2$ (a1) ‘the lugal is one who loves (or is beloved in) the Mušbar-temple’ 3.1.6.4, p. 155 n. 891, 185, 187
lugal-Muš$_3$-bar-ki-aĝa$_2$ gudu$_4$ ^{d}Eš$_3$-ir-nun ED IIIb/Lug. 4 Girsu *DP* 2/1 220 o. iii 5

lugal-na-de$_5$-ga (a≥1) ‘the lugal is pure (or instructed?) (?)’ 3.1.6.3, p. 152
lugal-na-de$_5$-ga ED IIIa Šuruppag *FTUM* 92 o. i 2’
lugal-na-de$_5$-ga ED IIIa Šuruppag *WF* 37 r. ii 2

lugal-na-nam (a1) ‘a lugal (he is) indeed’ 3.1.7.1, p. 161
lugal-na-nam ED IIIa-b Isin (?) OIP 104 14 r. vi 6

lugal-na$_2$-du$_{10}$ (a1/°1) ‘the lugal (on/of) the good bed’ 3.1.6.3, p. 150 n. 855
°lugal-na$_2$-du$_{10}$ ED IIIa Abū Ṣalābīḫ *IAS* 462 o. ii 4
lugal-na$_2$-du$_{10}$ ED IIIa Šuruppag M. Lambert, *Gs Unger*, p. 27–49 1 r. iii 4
lugal-na$_2$-du$_{10}$ ED IIIa Šuruppag M. Molina & H. Sanchiz, *StEL* 24 (2007), p. 1–15 2 o. iv 3
lugal-na$_2$-du$_{10}^{!}$ ED IIIa Šuruppag(“in Fara gekauft”) *WF* 135 o. i 2

lugal-na$_2$-du$_{10}$-ga (a1) ‘the lugal on/of the good bed’ 3.1.6.3, p. 150
lugal-na$_2$-du$_{10}$-ga ED IIIa Šuruppag *FTUM* 22 o. ii 1
lugal-[n]a$_2$-⸢du$_{10}$⸣-ga ED IIIa Šuruppag *FTUM* 23 o. i 3
lugal-na$_2$-du$_{10}$-ga s. Ur-^{d}En-lil$_2$, gal$_5$-la-gal ED IIIa Šuruppag M. Lambert, *Gs Unger*, p. 27–49 4 r. iv 4

lugal-nagar (a1) ‘the lugal (is) a carpenter’ 3.1.8, p. 180
lugal-nagar (lugal aša$_5$?) ED IIIb Umma-Zabala BIN 8 114 r. (!) i 9

lugal-nagar-zi (a2) ‘the lugal (is) a reliable carpenter’ 3.1.8, p. 180
lugal-nagar-zi MS-CS Adab CUSAS 13 42 o. 4
lugal-nagar-zi MS-CS Umma MAD 4 48 (translit. only) o. 12
lugal-nagar-zi MS-CS Umma MAD 4 57 (translit. only) r. 1
lugal-nagar-zi ugula MS-CS Umma MAD 4 142 o. 5
lugal-nagar-zi (ugula) MS-CS Umma MAD 4 167 (translit. only) o. 5
lugal-nagar-⸢zi⸣ f. [x-x(-x)] MS-CS Umma ? *TCVC* 730 o. ii 1
lugal-NA[GAR(-x)] ED IIIb-ES Umma B. R. Foster, *Fs Westenholz*, 127–137 6 o. ii 2

lugal-nam (a≥3) abbreviation 3.1.8, p. 180
lugal-nam ED IIIb/X Y 1 Girsu *DP* 2/2 453 o. i 2
lugal-nam ED IIIb/Lug. 1 Girsu VS 25 22 o. i 3
lugal-nam CS Girsu *STTI* 20 o. 5
lugal-nam nar CS Girsu CT 50 168 o. 7
lugal-nam f. Lu$_2$-zaḫ$_3$ (PN?) & Šeš-šeš CS Girsu *RTC* 96 o. i 10’
lugal-nam CS Adab CUSAS 13 2 r. 6
lugal-nam CS Adab CUSAS 13 2 r. 11
lugal-nam CS Adab *TCABI* 212 r. 1
⸢lugal⸣-nam CS Adab *TCABI* 231 r. 2
lugal-nam CS Adab *SIA* 658 o. 11

lugal-nam-dag (a1) ‘the lugal (removes?) sin’ 3.1.6.1, p. 110, 140
lugal-nam-dag s. Ur-temen, dumu Nibru^{ki}-me CS Girsu ITT 1 1100 o. 7

lugal-nam-DUB ? (a1) unkn. mng. 3.1.8, p. 180
lugal-nam-⸢DUB$^{?}$⸣ CS Adab *SIA* 1209 o. ii 10

[lugal]-nam-gu$_2$ (identical with lugal-nam-gu$_2$-su$_3$, gab$_2$-kas$_4$), p. 117 n. 637
[lugal]-nam-gu$_2$ gab$_2$-kas$_4$ ED IIIb/Lug. 3 Girsu *DP* 1/2 124 o. i 1

lugal-nam-gu$_2$-su$_3$ (a≥4) ‘the lugal is one who eradicates oppression’ 3.1.3.3, p. 110, 117
lugal-nam-gu$_2$-su$_3$ gab$_2$-kas$_4$ ED IIIb/Ukg. lugal 1 Girsu *Amherst* 2 o. i 1

lugal-nam-gu$_2$-su$_3$ ulu$_3$-di ED IIIb/Lug. 2 Girsu BIN 8 366 o. ii 5
lugal-⸢nam⸣-gu$_2$-⸢su$_3$⸣ ⸢gab$_2$-kas$_4$⸣ ED IIIb/Ukg. lugal 3 Girsu BIN 8 391 o. ii 3
lugal-nam-gu$_2$-su$_3$ ĝuruš, lu$_2$ u$_2$-rum, ^{d}Ba-u$_2$ ED IIIb/Ukg. lugal 6 Girsu *DP* 1/2 135 o. vii 8
lugal-nam-gu$_2$-su$_3$ sipa ED IIIb/Ukg. lugal 6 Girsu *DP* 1/2 135 r. v 6
lugal-nam-gu$_2$-su$_3$ aĝrig ED IIIb/Lug. 3 Girsu *DP* 1/1 59 o. v 15
lugal-nam-gu$_2$-su$_3$ (sipa) ED IIIb/Enz. ensi$_2$ 5 Girsu *DP* 1/2 94 o. iii 2
lugal-nam-gu$_2$-su$_3$ ulu$_3$-di ED IIIb/Lug. 5 Girsu *DP* 1/2 95 o. iii 3
lugal-nam-gu$_2$-su$_3$ ED IIIb/Lug. Y X Girsu E. Sollberger, *Genava* 26 (1948), p. 48–72 7 r. i 4
lugal-nam-gu$_2$-su$_3$ lu$_2$ e$_2$-nam ED IIIb Girsu Nik 1 14 r. i 5
lugal-nam-gu$_2$-su$_3$ sagi ED IIIb/Lug. 3 Girsu VS 14 79 o. ii 7
lugal-nam-gu$_2$-su$_3$ sagi ED IIIb/Lug. 4 Girsu VS 25 34 o. iii 3

lugal-nam-mu-šub-be$_2$ $^{(a1)}$ 'may the lugal not abandon me/you' 3.1.4.1, p. 124
lugal-nam-mu-šub-be$_2$ dub-sar, lu$_2$-ga[n$_2$-gid$_2$-da] ED IIIb/En. I ensi$_2$ Girsu OIP 104 23 o. xi 3

lugal-nam-mu-šub-e $^{(a1)}$ 'may the lugal not abandon me/you' 3.1.4.1, p. 124
lugal-nam-mu-šub-⸢e⸣ ED IIIb Nippur OSP 1 24 o. iii 2

°lugal-nam-nir $^{(°1)}$ 'the lugal … authority' 3.1.1.6, p. 100 n. 527, 255 n. 1500
°lugal-nam-nir ED IIIb Ebla ARET 5 25 o. ii 3

lugal-nam-nir-šum$_2$ $^{(a1/°1)}$ 'the lugal is granted authority' 3.1.1.6, p. 100, 255 n. 1500, 258
lugal-nam-nir:šum$_2$ lugal Kiš ED IIIa Girsu L. Heuzey, *RA* 3 (1894), p. 52–54 (AO 2675) 1
°lugal-nam-nir-šum$_2$ ED IIIb Ebla ARET 5 25 o. ii 4

lugal-nam-tar-re$_2$ $^{(a1)}$ 'the lugal is one who determines fates' 3.1.1.7, p. 104
lugal-nam-tar-re$_2$ CS/Śkś Y 2 Nippur OSP 2 100 r. i 15'

lugal-nam-zi-tar $^{(a1)}$ 'the lugal is one whose fate is reliably determined' 3.1.7.1, p. 160 n. 918
lugal-nam-zi-tar MS-CS Nippur OSP 2 136 o. 3

lugal-nam-zi-tar-ra $^{(a1)}$ 'the lugal is one (whose) fate is reliably determined' 3.1.7.1, p. 104, 160
lugal-nam-zi-tar-ra [U]⸢r⸣-i$_7$-da, lu$_2$ Lugal-nam-zi-tar-ra MS-CS Nippur OSP 2 120 o. 4'
lugal-nam-zi-tar-ra MS-CS Nippur OSP 2 134 o. 5
lugal-nam-zi-tar-ra MS-CS Nippur OSP 2 149 o. 2
lugal-nam-zi-tar-ra MS-CS Nippur OSP 2 154 o. 8

lugal-nam-zu $^{(a1)}$ 'the lugal knows all' 3.1.2, p. 105
lugal-nam-zu Šuruppag AN-nu-me ED IIIa *WF* 124 o. iii 12

lugal-nam$_2$ $^{(a1)}$ 'the lugal is a prince (?)' 3.1.1.1, p. 86
lugal-nam$_2$ s. Lugal-AB ES Ur UET 1 269 1

lugal-^{d}Nanna-ra-tum$_2$ $^{(a1)}$ 'the lugal is one who befits Nanna' 3.1.6.2, p. 143, 251 n. 1478, 258
lugal-^{d}Nanna-ra-tum$_2$ ED IIIb Ur UET 2 suppl. 12 Low. Edge

lugal-^{d}Nanše-mu-tu $^{(a1)}$ 'the lugal is one born by Nanše' 3.1.6.2, p. 144, 251 n. 1478, 258
lugal-^{d}Nanše-mu-tu nitaḫ, il$_2$ ED IIIb/Ukg. lugal 1? Girsu *AWAS* 123 o. v 5
lugal-^{d}Nanše-mu-tu nitaḫ, il$_2$ ED IIIb/Ukg. lugal 2 Girsu *DP* 1/2 113 o. vii 1

lugal-NE-nu-si $^{(a1)}$ unkn. mng. 3.1.8, p. 180
lugal-NE-nu-si ugula-ni ED IIIb Adab CUSAS 11 70 o. ii 2

lugal-NE-nu-um (a1) unkn. mng. 3.1.8, p. 180, 215
lugal-NE-nu-um engar ED IIIb/Ukg. lugal 5 Girsu Nik 1 3 o. i 4

lugal-ne-te-na (a1) 'a lord unto himself' 3.1.7.1, p. 161
lugal-ne-⸢te-na⸣ CS Umma *AAS* 204 o. 1'

lugal-nemur$_x$(PIRIĜ.TUR) (a≥7) 'the lugal is (like) a leopard' 3.1.7.6, p. 165, 207, 241
lugal-nemur$_x$ Ni$_3$-lu$_2$-nu-tum$_2$-da, e-da-se$_{12}$, simug ED IIIb/Ukg. lugal 6 Girsu *AWAS* 122 r. ii 6
lugal-⸢nemur$_x$⸣ ED IIIb Girsu BIN 8 378 o. ii 1
lugal-nemur$_x$ Ni$_3$-lu$_2$-nu-tum$_2$, simug ED IIIb/Ukg. lugal 5 Girsu *DP* 1/2 114 r. i 12
lugal-nemur$_x$ Ni$_3$-lu$_2$-⸢nu⸣-tum$_2$, simug ED IIIb/Ukg. lugal 6 Girsu *DP* 1/2 115 r. ii 1
lugal-nemur$_x$ simug ED IIIb/Ukg. lugal 6 Girsu HSS 3 18 o. ix 3'
lugal-nemur$_x$ Ni$_3$-lu$_2$-nu-tum$_2$, simug ED IIIb/Ukg. lugal 1 Girsu HSS 3 17 r. ii 5
lugal-nemur$_x$ ED IIIb/Enz. ensi$_2$ 3 Girsu ITT 5 9231 o. i 3
lugal-nemur$_x$ Ni$_3$-lu$_2$-[nu-tum$_2$], simug ED IIIb/Ukg. lugal 4 Girsu Nik 1 2 r. i 2'
lugal-nemur$_x$ Ur-ki-ḪAR-ra-ka ED IIIb/Dudu saĝa Girsu W. W. Hallo, *OrNS* 42 (1973), p. 228–238 r. ii 2
lugal-nemur$_x$ f. Ur-šu ED IIIb/Enz. ensi$_2$ X Girsu *RTC* 17 o. iii 9
lugal-nemur$_x$ saĝa ED IIIb/Enz. ensi$_2$ X Girsu *RTC* 57 r. i 3
lugal-nemur$_x$ Ni$_3$-[l]u$_2$-nu-tum$_2$, simug ED IIIb/Ukg. lugal 4 Girsu *TSA* 14 r. i 2
lugal-nemur$_x$ ⸢Ni$_3$⸣-lu$_2$-nu-tum$_2$, simug ED IIIb/Ukg. lugal 4 Girsu *TSA* 15 r. ii 3
lugal-[nemur$_x$] [simug] ED IIIb/Ukg. lugal 6 Girsu *TSA* 16 o. ix 9'
lugal-nemur$_x$ saĝa, E$_2$-babbar$_2$ ED IIIb/X Y 4 Girsu VS 14 45 o. ii 1
lugal-nemur$_x$ saĝa ⸢E$_2$⸣-babbar$_2$ ED IIIb/X Y 4 Girsu VS 14 125 o. i 3
lugal-nemur$_x$ ED IIIb/X Y 4 Girsu VS 27 88 r. ii 3
lugal-nemur$_x$(PIRIĜ.[TUR]) sim[ug] ED IIIb Nippur OSP 1 46 o. vi 1'
⸢lu:gal⸣-nemur$_x$ ED IIIb Nippur OSP 1 62 o. i 2
lu:gal-nemur$_x$ ED IIIb Nippur OSP 1 62 o. i 4
lugal-nemur$_x$ ED IIIb Nippur TMH 5 14 o. i 5'
lugal-nemur$_x$ ED IIIb/Luzag. ensi$_2$ 7 Umma-Zabala BIN 8 86 o. iii 10
lugal-nemur$_x$ ED IIIb/Luzag. ensi$_2$ 7 Umma-Zabala BIN 8 86 o. iv 6
lugal-nemur$_x$ ES Unknown BIN 8 36 o. i 2
lugal-nemur$_x$ sipa MS Adab *TCABI* 117 o. 3

lugal-nesaĝ (a≥4) 'the lugal (is just right for) the firstling offerings (or the sacristy?)' 3.1.6.3, p. 148 n. 831
lugal-nesaĝ ED IIIb Nippur OSP 1 49 o. i 1'
lugal-nesaĝ ED IIIb Nippur TMH 5 138 r. 3
lugal-nesaĝ ED IIIb-ES Umma-Zabala BIN 8 92 r. 1
lugal-nesaĝ MS-CS Umma BIN 8 317 o. 3
lugal-nesaĝ MS-CS Umma BIN 8 321 o. 3
lugal-nesaĝ MS-CS Umma BIN 8 334 o. 3
lugal-nesaĝ šeš Me-sag$_2$ šabra MS-CS Umma BIN 8 337 o. 2
lugal-nesaĝ MS-CS Umma BIN 8 339 o. 5
lugal-nesaĝ nu-banda$_3$ CS/Śkś Y 7 Umma CT 50 66 r. 13

lugal-nesaĝ-e (a≥4) 'the lugal (is just right for) the firstling offerings (or the sacristy?)' 3.1.6.3, p. 134, 148
lugal-nesaĝ-e CS Umma *AAS* 11 o. 2
lugal-nesaĝ-e nu-banda$_3$ CS Umma BARI S 2135 40 r. 8'
lugal-nesaĝ-e CS Umma W. Sommerfeld, K. Markina & N. Roudik, *Gs Diakonoff*, 225–231 4 r. 4
lugal-nesaĝ-e MS-CS Umma MesCiv 4 28 r. i 9
lugal-nesaĝ-e šabra CS Umma MVN 15 378 o. 8

lugal-nesaĝ-e ⸢nu-banda$_3$ gu$_4$ du$_7$⸣ CS Umma MVN 15 378 o. 9
lugal-nesaĝ-[e$^?$] s. Ur-es$_3$-sa$_2$ CS Umma *USP* 46 o. 2
lugal-nesaĝ-e s. Ur-lu$_2$, b. Lugal-^{ĝiš}gigir$_2$-e CS Umma *USP* 47 o. ii 10
lugal-nesaĝ-e šabra MS-CS Umma *USP* 53 o. 5
lugal-[nesaĝ(-e$^?$)] šabra MS-CS Umma *USP* 55 r. i 1
lugal-nesaĝ-e CS Unknown D. Snell & C. Lager, YOS 18 4 o. 2

lugal-NI-du$_8$ $^{(a1)}$ unkn. mng. 3.1.8, p. 180 w. n. 1100
lugal-NI-du$_8$ ES-MS Umma Nik 2 35 r. i 12'

lugal-NI:du$_{10}$ $^{(a1)}$ 'his king(ship) is good' 3.1.1.1, p. 83
lugal-NI:du$_{10}$ s. Ur-^{d}Ba-u$_2$ ED IIIb Girsu Nik 1 30 o. i 5

lugal-NI-i-MU $^{(a1)}$ unkn. mng. 3.1.8, p. 178 n. 1071, 180
lugal-NI-i-MU ED IIIa-b Unknown *L'uomo* 3 o. i 5

lugal-NI-KA $^{(a1)}$ (perhaps lugal-du$_{11}$(-ga)-ni: 'what the lugal says (?)') 3.1.1.4, p. 92 n. 469, 94
lugal-NI-KA ED I-II Ur UET 2 298 o. 5

lugal-NI-[x] lu$_2$-⸢u$_5$⸣ Ma-⸢x⸣^{ki} ED IIIb-ES Adab CUSAS 11 236 o. ii 1'
lugal-⸢NI⸣-[x] CS Nippur PBS 9 36 o. iii' 3'

°lugal-ni$_2$-bi-ak $^{(°1)}$ unkn. mng. 3.1.8, p. 180, 207 n. 1312
°lugal-ni$_2$-bi-ak LS-Ur III Unknown M. E. Cohen, *Fs Hallo*, p. 79–86 (YBC 2124) iv 11

lugal-NI$_2$-D[U$^?$] $^{(a1)}$ unkn. mng. 3.1.8, p. 180f. w. n. 1102
⸢lugal⸣-NI$_2$-D[U$^?$] ED I-II Ur UET 2 28 o. ii 3

lugal-ni$_2$-te-na $^{(a1)}$ 'a lord unto himself' 3.1.7.1, p. 161
lugal-ni$_2$-te-na ugula CS Umma Nik 2 69 o. 5

lugal-ni$_3$-a$_2$-zi-nu-ak $^{(a1)}$ 'the lugal is not one to commit a violent act' 3.1.3.3, p. 117
lugal-ni$_3$-a$_2$-zi-nu-ak lu$_2$ u$_2$-rum ^{d}Ba-u$_2$ ED IIIb/Ukg. lugal 2 Girsu *DP* 1/2 120 r. i 4
lugal-ni$_3$-a$_2$-zi-nu-ak ad-kup$_4$, lu$_2$ u$_2$-rum ^{d}Ba-u$_2$ ED IIIb/Ukg. lugal 5 Girsu Nik 1 3 r. iii 3'

lugal-ni$_3$-^{ba}bara$_3$-du$_{10}$ $^{(a4)}$ 'the lugal is one who makes joyous (things on) the bedspreads' 3.1.6.3, p. 150
lu[gal]-ni$_3$-^{ba}bara$_3$-du$_{10}$ ED IIIa Šuruppag *WF* 116 o. 2
lu[gal]-[ni$_3$]-^{ba}bara$_3$-du$_{10}$ [aš]gab ED IIIb Nippur OSP 1 46 o. i 3
lugal-ni$_3$-^{ba}bara$_3$-du$_{10}$ ED IIIb Umma-Zabala CUSAS 14 4 o. ii 6
lugal-ni$_3$-^{ba}bara$_3$-du$_{10}$ ED IIIb Umma-Zabala MVN 3 3 o. viii 3
lugal-ni$_3$-^{ba}bara$_3$-du$_{10}$ dam-gar$_3$ CS Umma MAD 4 51 r. 3'

lugal-ni$_3$-bara$_4$-du$_{10}$ $^{(a\geq16)}$ 'the lugal is one who makes joyous (things on) the bedspreads' 3.1.6.3, p. 150–151
lugal-ni$_3$-bara$_4$-du$_{10}$ ED IIIa-b Isin (?) OIP 104 14 o. iii 4
lugal-ni$_3$-bara$_4$-du$_{10}$ ED IIIa-b Unknown *L'uomo* 7 o. i 2
lugal-ni$_3$-bara$_4$-du$_{10}$ ED IIIb-ES Adab CUSAS 11 95 o. i 6
lugal-ni$_3$-bara$_4$-du$_{10}$ ED IIIb-ES Adab CUSAS 11 200 r. ii 1
lugal-ni$_3$-bara$_4$-du$_{10}$ s. Ur$^?$-apin$^?$ ED IIIb-ES Isin MVN 3 105 o. ii 4
lugal-ni$_3$-bara$_4$-du$_{10}$ ED IIIb-ES Isin MVN 3 105 r. i 3
lugal-ni$_3$-bara$_4$-du$_{10}$ saĝa ED IIIb/Urz. lugal Isin M. Lambert, *RA* 73 (1979), p. 5–6 o. ii 20
lugal-[ni$_3$]-bara$_4$-du$_{10}$ dam-gar$_3$(-ke$_4$) ED IIIb Nippur BE 1/2 96 3'
lugal-ni$_3$-bara$_4$-du$_{10}$ ED IIIb Nippur OSP 1 50 o. 3
lugal-ni$_3$-bara$_4$-du$_{10}$ ED IIIb Nippur OSP 1 71 o. 4
lugal-ni$_3$-bara$_4$-du$_{10}$ s. Zur-zur ED IIIb Nippur OSP 1 101 o. i 4

lugal-ni$_3$-bara$_4$-du$_{10}$ ED IIIb Nippur OSP 1 122 o. i 3'
lugal-ni$_3$-bara$_4$-du$_{10}$ ED IIIb Nippur OSP 1 132 o. 4
lugal-ni$_3$-bara$_4$-du$_{10}$ ED IIIb Nippur TMH 5 4 o. ii 4
lugal-ni$_3$-bara$_4$-du$_{10}$ ED IIIb Nippur TMH 5 11 o. i 5
lu:gal-ni$_3$-bara$_4$-du$_{10}$ sagi ED IIIb Nippur TMH 5 67 o. ii 7
lu:gal-ni$_3$-bara$_4$-du$_{10}$ muḫaldim ED IIIb Nippur TMH 5 67 o. iv 7
lugal-ni$_3$-bara$_4$-du$_{10}$ sagi ED IIIb Nippur TMH 5 83 o. 4
lugal-ni$_3$-bara$_4$-du$_{10}$ ED IIIb Nippur TMH 5 101 o. (!) ii 2'
lugal-ni$_3$-bara$_4$-du$_{10}$ Lugal-ni$_3$-bara$_4$-du$_{10}$, Ad-da-tur, bi-da ED IIIb Nippur TMH 5 159 r. i 11
lugal-ni$_3$-bara$_4$-du$_{10}$ ED IIIb Nippur TMH 5 167 o. iii 1
lugal-ni$_3$-bara$_4$-du$_{10}$ ma$_2$-laḫ$_4$ ES Adab CUSAS 11 306 o. ii 6
lugal-ni$_3$-bara$_4$-du$_{10}$ ES Adab *TCABI* 61 r. i 8'
lugal-ni$_3$-bara$_4$-du$_{10}$ ES-MS Adab *TCABI* 64 r. ii 7
lugal-ni$_3$-bara$_4$-du$_{10}$ sa$_{12}$-sug$_5$-be$_6$ ES-MS Nippur OSP 1 147 o. iii 1
lugal-ni$_3$-bara$_4$-du$_{10}$ ku$_3$-dim$_2$ ES Unknown MVN 3 88 o. 6
lugal-ni$_3$-bara$_4$-du$_{10}$ Ur-^{d}Šara$_x$(LAGAB×SIG$_7$.ME) …, x-la kalag-ga, Lugal-ni$_3$-bara$_4$-du$_{10}$ ildum$_x$(IGI.NAGAR)-k(e$_4$) MS Adab M. G. Biga, *Fs Klein*, p. 29–38 i 9
lugal-⌜ni$_3$⌝-bara$_4$-du$_{10}$ ugula MS Adab *TCABI* 77 o. 3
lu[gal]-ni$_3$-bara$_4$-du$_{10}$ MS Adab *TCABI* 189 o. i 1
lugal-ni$_3$-bara$_4$-du$_{10}$ ⌜x⌝ CS Adab CUSAS 13 152 r. 7
lugal-ni$_3$-bara$_4$-du$_{10}$ s. Ur-mes MS-CS Nippur TMH 5 52 r. i 5
lugal-ni$_3$-bara$_4$-du$_{10}$ h. Nin-maš-e, f. (?) [Du$_{11}$]-ga-ni MS-CS Nippur OSP 2 57 r. 2
lugal-ni$_3$-bara$_4$-du$_{10}$ MS-CS Nippur OSP 2 72 o. 1
lugal-ni$_3$-bara$_4$-du$_{10}$ f. Lugal-aĝrig-zi MS-CS Nippur TMH 5 92 o. 5
lugal-ni$_3$-bara$_4$-du$_{10}$? MS-CS Nippur OSP 2 96 o. ii 4
lugal-ni$_3$-bara$_4$-du$_{10}$ MS-CS Nippur OSP 2 118 r. 8'
lugal-ni$_3$-bara$_4$-du$_{10}$ MS-CS Nippur OSP 2 120 r. 8'
lugal-ni$_3$-bara$_4$-du$_{10}$ MS-CS Nippur OSP 2 125 r. 6
lugal-ni$_3$-bara$_4$-du$_{10}$ maškim-bi$_3$ MS-CS Nippur OSP 2 134 o. 6
lugal-ni$_3$-bara$_4$-du$_{10}$ sukkal I$_7$-da MS-CS Nippur OSP 2 136 r. 6'
lugal-⌜ni$_3$-bara$_4$⌝-du$_{10}$ MS-CS Nippur OSP 2 136 r. 14'
lugal-ni$_3$-bara$_4$-du$_{10}$ MS-CS Nippur OSP 2 139 r. 3'
lugal-ni$_3$-bara$_4$-du$_{10}$ gal-SAR MS-CS Nippur OSP 2 140 r. 8
lu[gal]-ni$_3$-bara$_4$-du$_{10}$ [sukkal] ^{d}I$_7$-da MS-CS Nippur OSP 2 141 o. 9
lugal-ni$_3$-[bara$_4$]-du$_{10}$ MS-CS Nippur OSP 2 141 r. 2
lugal-ni$_3$-bara$_4$-du$_{10}$ ašgab MS-CS Nippur OSP 2 149 r. 10
lugal-[ni$_3$-bara$_4$-du$_{10}$] MS-CS Nippur OSP 2 153 r. 6
lugal-ni$_3$-bara$_4$-du$_{10}$ MS-CS Nippur OSP 2 154 r. 8
lugal-ni$_3$-bara$_4$-du$_{10}$ MS-CS Nippur OSP 2 155 r. 5'
lugal-ni$_3$-bara$_4$-du$_{10}$ MS-CS Nippur OSP 2 156 r. 4'
⌜lugal-ni$_3$-bara$_4$-du$_{10}$⌝ MS-CS Nippur OSP 2 157 o. 7
lugal-ni$_3$-bara$_4$-du$_{10}$ MS-CS Nippur OSP 2 158 r. 1'
lugal-ni$_3$-bara$_4$-du$_{10}$ MS-CS Nippur OSP 2 159 r. 7'
⌜lugal⌝-[ni$_3$-bara$_4$-du$_{10}$] MS-CS Nippur OSP 2 160 r. 5
[lugal]-⌜ni$_3$⌝-bara$_4$-⌜du$_{10}$⌝ MS-CS Nippur OSP 2 164 r. 1'
lugal-ni$_3$-bara$_4$-du$_{10}$ MS-CS Nippur OSP 2 165 r. 2'
lugal-ni$_3$-bara$_4$-du$_{10}$ MS-CS Nippur OSP 2 167 edge
⌜lugal⌝-ni$_3$-bara$_4$-du$_{10}$ ki ⌜Lugal⌝-ni$_3$-bara$_4$-du$_{10}$, banšur du$_{10}$-ga-ta MS-CS Nippur OSP 2 170 o. 1
lugal-ni$_3$-bara$_4$-du$_{10}$ šeš šabra, maškim$_3$(-bi) MS-CS Nippur OSP 2 175 r. 2
lugal-ni$_3$-bara$_4$-du$_{10}$ ku$_3$-dim$_3$ CS/NS. Nippur PBS 9 25 r. 5

lugal-ni$_3$-da-sa$_2$ (a1) ‘what can compare with the lugal?’ 3.1.7.7, p. 167
lugal-ni$_3$-da-sa$_2$ ED IIIb/Il$_2$ ensi$_2$ Zabala *TCVBI* 1-1 r. i 2

lugal-ni$_3$-gur$_8$ (a1) unkn. mng. 3.1.8, p. 181
lugal-ni$_3$-gur$_8$ h. KA-TAR ED IIIb/Ukg. lugal 2 Girsu *DP* 1/2 128 o. iii 5
lugal-ni$_3$-gur$_8$ h. KA-TAR ED IIIb/Ukg. lugal 3 Girsu *DP* 1/2 129 o. iii 4
lugal-ni$_3$-gur$_8$ ‹h.› KA-TAR ED IIIb Ukg. UN:gal Girsu VS 27 33 o. iv 2

lugal-ni$_3$-ĝa$_2$ (a1) (abbreviation of the following) 3.1.1.1, p. 84 n. 407
lugal-ni$_3$-ĝa$_2$ šu-ku$_6$ ED IIIb Girsu *DP* suppl. 555 r. i 2

lugal-ni$_3$-ĝa$_2$-ni (a≥5) ‘the lugal … something of his’ 3.1.1.1, p. 84 n. 407
lugal-ni$_3$-ĝa$_2$-ni f. KUM-tuš-še$_3$ ED IIIb/Ukg. lugal 4 Girsu *DP* 1/2 138 o. iv 4
lugal-ni$_3$-ĝa$_2$-ni sipa, gab$_2$-ra ED IIIb/X Y 2 Girsu *RTC* 41 o. ii 1
lugal-ni$_3$-ĝa$_2$-ni šu-ku$_6$ ED IIIb Girsu Nik 1 120 o. i 2
lugal-ni$_3$-ĝa$_2$-ni Ur-šul, lu$_2$ Lugal-ni$_3$-ĝa$_2$-ni, …, ar$_3$-du$_2$ e$_2$-ša$_3$-ga ED IIIb/Ukg. lugal 2 Girsu Nik 1 230 o. i 6
lugal-ni$_3$-ĝa$_2$-ni ⸢gala⸣ ED IIIb/Lug. 6 Girsu VS 25 13 o. iii 1
lugal-ni$_3$-ĝa$_2$-ni CS Girsu CT 50 107 r. 2
lugal-ni$_3$-ĝa$_2$-ni f. ^{d}En-lil$_2$-la$_2$ MS-CS Unknown BIN 8 221 r. 2

lugal-ni$_3$-ĝa$_2$-ni-še$_3$ (a1) ‘the lugal … toward something of his’ 3.1.1.1, p. 83, 189
lugal-ni$_3$-ĝa$_2$-ni-še$_3$ engar CS Umma *USP* 46 r. 2’’

lugal-ni$_3$-kalag-ga (a1) ‘the lugal *is strong*’ 3.1.7.3, p. 163, 170 n. 992
lugal-ni$_3$-kalag-ga MS-CS Mesag BIN 8 264 o. 3

lugal-ni$_3$-lu-lu (a1) ‘the lugal is one who makes things thrive’ 3.1.5.3, p. 134, 254 n. 1492
lugal-ni$_3$-lu-lu ED IIIb/En. I ensi$_2$ Girsu OIP 104 23 u.e. x 34

°lugal-ni$_3$-lu-lu-a (a1) ‘the lugal is one who makes things thrive’ 3.1.5.3, p. 134, 237, 254 n. 1492
°lugal-ni$_3$-lu-lu-a CS Mugdan MAD 5 91 o. 2

lugal-ni$_3$-ni (a2) ‘the lugal … something of his’ 3.1.1.1, p. 84 n. 407, 147
lugal-ni$_3$-ni ED IIIa Šuruppag *FTUM* 30 o. i 4
lugal-ni$_3$-ni nu-banda$_3$-ni ES-MS Umma Nik 2 13 o. 5

lugal-ni$_3$-ni-še$_3$ (a≥2) ‘the lugal … toward something of his’ 3.1.1.1, p. 84 n. 407
lugal-ni$_3$-ni-⸢še$_3$⸣ ED IIIb-ES Umma-Zabala ? BIN 8 89 o. 2
⸢lugal-ni$_3$⸣-ni-še$_3$ ED IIIb/Il$_2$ ensi$_2$ Zabala *TCVBI* 1-1 r. i 4
lugal-ni$_3$-ni-še$_3$ [ugula-n]i MS-CS Umma ? *TCVC* 728 o. ii 16

lugal-ni$_3$-nidba$_2$-e (a1) ‘the lugal (is just right for) the nidba-offerings (?)’ 3.1.6.3, p. 147 n. 828
lugal-ni$_3$-nidba$_2$-e MS-CS Nippur OSP 2 51 o. 8

lugal-ni$_3$-nu-da-me (a1) ‘the lugal … nothing is beside (him)’ 3.1.7.7, p. 167–168
lugal-ni$_3$-nu-da-me ED IIIa Šuruppag *RTC* 13 o. v 3
⸢lugal⸣-ni$_3$-nu-da-me ED IIIa Šuruppag *WF* 35 o. v 2

lugal-ni$_3$-sa$_6$-ga (a4) ‘the lugal is something favourable’ 3.1.7.8, p. 170, 187
lugal-ni$_3$-sa$_6$-ga s. ^{d}En-lil$_2$-da, lu$_2$ tir ED IIIb Nippur OSP 1 109 o. ii 4
lu[gal]-⸢ni$_3$-sa$_6$⸣-ga CS/NS. Nippur TMH 5 7+184+201a r. ii 14’
lugal-ni$_3$-sa$_6$-ga f. LUL-gu-ak CS Umma *USP* 47 o. ii 8
lugal-ni$_3$-sa$_6$-ga nar MS-CS Unknown BIN 8 179 r. 1

lugal-ni$_3$-su (a1) ‘the lugal knows (every)thing’ 3.1.2, p. 105 n. 558
lugal-ni$_3$-su CS Unknown (Girsu$^?$) MVN 2 298 r. i 12

lugal-ni$_3$-U.TA (a≥3) ‘belonging of the lugal’ 3.1.1.1, p. 84

lugal-ni$_3$-U.TA s. E$_2$-gu$_3$-nun ED IIIb/Urz. lugal Isin M. Lambert, *RA* 73 (1979), p. 5–6 r. iv 4
lugal-ni$_3$-U.TA s. E$_2$-gu$_3$-nun ED IIIb/Urz. lugal Isin M. Lambert, *RA* 73 (1979), p. 5–6 r. v 20
lugal-ni$_3$-[U$^?$].TA ES-MS Nippur OSP 1 23 o. iv 21
lugal-ni$_3$-U.TA dam-gar$_3$ MS-CS Nippur OSP 2 45 r. i 5
lugal-ni$_3$-U.TA dam-gar$_3$ MS-CS Nippur OSP 2 48 o. ii 19
lugal-ni$_3$-U.TA h. Ama-na-nam CS Umma (?) MAD 4 37 r. 2
lugal-ni$_3$-U.TA MS-CS Umma MAD 4 162 (translit. only) o. 2

lugal-ni$_3$-UET2-276 (a1) unkn. mng. 3.1.8, p. 181
lugal-ni$_3$-UET2-276 ED I-II Ur UET 2 350 o. ii' 3'

lugal-ni$_3$-zu (a>20) 'the lugal knows (every)thing' 3.1.2, p. 104, 105–106, 236
lugal-ni$_3$-zu baḫar$_x$(BAR-LAK746) ED IIIa Šuruppag M. Lambert, *Gs Unger*, p. 27–49 3 o. v 1
lugal-ni$_3$-zu ED IIIb-ES Adab CUSAS 11 186 r. i 6
lugal-ni$_3$-zu Lugal-ni$_3$-zu, Ur$_2$-ni-bi$_3$-da ED IIIb Isin BIN 8 29 o. 1
lugal-ni$_3$-⸢zu⸣ s. Igi-bar, b. E$_2$-da-lu ED IIIb-ES Isin (?) BIN 8 170 o. 11
lugal-ni$_3$-zu (b. E$_2$-da-lu) ED IIIb-ES Isin (?) BIN 8 170 r. 12
lugal-ni$_3$-zu (b. E$_2$-da-lu) ED IIIb-ES Isin (?) BIN 8 170 r. 5
lugal-ni$_3$-zu s. Ur-li ED IIIb Isin TIM 9 96 o. i 2'
lugal-[ni$_3$-zu] ? ED IIIb Isin TIM 9 96 o. ii 2'
lugal-ni$_3$-zu ED IIIb Isin TIM 9 96 o. ii 8'
lugal-ni$_3$-zu (s.) Ur-li-ke$_4$ ED IIIb Isin TIM 9 100 r. 9'
lugal-ni$_3$-zu ED IIIb Nippur OSP 1 39 o. i 3'
lugal-ni$_3$-zu ED IIIb Nippur OSP 1 109 o. i 11
lugal-ni$_3$-zu Lugal-ki-gal-la, Lugal-ni$_3$-zu ED IIIb Nippur TMH 5 11 o. i 3
lugal-ni$_3$-zu s. Ur-ur, b. Giri$_3$-ni ED IIIb Nippur TMH 5 11 r. ii 8
⸢lugal⸣-ni$_3$-zu (s. Ur-ur) ED IIIb Nippur TMH 5 118 o. 5
⸢lugal⸣-ni$_3$-zu s. Ur-ur-ra ED IIIb Nippur TMH 5 118 r. 7
lugal-ni$_3$-zu maškim-bi ED IIIb Nippur TMH 5 159 o. vi 14'
lugal-ni$_3$-zu lu$_2$ Zi-mu ED IIIb Nippur TMH 5 171 o. 1
lugal-ni$_3$-zu ED IIIb-ES Unknown (Adab ?) BIN 8 27 o. ii 4
lugal-ni$_3$-zu ES Adab CUSAS 11 281 r. 1
lugal-ni$_3$-zu ? ensi$_2$-gal, …, ĝuruš, ir$_3$ dub-sar-ne ES-MS Umma *CHÉU* 54 o. i 11
lugal-ni$_3$-zu ES-MS Umma Nik 2 63 r. 5'
lugal-⸢ni$_3$⸣-zu engar CS Adab CUSAS 13 21 r. 8
lugal-ni$_3$-zu CS Adab *SIA* 868 o. 3
lugal-ni$_3$-zu CS Girsu *STTI* 104 o. 5'
lugal-ni$_3$-zu lu$_2$ ki Ma-ri$_2$-ka CS Girsu ITT 1 1241 r. 1
lugal-ni$_3$-zu dam-gar$_3$ CS Girsu ITT 1 1370 o. 3
lugal-ni$_3$-zu CS Girsu ITT 1 1448 o. ii 18
lugal-ni$_3$-zu f. Lugal-ezem CS Girsu *RTC* 81 o. 5
lugal-ni$_3$-zu f. Lu$_2$-^{d}Nin-ĝir-su CS Girsu MVN 3 113 o. ii 14
lugal-ni$_3$-zu MS-CS Isin ? MAD 4 155 o. 5
lugal-ni$_3$-zu MS-CS Isin ? MAD 4 155 o. 9
lugal-ni$_3$-zu f. KA-ku$_3$ MS-CS Isin ? MAD 4 150 r. 2
lugal-ni$_3$-zu f. KA-ku$_3$, ff. Ur-niĝin$_3$(UD.E$_2$) CS Isin ? MAD 4 169 r. 7
lugal-ni$_3$-zu f. Ur$_2$-ra-ni MS-CS Isin ? MVN 3 81 edge 2
lugal-ni$_3$-zu MS-CS Nippur TMH 5 127 o. 4
lugal-ni$_3$-zu dam-gar$_3$ MS-CS Nippur TMH 5 216 o. 1
lugal-ni$_3$-zu MS-CS Nippur OSP 2 55 o. 12

lugal-ni_3-zu MS-CS Nippur OSP 2 61 o. i 5
lugal-ni_3-zu MS-CS Nippur OSP 2 62 o. ii 10
lugal-ni_3-zu MS-CS Nippur OSP 2 63 o. ii 9
lugal-ni_3-zu MS-CS Nippur OSP 2 73 r. 5
lugal-ni_3-zu MS-CS Nippur OSP 2 84 o. i 7
lugal-ni_3-zu MS-CS Nippur OSP 2 96 o. i 14
lugal-[ni_3]-zu MS-CS Nippur OSP 2 96 o. ii 1
lugal-ni_3-zu MS-CS Nippur OSP 2 98 o. iii 2
lu[gal]-ni_3-zu MS-CS Nippur OSP 2 98 r. ii 12
lugal-ni_3-zu CS/Śkś Y 2 Nippur OSP 2 100 r. ii 6'
lugal-ni_3-zu CS/Śkś Y 2 Nippur OSP 2 100 r. iii 12'
lugal-ni_3-zu s. Ur-⌜^{d}Ḫendur-saĝ⌝ MS-CS Nippur OSP 2 128 r. ii 6
lugal-ni_3-zu ĝuruš-min MS-CS Nippur OSP 2 136 r. 2'
lugal-ni_3-zu MS-CS Nippur OSP 2 142 r. 10'
lugal-[ni_3-zu] ? ens[i_2] [Ni]ppur[^{ki}] CS/NS. (OB) Nippur A. Poebel., PBS 5 36 o. (?) v' 10'
lugal-ni_3-zu CS/NS. Nippur PBS 9 15+110 o. i 8
lugal-ni_3-zu CS Nippur PBS 9 36 o. ii' 5'
lugal-ni_3-zu$^!$(BA) $ensi_2$ Nibru^{ki}, saĝa ^{d}En-lil_2 CS/NS. Nippur PBS 15 82 1
lugal-⌜ni_3⌝-zu CS/NS. Nippur TMH 5 7+184+201a r. i 7'
lugal-ni_3-zu MS-CS Umma *CST* 9 o. 10
lugal-ni_3-zu saĝ-apin-na CS/Śkś Y 7 Umma CT 50 67 o. 5
lugal-ni_3-zu šitim, *be-lu bu-dim, in* Umma^{ki} CS Umma CT 50 188 r. i 8
lugal-⌜ni_3⌝-zu MS-CS Umma ? *TCVC* 727 o. i 9
lugal-ni_3-zu MS-CS Umma ? *TCVC* 728 o. iii 4
lugal-ni_3-zu s. ⌜E_2⌝-zi MS-CS Umma ? *TCVC* 730 r. i 5
[lugal-ni_3]-⌜zu⌝ ? saĝ-⌜apin⌝ MS-CS Umma ? *TCVC* 733 o. i' 6
lugal-ni_3-zu MS-CS Umma-Zabala ? R. D. Freedman, *The Cuneiform Tablets in St. Louis* 51 r. 1
lugal-[ni_3]-zu MS-CS Umma-Zabala ? R. D. Freedman, *The Cuneiform Tablets in St. Louis* 52 r. 1
lugal-ni_3-zu nu-kir[i_6] MS-CS Umma-Zabala ? R. D. Freedman, *The Cuneiform Tablets in St. Louis* 53 r. 5
lugal-ni_3-zu E_2-ma-al-za^{ki} MS-CS Unknown MesCiv 4 65 o. 2
lugal-ni_3-zu KUM-tuš-$še_3$ MS-CS Unknown MVN 3 103 o. 6
lugal-ni_3-zu MS-CS Unknown BIN 8 222 o. 3
lugal-ni_3-zu CS Unknown BIN 8 261 r. 1

lugal-Nibru^{ki} $^{(a2)}$ 'the lugal … Nippur' 3.1.6.4, p. 154 n. 884
lugal-Nibru^{ki} ED IIIa Šuruppag *TSŠ* 627 r. i' 1'
lugal-Nibru^{ki} dam-gar_3 ED IIIb-ES Nippur ? BIN 8 166 r. 7

lugal-$nidba_2$ $^{(a1)}$ 'the lugal (is just right for) the nidba-offerings (?)' 3.1.6.3, p. 147
lugal-$nidba_2$ ES-MS Nippur OSP 1 23 o. iii 2'

lugal-$nidba_2$-e $^{(a1)}$ 'the lugal (is just right for) the nidba-offerings (?)' 3.1.6.3, p. 147 n. 828, 256
lugal-$nidba_2$-e MS-CS Nippur OSP 2 48 o. i 4
lugal-$nidba_2$-e MS-CS Nippur OSP 2 52 o. 5
⌜lugal⌝-ni[dba_2-e] MS-CS Nippur OSP 2 53 r. (?) 1'
lugal-$nidba_2$-e MS-CS Nippur OSP 2 54 o. 5
lugal-$nidba_2$-e MS-CS Nippur OSP 2 63 r. ii 3

lugal-$NIĜ_2$ $^{(a>12)}$ abbreviation of a number of possible readings 3.1.8, p. 106, 181

lugal-NIĜ$_2$ ED IIIb-ES Adab CUSAS 11 102 o. i 4
lugal-NIĜ$_2$ ED IIIb-ES Adab CUSAS 11 102 o. ii 5
lugal-NIĜ$_2$ a-zu$_5$ ED IIIb-ES Adab CUSAS 11 186 o. iii 12
lugal-NIĜ$_2$ ED IIIb-ES Adab CUSAS 11 186 o. v 11
lugal-NIĜ$_2$ sip[a] ED IIIb Girsu CT 50 29 r. i 3
lugal-NIĜ$_2$ sipa ED IIIb Girsu OIP 14 57 r. ii 1
lugal-NIĜ$_2$ Lugal-NIĜ$_2$ Ama-bara$_2$-ge i$_3$-du$_8$ ED IIIb Umma-Zabala ? BIN 8 62 o. i 1
lugal-NIĜ$_2$ sipa ED IIIb/Luzag. Y 7 Umma-Zabala M. Powell, *HUCA* 49 (1978), p. 1–58 1 o. ii 1
lugal-NIĜ$_2$ ED IIIb Umma-Zabala M. Powell, *HUCA* 49 (1978), p. 1–58 15 o. i 4
lugal-NIĜ$_2$ s. E-⸢x⸣-[x], b. Ĝiš-ša$_3$, lu$_2$ aga$_3$ ma$_2$-gal ED IIIb Umma-Zabala M. Powell, *HUCA* 49 (1978), p. 1–58 18 r. i 11
lugal-NIĜ$_2$ ED IIIb Zabala M. Powell, *HUCA* 49 (1978), p. 1–58 8 o. ii 1
lugal-NIĜ$_2$ ES-MS Unknown *RIAA* 42 o. i 4
lugal-NIĜ$_2$ f. Nin-me CS Adab CUSAS 13 53 o. 2
lugal-NIĜ$_2$ dam-gar$_3$ CS Adab CUSAS 13 78 r. i 9
lugal-NIĜ$_2$ nagar CS Adab CUSAS 13 108 o. 14
lugal-NIĜ$_2$ MS-CS Adab OIP 14 156 o. 2
lugal-NIĜ$_2$ CS Adab *SIA* 674 o. 7 A 674
lugal-NIĜ$_2$ CS Adab *TCABI* 208 r. 4
lugal-NIĜ$_2$ ka-gur$_7$ CS Girsu CT 50 187 o. 4
lugal-NIĜ$_2$ ka-gur$_7$ CS/Śkś Girsu CT 50 172 r. ii 13
lugal-⸢NIĜ$_2$⸣ ku$_3$-dim$_2$ CS Girsu *RTC* 95 o. 4'
lugal-NIĜ$_2$ CS Girsu *RTC* 134 r. i 11'
lugal-⸢NIĜ$_2$⸣ MS-CS Isin BIN 8 156 o. 3
lugal-NIĜ$_2$ MS-CS Umma BIN 8 300 r. 3
lugal-NIĜ$_2$ MS-CS Umma BIN 8 313 o. 2
lugal-NIĜ$_2$ MS-CS Umma BIN 8 316 o. 7
lugal-NIĜ$_2$ f. ⸢Ad⸣-da, sur$_x$-re-ka-ke$_4$ ⸢e⸣-la$_2$ MS-CS Umma *CST* 11 o. 3
lugal-NIĜ$_2$ CS Umma Nik 2 84 r. 6
lugal-NIĜ$_2$ s. Ĝiš-ša$_3$ CS Umma Nik 2 84 r. 5
lugal-NIĜ$_2$ h. En-er$_2$-^{d}U[tu$^{?}$] MS-CS Unknown *DCS* 43 r. 1
lugal-NIĜ$_2$ OAkk Unknown MAD 4 26 (translit. only) o. 4
lugal-NIĜ$_2$ OAkk Unknown MAD 4 154 (translit. only) o. i 9

lugal-NIĜ$_2$-[x] ED I-II Ur UET 2 355 o. 2
lugal-NIĜ$_2$-⸢x⸣ ED IIIb-ES Umma B. R. Foster, *Fs Westenholz*, 127–137 6 o. i 4
lugal-NIĜ$_2$-[x(-x)] MS-CS Nippur OSP 2 86 o. i 11'
[lu]gal-NIĜ$_2$-⸢x⸣-[(x)] MS-CS Nippur OSP 2 95 o. iii 1
⸢lugal⸣-NIĜ$_2$-⸢x-x⸣ ? MS-CS Nippur OSP 2 96 o. ii 8

lugal-niĝir(LAK154) $^{(a\geq 6)}$ 'the lugal is a herald' 3.1.7.9, p. 88, 171, 188
lugal-niĝir lu$_2$ sar ED IIIb Adab *TCABI* 7 o. i 4
lugal-niĝir ED IIIb Nippur OSP 1 73 o. 2
lugal-niĝir ED IIIb Nippur TMH 5 170 o. i 5
lugal-niĝir ED IIIb Umma-Zabala BIN 8 111 r. i 1
lugal-niĝir ⸢Ur⸣-PA Lugal-niĝir ES-MS Isin BIN 8 154 left edge
lugal-niĝir s. Ša$_3$-dur$_2$-ba ES-MS Unknown MVN 3 98 r. i 5
lugal-niĝir *šu* ⸢Bar-ra-an⸣, ĝuruš CS Girsu *DPA* 43 (PUL 47) o. 7
lugal-niĝir f. Zi CS Girsu *STTI* 151 o. iii' 1'

lugal-nim-du $^{(a1)}$ 'the lugal goes (to) the highland' 3.1.3.3, p. 116 w. n. 629
lugal-nim-du saĝ-sug$_5$ ED IIIa Girsu PBS 9 2 o. iii 8
lugal-nim-du saĝ-sug$_5$ ED IIIa Girsu PBS 9 2 o. v 11

lugal-nir $^{(a3)}$ ‘the lugal is lord(ly)’ 3.1.1.6, p. 99
lugal-nir ugula e-me-a [x] ED IIIb/En. I ensi$_2$ 4 Lagaš BiMes 3 10 r. i 2
lugal-nir sipa CS Adab *TCABI* 236 o. 3
lugal-nir MS-CS Nippur OSP 2 80 o. ii 9

lugal-nir-ĝal$_2$ $^{(a\geq7/°1)}$ ‘the lugal is lord(ly)’ 3.1.1.6, p. 99
°lugal-nir-ĝal$_2$ ED IIIa Abū Ṣalābīḫ *IAS* 330 o. ii 2
lugal-[nir]-ĝal$_2$ ED IIIb-ES Adab CUSAS 11 201 o. iv 6
lugal-nir-ĝal$_2$ [x]-⸢a⸣, Lugal-nir-ĝal$_2$, E$_2$-zi, Ur-E$_2$-maḫ ED IIIb Adab Eig. ^{ni_3}ensi$_2$ OIP 14 49 r. ii’ 3’
°lugal-nir-ĝal$_2$ ED IIIb Ebla MEE 3 59 o. ii 2
lugal-nir-ĝal$_2$ maškim ED IIIb Isin ? BIN 8 17 o. ii 4
lugal-nir-ĝal$_2$ f. Lu$_2$-^{pa}pa$_3$-da, lu$_2$ *Im-lik*-e$_2$ ED IIIb-ES Isin MVN 3 53 o. ii 4
lugal-nir-ĝal$_2$ ugula nu-banda$_3$ ED IIIb Umma-Zabala M. Powell, *HUCA* 49 (1978), p. 1–58 23 o. i 1
lugal-⸢nir⸣-ĝal$_2$ sipa ED IIIb Zabala M. Powell, *HUCA* 49 (1978), p. 1–58 7 o. i 10
lugal-nir-ĝal$_2$ ensi$_2$ Adab^{ki}-ke$_4$ MS Adab *TCABI* 65 o. 6
⸢lugal-nir-ĝal$_2$⸣ MS-CS Adab OIP 14 168 r.(!) i 5’
lugal-nir-ĝal$_2$ (ugula) CS Girsu CT 50 105 r. 2
lugal-nir-ĝal$_2$ ugula CS Girsu *RTC* 127 r. v 11
⸢lugal⸣-[n]ir-ĝal$_2$ CS Girsu *RTC* 139 r. 7
⸢lugal⸣-nir-ĝal$_2$ f. [x]-^{d}Gu$_2$-la$_2$-ta MS-CS Nippur OSP 2 74 r. 3’
lugal-nir-ĝal$_2$ MS-CS Nippur PBS 9 28+34 r. i’ 6’
lugal-nir-ĝal$_2$ s. Ni$_3$-^{d}En-lil$_2$-le MS-CS Umma MesCiv 4 30 o. ii 22

lugal-nitaḫ-zi $^{(a\geq10)}$ ‘the lugal is a reliable man’ 3.1.7.9, p. 171
⸢lugal⸣-nitaḫ-zi umbisaĝ ED IIIa Unknown *RIAA* 44 r. i 10
lugal-nitaḫ-zi ED IIIb Adab CUSAS 11 40 r. ii 2
lugal-nitaḫ-zi ED IIIb-ES Adab CUSAS 11 139 o. ii 3
lugal-nitaḫ-zi ED IIIb-ES Adab CUSAS 11 162 o. ii 5
lugal-nitaḫ-zi lu$_2$ sar ED IIIb Adab *TCABI* 7 o. ii 1
lugal-nitaḫ-zi simug ED IIIb/Enz. ensi$_2$ 4 Girsu *DP* 1/2 92 r. ii 1
[lugal-nit]aḫ$^{?}$-zi ED IIIb Nippur OSP 1 27 o. i’ 12’
lugal-nitaḫ-zi ED IIIb Umma-Zabala CUSAS 14 164 o. ii 3
lugal-nitaḫ-zi ED IIIb Umma-Zabala CUSAS 14 276 o. ii 3
lugal-nitaḫ-zi ED IIIb/Luzag. ensi$_2$ 7 Umma-Zabala M. deJ. Ellis, *JCS* 31 (1979), p. 30–55 7 o. iii 16
lugal-nitaḫ-zi ED IIIb/Luzag. ensi$_2$ 7 Umma-Zabala M. deJ. Ellis, *JCS* 31 (1979), p. 30–55 7 r. ii 14
lugal-nitaḫ-zi ES Isin or Nippur ? MVN 3 45 r. iii 1
lugal-nitaḫ-zi Umma U$_3$-mu-NI#NI, lu$_2$ Lugal-nitaḫ-zi dam-gar$_3$-gal Zabala$_6^{ki}$ ES-MS Nik 2 19 o. ii 4
lugal-nitaḫ-zi En-ḪU-ĝal$_2$, lu$_2$ Lugal-nitaḫ-zi dam-gar$_3$-gal (Zabala$_6^{ki}$) ES-MS Umma Nik 2 19 o. ii 10
lugal-nitaḫ-zi CS Adab CUSAS 13 32 o. 10
lugal-nitaḫ-zi *Be-li$_2$-gu$_2$* CS Adab CUSAS 13 114 o. 4’
lugal-nitaḫ$^{?}$-zi MS-CS Adab MVN 3 62 o. 2
lugal-nitaḫ-zi CS Girsu MVN 3 51 o. 5
lugal-nitaḫ-zi CS Isin CUSAS 13 163 o. ii 2’

lugal-nitaḫ$_2$-zi $^{(a\geq2)}$ ‘the lugal is a reliable man’ 3.1.7.9, p. 171
lugal-nitaḫ$_2$-zi ES Adab CUSAS 11 329 o. 4
lugal-nitaḫ$_2$-zi utul MS Adab *TCABI* 68 o. 8
lu[gal]-nitaḫ$_2$-[zi$^{?}$] MS-CS Umma ? *TCVC* 729 r. 12’

lugal-nu-du$_{11}$-ga $^{(a\geq3)}$ 'was it not spoken by the lugal?' 3.1.1.4, p. 94
lugal-nu-du$_{11}$-ga ES Adab CUSAS 11 333 o. 3
lugal-nu-du$_{11}$-ga MS Adab *TCABI* 113 o. 4
lugal-nu-du$_{11}$-ga s. [x]-e CS Umma *USP* 47 o. i 2
lugal-nu-du$_{11}$-ga MS-CS Unknown *L'uomo* 15 r. 9
lugal-nu-du$_{11}$-ga b. Lugal-GU$_2$ CS Unknown Mesopotamia 9 2 o. 14'
lu[gal]-nu-du$_{11}$-[ga] b. Lugal-[GU$_2$] CS Unknown Mesopotamia 9 3 o. 14
lugal-nu-du$_{11}$-ga (b. Lugal-GU$_2$) CS Unknown Mesopotamia 9 4 o. 15

°lugal-nu-KI-SAĜ $^{(°3)}$ unkn. mng. 3.1.8, p. 181 w. n. 1103
°lugal-nu-KI-SAĜ ED IIIa Abū Ṣalābīḫ *IAS* 298 o. iii 15
°lugal-⌜nu⌝-KI-SAĜ ED IIIa Šuruppag *SF* 63 o. vi 4!
°lugal-nu-KI-SAĜ ED IIIa Unknown *RIAA* 44 o. iii' 10

lugal-nu-šilig(LAK650) $^{(a3/°3)}$ 'the lugal is untiring' 3.1.7.3, p. 163
°lugal-nu-šilig ED IIIa Abū Ṣalābīḫ *IAS* 298 o. iii 14
°lugal-nu-šilig ED IIIa Šuruppag *SF* 29 r. iii 10
°lugal-⌜nu-šilig⌝ ED IIIa Šuruppag *SF* 63 o. vi 3
lugal-nu-šilig ED IIIa Unknown F. Vukosavović, *JAC* 23 (2008), p. 37–54 2 o. ii 1
°lugal-nu-šilig$^!$(LAK648+SIG$_5$) ED IIIa Unknown *RIAA* 44 o. iii' 9
lugal-nu-šilig ED IIIa-b Girsu *RTC* 1 r. iv 3
lugal-nu-šilig ? ED IIIb Adab MVN 3 90 o. iii 3

lugal-numun-zi $^{(a\geq3)}$ 'the lugal (is a, or loves the) reliable offspring' 3.1.7.1, p. 160, 251 n. 1476
lugal-⌜numun⌝-zi ED IIIa-b Adab *TCABI* 3 r. i 2
lugal-numun-zi ED IIIb Adab BIN 8 6 o. ii 2
lugal-numun-zi ED IIIb Adab BIN 8 211 o. i 9
lugal-numun-zi ED IIIb Adab BIN 8 211 r. i 7
lugal-numun-zi ED IIIb Adab BIN 8 211 r. ii 1
lugal-numun-zi ED IIIb-ES Isin MVN 3 67 o. ii 7
lugal-numun-zi s. Ur-e$_2$-maḫ ED IIIb/Urz. lugal Isin M. Lambert, *RA* 73 (1979), p. 5–6 o. ii 3
lugal-numun-zi s. Ur-e$_2$-maḫ ED IIIb/Urz. lugal Isin M. Lambert, *RA* 73 (1979), p. 5–6 o. ii 22
lugal-numun-zi dub-sar ED IIIb/Urz. lugal Isin M. Lambert, *RA* 73 (1979), p. 5–6 o. xi 9
lugal-numun-zi [dub-sar$^?$] ED IIIb/Urz. lugal Isin M. Lambert, *RA* 73 (1979), p. 5–6 r. iv 25
lugal-numun-zi dub-sar ES Adab *TCABI* 32 o. ii 6

lugal-nun-DU $^{(a1)}$ unkn. mng. 3.1.8, p. 181
lugal-nun-DU sagi ED IIIa Šuruppag M. Lambert, *Gs Unger*, p. 27–49 4 r. i 4

°lugal-nun-pa$_3$ $^{(°1)}$ 'the lugal is one chosen by the noble one (?)' 3.1.6.2, p. 145
°lugal-nun-pa$_3$ ED IIIa Šuruppag *SF* 29 o. iv 16

lugal-pa-DU $^{(a1)}$ (probable defective writing of the following) 3.1.7.10, p. 174 n. 1017
lugal-pa-DU ED IIIb Marada ? *AAICAB* 1/1 (Ashm 1924-468) o. ii 4

lugal-pa-e$_3$ $^{(a\geq14)}$ 'the lugal is shining/splendid' 3.1.7.10, p. 173–174
lugal-pa-e$_3$ ED IIIa Adab CUSAS 11 4 o. i 1
lugal-pa-e$_3$ ED IIIa Šuruppag *WF* 66 o. v 2
⌜lugal⌝-pa-⌜e$_3$$^?$⌝ ED IIIa Šuruppag *WF* 149 r. ii 6'
lugal-pa-e$_3$ umbisaĝ ED IIIa Unknown *RIAA* 44 r. i 9
lugal-pa-e$_3$ si[pa šaḫ$_2$] ED IIIb/Ukg. lugal X Girsu *AWAS* 69 o. i 5
lugal-pa-e$_3$ sipa šaḫ$_2$ ED IIIb/Ukg. lugal X Girsu *AWAS* 70 r. iii' 1'

lugal-[pa]-e$_3$ [si]pa šaḫ$_2$ ED IIIb/Ukg. lugal 3 Girsu *AWAS* 118 r. i 5
lugal-pa-e$_3$ sipa šaḫ$_2$ ED IIIb/Ukg. lugal 1? Girsu *AWAS* 123 r. vi' 5
lugal-pa-e$_3$ sipa šaḫ$_2$ ED IIIb/Ukg. lugal 4 Girsu BIN 8 344 r. vi 3
lugal-pa-e$_3$ sipa šaḫ$_2$ ED IIIb/Ukg. lugal 3 Girsu BIN 8 345 r. v 7
lugal-pa-e$_3$ i$_3$-du$_8$ ED IIIb/Enz. ensi$_2$ 2 Girsu BIN 8 347 r. iv 5
lugal-pa-e$_3$ sipa udu s[iki]-ka ED IIIb/Lug. 1 Girsu BIN 8 372 o. iii 7
lugal-pa-e$_3$ (baḫar) ED IIIb/X Y 2 Girsu BIN 8 380 o. iii 1
[lugal]-⸢pa⸣-[e$_3$] sipa šaḫ$_2$ ED IIIb/Ukg. lugal 3 Girsu BIN 8 391 r. iv 12
lugal-pa-e$_3$ sipa šaḫ$_2$ ED IIIb/Ukg. lugal 4 Girsu CT 50 34 r. vii 9
lugal-pa-e$_3$ sipa šaḫ$_2$ ED IIIb/Ukg. lugal 5 Girsu *CTNMC* 3 r. iii 4
lugal-pa-e$_3$ ED IIIb/Ukg. lugal 3 Girsu Jacobsen *CTNMC* 4 r. vi 14
lu[gal]-[pa]-e$_3$ [si]pa šaḫ$_2$ ED IIIb Girsu *DCS* 2 r. vi 3'
lugal-pa-e$_3$ sipa šaḫ$_2$ ED IIIb Girsu *DCS* 3 r. vii 5
lugal-pa-e$_3$ sipa šaḫ$_2$ ED IIIb/Lug. [ensi$_2$] 3 Girsu *DCS* 6 r. i 3
lugal-pa-e$_3$ sipa šaḫ$_2$ ED IIIb/Ukg. lugal X Girsu *DCS* 7 r. iii 5'
lugal-pa-e$_3$ sipa šaḫ$_2$ ED IIIb/Lug. 1 Girsu *DCS* 8 r. iii 1
lugal-pa-e$_3$ engar ED IIIb/Lug. 5 Girsu *DP* 1/2 87 o. iii 2
lugal-pa-e$_3$ ED IIIb/Ukg. lugal 3 Girsu *DP* 1/2 130 o. v 7
lugal-pa-e$_3$ engar, ba-uš$_2$ ED IIIb/Ukg. lugal 4 Girsu *DP* 1/2 138 o. i 1
lugal-pa-e$_3$ s. Ur-dam, lu$_2$ luĝa ED IIIb/Lug. 4 Girsu *DP* suppl. 625 o. ii 3
lugal-pa-e$_3$ baḫar$_2$-bi ED IIIb/X Y 1 Girsu *DP* suppl. 637 r. i 1
lugal-pa-e$_3$ lu$_2$ ^{d}Ba-u$_2$ ED IIIb Girsu *DP* suppl. 568 o. i 1
lugal-pa-e$_3$ sipa šaḫ$_2$ ED IIIb/Ukg. Y X Girsu MVN 3 4 o. iv 3
lugal-pa-e$_3$ sipa šaḫ$_2$ ED IIIb/Ukg. lugal 6 Girsu MVN 3 7 o. iv 1'
lugal-pa-e$_3$ sipa šaḫ$_2$ ED IIIb/Ukg. lugal 2 Girsu Nik 1 1 r. v 13
lugal-pa-e$_3$ sipa [šaḫ$_2$] ED IIIb/Ukg. lugal 2 Girsu Nik 1 13 r. i 8
lugal-pa-e$_3$ A$_2$-kal-le, Lugal-pa-e$_3$ ED IIIb Umma MVN 3 106 o. i 5
lugal-pa-e$_3$$^{!}$(DIŠ.LIŠ.DU) ED IIIb Umma-Zabala ? BIN 8 51 o. 2
lugal-pa-e$_3$ ED IIIb/Luzag. (?) 7 Umma-Zabala BIN 8 55 o. ii 6
lugal-pa-e$_3$ nu-banda$_3$ ED IIIb Umma-Zabala ? BIN 8 58 o. 2
lugal-⸢pa-e$_3$⸣ ED IIIb Umma-Zabala ? BIN 8 64 o. i 3
lugal-pa-e$_3$ ED IIIb/Luzag. ensi$_2$ X Umma-Zabala BIN 8 82 o. iii 14
lugal-pa-e$_3$ ED IIIb Umma-Zabala BIN 8 111 o. i 5
lugal-pa-e$_3$ ED IIIb Umma-Zabala BIN 8 111 o. i 6
lugal-pa-e$_3$ ED IIIb/Luzag. ensi$_2$ [x] Umma-Zabala J. A. Brinkman, *Fs Kramer*, pl. III*-V* (W 2/7) o. iv 11'
lugal-pa-e$_3$ ED IIIb/X Y 29 Umma-Zabala M. Powell, *HUCA* 49 (1978), p. 1–58 6 o. ii 4
lugal-pa-e$_3$ ⸢KASKAL⸣ ES-MS Umma Nik 2 14 o. iii 1
lugal-pa-e$_3$ MS-CS Nippur OSP 2 81 r. 1
lugal-pa-e$_3$ CS Umma *AAS* 12 o. 4
lugal-pa-e$_3$ MS-CS Umma BIN 8 305 o. 2
lugal-pa-e$_3$ CS/Śkś Y 6 Umma CT 50 65 o. 2
lugal-pa-e$_3$ šitim, *be-lu bu-dim*, *in* Umma^{ki} CS Umma CT 50 188 r. i 10
lugal-pa-e$_3$ CS Umma *USP* 71 o. 1

lugal-pa$_3$ (a1/°1) 'the lugal is one chosen (by DN)' 3.1.6.2, p. 145 n. 817, 229, 246
lugal-pa$_3$ uĝken-gal ED I-II Ur UET 2 68b o. ii 4
°lugal-pa$_3$ ED IIIb Ebla ARET 5 25 r. i 3

lugal-pa$_3$-da (a2) 'the lugal is one chosen (by DN)' 3.1.6.2, p. 145 n. 817
lugal-pa$_3$:da f. Ad-da ED IIIb/X Y 5 Girsu *DP* suppl. 593 o. iii 7
lugal-pa$_3$-da f. Lum-ma-[(x)] CS Umma *USP* 47 o. ii 3

lugal-pa$_4$-zu $^{(a\geq1)}$ 'the lugal knows the uncle' 3.1.8, p. 181
lugal-pa$_4$-zu ED I-II Ur UET 2 297 o. i 2'
lugal-pa$_4$-zu ED I-II Ur UET 2 366 o. ii' 6

lugal-palil $^{(a2/°1)}$ 'the lugal is a vanguard' 3.1.3.1, p. 108
°lugal-palil ED IIIa Kiš MesCiv 14, pl. 23, 3: H+Y r.(?) ii' 2
lugal-palil ED IIIb Adab *TCABI* 12 o. i 2
lugal-palil lu$_2$ saĝa E$_2$-maḫ CS Adab CUSAS 13 70 r. 1

lugal-piriĝ $^{(a\geq8/°1)}$ 'the lugal is (like) a lion' 3.1.7.6, p. 165, 207, 241
°lugal-piriĝ ED IIIa Šuruppag *SF* 28 o. i 8
°lugal-piriĝ ED IIIa Šuruppag *SF* 29 o. i 8
lugal-piriĝ ED IIIa Šuruppag *TSŠ* 903 r. ii 2
lugal-piriĝ ED IIIb-ES Adab CUSAS 11 186 o. v 7
lugal-piriĝ šu-ku$_6$ ab-ba ED IIIb/Lug. X Girsu BIN 8 365 r. i 2
lugal-piriĝ šu-ku$_6$ ab-ba ED IIIb/Ukg. lugal 2 Girsu *DP* 2/1 171 r. v 17
lugal-piriĝ šu-ku$_6$ ab-ba ED IIIb Girsu *DP* 2/1 172 o. ii 3
lugal-piriĝ b., Lugal-ša$_3$-la$_2$-tuku, Saĝ-ḫab$_2$-ba, Aja$_2$-lu$_2$-lil-la, šu-ku$_6$ ab-ba ED IIIb/Ukg. lugal 3 Girsu *DP* 2/1 177 r. i 7
lugal-piriĝ šu-ku$_6$ ab-ba ED IIIb/Lug. 1 Girsu *DP* 2/1 191 r. iii 2
lugal-piriĝ šu-ku$_6$ e$_2$ saĝa-ka, šu-ku$_6$ ab-ba ED IIIb/Lug. 3 Girsu *DP* 2/2 279 r. i 3
lugal-piriĝ šu-ku$_6$ ab-ba ED IIIb/Enz. ensi$_2$ 2 Girsu *DP* 2/2 283 o. iii 5
lugal-piriĝ i$_3$-du$_8$ nam-dumu ED IIIb/Ukg. lugal 3 Girsu Nik 1 63 r. i 8
⸢lugal⸣-[pir]iĝ ⸢šu-ku$_6$ ab-ba⸣ ED IIIb/Ukg. lugal 2 Girsu Nik 1 272 o. ii 5
lu[gal]-piriĝ šu-ku$_6$ ab-ba ED IIIb/X Y 4 Girsu *RTC* 31 o. i 5
lugal-piriĝ šu-ku$_6$ e$_2$ saĝa-ka, šu-ku$_6$ ab-ba ED IIIb/Lug. 2 Girsu *RTC* 35 r. i 2
lugal-piriĝ lu$_2$ dun-a, Ne-saĝ-ĝa$_2$ ED IIIb/X Y 5 Girsu VS 27 55 o. i 3
lugal-piriĝ Ur-saĝ Lugal-p[iriĝ] ED IIIb/Luzag. ensi$_2$ 7 Umma-Zabala M. deJ. Ellis, *JCS* 31 (1979), p. 30–55 6 o. iv 16
lugal-piriĝ Ur-saĝ Lugal-piriĝ ED IIIb/Luzag. ensi$_2$ 7 Umma-Zabala M. deJ. Ellis, *JCS* 31 (1979), p. 30–55 6 o. v 6
lugal-⸢piriĝ⸣ Ur-saĝ [...] Lugal-⸢piriĝ⸣ ED IIIb Zabala BIN 8 75 o. 5
lugal-piriĝ mu-kiri$_6$ ^{d}Aš$_8$-gi$_4$-pa-e$_3$ ES Adab CUSAS 11 278 o. 2
lugal-piriĝ ab-ba nu-kiri$_6$ MS-CS Isin ? Nippur ? Adab ? A. Goetze, *JCS* 20 (1968), p. 126–127 o. 2
lugal-piriĝ s. Ur-en CS Girsu MVN 3 113 o. i 1
lugal-piriĝ CS Girsu *STTI* 25 r. 4'

lugal-ra $^{(a\geq14)}$ '… to the lugal' 3.1.8, p. 181
lugal-ra ED IIIb-ES Adab CUSAS 11 186 o. v 10
lugal-ra ED IIIb-ES Adab CUSAS 11 228 o. ii 8
lugal-ra ED IIIb Adab OIP 14 77 r. 2
lugal-ra h. GAN-ki ED IIIb/Ukg. lugal 2 Girsu *DP* 1/2 128 o. ii 7
lugal-ra h. GAN-ki ED IIIb/Ukg. lugal 3 Girsu *DP* 1/2 129 o. ii 7
lugal-ra s. U$_2$-da ED IIIb Girsu *DP* suppl. 555 r. i 4
lugal-ra b. Lugal-ušur$_3$ ED IIIb/X Y 5 Girsu *DP* suppl. 593 o. ii 1
lugal-ra s. U$_2$-da ED IIIb/X Y 5 Girsu Nik 1 101 o. i 2
lugal-ra ED IIIb/Ukg. lugal 4 Girsu *TSA* 47 o. iv 2
lugal-ra ED IIIb/Uru-KA UN:gal Girsu VS 27 33 o. iii 2
lugal-ra f. Lugal-ša$_3^{!?}$, nu-kiri$_6$ ED IIIb Nippur TMH 5 6 o. ii 3
lugal-ra AB$_2$-GAL ED IIIb Nippur TMH 5 16 o. 4
lugal-ra b. Ur-lu$_2$ ED IIIb Nippur TMH 5 17 o. i 5
lu:gal-ra ED IIIb Nippur TMH 5 41 r. ii 2'
⸢lugal-ra⸣ ED IIIb Nippur TMH 5 46 o. iii 6

lugal-ra ED IIIb Nippur TMH 5 53 o. i 2
lugal-ra ED IIIb Nippur TMH 5 53 o. i 7
lugal-ra ugula ED IIIb Nippur TMH 5 60 o. 2
lu:gal-ra ED IIIb Nippur TMH 5 67 r. i 1’
lugal-ra ED IIIb Nippur TMH 5 159 o. i 14’
lugal-ra maškim-bi ED IIIb Nippur TMH 5 159 o. v 6’
lugal-ra ED IIIb Nippur TMH 5 167 o. iii 6
lugal-ra ED IIIb Nippur OSP 1 34 o. i 1’
lugal-ra ED IIIb Nippur OSP 1 39 r. ii’ 5
lugal-ra simug ED IIIb Nippur OSP 1 46 o. i 7
lugal-ra ED IIIb Umma-Zabala ? BIN 8 18 r. 3
lugal-ra ED IIIb-ES Umma-Zabala BIN 8 92 r. 3
lugal-ra ES-MS Nippur OSP 1 23 o. ii 3’’
lugal-ra ES-MS Nippur OSP 1 23 o. v 34
lugal-ra ugula sagi-ne ES-MS Umma Nik 2 49 o. 5
lugal-ra CS Adab CUSAS 13 90 o. 10
lugal-ra CS/Śkś Girsu CT 50 51 r. 1
lugal-ra CS/Śkś Girsu CT 50 51 r. 4
lugal-ra CS Girsu *DPA* 12 (PUL 13) o. 3
lugal-ra CS Girsu *DPA* 14 (PUL 21) r. 10
lugal-ra CS Girsu *DPA* 23 (PUL 41) o. 5
lugal-ra CS Girsu *DPA* 48 (PUL 42) o. 3
lugal-ra CS Girsu *DPA* 49 (PUL 43) o. 3
lugal-ra nu-kiri$_6$? CS Girsu ITT 1 1374 o. ii 6
lu[gal]-r[a] MS-CS Nippur OSP 2 93 r. i 11’
lugal-ra MS-CS Nippur OSP 2 99 o. ii 6
lu[gal]-ra MS-CS Nippur OSP 2 121 o. 5
lugal-ra dumu nu-siki CS Nippur PBS 9 79 o. ii 4’
lugal-ra *Eb-um*, lu$_2$ Lugal-ra MS-CS Umma BIN 8 331 o. 6
lugal-ra MS-CS Umma ? *TCVC* 725 r. i 6’
lugal-ra MS-CS Unknown *DCS* 43 r. 9
lugal-ra *in* Ĝir$_2$-su^{ki} CS Unknown MAD 5 111 o. 2

lugal-ra-diri ? (a1) unkn. mng. 3.1.8, p. 181
lugal-ra-diri ? ED IIIa Šuruppag *WF* 37 o. ii 1’’

lugal-ra-mu-gi$_4$ (a≥2) ‘… answered the lugal’ 3.1.8, p. 177 n. 1051, 181 w. n. 1106
lugal-ra-mu-gi$_4$ ED IIIb/X Y 5 Girsu *DP* suppl. 593 o. v 7
lugal-ra-mu-gi$_4$ ED IIIb/X Y 5 Girsu *DP* suppl. 593 r. i 2
lugal-ra-mu-gi$_4$ ED IIIb Girsu *DP* suppl. 594 r. ii 2
lugal-ra-mu-gi$_4$ aga$_3$-us$_2$ ED IIIb/Lug. 3 Girsu Nik 1 17 o. ii 1
lugal-ra-mu-gi$_4$ ED IIIb Girsu Nik 1 36 o. ii 3
lugal-ra-mu-⸢gi$_4$⸣ ED IIIb Girsu Nik 1 41 r. i 5
lugal-ra-mu-gi$_4$ MS-CS Umma MAD 4 149 (translit. only) o. 6

lu:gal-RA-si ? (a1) unkn. mng. 3.1.8, p. 181
lu:gal-RA-⸢si$^?$⸣ ⸢lu$_2$ Ur$^?$⸣-[x-(x$^?$)] ED IIIb Nippur OSP 1 48 o. ii 5

lugal-ra-tum$_2$ (a1) perhaps ‘(he is) fit for a king!’ 3.1.6.2, p. 143, 161
lugal-ra-tum$_2$ ED IIIb Nippur TMH 5 53 o. ii 6
lugal-ra-[(x)] MS-CS Nippur PBS 9 50 o. 4’

°lugal-RU (°2) unkn. mng. 3.1.8, p. 181
°lugal-⸢RU⸣ ED IIIa Kiš MesCiv 14, pl. 23, 3: H+Y r.(?) i’ 3
°lugal-RU ED IIIa Šuruppag *SF* 29 o. ii 9

lu:gal-sa-par$_2$ $^{(a1)}$ ‘the lugal … the throw net’ 3.1.3.3, p. 113
lu:gal-sa-par$_2$ ED IIIb Nippur OSP 1 121 r. iii 2’

lugal-sa-par$_4$ $^{(a1)}$ ‘the lugal … the throw net’ 3.1.3.3, p. 113f. n. 611
⌜lugal-sa-par$_4$⌝ ED IIIa Kiš *AAICAB* 1/1 (Ashm 1928-431) o. i 2
lugal-sa-par$_4$ ED IIIa Kiš *AAICAB* 1/1 (Ashm 1928-431) r. ii 3

lugal-sa-šuš-gal $^{(a\geq2)}$ ‘the lugal … the throw net’ 3.1.3.3, p. 114, 185
lugal-sa-šuš-gal ED IIIb/Lug. 1 Girsu BIN 8 362 o. ii 1
lugal-sa-šuš-gal (lu$_2$ e$_2$-nam) ED IIIb/Ukg. lugal 5 Girsu *DP* 1/2 136 r. i 3
lugal-sa-šuš-gal lu$_2$ e$_2$-nam ED IIIb/Ukg. lugal 5 Girsu Nik 1 3 o. vi 19
lugal-sa-šuš-gal šeš kuš$_7$ ED IIIb Girsu Nik 1 116 o. i 3
lugal-sa-šuš-gal s. Lugal-uru ED IIIb/(Lug.) 1 Girsu Nik 1 160 o. i 2
lugal-sa-šuš-gal ED IIIb Girsu Nik 1 161 o. i 4
lugal-sa-šuš-gal ED IIIb Girsu Nik 1 161 r. i 5

lugal-sa$_6$ $^{(a\geq8)}$ ‘the lugal is favourable’ 3.1.7.8, p. 170, 188
lugal-sa$_6$ CS Adab CUSAS 13 145 o. 5
lugal-sa$_6$ CS Adab *SIA* 677 r. 3
lugal-sa$_6$ CS Girsu *DPA* 35 (PUL 48) o. 7
lugal-sa$_6$? CS Girsu *RTC* 96 o. i 12
lugal-sa$_6$ maškim MS-CS Nippur OIC 22 1 r. 4
lugal-sa$_6$ ^{ĝiš}dur-ĝar-la$_2$ MS-CS Nippur OSP 2 178 r. 5
lugal-sa$_6$ dub-sar MS-CS Nippur OSP 2 179 o. 4
lugal-sa$_6$ s. Me-^{sa}sag$_7$ MS-CS Nippur TMH 5 52 o. ii 16
lugal-sa$_6$ gal-sukkal, Nippur^{ki}-*u*$_3$ CS/NS. (OB) Nippur C. Wilcke, *ZA* 87 (1997), p. 11–32 (HS 1954+) o. iv 27’
lugal-sa$_6$ maškim CS Umma R. K. Englund, *ASJ* 14 (1992), p. 77–102 6 r. 7
lugal-sa$_6$ MS-CS Unknown MesCiv 4 71 r. 5
lugal-sa$_6$ MS Unknown MAD 4 70 r. 1
lugal-sa$_6$ CS Unknown Mesopotamia 9 4 r. 9

lugal-sa$_6$-ga $^{(a\geq6)}$ ‘the lugal is favourable’ 3.1.7.8, p. 170, 189
lugal-sa$_6$-ga ED IIIa-b Unknown *L’uomo* 3 r. ii 1
lugal-sa$_6$-ga ED IIIb/Eig. ^{ni_3}ensi$_2$ Adab OIP 14 49 o. iv 5
lugal-sa$_6$-ga Ur-^{d}Nin-ĝir$_2$-su ED IIIb Girsu J. Marzahn & H. Neumann, *AoF* 22 (1995), p. 111f. (VAT 6121) o. v 2’
lugal-sa$_6$-ga gudu$_4$ ED IIIb/Enz. ensi$_2$ 2 Girsu BIN 8 347 r. i 8
lugal-sa$_6$-ga Ur-^{d}Nin-ĝir$_2$-su ED IIIb Girsu CT 50 29 o. ii 1
lugal-sa$_6$-ga Ur-^{d}Nin-ĝir$_2$-su ED IIIb Girsu CT 50 30 o. ii’ 9
lugal-sa$_6$-ga sipa ED IIIb/Ukg. lugal 6 Girsu *DP* 1/2 135 r. v 20
lugal-sa$_6$-ga ED IIIb/Ukg. ensi$_2$ 1 Girsu *DP* suppl. 519 o. iii 3
lugal-sa$_6$-ga sipa ED IIIb/Ukg. lugal 4 Girsu *DP* suppl. 590 o. iv 10
lugal-sa$_6$-ga ED IIIb Girsu Nik 1 14 r. iii 1
lugal-sa$_6$-ga sipa ED IIIb/Lug. 3 Girsu Nik 1 195 r. i 3
lugal-sa$_6$-ga Ur-niĝ$_2$ ED IIIb Girsu OIP 14 57 o. ii 4
lugal-sa$_6$-ga ? (sipa$^{?}$) ED IIIb/Lug. 4 Girsu A. Deimel, *OrSP* 20, p. 28 (translit. only) o. ii 3
lugal-sa$_6$-ga (sipa) ED IIIb/Lug. 4 Girsu *RTC* 27 r. i 4
lugal-sa$_6$-ga ED IIIb Nippur OSP 1 26 r. i’ 3
lugal-sa$_6$-ga ED IIIb Nippur TMH 5 203 o. 4
lugal-sa$_6$-ga ED IIIb Nippur TMH 5 203 r. 2
lugal-sa$_6$-ga ED IIIb Umma-Zabala CUSAS 14 4 r. v 2

lugal-sa$_x$(ŠU$_2$.SA)-par$_4$ $^{(a1)}$ ‘the lugal … the throw net’ 3.1.3.3, p. 113f. n. 611

lugal-sa$_x$(ŠU$_2$.SA)-par$_4$ lu$_2$ Unug^{ki}, e-ra ED IIIb Umma-Zabala ? *L'uomo* 6 o. i 4

lugal-^{sa_2}sag$_7$ $^{(a1)}$ 'the lugal is one who vanquishes (evil portents?)' 3.1.8, p. 181
lugal-^{sa_2}sag$_7$ MS Adab *TCABI* 95 o. 5
lugal-^{sa_2}sag$_7$ CS Adab CUSAS 13 47 r. 3'
lugal-^{sa_2}sag$_7$ CS Adab CUSAS 13 48 o. 4

lugal-saĝ $^{(a\geq8)}$ 'the lugal is exalted' 3.1.7.7, p. 168
lugal-saĝ ED IIIb-ES Adab CUSAS 11 98 o. ii 6
lugal-saĝ ED IIIb-ES Adab CUSAS 11 100 o. i 5
lugal-saĝ sipa udu s[iki]-ka ED IIIb/Lug. 1 Girsu BIN 8 372 o. iii 9
lugal-saĝ ED IIIb/X Y 3 Girsu CT 50 43 o. iv 1
lugal-saĝ ED IIIb Girsu Nik 1 41 r. ii 9
lugal-saĝ i$_3$-du$_8$ ED IIIb/X Y 3 Girsu VS 25 56 o. i 6
lugal-saĝ ED IIIb-ES Nippur BIN 8 169 o. 4
lugal-saĝ ED IIIb Nippur OSP 1 24 o. ii 10
lugal-saĝ$^?$ ED IIIb/Luzag. ensi$_2$ [x] Umma-Zabala J. A. Brinkman, *Fs Kramer*, pl. III*-V* (W 2/7) o. v 6'
lugal-saĝ Lugal-saĝ ⸢lu$_2$⸣ ^{ĝiš}gi Lugal-⸢KA⸣-ke$_4$ ES-MS Umma *USP* 7 r. 5
lugal-saĝ MS Adab *TCABI* 148 o. 2
lugal-saĝ CS Adab CUSAS 13 21 o. 4'
lugal-saĝ f. Ur-NIĜ$_2$ CS Girsu MVN 3 113 o. ii 2
lugal-saĝ MS-CS Umma MAD 4 49 (translit. only) o. 4
lugal-saĝ MS-CS Umma MAD 4 72 (translit. only) o. 9
lugal-saĝ CS/NS. Unknown *RIAA* 79 o. 3

lugal-saĝ-bi-še$_{3\text{-}90°}$ $^{(a1)}$ 'the lugal takes precedence' 3.1.7.7, p. 169, 182 n. 1116
lugal-saĝ-bi-še$_{3\text{-}90°}$ ED IIIb Umma-Zabala MVN 3 3 o. viii 7

lugal-saĝ-du$_{10}$ $^{(a1)}$ unkn. mng. 3.1.8, p. 58 n. 280, 181 w. n. 1107
lugal-saĝ-du$_{10}$ ED IIIa Šuruppag L. Legrain, *RA* 32 (1935), p. 126 1 o. iii 2–3

°lugal-saĝ-kalam(LAK729) $^{(°1)}$ 'the lugal is exalted in the land' 3.1.1.6, p. 100, 248 n. 1468
°lugal-saĝ-kalam(LAK729) ED IIIa Šuruppag *SF* 63 r. iv 13

lugal-saĝ-rib $^{(a\geq1)}$ 'the lugal is preeminent' 3.1.7.7, p. 168
lugal-saĝ-rib aga$_3$-us$_2$ saĝa ED IIIb/Enz. 17 Girsu BIN 8 352 r. i 5
lugal-saĝ-rib s. Amar-šuba$_3$, dub-sar ED IIIb/Enz. or En. II Girsu ? *DP* 1/1 31 iv 13

lugal-si $^{(a1)}$ unkn. mng. 3.1.8, p. 181 w. n. 1108
lugal-si OAkk Unknown MAD 4 25 (translit. only) o. 7

lugal-SI.A $^{(a\geq1)}$ unkn. mng. 3.1.8, p. 175 n. 1027, 181
lugal-SI.A ED I-II Ur UET 2 224 o. ii 1
lugal-SI.A ED I-II Ur UET 2 224 r. i 3

lugal-si-DU$_6$-e $^{(a1)}$ unkn. mng. 3.1.8, p. 181
lugal-si-DU$_6$-e CS Girsu *STTI* 83 r. i 5'

lugal-si-ĝar $^{(a\geq3)}$ 'the lugal (is?) a door bolt' 3.1.3.3, p. 91 n. 466, 116, 251 n. 1477
lugal-si-ĝar ED IIIb/Ukg. lugal 6 Girsu *DP* 1/2 135 r. iii 10
lugal-si$^!$(MIN)-ĝar šu-ku$_6$ ab-ba ED IIIb/Ukg. lugal 4 Girsu *TSA* 47 o. i 4
lugal-si-ĝar f. E$_2$-zi MS-CS Adab *SIA* 705 r. i 7
lugal-si-ĝar sipa MS Adab *TCABI* 117 o. 4
lu‹g›al-si-ĝar b. Ga[la] CS Umma *AAS* 1 o. i 7
lugal-si-ĝar CS Umma *AAS* 1 o. ii 13
lugal-⸢si⸣-[ĝar] nu-banda$_3$-ni MS-CS Umma ? *TCVC* 725 r. i 5'

lugal-si-NE-e $^{(a\geq1)}$ unkn. mng. 3.1.8, p. 181
lugal-si-NE-[e] s. G[IR$_3$$^?$-x-x] MS-CS Umma *TCVC* 731 o. ii 19'

lugal-si-NE-e CS Umma W. Sommerfeld, K. Markina & N. Roudik, *Gs Diakonoff*, 225–231 4 o. 14

lugal-si-sa$_2$ (a≥10) 'the lugal is just' 3.1.3.3, p. 118, 241
lugal-si-sa$_2$ ED IIIa Šuruppag *TSŠ* 568 o. ii 2
lugal-si-sa$_2$ ED IIIa-b Unknown *L'uomo* 3 o. ii 5
lugal-si:sa$_2$ umbisaĝ ED IIIb Ebla ARET 5 21 r. vi 1''
lugal-si-sa$_2$ lu$_2$ ama sur$_x$ ED IIIb/Ukg. lugal 6 Girsu *DP* 1/2 135 r. v 6
lugal-si-sa$_2$ lu$_2$ dub-šen urudu ED IIIb/Lug. 2 Girsu VS 14 180 o. iii 5
lugal-si-sa$_2$ šu-i ED IIIb Nippur TMH 5 136 o. i 2
lugal-si-sa$_2$ sagi-maḫ ES-MS Umma Nik 2 14 o. iii 12
lugal-si-sa$_2$ nu-banda$_3$-bi ES-MS Umma Nik 2 19 r. i 11
lugal-si-sa$_2$ lu$_2$ uz-ga MS Adab *TCABI* 184 o. 5
lugal-⸢si⸣-sa$_2$ [x]-⸢x⸣ geme$_2$ Lugal-si-sa$_2$ CS Girsu ITT 5 6867 r. 4 (?)
lugal-si-sa$_2$ MS-CS Umma ? *TCVC* 727 o. i 10
lugal-si-sa$_2$ MS Unknown *L'uomo* 14 o. i 4

lugal-si-u$_4$-a (a1) 'the lugal in the high heavens (?)' 3.1.7.10, p. 172
lugal-si-u$_4$-a MS-CS Adab OIP 14 115 o. 5

lugal-sila(TAR)-si (a1) 'the lugal is just right for the road' 3.1.5.2, p. 130, 182 n. 1121
lugal-sila-si lugal Kiš ED IIIb Uruk CT 3, pl. 1 (BM 12155) 4

lugal-sipa (a≥8) 'the lugal is a shepherd' 3.1.3.3, p. 102 n. 540, 111, 151 n. 867, 253
lugal-sipa nitaḫ ED IIIb/Ukg. ensi$_2$ 1 Girsu *AWAS* 119 o. v 3
lugal-sipa nitaḫ ED IIIb/Ukg. lugal 4 Girsu *AWAS* 120 o. vi 3
lugal-sipa nitaḫ ED IIIb/[Ukg. lugal 3] Girsu *AWAS* 121 o. vi 3'
lugal-sipa nitaḫ ED IIIb/Ukg. lugal 6 Girsu *AWAS* 122 o. vi 14
lugal-sipa ⸢lu$_2$?⸣ u$_2$-bil$_2$ ED IIIb/Ukg. lugal 1? Girsu *AWAS* 123 o. iv 10
lugal-sipa [sagi] ED IIIb/Lug. ensi$_2$ [5] Girsu BIN 8 23 o. i' 2'
lugal-sipa ED IIIb Girsu *DCS* 4 o. v 5
lugal-sipa il$_2$ ED IIIb/Ukg. lugal 2 Girsu *DP* 1/2 113 o. vi 5
lugal-sipa (ugula) il$_2$ ED IIIb/Ukg. lugal 5 Girsu *DP* 1/2 114 o. vi 9
lugal-sipa sagi ED IIIb/Lug. 6 Girsu *DP* 2/1 157 o. i 4
lugal-sipa nitaḫ ED IIIb/Ukg. ensi$_2$ 1 Girsu MVN 3 2 o. v 13
lugal-sipa nitaḫ ED IIIb/Lug. 6 Girsu D. Charpin, *RA* 71 (1977), p. 97–105 o. v 3
lugal-sipa s. Lugal-la$_2$ ED IIIb Isin BIN 8 34 o. i 6
lu:gal-sipa ED IIIb Nippur TMH 5 11 o. iii 2
lugal-sipa Lu$_2$-inim-ku$_3$-ga-ni, lu$_2$ Lugal-sipa ED IIIb Nippur TMH 5 23 o. ii 3
lugal-sipa CS Girsu CT 50 169 o. i 15
lugal-sipa CS Girsu *STTI* 57 o. 2
lugal-sipa CS Girsu *STTI* 151 o. iii' 11'
lugal-sipa f. Uĝ$_3$!(LAK729)-IL$_2$, ⸢nagar⸣ CS/NS. Nippur TMH 5 7+184+201a r. ii 12'
lugal-sipa s. [x-x] MS-CS Umma ? *TCVC* 737 o. (?) 8'
lugal-sipa f. Ur-^{d}Šara$_2$ CS Umma *USP* 47 r. ii 1

lugal-su$_3$-aĝa$_2$ (a1) 'the lugal is brilliant' 3.1.7.10, p. 174
lugal-su$_3$-aĝa$_2$ dub-sar ES-MS Unknown *EGA* 406 (pl. 9 fig. 90)

lugal-su$_3$-še$_3$ (a1) probable defective writing of lugal-u$_4$-su$_3$-še$_3$ 3.1.7.7, p. 168 n. 976
lugal-su$_3$-še$_3$ ED IIIa Adab CUSAS 11 3 r. i 3

lugal-su$_{11}$-lum-ma-gub (a1) 'the lugal stands in the Date(-field)' 3.1.5.3, p. 133
lugal-su$_{11}$-lum-ma-gub šu-ku$_6$ a du$_{10}$-ga ED IIIb/Ukg. lugal 2 Girsu VS 27 13 r. ii 6

lugal-$^{su_{13}}$PA.SIKIL-nam-tar (a≥1) uncertain mng. 3.1.1.7, p. 103, 229, 246 n. 1450
lugal-$^{su_{13}}$PA.SIKIL-nam-tar ED I-II Ur UET 2 93 o. i 10

lugal-$^{su_{13}}$PA.SIKIL-nam-tar   ED I-II   Ur   UET 2   101   o. 2
lugal-$^{su_{13}}$PA.SIKIL-nam-tar   ED I-II   Ur   UET 2   101   o. 6
lugal-$^{su_{13}}$PA.SIKIL-nam-tar   ED I-II   Ur   UET 2   170   o. iii 1
lugal-$^{su_{13}}$PA.SIKIL-nam-tar   ED I-II   Ur   UET 2   224   o. i 4
lugal-⸢$^{su_{13}}$PA.SIKIL⸣-nam-tar   ED I-II   Ur   UET 2   224   r. i 5

°lugal-$^{su_{13}}$PA$^{!}$(MAŠ).SIKIL-nam-tar (°1)   uncertain mng.   3.1.1.7, p. 103
°lugal-$^{su_{13}}$PA$^{!}$(MAŠ).SIKIL-nam-tar   ED IIIa   Šuruppag ?   *SF*   53   o. ii 2

lugal-^{d}Sud$_{3}$-de$_{3}$ (a1)   'Sud … the lugal '   3.1.6.2, p. 144, 248 n. 1463
lugal-^{d}Sud$_{3}$-de$_{3}$ CS   Adab   *SIA*   1209   o. ii 9

lugal-^{d}Sud$_{3}$-ki-aĝ$_{2}$ (a1)   'Sud loves the lugal '   3.1.6.2, p. 144, 248 n. 1463
lugal-^{d}Sud$_{3}$-ki-aĝ$_{2}$ ED IIIa   Šuruppag   *RTC*   15   r. ii 4

lugal-⸢sukud$^{?}$⸣-[ra$_{2}^{?}$] (a1)   'the lugal is lofty'   3.1.7.7, p. 169 w. n. 984
lugal-⸢sukud$^{?}$⸣-[ra$_{2}^{?}$]   MS-CS   Unknown   MesCiv 4   53   o. 4

lugal-suluḫu$_{2}$(SIG$_{2}$.BU) (a1)   'the lugal wears a suluḫu-robe (?)'   3.1.1.3, p. 91, 230
lugal-suluḫu$_{2}$ CS   Girsu   ITT 1   1449   r. 11

lugal-sur$_{x}$(ERIM) (identical with lugal-sur$_{x}$(-re$_{2}$)-ki-aĝ$_{2}$, sukkal), p. 181
lugal-sur$_{x}$ sukkal   ED IIIb/Ukg. lugal 1?   Girsu   *AWAS*   123   o. v 18
lugal-sur$_{x}$ sukkal   ED IIIb/Ukg. lugal 2   Girsu   *DP* 1/2   113   o. viii 3

lugal-sur$_{x}$(ERIM) (a1)   unkn. mng.   3.1.8, p. 181
lugal-sur$_{x}$ ES-MS   Nippur   OSP 1   23   o. iv 17
lugal-sur$_{x}$ MS-CS   Adab   CUSAS 13   9   o. 5

lugal-sur$_{x}$(ERIM)-ki-aĝ$_{2}$ (identical with lugal-sur$_{x}$(-re$_{2}$-ki-aĝ$_{2}$), sukkal) , p. 181 n. 1111
lugal-sur$_{x}$-ki-aĝ$_{2}$ [sukkal]   ED IIIb/[Ukg. lugal 3]   Girsu   *AWAS*   121   o. vii 14'

lugal-sur$_{x}$(ERIM)-ra-sa$_{6}$ (a1)   unkn. mng.   3.1.8, p. 181
lugal-sur$_{x}$-ra-sa$_{6}$ ED IIIb/X Y 2   Girsu   Nik 1   114   o. ii 2

lugal-sur$_{x}$(ERIM)-re$_{2}$-ki-aĝ$_{2}$ (a1)   'the lugal is one who loves the (work) troops (?)'   3.1.8, p. 181
lugal-sur$_{x}$-re$_{2}$-ki-aĝ$_{2}$ sukkal   ED IIIb/Ukg. lugal 4   Girsu   *AWAS*   120   o. vii 10
lugal-sur$_{x}$-re$_{2}$-ki-aĝ$_{2}$ sukkal   ED IIIb/Ukg. lugal 6   Girsu   *AWAS*   122   o. viii 5
⸢lugal-sur$_{x}$⸣-re$_{2}$-[ki]-⸢aĝ$_{2}$⸣ ⸢sukkal$^{?}$⸣   ED IIIb   Girsu   *DCS*   5   o. vi' 3'
lugal-sur$_{x}$-re$_{2}$-ki-aĝ$_{2}$ sukkal   ED IIIb/Ukg. lugal 5   Girsu   *DP* 1/2   114   o. vii 16
lugal-sur$_{x}$-re$_{2}$-ki-aĝ$_{2}$ ⸢sukkal⸣   ED IIIb/Ukg. ensi$_{2}$ 1   Girsu   *DP* 2/1   227   o. v 6
lugal-sur$_{x}$-re$_{2}$-ki-aĝ$_{2}$ sukkal   ED IIIb/Ukg. ensi$_{2}$ 1   Girsu   HSS 3   15   o. vi 5
lugal-sur$_{x}$-re$_{2}$-ki-aĝ$_{2}$ sukkal   ED IIIb/Ukg. lugal 6   Girsu   HSS 3   18   o. vi 2
lugal-sur$_{x}$-re$_{2}$-ki-aĝ$_{2}$ sukkal   ED IIIb/Ukg. ensi$_{2}$ 1   Girsu   HSS 3   16   o. vi 8
lugal-sur$_{x}$-re$_{2}$-ki-aĝ$_{2}$ sukkal   ED IIIb/Ukg. ensi$_{2}$ 1   Girsu   MVN 3   2   o. vii 13
lugal-sur$_{x}$-re$_{2}$-ki-aĝ$_{2}$ sukkal   ED IIIb   Girsu   MVN 3   26   o. iii' 2'
lugal-sur$_{x}$-re$_{2}$-ki-aĝ$_{2}$ sukkal   ED IIIb/Ukg. lugal 4   Girsu   Nik 1   2   o. vii 9
lugal-sur$_{x}$-re$_{2}$-ki-aĝ$_{2}$ sukkal   ED IIIb/Ukg. ensi$_{2}$ 1(+X?)   Girsu   Nik 1   9   o. vi 10
lugal-sur$_{x}$-re$_{2}$-ki-aĝ$_{2}$ sukkal   ED IIIb/Ukg. lugal 4   Girsu   *TSA*   14   o. vii 10
lugal-sur$_{x}$-re$_{2}$-ki-aĝ$_{2}$ sukkal   ED IIIb/Ukg. lugal 4   Girsu   *TSA*   15   o. viii 7
[lugal-sur$_{x}$-re$_{2}$-ki-a]ĝ$_{2}$ sukkal   ED IIIb/Ukg. lugal 6   Girsu   *TSA*   16   o. vii 2
lugal-sur$_{x}$-re$_{2}$-ki-aĝ$_{2}$ sukkal   ED IIIb/[Ukg. lugal 6]   Girsu   *TSA*   17   o. vii 7'
lugal-sur$_{x}$-re$_{2}$-ki-aĝ$_{2}$ sukkal   ED IIIb/Lug. 6   Girsu   VS 25   11   o. vii 8
⸢lugal⸣-sur$_{x}$-re$_{2}$-⸢ki-aĝ$_{2}$⸣ sukkal   ED IIIb/Lug. 6   Girsu   VS 25   71   o. vii 10

lugal-ša$_{3}$ (a>27)   abbreviation   3.1.8, p. 122 n. 656, 181 w. n. 1112, 236
lugal-ša$_{3}$ ED IIIb   Adab   CUSAS 11   40   o. i' 1
lugal-ša$_{3}$ nu-banda$_{3}$ ED IIIb   Adab   CUSAS 11   42   o. i 4
lugal-ša$_{3}$ nu-banda$_{3}$ ED IIIb   Adab   CUSAS 11   57   o. i 1

lugal-ša$_3$ ED IIIb-ES Adab CUSAS 11 75 o. i 4

lugal-ša$_3$ ugula ED IIIb-ES Adab CUSAS 11 103 r. i 5

⸢lugal⸣-ša$_3$ ED IIIb-ES Adab CUSAS 11 221 r. i 3

lugal-ša$_3$ ED IIIb Adab *TCABI* 5 o. 4

lugal-ša$_3$ dub-sar ED IIIb/[Ukg. lugal 3] Girsu *AWAS* 121 r. i 5

lugal-ša$_3$ muḫaldim ED IIIb/Enz. ensi$_2$ 2 Girsu BIN 8 347 r. iii 2

lugal-ša$_3$ šu-ku$_6$ ab-ba ED IIIb/X Y 3 Girsu BIN 8 357 o. ii 1

lugal-ša$_3$ ugula-bi, šu-ku$_6$ ab-ba ED IIIb/X Y 5 Girsu *CTNMC* 2 r. ii 4

lugal-ša$_3$ nar-gal ED IIIb/Lug. ensi$_2$ Girsu *DP* 1/2 127 o. iii 8

lugal-«x»-ša$_3$ lu$_2$ dun-a ED IIIb/Ukg. lugal 4 Girsu *DP* 1/2 138 r. ii 10

lugal-ša$_3$ ED IIIb/Lug. 1 Girsu *DP* 2/1 191 o. iv 4

lugal-ša$_3$ ugula ED IIIb/Lug. 1 Girsu *DP* 2/1 191 o. iv 7

lugal-ša$_3$ muḫaldim ED IIIb Girsu *DP* suppl. 617 o. iii 1

lugal-ša$_3$ muḫaldim ED IIIb/X Y 3 Girsu *DP* suppl. 615 o. ii 1

lugal-ša$_3$ šu-ku$_6$ ab-ba ED IIIb Girsu *DP* 2/2 360 o. i 4

lugal-ša$_3$ dub-sar ED IIIb/Ukg. lugal 1 Girsu HSS 3 17 o. viii 14

lugal-ša$_3$ muḫaldim ED IIIb/Ukg. lugal 1 Girsu HSS 3 40 o. vi 13

lugal-ša$_3$ nar-gal ED IIIb/Enz. ensi$_2$ 2 Girsu ITT 5 9244 o. ii 1

lugal-ša$_3$ nar-gal ED IIIb/Enz. ensi$_2$ 1 Girsu ITT 5 9247 o. i 2

lugal-ša$_3$ lu$_2$ e$_2$-nam ED IIIb/Ukg. lugal 5 Girsu Nik 1 3 o. vi 13

lugal-ša$_3$ ED IIIb Girsu Nik 1 4 o. i 3

lugal-ša$_3$ lu$_2$-eš$_2$-gi[d$_2$] ED IIIb/Lug. 2 Girsu Nik 1 125 o. ii 11

lugal-ša$_3$ ED IIIb Girsu OIP 14 57 r. i 1

lugal-ša$_3$ ad-kup$_4$ ED IIIb/X Y 4 Girsu *TSA* 7 o. v 9

lugal-ša$_3$ dub-sar ED IIIb/Ukg. lugal 4 Girsu *TSA* 15 o. ix 14

lugal-ša$_3$ lu$_2$-eš$_2$-gid$_2$ ED IIIb/Lug. 2 Girsu VS 14 171 o. vi 10

lugal-ša$_3$ (šu-ku$_6$) ED IIIb Girsu VS 25 16 o. iii 5

lugal-ša$_3$ šu-ku$_6$ ab-ba ED IIIb/X Y 4 Girsu VS 25 52 o. ii 2

lugal-ša$_3$ šu-ku$_6$ ab-ba ED IIIb/Ukg. lugal 1 Girsu VS 25 70 o. iii 7

lugal-ša$_3$ h. Nin-PA-da ED IIIb Isin BIN 8 38 o. 5

lugal-[ša$_3$] f. KUM-⸢tuš⸣-[še$_3$] ED IIIb Isin BIN 8 38 r. 2

lugal-ša$_3$ ED IIIb Isin BIN 8 80 r. i 11

lugal-ša$_3$ s. AN.TUR, b. Ur-šul ED IIIb/Urz. lugal Isin M. Lambert, *RA* 73 (1979), p. 5–6 o. v 9

lugal-ša$_3$ s. Uzug$_x$(AN.⸢ZAG⸣)-še$_3$ ED IIIb/Urz. lugal Isin M. Lambert, *RA* 73 (1979), p. 5–6 o. v 21

lugal-ša$_3$ f. ⸢Ki⸣-ku$_3$ (⸢Dug$^?$⸣-ru^{ki}-ka) ED IIIb-ES Nippur ? BIN 8 166 r. 9

lugal-ša$_3$ ED IIIb Nippur OSP 1 25 "ii" 8'

lugal-ša$_3$ ED IIIb Nippur OSP 1 27 o. i' 7'

lugal-ša$_3$ nu-kiri$_6$ ED IIIb Nippur OSP 1 113 o. i 4'

lugal-⸢ša$_3$⸣ f. [Ur]-ur ED IIIb Nippur TMH 5 3 o. ii 1

lugal-ša$_3$ ED IIIb Nippur TMH 5 4 o. ii 1

lugal-ša$_3$ Ur-KID$_2$-ma, Lugal-ša$_3$, saĝ ⸢sa$_{10}$⸣-a ED IIIb Nippur TMH 5 11 r. ii 11

lugal-ša$_3$? s. Lugal-ra, nu-kiri$_6$ ED IIIb Nippur TMH 5 6 o. ii 2

lugal-ša$_3$ ED IIIb Nippur TMH 5 15 o. i 4

lugal-ša$_3$ TAR-ta, lu$_2$ Lugal-ša$_3$, nu-^{ki}kiri$_6$ ED IIIb Nippur TMH 5 17 o. ii 3

lugal-ša$_3$ (nu-^{ki}kiri$_6$) ED IIIb Nippur TMH 5 17 o. ii 8

lu:gal-ša$_3$ sipa anše ED IIIb Nippur TMH 5 67 o. iii 7

lugal-ša$_3$ s. Lugal-lu$_2$ ED IIIb Nippur TMH 5 69 o. ii 3

lugal-ša$_3$ ED IIIb Nippur TMH 5 113 r. 2

lugal-ša$_3$ engar ED IIIb Nippur TMH 5 134 o. ii 2

lugal-ša$_3$ s. Ur-saĝ-Utu, maškim-bi ED IIIb/Enšak. Y X Nippur TMH 5 158 r. 5

lugal-ša$_3$ engar ED IIIb Nippur TMH 5 159 o. ii 4’
lugal-ša$_3$ b. [x]-ra ED IIIb Nippur TMH 5 210 r. 1
lugal-ša$_3$ gudu$_4$-abzu ED IIIb/Luzag. (?) Y 7 Zabala BIN 8 61 o. i 2
lugal-ša$_3$ ED IIIb-ES Umma-Zabala ? BIN 8 88 o. 2
lugal-ša$_3$ ED IIIb-ES Umma-Zabala ? BIN 8 88 o. 4
lugal-ša$_3$ ugula nu-banda$_3$ ED IIIb-ES Umma-Zabala ? BIN 8 108 o. i 5
lugal-ša$_3$ ugula nu-banda$_3$ ED IIIb Umma-Zabala M. Powell, *HUCA* 49 (1978), p. 1–58 19 o. i 5
lugal-ša$_3$ ugula nu-banda$_3$ ED IIIb Umma-Zabala M. Powell, *HUCA* 49 (1978), p. 1–58 22 o. i 6
lugal-ša$_3$ ED IIIb/Luzag. ensi$_2$ 7 Umma-Zabala M. deJ. Ellis, *JCS* 31 (1979), p. 30–55 6 o. i 13
lugal-ša$_3$ ES Adab CUSAS 11 257 o. ii 1
lugal-ša$_3$ ES Adab CUSAS 11 271 o. 1
lugal-ša$_3$ (dam-gar$_3$?) ES Adab *TCABI* 32 r. ii 3
lugal-ša$_3$ ugula ES-MS Adab *TCABI* 64 o. iv 1
lugal-ša$_3$ Ur-DIM saĝ Lugal-ša$_3$ ES-MS Umma Nik 2 16 o. 2
lugal-ša$_3$ b. Ur-kal MS Adab *TCABI* 166 o. 3
lugal-ša$_3$ *šu*-gal$_5$ -la$_2$-*um* CS Adab CUSAS 13 57 r. 2
lugal-ša$_3$ CS Adab CUSAS 13 76 o. 2
lugal-ša$_3$ CS Adab CUSAS 13 79 r. 2
lugal-ša$_3$ CS Adab *TCABI* 239 r. 5
lugal-ša$_3$ f. ^{d}Nanna-⸢MU⸣ CS Girsu ITT 1 1350 o. 2
lugal-ša$_3$ *šu*-gal$_5$ *-la-um* CS Girsu ITT 1 1427 o. 7
lugal-ša$_3$ CS Girsu ITT 1 1441 o. 4’
lugal-ša$_3$ f. U$_2$-da CS Girsu MVN 3 113 o. ii 12
lugal-ša$_3$ MS-CS Isin ? MAD 4 80 r. 6
lugal-ša$_3$ MS-CS Lagaš BiMes 3 24 r. 4
lugal-ša$_3$ šabra MS-CS Mesag BIN 8 131 r. ii 7
lugal-ša$_3$ MS-CS Mesag BIN 8 342 o. 6
⸢lugal⸣-ša$_3$? MS-CS Nippur OSP 2 56 o. ii 3
lugal-ša$_3$ f. Ur$_2$-ni, ku$_3$-dim$_2$ MS-CS Nippur OSP 2 58 o. 6
lugal-ša$_3$ f. Da-da, ku$_3$-dim$_2$ MS-CS Nippur OSP 2 140 o. 7
lugal-ša$_3$ f. D[a$^{?}$-da$^{?}$] MS-CS Nippur OSP 2 168 o. 5’
lugal-⸢ša$_3$$^{?}$⸣ ? CS/NS. Nippur TMH 5 7+184+201a o. iii 8
lugal-ša$_3$ b. ugula E$_2$-sikil, gu$_4$-apin CS/NS. Nippur TMH 5 7+184+201a r. ii 7’
lugal-ša$_3$ MS-CS Nippur TMH 5 29 r. ii 12’
lugal-⸢ša$_3$$^{?}$⸣ [ugula$^{?}$]-b[i$^{?}$] MS-CS Nippur TMH 5 29 r. ii 19’
lugal-ša$_3$ f. Da-da MS-CS Nippur TMH 5 120 r. 1
lugal-ša$_3$ CS ? Susa MDP 14 20 o. 2’
lugal-⸢ša$_3$⸣ MS-CS Umma BIN 8 298 o. 2
lugal-ša$_3$ sipa CS Umma BIN 8 335 r. 1
lugal-ša$_3$ s. KA-ku$_3$ CS Umma *USP* 47 r. i 14
lugal-ša$_3$ b. Lugal-lama$_3$-zi CS Unknown BIN 8 213 o. 5
lugal-ša$_3$ MS-CS Unknown BIN 8 241 o. 5
lugal-ša$_3$ CS Unknown W. Sommerfeld, K. Markina & N. Roudik, *Gs Diakonoff*, 225–231 12 o. 3
lugal-ša$_3$? MS-CS Unknown MVN 3 56 edge i 2

lugal-ša$_3$-an-zu (a1) uncertain mng. 3.1.5.1, p. 128 n. 703, 129
lugal-ša$_3$-an-zu ED IIIa Šuruppag *RTC* 15 r. ii 1
lugal-ša$_3$-AN-[…] lu$_2$ ti[r] ED IIIb Adab *TCABI* 13 o. ii 5

lugal-ša$_3$-ENGUR $^{(a1)}$ unkn. mng. 3.1.8, p. 181

lugal-ša$_3$-ENGUR ensi$_2$ BUR$^?$-ŠIR-[LA^{ki} ?] ED IIIa Girsu Mesilim X L. Heuzey, *RA* 3 (1894), p. 55–58 (AO 2675) 7

lugal-ša$_3$-ga $^{(a1)}$ unkn. mng. 3.1.8, p. 122 n. 659, 181 w. n. 1114

lugal-ša$_3$-ga e$_2$:duru$_5$ Lugal-ša$_3$-ga OAkk Unknown MAD 4 140 (translit. only) o. 5

°lugal-ša$_3$-ge-ib$_2$-tu $^{(°1)}$ 'the lugal was born *in* the heart (of DN?)' 3.1.6.2, p. 144

°lugal-ša$_3$-ge-ib$_2$-tu LS-Ur III Unknown M. E. Cohen, *Fs Hallo*, p. 79–86 (YBC 2124) iii 3

lugal-ša$_3$-gid$_2$ $^{(a\geq8)}$ 'the lugal is considerate' (in non–Nippur cases, perhaps, to be read lugal-ša$_3$-su$_{13}$) 3.1.4.1, p. 118, 121f. w. n. 655

lugal-ša$_3$-gid$_2^!$(MUNU$_4$) ar$_3$-du$_2$ ED IIIa Larsa ? *AAICAB* 1/1 (Ashm 1924-455) o. ii 1
lugal-ša$_3$-gid$_2$ ED IIIa Nippur TMH 5 54 o. iii 2
lugal-ša$_3$-gid$_2$ ED IIIa Nippur TMH 5 54 o. iv 4
lugal-ša$_3$-gid$_2$ nagar ED IIIa Šuruppag ("gekauft") *WF* 33 o. iv 2
lugal-ša$_3$-gid$_2$ ED IIIa-b Isin (?) OIP 104 15 o. iv 6
lugal-ša$_3$-gid$_2$ ED IIIb Marada ? *AAICAB* 1/1 (Ashm 1924-468) r. i 2
lu:gal-ša$_3$-gid$_2$ ED IIIb Nippur OSP 1 38 o. ii 4
lugal-ša$_3$-gid$_2$ ED IIIb Nippur OSP 1 81 o. ii 2
lugal-ša$_3$-gid$_2$ ED IIIb Umma T. Ozaki, *JAC* 23 (2008), p. 55–64 2 o. iii 7
lugal-⸢ša$_3$⸣-gid$_2$ ⸢x⸣-GU ? ED IIIb-ES Umma-Zabala ? BIN 8 103 o. ii 2
lugal-ša$_3$-gid$_2$ MS-CS Nippur TMH 5 29 r. iii 8

°lugal-ša$_3$-⸢ĜA$_2$×X⸣ $^{(°1)}$ unkn. mng. 3.1.8, p. 181

°lugal-ša$_3$-⸢ĜA$_2$×X⸣ ED IIIa Abū Ṣalābīḫ *IAS* 330 o. i 3

lugal-ša$_3$-kuš$_2$ $^{(a1)}$ 'the lugal is sensible' 3.1.2, p. 106

lugal-ša$_3$-kuš$_2$ ED IIIa-b Girsu *RTC* 1 r. iv 2

lugal-ša$_3$-la$_2$-tuku $^{(a\geq13)}$ 'the lugal has compassion' 3.1.4.1, p. 118, 122, 181 n. 1112

lugal-ša$_3$-la$_2$-tuku šu-ku$_6$ ab-ba ED IIIb/X Y 4 Girsu *Amherst* 1 o. iv 5
[lugal]-ša$_3$-la$_2$-tuku dub-sar ED IIIb/Ukg. lugal 4 Girsu *AWAS* 120 o. viii 14
lugal-ša$_3$-la$_2$-tuku dub-sar ED IIIb/Ukg. lugal 6 Girsu *AWAS* 122 o. ix 14
lugal-ša$_3$-la$_2$-tuku ugula, šu-ku$_6$ ab-ba ED IIIb/X Y 5 Girsu *CTNMC* 2 o. ii 3
lugal-ša$_3$-la$_2$-tuku (ugula) šu-ku$_6$ ab-ba ED IIIb/X Y 5 Girsu *CTNMC* 2 r. i 4
lugal-ša$_3$-la$_2$-tuku muḫaldim ED IIIb/Lug. 1 Girsu *DCS* 8 o. iv 7
lugal-ša$_3$-la$_2$-tuku lu$_2$-eš$_3$-gid$_2$ ^{d}Nin-ĝir$_2$-su ED IIIb/Lug. 3 Girsu *DP* 1/1 59 o. ix 13
lugal-ša$_3$-la$_2$-tuku dub-sar ED IIIb/Ukg. lugal 5 Girsu *DP* 1/2 114 o. ix 7
lugal-ša$_3$-la$_2$-tuku b. Ur-pu$_2$-saĝ ED IIIb/Ukg. lugal 2 Girsu *DP* 1/2 120 r. i 3
lugal-ša$_3$-la$_2$-tuku s. En-kisal-si ED IIIb/Ukg. lugal 2 Girsu *DP* 1/2 120 r. iv 13
lugal-ša$_3$-la$_2$-tuku s. Šubur, ad-⸢kup$_4$⸣ ED IIIb/Ukg. lugal 2 Girsu *DP* 1/2 120 r. v 3
lugal-ša$_3$-la$_2$-tuku šu-ku$_6$ ab-ba ED IIIb/Ukg. lugal 3 Girsu *DP* 1/2 130 r. iv 6
lugal-ša$_3$-la$_2$-tuku bir$_3$ suḫ$_5$-ḫa ED IIIb/Ukg. lugal 6 Girsu *DP* 1/2 135 o. iii 16
lugal-ša$_3$-la$_2$-tuku ED IIIb/Ukg. lugal 6 Girsu *DP* 1/2 135 r. iii 6
lugal-ša$_3$-la$_2$-tuku sipa ED IIIb/Ukg. lugal 6 Girsu *DP* 1/2 135 r. vi 3
lugal-ša$_3$-la$_2$-tuku lu$_2$ Inim-ma-ni-zi, lu$_2$ e$_2$-nam ED IIIb/Ukg. lugal 5 Girsu *DP* 1/2 136 o. vii 1
lugal-ša$_3$-la$_2$-tuku ED IIIb/Ukg. lugal 3 Girsu *DP* 2/1 177 o. iv 1
lugal-ša$_3$-la$_2$-tuku ugula, b. Lugal-piriĝ, Saĝ-ḫab$_2$-ba & Aja$_2$-lu$_2$-lil-la ED IIIb/Ukg. lugal 3 Girsu *DP* 2/1 177 r. i 1
lugal-ša$_3$-la$_2$-tuku ugula ED IIIb/Ukg. lugal 3 Girsu *DP* 2/1 177 r. i 5
lugal-ša$_3$-la$_2$-tuku šu-ku$_6$, e$_2$-mi$_2$ ED IIIb/Lug. 2 Girsu *DP* 2/2 278 o. ii 1
lugal-ša$_3$-la$_2$-tuku ED IIIb/Ukg. lugal 4 Girsu *DP* suppl. 590 r. iii 7
lugal-ša$_3$-la$_2$-tuku ED IIIb Girsu ITT 5 9230 o. iii' 1'

lugal-ša$_3$-la$_2$-tuku nar-gal ED IIIb/Enz. ensi$_2$ 3 Girsu ITT 5 9231 r. i 1
lugal-ša$_3$-la$_2$-tuku ED IIIb Girsu MVN 3 26 o. iv' 7'
lugal-ša$_3$-la$_2$-tuku ad-kup$_4$ ED IIIb/Ukg. lugal 5 Girsu Nik 1 3 r. iii 7'
lugal-ša$_3$-la$_2$-tuku ma$_2$-laḫ$_5$ ED IIIb/Ukg. lugal 5 Girsu Nik 1 3 r. iv 11
lugal-ša$_3$-la$_2$-tuku muḫaldim ED IIIb/Lug. 4 Girsu VS 14 72 r. iii 1
lugal-ša$_3$-la$_2$-tuku šu-ku$_6$ ab-ba ED IIIb/X Y 1 Girsu VS 14 20 o. i 4
lugal-ša$_3$-la$_2$-tuku ? muḫaldim ED IIIb/Ukg. lugal 1 Girsu VS 25 70 r. iv 6
lugal-ša$_3$-la$_2$-tuku ED IIIb/Ukg. lugal 2 Girsu VS 27 13 o. vi 1
lugal-ša$_3$-la$_2$-tuku lu$_2$ Dam-diĝir-ĝu$_{10}$, RU-lugal ED IIIb/Ukg. lugal 2 Girsu VS 27 13 o. vii 7
lugal-ša$_3$-la$_2$-tuku gala ED IIIb/Lug. 4 Girsu VS 27 78 o. ii 6

lugal-ša$_3$-pa$_3$ (a2) 'the lugal is one chosen in the heart (of DN)' 3.1.6.2, p. 145, 248 n. 1463
lugal-ša$_3$-pa$_3$ ED IIIa Šuruppag *WF* 35 r. ii 3
⸢lugal-ša$_3$⸣-pa$_3$ s. E$_2$-me-nam-nun-ka ED IIIb Girsu En. I ensi$_2$ OIP 104 22 r. ii 36

lugal-ša$_3$-pa$_3$-da (a2) 'the lugal is one chosen in the heart (of DN)' 3.1.6.2, p. 145, 245, 258
lugal-ša$_3$-pa$_3$-da ED IIIa-b Ur UE 2 pl. 197 no. 63 1
lugal-ša$_3$-pa$_3$-da s. E$_2$-ib$^!$-zi-me, b. Lugal-u$_3$-ma ED IIIb/En. I ensi$_2$ 4 Lagaš BiMes 3 10 o. iii 3'

lugal-ša$_3$-su$_3$ (a3) 'the lugal is full of compassion' 3.1.4.1, p. 121f. n. 655, 122, 181 n. 1114, 253 n. 1490
lugal-ša$_3$-su$_3$ Girsu h. Nin-bur, lu$_2$-eš$_2$-gid$_2$ ED IIIb/X Y 6 *RTC* 44 r. i 6
lugal-ša$_3$-su$_3$ ED IIIb Umma-Zabala MVN 3 3 r. ii 6
lugal-ša$_3$-su$_3$ ES Ur UE 2 pl. 212 no. 311 1

lugal-ša$_3$-uru (a1) 'the lugal in the midst of the city' 3.1.8, p. 181
lugal-ša$_3$-uru nu-banda$_3$, Nippur^{ki}, nu-banda$_3$-*u*$_3$ CS/NS. (OB) Nippur C. Wilcke, *ZA* 87 (1997), p. 11–32 (HS 1954+) o. vi 3'

lugal-ša$_3$(-)za$_3$-[x] (a1) unkn. mng. 3.1.8, p. 181f. w. n. 1115
lugal-ša$_3$(-)za$_3$-[x] CS Adab *SIA* 692 r. 5'

lugal-ša$_3$-zu (a1) 'the lugal is a midwife (?)' 3.1.5.1, p. 128
lugal-⸢ša$_3$⸣-zu CS Nippur PBS 9 36 o. ii' 4'

lu:gal-ša$_3$-[(x)] ED IIIb Nippur TMH 5 41 r. i 3'
lugal-ša$_3$-[(x)] CS Adab *TCABI* 244 o. 4

lugal-šar$_2$-ur$_3$-e (a1) 'the lugal (answered? grasped?) Šarur' 3.1.3.3, p. 112, 258 n. 1522, 259
lugal-šar$_2$-ur$_3$-e nitaḫ, ĝuruš CS Girsu *DPA* 45 (PUL 22) r. 8

lugal-ŠE (a2) 'the lugal … grain (?)' 3.1.5.3, p. 133
lugal-ŠE (ugula) MS-CS Umma MAD 4 66 (translit. only) o. 9
lugal-ŠE ugula MS-CS Umma MAD 4 66 (translit. only) r. 3
lugal-ŠE (ugula) MS-CS Umma MAD 4 167 (translit. only) o. 5
lugal-ŠE MS-CS Umma MesCiv 4 13 o. 11

lugal-ŠE-[(x)] ED IIIb Girsu ITT 5 9201 o. i 5
lugal-ŠE-[(x)] ED IIIb Girsu ITT 5 9208 r. (?) ii 4

lugal-še-gu-na (a≥3) 'the lugal of grain (and) flax' 3.1.5.3, p. 50 n. 232, 133, 254 n. 1491, 259
lugal-še-gu-na ED IIIb Nippur OSP 1 138 o. ii 5
lugal-še-gu-na ES-MS Adab *TCABI* 64 o. v 1
lugal-še-gu-na ugula-bi$_3$ ES-MS Nippur OSP 1 23 o. iii 15'
lugal-še-gu-na CS Adab *SIA* 1209 o. ii 8

lugal-ŠE$_3$-saĝ (a1) unkn. mng. 3.1.8, p. 139, 181–182

lugal-ŠE$_3$-saĝ ED IIIa-b Girsu *RTC* 1 o. iv 3
lugal-ŠE$_3$-saĝ ED IIIa-b Girsu *RTC* 1 r. ii 4’

lugal-šembi$_3$ (a≥2/°2) ‘the lugal is ointment’ 3.1.7.8, p. 170
°lugal-šembi$_3$ aĝri[g] ED IIIa Abū Ṣalābīḫ *IAS* 61 o. vii 6
°⌜lugal⌝-šembi$_3$ lu$_2$ šakir ED IIIa Abū Ṣalābīḫ *IAS* 61 o. viii 17
°lugal-⌜šembi$_3$⌝ ⌜aĝrig⌝ ED IIIa Abū Ṣalābīḫ *IAS* 74 o. vi 2’
°lugal-šembi$_3$ l[u$_2$ ...] ED IIIa Abū Ṣalābīḫ *IAS* 74 o. vii 4’
lugal-šembi$_3$ Lugal-šembi$_3$, Ur-ur, maškim ED IIIa Šuruppag *NTSŠ* 296 o. ii 1
lugal-šembi$_3$ ^{d}Gibil$_6$ ED IIIa Šuruppag *TSŠ* 1 o. ii 2’
lugal-šembi$_3$ ^{d}Gibil$_6$ ED IIIa Šuruppag *TSŠ* 9+127 o. iv 7
lugal-šembi$_3$ ED IIIa Šuruppag *TSŠ* 14 r. v 5’
lugal-šembi$_3$ ED IIIa Šuruppag *TSŠ* 101 r. iii 4
lugal-šembi$_3$ ^{d}Gibil$_6$ ED IIIa Šuruppag *WF* 15 o. v 1
lugal-šembi$_3$ ED IIIa Šuruppag *WF* 57 o. i 2
lugal-šembi$_3$ ED IIIa Šuruppag *WF* 60 o. i 1
°lugal-šembi$_3$ ED IIIb Ebla MEE 3 59 o. ii 1
°lu[gal]-šembi$_3$ [l]u$_2$ usan$_3$ ED IIIb Ebla A. Archi, *RA* 78 (1984), p. 171–174 r. i 5
°lugal-šembi$_3$ aĝrig ED IIIb Ebla A. Archi, *StEb* 4 (1981), p. 177–204 o. viii 8

lugal-šembi$_3^!$(DUG×IGI) (a1) ‘the lugal is ointment’ 3.1.7.8, p. 170 n. 989
lugal-šembi$_3^!$ ^{d}Nin-PA ED IIIa Šuruppag *TSŠ* 794 o. ii 5’

lugal-šer$_2$-zi (a≥1) ‘the lugal is resplendent’ 3.1.7.10, p. 174 n. 1021
lugal-šer$_2$-zi ED IIIa Šuruppag *TSŠ* 536 r. iii 3
lugal-šer$_2$-zi ED IIIa Šuruppag *WF* 65 o. vi 2

lugal-šer$_7$-zi (a2/°1) ‘the lugal is resplendent’ 3.1.7.10, p. 174, 183 n. 1135, 255 n. 1500
°lu[gal]-šer$_7$-zi ED IIIa Abū Ṣalābīḫ *IAS* 330 o. i 2
lugal-⌜šer$_7$⌝-zi ED IIIa-b Girsu *RTC* 1 o. i 4
lugal-šer$_7$-zi ED IIIa-b Marada ? *AAICAB* 1/1 (Ashm 1924-467) o. ii 2

lugal-šeš (a5) ‘the lugal (is) a brother’ 3.1.1.2, p. 87
lugal-šeš ED IIIa-b Unknown *L’uomo* 3 o. iii 6
lugal-šeš E$_2$-šeš, Lugal-šeš ED IIIa-b Unknown *L’uomo* 3 r. i 7
lugal-šeš ED IIIb Adab *TCABI* 13 o. i 6
lugal-šeš ED IIIb Umma-Zabala CUSAS 14 4 o. vi 5
lugal-šeš$^?$ f. Šu-⌜na⌝ CS Girsu *STTI* 164 r. i 2’
lugal-šeš CS Unknown (Girsu$^?$) MVN 2 298 o. i 13

lugal-šilig (a1) ‘the lugal … the šilig-axe’ 3.1.3.3, p. 113 n. 606
lugal-šilig ES Adab CUSAS 11 330 o. 3

lugal-šilig-e (a1) ‘the lugal … the zilig-axe’ 3.1.3.3, p. 113 w. n. 606
lu‹g›al-šilig-e ugula MS-CS Umma MesCiv 4 30 o. ii 3

lugal-šita (a2) ‘the lugal … prayer’ 3.1.6.1, p. 140
lugal-šita ED IIIb-ES Adab CUSAS 11 118 o. i 4
lugal-šita f. KUM-tuš-še$_3$ MS-CS Unknown MVN 3 103 o. 3

lugal-šita-ĝu$_{10}$ (a1) ‘the lugal … my prayer’ 3.1.6.1, p. 140
lugal-[ši]ta-ĝu$_{10}$ ED IIIb-ES Adab CUSAS 11 120 o. iii 3’

lugal-šita-uru (a1) ‘the lugal … the prayer of the city’ 3.1.6.1, p. 140
lugal-šita-uru ES Adab CUSAS 11 288 o. 5
lugal-šita-uru ES Adab CUSAS 11 290 o. 4

lugal-šu (identical with lugal-šu-luḫ-ku$_3$-An-na, dub-sar), p. 150 n. 851
lugal-šu ED IIIb Ur UET 2 suppl. 47 o. i 3

lugal-šu (a≥6) abbreviation of a number of possible names 3.1.8, p. 182
lugal-šu ED IIIb/Ukg. lugal Girsu ? *DP* 1/1 32 iii 15
lugal-šu f. Ur-en-ĝe$_6$-dam & Lugal-u$_3$-ma ED IIIb/Ukg. lugal Girsu ? *DP* 1/1 32 v 1
lugal-šu f. Ur-šu-ga-lam-ma ED IIIb/Enz. ensi$_2$ 5 Girsu *DP* 2/2 274 o. ii 6
lugal-šu h. Nin-tur, [unu$_3$] ED IIIb/Lug. 1 Girsu Nik 1 53 r. i 7
lugal-šu unu$_3$ ED IIIb/Dudu saĝa Girsu W. W. Hallo, *OrNS* 42 (1973), p. 228–238 o. ii 10
lugal-šu f. Ur-šu-ga-lam-ma ED IIIb/Dudu saĝa Girsu W. W. Hallo, *OrNS* 42 (1973), p. 228–238 o. iv 2(!)
lugal-šu h. Nin-tur, unu$_3$ ED IIIb/Lug. 1 Girsu *RTC* 61 r. i 8
lugal-šu$^?$ s. E$_2$-gu$_3$-nun ED IIIb/Urz. lugal Isin M. Lambert, *RA* 73 (1979), p. 5–6 r. iv 22
lugal-šu zadim ugula, lu$_2$ Inim-^{d}Šara$_2$-zi ED IIIb Umma-Zabala M. Powell, *HUCA* 49 (1978), p. 1–58 18 r. ii 4
lugal-šu lu$_2$ Unug^{ki} e-ra ED IIIb Umma-Zabala ? *L'uomo* 6 o. ii 2
lugal-šu ED IIIb-ES Ur UET 2 suppl. 7 o. i 2
lugal-šu s. Ma-ma CS Isin *TCVBI* 1-57 o. 3*
lugal-šu ugula E$_2$-šu$_2$ E$_2$-⸢nar$^?$⸣-ka MS-CS Unknown BIN 8 181 r. 1

lugal-šu-du$_7$ (a1/°1) 'the lugal is perfect' 3.1.7.7, p. 169
°lugal-šu-du$_7$ šitim ED IIIa Abū Ṣalābīḫ *IAS* 62 o. ii 8
°lugal-[šu-du$_7$] [šitim] ED IIIa Abū Ṣalābīḫ *IAS* 64 o. ii' 7'
°⸢lugal⸣-šu-du$_7$ šitim ED IIIa Abū Ṣalābīḫ *IAS* 73 (o.) ii 1'
°lugal-šu-du$_7$ ⸢šitim⸣ ED IIIa Abū Ṣalābīḫ *IAS* 74 o. ii 4
lugal-šu-du$_7$ ED IIIa Šuruppag *TSŠ* 209 r. ii 2
lugal-šu-du$_7$ ED IIIa Šuruppag *WF* 16 r. i 2
°[lu]gal-š[u-du$_7$] [ši]tim ED IIIb Ebla A. Archi, *StEb* 4 (1981), p. 177–204 (translit. only) o. iii 7

lugal-šu-du$_7$-a (a1) 'the lugal is perfect' 3.1.7.7, p. 169
lugal-šu-du$_7$-a s. Diĝir-aja$_2$-ĝu$_{10}$, engar ED IIIb Girsu ? BIN 8 13 r. ii 3

lugal-šu-du$_{11}$ (a1) unkn. mng. 3.1.8, p. 163 n. 942, 182
lugal-šu-du$_{11}$ kurušda ? ED IIIb Umma-Zabala ? BIN 8 62 o. i 7
lugal-šu-du$_{11}$ kurušda ? ED IIIb/Luzag. Y 7 Umma-Zabala M. Powell, *HUCA* 49 (1978), p. 1–58 1 o. iv 6

lugal-šu-gi$_4$-gi$_4$ (a1) unkn. mng. 3.1.8, p. 182
lugal-šu-gi$_4$-gi$_4$ ED IIIb Umma-Zabala CUSAS 14 148 o. i 5

lugal-šu-ĝal$_2$ (PN ?) (a1) unkn. mng. 3.1.8, p. 182, 237
lugal-šu-ĝal$_2$ ED IIIa Abū Ṣalābīḫ *IAS* 494 o. iii 2

lugal-šu-luḫ-ku$_3$-An-na (a1) 'the lugal (is one befitting for) the holy handwashing rites of An' 3.1.6.3, p. 150, 233
lugal-šu-luḫ-ku$_3$-An-na dub-⸢sar⸣, ⸢maškim-bi⸣ ED IIIb Ur G. Visicato & A. Westenholz, *Kaskal* 2 (2005), 55–78 2 o. 3
lugal-šu-luḫ-ku$_3$-An-na dub-sar, maškim-bi ED IIIb Ur UET 2 suppl. 44 r. ii 4

lugal-šu-maḫ (a≥8) 'the lugal (is) forceful' 3.1.7.3, p. 163
lugal-šu-maḫ nagar ED IIIb/Ukg. lugal 6 Girsu *AWAS* 122 r. ii 14
lugal-šu-maḫ muḫaldim ED IIIb/Ukg. [lugal] 6 Girsu BIN 8 354 r. ii 7'
lugal-šu-maḫ nu-banda$_3$ ED IIIb/Ukg. lugal X Girsu *CTNMC* 1 o. iii 1
lugal-šu-maḫ nag[ar] ED IIIb Girsu *DCS* 5 r. i 4'
lugal-šu-maḫ nagar ED IIIb/Ukg. lugal 6 Girsu *DP* 1/2 115 r. ii 11
lugal-šu-maḫ f. Šubur ED IIIb Girsu *DP* suppl. 554 o. ii 2
lugal-šu-maḫ f. Šubur ED IIIb/X Y 5 Girsu *DP* suppl. 593 o. iii 10
lugal-šu-maḫ muḫaldim ED IIIb/Ukg. lugal 3(+X?) Girsu HSS 3 12 r. ii 12

lugal-šu-maḫ muḫaldim ED IIIb Girsu HSS 3 13 r. ii 11
lugal-šu-maḫ nagar ED IIIb/Ukg. lugal 6 Girsu HSS 3 18 o. ix 13'
lugal-šu-maḫ f. Šubur ED IIIb Girsu Nik 1 41 o. i 8
lugal-šu-maḫ simug ED IIIb/Ukg. lugal 5 Girsu Nik 1 3 r. ii 2'
lugal-šu-maḫ simug ED IIIb/Ukg. lugal 5 Girsu Nik 1 3 r. ii 3'
lugal-šu-maḫ simug ED IIIb/Ukg. lugal 3 Girsu Nik 1 32 r. i 9
lu[gal]-šu-maḫ nagar ED IIIb/Ukg. lugal 6 Girsu *TSA* 16 r. i 4'
lugal-šu-maḫ ⌜nagar⌝ ED IIIb/[Ukg. lugal 6] Girsu *TSA* 17 r. ii 10'
lugal-šu-maḫ simug ED IIIb/Ukg. lugal 2 Girsu VS 27 13 r. iii 7
lugal-šu-maḫ CS Girsu ITT 1 1460 o. 2
lugal-šu-maḫ muḫaldim CS Girsu ITT 5 6867 o. 9
lugal-⌜šu-maḫ⌝ f. Bar-ra-an, dub-sar CS Girsu *RTC* 81 r. 4
lugal-šu-maḫ f. Sa_2-d[u_{11}], lu_2 NINA^{ki} CS Girsu *RTC* 120 o. 2
lugal-šu-maḫ CS Girsu *STTI* 26 o. i 16'
lugal-šu-maḫ sipa MS-CS Umma MAD 4 60 (translit. only) o. 3
lugal-šu-maḫ MS-CS Unknown CT 50 77 o. 4
⌜lu⌝[gal]-šu-maḫ ? MS-CS Unknown L. J. Delaporte, *ZA* 18 (1904), p. 245–256 5 o. 6

lugal-šu-mu-gi$_4$ $^{(a1)}$ 'the lugal restored … (to someone)' 3.1.8, p. 163 n. 942, 182
lugal-šu-mu-gi$_4$ lu_2 u_5, Unug^{ki} ED IIIb/Urz. lugal Isin M. Lambert, *RA* 73 (1979), p. 5–6 o. i 19

lugal-šu-sikil $^{(a\geq1)}$ 'the lugal is the pure hand (of DN)' 3.1.6.3, p. 150
lugal-šu-sikil sagi CS Isin CUSAS 13 163 r. i 8
lugal-šu-sikil MS-CS Nippur OIP 97 7 o. 2

lugal-šu-[(x)] ED IIIb/Luzag. ensi$_2$ [x] Umma-Zabala J. A. Brinkman, *Fs Kramer*, pl. III*-V* (W 2/7) o. v 2'
lugal$^!$(MAŠ.LU$_2$)-ŠU$^?$-[(x)] ED IIIb Nippur PBS 15 9 1

lugal-ŠU$_2$ $^{(a1)}$ unkn. mng. 3.1.8, p. 182
lugal-ŠU$_2$ MS-CS Adab CUSAS 13 42 o. 3

lugal-šuba$_3$ $^{(a1)}$ unkn. mng. 3.1.8, p. 188
lugal-šuba$_3$ OAkk Ur M. Civil, *AulaOr* 6 (1988), 105 (U 4395, translit. only) o. 1

lugal-šuba$_3$-zi $^{(a1)}$ unkn. mng. 3.1.8, p. 182, 188
lugal-šuba$_3$-zi saĝa E$_2$-kiš-nu-ĝal$_2$, ^{d}Nanna-ka CS Ur A. Quentin, *Journal Asiatique* 1888, 287 1

lugal-šud$_3$ (identical with lugal-šud$_3$-de$_3$(-ba-ša$_4$) dub-sar-maḫ), p. 139 n. 772
lugal-šud$_3$ dub-sar maḫ ED IIIb/Ukg. lugal 1 Girsu *DP* suppl. 591 r. iv 14
lugal-šud$_3^!$(KA) dub-sar maḫ ED IIIb/X Y 2 Girsu *DP* suppl. 578 r. ii 6

lugal-šud$_3$ $^{(a\geq10)}$ 'the lugal … prayer' 3.1.6.1, p. 139, 215
lugal-šud$_3$ muš-laḫ$_5$ ED IIIb/Ukg. lugal Girsu? *DP* 1/1 32 v 19
lugal-⌜šud$_3$⌝ dumu engar ED IIIb Nippur OSP 1 44 o. 1
lugal-šud$_3$ ED IIIb Nippur OSP 1 86 o. 4
lugal-šud$_3$ s. ^{d}En-lil$_2$-da, lu_2 tir ED IIIb Nippur OSP 1 109 r. iii ' 4
lugal-šud$_3$ ED IIIb Nippur TMH 5 17 o. i 8
lugal-šud$_3$ ED IIIb Nippur TMH 5 167 r. i 2'
⌜lugal-šud$_3$⌝ ED IIIb Nippur TMH 5 169 o. iii 2
lugal-šud$_3$ ES-MS Nippur TMH 5 180 o. i 9'
lugal-šud$_3$ sagi MS Adab *TCABI* 162 o. 3
lugal-šud$_3$ ⌜sagi⌝ MS Adab *TCABI* 184 o. 8
lugal-šud$_3$ MS-CS Adab ? MesCiv 4 60 o. 5
lugal-šud$_3$ dub-sar MS-CS Isin ? MAD 4 150 r. 5

lugal-šud$_3$ f. [Ur]-en$_3$ MS-CS Nippur OSP 2 51 r. 7
lugal-šud$_3$ lu$_2$ ga:eš$_8$ MS-CS Nippur OSP 2 64 o. 8’
lugal-šud$_3$ MS-CS Nippur OSP 2 83 o. 9
lugal-šud$_3$? s. Ur-mes MS-CS Nippur TMH 5 52 o. ii 8
lugal-šud$_3$ šabra MS-CS Nippur TMH 5 63 o. i 6
lugal-šud$_3$ MS-CS Nippur TMH 5 120 r. 1
lugal-šud$_3$ CS Nippur TMH 5 186+202 o. i 2’
lugal-šud$_3$ dub-sar MS-CS Unknown OIP 47 pl. 6 no. 41 1

lugal-šud$_3$-de$_3$ (identical with lugal-šud$_3$(-de$_3$-ba-ša$_4$) dub-sar-maḫ), p. 139 n. 772
lugal-šud$_3$-de$_3$ dub-sar maḫ ED IIIb/Ukg. lugal 1 Girsu *DP* 1/2 133 r. i 7
lugal-šud$_3$-de$_3$ dub-sar maḫ ED IIIb/Enz. ensi$_2$ 3 Girsu *DP* 1/1 42 o. ii 11

lugal-šud$_3$-de$_3$ $^{(a\geq7)}$ ‘the lugal (stands by) for prayer’ 3.1.6.1, p. 139
lugal-šud$_3^{!}$(SAĜ×ŠU)-de$_3$ ED IIIa Girsu PBS 9 2 bottom
lugal-šud$_3$-de$_3$ (nam-dumu) ED IIIb/Ukg. lugal 4 Girsu *DP* suppl. 590 o. v 1
⸢lu:gal⸣-šud$_3$-[d]e$_3$ ED IIIb Nippur OSP 1 45 o. iii’ 3
lugal-šud$_3$-de$_3$? ED IIIb Nippur TMH 5 15 o. i 1
lugal-šud$_3$-de$_3$ Uru-saĝ-rig$_7^{ki}$ ED IIIb Nippur TMH 5 64 o. i 2
lugal-⸢šud$_3$⸣-de$_3$ ED IIIb Umma-Zabala CUSAS 14 107 o. i 4
lugal-šud$_3$-de$_3$ ED IIIb Ur G. Visicato & A. Westenholz, *Kaskal* 2 (2005), 55–78 3 o. 2
⸢lugal⸣-šud$_3$-de$_3$ ED IIIb Ur G. Visicato & A. Westenholz, *Kaskal* 2 (2005), 55–78 4 o. 2
lugal-⸢šud$_3$⸣-de$_3$ ED IIIb Ur G. Visicato & A. Westenholz, *Kaskal* 2 (2005), 55–78 5 o. 2
lu[gal]-šud$_3$-de$_3$ ED IIIb Ur UET 2 suppl. 36 o. 3
lugal-šud$_3$-de$_3$ dub-sar maškim(-bi) ED IIIb Ur UET 2 suppl. 43 o. 3
lugal-šud$_3$-de$_3$ (ugula) ĝuruš CS Girsu ITT 1 1352 o. 5

lugal-šud$_3$-de$_3$-ba-ša$_4$ $^{(a1)}$ ‘the lugal stands by for prayer’ 3.1.6.1, p. 138–139
lugal-šud$_3$-de$_3$-ba-ša$_4$ dub-sar maḫ ED IIIb/Lug. 3 Girsu *DP* 1/1 59 r. i 19

lugal-šud$_3$-du$_{10}$ $^{(a2)}$ ‘the lugal (of) a good prayer’ 3.1.6.1, p. 139 n. 774, 251 n. 1477
lugal-šud$_3$-du$_{10}$ ED IIIb Girsu ITT 5 9228 o. iii 4
lugal-šud$_3$-du$_{10}$ ED IIIb Umma-Zabala CUSAS 14 4 o. iv 3

lugal-šud$_3$-du$_{10}$-ga $^{(a2)}$ ‘the lugal of a *good* prayer’ 3.1.6.1, p. 139
lugal-šud$_3$-du$_{10}$-ga ED IIIb/Lug. 1 Girsu BIN 8 362 o. iii 10
lugal-šud$_3$-du$_{10}$-ga en ED IIIb/Ukg. ensi$_2$ 1 Girsu *DP* suppl. 519 o. iii 3
lugal-šud$_3^{!}$(KA)-du$_{10}$-ga en ED IIIb/Lug. Y X Girsu E. Sollberger, *Genava* 26 (1948), p. 48–72 7 r. i 1
lugal-šud$_3$-du$_{10}$-ga sipa ED IIIb/Lug. 3 Girsu Nik 1 175 o. iii 9
lugal-šud$_3$-du$_{10}$-ga (sipa?) ED IIIb/Lug. 4 Girsu A. Deimel, *OrSP* 20, p. 28 (translit. only) o. iii 4
lugal-šud$_3$-du$_{10}$-ga en ED IIIb/Lug. 4 Girsu *RTC* 27 o. iii 3
lugal-šud$_3$-du$_{10}$-ga en ED IIIb/Lug. 4 Girsu VS 14 65 o. ii 7
lugal-šud$_3$-du$_{10}$-ga sipa ED IIIb/X Y 3 Girsu VS 14 127 o. iv 6
lugal-šud$_3$-du$_{10}$-ga ED IIIb/Lug. [X] Girsu VS 25 36 o. v 7

lugal-šud$_3$-ĝiš-tuku $^{(a1)}$ ‘the lugal is one who hears prayers’ 3.1.6.1, p. 139
lugal-šud$_3$-ĝiš-tuku ED IIIa Šuruppag? G. Visicato & A. Westenholz, *Gs Cagni*, p. 1107–1133 3 o. v 3

lugal-tab (PN?) $^{(a1)}$ unkn. mng. 3.1.8, p. 182
lugal-tab me$_3$-ta DU ED IIIa Šuruppag *TSŠ* 782 r. i 8

lugal-TAR $^{(a1)}$ unkn. mng. 3.1.8, p. 182 w. n. 1121
lugal-TAR ED IIIb-ES Adab CUSAS 11 169 o. i 4

lugal-TAR ensi$_2$ Unug^{ki}-ga ED IIIb Girsu J. J. A. van Dijk, *Sumer* 15 (1959), 5–14 1 ii' 8'
lugal-TAR ED IIIb Nippur TMH 5 134 o. ii 7
⌜lugal-TAR⌝ ED IIIb Nippur TMH 5 149 o. ii 1
lugal-TAR ED IIIb Nippur TMH 5 165 o. 3
lugal-TAR ED IIIb Umma-Zabala CUSAS 14 223 r. i 6
lugal-TAR ES Adab CUSAS 11 303 r. 2
lugal-TAR f. Nin-ab-sa$_2$, en ^{d}Mes-saĝa-Unug^{ki} ES-MS Unknown *EGA* 1594 pl. 56 fig. 670 2
lugal-TAR CS Girsu ITT 2/1 4582 r. 10
lugal-TAR MS-CS Nippur TMH 5 191 r. 11
lugal-TAR MS-CS Umma MAD 4 104 (translit. only) o. 3
lugal-TAR$^{?}$ *Eš$_3$-me-qara$_4$* nu-banda$_3$-ni, ir$_{11}$ Lugal-T[AR$^{?}$] MS-CS Umma ? *TCVC* 728 o. iii 15
lugal-TAR lu$_2$ Ur-^{d}Šara$_2$, šitim(-me) CS Unknown CUSAS 13 200 o. 12
lugal-TAR f. Lu$_2$-^{d}Utu MS-CS Unknown BIN 8 279 o. 2
lugal-TAR Ur-me, mi$_2$-us$_2$-sa$_2$ Lugal-TAR MS-CS Unknown BIN 8 279 o. 4

lugal-TAR-me-te $^{(a1)}$ unkn. mng. 3.1.8, p. 182
lugal-TAR-me-te ED IIIa Šuruppag CUSAS 11 341 r. i 2
lugal-TAR-[(x)] ED IIIb-ES Adab CUSAS 11 182 r. i 1'

lugal-temen $^{(a\geq 2)}$ 'the lugal … the foundations' 3.1.6.4, p. 156 n. 900
lugal-temen ED IIIb-ES Adab CUSAS 11 163 o. i 3
lugal-temen ED IIIb-ES Adab CUSAS 11 163 o. i 6
lugal-temen Saĝ-mu-ab-tuku, šu-i$_2$-am$_6$, Lugal-temen-da, e-da-ti ED IIIb/Ukg. lugal 3 Girsu *AWAS* 124 o. vi 10
lugal-temen šu-i$_2$ ED IIIb/Enz. ensi$_2$ 2 Girsu BIN 8 347 r. iii 13
lugal-temen ED IIIb/Ukg. lugal 2 Girsu BIN 8 359 o. v 3'''
lugal-temen ED IIIb/Ukg. lugal 4 Girsu *DP* 1/2 116 o. i 5
lugal-temen šu-i$_2$ ED IIIb/Lug. Girsu *DP* 1/2 127 o. v 3
lugal-[temen] ED IIIb/Ukg. lugal 3 Girsu *TSA* 18 o. vi 2

lugal-temen-na $^{(a1)}$ 'the lugal … in/of the foundations' 3.1.6.4, p. 156 n. 900
lugal-temen-na [l]⌜u$_2$⌝ Inim-du$_{10}$-ga ED IIIb/Ukg. lugal X Girsu *Amherst* 3 2

lugal-teš$_2$ $^{(a2)}$ 'the lugal … well-being' 3.1.7.8, p. 85, 171, 175 n. 1028
lugal-teš$_2$ MS-CS Adab OIP 14 173 r. 4
lu[gal]-teš$_2$ muḫaldim MS Adab *TCABI* 184 o. 8
lugal-teš$_2$ muḫaldim? CS Adab *TCABI* 257 o. 7
lugal-teš$_2$ MS-CS Nippur OSP 2 98 r. ii 7

lugal-teš$_2$-ĝu$_{10}$ $^{(a\geq 13)}$ 'the lugal is my (source of) well-being' 3.1.7.8, p. 171
lu[gal]-teš$_2$-ĝu$_{10}$ ED IIIb-ES Adab CUSAS 11 89 o. i 3
lugal-teš$_2$-ĝu$_{10}$ ED IIIb-ES Adab CUSAS 11 126 o. i 3
lugal-teš$_2$-ĝu$_{10}$ ED IIIb-ES Adab CUSAS 11 252 o. i 5
lugal-teš$_2$-ĝu$_{10}$ ED IIIb Adab OIP 14 74 o. ii 8
lugal-teš$_2$-ĝu$_{10}$ lu$_2$ a-k[um$_2$] ED IIIb/Ukg. ensi$_2$ 1 Girsu *AWAS* 119 o. vii 3'
lugal-teš$_2$-ĝu$_{10}$ lu$_2$ a-kum$_2$ ED IIIb/Ukg. lugal 4 Girsu *AWAS* 120 o. viii 11
lugal-teš$_2$-ĝu$_{10}$ lu$_2$ Ur-ki, gab$_2$-kas$_4$ ED IIIb/Ukg. lugal 4 Girsu *AWAS* 120 r. iv 1
lugal-teš$_2$-ĝu$_{10}$ lu$_2$ a-kum$_2$ ED IIIb/[Ukg. lugal 3] Girsu *AWAS* 121 r. i 1
lugal-teš$_2$-ĝu$_{10}$ ED IIIb/[Ukg. lugal 3] Girsu *AWAS* 121 r. v 1
lugal-teš$_2$-ĝu$_{10}$ lu$_2$ a-kum$_2$ ED IIIb/Ukg. lugal 6 Girsu *AWAS* 122 o. ix 11
lugal-teš$_2$-ĝu$_{10}$ [lu$_2$ a-kum$_2$] ED IIIb/Ukg. lugal 1? Girsu *AWAS* 123 frag. g 1'
lugal-teš$_2$-ĝu$_{10}$ lu$_2$ igi-niĝin$_2$ ED IIIb/Enz. ensi$_2$ 3 Girsu *DP* 1/2 110 o. iii 5

lugal-teš$_2$-ĝu$_{10}$ ED IIIb/Ukg. lugal 2 Girsu *DP* 1/2 113 r. iii 11
lugal-teš$_2$-ĝu$_{10}$ ED IIIb/Ukg. lugal 2 Girsu *DP* 1/2 113 r. iii 12
lugal-teš$_2$-ĝu$_{10}$ nitaḫ ED IIIb/X ensi$_2$ 3 Girsu *DP* 2/1 176 o. iv 4
lugal-teš$_2$-ĝu$_{10}$ f. E-ta-[e$_{11}$$^{?}$] ED IIIb/Ukg. ensi$_2$ 1 Girsu *DP* suppl. 519 o. ii 2
lugal-teš$_2$-ĝu$_{10}$ ED IIIb/Lug. Y X Girsu E. Sollberger, *Genava* 26 (1948), p. 48–72 7 o. iii 4
lugal-teš$_2$-ĝu$_{10}$ lu$_2$ a-kum$_2$ ED IIIb/Ukg. lugal 1 Girsu HSS 3 17 o. viii 10
lugal-⌜teš$_2$⌝-ĝu$_{10}$ gab$_2$-kas$_4$ ED IIIb/Ukg. lugal 1 Girsu HSS 3 17 r. iv 14
lugal-teš$_2$-ĝu$_{10}$ gab$_2$-kas$_4$ ED IIIb/Ukg. lugal 1 Girsu HSS 3 17 r. iv 15
lugal-teš$_2$-ĝu$_{10}$ ED IIIb Girsu ITT 5 9202 r. ii 7
lugal-teš$_2$-ĝu$_{10}$ ED IIIb Girsu ITT 5 9215 r. 4
lugal-teš$_2$-ĝu$_{10}$ ED IIIb Girsu MesCiv 4 8 o. iii 1
lugal-teš$_2$-ĝu$_{10}$ lu$_2$ a-kum$_2$ ED IIIb/Ukg. ensi$_2$ 1 Girsu MVN 3 2 o. viii 5
lugal-teš$_2$-ĝu$_{10}$ lu$_2$ a-kum$_2$ ED IIIb Girsu MVN 3 26 o. iv' 4'
lugal-teš$_2$-ĝu$_{10}$ ED IIIb Girsu MVN 3 26 r. iii 5'
lugal-teš$_2$-ĝu$_{10}$ sipa anše sur$_x$-ka ED IIIb/Ukg. lugal 1 Girsu Nik 1 18 o. ii 4
lugal-teš$_2$-ĝu$_{10}$ sipa anše sur$_x$-ka ED IIIb/Ukg. lugal 1 Girsu Nik 1 18 o. ii 5
lugal-teš$_2$-ĝu$_{10}$ lu$_2$ a kum$_2$ ED IIIb/Lug. 6 Girsu D. Charpin, *RA* 71 (1977), p. 97–105 o. viii 6
lugal-teš$_2$-ĝu$_{10}$ nitaḫ ED IIIb/Ukg. lugal 4 Girsu *TSA* 14 o. viii 11
lugal-teš$_2$-ĝu$_{10}$ sa$_{10}$ Lugal-teš$_2$-ĝu$_{10}$, KA-TAR-kam ED IIIb/Urz. lugal Isin M. Lambert, *RA* 73 (1979), p. 5–6 o. ii 13
lugal-teš$_2$-ĝu$_{10}$ ED IIIb/Urz. lugal Isin M. Lambert, *RA* 73 (1979), p. 5–6 r. ii 13
lugal-teš$_2$$^{!}$(MA)-ĝu$_{10}$? ED IIIb/En. I Lagaš R. D. Biggs, *Fs Kramer*, p. 34–35 r. vi 7
lugal-teš$_2$-ĝu$_{10}$ lu$_2$ bappir$_3$ ED IIIb/X Y 3 Lagaš V. E. Crawford, *JCS* 29 (1977), 189–222 (4H-T38/4H 90) r. iv' 3'
lugal-teš$_2$-ĝu$_{10}$ ED IIIb Nippur OSP 1 51 o. 3
lugal-teš$_2$-ĝu$_{10}$ ED IIIb Nippur TMH 5 66 o. i 4
lugal-teš$_2$-ĝu$_{10}$ ED IIIb Nippur TMH 5 4 r. i 4
lugal-teš$_2$-ĝu$_{10}$ ED IIIb Nippur TMH 5 79 o. i 6
lugal-teš$_2$-ĝu$_{10}$ ED IIIb Nippur TMH 5 100 o. 2
lugal-teš$_2$-ĝu$_{10}$ ED IIIb Nippur TMH NF 1–2, suppl. 12 r. i 2
lugal-teš$_2$-ĝu$_{10}$ A.KA.DU$_3$ ED IIIb-ES Umma-Zabala ? BIN 8 98 o. i 3
lugal-teš$_2$-ĝu$_{10}$ ED IIIb Umma-Zabala M. Powell, *HUCA* 49 (1978), p. 1–58 12 o. i 4
lugal-teš$_2$-ĝu$_{10}$ ĝuruš, lu$_2$ gi sa$_{10}$-sa$_{10}$ ED IIIb Ur UET 2 suppl. 11 o. i 6
⌜lu:gal-teš$_2$-ĝu$_{10}$⌝ ES Nippur OSP 1 31 r. ii 1
⌜lugal⌝-teš$_2$-⌜ĝu$_{10}$⌝ CS Adab *SIA* 933 r. 1 A 933
lugal-teš$_2$-ĝu$_{10}$ MS-CS Nippur OSP 2 177 o. 3

lugal-ti (a2) unkn. mng. 3.1.8, p. 182
lugal-ti CS-LS Girsu *RTC* 254 o. i 6
lugal-ti dam-[gar$_3$] LS-Lagaš II Girsu *RTC* 221 r. iv 5 '
lugal-ti dam-gar$_3$ LS-Lagaš II Girsu *RTC* 222 r. iii 19

lugal-ti-da (a1) (phonetic writing of lugal-iti-da) 3.1.7.10, p. 172 n. 1004
lugal-ti-da šu-ku$_6$ ES Umma B. R. Foster, *Fs Westenholz*, 127–137 4 o. 1

lugal-ti-ma-nu$_2$ (a1) 'the lugal lies down in the sanctuary' 3.1.6.4, p. 158 n. 915, 172 n. 1004
lugal-ti-ma-nu$_2$ tug$_2$-du$_8$ ED IIIb Adab CUSAS 11 26 o. i 4

lugal-Ti-ra-aš$_2$-še$_3$ (a≥2) 'the lugal … by/toward the Tiraš-sanctuary' 3.1.6.4, p. 155 n. 889
lugal-Ti-ra-aš$_2$-še$_3$ CS Girsu *STTI* 91 o. 2
lu[gal]-Ti-ra-aš$_2$-še$_3$ CS/Śkś Girsu CT 50 50 o. 3
lugal-Ti-ra-aš$_2$-še$_3$ CS Girsu CT 50 106 r. i 15

lugal-ti-uš$_2$-da-kuš$_2$ (a1) perhaps 'the lugal is one who concerns himself with the living and the dead' 3.1.4.4, p. 126, 188
lugal-ti-uš$_2$-da-kuš$_2$ sipa ED IIIb/Ukg. lugal 6 Girsu *DP* 1/2 135 r. v 4

lugal-tigi$_x$(E$_2$.BALAĜ) (identical with lugal-tigi$_x$-mete šu-ku$_6$ ab-ba), p. 148 n. 835, 185
lugal-tigi$_x$ šu-ku$_6$ ab-ba ED IIIb/Lug. 1 Girsu *DP* 2/1 191 r. iv 2

lugal-tigi$_x$(E$_2$.BALAĜ)-mete(TE+ME) (a1) 'the Harp is befitting of the lugal' 3.1.6.3, p. 148, 185
lugal-tigi$_x$-mete šu-ku$_6$ ab-ba ED IIIb/Lug. 2 Girsu *DP* 2/2 278 o. iv 4

lugal-tigi$_x$(E$_2$.BALAĜ)-ni-du$_{10}$ (a1) 'the Harp of the lugal is pleasant-sounding' 3.1.6.3, p. 148, 185
lugal-tigi$_x$-ni-du$_{10}$ šu-ku$_6$ ab-ba ED IIIb/Enz. ensi$_2$ 2 Girsu *DP* 2/2 283 r. i 3

lugal-tir (a≥1) 'the lugal … the forest' 3.1.8, p. 182 2. n. 1123
lugal-tir ED IIIb-ES Umma B. R. Foster, *Fs Westenholz*, 127–137 6 o. i 4
lugal-tir MS-CS Umma MAD 4 45 (translit. only) o. 8

lugal-tir-a-DU (a1) 'the lugal stands (?) in the woods' 3.1.8, p. 182
lugal-tir-a-DU lu$_2$ igi-niĝin$_2$ ED IIIb/Enz. ensi$_2$ 3 Girsu *DP* 1/2 110 o. iii 2

lugal-^{d}Tu (a1) 'the lugal … (the goddess) Tu' 3.1.6.2, p. 144
lugal-^{d}Tu ED IIIb Umma-Zabala MVN 3 3 o. iv 15

lu:gal-tu$^{!?}$ (a1) 'the lugal is one born (by DN?)' 3.1.6.2, p. 144 n. 812
lu:gal-tu$^{!?}$ ES Nippur OSP 1 31 o. iii 4'

lugal-tug$_2$ (a1) (abbreviation of the following) 3.1.1.3, p. 91 n. 465
lu[gal]-tug$_2$ MS-CS Nippur OSP 2 80 o. i 3

lugal-tug$_2$-maḫ (a≥4) 'the lugal is (one wearing) a splendid robe' 3.1.1.3, p. 91, 230
lugal-tug$_2$-maḫ MS-CS Adab CUSAS 13 8 o. 5
lugal-tug$_2$-maḫ CS Adab CUSAS 13 32 o. 12
lugal-tug$_2$-maḫ CS Adab CUSAS 13 45 o. 5
lugal-tug$_2$-maḫ CS Adab CUSAS 13 66 o. 7
lugal-tug$_2$-maḫ CS Adab CUSAS 13 96 r. 1
lugal-tug$_2$-maḫ ? CS Adab CUSAS 13 153 o. 6
lugal-tug$_2$-maḫ MS-CS Adab OIP 14 79 o. 4
lugal-tug$_2$-maḫ CS Adab OIP 14 82 r. 2
lugal-tug$_2$-maḫ MS-CS Adab OIP 14 130 r. 2
lugal-tug$_2$-maḫ MS-CS Adab OIP 14 140 r. 2
lugal-tug$_2$-maḫ lu$_2$ Nibru^{ki} CS Adab *SIA* 1010 o. 2'
lugal-tug$_2$-maḫ ? CS Adab *SIA* 982 o. 2
lugal-tug$_2$-maḫ s. Za$_3$-mu CS Girsu CT 50 98 o. i 5
lugal-tug$_2$-maḫ Palil šandan MS-CS Isin ? MAD 4 78 o. 9
lugal-tug$_2$-maḫ ugula-ni MS-CS Isin ? MAD 4 158 o. 5'
lugal-tug$_2$-maḫ MS-CS Nippur OSP 2 68 o. 3
lugal-tug$_2$-maḫ MS-CS Nippur OSP 2 70 o. i 3
[lugal]-tug$_2$-⸢maḫ⸣ MS-CS Nippur OSP 2 98 r. i 1
lugal-tug$_2$-maḫ MS-CS Nippur OSP 2 126 o. i 1'
lugal-tug$_2$-maḫ MS-CS Nippur OSP 2 139 o. 6
lugal-tug$_2$-maḫ (maškim) MS-CS Nippur OSP 2 141 o. 4
lugal-tug$_2$-maḫ f. Nin-a-zu MS-CS Nippur TMH 5 39 o. iii 14'

lugal-TUR-x (a1) unkn. mng. 3.1.8, p. 182 w. n. 1124
lugal-TUR-⸢x⸣ ED IIIb-ES Ur UE 2 pl. 191 U. 13888 1

lugal-u$_2$ (identical with lugal-u$_2$-[tak$_4$] ma$_2$-GIN$_2$), p. 182 w. n. 1125
lugal-u$_2$ ma$_2$-GIN$_2$ ED IIIb/Lug. ⸢2+x⸣ Girsu VS 14 156 o. iii 4

lugal-u$_2$ $^{(a2)}$ unkn. mng. 3.1.8, p. 182
lugal-u$_2$ s. Lugal-ḫi-li CS Umma *USP* 46 o. 22
lugal-u$_2$ CS Unknown (Girsu ?) MVN 2 298 o. ii 12

lugal-u$_2$-dag-dag $^{(a1)}$ unkn. mng. 3.1.8, p. 182
lugal-u$_2$-dag-dag Adab^{ki} ED IIIb-ES Adab CUSAS 11 103 o. 1

lugal-u$_2$-tak$_4$ $^{(a2)}$ unkn. mng. 3.1.8, p. 182 w. n. 1125
lugal-u$_2$-tak$_4$ ED IIIb/Ukg. lugal 2 Girsu *DP* 1/2 120 r. ii 1
lugal-u$_2$-[tak$_4$] ma$_2$-GIN$_2$ ED IIIb/Lug. 1 Girsu *RTC* 61 r. iv 13

lugal-u$_3$-ma $^{(a\geq 11)}$ 'the lugal is victorious' 3.1.7.4, p. 164, 238
lugal-u$_3$-ma ED IIIa Šuruppag M. Lambert, *Gs Unger*, p. 27–49 4 r. i 2
lugal-⸢u$_3$⸣-ma ED IIIa Šuruppag? MVN 10 86 o. iv 6
⸢lugal⸣-u$_3$-ma ED IIIa Šuruppag > Nippur TMH 5 75 o. v 1'
lugal-u$_3$-ma ED IIIa Šuruppag *WF* 35 o. ii 4'
lugal-u$_3$-ma ED IIIa-b Isin (?) OIP 104 14 r. vi 15
lugal-u$_3$-ma baḫar ED IIIb-ES Adab CUSAS 11 93 o. ii' 2'
lugal-⸢u$_3$⸣-ma ED IIIb/Enz. 17 Girsu BIN 8 352 r. ii 8
lugal-u$_3$-ma s. Lugal-kur-dub$_2$ ED IIIb/Enz. or En. II Girsu ? *DP* 1/1 31 iii 21
lugal-u$_3$-ma ED IIIb/Ukg. lugal Girsu ? *DP* 1/1 32 iv 16
lugal-u$_3$-ma s. Lugal-šu, b. Ur-en-ĝe$_6$-dam ED IIIb/Ukg. lugal Girsu ? *DP* 1/1 32 iv 25
lugal-u$_3$-ma ED IIIb/Enz. ensi$_2$ 3 Girsu *DP* 1/2 110 o. iv 1
lugal-u$_3$-ma ED IIIb/Enz. ensi$_2$ 4 Girsu *DP* 1/2 111 o. i 7
lugal-u$_3$-ma ED IIIb Girsu ITT 5 9235 o. i 2
lugal-u$_3$-ma ED IIIb Girsu Nik 1 313 o. ii 3
lugal-u$_3$-ma s. Aja$_2$-abzu-si, b. Nin-ša$_3$-la$_2$-tuku & Ur-Ti-ra-aš$_2$ ED IIIb/Dudu saĝa Girsu W. W. Hallo, *OrNS* 42 (1973), p. 228–238 o. iv 6(!)
lugal-u$_3$-ma h. Ušur$_3$-ama-ĝu$_{10}$, UN:gal ED IIIb Girsu VS 14 106 o. i 7
lugal-u$_3$-ma ED IIIb/Urz. lugal Isin M. Lambert, *RA* 73 (1979), p. 5–6 o. vii 11
lugal-u$_3$-ma s. [...] ED IIIb ? Lagaš BiMes 3 9 i 1
lugal-u$_3$-ma s. E$_2$-ib$^!$-zi, b. Lugal-ša$_3$-pa$_3$-da ED IIIb/En. I ensi$_2$ 4 Lagaš BiMes 3 10 o. iii 4'
lugal-u$_3$-ma ED IIIb Umma-Zabala ? BIN 8 62 o. ii 4
lugal-u$_3$-ma ED IIIb Umma-Zabala M. Powell, *HUCA* 49 (1978), p. 1–58 15 o. i 2
lugal-u$_3$-ma ? ED IIIb/Luzag. ensi$_2$ [x] Umma-Zabala J. A. Brinkman, *Fs Kramer*, pl. III*-V* (W 2/7) o. iv 12'
lu[gal]-⸢u$_3$⸣-ma sagi ED IIIb Ur UET 2 suppl. 23 o. i 1
lugal-u$_3$-ma ED IIIb-ES Unknown MVN 3 91 o. 3
lugal-u$_3$-ma ES-MS Unknown MVN 3 85 r. 1

lugal-u$_3$-ma$_2$ $^{(a1)}$ 'the lugal is victorious' 3.1.7.4, p. 164 n. 947
lugal-u$_3$-ma$_2$ ED IIIb Zabala (?) BIN 8 46 o. iii 1

lugal-u$_4$-an $^{(a1)}$ 'the lugal is the light (of the) skies' 3.1.7.10, p. 172 n. 1009
lugal-u$_4$-an MS-CS Mesag BIN 8 255 o. 6
lugal-u$_4$-an-[(x)] i$_3$-du$_8$ MS-CS Nippur PBS 9 28+34 o. ii 10'

lugal-u$_4$-an-na $^{(a1)}$ 'the lugal is the light of the skies' 3.1.7.10, p. 172
lugal-u$_4$-an-na MS-CS Mesag BIN 8 237 o. 7

lugal-u$_4$-de$_3$ $^{(a\geq 2)}$ unkn. mng. 3.1.8, p. 182 w. n. 1126
lugal-u$_4$-de$_3$ ED IIIb-ES Adab CUSAS 11 102 obv, i 1
lugal-u$_4$-de$_3$ ED IIIb-ES Adab CUSAS 11 186 o. v 15
lugal-u$_4$-de$_3$ ED IIIb Girsu *DP* 1/1 57 o. iii 13
lugal-u$_4$-de$_3$ ED IIIb Girsu *DP* 1/1 57 o. v 13

lugal-u$_4$-de$_3$ ED IIIb Girsu *DP* 1/1 57 r. ii 2’

lugal-u$_4$-su$_3$-[(še$_3^?$)] (a1) ‘the lugal is (the greatest for) far off days’ 3.1.7.7, p. 168 n. 975
lugal-u$_4$-su$_3$-[(še$_3^?$)] CS Adab CUSAS 13 61 o. 2

lugal-u$_4$-su$_{13}$-še$_3$ (a≥2/°1) ‘the lugal is (the greatest) for far off days’ 3.1.7.7, p. 168
lugal-u$_4$-su$_{13}$-še$_3$ ED IIIa Šuruppag *FTUM* 40 o. i 2
lugal-u$_4$-su$_{13}$-še$_3$ [um$^?$]-mi-[a$^?$] ED IIIa Šuruppag *FTUM* 55 o. i 2
lugal-u$_4$-su$_{13}$-še$_3$ dub-sar ED IIIa Šuruppag *RTC* 14 o. v 1
lugal-u$_4$-su$_{13}$-še$_3$ f. Mes-e$_2$-zi-da ED IIIb Adab OIP 14 73 o. ii 2
°lugal-u$_4^?$-su$_{13}^?$-še$_3$ ED IIIb Ebla MEE 3 67 o. ii 3

lugal-u$_4$-suḫ̮$_3$(GU.GU)-gi$_4$ (a1) uncertain mng. 3.1.7.10, p. 173, 229, 246 n. 1450
lugal-u$_4$-suḫ̮$_3$(GU.GU)-gi$_4$ ED I-II Ur UET 2 41 o. i 3’

lugal-UD (a≥6/°1) (perhaps) ‘the lugal is (like) Utu’ 3.1.6.2, p. 62 n. 310, 146, 166 n. 959, 237, 253 n. 1487
lugal-UD ? ED IIIa Kiš *AAICAB* 1/1 (Ashm 1928-428) o. ii 2
lugal-UD s. Utu-mu-kuš$_2$ ED IIIa Šuruppag? MVN 10 82 o. v 4
lugal-UD s. Utu-mu-kuš$_2$ ED IIIa Šuruppag? MVN 10 83 o. iv 5
lugal-UD kin-nir ED IIIa Šuruppag *WF* 5 r. iv 1
lugal-UD kin-nir ED IIIa Šuruppag *WF* 6 r. iii 1
[lu]gal-⸢UD⸣ kin-⸢nir⸣ ED IIIa Šuruppag *WF* 15 r. v 3
lugal-UD ED IIIa Šuruppag *WF* 22 o. viii 11
lugal-⸢UD$^?$⸣ ? ED IIIa Šuruppag *WF* 41 o. iii 2
lugal-UD lugal ED IIIb Kiš EK 1 pl. 6 no. 1
°lugal-UD ED IIIb Ebla MEE 3 59 o. ii 5
lugal-UD f. Ur-[x] ED IIIb Girsu *DP* suppl. 555 o. iii 6
lugal-UD lugal ED IIIb Mari MAM 1 pl. 54 no. 413
lu:gal-UD ED IIIb Nippur TMH 5 132 o. i 2
lugal-UD ES-MS Nippur OSP 1 23 r. i 2’

lugal-UET2-300-si (a1) uncertain mng. 3.1.3.1, p. 108 n. 570
lugal-UET2-300-si ED I-II Ur UET 2 9 o. i 1

lugal-uĝ$_3$-e (identical with lugal-uĝ$_3$-ĝe$_{26}$ s. ^{d}Inana-ur-saĝ)
lugal-uĝ$_3$-e s. ^{d}Inana-⸢ur-saĝ⸣ ED IIIb Nippur TMH 5 171 o. 3

lugal-uĝ$_3$-e (a2) (abbreviation of *lugal-uĝ$_3$-e-du$_{10}$) 3.1.1.6, p. 100 n. 531
lugal-uĝ$_3$-e šu-i$_2$, maškim-bi ES-MS Isin BIN 8 154 r. i 7
[lugal]-uĝ$_3$-e CS-LS Uruk H. Neumann, *AoF* 15 (1988), 209–210 o. i 1
⸢lugal-uĝ$_3$-e⸣ f. [(x)] E$_2$ [(x)], ⸢dub⸣-sar CS-LS Uruk H. Neumann, *AoF* 15 (1988), 209–210 Seal: 1

lugal-uĝ$_3$(LAK730)/-uĝ$^!$(LAK729)-ĝe$_{26}$ (a≥6) (abbreviation of the following) 3.1.1.6, p. 100 n. 531
lu:gal-uĝ$_3^!$(LAK729)-ĝe$_{26}$ s. ^{d}Inana-ur-saĝ ED IIIb Nippur TMH 5 1 r. i 3
lugal-uĝ$_3$-ĝe$_{26}$ ES-MS Adab *TCABI* 64 r. iii 4
lugal-uĝ$_3$-ĝe$_{26}$ CS Girsu *RTC* 120 r. 5
lugal-⸢uĝ$_3$-ĝe$_{26}$⸣ s. ⸢Ur⸣-akkil$_x$(AB.KID.KID) MS-CS Isin ? MAD 4 78 r. 7
lugal-uĝ$_3$-ĝe$_{26}$ MS-CS Nippur OSP 2 45 r. i 9
lugal-uĝ$_3^!$(LAK729)-ĝe$_{26}$ MS-CS Nippur OSP 2 48 r. i 4
lugal-uĝ$_3$-ĝe$_{26}$ šu-ku$_6$ CS Unknown Mesopotamia 9 2 r. 9
lugal-uĝ$_3$-ĝe$_{26}$ šu-ku$_6$ CS Unknown Mesopotamia 9 3 r. 6’

lugal-uĝ$_3^!$(LAK729)-ĝe$_{26}$-du$_{10}$ (a1) ‘the lugal is one who does good for the people’ 3.1.1.6, p. 100–101, 188
lugal-uĝ$_3^!$-ĝe$_{26}$-du$_{10}$ ED IIIb/Lug. 4 Girsu VS 25 26 o. i 3

lugal-uĝken-ne$_2$ $^{(a\geq3)}$ 'the lugal (is just right for) the council (?)' 3.1.1.5, p. 94–95
lugal-uĝken-ne$_2$ ED IIIb Umma-Zabala CUSAS 14 272 o. i 2
lugal-uĝken-ne$_2$ CS Girsu CT 50 85 o. ii 18
lugal-uĝken-ne$_2$ a-zu CS/Śkś Girsu CT 50 172 r. i 7
lugal-uĝken-ne$_2$ Umma^{ki} CS Girsu ITT 1 1241 r. 3

lugal-uĝu$_3$(LAK730)-du$_{10}$ $^{(a1)}$ 'the lugal is one who does good for the people' 3.1.1.6, p. 100 n. 31, 186, 187
lugal-uĝu$_3$-du$_{10}$ ED IIIa-b Isin (?) OIP 104 14 r. ii 1

lugal-ul$_4$-gal $^{(a\geq4)}$ 'the lugal is a great thornbush' 3.1.3.1, p. 108
lugal-ul$_4$-gal ED I-II Ur UET 2 70 o. iii 2
lugal-ul$_4$-gal ED I-II Ur UET 2 104 o. i 3
lugal-ul$_4$-gal ED I-II Ur UET 2 128 o. ii' 1
lugal-[ul$_4$]-gal ? ED I-II Ur UET 2 145 o. ii 1
lugal-ul$_4$-gal ED I-II Ur UET 2 185 o. ii 4
lugal-ul$_4$-gal šu-ku$_6$ ED IIIb Girsu Nik 1 41 r. iii 1
lugal-ul$_4$-gal šu-ku$_6$ ED IIIb/X Y 6 Girsu Nik 1 105 o. ii 1
lu:gal-ul$_4$-gal ED IIIb Nippur TMH 5 74 o. i 2
lugal-ul$_4$-gal ED IIIb Nippur TMH 5 138 o. 6
lugal-⸢ul$_4$⸣-gal ES-MS Nippur OSP 1 23 r. ii 6'''
lu:gal-ul$_4$-gal ES Nippur OSP 1 31 r. ii 2
lugal-ul$_4$-gal CS Adab CUSAS 13 56 o. ii 7

lugal-ur-saĝ $^{(a\geq10/°2)}$ 'the lugal is a hero/warrior' 3.1.7.4, p. 164, 229, 238
lugal-ur-saĝ ED I-II Ur UET 2 5 o. ii 2
°lugal-ur-⸢saĝ⸣ ED IIIa Abū Ṣalābīḫ *IAS* 462 o. ii 2
lugal-ur-saĝ ED IIIa Nippur TMH 5 54 o. iii 4
lugal-ur-saĝ ED IIIa Nippur TMH 5 54 o. iv 6
lugal-ur-saĝ ED IIIa-b Girsu *RTC* 4 o. ii 4
°lugal-ur-saĝ ED IIIb Ebla MEE 3 67 o. i 2
lugal-ur-saĝ ED IIIb/Urz. lugal Isin M. Lambert, *RA* 73 (1979), p. 5–6 o. iii 21
lugal-ur-saĝ f. E$_2$-ERIM ED IIIb/Urz. lugal Isin M. Lambert, *RA* 73 (1979), p. 5–6 o. iv 17
lugal-ur-saĝ f. E$_2$-ERIM ED IIIb/Urz. lugal Isin M. Lambert, *RA* 73 (1979), p. 5–6 o. vi 20
lugal-ur-saĝ ED IIIb Marada ? *AAICAB* 1/1 (Ashm 1924-468) r. i 3
lugal-ur-saĝ s. Lugal-apin-du$_{10}$ ED IIIb Nippur TMH 5 11 o. i 6
lugal-ur-saĝ GAN$_2$-u$_2$-⸢OSP1-X$_6$⸣-ba^{ki} ED IIIb Nippur TMH 5 21 o. ii 6'
lu:gal-ur-[s]aĝ ED IIIb Nippur TMH 5 41 r. ii 2'
lu:gal-ur-saĝ ED IIIb Nippur OSP 1 121 r. iii 4'
lugal-ur-saĝ ? ED IIIb Ur UET 2 suppl. 12 o. 4
lugal-ur-saĝ lu$_2$ Umma^{ki} CS Girsu ITT 2/1 4455 o. 5'
lugal-ur-saĝ CS Unknown (Girsu ?) MVN 2 298 o. ii 20

lugal-ur$_2$-ra-ni $^{(a1)}$ 'the lugal … his (her?) lap' 3.1.7.2, p. 162, 189
lugal-ur$_2$-ra-ni ki Lugal-ur$_2$-ra-ni-ta LS-Lagaš II? Girsu *RTC* 221 r. iii 14'

lugal-uri$_3$ $^{(a\geq12)}$ 'the lugal … the standard' 3.1.6.3, p. 151
lugal-uri$_3$ ED I-II Ur UET 2 128 r. i 3
lu[gal]-uri$_3$ [šeš] lu$_2$ ED IIIa Šuruppag? G. Visicato & A. Westenholz, *Gs Cagni*, p. 1107–1133 5 (translit. only) o. iii 9
lugal-uri$_3$ s. Lugal-ĝeštu$_2$-su$_{20}$ ED IIIa Šuruppag? MVN 10 82 o. v 1
lugal-uri$_3$ s. Lugal-ĝeštu$_2$-su$_{20}$ ED IIIa Šuruppag? MVN 10 83 o. iii 10
lugal-uri$_3$ ED IIIa-b Nippur A. Goetze, *JCS* 23 (1970), p. 46 (7N-299) 1!
lugal-uri$_3^{!}$ ED IIIb Girsu *NFT*, p. 180 (bottom) o. iii 1
lugal-uri$_3$ saĝ-apin ED IIIb Girsu VS 27 29 o. i 1

lugal-uri$_3$ dub-sar ED IIIb Nippur A. Goetze, *JCS* 23 (1970), p. 54 (7N-238) 3
lugal-uri$_3$ ED IIIb Nippur OSP 1 24 o. iii 5
lugal-uri$_3$ ED IIIb-ES Nippur OSP 1 55 o. i 7
lugal-uri$_3$ ‹f.› Ur$_2$-ni, nu-kiri$_6$ ED IIIb Nippur TMH 5 6 o. i 4
lugal-uri$_3$ ED IIIb Nippur TMH 5 38 o. i 9
lugal-uri$_3$ ES-MS Nippur OSP 1 23 r. iv 8
lu:gal-uri$_3$ ES-MS Nippur OSP 1 129 o. i 6
lugal-uri$_3$ CS Adab *SIA* 640 o. i 14
lugal-⸢uri$_3$⸣ CS Adab *SIA* 806 r. 1
lugal-⸢uri$_3^?$⸣ ? CS Girsu ITT 1 1288 o. 6
lugal-uri$_3$ ma$_2$-laḫ$_5$ CS Mesag BIN 8 152 o. iii 7
lugal-uri$_3$ ma$_2$-laḫ$_5^!$, ĝuruš CS Mesag M. deJ. Ellis, *JCS* 31 (1979), p. 30–55 16 o. iii 5
lugal-uri$_3$ MS-CS Nippur OSP 2 82 o. 8
lugal-uri$_3$ MS-CS Nippur OSP 2 89 o. 8
lugal-uri$_3$ MS-CS Nippur OSP 2 96 o. i 10
lugal-uri$_3$ MS-CS Nippur OSP 2 96 o. ii 6
lugal-uri$_3$ MS-CS Nippur OSP 2 98 r. ii 11
lugal-uri$_3$ MS-CS Nippur OSP 2 107 r. 5
lugal-uri$_3$ sagi MS-CS Nippur OSP 2 129 o. ii 3’
lugal-uri$_3$ MS-CS Nippur OSP 2 174 o. 6
lugal-uri$_3$ f. Ur-^{d}E[n-x] CS/Śkś Y 2 Nippur OSP 2 100 o. iv 4
lugal-uri$_3$ CS/Śkś Y 2 Nippur OSP 2 100 o. iv 5
lugal-uri$_3$ f. E$_2$-ta MS-CS Nippur TMH 5 52 o. ii 15

lugal-uri$_3$-da $^{(a1)}$ ‘the lugal … by the standard’ 3.1.6.3, p. 151
lugal-uri$_3$-da s. U$_3$-mu-NI.NI ED IIIb Nippur OSP 1 85 r. 1

lugal-Urim$_2^{ki}$-e $^{(a1)}$ ‘the lugal … Ur’ 3.1.6.4, p. 154 n. 886
lu[gal]-Urim$_2^{ki}$-e CS Adab CUSAS 13 61 o. 5
lugal-Urim$_2^{ki}$-e CS Adab *TCABI* 227 o. 3

lugal-Urim$_x$(AB.URI$_3$)^{ki} $^{(a1)}$ ‘the lugal … Ur’ 3.1.6.4, p. 154 n. 886, 185
lugal-Urim$_x$(AB.URI$_3$)^{ki} CS Unknown MAD 4 36 r. 6

lugal-uru $^{(a\geq9)}$ unkn. mng. 3.1.8, p. 182
lugal-uru ED I-II Ur UET 2 112 o. vi’ 11
lugal-uru ED IIIb-ES Adab CUSAS 11 139 o. i 2
lugal-uru engar ĝuruš-ne-ka$^!$ ED IIIb/Ukg. lugal 1 Girsu *Amherst* 2 o. ii 6
lugal-uru A$_2$-ne$_2$-kur-ra ED IIIb/Enz. or En. II Girsu ? *DP* 1/1 31 iv 6
lugal-uru ED IIIb/Enz. ensi$_2$ 3 Girsu *DP* 1/2 110 o. iii 8
lugal-uru ED IIIb/Enz. ensi$_2$ 4 Girsu *DP* 1/2 111 o. i 5
lugal-uru ED IIIb Girsu ITT 5 9233 o. ii 1
lugal-uru f. Lugal-sa-šuš-gal ED IIIb/X Y 1 Girsu Nik 1 160 o. i 3
lugal-uru ⸢dub⸣-sar, lu$_2$ ki inim-[ma-bi] ED IIIb Girsu Nik 1 318 ii’ 4’
lugal-uru ED IIIb Girsu *TSA* 44 o. i 3
lugal-uru dub-sar ES Umma-Zabala E. Milone, *Sefarad* 62 (2002), 369–374 16 o. 2
lugal-uru utul MS Adab *TCABI* 68 o. 1
lugal-uru MS Adab *TCABI* 169 r. 1
lugal-uru ku$_3$-dim$_2$ CS Adab CUSAS 13 78 r. i 1
lugal-uru CS Girsu ITT 1 1404 o. 4
lugal-uru ĝu[ruš$^?$] CS Mesag BIN 8 152 o. iv 5
lugal-uru MS-CS Mesag BIN 8 276 o. ii 3
lugal-uru MS-CS Mesag E. Salgues, *Fs Westenholz*, 253–272 (RBC 2631) r. ii 5

lugal-uru ⌜sipa⌝ anš[e] MS-CS Mesag MesCiv 4 33 o. 15
lugal-uru h. Nin-maš-e MS-CS Unknown B. R. Foster, *JCS* 35 (1983), p. 147–175 8 o. 7

lugal-uru-da (a≥3) 'the lugal (is one who concerns himself) with the city' 3.1.4.2, p. 125
lu:gal-uru-da ED IIIb Nippur OSP 1 38 o. iii 2
lugal-uru-da ku_3-dim_2 ED IIIb Nippur OSP 1 46 o. ii 13
lugal-uru-da f. Lugal-kar, lu_2 Šuruppag^{ki} ED IIIb Nippur TMH 5 8 o. ii 1
lugal-uru-da CS-LS ? Girsu *RTC* 216 o. 3
lugal-uru-da CS-LS ? Girsu *RTC* 254 r. i 2

lugal-uru-da-[(x)] ED IIIa-b Girsu *RTC* 2 r. i 1

lugal-uru-na (a3) 'the lugal … in/of his city' 3.1.1.5, p. 96, 110 n. 587
⌜lugal-uru-na⌝ ED IIIb-ES Adab CUSAS 11 101 o. i 2
⌜lugal⌝-uru-na ED IIIb Adab MVN 3 90 o. iii 1
lugal-uru-na ED IIIb Umma-Zabala BIN 8 68 r. i 8
lugal-uru-na f. ⌜E_2⌝-ur_2 MS Isin ? MAD 4 170 3

lugal-uru-na-nu_2 (a3) 'the lugal lies down in his city' 3.1.1.5, p. 62, 96
lugal-uru-na-nu_2 ED IIIb Ur UET 2 suppl. 14 r. i 4

lugal-uru-si (a2) 'the lugal is just right for the city' 3.1.5.2, p. 130, 229
lugal-uru-si ED I-II Ur UET 2 112 o. iv' 1''
⌜lugal⌝-uru-si x x NE, ⌜*Im*$^?$-*li*$^?$⌝-*ik*, KI [x KIŠ.NI]TAH̰, Ki-[en]-gi k[i-u]ri, Lugal-uru-si CS/NS. (OB) Ur UET 1 276 r. i 5

lugal-URUDU-da (a1) unkn. mng. 3.1.8, p. 112, 182 w. n. 1128
lugal-URUDU-da ED IIIb Umma-Zabala MVN 3 3 o. vi 13

lugal-UŠ(ARAD) (a1) unkn. mng. 3.1.8, p. 182f. n. 1129
lugal-UŠ ED IIIa Šuruppag *WF* 125 r. i 6

lugal-UŠ (a1) unkn. mng. 3.1.8, p. 182f. n. 1129
lugal-UŠ s. Ur-lu_2, muhal[dim$^?$] ED IIIb-ES Adab CUSAS 11 150 o. i 2
lugal-UŠ ED IIIb-ES Adab CUSAS 11 162 o. ii 2
lugal-UŠ ED IIIb-ES Adab CUSAS 11 239 o. i 1
⌜lugal-UŠ⌝ ED IIIb Adab MVN 3 28 r. iii 12
lugal-UŠ ED IIIb Nippur TMH 5 46 o. ii 7
lugal-UŠ ad-kup_4 ED IIIb-ES Umma-Zabala ? BIN 8 257 o. 2

lugal-uš-su_{20} (a1) unkn. mng. 3.1.8, p. 182
lugal-uš-su_{20} dub-sar $aša_5$ ED IIIa Šuruppag? G. Visicato & A. Westenholz, *Gs Cagni*, p. 1107–1133 3 r. ii 1
lugal-uš-su_{20} ED IIIa Šuruppag L. Milano, *StEL* 3 (1986), p. 3–12 o. iii 7
lu[gal]-uš-su_{20} ED IIIa Šuruppag *WF* 37 o. iv 6
lugal-uš-su_{20} ED IIIa Šuruppag *WF* 40 o. i 3
lugal-uš-su_{20} ED IIIa Šuruppag *WF* 40 r. i 2

lugal-uš-su_x(MUŠ) (a≥5) unkn. mng. 3.1.8, p. 182f. n. 1130, 189
lugal-uš-su_x ED IIIa Adab ? BIN 8 15 o. i 4
lugal-uš-su_x ED IIIa Šuruppag? G. Visicato & A. Westenholz, *Gs Cagni*, p. 1107–1133 3 o. v 4
lugal-uš-su_x sipa g[u_4 tur-tur] ED IIIb/Ukg. lugal 3 Girsu *AWAS* 118 o. v 2
lugal-uš-su_x sipa amar ru-ga-[ka] ED IIIb/Ukg. lugal 4 Girsu *DP* 1/2 99 o. ii 6
lugal-uš-su_x ED IIIb/Ukg. lugal 5 Girsu *DP* 1/2 136 r. iii 4
lugal-uš-su_x sipa gu_4 ED IIIb/Ukg. lugal 2 Girsu *DP* 2/1 171 o. iii 16
lugal-uš-su_x sipa gu_4 tur-tur ED IIIb Girsu MVN 3 8 o. v 1'
lugal-uš-su_x ED IIIb/Ukg. lugal 5 Girsu Nik 1 3 o. iv 11

lugal-uš-su$_x$ sipa gu$_4$ tur-tur ED IIIb/X Y 4 Girsu Nik 1 68 o. ii 6
lugal-uš-su$_x$ f. Ad-da-tur, nu-kiri$_6$ ED IIIb Nippur TMH 5 6 r. i 2
lugal-uš-su$_x$ ES Adab CUSAS 11 306 o. i 6
lugal-uš-su$_x$ h. Šu-bar ES Adab CUSAS 11 306 o. ii 1

lugal-ušum-AN (a1) unkn. mng. 3.1.8, p. 183
lugal-ušum-AN ED IIIa Šuruppag CUSAS 11 341 o. ii' 3

lugal-ušumgal (a≥7) 'the lugal is a *fierce beast* (?)' 3.1.7.6, p. 166
lugal-ušumgal ⸢ĝiš-ru⸣ ED IIIa Kiš *AAICAB* 1/1 (Ashm 1928-429) o. ii 2'
lugal-ušumgal ED IIIa Nippur TMH 5 54 o. iii 5
lugal-ušumgal ED IIIa Nippur TMH 5 54 o. v 1
lugal-ušumgal baḫa[r] ED IIIb Umma-Zabala MVN 3 3 o. ii 9'
lugal-ušumgal baḫar ED IIIb Umma-Zabala MVN 3 3 o. iii 1
lugal-ušumgal CS Adab CUSAS 13 132 o. 4
lugal-ušumgal [e]nsi$_2$ CS Girsu *STTI* 155 o. 3
lugal-ušumgal ensi$_2$ CS Girsu ITT 1 1040 o. 2'
lugal-ušumgal CS Girsu ITT 1 1058 o. 6
lugal-ušumgal ensi$_2$ CS Girsu ITT 1 1062 r. 3
lugal-ušumgal [ens]i$_2$ CS Girsu ITT 1 1070 r. 2
lugal-ušumgal CS Girsu ITT 1 1080 r. 6'
lugal-ušumgal CS Girsu ITT 1 1088 o. 2
lugal-ušumgal ensi$_2$ Lagaš^{ki} CS Girsu ITT 1 1225 r. 5
lugal-ušumgal CS Girsu ITT 1 1291 o. 3
lugal-ušumgal ensi$_2$ Lagaš^{ki} CS Girsu ITT 1 1471 o. 4
lugal-ušumgal (ensi$_2$) CS Girsu ITT 1 1474 r. 5
lugal-ušumgal ensi$_2$ CS Girsu ITT 2/1 4516 r. 1
lugal-ušumgal ensi$_2$ Lagaš^{ki} CS Girsu ITT 2/1 4543 r. 2
lugal-ušumgal ensi$_2$ CS Girsu ITT 2/1 4578 o. 4
lugal-ušumgal CS Girsu ITT 2/2 5758 o. 3
lugal-ušumgal CS Girsu ITT 5 6682 o. 3
lugal-ušumgal ensi$_2$ CS Girsu ITT 5 9303 r. 1
lugal-ušumgal CS Girsu *RTC* 77 r. 1
lugal-ušumgal CS Girsu *RTC* 78 r. 4
lugal-ušumgal ensi$_2$ CS Girsu *RTC* 79 o. 3
lugal-⸢ušumgal⸣ ensi$_2$ Lagaš^{ki} CS Girsu *RTC* 80 o. 7
lugal-ušumgal ensi$_2$ CS Girsu *RTC* 81 o. 5
lugal-ušumgal Lagaš^{ki} CS Girsu *RTC* 117 o. 2
lugal-ušumgal CS Girsu *RTC* 119 o. 3
lugal-ušumgal CS Girsu *RTC* 121 r. 2
lugal-ušumgal CS Girsu *RTC* 136 r. iii 8'
lugal-ušumgal CS/Śkś Girsu *RTC* 161 o. 1
lugal-ušumgal ⸢ensi$_2$⸣ Lagaš^{ki} CS/Śkś Girsu *RTC* 162 Seal: ii 1
⸢lugal⸣-ušumgal CS/NS. Girsu *RTC* 165 Seal ii 2
lugal-ušumgal CS Girsu *RTC* 170 1
⸢lugal⸣-ušumgal CS Girsu *RTC* 179 Seal: 3
lugal-ušumgal CS Girsu *STTI* 1 r. 1
lugal-ušumgal CS Girsu *STTI* 2 r. 3'
lugal-ušumgal CS Girsu *STTI* 3 o. 3
lugal-ušumgal CS Girsu *STTI* 64 o. 3
lugal-ušumgal (ensi$_2$ Lagaš^{ki}) MS-CS Mesag BIN 8 214 r. 2
[lugal]-ušum[gal] nitaḫ MS-CS Nippur OSP 2 23 r. 2' 344
lugal-ušumgal ugula CS Umma CT 50 188 o. i 14

lugal-ušur$_3$(LAL$_2$+LAGAB) $^{(a\geq6)}$ unkn. mng. 3.1.8, p. 183
lugal-ušur$_3$ b. Lugal-ra ED IIIb/X Y 5 Girsu *DP* suppl. 593 o. i 10
lugal-⸢ušur$_3$⸣ ? MS-CS Adab CUSAS 13 38 o. 4
lugal-ušur$_3$ s. Nin-ĝa$_2$ CS Girsu CT 50 87 o. 1
lugal-ušur$_3$ lu$_2$ Ur-da CS Girsu CT 50 106 o. i 7’
lugal-ušur$_3$ CS-LS ? Girsu *RTC* 254 r. ii 20
lugal-ušur$_3$ CS Girsu *STTI* 105 o. 7’
lugal-ušur$_3$ s. Da-da CS Umma *USP* 47 o. ii 15
lugal-ušur$_3$ MS-CS Unknown MesCiv 4 63 r. 2

lugal-ušur$_3$-MU $^{(a\geq4)}$ unkn. mng. 3.1.8, p. 183
lugal-ušur$_3$-MU ED IIIb Nippur TMH 5 11 o. i 4
lugal-ušur$_3$-MU ED IIIb Nippur TMH 5 159 o. iii 16’
lugal-ušur$_3$-MU ED IIIb Nippur TMH 5 159 o. iv 10’
lugal-ušur$_3$-MU ES Adab *TCABI* 61 o. iii 8
lugal-ušur$_3$-MU ES-MS Umma Nik 2 67 o. i 3
lugal-ušur$_3$-MU CS Adab CUSAS 13 153 o. 7
lugal-ušur$_3$-MU CS Adab *TCABI* 225 o. 3

lugal-ušur$_3$-nu$_2$ (identical with lugal-ušur$_3$-ra-nu$_2$, nu-kiri$_6$), p. 183 n. 1131
lugal-ušur$_3$-nu$_2$ nu-kiri$_6$ ED IIIb/Lug. 6 Girsu *DP* 2/1 157 o. iv 8

lugal-ušur$_3$-ra $^{(a>7)}$ unkn. mng. 3.1.8, p. 183
lugal-[ušur$_3^?$]-ra dam-gar$_3$ ED IIIb Girsu J. Marzahn & H. Neumann, *AoF* 22 (1995), p. 111f. (VAT 6121) r. ii 4’
lugal-ušur$_3$-ra šagan-keš$_2$ ED IIIb Girsu J. Bauer, *AoN* 1 (1976) 1 (translit. only) r. ii 1
lugal-ušur$_3$-ra aga$_3$-us$_2$ saĝa ED IIIb/Enz. 17 Girsu BIN 8 352 r. i 9
lugal-ušur$_3$-ra u$_2$-DU udu ED IIIb Girsu CT 50 30 r. i 5
lugal-ušur$_3$-ra f. Ni$_3$-lu$_2$-nu-tum$_2$ ED IIIb/Ukg. lugal 2 Girsu *DP* 1/2 120 o. iii 2
lugal-ušur$_3$-ra h. Munus-sa$_6$-ga, saĝ-apin ED IIIb/Ukg. lugal 3 Girsu *DP* 1/2 129 r. ii 7
lugal-ušur$_3$-ra ama sur$_x$-kam ED IIIb/Ukg. lugal 6 Girsu *DP* 1/2 135 o. ii 17
lugal-ušur$_3$-ra ED IIIb/Ukg. lugal 6 Girsu *DP* 1/2 135 o. vi 8
lugal-ušur$_3$-ra šu-ku$_6$ ⸢a⸣ du$_{10}$-ga ED IIIb/Ukg. lugal 6 Girsu *DP* 1/2 135 r. ii 2
lugal-ušur$_3$-ra sipa ED IIIb/X Y 4 Girsu *DP* suppl. 587 o. i 6
lugal-ušur$_3$-ra apin-us$_2$ ED IIIb/Ukg. lugal 4 Girsu *DP* suppl. 590 o. iii 10
lugal-ušur$_3$-ra ED IIIb/Ukg. lugal 3 Girsu HSS 3 8 o. i 8
lugal-ušur$_3$-ra ED IIIb/Ukg. lugal 3 Girsu HSS 3 9 o. i 8
lugal-ušur$_3$-ra i$_3$-du$_8$ ^{d}Ba-u$_2$ ED IIIb Girsu Nik 1 102 o. i 4
lugal-ušur$_3$-ra šagan-keš$_2$ ED IIIb Girsu OIP 14 65 o. ii 1
lugal-ušur$_3$-ra niĝir ED IIIb/Lug. 1 Girsu *RTC* 75 o. i 4
lugal-ušur$_3$-ra ED IIIb/Lug. 1 Girsu *RTC* 75 o. iv 3
lugal-ušur$_3$-ra šu-ku$_6$ a du$_{10}$-ga ED IIIb/Ukg. lugal 4 Girsu *TSA* 47 o. iii 8

lugal-ušur$_3$-ra-nu$_2$ $^{(a>3)}$ unkn. mng. 3.1.8, p. 183
lugal-ušur$_3$-ra-nu$_2$ ED IIIb/Ukg. lugal 3 Girsu *AWAS* 68 o. i 8
lugal-ušur$_3$-ra-nu$_2$ lu$_2$ dili ED IIIb/Ukg. lugal 3 Girsu *AWAS* 118 o. i 8
lugal-ušur$_3$-ra-nu$_2$ a-da-ba ED IIIb/Ukg. ensi$_2$ 1 Girsu *AWAS* 119 r. ii 11’
lugal-ušur$_3$-ra-nu$_2$ šu-ku$_6$ ab-ba ED IIIb/X Y 5 Girsu *CTNMC* 2 o. i 3
lugal-ušur$_3$-ra-nu$_2$ ED IIIb/Ukg. lugal 4 Girsu *DP* 1/2 138 o. i 8
lugal-ušur$_3$-ra-nu$_2$ s. Ak-si$_4$ ED IIIb/X Y 3 Girsu *DP* 2/2 351 o. i 3
lugal-ušur$_3$-ra-nu$_2$ a-da-ba ED IIIb/Ukg. ensi$_2$ 1 Girsu MVN 3 2 r. v 6
lugal-⸢ušur$_3^!$(DIB)⸣-ra-nu$_2$ ED IIIb/Ukg. lugal 5 Girsu Nik 1 3 o. vii 14
lugal-ušur$_3$-ra-nu$_2$ a-da-ba, nar ED IIIb/Ukg. ensi$_2$ 1(+X?) Girsu Nik 1 9 r. iii 3

lugal-⌜ušur$_3$⌝-ra-nu$_2$ a-da-ba ED IIIb/Lug. 6 Girsu D. Charpin, *RA* 71 (1977), p. 97–105 r. iv 15
lugal-ušur$_3$-ra-nu$_2$ nu-kiri$_6$ ED IIIb/X Y 5 Girsu *RTC* 39 o. ii 7
lugal-[ušur$_3$-ra-nu$_2$] a-da-[ba] ED IIIb/Lug. 6 Girsu VS 25 11 r. iii 17
lugal-ušur$_3$-ra-nu$_2$ a-da-ba ED IIIb/Lug. 6 Girsu VS 25 71 r. iv 4
lugal-ušur$_3$-ra-nu$_2$ (lu$_2$) [Ur]-⌜^{d}⌝^{še_3}[šer$_7$]-da ED IIIb/Ukg. lugal 2 Girsu VS 27 13 o. i 4

lugal-ušur$_4$(LAL+LAGAB) $^{(a3)}$ unkn. mng. 3.1.8, p. 183
lugal-ušur$_4$ ED IIIb Uruk M. W. Green, *ZA* 72 (1982), p. 163–177 16 o. ii’ 4
lugal-⌜ušur$_4$⌝ CS Adab *SIA* 646 o. ii 2’
lugal-ušur$_4$ [simu]g$^?$ CS Adab *SIA* 951 o. 4

lugal-ušur$_4$-MU $^{(a\geq5)}$ unkn. mng. 3.1.8, p. 183
⌜lugal-ušur$_4$-MU⌝ ED IIIb Adab CUSAS 11 50 o. ii 5
lugal-ušur$_4$-MU ED IIIb-ES Adab CUSAS 11 95 o. i 4
lugal-ušur$_4$-MU ED IIIb-ES Adab CUSAS 11 98 o. ii 5
lugal-ušur$_4$-MU ED IIIb-ES Adab CUSAS 11 100 o. i 4
lugal-ušur$_4$-MU s. Ur-$^{d\ še_3}$šer$_7$-da sukkal ED IIIb-ES Adab CUSAS 11 103 o. i 1
lugal-ušur$_4$-MU ED IIIb-ES Adab CUSAS 11 115 o. i 3
lugal-ušur$_4$-MU ED IIIb-ES Adab CUSAS 11 200 o. i 7
lugal-ušur$_4$-MU ir$_{11}$ Ur-^{d}⌜ĜA$_2$×SIG$_7$$^?$⌝ ED IIIb Nippur TMH 5 20 r. 1
lu:gal-ušur$_4$-MU h. Za$_3$-mu ED IIIb Nippur TMH 5 132 o. ii 2
lu:gal-ušur$_4$-MU ED IIIb Nippur TMH 5 132 r. i 3
lugal-ušur$_4$-MU ED IIIb Umma-Zabala BIN 8 67 o. ii 11
lugal-ušur$_4$-MU ES Adab CUSAS 11 257 o. ii 4
lugal-ušur$_4$-MU ES Adab CUSAS 11 281 o. 2
⌜lugal⌝-ušur$_4$-MU MS-CS Unknown BIN 8 293 r. ii 7

lugal-ušur$_x$(LAL+KU) $^{(a1)}$ unkn. mng. 3.1.8, p. 183
lugal-ušur$_x$(LAL+KU) CS-LS ? Girsu *RTC* 254 r. ii 2

lugal-^{d}Utu $^{(a1)}$ ‘the lugal is (like) Utu’ 3.1.6.2, p. 146, 166 n. 959
lugal-^{d}Utu MS-CS Isin ? MVN 3 81 o. 4

lugal-Utu-gin$_7$-e$_3$ $^{(a\geq1)}$ ‘the lugal goes forth like Utu’ 3.1.7.10, p. 146, 166 n. 959, 173, 211 n. 1347
lugal-Utu-gin$_7$-⌜e$_3$⌝(UD.[DU]) ED IIIb Umma-Zabala CUSAS 14 140 r. 1
lugal-Utu-gin$_7$-[e$_3$] ED IIIb Umma-Zabala CUSAS 14 140 r. 3
lugal-Utu-gin$_7$-e$_3$ ED IIIb Umma-Zabala CUSAS 14 162 o. i 4
lugal-Utu-gin$_7$-e$_3$ ED IIIb Umma-Zabala CUSAS 14 280 r. i 3
lugal-Utu-gin$_7$$^!$-e$_3$ ED IIIb/X Y 28 Umma-Zabala *SAKF* 3 o. iii 5

lugal-uzug$_x$(AN.ZAG)-še$_3$ $^{(a4)}$ ‘the lugal … *towards* the cella’ 3.1.6.4, p. 158 n. 915, 183 n. 1137
lugal-uzug$_x$-še$_3$ nar-gal ED IIIa Šuruppag CUSAS 11 343 o. iii’ 3’
lugal-uzug$_x$-še$_3$ ED IIIa Nippur TMH 5 54 o. iii 3
lugal-uzug$_x$-še$_3$ ED IIIa-b Ur UE 3 512 1
lugal-uzug$_x$-še$_3$ gala ED IIIa-b Unknown K. Volk, *OrNS* 57 (1988), p. 206 o. 1

lugal-za-me $^{(a\geq1)}$ ‘you are (a) lord!’ 3.1.7.1, p. 161
lugal-za-me CS Girsu *RTC* 125 o. ii 5
lugal-za-me CS Girsu *RTC* 126 r. i 8
lugal-za-[me$^?$] sag[i] CS Girsu *STTI* 124 o. 2’
lugal-za-me CS Girsu *STTI* 163 o. 4

lugal-za$_3$ $^{(a1)}$ (abbreviation of the following) 3.1.6.4, p. 158 n. 915

lugal-za$_3$ DU-DU, lu$_2$ Lugal-za$_3$ ugula ES-MS Umma F. Thureau-Dangin, *RA* 8 (1911), p. 158 o. 2

lugal-za$_3$-ge $^{(a1)}$ (abbreviation of the following) 3.1.6.4, p. 158 n. 915
lugal-za$_3$-ge f. Ur-^{d}Nin-ma-da MS-CS Nippur TMH 5 52 r. i 5

lugal-za$_3$-ge-si $^{(a2)}$ 'the lugal is just right for the sanctuary' 3.1.6.4, p. 158 n. 915
lugal-za$_3$-ge-si Mes-ki-gal-la, e[ns]i$_2$ ⸢Adab^{ki}⸣, Lugal-za$_3$-ge-si lugal ED IIIb/Meskigala ensi$_2$ X/Luzag. lugal Adab BIN 8 26 r. ii 6
lugal-za$_3$-ge-si ensi$_2$ Umma^{ki} ED IIIb/Luzag. X E$_{11}$.KI RIME 1.12.7.1 i 3
lugal-za$_3$-ge-si ensi$_2$ Umma^{ki} ED IIIb/Ukg. lugal/Luzag. X Girsu *CIRPL* Ukg. 16 r. iii 11
lugal-za$_3$-ge-si lugal Unug^{ki}-ga, lugal kalam-ma ED IIIb/Luzag. X Nippur BE 1/2 87 i 3
lugal-za$_3$-ge-si (lugal Unug^{ki}-ga, lugal kalam-ma) ED IIIb/Luzag. X Nippur BE 1/2 87 i 38
lugal-za$_3$-ge-si lugal Unug^{ki}-ga, lugal kalam-ma ED IIIb/Luzag. X Nippur BE 1/2 87 iii 3
lugal-za$_3$-ge-si (lugal) ED IIIb/Luzag. Y 1 ? Nippur TMH 5 82 o. 7
lugal-za$_3$-ge-si ensi$_2$ ED IIIb/Luzag. ensi$_2$ X Umma-Zabala BIN 8 82 r. iii 5
lugal-za$_3$-ge-si ensi$_2$ ED IIIb/Luzag. ensi$_2$ 7 Umma-Zabala BIN 8 86 r. i 5
lugal-za$_3$-ge-si ensi$_2$ ⸢Šuruppag^{ki}⸣ CS Unknown MAD 4 168 o. 6

lugal-za$_3$-si $^{(a1)}$ 'the lugal is just right for the sanctuary' 3.1.6.4, p. 158 n. 915
lugal-za$_3$-si s. Lugal-en-nu-ĝu$_{10}$ ED IIIa Šuruppag M. Molina & H. Sanchiz, *StEL* 24 (2007), p. 1–15 2 o. ii 5

lugal-zi $^{(a\geq7)}$ 'the lugal is reliable (?)' or an abbreviation 3.1.8, p. 183 w. n. 1132
lugal-zi ED IIIb-ES Adab CUSAS 11 117 o. ii 5
lugal-zi ED IIIb-ES Adab CUSAS 11 252 o. ii 5
lugal-zi ED IIIb Umma-Zabala M. Powell, *HUCA* 49 (1978), p. 1–58 24 "o." i 5
lugal-zi ED IIIb/Luzag. ensi$_2$ 7 Umma-Zabala M. deJ. Ellis, *JCS* 31 (1979), p. 30–55 7 o. iii 4
lugal-zi ES Adab CUSAS 11 329 o. 2
lugal-zi ES Adab *TCABI* 25 o. i 4
lugal-zi ES Adab *TCABI* 32 o. i 8
lugal-zi CS Adab CUSAS 13 138 r. 1
lugal-zi CS Adab CUSAS 13 151 o. ii 13
lugal-zi CS Adab CUSAS 13 155 o. 3
lugal-zi MS-CS Adab ? MesCiv 4 60 r. 6
lugal-zi CS Adab *SIA* 685+734 o. 6
lugal-zi CS Girsu *DPA* 31 (PUL 23) r. 2
lugal-zi f. NIĜIN$_3$ CS Girsu ITT 2/1 4514 r. 3'
lugal-zi CS Girsu *STTI* 20 r. 3'
lugal-zi CS Girsu *STTI* 151 r. i' 8'
lugal-zi ir$_{11}$ ⸢x⸣-[x] CS Girsu *STTI* 168 o. ii 5'
lugal-zi [s.] (?) Ur-^{d}Iškur CS Girsu *STTI* 180 r. i 2
lugal-zi [p]alil-b[i] MS-CS Nippur OSP 2 49 r. i 7'
lugal-zi p[a]lil-b[i] MS-CS Nippur OSP 2 49 r. ii 7
lugal-zi f. Gala MS-CS Nippur OSP 2 64 r. 4
lugal-zi f. Aš$_{10}$-tar$_2$-*dan*, dub-sar CS-LS Unknown *EGA* 593 (translit. only) 3
lugal-zi f. Amar-su$_4$ MS-CS Unknown L. J. Delaporte, *ZA* 18 (1904), p. 245–256 3 r. 4

lugal-zi-de$_3$? $^{(a1)}$ unkn. mng. 3.1.8, p. 183
⸢lugal$^{?}$-zi⸣-de$_3$? f. [E$_2$-me-nam-nun] ED IIIb/En. I ensi$_2$ Girsu OIP 104 22 o. ii 2

lugal-zi-kalam(LAK729) $^{(al)}$ 'the lugal is the life of the land' 3.1.5.4, p. 137
lugal-zi-kalam umbisaĝ, dub mu-sar ED IIIa Šuruppag *TSŠ* 46 r. ii 5
lugal-zi-kalam ED IIIa Šuruppag *TSŠ* 605 o. i 2
lugal-[zi]-kalam ED IIIa Šuruppag *TSŠ* 605 o. iii 1

lugal-zi-ša$_3$-ĝal$_2$ $^{(al)}$ 'the lugal is one who establishes life' 3.1.5.4, p.136–137, 236
lugal-zi-ša$_3$-ĝal$_2$ nu-kiri$_6$ ED IIIa Šuruppag? MVN 10 82 r. i 3
lugal-zi-ša$_3$-ĝal$_2$ nu-kiri$_6$ ED IIIa Šuruppag? MVN 10 83 o. v 4

lugal-…
lugal-x$^{?}$-NI-SI$^{!?}$ ED I-II Ur UET 2 312 o. ? 1
lugal-x-si-x ? ED I-II Ur UET 2 28 o. i 6
lugal-x-ti ED I-II Ur UET 2 161 o. ii 1
⸢lugal⸣-[x-x] ? ED I-II Ur UET 2 139 o. 1'
lugal-[x] ED I-II Ur UET 2 361 r. 2'
°lugal-⸢x⸣ ED IIIa Abū Ṣalābīḫ *IAS* 462 o. ii 5
°lugal-⸢x⸣ ED IIIa Abū Ṣalābīḫ *IAS* 330 o. iii 4
lugal-⸢x⸣-du$_{10}$ ugula ED IIIa Adab CUSAS 11 6 o. ii 2
lu[gal]-[x-x] ED IIIa Adab CUSAS 11 6 o. i 3
lugal-x-x-(x?) ED IIIa-b Girsu *RTC* 5 r. i 4
lugal-x-da-kuš$_2$ ED IIIa Šuruppag *RTC* 15 r. i 6
⸢lugal$^{?}$⸣-x-ku$_3$ dam-gar$_3$, ⸢lu$_2$ aša$_5$ sa$_{10}$⸣ ED IIIa Šuruppag? G. Visicato & A. Westenholz, *Gs Cagni*, p. 1107–1133 4 (translit. only) r. ii 1
⸢lugal-x-si⸣ ? ED IIIa Šuruppag *TSŠ* 135 o. i 3
lugal-[x-(x)]-zi ED IIIa Šuruppag *TSŠ* 60 o. iii 5
lugal-⸢x⸣ ED IIIa Šuruppag CUSAS 11 368 r. i 3
lugal-x-[(x)] ED IIIa Šuruppag CUSAS 11 341 o. i' 9
lugal-⸢x⸣-[x] AN-nu-me ED IIIa Šuruppag *TSŠ* 14 o. v 5
lugal-x PN? ⸢Ur-Dumu-zi⸣, ugula, Lugal-⸢x⸣ ED IIIa Šuruppag *WF* 78 o. ii 5'
lugal-⸢x⸣-[x] E$_2$-saḫar-ta, šu-ku$_6$ ED IIIa Šuruppag *NTSŠ* 444 obv v 1
lugal-[(x)]-⸢x⸣ ^{d}GIR$_3$$^{?}$-me ED IIIa Šuruppag ("gekauft") *WF* 138 o. ii 4
lugal-⸢x⸣ ED IIIa Umma-Zabala CUSAS 11 348 o. ii 3
lugal-x-E$_2$-x GAG.TAR ED IIIa-b Unknown *L'uomo* 3 r. i 7
⸢lugal-x⸣-ĜA$_2$ ED IIIb Adab MVN 3 28 r. iii 11
lugal-[x(-x)]-ḫul$_2$ ED IIIb-ES Adab CUSAS 11 98 o. i 3'
lugal-[(x)]-lum-[x] ED IIIb Adab CUSAS 11 32 o. i 5
lugal-[x-x]-NI ED IIIb-ES Adab CUSAS 11 115 o. i 2
lugal-[x]-šu ED IIIb Adab CUSAS 11 50 o. iv 5
lugal-CUSAS11-X$_4$-⸢x⸣ ED IIIb-ES Adab CUSAS 11 101 o. ii 2
lugal-⸢x-x⸣ ED IIIb Adab BIN 8 8 r. i 4
lugal-[x] ED IIIb Adab CUSAS 11 29 o. ii 2
lugal-[x] ED IIIb Adab CUSAS 11 42 r. ii 3
lugal-[x] ED IIIb Adab CUSAS 11 58 o. i 2
lugal-[x] ED IIIb-ES Adab CUSAS 11 82 o. ii 3
lugal-[x(-x)] ED IIIb-ES Adab CUSAS 11 186 o. i 10
lugal-[x] ED IIIb-ES Adab CUSAS 11 186 r. i 14
°lu[gal]-[x-(x)] ED IIIb Ebla MEE 3 59 o. ii 7
lugal-⸢x⸣ ED IIIb Girsu ITT 5 9201 o. i 4
lugal-⸢x⸣ ED IIIb Girsu ITT 5 9208 r. (?) i 1
lugal-⸢x⸣-NI-[x] ED IIIb/En. I ensi$_2$ Girsu OIP 104 22 r. iv 45
⸢lugal⸣-[x-x] sipa ED IIIb Girsu *DP* suppl. 594 r. ii 2
lugal-[x-x] ED IIIb Girsu ITT 5 9202 r. i 5
lugal-[(x)]-⸢x⸣ ED IIIb Girsu *RTC* 18 ii 6

lugal-⸢x⸣-[x(-x)] s[ipa x x] ED IIIb/X Y 4 Girsu *RTC* 22 r. ii 1
lugal-⸢x⸣ gal-dam-gar$_3$ ED IIIb/Ukg. lugal 2 Girsu VS 14 43 r. i 3
lugal-[x(-x)] b. [x-x] ED IIIb Isin BIN 8 80 o. ii 10'
lugal-⸢x⸣-DU ED IIIb Nippur TMH 5 18 o. 2
lugal-[x]-DU ED IIIb Nippur TMH 5 167 r. iii 2'
lugal-⸢x⸣-NI ED IIIb Nippur OSP 1 138 o. iii 2
lugal-(x)-U$_2$-X ED IIIb Nippur AS 17 42 2'
lugal-[x-x]-du$_{10}$ ED IIIb Nippur OSP 1 25 "iii" 10'
lugal-⸢x-x⸣-ša$_3$ ED IIIb Nippur OSP 1 25 "iii" 9'
lugal-[x]-⸢x⸣ ED IIIb Nippur OSP 1 27 o. ii' 13'
lugal-[x] ED IIIb Nippur OSP 1 29 r. i 9
lugal-[x] ED IIIb Nippur OSP 1 29 r. i 10
lugal-[x] ED IIIb Nippur OSP 1 29 r. i 12
⸢lugal⸣-[x] ED IIIb Nippur OSP 1 99 o. i 5
⸢lugal⸣-[x(-x)] ED IIIb Nippur OSP 1 100 o. ii 4
lugal-⸢x⸣ ED IIIb Nippur OSP 1 142 r. 1
⸢lugal⸣-[x(-x)] ED IIIb Nippur TMH 5 9 o. iii 9
lugal-[x] ED IIIb Nippur TMH 5 12 r. 1
lugal-[x] ED IIIb Nippur TMH 5 14 o. i 1'
lugal-⸢x⸣-[(x)] ED IIIb Nippur TMH 5 36 o. ii 4
⸢lu:gal⸣-[x] ED IIIb Nippur TMH 5 41 r. i 1'
lu:gal-[x] ED IIIb Nippur TMH 5 45 o. ii 1'
⸢lugal⸣-[x]-⸢x⸣ ED IIIb Nippur TMH 5 93 r. 1
lugal-[x] ED IIIb Nippur TMH 5 125 o. 3
lugal-[x-x] ED IIIb Nippur TMH 5 164 o. ii 5
lugal-[x(-x)] ED IIIb Nippur TMH 5 203 o. 5
lugal-x-da ED IIIb/Meannedu 5 Umma T. Ozaki, *JAC* 23 (2008), p. 55–64 1 o. iii 4
lugal-⸢x⸣-NI ED IIIb Umma-Zabala CUSAS 14 94 o. ii 1
lugal-x-su ED IIIb/Luzag. ensi$_2$ 7 Umma-Zabala M. deJ. Ellis, *JCS* 31 (1979), p. 30–55 7 o. i 8
lugal-x-x-zi ?? ED IIIb Umma-Zabala M. Powell, *HUCA* 49 (1978), p. 1–58 13 r. i 1'
lugal-⸢x⸣-[(x)] (PN ?) ED IIIb Umma-Zabala ? BIN 8 52 o. 3
lugal-[x(-x)] ED IIIb/Luzag. ensi$_2$ X Umma-Zabala BIN 8 82 o. vi 6'
lugal-x-x ED IIIb Umma-Zabala CUSAS 14 4 r. i 2
lugal-⸢x⸣ ED IIIb Umma-Zabala CUSAS 14 118 o. ii 6
lugal-[x] ED IIIb Umma-Zabala CUSAS 14 118 o. ii 8
lugal-[x] ED IIIb Umma-Zabala CUSAS 14 118 r. i 1
lugal-⸢x⸣-[(x)] ED IIIb Umma-Zabala CUSAS 14 149 o. i 5
lugal-⸢x-x-x⸣ ED IIIb Umma-Zabala CUSAS 14 221 o. ii 1
lugal-⸢x⸣ ED IIIb Umma-Zabala CUSAS 14 223 r. i 9
lugal-⸢x⸣ ED IIIb-ES B. R. Foster, *Fs Westenholz*, 127–137 6 o. ii 4
lugal-[x-x] ED IIIb Umma-Zabala M. Powell, *HUCA* 49 (1978), p. 1–58 21 o. ii 2
lugal-⸢x⸣ ED IIIb Umma-Zabala M. Powell, *HUCA* 49 (1978), p. 1–58 23 o. ii 7
lugal-[x-x] ugula ? ED IIIb/Luzag. ensi$_2$ 7 Umma-Zabala M. deJ. Ellis, *JCS* 31 (1979), p. 30–55 6 o. i 6
lugal-[x-x] ED IIIb/Luzag. ensi$_2$ 7 Umma-Zabala M. deJ. Ellis, *JCS* 31 (1979), p. 30–55 6 r. i 1
lugal-x$^?$-du$_{10}$ ED IIIb Ur UET 2 suppl. 46 r. ii 6
lugal-⸢x-x⸣-e$_3$ ED IIIb Ur UET 2 suppl. 41 o. 5
lugal-x-da-x maškim-bi ED IIIb/Luzag. (?) Y 7 Zabala BIN 8 61 o. i 5
⸢lugal⸣-[x-x] ED IIIb Unknown TIM 9 98 o. 14
lugal-[x] ED IIIb-ES Unknown *L'uomo* 8 o. iii 4'

[lu]gal-[x] ED IIIb-ES Unknown *L'uomo* 8 o. iii 8'
⸢lugal⸣-[x]-⸢ŠIR.TI⸣ ⸢saĝa Isin[ki]-ke$_4$⸣ ES Adab *TCABI* 41 o. i 5
lugal-⸢x⸣ ES Adab CUSAS 13 2 r. 6
lugal-[x(-x)] b. Igi-⸢su$_4$[?]⸣ ES Adab *TCABI* 61 o. iii 4
⸢lugal⸣-[x(-x)] ES Adab *TCABI* 61 o. iii 10
lugal-[x(-x)] ES-MS Adab *TCABI* 64 r. iii 6
lugal-[x] f. (?) A-ba-[[d]En-lil$_2$[?]] ES-MS Isin ? MAD 4 152 o. ii 5
⸢lugal⸣-[x] ES-MS Isin ? MAD 4 152 o. ii 9
lugal-[x(-x)] ES Isin ? *TCVBI* 1-55 edge
⸢lugal⸣-[x-x] ES-MS Nippur OSP 1 23 o. iii 1''
lugal-[x] ES-MS Nippur OSP 1 23 o. vi 5
⸢lu:gal⸣-[x] ES Nippur OSP 1 31 o. iii 5'
⸢lu:gal⸣-[x] ES Nippur OSP 1 31 r. i 2
lugal-[x-x] ES Sippar ? OIP 104 41 o. ix 3'
lugal-[x] ES-MS Umma Nik 2 14 o. i 9'
lugal-[x-(x)] f. Ur-[ĝiš]gigir$_2$ ES Unknown *EGA* 230 pl. 17 fig. 293
lugal-⸢x-x⸣-e CS Adab CUSAS 13 137 r. 1
lugal-x-gi CS Adab *SIA* 677 o. 11
lugal-x-KAR CS Adab *SIA* 685+734 o. 18
lugal-x-x CS Adab CUSAS 13 62 o. 11
lugal-[x(-x)] CS Adab CUSAS 13 152 r. 2
lugal-[x(-x)] CS Adab CUSAS 13 66 o. 10
lugal-[x(-x)] MS-CS Adab CUSAS 13 3 r. 6'
lugal-[x] aga$_3$-us$_2$ MS-CS Adab CUSAS 13 38 o. 6
lugal-[x] CS Adab CUSAS 13 12 r. 5
l[u]gal-[x] CS Adab CUSAS 13 124 r. 3'
lugal-x CS Adab CUSAS 13 108 o. 11
lugal-⸢x⸣ CS Adab CUSAS 13 62 r. 11
lugal-⸢x⸣ CS Adab CUSAS 13 69 o. 6
lugal-[x] CS Adab OIP 14 78 o. iii' 8
lugal-[x] CS Adab OIP 14 78 o. iii' 13
lugal-[x] ni-is-ku MS-CS Adab OIP 14 138 o. 2
lugal-[x] sipa anše CS Adab *SIA* 639 o. ii 3
lugal-[x] CS Adab *SIA* 640 o. ii 1
lugal-[x(-x)] CS Adab *SIA* 640 r. i 1
lugal-⸢x⸣ CS Adab *SIA* 640 r. i 2
lugal-⸢x⸣-[x] s. Da-d[a[?]] MS-CS Adab *SIA* 705 o. ii 1
lugal-[x-(x)] f. Ur-PA MS-CS Adab *SIA* 705 r. i 12
lugal-[x(-x)] MS Adab *TCABI* 190 o. 3*
lugal-⸢x⸣ MS-CS Adab *TCABI* 196 o. ii 7
lugal-[x] MS-CS Adab *TCABI* 196 o. ii 8
⸢lugal-x⸣-[x] CS Adab *TCABI* 202 o. 5
⸢lugal-x-x⸣ CS Adab *TCABI* 202 r. 3
⸢lugal[?]⸣-[x-x] ? lu$_2$ Kin-⸢du$_3$[?]⸣ CS Adab *TCABI* 213 r. 3
lugal-[x(-x)] CS Adab *TCABI* 249 o. 4
lugal-x-DU ? f. Ur-[d]KA.DI CS Girsu MVN 3 113 r. iii 25'
lugal-x[?]-IG-X? CS Girsu ITT 2/1 3150 r. 10'
lugal-x-ni[?] Šu-na lu$_2$ Lugal-⸢x⸣-n[i[?]] CS Girsu *STTI* 105 o. 3'
lugal-⸢x⸣ dub-⸢sar⸣ CS Girsu *RTC* 177 Seal: 1
lugal-⸢x-x⸣ CS Girsu ? *DCS* 45 r. 1
lugal-⸢x⸣-([x]) CS Girsu ITT 1 1040 o. 4'
lugal-[x] CS Girsu ITT 1 1089 o. 1'

lugal-[x] CS Girsu ITT 1 1288 r. 1
lugal-[x] Ur-^{d}⸢K⸣[A.DI$^{?}$], ir$_{11}$ Lugal-[x] CS Girsu ITT 1 1463 o. 2’
lugal-[x] CS Girsu ITT 1 1472 o. ii 10’
lugal-⸢x⸣-[(x)] dub-sar CS Girsu ITT 1 1474 r. 1
lugal-[x] CS Girsu ITT 2/1 3130 r. 2
lugal-[x] CS Girsu ITT 2/1 4516 r. 6
lugal-[x-x] s. [x-x] CS Girsu MVN 3 113 r. ii 13’
lugal-[x-x] ki ga-[eš$_{8}$] CS Girsu *RTC* 91 r. i’ 4’
lugal-[x-x] nu-⸢banda$_{3}$⸣ CS Girsu *RTC* 92 r. i 1’
lugal-⸢x⸣ Ur-^{d}Ab-u$_{2}$, ⸢lu$_{2}$⸣ Lugal-⸢x⸣ CS Girsu *RTC* 94 o. 4’
lugal-⸢x⸣ ⸢ugula$^{?}$⸣ CS-LS ? Girsu *RTC* 239 r. i 4
lugal-⸢x⸣-[(x)] Umma^{ki} CS-LS ? Girsu *RTC* 254 o. iii 16
lugal-⸢x-x-x⸣ CS Girsu *RTC* 256 r. 8’
lugal-[x] f. U$_{2}$-t[a$_{2}$] CS Girsu *STTI* 164 r. i 4’
lugal-⸢x⸣ CS Girsu *STTI* 167 o. ii 6’
lugal-[x(-x)] CS Girsu *STTI* 178 o. ii 3’
lugal-x-da CS/Škś Isin B. R. Foster, *WO* 13 (1982), p. 15–24 6 o. 1
⸢lugal⸣-[x-x] MS-CS Isin ? BIN 8 158 o. ii 8’
lugal-[x] MS-CS Lagaš BiMes 3 24 r. 2
lugal-[x(-x)] ⸢ĝuruš⸣ MS-CS Mesag BIN 8 148 o. iii 15’
lugal-[x(-x)] s. [x-x] MS-CS Mesag BIN 8 148 o. iii 18’
lugal-⸢x-x⸣ Lugal-KA, ir$_{11}$ Lugal-⸢x-x⸣ n[ar$^{?}$] MS-CS Mesag BIN 8 267 r. ii 9
lugal-[x-x] CS Mesag BIN 8 273 r. i 8
lugal-[x(-x)] MS-CS Nippur OSP 2 14 o. ii 3’
lugal-[x(-x)] CS Nippur OSP 2 15 r. (?) 7’
lugal-[x] s. E$_{2}$-da MS-CS Nippur OSP 2 50 r. i 1
lugal-[x] MS-CS Nippur OSP 2 56 o. ii 4
lugal-[x] MS-CS Nippur OSP 2 80 r. i 7
⸢lugal⸣-[x-x] MS-CS Nippur OSP 2 86 r. i 8
lugal-[x] MS-CS Nippur OSP 2 87 o. 5
lugal-[x(-x)] MS-CS Nippur OSP 2 90 o. ii 13
lugal-[x] lu$_{2}$-bala MS-CS Nippur OSP 2 90 r. i 1’
lugal-[x] MS-CS Nippur OSP 2 91 o. 1’
⸢lugal⸣-[x] MS-CS Nippur OSP 2 91 o. 6’
lugal-[x] MS-CS Nippur OSP 2 93 o. ii 2’
⸢lugal⸣-[x] lu$_{2}$ [x] MS-CS Nippur OSP 2 93 o. ii 8’
lugal-[x] MS-CS Nippur OSP 2 93 o. i 9’
lugal-⸢x⸣-[(x)] MS-CS Nippur OSP 2 94 o. ii 3
lugal-[x(-x)] MS-CS Nippur OSP 2 95 r. ii 2’
lugal-[x] MS-CS Nippur OSP 2 96 o. i 15
lugal-⸢x⸣ MS-CS Nippur OSP 2 98 o. i 11
lugal-[x] MS-CS Nippur OSP 2 98 o. ii 1
lugal-[x] f. [U]r-⸢lugal$^{?}$⸣ CS/Škś Y 2 Nippur OSP 2 100 r. i 2’
lugal-[x] CS/Škś Y 2 Nippur OSP 2 100 r. i 5’
lu:gal-[x] MS-CS Nippur OSP 2 102 r. i’ 9’
lugal-[x-x] MS-CS Nippur OSP 2 118 r. 3’
⸢lugal⸣-[x(-x)] s. (?) [U]r$^{?}$-^{d}[x] MS-CS Nippur OSP 2 159 r. 5’
lugal-[x-(x)] saĝ-[sug$_{5}$$^{?}$] MS-CS Nippur PBS 9 28+34 r. i’ 1’
lugal-[x(-x)] s. [x-x-x] CS Nippur PBS 9 36 o. iii’ 9’
lugal-[x(-x)] MS-CS Nippur PBS 9 39 o. ii 6’
⸢lugal⸣-[x(-x)] MS-CS Nippur PBS 9 39 o. iii 2’
lugal-[x] MS-CS Nippur PBS 9 42 o. i 1’

lugal-⸢x-x-x⸣ MS-CS Nippur PBS 9 42 o. i 6’
lugal-[x(-x)] MS-CS Nippur PBS 9 42 o. i 13’
lugal-[x(-x)] MS-CS Nippur PBS 9 50 o. 7’
lugal-[x(-x)] CS Nippur PBS 9 77 o. iii 4’
lugal-[x] MS-CS Nippur TMH 5 29 o. iii 8’
lugal-[x-x] ugula-[bi] MS-CS Nippur TMH 5 29 o. iii 9’
⸢lugal⸣-[x-x] MS-CS Nippur TMH 5 29 o. iii 14’
⸢lugal⸣-[x(-x)] MS-CS Nippur TMH 5 29 r. ii 4’
⸢lugal⸣-[x(-x)] MS-CS Nippur TMH 5 29 r. ii 6’
lugal-[x(-x)] MS-CS Nippur TMH 5 29 r. ii 16’
⸢lugal⸣-[x] s. ⸢Lugal⸣-[x-(x)] MS-CS Nippur TMH 5 52 o. ii 6
⸢lugal⸣-[x-(x)] f. ⸢Lugal⸣-[x] MS-CS Nippur TMH 5 52 o. ii 7
lugal-[x] ugula CS Nippur TMH 5 186+202 o. ii 15’
lugal-⸢x-x⸣ MS-CS Nippur TMH 5 191 o. 14
lugal-[x]-da CS Sippar ? CT 44 48 r. 8
lugal-⸢x⸣ KA.GUR$_7$ MS-CS Susa MDP 14 19 r. 7
lugal-[x] CS ? Susa MDP 14 20 r. 2
lugal-[x] CS ? Susa MDP 14 20 r. 4
lugal-⸢x⸣ MS-CS Susa MDP 14 42 r. i’ 3’
lugal-x-mu-x MS-CS Umma *USP* 40 o. 4
lugal-x-na CS/Śkś Y 2 Umma CT 50 53 o. 7
lugal-⸢x⸣-N[E] CS Umma T. Donald, *MCS* 9 (1964) 238 o. ii 2
lugal-[x-x] MS-CS Umma BIN 8 323 r. 3
lugal-⸢x⸣ šitim, *be-lu bu-dim*, *in* Umma^{ki} CS Umma CT 50 188 r. i 6
lugal-[x] šitim, *be-lu bu-dim*, *in* Umma^{ki} CS Umma CT 50 188 r. i 17
lugal-[x] šitim, *be-lu bu-dim*, *in* Umma^{ki} CS Umma CT 50 188 r. i 18
lugal-⸢x⸣-[x] CS Umma MAD 4 32 r. 3’
[lu]gal-[x] (ugula) MS-CS Umma MAD 4 167 (translit. only) r. 3
lugal-[x] Ur-^{d}Nin-⸢x⸣-[x], lu$_2$ Lugal-[x] MS-CS Umma MesCiv 4 30 r. i 5
lugal-[x(-x)] CS Umma Nik 2 76 o. ii 7
lugal-⸢x⸣-[(x)] ES-MS Umma ? *SAKF* 1 r. 1
lugal-[x] ens[i$_2$-gal] MS-CS Umma ? *TCVC* 726 o. iii 10
lugal-⸢x⸣-[(x)] s. MIR-[x] MS-CS Umma ? *TCVC* 729 r. 4’
lugal-[x] f. Ur-en-[x] MS-CS Umma ? *TCVC* 729 r. 9’
lugal-[x(-x)] CS Umma *USP* 22 o. ii 1
lugal-[x(-x)] CS Umma *USP* 22 o. ii 3
lugal-[x(-x)] CS Umma *USP* 45 o. ii 20
lugal-⸢x⸣-[(x)] f. Ur-[x] CS Umma *USP* 45 r. i 4
lugal-[x-(x)] f. Ur-^{d}Dumu-[zi$^{?}$] CS Umma *USP* 45 r. i 24
lugal-⸢x-x⸣ s. Ur-mes, ir$_{11}$ Lugal-⸢iti⸣ CS Umma *USP* 50 o. 1
lugal-x-LA/RA-ni CS Ur UE 2 pl. 206 no. 201 1
lugal-x-x CS Ur UE 2 pl. 205 no. 181 2
lugal-[x-x] MS-CS Ur UET 2 suppl. 32 o. 6’
⸢lugal⸣-⸢x⸣-[(x)] MS-CS Ur UET 2 suppl. 48 o. ii 3
⸢lugal⸣-⸢(x$^{?}$)-x⸣-[(x)] MS-CS Ur UET 2 suppl. 48 o. ii 4
lugal-⸢x⸣-maḫ CS Unknown CUSAS 13 181 o. 5
lugal-⸢x⸣ (N[UN$^{?}$]) MS-CS Unknown MesCiv 4 68 o. 6
lugal-⸢x⸣ [li]bir(-me) CS Unknown CUSAS 13 179 r. 3’
lugal-[x] Ur-zu, ir$_{11}$ Lugal-[x], šitim(-me) CS Unknown CUSAS 13 200 o. 2
lugal-[x] ir$_{11}$ KA-[x], šitim(-me) CS Unknown CUSAS 13 200 o. 3
lugal-[x] MS-CS Unknown CT 50 77 r. 1’

lugal-[x(-x)] CS Unknown W. Sommerfeld, K. Markina & N. Roudik, *Gs Diakonoff*, 225–231 8 r. 6'
lugal-[x(-x)] s. DU-DU MS-CS Unknown MVN 3 64 o. ii 3'
lugal-[x-(x)] f. Ur-^{d}Nin-⌈ĝir$_2$⌉-su MS-CS Unknown MVN 3 64 o. ii 6'
lugal-[x(-x)] s. DU-[x] MS-CS Unknown MVN 3 64 o. ii 9'
lugal-[x-(x)] s. Lugal-[x-(x)] MS-CS Unknown MVN 3 64 r. i 8
lugal-[x-(x)] f. Lugal-[x-(x)] MS-CS Unknown MVN 3 64 r. i 9
lugal-[x(-x)] MS-CS Unknown T. Ozaki, SANTAG 7 4 o. 11
lugal-[x(-x)] ugula e$_2$-[(x$^?$-x$^?$)] MS-CS Unknown T. Ozaki, SANTAG 7 4 r. 7
lugal-[x] CS Unknown T. Ozaki, SANTAG 7 62 o. ii 12

maš-lugal (a≥3/°1) 'goat('s kid) of the lugal' 3.1.1.1, p.84, 229, 247 n. 1453
maš-lugal ED I-II Ur UET 2 53 o. ii 6
°maš-lugal ED IIIa Šuruppag *SF* 28 o. ii 4
°maš-lugal ED IIIa Šuruppag *SF* 29 o. i 13
maš-lugal ED IIIa Šuruppag *SF* 62 o. vi 2'
maš-lugal ED IIIa Šuruppag *TSŠ* 467 o. i 3
maš-lugal ^{d}Ad-DU ED IIIa Šuruppag *WF* 74 r. ii 9
maš-lugal ED IIIa Šuruppag *WF* 100 o. iii 8
maš-lugal s. Lugal-ezem ED IIIa-b Isin (?) OIP 104 14 o. iii 6

nam-lugal-ni (a1) (abbreviation of the following) 3.1.1.1, p. 83
nam-lugal-ni MS Adab *TCABI* 78 r. 5

nam-lugal-ni-du$_{10}$ (a2) 'his kingship is good' 3.1.1.1, p. 83
nam-[lu]gal-ni-du$_{10}$ ED IIIb Girsu ? BIN 8 12 r. ii 3
nam-lugal-ni-du$_{10}$ ED IIIb/En. I ensi$_2$ 4 Lagaš BiMes 3 10 r. iii 3

^{d}Nanše-ama-Lugal-AN-da (a1) 'Nanše is the mother of LugalANda' 3.1.6.2, p. 87 n. 436, 141 n. 788
^{d}Nanše-ama-Lugal-AN-da muḫaldim ED IIIb/Lug. 6 Girsu *DP* 2/1 157 o. i 8
^{d}Nanše-ama-Lugal-AN-da muḫaldim ED IIIb/Lug. 5 Girsu *RTC* 53 o. i 7
^{d}Nanše-ama-Lugal-AN-da muḫaldim ED IIIb/Lug. 5(+1?) Girsu VS 25 14 o. i 8

nu-gal (a≥3) (phonetic for lugal) 3.1.8, p. 183 w. n. 1133, 237
nu-gal f. *Ip-lul-Il$_3$*, dub-sar, lu$_2$-gan$_2$-gid$_2$-da ES/Man. Unknown (MO) OIP 104 40 C xiv' 8
nu-gal f. *Ip-lul-Il$_3$*, ff. *I-da-Il$_3$*, ĝuruš, Mar$_2$-da^{ki}, abba$_2$.abba$_2$ gan$_2$ ES/Man. Unknown (MO) OIP 104 40 C xvii' 29
nu-gal (PN?) MS-CS Adab CUSAS 13 11 o. 3
nu-gal ? CS Gasur HSS 10 158 r. i 5
nu-gal *ša-at* Nu-gal MS-CS Mesag E. Salgues, *Fs Westenholz*, 253–272 (RBC 2631) o. ii 7

nu-gal-AŠ$_2$-DA (a1) unkn. mng. 3.1.8, p. 183
nu-gal-AŠ$_2$-DA nar-nar Ma-ri$_2^{ki}$ ED IIIb Ebla A. Archi, *MARI* 4 (1985), p. 63–83 126 (translit. only) o. x 16bis

°nu-gal-en-nam-gal-ga (°1) (phonetic for lugal-inim-kalag) 3.1.1.4, p. 94 n. 481
°nu-gal-en-nam-gal-ga ED IIIb Ebla ARET 5 24 r. i 1

°nu-gal-ḫi-gal (°1) (phonetic for lugal-ḫe$_2$-ĝal$_2$) 3.1.5.3, p. 134
°nu-gal-ḫi-gal ED IIIb Ebla ARET 5 24 r. i 2

°nu-gal-ḪI-zi (°1) (phonetic for lugal-šer$_7$-zi (ḪI=šar$_2$) ? Compare lugal-ḪI-zi) 3.1.8, p. 183 w. n. 1135
°nu-gal-ḪI-zi ED IIIb Ebla ARET 5 24 r. ii 3

°nu-gal-me-'a$_3$-ma (°1) (phonetic for lugal-men$_x$-am/lugal-me-am) 3.1.1.3, p. 88 n. 445

°nu-gal-me-'a_3-ma ED IIIb Ebla ARET 5 24 r. ii 1

°nu-gal-me-ga-šu-u_3 (°1) (phonetic for lugal-mu-da-kuš) 3.1.4.1, p. 124
°nu-gal-me-ga-šu-u_3 ED IIIb Ebla ARET 5 24 r. i 5

nu-gal-mu-da-kaš$_2$ (a1) (phonetic for lugal-mu-da-kuš) 3.1.4.1, p. 124, 187
nu-gal-mu-da-kaš$_2$ nar tur Ma-ri$_2^{ki}$ ED IIIb Ebla ARET 1 7 r. i 24

°nu-gal-nam-URU (°1) (phonetic for lugal-nam-nir) 3.1.1.6, p. 100 n. 527
°nu-gal-nam-URU ED IIIb Ebla ARET 5 24 r. i 3

°nu-gal-nam-URU-šu-ma (°1) (phonetic for lugal-nam-nir-šum$_2$-ma) 3.1.1.6, p. 100 n. 527
°nu-gal-nam-URU-šu-ma ED IIIb Ebla ARET 5 24 r. i 4

nu-gal-NI-zi (a1) unkn. mng. 3.1.8, p. 183 w. n. 1136
nu-gal-NI-zi nar tur Ma-ri$_2^{ki}$ ED IIIb Ebla ARET 1 7 r. i 20
nu-gal-NI-zi nar-nar Ma-ri$_2^{ki}$ ED IIIb Ebla A. Archi, *MARI* 4 (1985), p. 63–83 126 (translit. only) o. x 16bis

°nu-gal-pa$_2$-da (°1) (phonetic for lugal-pa$_3$-da) 3.1.6.2, p. 145 n. 817
°nu-gal-pa$_2$-da ED IIIb Ebla ARET 5 24 r. ii 2

nu-gal-zi-ga (a1) unkn. mng. 3.1.8, p. 183 w. n. 1137
nu-gal-zi-ga nar tur Ma-ri$_2^{ki}$ ED IIIb Ebla ARET 1 7 r. i 6
nu-gal-zi-ga nar-nar Ma-ri$_2^{ki}$ ED IIIb Ebla A. Archi, *MARI* 4 (1985), p. 63–83 126 (translit. only) o. x 16bis

UD-lugal-le (PN?) (a1) unkn. mng. 3.1.8, p. 183
UD-lugal-le ES-MS Ur UET 2 suppl. 3 o. i' 1'

Umma$_2$(ḪI×DIŠ)^{ki}-lugal (a1) 'Umma is lord' 3.1.1.5, p. 95
Umma$_2^{ki}$-lugal ED IIIb Umma-Zabala BIN 8 111 o. ii 1
Umma$_2^{ki}$-lugal apin-u[s$_2^{?}$] ED IIIb/Luzag. ensi$_2$ [x] Umma-Zabala J. A. Brinkman, *Fs Kramer*, pl. III*-V* (W 2/7) o. i 17'

Umma$_2$(ḪI×DIŠ)^{ki}-lugal-ĝu$_{10}$ (a1) 'Umma is my lord' 3.1.1.5, p. 95, 259
Umma$_2$-lugal-ĝu$_{10}$ ED IIIb/Luzag. ensi$_2$ [x] Umma-Zabala J. A. Brinkman, *Fs Kramer*, pl. III*-V* (W 2/7) o. ii 12'

ur-lugal (a>15) '*man* of the lugal' 3.1.1.1, p. 63, 71, 81, 85, 86, 127 n. 695, 175 n. 1028, 229, 261
ur-lugal ED I-II Ur UET 2 6 o. i 2
ur-lugal ED I-II Ur UET 2 41 o. i 2'
ur-lugal ? ED I-II Ur UET 2 81a o. ii 3
u[r]-⸢lugal⸣ ED I-II Ur UET 2 266 o. 1
ur-lugal saĝ-nar$_x$ engar ED IIIa Šuruppag *WF* 77 l.e. 14
ur-lugal saĝa ED IIIb Adab BIN 8 6 o. i 3
ur-lugal kuš$_7$ ED IIIb Adab BIN 8 6 o. i 5
ur-lugal saĝa ED IIIb Adab BIN 8 211 o. i 4
ur-lugal kuš$_7$ ED IIIb Adab BIN 8 211 o. i 7
ur-lugal s. KA-TAR ED IIIb/Ukg. lugal Girsu ? *DP* 1/1 32 v 23
ur-lugal kuš$_7$ ED IIIb Isin BIN 8 37 o. i 2
ur-lugal ED IIIb-ES Isin BIN 8 39 r. ii 3
ur-lugal ED IIIb-ES Isin BIN 8 39 r. ii 7
ur-lugal sipa anše-k(e$_4$) ED IIIb Isin BIN 8 173 o. 7
ur-lugal ED IIIb-ES Isin MVN 3 13 o. iv 11
ur-lugal ED IIIb-ES Isin MVN 3 105 o. ii 4
ur-lugal ED IIIb Nippur TMH 5 4 o. ii 2
[u]r-lu:gal ? ED IIIb Nippur TMH 5 31 o. i 3
[u]r-lu:gal ? ED IIIb Nippur TMH 5 31 o. iii 9

ur-lugal ? ED IIIb Nippur TMH 5 56 o. iii 1
ur-lugal ED IIIb Nippur TMH 5 167 o. ii 4
ur-lugal h. Ar_3 (FPN?), niĝir ED IIIb Unknown BIN 8 28 o. ii 1
ur-lugal ES Nippur OSP 1 31 o. ii 3'
ur-lugal ES-MS Nippur OSP 1 120 o. i' 1
[ur$^?$]-lugal ? maškim-bi ES-MS Umma *CHÉU* 53 o. 6
ur-lugal ad-kup_4 MS-CS Adab CUSAS 13 13 r. 1
ur-lugal CS Adab CUSAS 13 65 r. 4'
ur-lugal CS Adab *SIA* 685+734 o. 21
ur-lugal CS Girsu *DPA* 40 (PUL 30) r. 5
ur-lugal s. Lugal-ḫ[$e_2^?$] CS Girsu MVN 3 113 o. iii 13
ur-lugal Ur-An-$šar_2$, Lugal-mas-su_2, lu_2 di-da Ur-lugal-me MS-CS Isin ? BIN 8 153 o. 6
ur-lugal MS-CS Isin BIN 8 155 o. 1
ur-⸢lugal⸣ MS-CS Isin BIN 8 157 o. 1
ur-lugal CS/NS. Isin BIN 8 164 o. 1
ur-lugal CS/NS. Isin BIN 8 164 r. 11'
ur-lugal CS Nippur ? BIN 8 177 r. 5
ur-lugal MS-CS Nippur OSP 2 95 r. ii 1''
[u]r-⸢lugal$^?$⸣ s. Lugal-[x] CS/Śkś Y 2 Nippur OSP 2 100 r. i 1'
ur-lugal s. Inim-ma-ni-zi MS-CS Nippur TMH 5 52 o. ii 10
ur-lugal CS/NS. Unknown BIN 8 162 o. 3
ur-lugal nar MS-CS Unknown BIN 8 253 o. 4
ur-lugal b. Lugal-ĝiš MS-CS Unknown B. R. Foster, *JCS* 35 (1983), p. 147–175 11 o. 5
°ur-lugal LS-Ur III Unknown M. E. Cohen, *Fs Hallo*, p. 79–86 (YBC 2124) iv 13

ur-^{d}Lugal$^!$-ba-$gara_2$? (a1) '*man* of Lugalbagara (?)' 3.1.1.1, p. 85 n. 420
ur-^{d}Lugal$^!$-ba-$gara_2$? ED IIIa-b Isin (?) OIP 104 14 r. ii 1

ur-^{d}Lugal-ban_3-da (a2) '*man* of Lugalbanda' 3.1.1.1, p. 85 n. 420
ur-^{d}Lugal-ban_3-da bir_3 suḫ$_5$-ḫa ED IIIb/Ukg. lugal 6 Girsu *DP* 1/2 135 o. i 10
ur-^{d}Lugal-ban_3-da Šeš-tur, ugula-bi ED IIIb/Ukg. lugal 6 Girsu *DP* 1/2 135 o. vi 6
ur-^{d}Lugal-ban_3-da CS Adab *SIA* 879 o. 3

ur-^{d}Lugal-DU (a1) '*man* of LugalDU' 3.1.1.1, p. 85 n. 420, 86 n. 424
ur-^{d}Lugal-DU šeš lu_2 ED IIIa Šuruppag T. Gomi, *Orient* 19 (1983), p. 2–3 o. iii 8
ur-^{d}Lugal-DU ED IIIa Šuruppag M. Molina & H. Sanchiz, *StEL* 24 (2007), p. 1–15 1 o. iii 4
ur-^{d}Lugal-DU ED IIIa Šuruppag *TSŠ* 526 o. iv 1

ur-Lugal-DU (a≥1) '*man* of LugalDU' 3.1.1.1, p. 85 n. 420, 86 n. 424
ur-Lugal-DU ED IIIa Šuruppag? CT 50 20 o. i 3'
ur-Lugal-DU ED IIIa Šuruppag *FTUM* 92 o. i 1'
ur-Lugal-DU ED IIIa Šuruppag *NTSŠ* 147 o. iv 11
ur-Lugal-DU ED IIIa Šuruppag *NTSŠ* 234 r. i 4
ur-⸢Lugal⸣-DU [sagi$^?$] ED IIIa Šuruppag *TSŠ* 8 o. iii 13
ur-Lugal-DU ED IIIa Šuruppag *TSŠ* 65+ o. iii 7
ur-Lugal-DU AN-nu-me ED IIIa Šuruppag *TSŠ* 102 o. iii 3
ur-[Lugal-DU] Pa-bil_x-ga [(engar$^?$)] ED IIIa Šuruppag *TSŠ* 130 r. i 4'
ur-Lugal-DU Pa-bil_x-ga engar ED IIIa Šuruppag *TSŠ* 130 r. iv 13'
ur-Lugal-DU ED IIIa Šuruppag *TSŠ* 158 o. iv 11
ur-Lugal-DU Pa-bi[l_x-ga] engar ED IIIa Šuruppag *TSŠ* 237 o. iv 5
ur-Lugal-DU engar ĝuruš ED IIIa Šuruppag *TSŠ* 522 o. i 7

ur-Lugal-DU ? ED IIIa Šuruppag *WF* 45 o. vi 8
ur-Lugal-DU AN-nu-me ED IIIa Šuruppag *WF* 53 o. ii 2
ur-Lugal-DU ED IIIa Šuruppag *WF* 77 o. iii 12
ur-Lugal-⌜DU⌝ engar ED IIIa Šuruppag *WF* 78 o. ii 8''
ur-Lugal-DU engar ED IIIa Šuruppag *WF* 78 o. iii 15
ur-Lugal-DU engar ED IIIa Šuruppag *WF* 78 o. iv 12
ur-Lugal-DU engar ED IIIa Šuruppag *WF* 78 o. v 4
ur-Lugal-DU engar ED IIIa Šuruppag *WF* 78 o. v 7
ur-Lugal-DU engar ED IIIa Šuruppag *WF* 78 o. v 11
ur-Lugal-⌜DU⌝ engar ED IIIa Šuruppag *WF* 78 o. v 16
ur-Lugal-DU ED IIIa Šuruppag *WF* 87 o. iii 7
ur-Lugal-DU [engar] ED IIIa Šuruppag *WF* 87 r. iii 1
ur-Lugal-DU AN-nu-me ED IIIa Šuruppag *WF* 124 o. v 4
ur-Lugal-DU ED IIIa Šuruppag *WF* 129 o. ii 5

ur-^{d}Lugal-eden (a1) '*man* of Lugaleden' 3.1.1.1, p. 85 n. 420, 97
ur-^{d}Lugal-eden CS-LS ? Girsu *RTC* 243 o. 5

ur-Lugal-eden (a1) '*man* of Lugaleden' 3.1.1.1, p. 85 n. 420, 97
ur-Lugal-eden CS Umma Nik 2 84 r. 4

ur-Lugal-eden-na (a1) '*man* of Lugaleden' 3.1.1.1, p. 85 n. 420, 97
ur-Lugal-eden-na (lu$_2$) Geme$_2$-^{d}Ba-u$_2$-ka, igi-nu-du$_8$, dumu URU.AZ^{ki}-ka ED IIIb/Ukg. lugal 4 Girsu *DP* 2/2 339 o. ii 1

ur-lugal-la$_2$ (a1) '*man* of the lugal' 3.1.1.1, p. 85
ur-lugal-la$_2$ CS/NS. Nippur TMH 5 7+184+201a r. i 4'

ur-Lugal-ra (a1) '*man* of Lugal-ra (?)' 3.1.1.1, p. 86
ur-Lugal-ra f. Ur-$^{d\ še_3}$Šer$_7$-da ED IIIb Nippur TMH 5 1 o. i 2

^{d}Utu-palil-Lugal-AN-da (a1) 'Utu is the vanguard of LugalANda' 3.1.6.2, p. 54, 108, 141 n. 788
^{d}Utu-palil-Lugal-AN-da nitah̬ ED IIIb/Ukg. ensi$_2$ 1 Girsu *AWAS* 119 o. iii 15
^{d}Utu-palil-Lugal-AN-da nitah̬, [il$_2^?$] ED IIIb/Ukg. ensi$_2$ 1 Girsu *DP* 2/1 228 o. iii 13
^{d}Utu-palil-Lugal-AN-da nitah̬, il$_2$ ED IIIb/Ukg. ensi$_2$ 1 Girsu HSS 3 15 o. iii 13
^{d}Utu-palil-Lugal-AN-da nitah̬, il$_2$ ED IIIb/Ukg. ensi$_2$ 1.6 Girsu HSS 3 16 o. iii 12
^{d}Utu-palil-Lugal-AN-da nitah̬ ED IIIb/Ukg. ensi$_2$ 1 Girsu MVN 3 2 o. iv 8
^{d}Utu-palil-Lugal-AN-da nitah̬, il$_2$ ED IIIb/Ukg. ensi$_2$ 1 Girsu Nik 1 9 o. iii 15
^{d}Utu-palil-Lugal-AN-da nitah̬ ED IIIb/Lug. 6 Girsu D. Charpin, *RA* 71 (1977), p. 97–105 o. iii 16
^{d}Utu-palil-Lugal-AN-da nitah̬ ED IIIb/Lug. 6 Girsu VS 25 11 o. iii 12
^{d}Utu-palil-Lugal-AN-da nitah̬, i[l$_2$] ED IIIb/Lug. 6 Girsu VS 25 71 o. iii 15

za-lugal (a1) unkn. mng. 3.1.8, p. 183
za-⌜lugal⌝ ašgab CS Girsu ITT 2/1 4508 r. 4'

[x]-lu[gal] (PN?) ED IIIb-ES Adab CUSAS 11 208 o. ii 7
⌜x⌝-lugal ES-MS Nippur OSP 1 83 r. ii 6
⌜x⌝-lu:gal MS-CS Nippur OSP 2 102 r. iii' 11'
[x-(x)]-lu[gal$^?$] MS-CS Kiš MAD 5 48 r. 1' Kish 1930-559c
[x]-lugal (PN ?) MS-CS Susa MDP 14 33 r. ii 3'

2. List of *śarrum*-names

Entries in the lists of attestations are provided with a heading in bold script. The heading provides the writing encountered in the previous chapters. A raised parenthesis signals the number of bearers (given as $^{(a\#)}$), and/or discrete entries in scholastic lists of PNN (given as $^{(\circ\#)}$). The translation suggested in discussions is then followed by the section or subheading under which the name was treated, followed by page references, including cross references.

Underneath the bold heading, the writing of the name, filiations (if any), date (with ruler and regnal year if known), provenience, publication data, column and line number follow. Attestations are organized according to date and provenience.

Entries are divided into the discrete time periods ED IIIa, ED IIIa-b, ED IIIb, and ES. Later Sargonic references are not further subdivided due to difficulties in assigning a precise date to texts belonging to the second half of the Sargonic period. A few later attestations are also included due in part to the same reasons, or if they form part of an earlier tradition, as in the case of a few scholastic texts. Hence, some references to texts dated to CS-LS, LS-Lagaš II, or LS-Ur III are also listed. Names taken from OB copies of older original inscriptions are marked as (OB) following the date of the original inscription. All names culled from transliterations only are so marked.

Multiple attestations of a name from the same period and place are organized alphabetically after publication. Each and every instance of *śarrum*-names in CS Girsu texts have not been entered in the list. See the introductory notes to the list of lugal-names.

Museum or excavation nos. are given under certain circumstances. Either the texts are not sequentially numbered (e.g. *AAICAB*), or the numbering of the illustrations follows a different sequence than the treatment of the texts in the monograph (*DPA*). In other cases, a plate may contain a number of figures, and museum numbers are then indicated to tell them apart.

Abbreviations used in notes on filiations are given in Technical Abbreviations.

AN-*śar* $^{(a1)}$ 'Ilum/the god is king' 3.2.7.6, p. 210 n. 1332
AN-*śar* MS-CS Tutub MAD 1 219 (translit. only) r. 12
AN-*śar* s. ^{d}Su'en-LUM CS Tutub MAD 1 232 o. ii 13

***bi-in-ka*$_3$*-li*$_2$-lugal-*re*$_2$** $^{(a1)}$ 'offspring of all *śarrums*' 3.2.7.1, p. 206, 259
bi-in-ka$_3$*-li*$_2$-lugal-*re*$_2$ s. ^{d}*Na-ra-am-*^{d}EN:ZU diĝir A-ka$_3$-de$_3$^{ki}, *A-bi*$_2$*-i-śar*, dub-sar, ir$_{11}$-*su*$_2$ CS/NS. Girsu R. M. Boehmer, *Fs Moortgat*, p. 42–56 13 ii 1
bi-in-ka$_3$*-li*$_2$-lugal-*re*$_2$ [*Ir*$_3^?$]-⸢*e*$^?$⸣-*u*[*m*], [*š*]*u Bi-*⸢*in-ka*$_3$⸣*-li*$_2$*-sar*$_3$*-re*$_2$ CS/NS. Tutub MAD 1 225 r. 3'
bi-in-ka$_3$*-li*$_2$-lugal-*re*$_2$ CS Tutub MAD 1 238 o. 6'
bi-in-ka$_3$*-li*$_2$-lugal-*re*$_2$ dumu lugal CS/NS. Unknown R. M. Boehmer, *Fs Moortgat*, p. 42–56 10 1

***bi-ka*$_3$*-li*$_2$-lugal-*re*$_2$** $^{(a1)}$ 'offspring of all *śarrums*' 3.2.7.1, p. 206 n. 1308
bi-ka$_3$*-li*$_2$-lugal-*re*$_2$ *Ib*-[x-x], ir$_{11}$ *Bi-ka*$_3$*-li*$_2$-lugal-*re*$_2$ CS Girsu *RTC* 94 o. 2'

***bi*$^!$*-ka*$_3$*-li*$_2$*-śar-*[*re*$_2$]** $^{(a1)}$ 'offspring of all *śarrums*' 3.2.7.1, p. 206 n. 1308
bi$^!$*-ka*$_3$*-li*$_2$*-śar-*[*re*$_2$] CS Girsu CT 50 146 o. 9

E$_2$-a-*śar* (a2) 'Ea is king' 3.2.7.6, p. 210 n. 1334
E$_2$-a-*śar* ugula CS-LS Kiš MAD 5 45 o. ii 12
E$_2$-a-*śar* s. *Ta$_2$-wi-ra*, ss. [x x] nagar, guruš, ir$_{11}$ ^{d}En-ki CS Kiš MAD 5 56 o. iii 5

E$_3$-a-*śar* (a1) 'Ea is king' 3.2.7.6, p. 210 n. 1334
E$_3$-a-*śar* ED IIIb Nippur TMH 5 38 r. i 5

***en-bu*-lugal** (a1) uncertain mng. 3.2.8, p. 212–213
en-bu-lugal *ra$^?$-x-a* CS Gasur HSS 10 34 o. ii 1

^{d}EN:ZU-*śar* (a1) 'Su'en is king' 3.2.7.6, p. 210 n. 1336
^{d}EN:ZU-*śar* MS-CS Tutub MAD 1 219 (translit. only) r. 7
^{d}EN:ZU-*śar* CS Tutub MAD 1 233 r. i 7
^{d}EN:ZU-*śar* MS-CS Tutub MAD 1 234 r. 6
^{d}EN:ZU-*śar* f. *Ma-ka$_3$-ka$_3$* CS Tutub MAD 1 254 o. i 7'

gal-zu-[*śar*]-*ru-śi*-[*in*] (a1) 'their *śarrum* is a wise one (?)' 3.2.2, p. 195
gal-zu-[*śar*]-*ru-śi*-[*in*] maškim [lu]gal CS Mugdan BIN 8 144 o. ii 9

***i-ba*-lugal** (a1) 'the *śarrum* drew near (?)' 3.2.8, p. 213
i-ba-lugal Ur-⌜Keš$_3^{ki}$⌝, *šu I-ba*-lugal MS-CS Unknown B. R. Foster, *JCS* 35 (1983), P. 147–175 16 r. 4

i-li$_2$-śar-ru (a2) 'a *śarrum* emerged (?)' 3.2.8, p. 213
i-li$_2$-śar-ru s. *I-di$_3$-śum*, šagina, lu$_2$ ĝiš-gid$_2$-da, dumu.dumu A-ka$_3$-de$_3^{ki}$ ES/Man. Unknown (MO) OIP 104 40 A xii 11
i-li$_2$-śar-ru s. *I-di$_3$-śum*, šagina, lu$_2$ ĝiš-gid$_2$-da, dumu.dumu A-ka$_3$-de$_3^{ki}$ ES/Man. Unknown (MO) OIP 104 40 B xvii 9
i-li$_2$-śar-ru s. *I-di$_3$-śum*, šagina, lu$_2$ ĝiš-gid$_2$-da, dumu.dumu A-ka$_3$-de$_3^{ki}$ ES/Man. Unknown (MO) OIP 104 40 C xxi' 8
i-li$_2$-śar-ru s. *I-di$_3$-śum*, šagina, lu$_2$ ĝiš-gid$_2$-da, dumu.dumu A-ka$_3$-de$_3^{ki}$ ES/Man. Unknown (MO) OIP 104 40 D ix' 10
i-li$_2$-śar-ru CS Girsu CT 50 126 r. 3'

i-mi-śar-ru (a1) 'the *śarrum* protected' 3.2.3.1, p. 197
i-mi-śar-ru šu AN-AB ES-MS Sippar CTMMA 1 7 r. i 5
i-mi-[*śar$^?$-ru$^?$*] f. ⌜E$_2^?$⌝-[x-x] CS Sippar CT 50 74 o. 2'

i-pu$_3$-śar (a2) unkn. mng. 3.2.8, p. 213
i-pu$_3^?$-śar ED IIIa Šuruppag *TSŠ* 750 o. 2
i-pu$_3$-śar dub-sar maḫ ED IIIb Mari MAM 3 8 1

i-śar-śar-ri$_2$ (a1) 'the *śarrum* is just' 3.2.7.9, p. 211, 239 n. 1428
i-śar-śar-ri$_2$ CS Girsu *RTC* 127 r. iv 3

i$_3$-lum-śar (a1) 'Ilum/the god is king' 3.2.7.6, p. 210 n. 1332
i$_3$-lum-śar f. *A-ḫu*-du$_{10}$ ES Sippar ? OIP 104 41 o. iii 20'

***ib-ni*-lugal** (a≥1) 'the *śarrum* created' 3.2.5.1, p. 20f. n. 70, 201
ib-ni-lugal s. *Ḫu*-[x-x] CS Girsu ITT 2/1 4578 o. 7
ib-ni-lugal MS-CS Umma ? BIN 8 151 o. 2
ib-ni-lugal CS Umma MVN 3 110 o. 3
ib-ni-lugal dub-sar CS Unknown R. M. Boehmer, *Fs Moortgat*, p. 42–56 31 4

il-lu-śar (a1) 'a *śarrum* indeed is the god' 3.2.7.6, p. 209
il-lu-śar ED IIIa Šuruppag *WF* 122 o. i 2

^{d}IM-*śar* (a1) 'Adad is king' 3.2.7.6, p. 210 n. 1335
^{d}IM-*śar* CS-LS Kiš MAD 5 21 o. 4
^{d}IM-*śar* f. [*Ku$^?$-r*]*u*-ur-saĝ CS-LS Kiš MAD 5 36 o. 2

iš-ṭup-śar (a1) 'the *śarrum* saved' 3.2.3.1, p. 197

iš-ṭup-śar lugal Ma-ri$_2$^{ki} ED IIIb Mari>Ebla ARET 13 4 o. v 3

lugal-*a-ba$_4$* $^{(a\geq1)}$ 'the *śarrum* is a father' 3.2.1.2, p. 192
lugal-*a-ba*$_4$ Ma-ri$_2$^{ki} ED IIIb Ebla ARET 2 12 o. iv 13
lugal-*a-ba*$_4$ ED IIIb Ebla ARET 7 89 o. i 2
lugal-*a-ba*$_4$ Ma-ri$_2$^{ki} ED IIIb Ebla ARET 8 3 o. x 14

lugal-*da-di$_3$* $^{(a1)}$ 'the *śarrum* is my favourite/the favourite (of DN)' 3.2.6.2, p. 204
lugal-*da-di*$_3$ MS-CS Ešnuna MAD 1 72 (translit. only) r. 4'
[lugal$^?$]-*da-di*$_3$? MS-CS Ešnuna MAD 1 103 (translit. only) o. i' 1'

lugal-gi $^{(a1)}$ 'the *śarrum* is dependable' 3.2.7.9, p. 211 n. 1344
lugal-gi URU.IM.KI, *u*$_3$ Lugal-gi MS-CS Unknown B. R. Foster, *JCS* 35 (1983), p. 147–175 4 o. 4

lugal-gi-pa-e$_3$ $^{(a1)}$ '*Śarrukēn* is famous (?)' 3.2.7.9, p. 211 n. 1344
⌜lugal⌝-gi-pa-e$_3$ dub-sar MS-CS Unknown B. R. Foster, *JCS* 35 (1983), p. 147–175 4 o. 9

°lugal-*ka-śer$_7$*(NIR) $^{(°1)}$ 'the *śarrum* is one who compensates (?)' 3.2.8, p. 212
°lugal-*ka-śer*$_7$(NIR) šagina ED IIIb Ebla A. Archi, *StEb* 4 (1981), p. 177–204 (translit. only) o. i 5

°lugal-*ka$_3$-śer$_7$*(NIR) $^{(°1)}$ 'the *śarrum* is one who compensates (?)' 3.2.8, p. 212
°lu[gal]-*ka*$_3$-*śer*$_7$(NIR) [ša]g[ina]([KI]š.[NITAḪ]) ED IIIa Abū Ṣalābīḫ *IAS* 62 o. i 10

lugal-*na-i-iš* $^{(a1)}$ 'the *śarrum* is a lion (?)' 3.2.7.3, p. 207, 241
lugal-*na-i-iš* s. EN Ma-nu-wa-ad^{ki} ED IIIb Ebla ARET 3 93 (translit. only) o. ii 4'
lugal-*na-i-iš* ED IIIb Ebla ARET 3 295 (translit. only) o. ii 2
lugal-*na-i-iš* ED IIIb Ebla ARET 3 421 (translit. only) o. iv 3
lugal-*na-i-iš* ED IIIb Ebla ARET 3 562 o. viii (?) 3'
lugal-*na-i-iš* ED IIIb Ebla ARET 3 595+631 (translit. only) o. v (?) 2'

lugal-*nu-ru* $^{(a1)}$ 'the *śarrum* is light (?)' 3.2.7.10, p. 211
lugal-*nu-ru* ES-MS Ur UET 2 suppl. 30 o. 2

lugal-OSP1-X$_5$ $^{(a1)}$ unkn. mng. 3.2.8, p. 213
lugal-OSP1-X$_5$ dumu nitaḫ ES-MS Nippur OSP 1 47 o. iii 8

lugal-*pa$_2$-luḫ* $^{(a1)}$ 'the *śarrum* is awe-inspiring' 3.2.7.3, p. 207 n. 1312
lu[gal]-*pa*$_2$-*luḫ* CS Girsu ITT 5 9259 r. 1

Ma-ma-*śa-ra-at* $^{(a1)}$ 'Mama is queen' 3.2.7.6, p. 210 n. 1337
Ma-ma-*śa-ra-at* MS-CS Ešnuna MAD 1 53 (translit. only) r. i' 4'
Ma-ma-*śa-ra-at* MS-CS Ešnuna MAD 1 163+165 o. i 33

***ṣi$_2$-la*-lugal** $^{(a1)}$ 'the *śarrum* is shade' 3.2.3.1, p. 197
ṣi$_2$-*la*-lugal lu$_2$ kar Ma-ri$_2$^{ki} ED IIIb Ebla A. Archi, *MARI* 4 (1985), p. 63–83 73 (translit. only) o. iii 17bis & iv 6bis

śar-a-‹ba$_4$› $^{(a1)}$ (defective writing of the following) 3.2.1.2, p. 192 n. 1243
śar-a-‹ba$_4$› lu$_2$ kar Ma-ri$_2$^{ki} ED IIIb Ebla ARET 8 5 o. ix 20

śar-a-ba$_4$ $^{(a\geq1/°1)}$ 'the *śarrum* is a father' 3.2.1.2, p. 192
°*śar-a-ba*$_4$ ED IIIb Ebla MEE 3 59 o. iii 8
śar-a-ba$_4$ ED IIIb Ebla ARET 9 64 o. i 3 (translit. only)
śar-a-ba$_4$ ED IIIb Ebla ARET 9 68 o. iii 13 (translit. only
śar-a-ba$_4$ ED IIIb Ebla ARET 9 106 o. ii 4 (translit. only

śar-a-Ti-Gu-Bi-śi-in $^{(a1)}$ unkn. mng. 3.2.8, p. 213 w. n. 1364
śar-a-Ti-Gu-Bi-śi-in Ilum-dan, ši Šu-i$_3$-*li*$_2$-*śu*, sa$_{12}$-sug$_5$, ir$_{11}$ *Ilum-ba-ni*, dam-gar$_3$, ir$_{11}$ *Śar-a-Ti-Gu-Bi-śi-in* LS MAD 5 22 r. 1 Kiš

śar-a-Ti-Gu-Bi-śi-in dumu lugal, Ur-sa$_6$, dub-sar, ir$_{11}$-*su*$_2$ LS Unknown *EGA* 798 i 1

°*śar*-bad$_3$ (a1) 'the *śarrum* is a fortress' 3.2.3.1, p. 197 n. 1271, 240
°*śar*-bad$_3$ ED IIIb Ebla MEE 3 59 o. iii 5

***śar-ḫa-lu-ub*$_2$** (a1) 'the *śarrum* … oak(tree) (?)' 3.2.5.3, p. 202
śar-ḫa-lu-ub$_2$ dumu nitaḫ ES-MS Nippur OSP 1 47 o. ii 7

***śar-iś-ta*$_2$*-kal*$_2$** (a1) 'rely on the *śarrum*!' 3.2.3.1, p. 196
śar-iś-ta$_2$*-kal*$_2$ f. ⸢*I*⸣*-da-ḫu-*⸢x⸣ CS Gasur HSS 10 210 r. 3'

***śar-ka*$_3$*-li*$_2$-lugal-*re*$_2$** (a1) '*śarrum* of all *śarrums*' 3.2.7.1, p. 206, 259
śar-ka$_3$*-li*$_2$-lugal-*re*$_2$ CS/Śkś Adab R. M. Boehmer, *Fs Moortgat*, p. 42–56 28 i 1
śar-ka$_3$*-li*$_2$-lugal-*re*$_2$ CS/Śkś Adab *SIA* 874 o. 6
śar-ka$_3$*-li*$_2$-lugal-*re*$_2$ CS/Śkś Girsu CT 50 50 r. 5'
śar-ka$_3$*-li*$_2$-lugal-*re*$_2$ CS/Śkś Girsu M. Çığ, *Fs Kramer*, p. 75–82 1 r. 5'
śar-ka$_3$*-li*$_2$-lugal-*re*$_2$ CS/Śkś Girsu ITT 1 1097 o. i' 2'
śar-ka$_3$*-li*$_2$-lugal-*re*$_2$ CS/Śkś Girsu ITT 1 1114 r. 5'
śar-ka$_3$*-li*$_2$-lugal-*re*$_2$ CS/Śkś Girsu ITT 1 1115 r. 3'
śar-ka$_3$*-li*$_2$-[lugal-*re*$_2$] CS/Śkś Girsu ITT 2/1 3078 r. 1'
śar-ka$_3$*-li*$_2$-lugal-*re*$_2$ CS/Śkś Girsu B. R. Foster, *JANES* 12 (1980), p. 29–42 1 o. ii 3'
śar-ka$_3$*-li*$_2$-lugal-*re*$_2$ CS/Śkś Girsu *RTC* 85 r. 2
śar-ka$_3$*-li*$_2$-lugal-*re*$_2$ CS/Śkś Girsu *RTC* 87 r. 2' (?)
śar-ka$_3$*-li*$_2$-lugal-*re*$_2$ CS Girsu *RTC* 97 o. 7
[*śar-k*]*a*$_3$*-li*$_2$-⸢lugal⸣-*re*$_2$ CSŚkś Girsu *RTC* 118 r. 3'
śar-ka$_3$*-li*$_2$-lugal-*re*$_2$ CS/Śkś Girsu *RTC* 124 r. ii 3
śar-ka$_3$*-li*$_2$-lugal-*re*$_2$ CS/Śkś Girsu *RTC* 130 r. i' 2'
śar-ka$_3$*-li*$_2$-lugal-*re*$_2$ CS/Śkś Girsu *RTC* 161 Seal 1: 1
śar-ka$_3$*-li*$_2$-lugal-*re*$_2$ CS/Śkś Girsu *RTC* 162 Seal: i 1
śar-ka$_3$*-li*$_2$-lugal-*re*$_2$ CS/Śkś Girsu *RTC* 163 Seal: i 1
śar-ka$_3$*-li*$_2$-lugal-*re*$_2$ CS/Śkś Isin MAD 4 15 o. 10
śar-ka$_3$*-li*$_2$-lugal-*re*$_2$ CS/Śkś Isin B. R. Foster, *WO* 13 (1982), p. 15–24 6 o. 4'
śar-ka$_3$-⸢*li*$_2$⸣-[lugal]-*re*$_2$ dumu ⸢lugal⸣, maškim CS/NS. Nippur OSP 2 16 o. iii 18'
śar-ka$_3$*-li*$_2$-lugal-*re*$_2$ CS/Śkś Y 2 Nippur OSP 2 100 r. iii 12'
śar-ka$_3$*-li*$_2$-lugal-*re*$_2$ CS/Śkś Y [1] Umma MesCiv 4 27 r. ii 12

^{d}*śar-ka*$_3$*-li*$_2$-lugal-*re*$_2$ (a1) '*śarrum* of all *śarrums*' 3.2.7.1, p. 204 n. 1305
^{d}*śar-ka*$_3$*-li*$_2$-lugal-*re*$_2$ SU CS/Śkś Girsu CT 50 51 r. 7
$^{[d]}$*śar-ka*$_3$*-li*$_2$-lugal-*re*$_2$ CS/Śkś Adab R. M. Boehmer, *Fs Moortgat*, p. 42–56 30a, b i 1
^{d}*śar-ka*$_3$*-li*$_2$-lugal-*re*$_2$ CS/Śkś Unknown R. M. Boehmer, *Fs Moortgat*, p. 42–56 31 1

***śar-ka*$_3$-lugal** (a1) '*śarrum* of all *śarrums*' 3.2.7.1, p. 206
śar-ka$_3$-lugal CS/Śkś Tell Ağrab MAD 1 268 (translit. only) r. 2

°*śar-Ku-Da* (°1) unkn. mng. 3.2.8, p. 213
°*śar-Ku-Da* ED IIIb Ebla MEE 3 59 o. iii 2

°*śar-ma* (°1) 'a *śarrum* indeed (…?)' 3.2.7.6, p. 209
°*śar-ma* ED IIIb Ebla MEE 3 59 o. iii 6

śar-ma-i*$_3$*-lum (a1/°1) 'a *śarrum* indeed is the god' 3.2.7.6, p. 209
śar-ma-i$_3$*-lum* ED IIIa-b Tutub OIP 53, p. 147 5 1
°*śar-ma-i*$_3$*-lum* ED IIIb Ebla MEE 3 59 o. iii 3

°*śar-ma*-NI (°1) 'a *śarrum* indeed is the god' 3.2.7.6, p. 209
°*śar-ma*-NI ED IIIb Ebla MEE 3 59 o. iii 7

śar-me-il (a1) 'a *śarrum* indeed is the god' 3.2.7.6, p. 209
śar-me-il ED IIIb Mari MAM 1 pl. 65 no. 1388

***śar-me*-NI** (a1) 'a *śarrum* indeed is my god' 3.2.7.6, p. 209
śar-me-NI MS-CS Ešnuna MAD 1 163+165 (translit. only) r. i' 5'

śar-mi-lu (a1) 'a *śarrum* indeed is the god' 3.2.7.6, p. 209
śar-mi-lu ED IIIb Ebla ARET 7 18 o. iii 6

°*śar*-NI-*sa* (°1) unkn. mng. 3.2.8, p. 213
°*śar*-NI-*sa* ED IIIb Ebla MEE 3 59 o. iii 4

śar-ri₂ (a1) 'my *śarrum*' 3.2.1.1, p. 191, 259
śar-ri₂ ED IIIb Ebla ARET 3 471 o. viii 9 (translit. only)

śar-ri₂-iś-ta₂-kal₂ (a1) 'rely on the *śarrum*!' 3.2.3.1, p. 196, 239, 257 n. 1519
śar-ri₂-iś-ta₂-kal₂ ᵈ*Na*-⸢*ra*⸣-*am*-ᵈZu:⸢en⸣, diĝir A-ka₃-de₃⸢ki⸣, *Śar-ri₂-iś-ta₂-kal₂*, dub-sar, ⸢ir₁₁⸣-*su₂* CS Girsu *RTC* 170 Seal: ii 1

śar-ru-al-śi-in (a1) 'the *śarrum* is their city (?)' 3.2.3.1, p. 197–198, 240, 258 n. 1524
śar-ru-al-śi-in CS Tutub MAD 1 233 o. i 5

śar-ru-ba-ni (a≥1) 'the *śarrum* is a creator/created (?)' 3.2.5.1, p. 210–202
śar-ru-ba-ni CS Girsu ITT 1 1372 o. 3
śar-ru-ba-ni *I₃-li₂*-[x], ⸢ir₁₁⸣ *Sar-ru-ba-ni* CS Girsu ITT 5 6867 o. 2
śar-ru-ba-ni šu-⸢i₂⸣ CS Girsu *RTC* 127 r. iii 21
śar-ru-ba-ni CS-LS Kiš MAD 5 5 r. 4

***śar-ru*-bad₃** (a1) 'the *śarrum* is a fortress' 3.2.3.1, p. 197 n. 1271, 240
śar-ru-bad₃ f. *Śar-ru-i₃-li₂*, ensi, dumu.dumu A-ka₃-de₃ᵏⁱ ES/Man. Unknown (MO) OIP 104 40 A xv 26
śar-ru-bad₃ f. *Śar-ru-i₃-li₂*, ensi, dumu.dumu A-ka₃-de₃ᵏⁱ ES/Man. Unknown (MO) OIP 104 40 B xxi 19
śar-ru-bad₃ f. *Śar-ru-i₃-li₂*, ensi, dumu.dumu A-ka₃-de₃ᵏⁱ ES/Man. Unknown (MO) OIP 104 40 C xxiv' 6
śar-ru-bad₃ f. *Śar-ru-i₃-li₂*, ensi, dumu.dumu A-ka₃-de₃ᵏⁱ ES/Man. Unknown (MO) OIP 104 40 D xiii' 22

śar-ru-da-di₃ (a1) 'the *śarrum* is my favourite/the favourite (of DN)' 3.2.6.2, p. 204
śar-ru-da-di₃ ⸢UN:gal⸣, [š]u-i CS Girsu *RTC* 127 r. ii 12

śar-ru-dan (a2) 'the *śarrum* is powerful' 3.2.7.3, p. 206
śar-ru-dan MS-CS Susa MDP 14 47 r. 2
śar-ru-dan CS Umma *AAS* 4 r. 1
śar-ru-dan CS Umma *CST* 5 r. 5

śar-ru-Du-Gul (a1) unkn. mng. 3.2.8, p. 213–214
śar-ru-Du-Gul MS-CS Ešnuna MAD 1 163+165 o. ii 32

śar-ru-du₂-ri₂ (a1) 'the *śarrum* is my fortress' 3.2.3.1, p. 197 n. 1271, 240
śar-ru-du₂-ri₂ MS-CS Adab OIP 14 116 o. 4

***śar-ru*-du₁₀** (a1) the' *śarrum* is good' 3.2.7.8, p. 210
śar-ru-du₁₀ CS/Śkś Girsu CT 50 172 o. i 12
śar-ru-du₁₀ CS Girsu ITT 1 1080 r. 5'
śar-ru-du₁₀ CS Girsu ITT 1 1472 o. i 3'
śar-ru-du₁₀ CS Girsu ITT 2/1 4566 o. 6
śar-ru-du₁₀ CS Girsu *RTC* 127 o. iv 21'
śar-ru-du₁₀ CS Girsu *RTC* 127 r. vi 1'
śar-ru-du₁₀ CS Girsu *RTC* 134 o. ii 7

***śar-ru*-gal-zu** (a1) 'the *śarrum* is a wise one' 3.2.2, p. 106, 195
śar-ru-gal-zu ugula CS Umma CT 50 188 o. i 11

***śar-ru*-gar₃** (a1) 'the *śarrum* is a hero' 3.2.7.4, p. 207, 208

śar-ru-gar$_3$ CS Gasur HSS 10 169 o. 2
śar-ru-gar$_3$ CS Gasur HSS 10 169 o. 6

***śar-ru*-gi** (a2) 'the *śarrum* is dependable' 3.2.7.9, p. 73, 212 n. 1343
śar-ru-gi En-ḫe$_2$-du$_7$-an-na, dumu *Śar-ru*-gi, Dingir-pal[il], kinda-n[i] ES-MS Ur R. M. Boehmer, *Fs Moortgat*, p. 42–56 2 i 2
śar-ru-gi ES-MS Ur R. M. Boehmer, *Fs Moortgat*, p. 42–56 5 2
śar-ru-gi zirru$_x$(MUNUS.NUNUZ.ZI.AN.ŠEŠ.KI), dam ^{d}Nanna, dumu, ⸢*Śar-ru*⸣-[gi] ES-MS Ur UET 1 23 5
śar-ru-gi [...]-na, [*Śar*]-⸢*ru*⸣-gi, [l]u[gal], Ki]š ES-MS Ur UET 8 10 2'
śar-ru-gi h. *Taš$_3$-lul-tum* ES/*Śk.* Unknown YOS 1 7 3–4
śar-ru-gi LS-Lagaš II Girsu *RTC* 83 o. 6'

śar-ru*-gi-*i$_3$-li$_2$ (a1) '*Śarrukēn* is my god' 3.2.4.1, p. 200, 257
śar-ru-gi-*i$_3$-li$_2$* s. BAL-*ga*, b. UD-ti-ru, *ši* nar, dumu.dumu A-ka$_3$-de$_3$^{ki} ES/Man. Unknown (MO) OIP 104 40 A xii 8
śar-ru-gi-*i$_3$-li$_2$* s. BAL-*ga*, b. UD-ti-ru, *ši* nar, dumu.dumu A-ka$_3$-de$_3$^{ki} ES/Man. Unknown (MO) OIP 104 40 B xvii 6
śar-ru-gi-*i$_3$-li$_2$* s. BAL-*ga*, b. UD-ti-ru, *ši* nar, dumu.dumu A-ka$_3$-de$_3$^{ki} ES/Man. Unknown (MO) OIP 104 40 C xxi' 5
śar-ru-gi-*i$_3$-li$_2$* s. BAL-*ga*, b. UD-ti-ru, *ši* nar, dumu.dumu A-ka$_3$-de$_3$^{ki} ES/Man. Unknown (MO) OIP 104 40 D ix' 7

***śar-ru*-gu$_2$** (a1) ' *śarrum* is a (river-)bank (?)' 3.2.3.1, p. 198
śar-ru-gu$_2$ *šu* sukkal-gal MS Kazallu BIN 8 121 o. ii 9

***śar-ru*-ḫur-saĝ** (a1) 'the *śarrum* is a mountain' 3.2.7.6, p. 167 n. 968, 210
śar-ru-ḫur-saĝ *I$_3$-li$_2$-dan*, *Il$_3$-ra-bi$_2$*, *šu-ut Śar-ru*-ḫur-saĝ *AIHA* Awal MS 3 r. ii 3

śar-ru-i-śar (a1) 'the *śarrum* is just' 3.2.7.9, p. 211, 241
śar-ru-i-śar Śar-ru-i-śar, *Na-ah-śum*-⸢*sa*⸣-*na*-[*a*]*t*, ⸢šabra⸣ [e$_2$$^?$], ĝiš-kin-t[i (x)] CS Girsu *RTC* 127 r. v 18

śar-ru-i$_3$-li$_2$ (a≥6) 'the *śarrum* is my god' 3.2.4.1, p. 73 n. 372, 199, 257, 259
śar-ru-i$_3$-li$_2$ s. *Śar-ru*-bad$_3$, ensi, dumu.dumu A-ka$_3$-de$_3$^{ki} ES/Man. Unknown (MO) OIP 104 40 A xv 25
śar-ru-i$_3$-li$_2$ s. *Śar-ru*-bad$_3$, ensi, dumu.dumu A-ka$_3$-de$_3$^{ki} ES/Man. Unknown (MO) OIP 104 40 B xxi 18
śar-ru-i$_3$-li$_2$ s. *Śar-ru*-bad$_3$, ensi, dumu.dumu A-ka$_3$-de$_3$^{ki} ES/Man. Unknown (MO) OIP 104 40 C xxiv' 5
śar-ru-i$_3$-li$_2$ s. *Śar-ru*-bad$_3$, ensi, dumu.dumu A-ka$_3$-de$_3$^{ki} ES/Man. Unknown (MO) OIP 104 40 D xiii' 21
śar-ru-i$_3$-li$_2$ MS Awal *AIHA* 8 o. 12
śar-ru-i$_3$-li$_2$ CS Adab CUSAS 13 116 r. 4
śar-ru-i$_3$-li$_2$ CS Adab CUSAS 13 119 r. 6
śar-ru-i$_3$-li$_2$ Ur-rin$_5$(LU$_2$-*šessig*), lu$_2$ *Śar-ru-i$_3$-li$_2$* CS Girsu ITT 1 1106 o. 2
śar-ru-i$_3$-li$_2$ *Śar-ru-i$_3$*-[*li$_2$*], nam-maškim ⸢x⸣ CS Girsu ITT 5 6753 o. 6
śar-ru-i$_3$-li CS Girsu *RTC* 121 o. 4
śar-ru-i$_3$-li$_2$ CS Girsu *RTC* 131 o. 5
śar-ru-i$_3$-li$_2$ CS Mugdan B. R. Foster, *ASJ* 4 (1982), p. 7–51 14 r. i 8
śar-ru-i$_3$-li$_2$ *šu* sukkal-*li* CS-LS Unknown *TCVBI* 1-60 o. 3*

***śar-ru-ki*-^{d}Utu** (a1) 'the *śarrum* is like Śamaś' 3.2.7.9, p. 173 n. 1013, 210, 211
śar-ru-ki-^{d}Utu CS Umma *CST* 6 o. 3
śar-ru-ki-^{d}Utu CS Umma *CST* 17 o. 4

śar-ru-la-ba (a1) 'the *śarrum* is a lion' 3.2.7.3, p. 207, 241 *śar-ru-la-ba* CS Girsu *RTC* 112 o. 3

śar-ru-mu-da (a2) 'the *śarrum* is a wise one' 3.2.2, p. 180 n. 1096, 195
śar-ru-mu-da *Qu₂-ra-dum*, dumu *A-ḫu-mu-*NE, *ši Sar-ru-mu-da* ES-MS Sippar CTMMA 1 7 o. ii 1
śar-ru-mu-da ugula e₂ ES-MS Umma Nik 2 53 o. ii 6

śar-ru-na? (a1) 'our *śarrum* (?)' 3.2.1.1, p. 191, 259
śar-ru-na? MS-CS Nagar ETB 2 26 1

***śar-ru-*NE** (a1) unkn. mng. 3.2.8, p. 178 n. 1072, 214
*śar-ru-*NE f. *Um-mi-*du₁₀ munus-balaĝ-di, *šu-‹ut›* abba₂*-bu-ut si-da-tim*, *i-mu-ru* CS Ešnuna MAD 1 336 r. 1

śar-ru-ni (a1) 'our *śarrum*' 3.2.1.1, p. 191, 259
[*śa*]*r-ru-ni* MS-CS Nagar ETB 2 25 (translit. only) 1

***śar-ru-*pa-[x]** (a1) unkn. mng. 3.2.8, p. 214
*śar-ru-*pa-[x] CS Girsu *STTI* 3 o. 2

śar-ru-pa₂-luḫ (a1) 'the *śarrum* is awe-inspiring' 3.2.7.3, p. 207
śar-ru-pa₂-luḫ CS Gasur HSS 10 126 o. 7'

śar-ru-ru (a≥3) unkn. mng. 3.2.8, p. 214
śar-ru-ru MS-CS Ešnuna MAD 1 46(+101) (translit. only) r. ii 11
śar-ru-ru CS-LS Kiš MAD 5 9 r. ii 1
śar-ru-ru CS-LS Kiš MAD 5 45 o. iii 14
śar-ru-ru MS-CS Umma *CST* 2 r. 6
śar-ru-ru CS/Škś Umma CT 50 57 o. 4
śar-ru-ru CS Umma *MCS* 9 (1964) 254 o. 6
śar-ru-ru CS Umma *MCS* 9 (1964) 256 o. 4
śar-ru-ru CS Umma *MCS* 9 (1964) 273 o. 4

***śar-ru-*sig₅** (a1) 'the *śarrum* is kind' 3.2.7.8, p. 210
*śar-ru-*sig₅ MS-CS Susa MDP 14 39 o. 5'

śar-ru-um (a1) abbreviation ? 3.2.8, p. 214
*śar-ru-um al-mu-*NE MS-CS Ur UET 2 suppl. 50 r. 3

***sar-ru-*ur-saĝ** (a1) 'the *śarrum* is a hero' 3.2.7.4, p. 208
*sar-ru-*ur-saĝ CS Unknown *EGA* 694 pl. 20 fig. 220 1

śar-ru-[x-x] CS Sippar CT 50 74 r. 2'

śar-ruₓ*(KU)*-ma-da (a1) 'the *śarrum* is a wise one' 3.2.2, p. 195 w. n. 1260
śar-ruₓ(KU)*-ma-da* ugula!(AŠ₂) ⸢e₂⸣ ES-MS Umma Nik 2 46 o. 6

***śar-rum₂-*gi** (a1) 'the *śarrum* is dependable' 3.2.7.9, p. 73, 211 n. 1343
*śar-rum₂-*gi ES/Šk. Adab *TCABI* 63 o. i 4

***śar-um-*gi** (a1) 'the *śarrum* is dependable' 3.2.7.9, p. 73, 211 n. 1343
*śar-um-*gi ES/Śk. Nippur OSP 1 145 r. 2
*śar-um-*gi ES/Śk. Nippur TMH 5 84 o. 5
*śar-um-*gi ES/Śk. Nippur TMH 5 85 o. ii 1; r. ii 1
*śar-um-*gi ES/Śk. Nippur TMH 5 86 o. 5
*śar-um-*gi ES/Śk. Nippur TMH 5 151 r. 5
*śar-um-*gi ES/Śk. Nippur TMH 5 181 r. 5

śar-um-i₃-li₂ (a1) 'the *śarrum* is my god' 3.2.4.1, p. 73 n. 372, 199 n. 1286
śar-um-i₃-li₂ MS-CS Umma MesCiv 4 25 r. 6

°*śar-*x*-tu* (°1) unkn. mng. 3.2.8, p. 214
°*śar-*x*-tu* ED IIIb Ebla MEE 3 59 o. iii 1

śu₂-ma-śar ⁽ᵃ¹⁾ 'he alone is king'   3.2.7.6, p. 210 n. 1333
śu₂-ma-śar   MS   Awal   *AIHA*   6   o. i 2

tu-ta₂-lugal-li-bi₂-iś ⁽ᵃ¹⁾ 'she found a *śarrum* of her liking'   3.2.6.2, p. 203, 204 w. n. 1302, 240, 260
tu-ta₂-lugal-*li-bi₂-iś*   CS   Ešnuna   MAD 1   292   o. 6
tu-ta₂-lugal-*li-bi₂-iś*   CS   Ešnuna   MAD 1   306   o. 5

tu-ta₂-śar-li-bi₂-iś ⁽ᵃ¹⁾ 'she found a *śarrum* of her liking'   3.2.6.2, p. 204, 240, 260
tu-ta₂-śar-li-bi₂-iś   nin   CS/Śkś   Adab   R. M. Boehmer, *Fs Moortgat*, p. 42–56   28   ii 1
tu-ta₂-śar-li-bi₂-iś   CS   Ešnuna   MAD 1   331   o. 5
tu-ta₂-śar-li-bi₂-iś   [na]-ⁱra-maⁱ-at lugal   CS/Śkś   Girsu   *RTC*   161   Seal 2:1

u-bi-in-lugal-re₂ ⁽ᵃ²⁾ unkn. mng.   3.2.8, p. 214
u-bi-in-lugal-re₂ s. Ur-ur, *ši* sukkal-gal-*li*, dumu.dumu A-ka₃-de₃ᵏⁱ   ES/Man.   Unknown (MO)   OIP 104   40   A xv 5
u-bi-in-lugal-re₂ s. BAL-E₂-a, Ir₁₁-da-niᵏⁱ, dumu.dumu A-ka₃-de₃ᵏⁱ   ES/Man.   Unknown (MO)   OIP 104   40   A xv 11
u-bi-in-lugal-re₂ s. Ur-ur, *ši* sukkal-gal-*li*, dumu.dumu A-ka₃-de₃ᵏⁱ   ES/Man.   Unknown (MO)   OIP 104   40   B xx 19
u-bi-in-lugal-re₂ s. BAL-E₂-a, Ir₁₁-da-niᵏⁱ, dumu.dumu A-ka₃-de₃ᵏⁱ   ES/Man.   Unknown (MO)   OIP 104   40   B xxi 4
u-bi-in-lugal-re₂ s. Ur-ur, *ši* sukkal-gal-*li*, dumu.dumu A-ka₃-de₃ᵏⁱ   ES/Man.   Unknown (MO)   OIP 104   40   C xxiii' 16
u-bi-in-lugal-re₂ s. BAL-E₂-a, Ir₁₁-da-niᵏⁱ, dumu.dumu A-ka₃-de₃ᵏⁱ   ES/Man.   Unknown (MO)   OIP 104   40   C xxiii' 22
u-bi-in-lugal-re₂ s. Ur-ur, *ši* sukkal-gal-li, dumu.dumu A-ka₃-de₃ᵏⁱ   ES/Man.   Unknown (MO)   OIP 104   40   D xiii' 1
u-bi-in-lugal-re₂ s. BAL-E₂-a, Ir₁₁-da-niᵏⁱ, dumu.dumu A-ka₃-de₃ᵏⁱ   ES/Man.   Unknown (MO)   OIP 104   40   D xiii' 7

ZU.EN-lugal ⁽ᵃ¹⁾ 'Su'en is king'   3.2.7.6, p. 210 n. 1336
ZU.EN-lugal   LU-UM sa₁₂-sug₅ AN.EN.AL   ED IIIa-b   Unknown   YOS 9   1   1

[x]-lu[gal?] ff. ⁱI₃ⁱ-*li₂-a-bi₂*, d. *Il₃-ra-bi₂*   MS-CS   Kiš   MAD 5   50   o. 5
[x x x]-*śar*   MS-CS   Tutub   MAD 1   237 (translit. only)   r. 3'

Indices

1. Sumerian names

The index contains references to names cited in discussions and notes, excluding lugal-names from the period investigated. For these, full page references are given in the list of attestations. The lugal-names which are included in the list are from later periods, or represent forms reconstructed from parallels, or names the readings of which are questionable. The latter two types are marked with a star symbol *. Names of persons discussed from a point of view of historical significance may be found in index 4, below.

A

a-ba-aja$_2$-da-sa$_2$, 167 n. 969
a-ba-AN-da-sa$_2$, 167 n. 969
A EN$_a$, 58 n. 280
A EN$_a$ DA$_a$, 58 n. 280
a-ša$_4$-ni, 168 n. 971
⸢a$_2$-gur-ra⸣, 162 n. 933
a$_2$(-ni)-kur-ra, 102 n. 546
a$_2$-na-mu-gub, 121 n. 653
a$_2$-šum$_2$-ma, 98 n. 514
a$_2$-tuku, 163 n. 942
a$_2$-zi-da, 109 n. 574
ab-ba-nir-ĝal$_2$, 99 n. 526
abzu:da, 153 n. 877
aga-zi, 88 n. 442
aga$_3$-zi, 88 n. 442
aja$_2$-aĝrig-zi, 129f. n. 715
aja$_2$-da-gal-di, 160 n. 920
aja$_2$-en-da, 58 n. 280
aja$_2$-en-ra-mu-gi$_4$, 181 n. 1106
aja$_2$-en-ra-tum$_2$, 143 n. 802
aja$_2$-ĝeštin, 169 n. 986
aja$_2$-ki-gal, 39 n. 182
aja$_2$-nir, 99 n. 526
AK, 60 w. n. 293, 127f. w. n. 696
AK EN$_a$ GAL$_a$, 58 n. 280
AK-^{d}Nin-gal, 58 n. 280
ama-ab-zu-da, 153 n. 877
ama-bara$_2$-ge-si, 65
(GAN$_2$) ama-bara$_2$-ge-si^{ki}, 65 n. 328
ama-bara$_2^!$(DARA$_4$)-ge, 58 n. 280
ama-bara$_2^!$(DARA$_4$)-si, 58 n. 280
ama-da-nu-sa$_2$, 177 n. 1050
ama-‹ĝeš›tin, 169 n. 986
ama-ig-gal, 116 n. 637
ama-kalam$^!$(LAK730)-ma, 100 n. 529
ama-lal$_3$, 169 n. 985
ama-lugal, 87 n. 436
ama-ne$_2$-al-sa$_6$, 175 n. 1033
ama-ni$_3$-kal-la, 163 n. 941
ama-numun-zi, 160 n. 921
ama-še-numun-⸢zi⸣, 160 n. 921
AMA UET2-370$_d$, 58 n. 280
amar-$^{(d)}$Nam-nir, 100 n. 528
amar-en-ne$_2$-il$_2$-la$_2$, 84 n. 410
amar-saĝa, 84 n. 416
*^{d}Amar-^{d}Su'en-a-kalam-ma, 102 n. 542
^{d}Amar-^{d}Su'en-igi-kalam-ma, 102 n. 542
^{d}Amar-^{d}Su'en-^{d}Lama$_3$-ĝu$_{10}$, 109 n. 580

^{d}Amar-^{d}Su'en-^{d}Ašnan-gin$_7$-zi-ša$_3$-ĝal$_2$-kalam-ma 137
^{d}Amar-^{d}Su'en-zi-kalam-ma, 137 n. 768
ambar-re$_2$-si, 176 n. 1036
AN-da-lu, 134 n. 745
an-dul$_3$-nu-me, 111f.
AN EN$_a$ DU, 58 n. 280
AN-i$_3$-kuš$_2$, 107 n. 567
AN-kalag-ga, 163
*AN-lugal, 184
AN-me-me-kalag-ga, 163 n. 939
AN-mud, 179 n. 1085
an-na-ḫe$_2$-ĝal$_2$, 137
an-ne$_2$-ba(-ab)-du$_7$, 53 n. 252, 142 n. 796
an-ta-ḫe$_2$-ĝal$_2$, 137
apin-ne$_2$, 131 n.. 727
$^{d\ aš}$aš$_7$-gi$_4$-da-lu, 134 n. 745
^{d}Aš$_8$-gi$_4$-pa-e$_3$, 174 n. 1018
aš$_{10}$-a-ni, 168 n. 971
aš$_{10}$-ša$_4$-ni, 168 n. 971

B

^{d}Ba-u$_2$-da-nir-ĝal$_2$, 99 n. 524
^{d}Ba-u$_2$-diĝir-ĝu$_{10}$, 120 n. 649
$^{i_7\ d}$Ba-u$_2$-ḫe$_2$-ĝal$_2$-su$_3$ (CN), 135 n. 751
^{d}Ba-u$_2$-i$_3$-kuš$_2$, 107 n. 568
^{d}Ba-u$_2$-ib$_2$-ta-e$_3$, 128 n. 701
^{d}Ba-u$_2$-lu$_2$-sa$_6$-ga, 123 n. 671
^{d}Ba-u$_2$-men$_x$(ĜA$_2$×EN)-zi-PAP.PAP, 89 w. n. 449
^{d}Ba-u$_2$-na-nam, 161 n. 924
^{d}Ba-u$_2$-nu-mu-šub-be$_2$, 124 n. 684
^{d}Ba-u$_2$-zi-kalam-ma, 137 n. 768
bad$_3$(LAK619b)-si-DU, 108 n. 570
bad$_3$-lugal-zi^{ki}, 183 n. 1132
BAḪAR$_{2a}$ EN$_a$, 58 n. 280
bara$_2$-ga-ne$_2$, 90 n. 458
bara$_2$-ge-si, 90n. 459
bara$_2$-zi-ša$_3$-ĝal$_2$, 137 n. 765
bu$_3$-la-ni, 176 n. 1042

D

da-da, 162 n. 933
dam-da-nu-sa$_2$, 177 n. 1050
DARA$_{4a1}$ SI, 58 n. 280
diĝir-ĝe$_{26}$-ab-be$_2$-en$_6$, 93 n. 478
diĝir-mu-daḫ, 128 n. 698
du$_{11}$-ga-ni-še$_3$, 92 n. 470
*dumu-lugal-nam, 184
DUN-NE(-nu-um), 215

E

e$_2$-da-ḫul$_2$, 177 n. 1057
e$_2$-da-lu, 134 n. 745, 177 n. 1057
e$_2$-da-sur-ra (FN), 177 n. 1057
e$_2$-di-de$_3$-ba-gub, 117 n. 640
E$_2$-Diĝir-ĜA$_2$-ab-be$_2$, 93 n. 477
e$_2$-eden-ne$_2$-si, 97 n. 502
e$_2$-en-ra, 143 n. 802
e$_2$-GAN$_2$-a, 132 n. 734
e$_2$-ĝissu-bi, 186 n. 1169
e$_2$-ḫa-lu-ub$_2$, 202 n. 1297
e$_2$-ḫur-saĝ, 167 n. 968
e$_2$-i$_3$-gara$_2$-sug$_4$, 122 n. 661
e$_2$-igi-nim-pa-e$_3$, 174 n. 1018
e$_2$-ki-be$_2$-gi$_4$, 179 n. 1083
e$_2$-ki-be$_6$-gi$_4$, 179 n. 1083
e$_2$-lu-be$_2$-dug, 88 n. 440
e$_2$-lu-be$_2$-zu, 88 n. 440
e$_2$-lu$_2$-be$_2$-du$_{10}$, 88 n. 440
e$_2$-lu$_2$-be$_2$-su, 88 n. 440
e$_2$-lu$_2$-be$_2$-zu, 88 n. 440
e$_2$-Ma-nu-gal, 237 n. 1422
e$_2$-mu-bi-du$_{10}$, 61 n. 300
E$_2$-muš$_3$-ša$_3$-bi-gal, 61
e$_2$-ni-še$_3$, 87 n. 438
e$_2$-sa$_x$(ŠU$_2$.SA)-par$_4$, 113 n. 611
e$_2$-su$_{13}$-aĝa$_2$, 174 n. 1022
e$_2$-šud$_3$-de$_3$, 139 n. 772
e$_2$-šud$_3$-du$_{10}$-ga, 139
e$_2$-ur$_2$-bi-du$_{10}$, 61, 188 n. 1201
e$_2$-Utu-gin$_7$-e$_3$, 173 n. 1012
e$_2$-zi-ĝal$_2$-kalam-ma (PN? TN?, 137 n. 765
e$_2$-zi-ša$_3$-ĝal$_2$, 137 n. 765
en-abzu-a-tum$_2$, 153 n. 878
en-abzu-ta-mud, 62
en-aga$_3$-zi-an-na, 89
en-an-na-tum$_2$, 77, 58 n. 280, 157
en-da-gal-di, 153 n. 878
en-da-nir-ĝal$_2$, 140, 183
en-eden-ne$_2$-si, 58 n. 280, 97 n. 502
en-en$_3$-tar-zi, 123 n. 666
en-ensi$_2$-gal, 129
en-⌜gu$_2$⌝-gal, 178 n. 1063
*en-ĝipar$_x$(KISAL)-re-si, 158 n. 912
en-ḫe$_2$-du$_7$-an-na, 55, 143 n. 803
en-il$_2$-⌜lu$_2^?$⌝-ni, 177 n. 1055

en-kisal-e-si, 158 n. 912
en-Kul-aba$_4$-si, 152 n. 872
^{d}En-lil$_2$-a$_2$-ĝu$_{10}$, 109
^{d}En-lil$_2$-a$_2$-maḫ, 98 w. n. 509
^{d}En-lil$_2$-al-sa$_6$, 175 n. 1033
^{d}En-lil$_2$-da-maḫ-di, 142 n. 789
^{d}En-lil$_2$-da-nir-ĝal$_2$, 142 n. 789
^{d}En-lil$_2$-gal-zu, 106 n. 562
^{d}En-lil$_2$-la$_2$, 59 n. 282
^{d}En-lil$_2$-la$_2$-al-sa$_6$, 175 n. 1033
^{d}En-lil$_2$-le, 175
^{d}En-lil$_2$-lu$_2$-sa$_6$-ga, 123 n. 671
^{d}En-lil$_2$-me-zi, 150 n. 850
^{d}En-lil$_2$-sipa, 60f.
en-lirum, 163
en-lu$_2$, 233
en-lu$_2$-sa$_6$-ga, 123 n. 671, 233
en-me-bara$_2$-si, 90f. n. 91
en-me-zi-An-na, 150 n. 850
en-me(n)-nun-na, 89 n. 446
en-^{d}Nanna-^{d}Amar-^{d}Su'en-ra-ki-aĝa$_2$, 55 n. 261
en-^{d}Nanše-mu-tu, 144 n. 806
en-ne$_2$-a-na-ak, 49 n. 230
en-ne$_2$-šu-du$_7$-a, 169 n. 983
en-ni$_3$-lu$_5$-la, 85 n. 421
en-ni$_3$-lu$_5$-la$_2$, 85 n. 421
en-ra-tum$_2$, 143 n. 802
en-saĝ, 169f. n. 979
en-sila-si, 130
en-sipa-zi-an-na, 111 n. 590
en-ša$_3$-kuš$_2$-An-na, 106
en-še-gu-na, 133 n. 742
en-šer$_7$-zi-an-na, 174 n. 1021
en-temen-na, 156 n. 900
en-u$_4$-su$_3$-še$_3$, 168 n. 976
*engar-du$_{10}$, 131 n. 725
engar-zi, 62
ereš-e-rib-ba-ni-gin$_7$-mi$_2$-zi(-du$_{11}$-ga), 49 n. 230
ereš-e-an-zu, 129 n. 706
ereš-še$_3$-an-su, 129 n. 706
G
gala, 60
GAN-ki, 179 n. 1081
geme$_2$-Bau, 71
geme$_2$-^{d}Dumu-zi, 60
^{ĝiš}gigir$_2$-du$_{10}$, 113 w. n. 605
GIR$_{3a/c}$ NI$_a$, 58 n. 280
giri$_3$-lugal-ĝa$_2$-i$_3$-dab$_5$, 175 n. 1025
giri$_3$-ni-ba-dab$_5$, 58 n. 280
gu$_3$-zi-de$_2$, 145 n. 815
gu$_3$-zi-de$_2$-a, 145 n. 815
Ĝ
ĝa$_2$-ka-na-nam-ḫe$_2$-ti, 161 n. 924
ĝi$_6$-par$_4$-e-ḫe$_2$-du$_7$, 143 n. 803
Ĝir$_2$-nun-zi-ša$_3$-ĝal$_2$, 137 n. 765
Ḫ
ḫa-la-^{d}Ba-u$_2$, 125 n. 689
ḫa-ma-ti, 121 n. 651
ḫi nin saĝ, 58 n. 280
ḫi saĝ e$_{2a}$, 58 n. 280
I
i$_3$-lu-lu-sila-si, 130 n. 717
i$_7$-de$_3$-ba-du$_7$, 53 n. 252
i$_7$-de$_3$-si, 118 n. 641
ib$_2$-ta-e$_3$, 128 n. 701
igi-AN-še$_3$, 61 n. 299
igi-AN-še$_3$-[(x$^?$)], 61 n. 299
igi-ĝu$_{10}$-AN-še$_3$-ĝal$_2$, 61, 119 n. 645
IL$_2$, 60 w. n. 288
^{d}Inana-ama-ĝu$_{10}$, 96 n. 496
^{d}Inana-diĝir-ĝu$_{10}$, 120 n. 649
^{d}Inana-men$_x$(ĜA$_2$×EN)-zi-PAP.PAP, 89
inim-du$_{11}$-du$_{11}$-ga-ni-an-dab$_5$, 92 n. 470
*inim-lugal-da-zi, 93 fn. 474
*inim-i$_3$-zi, 183 n. 1136
inim-ma-ni, 93 n. 474
inim-ni-zi, 183 n. 1136
inim-^{d}Nin-ĝir$_2$-su-ka-ib$_2$-ta-e$_3$, 128 n. 701
inim-^{d}Sud$_3$-da, 94 n. 480
inim-^{d}Sud$_3$-da-zi, 94 n. 480
inim-TAR-nin-ĝa$_2$, 118 n. 643
inim-Utu-zi, 93 n. 474
^{d}Iškur-ma-kuš$_2$, 124
K
KA-ni, 94 n. 484
KA-ni-ḫur-saĝ, 167 n. 968
ka$_5$-a, 60
ki-gal-du$_{10}$, 157 n. 903
ki-ni-ḫur-saĝ-še$_3$-maḫ, 167 n. 966
ki-saĝ-gam-gam, 181 n. 1103
ki-tuš-du$_{10}$, 125 n. 688
KISAL$_{b1}$ PAP$_a$ SI, 58 n. 280
KISAL$_{b1}$ SI AMA$_b$, 58 n. 280

kur-DA-bad, 102 n. 546
kur-da-lu-lu (FN), 134 n. 745
kur-giri$_{3}$-ni-še$_{3}$, 115f.
kur-mu-gam, 116 n. 626
kur-šu-ni-še$_{3}$, 115
L
Lagaš^{ki}-giri$_{3}$-na, 116 n. 626, 187
LAK611(EZEM×BAD)-si-DU, 108 n. 570
^{d}lama$_{3}$-zi-ĝu$_{10}$, 109 n. 579
*lu-ga-lu-mu-ug, 184
lu$_{2}$-a-ma-ru (lu⸢gal⸣-a-ma-ru), 112 n. 598
lu$_{2}$-aĝrig-zi, 129f. n. 715
lu$_{2}$-bi, 161 n. 924
lu$_{2}$-bi-na-nam, 161 n. 924
lu$_{2}^{!}$(LUGAL)-diĝir-ra, 177 n. 1052
lu$_{2}$-engar-zi, 132 n. 730
lu$_{2}$-gi-sa$_{3}$, 162 n. 931
lu$_{2}$-ḫi-li-su$_{3}$, 170 n. 995
lu$_{2}$-igi-sa$_{6}$, 162 n. 931
lu$_{2}$-inim-kalag, 94 n. 481
lu$_{2}$-na-nam, 161 n. 924
lu$_{2}$-nin-MU, 141 n. 786
lu$_{2}$-^{d}Nin-mu$_{2}$, 141 n. 786
lu$_{2}$-nu-mu-da-sa$_{2}$, 167 n. 969
*lu$_{2}$-Ti-ra-aš$_{2}$-še$_{3}$, 155 n. 889
lu$_{2}$-tuš-du$_{10}$, 125 n. 688
*lugal-a-maḫ, 184
lugal-a$_{2}$-da, 175 n. 1029
*lugal-a$_{2}$-gur-re$_{2}$, 184
*lugal-a$_{2}$-MUG.GU-pa$_{3}$, 184
*lugal-AB.URI$_{3}$.KI, 185
lugal-⸢aĝa$_{2}$⸣, 170 n. 994
*lugal-AN-da-maḫ-di, 141
*lugal-AN-da-nir-ĝal$_{2}$, 141
lugal-an-na-ab-tum$_{2}$, 143 n. 799
*lugal-an-na-igi-su-su, 185
lugal-an-na-tum$_{2}$, 65 n. 321
lugal-an-ne$_{2}$-ba-DU, 142 n. 796
lugal-bad$_{3}$-uru-na, 96 n. 499
lugal-da-nir-ĝal$_{2}$, 142 n. 790
*lugal-dam-me-ki-aĝ$_{2}$, 185
*lugal-dib-ra-na$_{2}$, 185
Lugaldiĝirda, 142 n. 791
*lugal-du$_{10}$-bar-SU, 185
lugal-du$_{11}$-ge-du$_{7}$, 93 n. 477
*lugal-dub-saĝ-ki, 185
*lugal-dumu-gir$_{15}$-ni, 18o n. 1088
lugal-dur$_{2}$-du$_{10}$, 125 n. 688
*lugal-e-a$_{2}$-na-mu-gub, 121
lugal-e$_{2}$-muš-e, 155
*lugal-e$_{2}$-ni-še$_{3}$-nu-kar$_{2}$-kar$_{2}$, 87f.
lugal-en-saĝ, 168f. n. 979
Lugal-^{d}EN.ZU^{ki}, 210 n. 1336
*lugal-engar-du$_{10}$, 131 n. 725
lugal-gaba-ri-nu-tuku, 142 n. 796
lugal-gu$_{4}$-e, 135 n. 754, 148 n. 837
lugal-ĝiskim-ti, 129 n. 714
lugal-ḫe$_{2}$-du$_{7}$-an-ki, 143 n. 803
lugal-ḫi-li-an-na, 170 n. 995
*lugal-ḫi-li-su$_{3}$, 170 n. 995
*lugal-i$_{3}$-zi, 183 n. 1136
lugal-igi-an-na, 142 n. 793
lugal-igi-sa$_{6}$-sa$_{6}$, 162 n. 932
[lugal]-im-ri-a, 179 n. 1079
lugal-^{d}KA.DI-gin$_{7}$-di-ku$_{5}$-da-pa-e$_{3}$, 146 n. 824
Lugal-kalam-ma$^{\langle ki \rangle}$, 100 n. 530
*lugal-ki-gub(-a)-ni-še$_{3}$-du$_{7}$-du$_{7}$, 155f
*lugal-ki-ni-še$_{13}$-du$_{7}$-du$_{7}$, 156 n. 896
lugal-kisal-e-si, 158 n. 912
lugal-kisal-le-si, 158 n. 912
lugal-ku$_{3}$-maḫ, 179 n. 1087
lugal-^{d}Lama$_{3}$-ĝu$_{10}$, 109
lugal-ma$_{2}$-gur$_{8}$-re, 102 n. 540
lugal-me-šu-du$_{7}$, 169 n. 982
lugal-me$_{3}$-a, 117
*lugal(-ak)-murum-ma(-ni)-du$_{10}$(-ga-am), 178
lugal-nam-tar-re, 104 n. 556
lugal-^{d}Nanše-ki-aĝ$_{2}$, 144 n. 805
lugal-ne-te-na, 161 w. n. 927
lugal-nesaĝ-e-si, 148 n. 831
lugal-ni$_{2}$-ri-a, 179 n. 1079
*lugal-ni$_{3}$-bara$_{4}$-ga, 187
*lugal-ni$_{3}$-bara$_{4}$-ge, 187
lugal-nidba-si$^{!}$ (?), 147 n. 828
lugal-Nina^{ki}-ta, 153 n. 881
lugal-nir, 99 n. 524
*lugal-ra-ni, 95 n. 487
lugal-sa-par$_{2}$-re, 114 w. n. 614
*lugal-saĝa-ni, 95 n. 487
lugal-suluḫu(SIG.SUD), 91 n. 466
lugal-ša$_{3}$-ga, 163, 224, 264
*lugal-ša$_{3}$-[ga]-su$_{3}$, 122 n. 660

lugal-ša$_3$-la$_2$-su$_3$, 122 n. 660
lugal-ša$_3$-su$_{13}$, 122 n. 655
lugal-ša$_3$-naĝa, 122 n. 657
lugal-Ti-⸢ra⸣-[aš$_2$-e], 155 n. 889
*lugal-tur(-nir), 182 n. 1124
*lugal-UD.DIM.E$_3$, 173 n. 1012
*lugal-uru-da-lugal, 125 n. 691
lugal-^{d}Utu-gin$_7$, 146 n. 824, 211 n. 1347
*lugal-zi-ga, 183 n. 1137
lugal-zi-ĝu$_{10}$, 183 n. 1132
LUM-ma-MU, 124 n. 678
M
*ma-ti-ra-aš$_2$, 155 n. 889
ma$_2$-gur$_8$-si, 135 n. 757
maš, 60
maš-gur-ra, 162 n. 935
maš-^{d}Nin-ĝir$_2$-su, 85 n 418
me-Eridu^{ki}-ta, 153 n. 880
me-ḫur-saĝ, 167 n. 968
*me-lugal-kur-dub$_2$, 115 n. 624
me-nun-si, 39 n. 182
me-šu-du$_7$, 169 n. 982
me-zi-pa-e$_3$, 150 n. 850
men-nun-na, 89 n. 446
^{d}Mes-an-du-lu$_2$-sa$_6$-ga, 123 n. 671
mes-en-ra-tum$_2$, 143 n. 802
mes-kalam-ne$_2$-du$_{10}$, 101 n. 532
mes-KALAM-NI-du$_{10}$, 101 n. 532
*mes-ki-aĝ$_2$-nun, 145 n. 818
mes-nun-ki-aĝ$_2$, 145 n. 818
*mes-uĝ$_3$-i$_3$-du$_{10}$, 101 n. 532
mes-uĝu$_3$-ne$_2$-du$_{10}$, 101 n. 532
mu-ni-da, 180 n. 1097
mu-ni-ḫur-saĝ, 167 n. 968
mu-ni-^{d}I$_7$-da, 180 n. 1097
mu-ni-kalam(-ma), 188 n. 1200
mu-ni-lal$_3$, 169 n. 985
mu-ni-uri$_3$, 151
*mug-gu-pa$_3$, 184 n. 1146
munus-alam-ak, 175 n. 1034
munus-en-da, 58 n. 280
munus-ĝeštin, 169 n. 986
munus-ig-gal, 116 n. 631
N
nam-dag-su$_3$, 140 n. 780
nam-egi-ni-du$_{10}$, 83 n. 403
nam-ku-li-ni-du$_{10}$, 83 n. 403
nam-lugal-ni-du$_{10}$, 83 n. 404
nam-nin-(a)-ni-du$_{10}$, 83 n. 403
nam-šita-ĝu$_{10}$-bi$_2$-du$_{11}$, 140 n. 784
nam-um-me-ga-ni, 83 n. 403
nam-ušur$_3$-ni-ŠE$_3$, 83 n. 403
Nanna^{na}, 59 n. 282, 172 n. 1007
^{d}Nanna-aĝa$_2$, 170 n. 994
Nanna-erim$_2$-ma, 172 n. 1007
^{d}Nanna-gal-zu, 106 n. 562
^{d}Nanna-lugal, 96 n. 496, 141
^{d}Nanna-⸢lugal⸣-dalla, 141 n. 785
^{d}Nanna-mu-daḫ, 128 n. 699
^{d}Nanna-sa$_6$-ga, 51
^{d}Nanna-uri$_3$, 151 n. 864
^{d}Nanna-za-me-en, 161 n. 925
^{d}Nanše-lu$_2$-sa$_6$-ga, 123 n. 671
^{d}Nanše-uri$_3$, 151 n. 864
ni$_2$-ḫur-saĝ, 167 n. 968
ni$_3$-ĝa$_2$-ni, 84 n. 407
ni$_3$-U.TA, 84 n. 409
Nibru^{ki}-da-lu, 134 n. 745
Nibru^{ki}-da-lu$_2$, 134 n. 745
NIĜ$_2$-da-lu, 134 n. 745
niĝir-me-te-na, 161 w. n. 929
nin-a$_2$-maḫ, 97f. w. n. 508
^{d}Nin-a$_2$-na^{ki}, 121 n. 653
nin-ab-ba-nir-ĝal$_2$, 99 n. 526
nin-aga$_3$-zi, 88 n. 442
nin-aĝrig-zi, 129f. n. 715
nin-an-dul$_3$, 108 n. 569
NIN AN GAL$_a$ AK$_a$, 58 n. 280
nin-bad$_3$-uru-na, 96 n. 499
nin-bara$_2$-ga-ne$_2$-du$_{10}$, 90 n. 458
nin-be$_2$-al-sa$_6$, 175 n. 1033
nin-da-nir, 99 n. 524
nin-da-nu-me-a, 111
nin-DAM-MU, 177 n. 1051
nin-di-de$_3$, 117f. n. 640
nin-e-a$_2$-na, 121 n. 653
nin-e$_2$-gal-le-si, 185
nin-e$_2$-gal-NI-si, 185 n. 1162
nin-e$_2$-ni-še$_3$-nu-kar$_2$-kar$_2$, 88 n. 439
nin-e$_2$-Unug^{ki}-ga-nir-ĝal$_2$, 99 n. 526, 152 n. 873
nin-eg$_2$-ge, 132 n. 732
nin-en-nu-ĝu$_{10}$, 108f. n. 573
nin-en-ra, 143 n. 802
nin-en$_3$-tar-ĝu$_{10}$, 163, 164
nin-engar-zi, 132 n. 730
nin-ensi$_2$, 37 n. 172

nin-ensi₂-uru-na, 37 n. 172
nin-ezem-ma-ne₂, 130f. n. 721
nin-ezem-ma-ne₂-ki-aĝ₂, 130f.
nin-gal-zu, 106 n. 562
nin-GAN₂-a, 132 n. 734
nin-gu₂-gal, 178 n. 1063
nin-ĝa₂-si, 136 n. 763
ᵈNin-ĝir₂-su-bad₃-uru-na, 96 n. 499
ᵈNin-ĝir₂-su-za-me, 161 n. 925
nin-ĝiskim-ti, 129 n. 714
nin-ĝissu, 186 n. 1169
nin-ĝissu-na-NI, 186 n. 1169
nin-ĝu₁₀-da-nu-me-a, 111 n. 593
nin-ĝu₁₀-niĝin-ĝu₁₀, 141 n. 786
nin-ĝu₁₀-nin-ĝu₁₀, 141 n. 786
nin-ḪAR-an-[x], 178 n. 1066
nin-i₃-kuš₂, 107 n. 568
nin-ib₂-ta-e₃, 128 n. 701
nin-ig-gal, 116 n. 631
nin-inim-ĝa₂-ka-bi, 93 n. 479
nin-inim-TAR, 118 n. 643
nin-kar-re, 136 n. 762
nin-kar-re₂, 136 n. 762
nin-ki-tuš-du₁₀, 125 n. 688
nin-kisal-si, 58 n. 280
ᵈNin-lil₂-zi-ša₃-ĝal₂, 137 n. 765
nin-lu₂-ni-nu-si-ge, 83 n. 401
nin-lu₂-ni-nu-ša-ge, 83 n. 401
*nin-lugal-ti-ti, 123 n. 669
nin-ma-de₆, 121 n. 654
nin-ma₂-gur₈-re-si, 136 n. 762
nin-maš-e, 148 n. 837
nin-me-du₁₀(-ga), 150 n. 848
nin-me-gal-gal, 149 n. 844
nin-me-sikil-An-na, 150 w. n. 849
nin-menₓ(ĜA₂×EN), 88 n. 444
nin-menz(ĜIŠ×EN), 88 n. 444
nin-MU-ba-daḫ, 128 n. 699
nin-mu-da-kuš₂, 124 n. 678
nin-mu-daḫ, 128 n. 699
nin-nam-dag-nu-tuku, 140 n. 780
nin-nam-mu-šub-be₂, 124 n. 684
nin-nam-mu-šub-e, 124 n. 683
nin-nam-tag-du₈, 140 n. 780
nin-namⁱ(MU)-tag-du₈, 140 n. 780
nin-ni₃-ni, 84 n. 407
nin-ni₃-sa₆-sa₆-ga, 170 n. 992
nin-ni₃-ša₃-An-na-ke₄-ba-du₁₀, 163 n. 941

nin-nu-mu-šub-e, 124 n. 684
nin-saĝ-e-ki-aĝ₂, 168f. n. 979
nin-saĝ-ĝe₂₆-tuku, 168f. n. 979
nin-si-ĝar-ab-ba, 49 n. 230, 116 n. 633
nin-ša₃-gid₂, 122 w. n. 658
nin-ša₃-la₂-tuku, 122 w. n. 658
nin-ša₃-su-ĝu₁₀, 129 n. 707
nin-ˢᵉ³šer₇-zi, 174 n. 1021
nin-šer₇-zi, 174 n. 1021
nin-tigiₓ-ni, 148 n. 836
nin-tigiₓ-ni-du₁₀, 148 n. 836
*nin-tug₂, 91 n. 465
nin-tug₂-maḫ, 91 w. n. 465
nin-uri₃, 151 n. 864
nin-uru-da-kuš₂, 125
nin-uru-ni-še₃-nu-kar₂-kar₂, 88 n. 439
nin-uru₁₆-ni-še₃-nu-kar₂-kar₂, 88 n. 439
nin-uru₁₆-še₃-nu-kar₂-kar₂, 88 n. 439
nin-za-me, 161 n. 925
*nin-za₃-ta-e₃, 120 n. 646
nin-zi-ša₃-ĝal₂, 137 n. 765
nir-AN-da-ĝal₂, 99 n. 524
numun-zi, 160 n. 921

P
PAP.PAP, 54, 89, 120 w. n. 649, 144 n. 806
PAP.PAP-ᵈBa-u₂-mu-tu, 144 n. 806
PAP.PAP-diĝir-ĝu₁₀, 120 n. 649
PAP.PAP-ᵈNanše-mu-tu, 144 n. 806

S
sa-a, 60
saĝ-be₆-e₃-a, 169 n. 981
saĝ-lugal-e-zu, 88 n. 440
saĝ-ᵈNanna-zu, 88 n. 440
saĝ-nin-e-zu, 88 n. 440
saĝ-ᵈUtu-zu, 88 n. 440
SI DARA₄ᵦ AMA, 58 n. 280
sila-si, 130 n. 717
sipa-lu₂-sa₆-ga, 123 n. 671
sipa-uru-da-kuš₂, 125 n. 690
su₆-mu₂, 215
ᵈSud₃-a₂-maḫ, 98 w. n. 509
ᵈSud₃-šer₇-zi, 174 n. 1021

Š
ša₃-AN, 129 n. 706
ša₃-AN-[x], 129 n. 706

2. Akkadian names

The index contains references to names cited in discussions and notes, excluding *śarrum*-names from the period investigated. The list also includes names from later periods. Forms which have been thought of as containing the appellative *śarrum* and names the readings of which are questionable, are all marked with a star symbol *. Names of persons discussed from a point of view of historical significance may also be found in index number 4, below.

A

a-ḫu-ni, 191 n. 1238
Aḫa-arši, 51f.
a$_2$*-bi*$_2$*-la-ša*, 95
a-bi$_3$*-la-ša*, 95
^{d}Adad-*šar-ru-um*, 210 n. 1335
al-mu-NE, 215
AN-*al-śu*, 197 n. 1273
**aś-ma*$_2$$^{!}$(SI)-*śar*, 214
Aš$_{10}$-tar$_2$-*al-śu*, 197 n. 1273
Aš$_{10}$-tar$_2$-*ni-sa*, 213 n. 1366

B

ba-al-li$_2$, 202 n. 1294
be-la-ma-AN, 209 n. 1327
be-la-śu-nu, 18 n. 64
be-le-su$_2$*-nu*, 18 n. 64
be-let-su-nu, 18 n. 64
be-li$_2$, 191 n. 1237
be-li$_2$*-ba-ni*, 202 n. 1294
be-li$_2$-bad$_3$, 197 n. 1271
be-li$_2$-bad$_3$-*ri*$_2$, 197 n. 1272
be-li$_2$-bara$_2$, 91
be-li$_2$*-dan*, 206 n. 1309
be-li$_2$-*Du-Gul*, 214 n. 1367
be-li$_2$*-du*$_2$*-ri*$_2$, 197 n. 1271, 214 n. 1367
be-li$_2$-du$_{10}$, 210 n. 1339
be-li$_2$-gal-zu, 195
be-li$_2$-gar$_3$, 207 n. 1315
be-li$_2$-gi, 211 n. 1343
be-li$_2$*-gu*$_2$, 198 n. 1278
be-li$_2$*-iś-ta*$_2$*-kal*$_2$, 196 n. 1264
be-li$_2$-kara$_6$(GUR$_7$), 208 n. 1324
be-li$_2$*-la-ba*, 207 n. 1311
be-li$_2$*-me-li*$_2$, 209 n. 1330
be-li$_2$*-mu-da*, 195
be-li$_2$-NE, 178 n. 1072
be-li$_2$*-nu-ri*$_2$, 211 n. 1348
be-li$_2$*-pa*$_2$*-luḫ*, 207 n. 1312
be-li$_2$*-tu*$_3$*-kul*$_2$*-ti*, 199
be-li$_2$-^{d}Utu$^{\acute{s}i}$, 239 n. 1429
be-lu-gu$_2$, 198 n. 1278
be-lum-gu$_2$, 198 n. 1278
be-*su*$_{13}$-bad$_3$, 197 n. 1271
be$_2$*-lat-su-nu*, 18 n. 64

D

da-na-LUGAL, 121 n. 653
da-ni-LUGAL, 121 n. 653
dan-ma-ḫum, 209 n. 1327
dan-ma-šeš, 209 n. 1327
dan-nu-šarru, 206 n. 1309

E

E$_2$-a-ba-ni, 202 n. 1295
E$_2$-a-*šar-rum*, 210 n. 1334
en-bi$_2$-Aš$_{10}$-tar$_2$, 213
eś$_3$*-me-qara*$_4$(GA*gunû*), 207 w. n. 1318
eś$_3$*-me-qara*$_4$*-ad*, 208
EZEM-*qar-ra-ad*, 208

G

gal-zu-sipa-*ni*, 199

I

i-da-be, 195
i-da-be-li$_2$, 195
I-da-AN, 73 n. 367
i-di$_3$-DN/DN-*iddinam*, 121
i-ku^{ku_8}*-il*, 232 n. 1399
i-mi$^{!}$(DUGUD)-*i*$_3$*-lum*, 197 n. 1268
i-na-ša-me-e-wu-sum$_2$, 143 n. 803
i-śar-be-li$_2$, 215
i-śar-ru-um, 215 n. 1395
i-šar-le-e, 214 n. 1378
ib-ni-ba-li$_2$, 201 n. 1292
ib-ni-be$_6$*-li*$_2$, 201 n. 1292

iḫ-bu-ut-al-śi-in, 198 n. 1275
Ikšud-appašu, 52
il-śu$_3$-gar$_3$, 207 n. 1317
il$_2$*-e-i-śar*, 214
**il*$_2$*-e-śar*, 214
Il$_3$-a-ba$_4$-*al-śu*, 197 n. 1273
il$_3$*-śu*-gar$_3$, 207 w. n. 1317
il$_3$*-śu-la-ba*, 207 n. 1311
il$_3$*-śu-qa*$_2$*-ra-ad*, 207 w. n. 1317
il$_3$*-śu-qara*$_4$(GAgunû)*-ad*, 207
ʾIlak-nuʾʾid, 73
ʾIliś-takal, 73
iś$_2$*-ma*$_2$*-qar-du*, 208
Ištaran-*dābibī*, 93f. n. 479
iš-ṭup-be, 197 n. 1269
iš-ṭup-il, 197 n. 1269
K
ka$_3$*-la-ab*-E$_2$-a, 238
^{giš}tukul^{ka_3}*-śu-al-śi-in*, 197 n. 1274
kal$_2$*-bu*$_3$-Aš$_{10}$-tar$_2$, 213 n. 1356
**ki-śar*, 214
Ku-Da-Al$^?$-la, 213 n. 1365
ku$_8$*-li*-SAR, 171 n. 997
ku$_8$*-ru*$_x$(KU)*-ub-e-la-ak*, 195 n. 1260
L
li-pi$_5$*-it-i*$_3$*-le*, 182
*lugal-*a-mi*, 214f.
*lugal-*bi*$_2$*-nu-um*, 180 n. 1099, 215
*lugal-*na-da*, 215
*lugal-*pu*$_5$ (KA), 193, 215
*lugal-*pum*, 193, 215
M
^{d}Ma-lik-*zi-in-śu*, 73 w. n. 367
Ma-ma-ḫur-saĝ, 210 n. 1338
Ma-mi-*šar-ra-at*, 210 w. n. 1337
mār-ūmi-ešrā, 52 n. 247
Mīn-arnī, 52
N
na-aḫ-śum-śa-na-at, 73
na-ḫaś$_2$*-śi-na-at*, 73
^{d}*Na-ra-am*-^{d}EN.ZU-*i*$_3$*-li*$_2$, 55, n. 262, 200 n. 1287
P
pu$_3$-AD, 115 n. 621
**pu*$_3$*-śar*, 193, 215
pu$_3$*-śu*-gi, 93
R
ra-am-ra-zu-en-zu, 83 n. 404
S
sipa-*ni-śe*$_2$, 198f.
sipa-*śi-in*, 198
^{d}Su'en-*al-śu*, 197 n. 1273
Ś
**śar-be-li*$_2$, 215
śar-ru-URU.KI^{li_2}, 197 n. 1273
**śar-ru-um*-Dilmun-*mu-bi*$_2$, 215
**śar-ru-um*-maḫ$_2$*-mu-pi*$_5$, 215
śi-ḫur-saĝ, 192 n. 1244, 210 n. 1338
śu-ma-a-ba$_4$, 210 n. 1333
śu-mi-ig-ri$_2$, 55 n. 260
Š
šar-ma-^{d}Adad, 209 n. 1327
šar-na-an, 209 n. 1328
šar-ri-ni, 191 n. 1240
Šarru-kīn(*u*), 210 n. 1341
Šarru-nūri, 211 n. 1348
šar-ru-su$_2$*-ṭa-bat*$_3$, 83 n. 405
Šēpēt-Ninlil-*aṣbat*, 53
Šikkû, 52
šu-ʿAštar, 73
^{d}*Šu*-^{d}Su'en-*wu-su*$_2$*-um-i-šar-ri*, 143 n. 803
T
tar$_2$*-am*$_3$-A-ka$_3$-de$_3$^{ki}, 55 n. 260
taš$_2$*-ṭup*-AN.AN, 232 n. 1399
taš$_3$*-lul-tum*, 38 n. 178
Ṭ
ṭa$_3$*-ab-e-li-ma-ti-šu*, 101 n. 533
ṭa$_3$*-ab-e-li-um-ma-ni-šu*, 101 n. 533
U
u-bil-Aš$_{10}$-tar$_2$, 55 n. 260
^{d}Utu-*i-in*-^{d}En-lil$_2$, 142 n. 793
W
wu-sum$_2$-^{d}Šul-gi, 143 n. 803
Y
yirʿeum, 72f.

3. Persons

The following names represent persons mentioned in the text, and whose names are not necessarily of primary interest to the main lines of the investigation itself.

A

Abī-simtī, 56 n. 266
Ajašurmen, 38 n. 178
AK-Utu, 89 n. 446
Amat-Bau, 52
Amat-Eššešim, 52, 131 n. 723

B

Bilgames, 47 n. 218, 163 n. 938, 202 n. 1296
bil$_2$-lal$_3$-la, 61 n. 300

E

Eanatum, 6 n. 16, 12 n. 44, 40 n. 191, 44 n. 211, 48, 50, 68 n. 339, 98 n. 516, 106, 109 n. 575, 114, 115, 128 n. 702, 145 nn. 813 & 816, 164 n. 950, 167, 176 n. 1044, 251
Enanatum I, 6 n. 16, 38 n. 178, 54, 111, 116
Enanatum-sipa-zi, 54, 111
Enentarzi, 41 n. 195, 186
Enḫeduana, 143 n. 803, 208 n. 1326
Enmenana, 89
en-me(n)-nun-na, 89 n. 446
Enšakušana, 39 n. 185, 182 n. 1119
Erriduwizir, 44 n. 210

G

gan-saman$_3$(ŠE.ŠE$_3$.BU.NUN)-nu, 115 n. 621
Gudea, 44, 105 n. 557, 109 n. 575, 119 n. 644, 120, 129, 130, 140, 149, 151, 157 n. 910, 158 n. 913, 162 n. 936, 165–166 w. n. 956

Ĝ

Ĝišakidu, 38 n. 174, 99 n. 520

Ḫ

Ḫammurapi, 33, 43

I

Ipḫur-Kiš, 55, 217, 244
ir$_{11}$-ĝu$_{10}$, 56
ir$_{11}$-^{d}Nanna, 56

L

Lugalanatum, 44 n. 210
LugalANda, 54, 87 n. 436, 92 n. 469, 108, 111 n. 593, 120, 141–142, 158 n. 913, 180 n. 1093, 216, 217, 224, 226, 253 n. 1488
Lugajaĝu, 41 n. 195
Lugalanemundu, 248 n. 1458
Lugalbanda, 106, 151 n. 858
Lugalkigubnišedudu, 156, 250 n. 1472
Lugalušumgal, 257 n. 1518
Lugalzagesi, 39 n. 185, 41, 50 n. 236, 68 n. 342, 91, 95, 98, 100 n. 529, 102 n. 544, 129, 140 n. 784, 147 n. 829, 150 n. 854, 158 n. 915, 160 n. 919, 164 n. 950, 221, 224, 250 n. 1473, 252
Lu$_2$-^{d}Utu, 157

M

Maništūšu, 43, 193 n. 1249, 257
Mār-Ištar, 52, 87 n. 428
Mebarasi, 39, 247 n. 1454
me-nun-si, 39 n. 182
men-nun, 89 n. 446
men-nun-na, 89 n. 446
Mesilim, 39

N

Naḫśum-śanat, 73
Narām-Su'en, 33, 44 n. 209, 55, 72 n. 362, 83 n. 404, 89, 111 n. 592, 182 n. 1117, 192, 193, 194, 198 n. 1282, 201, 203, 206, 208, 244, 255 n. 1501, 257

P

Puzur-Mama, 44, 105 n. 557

R

Rīm-Sîn-Šala-*bāštašu*, 165 n. 951
Rīmuś, 43, 106, 147 n. 827, 208
Ruttīya, 52

S
Samsuditana, 52 n. 246
Samsuiluna, 172 n. 1005
Si-u_3-um, 44 n. 210
Ś
Śarkaliśarrē, 55, 192, 201, 204, 206, 257, 259
Śarrukēn, 23, 38 n. 178, 41 n. 192, 43, 73, 76, 114 n. 612, 129 n. 708, 143 n. 803, 147 n. 829, 150 n. 854, 192–193, 200, 203, 204, 205–206, 210–211, 221, 225, 250, 255–256, 257
Śuā(i)ś-takal, 196 w. n. 1266
Š
Šulgi, 56–57, 84 n. 414, 94, 98, 106 n. 562, 109, 134 n. 748, 143 n. 803, 164 n. 946, 173, 241
Šulgi-*simtī*, 56 n. 266
Šutruk-Naḫḫunte, 33
T
Tarām-Akkade, 55 n. 260, 217
Tašlultum, 38 n. 178
Tūtaʾ-śar-libbīś, 55 n. 260, 215, 240
Tuṭṭanābśum, 55 n. 260, 72 n. 362
U
U'u, 41 n. 193
Ur-Bau, 162 n. 936
Ur-Namma, 79, 98, 132 n. 729, 180 n. 1092
UruKAgina, 12 n. 44, 41, 54, 61 n. 305, 89 n. 450, 103, 139 n. 773, 153 n. 880, 168 n. 978, 256 n. 1507

4. Deities

The index cites page and footnote references to divinities forming part of discussions. For some deities, there is a certain overlap with the indices of Sumerian and Akkadian PNN as many of them are discussed when appearing as theophore elements in names.

A
Alla, 113 n. 610, 213 n. 1365
Amaušumgal(ana), 166 n. 962, 172 n. 1006
^{d}Am-gal-KIŠ, 175 n. 1035
^{d}Am-gal-nun, 175 n. 1035
Anzu, 103, 114–115, 165–167
Asalluḫi, 70 n. 356, 129 n. 705
Ašgi, 134 n. 745, 174, 250
Ašnan, 137
B
Bau, 37 n. 172, 44, 49, 52, 71, 89, 110 n. 584, 99 n. 524, 107 n. 568, 118 n. 643, 120 n. 649, 122 n. 661, 123 n. 671, 124 n. 684, 125 n. 689, 128 n. 701, 135 n. 751, 137 n. 768, 139 n. 773, 141 n. 788, 144 n. 806, 161 nn. 924–925, 234
D
Dagān, 192, 203
Dumuzi, 60, 68 n. 337, 91 n. 465–466, 113 n. 610, 139 n. 776, 146, 155, 174 n. 1018, 217, 229
E
Enki, 68 n. 336, 69, 70 n. 352, 77, 96 n. 494, 105 n. 557, 127 n. 694, 136 n. 759, 143 n. 798, 147 w. n. 826, 152, 153 nn. 877 & 879, 160 n. 916, 177 n. 1048, 217, 229, 248 n. 1460, 249, 252
Enkimdu, 132 n. 733
Enlil, 38 n. 175, 43, 54, 55 n. 260, 59 n. 282, 60, 63, 67 n. 333, 68–69, 70 n. 352, 71, 77, 86, 92 n. 468, 96 n. 498, 97 n. 506, 98, 99 nn. 520 & 522, 102 n. 544, 106 n. 562, 106f. n. 566, 109, 111, 112 n. 597, 119 n. 644, 123 n. 671, 129, 140 n. 784, 142–143, 145, 146, 147 n. 829, 148 n. 837, 149, 150, 154, 160, 168, 175 n. 1033, 176 n. 1037, 192, 193, 194, 203, 204,

217, 224, 226, 229, 233, 237, 248 n. 1459, 249, 252, 253, 255, 257
Ereškigal, 157
Erra, 68 n. 338, 197
$Eš_3$-ir-nun, 155 n. 891
I
Ilaba, 192, 197 n. 1273
^{d}Inana-kur-si, 103 n. 550
L
Lugal-amaru, 112 n. 597
^{d}Lugal:ambar, 176 n. 1036
^{d}Lugal-agrun-na, 158 n. 914
Lugal-dur(a), 180 n. 1090
Lugal-eden(-na), 85 n. 420, 97 w. n. 503
^{d}Lugal-eg_2-ga, 132 n. 732
^{d}Lugal-ḫe_2-ĝal_2(-la), 134 n. 749
^{d}Lugal-ḫur-saĝ, 167 n. 967
Lugal-idda, 178 n. 1073
Lugal-ilduma, 179 n. 1077
Lugal-inimgina, 93 n. 471
Lugal-KA-gin_6-na, 93 n. 471
Lugal-kalag-ga, 163 n. 938
Lugal-kalam-ma-u_3-tu-ud, 101 n. 535
Lugal-kurra, 103 n. 549
^{d}Lugal-LAK545, 180 n. 1090
Lugal-ma_2-gur_8-ra, 135 n. 757
Lugalmarad, 102 n. 542
Lugal-nam-tar-ra, 104 n. 556
^{d}Lugal-nir-ĝal_2, 99 n. 525
Lugal-nitaḫ-zi, 171 n. 1001
Lugal-sa-par_4, 113 n. 607
Lugal-si, 181 n. 1108
Lugal-sisa, 118 n. 642
^{d}Lugal-sukud-ra_2, 169 n. 984
Lugal-šudde, 139 n. 776
Lugal-UD, 69 n. 348
Lugal-uru, 182 n. 1127
Lugal-uru_{11}(URU×KAR_2), 182 n. 1127
Lugal-uru-bar(-ra), 182 n. 1127
M
^{d}Ma-ni, 209 n. 1329
^{d}Men_x(ĜA_2×EN), 89
^{d}Men_x(ĜA_2×EN)-bar, 89
^{d}Mes-nun-sa_6-aĝ$_2$, 145 n. 818
^{d}Mes-saĝa-uru_{16}, 68 n. 336
N
^{d}$Nam_{(2)}$-nir, 100 n. 528
Nanna/Su'en, 51, 55, 56, 59 n. 282, 63, 69, 70, 77, 88 n. 440, 89, 96 n. 496, 104, 106 n. 562, 106f. n. 566, 114 n. 613, 128 n. 699, 135 n. 755, 137 n. 765, 141, 143, 150, 151, 154 n. 886, 161 n. 925, 168, 170 n. 994, 172, 173, 189, 197, 208, 210, 217, 225, 229, 236, 238, 240, 247 n. 1454, 249–250, 251 n. 1478, 252, 253 n. 1486, 254, 256, 258, 259, 261
Nanše, 41 n. 192, 50 n. 237, 54, 87 n. 436, 99 n. 526, 118 n. 643, 123 n. 671, 130, 133, 141 n. 788, 144, 145 n. 816, 151, 176 n. 1045, 216, 217, 225, 226, 246 n. 1448, 251 n. 1478, 258
Nergal, 146 n. 822, 163 n. 938, 192, 258
Ningirsu, 41 n. 195, 54, 67, 85 n. 418, 96 n. 499, 99 n. 525, 112, 115, 118 n. 642, 119 n. 644, 128 n. 701, 132 n. 728, 133 n. 735, 149, 151 n. 865, 153 n. 881, 161 n. 925, 162 nn. 930 & 936, 164 n. 947, 165 n. 953, 166, 167 n. 964, 168 n. 976, 175 n. 1035, 182 n. 1128, 189, 249, 250, 251f. n. 1480, 258, 259, 261, 263
Ningišzida, 113 n. 610, 139 n. 776
Ningublaga, 172 n. 1009
Ninḫursaĝ, 50, 70 n. 352, 154, 167, 176 n. 1039
^{d}Nin-me-šu-du_7, 169 n. 982
^{d}Nin-su_{13}-aĝa_2, 174 n. 1022
Ninsun(a), 109 n. 578, 161 n. 923, 163 n. 938, 171 n. 1001
Ninur, 38 n. 174
Ninurta, 43 n. 207, 68, 77, 111, 112, 113, 115 n. 625, 117, 132 n. 728, 133 n. 735, 139 n. 776, 149, 163 n. 940, 167 n. 965, 175 n. 1035, 250, 259, 261, 263
^{d}Nin-uru-si, 130 n. 718
Nisaba, 41 n. 193, 77, 250 n. 1473
^{d}Nu-gal, 183 n. 1133
Nunamnir, 99 n. 522

Numušda, 162 n. 930
S
Śamaś, 70, 77, 116 n. 633, 197, 208, 210, 211, 217, 239, 240, 241, 254, 255, 256, 258, 259
$^{(ĝiš)}$Šar$_2$-ur$_3$, 109 n. 575, 112, 182 n. 1128, 217, 225, 259
U
^{d}Uĝken-du$_{10}$, 95 n. 486
Uttu, 89 n. 447
Utu, 50 n. 236, 54, 62 n. 310, 63 n. 315, 69, 70, 77, 88 n. 440, 89, 93 n. 474, 98, 107 n. 568, 109, 111 nn. 593–594, 117 n. 640, 118, 123 n. 671, 124, 134, 141 n. 788, 142, 143, 144 n. 804, 146, 151, 166 n. 959, 171 n. 1001, 172f. n. 1009, 173, 174, 176, 179 n. 1078, 180 n. 1096, 211, 217, 229, 240, 241, 249, 250, 252, 253 n. 1487, 254, 255
Z
Zu-i-nu, 210 n. 1336

5. Sumerian words, phrases and signs

The list is a selection of key terms discussed in relation with the reading or interpretation of specific names. Other lemmas can be found by browsing through the tables 4.2–4.4 on pages 220–225 and following the page references in the list of attestations for lugal-names.

A
a ĝe$_6$, 112 w. n. 596
a$_2$ maḫ, 97–98
a$_2$ šum(-ma), 98, 258
a$_2$ tuku, 98–99
a$_2$ zi-da, 109 w. n. 575
(a-)ab-ba 49 n. 230, , 87 n. 432, 99 w. n. 526, 112 w. n. 596
abba (and ab-ba), 68 n. 341, 87, 144, 177 n. 1056, 189, 192
ab-ba uru (and abba$_2$ uru), 95, 144 n. 804
abba$_2$, 87 w. n. 433, 144, 189
ad gi$_4$-gi$_4$, 167 n. 965
adda (and ad-da), 186 n. 1172, 192
aga$_{(3)}$ (zi), 88 w. nn. 442–443, 89, 171, 188, 189, 230
aga-ni$_3$-g[i-na$^?$], 188 n. 1206
aga-ni$_3$-z[i-da$^?$], 188 n. 1206
aga-šilig, 113 nn. 607–608
aĝrig, 54, 129–130
aja$_2$, 55 n. 261, 160, 192, 238, 264
AK, 60 w. n. 293, 127f. w. n. 696
am gal kur-[ra$^?$], 175 n. 1035
-am$_3$(A.AN)/-am$_6$(AN), 62 n. 308
ama, 49, 55 n. 261, 65, 87 n. 436, 116 n. 631, 122 n. 661, 161 n. 923, 163 n. 941, 189 n. 1225, 238, 264
amar, 49, 84–86, 97, 106f. n. 566, 131, 135, 166, 238
(lugal) an-ki, 168 n. 972, 176 n. 1037
B
bara$_2$, 90–91, 229
D
da-ri$_2$, 164, 165
diĝir uru-na, 120 n. 650
DN-ma-an-šum$_2$, 121
dugin$_2$(EZEM×MIR), 154 n. 888
E
e$_2$, 86, 87–88, 97, 113 n. 611, 136, 137 n. 765, 173 n. 1012, 186, 235–236, 237
E$_2$.NUN, 158 n. 914
e$_2$-gal, 35, 40, 185, 201
E$_2$-igi-nim, 174 n. 1018
E$_2$-maš, 155 w. n. 892
E$_2$-muš$_3$(-kalam-ma), 61, 68 n. 337, 136 n. 759, 155 w. n. 890
E$_2$-ul-maš, 203 w. n. 1298
e$_3$, 100 n. 531, 128, 173
eden, 96–97
eger tu-da, 51
en, 4, 37–38, 55 w.nn. 260–261, 89, 129, 152, 233–235, 244, 248 n. 1460, 258, 264
en$_{3/8}$-tar, 122–123

Eninnu, 142 n. 792, 158 n. 913, 162 n. 936, 164 n. 947, 165–166
en-nu(n), 107, 110
ensi$_2$, 29, 36–38, 39, 41, 43 n. 205, 44 nn. 210–211, 83 n. 404, 89 n. 446, 90, 91 n. 462, 94, 120, 129 n. 712, 141, 157, 172 w. n. 172, 185 n. 1158, 200, 244, 245, 250 n. 1473, 251, 252, 256, 257 n. 1518
ensi$_2$-gal, 37 n. 172, 43 n. 205, 129, 252
Eridu, 68 n. 336, 69, 115 n. 625, 152–153
EZEM×GAL^{ki}, 154 n. 888
EZEM×SIG$_7$, 154 n. 888

G

gal-zu, 106
gal$_5$-la$_2$, 167 n. 965

Ĝ

ĝi$_6$-par$_4$/ĝipar$_x$(KISAL), 143 n. 803, 158 n. 912
ĝidri, 90, 229
Ĝir$_2$-nun, 137, 158 n. 913

Ḫ

ḫuĝ, 141 n. 787

I

ig(-gal), 116, 182 n. 1128
igi ^{d}Utu-ka, 119 n. 644
igi ^{d}Utu-še$_3$, 119 n. 644
igi kalam-ma, 102 w. n. 544
igi-X-še$_3$, 119 n. 644
im-ri/-ru, 179 n. 1079
IM-ru, 179 n. 1078
ir$_{11}$, 82 w. n. 298

K

kalam(LAK729)/kalam(LAK730), 100 n. 529, 102 n. 542, 187f. w. n. 1200
Keš, 154, 247
KI.LUGAL.GUB, 155
ki-gal, 156–157
kisal, 157–158
kisig$_2$(EZEM×SIG$_7$), 154 n. 888
kur$_2$, 92 w. n. 469

L

LAK611, 108 n. 570
LAK617, 108 n. 570
LAK619b, 108 n. 570
lu, 101–102
LU (for LU$_2$), 79, 101, 110
lu$_2$, 79, 85 n. 419, 94 n. 481, 101–102, 112 n. 598, 123, 131 n. 727, 244 n. 1438, 246
LU$_2$ (for LU), 134 n. 745
LUGAL BE:E$_2$, 192 n. 1243
lugal E$_2$-muš$_3$-a, 68 n. 337
lugal Eridu^{ki}, 68 n. 336
lugal kur-kur-ra, 68 nn. 341–342, 102 n. 544, 143 n. 798, 252
lugal Mes-lam-ma, 68 n. 338
lugal ša$_3^!$(ŠA$_3$×TAB) an-su, 129 n. 706
lugal-ĝu$_{10}$, 71

M

maš, 60, 84 w. n. 411, 85, 97, 229
maš$_2$, 84 n. 411
maškim(-gi$_4$), 90, 193, 180 n. 1092, 193
me gal-gal (an-ki), 149
men an (ki/uraš)-a, 89 w. n. 453
mes, 65, 264
mu, (and MU) 6 n. 16, 10, 47, 50 n. 234, 114, 123, 128, 140, 141, 164–165
mu an-na, 11 n. 37
mu nu-tuku, 47 n. 217
mu$_4$, 91 n. 465
mu$_6$, 90 n. 455
mud, 62 n. 306
munus zi, 133 n. 735
Muš$_3$-bar, 155 n. 891

N

nagar, 182 n. 1123
nam, 83, 105, 140 n. 784
nam-lugal, 36, 40, 66, 69f. n 351, 81, 83, 88, 96, 97, 98, 100 n. 529, 102 n. 544, 116 n. 628, 141, 142, 146, 245, 246, 250, 263
nam-nir, 99f. w. n. 527, 255 n. 1500, 258
nemur$_x$(PIRIĜ.TUR), 165–166
nesaĝ, 148
ni$_3$/NIĜ$_2$, 105, 134, 163, 187, 189 n. 1235
ni$_3$-a$_2$-zi(-g), 117
nin, 4, 17 n. 61, 21 n. 73, 22, 38, 55 n. 261, 64–65, 80, 90 n. 458, 91, 94, 98, 106 n. 562, 110, 111, 125

n. 688, 135, 137 n. 765, 141, 176 n. 1039, 186, 189 n. 1235, 233–236, 258, 262, 264
nin$_{(9)}$, 38, 64f. w. n. 324, 189
Nina^{ki}, 153 n. 881
nir, /NIR, 99 w. n. 524, 100, 212
nir-ĝal$_2$, 99
nitaḫ$_{(2)}$, 10 n. 36, 49, 171 w. n. 1001, 202 n. 1297, 244 n. 1438
nu-banda$_3$, 95, 175 n. 1034
nu-gal, 68 n. 336, 80, 183 n. 1133, 190, 236–237, 254 w. n. 1494
P
pirĝ (banda$_3$/gal/tur ban$_3$-da), 165 n. 954
S
sa$_4$, 47
SAR.A.GU$_2$, 198 n. 1280
sa$_x$(ŠU$_2$.SA)-par$_4$, 113 n. 611
si/SI, 58, 65, 97, 100 n. 531, 108 n. 578, 113, 116 n. 633, 131 n. 726, 137 n. 768, 147, 148 n. 831, 157, 158 n. 915, 214
sipa, 90, 111, 123, 198–199
$^{su_{13}}$sug$_x$(PA.SIKIL), 104
su$_3$, 58 n. 277, 117 n. 637, 122, 134f. w. nn. 749–750 & 753
su$_x$(TAG), 58 n. 277, 134f. n. 750
Š
ša$_3$–kuš$_2$(-u$_3$), 106 w. n. 565, 107 w. n. 567, 124 n. 673
ša$_3$(-še$_3$) gid$_2$, 121f. n. 655
šabra, 90
šar$_2$-gaz, 182 n. 1128
še$_{21}$, 6 n. 16, 47, 69f. n. 351
šeš, 55 n. 261, 65 w. n. 323
šuba$_2$, 94 w. n. 483
šud$_3$(–ša$_4$), 138–139, 203 w. n. 1299
šul, 65, 264
T
temen, 156, 157
teš$_2$, 171
ti-da (iti-da), 172 n. 1004
ti-ma (itima), 158 n. 915
tigi$_x$(E$_2$.BALAĜ), 148, 185
tir/TIR, 182 w. n. 1123
tug$_2$ maḫ, 91
U
u$_2$-si-na, 104
u$_3$-ma(-ni) gub-gub, 164
u$_4$-de$_3$, 182 n. 1126
ud(i)nim(EZEM×SIG$_7$), 154 n. 888
UET2-300, 108 n. 570
uĝ$_3$(LAK730)/uĝ$_3^!$(LAK729), 100 nn. 529–530, 101 n. 532
uĝken, 94–95
urudu ni$_3$-kalag-ga, 163 n. 940
URUDU-da, 182 n. 1128
UŠ, 171 n. 1001, 182f. n. 1129
uš$_2$(TIL), 126 n. 693
ušumgal, 113 n. 608, 166–167
Z
zi(-d), 65, 94 n. 480, 109 n. 579, 132, 136, 137, 145, 160, 171, 188, 202, 229, 241, 244, 252, 255
zi ša$_3$ ĝal$_2$, 136–137

6. Akkadian words and phrases

The list gives a selection of key Akkadian words which form part of names discussed or which may serve to illustrate points in relation to specific names or ideas. Most are listed under their Old Babylonian citation forms.

A
agārum, 141 n. 787
ʿal (eli), 197 w. n. 1274
ālum, 197f. w. n. 1275, 221
amûm, 197 w. n. 1267, 227
apālum, 213 n. 1362
ašarēdum, 108, 178 n. 1063
B
balālum, 101 w. n. 538
banûm, 127, 195f., 201f., 227
bānû(m), 101 n. 535, 201f., 221
baʿlum, 4, 22 w. n. 78, 76 w. n. 383, 190, 191, 192, 194, 195, 196, 198, 201, 233, 238, 262
bêlum, 22 n. 78

D
dādum, 204, 221
danānum, 121 n. 653
dūrum, 197, 221, 240
duššûm, 101f.
E
edûm, 195
elûm, 213 w. n. 1361, 227
emēdum, 197 n. 1267
enēnum, 213 n. 1355
ēniqtu, 53
ennum, 110 n. 586
epēšum, 213 n. 1362, 227
ešērum, 211, 214
eśme$_x$(EZEM), 208
eṭlum, 90 n. 455
Ḫ
ḫabātum, 198 n. 1275
I
iltum, 75 w. n. 380
ilum (*ʾilum*), 75 w. n. 380, 192, 196, 200, 201, 208, 209 n. 1327, 210
ina maḫar [d]Šamaš, 119 n. 644
inbum (*ʿenbum*), 212f.
išarum (*yiśarum*), 211, 225
K
kašārum, 212
kibrum, 198
kigallu, 157
kišādum, 198
kullum, 171 n. 997
L
lābum/*labʾum*, 207 w. n. 1311, 221
lapātum, 182 n. 1117
leʾûm, 214
M
malkum, 4, 190
mūdûm, 195 w. n. 1256, 221
N
nabûm, 47, 213
naṣārum, 110 n. 586
nišū (*niśū*), 198, 199 w. n. 1283
P
pāqidum, 122 n. 663
parakkum, 91
pu$_5$(KA), 215
Q
qara$_4$(GA*gunû*), 207f.
qara$_x$(GUR$_7$), 208 n. 1324
qarrād(*um*), 166 n. 957, 207, 208 n. 1324, 221
qurād(*um*), 166 n. 957, 208
R
ramûm, 179 n. 1079
reʾûm, 73, 196
rēʾûm, 198
riābum, 212 w. n. 1352
S
sanāqum, 93
Š
šarārum (**śarārum*), 76
šarrum, 77, 191, 204, 206, 259
šarrum rēmēnûm, 122 n. 662
šaṭāpum, 197, 227
šaʾālum, 122 n. 663
šemûm, 208
šerrum, 77, 191, 204, 206, 259
šībum, 87 n. 433
šitūlum, 122 n. 663
šumu(*m*), 6 n. 16, 10 w. n. 36, 47 w. n. 218
šūpûm (*śūpiʾum*), 211
šutukkum, 158 n. 914
T
tem(*m*)*ennu*, 156 n. 899
W
waqārum, 207 n. 1315
wasāmum, 143 n. 803

7. Texts and text passages

Text references to single name entries are as a rule not entered in the list below, but primarily only larger quotations or references which serve to illustrate a point in discussions or notes to a specific name or lemma, over and above plain references to parallels or the existence of a name in a subsequent time period.

A
Angim 28, 175 n. 1035
Angim 133, 113 n. 608
ARET 5 6 o. v 5, 208 n. 1324
ARET 5 6 r. ii 4, 70
ARET 8 21 o. iii 2–3, 192 n. 1243
ArOr 39 (1971), p. 14 o. iii 3, 146 n. 823
B
BE 1/1 2 i 2, 204 w. n. 1305
BE 1/1 2 i 4–8, 192
BE 1/1 13, 147 w. n. 827
BE 1/2 87 i 6, 150 n. 854
BE 1/2 87 i 19–33, 50 n. 236
BE 1/2 87 i 36–43, 102 n. 544
BE 1/2 87 i 39–40, 42, 100 n. 529
BE 1/2 87 ii 21–22, 91 w. n. 462
BE 1/2 87 ii 38–42, 98 w. n. 510
BE 1/2 87 iii 7–12, 147 n. 829
BE 1/2 87 iii 17–18, 140 n. 784
BE 1/2 87 iii 32–33, 160 n. 919
BE 1/2 87 iii 36, 164 n. 950
BE 1/2 87 iii 38–39, 68 n. 339
BiMes 3 14 r. i 1, 175 n. 1034
BiMes 3 27 r. ii 4 (=28 r. i 4), 156 n. 900
BIN 8 12, 83 n. 404
BIN 8 242, 86 n. 422
C
CIRPL Ean. 1 o. iv 18–v 29, 50 n. 235
CIRPL Ean. 1 o. v 21, 98 n. 516
CIRPL Ean. 1 o. vi 1, 98 n. 516
CIRPL Ean. 1 o. vii 6–8, 109 n. 575
CIRPL Ean. 1 o. xvi 21–22, 176 n. 1037
CIRPL Ean. 1 o. xx 16, 164 n. 950
CIRPL Ean. 1 r. x 23–25, 50 n. 234
CIRPL Ean. 2 vi 21–vii 2, 251f. n. 1480
CIRPL Ean. 6 iv 7–10, 50 n. 237
CIRPL Ean. 60 i 6–8, 145 n. 816
CIRPL Ean. 63+N. 5 ii' 2'–3', 167 n. 964
CIRPL Ent. 28 i 1–3, 68 w. n. 341
CIRPL Ent. 28 i 10, 70 n. 354
CIRPL Ent. 28 ii 3, 128 w. n. 702
CIRPL Ent. 28 iii 28–29, 41 n. 195, 60 n. 288
CIRPL Ent. 32 i 4''–8'', 154 n. 885
CIRPL Ent. 45–73, 250 n. 1472
CIRPL Ukg. 9 i' 6'–7', 141 n. 788
CIRPL Ukg. 14 ii' 6', 117 n. 638
CIRPL Ukg. 17–33, 110 n. 585
CIRPL Ukg. 36, 153 n. 880
CIRPL Ukg. 41, 93 n. 476
CIRPL Ukg. 54–55 1–3, 139 w. n. 773
CIRPL Urn. 24 iii 3–6, 41 n. 192, 246 n. 1448
CT 32 pl. 7–8 o. iii' 4–5, 232 n. 1399
CT 32 pl. 7–8 r. iii' 4, 100 n. 530
CT 36 pl. 2 (BM 114684) l. 23, 89
CT 36 pl. 33f. (BM 96739) r. 17–18, 172
Curse of Akkade l. 40, 111 n. 592
CUSAS 17 10, 83 n. 404
CUSAS 17 13, 248 n. 1457
CUSAS 17 13 i 1–4, 41 n. 195
D
DP 1/1 31 i 4–5, 41 n. 195
DP 2/1 163 o. iv 10–r. i 1, 155 n. 889
E
ED Lu C 44, 177 n. 1055
G
Gudea Cyl. A i 3, 119 n. 644
Cyl. A i 20, 149 n. 845
Cyl. A ix 1–2, 129 n. 705
Cyl. A xii 21–xiii 15, 140
Cyl. A xv 23, 109 n. 575
Cyl. A xvi 26–27, 165f. w. n. 956
Cyl. A xx 1, 151 w. n. 865
Cyl. A xxiii 9, 157 n. 910
Cyl. A xxiv 5, 142 n. 792
Cyl. B i 12–15, 120
Cyl. B iv 17–19, 166 w. n. 961
Cyl. B x 9–15, 148 n. 836
Cyl. B xviii 16, 161 n. 926
Cyl. B xxiii 19–20, 161 n. 923
I
IAS 33 o. xi 7', 113 n. 606
IAS 82, 249f.
IAS 83 o. iii' 6', 183 n. 1133
IAS 84 o. i' 4', 183 n. 1133
IAS 86 o. ii 4, iii 1, 175 n. 1035
IAS 90 o. ii' 2', 103 n. 550

IAS 113 o. ii 13, 38 n. 175
IAS 114 o. iv 1', 69f. n. 351
IAS 124 o. iv' 8'–10', 38 n. 175
IAS 137 o. ii 2'–3', 68 w. n. 341
IAS 247 ii' 1'–8', 248 n. 1460
IAS 256 r. iv 6–7, 99 n. 521
IAS 326+ o. iii 14, 208 n. 1324
IAS 357 o. ii' 2', 108 n. 569
IAS 392 o. iv' 3'–4', 136 w. n. 759
IAS 397, o. ii' 5'–6', 109 n. 578
IAS 504 r. 1, 152 n. 872
IAS 505 r. i' 4'–5', 152 n. 872
Iraq 36 (1974), 32 fig. 4 (3H T7) r. 1, 68 n. 339
Iraq 36 (1974), 34 fig. 15 (3H T14) 2'–5', 38 n. 178
ITT 1 1081, 201 n. 1289
J
JANES 12 (1980), 30 no. 1 o. ii 2', 147 n. 828
JAOS 83 (1963), 171f. (YBC 3654) o. ii 9, 112 n. 601
JAOS 83 (1963), 171f. (YBC 3654) r. i 9, 116 n. 633
JAOS 88 (1968), 57 (6N-T658) o. i 1–5, 204 w. n. 1305
K
Keš Temple Hymn 79, 37 n. 172
L
Lipit-Ištar A 1, 160 n. 922
M
MAD 1 172 o. 10', 68 n. 336
MAD 1 191 o. 1–8, 192 n. 1244
MAD 4 92 o. 1–5, 63 n. 315
MAD 4 100 o. 5–r. 3, 63 n. 315
MAD 4 109 o. 1–4, 63 n. 315
Mesopotamia 8, 67–75 o. ii 7, 89 n. 447
MLVS 1, 8 no. 10 o. i 3–4, 113 n. 605
N
NATN 761, 51
O
OIP 99, 46–53 6–7, 99 n. 522
OIP 99, 46–53 8–10, 92 n. 468
OIP 99, 46–53 11–14, 68 w. n. 343
OIP 99, 46–53 36, 69 w. n. 347
OIP 99, 46–53 38, 69 w. n. 348
OIP 99, 46–53 87, 133 n. 742
OIP 104 279, 51
OrNS 28 (1959), 339 i 3'–4', 99 n. 520
OrNS 28 (1959), 339 i 4', 8', 10', 38 n. 174
OrNS 54 (1985), 57 r. 2, 120 n. 648
OrNS 54 (1985), 57 r. 8, 176 n. 1045
P
PBS 5 34+PBS 15 41 o. v 14'–19', 203 w. n. 1299
PBS 5 34+PBS 15 41 o. vi 19'–26', 203 w. n. 1299
PBS 5 36 r. iii' 18'–20', 99 n. 520
PBS 5 66 o. i 1–3, 168 n. 972
PBS 15 41 o. x 3''–6'', 203 w. n. 1301
R
RIME 3/2.1.4.1 iii 24–25, 169 n. 981
RTC 196 o. ii 2–6, 182 n. 1128
S
SAT 2 445 r. 1–3, 114 n. 614
SF 1 o. i 5–8, 89
SF 1 o. i 15, 109 n. 578
SF 1 o. iv 17', 174 n. 1022
SF 1 o. vii 17, 100 n. 528
SF 1 r. ii 25, 95 n. 486
SF 1 r. iv 4''', 176 n. 1036
SF 28 o. iii 6–7, 176 n. 1040
SF 28 r. ii 9, 102 n. 546
SF 29 o. ii 10, 176 n. 1040
SF 29 o. iv 6, 102 n. 546
SF 29 r. i 9, 175 n. 1034
SF 37 o. iv 19'–20', 69 w. n. 351
SF 38 o. iii 1–2, 69 w. n. 351
SF 77 o. vii 2, 177 n. 1051
SIA 640 o. ii 1, 189
SIA 1026 o. 2, 189 n. 1228
STTI 185 r. 6'–7', 197f. n. 1274
Sumer 29 (1973), 30 (En. I 33) iii 1–8, 116 w. n. 628
Š
Šulgi A 55, 134 n. 748
Šulgi A 90, 98, 98 w. n. 512
Šulgi C 3, 173 w. n. 1015
Šulgi D 6, 165 n. 954
Šulgi D 29, 175 n. 1035
Šulgi D 191, 176 n. 1047

Šulgi D 295, 89 n. 448
Šulgi D 299, 175 n. 1035
Šulgi D 344–345, 112 n. 601
Šulgi D 366–367, 185 n. 1160
Šulgi D 390, 88 n. 443
T
TCABI 8, 184 w. n. 1138
TH 176, 69 n. 349, 246 n. 1449
TH 218, 68 n. 337, 246 n. 1449
TH 251–252, 162 n. 930
TH 256, 246 n. 1449
TH 258, 164 n. 947,
TH 264, 110 n. 584
TH 267, 122 n. 661
TH 289, 112 n. 596
TH 332, 133 n. 742
TH 338, 112 n. 600
TH 407, 102 n. 542
TH 431, 246 n. 1449
TH 440, 246 n. 1449
TH 445, 246 n. 1449
TH 454, 246 n. 1449
TH 463–464, 68 n. 338
TH 491, 69 n. 349, 246 n. 1449
TM.75.G.1917, 183 n. 1136–1137
TM.75.G.2429 o. xx 4–12, 236f.
TSŠ 627, 154 n. 884
U
UET 1 71, 114 n. 613
UET 3 26 (=OIP 104 281), 51 w. n. 239
UET 8 2, 115 n. 621
Urnamma A 25, 132 n. 733
Urnamma A 98, 91 n. 466
Urnamma A 209, 92 n. 469
Urnamma B 59, 61, 117 n. 637
Urnamma C 13, 155 n. 893
Urnamma C 22–23, 160 n. 916
Urnamma C 53, 94 n. 483
Urnamma D 41', 164 n. 950
Urnamma EF 35, 180 n. 1092
Urnamma G 11, 131 n. 725
Urnamma G 19–20, 131 n. 724
V
VE238, 158 n. 914
VE908, 110 n. 585
VE1043, 65 n. 323
VE1044, 65 n. 322
VE1161, 204 n. 1304
VE1183, 65 n. 324
VE0371, 128 n. 704
W
WF 41 o. viii 6, 146 n. 823
Y
YOS 1 14 1–9, 157 w. n. 905
YOS 1 20 i 7–11, 150 n. 854
YOS 9 31, 165 n. 951
YOS 13 192, 52 w. n. 246